A HISTORY OF
THE
GREAT REVOLT

A HISTORY OF THE GREAT REVOLT

(In Three Volumes)

Volume I

JOHN WILLIAM KAYE

GYAN PUBLISHING HOUSE

New Delhi - 110002

A History of The Great Revolt

ISBN: 81-212-0194-2 (Set)
ISBN: 81-212-0195-0 (Vol. 1)

Reprinted in 2011 in India by
Gyan Publishing House
23, Main Ansari Road, Daryaganj,
New Delhi - 110002
Phone : 23282060, 23261060
Fax : (011) 23285914
e-mail : books@gyanbooks.com
gyanbook@vsnl.com
website : gyanbooks.com

Printed at : G. Print Process, Delhi

CONTENTS OF VOL. I

BOOK I.—INTRODUCTORY.

CHAPTER I.

THE CONQUEST OF THE PUNJAB AND PEGU.

CHAPTER II.

THE "RIGHT OF LAPSE."

CHAPTER III.

THE ANNEXATION OF OUDE.

CHAPTER IV

PROGRESS OF ENGLISHISM.

BOOK II.—THE SEPOY ARMY: ITS RISE, PROGRESS, AND DECLINE.

CHAPTER I.

EARLY HISTORY OF THE NATIVE ARMY.

CHAPTER II.

DETERIORATING INFLUENCES.

CHAPTER III.

THE SINDH MUTINIES.

CHAPTER IV.

THE PUNJAB MUTINIES.

CHAPTER V.

DISCIPLINE OF THE BENGAL ARMY.

BOOK III.—THE OUTBREAK OF THE MUTINY.

CHAPTER I.

LORD CANNING AND HIS COUNCIL.

CHAPTER II.

THE OUDE ADMINISTRATION AND THE PERSIAN WAR.

CHAPTER III.

THE RISING OF THE STORM.

CHAPTER IV

THE FIRST MUTINY.

CHAPTER V.

PROGRESS OF MUTINY.

CHAPTER VI.

EXCITEMENT IN UPPER INDIA.

CHAPTER VII.

BURSTING OF THE STORM.

PREFACE.

It was not without much hesitation that I undertook to write this narrative of the events, which have imparted so painful a celebrity to the years 1857-58, and left behind them such terrible remembrances. Publicly and privately I had been frequently urged to do so, before I could consent to take upon myself a responsibility, which could not sit lightly on any one capable of appreciating the magnitude of the events themselves and of the many grave questions which they suggested. If, indeed, it had not been that, in course of time, I found, either actually in my hands or within my reach, materials of history such as it was at least improbable that any other writer could obtain, I should not have ventured upon so difficult a task. But having many important collections of papers in my possession, and having received promises of further assistance from surviving actors in the scenes to be described, I felt that, though many might write a better history of the Sepoy War, no one could write a more truthful one.

So, relying on these external advantages to compensate all inherent deficiencies, I commenced what I knew must be a labour of years, but what I felt would be also a labour of love. My materials were too ample to be otherwise than most sparingly displayed. The prodigal citation of authorities has its advantages; but it encumbers the text, it impedes the narrative, and swells to inordinate dimensions the record of historical events. On a former occasion, when I laid before the public an account of a series of important transactions, mainly derived from original documents, public and private, I quoted those documents freely both in the text and in the notes. As I was at that time wholly unknown to the public, it was necessary that I should cite chapter and verse to obtain credence for my statements. There was no ostensible reason why I should have known more about those transactions than any other writer (for it was merely the accident of private friendships and associations that placed such profuse materials in my possession), and it seemed to be imperative upon me therefore to produce my credentials. But, believing that this necessity no longer exists, I have in the present work abstained from adducing my authorities, for the mere purpose of substantiating my statements. I have quoted the voluminous correspondence in my possession only where there is some dramatic force and propriety in the words cited, or when they appear calculated, without impeding the narrative, to give colour and vitality to the story.

And here I may observe that, as on former occasions, the historical materials which I have moulded into this narrative are rather of a private than of a public character. I have made but little use of recorded official documents. I do not mean that access to such documents has not been extremely serviceable to me; but that it has rather afforded the means of verifying or correcting statements received from other sources than it has supplied me with original materials. So far as respects the accumulation of facts, this History would have differed but slightly from what it is, if I had never passed the door of a public office; and, generally, the same may be said of the opinions which I have expressed. Those opinions, whether sound or unsound, are entirely my own personal opinions—opinions in many instances formed long ago, and confirmed by later events and more mature consideration. No one but myself is responsible for them; no one else is in any way identified with them. In the wide range of inquiry embraced by the consideration of the manifold causes of the great convulsion of 1857, almost every grave question of Indian government and administration presses forward, with more or less importunity, for notice. Where, on many points, opinions widely differ, and the policy, which is the practical expression of them, takes various shapes, it is a necessity that the writer of cotemporary history, in the exercise of independent thought, should find himself dissenting from the doctrines and disapproving the actions of some authorities, living and dead, who are worthy of all admiration and respect. It is fortunate, when, as in the present instance, this difference of opinion involves no diminution of esteem, and the historian can discern worthy motives, and benevolent designs, and generous strivings after good, in those whose ways he may think erroneous and whose course of action he may deem unwise.

Indeed, the errors of which I have freely spoken were, for the most part, strivings after good. It was in the over-eager pursuit of Humanity and Civilisation that Indian statesmen of the new school were betrayed into the excesses which have been so grievously visited upon the nation. The story of the Indian Rebellion of 1857 is, perhaps, the most signal illustration of our great national character ever yet recorded in the annals of our country. It was the vehement self-assertion of the Englishman that produced this conflagration; it was the same vehement self-assertion that enabled him, by God's blessing, to trample it out. It was a noble egotism, mighty alike in doing and in suffering, and it showed itself grandly capable of steadfastly confronting the dangers which it had brought down upon itself. If I have any predominant theory it is this: Because we were too English the great crisis arose; but it was only because we were English that, when it arose, it did not utterly overwhelm us.

It is my endeavour, also, to show how much both of the dangers which threatened British dominion in the East, and of the success with which they were encountered, is assignable to the individual characters of a few eminent men. With this object I have sought to bring the reader face to face with the principal actors in the events of the Sepoy War, and to take a personal interest in them. If it be true that the best history is that which most nearly resembles a bundle of biographies, it is especially true when said with reference to Indian history; for nowhere do the characters of individual Englishmen impress themselves with a more vital reality upon the annals of the country in which they live; nowhere are there such great opportunities of independent action; nowhere are developed such capacities for evil or for good, as in our great Anglo-Indian Empire. If, then, in such a work as this, the biographical element were not prominently represented—if the individualities of such men as Dalhousie and Canning, as Henry and John Lawrence, as James Outram, as John Nicholson, and Herbert Edwardes, were not duly illustrated, there would be not only a cold and colourless, but also an unfaithful, picture of the origin and progress of the War. But it is to be remarked that, in proportion as the individuality of the English leaders is distinct and strongly marked, that of the chiefs of the insurrectionary movement is faint and undecided. In the fact of this contrast we see the whole history of the success which, by God's providence, crowned the efforts of our countrymen. If the individual energies of the leaders of the revolt had been commensurate with the power of the masses, we might have failed to extinguish such a conflagration. But the whole tendency of the English system had been to crush out those energies; so again, I say, we found in the very circumstances which had excited the rebellion the very elements of our success in suppressing it. Over the Indian Dead Level which that system had created, the English heroes marched triumphantly to victory.

In conclusion, I have only to express my obligations to those who have enabled me to write this History by supplying me with the materials of which it is composed. To the executors of the late Lord Canning, who placed in my hands the private and demi-official correspondence of the deceased statesman, extending over the whole term of his Indian administration, I am especially indebted. To Sir John Lawrence and Sir Herbert Edwardes, who have furnished me with the most valuable materials for my narrative of the rising in the Punjab and the measures taken in that province for the re-capture of Delhi; to the family of the late Colonel Baird Smith, for many interesting papers illustrative of the operations of the great siege; to Sir James Outram, who gave me before his death his correspondence relating to the brilliant operations in Oude; to Sir Robert Hamilton, for much valuable matter in elucidation of the history of the Central Indian Campaign; and to Mr. E. A. Reade, whose comprehensive knowledge of the progress of events in the North-Western Provinces has been of material service to me, my warmest acknowledgments are due. But to no one am I more indebted than to Sir Charles Wood, Secretary of State for India, who has permitted me to consult the official records of his Department—a privilege which has enabled me to make much better use of the more private materials in my possession. No one, however, can know better or feel more strongly than myself, that much matter of interest contained in the multitudinous papers before me is unrepresented in my narrative. But such omissions are the necessities of a history so full of incident as this. If I had yielded to the temptation to use my illustrative materials more freely, I should have expanded this work beyond all acceptable limits.

London, October, 1864.

. . . FOR TO THINK THAT AN HANDFUL OF PEOPLE CAN, WITH THE GREATEST COURAGE AND POLICY IN THE WORLD, EMBRACE TOO LARGE EXTENT OF DOMINION, IT MAY HOLD FOR A TIME, BUT IT WILL FAIL SUDDENLY.—*Bacon.*

. . . AS FOR MERCENARY FORCES (WHICH IS THE HELP IN THIS CASE), ALL EXAMPLES SHOW THAT, WHATSOEVER ESTATE, OR PRINCE, DOTH REST UPON THEM, HE MAY SPREAD HIS FEATHERS FOR A TIME, BUT HE WILL MEW THEM SOON AFTER.—*Bacon.*

IF THERE BE FUEL PREPARED, IT IS HARD TO TELL WHENCE THE SPARK SHALL COME THAT SHALL SET IT ON FIRE. THE MATTER OF SEDITIONS IS OF TWO KINDS, MUCH POVERTY AND MUCH DISCONTENTMENT. IT IS CERTAIN, SO MANY OVERTHROWN ESTATES, SO MANY VOTES FOR TROUBLES. . . . THE CAUSES AND MOTIVES FOR SEDITION ARE, INNOVATIONS IN RELIGION TAXES, ALTERATION OF LAWS AND CUSTOMS, BREAKING OF PRIVILEGES, GENERAL OPPRESSION, ADVANCEMENT OF UNWORTHY PERSONS, STRANGERS, DEATHS, DISBANDED SOLDIERS, FACTIONS GROWN DESPERATE; AND WHATSOEVER IN OFFENDING PEOPLE JOINETH AND KNITTETH THEM IN A COMMON CAUSE.—*Bacon.*

HISTORY OF THE SEPOY WAR.

BOOK I.—INTRODUCTORY.

[1846—1856.]

CHAPTER I.

THE ADMINISTRATION OF LORD DALHOUSIE—HIS FAREWELL MINUTE—RETROSPECT OF THE FIRST SIKH WAR—THE MILITARY OCCUPATION OF THE PUNJAB—THE COUNCIL OF REGENCY—THE SECOND SIKH WAR—THE ANNEXATION OF THE PUNJAB—ITS ADMINISTRATION UNDER THE LAWRENCES—THE CONQUEST OF PEGU.

BROKEN in bodily health, but not enfeebled in spirit, 1856.
by eight years of anxious toil, beneath an Indian sun, Lord Dalhousie laid down the reins of government and returned to his native country to die. Since the reign of Lord Wellesley, so great in written history, so momentous in practical results, there had been no such administration as that of Lord Dalhousie; there had been no period in the annals of the Anglo-Indian Empire surcharged with such great political events, none which nearly approached it in the rapidity of its administrative progress. Peace and War had yielded their fruits with equal profusion.

On the eve of resigning his high trust to the hands of another, Lord Dalhousie drew up an elaborate state-

1856. paper reviewing the eventful years of his government. He had reason to rejoice in the retrospect; for he had acted in accordance with the faith that was within him, honestly and earnestly working out his cherished principles, and there was a bright flush of success over all the apparent result. Peace and prosperity smiled upon the empire. That empire he had vastly extended, and by its extension he believed that he had consolidated our rule and imparted additional security to our tenure of the country.

Of these great successes some account should be given at the outset of such a narrative as this; for it is only by understanding and appreciating them that we can rightly estimate the subsequent crisis. It was in the Punjab and in Oude that many of the most important incidents of that crisis occurred. Lord Dalhousie found them Foreign States; he left them British Provinces.

1845-46. First occupation of the Punjab.

Lord Hardinge conquered the Sikhs; but he spared the Punjab. Moderate in victory as resolute in war, he left the empire of Runjeet Singh, shorn only of its outlying provinces, to be governed by his successors, and strove to protect the boy-prince against the lawlessness of his own soldiers. But it was felt that this forbearance was only an experimental forbearance; and the proclamation which announced the restoration of the Punjab to the Maharajah Duleep Singh sounded also a note of warning to the great military autocracy which had well-nigh overthrown the State. "If this opportunity," said the victor, "of rescuing the Sikh nation from military anarchy and misrule be neglected, and hostile opposition to the British army be renewed, the Government of India will make such other arrangements for the future government of the Punjab as the interests and security of the British power may render just and expedient." Thus was the doubt expressed; thus were the consequences foreshadowed. It did not seem likely that the experiment would succeed; but it was not less right to make it. It left the future destiny of the empire, under Providence, for the Sikhs themselves to determine. It taught them how to preserve their national independence, and left them to work out the problem with their own hands. 1846.

But Hardinge did more than this. He did not interfere with the internal administration, but he established a powerful military protectorate in the Punjab. He left the Durbar to govern the country after its own fashion, but he protected the Government against the lawless domination of its soldiery. The Sikh army was overawed by the presence of the British battalions; and if the hour had produced the man—if there had been any wisdom, any love of country, in the councils of the nation—the Sikh Empire might have survived the great peril of the British military protectorate. But there was no one worthy to rule; no one able to govern. The mother of the young Maharajah was nominally the Regent. There have been great queens in the East as in the West—women who have done for their people what men have been incapable of doing. But the mother of Duleep Singh was not one of these. To say that she loved herself better than her country is to use in courtesy the mildest words, which do not actually violate truth. She was, indeed, an evil presence in the nation. It rested with her to choose a minister, and the choice which she made was another great suicidal blow struck at the life of the Sikh Empire. It may have been difficult in this

1846. emergency to select the right man, for, in truth, there were not many wise men from whom a selection could be made. The Queen-Mother cut through the difficulty by selecting her paramour.

Lal Singh was unpopular with the Durbar; unpopular with the people; and he failed. He might have been an able and an honest man, and yet have been found wanting in such a conjuncture. But he was probably the worst man in the Punjab on whom the duty of reconstructing a strong Sikh Government could have devolved. To do him justice, there were great difficulties in his way. He had to replenish an exhausted treasury by a course of unpopular retrenchments. Troops were to be disbanded and Jagheers resumed. Lal Singh was not the man to do this, as one bowing to a painful necessity, and sacrificing himself to the exigencies of the State. Even in a country where political virtue was but little understood, a course of duty consistently pursued for the benefit of the nation might have ensured for him some sort of respect. But whilst he was impoverishing others, he was enriching himself. It was not the public treasury, but the private purse that he sought to replenish, and better men were despoiled to satisfy the greed of his hungry relatives and friends. Vicious among the vicious, he lived but for the indulgence of his own appetites, and ruled but for his own aggrandisement. The favourite of the Queen, he was the oppressor of the People. And though he tried to dazzle his British guests by rare displays of courtesy towards them, and made himself immensely popular among all ranks of the Army of Occupation by his incessant efforts to gratify them, he could not hide the one great patent fact, that a strong Sikh Government could never be established under the wuzeerat of Lal Singh. 1846.

But the British were not responsible for the failure. The Regent chose him; and, bound by treaty not to exercise any interference in the internal administration of the Lahore State, the British Government had only passively to ratify the choice. But it was a state of things burdened with evils of the most obtrusive kind. We were upholding an unprincipled ruler and an unprincipled minister at the point of our British bayonets, and thus aiding them to commit iniquities which, without such external support, they would not have long been suffered to perpetrate. The compact, however, was but for the current year; and even for that brief period there seemed but little probability of Lal Singh tiding over the difficulties and dangers which beset his position.

Very soon his treachery undid him. False to his own country, he was false also to the British Government. The province of Cashmere, which was one of the outlying dependencies taken by the British in payment of the war-charges, had been made over to Gholab Singh, chief of the great Jummoo family, who had paid a million of money for the cession. But the transfer had been resisted by the local governor, who had ruled the province under the Sikh Rajahs, and covertly Lal Singh had encouraged the resistance. The nominal offender was brought to public trial, but Dec. 1846.
it was felt that the real criminal was Lal Singh, and that upon the issue of the inquiry depended the fate of the minister. It was soon apparent that he was a traitor, and that the other, though for intelligible reasons of his own, reluctant to render an account of his stewardship, was little more than a tool in his

1846. hands. The disgrace of the minister was the immediate result of the investigation. He left the Durbar tent a prisoner under a guard, an hour before his own body-guard, of Sikh soldiers; and the great seal of the Maharajah was placed in the hands of the British Resident. So fell Lal Singh; and so fell also the first experiment to reconstruct a strong Sikh Government on a basis of national independence.

Another experiment was then to be tried. There was not a native of the country to whose hands the destinies of the empire could be safely entrusted. If the power of the English conqueror were demanded to overawe the turbulent military element, English wisdom and English integrity were no less needed, in that conjuncture, to quicken and to purify the corrupt councils of the State. Sikh statesmanship, protected against the armed violence of the Prætorian bands, which had overthrown so many ministries, had been fairly tried, and had been found miserably wanting. A purely native Government was not to be hazarded again. Averse as Hardinge had been, and still was, to sanction British interference in the internal administration of the Punjab, there was that in the complications before him which compelled him to overcome his reluctance. The choice, indeed, lay between a half measure, which might succeed, though truly there was small hope of success, and the total abandonment of the country to its own vices, which would have been speedily followed, in self-defence, by our direct assumption of the Government on our own account. Importuned by the Sikh Durbar, in the name of the Maharajah, Hardinge tried the former course. The next effort, therefore, to save the Sikh Empire from self-destruction, embraced the idea of a native Government, presided over by a British statesman. A Council of Regency was instituted, to be composed of Sikh chiefs, under the superintendence and control of the Resident; or, in other words, the British Resident became the virtual ruler of the country. 1846.

And this time the choice, or rather the accident, of the man was as propitious, as before it had been untoward and perverse. The English officer possessed well-nigh all the qualities which the Sikh Sirdar so deplorably lacked. A captain of the Bengal Artillery, holding the higher rank of colonel by brevet for good service, Henry Lawrence had graduated in Punjabee diplomacy under George Clerk, and had accompanied to Caubul the Sikh Contingent, attached to Pollock's 1842.
retributory force, combating its dubious fidelity, and controlling its predatory excesses on the way. After the return of the expedition to the British provinces, he had been appointed to represent our interests in Nepaul; and there—for there was a lull in the sanguinary intrigues of that semi-barbarous Court—immersed in his books, and turning to good literary purpose his hours of leisure, he received at Catamandoo intelligence of the Sikh invasion, and of the death of George Broadfoot, and was summoned to take the place of that lamented officer as the agent of the Governor-General on the frontier. In the negotiations which followed the conquest of the Khalsa army, he had taken the leading part, and, on the restoration of peace, had been appointed to the office of British Resident, or Minister, at Lahore, under the first experiment of a pure Sikh Government hedged in by British troops.

If the character of the man thus placed at the head of affairs could have secured the success of this great compromise, it would have been successful far beyond

1846. the expectations of its projectors. For no man ever undertook a high and important trust with a more solemn sense of his responsibility, or ever, with more singleness of purpose and more steadfast sincerity of heart, set himself to work, with God's blessing, to turn a great opportunity to great account for the benefit of his fellows. In Henry Lawrence a pure transparent nature, a simple manliness and truthfulness of character, were combined with high intellectual powers, and personal energies which nothing earthly could subdue. I may say it here, once for all, at the very outset of my story, that nowhere does this natural simplicity and truthfulness of character so often as in India survive a long career of public service. In that country public men are happily not exposed to the pernicious influences which in England shrivel them so fast into party leaders and parliamentary chiefs. With perfect singleness of aim and pure sincerity of purpose, they go, with level eyes, straight at the public good, never looking up in fear at the suspended sword of a parliamentary majority, and never turned aside by that fear into devious paths of trickery and finesse. It may be that ever since the days of Clive and Omichund an unsavoury odour has pervaded the reputation of Oriental diplomacy; but the fact is, that our greatest successes have been achieved by men incapable of deceit, and by means which have invited scrutiny. When we have opposed craft to craft, and have sought to out-juggle our opponents, the end has been commonly disastrous. It is only by consummate honesty and transparent truthfulness that the Talleyrands of the East have been beaten by such mere children in the world's ways as Mountstuart Elphinstone, Charles Metcalfe, James Outram, and Henry Lawrence.

Henry Lawrence, indeed, was wholly without guile. 1846.
He had great shrewdness and sagacity of character, and he could read and understand motives, to which his own breast was a stranger, for he had studied well the Oriental character. But he was singularly open and unreserved in all his dealings, and would rather have given his antagonist an advantage than have condescended to any small arts and petty trickeries to secure success. All men, indeed, trusted him; for they knew that there was nothing selfish or sordid about him; that the one desire of his heart was to benefit the people of the country in which it had pleased God to cast his lot. But he never suffered this plea of beneficence to prevail against his sense of justice. He was eminently, indeed, a just man, and altogether incapable of that casuistry which gives a gloss of humanity to self-seeking, and robs people for their own good. He did not look upon the misgovernment of a native State as a valid reason for the absorption of its revenues, but thought that British power might be exercised for the protection of the oppressed, and British wisdom for the instruction and reformation of their oppressors, without adding a few more thousand square miles to the area of our British possessions, and a few more millions of people to the great muster-roll of British subjects in the East.

Above the middle height, of a spare, gaunt frame, and a worn face bearing upon it the traces of mental toil and bodily suffering, he impressed you, at first sight, rather with a sense of masculine energy and resolution than of any milder and more endearing qualities. But when you came to know him, you saw at once that beneath that rugged exterior there was a heart gentle as a woman's, and you recognised in his words and in his manner the kindliness of nature,

1846. which won the affection of all who came within its reach, and by its large and liberal manifestations made his name a very household word with thousands, who had never felt the pressure of his hand or stood in his living presence. But, with all this, though that name was in men's mouths and spoken in many languages, no unknown subaltern had a more lowly mind or a more unassuming deportment.

Such was the man who now found himself the virtual sovereign of the empire of Runjeet Singh. The new protectorate, established at the end of 1846, gave to Henry Lawrence "unlimited authority," "to direct and control every department of the State." He was to be assisted in this great work by an efficient establishment of subordinates, but it was no part of the design to confer upon them the executive management of affairs. The old officers of the Sikh Government were left to carry on the administration, guided and directed by their British allies. Under such a system corruption and oppression could no longer run riot over the face of the land. It was a protectorate for the many, not for the few; and for a while it seemed that all classes were pleased with the arrangement. Outwardly, indeed, it did not seem that feelings of resentment against the British Government were cherished by any persons but the Queen-Mother and her degraded paramour.

1847. And so, in the spring of 1847, the political horizon was almost unclouded. The Council of Regency, under the control of Henry Lawrence, seemed to be carrying on the government with a sincere desire to secure a successful result. Tranquillity had been restored; confidence and order were fast returning. The Sikh soldiery appeared to be contented with their lot, and to be gradually acquiring habits of discipline and obedience, under a system which rendered them dependent on the British officers for whatever most promoted their interests and contributed to their comforts. But it did not escape the sagacious mind of the Resident, that serene as was the aspect of affairs, and promising as were the indications of continued repose, there were, beneath all this surface-calm, dangerous elements at work, waiting only for time and circumstance to call them into full activity. The memory of frequent defeat was still too fresh in the minds of the humbled Khalsa to suffer them to indulge in visions of at once re-acquiring their lost supremacy. But as time passed and the impression waxed fainter and fainter, it was well-nigh certain that the old hopes would revive, and that outbursts of desperate Asiatic zeal might be looked for in quarters where such paroxysms had long seemed to be necessary to the very existence of a lawless and tumultuous class. It is a trick of our self-love—of our national vanity—to make us too often delude ourselves with the belief that British supremacy must be welcome wheresoever it obtrudes itself. But Henry Lawrence did not deceive himself in this wise. He frankly admitted that, however benevolent our motives, and however conciliatory our demeanour, a British army could not garrison Lahore, and a British functionary supersede the Sikh Durbar, without exciting bitter discontents and perilous resentments. He saw around him, struggling for existence, so many high officers of the old Sikh armies, so many favourites of the old line of Wuzeers now cast adrift upon the world, without resources and without hope under the existing system, that when he remembered their lawless 1847.

1847. habits, their headstrong folly, their desperate suicidal zeal, he could but wonder at the perfect peace which then pervaded the land.

But whatsoever might be taking shape in the future, the present was a season of prosperity—a time of promise—and the best uses were made by the British functionaries of the continued calm. Interference in the civil administration of the country was exercised only when it could be turned to the very apparent advantage of the people. British authority and British integrity were then employed in the settlement of long-unsettled districts, and in the development of the resources of long-neglected tracts of country. The subordinate officers thus employed under the Resident were few, but they were men of no common ability and energy of character—soldiers such as Edwardes, Nicholson, Reynell Taylor, Lake, Lumsden, Becher, George Lawrence, and James Abbott; civilians such as Vans Agnew and Arthur Cocks—men, for the most part, whose deeds will find ample record in these pages. They had unbounded confidence in their chief, and their chief had equal confidence in them. Acting, with but few exceptions, for the majority were soldiers, in a mixed civil and military character, they associated with all classes of the community; and alike by their courage and their integrity they sustained the high character of the nation they represented. One common spirit of humanity seemed to animate the Governor-General, the Resident, and his Assistants. A well-aimed blow was struck at infanticide, at Suttee, and at the odious traffic in female slaves. In the agricultural districts, a system of enforced labour, which had pressed heavily on the ryots, was soon also in course of abolition. The weak were everywhere protected against the strong. An

entire revision of the judicial and revenue systems of 1847.
the country—if systems they can be called, where system there was none—was attempted, and with good success. New customs rules were prepared, by which the people were greatly gainers. Every legitimate means of increasing the revenue, and of controlling unnecessary expenditure, were resorted to, and large savings were effected at no loss of efficiency in any department of the State. The cultivators were encouraged to sink wells, to irrigate their lands, and otherwise to increase the productiveness of the soil, alike to their own advantage and the profit of the State. And whilst everything was thus being done to advance the general prosperity of the people, and to ensure the popularity of British occupation among the industrial classes, the Army was propitiated by the introduction of new and improved systems of pay and pension, and taught to believe that what they had lost in opportunities of plunder, and in irregular largesses, had been more than made up to them by certainty and punctuality of payment, and the interest taken by the British officers in the general welfare of their class.

As the year advanced, these favourable appearances rather improved than deteriorated. In June, the Resident reported that a large majority of the disbanded soldiers had returned to the plough or to trade, and that the advantages of British influence to the cultivating classes were every day becoming more apparent. But still Lawrence clearly discerned the fact that although the spirit of insurrection was at rest in the Punjab, it was not yet dead. There were sparks flying about here and there, which, alighting on combustible materials, might speedily excite a blaze. "If every Sirdar and Sikh in the Punjab," he

1847. wrote, with the candour and good sense which are so conspicuous in all his communications, "were to avow himself satisfied with the humbled position of his country, it would be the extreme of infatuation to believe him, or to doubt for a moment that among the crowd who are loudest in our praise there are many who cannot forgive our victory, or even our forbearance, and who chafe at their own loss of power in exact proportion as they submit to ours." People were not wanting even then, in our camp, to talk with ominous head-shakings of the "Caubul Catastrophe," and to predict all sorts of massacres and misfortunes. But there was no parallel to be drawn between the two cases, for an overweening sense of security had not taken possession of the British functionaries at Lahore. They had not brought themselves to believe that the country was "settled," or that British occupation was "popular" among the chiefs and people of the Punjab. With God's blessing they were doing their best to deserve success, but they knew well that they might some day see the ruin of their hopes, the failure of their experiments, and they were prepared, in the midst of prosperity, at any hour to confront disaster.

Even then, fair as was the prospect before us, there was one great blot upon the landscape; for whilst the restless nature of the Queen-Mother was solacing itself with dark intrigues, there was a continual source of disquietude to disturb the mind of the Resident with apprehensions of probable outbreaks and seditions. She hated the British with a deadly hatred. They had deprived her of power. They had torn her lover from her arms. They were training her son to become a puppet in their hands. To foment hostility against them, wheresoever there seemed to be any hope of successful revolt, and to devise a plot for the murder of the Resident, were among the cherished objects by which she sought to gratify her malice. But she could not thus labour in secret. Her schemes were detected, and it was determined to remove her from Lahore. The place of banishment was Sheikopoor, in a quiet part of the country, and in the midst of a Mussulman population. When the decision was communicated to her by her brother, she received it with apparent indifference. She was not one to give her enemies an advantage by confessing her wounds and bewailing her lot. She uttered no cry of pain, but said that she was ready for anything, and at once prepared for the journey. 1847.

The autumn passed quietly away. But an important change was impending. Lord Hardinge was about to lay down the reins of government, and Colonel Lawrence to leave the Punjab for a time. The health of the latter had long been failing. He had tried in August and September the effect of the bracing hill air of Simlah. It had revived him for a while, but his medical attendants urged him to resort to the only remedy which could arrest the progress of disease; and so, with extreme reluctance, he consented to quit his post, and to accompany Lord Hardinge to England. He went; and Sir Frederick Currie, a public servant of approved talent and integrity, who, in the capacity of Political Secretary, had accompanied the Governor-General to the banks of the Sutlej, and who had been subsequently created a baronet and appointed a member of the Supreme Council of India, was nominated to act as Resident in his place.

Meeting the stream of European revolution as they journeyed homewards, Hardinge and Lawrence came

1848. overland to England in the early spring of 1848. Brief space is allowed to me for comment; but before I cease to write Lord Hardinge's name in connexion with Sikh politics and history, I must give expression, if only in a single sentence, to the admiration with which I regard his entire policy towards the Punjab. It was worthy of a Christian warrior: it was worthy of a Christian statesman. It is in no wise to be judged by results, still less by accidents not assignable to errors inherent in the original design. What Hardinge did, he did because it was right to do it. His forbearance under provocation, his moderation in the hour of victory foreshadowed the humanity of his subsequent measures. It was his one desire to render British connexion with the Punjab a blessing to the Sikhs, without destroying their national independence. The spirit of Christian philanthropy moved at his bidding over the whole face of the country—not the mere image of a specious benevolence disguising the designs of our ambition and the impulses of our greed, but an honest, hearty desire to do good without gain, to save an Empire, to reform a people, and to leave behind us the marks of a hand at once gentle and powerful—gentle to cherish and powerful only to sustain.

Conquest of the Punjab. The portfolio of the Indian Government now passed into the hands of Lord Dalhousie, a young statesman of high promise, who, in the divisions of party politics at home, had been ranged among the followers of Sir Robert Peel, and professed the newly-developed liberalism of that great parliamentary chief. Held in esteem as a man of moderate views, of considerable administrative ability, and more than common assi-

duty in the public service, his brief career as an 1848.
English statesman seemed to afford good hope that, in the great descriptive roll of Indian Viceroys, his name would be recorded as that of a ruler distinguished rather for the utility than for the brilliancy of his administration. And so, doubtless, it seemed to himself. What India most wanted at that time was Peace. Left to her repose, even without external aid, she might soon have recovered from the effects of a succession of wasting wars. But, cherished and fostered by an unambitious and enlightened ruler, there was good prospect of a future of unexampled prosperity—of great material and moral advancement—of that oft-promised, ever realisable, but still unrealised blessing, the "development of the resources of the country." The country wanted Railroads, and the people Education, and there was good hope that Dalhousie would give them both.

When he looked beyond the frontier he saw that everything was quiet. The new year had dawned auspiciously on the Punjab. The attention of the British functionaries, ever earnest and active in well-doing—for the disciples of Henry Lawrence had caught much of the zealous humanity of their master—was mainly directed to the settlement of the Land Revenue and the improvement of the judicial system of the country. They had begun codifying in good earnest, and laws, civil and criminal, grew apace under their hands. In a state of things so satisfactory as this there was little to call for special remark, and the Governor-General, in his letters to the Home Government, contented himself with the simple observation, that he "forwarded papers relating to the Punjab." But early in May intelligence had reached Calcutta which impelled him to indite a more stirring

1848. epistle. The Punjab was on the eve of another crisis.

In September, 1844, Sawun Mull, the able and energetic Governor* of Mooltan, was shot to death by an assassin. He was succeeded by his son Moolraj, who also had earned for himself the reputation of a chief with just and enlightened views of government, and considerable administrative ability. But he had also a reputation very dangerous in that country: he was reputed to be very rich. Sawun Mull was believed to have amassed immense treasures in Mooltan; and on the instalment of his son in the government, the Lahore Durbar demanded from him a succession-duty† of a million of money. The exorbitant claim was not complied with; but a compromise was effected, by which Moolraj became bound to pay to Lahore less than a fifth of the required amount. And this sum would have been paid, but for the convulsions which soon began to rend the country, and the disasters which befel the Durbar.

On the re-establishment of the Sikh Government the claim was renewed. It was intimated to the Dewan that if the stipulated eighteen lakhs, with certain amounts due for arrears, were paid into the Lahore Treasury, he would be allowed to continue in charge of Mooltan; but that if he demurred, troops would be sent to coerce him. He refused payment of the money, and troops were accordingly sent against him. Thus threatened, he besought the British Government to interfere in his favour, and consented to adjust the matter through the arbitration of the Resident. The result was, that he went to Lahore in the

* I have used the word most intelligible to ordinary English readers, but it does not fitly represent the office held by the "Dewan," who was financial manager or revenue-farmer of the district, with the control of the internal administration.

† Nuzzurana.

autumn of 1846; promised to pay by instalments the money claimed; and was mulcted in a portion of the territories from which he had drawn his revenue. The remainder was farmed out to him for a term of three years. With this arrangement he appeared to be satisfied. He was anxious to obtain the guarantee of the British Government; but his request was refused, and he returned to Mooltan without it. 1848.

For the space of more than a year, Moolraj remained in peaceful occupation of the country which had been leased out to him. There was no attempt, on the part of the British functionaries, to interfere with the affairs of Mooltan. That territory was especially exempted from the operation of the revenue settlement, which had taken effect elsewhere, and of the new customs regulations which had been established in other parts of the Punjab. But the compact which had been entered into with the Lahore Durbar did not sit easily upon him. He thought, or affected to think, that its terms were too rigorous; and accordingly, about the close of 1847, he repaired to the capital to seek some remission of them. He soon began intriguing with the Durbar for the reduction of the stipulated rents; and not coming to any satisfactory arrangement, intimated his wish to resign a charge which he had found so little profitable. He was told that his resignation, when formally tendered, would be accepted; but was recommended to reflect upon the subject before finally coming to a determination, which could not be subsequently revoked. Moolraj quitted Lahore; and sent in first a somewhat vague, and afterwards a more distinct, resignation of his office; and the Durbar at once appointed a successor. Sirdar Kan Singh, who was described as "a brave soldier and intelligent man," was nominated to

1848. the Governorship of Mooltan, on a fixed annual salary. At the same time, Mr. Vans Agnew, a civil servant of the Company, and Lieutenant Anderson, of the Bombay army, were despatched to Mooltan with the new Governor, and an escort of five hundred men, to receive charge of the place. On their arrival before the city there were no symptoms of any hostile intentions on the part of its occupants. Moolraj himself waited on the British officers on the 18th of April, and was peremptorily called upon to give in his accounts. Disconcerted and annoyed, he quitted their presence, but next morning he met them with a calm aspect, and conducted them through the fort. Two companies of Goorkhas and some horsemen of the escort were placed in possession of one of the fort-gates. The crisis was now at hand. Moolraj formally gave over charge of the fort; and as the party retired through the gate, the British officers were suddenly attacked and severely wounded. Moolraj, who was riding with them at the time, offered no assistance, but, setting spurs to his horse, galloped off in the direction of his garden-house, whilst the wounded officers were carried to their own camp by Kan Singh and a party of the Goorkhas.

In the course of the following day all the Mooltanee troops were in a state of open insurrection. Moolraj himself, who may not have been guilty in the first instance of an act of premeditated treachery, and who subsequently pleaded that he was coerced by his troops, sent excuses to Vans Agnew, who, with the generous confidence of youth, acquitted him of all participation in the outrage. But he was soon heart and soul in the work; and his emissaries plied their trade of corruption with unerring effect. Before nightfall, the commandant of the escort, with all his men, went over to the enemy. The building in which the wounded officers lay was surrounded. A motley crew of ruffians—soldiers and citizens—men of all classes, young and old, moved by one common impulse, one great thirst of blood, came yelling and shouting around the abode of the doomed Feringhees. In they rushed, with a savage cry, and surrounded their victims. The wounded officers lay armed on their beds, and helpless, hopeless as they were, put on the bold front of intrepid Englishmen, and were heroes to the last. Having shaken hands, and bade each other a last farewell, they turned upon their assailants as best they could; but overpowered by numbers, they fell, declaring in the prophetic language of death, that thousands of their countrymen would come to avenge them. The slaughter thoroughly accomplished, the two bodies were dragged out of the mosque, and barbarously mutilated by the murderers, with every indignity that malice could devise. 1848.

Irretrievably committed in the eyes both of our countrymen and his own, Moolraj now saw that there was no going back; he had entered, whether designedly or not, on a course which admitted of no pause, and left no time for reflection. All the dormant energies of his nature were now called into full activity. He took command of the insurgents—identified himself with their cause—bestowed largesses upon the men who had been most active in the assault upon the British officers, retained all who would take service with him, laid in stores, collected money, and addressed letters to other chiefs urging them to resistance. He had never been looked upon by others—never regarded himself—as a man to become the leader of a great national movement; but now circumstances

1848. had done for him what he would never willingly have shaped out for himself; so he bowed to fate, and became a hero.

Thus was the second Sikh War commenced. Outwardly, it was but the revolt of a local government—the rebellion of an officer of the Sikh State against the sovereign power of the land. But, rightly considered, it was of far deeper significance. Whether Moolraj had been incited to resistance by the promptings of a spirit far more bitter in its resentments, and more active in its malignity than his own, is not very apparent. But it is certain that when he raised the standard of rebellion at Mooltan, he did but anticipate a movement for which the whole country was ripe. Already had ominous reports of ill-concealed disaffection come in from some of the outlying districts, and though the mortifying fact was very reluctantly believed, it is certain that the state of things which Henry Lawrence had predicted was already a present reality, and that the Sikhs, chafing under the irritating interference of the European stranger, were about to make a common effort to expel him. A finer body of officers than those employed under the British Resident in the Punjab seldom laboured for the good of a people. That they worked, earnestly and assiduously, animated by the purest spirit of Christian benevolence, is not to be doubted. But it was not in the nature of things that even if the thing done had been palatable to the Sikhs, they would have reconciled themselves to the doers of it. Habituated to rule in all parts of the world, and to interfere in the affairs of people of all colours and creeds, Englishmen are slow to familiarise themselves with the idea of the too probable unpopularity of their interference. They think that if they mean well they must secure confidence. They do not consider that our beneficent ways may not be more in accordance with the national taste than our round hats and stiff neckcloths; and that even if they were, alien interference must in itself be utterly distasteful to them. It is not to be doubted, I say, that the young Englishmen first employed in the Punjab laboured earnestly for the good of the people; but their very presence was a sore in the flesh of the nation, and if they had been endowed with superhuman wisdom and angelic benevolence, it would have made no difference in the sum total of popular discontent. 1848.

But it is probable that some mistakes were committed—the inevitable growth of benevolent ignorance and energetic inexperience—at the outset of our career as Punjabee administrators. The interference appears to have been greater than was contemplated in the original design of the Second Protectorate. At that time the God Terminus was held by many of our administrators in especial veneration. The Theodolite, the Reconnoitring Compass, and the Measuring Chain were the great emblems of British rule. And now these mysterious instruments began to make their appearance in the Punjab. We were taking sights and measuring angles on the outskirts of civilisation; and neither the chiefs nor the people could readily persuade themselves that we were doing all this for their good; there was an appearance in it of ulterior design. And, as I have hinted, the agents employed were sometimes wholly inexperienced in business of this kind. "My present *rôle*," wrote a young ensign* of two years' standing in the service, whose later exploits will be recorded in these pages, "is to survey a part

* W. R. Hodson ("Hodson of Hodson's Horse"), January, 1848. This young officer narrowly escaped the fate of Anderson at Mooltan, for he had been selected in the first instance to accompany Vans Agnew.

1848. of the country lying along the left bank of the Ravee and below the hills, and I am daily and all day at work with compasses and chain, pen and pencil, following streams, diving into valleys, burrowing into hills, to complete my work. I need hardly remark, that having never attempted anything of the kind, it is bothering at first. I should not be surprised any day to be told to build a ship, compose a code of laws, or hold assizes. In fact, 'tis the way in India; every one has to teach himself his work, and to do it at the same time." Training of this kind has made the finest race of officers that the world has ever seen. But the novitiate of these men may have teemed with blunders fatal to the people among whom they were sent, in all the self-confidence of youth, to learn their diversities of work. As they advance in years, and every year know better how difficult a thing it is to administer the affairs of a foreign people, such public servants often shudder to think of the errors committed, of the wrong done, when they served their apprenticeship in government without a master, and taught themselves at the expense of thousands. The most experienced administrators in the present case might have failed from the want of a right understanding of the temper of the people. But it was the necessity of our position that some who were set over the officers of the Sikh Government knew little of the people and little of administration. They were able, indefatigable, and conscientious. They erred only because they saw too much and did too much, and had not come to understand the wise policy of shutting their eyes and leaving alone.

And so, although the rebellion of Moolraj was at first only a local outbreak, and the British authorities were well disposed to regard it as a movement against the Sikh Government, not as an outrage especially directed against ourselves, that fiction could not be long maintained—for every day it became more and more apparent that the whole country was ripe for another war with the intruding Feringhee. The Durbar officers did not hesitate to express their conviction that to send Sikh troops to act against Moolraj would only be to swell the number of his adherents. To have despatched with them a small English force would have been to risk its safety and precipitate the conflict. An overwhelming display of force, on the part of the British Government, might have crushed the rebellion at Mooltan and retarded the general rising of the country. But the season was far advanced; the responsibility was a great one. The Commander-in-Chief of the British army in India was not far distant. Currie, therefore, though his own judgment inclined to the commencement of immediate hostilities, rightly referred the momentous question to the military chief. Lord Gough was against immediate action; and the head of the Indian Government unreservedly endorsed the decision. 1848.

The remnant of the old Khalsa army eagerly watched the result, and were not slow to attribute our inactivity, at such a moment, to hesitation—to fear—to paralysis. I am not writing a military history of the Second Sikh War, and the question now suggested is one which I am not called upon to discuss. But I think that promptitude of action is often of more importance than completeness of preparation, and that to show ourselves confident of success is in most cases to attain it. The British power in India cannot afford to be quiescent under insult and outrage. Delay is held to be a sign of weakness. It encourages enmity and confirms vacillation. It is a disaster in

1848. itself—more serious, often, than any that can arise from insufficient preparation, and that great bugbear the inclemency of the season. On the other hand, it is not to be forgotten that to despise our enemies is a common national mistake, and that sometimes it has been a fatal one. We have brought calamities on ourselves by our rashness, as we have by our indecision. The History of India teems with examples of both results; the most profitable lesson to be learnt from which is, that, however wise we may be after the event, criticism in such a case ought to be diffident and forbearing.

But whilst the Commander-in-Chief, in the cool mountain air of Simlah, was deciding on the impossibility of commencing military operations, a young lieutenant of the Bengal army, who had been engaged in the Revenue settlement of the country about Bunnoo, was marching down upon Mooltan with a small body of troops, to render assistance to his brother-officers in their perilous position, and to support the authority of the Lahore Durbar. A letter from Vans Agnew, dictated by the wounded man, had providentially fallen into his hands. He saw at once the emergency of the case; he never hesitated; but abandoning all other considerations, improvised the best force that could be got together, and, with fifteen hundred men and two pieces of artillery, marched forth in all the eager confidence of youth, hoping that it might be his privilege to rescue his countrymen from the danger that beset them.

The name of this young officer was Herbert Edwardes. A native of Frodley, in Shropshire, the son of a country clergyman, educated at King's College, London, he had entered the Company's service as a cadet of infantry, at an age somewhat more advanced

than that which sees the initiation into military life 1848.
of the majority of young officers. But at an age much earlier than that which commonly places them in possession of the most superficial knowledge of the history and politics of the East, young Edwardes had acquired a stock of information, and a capacity for judging rightly of passing events, which would have done no discredit to a veteran soldier and diplomatist. He had served but a few years, when his name became familiar to English readers throughout the Presidency to which he belonged, as one of the ablest anonymous writers in the country. His literary talents, like his military qualities, were of a bold, earnest, impulsive character. Whatever he did, he did rapidly and well. He was precisely the kind of man to attract the attention and retain the favour of such an officer as Henry Lawrence, who, with the same quiet love of literature, combined a keen appreciation of that energy and fire of character which shrink from no responsibility, and are ever seeking to find an outlet in dashing exploits. In one of the earliest and most striking scenes of the Punjabee drama, Edwardes had acted a distinguished part. When the insurrection broke out in Cashmere, he was despatched to Jummoo, to awaken Gholab Singh to a sense of his duty in that conjuncture; and there are few more memorable and impressive incidents in Sikh history than that which exhibited a handful of British officers controlling the movements of large bodies of foreign troops,—the very men, and under the very leaders, who, so short a time before, had contested with us on the banks of the Sutlej the sovereignty of Hindostan.

On the reconstruction of the Sikh Government, after the deposition of Lal Singh, Herbert Edwardes

1848. was one of the officers selected to superintend the internal administration of the country; and he had just completed the Revenue settlement of Bunnoo, when the startling intelligence of the Mooltanee outbreak reached his camp. He marched at once to succour his brother-officers; crossed the Indus, and took possession of Leia, the chief city in the Sindh Saugor Doab. But tidings by this time had reached him of the melancholy fate of Agnew and Anderson, and there was then no profit in the immediate movement on Mooltan to compensate for its certain danger. But the demonstration still had its uses. It was something that there was a force in the field with a British officer at the head of it to assert the cause of order and authority in the name of the Maharajah of the Punjab. Such a force might, for a time at least, hold rebellion in check in that part of the country. But Edwardes dreamt of higher service than this. To the south of Mooltan, some fifty miles, lies Bahwulpore, in the chief of which place we believed that we had a staunch ally. In the name of the British Government, Edwardes called upon him to move an auxiliary force upon Mooltan; and he had little doubt that, after forming a junction with these troops, he could capture the rebel stronghold. The confidence of the young soldier, stimulated by a victory which he gained over a large body of rebels on the great anniversary of Waterloo, saw no obstacle to this enterprise which could not be overcome if the Resident would only send him a few heavy guns and mortars, and Major Napier, of the Engineers, to direct the operations of the siege. He knew the worth of such a man in such a conjuncture, and every year that has since passed has made him prouder of the youthful forecast which he then evinced.

The Bahwulpore troops were sent, the junction was formed, and the forces marched down upon Mooltan. Placing himself at the head of a considerable body of men, the rebel chief went out to give them battle, but was beaten by Edwardes, aided by Van Cortlandt, a European officer in Sikh employ, who has since done good service to the British Government, and Edward Lake, a gallant young officer of Bengal Engineers, directing the Bahwulpore column, who has abundantly fulfilled, on the same theatre of action, the high promise of his youth. But much as irregular levies, so led, might do in the open field, they were powerless against the walls of Mooltan. Again, therefore, Edwardes urged upon the Resident the expediency of strengthening his hands, especially in respect of the ordnance branches of the service. Only send a siege train, some Sappers and Miners, with Robert Napier to direct the siege, and—this time, for the difficulties of the work had assumed larger proportions in his eyes—a few regular regiments, under a young brigadier, and we shall "close," he said, "Moolraj's accounts in a fortnight, and obviate the necessity of assembling fifty thousand men in October." 1848.

In the early part of July this requisition was received at Lahore. The interval which had elapsed, since the disastrous tidings of the rebellion of Moolraj had reached the Residency, had not been an uneventful one at the capital. Early in May, discovery was made of an attempt to corrupt the fidelity of our British Sepoys. The first intimation of the plot was received from some troopers of the 7th Irregular Cavalry, who communicated the circumstance to their commanding officer. The principal conspirators were one Kan Singh, an unemployed general of the Sikh army, and Gunga Ram, the confidential Vakeel of the

1848. Maharanee. These men, and two others, were seized, tried, and convicted. The two chief conspirators were publicly hanged, and their less guilty associates transported. That they were instruments of the Maharanee was sufficiently proved. The conspirators acknowledged that she was the prime instigator of the treacherous attempt, and her letters were found in their possession. With this knowledge, it could no longer be a question with the Resident as to what course it behoved him to adopt. The mother of the Maharajah and the widow of Runjeet Singh could no longer be suffered to dwell among the Sikhs. She had already been removed from Lahore to Sheikopoor. It now became necessary to remove her from the Punjab. Accordingly, certain accredited agents of the Lahore Durbar, accompanied by two British officers, Captain Lumsden and Lieutenant Hodson, were despatched to Sheikopoor, with a mandate under the seal of the Maharajah, directing her removal from that place. Without offering any resistance, or expressing any dissatisfaction, she placed herself under the charge of the deputation; and, when it became clear to her that she was on her way to the British frontier, she desired—not improbably with that blended irony and bravado which she so well knew how to employ—that her thanks might be conveyed to the Resident for removing her to the Company's dominions, out of the reach of the enemies who would destroy her. With a considerable retinue of female attendants, she was conveyed to Ferozepore, and eventually to Benares, where she was placed under the charge of Major George Macgregor, an Artillery officer of high personal character and great diplomatic experience, who had well sustained in the Punjab the brilliant reputation which he had earned at Jellalabad.

Such was the apparent growth visible at the British Residency, recognised in our State-papers, of those three months in the Punjab. But in the hands of a Sikh historian these incidents would form but a small part of the national annals, for all over the country the great chiefs were actively maturing the plan of their emancipation, calling upon all true Sikhs, in the name of the great Founder of their Faith, to exterminate the Christian usurpers, and even those nearest to the throne were among the arch-promoters of the movement. The daughter of Chuttur Singh and the sister of Shere Singh was the betrothed wife of the Maharajah; but these Sirdars, though anxious to veil their designs until the whole country was ripe for a simultaneous rising, were intriguing and plotting for our overthrow. The former was in the Hazareh, where his fidelity had been for some time suspected by James Abbott—another officer of the Bengal Artillery, friend and comrade, of Henry Lawrence, who had been settling that part of the country—one of those men whose lot in life it is never to be believed, never to be appreciated, never to be rewarded; of the true salt of the earth, but of an unrecognised savour; chivalrous, heroic, but somehow or other never thoroughly emerging from the shade. He was not one to estimate highly the force of the maxim that "speech is silver, silence is gold;" and his suspicions are said not to have been acceptable at Lahore. But though it may be good to suspect, it is doubtless good, also, not to appear to suspect. And if Currie, in that conjuncture, had betrayed a want of confidence in the Sikh Sirdars, he would have precipitated the collision which it was sound policy to retard. So, whatever may have been his genuine convictions, he 1848.

1848. still appeared to trust the chiefs of the Regency; and Shere Singh, with a strong body of Sikh troops, was sent down to Mooltan. It was wise to maintain, as long as possible, the semblance of the authority of the Sikh Durbar—wise to keep up the show of suppressing a rebellion by the hand of the native Government. To send down that undeveloped traitor to the great centre of revolt may have been a hazardous experiment, but it was hazardous also to keep him where he was; and the master-passion of the Sikh soldiery for plunder might have kept his battalions nominally on the side of authority, until they had glutted themselves with the spoils of Mooltan, and preparations had, meanwhile, been made in the British provinces for the commencement of military operations on a scale befitting the occasion. But the repeated requisitions of Edwardes for British aid at last wrought upon the Resident, and Currie determined to send a force to Mooltan, with a siege-train for the reduction of the fortress. In General Samson Whish, of the Artillery, under whose command the force was despatched, there was not literally what Edwardes had asked for—"a young brigadier"—but there was a general officer of unwonted youthfulness of aspect and activity of body, who could sit a horse well, could ride any distance at a stretch, and was generally esteemed to be one of the best artillery officers in the service. This forward movement was not countenanced in high places. The Commander-in-Chief shook his head. The Governor-General shook his head. But the Resident had ordered it, and it could not be countermanded, without encouraging a belief that there was a want of unanimity in British councils.

So the besieging force marched upon Mooltan, and

arrived before the city in high health and excellent spirits. On the 5th of September, in the name of the Maharajah and Queen Victoria, the British General summoned the garrison to surrender. No answer was returned to the summons, and the siege commenced. But on the 14th, when our guns were within breaching distance of the walls of the town, Whish, to his bitter mortification, was compelled to abandon the siege. The Sikh force under Shere Singh had gone over to the enemy. 1848.

This event had long been matter of anxious speculation in the British camp, and now took no one by surprise. It was known that the hearts of the soldiery were with Moolraj; but there was something of a more doubtful character in the conduct of the Rajah himself, who had on more than one occasion testified his zeal and loyalty by voluntary acts of service in our cause. In his own camp, the Khalsa troops said contemptuously, that he was a Mussulman. With Edwardes he was outwardly on the best possible terms; spoke freely of the conduct of his father, Chuttur Singh; declared that he washed his hands of all the old man's rebellious projects; and candidly avowed his mistrust of the Sikh troops. But in all this he was playing a part. He had written to his brother to say that he intended to go over to the enemy on that very 14th of September, and he kept his word to the letter. On the morning of that day, the whole Durbar force sought entrance into the city. Doubtful of the real nature of the movement, Moolraj at first refused them admittance; but soon satisfied of their intentions, he opened his gates; the long dreaded and fatal junction was effected; and the British General was under the mortifying necessity of raising the siege of Mooltan.

1848. The whole truth was now visible before the world. It was impossible any longer to maintain the fiction of a local rebellion, to pretend that the Lahore Government, assisted by British troops, was endeavouring to coerce a refractory subject. The very heads of that Government were in open hostility to the British, raising the standard of nationality in the name of the Maharajah. It was obvious that the war now about to be waged, was between the British and the Sikhs. Some hope was at one time to be drawn from the fact of long-standing feuds among the different Sikh families. Then there was the not unreasonable conviction that the Mahomedan population of the Punjab might easily be kept in a state of enmity with the Sikhs. But these assurances soon melted away. Hostile families and hostile religions were content to unite for the nonce against the Feringhees; and the Commander-in-Chief, as the cold weather approached, was gratified by finding that there had been no premature birth of victory—that the work was yet to be done—and that an army of twenty thousand men, under his personal command, was required to take the field.

And from that time Mooltan ceased to be the focus of rebellion and the head-quarters of the war. In the Hazareh country Chuttur Singh had thrown off all vestments of disguise, and plunged boldly into the troubled waters that lay before him. The thoughts of Shere Singh soon began to turn towards that quarter—indeed, such had been his desire from the first—and before the second week of October had passed away, he had marched out of Mooltan to join his father. The whole country was now rising against us. Having used the name of the Maharajah, the Sikh leaders were eager to possess themselves of

the person of the boy-King, and but for the vigilance 1848.
of the Resident they would have achieved an object which would have added a new element of strength to the national cause. Duleep Singh remained in our hands virtually a prisoner at Lahore.

All this time the Governor-General was at Calcutta, watching from a distance the progress of events, and betraying no eagerness to seize a favourable opportunity for the conquest of the Punjab. Indeed, it has been imputed to him, as a grave political error, that he did not at an earlier period make due preparation for the inevitable war. But, it would seem that in the summer of 1848, his desire was to recognise as long as possible only internal rebellion in the Sikh country—to see, not the rising of a nation against a foreign intruder, but the revolt of a few unloyal chiefs against their own lawful sovereign. But with the first breath of the cool season there came a truer conception of the crisis, and Lord Dalhousie prepared himself for the conflict. "I have wished for peace," he said, at a public entertainment, early in October; "I have longed for it; I have striven for it But if the enemies of India determine to have war, war they shall have, and on my word they shall have it with a vengeance." A few days afterwards he turned his back upon Calcutta, and set his face towards the north-west. All the energies of his mind were then given to the prosecution of the war.

The British army destined for the re-conquest of the Punjab assembled at Ferozepore, and crossed the Sutlej in different detachments. On the 13th of November the head-quarters reached Lahore. At that time it could hardly be said that British influence extended a rood beyond the Residency walls. In all parts of the country the Sikhs had risen against

1848. the great reproach of the English Occupation. In many outlying places, on the confines of civilisation, our English officers were holding out, in the face of every conceivable difficulty and danger, with constancy and resolution most chivalrous, most heroic, hoping only to maintain, by their own personal gallantry, the character of the nation they represented. There was, indeed, nothing more to be done. We had ceased to be regarded as allies. So eager and so general was the desire to expel the intruding Feringhee, that the followers of Govind sank for a time all feelings of national and religious animosity against their Afghan neighbours, and invoked Mahomedan aid from the regions beyond the passes of the Khyber.

On the 21st of November, Lord Gough joined the army on the left bank of the Sutlej. A veteran commander, who within the space of a few years had fought more battles in different parts of the world than were crowded into the lives of most living warriors—a general whose uniform good fortune had glossed over his want of forecast and science, and whose repeated successes had silenced criticism—he was now about to engage in military operations greater than those of his antecedent campaigns, with, perhaps, even less knowledge of the country and less consideration of the probable contingencies of the war. But all men had confidence in him. India had been won by a series of military mistakes that would have disgraced an ensign before the examination period, and, perhaps, would not have been won at all if we had infused into our operations more of the pedantry of military science. He was a soldier, and all who fought under him honoured his grey hairs, and loved him for his manly bearing, his fine frank character, and

even for the impetuosity which so often entangled 1848.
his legions in difficulties, and enhanced the cost of the victories he gained.

The arrival of the Commander-in-Chief was the signal for the immediate commencement of hostilities. The force then under his personal command consisted of upwards of twenty thousand men, with nearly a hundred pieces of artillery, and Gough was in no temper for delay. On the day after his arrival in camp was fought the battle of Ramnuggur, the first of those disastrous successes which have given so gloomy a character to the campaign. The enemy had a strong masked battery on the other side of the river, and very cleverly contrived to draw the British troops into an ambuscade. The operations of the Commander-in-Chief, commenced with the object of driving a party of the rebels, who were on his side of the Chenab, across the river, had the effect of bringing his cavalry and artillery within reach of these concealed guns; and twenty-eight pieces of ordnance opened upon our advancing columns. The cavalry were ordered to move forward to the attack as soon as an opportunity presented itself. They found an opportunity, and charged a large body of the enemy, the Sikh batteries pouring in their deadly showers all the while. Many fell under the fire of the guns, many under the sabre-cuts of the Sikh swordsmen, many under the withering fire of a body of matchlockmen, who, taking advantage of the nature of the ground, harassed our horsemen sorely. Nothing was gained by our "victory;" but we lost many brave and some good soldiers; and our troops returned to camp weary and dispirited, asking what end they had accomplished, and sighing over the cost.

Some days afterwards a force under General Thack-

1848. well was sent out to cross the river, but being scantily supplied with information, and grievously hampered by instructions, it succeeded only in losing a few men and killing several of the enemy. No great object was gained, but great opportunities were sacrificed. The Commander-in-Chief pompously declared that "it had pleased Almighty God to vouchsafe to the British arms the most successful issue to the extensive combinations rendered necessary for the purpose of effecting the passage of the Chenab, the defeat and dispersion of the Sikh force under the insurgent Rajah Shere Singh and the numerous Sikh Sirdars who had the temerity to set at defiance the British power." These "events, so fraught with importance," were to "tend to most momentous results." The results were, that the field of battle was shifted from the banks of the Chenab to the banks of the Jhelum. The enemy, who might have been taken in rear, and whose batteries might have been seized, if Thackwell had been free to carry out the most obvious tactics, escaped with all their guns; and on the 13th of January bore bloody witness to the little they had suffered, by fighting one of the greatest and most sanguinary battles in the whole chronicle of Indian warfare.

By this time Henry Lawrence had returned to the Punjab. The news of the outbreak at Mooltan had reached him in England, whilst still in broken health, and had raised within him an incontrollable desire, at any hazard, to return to his post. He had won his spurs, and he was eager to prove that he was worthy of them, even at the risk of life itself. It has been said that he ought not to have quitted the Punjab, and that if he had been at Lahore in the spring of 1848, the war would not then have been precipitated by the rebellion of Moolraj, for "any one but a civilian would have foreseen that to send Vans Agnew and Anderson down to Mooltan at the time and in the manner selected was almost sure to produce an ebullition of feeling and violence." But if Lawrence had not gone to England at that time, he would, in all human probability, have died; and though he might not have sent the same men to Mooltan, he would have sent a mission there for the same purpose. "I meant to have sent Arthur Cocks," was his remark to the present writer, when the disastrous news reached us in London. He saw at once that the Mooltanee revolt was but the prelude to a great national outbreak, and though his friends trembled for his safety and counselled delay, his strong sense of duty to the State overruled all personal considerations, and so he carried back his shattered frame and his inexhaustible energies to the scene of the coming conflict. Leaving London at the end of October, he reached Bombay early in December, and pushing up the Indus with characteristic rapidity of movement, joined the camp of General Whish, before the walls of Mooltan, two days after the great festival of Christmas. 1848. Calcutta Review.

On the second day of the new year, Whish, reinforced from Bombay, carried the city of Mooltan. Long and obstinate had been the resistance of the besieged; and now that our storming columns entered the breach, the garrison still, at the bayonet's point, showed the stuff of which they were made. Frightful had been the carnage during the siege. Heaps of mangled bodies about the battered town bore ghastly witness to the terrible effects of the British ordnance. But many yet stood to be shot down or bayoneted in the streets; and the work of the besieging force was 1849.

1849. yet far from its close. Moolraj was in the citadel with some thousands of his best fighting-men; and the fort guns were plied as vigorously as before the capture of the town. The strength of this formidable fortress seemed to laugh our breaching batteries to scorn. Mining operations were, therefore, commenced; but carried on as they were, beneath a constant discharge from our mortars, it seemed little likely that the enemy would wait to test the skill of the engineers. The terrible shelling to which the fortress was exposed dismayed the pent-up garrison. By the 21st of January they were reduced to the last extremity. Moolraj vainly endeavoured to rally his followers. Their spirit was broken. There was nothing left for them but to make a desperate sally and cut their way through the besiegers, or to surrender at once. The nobler alternative was rejected. Asking only for his own life and the honour of his women, Moolraj tendered on that day his submission to the British General. Whish refused to guarantee the first, but promised to protect the women; and on the following morning the garrison marched out of Mooltan, and Dewan Moolraj threw himself upon the mercy of the British Government.

Meanwhile, Henry Lawrence, having witnessed the fall of the city of Mooltan, hastened upwards to Ferozepore, conveyed to Lord Dalhousie the first welcome tidings of that event, took counsel with the Governor-General, made himself master of the great man's views, then hurried on to Lahore, communicated with the Resident, and on the same evening pushed on to the camp of the Commander-in-Chief, which he reached on the night of the 10th of January. He was there in no recognised official position, for Currie's tenure of office did not expire until the beginning of the ensuing month; but he was ready for any kind of service, and he placed himself at Lord Gough's disposal, as an honorary aide-de-camp, or any other subordinate officer, in the fine army which was now stretching out before him. 1849.

Three days after Lawrence's arrival in camp the battle of Chillianwallah was fought. The time had arrived when a far less impetuous general than Gough might have deemed it incumbent on him to force the Sikh army into a general action. It is true that the final reduction of the fortress of Mooltan would have liberated a large portion of Whish's column, and greatly have added to the strength of the British army on the banks of the Jhelum. But the Sikh Sirdars, on this very account, were eager to begin the battle, and would not have suffered us to wait for our reinforcements. Gough already had a noble force under him, equal to any service. It was panting for action. There had been a lull of more than a month's duration, and all through India there was a feeling of impatience at the protracted delay. Gough, therefore, prepared for action. Ascertaining the nature of the country occupied by the Sikh army, and the position of their troops, he planned his attack upon sound tactical principles, and fully instructed his generals in the several parts which they were called upon to play. On the afternoon of the 13th everything was ready, and the battle was to have been commenced early on the following morning. But, unwilling to give the British General the long hours of the morrow's light, from daybreak to sunset, that he wanted, to fight his battle according to approved principles of modern warfare, the Sikh leaders, when the day was far spent, determined, if possible, to aggravate him into an immediate encounter. They

1849. knew their man. So they advanced a few guns, and sent some round-shot booming in the direction of the British camp. The bait took. The warm Hibernian temperament of the British leader could not brook the insult. He moved up his heavy guns, responded with some chance shots at the invisible enemy, and then, there being little of the day left for his operations, gave the command for his line to advance.

The story of what followed has been often told, and it is not so gratifying a page of history that I need care to repeat it. Night closed upon the fearful carnage of that terrible engagement, and both armies claimed the victory. What it cost us is written in the Gazette. Never was an official bulletin received in England with a wilder outcry of pain and passion. The past services, the intrepid personal courage, the open honest character, the many noble qualities of the veteran Commander were forgotten in that burst of popular indignation, and hundreds of English families turned from the angry past to the fearful future, and trembled as they thought that the crowning action with that formidable enemy had yet to be fought by a General so rash, so headstrong, and so incompetent.

In the high places of Government there was universal discomposure, and the greatest military authority in the country shook his head with an ominous gesture of reproach. Then arose a wild cry for Napier. The conqueror of the Beloochees was sent out in hot haste to India to repair the mischief that had been done by Gough, and to finish off the war with the Sikhs in a proper workmanlike manner. But the hottest haste could not wholly annihilate time and space, and though this sudden supersession of the brave old chief, who had fought so many battles and won so many victories, might shame his grey hairs, it could not bring the war to a more rapid or a more honourable close. The carnage of Chillianwallah shook for a time the confidence of the army in their chief, but it did not shake the courage of our fighting-men, or destroy their inherent capacity for conquest. It was a lesson, too, that must have scored itself into the very heart of the British chief, and made him a sadder man and a wiser commander. The errors of the 13th of January were to be atoned for by a victory which any leader might contemplate with pride, and any nation with gratitude. Scarcely had his appointed successor turned his back upon England when Gough fought another great battle, which neither Napier, nor Wellington himself, who talked of going in his place, could have surpassed in vigour of execution or completeness of effect. 1849.

Anxiously was intelligence of the surrender of Moolraj looked for in the camp of the Commander-in-Chief. Since that disastrous action at Chillianwallah, Gough had been entrenching his position, and waiting reinforcements from Mooltan. The surrender of that fortress set free some twelve thousand men, and Whish, with unlooked-for rapidity, marched to the banks of the Jhelum to swell the ranks of the grand army. A great crisis was now approaching. Thrice had the British and Sikh forces met each other on the banks of those classical rivers which had seen the triumphs of the Macedonian—thrice had they met each other only to leave the issue of the contest yet undecided. A great battle was now about to be fought—one differing from all that had yet been fought since the Sikhs first crossed the Sutlej, for a strange but not unlooked-for spectacle was about to present itself—Sikhs and Afghans, those old heredi-

1849. tary enemies, fighting side by side against a common foe. The Sikh Sirdars, I have said, had been intriguing to secure the assistance of the Ameer of Cabool. For some time there appeared little likelihood that old Dost Mahomed, whose experience ought to have brought wisdom with it, would lend himself to a cause which, in spite of temporary successes, was so sure to prove hopeless in the end. But neither years, nor experience, nor adversity had taught him to profit by the lessons he had learned. The desire of repossessing himself of Peshawur was the madness of a life. The bait was thrown out to him, and he could not resist it. He came through the Khybur with an Afghan force, marched upon the Indus, and threatened Attock, which fell at his approach; despatched one of his sons to the camp of Shere Singh, and sent a body of Douranee troops to fight against his old Feringhee enemy, who for years had been the arbiter of his fate. How deplorable an act of senile fatuity it was, the events of the 21st of February must have deeply impressed upon his mind. On that day was fought an action—was gained a victory, in the emphatic words of the Governor-General, "memorable alike from the greatness of the occasion, and from the brilliant and decisive issue of the encounter. For the first time, Sikh and Afghan were banded together against the British power. It was an occasion which demanded the putting forth of all the means at our disposal, and so conspicuous a manifestation of the superiority of our arms as should appal each enemy, and dissolve at once their compact by fatal proof of its futility. The completeness of the victory which has been won equals the highest hopes entertained." And there was no official exaggeration in this; none of the vain boasting of the interested despatch-writer. At Goojrat, to which place the enemy had unexpectedly moved their camp, Lord Gough fought a great battle as a great battle ought to be fought, coolly and deliberately, by a British Commander. Every arm of his fine force was brought effectively into play; each in its proper place, each supporting and assisting the others, and each covering itself with glory. From the early dawn of that clear bright morning the cannonade commenced. Never had the Bengal Artillery made a nobler display; never had it been worked with more terrible effect. Resolute and well handled as was the Sikh army, it could not stand up against the steady fire of our guns. By noon the enemy were retreating in terrible disorder, "their position carried, their guns, ammunition, camp equipage, and baggage captured, their flying masses driven before their victorious pursuers, from mid-day receiving most severe punishment in their flight." And all this was accomplished with but little loss of life on the side of the victorious army. It pleased the Almighty that the bloody lessons of the Chenab and the Jhelum should not be thrown away. 1849

A division under Sir Walter Gilbert, an officer of great personal activity, unequalled in the saddle, was ordered to follow up the success of Goojrat, and to drive the Afghans from the Punjab. And well did he justify the choice of his chief. By a series of rapid marches, scarcely excelled by any recorded in history, he convinced the enemy of the hopelessness of all further resistance. The Barukzye force fled before our advancing columns, and secured the passage of the Khybur before British influence could avail to close it against the fugitives. By the Sikhs themselves the game had clearly been played out. The

1849. Khalsa was now quite broken. There was nothing left for Shere Singh and his associates but to trust themselves to the clemency of the British Government. On the 5th of March, the Rajah sent the British prisoners safely into Gilbert's camp. On the 8th, he appeared in person, to make arrangements for the surrender of his followers; and on the 14th, the remnant of the Sikh army, some sixteen thousand men, including thirteen Sirdars of note, laid down their arms at the feet of the British General.

The military chief had now done his work, and it was time for the appearance of the Civil Governor on the scene. Lord Dalhousie was on the spot prepared for immediate action. Already was his portfolio weighty with a proclamation which was to determine the fate of the empire of Runjeet Singh. I do not suppose that a moment's doubt ever obscured the clear, unsullied surface of the Governor-General's resolution. It was a case which suggested no misgivings and prompted no hesitation. The Sikhs had staked everything on the issue of the war, and they had lost it in fair fight. They had repaid by acts of treachery and violence the forbearance and moderation of the British Government. We had tried to spare them; but they would not be spared. First one course, then another, had been adopted in the hope that eventually a strong native Government might be established, able to control its own subjects, and willing to live on terms of friendly alliance with its neighbours. Our policy had from the first been wholly unaggressive. There was no taint of avarice or ambition in it. But it had not been appreciated; it had not been successful. The whole system had collapsed. And now that again a British ruler was called upon to solve the great problem of the Future of the

Punjab, he felt that there was no longer any middle course open to him; that there was but one measure applicable to the crisis that had arisen; and that measure was the annexation of the country to the territories of the British Empire. So a Proclamation was issued announcing that the kingdom founded by Runjeet Singh had passed under British rule; and the wisdom and righteousness of the edict few men are disposed to question. 1849.

The last Sikh Durbar was held at Lahore. The fiat of the British conqueror was read aloud, in the presence of the young Maharajah, to the remnant of the chiefs who had not committed themselves by open rebellion; and a paper of Terms was then produced by which the British Government bound themselves to pay the annual sum of forty or fifty thousand pounds to the boy-Prince and his family,* so long as he should remain faithful to his new master and abide by his sovereign will. It was a happy change for Duleep Singh, born as he was for the Sikh shambles; for in his new state he had abundant wealth, perfect safety, freedom from all care, and the insurpassable blessing of a saving faith. Becoming, in his twelfth year, the ward of the Governor-General, he was placed under the immediate tutelage of an Assistant-Surgeon of the Bengal Army,† who was so fit a man for the office, so worthy of the confidence reposed in him, that the little Sikh Prince, under his wise ministrations, developed into a Christian gentleman, an English courtier, and a Scotch laird. And it may be recorded here, before I pass on to the history of British rule in the Punjab, that the mother March 29, 1849.

* This is not the loose diction of doubt. The agreement was, that the British Government should pay not less than four, or more than five, lakhs of rupees.

† Afterwards Sir John Login.

1849. of Duleep Singh, the widow of old Runjeet, that restless, turbulent Chund Kowr, whose intrigues did so much to precipitate the fall of the Sikh Empire, after a series of strange romantic vicissitudes, prematurely old, well-nigh blind, broken and subdued in spirit, found a resting-place at last under the roof of her
1863. son, in a quiet corner of an English castle, and died in a London suburb.

1849. Administration of the Punjab.

The Proclamation which turned the Punjab into a British province was not the only weighty State-paper in the portfolio of the Governor-General. Whilst Gough had been preparing to strike the last crushing blow at the military power of the Khalsa, Dalhousie, with Henry Elliot at his elbow, never doubting the issue, was mapping out the scheme of administration under which it seemed good to him to govern the country which was about to pass under our rule. The crowning victory of Goojrat found everything devised and prepared to the minutest detail. The men were ready; the measures were defined. There was no hurry, therefore—no confusion. Every one fell into his appointed place, and knew what he had to do. And never had any Governor better reason to place unbounded confidence in the men whom he employed; never was any Governor more worthily served.

The country which had thus fallen by right of conquest into our hands embraced an area of fifty thousand square miles, and contained a population of four millions of inhabitants. These inhabitants were Hindoos, Mahomedans, and Sikhs. The last were a new people—a sect of reformed Hindoos, of a purer faith than the followers of the Brahminical superstitions. It was a Sikh Government that we had supplanted; and mainly a Sikh army that we had conquered; but it must not be supposed that Punjabee is synonimous with Sikh, that the country was peopled from one end to the other with the followers of Nanuk and Govind, or that they were the ancient dwellers on the banks of those five legendary rivers. The cities of the Punjab were Mahomedan cities; cities founded, perhaps, ere Mahomed arose, enlarged and beautified by the followers of the Ghuznivite. The monuments were mainly Mahomedan monuments, with traces here and there of Grecian occupation and Bactrian rule. Before Delhi had risen into the imperial city of the Moguls, Lahore had been the home of Indian kings. But the rise of the Sikh power was cotemporaneous with our own, and the apostles of the new Reformation had not numbered among their converts more than a section of the people. And as was the population, so was the country itself, of a varied character. Tracts of rich cultivated lands, the corn-field and the rose-garden, alternated with the scorched plain and the sandy desert. Here, as far as the eye could reach, a dreary level of jungle and brushwood; there, a magnificent panorama, bounded by the blue ranges and the snowy peaks of the Himalayah. And ever the great rivers as they flowed suggested to the cultured mind of the English scholar thoughts of that grand old traditionary age, when Porus fought, and Alexander conquered, and Megasthenes wrote, and the home-sick Argive, on the banks of those fabulous streams, sighed for the pleasant country he had left, and rebelled against his leader and his fate. It was a country full of interest and full of opportunity; and it grew at once into the pet province of the 1849.

1849. British Viceroy, the youngest and the most hopeful of all.

That a country so situated, so circumstanced, and so peopled, should not be brought under the system of administration prevailing in our long-settled provinces was a mere matter of course. But Dalhousie had no disposition to rush into the opposite extreme of a purely military government. He had at no time of his career any class prejudices, and he did not see why soldiers and civilians should not work harmoniously together in the administrative agency of the province. He had faith in both; each in his appointed place; for there was rough soldiers' work to be done, and much also that needed the calm judgment and the tutored eye of the experienced civilian. So he called in the aid of a mixed Staff of civil and military officers, and at the head of this he placed a Board of Administration, presided over by Henry Lawrence.*

The Board was to consist of three members, with secretaries to do the pen-work of the administration, and to scatter its instructions among the subordinate functionaries of the province. It was not a controlling authority which a man of Dalhousie's stamp was likely to affect; scarcely, indeed, could he be supposed to tolerate it. But he could not set aside the great claims of Henry Lawrence, nor, indeed, could he safely dispense with his services in such a conjuncture; yet he was unwilling to trust to that honest, pure-minded, soldier-statesman the sole direction of affairs. The fact is that, with a refinement of the justice and moderation which were such conspicuous features of Henry's character, he dissented from the

* Sir Frederick Currie had by this time resumed his seat in the Supreme Council of India.

policy of annexation. He thought that another effort 1849.
might have been made to save the Sikh Empire from destruction. Out of this difficulty arose the project of the Board. It was natural that Dalhousie should have desired to associate with one thus minded some other statesman whose views were more in harmony with his own. A Board of two is, under no circumstances, a practicable institution; so a Triumvirate was established. But sentence of death was written down against it from the very hour of its birth.

The second seat at the Board was given to the President's brother, John Lawrence. An officer of the Company's Civil Service, he had achieved a high reputation as an administrator; as one of those hard-working, energetic, conscientious servants of the State, who live ever with the harness on their back, to whom labour is at once a duty and a delight, who do everything in a large unstinting way, the Ironsides of the Public Service. He had taken, in the earlier stages of his career, an active part in the Revenue Settlement of the North-Western Provinces, and had subsequently been appointed Magistrate of the great imperial city of Delhi, with its crowded, turbulent population, and its constant under-current of hostile intrigue. In this post, winning the confidence of men of all classes and all creeds, Lord Hardinge found him when, in 1845, he journeyed upwards to join the army of the Sutlej. There was an openness, a frankness about him that pleased the old soldier, and a large-hearted zeal and courage which proclaimed him a man to be employed in a post of more than common difficulty, beyond the circle of ordinary routine. So, after the campaign on the Sutlej, when the Jullindur Doab was taken in part payment of the charges of the war, John Lawrence was appointed to superintend the administration of

1849. that tract of country; and on more than one occasion, during the enforced absence of Henry from Lahore, in the first two years of the British Protectorate, he had occupied his brother's seat at the capital, and done his work with unvaried success. That there were great characteristic differences between the two Lawrences will be clearly indicated as I proceed; but in unsullied honesty and intrepid manliness, they were the counterparts of each other. Both were equally without a stain.

The third member of the Lahore Board of Administration was Mr. Charles Grenville Mansel, also a covenanted civilian, who had earned a high reputation as one of the ablest financiers in India, and who supplied much of the knowledge and experience which his colleagues most lacked. His honesty was of as fine a temper as theirs, but he was a man rather of thought than of action, and wanted the constitutional robustness of his associates in office. Perhaps his very peculiarities, rendering him, as it were, the complement of the other two, especially marked him out as the third of that remarkable triumvirate. Regarded as a whole, with reference to the time and circumstances of its creation, the Board could not have been better constituted. It did honour to the sagacity of Lord Dalhousie, and fully justified the choice of agents he had made.

The system was one of divided labour and common responsibility. On Henry Lawrence devolved what was technically called the "political" work of the Government. The disarming of the country, the negotiations with the chiefs, the organisation of the new Punjabee regiments, the arrangements for the education of the young Maharajah, who had now become the ward of the British Government, were among the immediate duties to which he personally devoted himself; the chief care of John Lawrence was the civil administration, especially the settlement of the Land Revenue; whilst Mansel superintended the general judicial management of the province; each, however, aiding the others with his advice, and having a potential voice in the general Council. Under these chief officers were a number of subordinate administrators of different ranks, drawn partly from the civil and partly from the military service of the Company. The province was divided into seven divisions, and to each of these divisions a Commissioner was appointed. Under each of these Commissioners were certain Deputy-Commissioners, varying in number according to the amount of business to be done; whilst under them again were Assistant-Commissioners and Extra Assistants, drawn from the uncovenanted servants of Government—Europeans, Indo-Britons, or natives of pure descent. 1849.

The officers selected for the principal posts under the Lahore Board of Administration were the very flower of the Indian services. Dalhousie had thrown his whole heart into the work which lay before him. Resolved that it should not be marred by the inefficiency of his agents, he looked about him for men of mark and likelihood, men in the vigour of their years, men of good performance for the higher posts, and sturdy, eager-spirited youths of good promise for the lower. It mattered not to him whether the good stuff were draped in civil black or military red. Far above all petty prejudices of that kind, the Governor-General swept up his men with an eye only to the work that was in them, and sent them forth to do his bidding. Some had already graduated in Punjabee administration under the Protectorate; others crossed

1849. the Sutlej for the first time with honours taken under Thomason and his predecessors in the North-West Provinces. And among them were such men as George Edmonstone, Donald Macleod, and Robert Montgomery from the one service; Frederick Mackeson and George Macgregor from the other; such men, besides those already named,* as Richard Temple, Edward Thornton, Neville Chamberlain, George Barnes, Lewin Bowring, Philip Goldney, and Charles Saunders; soldiers and civilians working side by side, without a feeling of class jealousy, in the great work of reconstructing the administration of the Punjab and carrying out the executive details; whilst at the head of the department of Public Works was Robert Napier, in whom the soldier and the man of science met together to make one of the finest Engineer officers in the world.

They found much to do, but little to undo. The Government of Runjeet Singh had been of a rude, simple, elementary character; out of all rule; informal; unconstitutional; unprincipled; one great despotism and a number of petty despotisms; according to our English notions, reeking with the most "frightful injustice." But somehow or other it had answered the purpose. The injustice was intelligible injustice, for it was simply that of the strong will and the strong hand crushed down in turn by one still stronger. Petty governors, revenue-farmers, or kardars might oppress the people and defraud the State, but they knew that, sooner or later, a day of reckoning would come when their accounts would be audited by the process of compulsory disgorgement,

* *Ante*, p. 42. I have here named only those distinguished during the earlier period of our Punjabee career. Others there were, appointed at a later period, equally entitled to honourable mention.

or in some parts of the country settled in the noose of 1849.
the proconsular gibbet. No niceties of conscience and no intricacies of law opposed an obstacle to these summary adjustments. During the existence of that great fiction the Council of Regency, we had begun to systematise and to complicate affairs; and as we had found—at least, as far as we understood the matter—a clear field for our experiments, we now, on assuming undisguisedly the administration of the country, had a certain basis of our own to operate upon, and little or nothing to clear away.

The system of administration now introduced into the Punjab, formal and precise as it may have been when compared with the rude simplicity of the old Sikh Government, was loose and irregular in comparison with the strict procedure of the Regulation Provinces. The administrators, whether soldiers or civilians, were limited to the discharge of no particular departmental functions. They were judges, revenue-collectors, thief-catchers, diplomatists, conservancy officers, and sometimes recruiting serjeants and chaplains, all in one. Men trained in such a school as this, and under such masters as the Lawrences, became equal to any fortune, and in no conjuncture, however critical, were ever likely to fail. There was hardly one among them who did not throw his whole heart into his work; who ever thought of ease, or leisure, or any personal enjoyment beyond that which comes from an honest sense of duty done. They lived among the people of the country, their tents open to all the points of the compass;* and

* Sir John Malcolm used to say that the only way to govern the people of a newly-acquired country was by means of *char durwaseh kolah*, or four doors open. That the Punjabee officials well understood this, here is a pleasant illustrative proof, from a paper written by one of them:—"For eight months in the year the tent is the proper home of him who loves his duties and his people. Thus he comes to know and be known of

1849. won by their personal bearing the confidence and the admiration of all who came within their reach.

And so, far sooner than even sanguine men ventured to predict, the Punjab began to settle down under its new rulers. Even the old Khalsa fighting-men accepted their position, and with a manly resignation looking cheerfully at the inevitable, confessed that they had been beaten in fair fight, and submitted themselves to the English conqueror. Some were enlisted into the new Punjabee Irregular Regiments, which were raised for the internal defence of the province. Others betook themselves, with the pensions or gratuities which were bestowed upon them, to their fields, and merged themselves into the agricultural population. There was no fear of any resurrection of the old national cause. For whilst the people were forced to surrender all their weapons of war—their guns, their muskets, their bayonets, their sabres, their spears—the whole province was bristling with British arms. An immense military force was maintained in the Punjab. It was a happy circumstance that, as the Indus had now become our boundary and the country of the Sikhs our frontier province, it was necessary for purposes of external defence, after the apparent settling down of our newly-acquired territories, still to keep our regular troops, European and native, at a strength more than sufficient to render utterly harmless all the turbulent elements of Punjabee society. Had the British army been withdrawn

them; thus personal influence and local knowledge give him a power not to be won by bribes or upheld by bayonets. The notables of the neighbourhood meet their friend and ruler on his morning march; greybeards throng round his unguarded door with presents of the best fruits of the land, or a little sugar, spices, and almonds, according to the fashion of their country, and are never so happy as when allowed to seat themselves on the carpet and talk over old times and new events—the promise of the harvest and the last orders of the rulers."—*Calcutta Review*, vol. xxxiii.

from the Punjab, as at a later period it was from Oude it is hard to say what might not have resulted from our confidence and incaution. 1849.

On the acquisition of a new country and the extinction of an old dynasty, it has commonly happened that the chief sufferers by the revolution have been found among the aristocracy of the land. The great masses of the people have been considerately, indeed generously treated; but the upper classes have been commonly prostrated by the annexing hand, and have never recovered from the blow. This may be partly attributed to what is so often described as the "inevitable tendency" of such a change from a bad to a good government. It has been assumed that the men whom we have found in the enjoyment of all the privileges of wealth and social position, have risen to this eminence by spoliation and fraud, and maintained it by cruelty and oppression. And it is true that the antecedents of many of them would not bear a very jealous scrutiny. Now, so far as the substitution of a strong and pure for a weak and corrupt government must necessarily have checked the prosperous career of those who were living on illicit gains and tyrannous exactions, it was, doubtless, the inevitable tendency of the change to injure, if not to ruin them, as the leaf must perish when the stem dies. But it must be admitted that for some years past the idea of a native aristocracy had been an abomination in the eyes of English statesmen in India; that we had desired to see nothing between the Sircar, or Government, and the great masses of the people; and that, however little we might have designed it, we had done some great wrongs to men, whose misfortune, rather than whose fault, it was that they were the growth of a corrupt system. There was at the bottom of this a

1849. strong desire for the welfare of the people—an eager and a generous longing to protect the weak gainst the tyranny of the strong; but benevolence, like ambition, sometimes overleaps itself, and falls prostrate on the other side, and out of our very love of justice come sometimes unjust deeds.

To the great chiefs of the Punjab the annexation of the country to the British Empire was a source of sore disquietude.* Mercy to the vanquished in the hour of victory was not one of the weaknesses they had been accustomed to contemplate. They had played for a great stake, and they had lost. They had brought their losses on themselves. They had invited by their own acts the conflict which had ruined them. In no one instance had our policy been aggressive. We had not coveted the possession of the Punjab. We had not invited either the first or the second great conflict between the British and the Sikh armies. A brave nation fighting for its independence is one of the noblest spectacles of humanity; and the leaders of such a movement have just claim to sympathy and respect. But these men had risen against us whilst they pretended to be our friends. They had soiled their patriotism by treachery, and forfeited their honour by falsehood and deceit. Still, to a man of large mind and catholic spirit like Henry Lawrence, it could not seem right to judge these Sirdars as he would the

* This was admitted in the first Punjab Report, the following passage of which may be advantageously quoted :—"A great revolution cannot happen without injuring some classes. When a State falls, its nobility and its supporters must to some extent suffer with it; a dominant sect and party once moved by political ambition and religious enthusiasm, cannot return to the ordinary level of society and the common occupations of life without feeling some discontent and some enmity against their powerful but humane conquerors. But it is probable that the mass of the people will advance in material prosperity and in moral elevation under the influence of British rule."

flower of European chivalry. So he dealt gently 1849.
with their offences; and when he came to consider their position under the new Government, he respected their fallen fortunes, and laid a lighter hand upon their tenures than higher authority was altogether willing to sanction. That a large portion of the revenue would be alienated by grants to military chiefs and to priestly sinecurists was certain; not less certain did it appear that the money might be better bestowed. Still, it might be politic, even in a financial aspect, to tolerate for a time abuses of this kind, as not the most expensive means of reconciling the influential classes to our rule. Thus argued Henry Lawrence. So these privileged classes received from him, in many instances, though not all that he wished to give, more perhaps than they had dared to expect. Existing incumbents were generally respected; and the privileges enjoyed by one generation were to be only partially resumed in the next.

Thus, by a well-apportioned mixture of vigour and clemency, the submission, if not the acquiescence, of the more dangerous classes was secured; and our administrators were left, undisturbed by the fear of internal revolt, to prosecute their ameliorative measures. It would be beyond the scope of such a narrative as this to write in detail of the operations which were carried out, under the Lahore Board, at once to render British rule a blessing to the people, and the possession of the Punjab an element of strength and security to the British Empire. These great victories of peace are reserved for others to record. That the measures were excellent, that the men were even better than the measures, that the administration of the Punjab was a great fact, at which Englishmen pointed with pride and on which

1849. foreigners dwelt with commendation, is freely admitted, even by those who are not wont to see much that is good in the achievements of the British Government in India. Under the fostering care of the Governor-General, who traversed the country from one end to the other, and saw everything with his own eyes, the "Punjab system" became the fashion, and men came to speak and to write of it as though it were a great experiment in government originated by Lord Dalhousie. But it was not a new system. It had been tried long years before, with marked success, and was still in force in other parts of India, though it had never been carried out on so large a scale, or in so fine a country, or been the darling of a viceroy. The only novelty in the construction of the administration was the Lahore Board, and that was abandoned as a failure.

I do not say that it *was* a failure; but it was so regarded by Lord Dalhousie, who, in 1853, remorselessly signed its death-warrant. A delicate operation, indeed, was the breaking up of the Punjabee Cabinet and the erection of an autocracy in its place. It was the will of the Governor-General that the chief direction of affairs should be consigned to the hands, not of many, but of one. And when the rumour of this resolution went abroad, there was scarcely a house, or a bungalow, or a single-poled tent occupied by an English officer, in which the future of the Punjab—the question of the Lawrences—was not eagerly discussed. Was Henry or was John Lawrence to remain supreme director of affairs? So much was to be said in favour of the great qualities of each brother, that it was difficult to arrive at any anticipatory solution of the question. But it was in the character of the Governor-General himself that the key to the difficulty should have been sought. Lord Hardinge would have chosen Henry Lawrence. Lord Dalhousie chose John. No surprise is now expressed that it was so; for, in these days, the character and policy of Dalhousie are read by the broad light of history. No regret is now felt that it was so; for, when the great hurricane of which I am about to write swept over India, each of those two great brothers was, by God's providence, found in his right place. But there were many at the time who grieved that the name of Henry Lawrence, who had been for so many years associated with all their thoughts of British influence in the Sikh country, and who had paved the way to all our after successes, was to be expunged from the list of Punjabee administrators. It was said that he sympathised overmuch with the fallen state of Sikhdom, and sacrificed the revenue to an idea; that he was too eager to provide for those who suffered by our usurpation; whilst Dalhousie, deeming that the balance-sheet would be regarded as the great test and touchstone of success, was eager to make the Punjab pay. John Lawrence, it was said, better understood the art of raising a revenue. He was willing, in his good brotherly heart, to withdraw from the scene in favour of Henry; but the Governor-General needed his services. So he was appointed Chief-Commissioner of the Punjab, and a new theatre was found for the exercise of Henry Lawrence's more chivalrous benevolence among the ancient states of Rajpootana. 1853.

Outwardly, authoritatively, and not untruthfully, the explanation was, that the work of the soldier-statesman was done, that the transition-period in which

1853. Henry Lawrence's services were so especially needed had passed; that the business of internal administration was principally such as comes within the range of the civil officer's duties; and that a civilian with large experience, especially in revenue matters, was needed to direct all the numerous details of the Executive Government. Dalhousie never liked the Board. It was not a description of administrative agency likely to find favour in his eyes; and it is not impossible that he placed, with some reluctance, at the head of it a man who had not approved the original policy of annexation. But he could not have read Henry Lawrence's character so badly as to believe for a moment that, on that account, the policy once accomplished, he could have been less eager for its success, or less zealous in working it out. There was the indication, however, of a fundamental difference of opinion, which as time advanced became more and more apparent, for Henry's generous treatment of his fallen enemies came from that very source of enlarged sympathy which rendered the policy of annexation distasteful to him. It was natural, therefore, that the Governor-General, who had resolved to rid himself of the Board on the first fitting opportunity, should have selected as the agent of his pet policy, the administrator of his pet province, the civilian who concurred with, rather than the soldier who dissented from, his views. The fitting opportunity came at last, for there was a redistribution of some of the higher political offices;* and Dalhousie then

* The Hyderabad Residency was about to be vacated. It was an office that had been held by Sir Charles Metcalfe and other eminent men. I believe that Henry Lawrence suggested (for the days of the Board had been for some time numbered) that either he or his brother should be sent to Hyderabad. Lord Dalhousie, however, sent General Low to the Court of the Nizam, and gave Henry Lawrence the scarcely less honourable appointment of Governor-General's agent in Rajpootana.

swept away the obnoxious institution, and placed the administration of the Punjab in the hands of a single man. 1853.

Henry Lawrence bowed to the decision, but was not reconciled to it. He betook himself to his new duties a sadder and a wiser man. He did not slacken in good service to the State; but he never again had the same zest for his work. Believing that he had been unfairly and ungratefully treated, he had no longer his old confidence in his master, and as the Dalhousie policy developed itself, under the ripening influence of time, he saw more clearly that he was not one to find favour in the eyes of the Governor-General. Much that he had before but dimly seen and partly understood now became fully revealed to him in the clear light of day. Once, and once only, there was any official conflict; but Henry Lawrence saw much that whilst he deplored he could not avert, and he sighed to think that his principles were out of date and his politics out of fashion.

In the mean while, John Lawrence reigned in the Punjab. The capacity for administration, which he had evinced as a Member of the Board, had now free scope for exercise, and was soon fully developed. His name became great throughout the land, and he deserved the praise that was lavished upon him. Right or wrong he did all in accordance with the faith that was in him. He was a fitting agent of Dalhousie's policy, only because he believed in that policy. And happily the greater part of his work lay along the straight road of undebatable beneficence. How he worked, day after day, early and late, and how all men worked under him, is a history now well known. He was emphatically a man without a weakness. Strong himself, bone and muscle, head and heart, of

1853. adamantine strength, that would neither bend nor break, he expected others to be equally strong. They sighed, perhaps they inwardly protested, but they knew that the work he exacted from them he gave, in his own person, unstintingly to the State; and they could not regard as a hard task-master one who tasked himself hardest of all. From moral infirmities of all kinds he appeared to be equally free. He did not even seem to be ambitious. Men said that he had no sentiment, no romance. We so often judge our neighbours wrongly in this, that I hesitate to adopt the opinion; but there was an intense reality about him such as I have never seen equalled. He seemed to be continually toiling onwards, upwards, as if life were not meant for repose, with the grand princely motto, "*I serve*," inscribed in characters of light on his forehead. He served God as unceasingly as he served the State; and set before all his countrymen in the Punjab the true pattern of a Christian gentleman.

And it was not thrown away. The Christian character of British administration in the Punjab has ever been one of its most distinguishing features. It is not merely that great humanising measures were pushed forward with an alacrity most honourable to a Christian nation—that the moral elevation of the people was continually in the thoughts of our administrators; but that in their own personal characters they sought to illustrate the religion which they professed. Wherever two or three were gathered together, the voice of praise and prayer went up from the white man's tent. It had been so during the Protectorate, when, in the wildest regions and in the most stirring times, men like the Lawrences, Reynell Taylor, and Herbert Edwardes, never forgot the

Christian Sabbath.* And now that peace and order reigned over the country, Christianity asserted itself more demonstratively, and Christian churches rose at our bidding. There was little or none, too, of that great scandal which had made our names a hissing and a reproach in Afghanistan. Our English officers, for the most part, lived pure lives in that heathen land; and private immorality under the administration of John Lawrence grew into a grave public offence. 1853

Conquest of Pegu.

And so the Punjab administration flourished under the Chief-Commissioner and his assistants;† and the active mind of Lord Dalhousie was enabled to direct itself to new objects. Already, far down on the south-eastern boundary of our empire—at the point farthest removed of all from the great country whose destinies we have been considering—the seeds of war had been sown broad-cast. Ever since 1826, when the first contest with Ava had been brought to a close by the surrender to the English of certain tracts of country in which no Englishman could live, our relations with the Burmese had been on an unsatisfactory footing. In truth, they were altogether a very unsatisfactory people; arrogant and pretentious, blind to reason, and by no means anxious to manifest their appreciation of the nice courtesies of diplomatic in-

* Many will remember that delightful little story, so pleasantly told in Edwardes's "Year on the Punjab Frontier," of Reynell Taylor's invitation to prayer on a Sunday morning in February, 1848, and of the question whether the half-caste colonel, "John Holmes," who had "always attended prayers at Peshawur" in George Lawrence's house. was sufficiently a Christian to be admitted to swell the two or three into three or four.

† On the abolition of the Board, Mr. Montgomery, who had succeeded Mr. Mansel as third member, became Judicial Commissioner, and Mr. Macleod was appointed Financial Commissioner.

1849. tercourse. To find just cause, according to European notions, for chastising these people would at any time have been easy. But their insolence did us very little harm. We could tolerate, without loss of credit or of prestige, the discourtesies of a barbarian Government on the outskirts of civilisation. An insult on the banks of the Irrawaddy was very different from an insult on the banks of the Jumna. The Princes and chiefs of India knew nothing and cared nothing about our doings far out beyond the black waters of the Bay of Bengal. But at last these discourtesies culminated in an outrage which Lord Dalhousie thought it became the British Government to resent. Whether, under more discreet management, redress might have been obtained and war averted, it is now of little moment to inquire. A sea-captain was appointed to conduct our diplomacy at Rangoon, and he conducted it successfully to a rupture. A war ensued, to which the future historian of India may devote a not very inviting chapter, but its details have nothing to do with the story of this book. English arms were triumphant, and the province of Pegu lay at our feet. Dalhousie annexed it to the British Empire, "in order that the Government of India might hold from the Burmese State both adequate compensation for past injury, and the best security against future danger." Thus did the British Empire, which had so recently been extended to the north-west, stretch itself out to the south-east; and the white man sat himself down on the banks of the Irrawaddy as he had seated himself on the banks of the Indus. There were not wanting those who predicted that the whole of Burmah would soon become British territory, and that then the "uncontrollable principle," by reference to which a great English statesman justified the seizure of Sindh, would send the English conqueror to grope his way through the Shan States and Siam to Cochin-China. But these apprehensions were groundless. The administrator began his work in Pegu, as he had begun his work in the Punjab, and there was no looking beyond the frontier; but, on the other hand, a desire to avoid border disputes, or, if they could not be avoided, to treat them as matters of light account, inevitable and soon to be forgotten. There was a military officer, admirably fitted for the work, who had served long and successfully, as a civil administrator, in Arracan; who knew the Burmese language and the Burmese people, and had a great name along the eastern coast. Those isolated regions beyond the Bay of Bengal are the grave of all catholic fame. Whilst the name of Lawrence was in all men's mouths, Phayre was pursuing the even tenor of his way, content with a merely local reputation. But the first, and as I write the only commissioner of Pegu, is fairly entitled to a place in the very foremost rank of those English administrators who have striven to make our rule a blessing to the people of India, and have not failed in the attempt. 1849.

In India the native mind readily pervades vast distances, and takes little account of space that the foot can travel. But it is bewildered and confused by the thought of the "black water." The unknown is the illimitable. On the continent of India, therefore, neither our war-successes nor our peace-successes in the Burmese country stirred the heart of Indian society. In the lines of the Sepoy or the shops of the money-changer they were not matters of eager interest and voluble discourse. We might have sacked the cities of Ava and Amarapoora, and caused their sovereign lord to be trodden to death by one of his

1849. white elephants without exciting half the interest engendered by a petty outbreak in Central India, or the capture of a small fort in Bundelkund. The Princes and chiefs of the great continent of Hindostan knew little and cared less about a potentate, however magnificent in his own dominions, who neither worshipped their gods nor spoke their language, and who was cut off from their brotherhood by the intervention of the great dark sea. We gained no honour, and we lost no confidence, by the annexation of this outlying province; but it opened to our Native Soldiery a new field of service, and unfortunately it was beyond the seas.

CHAPTER II.

THE ADMINISTRATION OF LORD DALHOUSIE—ADOPTION—THE "RIGHT OF LAPSE"—SATTARAH—NAGPORE—JHANSI—KEROWLEE—THE CARNATIC—TANJORE—THE CASE OF THE PEISHWAH—DUNDOO PUNT, NANA SAHIB—SUMBHULPORE.

So, three years after his arrival in India, Dalhousie 1848-1856.
had brought to a close two great military campaigns, and had captured two great provinces. He had then done with foreign wars; his after-career was one of peaceful invasion. Ere long there was a word which came to be more dreaded than that of Conquest. The native mind is readily convinced by the inexorable logic of the sword. There is no appeal from such arbitration. To be invaded and to be conquered is a state of things appreciable by the inhabitant of India. It is his "kismut;" his fate; God's will. One stronger than he cometh and taketh all that he hath. There are, however, manifest compensations. His religion is not invaded; his institutions are not violated. Life is short, and the weak man, patient and philosophical, is strong to endure and mighty to wait. But LAPSE is a dreadful and an appalling word; for it pursues the victim beyond the grave. Its significance in his eyes is nothing short of eternal condemnation.

1848-1856. "The son," says the great Hindoo lawgiver, "delivers his father from the hell called Put." There are, he tells us, different kinds of sons; there is the son begotten; the son given; the son by adoption; and other filial varieties. It is the duty of the son to perform the funeral obsequies of the father. If they be not performed, it is believed that there is no resurrection to eternal bliss. The right of adoption is, therefore, one of the most cherished doctrines of Hindooism. In a country where polygamy is the rule, it might be supposed that the necessity of adopting another man's offspring, for the sake of these ceremonial ministrations, or for the continuance of an ancestral name, would be one of rare occurrence. But all theory on the subject is belied by the fact that the Princes and chiefs of India more frequently find themselves, at the close of their lives, without the solace of male offspring than with it. The Zenana is not an institution calculated to lengthen out a direct line of Princes. The alternative of adoption is one, therefore, to which there is frequent resort; it is a source of unspeakable comfort in life and in death; and politically it is as dear to the heart of a nation as it is personally to the individual it affects.

It is with the question of Adoption only in its political aspects that I have to do in this place. There is a private and personal, as there is a public and political, side to it. No power on earth beyond a man's own will can prevent him from adopting a son, or can render that adoption illegal if it be legally performed. But to adopt a son as a successor to private property is one thing, to adopt an heir to titular dignities and territorial sovereignty is another. Without the consent of the Paramount State no adoption of the latter kind can be valid. Whether in this case of a titular Prince or a possessor of territorial rights, dependent upon the will of the Government, Hindooism is satisfied by the private adoption and the penalties of the sonless state averted, is a question for the pundits to determine; but no titular chief thinks the adoption complete unless he can thereby transmit his name, his dignities, his rights and privileges to his successor, and it can in no wise be said that the son takes the place of his adoptive father if he does not inherit the most cherished parts of that father's possessions. 1848-1856.

But whether the religious element does or does not rightly enter into the question of political adoptions, nothing is more certain than that the right, in this larger political sense, was ever dearly prized by the Hindoos, and was not alienated from them by the Lords-Paramount who had preceded us. The imperial recognition was required, and it was commonly paid for by a heavy "nuzzurana," or succession-duty, but in this the Mogul rulers were tolerant. It was reserved for the British to substitute for the right of adoption what was called "the right of lapse," and in default of male heirs of the body lawfully begotten to absorb native principalities into the great amalgam of our British possessions. "In 1849," wrote Lord Dalhousie, in his elaborate farewell minute, "the principality of Sattarah was included in the British dominions by right of lapse, the Rajah having died without male heir." The Princes of Sattarah were the descendants of Sevajie, the founder and the head of the Mahratta Empire. Their power and their glory had alike departed. But they were still great in tradition, and were looked up to with respect by the 1848. Sattarah.

1848. Mahrattas of Western India. In April, 1848, the last Rajah died;* and a question arose as to whether, no direct male heir of the body having been left by the deceased, a son by adoption, or a collateral member of the family, should be permitted to succeed him, or whether the rights and titles of the principality should be declared to be extinct. Sir George Clerk was then Governor of Bombay. He looked at the Treaty of 1819; saw that "the British Government agreed to cede in perpetual sovereignty to the Rajah of Sattarah, his heirs and successors," the territories which he had held, and at once declared himself in favour of the continuance of the native Raj. The members of his Council looked upon the question as purely one of expediency, and considered it the duty of the British Government to decide it in the manner most advantageous to ourselves. But the Governor refused to admit any secondary considerations, saying, "If it be inconsistent with justice to refuse confirmation to the act of adoption, it is useless to inquire whether it is better for the interests of the people or of the empire at large to govern the Sattarah territories through the medium of a native Rajah, or by means of our own administration." The trumpet of that statesman was not likely to give an uncertain sound.

When this question first arose, the Governor-General was in his novitiate. But new as he was to the consideration of such subjects, he does not appear to have faltered or hesitated. The opinions, the practical expression of which came subsequently to be called

* Appa Sahib. He had succeeded his brother, who in 1839 was deposed, and, as I think, very rightly, on account of a series of intrigues against the British Government, equally foolish and discreditable. It is worthy of remark, that Sir Robert Grant, being satisfied of the Rajah's guilt, proposed to punish him in the manner least likely to be advantageous to ourselves.

the "policy of annexation," were formed at the very outset of his career, and rigidly maintained to its close. Eight months after his first assumption of the Government of India, he placed on record a confession of faith elicited by this agitation of the Sattarah question. Subsequent events of far greater magnitude dwarfed that question in the public mind, and later utterances of the great minute-writer caused this first manifesto to be comparatively forgotten; but a peculiar interest must ever be associated with this earliest exposition of Dalhousie's political creed, and therefore I give it in the words of the statesman himself: "The Government," he wrote on the 30th August, 1848, "is bound in duty, as well as policy, to act on every such occasion with the purest integrity, and in the most scrupulous observance of good faith. Where even a shadow of doubt can be shown, the claim should at once be abandoned. But where the right to territory by lapse is clear, the Government is bound to take that which is justly and legally its due, and to extend to that territory the benefits of our sovereignty, present and prospective. In like manner, while I would not seek to lay down any inflexible rule with respect to adoption, I hold that, on all occasions, where heirs natural shall fail, the territory should be made to lapse, and adoption should not be permitted, excepting in those cases in which some strong political reason may render it expedient to depart from this general rule. There may be conflict of opinion as to the advantage or the propriety of extending our already vast possessions beyond their present limits. No man can more sincerely deprecate than I do any extension of the frontiers of our territory which can be avoided, or which may not become indispensably necessary from

1848.

1849. considerations of our own safety, and of the maintenance of the tranquillity of our provinces. But I cannot conceive it possible for any one to dispute the policy of taking advantage of every just opportunity which presents itself for consolidating the territories that already belong to us, by taking possession of States that may lapse in the midst of them; for thus getting rid of these petty intervening principalities, which may be made a means of annoyance, but which can never, I venture to think, be a source of strength, for adding to the resources of the public Treasury, and for extending the uniform application of our system of government to those whose best interests, we sincerely believe, will be promoted thereby. Such is the general principle that, in our humble opinion, ought to guide the conduct of the British Government in its disposal of independent States, where there has been a total failure of heirs whatsoever, or where permission is asked to continue by adoption a succession which fails in the natural line."

The Court of Directors of the East India Company confirmed the decision of the Governor-General, and Sattarah was annexed. There were men, however, in the Direction who protested against the measure as an act of unrighteous usurpation. "We are called upon," said Mr. Tucker, ever an opponent of wrong, "to consider and decide upon a claim of right, and I have always felt that our best policy is that which most closely adheres to the dictates of justice." "We ought not to forget," said Mr. Shepherd, who, on great questions of this kind, was commonly to be found side by side with his veteran friend, contending for the rights of the native Princes of India, "that during the rise and progress of our empire in the East, our Governments have continued to announce and proclaim to the people of India that not only should all their rights and privileges which existed under preceding Governments be preserved and maintained, but that their laws, habits, customs, and prejudices should be respected."* And what right more cherished, what custom more honoured, than the right and custom of adoption? But the majority of the Court of Directors supported the views of the Governor-General. They had heard the voice of the charmer. And from that time the policy of Dalhousie became the policy of Leadenhall-street, and the "Right of Lapse" was formally acknowledged. 1849.

And it was not, for reasons which I have already given, likely long to remain a dead letter. Soon another of the great Mahratta chiefs was said to be dying, and in a few days news came to Calcutta that he was dead. It was the height of the cold season of 1853—a few days before Christmas—when the slow booming of minute guns from the Saluting Battery of Fort William announced the death of Ragojee Bonslah, Rajah of Nagpore. At the age of forty-seven he succumbed to a complication of disorders, of which debauchery, cowardice, and obstinacy were the chief. There have been worse specimens of royalty, both in Eastern and Western Palaces, than this poor, worn-out, impotent sot; for although he was immoderately addicted to brandy and dancing-girls, he rather liked his people to be happy, and was not incapable of kindness that caused no trouble to himself. He had no son to succeed him; a posthumous son was an impossibility; and he had not adopted an heir. 1853. Nagpore.

It may seem strange and contradictory that if the

* Colonel Oliphant and Mr. Leslie Melville recorded minutes on the same side.

1853. right of adoption as sanctioned by religion and prescribed by ancestral usage be so dear to the people of India, they should ever fail to adopt in default of heirs of their body. But we know that they often do; and the omission is readily explicable by a reference to the ordinary weaknesses of humanity. We know that even in this country, with all the lights of civilisation and Christianity to keep us from going astray, thousands of reasoning creatures are restrained from making their wills by a vague feeling of apprehension that there is something "unlucky" in such a procedure; that death will come the sooner for such a provision against its inevitable occurrence. What wonder, then, that in a country which is the very hotbed of superstition, men should be restrained by a kindred feeling from providing against the event of their dissolution? But in this case there is not only the hope of life, but the hope of offspring, to cause the postponement of the anticipatory ceremony. Men, under the most discouraging circumstances, still cling to the belief that by some favourable reaction of nature they may, even when stricken in years, beget an heir to their titles and possessions. In this sense, too, adoption is held to be unlucky, because it is irreligious. It is like a surrender of all hope, and a betrayal of want of faith in the power and goodness of the Almighty. No man expects to beget a son after he has adopted one.

In the case, too, of this Mahratta Prince, there were special reasons why he should have abstained from making such a provision for the continuance of his House. According to the law and usage of his country, an adoption by his widow would have been as valid as an adoption by himself. It was natural, therefore, and assuredly it was in accordance with

the character of the man, who was gormandising and 1853.
dallying with the hand of death upon him, that he should have left the ceremony to be performed by others. Whether it was thus vicariously performed is not very clearly ascertainable. But it is certain that the British Resident reported that there had been no adoption. The Resident was Mr. Mansel, who had been one of the first members of the Lahore Board of Administration—a man with a keen sense of justice, favourable to the maintenance of native dynasties, and therefore, in those days, held to be crotchety and unsound. He had several times pressed the Rajah on the subject of adoption, but had elicited no satisfactory response. He reported unequivocally that nothing had been done, and asked for the instructions of the Supreme Government.

Lord Dalhousie was then absent from Calcutta. He was making one of his cold-weather tours of inspection—seeing with his own eyes the outlying province of Pegu, which had fallen by right of conquest into his hands. The Council, in his absence, hesitated to act, and all the instructions, therefore, which they could send were to the effect that the Resident should provide for the peace of the country, and keep things quiet until further orders. There was no doubt about Dalhousie's decision in such a case. Had the Rajah adopted a son, there was little likelihood of the Governor-General's sanction of the adoption; but as he had wilfully failed to perform the ceremony, it appeared to be as clear as noon-day that the great organ of the Paramount State would pronounce the fatal sentence of Lapse.

Dalhousie returned to Calcutta, and with characteristic energy addressed himself to the mastery of the whole question. Before the first month of the

Jan. 28, 1854. new year had worn to a close, he attached his signature to an elaborate minute, in which he exhausted all the arguments which could be adduced in favour of the annexation of the country. Printed at full length, it would occupy fifty pages of this book. It was distinguished by infinite research and unrivalled powers of special pleading. It contended that there had been no adoption, and that if there had been, it would be the duty of the British Government to refuse to recognise it. "I am well aware," he said, "that the continuance of the Raj of Nagpore under some Mahratta rule, as an act of grace and favour on the part of the British Government, would be highly acceptable to native sovereigns and nobles in India; and there are, doubtless, many of high authority who would advocate the policy on that special ground. I understand the sentiment and respect it; but remembering the responsibility that is upon me, I cannot bring my judgment to admit that a kind and generous sentiment should outweigh a just and prudent policy."

Among the members of the Supreme Council at that time was Colonel John Low. An old officer of the Madras army, who long years before, when the Peishwah and the Bonslah were in arms against the British, had sate at the feet of John Malcolm, and had graduated in diplomacy under him, he had never forgotten the lessons which he had learnt from his beloved chief; he had never ceased to cherish those "kind and generous sentiments" of which the Governor-General had spoken in his minute. His whole life had been spent at the Courts of the native Princes of India. He had represented British interests long and faithfully at the profligate Court of Lucknow. He had contended with the pride, the obstinacy, and

the superstition of the effete Princes of Rajpootana. 1854.
He had played, and won, a difficult game, with the bankrupt State of Hyderabad. He knew what were the vices of Indian Princes and the evils of native misrule. But he had not so learnt the lesson presented to him by the spectacle of improvident rulers and profligate Courts; of responsibilities ignored and opportunities wasted; as to believe it to be either the duty or the policy of the Paramount Government to seek "just occasions" for converting every misgoverned principality into a British province. Nor had he, knowing as he did, better perhaps than any of his countrymen, the real character of such misgovernment, ever cherished the conviction that the inhabitants of every native State were yearning for the blessings of this conversion. There were few such States left—Hindoo or Mahomedan—but what remained from the wreck of Indian dynasties he believed it to be equally just and politic to preserve. And entertaining these opinions, he spoke them out; not arrogantly or offensively, but with what I believe may be described as the calm resolution of despair. He knew that he might speak with the tongue of angels, and yet that his speech would no more affect the practical result than a sounding brass or a tinkling cymbal. What am I against so many? he said; nay, what am I against one? Who will listen to the utterance of my ideas when opposed to the "deliberately-formed opinion of a statesman like the Marquis of Dalhousie, in whose well-proved ability and judgment and integrity of purpose they have entire confidence?"* But great statesmen in times past had thought that the extension of British rule in India was, for our own sakes, to be arrested rather than accelerated; that the

* Minute of Colonel John Low. February 10, 1854.

1854. native States were a source to us of strength rather than of weakness, and that it would go ill with us when there were none left.*

Strong in this belief, Colonel Low recorded two minutes, protesting against the impolicy and the injustice of the proposed annexation of Nagpore. He said that already the annexation of Sattarah had in many parts of India had a bad moral effect;† that it had shaken the confidence of the people in the justice and good faith of the British Government; that people had asked what crime Sattarah had committed that sentence of political death should thus have been pronounced against it; that throughout India acquisition by conquest was well understood, and in many cases admitted to be right; that the annexation of the Punjab, for example, had not been regarded as a wrong, because the chiefs and people had brought it on themselves, but that the extinction of a loyal native State, in default of heirs, was not appreciable in any part of India, and that the exercise of the alleged right of lapse would create a common feeling of uncertainty and distrust at every Durbar in the

* "If Great Britain shall retain her present powerful position among the States of Europe, it seems highly probable that, owing to the infringement of their treaties on the part of native Princes and other causes, the whole of India will, in the course of time, become one British province; but many eminent statesmen have been of opinion that we ought most carefully to avoid unnecessarily accelerating the arrival of that great change; and it is within my own knowledge that the following five great men were of that number—namely, Lord Hastings, Sir Thomas Munro, Sir John Malcolm, the Hon. Mountstuart Elphinstone, and Lord Metcalfe."—*Minute, Feb.* 10, 1854.

† "When I went to Malwa, in 1850, where I met many old acquaintances, whom I had known when a very young man, and over whom I held no authority, I found these old acquaintances speak out much more distinctly as to their opinion of the Sattarah case; so much so, that I was, on several occasions, obliged to check them. It is remarkable that every native who ever spoke to me respecting the annexation of Sattarah, asked precisely the same question: 'What crime did the late Rajah commit that his country should be seized by the Company?' Thus clearly indicating their notions, that if any crime had been committed our act would have been justifiable, and not otherwise." *Minute of Colonel Low, Feb.* 10, 1854.

country. He dwelt upon the levelling effects of British dominion, and urged that, as in our own provinces, the upper classes were invariably trodden down, it was sound policy to maintain the native States, if only as a means of providing an outlet for the energies of men of good birth and aspiring natures, who could never rise under British rule. He contended that our system of administration might be far better than the native system, but that the people did not like it better; they clung to their old institutions, however defective, and were averse to change, even though a change for the better. "In one respect," he said, "the natives of India are exactly like the inhabitants of all parts of the known world; they like their own habits and customs better than those of foreigners." 1854.

Having thus in unmeasured opposition to the Dalhousie theory flung down the gauntlet of the old school at the feet of the Governor-General, Low ceased from the enunciation of general principles, and turned to the discussion of the particular case before him. He contended that the treaty between the British Government and the late Rajah did not limit the succession to heirs of his body, and that, therefore, there was a clear title to succession in the Bonslah family by means of a son adopted by either the Rajah himself or by his eldest widow, in accordance with law and usage. The conduct, he said, of the last Prince of Nagpore had not been such as to alienate this right; he had been loyal to the Paramount State, and his country had not been misgoverned; there had been nothing to call for military interference on our part, and little to compel grave remonstrance and rebuke. For what crime, then, was his line to be cut off and the honours of

1854. his House extinguished for ever? To refuse the right of adoption in such a case would, he alleged, be entirely contrary to the spirit, if not to the letter, of the treaty—But how was it to be conceded when it was not claimed; when no adoption had been reported; when it was certain that the Rajah had not exercised his right, and there had been no tidings of such a movement on the part of his widow? The answer to this was, that the Government had been somewhat in a hurry to extinguish the Raj without waiting for the appearance of claimants, and that if they desired to perpetuate it, it was easy to find a fitting successor.

Of such opinions as these Low expected no support in the Council-chamber of Calcutta—no support from the authorities at home. It little mattered, indeed, what the latter might think, for the annexation of Nagpore was decreed and to be accomplished without reference to England. As the extinction of the Sattarah State had been approved by the Company, in the face of an undisputed adoption asserted at the right time, Dalhousie rightly judged that there would be no straining at a gnat in the Nagpore case, where there had been no adoption at all. Indeed, the general principles upon which he had based his proceedings towards Sattarah, in the first year of his administration, having been accepted in Leadenhall-street, there could be no stickling about so mild an illustration of them as that afforded by the treatment of Nagpore. The justification of the policy in the latter instance is to be found in the fact that there was no assertion of an adoption—no claim put forward on behalf of any individual—at the time when the British Government was called upon to determine the course to be pursued. It is true that the provisional Government might, for a time, have been vested in the eldest widow of the deceased Prince, adoption by whom would have been recognised by Hindoo law and Mahratta usage; but it was not probable that the British Government would have thus gone out of its way to bolster up a decayed Mahratta dynasty, when the head of that Government conscientiously believed that it was the duty of the Paramount State to consolidate its dominions by recognising only among these effete Princes succession by direct heirship of the body. Cherishing the faith which he did, Dalhousie would have gone grievously wrong, and he would have stood convicted of a glaring inconsistency, if he had adopted any other course; so the kingdom of Berar was declared to have lapsed to the British Government, and the family of the Bonslah was extinct. 1854.

The country passed under British rule, and the people became British subjects, without an audible murmur of discontent except from the recesses of the palace. There the wretched ladies of the royal household, at first dismayed and paralysed by the blow which had fallen upon them, began, after a little space, to bestir themselves and to clamour for their asserted rights. Liberal pensions had been settled upon them; but their family was without a head, and that which might soon have faded into an idea was rendered a galling and oppressive reality by the spoliation of the palace, which followed closely upon the extinction of the Raj. The live stock and dead stock of the Bonslah were sent to the hammer. It must have been a great day for speculative cattle-dealers at Seetabaldee when the royal elephants,

1854. horses, and bullocks were sold off at the price of carrion;* and a sad day, indeed, in the royal household, when the venerable Bankha Baee,† with all the wisdom and moderation of fourscore well-spent years upon her, was so stung by a sense of the indignity offered to her, that she threatened to fire the palace if the furniture were removed. But the furniture was removed, and the jewels of the Bonslah family, with a few propitiatory exceptions, were sent to the Calcutta market. And I have heard it said that these seizures, these sales, created a worse impression, not only in Berar, but in the surrounding provinces, than the seizure of the kingdom itself.‡

But even in the midst of their degradation, these unfortunate ladies clung to the belief that the Bonslah family would some day be restored and rehabilitated. The Governor-General had argued that the widow, knowing that her husband was disinclined to adopt, had, for like reasons, abstained from adoption. He admitted the right according to Mahratta usage, but declared that she was unwilling to exercise it. He contended, too, that the Bankha Baee, the most influential of the royal ladies, would naturally be averse to a measure which would weaken her own authority in the palace. But his logic halted, and

* Between five and six hundred elephants, camels, horses, and bullocks were sold for 1300*l*. The Ranees sent a protest to the Commissioner, and memorialised the Governor-General, alleging, in the best English that the Palace could furnish, that "on the 4th instant (Sept.) the sale of animals, viz. bullocks, horses, camels, and elephants, commenced to sell by public auction and resolution—a pair her hackery bullocks, valued 100 rupees, sold in the above sale for 5 rupees."

† The Bankha Baee was a widow of the deceased Rajah's grandfather.

‡ I know that the question of public and private property, in such cases, is a very difficult one, and I shall not attempt to decide it here. I only speak of the intense mortification which these sales create in the family itself, and the bad impression which they produce throughout the country. Rightly or wrongly, they cast great discredit on our name; and the gain of money is not worth the loss of character.

his prophecy failed. Both the elder and the younger lady were equally eager to perpetuate the regal dignities of their House. Mr. Mansel had suggested a compromise, in the shape of an arrangement somewhat similar to that which had been made with the Newabs of the Carnatic, by which the title might be maintained, and a certain fixed share of the revenue set apart for its dotation. But he had been severely censured for his indiscretion, and had left Nagpore in disgrace. He was, perhaps, the best friend that the Ranees had in that conjuncture; but—such is the value of opinion—they accused him, in the quaint Palace-English of their scribe, of "endeavouring to gain baronetage and exaltation of rank by reporting to the Governor-General that the late Rajah was destitute of heirs to succeed him, with a view to his Lordship being pleased to order the annexation of the territory."* But there was not a man in the country less disposed to annex provinces and to humour Governors than Charles Mansel, and instead of being exalted in rank, he sacrificed his prospects to his principles and retired from the Service. 1854.

Failing altogether to move the Governor-General, the Ranees sent agents to London, but with no better

* Lord Dalhousie, in his Nagpore Minute, says that the Rajah did not adopt, partly because he did not like to acknowledge his inability to beget a son, and partly because he feared that the existence of an adopted son might some day be used as a pretext for deposing him. He then observes: "The dislike of the late Rajah to the adoption of a successor, was of course known to his widow; and although the custom of the Mahrattas exempts her from that necessity for having the concurrence of her husband in adoption, which general Hindoo law imperatively requires, in order to render the act of adoption valid, still the known disinclination of the Rajah to all adoption could not fail to disincline his widow to have recourse to adoption after his decease." It will be seen at once that the ordinary logical acumen of the Governor-General failed him in this instance, for the very reasons given by the writer himself for the failure of adoption by the Rajah ceased altogether to be operative, *ipso facto*, "after his decease."

1854 result. After the manner of native emissaries from Indian Courts, they spent large sums of money in feeing lawyers and printing pamphlets, without making any impression on Leadenhall-street or Cannon-row, and at last, being recalled by their employers, and having nothing wherewith to pay their debts, they flung themselves on the generosity of their opponents, and were sent home by the help of the great Corporation whom they had reviled. Meanwhile, the elder widow of the late Rajah died, and a boy, of another branch, whom the Ranees called Janojee Bonslah, and in whose person they desired to prolong the Nagpore dynasty, was formally adopted by the dying lady. Clutching at any chance, however desperate, an attempt was made to revive the question of the political adoption; but the sagacity of the Bankha Baee must have seen that it was too late, and that nothing but the private property of the deceased Princess could be thus secured to the adopted heir. The country of the Bonslahs had become as inalienably a part of the Company's possessions as the opium go-downs of Patna, or the gun-factory at Cossipore.

Thus, within a few years of each other, the names of two of the great rulers of the Mahratta Empire ceased from off the roll of Indian Princes; and the territories of the Company were largely increased. Great in historical dignity as was the Sattarah Raj, it was comparatively limited in geographical extent, whilst the Bonslah, though but a servant in rank, owned rich and productive lands, yielding in profusion, among other good gifts, the great staple of our English manufactures.* Whilst the annexation of

* Lord Dalhousie put forth the cotton-growing qualities of the Berar country as one of the many arguments which he adduced in favour of the annexation of the territory.

the Punjab and of Pegu extended the British Empire at its two extreme ends, these Mahratta acquisitions helped to consolidate it. Some unseemly patches, breaking the great rose-hued surface, which spoke of British supremacy in the East, were thus effaced from the map; and the Right of Lapse was proclaimed to the furthermost ends of our Indian dominions. 1854.

There is a circumstantial difference between these two cases, inasmuch as that, in the one, there was an actual and undisputed adoption by the deceased Rajah, and in the other there was none; but as Dalhousie had frankly stated that he would not have recognised a Nagpore adoption had there been one, the two resumptions were governed by the same principle. And this was not a mere arbitrary assertion of the power of the strong over the weak, but was based, at all events, on a plausible substratum of something that simulated reason and justice. It was contended that, whenever a native Prince owed his existence as a sovereign ruler to the British Government, that Government had the right, on failure of direct heirs, to resume, at his death, the territories of which it had originally placed him in possession. The power that rightly gives, it was argued, may also rightfully take away. Now, in the cases both of Sattarah and Nagpore, the Princes, whom the British Government found in possession of those States, had forfeited their rights: the one by hidden treachery and rebellion, the other by open hostility. The one, after full inquiry, had been deposed; the other, many years before, had been driven into the jungle, and had perished in obscurity a fugitive and an outcast.* In

* It is to be observed, too, with respect to Sattarah, that not only had the last Rajah been elevated by the British Government, but that the Raj itself had been resuscitated by us in the person of his predecessor. We had found the Rajah prostrate and a prisoner, almost, it may be

1854. both cases, therefore, the "crime" had been committed which the natives of India are so willing to recognise as a legitimate reason for the punishment of the weaker State by the stronger. But the offence had been condoned, and the sovereignty had been suffered to survive; another member of the reigning family being set up by the Paramount State in place of the offending Prince. Both Pertaub Singh and Ragojee Bonslah, as individuals, owed their sovereign power to the grace and favour of the British Government. All this is historical fact. It may be admitted, too, that when the crimes of which I have spoken were committed by the heads of the Sattarah and Nagpore families, the British Government would have been justified in imposing conditions upon the restoration of the Raj, to the extent of limiting the succession to heirs of the body, or even in making a personal treaty with the favoured Prince conferring no absolute right of sovereignty upon his successors. But the question is whether, these restrictions not having been penally imposed, at the time of forfeiture, the right which then might have been exercised could be justly asserted on the occurrence of a subsequent vacancy created by death? Lord Dalhousie thought that it could—that the circumstances under which the Sattarah and Nagpore Princes had received their principalities as free gifts from the British Government conferred certain rights of suzerainty on that Government, which otherwise they could not have properly asserted. But, on the other hand, it is contended that both principalities, what-

said, at his last gasp; we had rescued him from his enemies, and set him up in a principality of his own; a fact which, assuming the validity of the argument against adoption, necessarily imparted additional force to it. The same may be said of the Nagpore Raj. It was "resuscitated" by the British Government.

soever might have been the offences committed years before by their rulers, had been re-established in their integrity—that no restrictions as to their continuance had then been imposed—that treaties had been concluded containing the usual expressions with respect to succession—in a word, that the condonation had been complete, and that both the Sattarah and the Nagpore Houses really possessed all the rights and privileges which had belonged to them before the representative of the one compromised himself by a silly intrigue, and the head of the other, with equal fatuity, plunged into hostilities which could result only in his ruin. 1854.

This justificatory plea, based upon the alleged right of the British Government to resume, in default of direct heirs, tenures derived from the favour of the Lord Paramount, was again asserted about the same time, but with some diversity of application. Comparatively insignificant in itself, the case claims especial attention on account of results to be hereafter recorded in these pages. In the centre of India, among the small principalities of Bundelkund, was the state of Jhansi, held by a Mahratta chief; originally a vassal of the Peishwah. But on the transfer to the British Government of that Prince's possessions in Bundelkund, the former had resolved "to declare the territory of Jhansi to be hereditary in the family of the late Sheo Rao Bhow, and to perpetuate with his heirs the treaty concluded with the late Bhow;" and, accordingly, a treaty was concluded with the ruling chief, Ram Chand, then only a Soubahdar, constituting "him, his heirs and successors," hereditary rulers of the territory. Loyal and well disposed, he won the favour of the British Government, who, fifteen years after the conclusion of

Jhansi.

1854. the treaty, conferred upon him the title of Rajah, which he only lived three years to enjoy.

For all purposes of succession he was a childless man; and so various claimants to the chiefship appeared. The British agent believed that the most valid claim was that of the late Rajah's uncle, who was at all events a direct lineal descendant of one of the former Soubahdars. He was a leper, and might have been rejected, but, incapable as he was, the people accepted him, and, for three years, the administration of Jhansi was carried on in his name. At the end of those three years he died, also without
1838. heirs of the body, and various claimants as before came forward to dispute the succession. Having no thought of absorbing the State into our British territories, Lord Auckland appointed a commission of British officers to investigate and report upon the pretensions of the several claimants; and the result was, that Government, rightly considering that if the deceased Rajah had any title to the succession, his brother had now an equally good title, acknowledged Gungadhur Rao's right to succeed to the hereditary chiefship.

Under the administration of Ragonath the Leper the country had been grossly mismanaged, and as his successor was scarcely more competent, the British Government undertook to manage the State for him, and soon revived the revenue which had dwindled down under the native rulers. But, in 1843, after the amputation of a limb of the territory for the support of the Bundelkund Legion, the administration was restored to Gungadhur Rao, who carried on the government for ten years, and then, like his predecessors, died childless.

Then again arose the question of succession; but

the claims of the different aspirants to the Raj were 1853.
regarded with far other eyes than those which had scrutinised them in times past. The Governor-General recorded another fatal minute, by which the death-warrant of the State was signed. It was ruled that Jhansi was a dependent State, held by the favour of the Peishwah, as Lord Paramount, and that his powers had devolved upon the British Government. A famous minute recorded, in 1837, by Sir Charles Metcalfe, was cited to show the difference between Hindoo sovereign Princes and "chiefs who hold grants of land or public revenue by gift from a sovereign or paramount Power," and to prove that, in the latter case, "the Power which made the grant, or that which by conquest or otherwise has succeeded to its rights, is entitled to limit succession," and to "resume on failure of direct heirs of the body."* To demonstrate the right to resume was in those days tantamount to exercising it. So Jhansi was resumed. In vain the widow of the late Rajah, whom the Political Agent described as "a lady bearing a high character, and much respected by every one at Jhansi," protested that her husband's House had ever been faithful to the British Government—in vain she dwelt upon services rendered in former days to that Government, and the acknowledgments which they had elicited from our rulers—in vain she pointed to the terms of the treaty, which did not, to her simple understanding, bar succession in accordance with the laws and usages of her country—in vain she quoted

* But what Sir Charles Metcalfe really said was, that the paramount Power was "entitled to limit succession *according to the limitations of the grant*, which in general confirms it to heirs male of the body, and consequently precludes adoption. *In such cases*, therefore, the Power which granted, or the Power standing in its place, would have a right to resume on failure of heirs male of the body." This passage is very fairly quoted in Lord Dalhousie's Minute.

1853. precedents to show that the grace and favour sought for Jhansi had been yielded to other States. The fiat was irrevocable. It had been ruled that the interests both of the Jhansi State and the British Government imperatively demanded annexation. "As it lies in the midst of other British districts," said Lord Dalhousie, "the possession of it as our own will tend to the improvement of the general internal administration of our possessions in Bundelkund. That its incorporation with the British territories will be greatly for the benefit of the people of Jhansi a reference to the results of experience will suffice to show." The results of experience have since shown to what extent the people of Jhansi appreciated the benefits of that incorporation.

Kerowlee. Whilst this question was being disposed of by Lord Dalhousie and his colleagues, another lapse was under consideration, which had occurred some time before, but regarding which no final decision had been passed. In the summer of 1852, the young chief of Kerowlee, one of the smaller Rajpoot States, had died, after adopting another boy, connected with him by ties of kindred. At that time Colonel Low represented the British Government in Rajpootana, and he at once pronounced his opinion that the adoption ought immediately to be recognised.

The Governor-General hesitated. It appeared to him that Kerowlee might, rightly and expediently, be declared to have lapsed. But his Council was divided; his Agent in Rajpootana had declared unequivocally for the adoption; and the case differed in some respects from the Sattarah question, which had already been decided with the sanction and approval of the Home Government. How great the difference really was appeared far more clearly to the experienced eye of Sir Frederick Currie than to the vision of the Governor-General, clouded as it was by the film of a foregone conclusion.* The name of Sattarah had, by the force of accidental circumstances, become great throughout the land, both in India and in England; it was a familiar name to thousands and tens of thousands who had never heard of Kerowlee. With the Mahrattas, too, the House of Sivajee had been held in high veneration; but the Mahrattas could only boast of recent sovereignty; their high estate was one of modern usurpation. Their power had risen side by side with our own, and had been crushed down by our greater weight and greater vigour. But the Houses of Rajpootana had flourished centuries before the establishment of British rule; and the least of them had an ancestral dignity respected throughout the whole length and breadth of Hindostan, and treaty rights not less valid than any possessed by the greatest of territorial Princes. To men who had graduated, from boyhood upwards, in Indian statesmanship, there was something almost sacrilegious in the idea of laying a destroying hand even upon the least of the ancient Houses of Rajpootana—of destroying titles that had been honoured long years before the face of the white man had been seen in the country. But impressions of this kind are the growth of long intercourse with the people themselves, and we cannot be surprised that, after a year or two of Indian government, Lord Dalhousie, with all his unrivalled quickness of perception, should not have thoroughly understood the vital differences between the various 1852.

* Sir Frederick Currie's Minute on the Kerowlee question is an admirable state-paper—accurate in its facts, clear in its logic, and unexceptionable in its political morality.

1852. races inhabiting the great continent of India. Had he done so, he would at once have sanctioned the proposed adoption; as it was, he referred the question to the final decision of the Home Government.

Eager as they were at that time to support the policy of Lord Dalhousie, and entire as was the faith of many of them in his wisdom, the Directors could not look with favour upon a proposal to commence the gradual extinction of the ancient principalities of Rajpootana.

Jan. 26, 1853. "It appears to us," they said, "that there is a marked distinction in fact between the case of Kerowlee and Sattarah, which is not sufficiently adverted to in the Minute of the Governor-General. The Sattarah State was one of recent origin, derived altogether from the creation and gift of the British Government, whilst Kerowlee is one of the oldest of the Rajpoot States, which has been under the rule of its native Princes from a period long anterior to the British power in India. It stands to us only in the relation of protected ally, and probably there is no part of India into which it is less desirable, except upon the strongest grounds, to substitute our government for that of the native rulers. In our opinion, such grounds do not exist in the present case, and we have, therefore, determined to sanction the succession of Bhurt Pal."

But before the arrival of the despatch expressing these just sentiments and weighty opinions, all chance of the succession of Bhurt Pal had passed away. Had the adoption been granted at once, it would, in all probability, have been accepted by the members of the late Rajah's family, by the principal chiefs, and by the people of the country. But it is the inevitable tendency of delay in such a case to unsettle the public mind, to raise questions which but for this suspense would not have been born, and to excite hopes and stimulate ambitions which otherwise would have lain dormant. So it happened that whilst London and Calcutta were corresponding about the rights of Bhurt Pal, another claimant to the sovereignty of Kerowlee was asserting his pretensions in the most demonstrative manner. Another and a nearer kinsman of the late Prince—older, and, therefore, of a more pronounced personal character—stood forward to proclaim his rights, and to maintain them by arms. The ladies of the royal family, the chiefs, and the people, supported his claims; and the representative of the British Government in Rajpootana recognised their validity. That representative was Sir Henry Lawrence. Succeeding General Low in the Agency, he cherished the same principles as those which had ever been so consistently maintained by that veteran statesman; but circumstances had arisen which moved him to give them a different application. This new pretender to the throne had better claims on the score of consanguinity than Bhurt Pal, but Adoption overrides all claims of relationship, and, if the adoption were valid, the latter was legally the son and heir of the deceased. In this view, as consonant with the customs of the country, Henry Lawrence would have supported the succession of Bhurt Pal; but, on investigation, it appeared that all the requirements and conditions of law and usage had not been fulfilled, and that the people themselves doubted the validity of the adoption. It appeared to him, therefore, that the British Government would best discharge its duty to Kerowlee by allowing the succession of Muddun Pal. Even on the score of adoption his claims were good, for he had been adopted by the eldest of the late Rajah's widows, which, in default of adoption by

1853.

1853. the Rajah himself, would have been good against all claimants. But, in addition to this, it was to be said of the pretensions of this man that he was older than the other; that a minority would thus be avoided altogether; that he had some personal claims to consideration; and that the voice of the chiefs and the people had decided in his favour. As the succession, therefore, of Bhurt Pal had not been sanctioned, and as the decision of the Home Government in his favour had not been published, there would be no wrong to him in this preference of his rival, so Henry Lawrence recommended, and the Government of Lord Dalhousie approved, the succession of Muddun Pal to the sovereignty of Kerowlee.

So Lapse, in this instance, did not triumph; and the ancient Houses of Rajpootana, which, during these two years of suspense, had awaited the issue with the deepest interest, felt some temporary relief when it was known that the wedge of annexation had not been driven into the time-honoured circle of the States. But it is not to be supposed that because no wrong was done at last no injury was done by the delay. Public rumour recognises no Secret Department. It was well known at every native Court, in every native bazaar, that the British Government were discussing the policy of annexing or not annexing Kerowlee. The mere fact that there was a question to be discussed, in such a case, was sufficient to fill the minds of the people with anxiety and alarm. For two years Kerowlee was without any other ruler than the Political Agent of the British Government; and this was a significant fact, the impression of which was not to be removed by the subsequent decision. The Rajpoot Princes lost their confidence in the good faith of the British Government. Kerowlee had been spared, they scarcely knew how; some were fain to attribute it to the well-known justice and liberality of Henry Lawrence. But the same moderation might not be displayed again; there were childless men amongst them; and from that time a restless, uneasy feeling took possession of them, and no man felt sure that his House would not perish with him. It was not strange, indeed, that a year or two afterwards there should have been in circulation all over the country ominous reports to the effect that the policy of Lord Dalhousie had eventually triumphed, and that the gradual absorption of all the Rajpoot States had been sanctioned by the Home Government. It was a dangerous lie; and even the habitual reticence of the Court of Directors was not proof against the grossness of the calumny; so it was authoritatively contradicted. But not before it had worked its way in India, and done much to undermine the foundations of that confidence which is one of the main pillars of our strength. 1853.

There is one other story of territorial annexation yet to be told—briefly, for it was not thought at the time to be of much political importance, and now is held but little in remembrance. Beyond the south-western frontier of Bengal was the territory of Sumbhulpore. It had formerly been an outlying district of the Nagpore principality, but had been ceded by the Bonslah family, and had been bestowed by the British on a descendant of the old Sumbhulpore Rajahs, under terms which would have warranted the resumption of the estate on the death of the first incumbent. But twice the sovereign rights had been bestowed anew upon members of the family, and not until 1849, when Narain Singh lay at the point of death, was it determined to annex the territory to Sumbhulpore 1849.

1849. the British dominions. There were no heirs of the body; no near relatives of the Rajah. No adoption had been declared. The country was said to have been grievously misgoverned. And so there seemed to be a general agreement that the Lapse was perfect, and that annexation might be righteously proclaimed. Dalhousie was absent from the Presidency; but the case was clear, and the Government neither in India nor in England hesitated for a moment. And, perhaps, though it was not without its own bitter fruit, there is less to be said against it, on the score of abstract justice, than against anything of which I have written in this division of my work.

But there were lapses of another kind, lapses which involved no gain of territory to the British Government, for the territory had been gained before. There were several deposed princes in the land, representatives of ancient Houses, whose sceptres had passed by conquest or by treaty into the white man's hand, but who still enjoyed the possession of considerable revenues, and maintained some semblance of their former dignity and state. It happened that, whilst Dalhousie reigned in India, three of these pensioned princes died. Of the story of one of them I must write in detail. There had once been three great Mahratta Houses: the Houses of Sattarah, of Nagpore, and of Poonah. It has been told how Dalhousie extinguished the two first; the third had been for some thirty years territorially extinct, when he was sent out to govern India. In 1818, at the close of the second great Mahratta war, the Peishwah, Badjee Rao, surrendered to Sir John Malcolm. He had been betrayed into hostility, and treacherous hostility; he had appealed to the sword, and he had been fairly beaten; and there was nothing

The story of the Peishwah.

left for him but to end his days as an outcast and a fugitive, or to fling himself upon the mercy of the British Government. He chose the latter course; and when he gave himself to the English General, he knew that he was in the hands of one who sympathised with him in his fallen fortunes, and would be a generous friend to him in adversity. Malcolm pledged the Government to bestow upon the Peishwah, for the support of himself and family, an annual pension of not less than eight lakhs of rupees. The promise was said to be an over-liberal one; and there were those who at the time condemned Malcolm for his profuseness. But he replied, that "it had been the policy of the British Government, since its first establishment in India, to act towards princes, whose bad faith and treachery had compelled it to divest them of all power and dominion, with a generosity which almost lost sight of their offences. The effect of this course of proceeding in reconciling all classes to its rule had been great. The liberality and the humanity which it had displayed on such occasions had, I was satisfied, done more than its arms towards the firm establishment of its power. It was, in fact, a conquest over mind, and among men so riveted in their habits and prejudices as the natives of their country, the effect, though unseen, was great beyond calculation." It was a solace to him to think that these sentiments were shared by such men as Mountstuart Elphinstone, David Ochterlony, and Thomas Munro. 1818.

So Badjee Rao went into honourable seclusion, and an asylum was found for him at Bithoor, distant some twelve miles from the great military station of Cawnpore, in the North-Western Provinces of India. He was not then an old man, as age is calcu-

1818-51. lated by years, but he was said to be of debauched habits and feeble constitution; and no one believed that he would very long survive to be a burden upon the Company. But he outlived his power for a third part of a century, living resignedly, if not contentedly, in his new home, with a large body of followers and dependents, mostly of his own race, and many others of the outward insignia of state. From the assemblage, under such circumstances, of so large a body of Mahrattas, some feeling of apprehension and alarm might have arisen in the mind of the British Government, especially in troubled times; but the fidelity of the ex-Peishwah himself was as conspicuous as the good conduct and the orderly behaviour of his people. Nor was it only a passive loyalty that he manifested; for twice in critical conjunctures, when the English were sore-pressed, he came forward with offers of assistance. When the War in Afghanistan had drained our Treasury, and money was grievously wanted, he lent the Company five lakhs of rupees; and when, afterwards, our dominions were threatened with an invasion from the Punjab, and there was much talk all over the country of a hostile alliance between the Sikhs and the Mahrattas, the steadfastness of his fidelity was evidenced by an offer made to the British Government to raise and to maintain at his own cost a thousand Horse and a thousand Foot. As he had the disposition, so also had he the means to serve us. His ample pension more than sufficed for the wants even of a retired monarch; and as years passed, people said that he had laid by a great store of wealth, and asked who was to be its inheritor? For it was with him, as it was with other Mahratta princes, he was going down to the grave leaving no son to succeed him. So he adopted a son, from his own family stock,* and, some years before his death, sought the recognition of the British Government for an adoption embracing more than the right of succession to his savings (for this needed no sovereign sanction) the privilege of succeeding to the title and the pension of the Peishwah. The prayer was not granted; but the Company did not shut out all hope that, after the death of Badjee Rao, some provision might be made for his family. The question was reserved for future consideration—that is, until the contingency of the ex-Peishwah's death should become an accomplished reality; and as at this time the old man was feeble, paralytic, and nearly blind, it was not expected that his pension would much longer remain a burden on the Indian revenues. 1818-51.

Death of Badjee Rao.

But not until the 28th of January, 1851, when there was the weight of seventy-seven years upon him, did the last of the Peishwahs close his eyes upon the world for ever. He left behind him a will, executed in 1839, in which he named as his adopted son, "to inherit and be the sole master of the Guddee of the Peishwah, the dominions, wealth, family possessions, treasure, and all his real and personal property," a youth known as Doondoo Punt, Nana Sahib. When Badjee Rao died, the heir was twenty-seven years old; described as "a quiet, unostentatious young man, not at all addicted to any extravagant habits, and invariably showing a ready disposition to attend to the advice of the British Commissioner."

The Nana Sahib.

* Strictly it should be said that he adopted three sons and a grandson. His will says: "That Doondoo Punt, Nana, my eldest son, and Gungadhur Rao, my youngest and third son, and Sada-Sheo Punt Dada, son of my second son, Pundoo Rung Rao, my grandson; these three are my sons and grandson. After me Doondoo Punt, Nana, my eldest son, Mookh Perdan, shall inherit and be the sole master of the Guddee of the Peishwah, &c."—*MS. Records.*

1851. What he was safe to inherit was about 300,000*l.*, more than one-half of which was invested in Government securities;* but there was an immense body of dependents to be provided for, and it was thought that the British Government might appropriate a portion of the ex-Peishwah's stipend to the support of the family at Bithoor. The management of affairs was in the hands of the Soubahdar Ramchunder Punt, a faithful friend and adherent of Badjee Rao, who counselled his master with wisdom, and controlled his followers with vigour; and he now, with all due respect for the British Government, pleaded the cause of the adopted son of the Peishwah. "Nana Sahib," he said, "considering the Honourable Company in the room of the late Maharajah as his protector and supporter, is full of hopes and free of care on this subject. His dependence in every way is on the kindness and liberality of the British Government, for the increase of whose power and prosperity he has ever been, and will continue to be, desirous." The British Commissioner at Bithoor† supported the appeal in behalf of the family, but it met with no favour in high places. Mr. Thomason was then Lieutenant-Governor of the North-Western Provinces. He was a good man, an able man, a man of high reputation, but he was one of the leaders of the New School, and was no friend to the princes and nobles of the land; and he told the Commissioner to discourage all hopes of further assistance in the breasts

* The official report of the Commissioner said, 16 lakhs of Government paper, 10 lakhs of jewels, 3 lakhs of gold coins, 80,000 rupees gold ornaments, 20,000 rupees silver plate.

† It should rather be said, "two British Commissioners." Colonel Manson was Commissioner when the Peishwah died, but he left Bithoor shortly afterwards, and Mr. Morland, then magistrate at Cawnpore, took his place, and on him devolved the principal business of the settlement of the ex-Peishwah's affairs.

of the family, and to "strive to induce the numerous retainers of the Peishwah speedily to disperse and return to the Deccan." Lord Dalhousie was Governor-General; and, in such a case, his views were little likely to differ from those of his Lieutenant. So he declared his opinion that the recommendations of the Commissioner were "uncalled for and unreasonable." "The Governor-General," it was added, "concurs in opinion with his Honour (Mr. Thomason) in thinking that, under any circumstances, the Family have no claim upon the Government; and he will by no means consent to any portion of the public revenues being conferred on them. His Lordship requests that the determination of the Government of India may be explicitly declared to the Family without delay." And it was so declared; but with some small alleviation of the harshness of the sentence, for the Jagheer, or rent-free estate, of Bithoor was to be continued to the Nana Sahib, but without the exclusive jurisdiction which had been enjoyed by the ex-Peishwah. 1851.

When Doondoo Punt learnt that there was no hope of any further assistance to the family at Bithoor from the liberality of the Government of India, he determined to appeal to the Court of Directors of the East India Company. It had been in contemplation during the lifetime of Badjee Rao to adopt such a course, and a son of the Soubahdar Ramchunder had been selected as the agent who was to prosecute the appeal. But discouraged by the Commissioner, the project had been abandoned, and was not revived until all other hope had failed after the ex-Peishwah's death. Then it was thought that a reversal of the adverse decision might be obtained by memorialising the authorities in England, and a Memorial of the Nana.

December 29, 1852. memorial was accordingly drawn up and despatched, in the usual manner, through the Government in India. "The course pursued by the local governments," it was said, "is not only an unfeeling one towards the numerous family of the deceased prince, left almost entirely dependent upon the promises of the East India Company, but inconsistent with what is due to the representative of a long line of sovereigns. Your memorialist, therefore, deems it expedient at once to appeal to your Honourable Court, not merely on the ground of the faith of treaties, but of a bare regard to the advantages the East India Company have derived from the last sovereign of the Mahratta Empire. . . . . It would be contrary to the spirit of all treaties hitherto concluded to attach a special meaning to an article of the stipulations entered into, whilst another is interpreted and acted upon in its most liberal sense." And then the memorialist proceeded to argue, that as the Peishwah, on behalf of his heirs and successors, had ceded his territories to the Company, the Company were bound to pay the price of such cession to the Peishwah and his heirs and successors. If the compact were lasting on one side, so also should it be on the other. "Your memorialist submits that a cession of a perpetual revenue of thirty-four lakhs of rupees in consideration of an annual pension of eight lakhs establishes a *de facto* presumption that the payment of one is contingent upon the receipt of the other, and hence that, as long as those receipts continue, the payment of the pension is to follow." It was then argued that the mention, in the treaty, of the "Family" of the Peishwah indicated the hereditary character of the stipulation, on the part of the Company, as such mention would be unnecessary and unmeaning in its application to a mere life-grant, "for a provision for the support of the prince necessarily included the maintenance of his family;" and after this, from special arguments, the Nana Sahib turned to a general assertion of his rights as based on precedent and analogy. "Your memorialist," it was said, "is at a loss to account for the difference between the treatment, by the Company, of the descendants of other princes and that experienced by the family of the Peishwah, represented by him. The ruler of Mysore evinced the most implacable hostility towards the Company's government; and your memorialist's father was one of the princes whose aid was invoked by the Company to crush a relentless enemy. When that chieftain fell, sword in hand, the Company, far from abandoning his progeny to their fate, have afforded an asylum and a liberal support to more than one generation of his descendants, without distinction between the legitimate and the illegitimate. With equal or even greater liberality the Company delivered the dethroned Emperor of Delhi from a dungeon, re-invested him with the insignia of sovereignty, and assigned to him a munificent revenue, which is continued to his descendants to the present day. Wherein is your memorialist's case different? It is true that the Peishwah, after years of amity with the British Indian Government, during which he assigned to them revenues to the amount of half a crore of rupees, was unhappily engaged in war with them, by which he perilled his throne. But as he was not reduced to extremities, and even if reduced, closed with the terms proposed to him by the British Commander, and ceded his rich domains to place himself and his family under the fostering care of the Company, and as the Company still profit by the revenues 1852

1852. of his hereditary possessions, on what principle are his descendants deprived of the pension included in those terms and the vestiges of sovereignty? Wherein are the claims of his family to the favour and consideration of the Company less than those of the conquered Mysorean or the captive Mogul?" Then the Nana Sahib began to set forth his own personal claims as founded on the adoption in his favour; he quoted the best authorities on Hindoo law to prove that the son by adoption has all the rights of the son by birth; and he cited numerous instances, drawn from the recent history of Hindostan and the Deccan, to show how such adoptions had before been recognised by the British Government. "The same fact," he added, "is evinced in the daily practice of the Company's Courts all over India, in decreeing to the adopted sons of princes, of zemindars, and persons of every grade, the estates of those persons to the exclusion of other heirs of the blood. Indeed, unless the British Indian Government is prepared to abrogate the Hindoo Sacred Code, and to interdict the practice of the Hindoo religion, of both of which adoption is a fundamental feature, your memorialist cannot understand with what consistency his claim to the pension of the late Peishwah can be denied, merely on the ground of his being an adopted son."

Another plea for refusal might be, nay, had been, based upon the fact that Badjee Rao, from the savings of his pension, had accumulated and left behind him a large amount of private property, which no one could alienate from his heirs. Upon this the Nana Sahib, with not unreasonable indignation, said: "That if the withholding of the pension proceeded from the supposition that the late Peishwah had left a sufficient provision for his family, it would be altogether foreign to the question, and unprecedented in the annals of the History of British India. The pension of eight lakhs of rupees per annum has been agreed upon on the part of the British Government, to enable his Highness the late Badjee Rao to support himself and family; it is immaterial to the British Government what portion of that sum the late prince actually expended, nor has there been any agreement entered into to the effect that his Highness the late Badjee Rao should be compelled to expend every fraction of an annual allowance accorded to him by a special treaty, in consideration of his ceding to the British Government territories yielding an annual and perpetual revenue of thirty-four lakhs of rupees. Nobody on earth had a right to control the expenditure of that pension, and if his Highness the late Badjee Rao had saved every fraction of it, he would have been perfectly justified in doing so. Your memorialist would venture to ask, whether the British Government ever deigned to ask in what manner the pension granted to any of its numerous retired servants is expended? or whether any of them saves a portion, or what portion, of his pension? and, furthermore, in the event of its being proved that the incumbents of such pensions had saved a large portion thereof, it would be considered a sufficient reason for withholding the pension from the children in the proportions stipulated by the covenant entered into with its servant? And yet is a native prince, the descendant of an ancient scion of Royalty, who relies upon the justice and liberality of the British Government, deserving of less consideration than its covenanted servants? To disperse, however, any erroneous impression that 1852.

1852. may exist on the part of the British Government on that score, your memorialist would respectfully beg to observe that the pension of eight lakhs of rupees, stipulated for by the treaty of 1818, was not exclusively for the support of his Highness the late Badjee Rao and his family, but also for the maintenance of a large retinue of faithful adherents, who preferred following the ex-Peishwah in his voluntary exile. Their large number, fully known to the British Government, caused no inconsiderable call upon the reduced resources of his Highness; and, furthermore, if it be taken into consideration the appearance which Native princes, though rendered powerless, are still obliged to keep up to ensure respect, it may be easily imagined that the savings from a pension of eight lakhs of rupees, granted out of an annual revenue of thirty-four lakhs, could not have been large. But notwithstanding this heavy call upon the limited resources of the late Peishwah, his Highness husbanded his resources with much care, so as to be enabled to invest a portion of his annual income in public securities, which, at the time of his death, yielded an income of about eighty thousand rupees. Is then the foresight and the economy on the part of his Highness the late Badjee Rao to be regarded as an offence deserving to be visited with the punishment of stopping the pension for the support of his MS. Records. family guaranteed by a formal treaty?"

But neither the rhetoric nor the reasoning of the Nana Sahib had any effect upon the Home Government. The Court of Directors of the East India Company were hard as a rock, and by no means to be moved to compassion. They had already expressed an opinion that the savings of the Peishwah were sufficient for the maintenance of his heirs and dependents;* and when the memorial came before them, they summarily rejected it, writing out to the Government to "inform the memorialist that the pension of his adoptive father was not hereditary, that he has no claim whatever to it, and that his application is wholly inadmissible." Such a reply as this must have crushed out all hope from the Bithoor Family, and shown the futility of further action; but it happened that, before this answer was received, the Nana Sahib had sent an agent to England to prosecute his claims. This agent was not the son of the old Mahratta Soubahdar, to whom the mission first contemplated was to have been entrusted, but a young and astute Mahomedan, with a good presence, a plausible address, and a knowledge of the English language. His name was Azim-oollah Khan. In the summer of 1853 he appeared in England, and in conjunction with an Englishman, named Biddle, prosecuted the claims of the Nana, but with no success. Judgment had already been recorded, and nothing that these agents could say or do was likely to cause its reversal.

1853. Decision of the Company.

May 4, 1853.

So Azim-oollah Khan, finding that little or nothing could be done in the way of business for his employer, devoted his energies to the pursuit of pleasure on his own account. Passing by reason of his fine clothes for a person of high station, he made his way into good society, and is said to have boasted of favours received from English ladies. Outwardly he was a gay, smiling, voluptuous sort of person; and

* "*May* 19, 1852.—We entirely approve of the decision of the Governor-General that the adopted son and dependents on Badjee Rao have no claim upon the British Government. The large pension which the ex-Peishwah enjoyed during thirty-three years afforded him the means of making an abundant provision for his family and dependents, and the property, which he is known to have left, is amply sufficient for their support."—*The Court of Directors to the Government of India.—MS.*

1853. even a shrewd observer might have thought that he was intent always upon the amusement of the hour. There was one man, however, in England at that time, who, perhaps, knew that the desires of the plausible Mahomedan were not bounded by the enjoyment of the present. For it happened that the agent, who had been sent to England by the deposed Sattarah Family, in the hope of obtaining for them the restoration of their principality, was still resident in the English metropolis. This man was a Mahratta named Rungo Bapojee. Able and energetic, he had pushed his suit with a laborious, untiring conscientiousness, rarely seen in a Native envoy; but though aided by much soundness of argument and much fluency of rhetoric expended by others than hired advocates, upon the case of the Sattarah Princes, he had failed to make an impression on their judges. Though of different race and different religion, these two men were knit together by common sympathies and kindred tasks, and in that autumn of 1853, by like failures and disappointments to brood over and the same bitter animosities to cherish. What was said and what was done between them no Historian can relate. They were adepts in the art of dissimulation. So the crafty Mahratta made such a good impression even upon those whom his suit had so greatly troubled, that his debts were paid for him, and he was sent back at the public expense to Bombay with money in his pocket from the Treasury of the India House;* whilst the gay Mahomedan floated about the surface of society and made a conspicuous figure at crowded watering-places, as if he dearly loved England and the English, and could not per-

* Rungo Bapojee returned to India in December, 1853. The East India Company gave him 2500*l.* and a free passage.

suade himself to return to his own dreary and benighted land. 1853.

So little material are they to this History that I need not write in detail of the circumstances attending the extinction of the titular sovereignties of the Carnatic and Tanjore, two ancient Houses, one Mahomedan, the other Hindoo, that had once flourished in the Southern Peninsula. Lord Wellesley had stripped them of territorial power. It remained, therefore, only for Lord Dalhousie, when the Newab of the Carnatic and the Rajah of Tanjore died without heirs of the body, to abolish the titular dignities of the two Families and "to resume the large stipends they had enjoyed, as Lapses to Government." Pensions were settled upon the surviving members of the two Families; but in each case, the head of the House made vehement remonstrance against the extinction of its honours, and long and loudly clamoured for restitution. There were many, doubtless, in Southern India who still clung with feelings of veneration to these shadowy pageants, and deplored the obliteration of the royal names that they had long honoured; and as a part of the great system of demolition these resumptions made a bad impression in more remote places. But empty titular dignities are dangerous possessions, and it may be, after all, only mistaken kindness to perpetuate them when the substance of royalty is gone.

Carnatic and Tanjore.

1854.

1855.

*** In this chapter might have been included other cases of Lapse, as those of the Pergunnah, of Odeipoor, on the South-Western Frontier, and of Jeitpore, in Bundlekhund; but, although every additional absorption of territory tended to increase, in some measure, the feeling of insecurity in men's minds, they were comparatively of little political importance; and Lord Dalhousie did not think them worth a paragraph in his Farewell Minute.

CHAPTER III.

THE ANNEXATION OF OUDE—EARLY HISTORY OF THE PROVINCE—THE TREATY OF 1801—EFFECTS OF THE DOUBLE GOVERNMENT—CREATION OF THE KINGSHIP—PROGRESS OF MISRULE—REPEATED WARNINGS—THE UNRATIFIED TREATY—COLONEL SLEEMAN'S REPORTS—LORD DALHOUSIE'S MINUTE—VIEWS OF THE COURT OF DIRECTORS—SIR JAMES OUTRAM RESIDENT—ANNEXATION PROCLAIMED.

1856. THERE was still another province to be absorbed into the British Empire under the administration of Lord Dalhousie; not by conquest, for its rulers had ever been our friends, and its people had recruited our armies; not by lapse, for there had always been a son or a brother, or some member of the royal house, to fulfil, according to the Mahomedan law of succession, the conditions of heirship, and there was still a king, the son of a king, upon the throne; but by a simple assertion of the dominant will of the British Government. This was the great province of Oude, in the very heart of Hindostan, which had long tempted us, alike by its local situation and the reputed wealth of its natural resources.

It is a story not to be lightly told in a few sentences. Its close connexion with some of the more important passages of this history fully warrants some amplitude of narration. Before the British settler had established himself on the peninsula of India, Oude was

a province of the Mogul Empire. When that empire 1756-1796.
was distracted and weakened by the invasion of Nadir Shah, the treachery of the servant was turned against the master, and little by little the Governor began to govern for himself. But holding only an official, though an hereditary title, he still acknowledged his vassalage; and long after the Great Mogul had shrivelled into a pensioner and a pageant, the Newab-Wuzeer of Oude was nominally his minister.

Of the earliest history of British connexion with the Court of the Wuzeer, it is not necessary to write in detail. There is nothing less creditable in the annals of the rise and progress of the British power in the East. The Newab had territory; the Newab had subjects; the Newab had neighbours; more than all, the Newab had money. But although he possessed in abundance the raw material of soldiers, he had not been able to organise an army sufficient for all the external and internal requirements of the State, and so he was fain to avail himself of the superior military skill and discipline of the white men, and to hire British battalions to do his work. At first this was done in an irregular, desultory kind of way, job-work, as in the infamous case of the Rohilla massacre; but afterwards it assumed a more formal and recognised shape, and solemn engagements were entered into with the Newab, by which we undertook, in consideration of certain money-payments, known as the Subsidy, to provide a certain number of British troops for the internal and external defence of his Excellency's dominions.

In truth it was a vicious system, one that can hardly be too severely condemned. By it we established a Double Government of the worst kind. The Political and Military government was in the hands

1796. of the Company; the internal administration of the Oude territories still rested with the Newab-Wuzeer. In other words, hedged in and protected by the British battalions, a bad race of Eastern Princes were suffered to do, or not to do, what they liked. Under such influences it is not strange that disorder of every kind ran riot over the whole length and breadth of the land. Never were the evils of misrule more horribly apparent; never were the vices of an indolent and rapacious Government productive of a greater sum of misery. The extravagance and profligacy of the Court were written in hideous characters on the desolated face of the country. It was left to the Nabob's Government to dispense justice: justice was not dispensed. It was left to the Nabob's Government to collect the revenue; it was wrung from the people at the point of the bayonet. The Court was sumptuous and profligate; the people poor and wretched. The expenses of the royal household were enormous. Hundreds of richly-caparisoned voracious elephants ate up the wealth of whole districts, or carried it in glittering apparel on their backs. A multitudinous throng of unserviceable attendants; bands of dancing-girls; flocks of parasites; costly feasts and ceremonies; folly and pomp and profligacy of every conceivable description, drained the coffers of the State. A vicious and extravagant Government soon beget a poor and a suffering people; a poor and a suffering people, in turn, perpetuate the curse of a bankrupt Government. The process of retaliation is sure. To support the lavish expenditure of the Court the mass of the people were persecuted and outraged. Bands of armed mercenaries were let loose upon the ryots in support of the rapacity of the Aumils, or Revenue-farmers, whose appearance was a terror to the people. Under such a system of cruelty and extortion, the country soon became a desert, and the Government then learnt by hard experience that the prosperity of the people is the only true source of wealth. The lesson was thrown away. The decrease of the revenue was not accompanied by a corresponding diminution of the profligate expenditure of the Court, or by any effort to introduce a better administrative system. Instead of this, every new year saw the unhappy country lapsing into worse disorder, with less disposition, as time advanced, on the part of the local Government to remedy the evils beneath which it was groaning. Advice, protestation, remonstrance were in vain. Lord Cornwallis advised, protested, remonstrated: Sir John Shore advised, protested, remonstrated. At last a statesman of a very different temper appeared upon the scene. 1798.

Lord Wellesley was a despot in every pulse of his heart. But he was a despot of the right kind; for he was a man of consummate vigour and ability, and he seldom made a mistake. The condition of Oude soon attracted his attention; not because its government was bad and its people were wretched, but because that country might either be a bulwark of safety to our own dominions, or a sea of danger which might overflow and destroy us. That poor old blind ex-King, Shah Zemaun, of the Suddozye family of Caubul, known to the present generation as the feeble appendage of a feeble puppet, had been, a little while before the advent of Lord Wellesley, in the heyday of his pride and power, meditating great deeds which he had not the ability to accomplish, and keeping the British power in India in a chronic state of unrest. If ever there had been any real peril, it had passed away before the new century was a year old But it

1799. might arise again. Doubtless the military strength of the Afghans was marvellously overrated in those days; but still there was the fact of a minatious Mahomedan power beyond the frontier, not only meditating invasion, but stirring up the Mahomedan Princes of India to combine in a religious war against the usurping Feringhee. Saadut Ali was then on the musnud of Oude; he was the creature and the friend of the English, but Vizier Ali, whom he had supplanted, had intrigued with Zemaun Shah, and would not only have welcomed, but have subsidised also an Afghan force in his own dominions. At the bottom of all our alarm, at that time, were some not unreasonable apprehensions of the ambitious designs of the first Napoleon. At all events, it was sound policy to render Oude powerful for good and powerless for evil. To the accomplishment of this it was necessary that large bodies of ill-disciplined and irregularly paid native troops in the service of the Newab-Wuzeer --lawless bands that had been a terror alike to him and to his people—should be forthwith disbanded, and that British troops should occupy their place. Now, already the Wuzeer was paying seventy-six lakhs of rupees, or more than three-quarters of a million of money, for his subsidised British troops, and though he was willing to disband his own levies, and thereby to secure some saving to the State, it was but small in proportion to the expense of the more costly machinery of British military defence now to be substituted for them. The additional burden to be imposed upon Oude was little less than half a million of money, and the unfortunate Wuzeer, whose resources had been strained to the utmost to pay the previous subsidy, declared his inability to meet any further demands on his treasury. This was what Lord Wellesley expected—nay, more, it was what he wanted. If the Wuzeer could not pay in money, he could pay in money's worth. He had rich lands that might be ceded in perpetuity to the Company for the punctual payment of the subsidy. So the Governor-General prepared a treaty ceding the required provinces, and with a formidable array of British troops at his call, dragooned the Wuzeer into sullen submission to the will of the English Sultan. The new treaty was signed; and districts then yielding a million and a half of money, and now nearly double that amount of annual revenue, passed under the administration of the British Government. 1800.

Now, this treaty—the last ever ratified between the two Governments—bound the Newab Wuzeer to "establish in his reserved dominions such a system of administration, to be carried on by his own officers, as should be conducive to the prosperity of his subjects, and be calculated to secure the lives and properties of the inhabitants," and he undertook at the same time "always to advise with and to act in conformity to the counsels of the officers of the East India Company." But the English ruler knew well that there was small hope of these conditions being fulfilled. "I am satisfied," he said, "that no effectual security can be provided against the ruin of the province of Oude until the exclusive management of the civil and military government of that country shall be transferred to the Company under suitable provisions for the maintenance of his Excellency and his family." He saw plainly before him the breakdown of the whole system, and believed that in the course of a few years the entire administration of the province would be transferred to the hands of our British officers. There was one thing, however, on 1801.

1801-17. which he did not calculate—the moderation of his successors. He lived nearly half a century after these words were written, and yet the treaty outlived him by many years.

If there was, at any time, hope for Oude, under purely native administration, it was during the wuzeership of Saadut Ali, for he was not a bad man, and he appears to have had rather enlightened views with respect to some important administrative questions.* But the opportunity was lost; and whilst the counsels of our British officers did nothing for the people, the bayonets of our British soldiers restrained them from doing anything for themselves. Thus matters grew from bad to worse, and from worse to worst. One Governor-General followed another; one Resident followed another; one Wuzeer followed another: but still the great tide of evil increased in volume, in darkness, and in depth.

But, although the Newab-Wuzeers of Oude were, doubtless, bad rulers and bad men, it must be admitted that they were good allies. False to their people —false to their own manhood—they were true to the British Government. They were never known to break out into open hostility, or to smoulder in hidden treachery against us; and they rendered good service, when they could, to the Power to which they owed so little. They supplied our armies, in time of war, with grain, they supplied us with carriage-cattle; better still, they supplied us with cash. There was money in the

* Sir Henry Lawrence says that he was "in advance of the Bengal Government of the day on revenue arrangements," and gives two striking instances of the fact. With characteristic candour and impartiality, Lawrence adds that Saadut Ali's mal-administration was "mainly attributable to English interference, to the resentment he felt for his own wrongs, and the bitterness of soul with which he must have received all advice from his oppressors, no less than to the impunity with which they enabled him to play the tyrant."—*Calcutta Review*, vol. iii. See also Lawrence's Essays, in which this paper is printed.

Treasury of Lucknow, when there was none in the Treasury of Calcutta; and the time came when the Wuzeer's cash was needed by the British ruler. Engaged in an extensive and costly war, Lord Hastings wanted more millions for the prosecution of his great enterprises. They were forthcoming at the right time; and the British Government were not unwilling in exchange to bestow both titles and territories on the Wuzeer. The times were propitious. The successful close of the Nepaul war placed at our disposal an unhealthy and impracticable tract of country at the foot of the Hills. This "terai" ceded to us by the Nepaulese was sold for a million of money to the Wuzeer, to whose domains it was contiguous, and he himself expanded and bloomed into a King under the fostering sun of British favour and affection.* The interest of the other million was paid away by our Government to a tribe of Oude pensioners, who were not sorry to exchange for a British guarantee the erratic benevolence of their native masters. 1817.

It would take long to trace the history of the progressive misrule of the Oude dominions under a succession of sovereigns all of the same class—passive permitters of evil rather than active perpetrators of iniquity, careless of, but not rejoicing in, the sufferings of their people. The rulers of Oude, whether Wuzeers or Kings, had not the energy to be tyrants.

* Sir John Malcolm said that the very mention of "his Majesty of Oude" made him sick. "Would I make," he said, "a golden calf, and suffer him to throw off his subordinate title, and assume equality with the degraded representative of a line of monarchs to whom his ancestors have been for ages really or nominally subject?" Sir Henry Lawrence seems to have thought that this was precisely what was intended. "The Newab Ghazee-ood-deen Hyder," he wrote, "was encouraged to assume the title of King; Lord Hastings calculated on this exciting a rivalry between the Oude and Delhi Families."—*Calcutta Review*, vol. iii.; and Essays, page 119.

1817. They simply allowed things to take their course. Sunk in voluptuousness and pollution, often too horribly revolting to be described, they gave themselves up to the guidance of pandars and parasites, and cared not so long as these wretched creatures administered to their sensual appetites. Affairs of State were pushed aside as painful intrusions. Corruption stalked openly abroad. Every one had his price. Place, honour, justice—everything was to be bought. Fiddlers and barbers, pimps and mountebanks, became great functionaries. There were high revels at the capital, whilst, in the interior of the country, every kind of enormity was being exercised to wring from the helpless people the money which supplied the indulgences of the Court. Much of the land was farmed out to large contractors, who exacted every possible farthing from the cultivators; and were not seldom, upon complaint of extortion, made, unless inquiry were silenced by corruption, to disgorge into the royal treasury a large portion of their gains. Murders of the most revolting type, gang-robberies of the most outrageous character, were committed in open day. There were no Courts of Justice except at Lucknow; no Police but at the capital and on the frontier. The British troops were continually called out to coerce refractory landholders, and to stimulate revenue-collection at the point of the bayonet. The sovereign—Wuzeer or King—knew that they would do their duty; knew that, under the obligations of the treaty, his authority would be supported; and so he lay secure in his Zenana, and fiddled whilst his country was in flames.

And so years passed; and ever went there from the Residency to the Council-chamber of the Supreme Government the same unvarying story of frightful misrule. Residents expostulated, Governors-General protested against it. The protests in due course became threats. Time after time it was announced to the rulers of Oude that, unless some great and immediate reforms were introduced into the system of administration, the British Government, as lords-paramount, would have no course left to them but to assume the direction of affairs, and to reduce the sovereign of Oude to a pensioner and a pageant. 1831.

By no man was the principle of non-interference supported more strenuously, both in theory and in practice, than by Lord William Bentinck. But in the affairs of this Oude State he considered that he was under a righteous necessity to interfere. In April, 1831, he visited Lucknow; and there, distinctly and emphatically told the King that "unless his territories were governed upon other principles than those hitherto followed, and the prosperity of the people made the principal object of his administration, the precedents afforded by the principalities of the Carnatic and Tanjore would be applied to the kingdom of Oude, and to the entire management of the country, and the King would be transmuted into a State prisoner." This was no mere formal harangue, but the deliberate enunciation of the Government of India; and to increase the impression which it was calculated to make on the mind of the King, the warning was afterwards communicated to him in writing. But, spoken or written, the words were of no avail. He threw himself more than ever into the arms of parasites and pandars; plunged more deeply into debauchery than before, and openly violated all decency by appearing drunk in the public streets of Lucknow.* With the corruption of the Court the

* This was Nussur-ood-deen Hyder—the second of the Oude kings, and perhaps the worst. I speak dubiously, however, of their comparative merits. Colonel Sleeman seems to have thought that he might have extracted more good out of Nussur-ood-deen than out of any of the rest.

1831. disorders of the country increased. The crisis seemed now to have arrived. A communication was made to the Court of Oude, that "instructions to assume the government of the country, if circumstances should render such a measure necessary, had arrived, and that their execution was suspended merely in the hope that the necessity of enforcing them might be obviated."

But in what manner was the administration to be assumed—in what manner was the improvement of the country to be brought about by the intervention of the British Government? There were different courses open to us, and they were all diligently considered. We might appoint a Minister of our own selection, and rule through him by the agency of the Resident. We might depose the ruling sovereign, and set up another and more hopeful specimen of royalty in his place. We might place the country under European administration, giving all the surplus revenues to the King. We might assume the entire government, reducing the King to a mere titular dignitary, and giving him a fixed share of the annual revenues. Or we might annex the country outright, giving him so many lakhs of rupees a year, without reference to the revenues of the principality. The ablest and most experienced Indian statesmen of the day had been invited to give their opinions. Malcolm and Metcalfe spoke freely out. The first of the above schemes seemed to represent the mildest form of interference; but both the soldier and the civilian unhesitatingly rejected it as the most odious, and, in practice, the most ruinous of all interposition. Far better, they said, to set up a new King, or even to assume the government for ourselves. But those were days when native dynasties were not considered unmixed evils, and native institutions were not pure abominations in our eyes. And it was thought that we might assume the administration of Oude, but not for ourselves. It was thought that the British Government might become the guardian and trustee of the King of Oude, administer his affairs through native agency and in accordance with native institutions, and pay every single rupee into the royal treasury. 1832.

This was the scheme of Lord William Bentinck, a man of unsurpassed honesty and justice; and it met with favourable acceptance in Leadenhall-street. The Court of Directors at that time, true to the old traditions of the Company, were slow to encourage their agents to seek pretexts for the extension of their dominions. The despatches which they sent out to India were for the most part distinguished by a praiseworthy moderation; sometimes, indeed, by a noble frankness and sincerity, which showed that the authors of them were above all disguises and pretences. They now looked the Oude business fairly in the face, but hoping still against hope that there might be some amelioration, they suffered, after the receipt of Lord William Bentinck's report, a year to pass away, and then another year, before issuing authoritative orders, and then they sent forth a despatch, which was intended to bring the whole question to a final issue. They spoke of the feelings July 16, 1834. which the deplorable situation of a country so long and so nearly connected with them had excited in their minds—of the obligations which such a state of things imposed upon them—of the necessity of finding means of effecting a great alteration. They acknowledged, as they had acknowledged before, that our connexion with the country had largely contributed to the sufferings of the people, inasmuch as it had afforded protection to tyranny, and rendered

1834. hopeless the resistance of the oppressed.* This made it the more incumbent upon them to adopt measures for the mitigation, if not the removal, of the existing evil. They could no look on whilst the ruin of the country was consummated. It was certain that something must be done. But what was that something to be? Then they set in array before them, somewhat as I have done above, the different measures which might be resorted to, and, dwelling upon the course which Bentinck had recommended, placed in the hands of the Governor-General a discretionary power to carry the proposed measure into effect at such period, and in such a manner as might seem advisable, but with the utmost possible consideration for the King, whose consent to the proposed arrangement was, if possible, to be obtained. It was suggested that all the titles and honours of sovereignty should remain with his Majesty as before; that the revenues should be mainly expended in the administration and the improvement of the country, and that either the surplus, or a fixed stipend, should be assigned to the King. But, at the same time, the Government were instructed, in the event of their proceeding to assume the administration of the country, distinctly to announce that, so soon as the necessary reforms should have been effected, the administration of the country, as in the case of Nagpore, would be restored to its native rulers.

Colonel John Low, of whose character and career I have already spoken, was then Resident at Luck-

* For a long time, as we have said, our troops were employed by the King's officers to aid them in the collection of the revenue; thereby active, as the Court frankly described it, as "instruments of extortion and vengeance." This scandal no longer existed; but our battalions were still stationed in the country, ready to dragoon down any open insurrection that might result from the misgovernment of Oude.

now. The despatch of the Court of Directors, authorising the temporary assumption of the Government of Oude, was communicated to him, and he pondered over its contents. The scheme appeared in his eyes to be distinguished by its moderation and humanity, and to be one of a singularly disinterested character. But he was convinced that it would be misunderstood. He said that, however pure the motives of the British Government might be, the natives of India would surely believe that we had taken the country for ourselves. So he recommended the adoption of another method of obtaining the same end. Fully impressed with the necessity of removing the reigning King, Nussur-ood-deen, he advised the Government to set up another ruler in his place; and in order that the measure might be above all suspicion, to abstain from receiving a single rupee, or a single acre of ground, as the price of his elevation. "What I recommend is this," he said, "that the next heir should be invested with the full powers of sovereignty; and that the people of Oude should continue to live under their own institutions." He had faith in the character of that next heir; he believed that a change of men would produce a change of measures; and, at all events, it was but bare justice to try the experiment. 1835.

But, before anything had been done by the Government of India, in accordance with the discretion delegated to them by the Court of Directors, the experiment which Low had suggested inaugurated itself. Not without suspicion of poison, but really, I believe, killed only by strong drink, Nussur-ood-deen Hyder died on a memorable July night. It was a crisis of 1837. no common magnitude, for there was a disputed succession; and large bodies of lawless native troops in Lucknow were ready to strike at a moment's notice.

1837. The cool courage of Low and his assistants saved the city from a deluge of blood. An uncle of the deceased Prince—an old man and a cripple, respectable in his feebleness—was declared King, with the consent of the British Government; and the independence of Oude had another lease of existence.

Lord Auckland was, at that time, Governor-General of India. The new King, who could not but feel that he was a creature of the British, pledged himself to sign a new treaty. And soon it was laid before him. That the engagements of the old treaty had been violated, day after day, year after year, for more than a third part of a century, was a fact too patent to be questioned. The misgovernment of the country was a chronic breach of treaty. Whether the British or the Oude Government were more responsible for it was somewhat doubtful to every clear understanding and every unprejudiced mind. The source of the failure was in the treaty itself, which the author of it well knew from the first was one of impossible fulfilment. But it was still a breach of treaty, and there was another in the entertainment of vast numbers of soldiers over and above the stipulated allowance. Those native levies had gradually swollen, according to Resident Low's calculations, to the bulk of seventy thousand men. Here was an evil not to be longer permitted; wonder, indeed, was it that it should have been permitted so long. This the new treaty was to remedy; no less than the continued mal-administration of the country by native agency. It provided, therefore, that in the event of any further-protracted misrule, the British Government should be entitled to appoint its own officers to the management of any part, small or great, of the province; that the old native levies should be abandoned, and a new force, commanded by British officers, organised in its place, at the cost of the Oude Government. But there was no idea of touching, in any other way, the revenues of the country. An account was to be rendered of every rupee received and expended, and the balance was to be paid punctually into the Oude Treasury. 1837.

This was the abortion, often cited in later years as the Oude Treaty of 1837. Authentic history recites that the Government of India were in throes with it, but the strangling hand of higher authority crushed all life out of the thing before it had become a fact. The treaty was wholly and absolutely disallowed by the Home Government.* They took especial exception to the establishment of the new auxiliary force, which was to cost the Oude Treasury sixteen lakhs of rupees a year; for, with all the pure logic of honesty, they said that the treaty of 1801 had made it compulsory on the British Government to provide for the defence of the country, and that a large tract of territory had been ceded with the express object of securing the payment of the troops necessary for this purpose. If, then, it were expedient to organise a fresh force under British officers, it was for the Company, not for the Oude Government, to defray the expenses of the new levy. But not only on these grounds did they object to the treaty. It is true that, a few years before, they had given the Governor-General discretionary power to deal, as he thought best, with the disorders of Oude, even to the extent of a temporary assumption of the government; but this authority had been issued at a time when Nussur-ood-deen, of whose vicious incapacity they had had

* That is to say, by the Secret Committee, who had, by Act of Parliament, special powers in this matter of Treaty-making.

1838. many years' experience, sat upon the throne; and the Home Government were strongly of opinion that the new King, of whose character they had received a favourable account, ought to be allowed a fair trial, under the provisions of the treaty existing at the time of his accession to the throne. They therefore directed the abrogation, not of any one article, but of the entire treaty. Wishing, however, the annulment of the treaty to appear rather as an act of grace from the Government of India than as the result of positive and unconditional instructions from England, they gave a large discretion to the Governor-General as to the mode of announcing this abrogation to the Court of Lucknow.

The receipt of these orders disturbed and perplexed the Governor-General. Arrangements for the organisation of the Oude auxiliary force had already advanced too far to admit of the suspension of the measure. It was a season, however, of difficulty and supposed danger, for the seeds of the Afghan war had been sown. Some, at least, of our regular troops in Oude were wanted to do our own work; so, in any view of the case, it was necessary to fill their places. The Auxiliary Force, therefore, was not to be arrested in its formation, but it was to be maintained at the Company's expense. Intimation to this effect was given to the King in a letter from the Governor-General, which, after acquainting his Majesty that the British Government had determined to relieve him of a burden which, in the existing state of the country, might have imposed heavier exactions on the people than they were well able to bear, expressed a strong hope that the King would see, in the relaxation of this demand, good reason for applying his surplus revenues firstly to the relief of oppressive taxation, and, secondly, to the prosecution of useful public works. But nothing was said, in this letter, about the abrogation of the entire treaty, nor was it desired that the Resident, in his conferences with the King or his minister, should say anything on that subject. The Governor-General, still hoping that the Home Government might be induced to consent to the terms of the treaty (the condition of the auxiliary force alone excluded), abstained from an acknowledgment which, he believed, would weaken the authority of his Government. But this was a mistake, and worse than a mistake. It betrayed an absence of moral courage not easily to be justified or forgiven. The Home Government never acknowledged the validity of any later treaty than that which Lord Wellesley had negotiated at the commencement of the century. 1838.

Such is the history of the treaty of 1837. It was never carried out in a single particular, and seldom heard of again until after a lapse of nearly twenty years, except in a collection of treaties into which it crept by mistake.* And, for some time, indeed,

* Much was attempted to be made out of this circumstance—but the mistake of an under Secretary cannot give validity to a treaty which the highest authorities refused to ratify. If Lord Auckland was unwilling to declare the nullity of the treaty because its nullification hurt the pride of his Government, the Home Government showed no such unwillingness, for, in 1838, the following return was made to Parliament, under the signature of one of the Secretaries of the Board of Control:

"There has been no treaty concluded with the present King of Oude, which has been ratified by the Court of Directors, with the approbation of the Commissioners for the affairs of India. (Signed) "R. GORDON.

"India Board, 3rd July, 1838."

It must, however, be admitted, on the other hand, that, years after this date, even in the Lucknow Residency, the treaty was held to be valid. In October, 1853, Colonel Sleeman wrote to Sir James Hogg: "The treaty of 1837 gives our Government ample authority to take the whole administration on ourselves." And again, in 1854, to Colonel Low: "Our Government would be fully authorised at any time to enforce the penalty prescribed in your treaty of 1837." This was doubly a mistake. The treaty was certainly not Low's.

1838-46. little was heard of Oude itself. A Native State is never so near to death, but that it may become quite hale and lusty again when the energies and activities of the British are engrossed by a foreign war. Now, it happened that, for some time to come, the British had quite a crop of foreign wars. First, the great Afghanistan war of Auckland, which made him wholly forgetful of Oude—her People and her King—her sorrows and her sensualities. Then there was the Sindh war of Ellenborough, intended to wash out by a small victory the stain of a great defeat, but fixing a still deeper stain upon the character of the nation; and next the fierce Mahratta onslaught, which followed closely upon it. Then there was the invasion from beyond the Sutlej, and the first Sikh war, in which Hardinge was most reluctantly immersed. Altogether, some eight years of incessant war, with a prospect of further strife, kept the sword out of the scabbard and the portfolio out of the hand. Then Oude was safe in its insignificance and obscurity. Moreover, Oude was, as before, loyal and sympathising, and, although the hoardings of Saadut Ali had long since been squandered, there was still money in the Treasure-chests of Lucknow. But peace came, and with it a new birth of danger to the rulers of that misruled province. There had been no change for the better; nay, rather there had been change for the worse, during the years of our conflicts beyond the frontier. One Prince had succeeded another only to emulate the vices of his ancestors with certain special variations of his own. And when Lord Hardinge, in the quiet interval between the two
1847. Sikh wars, turned his thoughts towards the kingdom of Oude, he found Wajid Ali Shah, then a young man in the first year of his reign, giving foul pro-

mise of sustaining the character of the Royal House.* 1847

With the same moderation as had been shown by Lord William Bentinck, but also with the same strong sense of the paramount duty of the British Government to arrest the disorders which had so long been preying upon the vitals of the country, Lord Hardinge lifted up his voice in earnest remonstrance and solemn warning; and the young King cowered beneath the keen glance of the clear blue eyes that were turned upon him. There were no vague words in that admonition; no uncertain sound in their utterance. Wajid Ali Shah was distinctly told that the clemency of the British Government would allow him two years of grace; but that if at the end of that period of probation there were no manifest signs of improvement, the British Government could, in the interests of humanity, no longer righteously abstain from interfering peremptorily and absolutely for the introduction of a system of administration calculated to restore order and prosperity to the kingdom of Oude. The discretionary power had years before been placed in the hands of the Governor-General, and these admonitions failing, it would assuredly be exercised. A general outline of the means, by which the administration might be reformed, was laid down in a memorandum read aloud to the King; and it was added that, if his Majesty cordially entered into the plan, he might have the satisfaction,

* There was something in the number *seven* fatal to the Princes of Oude. Ghazee-ood-deen Hyder died in 1827; Nussur-ood-deen in 1837; and Umjid Ali Shah in 1847. The last named succeeded, in 1842, the old King, whom we had set up, and from whose better character there appeared at one time to be some hope of an improved administration. But, *capax imperii nisi imperasset*, he was, for all purposes of government, as incompetent as his predecessors. His besetting infirmity was avarice, and he seemed to care for nothing so long as the treasure-chest was full.

1847. within the specified period of two years, of checking and eradicating the worst abuses, and, at the same time, of maintaining his own authority and the native institutions of his kingdom unimpaired—but that if he should adhere to his old evil ways, he must be prepared for the alternative and its consequences.

Nervous and excitable at all times, and greatly affected by these words, the King essayed to speak; but the power of utterance had gone from him. So he took a sheet of paper and wrote upon it, that he thanked the Governor-General, and would regard his counsels as though they had been addressed by a father to his son. There are no counsels so habitually disregarded; the King, therefore, kept his word. Relieved from the presence of the Governor-General his agitation subsided, and he betook himself, without a thought of the future, to his old courses. Fiddlers and dancers, singing men and eunuchs, were suffered to usurp the government and to absorb the revenues of the country. The evil influence of these vile panders and parasites was felt throughout all conditions of society and in all parts of the country. Sunk in the uttermost abysses of enfeebling debauchery, the King pushed aside the business which he felt himself incapable of transacting, and went in search of new pleasures. Stimulated to the utmost by unnatural excitements, his appetites were satiated by the debaucheries of the Zenana, and, with an understanding emasculated to the point of childishness, he turned to the more harmless delights of dancing, and drumming, and drawing, and manufacturing small rhymes. Had he devoted himself to these pursuits in private life, there would have been small harm in them, but overjoyed with his success as a musician, he went about the crowded streets of Lucknow with a big drum round his neck, striking as much noise out of it as he could, with all the extravagance of childish delight. 1849.

The two years of probation had passed away, and the British Resident reported that "the King had not, since the Governor-General's visit in October, 1847, shown any signs of being fully aware of the responsibility he incurred." "In fact," he added, "I do not think that his Majesty can ever be brought to feel the responsibilities of sovereignty strongly enough to be induced to bear that portion of the burden of its duties that must necessarily devolve upon him; he will always confide it to the worthless minions who are kept for his amusements, and enjoy exclusively his society and his confidence." So the time had arrived when the British Government might have righteously assumed the administration of Oude. The King had justly incurred the penalty, but the paramount power was in no haste to inflict it. Lord Dalhousie was Governor-General of India; but again the external conflicts of the British were the salvation of the sovereignty of Oude. The Punjab was in flames, and once more Lucknow was forgotten. The conquest of the Sikhs; the annexation of their country; the new Burmese war and its results; the lapses of which I have spoken in my last chapter; and many important affairs of internal administration of which I have yet to speak, occupied the ever-active mind of Lord Dalhousie until the last year of his reign; but it was felt by every one, who knew and pondered over the wretched state of the country, that the day of reckoning was approaching, and that the British Government could not much longer shrink from the performance of a duty imposed upon it by every consideration of humanity.

1849-50. Colonel Sleeman was then Resident at Lucknow. He was a man of a liberal and humane nature, thoroughly acquainted with the character and feelings, the institutions and usages of the people of India. No man had a larger toleration for the short-comings of native Governments, because no one knew better how much our own political system had aggravated, if they had not produced, the evils of which we most complained. But he sympathised at the same time acutely with the sufferings of the people living under those native Governments; and his sympathy overcame his toleration. Having lived all his adult life in India—the greater part of it in, or on the borders of, the Native States—he was destitute of all overweening prepossessions in favour of European institutions and the "blessings of British rule." But the more he saw, on the spot, of the terrible effects of the misgovernment of Oude, the more convinced he was of the paramount duty of the British Government to step in and arrest the atrocities which were converting one of the finest provinces of India into a moral pest-house. In 1849 and 1850 he made a tour through the interior of the country. He carried with him the prestige of a name second to none in India, as that of a friend of the poor, a protector of the weak, and a redresser of their wrongs. Conversing freely and familiarly in the native languages, and knowing well the character and the feelings of the people, he had a manner that inspired confidence, and the art of extracting from every man the information which he was best able to afford. During this tour in the interior, he noted down, from day to day, all the most striking facts which were brought to his notice, with the reflections which were suggested by them; and the whole presented a revolting picture of the worst type of misrule—of a feebleness worse than despotism, of an apathy more productive of human suffering than the worst forms of tyrannous activity. In the absence of all controlling authority, the strong carried on everywhere a war of extermination against the weak. Powerful families, waxing gross on outrage and rapine, built forts, collected followers, and pillaged and murdered at discretion, without fear of justice overtaking their crimes. Nay, indeed, the greater the criminal the more sure he was of protection, for he could purchase immunity with his spoil. There was hardly, indeed, an atrocity committed, from one end of the country to the other, that was not, directly or indirectly, the result of the profligacy and corruption of the Court.* 1850.

Such was Colonel Sleeman's report of the state of the Oude country; such was his account of what he had seen with his own eyes or heard with his own ears. There was not a man in the Two Services who was more distressed by the fury for annexation which

* "The Talookdars keep the country in a perpetual state of disturbance, and render life, property, and industry, everywhere insecure. Whenever they quarrel with each other, or with the local authorities of the Government, from whatever cause, they take to indiscriminate plunder and murder—over all lands not held by men of the same class—no road, town, village, or hamlet, is secure from their merciless attacks—robbery and murder become their diversion, their sport, and they think no more of taking the lives of men, women, and children, who never offended them, than those of deer and wild hogs. They not only rob and murder, but seize, confine, and torture all whom they seize, and suppose to have money or credit, till they ransom themselves with all they have, or can beg or borrow. Hardly a day has passed since I left Lucknow, in which I have not had abundant proof of numerous atrocities of this kind committed by landholders within the district through which I was passing, year by year, up to the present day." And again: "It is worthy of remark that these great landholders, who have recently acquired their possessions by the plunder and the murder of their weaker neighbours, and who continue their system of plunder in order to acquire the means to maintain their gangs and add to their possessions, are those who are most favoured at Court, and most conciliated by the local rulers, because they are more able and more willing to pay for the favour of the one and set at defiance the authority of the other."—*Sleeman's Diary*.

1852. was at that time breaking out in the most influential public prints and the highest official circles. He saw clearly the danger into which this grievous lust of dominion was hurrying us, and he made a great effort to arrest the evil;* but he lifted up a warning voice in vain. The letters which he addressed to the Governor-General and to the Chairman of the East India Company appear to have produced no effect. He did not see clearly, at that time, that the principles which he held in such abhorrence were cherished by Lord Dalhousie himself, and he did not know that the Court of Directors had such faith in their Governor-General that they were content to substitute his principles for their own. But, utterly distasteful to him as were the then prevailing sentiments in favour of absorption and confiscation, Sleeman never closed his eyes against the fact that interference in the affairs of Oude, even to the extent of the direct assumption of the government, would be a righteous interference. Year after year he had pressed upon the Governor-General the urgent necessity of the measure. But, perhaps, had he known in what manner his advice was destined to be followed, and how his authority would be asserted in justifica-

* See Sleeman's Correspondence, *passim*. *Exempli gratiâ:* "In September, 1848, I took the liberty to mention to your Lordship my fears that the system of annexing and absorbing Native States—so popular with our Indian Services, and so much advocated by a certain class of writers in public journals—might some day render us too visibly dependent upon our Native Army; that they might see it, and that accidents might occur to unite them, or too great a portion of them, in some desperate act."—(*Colonel Sleeman to Lord Dalhousie*, April, 1852.) And again: "I deem such doctrines to be dangerous to our rule in India, and prejudicial to the best interests of the country. The people see that these annexations and confiscations go on, and that rewards and honorary distinctions are given for them and for the victories which lead to them, and for little else; and they are too apt to infer that they are systematic and encouraged and prescribed from home. The Native States I consider to be breakwaters, and when they are all swept away we shall be left to the mercy of our Native Army, which may not always be sufficiently under our control."—*Colonel Sleeman to Sir James Hogg*, January, 1853.

tion of an act which he could never countenance, he 1852.
would rather have suffered the feeble-minded debauchee who was called King of Oude still to remain in undisturbed possession of the throne, than have uttered a word that might hasten a measure so at variance with his sense of justice, and so injurious as he thought to our best interests, as that of which the interference of Government eventually took the shape.

Sleeman's advice had been clear, consistent, unmistakable. "Assume the administration," he said, "but do not grasp the revenues of the country." Some years before the same advice had been given by Henry Lawrence,* between whom and Sleeman there was much concord of opinion and some similitude of character. The private letters of the latter, addressed to the highest Indian functionaries, and, therefore, having all the weight and authority of public documents, were as distinct upon this point as the most emphatic words could make them. "What the people want, and most earnestly pray for," he wrote to the Governor General, "is that our Government should take upon itself the responsibility of governing them well and permanently. All classes, save the knaves, who now surround and govern the King, earnestly pray for this—the educated classes, because they would then have a chance of respectable employment, which none of them now have; the middle classes, because they find no protection or encouragement, and no hope that their children will be permitted to inherit

* "Let the management," he said, "be assumed under some such rules as those which were laid down by Lord William Bentinck. Let the administration of the country, as far as possible, be native. *Let not a rupee come into the Company's coffers.*" (The italics are Lawrence's.) "Let Oude be at last governed, not for one man, the King, but for him and his people."—*Calcutta Review*, vol. iii. (1845); and Lawrence's Essays, p. 132.

1853. the property they leave, not invested in our Government Securities; and the humbler classes, because they are now abandoned to the merciless rapacity of the starving troops and other public establishments, and of the landholders driven or invited to rebellion by the present state of misrule." But he added: "I believe that it is your Lordship's wish that the whole of the revenues of Oude should be expended for the benefit of the Royal Family and People of Oude, and that the British Government should disclaim any wish to derive any pecuniary advantage from assuming to itself the administration." And again, about the same time, he had written to the Chairman of the Court of Directors, urging the expediency of assuming the administration, but adding: "If we do this, we must, in order to stand well with the rest of India, honestly and distinctly disclaim all interested motives, and appropriate the whole of the revenues for the benefit of the People and Royal Family of Oude. If we do this, all India will think us right." And again, a few months later, writing to the same high authority, he said, mournfully and prophetically, that to annex and confiscate the country, and to appropriate the revenues to ourselves, would "be most profitable in a pecuniary view, but most injurious in a political one. It would tend to accelerate the crisis which the doctrines of the absorbing school must sooner or later bring upon us."*

Such was the counsel Sleeman gave; such were the warnings he uttered. But he did not remain in India, nay, indeed he did not live, to see his advice ignored, his cautions disregarded. After long years of arduous and honourable service, compelled to retire in broken

* Private correspondence of Sir W. H. Sleeman, printed at the end of the English edition of his "Diary in Oude."

health from his post, he died on his homeward voyage, 1853.
leaving behind him a name second to none upon the roll of the benefactors and civilisers of India, for he had grappled with her greatest abomination, and had Thuggee. effectually subdued it. Some solace had it been to him when he turned his back upon the country to know that his place would be well and worthily filled. "Had your Lordship left the choice of a successor to me," he wrote to the Governor-General, "I should September, 1854. have pointed out Colonel Outram; and I feel very much rejoiced that he has been selected for the office, and I hope he will come as soon as possible."

An officer of the Company's army on the Bombay establishment, James Outram had done good service to his country, good service to the people of India, on many different fields of adventure; and had risen, not without much sore travail and sharp contention, to a place in the estimation of his Government and the affections of his comrades, from which he could afford to look down upon the conflicts of the Past with measureless calmness and contentment. Versed alike in the stern severities of war and the civilising humanities of peace, he was ready at a moment's notice to lead an army into the field or to superintend the government of a province. But it was in rough soldier's work, or in that still rougher work of mingled war and diplomacy which falls to the share of the Political officer in India, that Outram's great and good qualities were most conspicuously displayed. For in him, with courage of the highest order, with masculine energy and resolution, were combined the gentleness of a woman and the simplicity of a child. No man knew better how to temper power with mercy and forbearance, and to combat intrigue and perfidy with pure sincerity and stainless truth. This truth-

1854. fulness was, indeed, perhaps the most prominent, as it was the most perilous, feature of his character. Whatsoever he might do, whatsoever he might say, the whole was there before you in its full proportions. He wore his heart upon his sleeve, and was incapable of concealment or disguise. A pure sense of honour, a strong sense of justice, the vehement assertions of which no self-interested discretion could hold in restraint, brought him sometimes into collision with others, and immersed him in a sea of controversy. But although, perhaps, in his reverential love of truth, he was over-eager to fight down what he might have been well content to live down, and in after life he may have felt that these wordy battles were very little worth fighting, he had still no cause to regret them, for he came unhurt from the conflict. It was after one of these great conflicts, the growth of serious official strife, which had sent him from an honourable post into still more honourable retirement, that, returning to India with strong credentials from his masters in Leadenhall-street, Lord Dalhousie selected him to succeed Sleeman as Resident at Lucknow.

The choice was a wise one. There was work to be done which required a hand at once gentle and strong. The fame of Outram was not the fame of a spoliator, but of a just man friendly to the native Princes and chiefs of India, who had lifted up his voice against wrongs done to them in his time, and who would rather have closed his public career than have been the agent of an unrighteous policy. But a measure which Low, and Sleeman, and Henry Lawrence had approved, nay, which in the interests of humanity they had strenuously recommended, was little likely to be an unrighteous one, and Outram, whilst rejoicing that his past career had thus been stamped by

his Government with the highest practical approval, 1854.
accepted the offer in the full assurance that he could fulfil its duties without a stain upon his honour or a burden upon his conscience.*

Making all haste to join his appointment, Outram quitted Aden, where the summons reached him, and took ship for Calcutta, where he arrived in the first month of the cold season. His instructions were soon November, 1854.
prepared for him; they were brief, but they suggested the settled resolution of Government to wait no longer for impossible improvements from within, but at once to shape their measures for the assertion, in accordance with Treaty, of the authority of the Paramount State. But it was not a thing to be done in a hurry. The measure itself was to be deliberately carried out after certain preliminary formalities of inquiry and reference. It was Outram's part to inquire. A report upon the existing state of Oude was called for from the new Resident, and before the end of March it was forwarded to Calcutta. It was 1855.
an elaborate history of the misgovernment of Oude from the commencement of the century, a dark catalogue of crime and suffering "caused by the culpable apathy of the Sovereign and the Durbar." "I have shown," said the new Resident, in conclusion, "that the affairs of Oude still continue in the same state, if not worse, in which Colonel Sleeman from time to time described them to be, and that the improvement which Lord Hardinge peremptorily demanded, seven years ago, at the hands of the King, in pursuance of the Treaty of 1801, has not, in any degree, been effected. And I have no hesitation in declaring my opinion,

* I speak, of course, of the mere fact of the assumption of the administration. The manner of carrying out the measure had not then been decided.

1855. therefore, that the duty imposed on the British Government by that treaty, cannot any longer admit of our 'honestly indulging the reluctance which the Government of India has felt heretofore to have recourse to those extreme measures which alone can be of any real efficiency in remedying the evils from which the state of Oude has suffered so long.'"

To this report, and to much earlier information of the same kind with which the archives of Government were laden, the Governor-General gave earnest and sustained attention amidst the refreshing quiet of the Blue Mountains of Madras. The weighty document had picked up, on its road through Calcutta, another March 28, 1855. still more weighty, in the shape of a minute written by General Low. Few as were the words, they exhausted all the arguments in favour of intervention, and clothed them with the authority of a great name. No other name could have invested them with this authority, for no other man had seen so much of the evils of native rule in Oude, and no man was on principle more averse to the extinction of the native dynasties of India. All men must have felt the case to be very bad when John Low, who had spoken the brave words in defence of the Princes and chiefs of India which I have cited in the last chapter, was driven to the forcible expression of his conviction that it was the paramount duty of the British Government to interfere at once for the protection of the people of Oude.*

* Low said that he was in favour of interference, "because the public and shameful oppressions committed on the people by Government officers in Oude have of late years been constant and extreme; because the King of Oude has continually, during many years, broken the Treaty by systematically disregarding our advice, instead of following it, or even endeavouring to follow it; because we are bound by *Treaty* (quite different in that respect from our position relatively to most of the great Native States) to prevent serious interior misrule in Oude; because it has

It was not possible to add much in the way of fact to what Outram had compiled, or much in the way of argument to what Low had written. But Dalhousie, to whom the fine bracing air of the Neilgherries had imparted a new-born capacity for sustained labour, sat himself down to review the whole question in a gigantic minute. He signed it on the 18th June; and, indeed, it was his Waterloo—the crowning victory of annexation. It is not necessary to repeat the facts, for I have stated them, or the arguments, for I have suggested them. No reader can have followed me thus far, without a strong assurance on his mind that it would have been a grievous wrong done to humanity to have any longer abstained from interference. But what was the interference to be? Here was a question for the Governor-General to solve in the invigorating atmosphere of Ootacamund—a question, the solution of which was to yield the crowning measure of his long vice-regal career. 1855.

There may have been many ways of working out the practical details of this measure; but there was only one uncertain point which was of much substantial importance. All men agreed that the Treaty of 1801 might rightfully be declared to have ceased by reason of repeated violations, and that with the consent of the King, if attainable, or without it, if unattainable, the Government of the country might be transferred to the hands of European administrators. That the King must be reduced to a mere cypher was

been fully proved that we have not prevented it, and that we cannot prevent it by the present mode of conducting our relations with that State; and because no man of common sense can entertain the smallest expectation that the present King of Oude can ever become an efficient ruler of his country." And he added to these pungent sentences an expression of opinion that the unfulfilled threats of Lord Hardinge had increased the evil, inasmuch as that they had produced an impression in Oude that the Indian Government were restrained from interference by the orders of higher authority at home.

1855. certain; it was certain that all possible respect ought to be shown to him in his fallen fortunes, and that he and all his family ought to be splendidly endowed; no question could well be raised upon these points. The question was, what was to be done with the surplus revenue after paying all the expenses of administration? Just and wise men, as has been shown, had protested against the absorption of a single rupee into the British Treasury. They said that it would be as politic as it would be righteous, to demonstrate to all the States and Nations of India, that we had not deposed the King of Oude for our own benefit—that we had done a righteous act on broad principles of humanity, by which we had gained nothing. But Lord Dalhousie, though he proposed not to annex the country, determined to take the revenues.

It is not very easy to arrive at a just conception of his views: "The reform of the administration," he said, "may be wrought, and the prosperity of the people may be secured, without resorting to so extreme a measure as the annexation of the territory and the abolition of the throne. I, for my part, therefore, do not recommend that the province of Oude should be declared to be British territory." But he proposed that the King of Oude, whilst retaining the sovereignty of his dominions, should "vest all power, jurisdiction, rights and claims thereto belonging, in the hands of the East India Company," and that the surplus revenues should be at the disposal of the Company. What this territorial sovereignty was to be, without territorial rights or territorial revenues, it is not easy to see. When the Newab of the Carnatic and the Rajah of Tanjore were deprived of their rights and revenues, they were held to be not territorial, but titular sovereigns. The Nizam, on the other hand, might properly be described as "territorial sovereign" of the Assigned Districts, although the administration had been taken from him, because an account of the revenue was to be rendered to him, and the surplus was to be paid into his hands. But the King of Oude, in Dalhousie's scheme, was to have had no more to do with his territories, than the titular sovereigns of the Carnatic and Tanjore; and yet he was to be told that he was "to retain the sovereignty of all the territories" of which he was then in possession. 1855.

Strictly interpreted to the letter, the scheme did not suggest the annexation of Oude. The province was not to be incorporated with the British dominions. The revenues were to be kept distinct from those of the empire; there was to be a separate balance-sheet; and thus far the province was to have a sort of integrity of its own. This is sufficiently intelligible in itself; and, if the balance being struck, the available surplus had been payable to the King of Oude, the rest of the scheme would have been intelligible also, for there would have been a quasi-sovereignty of the territories thus administered still remaining with the King. But the balance being payable into the British Treasury, it appears that Oude, in this state of financial isolation, would still have substantially been British territory, as much as if it had become a component part of the empire. Again, under the proposed system, Oude would have been beyond the circle of our ordinary legislation, in which respect it would not have differed much from other "Non-Regulation Provinces;" and if it had, even this Legislative segregation superadded to the Financial isolation of which I have spoken, would not have made it any the less British territory. The Channel Islands have a separate

1855. Budget and distinct laws of their own, but still they are component parts of the British Empire, although they do not pay their surplus into the British Treasury. But in everything that really constitutes Kingship, the Bailiff of Jersey is as much the territorial sovereign of that island as Wajid Ali would have been territorial sovereign of Oude under Lord Dalhousie's programme of non-annexation.

But this transparent disguise was not to be worn; this distinction without a difference was not to be asserted, anywhere out of Lord Dalhousie's great Minute. The thing that was to be done soon came to take its proper place in the Councils of the Indian Empire as the Annexation of Oude; and it was as the annexation of Oude that the measure was considered by the Government at home. The Court of Directors consented to the annexation of Oude. The Board of Control consented to the annexation of Oude. The British Cabinet consented to the annexation of Oude. The word was not then, as it since has been, freely used in official documents, but it was in all men's minds, and many spoke it out bluntly instead of talking delicately about "assuming the Government of the Country." And, whether right or wrong, the responsibility of the measure rested as much with the Queen's Ministers as with the Merchant Company. That the Company had for long years shown great forbearance is certain. They had hoped against hope, and acted against all experience. So eager, indeed, had they been to give the native Princes of India a fair trial, that they had disallowed the proposed treaty of 1837, and had pronounced an authoritative opinion in favour of the maintenance of the then existing Native States of India. But twenty more years of misrule and anarchy had raised in their minds a feeling of wondering self-reproach at the thought of their own patience; and when they responded to the reference from Calcutta, they said that the doubt raised by a survey of the facts before them, was not whether it was then incumbent upon them to free themselves from the responsibility of any longer upholding such a Government, but whether they could excuse themselves for not having, many years before, performed so imperative a duty. 1855.

The despatch of the Court of Directors was signed in the middle of November. At midnight on the 2nd of January, the Governor-General mastered its contents. Had he thought of himself more than of his country he would not have been there at that time. The energies of his mind were undimmed; but climate, and much toil, and a heavy sorrow weighing on his heart, had shattered a frame never constitutionally robust, and all men said that he was "breaking." Without any failure of duty, without any imputation on his zeal, he might have left to his successor the ungrateful task of turning into stern realities the oft-repeated menaces of the British rulers who had gone before him. But he was not one to shrink from the performance of such a task because it was a painful and unpopular one. He believed that by no one could the duty of bringing the Oude Government to solemn account be so fitly discharged as by one who had watched for seven years the accumulation of its offences, and seen the measure of its guilt filled to the brim. He had intimated, therefore, to the Court of Directors his willingness to remain at his post to discharge this duty, and in the despatch, which he read in the quiet of that January night, he saw on official record the November 19, 1855.

1856. alacrity with which his offer was accepted, and he girded himself for the closing act of his long and eventful administration.*

Next morning he summoned a Council. It was little more than a form. Dalhousie had waited for the authoritative sanction of the Home Government; but he knew that sanction was coming, and he was prepared for its arrival. The greater part of the work had, indeed, been already done. The instructions to be sent to the Resident; the treaty to be proposed to the King; the proclamation to be issued to the people had all been drafted. The whole scheme of internal government had been matured, and the agency to be employed had been carefully considered. The muster-roll of the new administration was ready, and the machinery was complete. The system was very closely to resemble that which had been tried with such good success in the Punjab, and its agents were, as in that province, to be a mixed body of civil and military officers, under a Chief Commissioner. All the weighty documents, by which the revolution was to be effected, were in the Portfolio of the Foreign Secretary; and now, at this meeting of the Council, they were formally let loose to do their work.

The task which Outram was commissioned to perform was a difficult, a delicate, and a painful one. He was to endeavour to persuade the King of Oude formally to abdicate his sovereign functions, and to make over, by a solemn treaty, the government of his territories to the East India Company. In the event of his refusal, a proclamation was to be issued, declaring the whole of Oude to be British territory.

* The Court of Directors to the Government of India, November 19, 1855. Paragraph 19.

By a man of Outram's humane and generous nature no counsel from his Government was needed to induce him to do the work entrusted to him in the manner least likely to wound the feelings of the King. But it was right that such counsel should be given. It was given; but the decree of the Paramount State, tempered as it might be by outward courtesy of manner, was still to be carried out, with stern and resolute action. No protests, no remonstrances, no promises, no prayers were to be suffered to arrest the retributive measure for a day. It need not be added that no resistance could avert it. A body of British troops, sufficient to trample down all possible opposition, had been moved up into a position to overawe Lucknow, and for the doomed Government of Oude to attempt to save itself by a display of force would have been only to court a most useless butchery. 1856.

Outram received his instructions at the end of January. On the last day of the month he placed himself in communication with the Oude Minister, clearly stated the orders of the British Government, and said that they were final and decisive. Four days were spent in preliminary formalities and negotiations. In true Oriental fashion, the Court endeavoured to gain time, and, appealing to Outram, through the aged Queen Mother—a woman with far more of masculine energy and resolution than her son—importuned him to persuade his Government to give the King another trial, to wait for the arrival of the new Governor-General, to dictate to Wajid Ali any reforms to be carried out in his name. All this had been expected; all this provided for. Outram had but one answer; the day of trial, the day of forbearance was past. All that he could now do was to deliver his message to the King.

1856. On the 4th of February, Wajid Ali announced his willingness to receive the British Resident; and Outram, accompanied by his lieutenants, Hayes and Weston, proceeded to the palace. Strange and significant symptoms greeted them as they went. The guns at the palace-gates were dismounted. The palace-guards were unarmed. The guard of honour, who should have presented arms to the Resident, saluted him only with their hands. Attended by his brother and a few of his confidential Ministers, the King received the English gentlemen at the usual spot; and after the wonted ceremonies, the business commenced. Outram presented to the King a letter from the Governor-General, which contained, in terms of courteous explanation, the sentence that had been passed upon him, and urged him not to resist it. A draft of the proposed treaty was then placed in his hands. He received it with a passionate burst of grief, declared that treaties were only between equals; that there was no need for him to sign it, as the British would do with him and his possessions as they pleased; they had taken his honour and his country, and he would not ask them for the means of maintaining his life. All that he sought was permission to proceed to England, and cast himself and his sorrows at the foot of the Throne. Nothing could move him from his resolution not to sign the treaty. He uncovered his head; placed his turban in the hands of the Resident, and sorrowfully declared that title, rank, honour, everything were gone; and that now the British Government, which had made his grandfather a King, might reduce him to nothing, and consign him to obscurity.

In this exaggerated display of helplessness there was something too characteristically Oriental for any

part of it to be assigned to European prompting. But 1856.
if the scene had been got up expressly for an English audience, it could not have been more cunningly contrived to increase the appearance of harshness and cruelty with which the friends of the King were prepared to invest the act of dethronement. No man was more likely than Outram to have been doubly pained, in the midst of all his painful duties, by the unmanly prostration of the King. To deal harshly with one who declared himself so feeble and defenceless, was like striking a woman or a cripple. But five millions of people were not to be given up, from generation to generation, to suffering and sorrow, because an effeminate Prince, when told he was no longer to have the power of inflicting measureless wrongs on his country, burst into tears, said that he was a miserable wretch, and took off his turban instead of taking out his sword.

There was nothing now left for Outram but to issue a proclamation, prepared for him in Calcutta, declaring the province of Oude to be thenceforth, for ever, a component part of the British Indian Empire. It went forth to the people of Oude; and the people of Oude, without a murmur, accepted their new masters. There were no popular risings. Not a blow was struck in defence of the native dynasty of Oude. The whole population went over quietly to their new rulers, and the country, for a time, was outwardly more tranquil than before.

This was the last act of Lord Dalhousie's Ministry. When he placed the Portfolio of Government in the hands of Lord Canning, the British officers to whom had been entrusted the work of reforming the administration of Oude, were discharging their prescribed duties with an energy which seemed to

1856. promise the happiest results. The King was still obstinate and sullen. He persisted in refusing to sign the treaty or to accept the proposed stipend of £120,000 twelve lakhs; and though he had thought better of the idea of casting himself at the foot of the British Throne, he had made arrangements to send his nearest kindred—his mother, his brother, and his son—to England to perform a vicarious act of obeisance, and to clamour for his rights.

With what result the administration, as copied closely from the Punjabee system, was wrought out in detail, will be shown at a subsequent stage of this narrative. It was thought, as the work proceeded in quietude and in seeming prosperity, that it was a great success; and it gladdened the heart of the Government in Leadenhall-street, to think of the accomplishment of this peaceful revolution. But that the measure itself made a very bad impression on the minds of the people of India, is not to be doubted; not because of the deposition of a King who had abused his powers; not because of the introduction of a new system of administration for the benefit of the people; but because the humanity of the act was soiled by the profit which we derived from it; and to the comprehension of the multitude it appeared that the good of the people, which we had vaunted whilst serving ourselves, was nothing more than a pretext and a sham; and that we had simply extinguished one of the few remaining Mahomedan States of India that we might add so many thousands of square miles to our British territories, and so many millions of rupees to the revenues of the British Empire in the East. And who, it was asked, could be safe, if we thus treated one who had ever been the most faithful of our allies?

CHAPTER IV.

DESTRUCTION OF THE NATIVE ARISTOCRACY — RETROSPECT OF REVENUE ADMINISTRATION—THE SETTLEMENT OF THE NORTH-WEST PROVINCES—THE OUSTING OF THE TALOOKHDARS—RESUMPTION OPERATIONS—THE INAM COMMISSION—DECAY OF PRIESTLY POWER—SOCIAL REFORMS—MORAL AND MATERIAL PROGRESS.

WHILST great principalities were thus being absorbed and ancient sovereignties extinguished, a war of extermination no less fatal in its effects, but more noiseless in its operations, was being waged against the nobility and gentry of the country. The original proclamation of this war did not emanate from Lord Dalhousie. The measures by which the native aristocracy were destroyed were not primarily his measures. It was the policy of the times to recognise nothing between the Prince and the Peasant; a policy which owed its birth not to one but to many; a policy, the greatest practical exposition of which was the Settlement of the North-West Provinces. It was adopted in pure good faith and with the most benevolent intentions. It had the sanction of many wise and good men. It was not the policy by which such statesmen as John Malcolm, George Clerk, and Henry Lawrence, sought to govern the people; but it was sanctified by the genius of John Lawrence, and of the Gamaliel at whose feet he had sat, the virtuous, pure-minded James Thomason.

1806 1856.

1806-56. To bring the direct authority of the British Government to bear upon the great masses of the people, without the intervention of any powerful section of their own countrymen—to ignore, indeed, the existence of all governing classes but the European officers, who carried out the behests of that Government—seemed to be a wise and humane system of protection. It was intended to shelter the many from the injurious action of the interests and the passions of the few. The utter worthlessness of the upper classes was assumed to be a fact; and it was honestly believed that the obliteration of the aristocracy of the land was the greatest benefit that could be conferred on the people. And thus it happened that whilst the native sovereigns of India were one by one being extinguished, the native aristocracy had become well-nigh extinct.

Doubtless, we started upon a theory sound in the abstract, intent only on promoting the greatest happiness of the greatest number; but if we had allowed ourselves to understand the genius and the institutions of the people, we should have respected the rights, natural and acquired, of all classes of the community, instead of working out any abstract theory of our own. It was in the very nature of things necessary, inevitable, that the extension of British rule, followed always by a reconstruction of the administration, and a substitution of civil and military establishments fashioned upon our own models and composed of our own people, should have deprived many of the chief people of their official rank and official emoluments, and cast them adrift upon the world, either to seek new fields of adventure in the unabsorbed Native States, or to fester into a disaffected and dangerous class sullenly biding their time. This is an old story; an old complaint. Half a century before the time of which I am now writing, it had been alleged to be one of the main causes of that national outburst in Southern India known as the mutiny of Vellore. But this very necessity for the extinction of the old race of high native functionaries, often hereditary office-bearers, ought to have rendered us all the more desirous to perpetuate the nobility whose greatness was derived from the Land. It is true that the titles of the landed gentry whom we found in possession were, in some cases, neither of very ancient date nor of very unquestionable origin. But, whatsoever the nature of their tenures, we found them in the possession of certain rights or privileges allowed to them by the Governments which we had supplanted, and our first care should have been to confirm and secure their enjoyment of them. We might have done this without sacrificing the rights of others. Indeed, we might have done it to the full contentment of the inferior agricultural classes. But many able English statesmen, especially in Upper India, had no toleration for any one who might properly be described as a Native Gentleman. They had large sympathies and a comprehensive humanity, but still they could not embrace any other idea of the Native Gentry of India than that of an institution to be righteously obliterated for the benefit of the great mass of the people. 1806-56.

There were two processes by which this depression of the privileged classes was effected. The one was known by the name of a Settlement, the other was called Resumption. It would be out of place here, if I had the ability, to enter minutely into the difficult question of landed tenures in India. It is an old story now, that when that clever coxcomb, Victor Jacque-

1806-56. mont, asked Holt Mackenzie to explain to him in a five minutes' conversation the various systems of Land Revenue obtaining in different parts of the country, the experienced civilian replied that he had been for twenty years endeavouring to understand the subject and had not mastered it yet. Such a rebuke ought to be remembered. The little that I have to say on the subject shall be said with the least possible use of technical terms, and with the one object of making the general reader acquainted with the process by which the substance of the great landholders in Upper India was diminished by the action of the British Government.

Settlement Operations.

In the Literature of India the word "Settlement" is one of such frequent occurrence, and to the Indian resident it conveys such a distinct idea, that there is some danger of forgetting that the general reader may not be equally conversant with the exact meaning of the term. It may therefore, perhaps, be advantageously explained that as the Indian Revenue is mainly derived from the land, it is of the first importance, on the acquisition of new territory, clearly to ascertain the persons from whom the Government dues are to be exacted, and the amount that is payable by each. We may call it Rent or we may call it Revenue, it little matters. The adjustment of the mutual relations between the Government and the agriculturists was known as the Settlement of the Revenue. It was an affair of as much vital interest and concernment to the one as to the other, for to be charged with the payment of the Revenue was to be acknowledged as the proprietor of the land.

When we first took possession of the country ceded by the Newab-Wuzeer of Oude, or conquered from the Mahrattas, all sorts of proprietors presented themselves, and our officers, having no special theories and no overriding prejudices, were willing to consider the claims of all, whether small or great holders, whom they found in actual possession; and brief settlements or engagements were made with them, pending a more thorough investigation of their rights. There was, doubtless, at first a good deal of ignorance on our part, and a good deal of wrong-doing and usurpation on the part of those with whom we were called upon to deal. But the landed gentry of these Ceded and Conquered Provinces, though they suffered by the extension of the British Raj, were not deliberately destroyed by a theory. It was the inevitable tendency of our Regulations, especially of that great Mystery of Iniquity, the Sale Law, and of the immigration of astute native functionaries from the Lower Provinces, which inaugurated our rule, to subvert the supremacy of the old landholders. Under the system, which we introduced, men who had been proprietors of vast tracts of country as far as the eye could reach, shrivelled into tenants of mud-huts and possessors only of a few cooking-pots. The process, though certain in its results, was gradual in its operation; and the ruin which it entailed was incidental, not systematic. It was ignorantly suffered, not deliberately decreed. But, at a later period, when a new political creed had grown up among our British functionaries in India, and upon officers of this new school devolved the duty of fixing the relations of the agricultural classes with the British Government, the great besom of the Settlement swept out the remnant of the landed gentry from their baronial possessions, and a race of peasant-proprietors were recognised as the legitimate inheritors of the soil. 1806-56.

How this happened may be briefly stated. A Per-

1806-56. manent Settlement on the Bengal model had been talked of, ordered and counter-ordered; but for nearly a third part of a century, under a series of brief engagements with holders of different kinds, uncertainty and confusion prevailed, injurious both to the Government and to the People. But in the time
1833. of Lord William Bentinck an order went forth for the revision of this system or no-system, based upon a detailed survey and a clearly recorded definition of rights, and what is known in History as the Settlement of the North-West Provinces, was then formally commenced.

That it was benevolently designed and conscientiously executed, is not to be doubted. But it was marred by a Theory. In the pursuit of right, the framers of the settlement fell into wrong. Striving after justice, they perpetrated injustice. Nothing
1845. could be sounder than the declared principle that "it was the duty of the Government to ascertain and protect all existing rights, those of the poor and humble villager as well as those of the rich and influential Talookhdar."* It was said that this principle had been not only asserted, but acted upon. But the fact is, that the practice halted a long way behind the principle. Such were the feelings with which many of our officers regarded the great landholders, that equal justice between the conflicting claims and interests of the two classes was too often ignored. There were scales over the eyes of commonly clear-sighted men when they came to look at this question in the face, and therefore the "poor and humble villager"

* See letter of Mr. John Thornton, Secretary to Government, North-West Provinces, to Mr. H. M. Elliot, Secretary to Board of Revenue, April 30, 1845. It is added, with undeniable truth, that "in so far as this is done with care and diligence will the measure be successful in placing property on a healthy and sound footing."

had a full measure of justice, pressed down and running over, whilst the "rich and influential Talookhdar" had little or none. 1836-46.

There are few who have not become familiar with this word *Talookhdar;* who do not know that an influential class of men so styled in virtue of certain rights or interests in the land, were dispossessed of those rights or interests and reduced to absolute ruin. It must be understood, however, that the proprietary rights of which I speak were very different from the rights of landed property in England. The Talookhdar was little more than an hereditary revenue-contractor. His right was the right to all the just rents paid by the actual occupants, after satisfaction of the Government claims. His property was the rent *minus* the revenue of a particular estate. This Talookhdaree right, or right of collection, was distinct from the Zemindaree right, or proprietary right in the soil. The Talookhdar, who paid to Government the revenue of a large cluster of villages, had, perhaps, a proprietary right in some of these small estates; perhaps, in none. The proprietary right, in most instances, lay with the village communities. And it was the main effort of the English officers, engaged in the Settlement of the North-West Provinces, to bring these village occupants into direct relations with the Government, and to receive from them the amount of the assessment fixed upon their several estates.

Now it was a just and fitting thing that the rights of these village proprietors should be clearly defined. But it was not always just that the Government should enter into direct engagements with them and drive out the intervening Talookhdar. The actual occupants might, in a former generation, have been a con-

1836-46. sequence only of a pre-existing Talookhdaree right, as in cases where cultivators had been located on waste lands by a contractor or grantee of the State; or the Talookhdar might have acquired his position by purchase, by favour, perhaps by fraud, after the location of the actual occupants; still it was a proprietary interest, perhaps centuries old. Let us explain their position as we may, these Talookhdars constituted the landed aristocracy of the country; they had recognised manorial rights; they had, in many instances, all the dignity and power of great feudal barons, and, doubtless, often turned that power to bad account. But whether for good or for evil, in past years, we found them existing as a recognised institution; and it was at the same time a cruel wrong and a grievous error to sweep it away as though it were an incumbrance and an usurpation.

The theory of the Settlement officers was that the village Zemindars had an inalienable right in the soil, and that the Talookhdar was little better than an upstart and an impostor. All the defects in his tenure were rigidly scanned; all the vices of his character were violently exaggerated. He was written down as a fraudulent upstart and an unscrupulous oppressor. To oust a Talookhdar was held by some young Settlement officers to be as great an achievement as to shoot a tiger; and it was done, too, with just as clear a conviction of the benefit conferred upon the district in which the animal prowled and marauded. It was done honestly, conscientiously, laboriously, as a deed entitling the doer to the gratitude of mankind. There was something thorough in it that wrung an unwilling admiration even from those who least approved. It was a grand levelling system, reducing everything to first principles and a delving Adam. Who was a gentleman and a Talookhdar, they asked, when these time-honoured Village Communities were first established on the soil? So the Settlement Officer, in pursuit of the great scheme of restitution, was fain to sweep out the Landed Gentry and to applaud the good thing he had done.* 1836-46

And if one, by happy chance, was brought back by a saving hand, it was a mercy and a miracle; and the exception which proved the rule. The chances against him were many and great, for he had divers ordeals to pass through, and he seldom survived them all. It was the wont of many Settlement officers to assist the solution of knotty questions of proprietary right by a reference to personal character and conduct, so that when the claims of a great Talookhdar could not be altogether ignored, it was declared that he was a rogue or a fool—perhaps, an atrocious compound of both—and that he had forfeited, by oppressions and cruelties, or by neglects scarcely less cruel, all claim to the compassion of the State. They gave the man a bad name, and straightway they went out to ruin him. A single illustration will suffice. One of the great landholders thus consigned to perdition was the Rajah of Mynpooree. Of an old and honoured family, distinguished for loyalty and good service to the British Government, he was the Talookhdar of a large estate comprising nearly two hundred villages, and was amongst the most influential of the landed aristocracy of that part of the country. The Settlement officer was one of

* In sober official language, described by Lieutenant-Governor Robertson as "the prevailing, and perhaps excessive, readiness to reduce extensive properties into minute portions, and to substitute, whenever there was an opportunity, a village community for an individual landholder."

1836-46. Mr. G. Edmonstone.

the ablest and best of his class. Fulfilling the great promise of his youth, he afterwards attained to the highest post in those very Provinces, an eminence from which he might serenely contemplate the fact that the theory of the Dead-Level is against nature, and cannot be enforced without a convulsion. But, in the early days of which I am speaking, a great Talookhdar was to him what it was to others of the same school; and he represented that the Rajah, himself incompetent almost to the point of imbecility, was surrounded by agents of the worst character, who in his name had been guilty of all kinds of cruelty and oppression. Unfit as he was said to be for the management of so large an estate, it would, according to the prevailing creed, have been a righteous act to exclude him from it; but it was necessary, according to rule, to espy also a flaw in his tenure; so it was found that he had a just proprietary right in only about a fourth of the two hundred villages.* It was proposed, therefore, that his territorial greatness should to this extent be shorn down in the future Settlement, and that the bulk of the property should be settled with the village communities, whose rights, whatever they might originally have been, had lain for a century in abeyance.

Above the Settlement officer, in the ascending scale of our Administrative Agency, was the Commissioner; above the Commissioner, the Board of Revenue; above the Board of Revenue, the Lieutenant-Governor. In this cluster of graduated authorities the Old and New School alternated like the Black and White of a chess-board. The recommen-

* The exact number was 189, of which it was ruled that the Rajah could justly be recorded as proprietor only of 51. A money-compensation, in the shape of a percentage, was to be given him for the loss of the rest.

dations of George Edmonstone were stoutly opposed by Robert Hamilton. The sharp, incisive logic of the Commissioner cut through the fallacious reasoning of the Settlement officer. "He was of opinion that the value of landed possessions and the importance attached to them could never be made up by a money allowance; that the imbecility of the Rajah, if affording a justification for his being relieved from the management of his estate, could be none for depriving his family of their inheritance; and that it was inconsistent to denounce as oppressive in a native ruler the same measures of sale and dispossession which were adopted by our own Government towards Revenue defaulters."* But the Board, of which the living principle was Robert Bird, dissented from the views of the Commissioner, and upheld the levelling processes of the Settlement officer. Then Lieutenant-Governor Robertson appeared upon the scene, and the decision of the Board was flung back upon them as the unjust growth of a vicious, generalising system, which would break up every large estate in the country into minute fractions, and destroy the whole aristocracy of the country. He could not see that, on the score either of invalidity of tenure or of administrative incapacity, it would be just to pare down the Rajah's estate to one-fourth of its ancestral dimensions; so he ruled that the settlement of the whole ought rightly to be made with the Talookhdar.† But the vicissitudes of the case were not even then at an 1836-46.

* Despatch of Court of Directors, August 13, 1851.

† "The Lieutenant-Governor recorded his opinion, that no proof of the Rajah's mismanagement, such as could justify his exclusion, had been adduced; that the evidence in support of the proprietary claims of the Zemindars was insufficient and inconclusive; that if the Zemindars ever possessed the rights attributed to them, they had not been in the active enjoyment of them for upwards of a century, while the Rajah's claims had been admitted for more than four generations; that, admitting the inconvenience which might sometimes result from the recognition of

1836-46. end. The opposition of the Board caused some delay in the issue of the formal instructions of Government for the recognition of the Talookhdar, and before the settlement had been made with the Rajah, Robertson had resigned his post to another. That other was a man of the same school, with no greater passion than his predecessor for the subversion of the landed gentry; but sickness rendered his tenure of office too brief, and, before the close of the year, he was succeeded by one whose name is not to be mentioned without respect—the honoured son of an honoured father—the much-praised, much-lamented Thomason. He was as earnest and as honest as the men who had gone before him; but his strong and sincere convictions lay all in the other way. He was one of the chief teachers in the New School, and so strong was his faith in its doctrines that he regarded, with feelings akin to wondering compassion, as men whom God had given over to a strong delusion that they should believe a lie, all who still cherished the opinions which he had done so much to explode.*

Mr. George Clerk.

1844.

Mr. Thomason.

the superior malgoosar, it would not be reconcilable with good feeling or justice to deal as the Board proposed to do, with one found in actual and long-acknowledged possession. He condemned the practice of deciding cases of this nature on one invariable and generalising principle; stated that he could discover no sufficient reason for excluding the Rajah of Mynpooree from the management of any of the villages composing the Talook of Minchunnah; and finally withheld his confirmation of the settlement concluded with the village Zemindars, directing the engagements to be taken from the Talookhdar."—*Despatch of Court of Directors, August* 13, 1851.

* See, for example, his reflections on the contumacy of Mr. Boulderson, of whom Mr. Thomason says: "With much honesty of principle he is possessed of a constitution of mind which prevents him from readily adopting the principles of others, or acting upon their rules. A great part of his Indian career has been passed in opposition to the prevailing maxims of the day, and he finds himself conscientiously adverse to what has been done." With respect to these prevailing maxims, Mr. F. H. Robinson, of the Civil Service, in a pamphlet published in 1855, quotes the significant observation of an old Ressaldar of Gardener's Horse, who said to him: "No doubt the wisdom of the new gentlemen had shown them the folly and the ignorance of the gentlemen of the old time, on whom it pleased God, nevertheless, to bestow the government of India."

Supreme in the North-West Provinces, he found the 1836-46.
case of the Mynpooree Rajah still formally before the Government. No final orders had been issued, so he issued them. The besom of the Settlement swept the great Talookhdar out of three-fourths of the estate, and the village proprietors were left to engage with Government for all the rest in his stead.

It is admitted now, even by men who were personally concerned in this great work of the Settlement of Northern India, that it involved a grave political error. It was, undoubtedly, to convert into bitter enemies those whom sound policy would have made the friends and supporters of the State. Men of the Old School had seen plainly from the first that by these measures we were sowing broadcast the seeds of future trouble. Foremost among these was the veteran Director Tucker, who had been engaged in the first settlement of the Ceded and Conquered Provinces, and who knew as well as any man what rights existed on our original assumption of the government of those territories. "The way to conciliate the peasantry," 1832.
he wrote, "or to improve their condition, is not, I think, by dissolving the connexion between them and the superior Talookhdars, or village Zemindars. The one we have, I fear, entirely displaced; but we cannot destroy the memory of their past or the consciousness of their present state. They were once prosperous, and they and their descendants must feel that they are no longer so. They are silent, because the natives of India are accustomed to endure and to submit to the will of their rulers; but if an enemy appear on our Western frontier, or if an insurrection unhappily take place, we shall find these Talookhdars, I apprehend, in the adverse ranks, and their ryots and retainers ranged under the same standard." And a quarter of

1836-46. a century later, one who had received the traditions of this school unbroken from Thomas Campbell Robertson, at whose feet he had sat, wrote that he had long been pointing out that, "although the old families were being displaced fast, we could not destroy the memory of the past, or dissolve the ancient connexion between them and their people ; and said distinctly that, in the event of any insurrection occurring, we should find this great and influential body, through whom we can alone hope to keep under and control the rural masses, ranged against us on the side of the enemy, with their hereditary followers and retainers rallying around them, in spite of our attempts to separate their interests." "My warnings," he added, "were unheeded, and I was treated as an alarmist, who, having hitherto served only in the political department of the State, and being totally inexperienced in Revenue matters, could give no sound opinion on the subject."*

Treatment of the native gentry.

Warnings of this kind were, indeed, habitually disregarded; and the system, harsh in itself, was carried out, in some cases harshly and uncompromisingly, almost indeed as though there were a pleasure in doing it. It is true that men deprived of their vested interests in great estates were recommended for money-payments direct from the Treasury ; but this was no compensation for the loss of the land, with all the dignity derived from manorial rights and baronial privileges, and it was sometimes felt to be an insult. It was not even the fashion in those days to treat the Native Gentry with personal courtesy and conciliation. Some of the great masters

* Personal Adventures during the Indian Rebellion. By William Edwards, B.C.S., Judge of Benares, and late Magistrate and Collector of Budaon, in Rohilcund.

of the school, men of the highest probity and benevolence, are said to have failed in this with a great failure, as lamentable as it was surprising. "In the matter of discourtesy to the native gentry," wrote Colonel Sleeman to John Colvin, "I can only say that Robert Mertins Bird insulted them, whenever he had an opportunity of doing so; and that Mr. Thomason was too apt to imitate him in this as in other things. Of course their example was followed by too many of their followers and admirers."* 1836-46

Rent-free tenures.

And whilst all this was going on, there was another process in active operation by which the position of the privileged classes was still further reduced. There is not one of the many difficulties, which the acquisition of a new country entails upon us, more serious than that which arises from the multiplicity of privileges and prescriptions, territorial and official, which, undetermined by any fixed principle, have existed under the native Government which we have supplanted. Even at the outset of our administrative career it is difficult to deal with these irregular claims, but the difficulty is multiplied tenfold by delay. The action of our Government in all such cases should be prompt and unvarying. Justice or Injustice should be quick in its operation and equal in its effects. Accustomed to revolutions of empire and mutations of fortune, the native mind readily comprehends the idea of confiscation as the immediate result of conquest. Mercy and forbearance at such time are not expected, and are little understood. The descent of the strong hand of the conqueror upon all existing rights and privileges is looked for with a

* See Correspondence annexed to published edition of Sleeman's Oude Diary. I have been told by men whose authority is entitled to respect, that the statement is to be received with caution.

1836-46. feeling of submission to inevitable fate; and at such a time no one wonders, scarcely any one complains, when the acts of a former Government are ignored, and its gifts are violently resumed.

Under former Governments, and indeed, in the earlier days of our own, there had been large alienations of revenue in favour of persons who had rendered good service to the State, or had otherwise acquired the favour of the rulers of the land. These rent-free tenures were of many different kinds. A volume might be filled with an account of them. Some were burdened with conditions; some were not. Some were personal life-grants; some were hereditary and perpetual. Some were of old standing; some were of recent origin. Some had been fairly earned or justly acquired; others were the vile growth of fraud and corruption. They varied no less in the circumstances of their acquisition than in their intrinsic character and inherent conditions. But anyhow they were for some time a part of our system, and had come to be regarded as the rights of the occupants. Every year which saw men in undisturbed possession seemed to strengthen those rights. An inquiry, at the outset of our career of administration, into the validity of all such tenures would have been an intelligible proceeding. Doubtless, indeed, it was expected. But years passed, and the danger seemed to have passed with them. Nay, more, the inactivity, seemingly the indifference of the British Government, with respect to those whom we found in possession, emboldened others to fabricate similar rights, and to lay claim to immunities which they had never enjoyed under their native masters.

Bengal. In Bengal this manufacture of rent-free tenures

was carried on to an extent that largely diminished 1836-46. the legitimate revenue of the country. A very considerable portion of these tenures was the growth of the transition-period immediately before and immediately after our assumption of the Dewanee, or Revenue - Administration, of Bengal, Behar, and Orissa. 1793. At the time of the great Permanent Settlement the rent-free holders were called upon to register their claims to exemption from the payment of the Government dues, and their grounds of exemption; and as they still remained in possession, they believed that their rights and privileges had been confirmed to them. The Permanent Settlement, indeed, was held to be the Magna Charta of the privileged classes; and for more than forty years men rejoiced in their freeholds, undisturbed by any thoughts of invalidity of title or insecurity of tenure.

Resumption operations.

But after this lapse of years, when Fraud itself might reasonably have pleaded a statute of limitations, the English revenue-officer awoke to a sense of the wrongs endured by his Government. So much revenue alienated; so many worthless sinecurists living in indolent contentment at the cost of the State, enjoying vast privileges and immunities, to the injury of the great mass of the People. Surely it was a scandal and a reproach! Then well-read, clever secretaries, with a turn for historical illustration, discovered a parallel between this grievous state of things in Bengal and that which preceded the great revolution in France, when the privileges of the old nobility pressed out the very life of the nation, until the day of reckoning and retribution came, with a more dire tyranny of its own. Viewed in this light,

1836-46. it was held to be an imperative duty to Colbertise the Lakhirajdars of the Lower Provinces.* So the resumption-officer was let loose upon the land. Titles were called for; proofs of validity were to be established, to the satisfaction of the Government functionary. But in families, which seldom last a generation without seeing their houses burnt down, and in a climate, which during some months of the year is made up of incessant rains, and during others of steamy exhalations—where the devouring damp, and the still more devouring insect, consume all kinds of perishable property, even in stout-walled houses, it would have been strange if genuine documentary evidence had been forthcoming at the right time. It was an awful thing, after so many years of undisturbed possession, to be called upon to establish proofs, when the only proof was actual incumbency. A reign of terror then commenced. And if, when thus threatened, the weak Bengalee had not sometimes betaken himself in self-defence to the ready weapons of forgery, he must have changed his nature under the influence of his fears. That what ensued may properly be described as wholesale confiscation is not to be doubted. Expert young revenue-officers settled scores of cases in a day; and families, who had held possession of inherited estates for long years, and never doubted the security of their tenure, found

* "In a memoir of the Great Colbert I read the following words, which are exactly descriptive of the nature of the pretensions of the great mass of the Lakhirajdars, and of the present measures of the Government: 'Under the pernicious system which exempted the nobility from payment of direct taxes, a great number of persons had fraudulently assumed titles and claimed rank, while another class had obtained immunity from taxation by the prostitution of Court favour, or the abuse of official privileges. These cases Colbert caused to be investigated, and those who failed in making out a legal claim to immunity were compelled to pay their share of the public burdens, to the relief of the labouring classes, on whom nearly the whole weight of taxation fell.'"—*See Letters of* GAUNTLET, *addressed to the Calcutta Papers of* 1838.

themselves suddenly deprived of their freeholds and compelled to pay or to go. That the State had been largely defrauded, at some time or other, is more than probable. Many, it is admitted, were in possession who had originally no good title to the exemption they enjoyed. But many also, whose titles were originally valid, could produce no satisfactory evidence of their validity; so the fraudulent usurper and the rightful possessor were involved in one common ruin. 1836-46.

The success of these operations was loudly vaunted at the time. A social revolution had been accomplished, to the manifest advantage of the State, and at no cost, it was said, of popular discontent. The Bengalee is proverbially timid, patient, and long-suffering. But there were far-seeing men who said, even at that time, that though a strong Government might do this with impunity in those lower provinces, they must beware how they attempt similar spoliation in other parts of India, especially in those from which the Native Army was recruited. If you do, it was prophetically said, you will some day find yourselves holding India only with European troops. The probability of alienating by such measures the loyalty of the military classes was earnestly discussed in the European journals of Calcutta;* and it was said, by those who defended the measure, that it was not intended to extend these resumption operations to other

* The following, written a quarter of a century ago, affords a curious glimpse of the apprehensions even then entertained by far-seeing men: "We would just hint by the way to those who have planned this very extraordinary attack upon vested rights, that the Sepoys are almost all landholders, many of them Brahmins, whose families are supported by the charitable foundations which it is now sought to confiscate and destroy. The alarm has not yet, we believe, spread to the Army, but it has not been without its causes of complaints; and we would very calmly and respectfully put it to our rulers, whether it is wise or prudent to run the risk to which this Resumption measure would sooner or later in-

1836-46. parts of the country. But scarcely any part of the country escaped; scarcely any race of men, holding rent-free estates of any kind, felt secure in the possession of rights and privileges which they had enjoyed under Mogul and Mahratta rule, and had believed that they could still enjoy under the Raj of the Christian ruler.

North-West Provinces.

In the North-West Provinces it was part of the duty of the Settlement officer to inquire into rent-free tenures, and to resume or to release from assessment the lands thus held. The feelings with which the task imposed upon him was regarded varied with the character and the opinions of the functionary thus employed; but whilst those who were disposed to look compassionately upon doubtful claims, or believed that it would be sound policy to leave men in undisturbed possession even of what might have been in the first instance unrighteously acquired, were few, the disciples of Bird and Thomason, who viewed all such alienations of revenue as unmixed evils, and considered that any respect shown to men who were described as "drones who do no good in the public hive" was an injury done to the tax-paying community at large, were many and powerful, and left their impression on the land. Rejoicing in the great principle of the Dead-Level, the Board commonly supported the views of the resumptionist; and but for the intervention of Mr. Robertson, the Lieutenant-

fallibly lead. The native soldier has long been in the habit of placing implicit reliance upon British faith and honour; but let the charm once be broken, let the confiscation of rent-free land spread to those provinces out of which our Army is recruited, and the consequences may be that we shall very soon have to trust for our security to British troops alone. The Government may then learn rather late that revenue is not the only thing needful, and that their financial arithmetic, instead of making twice two equal to one, as Swift says was the case in Ireland, may end by extracting from the same process of multiplication just nothing at all."—*Englishman, November* 2, 1838.

Governor, there would scarcely, at the end of the Settlement operations, have been a rent-free tenure in the land. There was sometimes a show of justice on the side of resumption, for the immunity had been granted, in the first instance, as payment for service no longer demanded, or what had been originally merely a life-grant had assumed the character of an hereditary assignment. Perhaps there was sometimes more than suspicion that in unsettled times, when there was a sort of scramble for empire, privileges of this kind had been fabricated or usurped; but in other instances strong proofs of validity were ignored, and it has been freely stated, even by men of their own order, that these earnest-minded civilians "rejected royal firmans and other authentic documents," and brought upon the great rent-roll of the Company lands which had been for many generations free from assessment. Nay, even the highest authority, in the great Settlement epoch, declared that "the Settlement officer swept up, without inquiry, every patch of unregistered land; even those exempted by a subsequent order, which did not come out until five-sixths of the tenures had been resumed." In one district, that of Furruckabad, "the obligations of a treaty and the direct orders of Government were but lightly dealt with; and in all, a total disregard was evinced for the acts even of such men as Warren Hastings and Lord Lake."* In every case what was done was done conscientiously, in the assured belief that it was for the general good of the people; but the very knowledge that was most vaunted, a knowledge of the institutions and the temper of the natives,

1836-46.

* Minute of Mr. Robertson, Lieutenant-Governor of the North-West Provinces, quoted in Despatch of the Court of Directors, August 13, 1851.

1836-46. was that which they most lacked. They were wrecked upon the dangerous coast of Little Learning.

There were, however, it has been said, some men engaged in those great Settlement operations who were not smitten with this unappeasable earth-hunger, and who took altogether another view both of the duty and of the policy of the State. Mr. Mansel, of whose eager desire, so honourably evinced at a later period, to uphold the Native States of India I have already spoken, was the principal exponent of these exceptional opinions. "If it be of importance," he wrote, in his Report on the Settlement of the Agra District, "to conciliate the affections of the people, as well as to govern by the action of naked penal laws; if it be important that the natural tendency of every part of native society in these provinces, to sink into one wretched level of poverty and ignorance, should, as a principle, be checked as far as possible by the acts of Government; if it be important that the pride of ancestry and nobility, the valour of past times, and the national character of a country, should be cherished in recollection, as ennobling feelings to the human mind, I know of no act to which I could point with more satisfaction, as a zealous servant of Government, than the generous manner in which the restoration of the family of the Buddawar Rajah to rank and fortune was made by the Lieutenant-Governor of Agra; and I cannot refrain from allowing myself to echo, for the inhabitants of this part of the country, that feeling, in a report of necessity, largely connected with the welfare and happiness of the district of Agra." Mr. Robertson had granted the Buddawar Jagheer to the adopted son of the deceased Rajah, and it was the recognition of this adoption which so rejoiced the heart of the sympathising Settlement officer.

As the events of which I am about to write occurred, for the most part, in Northern India, it is to the disturbing causes in that part of the country that the introductory section of this book is mainly devoted. But before it passes altogether away from the subject of Resumption, something should be said about the operations of that great confiscatory Tribunal known as the Inam Commission of Bombay. This was but the supplement of a series of measures, of which it would take a long time to write in detail. A great part of the territory, now constituting the Presidency of Bombay, was in 1817 conquered from the Peishwah. With conquest came the old difficulty, of which I have spoken*—the difficulty of dealing with the privileges and prescriptions, the vested interests of all kinds, territorial and official, derived from the Mahratta Government. As in Bengal and in the North-Western Provinces, these difficulties were greatly aggravated by delay. Had we instituted a searching inquiry at once, and resumed every doubtful tenure; had we cancelled even the undoubted grants of former governments, and suddenly annulled all existing privileges, such proceedings in the eyes of the people would have been the intelligible tyranny of the conqueror, and, at all events, in accordance with the custom of the country. But our very desire to deal justly and generously with these privileged classes generated delaid and unequal action. At different times, and in different parts of Western India, these old alienations of Revenue were dealt with after different fashions; and it was a source of bitter discontent that, under like circumstances, claims were settled by Government with far greater rigour in one part of the country than in another.

1817-52.

The Inam Commission of Bombay

* *Ante*, page 167.

1852. Years passed, various regulations were framed, for the most part of restricted operation; and still, after the country had been for more than a third of a century under British rule, the great question of alienated revenue had only been partially adjusted. So in 1852 an act was passed, which empowered a little body of English officers, principally of the military profession—men, it was truly said, "not well versed in the principles of law, and wholly unpractised in the conduct of judicial inquiries"—to exercise arbitrary jurisdiction over thousands of estates, many of them held by men of high family, proud of their lineage, proud of their ancestral privileges, who had won what they held by the sword, and had no thought by any other means of maintaining possession. In the Southern Mahratta country there were large numbers of these Jagheerdars, who had never troubled themselves about title-deeds, who knew nothing about rules of evidence, and who had believed that long years of possession were more cogent than any intricacies of law. If they had ever held written proofs of the validity of their tenures, they had seldom been so provident as to preserve them. But, perhaps, they had never had better proof than the memory of a fierce contest, in the great *gurdee-ka-wukht*, or time of trouble, which had preluded the dissolution of the Mahratta power in Western India, and placed the white man on the Throne of the Peishwah.* Year after year had

* See the admirably-written memorial of Mr. G. B. Seton-Karr: "Chiefs, who had won their estates by the sword, had not been careful to fence them in with a paper barrier, which they felt the next successful adventurer would sweep away as unceremoniously as themselves. Instead of parchments, they transmitted arms and retainers, with whose aid they had learnt to consider mere titles superfluous, as without it they were contemptible. In other instances, men of local influence and energetic character having grasped at the lands which lay within their reach in the general scramble which preceded the down-

passed, one generation had followed another in undisturbed possession, and the great seal of Time stood them in stead of the elaborate technicalities of the Conveyancer. But the Inam Commission was established. The fame of it went abroad throughout the Southern Mahratta country. From one village to another passed the appalling news that the Commissioner had appeared, had called for titles that could not be produced, and that nothing but a general confiscation of property were likely to result from the operations of this mysterious Tribunal. "Each day," it has been said, "produced its list of victims; and the good fortune of those who escaped but added to the pangs of the crowd who came forth from the shearing-house, shorn to the skin, unable to work, ashamed to beg, condemned to penury."* The titles of no less than thirty-five thousand estates, great and small, were called for by the Commission, and during the first five years of its operations, three-fifths of them were confiscated.† 1852. 1852-57.

Operation of the Civil Courts.

Whilst the operations of the Revenue Department were thus spreading alarm among the privileged classes in all parts of the country, the Judicial Department was doing its duty as a serviceable ally in the great war of extermination. Many of the old landed proprietors were stripped to the skin by the decrees of our civil courts. The sale of land in satisfaction of these decrees was a process to which recourse was often had among a people inordinately

fal of the Peishwah's Government, had transmitted their acquisitions to the children, fortified by no better titles than entries in the village account-books, which a closer examination showed to be recent or spurious. Roused from the dreams of thirty years, these proprietors of precarious title, or of no title at all, found themselves suddenly brought face to face with an apparatus, which, at successive strokes, peeled away their possessions with the harsh precision of the planing machine."

* Memorial of G. B. Seton-Karr.

† Ibid.

1836-56. addicted to litigation. We must not regard it altogether with English eyes; for the Law had often nothing else to take. There was many a small landed proprietor whose family might have been established for centuries on a particular estate, with much pride of birth and affection for his ancestral lands, but possessing movable goods and chattels not worth more than a few rupees. He might have owned a pair of small bullocks and a rude country cart consisting of two wheels and a few bamboos, but beyond such aids to husbandry as these, he had nothing but a drinking-vessel, a few cooking-pots, and the blankets which kept the dews off at night. Justice in his case might not be satisfied without a surrender of his interests in the land, which constituted the main portion of his wealth.* So a large number of estates every year were put up to sale, under the decrees of the courts, in satisfaction of debts sometimes only of a few shillings, and bought by new men, perhaps from different parts of the country, not improbably the agents or representatives of astute native functionaries from the lower provinces; whilst the ancient proprietors, still rooted to the soil, shrunk into small farmers or under-tenants on their old ancestral domains. Thus a revolution of landed property was gradually brought about by means of English application, which, acting coincidentally with the other agencies of which I have spoken, swelled the number

* I have stated here the principle upon which the law was based. But I believe that in many cases no pains were taken to ascertain in the first instance what were the movable goods of the debtor. Recourse was had to the register of landed property, even when the debt amounted to no more than four or five rupees. "I have seen," says an officer of the Bengal Civil Service, in a Memorandum before me, "estates put up for sale for four rupees (eight shillings), which appears to me just the same as if an English grocer, getting a decree in a small-debt court against a squire for half a sovereign, put up his estate in Cheshire for the same, instead of realising the debt by the sale of his silk umbrella."

of the disaffected, dangerous classes, who traced their downfal to the operations of British rule, and sullenly bided their time for the recovery of what they had lost, in some new revolutionary epoch. 1836-56.

This general system of depression, which, thus assuming many different forms and exercising itself in many different ways, struck with uniform precision at the most cherished privileges of the upper classes, had not its origin in the fertile brain of Lord Dalhousie. He only confirmed and extended it; confirmed it in our older provinces, and extended it to those which he had himself acquired. In the Punjab it sorely disquieted some few of our more chivalrous English officers connected with the Administration,* and it was carried into the Oude dominions, as will hereafter be shown, with a recklessness which in time brought down upon us a terrible retribution. Every new acquisition of territory made the matter much worse. Not merely because the privileged classes were in those territories struck down, but because the extension of the British Raj gradually so contracted the area on which men of high social position, expelled by our system from the Company's provinces, could find profitable and honourable employment, that it seemed as though every outlet for native enterprise and ambition were about to be closed against them. It was this, indeed, that made the great difference between

* Sir Herbert Edwardes, in a Memorandum quoted by Mr. Charles Raikes in his graphic "Notes of the Revolt of the North-West Provinces of India," says of Arthur Cocks, that he "imbibed Sir Henry Lawrence's feelings, and became greatly attached to the chiefs and people. He hardly stayed a year after annexation, and left the Punjab because he could not bear to see the fallen state of the old officials and Sirdars." Of Henry Lawrence himself, Mr. Raikes says: "He fought every losing battle for the old chiefs and Jagheerdars with entire disregard for his own interest, and at last left the Punjab, to use Colonel Edwardes's words, dented all over with defeats and disappointments, honourable scars in the eyes of the bystanders."

1836-56. resumptions of rent-free estates under the Native Governments and under our own. It has been said that under the former there was no security of tenure; and it is true that the Native Princes did not consider themselves bound to maintain the grants of their predecessors, and often arbitrarily resumed them. But the door of honourable and lucrative employment was not closed against the sufferers. All the great offices of the State, civil and military, were open to the children of the soil. But it was not so in our British territories. There the dispossessed holder, no longer suffered to be an unprofitable drone, was not permitted to take a place among the working bees of the hive. And what place was there left for him, in which he could serve under other masters? We had no room for him under us, and we left no place for him away from us. And so we made dangerous enemies of a large number of influential persons, among whom were not only many nobles of royal or princely descent, many military chiefs, with large bodies of retainers, and many ancient landholders for whom a strong feudal veneration still remained among the agricultural classes, but numbers of the Brahminical, or priestly order, who had been supported by the alienated revenue which we resumed, and who turned the power which they exercised over the minds of others to fatal account in fomenting popular discontent, and instilling into the minds of the people the poison of religious fear.

The Priesthood.

Other measures were in operation at the same time, the tendency of which was to disturb the minds and to inflame the hatred of the Priesthood. It seemed as though a great flood of innovation were about to sweep away all their powers and their privileges. The pale-faced Christian knight, with the great Excalibar of Truth in his hand, was cleaving right through all the most cherished fictions and superstitions of Brahminism. A new generation was springing up, without faith, without veneration; an inquiring, doubting, reasoning race, not to be satisfied with absurd doctrines or captivated by grotesque fables. The literature of Bacon and Milton was exciting a new appetite for Truth and Beauty; and the exact sciences of the West, with their clear, demonstrable facts and inevitable deductions, were putting to shame the physical errors of Hindooism. A spirit of inquiry had been excited, and it was little likely ever to be allayed. It was plain that the inquirers were exalting the Professor above the Pundit, and that the new teacher was fast displacing the old. 1848-56.

Rightly to understand the stake for which the Brahmin was playing, and with the loss of which he was now threatened, the reader must keep before him the fact that Brahminism is the most monstrous system of interference and oppression that the world has ever yet seen, and that it could be maintained only by ignorance and superstition of the grossest kind. The people had been taught to believe that in all the daily concerns of life Brahminical ministrations were essential to worldly success. The Deity, it was believed, could be propitiated only by money-payments to this favoured race of holy men. "Every form and ceremony of religion," it has been said; "all the public festivals; all the accidents and concerns of life; the revolutions of the heavenly bodies; the superstitious fears of the people; births, sicknesses, marriages, misfortunes; death; a future state—have all been seized as sources of revenue to the Brahmins."

1848-56. "The farmer does not reap his harvest without paying a Brahmin to perform some ceremony; a tradesman cannot begin business without a fee to a Brahmin; a fisherman cannot build a new boat, nor begin to fish in a spot which he has farmed, without a ceremony and a fee."* "The Brahmin," says another and more recent writer, "does not only stand in a hierarchical, but also in the highest aristocratical position; and he has an authoritative voice in all pursuits of industry. All processes in other arts, as well as agriculture, are supposed to have been prescribed and imparted through the Brahmins. Every newly-commenced process of business, every new machine, or even repair of an old one, has to go through the ceremony of 'poojah,' with a feeing of the Brahmin."† And as the Brahmin was thus the controller of all the ordinary business concerns of his countrymen, so also was he the depositary of all the learning of the country, and the regulator of all the intellectual pursuits of the people. There was, indeed, no such thing among them as purely secular education. "It is a marked and peculiar feature in the character of Hindooism," says another writer, himself by birth a Hindoo, "that instead of confining itself within the proper and lawful bounds prescribed to every theological system, it interferes with and treats of every department of secular knowledge which human genius has ever invented; so that grammar, geography, physics, law, medicine, metaphysics, &c., do each form as essential a part of Hindooism as any religious topic with which it is concerned. . . . In their religious works they have treated of all the branches of secular

* Ward on the Hindoos.

† Jeffreys on the "British Army in India," Appendix, in which there is much interesting and valuable matter.

knowledge known among them, in a regular, systematic manner; and have given them out to the world in a tone of absolute authority, from which there could be no appeal."* But the English had established a Court of Appeal of the highest order, and Brahminism was being continually cast in it. In a word, the whole hierarchy of India saw their power, their privileges, and their perquisites rapidly crumbling away from them, and they girded themselves up to arrest the devastation. 1845-56

All this had been going on for years; but the progress of enlightenment had been too slow, and its manifestations too little obtrusive, greatly to alarm the sacerdotal mind. As long as the receptacles of this new wisdom were merely a few clever boys in the great towns, and the manhood of the nation was still saturated and sodden with the old superstition, Brahminism might yet flourish. But when these boys grew up in time to be heads of families, rejoicing in what they called their freedom from prejudice, laughing to scorn their ancestral faith as a bundle of old wives' fables, eating meat and drinking wine, and assuming some at least of the distinguishing articles of Christian apparel, it was clear that a very serious peril was beginning to threaten the ascendancy of the Priesthood. They saw that a reformation of this kind once commenced, would work its way in time through all the strata of society. They saw that, as new provinces were one after another brought under British rule, the new light must diffuse itself more and more, until there would scarcely be a place for Hindooism to lurk unmolested. And some at least, confounding cause and effect, began to argue that all this annexation and absorption was brought about for the

* *Calcutta Review*, vol. xi. Article: "Physical Errors of Hindooism."

1848-56. express purpose of overthrowing the ancient faiths of the country, and establishing a new religion in their place.

Education. Every monstrous lie exploded, every abominable practice suppressed, was a blow struck at the Priesthood; for all these monstrosities and abominations had their root in Hindooism, and could not be eradicated without sore disturbance and confusion of the soil. The murder of women on the funeral-pile, the murder of little children in the Zenana, the murder of the sick and the aged on the banks of the river, the murder of human victims, reared and fattened for the sacrifice, were all religious institutions, from which the Priesthood derived either profit, power, or both. Nay, even the wholesale strangling of unsuspecting travellers was sanctified and ceremonialised by religion. Now all these cruel rites had been suppressed, and, what was still worse in the eyes of the Brahmins, the foul superstitions which nurtured them were fast disappearing from the land. Authority might declare their wickedness, and still they might exist as part and parcel of the faith of the people. But when Reason demonstrated their absurdity, and struck conviction into the very heart of the nation, there was an end of both the folly and the crime. The Law might do much, but Education would assuredly do much more to sweep away all these time-honoured superstitions. Education, pure and simple in its secularity, was quite enough in itself to hew down this dense jungle of Hindooism; but when it was seen that the functions of the English schoolmaster and of the Christian priest were often united in the same person, and that high officers of the State were present at examinations conducted by chaplains or missionaries, a fear arose lest even secular education might be the mask of proselytism, and so the Brahmins began to alarm the minds of the elder members of the Hindoo community, who abstained, under priestly influence, from openly countenancing what they had not the energy boldly to resist.* 1848-56.

And, every year the danger increased. Every year were there manifestations of a continually increasing desire to emancipate the natives of India from the gross superstitions which enchained them. One common feeling moved alike the English Government and the English community. In other matters of State-policy there might be essential changes, but in this there was no change. One Governor might replace another, but only to evince an increased hostility to the great Baal of Hindooism. And in no man was there less regard for time-honoured abominations and venerable absurdities—in no man did the zeal of iconoclasm work more mightily than in Lord Dalhousie. During no former administration had the vested interests of Brahminism in moral and material error been more ruthlessly assailed. There was nothing systematic in all this. Almost, indeed, might it be said that it was unconscious. It was simply the manifestation of such love as any clear-sighted, strong-headed man may be supposed to have for truth above error, for intelligent progress above ignorant stagnation. From love of this kind, from the assured conviction that it was equally humane and politic to substitute the strength and justice of British administration for what he regarded as the effete tyrannies of the East, had emanated the annexations which had distinguished

* The English journalists sometimes remarked in their reports of these school-examinations upon the absence of the native gentry—*e. g.*: "We cannot help expressing great surprise at the absence of natives of influence."—*Bengal Hurkaru, March 14*, 1853.

1848-56. his rule. And as he desired for the good of the people to extend the territorial rule of Great Britain, so he was eager also to extend her moral rule, and to make those people subject to the powers of light rather than of darkness.' And so he strove mightily to extend among them the blessings of European civilisation, and the Priesthood stood aghast at the sight of the new things, moral and material, by which they were threatened.

Many and portentous were these menaces. Not only was Government Education, in a more systematised and pretentious shape than before, rapidly extending its network over the whole male population of the country, but even the fastnesses of the female apartments were not secure against the intrusion of the new learning and new philosophy of the West. England had begun to take account of its short-comings, and, among all the reproaches heaped upon the Company, none had been so loud or so general as the cry that, whilst they spent millions on War, they grudged hundreds for purposes of Education. So, in obedience to this cry, instructions had been sent out to India, directing larger, more comprehensive, more systematic measures for the instruction of the people, and authorising increased expenditure upon them. Whilst great Universities were to be established, under the immediate charge of the Government, the more humble missionary institutions were to be aided by grants of public money, and no effort was to be spared that could conduce to the spread of European knowledge. It was plain to the comprehension of the guardians of Eastern learning, that what had been done to unlock the flood-gates of the West, would soon appear to be as nothing in comparison with the great tide of European civilisation which was about to be poured out upon them. 1848-56.

Female Education.

Most alarming of all were the endeavours made, during Lord Dalhousie's administration, to penetrate the Zenana with our new learning and our new customs. The English at the large Presidency towns began to systematise their efforts for the emancipation of the female mind from the utter ignorance which had been its birthright, and the wives and daughters of the white men began to aid in the work, cheered and encouraged by the sympathies of their sisters at home. For the first time, the education of Hindoo and Mahomedan females took, during the administration of Lord Dalhousie, a substantial recognised shape. Before it had been merely a manifestation of missionary zeal addressed to the conversion of a few orphans and castaways. But now, if not the immediate work of the Government in its corporate capacity, it was the pet project and the especial charge of a member of the Government, and, on his death, passed into the hands of the Governor-General himself, and afterwards was adopted by the Company's Government. Some years before, the Priesthood, secure in the bigotry and intolerance of the heads of families, might have laughed these efforts to scorn. But now young men, trained under English Professors, were becoming fathers and masters, sensible of the great want of enlightened female companionship, and ill-disposed to yield obedience to the dogmas of the Priests. So great, indeed, was this yearning after something more attractive and more satisfying than the inanity of the Zenana, that the courtesans of the Calcutta Bazaars taught themselves to play on instruments, to sing songs, and to read poetry, that thereby they might lure from the dreary environ-

Mr. Bethune.

1855-56. ments of their vapid homes the very flower of Young Bengal.

Re-marriage of Hindoo Widows.

About the same time the wedge of another startling innovation was being driven into the very heart of Hindoo Society. Among the many cruel wrongs to which the womanhood of the nation was subjected was the institution which forbade a bereaved wife ever to re-marry. The widow who did not burn was condemned to perpetual chastity. Nay, it has been surmised that the burning inculcated in the old religious writings of the Hindoos was no other than that which, centuries afterwards, the great Christian teacher forbade, saying that it is better to marry than to burn. Be this as it may, the re-marriage of Hindoo widows was opposed both to the creeds and the customs of the land. It was an evil and a cruel thing itself, and the prolific source of other evils. Evil and cruel would it have been in any country and under any institutions, but where mere children are married, often to men advanced in years, and are left widows, in tender youth, when they have scarcely looked upon their husbands, its cruelty is past counting. To the more enlightened Hindoos, trained in our English colleges and schools, the evils of this prohibition were so patent and so distressing, that they were fain to see it abrogated by law. One of their number wrote a clever treatise in defence of the re-marriage of widows, and thousands signed a petition, in which a belief was expressed that perpetual widowhood was not enjoined by the Hindoo scriptures. But the orthodox party, strong in texts, greatly outnumbered, and, judged by the standard of Hindooism, greatly outargued them. The Law and the Prophets were on their side. It was plain that the innovation would inflict another deadly blow on the old Hindoo law of inheritance. Already had dire offence been given to the orthodoxy of the land by the removal of those disabilities which forbade all who had forsaken their ancestral faith to inherit ancestral property. A law had been passed, declaring the abolition of "so much of the old law or usage as inflicted on any person forfeiture of rights or property, by reason of his or her renouncing, or having been excluded from, the communion of any religion." Against this the old Hindoos had vehemently protested, not without threats, as a violation of the pledges given by the British Government to the natives of India; pledges, they said, issued in an hour of weakness and revoked in an hour of strength.* But Lord Dalhousie had emphatically recorded his opinion "that it is the duty of the State to keep in its own hands the right of regulating succession to property," and the Act had been passed. And now there was further authoritative interference on the part of the State, for it was proposed to bestow equal rights of inheritance on the offspring of what the old-school Hindoos declared to be an illicit, God-proscribed connexion. This, however, was but a part of the evil. Here was another step towards the complete emancipation of woman; and Hindoo orthodoxy believed, or professed to believe, that if widows were encouraged to marry new husbands instead of burning with the corpses of the old, 1855-56.

* The Bengal Memorial said: "Your memorialists will not conceal that from the moment the proposed act becomes a part of the law applicable to Hindoos, that confidence which they hitherto felt in the paternal character of their British rulers will be most materially shaken. No outbreak, of course, is to be dreaded; but the active spirit of fervent loyalty to their sovereign will be changed into sullen submission to their will, and obedience to their power." The Madras Memorial was couched in much stronger language. It denounced the measure as a direct act of tyranny, and said that the British Government, "treading the path of oppression," "would well deserve what it will assuredly obtain—the hatred and detestation of the oppressed."

1855-56. wives would be induced to make themselves widows by poisoning or otherwise destroying their lords. It was apprehended, too—and not altogether without reason*—that the re-marriage of Hindoo widows would soon be followed by a blow struck at Hindoo polygamy, especially in its worst but most honoured form of Kulinism; and so the Brahmin, discomfited and alarmed by these innovations, past, present, and prospective, strove mightily to resist the tide, and to turn the torrent of destruction back upon their enemies.†

The Railway and the Telegraph.

Nor was it only by the innovations of moral progress that the hierarchy of India were alarmed and offended. The inroads and encroachments of physical science were equally distasteful and disquieting. A privileged race of men, who had been held in veneration as the depositaries of all human knowledge, were suddenly shown to be as feeble and impotent as babes and sucklings. It was no mere verbal demonstration; the arrogant self-assertion of the white man, which the Hindoo Priesthood could contradict or explain away. There were no means of contradicting or explaining away the railway cars,

* See the following passage of a speech delivered by Mr. Barnes Peacock, in the Legislative Council, July 19, 1856: "There was a great distinction between preventing a man from doing that which his religion directed him to do, and preventing him from doing that which his religion merely allowed him to do. If a man were to say that his religion did not forbid polygamy, and therefore that he might marry as many wives as he pleased, when it was impossible for him to carry out the contract of marriage, it would be no interference with his religion for the Legislature to say that the marrying of a hundred wives, and the subsequent desertion of them, was an injury to society, and therefore that it should be illegal to do so. He" (Mr. Peacock) "maintained that it was the duty of the Legislature, in such a case, to prevent him from doing that which his religion merely permitted, but did not command him to do."

† The "Bill to remove all legal obstacles to the marriage of Hindoo widows," though introduced and discussed during the administration of Lord Dalhousie, was not finally passed till after his retirement. It received the assent of Lord Canning in July, 1856.

which travelled, without horses or bullocks, at the rate of thirty miles an hour, or the electric wires, which in a few minutes carried a message across the breadth of a whole province. 1848-56

These were facts that there was no gainsaying. He who ran might read. The prodigious triumphs over time and space achieved by these "fire-carriages" and "lightning-posts," put to shame the wisdom of the Brahmins, and seemed to indicate a command over the supernatural agencies of the Unseen World, such as the Pundits of the East could never attain or simulate. They, who for their own ends had imparted a sacred character to new inventions, and had taught their disciples that all improvements in art and science were derived from the Deity through their especial intercession, and were to be inaugurated with religious ceremonies attended with the usual distribution of largesses to the priests, now found that the white men could make the very elements their slaves, and call to their aid miraculous powers undreamt of in the Brahminical philosophy. Of what use was it any longer to endeavour to persuade the people that the new knowledge of the West was only a bundle of shams and impostures, when any man might see the train come in at a given moment, and learn at Benares how many pounds of flour were sold for the rupee that morning in the bazaars of Delhi and Calcutta?

To the introduction into India of these mysterious agencies the Hour and the Man were alike propitious. When Lord Dalhousie went out to India, England was just recovering from the effects of that over-activity of speculation which had generated such a disturbance of the whole financial system of the country. She had ceased to project lines of Railway

1848-56. between towns without Traffic, and through countries without Population, and had subsided, after much suffering, into a healthy state of reasonable enterprise, carefully estimating both her wants and her resources. As President of the Board of Trade, Dalhousie had enjoyed the best opportunities of acquainting himself with the principles and with the details of the great question of the day, at the one central point to which all information converged, and he had left England with the full determination, God willing, not to leave the country of his adoption until he had initiated the construction of great trunk-roads of iron between all the great centres of Government and of Commerce, and had traversed, at railway speed, some at least of their first stages. A little while before, the idea of an Indian railway had, in the estimation of the greater number of English residents, been something speculative and chimerical, encouraged only by visionaries and enthusiasts. A few far-seeing men, foremost among whom was Macdonald Stephenson, predicted their speedy establishment, and with the general acceptance of the nation; but even after Dalhousie had put his hand to the work, and the Company had responded to his efforts, it was the more general belief that railway communication in India would be rather a concern of Government, useful in the extreme for military purposes, than a popular institution supplying a national want. It was thought that Indolence, Avarice, and Superstition would keep the natives of the country from flocking to the Railway Station. But with a keener appreciation of the inherent power of so demonstrable a benefit to make its own way, even against these moral obstructions, Dalhousie had full faith in the result. He was right. The people now learnt to estimate at its full worth the great truth that Time is Money; and having so learned, they were not to be deterred from profiting by it by any tenderness of respect for the feelings of their spiritual guides. 1848-56.

That the fire-carriage on the iron road was a heavy blow to the Brahminical Priesthood is not to be doubted. The lightning post, which sent invisible letters through the air and brought back answers, from incredible distances, in less time than an ordinary messenger could bring them from the next street, was a still greater marvel and a still greater disturbance. But it was less patent and obtrusive. The one is the natural complement of the other; and Dalhousie, aided by the genius of O'Shaughnessy, had soon spread a network of electric wires across the whole length and breadth of the country. It was a wise thing to do; a right thing to do; but it was alarming and offensive to the Brahminical mind. It has been said, that as soon as we had demonstrated that the earth is a sphere revolving on its axis, there was an end to the superstitions of Hindooism. And so there was—in argument, but not in fact. The Brahminical teachers insisted that the new doctrines of Western civilisation were mere specious inventions, with no groundwork of eternal truth, and as their disciples could not bring the test of their senses to such inquiries as these, they succumbed to authority rather than to reason, or perhaps lapsed into a state of bewildering doubt. But material experiments, so palpable and portentous that they might be seen at a distance of many miles, convinced whilst they astounded. The most ignorant and unreasoning of men could see that the thing was done. They knew that Brahminism had never done it. They saw plainly

1848-56. the fact that there were wonderful things in the world which their own Priests could not teach them—of which, indeed, with all their boasted wisdom, they had never dreamt; and from that time the Hindoo Hierarchy lost half its power, for the People lost half their faith.

Caste. But clear as was all this, and alarming as were the prospects thus unfolded to the Pundits, there was something more than this needed to disturb the popular mind. Hindooism might be assailed; Hindooism might be disproved; and still men might go about their daily business without a fear for the future or a regret for the past. But there was something about which they disturbed themselves much more than about the abstract truths of their religion. The great institution of Caste was an ever-present reality. It entered into the commonest concerns of life. It was intelligible to the meanest understanding. Every man, woman, and child knew what a terrible thing it would be to be cast out from the community of the brotherhood, and condemned to live apart, abhorred of men and forsaken by God. If, then, the people could be taught that the English by some insidious means purposed to defile the Hindoos, and to bring them all to a dead level of one-caste or of no-caste, a great rising of the Natives might sweep the Foreigners into the sea. This was an obvious line of policy; but it was not a policy for all times. It needed opportunity for its successful development. Equally patient and astute, the Brahmin was content to bide his time rather than to risk anything by an inopportune demonstration. The English were loud in their professions of toleration, and commonly cautious in their practice. Still it was only in the nature of things that they should some day make a false step.

As the Brahmin thus lay in wait, eager for his

1845-56.

The Messing System in Gaols.

opportunity to strike, he thought he espied, perhaps in an unexpected quarter, a safe point of attack. It required some monstrous invention, very suitable to troubled times, but only to be circulated with success after the popular mind, by previous excitement, had been prepared to receive it, to give any colour of probability to a report that the Government had laid a plot for the defilement of the whole mass of the people. But there were certain classes with which Government had a direct connexion, and whose bodies and souls were in the immediate keeping of the State. Among these were the inmates of our gaols. As these people were necessarily dependent upon Government for their daily food, it appeared to be easy, by a well-devised system of Prison Discipline, either to destroy the caste of the convicts or to starve them to death. The old tolerant regulations allowed every man to cater and to cook for himself. A money-allowance was granted to him, and he turned it into food after his own fashion. But this system was very injurious to prison discipline. Men loitered over their cooking and their eating and made excuses to escape work. So the prisoners were divided into messes, according to their several castes; rations were issued to them, and cooks were appointed to prepare the daily meals at a stated hour of the day. If the cook were of a lower caste than the eaters, the necessary result was the contamination of the food and loss of caste by the whole mess. The new system, therefore, was one likely to be misunderstood and easily to be misinterpreted. Here, then, was one of those openings which designing men were continually on the alert to detect, and in a fitting hour it was turned to account. Not merely the inmates of the gaols, but the inhabitants of the towns in which pri-

1845-56. sons were located, were readily made to believe that it was the intention of the British Government to destroy the caste of the prisoners, and forcibly to convert them to Christianity. It mattered not whether Brahmin cooks had or had not, in the first instance, been appointed. There might be a Brahmin cook to-day; and a low-caste man in his place to-morrow. So the lie had some plausibility about it; and it went abroad that this assault upon the gaol-birds was but the beginning of the end, and that by a variety of different means the religions of the country would soon be destroyed by the Government of the Feringhees.

Reports of this kind commonly appear to be of Hindoo origin; for they are calculated primarily to alarm the minds of the people on the score of the destruction of caste. But it seldom happens that they are not followed by some auxiliary lies expressly designed for Mahomedan reception. The Mahomedans had some especial grievances of their own. The tendency of our educational measures, and the all-pervading Englishism with which the country was threatened, was to lower the dignity of Mahomedanism, and to deprive of their emoluments many influential people of that intolerant faith. The Moulavees were scarcely less alarmed by our innovations than the Pundits. The Arabic of the one fared no better than the Sanskrit of the other. The use of the Persian language in our law courts was abolished; new tests for admission into the Public Service cut down, if they did not wholly destroy, their chances of official employment. There was a general inclination to pare away the privileges and the perquisites of the principal Mahomedan seats of learning. All the religious endowments of the great Calcutta

Madrissa were annihilated; and the prevalence of the English language, English learning, and English law, made the Mahomedan doctors shrink into insignificance, whilst the resumption of rent-free tenures, which, in many instances, grievously affected old Mussulman families, roused their resentments more than all the rest, and made them ripe for sedition. A more active, a more enterprising, and a more intriguing race than the Hindoos, the latter knew well the importance of associating them in any design against the State.* So their animosities were stimulated, and their sympathies were enlisted, by a report, sedulously disseminated, to the effect that the British Government were about to issue an edict prohibiting circumcision, and compelling Mahomedan women to go abroad unveiled. 1845-56.

Small chance would there have been of such a lie as this finding a score of credulous Mussulmans to believe it, if it had not been for the little grain of truth that there was in the story of the messing-system in the gaols. The innovation had been originated some years before Lord Dalhousie appeared upon the scene. At first it had been introduced with

* It must be admitted, however, that it is a moot question, in many instances, whether the first movement were made by the Hindoos or the Mahomedans. Good authorities sometimes incline to the latter supposition. Take, for example, the following, which has reference to a seditious movement at Patna in the cold season of 1845-46: "From inquiries I have made," wrote Mr. Dampier, Superintendent of Police in the Lower Provinces, "in every quarter, I am of opinion that the Mahomedans of these parts, amongst whom the resumption of the Maafee Tenures, the new educational system, and the encouragement given to the English language, have produced the greatest discontent and the bitterest animosity against our government, finding that the enforcement of the messing-system in the gaols had produced a considerable sensation amongst the people, were determined to improve the opportunity, especially as our troops were weak in numbers, and we were supposed to be pressed in the North-West." Of the event to which this refers, more detailed mention will be found in a subsequent chapter of this work, in connexion with the attempt then made to corrupt the regiments at Dinapore.

1845-46. a discretion signifying a full knowledge of the lurking danger;* but, as time advanced, one experiment followed another, and some of the old caution was perhaps relaxed. So in many places the prisoners broke into rebellion and violently resisted the proposed change. Eager and excited, under the influence of a common alarm, the townspeople cheered them on, and were ready to aid them, with all their might, in what they believed to be the defence of their religion. At Shahabad, Sarun, Behar, and Patna, there were serious disturbances, and at a later
1852. period, Benares, the very nursery and hotbed of Hindooism, the cherished home of the Pundits, was saved only by prudential concessions, from becoming the scene of a sanguinary outbreak.

he Hindoo nd his Lotah. The experience thus gained of the extreme sensitiveness of the native mind, given up as it was to gross delusions, does not appear to have borne the fruit of increased caution and forbearance. For not long afterwards another improvement in prison discipline again stirred up revolt in the gaols; and, for the same reason as before, the people sided with the convicts. A Hindoo, or a Hindooised Mahomedan, is nothing without his Lotah. A Lotah is a metal drinking-vessel, which he religiously guards against defilement, and which he holds as a cherished possession when he has nothing else belonging to him in the world. But a brass vessel may be put to other uses than that of holding water. It may brain a magistrate,† or flatten the face of a gaoler, and truly

* See Circular Orders of Lieutenant-Governor of the North-West Provinces, July, 1841:—"Government are of opinion that these measures ought not to be compulsorily enforced, if there be any good ground to believe that they will violate or offend the religious prejudices of the people, or injure the future prospects of those who may be subjected to temporary imprisonment."

† My earliest recollection of India is associated with the sensation created in Calcutta, in April, 1834,

it was a formidable weapon in the hands of a desperate man. So an attempt was made in some places to deprive the prisoners of their lotahs, and to substitute earthenware vessels in their place. Here, then, in the eyes of the people, was another insidious attempt to convert prison discipline into a means of religious persecution—another attempt covertly to reduce them all to one caste. So the prisoners resisted the experiment, and in more than one place manifested their resentment with a fury which was shared by the population of the towns. At Arrah the excitement was so great that the guards were ordered to fire upon the prisoners, and at Mozufferpore, in Tirhoot, so formidable was the outburst of popular indignation, that the magistrate, in grave official language, described it as "a furious and altogether unexpected outbreak on the part of the people of the town and district in support and sympathy with the prisoners." The rioters, it was said, "included almost all the inhabitants of the town, as well as a vast number of ryots, who declared that they would not go away until the lotahs were restored;" and so great was the danger of the prisoners escaping, of their plundering the Treasury and pillaging the town, before the troops which had been sent for could be brought up, that the civil authorities deemed it expedient to pacify the insurgents by restoring the lotahs to the people in the gaols. And this was not held at the time to be a sudden outburst of rash and misguided ignorance, but the deliberate work of some of the rich native inhabitants of the town, and some of the higher native functionaries of our Civil Courts. 1855.

when Mr. Richardson, magistrate of the 24 Pergunnahs, was killed in Alipore gaol by a blow from a brass lotah.

1856. It was clear, indeed, that the inflammability of the native mind was continually increasing; and that there were many influential persons, both Hindoo and Mahomedan, running over with bitter resentments against the English, who were eagerly awaiting a favourable opportunity to set all these combustible materials in a blaze. The gaol-business was an experiment, and, as far as it went, a successful one. But it was not by an outbreak of the convict population that the overthrow of the English was to be accomplished. There was another class of men, equally under the control of the Government, whose corruption would far better repay the labours of the Moulavees and the Pundits.

BOOK II.—THE SEPOY ARMY.

[1756—1856.]

CHAPTER I.

THE SEPOY ARMY OF THE COMPANY—ITS RISE AND PROGRESS—THE FIRST MUTINY IN BENGAL—DETERIORATING INFLUENCES—DEGRADATION OF THE NATIVE OFFICER—THE REORGANISATION OF 1796—PROGRESS OF INNOVATION—THE MUTINY OF VELLORE—LATER SIGNS OF DISAFFECTION—CAUSES OF THE MUTINY.

WHILST the hearts of the Aristocracy and of the Priesthood of the country were thus turned against the government of the English, there was a third great class, esteemed to be more powerful than all, whom it was believed that our policy had propitiated. There was security in the thought that the Soldiery were with us. It was the creed of English statesmen that India had been won by the Sword, and must be retained by the Sword. And so long as we held the sword firmly in our hands, there was but little apprehension of any internal danger. The British power in the East was fenced in and fortified by an army of three hundred thousand men. 1856.

A small part only of this Army was composed of our own countrymen. Neither the manhood of England nor the revenues of India could supply the means of defending the country only with British troops. A large majority of our fighting-men were, therefore, natives of India, trained, disciplined, and

1756-1856. equipped after the English fashion. We had first learnt from the French the readiness with which the "Moors" and the "Gentoos" could be made to adapt themselves to the habits and forms of European warfare, and, for a hundred years, we had been improving on the lesson. Little by little, the handful of Blacks which had helped Robert Clive to win the battle of Plassey had swollen into the dimensions of a gigantic army. It had not grown with the growth of the territory which it was intended to defend; but still, nerved and strengthened by such European regiments as the exigencies of the parent state could spare for the service of the outlying dependency, it was deemed to be of sufficient extent to support the Government which maintained it against all foreign enmity and all intestine revolt.

It was, doubtless, a strange and hazardous experiment upon the forbearance of these disciplined native fighting-men, held only by the bondage of the Salt in allegiance to a trading Company which had usurped the authority of their Princes and reduced their countrymen to subjection. But it was an experiment which, at the date of the commencement of this history, had stood the test of more than a century of probation. The fidelity of the Native Army of India was an established article of our faith. Tried in many severe conjunctures, it had seldom been found wanting. The British Sepoy had faced death without a fear, and encountered every kind of suffering and privation without a murmur. Commanded by officers whom he trusted and loved, though of another colour and another creed, there was nothing, it was said, which he would not do, there was nothing which he would not endure. In an extremity of hunger, he had spontaneously offered his scanty food to sustain the robuster energies of his English comrade. He had planted the colours of his regiment on a spot which European valour and perseverance had failed to reach. He had subscribed from his slender earnings to the support of our European wars. He had cheerfully consented, when he knew that his Government was in need, to forego that regular receipt of pay, which is the very life-blood of foreign service. History for a hundred years had sparkled with examples of his noble fidelity; and there were few who did not believe, in spite of some transitory aberrations, that he would be true to the last line of the chapter. 1756-1856.

If there were anything, therefore, to disturb the mind of Lord Dalhousie when he laid down the reins of government on that memorable spring morning, the trouble which oppressed him was not the growth of any mistrust of the fidelity of the Sepoy. "Hardly any circumstance of his condition," he said, in his Farewell Minute, "is in need of improvement." And there were few who, reading this passage, the very slenderness of which indicated a more settled faith in the Sepoy than the most turgid sentences could have expressed, did not feel the same assurance that in that direction there was promise only of continued repose. It was true that Asiatic armies were ever prone to revolt—that we had seen Mahratta armies and Sikh armies, Arab armies and Goorkha armies, all the military races of India indeed, at some time or other rising in mutiny against their Government, and perhaps overthrowing it. But fifty years had passed away since the minds of our British rulers had been seriously disturbed by a fear of military revolt, and that half century, it was believed, had brought full conviction home to the understanding of the Sepoy 1856.

1856. that the Company was a good and generous master, whose colours it was a privilege to bear. Outwardly, there was only a great calm; and it was not thought that beneath that smooth surface there were any latent dangers peculiar to the times. The Sepoy was esteemed to be "faithful to a proverb;" and his fidelity was the right arm of our strength.

First Sepoy Levies in Bombay and Madras.

Our first Sepoy levies were raised in the Southern Peninsula, when the English and the French powers were contending for the dominant influence in that part of the country. They were few in number, and at the outset commonly held in reserve to support our European fighting-men. But, little by little, they proved that they were worthy to be entrusted with higher duties, and, once trusted, they went boldly to the front. Under native commandants, for the most part Mahomedans or high-caste Rajpoot Hindoos, but disciplined and directed by the English captain, their pride was flattered and their energies stimulated by the victories they gained. How they fought in the attack of Madura, how they fought in the defence of Arcot, how they crossed bayonets, foot to foot, with the best French troops at Cuddalore, historians have delighted to tell. All the power and all the responsibility, all the honours and rewards, were not then monopolised by the English captains. Large bodies of troops were sometimes despatched, on hazardous enterprises, under the independent command of a native leader, and it was not thought an offence to a European soldier to send him to fight under a black commandant. That black commandant was then a great man, in spite of his colour. He rode on horseback at the head of his men, and a mounted staff-officer, a native adjutant, carried his commands to the Soubahdars of the respective companies. And a brave man or a skilful leader was honoured for his bravery or his skill as much under the folds of a turban as under a round hat. 1756-57.

The Bengal Army.

When the great outrage of the Black Hole called Clive's retributory army to Bengal, the English had no Sepoy troops on the banks of the Hooghly. But there were fourteen native battalions in Madras, numbering in all ten thousand men, and Clive took two of these with him, across the black water, to Calcutta. Arrived there, and the first blow struck, he began to raise native levies in the neighbourhood, and a battalion of Bengal Sepoys fought at Plassey side by side with their comrades from Madras. Eight years after this victory, which placed the great province of Bengal at our feet, the one battalion had swollen into nineteen, each of a thousand strong. To each battalion three English officers were appointed —picked men from the English regiments.* The native element was not so strong as in the Southern Army; but a good deal of substantive authority still remained with the black officers.

And that the Bengal Sepoy was an excellent soldier, was freely declared by men who had seen the best troops of the European powers. Drilled and disciplined in all essential points after the English model, the native soldier was not called upon to divest himself of all the distinctive attributes of his race. Nothing that his creed abhorred or his caste rejected was forced upon him by his Christian masters. He lived apart, cooked apart, ate apart, after the fashion of his tribe. No one grudged him

* In 1765, the number was increased to five. There were then a native commandant and ten Soubahdars to each battalion.—*Broome.*

1757. his necklace, his ear-rings, the caste-marks on his forehead, or the beard which lay upon his breast. He had no fear of being forcibly converted to the religion of the white men, for he could not see that the white men had any religion to which they could convert him. There was no interference from the Adjutant-General's office, no paper government, no perpetual reference to order-books bristling with innovations; and so he was happy and contented, obedient to the officers who commanded him, and faithful to the Government he served.

His predominant sentiment, indeed, was fidelity to his Salt, or, in other words, to the hand that fed him. But if he thought that the hand was unrighteously closed to withhold from him what he believed his due, he showed himself to be most tenacious of his rights, and he resolutely asserted them. This temper very soon manifested itself. The Bengal Army was but seven years old, when it first began to evince some symptoms of a mutinous spirit. But in this instance the contagion came from the Europeans. The white troops had mutinied because the promise of a donation to the Army from Meer Jaffier had halted on the way to performance; and when the money came, the Sepoys followed their example, because they thought that they were denied their rightful share of the Prize. They had just ground of complaint in this instance, and they were soothed by a reasonable concession.* But the fire had not burnt itself out; and before the close of the year some regiments were again in rebellion. One battalion seized and imprisoned its English officers, and vowed that it would serve no more. It was one of those childish ebullitions, of which we have since

1764. The First Mutiny in Bengal.

* Whilst a private of the European Army was to receive forty rupees, it was proposed to give a Sepoy six. The share of the latter was afterwards fixed at twenty rupees.

seen so many in the Bengal Army. But it was plain that the evil was a growing one, and to be arrested with a strong hand. So twenty-four Sepoys were tried, at Chuprah, by a drum-head Court-Martial, for mutiny and desertion, found guilty, and ordered to be blown away from the guns. 1764.

A century has passed since the order was carried into execution, and many strange and terrible scenes have been witnessed by the Sepoy Army; but none stranger or more terrible than this. The troops were drawn up, European and Native, the guns were loaded, and the prisoners led forth to suffer. Major Hector Munro, the chief of the Bengal Army, superintended that dreadful punishment parade, and gave the word of command for the first four of the criminals to be tied up to the guns. The order was being obeyed; the men were being bound; when four tall, stately Grenadiers stepped forward from among the condemned, and represented that as they had always held the post of honour in life, it was due to them that they should take precedence in death. The request was granted; a brief reprieve was given to the men first led to execution; the Grenadiers were tied to the guns, and blown to pieces at the word of command.

Then all through the Sepoy battalions on that ghastly parade, there ran a murmur and a movement, and it seemed that the black troops, who greatly outnumbered the white, were about to strike for the rescue of their comrades. There were signs and sounds not to be misunderstood; so the officers of the native regiments went to the front and told Munro that their men were not to be trusted; that the Sepoys had resolved not to suffer the execution to proceed. On the issue of that reference depended the fate of the Bengal Army. The English troops on that parade were few.

1764. There was scarcely a man among them not moved to tears by what he had seen; but Munro knew that they could be trusted, and that they could defend the guns, which once turned upon the natives would have rendered victory certain. So he closed the Europeans on to the battery; the Grenadiers upon one side, the Marines on the other, loaded the pieces with grape, and sent the Sepoy officers back to their battalions. This done, he gave the word of command to the native regiments to ground arms. In the presence of those loaded guns, and of the two lines of white troops ready to fire upon them, to have disobeyed would have been madness. They moved to the word of command, laid down their arms, and when another word of command was given, which sent the Sepoys to a distance from their grounded muskets, and the Europeans with the guns took ground on the intervening space, the danger had passed away. The native troops were now completely at Munro's mercy, and the execution went on in their presence to its dreadful close. Twenty men were blown away from the guns at that parade. Four were reserved for execution at another station, as a warning to other regiments, which appeared to be mutinously disposed, and six more, tried and sentenced at Bankepore, were blown away at that place. Terrible as was this example, it was the act of a merciful and humane man, and Mercy and Humanity smiled sorrowfully, but approvingly, upon it. It taught the Sepoy Army that no British soldier, black or white, can rebel against the State without bringing down upon himself fearful retribution, and by the sacrifice of a few guilty forfeited lives checked the progress of a disease which, if weakly suffered to run its course, might have resulted in the slaughter of thousands.

The lesson was not thrown away. The Sepoy learnt to respect the stern authority of the Law, and felt that the Nemesis of this new Government of the British was certain in its operations, and not to be escaped. And the time soon came when his constancy was tested, and found to have the ring of the true metal. The European officers broke into rebellion; but the natives did not falter in their allegiance. Conceiving themselves aggrieved by the withdrawal of the extraordinary allowances which they had enjoyed in the field, the former determined to remonstrate against the reduction, and to clamour for what they called their rights. In each brigade meetings were called, consultations were held, and secret committees were formed, under the disguise of Freemasons' Lodges. Headstrong and obstinate, the officers swore to recover the double batta which had been taken from them, or to resign the service in a body. Large sums of money were subscribed, and the Company's civilians contributed to the fund, which was to enable their military brethren to resist the authority of their common masters. It was a formidable conjuncture, and one to try the courage even of a Clive. The orders of the Company were peremptory; and he was not a man to lower the authority of Government by yielding to a threat. But he could not disguise from himself that there were contingencies which might compel him to make a temporary concession to the insubordinates; one was an incursion of the Mahrattas,* the other the defection of the Sepoys. Had the native soldiers sympathised with and supported the English officers, the impetus

1766.

Mutiny of the Bengal Officers.

* "In case the Mahrattas should still appear to intend an invasion, or in case you apprehend a mutiny among the troops, but in no other case, you have authority to make terms with the officers of your brigade."—*Lord Clive to Col. Smith, May 11, 1766.* [See also following note.]

1766. thus given to the movement would have overborne all power of resistance, and Government must have succumbed to the crisis. In this emergency, Clive saw clearly the importance of securing "the fidelity and attachment of the Soubahdars, or commanding officers of the black troops," and he wrote urgently to his lieutenants, Smith and Fletcher, instructing them to attain this end. But the Sepoys had never wavered. True to their colours, they were ready at the word of command to fire on the white mutineers. Assured of this, Clive felt that the danger was over—felt that he could hold out against the mutiny of the English officers, even though the European troops should break into revolt.*

The founders of the Native Army had conceived the idea of a force recruited from among the people of the country, and commanded for the most part by men of their own race, but of higher social position—men, in a word, of the master-class, accustomed to exact obedience from their inferiors. But it was the inevitable tendency of our increasing power in India to oust the native functionary from his seat, or to lift him from his saddle, that the white man might fix himself there, with all the remarkable tenacity of his race. An Englishman believes that he can do all things better than his neighbours, and, therefore, it was doubt-

* "The black Sepoy officers, as well as men, have given great proofs of fidelity and steadiness upon this occasion, and so long as they remain so, nothing is to be apprehended from the European soldiery, even if they should be mutinously inclined." —*Clive to Smith, May* 15, 1760, *MS. Records.*—They had just afforded a striking proof that they were prepared, if necessary, to fire upon the Europeans. See Broome's History of the Bengal Army, vol. i. 589: "The European battalion had got under arms, and were preparing to leave the fort and follow their officers, and the artillery were about to do the same, but the unexpected appearance of this firm line of Sepoys, with their bayonets fixed and arms loaded, threw them into some confusion, of which Captain Smith took advantage, and warned them, that if they did not retire peaceably into their barracks, he would fire upon them at once."

less with a sincere conviction of the good we were doing that we gradually took into our own hands the reins of office, civil and military, and left only the drudgery and the dirty work to be done by the people of the soil. Whether, if we had fairly debated the question, it would have appeared to us a safer and a wiser course to leave real military power in the hands of men who might turn it against us, than to cast upon the country a dangerous class of malcontents identifying the rise of the British power with their own degradation, it may now be difficult to determine. But any other result than that before us would have been utterly at variance with the genius of the English nation, and, theorise as we might, was not to be expected. So it happened, in due course, that the native officers, who had exercised real authority in their battalions, who had enjoyed opportunities of personal distinction, who had felt an honourable pride in their position, were pushed aside by an incursion of English gentlemen, who took all the substantive power into their hands, and left scarcely more than the shadow of rank to the men whom they had supplanted. An English subaltern was appointed to every company, and the native officer then began to collapse into something little better than a name. 1784.

Increase of English Officers.

As the degradation of the native officer was thus accomplished, the whole character of the Sepoy army was changed. It ceased to be a profession in which men of high position, accustomed to command, might satisfy the aspirations and expend the energies of their lives. All distinctions were effaced. The native service of the Company came down to a dead level of common soldiering, and rising from the ranks by a painfully slow process to merely nominal

1784-96. command. There was employment for the many; there was no longer a career for the few. Thenceforth, therefore, we dug out the materials of our army from the lower strata of society, and the gentry of the land, seeking military service, carried their ambitions beyond the red line of the British frontier, and offered their swords to the Princes of the Native States.

But in those lower strata there were elementary diversities of which in England we know nothing. The lower orders amongst us are simply the lower orders—all standing together on a common level of social equality; we recognise no distinctions among them except in respect of the callings which they follow. Thus one common soldier differs only from another common soldier in the height of his stature, or the breadth of his shoulders, or the steadiness of his drill. But in India the great institution of Caste—at once the most exclusive and the most levelling system in the world—may clothe the filthiest, feeblest mendicant with all the dignities and powers of the proudest lord. So, in our native army, a Sepoy was not merely a Sepoy. He might be a Brahmin, or he might be a Pariah; and though they might stand beside each other shoulder to shoulder, foot to foot, on the parade-ground, there was as wide a gulf between them in the Lines, as in our own country yawns between a dustman and a duke.

Caste.

In the Bengal Army the Sepoys were chiefly of high Caste. Deriving its name from the country in which it was first raised, not from the people composing it, it was recruited in the first instance from among the floating population which the Mahomedan conquest had brought from the northern provinces—from Rohilcund, from Oude, from the country between the two rivers; men of migratory habits, and martial instincts, and sturdy frames, differing in all respects, mind and body, from the timid, feeble denizens of Bengal. The Jat, the Rajpoot, and the priestly Brahmin, took service, with the Patan, under the great white chief, who had humbled the pride of Soorajah Dowlah. And as time advanced, and the little local militia swelled into the bulk of a magnificent army, the aristocratic element was still dominant in the Bengal Army. But the native troops of Madras and Bombay were made up from more mixed and less dainty materials. There were men in the ranks of those armies of all nations and of all castes, and the more exclusive soon ceased from their exclusiveness, doing things which their brethren in the Bengal Army shrunk from doing, and solacing their pride with the reflection that it was the "custom of the country." Each system had its advocates. The Bengal Sepoy, to the outward eye, was the finest soldier; tallest, best-formed, and of the noblest presence. But he was less docile and serviceable than the Sepoy of the Southern and the Western Armies. In the right mood there was no better soldier in the world, but he was not always in the right mood; and the humours which he displayed were ever a source of trouble to his commanders, and sometimes of danger to the State. 1784-96.

In an army so constituted, the transfer of all substantive authority to a handful of alien officers might have been followed by a fatal collapse of the whole system, but for one fortunate circumstance, which sustained its vitality. The officers appointed to command the Sepoy battalions were picked men; men chosen from the European regiments, not merely as good soldiers, skilled in their professional duties, The Sepoy Officer.

1784-96. but as gentlemen of sound judgment and good temper, acquainted with the languages and the habits of the people of the country, and prone to respect the prejudices of the soldiery. The command of a native battalion was one of the highest objects of ambition. It conferred large powers and often great wealth upon the Sepoy officer; and though the system was one pregnant with abuses, which we see clearly in these days, it contained that great principle of cohesion which attached the English officer and the native soldier to each other—cohesion, which the refinements of a later civilisation were doomed rapidly to dissolve.

1796. It lasted out the century, but scarcely survived it.* The English Sepoy-officer having become a great substantive fact, not a mere excrescence upon the general body of the English Army, it became necessary to define his position. He had many great advantages, but he had not rank; and the Company's officer found himself continually superseded by younger men in the King's army. Very reasonably, if not always very temperately, he began then to assert his rights; and the result was an entire reor-

* That the national basis, which had originally distinguished the foundation of the Madras Army, did not very long survive the establishment of the reformed system of Bengal, and that the native officers soon lost the power and the dignity in which they had once rejoiced, may be gathered from an early incident in the Life of Sir John Malcolm. It was in 1784, when an exchange of prisoners with Tippoo had been negotiated, that a detachment of two companies of Sepoys was sent out from our side of the Mysore frontier to meet the escort under Major Dallas conveying the English prisoners from Seringapatam. "In command of this party," says the biographer, "went Ensign John Malcolm. This was his first service; and it was long remembered by others than the youthful hero himself. When the detachment met the prisoners' escort, a bright-faced, healthy English boy was seen by the latter riding up to them on a rough pony. Dallas asked him after his commanding officer. '*I* am the commanding officer,' said young Malcolm." As Malcolm was born in 1769, he must at this time have been a boy of fifteen; yet he commanded a detachment of two companies of Sepoys, and all the old native officers attached to them.

ganisation of the Company's army, which greatly improved the status of its old officers and opened a door for the employment of a large number of others. By the regulations then framed, two battalions of Sepoys were formed into one regiment, to which the same number of officers were posted as to a regiment in the King's army, and all took rank according to the date of their commissions. It was believed that the increased number of European officers would add to the efficiency of the Native Army. But it was admitted, even by those who had been most active in working out the new scheme, that it did not develop all the good results with which it was believed to be laden. The little authority, the little dignity, which still clung to the position of the native officers was then altogether effaced by this new incursion of English gentlemen;* and the discontent, which had been growing up in the minds of the soldiery, began then to bear bitter fruit. 1796.

But this was not all. The new regulations, which so greatly improved the position of the Company's officers, and in no respect more than in that of the pensions which they were then permitted to enjoy, held out great inducements to the older officers of the Company's army to retire from active service, and to spend the remainder of their days at home. Many of the old commandants then prepared to leave the battalions over which they had so long exercised paternal authority, and to give up their places to strangers. Not only was there a change of men, but a change also of system. The English officer rose by seniority to command. The principle of selection

* It was alleged to be an advantage of the new system that the increased number of English officers would obviate the necessity of ever sending out a detachment under native command.

1796 was abandoned. And men, who could scarcely call for a glass of water in the language of the country, or define the difference between a Hindoo and a Mahomedan, found themselves invested with responsibilities which ought to have devolved only on men of large local experience and approved good judgment and temper.

The Mysore and Mahratta Wars.

But the evil results of the change were not immediately apparent. The last years of the eighteenth, and the first years of the nineteenth century were years of active Indian warfare. In the Mysore and in the Mahratta countries the Sepoy had constant work, under great generals whom he honoured and trusted; he had strong faith in the destiny of the Company; and his pride was flattered by a succession of brilliant victories. But it is after such wars as those of Harris, Lake, and Wellesley, when a season of stagnation succeeds a protracted period of excitement, that the discipline of an army, whether in the East or in the West, is subjected to its severest trials. All the physical and moral properties which have so long sustained it in high health and perfect efficiency then seem to collapse; and the soldier, nerveless and languid, readily succumbs to the deteriorating influences by which he is surrounded. And so it was with the Sepoy after those exhausting wars. He was in the state which, of all others, is most susceptible of deleterious impressions. And, unhappily, there was one especial source of annoyance and alarm to irritate and disquiet him in the hour of peace. Amidst the stern realities of active warfare, the European officer abjures the pedantries of the drill-sergeant and the fopperies of the regimental tailor. He has no time for small things; no heart for trifles. It is enough for him that his men are in a condition to fight battles and to win them. But in Peace he sometimes shrivels into an Arbiter of Drill and Dress, and worries in time the best of soldiers into malcontents and mutineers. 1805.

And so it was that, after the fierce excitement of the Mysore and Mahratta wars, there arose among our English officers an ardour for military improvement; and the Sepoy, who had endured for years, without a murmur, all kinds of hardships and privations, under canvas and on the line of march, felt that life was less endurable in cantonments than it had been in the field, and was continually disturbing himself, in his matted hut, about the new things that were being forced upon him. All sorts of novelties were bristling up in his path. He was to be drilled after a new English fashion. He was to be dressed after a new English fashion. He was to be shaved after a new English fashion. He was not smart enough for the Martinets who had taken him in hand to polish him up into an English soldier. They were stripping him, indeed, of his distinctive Oriental character; and it was not long before he began to see in these efforts to Anglicise him something more than the vexatious innovations and crude experiments of European military reform.

To these annoyances and vexations the Madras Army were especially subjected. Composed as were its battalions of men of different castes, and not in any way governed by caste principles, they were held to be peculiarly accessible to innovation; and, little by little, all the old outward characteristics of the native soldier were effaced, and new things, upon the most approved European pattern, substituted in their place. Mutiny of the Coast Army.

1805-6. At last the Sepoy, forbidden to wear the distinguishing marks of Caste on his forehead, stripped of his ear-rings, to which, by ties alike of vanity and superstition, he was fondly attached,* and ordered to shave himself according to a regulation cut,† was put into a stiff round hat, like a Pariah drummer's, with a flat top, a leather cockade, and a standing feather. It was no longer called a "turband;" it was a hat or cap; in the language of the natives, a *topi;* and a *topi-wallah*, or hat-wearer, was in their phraseology a synonym for a Feringhee or Christian.

The Sepoy is not logical, but he is credulous and suspicious. It was not difficult to persuade him that there were hidden meanings and occult designs in all this assimilation of the native soldier's dress to that of the European fighting-man. The new hat was not merely an emblem of Christianity, and therefore possessed of a grave moral significance, but materially, also, it was discovered to be an abomination. It was made in part of leather prepared from the skin of the unclean hog, or of the sacred cow, and was, therefore, an offence and a desecration alike to Mahomedan and Hindoo. The former had no distinguishing marks of caste to be rubbed off on parade with a dirty stick, but he venerated his beard and his ear-rings, and, under the force of contact and example, he had developed many strong generic resemblances to the caste-observing Hindoo. The Mahomedan of India differs

* By the Mahomedan Sepoy the ear-ring was often worn as a charm. It was given to him at his birth, and dedicated to some patron saint.

† See the following, Para. 10, Sec. 11, Standing Orders of Madras Army: "It is ordered by the Regulations that a native soldier shall not mark his face to denote his caste, or wear ear-rings when dressed in his uniform; and it is further directed, that at all parades, and on all duties, every soldier of the battalion shall be clean-shaved on the chin. It is directed, also, that uniformity shall, as far as is practicable, be preserved in regard to the quantity and shape of the hair on the upper lip."

greatly in his habits and his feelings from the Mahomedan of Central Asia or Arabia; he accommodates himself, in some sort, to the usages of the country, and being thus readily acclimatised, he strikes strong root in the soil. Christianity does not differ more than Mahomedanism, doctrinally or ethically, from the religion of the Hindoos; but in the one case there may be social fusion, in the other it is impossible. Even in the former instance, the fusion is imperfect, and there is in this partial assimilation of races one of the chief elements of our security in India. But the security derived from this source is also imperfect; and circumstances may at any time, by an unfortunate coincidence, appeal to the ethnical resemblances and the common instincts of different nationalities, in such a manner as to excite in both the same fears and to raise the same aspirations, and so to cause all diversities to be for a time forgotten. And such a coincidence appears now to have arisen. Different races, moved by the sense of a common danger, and roused by a common hope, forgot their differences, and combined against a common foe. 1806.

And so it happened that in the spring of 1806, the Hindoo and Mahomedan Sepoy in the Southern Peninsula of India were talking together, like caste-brothers, about their grievances, and weaving plots for their deliverance. It is partly by accident, partly by design, that such plots ripen in the spring. By accident, because relieved from cold-weather exercises, parades, field-days, and inspections, the soldier has more leisure to ruminate his wrongs, and more time to discuss them. By design, because the coming heats and rains paralyse the activities of the white man, and are great gain to the native mutineer. In April and

1806. May the English officer sees little of his men; his visits to the Lines are few; few are his appearance on parade. He is languid and prostrate. The morning and evening ride are as much as his energies can compass. The Sepoy then, disencumbered of dress and dismissed from drill, can afford to snatch some hours from sleep to listen to any strange stories, told by wandering mendicants, with the odour of sanctified filth about them, and to discuss the most incredible fables with all the gravity of settled belief. There is always more or less of this vain talk. It amuses the Sepoy and for a while excites him with a visionary prospect of higher rank and better pay, under some new dispensation. But he is commonly content to regard this promised time as a far-off Hegira, and, as he turns himself round on his charpoy for another nap, he philosophically resolves in the mean while to eat the Company's salt in peace, and to wait God's pleasure in quietude and patience.

But there was at this time something more to excite the imagination of the Sepoy in Southern India than the ordinary vain talk of the Bazaars and the Lines. The travelling fakeers were more busy with their inventions; the rumours which they carried from place to place were more ominous; the prophecies which they recited were more significant of speedy fulfilment. There was more point in the grotesque performances of the puppet-shows — more meaning in the rude ballads which were sung and the scraps of verse which were cited. Strange writings were dropped by unseen hands, and strange placards posted on the walls. At all the large military stations in the Carnatic and in the Deccan there was an uneasy feeling as of something coming. There were manifold signs which seemed to indicate that the time to strike had arrived, and so the Sepoy began to take stock of his grievances and to set before him all the benefits of change. 1806.

The complaints of the Sepoy were many. If he were to pass his whole life in the Company's service and do what he might, he could not rise higher than the rank of Soubahdar; there had been times when distinguished native soldiers had been appointed to high and lucrative commands, and had faithfully done their duty; but those times had passed, and, instead of being exalted, native officers were habitually degraded. A Sepoy on duty always presented or carried arms to an English officer, but an English soldier suffered a native officer to pass by without a salute. Even an English Sergeant commanded native officers of the highest rank. On parade, the English officers made mistakes, used the wrong words of command, then threw the blame upon the Sepoys and reviled them. Even native officers, who had grown grey in the service, were publicly abused by European striplings. On the line of march the native officers were compelled to live in the same tents with the common Sepoys, and had not, as in the armies of native potentates, elephants or palanquins assigned to them for their conveyance, how great soever the distance which they were obliged to traverse. And if they rode horses or ponies, purchased from their savings, the English officer frowned at them as upstarts. "The Sepoys of the Nizam and the Mahratta chiefs," they said, "are better off than our Soubahdars and Jemidars." Then it was urged that the Company's officers took the Sepoys vast distances from their homes, where they died in strange places, and that their wives and children were left to beg their bread; that native Princes, when they conquered new

1806 countries, gave grants of lands to distinguished soldiers, but that the Company only gave them sweet words; that the concubines of the English gentlemen were better paid than the native officers, and their grooms and grass-cutters better than the native soldiers; that the English officers could import into their Zenanas the most beautiful women in the country, whilst the natives hardly dared look at the slave-girls; and, to crown all, it was declared that General Arthur Wellesley had ordered his wounded Sepoys to be mercilessly shot to death.

Preposterous as were some of the fables with which this bill of indictment was crusted over, there was doubtless beneath it a large substratum of truth. But the alleged grievances were, for the most part, chronic ailments which the Sepoy had been long enduring, and might have endured still longer, patiently and silently, had they not culminated in the great outrage of the round hat, with its auxiliary vexations of the shorn beard, the effaced caste-marks, and the despoiled ear-rings. Then, it was not difficult to teach him that this aggregation of wrongs had become intolerable, and that the time had come for him to strike a blow in defence of his rights. And the teacher was not far distant. The great Mahomedan usurpation of Mysore had been overthrown, but the representatives of the usurper were still in the country. The family of the slain Sultan were living in the fort of Vellore, as the clients rather than the captives of the English, with abundant wealth at their command, and a numerous body of Mussulman attendants. But generous as was the treatment they had received, and utterly at variance with their own manner of dealing with fallen enemies, they had not ceased to bewail the loss of the sovereign power which had passed from their House, or to hate the conquerors who had unkinged them. In the luxurious idleness of Vellore they dreamed of the recovery of their lost empire. There was but one way to the attainment of that cherished object, and that way was through the corruption of the Sepoy. The time was propitious, and the work commenced. 1806.

It ought not to have been easy work, but so it was. If there had been relations of confidence between the English officer and the native soldier, the corruption of the latter would have been a task of sore difficulty and danger; but those relations were not what they had been a few years before. It was not that the officers themselves had deteriorated, but that a new system had been introduced, which, greatly improving their state and prospects, and, it may be said, permanently increasing their efficiency as a body, still caused some temporary relaxation of the ties which bound them to the soldiery of the country. The new regulations of 1796, it has been said, opened out to the elder generation of officers a door by which they might retire on advantageous terms from the service. Some took their pensions at once; but a period of active warfare supervened, and many veteran officers waited for the restoration of peace to take advantage of the boon that was offered. They went; and a new race of men, young and inexperienced, took their places. And so, for a time, the Sepoy did not know his officer, nor the officer his men; they met almost as strangers on parade, and there was little or no communion between them. It was a transition-period of most untoward occurrence, when so many other adverse influences were destroying the discipline of the army; and, therefore, again

1806. I say the hour was propitious, and the work of corruption commenced.

May 7. Progress of the Mutiny.

At the end of the first week of May, as Adjutant-General Agnew was rising from his work, in the white heat of Fort St. George, there came tidings to his office of general disaffection among the native troops at Vellore. One battalion, at least, already had broken into open mutiny. The chief of the Madras army, Sir John Cradock, had retired for the evening to his garden-house in the pleasant suburbs of Madras, so Agnew drove out to see him with the important missive in his hand. A few days afterwards, Cradock was posting to Vellore. Arrived there, he found that there had been no exaggeration in the reports which had been furnished to him, but that more judicious treatment at the outset might have allayed the excitement among the troops, and restored the confidence of the Sepoy. So said a Court of Inquiry; so said the Commander-in-Chief. A gentle sudorific, almost insensibly expelling the pent-up humours, may suffice at the beginning, though only much blood-letting can cure at the end. But ailments of this kind, in the military body, seldom reveal themselves in their full significance until the time for gentle treatment is past. When Cradock went to Vellore no mere explanations could repair the mischief that had been done. The mutinous troops were sent down to the Presidency, and others substituted for them. Military discipline was vindicated for the time by a court-martial, and two of the ringleaders were sentenced to be—flogged. But the infection still clung to Vellore. The whole native garrison was tainted and corrupted.

Nor was it a mere local epidemic. At other military stations in the Carnatic there was similar excitement.

Midnight meetings were being held in the Lines; oaths of secresy were being administered to the Sepoys; threats of the most terrible vengeance were fulminated against any one daring to betray them. The native officers took the lead, the men followed, some roused to feelings of resentment, others huddling together like sheep, under the influence of a vague fear. In the bungalows of the English captains there was but small knowledge of what was passing in the Sepoys' Lines, and if there had been more, discretion would probably have whispered that in such a case "silence is gold." For when in the high places of Government there is a general disinclination to believe in the existence of danger, it is scarcely safe for men of lowlier station to say or to do anything indicating suspicion and alarm. 1806.

At Vellore, after the first immature demonstration, there was a lull; and the quietude had just the effect that it was intended to have; it disarmed the suspicion and suspended the vigilance of the English. The most obvious precautions were neglected. Even the significant fact that the first open manifestation of disaffection had appeared under the shadow of the asylum of the Mysore Princes, had not suggested any special associations, or indicated the direction in which the watchful eye of the British Government should be turned. Nothing was done to strengthen the European garrison of Vellore.* No pains were taken to cut off the perilous intercourse which existed be-

* "That neither the Government nor the Commander-in-Chief entertained any serious apprehensions from the agitation having first occurred at Vellore, is obvious. The battalion that most opposed the innovation was, indeed, ordered to Madras, but nothing was directed indicative of any jealousy of the Princes. No precautions seem to have been taken within the Fort, and notwithstanding the discontent manifested by the native troops, the garrison was still left with only four companies of Europeans."—*Barry Close to John Malcolm. Poonah, Aug.* 12, 1806. *MS. Correspondence.*

1806. tween the native soldiery and the occupants of the Palace. So the latter went about the Fort jeering the Sepoys, and telling them that they would soon be made Christians to a man. The different parts of their uniform were curiously examined, amidst shrugs and other expressive gestures, and significant "Wah-wahs!" and vague hints that everything about them in some way portended Christianity. They looked at the Sepoy's stock, and said, "What is this? It is leather! Well!" Then they would look at his belt, and tell him that it made a cross on his breast, and at the little implements of his calling, the turnscrew and worm, suspended from it, and say that they also were designed to fix the Christian's cross upon his person. But it was the round hat that most of all was the object of the taunts and warnings of the people from the Palace. "It only needed this," they said, "to make you altogether a Feringhee. Take care, or we shall soon all be made Christians—Bazaar-people, Ryots, every one will be compelled to wear the hat; and then the whole country will be ruined." Within the Fort, and outside the Fort, men of all kinds were talking about the forcible conversion to Christianity which threatened them; and everywhere the round hat was spoken of as the instrument by which the Caste of the Hindoo was to be destroyed, and the faith of the Mussulman desecrated and demolished.

But all this was little known to the officers of the Vellore garrison, or, if known, was little heeded. So unwilling, indeed, were they to believe that any danger was brewing, that a Sepoy who told his English officer that the regiments were on the eve of revolt was put in irons as a madman. The native officers declared that he deserved condign punishment for blackening the faces of his corps, and they were readily believed. But the time soon came when the prophecy of evil was verified, and the prophet was exalted and rewarded. Deeply implicated as he was said to be in the plot—a traitor first to the English, and then to his own people—his name became an offence and an abomination to the Army, and the favour shown to him a source of the bitterest resentment. "The disposition of the gentlemen of the Company's service," they said, "and the nature of their government, make a thief happy, and an honest man afflicted."* 1806.

On the 10th of July the mine suddenly exploded. It was remembered afterwards that on the preceding afternoon an unusual number of people had passed into the Fort, some mounted and some on foot, seemingly on no especial business; all with an insolent, braggart air, laughing and rollicking, making mimic battle among themselves, and otherwise expressing a general expectancy of something coming. It was remembered, too, that on that evening there had been more than the common tendency of the times to speak abusively of the English. The Adjutant of a Sepoy regiment had been called, to his face, by the vilest term of reproach contained in the language of the country.† But it has been doubted whether the day and hour of the outburst were those fixed for the development of the plot. The con- Vellore, July 10, 1806.

* From a paper in Hindostanee, transmitted to Adjutant-General Agnew from the Hyderabad Subsidiary Force: "In the affair at Vellore," said the Sepoys, "when the mutiny first commenced, it was on account of Mustapha Beg; and the gentlemen of the Company's Government have bestowed upon him a reward of two thousand pagodas from the public treasury, with the rank of Soubahdar. The same Mustapha Beg, Sepoy, was the man who gave the signal for revolt to the people at Vellore, and this is the man whom the Company have distinguished by their favour."

† Unhappily it is one of the first words which the Englishman in India learns to speak, and by which many young officers, when displeased, habitually call their native servants.

1806. spirators, it is said, were not ripe for action. Two or three days later, the first blow was to have been struck, but that a Jemadar, inflamed with strong drink, could not control the passionate haste within him, and he precipitated the collision which it was the policy of his party to defer.* Numbers thus suddenly roused to action were unprepared to play their parts; and letters which had been written to disaffected polygars and others in Mysore had not yet been despatched. It was confidently believed that in a few days ten thousand faithful adherents of the House of Hyder would rally round the standard of the Mussulman Princes. All that was required of the Sepoys was, that they should hold Vellore for a week. At the end of that time it was believed that the whole country would be in the hands of the insurgents.

His Majesty's 69th.

The European garrison of Vellore, at this time, consisted only of four companies of a Line regiment. To fall suddenly, in the dead of the night, on all who might happen to be on guard, to overpower them by numbers, and then to murder the rest in their beds, was apparently an easy task. Two hours after midnight the work commenced. The sentries were shot down. The soldiers on main guard were killed as they lay on their cots, and the white men in the

* In the private correspondence of the time, it is stated that the day fixed for the outbreak was the 14th. It appeared, however, in the evidence of the first Committee of Inquiry assembled at Vellore, that it was agreed that the first blow should be struck fifteen days after the Mysore standard, prepared in the Palace, was ready to be hoisted, and that thirteen days had then passed. The story of the drunken Jemadar appears in Madras Secret Letter, Sept. 30, 1806. It happened, too, that the European officer commanding the native guard fell sick, that the Soubahdar was also indisposed, and that Jemadar Cossim Khan, one of the most active of the mutineers, was eager to go the grand rounds; and it is possible that this accident helped to precipitate the crisis. On the other hand, it is to be observed that Major Armstrong, who had been absent from Vellore, and who returned on the night of the 10th, was warned by people outside the Fort not to enter, as something was about to happen.

hospital were ruthlessly butchered. There was then a scene of unexampled confusion. Roused from their beds by the unaccustomed sound of firing in the Fort, the English officers went out to learn the cause of the commotion, and many of them were shot down by the mutineers in the first bewilderment of surprise. The two senior officers of the garrison were among the first who fell. On the threshold of his house, Fancourt, who commanded the garrison, was warned, for dear life's sake, not to come out, but answering with the Englishman's favourite formula of "Never mind," he made for the Main Guard, and was shot with the "Fall in!" on his lips. Of the survivors two or three made their way to the barracks, and took command of such of the Europeans as had escaped the first murderous onslaught of the Sepoys. But it was little that the most desperate resolution could do in this extremity to stem the continually increasing tide of furious hostility which threatened to overwhelm them. It was no mere military revolt. The inmates of the Palace were fraternising with the Sepoys. From the apartments of the Princes went forth food to refresh the weary bodies of the insurgents, and vast promises to stimulate and sustain the energies of their minds. One of the Princes, the third son of Tippoo, personally encouraged the leaders of the revolt. With his own hands he gave them the significant bhetal-nut. With his own lips he proclaimed the rewards to be lavished upon the restorers of the Mahomedan dynasty. And from his apartments a confidential servant was seen to bring the tiger-striped standard of Mysore, which, amidst vociferous cries of "Dheen! Dheen!" was hoisted above the walls of the Palace. But the family of the Sultan were soon forgotten. There was no combination to aid their escape. The Sepoys at

1806.

Prince Moiz-ood-deen.

1806. first gave themselves up to the work of massacre. The people from the Palace, following in their wake, gorged themselves with the plunder of the white men, and aided the mutineers without sharing their danger. After a time the Sepoys betook themselves also to plunder; and the common object was forgotten under the excitement of personal greed. The white women in the Fort were spared. The tender mercies of the wicked, with a refined cruelty, preserved them for a worse fate than death. The people from the Palace told the Sepoys not to kill them, as all the English would be destroyed, and the Moormen might then take them for wives.*

But whilst these terrible scenes were being enacted, and the sons of Tippoo were swelling with the proud certainty of seeing the rule of the Sultan again established in Mysore, retribution swift and certain was overtaking the enterprise. An officer of the English regiment, who happened to be on duty outside the Fort, heard the firing, thoroughly apprehended the crisis, and, through the darkness of the early morning, made his way to Arcot, to carry thither the tidings of insurrection, and to summon succours to the aid of the imperilled garrison. There was a regiment of British Dragoons at Arcot, under the command of Colonel Gillespie. By seven o'clock Coats had told his story. Fifteen minutes afterwards, Gillespie, with a squadron of his regiment, was on his way to Vellore. The rest were saddling and mounting; the galloper-guns were being horsed and limbered; and a squadron of Native Cavalry was responding to the trumpet-call with as much alacrity

Major Coats.

The 19th Dragoons.

* The massacre included fourteen officers and ninety-nine soldiers killed. There were, moreover, several officers and men wounded, some of the latter mortally.

as the British Dragoons. The saving virtues of promptitude and preparation were never more conspicuously manifested. A little vacillation, a little blundering, a little delay, the result of nothing being ready when wanted, and all might have been lost. Never had the sage precept of Hyder Ali, that the English should keep their white soldiers like hunting-leopards in cages, and slip them suddenly and fiercely at the enemy, been wrought into practice with more terrible effect, than now against the followers and supporters of his descendants. 1806.

Once under the walls of Vellore, Gillespie was eager to make his way into the Fort, that he might rally the remnant of the European garrison and secure the safe admission of his men. The outer gates were open, but the last was closed, and in possession of the enemy. There was no hope of forcing it without the aid of the guns. But these were now rapidly approaching. There were good officers with the relieving force, to whom the conduct of external operations might be safely entrusted; and Gillespie longed to find himself with the people whom he had come to save. So, whilst preparations were being made for the attack, he determined to ascend alone the walls of the Fort. In default of ladders, the men of the 69th let down a rope, and, amidst the shouts of the delighted Europeans, he was drawn up, unhurt, to the crest of the ramparts, and took command of the survivors of the unhappy force. Quickly forming at the word of command, they came down eagerly to the charge, and, cheered by the welcome sound of the guns, which were now clamouring for admission, and not to be denied, they kept the mutineers at a distance till the gates were forced; and then the cavalry streamed in, and victory was easy.

1806. The retribution was terrible, and just. Hundreds fell beneath the sabres of the Dragoons and of the native horsemen, who emulated the ardour of their European comrades. Hundreds escaped over the walls of the Fort, or threw down their arms and cried for mercy. But the excited troopers, who had seen Tippoo's tiger-standard floating over the citadel of Vellore, could not, after that hot morning-ride, believe that they had done their work until they had destroyed the "cubs." They were eager to be led into the Palace, and there to inflict condign punishment on those whom they believed to be the real instigators of the butchery of their countrymen. For a moment there was a doubt in Gillespie's mind; but an appeal from Colonel Marriott, in whose charge was the Mysore family, removed it; and he put forth a restraining hand. He would not soil his victory with any cruel reprisals. The members of Tippoo's family were now at his mercy, and the mercy which he showed them was that which the Christian soldier delights to rain down upon the fallen and the helpless.*

* For all the facts given in the text, I have the authority of a mass of official, semi-official, and private contemporary correspondence, which I have very carefully collated. In doing so, I have been compelled to reject some personal incidents which have hitherto generally formed part of the narrative of the "Massacre of Vellore," but which, however serviceable they may be for purposes of effective historical writing, are, I am sorry to say, at best apocryphal. It has been said that the officer who carried the tidings to Arcot escaped through a sally-port, and swam the ditch of the Fort so famous for the number and size of its alligators. Sober official correspondence states that Major Coats, who was bearer of the news, was outside the Fort at the time of the outbreak. It is very generally stated, too, that when Gillespie wished to enter the Fort in advance of his men, as there were no ladders and no ropes, the survivors of the 69th fastened their belts together, and thus drew him up the walls. But I have before me two letters, signed "R. Gillespie," which state that he was drawn up by a rope. Among the fictitious incidents of the mutiny may be mentioned the whole of the stories which tell of the foul murder of English women, and the braining of little children before their mothers' eyes.

But the storm had not expended itself in this fierce convulsion. Taught by so stern a lesson, the Government resolved that "all orders which might be liable to the objection of affecting the usages of the troops," should be abandoned. But the obnoxious hats might have been burnt before the eyes of the troops, and the caste-marks and ear-rings restored on parade, in the presence of the Governor, the Commander-in-Chief, and all the magnates of the land; and still a return to quietude and contentment might have been far distant. Individual causes of anger and bitterness might be removed, but still there would remain, together with the mistrust they had engendered, all the vague anxieties on the one side, and the indefinite expectations on the other, which designing men had excited in the minds of the soldiery.* Rebellion had been crushed for a time at its Head-Quarters. The British flag floated again over Vellore; but there were other strong posts, which it had been intended to seize, and efforts might yet be made to establish revolt in other parts of the Southern Peninsula. 1806.

Nor was it only in Mysore and the Carnatic that the spirit of disaffection was rife. In the Deccan, also, it was manifesting itself in a manner which, for a while, created serious alarm. At Hyderabad, the capital of the Nizam's dominions, there was a high Hyderabad.

* "The subversion of the British Empire in India by foreign invasion and domestic revolt, seems to have been the common theme of discourse all over the country, and opinions have generally prevailed that such a revolution was neither an enterprise of great difficulty, nor that the accomplishment of it was far distant. . . . . . A most extraordinary and unaccountable impression has been made upon the Sepoys, which has been fomented by prophecies and predictions inducing a belief that wonderful changes are about to take place, and that the Europeans are to be expelled from India."—*General Hay Macdowall. Nundydroog, Oct. 31. MS. Correspondence.*

1806. tide of excitement. It was apprehended that the native troops of the Subsidiary Force, encouraged and aided by some of the chief people of this Mahomedan State, if not by the Nizam himself, would break out into revolt. They were wrought upon by nearly the same influences as had destroyed the loyalty of the troops in Mysore, with some peculiar aggravations of their own. A new commanding

Colonel Montresor. officer had recently been placed over them—a smart disciplinarian of the most approved European pattern. They had been worried and alarmed before his arrival. Montresor's appearance soon made matters worse. Knowing little or nothing of the habits and feelings of the people of the country, he enforced the new orders with more than common strictness, and supplemented them with some obnoxious regulations of his own. An order had been issued just before his arrival forbidding the Sepoy to leave his Guard and to divest himself of his uniform during his period of duty; and now the new English commandant prohibited the beating of taum-taums in the bazaars. It was not seen that these prohibitions were, in effect, orders that the Hindoo Sepoy should take no sustenance on duty, and that there should be no marriage and no funeral processions. When the discovery was made, the new local regulations were rescinded; but it was not possible to rescind the mischief that was done. There was a profound conviction among the Sepoys that it was the intention of the English to destroy their caste, to break down their religion, and forcibly to convert them to Christianity. And all through the long straggling lines of Hyderabad there was a continual buzz of alarm, and the Sepoys were asking each other if they had heard

how the English General, Wemyss Sahib, at Colombo, 1806.
had marched his native soldiers to Church.*

That the feeling of mingled fear and resentment, which had taken possession of the minds of the soldiery, was much fomented by emissaries from the city of Hyderabad, is not to be doubted. Many leading men, discontented and desperate, at all times prone to intrigue and ripe for rebellion, looked eagerly for a crisis out of which might have come some profit to themselves. It is probable that they were in communication with dependents of the House of Tippoo. It is certain that they fostered the resentments and stimulated the ambition of the native officers, and that a programme of action had been agreed upon, of which murder and massacre were the prelude.† But happily the Nizam and his minister, Meer Allum—the one in word, the other in spirit—were true to the English alliance. Wisely, in that conjuncture, did Sydenham confide all his troubles to them. It is a sad necessity to be compelled to communicate to a native Prince, the belief of the English Government that their troops are not to be trusted. But concealment in such a case is impossible, and any attempt to disguise the truth helps

* "It is astonishing how strong and how general the impression was of a systematic design to enforce the conversion of the Sepoys to Christianity. The men here heard, and talked of the late arrival of some clergymen from England, and of the story of General Wemyss marching the Sepoys to church at Colombo."—*Captain Thomas Sydenham* (*Resident at Hyderabad*) *to Mr. Edmonstone, July* 27, 1806. *MS. Correspondence.*

† Captain Sydenham wrote that, from the best information he could obtain at Hyderabad, it appeared that "the native troops had been invited to desert their colours, to break out in open mutiny, and to murder their officers. It was intended that a commotion should have taken place in the city at the moment of the insurrection in cantonments; that Meer Allum, and all those in the interests of the English, were to be destroyed; that the Soubahdar (Nizam) was to be confined, and Feridoom Jah either made Dewan or placed on the musnud, as circumstances might suggest."—*MS. Correspondence.*

1806. others to exaggerate and to distort it. The Nizam knew all that had been going on, perhaps before the British Resident had even a suspicion of it. Eager for his support, and willing to raise the standard of revolt in his name, the conspirators had conveyed to him a written paper signifying their wishes. He did not answer it. He did not give it to the Resident. He simply waited and did nothing. It was not in the nature of the man to do more. He knew the power of the English; but he secretly hated them, and naturally shrank from opposing or betraying a cause which appealed to him in the name of his religion. Perhaps it is hardly fair to expect from a native Prince, under such conflicting circumstances, more than this negative support.

The feeling among the native troops was so strong, the danger appeared to be so imminent, that Montresor was besought by some old Sepoy officers not to enforce the obnoxious regulations. But he replied that he had been selected for that especial command as a fitting agent for their enforcement, and how could he turn his back upon his duty? But when tidings of the massacre at Vellore reached Hyderabad, he saw at once that concession must be made to the prejudices of the Sepoy, and the orders were revoked in
July 22, 1806. anticipation of instructions from the Madras Government. Still the troops were not satisfied. Having gained one victory they determined to attempt another. So they fell back upon the old grievance of the leather stock, and the men of some of the battalions, encouraged by their native officers, were seen disencumbering themselves of this article of their uniform on parade, and casting it contemptuously on the ground. A display of vigour at the right time crushed the mutiny ere it was matured. On the

14th of August, the troops at Hyderabad were ordered under arms. The English regiment was posted near the park of artillery, and the cavalry were drawn up *en potence* on both flanks. Then four Soubahdars of Native Infantry, who were believed to be the ringleaders in the mutinous movement, were called to the front and marched off under a guard of thirty Europeans and a company of Sepoys. Under this escort they were sent to Masulipatam. This movement had the best possible effect both in the cantonment and the city. Mutiny was awe-struck; sedition was paralysed; conciliatory explanations and addresses, which had before failed, were now crowned with success, and early in the following month Sydenham wrote from Hyderabad that everything was "perfectly tranquil, both in the city and the cantonments." "The Sepoys," it added, "appear cheerful and contented, and the Government goes on with considerable vigour and regularity."

1806.

H.M.'s 33rd Regiment.

But ere long the anxieties of the Government again turned towards the old quarter. It was clear that, in the former domains of the Sultan, the fire, though suppressed for a time, had not been extinguished. At Nundydroog, in the heart of the Mysore territory, there had been symptoms of uneasiness from the commencement of the year. The native troops were few; but the fortress, built upon a high scarped rock, was one of uncommon strength, and, well defended, might have defied attack. In itself, therefore, a coveted possession for the rebel force, it was rendered doubly important by its position. For it was within a night's march of the great station of Bangalore, and the mutineers from that post would have flocked to it as a rallying-point and a stronghold, admirably suited

Nundydroog.

1806. for the Head-Quarters of Rebellion.* The influences, therefore, of which I have spoken—the fakeers, the conjurors, the puppet-showmen, the propagators of strange prophecies—were more than commonly operative in that direction, and had success attended the first outbreak at Vellore, the Nundydroog garrison would then have turned upon their officers, hoisted the rebel flag on the walls of the Fort, and displayed signals which might have been seen at Bangalore. But a season of suspended activity naturally followed this failure; and it was not until the month of October that they ventured to resolve on any open demonstration. Then the Mahomedan and Hindoo Sepoys feasted together, bound themselves by solemn engagements to act as brethren in a common cause, and swore that they would rise against and massacre their English officers.

October 18, 1806. The day and the hour of the butchery were fixed. The native soldiery had quietly sent their families out of the Fort, and otherwise prepared for the struggle.† Two hours before midnight on the 18th of October the Sepoys were to have rushed upon their English officers, and not left a white man living in the place. Capt. Baynes. But about eight o'clock on that evening an English officer galloped up to the house of the Commandant Cuppage, and told him that no time was to be lost; that the Sepoys were on the point of rising, and that

* Mark Wilks wrote to Barry Close, with reference to this movement at Nundydroog: "I do not know what to make of all this; men who had any great combination in view could scarcely have any design to act on so small a scale." But Barry Close, taking a more comprehensive view, replied: "The great object of the Insurgents at Vellore seems to have been to secure to themselves a strong post on which to assemble in force. Cuppage's garrison, though small, may have had it in view to seize on Nundydroog. Possessed of this strong post, the conspirators would have probably assembled upon it in force, and proceeded to act against us openly."—*MS. Correspondence.*

† Colonel Cuppage to Barry Close.—*MS. Correspondence.*

means of safety must at once be sought. Scarce had the story been told, when an old and distinguished native officer came breathless with the same intelligence. There was no room for doubt; no time for delay. An express, calling for reinforcements, was despatched to Bangalore; and the officers, selecting one of their houses in the Pagoda-square, which seemed best adapted to purposes of defence, took post together and waited the issue. The night passed without an attack; and on the morrow afternoon safety came in the shape of a squadron of Dragoons from Bangalore. Colonel Davis had received the tidings soon after daybreak, and by three o'clock his troopers were clattering into Nundydroog. 1806.

November came, and with it came new troubles. Far down the coast, not many leagues removed from the southernmost part of the Peninsula, lies the station of Pallamcottah. There Major Welsh, with six European officers under him, commanded a Sepoy battalion, in which many relatives of the mutineers cut up at Vellore were brooding over their loss of kindred. Towards the end of the third week of the month, it was believed that the Mahomedan Sepoys were about to rise and to massacre all the Europeans in the place. The story ran that, rejecting with contempt the idea of banding themselves with the Hindoos, they had met at a mosque and concerted their murderous plans. Some buildings were to be fired in the cantonment to draw the English officers from their homes. In the confusion, the whole were to be slain, the Fort was to be seized, and the rebel flag hoisted on the ramparts. Scenting the plot, a Malabar-man went to the mosque in disguise, and carried tidings of it to the English Commandant. The danger appeared to be imminent, and Welsh at once took his measures to avert it. Pallamcottah.

1806. Whatever may have been the judgment and discretion of the man, his courage and determination were conspicuous; and his comrades were of the same temper. Assuming the bold, intrepid front, which has so often been known to overawe multitudes, this little handful of undaunted Englishmen seized and confined thirteen native officers, and turned five hundred Mussulman Sepoys out of the Fort. That they were able to accomplish this, even with the support of the Hindoos, was declared to be a proof that no desperate measures had really been designed. But the premature explosion of a plot of this kind always creates a panic. In a state of fear and surprise, men are not capable of reasoning. There is a vague impression that boldness presages power; that there is something behind the imposing front. A single man has ere now routed a whole garrison. I am not sure, therefore, that there was no danger, because it was so easily trodden out.

Two days afterwards Colonel Dyce, who commanded the district of Tinnivelly, threw himself into Pallamcottah; assembled the Hindoo troops; told them that he had come there to maintain the authority of the Company, or to die in the defence of the colours which he had sworn to protect. He then called upon those who were of the same mind to approach the British flag for the same purpose, but if not, to depart in peace. They went up and took the oath to a man, presented arms to the colours, gave three unbidden cheers in earnest of their unshaken loyalty, and fell in as on a muster-parade.

On the first appearance of danger, Welsh had despatched a letter by a country-boat to Ceylon, calling for European troops, and the call was responded to with an alacrity beyond all praise. But so effectual were the measures which had been already adopted, or so little of real danger had there been, that when the succour which had been sent for arrived from Trichinopoly, the alarm had passed, and the work was done. 1806.

Told as I have told this story—a simple recital of facts, as written down in contemporary correspondence—it would appear to afford an instructive example of the virtue of promptitude and vigour. But this is not the only lesson to be learnt from it. It is more instructive still to note that Major Welsh was severely condemned as an alarmist, the tendency of whose precipitate action was to destroy confidence and to create irritation. Another officer,* who, apprehending danger, had disarmed his regiment as a precaution, was denounced with still greater vehemence.† Apprehensions of this kind were described as "disgraceful and groundless panics;" and political officers chuckled to think that it was proposed at Madras to remove from their commands and to bring to Courts-Martial the officers who had considered it their duty not to wait to be attacked.‡ With these lessons before

* Lieutenant-Colonel Grant.

† I find this fact recorded in the correspondence of the day with three notes of exclamation: "With regard to Colonel Grant," wrote Major Wilks from Mysore, "it appears that he disarmed his troops simply as a measure of precaution!!! Whether we are in danger from our own misconduct, or from worse causes, the danger is great. . . . I conclude that Chalmers will be sent to supersede Grant, and Vesey to Pallamcottah, and my best hope is that there will be found sufficient grounds for turning Welsh and Grant out of the service, but this will not restore the confidence of the Sepoys."—*M.S. Correspondence.* Grant's conduct was at once repudiated in a general order, and he and Welsh ordered for Court-Martial. Both were honourably acquitted.

‡ Many years after the occurrence of these events, Major, then Colonel Welsh, published two volumes of Military Reminiscences. Turning to these for some account of the affair at Pallamcottah, I was disappointed to find only the following scanty notice of it: "Towards the end of the year an event took place, which, although injurious to my own prospects and fortune, under the signal blessing of Providence terminated fortunately. Time has now spread his oblivious wings over the whole occurrence, and I will not attempt to remove the veil."

1806. us, we cannot wonder that men, in such conjunctures, should hesitate to strike the blow which any one may declare uncalled-for, and the wisdom of which no one can prove—should pause to consider whether they are more likely to develop the evil by an assertion of strength, or to encourage its growth by the feebleness of inaction.*

Wallajahabad. But it was plain that, whatsoever might be the wisest course in such a conjuncture, the Government of Lord William Bentinck was all in favour of the milder and more sedative mode of treatment. In remarkable contrast to the manner in which the symptoms of coming mutiny were grappled with at Pallamcottah stands the story of Wallajahabad. Some of the earliest signs of disaffection, on the score of the turban, had manifested themselves at that place; and Gillespie, with his dragoons, had been despatched thither at the end of July, not without a murmur of discontent at the thought of his "poor hard-worked fellows" being sent to counteract what appeared to him a doubtful danger. It was believed, however, that the uneasiness had passed away, and for some months there had been apparent tranquillity. But in November the alarm began to revive; and a

* The difficulties of the English officer at that time were thus described by a contemporary writer, in a passage which I have chanced upon since the above was written: "The massacre at Vellore had naturally created a great degree of mistrust between the European officers and the Sepoys throughout the Army; and the indecision of measures at Head-Quarters seemed further to strengthen this mistrust. If an officer took *no* precautionary measures on receiving information of an intended plot, he was liable to the severest censure, as well as responsible for his own and the lives of his European officers. On the contrary, if he took precautionary measures he was accused of creating unnecessary distrust; and equally censured for being premature and not allowing the mutiny to *go on* till satisfactorily proved, when it would have been too late to prevent."—*Strictures on the present Government of India, &c. In a Letter from an Officer resident on the spot. Trichinopoly,* 1807; *London,* 1808.

detailed statement of various indications of a coming outbreak, drawn up by Major Hazlewood, was sent to the authorities. On the morning of the 2nd of December the members of the Madras Government met in Council. Hazlewood's statement was laid before them and gravely discussed; but with no definite result. The Council broke up without a decision, but only to meet again, refreshed by the sea-breeze and the evening ride. Then it was resolved that a discreet officer, in the confidence of Government, should be sent to Wallajahabad to inquire into and report on the state of affairs; and on the same evening Colonel Munro, the Quartermaster-General, received his instructions, and prepared to depart. The event appeared to justify this cautious line of action; but one shudders to think what might have happened at Wallajahabad whilst Government were deliberating over written statements of danger, and drafting instructions for a Staff-officer in the Council-Chamber of Madras. 1806.

Six months had now passed since the Madras Government had been made acquainted with the state of feeling in the Native Army, and understood that a vague apprehension of the destruction of caste and of "forcible conversion to Christianity" had been one of the chief causes of the prevailing disquietude. The obnoxious regulations had been abandoned, but this was a concession obviously extorted from fear; and nothing had yet been done to reassure the minds of the soldiery by a kindly paternal address to them from the fountain-head of the local Government. But at last Bentinck and his colleagues awoke to a sense of the plain and palpable duty which lay before them; and at this Council of the 2nd of December a Proclamation was agreed upon, Dec., 1806.

1806. and on the following day issued, which, translated into the Hindostanee, the Tamul, and Telegoo dialects, was sent to every native battalion in the Army, with orders to commanding officers to make its contents known to every native officer and Sepoy under their command. After adverting to the extraordinary agitation that had for some time prevailed in the Coast Army, and the reports spread for malicious purposes, by persons of evil intention, that it was the design of the British Government to convert the troops by forcible means to Christianity, the Proclamation proceeded to declare that the constant kindness and liberality at all times shown to the Sepoy should convince him of the happiness of his situation, "greater than what the troops of any other part of the world enjoy," and induce him to return to the good conduct for which he had been distinguished in the days of Lawrence and Coote, and "other renowned heroes." If they would not, they would learn that the British Government "is not less prepared to punish the guilty than to protect and distinguish those who are deserving of its favour." But this was something more than the truth. The British Government did not show itself, in this conjuncture, to be "prepared to punish the guilty" in a manner proportionate to the measure of their offences. Lord William Bentinck and his Councillors were all for clemency. Sir John Cradock counselled the adoption of more vigorous punitory measures, and the Supreme Government were disposed to support the military chief. Something of a compromise then ensued, the result of which was a very moderate instalment of the retribution which was justly due. A few only of the most guilty of the murderers were executed; whilst others, clearly convicted of taking part in the sanguinary revolt, were merely dismissed the service. And if it had not been for the overruling authority of the Government at Calcutta—that is, of Sir George Barlow, with Mr. Edmonstone at his elbow*—the numbers of the assassin-battalions would not have been erased from the Army List. But penal measures did not end here. The higher tribunals of the Home Government condemned the chief authorities of Madras, and, justly or unjustly, the Governor, the Commander-in-Chief, and the Adjutant-General, were summarily removed from office. 1806.

1807.

Alleged causes of the Revolt.

The mutiny died out with the old year; the active danger was passed; but it left behind it a flood of bitter controversy which did not readily subside. What was the cause of the revolt? Whose fault was it? Was it a mere military mutiny, the growth of internal irritation, or was it a political movement fomented by agitators from without? The controversialists on both sides were partly wrong and partly right—wrong in their denials, right in their assertions. It is difficult in such a case to put together in proper sequence all the links of a great chain of events terminating even in an incident of yesterday, so little do we know of what is stirring in the occult heart of native society. After a lapse of half a century it is impossible. There is often in the Simultaneous, the Coincidental, an apparent uniformity of tendency, which simulates design, but which, so far as human agency is concerned, is wholly fortuitous. We see

* Many years afterwards, Sir George Barlow gracefully acknowledged the valuable assistance which, in this conjuncture, Mr. Edmonstone had rendered to him, saying that his "unshaken firmness and resolution in times of internal difficulty and danger" were "signally displayed on the discovery of the conspiracy formed at Vellore." "His wise and steady counsel," added Barlow, "afforded me important aid and support in carrying into effect the measures necessary for counteracting the impressions made by that alarming event, which threatened the most serious consequences to the security of our power."—*MS. Documents.*

1807. this in the commonest concerns of life. We see it in events affecting mightily the destinies of empires. Under a pressure of concurrent annoyances and vexations, men often cry out that there is a conspiracy against them, and the historical inquirer often sees a conspiracy when in reality there is only a coincidence. A great disaster, like the massacre at Vellore, acts like iodine upon hidden writings in rice-water. Suddenly is proclaimed to us in all its significance what has long been written down on the page of the Past, but which, for want of the revealing agent, has hitherto lain illegibly before us. Doubtless, many hidden things were disclosed to us at this time; but whether they were peculiar to the crisis or of a normal character, at any period discernible, had we taken proper steps to develop them, was matter of grave dispute. The political officers, headed by Mark Wilks, the historian of Southern India, who was then representing British interests in Mysore, laughed to scorn the discoveries of the military officers, and said that the things which they spoke of as so portentous were in reality only phenomena of every-day appearance, familiar to men acquainted with the feelings and habits of the people. He derided all that had been said about seditious conversations in the Bazaars and the Lines, the wild prophecies and mysterious hints of wandering Fakeers, and the suggestive devices of the puppet-shows.* There was nothing in all this, he contended, of an exceptional character, to be regarded as the harbingers of mutiny and massacre. And his arguments culminated in the chuckling assertion that the military authorities had discovered

* There were two subjects which the *Kootpootlee-Wallahs* extremely delighted to illustrate—the degradation of the Mogul, and the victories of the French over the English, the one intended to excite hatred, the other contempt, in the minds of the spectators.

a cabalistic document of a most treasonable character, 1807.
which appeared to their excited imaginations to be a plan for partitioning the territory to be wrested from the English, but which, in reality, was nothing more portentous than the scribblement of the Dervish Bazee, or "royal game of goose."

With equal confidence on the other hand, the military authorities protested that the new regulations had nothing to do with the mutiny—that it was altogether a political movement. The new cap, they said, had been accepted and worn by the Sepoys. Three representative men, types of the principal nationalities composing the Coast Army, had signified their satisfaction with the new head-dress, and one or two regiments *en masse* had been paraded in it without a murmur. The fact, they alleged, was that the movement had emanated solely from the deposed family of Tippoo Sultan; that its object was to restore, in the first instance, the Mahomedan dynasty in Southern India, and eventually to recover the imperial throne for the Mogul. If proper precautions had been taken by Government—if Tippoo's family, eager for a taste of blood, had not been left to disport themselves at will in Vellore—if they had not been gorged with money, and attended by countless Mussulman followers eager to recover the posts and the privileges which they had lost, there would, said the military leaders, have been no massacre and no mutiny, and, some said, not even a murmur of discontent. But the military critic was as wrong as the political, and for the same reason. Each was blinded by professional interests and professional prejudices. Each argued in self-defence. The truth, as it commonly does in such cases, lay midway between the two extremes. But for the intrigues of Tippoo's family

1807, there would have been no outbreak at that time, and but for the new military regulations they might have intrigued in vain. It so happened that the political and military influences were adverse to us at the same moment, and that from the conjuncture arose the event known in history as the Massacre of Vellore, but which was in reality a much more extensive military combination, prevented only by repeated local failures from swelling into the dimensions of a general revolt of the Coast Army.

Nor is it to be forgotten that there was a third party, which attributed the calamity less to political and to military causes than to the general uneasiness, which had taken possession of the native mind in consequence of the supposed activity of Christian missionaries and of certain "missionary chaplains." The dread of a general destruction of Caste and forcible conversion to Christianity was not confined to the Sepoys. The most preposterous stories were current in the Bazaars. Among other wild fables, which took firm hold of the popular mind, was one to the effect that the Company's officers had collected all the newly-manufactured salt, had divided it into two great heaps, and over one had sprinkled the blood of hogs, and over the other the blood of cows; that they had then sent it to be sold throughout the country for the pollution and the desecration of Mahomedans and Hindoos, that all might be brought to one caste and to one religion like the English. When this absurd story was circulated, some ceased altogether to eat salt, and some purchased, at high price, and carefully stored away, supplies of the necessary article, guaranteed to have been in the Bazaars, before the atrocious act of the Feringhees had been committed. Another story was that the Collector of

Trincomalee had, under the orders of Government, laid the foundation of a Christian Church in his district close to the great Pagoda of the Hindoos; that he had collected all the stone-cutters and builders in the neighbourhood; that he was taxing every household for the payment of the cost of the building; that he had forbidden all ingress to the Pagoda, and all worshipping of idols; and that to all complaints on the subject he had replied that there was nothing extraordinary in what he was doing, as Government had ordered a similar building to be erected in every town and every village in the country. In India, stories of this kind are readily believed. The grosser the lie the more eagerly it is devoured.* They are circulated by designing persons with a certainty that they will not be lost. That the excitement of religious alarm was the principal means by which the enemies of the British Government hoped to accomplish their objects is certain; but if there had not been a foregone determination to excite this alarm, nothing in the actual progress of Christianity at that time would have done it. A comparison, indeed, between the religious status of the English in India and the wild stories of forcible conversion, which were then circu- 1807.

* Not immediately illustrating this point of inquiry, but even more preposterous in itself than the rumours cited in the text, was a story which was circulated at Hyderabad. It was stated that an oracle in a neighbouring Pagoda had declared that there was considerable treasure at the bottom of a well in the European barracks, which was destined not to be discovered until a certain number of human heads had been offered up to the tutelar deity of the place; and that accordingly the European soldiers were sacrificing the necessary number of victims with all possible despatch. It happened that the dead body of a native without a head was found near the Residency, and that a drunken European artilleryman, about the same time, attacked a native sentry at his post. These facts gave new wings to the report, and such was the alarm that the natives would not leave their homes or work after dark, and it was reported both to the Nizam and his minister that a hundred bodies without heads were lying on the banks of the Moose River.—*Captain Sydenham to the Government of India. MS. Records.*

1807. lated, seemed openly to give the lie to the malignant inventions of the enemy. There were no indications on the part of Government of any especial concern for the interests of Christianity, and among the officers of the Army there were so few external signs of religion that the Sepoys scarcely knew whether they owned any faith at all.* But in a state of panic men do not pause to reason; and if at any time the doubt had been suggested, it would have been astutely answered that the English gentlemen cared only to destroy the religions of the country, and to make the people all of one or of no caste, in order that they might make their soldiers and servants do everything they wished.

Views of the Home Government.

The authoritative judgment of a Special Commission appointed to investigate the causes of the outbreak confirmed the views of the more moderate section of the community, which recognised, not one, but many disturbing agencies; and the Home Government accepted the interpretation in a candid and impartial spirit. That "the late innovations as to the dress and appearance of the Sepoys were the leading cause of the mutiny, and the other was the residence of the family of the late Tippoo Sultan at Vellore," was, doubtless, true as far as it went. But the merchant-rulers of Leadenhall-street were disposed to sound the lower depths of the difficulty. Those were not days when the numerous urgent claims of the Present imperatively forbad the elaborate investigation of the Past. So the Directors began seriously to consider what had been the more remote predisposing causes of the almost general disaffection

* Sir John Cradock said, after the occurrence of these events, that "from the total absence of religious establishments in the interior of the country, from the habits of life prevalent among military men, it is a melancholy truth that so unfrequent are the religious observances of officers doing duty with battalions, that the Sepoys have not, until very lately, discovered the nature of the religion professed by the English."

of the Coast Army. And the "Chairs," in a masterly letter to Mr. Dundas, freighted with the solid intelligence of Charles Grant, declared their conviction that the general decline of the fidelity of the Army and of the attachment of the People to British rule, was to be traced to the fact that a new class of men, with little knowledge of India, little interest in its inhabitants, and little toleration for their prejudices, had begun to monopolise the chief seats in the Government and the chief posts in the Army; that the annexations of Lord Wellesley had beggared the old Mahomedan families, and had shaken the belief of the people in British moderation and good faith; and that the whole tendency of the existing system was to promote the intrusion of a rampant Englishism, and thus to widen the gulf between the Rulers and the Ruled.* 1807.

* The Chairman and Deputy-Chairman of the East India Company (Mr. Parry and Mr. Grant) to the President of the Board of Control (Mr. Dundas).—*May* 18, 1807. *MS. Records.*

CHAPTER II.

SUBSIDENCE OF ALARM—THE SOLDIER IN ENGLAND AND IN INDIA—THE SEPOY AND HIS OFFICER—DETERIORATING INFLUENCES—THE DRAINAGE OF THE STAFF—PROGRESS OF CENTRALISATION—THE REORGANISATION OF 1824—THE BARRACKPORE MUTINY—THE HALF-BATTA ORDER—ABOLITION OF CORPORAL PUNISHMENT.

1807-1809.

IT was not strange that for some time after the occurrence of these events in the Coast Army, the English in Southern India should have been possessed by a common sense of anger, and that this feeling should have spread to some other parts of the country. For a while the white man saw a conspirator beneath the folds of every turban, and a conspiracy in every group of people talking by the wayside. In every laugh there was an insult, and in every shrug there was a menace. English officers pillowed their heads on loaded fire-arms, and fondled the hilts of their swords as they slept. But gradually they lived down the sensitiveness that so distressed them. Other thoughts and feelings took possession of the bungalow; other subjects were dominant in the mess-room. And ere long a new grievance came to supersede an old danger; and the officers of the Madras Army forgot the rebellion of the Sepoys as they incubated a rebellion of their own. How the mutiny of the officers grew out of the mutiny of the men of the Coast Army, it would not be difficult to show; but the chapter of

Mutiny of Madras Officers, 1809.

ndian history which includes the former need not be 1807-1809.
re-written here. The objects for which the officers contended were altogether remote from the interests and sympathies of the Sepoys; and although the latter, in ignorance, might at first have followed their commanders, it is not probable that they would have continued to cast in their lot with the mutineers, after the true character of the movement had been explained to them, and an appeal made to their fidelity by the State. But they were not unobservant spectators of that unseemly strife; and the impression made upon the Sepoy's mind by this spectacle of disunion must have been of a most injurious kind. There is nothing so essential to the permanence of that Opinion, on which we so much rely, as a prevailing sense that the English in India are not Many but One.

Nor was it strange that, after these unfortunate events, the fame of which went abroad throughout the whole country, there should have been for a little space less eagerness than before to enlist into the service of the Company. But the reluctance passed away under the soothing influence of time. In the prompt and regular issue of pay, and in the pensions, which had all the security of funded property, there were attractions, unknown to Asiatic armies, not easily to be resisted. And there were other privileges, equally dear to the people of the country, which lured them by thousands into the ranks of the Company's Army. As soon as his name was on the muster-roll, the Sepoy, and through him all the members of his family, passed under the special protection of the State.

The English Soldier.

It is difficult to conceive two conditions of life more dissimilar in their social aspects than soldiering

1807-1809. in India and soldiering in England. In England, few men enlist into the Army as an honourable profession, or seek it as an advantageous source of subsistence. Few men enter it with any high hopes or any pleasurable emotions. The recruit has commonly broken down as a civilian. Of ruined fortune and bankrupt reputation, he is tempted, cheated, snared into the Army. Lying placards on the walls, lying words in the pot-house, the gaudy ribbons of Sergeant Kite, the drum and the fife and the strong drink, captivate and enthral him when he is not master of himself. He has quarrelled with his sweetheart or robbed his employer. He has exhausted the patience of his own people, and the outer world has turned its back upon him. And so he goes for a soldier. As soon as he has taken the shilling, he has gone right out of the family circle and out of the circle of civil life. He is a thousandth part of a regiment of the Line. Perhaps he has changed his name and stripped himself of his personal identity. Anyhow, he is as one dead. Little more is heard of him; and unless it be some doting old mother, who best loves the blackest sheep of the flock, nobody much wishes to hear. It is often, indeed, no greater source of pride to an English family to know that one of its members is serving the Queen, in the ranks of her Army, than to know that one is provided for, as a convict, at the national expense.

The Indian Soldier.

But the native soldier of India was altogether of a different kind. When he became a soldier, he did not cease to be a civilian. He severed no family ties; he abandoned no civil rights. He was not the outcast, but the stay and the pride of his house. He visited his home at stated times. He remitted to it a large part of his pay. It was a decorous boast in many families that generation after generation had eaten the Company's salt. Often, indeed, in one household you might see the Past, the Present, and the Future of this coveted military service. There was the ancient pensioner under the shade of the banyan-tree in his native village, who had stories to tell of Lawrence, Coote, and Medows; of battles fought with the French; of the long war with Hyder and the later struggles with his son. There was the Sepoy, on furlough from active service, in the prime of his life, who had his stories also to tell of "the great Lord's brother," the younger Wellesley, of Harris and Baird, perhaps of "Bikrum Sahib" and Egypt, and how "Lick Sahib," the fine old man, when provisions were scarce in the camp, had ridden through the lines, eating dried pulse for his dinner. And there was the bright-eyed, supple-limbed, quick-witted boy, who looked forward with eager expectancy to the time when he would be permitted to take his father's place, and serve under some noted leader. It was no fond delusion, no trick of our self-love, to believe in such pictures as this. The Company's Sepoys had a genuine pride in their colours, and the classes from which they were drawn rejoiced in their connexion with the paramount State. It was honourable service, sought by the very flower of the people, and to be dismissed from it was a heavy punishment and a sore disgrace.

1807-1809.

Abercrombie and Lake.

Strong as were these ties, the people were bound to the military service of the Company by the still stronger ties of self-interest. For not only were the Sepoys, as has been said, well cared-for as soldiers —well paid and well pensioned—but, as civilians, they had large privileges which others did not enjoy. Many of them, belonging to the lesser yeomanry of

Civil privileges of the Sepoy.

1807-1809. the country, were possessors of, or shareholders in, small landed estates. And thus endowed, they rejoiced greatly in a regulation which gave the Sepoy on furlough a right to be heard before other suitors in our civil courts.* In a country whose people are inordinately given to litigation, and where justice is commonly slow-paced, this was so prodigious a boon, that entrance to the service was often sought for the express purpose of securing this valuable precedence, and the soldier-member of the family thus became the representative of his whole house. In this connexion of the soldiery with hereditary rights in the soil, there was an additional guarantee for his loyalty and good conduct. He was not merely a soldier—a component unit of number two company, third file from the right; he was an important member of society, a distinct individuality in his native village no less than in his cantonment Lines. He retained his self-respect and the respect of others; and had a personal interest in the stability of the Government under which his rights were secured.

The Sepoy and his Officer.

And whilst these extraneous advantages were attached to his position as a soldier of the Company, there was nothing inherent in the service itself to render it distasteful to him. His officers were aliens of another colour and another creed; but the Hindoo was accustomed to foreign supremacy, and the Mahomedan, profoundly impressed with the mutabilities of fortune, bowed himself to the stern necessities of fate. As long as the Sepoy respected the personal

* This was a part only of the civil privileges enjoyed by the native soldier. A memorandum in the Appendix will show the full extent of the advantages conferred upon him by this class-legislation. Sir Jasper Nicolls, in his evidence before the Parliamentary Committee of 1832, said that the withdrawal of these privileges had been regarded as an especial grievance by the Sepoys—but I have failed to discover that they ever were withdrawn.

qualities of the English officer, and the English officer 1809-1822.
felt a personal attachment for the Sepoy, the relations between them were in no degree marred by any considerations of difference of race. There was a strong sense of comradeship between them, which atoned for the absence of other ties. The accidental severance of which I have spoken was but short-lived.* In that first quarter of the present century, which saw so much hard fighting in the field, the heart of the Sepoy officer again turned towards his men, and the men looked up and clung to him with child-like confidence and affection. To command a company, and, in due course, a regiment of Sepoys, was still held to be a worthy object of professional ambition. The regiment, in those days, was the officer's home, whether in camp, or cantonment, or on the line of march. There was but little looking beyond; little hankering to leave it. To interest himself in the daily concerns of the Sepoys, to converse with them off parade, to enter into their feelings, to contribute to their comforts, were duties, the performance of which occupied his time, amused his mind, and yielded as much happiness to himself as it imparted to others. There was, in truth, little to divert him from the business of his profession or to raise up a barrier between him and his men. Intercourse with Europe was rare and difficult. Neither the charms of English literature nor the attractions of English womanhood alienated his affections from the routine of

* There had certainly been, before the mutiny in Southern India, a very culpable want of kindly consideration on the part of our English officers for the native officers and men of the Sepoy army. In the letter, written by the Chairman and Deputy-Chairman of the East India Company, to Mr. Dundas, referred to above, this is alleged to have been one of the remote causes of the mutiny. It is stated that the English had ceased to offer chairs to their native officers when visited by them. A favourable reaction, however, seems afterwards to have set in.

1809-22. military life, and made its details dull and dreary in his sight. He had subdued his habits, and very much his way of thinking, to the Orientalism by which he was surrounded. He was glad to welcome the native officer to his bungalow, to learn from him the news of the Lines and the gossip of the Bazaar, and to tell him, in turn, what were the chances of another campaign and to what new station the regiment was likely to be moved at the approaching annual Relief. If there were any complaints in the regiment, the grievance was stated with freedom on the one side, and listened to with interest on the other. If the men were right, there was a remedy; if they were wrong, there was an explanation. The Sepoy looked to his officer as to one who had both the power and the will to dispense ample justice to him. In every battalion, indeed, the men turned to their commandant as the depository of all their griefs, and the redresser of all their wrongs. They called him their father, and he rejoiced to describe them as his "babalogue"—his babes.

Progress of Centralisation.

But in time the power was taken from him, and with the power went also the will. A variety of deteriorating circumstances occurred—some the inevitable growth of British progress in the East, and some the results of ignorance, thoughtlessness, or miscalculation on the part of the governing body. The power of the English officer was curtailed and his influence declined. The command of a regiment had once been something more than a name. The commanding-officer could promote his men, could punish his men, could dress them and discipline them as he pleased. The different battalions were called after the commander who had first led them to victory, and they rejoiced to be so distinguished. But, little by little, this power, by the absorbing action of progressive centralisation, was taken out of his hands; and he who, supreme in his own little circle, had been now a patriarch and now a despot, shrivelled into the mouthpiece of the Adjutant-General's office and the instrument of Head-quarters. The decisions of the commanding officer were appealed against, and frequently set aside. In the emphatic language of the East, he was made to eat dirt in the presence of his men. The Sepoy, then, ceased to look up to him as the centre of his hopes and fears, and the commanding officer lost much of the interest which he before took in his men, when he knew how much their happiness and comfort depended upon his individual acts, and how the discipline and good conduct of the corps were the reflexion of his personal efficiency. 1822-1835.

England in India.

And it happened that, about the same time, new objects of interest sprung up to render more complete the severance of the ties which had once bound the English officer to the native soldier. The second quarter of the nineteenth century in India was a period of progressive reform. We reformed our Government and we reformed ourselves. Increased facilities of intercourse with Europe gave a more European complexion to society. English news, English books, above all, English gentlewomen, made their way freely and rapidly to India. The Overland Mail bringing news scarcely more than a month old of the last new European revolution; the book-club yielding its stores of light literature as fresh as is commonly obtained from circulating libraries at home; and an avatar of fair young English maidens, with the bloom of the Western summer on their cheeks, yielded attractions beside which the gossip of the lines and the feeble garrulity of the old Soubahdar

1822-35. were very dreary and fatiguing. Little by little, the Sepoy officer shook out the loose folds of his Orientalism. Many had been wont, in the absence of other female society, to solace themselves with the charms of a dusky mate, and to spend much time in the recesses of the Zenana. Bad as it was, when tried in the crucible of Christian ethics, it was not without its military advantages. The English officer, so mated, learnt to speak the languages of the country, and to understand the habits and feelings of the people; and he cherished a kindlier feeling for the native races than he would have done if no such alliances had been formed. But this custom passed away with the cause that produced it. The English wife displaced the native mistress. A new code of morals was recognised; and the Zenana was proscribed. With the appearance of the English gentlewoman in the military cantonment there grew up a host of new interests and new excitements, and the regiment became a bore.

Staff employment.

Whilst these influences were sensibly weakening the attachment which had existed between the native soldier and his English officer, another deteriorating agent was at work with still more fatal effect. The Staff was carrying off all the best officers, and unsettling the rest. As the red line of British Empire extended itself around new provinces, and the administrative business of the State was thus largely increased, there was a demand for more workmen than the Civil Service could supply, and the military establishment of the Company was, therefore, indented upon for officers to fill the numerous civil and political posts thus opened out before them. Extensive surveys were to be conducted, great public works were to be executed, new irregular regiments were to be raised, and territories not made subject to the "regulations" were, for the most part, to be administered by military men. More lucrative, and held to be more honourable than common regimental duty, these appointments were eagerly coveted by the officers of the Company's army. The temptation, indeed, was great. The means of marrying, of providing for a family, of securing a retreat to Europe before enfeebled by years or broken down by disease, were presented to the officer by this detached employment. And if these natural feelings were not paramount, there was the strong incentive of ambition or the purer desire to enter upon a career of more active utility. The number of officers with a regiment was thus reduced; but numbers are not strength, and still fewer might have sufficed, if they had been a chosen few. But of those who remained some lived in a state of restless expectancy, others were sunk in sullen despair. It was not easy to find a Sepoy officer, pure and simple, with no aspirations beyond his regiment, cheerful, content, indeed, proud of his position. All that was gone. The officer ceased to rejoice in his work, and the men saw his heart was not with them. 1822-35.

There were some special circumstances, too, which at this time—during the administrations of Lord Amherst and Lord William Bentinck—tended to aggravate these deteriorating influences both upon the officers and the men of the Sepoy regiments. Since the subsidence of the spirit of disaffection, which had pervaded the Coast Army in 1806, there had been no obtrusive manifestations of discontent in the Sepoy's mind. He had done his duty faithfully and gallantly in the great wars, which Lord Hastings

1822 had conducted to a triumphant issue; but when peace came again, he again, after a while, began to take stock of his troubles and to listen to strange reports. One more illustration may be drawn from Madras, before the Bengal Army claims a monopoly of the record. In the early spring of 1822, a paper was dropped in the Cavalry Lines of Arcot, setting forth that the followers of Mahomed, having been subjected to the power of the English, suffered great hardships—that being so subjected, their prayers were not acceptable to the Almighty, and that, therefore, in great numbers they were dying of cholera morbus—that the curse of God was upon them; and that, therefore, it behoved them to make a great effort for the sake of their religion. There were countless Hindoos and Mussulmans between Arcot and Delhi. But the Europeans being few, it would be easy to slay the whole in one day. Let them but combine, and the result would be certain. There was no time, it said, to be lost. The English had taken all the Jagheers and Inams of the people of the soil, and now they were about to deprive them of employment. A number of European regiments had been called for, and in the course of six months all the native battalions would be disbanded. Let, then, the senior Soubahdar of each regiment instruct the other Soubahdars, and let them instruct the Jemadars, and so on, till all the Sepoys were instructed, and the same being done at Vellore, at Chittore, at Madras, and other places, then, on a given signal, the whole should rise on one day. The day fixed was Sunday, the 17th of March. A Naick and ten Sepoys were to proceed at midnight to the house of each European, and kill him, without remorse, in his bed. This done, the regiments would be placed under the

Mahomedan Grievances.

command of the native officers, and the Soubahdars should have the pay of Colonels. It was always thus. It is always thus. A little for the Faith, and all for the Pocket. 1822.

From whomsoever this paper may have emanated, the attempt to corrupt the Sepoys was a failure. It was picked up in the Lines of the Sixth Cavalry, and another nearly resembling it was dropped in the Lines of the Eighth—but both were carried at once to the commanding officer of the station. Colonel Foulis took his measures with promptitude and vigour. He assembled the regimental commanders, imparted to them the contents of the paper, and desired them to place themselves in communication with the native officers whom they most trusted. Having done this, he wrote to the commandants of the several stations named in the paper. But they could see no signs of disaffection; and the appointed day passed by without even an audible murmur of discontent. But not many days afterwards, the Governor of Madras received by the post a letter in Hindostanee, purporting to come from the principal native officers and Sepoys of the Army, setting forth the grievances under which they suffered as a body The complaint was that all the wealth and all the honour went to the white Sirdars, especially to the civilians, whilst for the soldier there was nothing but labour and grief. "If we Sepoys take a country," they said, "by the sword, these whore-son cowardly civil Sirdars enter that country and rule over it, and in a short time fill their coffers with money and go to Europe—but if a Sepoy labour all his life, he is not five couries the better." Under the Mahomedan Government, it had been different, for when victories were gained, Jagheers were given to the soldiers, and high offices

Sir Thomas Munro.

1822. distributed among them. But under the Company, everything was given to the Civil Service. "A single Collector's peon has an authority and greatness in the country which cannot be expressed. But that peon does not fight like a Sepoy." Such, in effect, was the plaint of the native soldiery, as conveyed to Governor Munro. It may have been the work of an individual, as might have been also the papers picked up in the lines of Arcot; but it is certain that both documents expressed sentiments which may be supposed at all times to lie embedded in the Sepoy's mind, and which need but little to bring them, fully developed, above the surface.*

The relations between the English officer and the native soldier were better then than they had been sixteen years before. But these relations were sadly weakened, and a heavy blow was given to the discipline and efficiency of the Indian army, when, two years later, the military establishments of the Three Presidencies were reorganised. Then every regiment of two battalions became two separate regiments, and the officers attached to the original corps were told off alternately to its two parts—"all the odd or uneven numbers," said the General Order, "to the first, and the even numbers to the second;" by which process it happened that a large number of officers were detached from the men with whom they had been associated throughout many years of active service. The evil of this was clearly seen at the time, and a feeble compromise was attempted. "It is not intended," said the General Order, "that in carrying the present orders into effect, officers should be permanently removed from the particular battalion in which they

The Reorganisation.

May 6, 1824.

* It was to this event that Sir Thomas Munro alluded in his remarkable minute on the dangers of a Free Press in India.

may long have served and wished to remain, provided that by an interchange between officers standing the same number of removes from promotion, each could be retained in his particular battalion, and both are willing to make the exchange." In effect, this amounted to little or nothing, and a large number of officers drifted away from the battalions in which they had been reared from boyhood, and strangers glided into their place. 1824.

The Burmese War.

Bad as at any time must have been such a change as this, in its influence upon the morale of the Sepoy army, the evil was greatly enhanced by falling upon evil times. The best preservative, and the best restorative of military spirit and discipline, is commonly a good stirring war. But the Sepoy, though not unwilling to fight, was somewhat dainty and capricious about his fighting-ground. A battle-field in Hindostan or the Deccan was to his taste; but he was disquieted by the thought of serving in strange regions, of which he had heard only vague fables, beyond inaccessible mountain-ranges, or still more dreaded wildernesses of water. With the high-caste, fastidious Bengal Sepoy the war with Burmah was not, therefore, a popular war. The Madras Sepoy, more cosmopolitan and less nice, took readily to the transport vessel; and a large part of the native force was drawn from the Coast Army. But some Bengal regiments were also needed to take part in the operations of the war, and then the system began to fail us. To transport troops by sea from Calcutta to Rangoon would have been an easy process. But the Bengal Sepoy had enlisted only for service in countries to which he could march; to take ship was not in his bond. The regiments, therefore, were marched to the frontier station of Chittagong, and there as-

1824. sembled for the landward invasion of the Burmese country.

The Mutiny at Barrackpore.

Without any apparent symptoms of discontent, some corps had already marched, when, in October, the incident occurred of which I am about to write, an incident which created a most powerful sensation from one end of India to the other, and tended greatly to impair the loyalty and discipline of the Bengal Sepoy. The Forty-seventh Regiment had been warned for foreign service, and was waiting at Barrackpore, a few miles from the Presidency, whilst preparations were being made for its march in the cold weather. To wait is often to repent. Inactive in cantonments during the rainy season, and in daily intercourse with the men of other regiments, who had been warned for the same service, the Forty-seventh, uninfluenced by any other external causes, would have lost any ardour which might have possessed them when first ordered to march against a barbarous enemy who had insulted their flag. But it happened that ominous tidings of disaster came to them from the theatre of war. The British troops had sustained a disaster at Ramoo, the proportions of which had been grossly exaggerated in the recital, and it was believed that the Burmese, having cut up our battalions, or driven them into the sea, were sweeping on to the invasion of Bengal. The native newspapers bristled with alarming announcements of how the Commander-in-Chief had been killed in action and the Governor-General had poisoned himself in despair; and there was a belief throughout all the lower provinces of India that the rule of the Company was coming to an end. The fidelity of the Sepoy army requires the stimulus of continued success. Nothing tries it so fatally as disaster. When, therefore, news came that the war had opened with a great failure, humiliating to the British power, and all kinds of strange stories relating to the difficulties of the country to be traversed, the deadliness of the climate to be endured, and the prowess of the enemy to be encountered, forced their way into circulation in the Bazaars and in the Lines, the willingness which the Sepoys had once shown to take part in the operations beyond the frontier began to subside, and they were eager to find a pretext for refusing to march on such hazardous service. And, unhappily, one was soon found. There was a scarcity of available carriage-cattle for the movement of the troops. Neither bullocks nor drivers were to be hired, and fabulous prices were demanded from purchasers for wretched starvelings not equal to a day's journey. For the use of the regiments which had already marched, Bengal had been well-nigh swept out, and the reports which had since arrived rendered it difficult to persuade men voluntarily to accompany as camp-followers an expedition fraught with such peculiar perils. All the efforts of the Commissariat failed to obtain the required supply of cattle; and so the Sepoys were told to supply themselves. In this conjuncture, it would seem that a new lie was circulated through the Lines of Barrackpore. It was said that as the Bengal regiments could not, for want of cattle, be marched to Chittagong, they would be put on board ship and carried to Rangoon, across the Bay of Bengal. Murmurs of discontent then developed into oaths of resistance. The regiments warned for service in Burmah met in nightly conclave, and vowed not to cross the sea. 1824.

Still foremost in this movement, the Forty-seventh Regiment was commanded by Colonel Cartwright.

1824. Rightly measuring the difficulty, and moved with compassion for the Sepoy, who really had just ground of complaint, he offered to provide cattle from his private funds; and all the refuse animals, either too old or too young for service, were got together, and the Government offered to advance money for their purchase. But the terrible ban of "Too Late" was written across these conciliatory measures. The regiment was already tainted with the ineradicable virus of mutiny, which soon broke out on parade. The Sepoys declared that they would not proceed to Burmah by sea, and that they would not march unless they were guaranteed the increased allowances known in the jargon of the East as "double batta." This was on the 30th of October. On the 1st of November, another parade was summoned. The behaviour of the Sepoys was worse than before—violent, outrageous, not to be forgiven; and they remained masters of the situation throughout both the day and night. Then the Commander-in-Chief appeared on the scene. A hard, strict disciplinarian, with no knowledge of the native army, and a bitter prejudice against it, Sir Edward Paget was a man of the very metal to tread down insurrection with an iron heel, regardless both of causes and of consequences. He carried with him to Barrackpore two European regiments, a battery of European artillery, and a troop of the Governor-General's Body-guard. Next morning the native regiments found themselves in the presence of the English troops; but still they did not know the peril that awaited them, and, with a child-like obstinacy, they were not to be moved from their purpose of resistance. Some attempt was made at explanation—some attempt at conciliation. But it was feeble and ineffectual; perhaps not understood.

They were told, then, that they must consent to 1824.
march, or to ground their arms. Still not seeing the danger, for they were not told that the Artillery guns were loaded with grape, and the gunners ready to fire,* they refused to obey the word; and so the signal for slaughter was given. The guns opened upon them. The mutineers were soon in panic flight. Throwing away their arms and accoutrements, they made for the river. Some were shot down; some were drowned. There was no attempt at battle. None had been contemplated. The muskets with which the ground was strewn were found to be unloaded.

Then the formalities of the military law were called in to aid the stern decisions of the grape-shot. Some of the leading mutineers were convicted, and hanged; and the regiment was struck out of the Army List. But this display of vigour, though it checked mutiny for the time, tended only to sow broadcast the seeds of future insubordinations. It created a bad moral effect throughout the whole of the Bengal army. From Bazaar to Bazaar the news of the massacre ran with a speed almost telegraphic. The regiments, which had already marched to the frontier, were discussing the evil tidings with mingled dismay and disgust before the intelligence, sent by special express, had reached the ears of the British chiefs. "They are your own men whom you have been destroying," said an old native officer; and he could not trust
himself to say more.† The Bengal regiments, with 1825.
the expeditionary force, had soon a grievance of their own, and the remembrance of this dark tragedy

* It is doubtful, indeed, whether they knew that the guns were in the rear of the European regiments.

† "Political Incidents of the first Burmese War." By T. C. Robertson to whom was entrusted the political conduct of the war.

1825. increased the bitterness with which they discussed it. The high-caste men were writhing under an order which, on the occupation of Arracan, condemned the whole body of the soldiery to work, as labourers, in the construction of their barracks and lines. The English soldier fell to with a will; the Madras Sepoy cheerfully followed his example. But the Bengal soldier asked if Brahmins and Rajpoots were to be treated like Coolies, and, for a while, there was an apprehension that it might become necessary to make another terrible example after the Barrackpore pattern. But this was fortunately averted. General Morrison called a parade, and addressed the recusants. The speech, sensible and to the point, was translated by Captain Phillips; and so admirable was his free rendering of it, so perfect the manner in which he clothed it with familiar language, making every word carry a meaning, every sentence strike some chord of sympathy in the Sepoy's breast, that when he had done, the high-caste Hindostanees looked at each other, understood what they read in their comrades' faces, and forthwith stripped to their work.

Thus was an incipient mutiny checked by a few telling words. And the sad event which had gone before might have been averted also if there had been as much tact and address as "promptitude and decision." A few sentences of well-chosen, well-delivered Hindostanee, on that fatal November morning, might have brought the Sepoys back to reason and to loyalty. But they had the benefit of neither wise counsel from within nor kindly exhortation from without. Deprived, by the reconstruction of the Army, of the officers whom they had long known and trusted, they were more than ever in need of external aid to bring them back to a right state of feeling.

They wanted a General of Division, such as Malcolm or Ochterlony, to reawaken their soldierly instincts—their pride in their colours, their loyalty to their Salt. But, instead of such judicious treatment as would have shown them their own folly, as in a glass, the martinets of the Horse Guards, stern in their unsympathising ignorance, their ruthless prejudices, had, in our own territories, at the very seat of government, in the presence of no pressing danger, no other lessons to teach, no other remedies to apply, than those which were to be administered at the bayonet's point and the cannon's mouth. 1825-35.

The Half-Batta Order.

With the return of peace came new disquietudes. A reign of Retrenchment commenced. Alarmed by the expenses of their military establishments, the Company sent out imperative orders for their reduction—orders more than once issued before, more than once disobeyed. Blows of this kind commonly fall upon the weakest—upon those least able to endure them. So it happened that the condition of the regimental officer having, by a variety of antecedent circumstances, been shorn of well-nigh all its advantages, was rendered still more grievous and intolerable by the curtailment of his pecuniary allowances. An order, known in military history as the Half-Batta Order, was passed, by which all officers stationed within a certain distance from the Presidency were deprived of a large per-centage of their pay.* The order excited the utmost dismay throughout the Army; but the discontent which it engendered vented itself in words. Twice before the officers of the Company's army had resented similar encroachments, and

* Or, in strict professional language, his allowances. The gross salary of an Indian officer was known as his "pay and allowances." The former, which was small, was enhanced by several substantial accessories, as tentage, house-rent, and batta, or field allowance.

1825-35. had been prepared to strike in defence of their asserted rights. But this last blow did not rouse them to rebellion. Never before had justice and reason been so clearly upon their side; but, keenly as they felt their wrongs, they did not threaten the Government they served, but loyally protested against the treatment to which they had been subjected. The humours of which their memorials could not wholly relieve them, a Press, virtually free, carried off like a great conduit. The excitement expended itself in newspaper paragraphs, and gradually subsided. But it left behind it an after-growth of unanticipated evils. The little zeal that was left in the regimental officer was thus crushed out of him, and the Sepoy, who had watched the decline, little by little, of the power once vested in the English captain, now saw him injured and humiliated by his Government, without any power of resistance; saw that he was no longer under the special protection of the State, and so lost all respect for an instrument so feeble and so despised.

Abolition of Corporal Punishment.

And as though it were a laudable achievement thus to divest the native soldier of all fear of his European officer, another order went forth during the same interval of peace, abolishing the punishment of the lash throughout the Sepoy army in India. So little was he a drunkard and a ruffian, that it was a rare spectacle to see a black soldier writhing under the drummer's cat. But when the penalty, though still retained in the European army, became illegal and impossible among them, the native soldiery felt that another blow was struck at military authority—another tie of restraint unloosed. It was looked upon less as a boon than as a concession—less as the growth of our humanity than of our fear. So the Sepoy did not love us better, but held us a little more in contempt.

There were great diversities of sentiment upon this point, and some, whose opinions were entitled to respect, believed in the wisdom of the measure. But the weight of authority was against it,* and, some ten years afterwards, Hardinge revived what Bentinck had abolished. But even before the act of abolition, by a variety of concurrent causes, the character and the conduct of the Sepoy Army were so impaired, that an officer who had served long with them, and knew them well, declared, in his evidence before a Committee of Parliament, that "in all the higher qualifications of soldiers, in devotedness to the service, readiness for any duty they may be called upon to perform, cheerfulness under privations, confidence and attachment to their officers, unhesitating and uncalculating bravery in the field, without regard either to the number or the character of the enemy, the native soldier is allowed by all the best-informed officers of the service, by those who have most experience, and are best acquainted with their character, to have infinitely deteriorated."† 1832.

* Numerous illustrations might be cited, but none more significant than the following anecdote, told by Mr. Charles Raikes: "I recollect a conversation which I had in 1839 with an old pensioned Soubahdar. I inquired of him how the measure would work. He replied, that the abolition of the punishment would induce some classes to enter the Army who had not done so before. 'But, Sahib,' said the old man, '*Fouj-beh-durr hogya.*' (The Army has ceased to fear.)" Another native officer said: "The English, to manage us rightly, should hold the whip in one hand and the *mehtoys* (sweetmeats) in the other. You have dropped the whip, and now hold out sweets to us in both hands."

† Evidence of Captain Macan in 1832.

CHAPTER III.

THE WAR IN AFGHANISTAN—PERNICIOUS EFFECTS OF DEFEAT—THE ANNEXATION OF SCINDE—RESULTS OF EXTENSION OF EMPIRE—THE INDUS ALLOWANCES—MUTINY OF THE THIRTY-FOURTH REGIMENT—EMBARRASSMENTS OF GOVERNMENT—THE MARCH OF THE SIXTY-FOURTH—MUTINY AT SHIKARPORE—DISAFFECTION IN THE MADRAS ARMY.

The War in Afghanistan, 1838.

PEACE is never long-lived in India, and the Army was soon again in the bustle and excitement of active service. There was a long war; and, if it had been a glorious one, it might have had a salutary effect upon the disposition of the Sepoy. But when all his soldierly qualities were thus, as it were, at the last gasp, the War in Afghanistan came to teach him a new lesson, and the worst, at that time, which he could have been taught. He learnt then, for the first time, that a British army is not invincible in the field; that the great "Ikhbal," or Fortune, of the Company, which had carried us gloriously through so many great enterprises, might sometimes disastrously fail us; he saw the proud colours of the British nation defiled in the bloody snows of Afghanistan, and he believed that our reign was hastening to a close. The charm of a century of conquest was then broken. In all parts of Upper India it was the talk of the Bazaars that the tide of victory had turned against the Feringhees, and that they would soon be driven into the sea. Then the Sikh arose and the Mahratta bestirred himself, rejoicing in our humiliation, and eagerly watching the next move. Then it was that those amongst us, who knew best what was seething in the heart of Indian society, were "ashamed to look a native in the face." The crisis was a perilous one, and the most experienced Indian statesmen regarded it with dismay, not knowing what a day might produce. They had no faith in our allies, no faith in our soldiery. An Army of Retribution, under a wise and trusted leader, went forth to restore the tarnished lustre of the British name; but ominous whispers soon came from his camp that that Army was tainted—that the Sepoy regiments, no longer assured and fortified by the sight of that ascendant Star of Fortune which once had shone with so bright and steady a light, shrunk from entering the passes which had been the grave of so many of their comrades. It was too true. The Sikhs were tampering with their fidelity. Brahmin emissaries were endeavouring to swear them on the Holy Water not to advance at the word of the English commander. Nightly meetings of delegates from the different regiments were being held; and, perhaps, we do not even now know how great was the danger. But the sound discretion and excellent tact of Pollock, aided by the energies of Henry Lawrence and Richmond Shakespear, brought the Sepoys to a better temper, and, when the word was given, they entered the dreaded passes, and, confiding in their leader, carried victory with them up to the walls of the Afghan capital.

1841-42.

1842.

The Sepoy did his duty well under Pollock. He had done his duty well under Nott, who spoke with admiration of his "beautiful regiments," and man-

1843. fully resented any imputation cast upon them. And when, after the British Army had been disentangled from the defiles of Afghanistan, war was made against the Ameers of Scinde, the Sepoy went gallantly to the encounter with the fierce Belloochee fighting-man, and Napier covered him with praise. Then there was another war, and the native regiments of the Company went bravely up the slopes of Maharajpore, and turned not aside from the well-planted, well-manned batteries of the turbulent Mahrattas. But peace came, and with peace its dangers. Scinde had become a British province, and the Sepoy, who had helped to conquer, had no wish to garrison the country.

Results of the Conquest of Scinde.

The direct and immediate result of well-nigh every annexation of Territory, by which our Indian empire has been extended, may be clearly discerned in the shattered discipline of the Sepoy Army. To extend our empire without increasing our means of defence was not theoretically unreasonable; for it might have been supposed that as the number of our enemies was reduced by conquest and subjection, the necessity for the maintenance of a great standing army was diminished rather than increased. These annexations, it was said, consolidated our own territories by eradicating some native principality in the midst of them, or else substituted one frontier, and perhaps a securer one, for another. But the security of our empire lay in the fidelity of our soldiery. To diminish the number of our enemies, and to extend the area of the country to be occupied by our troops, was at the same time to diminish the importance of the Sepoy, and to render his service more irksome to him; for it sent him to strange places far away from his home, to do the work of military Police. It frittered away in small detached bodies the limited European force at the disposal of the Indian Government, or massed large ones on a distant frontier. This extension of territory, indeed, whilst it made us more dependent upon our native troops, made that dependence more hazardous. The conversion of Scinde into a British province, by which our long line of annexations was commenced, had burnt this truth into our history before Lord Dalhousie appeared upon the scene. For indeed it was a sore trial to the Sepoy to be posted in a dreary outlying graveyard of this kind, far away from his home and his people—far beyond the limits of the empire in which he had enlisted to serve. And when it was proposed to take from him the additional allowances, which had been issued to the troops, on active service in an enemy's country, on the plea that they had subsided into the occupation of British cantonments, he resented this severe logic, and rose against the retrenchment. He did not see why, standing upon the same ground, he should not receive the same pay, because the red line of the British boundary had been extended by a flourish of the pen, and the population of the country had by the same magic process been converted into British subjects; and still less easily could he reconcile himself to the decision when he thought that the Sepoy himself had contributed to bring about the result that was so injurious to him; that he had helped to win a province for his employers, and, in return for this good service, had been deprived of part of his pay. In the old time, when the Company's troops conquered a country, they had profited in many ways by the achievement, but now they were condemned to suffer as though gallantry were a crime. 1843-44

In more than a camel-load of documents the story

1844. lies recorded; but it must be briefly narrated here.

Mutiny of the Thirty-fourth. In the month of February, 1844, Governor-General Ellenborough, being then absent from his Council in the Upper Provinces, received the disheartening intelligence that the Thirty-fourth Sepoy Regiment of Bengal, which had been warned for service in Scinde, had been halted at Ferozepore. It had refused to enter our newly-acquired province, unless its services were purchased by the grant of the additional allowances given to the soldiery beyond the Indus in time of war. The distressing character of the intelligence was aggravated by many circumstances of time and place. In a moment, Ellenborough's quick perceptions had grappled the whole portentous truth. Our troops were mutinying for pay, on the Punjab frontier, almost in the presence of the disorderly masses of Sikh troops, who, gorged with the donatives they had forced from a weak Government, were then dominating the empire. Other regiments were coming up, on the same service, who might be expected to follow the rebellious lead of the Thirty-fourth; and so Ellenborough and Napier might have found themselves with the province they had just conquered on their hands, and no means of securing its military occupation, without destroying the authority of Government by humiliating concessions.

In this conjuncture, the first thing that Ellenborough did was the best that could have been done. He delegated to the Commander-in-Chief the full powers of the Governor-General in Council for the suppression of mutiny in the Army. But, how were those powers to be exercised? Doubt and perplexity, and something nearly approaching consternation, pervaded Army Head-Quarters. The Seventh Bengal Cavalry, on the line of march to the frontier, had broken into open mutiny, and in spite of all the efforts of their officers, who had guaranteed to pay them from their own funds the allowances they demanded, the troopers had refused to obey the trumpet-call to march, and were halted, therefore, sullen and obstinate, in the neighbourhood of Ferozepore. Some companies of Native Artillery had already refused to march, and there were rumours of other regiments being on the eve of declaring their refusal. The most obvious course, under such circumstances, was to march the recusant regiments back to one or more of the large stations, as Loodhianah and Meerut, where European troops were posted, and there to disband them. But sinister whispers were abroad that the sympathies of the Europeans, in this instance, were with the native soldiery. One regiment of the Line, it was reported, had openly declared that it would not act against the Sepoys, who were demanding no more than their rights. There were Sikh emissaries from beyond the Sutlej doing their best to debauch the Sepoys by offering both their sympathy and their assistance. Dick, the General of Division, declared his belief that an order to the mutineers to march back for disbandment would not be obeyed; and a violent collision at such a time would have set the whole frontier in a blaze. The project of disbandment was, therefore, suspended; and all the more readily, as even at Head-Quarters there was a belief that, although the recusant troops might have had no reasonable ground of complaint, the actual state of the case with respect to the Scinde pay and allowances had not been properly explained to them.* 1844.

* The extraordinary allowances—the withdrawal of which had created all this ill feeling—were originally granted when the troops crossed the Indus in 1838, on their march to Candahar and Caubul. They were withdrawn from the troops in Scinde early in 1840, when there seemed to

1844. Uncondemned, the mutinous regiments were ordered back to the stations from which they had marched, to await the result of a reference to the Governor-General; and other corps, warned for the Scinde service, came up to the frontier. Dick's first and wisest impulse had been to halt the regiments marching to Ferozepore, in order that they might not run the risk of contamination by the tainted corps, or the corrupting influence of the Sikhs. But, by some strange fatality, this judicious measure had been revoked; the regiments marched to the frontier; and Dick's difficulties increased. The Sixty-ninth refused to embark, unless the old Indus allowances were guaranteed to them. By the exertions of the officers, one-half of the regiment was afterwards brought round to a sense of their duty; they loaded their carriage cattle, marched to the banks of the river, and declared their willingness to embark on the boats. They ought to have been embarked at once with the colours of their regiment. Their comrades would then have followed them; and other regiments, moved by the good example, might also have asserted their fidelity. But the golden opportunity was lost; and all example was in the way of evil. The Fourth Regiment, trusted overmuch by its commanders, followed the Sixty-ninth into mutiny at Ferozepore, and such was the conduct of the Sepoys, that Philip Goldney, a man of equal courage and capacity, suddenly called to the scene of tumult, drew upon one of the foremost of the mutineers, and a younger officer, moved to passion

The Sixty-ninth and the Fourth.

be no longer any extraordinary duties to be performed by them. When the insurrection broke out in Afghanistan, and retributory operations were commenced, the allowances were restored; but they were again reduced from the 1st of July, 1843, after the close of the war in Afghanistan and the conquest of Scinde.

by their violence, struck out with a bayonet, and wounded two soldiers in the face. Those were days when mutiny did not mean massacre, and the Sepoy did not turn upon his officer. But neither regiment would march. On many hard-fought fields Sir Robert Dick had proved himself to be a good soldier, but he was not equal to such a crisis as this: so Ellenborough at once ordered him to be cushioned in some safer place. 1844.

In the mean while, aid to the embarrassed Government was coming from an unexpected quarter. The Sixty-fourth Regiment of Sepoys had formed part of that unfortunate detachment known in history as Wilde's Brigade, which had been sent, before Pollock's arrival at Peshawur, to carry the Khybur Pass, without guns and without provisions. It had afterwards served with credit during the second Afghan campaign, since the close of which it had been cantoned at the frontier station of Loodhianah. The Sepoys had manifested a strong reluctance to serve in Scinde, and had addressed to the Adjutant-General more than one *urzee*, or petition, couched in language of complaint almost akin to mutiny. From Loodhianah the regiment had been ordered down to Benares. On the 15th of February it reached Umballah, then become the Head-Quarters of the Sirhind division of the Army, which General Fast, an old officer of the Company's service, commanded. Well able to converse in the language of the country, and knowing, from long intercourse with them, the character and feelings of the native soldiery, Fast believed that something might still be done to bring the regiment back to its allegiance. So he halted the Sixty-fourth at Umballah, and summoned the native officers to his presence. Questioned as to the disposition of the

The Sixty-fourth.

1844. regiment, they one and all declared that the men had never refused to march to Scinde; that they were still willing to march; that only on the evening before the native officers had severally ascertained the fact from their respective companies; that the matter of the allowances would not influence the Sepoys; and that the mutinous *urzees* had emanated only from a few bad characters in the regiment; perhaps, it was added, from a Sepoy who had been already dismissed. From these and other representations, it appeared to the General that the Sixty-fourth really desired to wipe out the stain, which the *urzees* had fixed upon their character, and, believing in this, he recommended that they should be permitted to march to Scinde. Under certain stringent conditions, the Commander-in-Chief adopted the recommendation; and so Moseley, with his Sepoys, again turned his face towards the Indus.

The disposition of the regiment now seemed to be so good; it was marching with such apparent cheerfulness towards the dreaded regions, and setting so good an example to others, that the Commander-in-Chief was minded to stimulate its alacrity, and to reward its returning fidelity, by a voluntary tender of special pay and pension, and relaxations of the terms of service.* The language of these instructions was somewhat vague, and Moseley, eager to convey glad

* "In addition to the full or marching batta always allowed to regiments serving in Scinde, still higher advantages in regard to pay, together with the benefits of the regulated family pension to the heirs of those who may die from disease contracted on service." The commanding officer was also instructed "to make known to the corps that it shall be brought back to a station in the provinces in one year in the event of the ensuing season proving unhealthy, and under no circumstances be kept in Scinde beyond two years, while the indulgence of furlough to visit their homes will, in the latter case, be extended to the men in the proportion enjoyed by corps located at stations within the British frontier." — [*The Adjutant-General to Colonel Moseley, March* 15, 1844.] Scinde, however, had become a British "province," and was "within the British frontier."

tidings to his men, turned the vagueness to account by exaggerating the boon that was offered to them. And so the error of Head-Quarters was made doubly erroneous, and the Governor-General was driven wild by the blunder of the Commander-in-Chief. 1844.

Whatsoever Head-Quarters might have intended to grant, was contingent upon the good conduct of the regiment. But before the letter had been received by Moseley, on the line of march, mutiny had again broken out in the ranks of the Sixty-fourth. At Moodkhee, now so famous in the annals of Indian warfare, the regiment, not liking the route that had been taken, assumed a threatening front, and attempted to seize the colours.* The petulance of the hour was suppressed, and next day the regiment resumed its march. But transitory as was the outbreak, it was mutiny in one of its worst forms. On the second day, the Colonel received, at Tibbee, the letter from Head-Quarters, on the subject of the additional allowances. The outbreak at Moodkhee had converted it into an historical document, to be quietly put aside for purposes of future record. It was, indeed, a dead letter. The fatal words "too late" were already written across the page. But Moseley laid eager hands upon it, as a living reality, for present uses. The Sixty-fourth was plainly in an excitable state. It had mutinied once on the march, and, without the application of some very powerful sedative, it might mutiny again. The outbreak at Moodkhee had not been reported to Head-Quarters. It might pass into oblivion as an ugly dream of the past; and the future might be rendered peaceful and prosperous by the letter of the Adjutant-General. So

* It was advisable to march the troops proceeding to Scinde along a route which would not bring them into contact with other regiments, either coming from that province or stationed on the frontier; and it was especially desirable to mask Ferozepore.

1844. Moseley, having caused it to be translated into Hindostanee, summoned a parade, and ordered it to be read aloud to his men.

Tremendous as was this error—for it tendered to the mutinous the reward intended only for the faithful—its proportions were dwarfed by the after-conduct of the infatuated Colonel. He put a gloss of his own on the Head-Quarters' letter, and told the regiment that they would receive the old Indus allowances given to Pollock's Army.* Upon which they set up a shout of exultation. And then the Sixty-fourth pursued its journey to Scinde.

The horrible mistake which had thus been committed soon began to bear bitter fruit. The inevitable pay-day came; and Moseley, like a man who has silenced the clamorous demands of the Present by drawing a forged bill upon the Future, now saw his gigantic folly staring him in the face. The crisis came at Shikarpore. The Indus war-allowances were not forthcoming, and the Sixty-fourth refused in a body to receive their legitimate pay.

George Hunter. There was then, under Governor Napier, commanding the troops in Scinde, an old Sepoy officer, familiarly and affectionately known throughout the Army as George Hunter. Of a fine presence, of a kindly nature, and of a lively temperament, he led all men captive by the sunny influences of his warm heart and his flowing spirits; whilst his manly courage and resolution commanded a wider admiration and respect. Of his conspicuous gallantry in action he carried about with him the honourable insignia in an arm maimed and mutilated by the crashing downward blow of a Ját swordsman, as he was forcing one of

* This was known among the Sepoys as "Pollock's Batta." It made up the soldier's pay to twelve rupees a month.

the gates of Bhurtpore. In the whole wide circle of the Army, there was scarcely one man whom the Sepoy more loved and honoured; scarcely one whose appearance on the scene at this moment could have had a more auspicious aspect. But there are moods in which we turn most angrily against those whom we most love; and General Hunter in this emergency was as powerless as Colonel Moseley. 1844.

Mutiny of the Sixty-fourth.

George Hunter was not a man to coquet with mutiny. He saw at a glance the magnitude of the occasion, and he was resolute not to encourage its further growth by any inopportune delay. The short twilight of the Indian summer was already nearly spent when news reached him that the regiment had refused to receive its pay. Instantly calling a parade, he declared his intention of himself paying the troops. Darkness had now fallen upon the scene; but lamps were lit, and the General commenced his work. The light company, as the one that had evinced the most turbulent spirit, was called up first; the Sepoys took their pay to a man, and were dismissed to their Lines. Of the company next called, four men had refused to receive their pay, when Moseley went up to the General, and told him that the whole regiment would take their money quietly, if disbursed to them by their own officers. Hunter had once refused this, but now he consented, and again the effort to flatter the corps into discipline was miserably unsuccessful. No sooner was this reluctant consent wrung from the General, than the parade was broken up with a tumultuous roar. Filling the air with shouts, sometimes shaped into words of derision and abuse, the Sepoys flocked to their Lines. In vain Hunter ordered them to fall in; in vain he implored them to remember that they were soldiers. They turned upon

1844. him with the declaration that they had been lured to Scinde by a lie; and when he still endeavoured to restore order and discipline to the scattered rabble into which the regiment had suddenly crumbled, they threw stones and bricks at the fine old soldier and the other officers who had gone to his aid.

Nothing more could be done on that night; so Hunter went to his quarters, and waited anxiously for the dawn. A morning parade had been previously ordered, and when the General went to the ground, he saw, to his exceeding joy, that the Sixty-fourth were already drawn up—"as fine-looking and steady a body of men," he said, "as he could wish to see." No signs of disorder greeted him; and as he inspected company after company, calling upon all who had complaints to make to come forward, the regiment preserved its staid and orderly demeanour, and it seemed as if a great shame held them all in inactivity and silence.* Returning then to the head of the column, drawn up left in front, Hunter proceeded to resume the work which had been broken off so uproariously on the preceding evening. Ten men of one company refused their pay, but none others followed their example. All now seemed to be proceeding to a favourable issue; and Hunter believed that the favourable disposition which had begun to show itself might be confirmed by a suitable address. So he prepared himself to harangue them.

The ways of the Sepoy are as unaccountable as the ways of a child. It is impossible to fix the limits of his anger, or rightly to discern the point at which his good temper has really returned. Unstable and inconsistent, his conduct baffles all powers of human

* Only one man came forward, and his complaint was that he had been passed over in promotion.

comprehension. So it happened that just on the seeming verge of success the ground crumbled away under Hunter's feet. As each company had been called up to receive its pay, the men had piled their arms to the word of command. But when the word was given to un-pile, there was an immediate shudder of hesitation, which seemed to be caught by one company from another, until it pervaded the whole regiment. Each man seemed to read what was in his neighbour's heart, and without any previous concert, therefore, they clung to each other in their disobedience. Three Grenadier Sepoys took their muskets, and were promoted on the spot; but not another man followed their example. The regiment had again become a rabble. Nothing now could reduce them to order. 1844.

Until the blazing June sun was rising high in the heavens, Hunter and the regimental officers remained on the parade-ground, vainly endeavouring to persuade the Sepoys to return to their duty. They had only one answer to give—their Colonel and their Adjutant had promised them what they had not received. If the General would guarantee them the old Indus war-allowances, they would serve as good soldiers; if not, they wished to be discharged, and return to their homes. All through the day, and all through the night, without divesting themselves of their uniform, without going to their Lines to cook or to eat, the mutineers remained on the ground, sauntering about in the neighbourhood of their piled arms, and discussing their wrongs.

Day broke, and found them still on the ground. But hunger and fatigue had begun to exhaust the energies of their resistance, and when Hunter appeared again on the scene, accompanied only by his

1844. aide-de-camp, and beat to arms, the men fell in, took their muskets, and evinced some signs of contrition. Then the General spoke to them, saying that he would receive at his quarters a man from each company, and hear what he had to say on the part of his comrades. Satisfied with this promise, and being no longer irritated by the presence of the officers who had deceived them, the Sixty-fourth allowed the parade to be quietly dismissed, and went to their Lines. At the appointed hour, the delegates from the several regiments waited on the General, and each man told the same story of the deception that had been practised upon the regiment. They had been promised "General Pollock's Batta," and the twelve rupees which they had expected had dwindled down into eight.

With this evidence before him, the General removed Colonel Moseley from the command of the station and from the command of the regiment,* and ordered the Sixty-fourth to march to Sukkur, on their way back to our older provinces. It was an anxious time; a hazardous march. So Hunter went with them. But the hot stage of the fever had passed, and the paroxysm seemed to have left them feeble and June 25, 1844. sore-spent. Unresistingly they went to Sukkur, and encamped in the presence of European troops; and George Hunter, thanking God that the peril was over, and that not a drop of blood had been shed, then took upon himself the responsibility of pardoning the regiment as a body, and bringing to punishment only the worst of the individual offenders.† Such moderation could hardly be misunderstood at a time

* Colonel Moseley was afterwards tried by court-martial, and cashiered.

† Thirty-nine prisoners were sent to trial, of whom one only was acquitted. Six were ordered for capital punishment, and the sentence of death passed upon the others was commuted to imprisonment and hard labour for various terms.

when there was present power to enforce the decrees of a sterner justice. So he addressed the regiment on parade, told them that he pardoned all but the leading mutineers, who would be tried by Court-martial; and he trusted that the mercy thus shown to them would not be thrown away, that they would repent of their misconduct and return to their allegiance. And perhaps the provocation which they had received was ample warrant for the leniency of their treatment.* 1844.

But the embarrassments of the Government did not end here. Whatsoever might be the punishment of the offence, it could not afford a remedy for the evil. The mutinous regiments might be disbanded, and their ringleaders might be hanged by the neck, or blown to atoms from the guns; but still there would be no answer to the question of how was Scinde to be garrisoned with British troops? It had been the design of the Government to employ only Bengal regiments on that service, seeking aid in other quarters from Madras. But the Bengal Army had broken down under the experiment; and there was small hope, after what had passed, of its ever being induced, except by humiliating concessions, to look that hated province in the face. There were, however, two other Presidencies, and two other Armies, not so nice as Bengal; and the defence of Scinde might be entrusted to Bombay or Madras regiments. If such had been the design in the first instance, it might, under judicious management, have been suc-

* There is something very touching in the humility which pervades the letters written at this time by George Hunter to Lord Ellenborough and Sir Charles Napier. He asks to be pardoned for all short-comings, in consideration of the difficulty of the circumstances. "I never could write," he says at the end of one letter, "and old age does not improve a man in any way, except, I trust, in seeing his own failings and praying for mercy."

1843. cessfully carried into effect. But after such an example as had been set by the Bengal regiments, there was small consolation to be drawn from the prospect of loyal service to be rendered by their comrades. Already, indeed, were there signs that the disposition to strike for higher pay which had manifested itself among the Bengal troops was not confined to the Sepoys of that "pampered and petted" Army. The Bombay regiments were untainted;* but a mutinous spirit had again displayed itself among the native soldiery of the Coast Army.†

Mutiny of the Sixth Madras Cavalry.

The first symptom of this was in a Cavalry regiment at Jubbulpore. Among the results of an extension of empire without a corresponding augmentation of our military force, are frequent violations of old Presidential limits in the location of our troops, which, however unobjectionable they may appear at the Adjutant-General's office, are seldom carried out without some disturbance of our military system. It might seem to be of small consequence whether the station at which a regiment was posted were within the limits of one Presidency or another; but if a Madras regiment were called upon to serve in the Bengal Presidency, or a Bombay regiment in Madras, or any other departure from ordinary rule were decreed, the Government was fortunate if it were not seriously perplexed and embarrassed by the results. Now, the Madras Army, though, as has been

* The Bombay Army was said at that time to have more duty on its hands than it could perform without a severe strain, and the Bombay Government were clamouring for an augmentation.

† There had been several recent instances of extreme insubordination, amounting, indeed, to mutiny, in the Madras Army. The 52nd Native Infantry had mutinied at Asseeghur and Mallegaum; there had been a mutiny of the Madras troops at Secunderabad; and the 2nd and 41st Regiments had shown a bad spirit, when ordered to embark for China. The 3rd and 4th Native Cavalry regiments had also mutinied; the former in 1838, the latter in 1842.

said, more cosmopolitan and less nice than that of Bengal, and not deterred by caste prejudices from proceeding to strange places, suffered even more than the Bengal troops from being ordered to distant stations, because the family of the Madras soldier followed his regiment, whilst the belongings of his Bengal comrade remained in their native village. The removal of the family from one station to another was a sore trouble and a heavy expense to the Madras Sepoy; and whatever increased the distance to be traversed was, therefore, a grievance to him. 1843.

To the Cavalry it was especially a grievance, for the troopers were principally well-born Mahomedans, and the rigid seclusion in which their women were kept greatly increased the cost of their conveyance from one station to another. The Sixth Cavalry had been more than commonly harassed in this respect, when, towards the close of 1843, just as they were expecting to get their route for the favourite cavalry station of Arcot, they received orders to march from Kamptee to Jubbulpore, in the valley of the Nerbudda, which, in consequence of the demand for Bengal troops on the Indus, it had been necessary to occupy with regiments from Madras. The sharp disappointment, however, was in some measure mitigated by the assurance that the service on which they were required was but temporary, and that they would soon return within the proper limits of their own Presidency. They went, therefore, leaving their families behind them; but when they reached Jubbulpore, they found that they were to be permanently located there upon lower allowances than they had expected, that they must send for their families from Kamptee, and that their next march would be nine hundred miles southward to Arcot.

1843. Only by savings from their pay at the higher rates could the troopers hope to defray these extraordinary expenses. On the lower rates of pay it was impossible; for the greater part of their earnings was remitted for the support of their absent families, and what remained was barely enough to keep together body and soul. When, therefore, they found that they were to receive these lower rates at Jubbulpore, they broke into open manifestations of discontent, and bound themselves by oaths to stand by each other whilst they resisted the unjust decree. The first few days of December were, therefore, days of sore vexation and disturbance to the officers of the Sixth, and most of all to the Commandant, Major

Major Litchfield. Litchfield, to whose want of personal sympathy with their sufferings the Sepoys, reasonably or unreasonably, attributed a great part of their affliction. The conduct of the men was violent and outrageous. They were with difficulty induced to saddle and mount for exercise; and when the trumpet sounded for the canter, they loosened rein, urged their horses forward at a dangerous pace, and raising the religious war-cry of "Deen! deen!" broke into tumultuous disorder. Brought back to something like discipline, the regiment was dismissed; but throughout the day the greatest excitement prevailed among them, and a large body of troopers marched in a defiant manner

Capt. Byng. through the Lines to the tent of a favourite officer, declaring that they would obey his orders, and serve under him, and beseeching him to place himself at their head. On the following day the excitement had increased. The troop-officers went among their men, endeavouring to pacify them. But they could report nothing more satisfactory than that the troopers were in a frantic state, and that if Litchfield ventured on parade next morning the result would be fatal to him. 1843.

Undeterred by this, the Major would have held the parade, but the Brigadier commanding the station, to whom, in due course, all the circumstances were reported, caused it to be countermanded, and an Inspection Parade, under his own command, ordered in its stead. To this the regiment sullenly responded; and when the Brigadier addressed them, saying that he was willing to hear their complaints, many of the men stepped forward and presented him with petitions, which were given over to the troop-officers, to be forwarded to him through the regular official channels. But, although it was plain that there was a bitter feeling of resentment against Litchfield, no act of violence was committed at that parade. And it happened that before its dismissal a letter reached the Brigadier announcing that the higher allowances were to be given to the men; and so the active danger was passed. But the disturbance which had been engendered did not soon pass away; the Sepoys remained sullen and discontented, and for some days it appeared to the Brigadier not improbable that he would be compelled to call the Infantry and the Artillery to his assistance. But the Madras Army was spared this calamity of bloodshed; and after a little while the regiment returned to the quiet and orderly performance of its duty.

As the old year closed upon the scene of mutiny in 1843-44. the Madras Cavalry, so, very soon, the new year opened upon a kindred incident in the Madras Infantry. When it was found that the Bengal troops were reluctant to serve, under the proposed terms, in the Scinde province, and serious embarrassment was, thereby, likely to be occasioned to the Supreme Government, the

1843-44. Madras authorities, believing that the crisis was one in which it behoved every one to do his best, promptly and vigorously, for the salvation of the State, determined, on a requisition from the Government of Bombay, to send two infantry regiments to Scinde.* The Sepoys were to embark on board transport vessels at Madras, to touch at Bombay, and thence to proceed to Kurrachee. One of these regiments, the Forty-seventh, was in orders for Moulmein, on the eastern coast of the Bay of Bengal—a station at which, being beyond Presidential limits, extra allowances, known as field-batta and rations, were paid to the troops. Ignorant, it would appear, of the Bengal regulations, the Madras Government, represented by the Marquis of Tweedale, who held the double office of Governor and Commander-in-Chief, guaranteed to the regiments ordered to Scinde the allowances received at Moulmein; and under these conditions the Forty-seventh embarked for Bombay.

Mutiny of the Madras Forty-seventh.

Meanwhile, the Supreme Government had been advised of the unauthorised measures of the Madras authorities. Chafing under such usurpation of the powers and prerogatives of the Governor-General, Ellenborough sent orders for the detention of the Madras regiment at Bombay, and it was disembarked on its arrival.† There the Madras Sepoys learnt that the advantages of foreign service, promised to them at Madras, and on the faith of which they had set their faces towards Scinde, were disallowed. The greater part of their pay up to the end of March had already

* Sir Charles Napier had made an urgent call on Bombay, which, Bombay not being able to comply with it, passed on to Madras.

† Intelligence of the change of destination was communicated to the officers during the voyage. It should be stated that one detachment of the regiment mutinied on board the *John Line* transport vessel; but the discontent then manifested arose from circumstances unconnected with the after-causes of disaffection.

been disbursed to them, for the benefit of the families whom they left behind, and now they found, in the middle of February, that the scanty residue, on which they had relied for their own support, was by these retrenchments taken from them, and that, far away from their homes, starvation stared them in the face. It was not strange that they should have regarded this as a cruel breach of faith; and that they should have resented it. They had been promised rations, and they asked for them, and when they found they were not likely to be supplied, they manifested their discontent, after the wonted fashion, by breaking out on parade. When the word of command was given for them to march to their Lines, by fours from the left, they stood fast. The word was repeated, but still they stood fast; and when the Adjutant rode up to the leading section and asked the men if they had not heard the word of command, they answered sullenly that they had heard it; and when a Native officer asked them why they did not move, they told him that they wanted food, and that they would not stir without it. 1843-44. Feb. 19, 1844.

When the order to advance was again given, the regiment moved off; but only to renew on the following morning the exhibition of disobedience and discontent. Paraded before the General commanding the garrison, the regiment soon evinced signs of being in the same mood. After inspection, when the order was given to march by companies to their respective Lines, the Grenadiers stepped off, but presently wavered and halted; and when their captain, having ordered their arms, went off to report their conduct to the commanding officer, they insisted on following him in a body, declaring that if they then lost their chance of representing their hard case to the General, they

1844. might never find it again. Another company was even more violent in its demands. When the word of command was given to advance at the quick march, a man from the ranks cried out, "Right about face," and the whole company stood fast, as did other parts of the column. Taken in the act of flagrant mutiny, the Sepoy was disarmed, and sent to the guard, whither the greater part of the company followed, declaring that they also would go to the guard, that they wanted rice, and must have it.

After a while order was restored. The General addressed the European and Native officers, and told them to assure the men, that any complaints advanced in a soldierly manner would be inquired into and any grievances redressed, but that such conduct as had been displayed on parade could not be overlooked. The regiment was then moved off to its Lines, some of the ringleaders being carried off as prisoners; and an advance of money, at first reluctantly received, stifled the further progress of mutiny. Here, then, the story may end. The Madras Army was not destined to supply the want accruing from the defective loyalty of Bengal. It broke down at a critical time; but only under such a weight of mismanagement as might have crushed out the fidelity of the best mercenaries in the world.

In these, as in instances above cited, by conflicts of authority and variations of system, the Sepoy was not unreasonably alarmed for the integrity of his pay; and although we may condemn the manner in which he manifested his discontent, we must not think too harshly of the tenacity with which he asserted his rights. If an English soldier strikes for more pay, it is in most cases only another name for more drink. He seeks it, too often, as a means of personal indulgence.

There is nothing to render less greedy his greed. But the avarice of the Sepoy was purified by domestic affection, by a tender regard for the interests of others, and that strong feeling of family honour which in India renders Poor Laws an useless institution. He had so many dependents with whom to divide his slender earnings, that any unexpected diminution of his pay excited alarm lest those who were nearest and dearest to him should in his absence be reduced to want. The honour of his family was threatened; he chafed under the thought; and if he took unsoldierly means of asserting his rights, we must remember the provocation, and not forget those peculiarities of national sentiment which lighten the dark colours in which all such resistance of authority presents itself to European eyes. 1844.

Eventually Bombay troops were sent to garrison Scinde, and the province became a part of the Bombay Presidency. But it is hard to say how much these first abortive attempts to provide for its defence shook the discipline of the Sepoy Army. For the evil was one to which it was difficult to apply a remedy; and the authorities were greatly perplexed and at variance one with another. The disbandment of a mutinous regiment is, in such a case, the most obvious, as it is the easiest measure, to which Government can resort; but it may often be unjust in itself and dangerous in its results. It falls alike on the innocent and on the guilty. It fills the country with the materials of which rebellions are made, or sends hundreds of our best fighting-men, with all the lessons we have taught them, into the enemy's ranks. To be effective, it should follow closely on the commission of the crime which it is intended to punish; but it can rarely be accomplished with this essential promptitude, for it is Penal Measures.

1844. only under certain favouring circumstances that an order to reduce to penury and disgrace a thousand trained soldiers can be carried out with safety to the State. To delay the execution of the punishment is outwardly to condone the offence. It was not strange, therefore, that when the Thirty-fourth Infantry and the Seventh Cavalry of Bengal mutinied on the frontier, almost in the presence of the Sikh Army, there should have been obstinate questionings at Head-Quarters as to the expediency of disbandment on the spot, or at some safer place remote from the scene of their crimes. It was the opinion of Lord Ellenborough, at the time, that a regiment of Europeans and a troop of European artillery should have been summoned with all haste from Loodhianah to Ferozepore, and that, in presence of this force, the mutinous corps should have been at once disbanded. But a reference, it has been said, was made to Government, and the mutinous regiments were marched down, unsentenced, to Loodhianah and Meerut, there to await the decision of supreme authority. The orders given left some discretion with the Commander-in-Chief. The Seventh Cavalry had not mutinied in a body. The Native officers and nearly two hundred troopers were true to their Salt. Discipline might, therefore, be vindicated by ordinary processes of law without involving the innocent and the guilty alike in one common ruin. But the Thirty-fourth, Native officers and Sepoys, were all tainted; so, with every mark of infamy, in the presence of all the troops, European and Native, at Meerut, the regiment was broken up, the British uniform was stripped from the backs of the mutineers, and the number of the regiment was erased from the Army List.*

* Two or three years afterwards the gap was filled up by the raising of a new regiment, in no degree better than the old.

Propinquity to an overawing European force removes the chief difficulties which oppose themselves to the sudden dissolution of a Native regiment. But under no other circumstances is it to be counselled. The question of disbandment, therefore, perplexed the Madras authorities even more than those of Bengal. To march a regiment, with arms in its hands, some hundreds of miles across the country, to receive its services, and perhaps to witness its repentance during a period of many weeks, all that time concealing the fate that is in store for it, and then having caged it in a safe place, pinioned it, as it were, beyond all hope of resistance, to visit it with all the terrors of a long-hidden, long-delayed retribution, is altogether abhorrent to the generous nature of an English officer. To have disbanded, for example, the Sixth Madras Cavalry at Jubbulpore would have been cruel and dangerous. To have marched it to Arcot in ignorance of its fate, would have been cruel and dastardly. To have broken it up at Kamptee would have been to incur, only in a less degree, the evil of both courses. And nothing else appeared possible; for it was not to be supposed that all those indignant Mahomedans, men with whom revenge is a virtue, would have quietly gone down, mounted on good horses, and with sharpened sabres at their sides, in full knowledge of their destiny, to the disgraceful punishment awaiting them. With these considerations before them, it was not strange that the Madras authorities hesitated to carry out the comprehensive penalty of disbandment, and that, as a choice of difficulties, it should have suffered many guilty men to escape. 1844.

In this instance, Lord Ellenborough was eager for disbandment. He said that the conduct of the regiment had been equally bad in itself and pernicious in

1844. its results, for that the disturbed state of Bundelkund rendered it little short of mutiny before the enemy, and it had disconcerted all the arrangements of his Government for the general defence of the country. But it was not his, either on principle or in practice, to deal harshly with the errors and delusions of the Native Army, and there were few men living who had a more kindly appreciation of the good qualities of the Sepoy, or who could more readily sympathise with him. If he did not know precisely how to deal with a mutiny of that Army; if he could not, with accurate calculation of the results, so apportion the just measures of leniency and severity as in no case to encourage by the one or to exasperate by the other, he only failed where no one had yet succeeded, and need not have blushed to find himself mortal. He often said that a general mutiny of the Native Army was the only real danger with which our empire in India was threatened; and he believed that the surest means of maintaining the fidelity of the Sepoy was by continually feeding his passion for military glory. In this he was right. But the passion for military glory cannot always be fed without injustice, and the evils of conquest may be greater than its gains. He had much faith, too, in the good effect of stirring addresses, appealing to the imaginations of the soldiery, and in the application of donatives promptly following good service. And, although in working out his theory he was sometimes impelled to practical expressions of it, which caused people to smile, as in the famous Somnauth Proclamation, and in the distribution of the "favourite *mehtoys*" to the Sepoys after the battle of Maharajpore, there was, doubtless, sound philosophy at the bottom of it. But such light as this only served to show more clearly the many

Sweetmeats.

and great difficulties with which the whole question of the Sepoy Army was beset, and to convince reflecting minds that, though human folly might accelerate the break-down of the whole system, human wisdom could not so fence it around with safeguards as to give it permanent vitality and strength. 1844.

That the treatment to which the mutinies arising out of the annexation of Scinde were subjected by the Government of the day was nothing more than a series of expedients is a fact, but one which may be recorded without censure. The disbandment of one regiment, the punishment of a few ringleaders in others, the forgiveness of the rest; the dismissal of an officer or two for culpable mismanagement, and a liberal issue of donatives to all who during the preceding year had either done well, or suffered much, in the service of the State, were so many palliatives, born of the moment, which did not touch the seat of the disease, or contribute to the future healthy action of the system. But there were circumstances, both intrinsic and extrinsic, which seemed to forbid, on grounds alike of justice and of policy, the application of more vigorous remedies. The fact, indeed, that the misconduct of the soldiery had, in a great measure, been the direct growth of the injuries which they had sustained at the hands of the Government, would have made severity a crime. But it was no less certain that leniency was a blunder. If an Army once finds that it can dictate to Government the amount of its pay, there is an end to the controlling power of the latter. What the State ought to have learnt from this lesson was the paramount obligation which rested upon it of clearly explaining to its troops all regulations affecting their pay and allowances, and especially such as entailed upon them any loss of privileges

1844. antecedently enjoyed. Under any circumstances a reduction of pay is a delicate and hazardous operation. Even the loyalty of European officers is not always proof against such a trial. But the absence of explanation aggravates it, in the Sepoy's eyes, into a breach of faith; he believes that he is only asserting his rights when he strikes for the restoration of that of which he has been, in his own eyes unjustly, deprived; and the Government then, perplexed in the extreme, has only a choice of evils before it, and either on the side of leniency or severity is too likely to go lamentably wrong.

CHAPTER IV.

THE WAR ON THE SUTLEJ—THE PATNA CONSPIRACY—ATTEMPT TO CORRUPT THE SEPOYS AT DINAPORE—THE OCCUPATION OF THE PUNJAB—ANNEXATION AND ITS EFFECTS—REDUCTION OF THE SEPOY'S PAY—THE MUTINIES AT RAWUL PINDEE AND GOVINDGHUR—LORD DALHOUSIE AND SIR CHARLES NAPIER.

IT was fortunate, perhaps, for the rulers of that day that Peace was but of short duration, and that the "passion for military glory" had again something to feed upon. The Sikh Army, having risen against its own leaders, was vapouring on the banks of the Sutlej, and threatening to cross the British frontier. No war could have been more welcome to the Sepoy than a war with the Sikhs. For they were an insolent and minacious race, and it was known that they had talked of overrunning Hindostan, and pouring on to the sack of Delhi and the pillage of Calcutta. They took the first step, and the war commenced. 1845.

The Patna Conspiracy.

Whilst the Governor-General and the Commander-in-Chief were at the head of the Army on the frontier, and all eyes were turned towards the scene of that sanguinary conflict on the Sutlej, lower down, on the banks of the Ganges, four hundred miles from Calcutta, an incident was occurring, which, in quiet times, might have made itself heard all over the country, but which, lost in the din of battle in that

1845-46. momentous winter, gave only a local sound. Discovery was made of an organised attempt to corrupt the soldiery in the Lower Provinces. On Christmas-eve the magistrate of Patna received a letter from Major Rowcroft, informing him that the Moonshee of his regiment—the First Native Infantry—was in treasonable correspondence with a rich and influential landholder in the neighbourhood, who had been tampering with the allegiance of the Native officers and Sepoys in the contiguous station of Dinapore.

Of the truth of the story there was no doubt. To what dimensions the conspiracy really extended, and from what central point it radiated, is not known, and now never will be known. It was a season of considerable popular excitement, aggravated in the neighbourhood of Patna by local causes, and eager efforts had been made to prepare the people for revolt. Reports had been for some time current to the effect that the British Government purposed to destroy the caste of the Hindoos, and to abolish Mahomedanism by forbidding the initial ceremony through which admission is obtained to the number of the Faithful. And to this was added another lie, scarcely less alarming, that the Purdah was also to be prohibited, and that Mahomedan females of all ranks were to be compelled to go about unveiled. Stories of this kind, it has been observed, however monstrous in themselves, are readily believed, if there be but only a very little truth to give them currency. The truth may be from within or it may be from without. It may be direct proof or indirect confirmation. It little matters so long as there is something which men may see and judge for themselves. There had been many exciting causes at this time, to rouse the resentments and to stimulate the activities of the Moulavees and the Pundits, such as the new law of inheritance and the new educational measures; and now the introduction of the messing-system into the gaols was a patent fact which all might understand. It was an incident, moreover, of untoward occurrence, that about this time, when designing men were eagerly looking out for some false move on the part of the Government, the Magistrate of Patna, at the request of the Principal of the College, alarmed the inhabitants of the city by instituting inquiries enabling him to form something of a census of the population, showing their different castes, professions, and employments—a movement which was at once declared to be a part of the great scheme of the Government for the forcible conversion of the people. 1845-46

But it was necessary that the soldiery should be gained over by some alarming fiction of especial application to the Sepoy himself. Already had indirect agency been set at work for his corruption. He found the lie in full leaf in his native village. When he went on furlough, his relatives told him that if he did not make a stand for his religion he would soon have to fight against his brethren and kinsmen.* When he returned to his regiment he found that every one was talking on the same subject, and that it was currently believed that the introduction of the messing-system into the gaols was to be followed by its introduction into the Army, and that the Sepoy was not much longer to be allowed to have uncontrolled dominion over his own cooking-pot.

* Some of the men of the First Regiment told Major Rowcroft that the villagers had said, "Our village furnishes 500 men to your Army; but if you will not listen to us, we will send 2000 juwans (young men) to oppose you."

1845-46. If, then, there had been nothing more than this, the time would have been propitious, and plotters might reasonably have thought that the opportunity was ripe. But in that winter of 1845-46 a seditious enterprise of this kind in the Lower Provinces was favoured by the circumstances of the great war with the Sikhs, which was drawing all the resources of the Government to the North-Western frontier. There was a vague belief that lakhs of Punjabee fighting-men would soon be streaming over the country, and that the English would be driven into the sea. Many, then, with eager cupidity, bethought themselves of gutting the opium godowns of Patna, where a million and a half of Government property lay stored; and all the dangerous classes of the city were ripe and ready for pillage and for slaughter. A rising of the Sepoys at such a time, or their acquiescence in a rising of the people, might have been fatal to the continued supremacy of Government in that part of the country. The plotters scarcely hoped to accomplish more than the latter of these two means of overthrowing the English. At all events, it was safer to begin with the milder experiment on the fidelity of the Sepoy. So delegates went about in the Lines saying that the great King of Delhi had sent a confidential agent to give a month's pay to every Native officer and soldier in the regiments in order that if any outbreak should occur in their part of the country they should not lift a hand in support of the Government. All the landholders, and the cultivators, and the townspeople were ready, it was said, to rise; and if the soldiery would only remain inactive, the British power might be destroyed before it could perpetrate the outrages by which it sought to overturn the religions of the country.

A Jemadar of the First Regiment heard this story, gravely listened to all that was urged by the emissary of sedition, and said that he would consider of the matter.* Then he repeated all that had happened to his commanding officer, and measures were soon taken to test the reality of the plot. There was at all events one substantial proof that the story was no fiction. There was money counted out for the work of corruption, and tied up in bags ready for immediate delivery. It was agreed that the Jemadar and another officer in Rowcroft's confidence should take the money, and matters were soon conveniently arranged so as to bring about the disclosure. A detachment of the regiment was about to proceed to Gya; with this went the two faithful Jemadars. On the way they met or were overtaken by two well-dressed Mahomedans in an ecka, or native wheeled-carriage, who gave them the money, saying that others had taken it, and that larger supplies were forthcoming for the same purpose. Nothing could stamp the reality of the design more surely than this. Men are in earnest when they part with their money. 1845-46

Another Native officer of the First traitorously took the corrupting coin, and a Moonshee of the regiment was found to be deeply implicated in the plot. But Rowcroft's opportune discovery of the attempt to debauch his men, and the measures which he wisely adopted, rendered the further efforts of the conspirators utterly futile and hopeless. The military offenders were soon in confinement; the civil magistrate was tracking down the instigators of sedition; and if no great success then attended the attempt

* The Jemadar was a Brahmin, by name Mootee-Missur. He had been pay-havildar to Rowcroft, when the latter was adjutant of the regiment, and was greatly attached to him.

1845-46. to bring the necks of the most guilty to the gallows, it was sufficient for the public peace that the plot was discovered. What the amount of real danger then was it is difficult to determine. Two other Native regiments at Dinapore were tampered with in like manner, but the discovery of the plot in Rowcroft's corps rendered other efforts abortive. Many great names were used by the agents of sedition, but upon what authority can only be conjectured. It was stated that a royal mandate had come from the King of Delhi; that the Rajah of Nepaul was ready to send a great army sweeping down to the plains; and again it was said that the Sikhs were the prime movers of the plot.* All this can be only obscurely shadowed on the page of history. But it is certain that a scroll was found, described by a witness as being many cubits long, on which the names of some hundred of respectable inhabitants of Patna, Hindoos and Mahomedans, were attached to a solemn declaration binding them to die in defence of their religion, and that it was honestly believed by large numbers of the educated no less than the ignorant people of that part of the country, that the one cherished object of the British Government was to reduce all the people of India to the no-caste state of the Feringhees. Of the reality of this belief there was no doubt; so a Proclamation was put forth by the Governor of Bengal, declaring that as the British Government never had interfered, so the people

* The principal actor in the Patna conspiracy was one Khojah Hassan Ali Khan. It seems that at the Sonepore Fair, a short time before, he had appeared in great state, and received a considerable number of influential people in his tent, with the object of instilling into them a fear of religious conversion, and encouraging their determination to resist. He escaped for want of evidence. There was also a wandering bookseller, who, on the plea of selling Persian volumes to the Moonshees of regiments, readily gained access to them without exciting suspicion.

might be assured that it never would interfere in any way with the religions of the country. 1845-46.

The Jemadar and the Moonshee of the First Regiment, who had been seduced into traitorous courses, were tried by court-martial, and sentenced to death, with the usual reluctance manifested by a tribunal composed only of Native officers.* But it was not necessary to strike terror into the minds of an army hovering on the brink of general mutiny; so the sentence was not carried out. Whatever danger there may have been had passed away.† The victories of Hardinge and Gough had a grand moral effect from one end of the country to the other, for it had been believed that the British were sore pressed, and that their power would be shaken to the centre by this collision with the Sikhs. Victory made all things right again, and for a while we heard nothing more of mutiny or sedition. With intervals of comparative repose, distinguished by an occupation of the Sikh country, very flattering to the Sepoy's pride, and very profitable to his purse, the operations which resulted in the fall of the Sikh empire then lasted for more than three years. The story has been told in the first chapter of this work. The Punjab, like Scinde, was turned by a stroke of the pen into a British province, and the same difficulties bristled up in the path of

* Not long after the discovery of this plot, Major Rowcroft was seized with severe illness, not without suspicion of poison, and obliged to proceed to England. Jemadar Mootee-Missur told him that on his return to India, he would, doubtless, be able to lay before the Major further facts illustrative of the extent of the conspiracy. But when Rowcroft rejoined the regiment both Mootee-Missur and the other faithful Jemadar were dead.

† It is stated in an interesting pamphlet, published by Mr. Stocqueler, in 1857, that it was said at Dinapore, after the discovery of this conspiracy, that although the English had then escaped, there would be, in 1857, when they had ruled a hundred years, such a *tomasha* as the country had never seen. I can find no trace of this in any contemporary documents, nor have my inquiries from officers who were then at Dinapore enabled me to confirm the truth of the story.

1845-46. the Annexer. The Sepoy, called to serve in the Punjab, had no longer the privileges of foreign service; and, in spite of the lesson taught by the Scinde annexation, he could not understand why the conquest of the country should be inaugurated by the reduction of his pay.

Mutiny in the Punjab. 1849-50. And so the regiments in the Punjab at that time, and those which were moved across the Sutlej from our older provinces, determined to refuse the reduced rates, and to stand out boldly for the higher allowances. All the regiments, suffering or soon to suffer from the incidence of the reduction, took counsel with each other, and promised mutual support. Delegates from the several corps went about from station to station, and letters were exchanged between those at a distance. The first manifestation of open discontent was at Rawul Pindee. There, one morning in July, Sir Colin Campbell, a soldier of the highest promise, already budding into fame—the "war-bred Sir Colin," as Napier then called him—received the significant
July, 1849. intelligence that the Twenty-second Regiment had refused to receive their pay. Outwardly, the Sepoys were calm and respectful; but their calmness indicated a sense of strength, and Campbell felt that all the other Native regiments in the Punjab would probably follow their example. Such a combination at any time and in any place would have been dangerous and alarming; but the peril was greatly aggravated by the peculiar circumstances of the times. For it had grown up in a newly-conquered country, swarming with the disbanded fighting-men of the old Sikh Army, and it was believed that our discontented Sepoys, if they had once broken into rebellion, would have soon found their ranks swollen by recruits from the Kalsa soldiery, eager to profit by the crisis, and

again to strike for the recovery of their lost dominion. We had just seen the downfal of an empire precipitated by the lawlessness of an army, driven onward by the impulses of its greed; and now it seemed as though our own soldiery, having caught the contagion, were clamouring for donatives, and that it required very careful steering to save us from being wrecked upon the same rock. 1849.

Sir Charles Napier had, at that time, just appeared upon the stage. He had hastened from Calcutta to Simlah to meet the Governor-General, who was refreshing himself with the cool mountain air; and there the news reached him, not that one, but that two regiments at Rawul Pindee had refused to take their pay, and that there was every prospect of four more regiments at Wuzeerabad, and two at the intermediate station of Jhelum, following their example. Then Dalhousie and Napier took counsel together, with some of their staff-officers, and it was debated whether it would not be wise to strike a vigorous blow at the incipient mutiny by disbanding the regiments which had already refused to accept their pay. To this course, proposed by Colonel Benson, an old officer of the Company's service, held in deserved regard by many successive Governors-General, Napier resolutely objected, and Dalhousie concurred with the Chief. Hoping for the best, but still prepared for the worst, the old soldier instructed Campbell to point out to the recusant regiments the folly and wickedness of their course; but he wrote privately to him that in the event of their obduracy, he and other commanding officers must bring the power of the European regiments in the Punjab to bear upon the coercion of the mutinous Sepoys. But before these letters arrived, Campbell had tided over the difficulty. "The com-

1849. bination amongst the men of the Thirteenth and Twenty-second Regiments," he wrote to Napier, on the 26th of July, "gave way to fear on the 18th, the day before your prescription for bringing them to their senses was despatched from Simlah." The fact is that, at that time, they were not ready; they were not strong enough for the resistance of authority; and they were not prepared to be the protomartyrs in such a cause. There was a European regiment at Rawul Pindee; there were European regiments at other stations not far removed; and so it was held to be a wiser course to wait until the new regiments should arrive from the older provinces and unite with them in the dangerous work of military rebellion.

That these regiments were prepared to resist was soon too apparent. From Simlah, Napier proceeded on a tour of inspection to the principal military stations in the Northern Provinces of India; and at Delhi he found unmistakable signs of a confederation of many regiments determined not to serve in the Punjab except on the higher pay. One regiment there, warned for service beyond the Sutlej, declared its intention not to march; but it was conciliated by a liberal grant of furloughs, which had before been withheld; and it went on to its destination. Napier believed that the spirit of disaffection was wide-spread. He had heard ominous reports of twenty-four regiments prepared to strike, and when he entered the Punjab, he was not surprised to find that mutiny was there only in a state of suspended activity, and that at any moment it might burst out, all the more furiously for this temporary suppression.

At Wuzeerabad it soon openly manifested itself. In command of that station was one of the best soldiers of the Company's service. At an early age John

Hearsey had earned a name in History, as one of the heroes of Seetabuldee, and thirty years of subsequent service had thoroughly ripened his experience, so that at this time he had perhaps as large a knowledge of the Sepoy, of his temper, of his habits, of his language, as any officer in the Native Army. With this large knowledge dwelt also in him a large sympathy. It commonly happened in those days that the man who best knew the Sepoy best loved him; and Hearsey, who had seen how good a soldier he could be, before the enemy, respected his good qualities, and looked leniently on his bad. He believed that, with good management, a Sepoy regiment might be kept, under almost any circumstances, in the right temper, and he had great faith in the magic efficacy of a good speech. When, therefore, one of the regiments at Wuzeerabad openly refused its pay, Hearsey drew up the men on parade, and addressed them in language so touching, so forcible, and so much to the point, that many hung down their heads, ashamed of what they had done, and some even shed tears of penitence. The pay was then offered to them again. The first four men who refused were tried at once, and sentenced to imprisonment with hard labour. The whole brigade was then turned out to see the sentence carried into effect. There were four Native regiments at Wuzeerabad; but there was also a Regiment of the Line and detachments of European Artillery, Horse and Foot. In the presence of this force, the convicted Sepoys were manacled as felons and sent off to work on the roads. After this, there were no more refusals; the men took their pay and did their work. 1849.

But discipline had not yet been fully vindicated. Three ringleaders, who had been known to go from company to company, instigating and fomenting re-

1849. bellion, were tried by court-martial, and sentenced to fourteen years' imprisonment. But Napier, who regarded in a far stronger light both the enormity of the offence and the magnitude of the danger, ordered a revision of the sentence, and death was recorded against the culprits; and against two others who were tried for the same offence by the same Court.* Then justice was satisfied, and mercy might stretch forth its hand. The sentence was commuted to transportation for life. "In eternal exile," said Napier, in
January 25, 1850. his general order to the troops, "they will expiate their crimes. For ever separated from their country and their relations, in a strange land beyond the seas, they will linger out their miserable lives. It is a change, but I do not consider it an amelioration of their punishment. They will remain living examples of the miserable fate which awaits traitors to their colours."

But the spirit of disaffection was not suppressed, though locally for a time it was subdued. It was declared that the Post-office runners laboured under the weight of the Sepoys' letters, which were then passing from cantonment to cantonment; but a large number of these letters were seized and examined, and they were found to contain nothing on the subject of the allowances.† Napier, however, anticipated a crisis, and was prepared for it. Taking post at Peshawur, the extremest corner of our new Punjab territory, where was a strong European force, he believed that he would ere long be compelled to sweep down with the English regiments, picking up reinforcements as he went from station to station, and to

* Sir Charles Napier, in his Indian Misgovernment, says that four were tried at first, and one afterwards; but the fact is as stated in the text.

† Sir Henry Lawrence, in *Calcutta Review*, vol. xxii. The statement is made on the authority of Major W. Mayne, President of the Govindghur Court of Enquiry.

crush a general rising of the Sepoy troops. And soon it appeared to him that the crisis had come. The Sixty-sixth Regiment broke into mutiny at Govindghur. Bursting out, on parade, with vehement shouts of disapprobation, they attempted to seize the gates of the Fort, so as to cut off all communication with the loyal troops outside the walls. There was no European regiment at Govindghur, but the First Native Cavalry, under Bradford, were faithful among the faithless, and, aided by the cool courage of Macdonald, of the Sixty-sixth, they made good their entrance through the gate.* The Fort was saved. The European officers were saved. And the guilty regiment was doomed to a moral death. The Sixty-sixth was struck out of the Army List. The men were disbanded in a body, and their colours given to a corps of Goorkhas, from the hill-tracts of Nepaul, who were known to be good soldiers, with no Brahminical daintiness about them, and a general fidelity to their Salt. 1850.

"When the Sixty-sixth was disbanded," says Sir Charles Napier, "the mutiny ceased entirely. Why? The Brahmins saw that the Goorkhas, another race, could be brought into the ranks of the Company's Army—a race dreaded, as more warlike than their own. Their religious combination was by that one stroke rendered abortive." But, far other causes than this helped to subdue the spirit of disaffection which was then ripening in the Punjab. The Sepoys had struck for higher allowances than those which had been granted to them by the strict letter of the Regulations; but Napier thought, that however unsoldierly, however culpable their conduct might be,

* An opportune blow from Macdonald's sword appears to have caused the gate to be opened. See statement published by Sir H. Lawrence in *Calcutta Review*, vol. xxii.

1850. some grounds of dissatisfaction existed. The change, which the Sepoys resented, was declared by the Chief to be "impolitic and unjust;" and, pending a reference to Government, orders were issued for the payment of compensation to the troops,—on a higher scale than that sanctioned by the latest regulations.*

Dalhousie and Napier.

Then arose that memorable conflict between Napier and Dalhousie, which ended in the resignation by the former of an office which many had predicted that he could not long continue to hold. Both were men of imperious temper, and a collision between them was, from the first, clearly foreseen. When the Military Chief took upon himself to readjust the allowances of the troops in the Punjab, the Civil Go-

* The bare statement in the text will suffice for the general reader, but not, perhaps, for the professional one. It may be stated, therefore, that it had been for many years the rule of the Indian Government, whenever the prices of the common articles of consumption used by the Native soldiery exceeded a certain fixed price, to grant them compensation proportionate to the additional cost of supplies. This bounty seems first to have been bestowed in the year 1821 on the Native troops serving in the Western Provinces, and was limited to the single article of ottah, or flour. Whenever ottah was selling at less than fifteen seers (or thirty pounds) the rupee, a proportionate compensation was granted. But, subsequently, in 1844, the application of this order was extended by Lord Ellenborough, and compensation also was granted to the Native troops serving in Scinde, when certain minor articles of consumption were selling at a high price. In the following year a new order relative to this same subject of compensation-money was issued by Lord Hardinge, who had by this time succeeded to the government. Instead of granting a separate money-compensation for each particular high-priced article of consumption, all the several articles were massed, and some being cheaper than elsewhere, a general average was struck. It was then officially announced that thenceforth compensation would be granted to the Sepoys "whenever the price of provisions, forming the Native soldier's diet, should exceed 3 rupees and 8 annas, the aggregate of the rates for the several articles laid down in the General Orders of the 26th of February, 1844." Whenever, in other words, the Sepoy was unable to obtain his daily rations at a cost of 3 rupees 8 annas a month (which cost was calculated in accordance with the aggregate fixed rates of the prices of provisions, beyond which compensation, under the old regulations, was granted for each article), the excess was to be defrayed by the Government. The regulation of 1845 was not so favourable to the troops as that of 1844, and Sir Charles Napier, believing that the application of the former rule to the troops in the Punjab was a mistake, directed the regulation of 1844 again to be brought into force.

vernor was at sea beyond the reach of an official reference. He returned to find what had been done, and he resented such an encroachment upon the prerogative of the Government. Napier had justified the exercise of an authority not constitutionally belonging to his office, by the assertion that the danger was pressing, and that action, in such an emergency, did not admit delay. Dalhousie denied the premises; he insisted that there had been no danger. "I cannot sufficiently express," he wrote, in an elaborate Minute on Napier's proceedings, "the astonishment with which I read, on the 26th of May, the intimation then made to the Government by the Commander-in-Chief, that in the month of January last a mutinous spirit pervaded the army in the Punjab, and that insubordination had risen so high and spread so wide, as to impress his Excellency with the belief that the Government of the country was placed at that time in a position of 'great peril.' I have carefully weighed the statements which his Excellency has advanced. I have examined anew the records that bear on the state of public affairs at that period, and I have well reflected upon all that has passed. While I do not seek to question in any way the sincerity of the convictions by which Sir Charles Napier has been led to declare that the army was in mutiny and the empire in danger, I, on my part, am bound to say that my examination and reflection have not lessened in any degree the incredulity with which I first read the statements to which I have referred." "There is no justification," continued his Lordship, "for the cry that India was in danger. Free from all threat of hostilities from without, and secure, through the submission of its new subjects, from insurrection within, the safety of India has never for one moment 1850.

1850 been imperilled by the partial insubordination in the ranks of its army. I have confronted the assertions of the Commander-in-Chief on this head with undisputed facts, and with the authority of recorded documents, and my convictions strengthened by the information which the Government commands, I desire to record my entire dissent from the statement that the army has been in mutiny, and the empire in danger."

This was, doubtless, the popular view of the matter; and it was readily accepted at the time. What amount of danger really existed was never known, and now never will be known. Whatever it may have been, it was tided over; and the quietude that followed this temporary explosion seemed to warrant the confidence which the Governor-General had expressed. But Napier held to his opinion with as much tenacity as Dalhousie. Nothing could shake the belief of the old soldier that the exceptional course he had adopted was justified by the exceptional circumstances of the times. Still he knew the duty of obedience; he knew that in a conflict between two authorities the lower must yield to the higher, and that he had no right to complain if the latter asserted the power vested in him by the Law. "And I do not complain," he emphatically added. But, strong in his conviction of right, and master of himself, though not of the situation, he felt that he could retire with dignity from a position which he could not hold with profit to the State. And he did retire. On the 22nd of May, he addressed a letter to the Horse-Guards, requesting that the Duke of Wellington would obtain her gracious Majesty's permission for him to resign the chief command of the Indian Army. "And the more so," he added, "as being now nearly seventy years of age—during the last ten years of which I have gone through considerable fatigue of body and mind, especially during the last year—my health requires that relief from climate and business which public service in India does not admit." 1850.

But there is no blame, in such a case, to be recorded against the Governor-General. When an old and distinguished soldier—a warrior of high repute, and a man of consummate ability—deliberately declares that he regards the system under which he has been called upon to command an army as a system at once faulty and dangerous; that he conceives the power of the civil magistrate to be so absolute that the arm of the chief soldier is paralysed; and that, so enervated and emasculated by restrictions imposed upon him by law, he cannot wield the sword with honour to himself or advantage to the State, and that, therefore, he desires to lay it down, he utters words which, whether he be right or wrong in his estimate of what ought to be the just balance between the civil and the military power, are honest, manly, dignified words, and ought everywhere to be received with respect. Few men had a better right than Sir Charles Napier to criticise an Act of Parliament. He had a right to think that the law was a bad law; and he had a right to say that it was bad. But the law, whether good or bad, was not made by Lord Dalhousie, but by the British Parliament. It was Dalhousie's business to administer that law, and to maintain the authority vested in him by the Imperial Legislature. Of this Napier had no right to complain; and he declared that he did not complain. But the contest was on every account an unseemly and an unfortunate one. It was another and a culminating instance of that excessive centralisation which weakened the authority

1850 and degraded the character of the military arm, and taught the soldiery that the greatest chief whom England could send them was as much a subaltern of the civil governor as the youngest ensign on the Army List.

And it taught even more than this. It taught thinking men, not for the first time, that even the chief members of the Government were at war among themselves, and the lesson shook their faith in the stability of a power thus disunited, thus incoherent. "I am now sixty years of age," wrote an intelligent native official to Sir George Clerk. "I have heard three sayings repeated by wise men, and I myself have also found out, from my own experience, that the sovereignty of the British Government will not be overthrown save by the occurrence of three objectionable circumstances." And the first of these circumstances he thus stated: "Formerly the high, dignified Sahibs had no enmity among themselves, or at least the people of India never came to know that they had enmity. Now enmity exists among them, and it is as well seen as the sun at noonday that they calumniate and bear malice against each other."* Such conflicts of authority are keenly watched and volubly discussed; and a significance is attached to them out of all proportion to the importance with which amongst us like contentions are invested. The natives of India know that we are few; but they feel that union makes us many. Seen to be at discord among ourselves, we shrivel into our true proportions, and it is believed that our power is beginning to crumble and decay.

During the administration of Lord Ellenborough there had been disunion among the higher authorities, arising out of nearly similar causes. The unauthorised

* MS. Correspondence, translated from the Persian.

promises given by the Commander-in-Chief to the Native troops proceeding to Scinde had stirred the resentment of the Governor-General, and his grave displeasure was excited by the zealous indiscretions of the Madras Government. But he had studiously veiled from the public eye the differences that had arisen. There was nothing to which he was more keenly alive than to the necessity, especially in troubled times, of maintaining a show of union and co-operation in the high places of Government. It was his hard fate at last to be compelled, by the fiat of a higher power, to exhibit to the people of India, in his own person, the very spectacle which he had striven to conceal from them, and to declare, trumpet-tongued, that the English were vehemently contending among themselves. But so long as he exercised the supreme control he was careful not to reveal the local dissensions of the Government, lest he should weaken the authority it was so essential to uphold; and little even is now known of the strife that raged at the time, when the great difficulty of garrisoning Scinde was filling the minds of the rulers of the land. But the strife between Dalhousie and Napier was proclaimed, almost as it were by beat of drum, in all the Lines and Bazaars of the country; and all men knew that the English, who used so to cling to one another, that it seemed that they thought with one strong brain and struck with one strong arm, were now wasting their vigour by warring among themselves, and in their disunion ceasing to be formidable. 1850.

This was apparent to all men's eyes; but the Sepoy had his own particular lesson to learn, and did not neglect it. How it happened that the bitter experience which the English Government had gained, on the annexation of Scinde, made no impression upon

1850. the minds of those whose duty it was to provide against the recurrence of similar disasters, it is impossible to explain. All we know is, that five years after a misunderstanding between the Government and the Army with respect to the rates of pay and allowance to be disbursed to the Sepoy, in a newly-acquired country, had driven into mutiny a large number of Native regiments, and greatly perplexed the rulers of the day, a similar conjuncture arose, and there was a similar misunderstanding, with similar results.* The Sepoy had not learnt to reconcile himself to the British theory of Annexation, and so he resented it in the Punjab as he had before resented it in Scinde. In the latter country the excitement was far greater, and the danger more serious, than in the former; but in both there was an outburst on the one side, and a concession on the other. That was given to the mutinous soldier, not without loss of character by Government, which might before have been given to the loyal one with befitting dignity and grace. When the emergency arises, it is hard to say whether there be greater evil in concession or in resistance. Napier thought the

* This uncertainty with respect to the pay and allowances of different branches and different ranks of the Indian Army was emphatically commented upon by Sir Henry Lawrence in an article bearing his name in the *Calcutta Review:* "Of all the wants of the Army, perhaps the greatest want is a simple pay-code, unmistakably showing the pay of every rank, in each branch, under all circumstances. At present there are not three officers in the Bengal Army who could, with certainty, tell what they and the people under them are entitled to in every position in which they are liable to be placed. The Audit-office seldom affords help. It is considered an enemy ready to take advantage of difficulties, not an umpire between man and man. During the last thirty years, I have seen much hardship on officers in matters of accounts, and of the several instances of discontent that I have witnessed in the Native Army, all were more or less connected with pay, and in almost every instance the men only asked for what they were by existing rules entitled to. Half a sheet of paper ought to show every soldier his rate of pay, by sea, by land, on leave, on the staff, in hospital, on duty, &c. There ought to be no doubt on the matter. At present there is great doubt, though there are volumes of Pay and Audit Regulations."

one thing, Dalhousie thought the other; and each 1850
had strong argument on his side. But both must have bitterly regretted that the contingency was ever suffered to arise, that no one in authority, warned by the lessons of the Past, had learnt to look at the consequences of Annexation with a Sepoy's eyes, and anticipated, by small concessions, the not irrational expectations which, at a later stage developing into demands, had all the force and significance of mutiny. Had this been done; had the Sepoy been told that in consideration of increased distance from home, and other circumstances rendering service in Scinde and the Punjab more irksome to him than in our older provinces, certain especial advantages would be conferred upon him—advantages which might have been bestowed at small cost to the State—he would have received the boon with gratitude, and applauded the justice of his masters; but after he had struck for it, he saw not their justice, but their fear, in the concession, and he hugged the feeling of power, which lessons such as these could not fail to engender.

CHAPTER V

CHARACTER OF THE BENGAL SEPOY—CONFLICTING OPINIONS—CASTE—THE SENIORITY SYSTEM—THE OFFICERING OF THE ARMY—REGULAR AND IRREGULAR REGIMENTS—WANT OF EUROPEANS—THE CRIMEAN WAR—INDIAN PUBLIC OPINION—SUMMARY OF DETERIORATING INFLUENCES.

1851-56. AFTER this, there was again a season of quiet. The remaining years of Lord Dalhousie's administration passed away without any further military outbreaks to disturb his rooted conviction of the fidelity of the Sepoy. There were not wanting those who declared that there was an ineradicable taint in the constitution of the Bengal Army, that it was rotten to the very core. But the angry controversies which arose —the solemn warnings on the one side, and the indignant denials on the other—proved nothing more than that among men, entitled to speak with authority on the subject, there were vast diversities of opinion. Much of this was attributed to class prejudices and professional jealousies. One voice, very loud and very earnest, pealing from the West, sustained for years a continual remonstrance against the laxities of the Bengal System. But Bengal resented the outrage. A genuine man, above all pettiness, John Jacob, was declared to be the exponent only of small Presidential envyings and heart-burnings. The voice of Truth was proclaimed to be the voice of

Bombay. And when officers of the Bengal Army wrote, as some did most wisely, of the evil symptoms which were manifesting themselves, and of the dangers which appeared to be looming in the distance, they were denounced as defilers of their own nest, and as feeble-minded alarmists, to whose utterances no heed should be given. There was a general unwillingness to believe in the decay of discipline throughout one of the finest armies of the world; and in the absence of any outward signs of mischief, we willingly consented not to look beneath the surface for the virus of undeveloped disease. 1851-56.

There is nothing that is strange, and little that is blamable in this. The Bengal Sepoy had evinced signs of a froward, petulant nature, and he had, on several occasions, broken out after a fashion which, viewed by European military eyes, is criminality of the deepest dye. But these aberrations were merely a few dark spots upon a century of good service. It was not right that rare exceptions of this kind should cancel in our minds all the noble acts of fidelity which were chronicled in the history of our empire. Nor was it to be forgotten that, in most instances, the criminality of the Sepoy had been the direct growth of some mismanagement on the part either of the officers whom he followed or the Government which he served. To have looked with suspicion on the Sepoy, because from time to time some component parts of our Army had done that, which the Armies of every Native State had done, with their whole accumulated strength, would have been equally unwise and unjust. For although it might be said that the examples, which those Native States afforded, ought to have taught us to beware of the destroying power of a lawless soldiery, the English were justified in be-

1851-56. lieving that there were special reasons why their own mercenaries should not tread in the footsteps of the Mahratta and Sikh Armies. They did not believe in the love of the Sepoy; but they believed in his fidelity to his Pay.

Character of the Sepoy.

Whilst it was natural, and indeed commendable, that the remembrance of all the good service which the Native soldiery had done for their English masters, should have sustained our confidence in them as a body, there was nothing in the individual character of the Sepoy to subvert it. Even his outbreaks of rebellion had recently partaken more of the naughtiness of the child than of the stern resolution of manhood. He had evinced a disposition, indeed, rather to injure himself than to injure others; and it was not easy for those who knew him to believe that he was capable of any violent and sanguinary excesses. His character was made up of inconsistencies, but the weaker and less dangerous qualities appeared to have the preponderance; and though we knew that they made him a very difficult person to manage, we did not think that they made him a dangerous one. From the time when, in the very infancy of the Sepoy Army, a Madras soldier cut down Mr. Haliburton, and was immediately put to death by his own comrades, to the day when Colin Mackenzie was well-nigh butchered at Bolarum by troopers of his own brigade, there had been ever and anon some murderous incidents to disfigure the Military History of our Indian Empire.* But outrages of this kind are common to all armies; and there was no reason to regard them in any other light than that of exceptional aberrations. It was not to

* See Williams's Bengal Army and Mackenzie's Narrative of the Mutiny at Bolarum; compare also section on the Sepoy Army in Sutherland's Sketches of the Native States of India.

be said that the Sepoy was a ruffian because he had done some ruffianly deeds. 1851-56.

He was, indeed, altogether a paradox. He was made up of inconsistencies and contradictions. In his character, qualities, so adverse as to be apparently irreconcilable with each other, met together and embraced. He was simple and yet designing; credulous and easily deceived by others, and yet obstinately tenacious of his own in-bred convictions; now docile as a child, and now hard and immovable in the stubbornness of his manhood. Abstemious and yet self-indulgent, calm and yet impetuous, gentle and yet cruel, he was indolent even to languor in his daily life, and yet capable of being roused to acts of the most desperate energy. Sometimes sportive, and sometimes sullen, he was easily elevated and easily depressed; but he was for the most part of a cheerful nature, and if you came suddenly upon him in the Lines you were more likely to see him with a broad grin upon his face than with any expression of moroseness or discontent. But light-hearted as was his general temperament, he would sometimes brood over imaginary wrongs, and when a delusion once entered his soul it clung to it with the subtle malevolence of an ineradicable poison.

And this, as we now understand the matter, was the most dangerous feature of his character. For his gentler, more genial qualities sparkled upon the surface and were readily appreciated, whilst all the harsher and more forbidding traits lay dark and disguised, and were not discernible in our ordinary intercourse with him. There was outwardly, indeed, very much to rivet the confidence of the European officer, and very little to disturb it. It is true that if we reasoned about it, it did not seem to be alto-

1851-56. gether reasonable to expect from the Sepoy any strong affection for the alien officer who had usurped all the high places of the Army, and who kept him down in the dead level of the dust. But Englishmen never reason about their position in the midst of a community of strangers; they take their popularity for granted, and look for homage as a thing of course. And that homage was yielded to the British officer, not for his own sake, for the Sepoy hated his colour and his creed, his unclean ways, and his domineering manners; but because he was an embodiment of Success. It was one of the many inconsistencies of which I have spoken, that though boastful and vain-glorious beyond all example, the Native soldier of India inwardly acknowledged that he owed to the English officer the aliment which fed his passion for glory and sustained his military pride. This, indeed, was the link that bound class to class, and resisted the dissolving power of many adverse influences. It was this that moved the Sepoy to light up the tomb of his old commanding officer; it was this that moved the veteran to salute the picture of the General under whom he had fought. But there was a show also of other and gentler feelings, and there were instances of strong personal attachment, of unsurpassed fidelity and devotion, manifested in acts of charity and love. You might see the Sepoy of many fights, watchful and tender as a woman, beside the sick-bed of the English officer, or playing with the pale-faced children beneath the verandah of his captain's bungalow. There was not an English gentlewoman in the country who did not feel measureless security in the thought that a guard of Sepoys watched her house, or who would not have travelled, under such an escort, across the whole length and breadth of the land. What was lurking beneath the fair surface we knew not. We saw only the softer side of the Sepoy's nature; and there was nothing to make us believe that there was danger in the confidence which we reposed in those outward signs of attachment to our rule. 1851-56.

Defects in the System.

But whilst cherishing this not unreasonable confidence in the general good character of the Sepoy, the British Government might still have suffered some doubts and misgivings to arise when they looked into the details of the System. They might, it has been urged, have believed in the soundness of the whole, but admitted the defectiveness of parts, and addressed themselves earnestly and deliberately to the details of the great work of Army Reform. Instead of boasting that the condition of the Native soldier left nothing to be desired, Lord Dalhousie, it is said, ought to have looked beneath the surface, to have probed all the vices of the existing system, and to have striven with all his might to eradicate them. Information was not wanting. "Officers of experience" were at all times ready to tell him what it behoved him to do. But in the multitude of counsellors there was inextricable confusion. As with the whole, so with the parts. The forty years' experience of one greybeard belied the forty years' experience of another. And when the responsible ruler had been almost persuaded to see a blot and to promise to erase it, another adviser came, straightway declared it to be a beauty, and besought him to leave it as it was. Thus distracted by the conflicting judgments of the best military critics, Dalhousie did, as others had done before him; he admitted that if he had then for the first time to construct a Native Army it would in some respects differ from that

1851-56. which he saw before him, the growth not of systems and theories but of circumstances; but that as it had grown up, so on the whole it was better to leave it, as Change is sometimes dangerous, and almost always misunderstood.

That, indeed, there was no more difficult question to understand than that of the Sepoy Army, was a fact which must have been continually forced upon the mind of the Governor-General, by the discordant opinions which were pronounced on points vitally affecting its fidelity and efficiency. Even on the great question of Caste, men differed. Some said it was desirable that our Native regiments should be composed mainly of high-caste men; because in such men were combined many of the best qualities, moral and physical, which contribute to the formation of an accomplished soldier. The high-caste man had a bolder spirit, a purer professional pride, a finer frame, and a more military bearing, than his countryman of lower social rank. Other authorities contended that the Native soldiery should be enlisted indiscriminately, that no account should be taken of Caste distinctions, and that the smaller the proportion of Brahmins and Rajpoots in the service the better for the discipline of the Army.* Comparisons were drawn between the Bengal and the Bombay Armies. There was a strong and not unnatural prejudice in favour of the Bengal Sepoy; for he was a fine, noble-looking fellow, and in comparison with his comrades from the Southern and Western Presidencies, was said to be quite a gentleman; but there were those who alleged that he was more a gentleman than a soldier; and it was urged that the normal state of the Bengal Army was Mutiny, because in an Army so constituted Caste was ever

Caste.

* For the statistics of Caste in the Sepoy Army, see Appendix.

stronger than Discipline; and the social institutions of the Sepoy domineered over the necessities of the State. 1851-56.

It was contended, for this reason, that the Bengal Army required a larger infusion of low-caste men. But it was alleged, on the other hand, that this very mixture of castes tended to destroy the discipline of which it was proposed to make it the preservative; for that military rank was held to be nothing in comparison with Brahminical Elevation, and that the Sepoy was often the "master of the officer."* To this it was replied that the presumption of Caste was favoured and fostered by the weakness and indulgence of the officers of the Bengal Army; that, in the armies of Madras and Bombay, Caste had found its level; that it had neither been antagonistic to good service, nor injurious to internal discipline; that high-caste men in those armies did cheerfully what they refused to do in Bengal, and that low-caste native officers met with all the respect from their social superiors due to their superior military rank. It was asserted, indeed, that Brahminism was arrogant and exacting in Bengal, because it saw that it could play upon the fears of the English officers. To this it was replied, that disregard Caste as we might, we could never induce the natives to disregard it. And then again the rejoinder was, that in the other Presidencies we had taught them to disregard it, why, then, might not the same lesson be taught in Bengal? The answer to this was, that men will often do in other countries what they cannot be persuaded to do

* "I cannot conceive the possibility of maintaining discipline in a corps where a low-caste non-commissioned officer will, when he meets off duty a Brahmin Sepoy, crouch down to him with his forehead on the ground. I have seen this done. The Sepoy thus treated is the master of the officer."—*Evidence of Major-General Birch.*

1851-56. in their own; that high-caste Hindostanees enlisting into the Bombay or Madras Armies were, to a great extent, cut off from the brotherhood, that they were greatly outnumbered in their several regiments, that it was convenient to conform to the custom of the country, and that what he did in a foreign country among strangers was little known at home. In a word, when he took service in the Bombay Army, he did what was done in Bombay; just as among ourselves, men who, fearful of losing caste, would on no account be seen to enter a London hell, think nothing of spending whole days in the gambling-rooms of Homburg or Baden-Baden.

Nationalities. Of a kindred nature was the question hotly discussed, whether it were wiser to compose each regiment of men of the same race, or to mix up different races in the same corps. On the one hand, it was alleged that the fusion of different nationalities had a tendency to keep internal combinations in check; but that if men of one tribe were formed into separate regiments; if we had Patan regiments and Goorkha regiments, Sikh regiments and Mahratta regiments, facilities for mutinous combinations would be greatly increased. On the other hand, it was contended that the fusion of different tribes and castes in the several regiments encouraged external combinations by imparting common interests to the whole Army; that if safety were to be sought in the antagonism of nationalities, it was more likely to be attained by keeping them apart than by fusing them into a heterogeneous mass; that it was easier to keep one regiment from following the example of another composed of different materials, raised and stationed in a different part of the country, than to keep one half of a regiment from following the example of the other; easier to make men fight against those whom they had never seen, than against those with whom they had long lived, if not in brotherhood of caste, at least in brotherhood of service. 1851-56.

Local and General Service.

Again, men discussed, with reference to this question of combination, the relative advantages and disadvantages of localisation and distribution. Whilst some contended that the different Sepoy regiments should serve respectively only in certain parts of the country, except under any peculiar exigencies of war —in other words, that they should be assimilated as much as possible to a sort of local militia—others were in favour of the existing system, under which there were periodical reliefs, and regiments marched from one station to another, often many hundreds of miles apart. On the one hand it was argued that there was much danger in the local influence which would be acquired by men long resident in the same place, and that intrigues and plots, rendered perilous by the fusion of the civil and military classes, might result from this localisation; and, on the other, it was urged that it was far more dangerous to suffer the Sepoy regiments to become extensively acquainted with each other, for the men to form friendships, and therefore to have correspondents in other corps, and thus to afford them the means, in times of excitement, of forming extensive combinations, and spreading, as it were, a network of conspiracy over the whole face of the country. Thus, again, men of wisdom and experience neutralised one another's judgments, and from amongst so many conflicting opinions it was impossible to evolve the truth.

Families.

It was a question also much debated whether the fidelity and efficiency of the Sepoy were best maintained by keeping him apart from his family, or by

1851-56. suffering the wives, the children, and the dependents of the soldier to attach themselves to his regiment, and to follow his fortunes. The former was the system in the Bengal Army; the latter, in the Army of Madras, and partially in that of Bombay. Each system had its advocates; each its special advantages. The Bengal Sepoy visited his family at stated times, and remitted to them a large part of his pay. If he failed to do this he was a marked man in his regiment; and, it was said, that the knowledge that if he failed in his duty as a soldier, a report of his misconduct would surely reach his native village, and that his face would be blackened before his kindred, kept him in the strict path of his duty. The presence of the Family led to much inconvenience and embarrassment, and the necessity of moving it from one station to another, when the regiments were relieved, strained the scanty resources of the Sepoy, and developed grievances out of which mutiny might arise.* It was said, indeed, that there was "hardly a Native regiment in the Bengal Army in which the twenty drummers, who were Christians, and had their families with them, did not cause more trouble to their officers than the whole eight hundred Sepoys."† On the other hand, it was urged that the presence of the Family afforded the best guarantee for the fidelity and good conduct of the Sepoy. His children were hostages in our hands; the honour of his women was in our keeping. These were held to be safeguards against mutiny and massacre. It was urged, too, that the system tended more to keep them, as a race, apart from the general mass of their countrymen; that the ties which bound them to the country were

* See the case of the Sixth Madras Cavalry, *ante*, page 291.

† Sleeman on the Spirit of Discipline in the Native Army.

thus weakened, and their interests more indissolubly associated with the State. They were less representative men than their brethren of the Bengal Army, and more a part of the machinery of Government. And so each system had its advocates, and each was left to work itself out and develop its own results. 1851-56.

Great, also, was the difference of opinion with respect to Promotion. Some said that the Bengal Army was destroyed by the Seniority system, which gave to every Sepoy in the service an equal chance of rising to the rank of a Commissioned Officer.* Others maintained that this was the very sheet-anchor which enabled it to resist all adverse influences. Strong arguments were adduced, and great names were quoted upon both sides. It was said that under such a system there was no incentive to exertion; that the men were independent of their officers, that they had no motive to earn the good opinion of their superiors, that it was enough for them to drowse through a certain number of years of service, to slide quietly into a commission, and then to end their military lives in a state of senile somnolence and apathy. The Native officers of the Bengal Army were, therefore, for the most part, respectable, worn-out, feeble-minded old men, with no influence in their regiments, and no desire beyond that of saving themselves as much trouble as possible, and keeping things as quiet as they could. On the other hand, it was alleged that the seniority system was the very prop and support of the Sepoy service; that all men were happy and contented, and had some aliment of hope, so long as they felt that nothing but their own misconduct could deprive them of the right of succession to the highest grades of the Promotion.

* To every regiment of Native infantry were attached one Soubahdar-major, ten Soubahdars, and ten Jemadars.

1851-56. Native Army. It was said that to pass over a man at the head of the list, and to give promotion to others of shorter service, would be to flood the regiments with desperate malcontents, or else with sullen, broken-spirited idlers. Whilst Henry Lawrence and John Jacob were descanting on the evil of filling the commissioned ranks of the Sepoy Army with "poor old wretches, feeble in body and imbecile in mind,"* Charles Napier was peremptorily commanding that "the fullest attention and consideration should invariably be given to the claim of seniority in every grade" of the Native Army, and William Sleeman was asserting, not less emphatically, in his published writings, that "though we might have in every regiment a few smarter Native officers, by disregarding the rule of promotion than by adhering to it, we should, in the diminution of good feeling towards the European officers and the Government, lose a thousand times more than we gained."† What wonder, then, that Governor-General after Governor-General was perplexed and bewildered, and left things, when he passed away from the scene, as he found them on his first arrival.

* *Views and Opinions of General John Jacob*, p. 120; compare also Sir Henry Lawrence's *Essays, Military and Political*, p. 24 *et seq.*

† Sleeman relates, that "an old Soubahdar, who had been at the taking of the Isle of France, mentioned that when he was the senior Jemadar of his regiment, and a vacancy had occurred to bring him in as Soubahdar, he was sent for by his commanding officer, and told that by orders from Head-Quarters he was to be passed over, on account of his advanced age and supposed infirmity. 'I felt,' said the old man, 'as if I had been struck by lightning, *and fell down dead.* The Colonel was a good man, and had seen much service. He had me taken into the open air, and when I recovered he told me that he would write to the Commander-in-Chief and represent my case. He did so immediately, and I was promoted, and I have since done my duty as Soubahdar for ten years.'" But, it may be asked, *how?* It must be borne in mind, too, that Sleeman speaks here of the effect of supersession under a Seniority system. Under a system of selection such results would not be apparent, because there would not be the same disgrace in being passed over.

1851-56.

European Officers.

Then, again, there were wide diversities of opinion with respect to the European officering of regiments. There were those who contended for the Irregular and those who were loud in their praises of the Regular system; some who thought it better to attach to each regiment a few select officers, as in the old times, giving them some power and authority over their men; and others who believed it to be wiser to officer the regiments after the later English system, like regiments of the Line, with a large available surplus for purposes of the General Staff, and to leave all the centralised power and authority in the hands of the Adjutant-General of the Army.* There was a continual cry, not always, it must be admitted, of the most unselfish character, for "more officers;" and yet it was plain that the Irregular regiments, to which only three or four picked officers were attached, were in a perfect state of discipline in peace, and capable of performing admirable service in war. It was said that in action the Sepoys, losing their officers, killed or carried wounded to the rear, lost heart, and were soon panic-struck; and that if officers were so few, this contingency must often happen. To this, however, it was replied, that if the Native officers were of the right class, they would keep their men together, and still do good service; but if they were worn-out imbeciles, or over-corpulent and scant of breath, of course disorder and ruin must follow the fall of the English officers. Then, hearing this, the disputant on the other side would triumphantly ask how many years' purchase our empire in India were worth, if our Native officers were as efficient as

* A regiment of Native Infantry in March, 1856, was officered by 1 colonel, 1 lieutenant-colonel, 1 major, 6 captains, 10 lieutenants, and 5 ensigns. A few months afterwards another captain and another lieutenant were added to each regiment.

1851-56. ourselves. It was often argued, indeed, that our instructions might some day return to plague the inventor; that to make men qualified to lead our battalions to battle against our enemies is to qualify them to command troops to fight against ourselves. But there were others, and chief among them Henry Lawrence, who, taking a larger and more liberal view of the question, contended that it was sound policy to give to every man, European and Native, a motive for exertion; who declared that it was one of the crying wants of our system that it afforded no outlet for the energies of Native soldiers of superior courage and ability, and urged that we could not expect to have an efficient Native Army so long as we rigidly maintained in it the theory of the Dead Level, and purposely excluded every possible inducement to superior exertion.

Nor less curious were the fundamental diversities of opinion which manifested themselves, when thinking men began to consider whether the English in India carried into their daily lives too much or too little of their nationality. It was asserted on the one side that the English officer was too stiff-necked and exclusive, that he dwelt apart too much, and subdued himself too little to surrounding influences; and on the other side, that he fell too rapidly into Oriental habits, and soon ceased to be, what it should have been his ambition to remain to the last, a model of an English Gentleman. It was urged by some that increased facilities of intercourse with Europe rendered men more dissatisfied with the ordinary environments of Eastern life and professional duty, whilst others declared that one of the most serious defects in the Indian Military System was the difficulty with which the English officer obtained furlough to Europe.* The stringency of the Furlough Regulations had, however, been greatly relaxed during the administration of Lord Dalhousie, and the establishment of regular steam-communication between the two countries had made the new rules practical realities. But whatsoever increased intercourse with Europe may have done to promote the application of Western science to our Indian Military System, it did not improve the regimental officer. It was contended that he commonly returned to his duty with increased distaste for cantonment life; and that he obeyed the mandate, "Let it be the fashion to be English," by suffering a still greater estrangement to grow up between him and the Native soldier. 1851-56.

Indeed, there was scarcely a single point, in the whole wide range of topics connected with the great subject of the efficiency of the Native Indian Army, which did not raise a doubt and suggest a controversy. And there was so much of demonstrable truth in the assertions, and so much cogency in the arguments adduced, on both sides, that in the eyes of the looker-on it was commonly a drawn battle between the two contending parties; and so, as it was the easier and perhaps the safer course to leave things as they were, the changes which Army Reformers so earnestly advocated were practically rejected, and we clung to evils which had grown up in the system rather than we would incur the risk of instituting others of our own.

Intermixture of European Troops.

But perplexing as were these practical details, there was nothing so difficult of solution as the great doubt which arose as to the amount of confidence in the Sepoy Army which it was expedient outwardly to manifest. It was said, upon the one hand, that any

* *Views and Opinions of Brigadier-General John Jacob.*

1851-56. diminution of our confidence would be fatal to our rule, and, on the other, that our confidence was leading us onward to destruction. Some said that the Native Army should be narrowly watched, and held in control by sufficient bodies of European soldiery; others contended that we could commit no more fatal mistake than that of betraying the least suspicion of the Sepoy, and suggesting even a remote possibility of one part of our Army ever being thrown into antagonism to the other. This controversy was half a century old. When, after the Massacre of Vellore, the Madras Government urged upon the Supreme Authority in Bengal the expediency of sending some reinforcements of European troops to the Coast, the latter refused to respond to the call, on the ground that such a movement would betray a general want of confidence in the Native Army, and might drive regiments still loyal into rebellion under an impulse of fear. There was force in this argument, which will be readily appreciated by all who understand the character of the Sepoy Army; and its cogency was not diminished by the fact put forth by the Madras Government that the European troops under their command were fewer by two thousand men than they had been before the recent large extension of territory. But a great lesson was to be learnt from the embarrassment which then arose; a lesson which ought to have been taken to the hearts of our rulers from one generation to another. It was then clearly revealed, not merely that "prevention is better than cure," but that prevention may be possible when cure is not; that we may hold danger in check by quietly anticipating it, but that, when it has arisen, the measures, to which we might have resorted before the fact, cannot be pursued, after it, without increasing the evil. If anything should teach us the wisdom of never suffering our European force, even in the most tranquil times, to decline below what we may call "the athletic standard," it is the fact that, when the times cease to be tranquil, we cannot suddenly raise it to that standard without exciting alarm and creating danger. 1851-56.

But this lesson was not learnt. Or, if Indian statesmen ever took it to their hearts, it was remorselessly repudiated in the Councils of the English nation. Other considerations than those of the actual requirements of our Indian Empire were suffered to determine the amount of European strength to be maintained on the Company's establishment. Stated in round numbers, it may be said that the normal state of things, for some years, had been that of an Army of three hundred thousand men, of which forty thousand were European troops.* Of these, roughly calculated, about one-third were the local European troops of the Company, raised exclusively for Indian service; the rest were the men of royal regiments, Horse and Foot, periodically relieved according to the will of the Imperial Government, but paid out of the Revenues of India. In the five years preceding the departure of Lord Dalhousie from India, the strength of the Company's European troops had been somewhat increased, but the force which England lent to India was considerably reduced. In 1852, there were twenty-nine Royal regiments in the three Presidencies of India, mustering twenty-eight thousand men; in 1856, there were twenty-four Royal regiments, mustering twenty-three thousand men. During those five years there had been a vast extension of empire; but the aggregate European strength was lower in

* For the details of the Native Army of India, see Tables in Appendix.

1851-56. 1856 than in 1852 by nearly three thousand men. Between those two dates England had been engaged in a great war, and she wanted her troops for European service.

The Crimean War. We deceive ourselves, when we think that European politics make no impression on the Indian Public. The impression may be very vague and indistinct; but ignorance is a magnifier of high power, and there are never wanting a few designing men, with clearer knowledge of the real state of things, to work upon the haziness of popular conceptions, and to turn a little grain of truth to account in generating a harvest of lies. That a number of very preposterous stories were industriously circulated, and greedily swallowed, during the Crimean war, and that these stories all pointed to the downfal of the British power, is not to be doubted. It was freely declared that Russia had conquered and annexed England, and that Queen Victoria had fled and taken refuge with the Governor-General of India. The fact that the war was with Russia gave increased significance to these rumours; for there had long been a chronic belief that the Russlogue would some day or other contend with us for the mastery of India; that, coming down in immense hordes from the North, and carrying with them the intervening Mahomedan States, they would sweep us, broken and humbled, into the sea. And it required no great acuteness to perceive that if a popular insurrection in India were ever to be successful, it was when the military resources of the empire were absorbed by a great European war. It is at such times as these, therefore, when there is always some disturbance of the public mind, that especial care should be taken to keep the European strength in India up to the right athletic standard. But, in these very times, the dependency is called upon to aid the empire, and her European regiments are reluctantly given up at the critical moment when she most desires to retain them. "The idea broached in Parliament," said a Native gentleman, "of drawing troops from India for the Crimean War, took intelligent natives of India by surprise." They saw plainly the folly of thus revealing our weakness to the subject races; for we could not more loudly proclaim the inadequacy of our resources than by denuding ourselves in one quarter of the world in order that we might clothe ourselves more sufficiently in another. 1851-56.

Nor was it this alone that, during the last years of Lord Dalhousie's administration, "took intelligent natives of India by surprise." They saw us increasing our territory, in all directions, without increasing our European force. There were those who argued that territorial increase did not necessarily demand increased means of defence, as it might be a change, not an extension of frontier; indeed, that the consolidation of our empire, by diminishing the numbers of our enemies, ought rather to be regarded as a reason for the diminution of our military strength. And this, in respect to our external enemies, it has already been observed, was not untrue.* But our dangers were from within, not from without; and it was forgotten that false friends might be more dangerous than open enemies. The English in India were, indeed, continually in a state of siege, and the conquest of their external enemies increased the perils of their position, for it deprived them of those safety-valves which had often before arrested a ruinous explosion. We were far too sanguine in our estimates of the results of conquest or annexation. We saw everything as we wished

* *Ante*, p. 276.

1851-56. to see it. We saw contentment in submission, loyalty in quiescence; and took our estimate of national sentiment from the feelings of a few interested individuals who were making money by the change. But "intelligent natives" seeing clearly our delusion, knowing that we believed a lie, wondered greatly at our want of wisdom in suffering vast tracts of territory, perhaps only recently brought under British rule, to lie naked and defenceless, without even a detachment of English fighting men to guard the lives of the new masters of the country. And little as we gave them credit for sagacity in such matters, they touched the very kernel of our danger with a needle's point, and predicted that our confidence would destroy us.

It was fortunate that, when we conquered the Punjab, it was impossible to forget that Afghanistan, still festering with animosities and resentments born of the recent invasion, lay contiguous to the frontier of our new province. It was fortunate, too, that Henry Lawrence, being a man of a quick imagination, could feel as a Sikh chief or a Sikh soldier would feel under the new yoke of the Feringhee, and could therefore believe that we were not welcomed as deliverers from one end of the country to the other. But it was not fortunate that the obvious necessity of garrisoning this frontier Province with a strong European force should have been practically regarded as a reason for denuding all the rest of India of English troops. Acting in accordance with the old traditions, that the only danger with which our position in India is threatened, is danger coming from the North-West, we massed a large body of Europeans in the Punjab, and scattered, at wide intervals, the few remaining regiments at our disposal over other parts of our extended dominions. Thus we visibly became more and more dependent on our Native Army; and it needed only the declaration of weakness made, when England called on India for regiments to take part in the Crimean war, to assure "intelligent natives" that the boasted resources of England were wholly insufficient to meet the demands made upon them from different quarters, and that we could only confront danger in one part of the world by exposing ourselves to it in another.* 1851-56.

Effects of the Annexation of Oude.

And this impression was strengthened by the fact that when Oude was annexed to our British territories, although the province was thereby filled with the disbanded soldiery of the destroyed Native Government, and with a dangerous race of discontented nobles, whom the revolution had stripped of their privileges and despoiled of their wealth, the English appeared not to possess the means of garrisoning with European troops the country which they had thus seized. As Oude was not a frontier province, there was no necessity to mass troops there, as in the Punjab, for purposes of external defence; and the English, emboldened by success, were stronger than ever in their national egotism, and believed that, as they could not be regarded in Oude in any other light than that of deliverers, there was small need to make provision against the possibility of internal disturbance. They left the province, therefore, after annexation had been proclaimed, with only a small handful of European fighting men; and "intelligent natives" were again surprised to see that the English gentlemen were carrying out their new scheme of administration, to the ruin of almost every pre-existing interest

* It has been alleged, too, that the subscriptions raised towards the support of the Patriotic Fund, during the Crimean War, impressed intelligent natives with the belief that we were as short of money as we were of men.

1851-56. in the country, with as much confidence as if every district of Oude were bristling with British bayonets. They saw, too, that the English had absorbed one of the last remaining Mahomedan States of India; and they felt that not only would this prodigious appropriation be regarded from one end of India to the other as the precursor of new seizures, and that it would thus greatly disturb the public mind, but that the very class of men on whom we appeared to rely for the continued security of our position were, of all others, most likely to resent this act of aggression.

For the annexation of Oude had some results injurious to the Sepoy. A very large portion of the Bengal Army was drawn from that province. In every village were the families of men who wore the uniform and bore the arms of the English. Being for the most part high-caste Hindoos, they might not have regarded the peaceful revolution by which a Mahomedan monarchy was destroyed with any strong feelings of national resentment; and it is certain that this extension of territory was not provocative of the feelings of aversion and alarm with which they regarded those other seizures which had sent them to rot in the charnel-house of Scinde, or to perish in exile on the frontiers of Afghanistan. Their griefs were of another kind. The old state of things had suited them better. They had little sympathy, perhaps, with Wajid Ali, and service in Oude brought them nearer to their homes. But so long as it was a foreign province, they derived certain special privileges and advantages from their position as the servants of the Company, and increased importance in the eyes of the people of the province. They had, indeed, been a favoured race, and as such the Sepoy families had held up their heads above those of their countrymen who had no such bonds of privilege and protection to unite them to the Paramount State. "The Sepoy," wrote the man who had studied the character and probed the feelings of the Native more deeply and philosophically perhaps than any of his contemporaries—"the Sepoy is not the man of consequence he was. He dislikes annexations; among other reasons, because each new province added to the Empire widens his sphere of service, and at the same time decreases our foreign enemies and thereby the Sepoy's importance. . . . . The other day, an Oude Sepoy of the Bombay Cavalry at Neemuch, being asked if he liked annexation, replied, 'No; I used to be a great man when I went home. The best in my village rose as I approached. Now the lowest puff their pipes in my face.' "* Under the all-prevailing lawlessness and misrule, which had so long overridden the province, the English Sepoy, whatever might be the wrongs of others, was always sure of a full measure of justice on appeal to the British Resident. If he himself were not, some member of his family was, a small yeoman, with certain rights in the land—rights which commonly among his countrymen were as much a source of trouble as a source of pride—and in all the disputes and contentions in which these interests involved him, he had the protection and assistance of the Resident, and right or wrong carried his point. In the abstract it was, doubtless, an evil state of things, for the Sepoys' 1851-56.

* Sir Henry Lawrence to Lord Canning, MS. Correspondence. I may give here in a note the words omitted in the text, as bearing, though not immediately, upon the Oude question, and upon the general subject of annexation: "Ten years ago, a Sepoy in the Punjab asked an officer what we would do without them. Another said, 'Now you have got the Punjab, you will reduce the Army.' A third remarked, when he heard that Scinde was to be joined to the Bengal Presidency, 'Perhaps there will be an order to join London to Bengal.'"

1851-56. privileges were often used as instruments of oppression, and were sometimes counterfeited with the help of an old regimental jacket and pair of boots, by men who had never gone right-face to the word of command. But for this very reason they were dearly valued; and when the Sepoys were thus brought down by annexation to the dead level of British subjects, when the Residency ceased to be, and all men were equally under the protection of the Commissioner, the Sepoy families, like all the other privileged classes in Oude, learnt what the revolution had cost them, and, wide apart as their several grievances lay from each other, they joined hands with other sufferers over a common grief.

Summary of deteriorating influences.

Looking, then, at the condition of the Native Army of India, and especially at the state of the Bengal regiments, as it was in the spring of 1856, we see that a series of adverse circumstances, culminating in the annexation of Oude, some influencing him from without and some from within, had weakened the attachment of the Sepoy to his colours. We see that, whilst the bonds of internal discipline were being relaxed, external events, directly or indirectly affecting his position, were exciting within him animosities and discontents. We see that as he grew less faithful and obedient, he grew also more presuming; that whilst he was less under the control of his officers and the dominion of the State, he was more sensible of the extent to which we were dependent upon his fidelity, and therefore more capricious and exacting. He had been neglected on the one hand, and pampered on the other. As a soldier, he had in many ways deteriorated, but he was not to be regarded only as a soldier. He was a representative man, the embodiment of feelings and opinions shared by large classes of his countrymen, and circumstances might one day render him their exponent. He had many opportunities of becoming acquainted with passing events and public opinion. He mixed in cantonments, or on the line of march, with men of different classes and different countries; he corresponded with friends at a distance; he heard all the gossip of the Bazaars, and he read, or heard others read, the strange mixture of truth and falsehood contained in the Native newspapers. He knew what were the measures of the British Government, sometimes even what were its intentions, and he interpreted their meanings, as men are wont to do, who, credulous and suspicious, see insidious designs and covert dangers in the most beneficent acts. He had not the faculty to conceive that the English were continually originating great changes for the good of the people; our theories of government were beyond his understanding, and as he had ceased to take counsel with his English officer, he was given over to strange delusions, and believed the most dangerous lies. 1851-56.

But in taking account of the effect produced upon the Sepoy's mind by the political and social measures of the British Government, we must not think only of the direct action of these measures—of the soldier's own reading of distant events, which might have had no bearing upon his daily happiness, and which, therefore, in his selfishness he might have been content to disregard. For he often read these things with other men's eyes, and discerned them with other men's understandings. If the political and social revolutions, of which I have written, did not affect him, they affected others, wiser in their generation, more astute,

1851-56. more designing, who put upon everything that we did the gloss best calculated to debauch the Sepoy's mind, and to prepare him, at a given signal, for an outburst of sudden madness. Childish, as he was, in his faith, there was nothing easier than to make him believe all kinds and conditions of fictions, not only wild and grotesque in themselves, but in violent contradiction of each other. He was as ready to believe that the extension of our territory would throw him out of employment, as that it would inflict upon him double work. He did not choose between these two extremes; he accepted both, and took the one or the other, as the humour pleased him. There were never wanting men to feed his imagination with the kind of aliment which pleased it best, and reason never came to his aid to purge him of the results of this gross feeding.

Many were the strange glosses which were given to the acts of the British Government; various were the ingenious fictions woven with the purpose of unsettling the minds and uprooting the fidelity of the Sepoy. But diverse as they were in many respects, there was a certain unity about them, for they all tended to persuade him that our measures were directed to one common end, the destruction of Caste, and the general introduction of Christianity into the land. If we annexed a province, it was to facilitate our proselytising operations, and to increase the number of our converts. Our resumption operations were instituted for the purpose of destroying all the religious endowments of the country. Our legislative enactments were all tending to the same result, the subversion of Hindooism and Mahomedanism. Our educational measures were so many direct assaults upon the religions of the country. Our penal system,

according to their showing, disguised a monstrous 1851-56.
attempt to annihilate caste, by compelling men of all denominations to feed together in the gaols. In the Lines of every regiment there were men eager to tell lies of this kind to the Sepoy, mingled with assurances that the time was coming when the Feringhees would be destroyed to a man; when a new empire would be established, and a new military system inaugurated, under which the high rank and the higher pay monopolised by the English would be transferred to the people of the country. We know so little of what is stirring in the depths of Indian society; we dwell so much apart from the people; we see so little of them, except in full dress and on their best behaviour, that perilous intrigues and desperate plots might be woven, under the very shadow of our bungalows, without our perceiving any symptoms of danger. But still less can we discern that quiet under-current of hostility which is continually flowing on without any immediate or definite object, and which, if we could discern it, would baffle all our efforts to trace it to its source. But it does not the less exist because we are ignorant of the form which it assumes, or the fount from which it springs. The men, whose business it was to corrupt the minds of our Sepoys, were, perhaps, the agents of some of the old princely houses, which we had destroyed,* or members of old baronial families which we had brought to poverty and disgrace. They were, perhaps, the emissaries of Brahminical Societies, whose precepts we were turning into folly, and whose power we were setting at naught. They were, perhaps, mere visionaries and enthusiasts, moved only by their

* It was asserted at the time of the "Mutiny of Vellore," that not only were agents of the House of Tippoo busy in all the Lines of Southern India, but that there was scarcely a regiment into which they had not enlisted.

1851-56. own disordered imaginations to proclaim the coming of some new prophet or some fresh avatar of the Deity, and the consequent downfal of Christian supremacy in the East. But whatsoever the nature of their mission, and whatsoever the guise they assumed, whether they appeared in the Lines as passing travellers, as journeying hawkers, as religious mendicants, or as wandering puppet-showmen, the seed of sedition which they scattered struck root in a soil well prepared to receive it, and waited only for the ripening sun of circumstance to develop a harvest of revolt.

BOOK III.—THE OUTBREAK OF THE MUTINY.

[1856–1857.]

CHAPTER I.

DEPARTURE OE LORD DALHOUSIE—HIS CHARACTER—THE QUESTION OF SUCCESSION—ARRIVAL OF LORD CANNING—HIS EARLY CAREER—COMMENCEMENT OF HIS ADMINISTRATION—HIS FELLOW-COUNCILLORS—GENERAL LOW—MR. DORIN—MR. GRANT—MR. BARNES PEACOCK—THE COMMANDER-IN-CHIEF.

WHEN, on the last day of February, 1856, "the 1856.
Most Noble" the Marquis of Dalhousie placed the Portfolio of the Indian Empire in the hands of his successor, all men said that a great statesman and a great ruler was about to depart from the land. The praises that were bestowed upon him had been well earned. He had given his life to the public service; and many feared, as they sorrowfully bade him farewell, that he had given it up for the public good.

He stood before men at that time as the very embodiment of Success. Whatsoever he had attempted to do he had done with his whole heart, and he had perfected it without a failure or a flaw. The policy which during those eventful eight years had been so consistently maintained was emphatically his policy. The success, therefore, was fairly his. No man had ever stamped his individuality more clearly upon the public measures of his times. There are periods when the Government fades into an impersonality; when

1856. men cease to associate its measures with the idea of one dominant will. But during the reign then ended we heard little of "the Government;" in every one's mouth was the name of the individual Man.

Character of Lord Dalhousie.

And in this remarkable individual manhood there was the very essence and concentration of the great national manhood; there was an intense Englishism in him such as has seldom been equalled. It was the Englishism, too, of the nineteenth century; and of that particular epoch of the nineteenth century when well-nigh every one had the word "progress" on his lips, and stagnation was both disaster and disgrace. A man of strong convictions and extraordinary activity of mind, he laid fast hold of the one abstract truth that English government, English laws, English learning, English customs, and English manners, are better than the government, the laws, the learning, the customs, and the manners of India; and with all the earnestness of his nature and all the strength of his understanding he wrought out this great theory in practice. He never doubted that it was good alike for England and for India that the map of the country which he had been sent to govern should present one surface of Red. He was so sure of this, he believed it so honestly, so conscientiously, that, courageous and self-reliant as he was, he would have carried out this policy to the end, if all the chief officers and agents of his government had been arrayed against him. But he commenced his career at a time when the ablest of our public functionaries in India, with a few notable exceptions, had forsaken the traditions of the old school—the school of Malcolm, of Elphinstone, and of Metcalfe—and stood eager and open-armed to embrace and press closely to them the very doctrines of which they perceived in

Dalhousie so vigorous an exponent. He did not found the school; neither were his opinions moulded in accordance with its tenets. He appeared among them and placed himself at their head, just at the very time when such a coming was needed to give consistency to their faith, and uniformity to their works. The coincidence had all the force of a dispensation. No prophet ever had more devoted followers. No king was ever more loyally served. For the strong faith of his disciples made them strive mightily to accomplish his will; and he had in a rare degree the faculty of developing in his agents the very powers which were most essential to the fitting accomplishment of his work. He did not create those powers, for he found in his chief agents the instincts and energies most essential to his purpose; but he fostered, he strengthened and directed them, so that what might have run to weed and waste withou this cherishing care, yielded under his culture, in ripe profusion, a harvest of desired results. 1856.

As his workmen were admirably suited to his work, so also was the field, to which he was called, the one best adapted to the exercise of his peculiar powers. In no other part of our empire could his rare administrative capacity have found such scope for development. For he was of an imperious and despotic nature, not submitting to control, and resenting opposition; and in no situation could he have exercised a larger measure of power in the face of so few constitutional checks. His capacities required free exercise, and it may be doubted whether they would have been fully developed by anything short of this absolute supremacy. But sustained and invigorated by a sense of enormous power, he worked with all the energies of a giant. And he was successful beyond all

1856. example, so far as success is the full accomplishment of one's own desires and intentions. But one fatal defect in his character tainted the stream of his policy at the source, and converted into brilliant errors some of the most renowned of his achievements. No man who is not endowed with a comprehensive imagination can govern India with success. Dalhousie had no imagination. Lacking the imaginative faculty, men, after long years of experience, may come to understand the national character; and a man of lively imagination, without such experience, may readily apprehend it after the intercourse of a few weeks. But in neither way did Dalhousie ever come to understand the genius of the people among whom his lot was cast. He had but one idea of them —an idea of a people habituated to the despotism of a dominant race. He could not understand the tenacity of affection with which they clung to their old traditions. He could not sympathise with the veneration which they felt for their ancient dynasties. He could not appreciate their fidelity to the time-honoured institutions and the immemorial usages of the land. He had not the faculty to conceive that men might like their own old ways of government, with all their imperfections and corruptions about them, better than our more refined systems. Arguing all points with the preciseness of a Scotch logician, he made no allowance for inveterate habits and ingrained prejudices, and the scales of ignorance before men's eyes which will not suffer them rightly to discern between the good and the bad. He could not form a true dramatic conception of the feelings with which the representative of a long line of kings may be supposed to regard the sudden extinction of his royal house by the decree of a stranger and an infidel, or

the bitterness of spirit in which a greybeard chief, 1856.
whose family from generation to generation had enjoyed ancestral powers and privileges, might contemplate his lot when suddenly reduced to poverty and humiliation by an incursion of aliens of another colour and another creed. He could not see with other men's eyes; or think with other men's brains; or feel with other men's hearts. With the characteristic unimaginativeness of his race he could not for a moment divest himself of his individuality, or conceive the growth of ancestral pride and national honour in other breasts than those of the Campbells and the Ramsays.

And this egotism was cherished and sustained by the prevailing sentiments of the new school of Indian politicians, who, as I have said, laughed to scorn the doctrines of the men who had built up the great structure of our Indian Empire, and by the utterances of a Press, which, with rare ability, expounded the views of this school, and insisted upon the duty of universal usurpation. Such, indeed, was the prevailing tone of the majority, in all ranks from the highest to the lowest, that any one who meekly ventured to ask, "How would you like it yourself?" was reproached in language little short of that which might be fitly applied to a renegade or a traitor. To suggest that in an Asiatic race there might be a spirit of independence and a love of country, the manifestations of which were honourable in themselves, however inconvenient to us, was commonly to evoke as the very mildest result the imputation of being "Anti-British," whilst sometimes the "true British feeling" asserted itself in a less refined choice of epithets, and those who ventured to sympathise in any way with the people of the East were at once de-

1856. nounced as "white niggers." Yet among these very men, so intolerant of anything approaching the assertion of a spirit of liberty by an Asiatic people, there were some who could well appreciate and sympathise with the aspirations of European bondsmen, and could regard with admiration the struggles of the Italian, the Switzer, or the Pole to liberate himself, by a sanguinary contest, from the yoke of the usurper. But the sight of the dark skin sealed up their sympathies. They contended not merely that the love of country, that the spirit of liberty, as cherished by European races, is in India wholly unknown, but that Asiatic nations, and especially the nations of India, have no right to judge what is best for themselves; no right to revolt against the beneficence of a more civilised race of white men, who would think and act for them, and deprive them, for their own good, of all their most cherished rights and their most valued possessions.

So it happened that Lord Dalhousie's was a strong Government; strong in everything but its conformity to the genius of the people. It was a Government admirably conducted in accordance with the most approved principles of European civilisation, by men whose progressive tendencies carried them hundreds of years in advance of the sluggish Asiatics, whom they vainly endeavoured to bind to the chariot-wheels of their refined systems. There was everything to give it complete success but the stubbornness of the national mind. It failed, perhaps, only because the people preferred darkness to light, folly to wisdom. Of course the English gentlemen were right and the Asiatics lamentably wrong. But the grand scriptural warning against putting new wine into old bottles was disregarded. The wine was good wine, strong wine; wine to gladden the heart of man. But poured into those old bottles it was sure, sooner or later, to create a general explosion. They forgot that there were two things necessary to successful government: one, that the measures should be good in themselves; and the other, that they should be suited to the condition of the recipients. Intent upon the one, they forgot the other, and erred upon the side of a progress too rapid and an Englishism too refined. 1856.

But at the bottom of this great error were benign intentions. Dalhousie and his lieutenants had a strong and steadfast faith in the wisdom and benevolence of their measures, and strove alike for the glory of the English nation and the welfare of the Indian people. There was something grand and even good in the very errors of such a man. For there was no taint of baseness in them; no sign of anything sordid or self-seeking. He had given himself up to the public service, resolute to do a great work, and he rejoiced with a noble pride in the thought that he left behind him a mightier empire than he had found, that he had brought new countries and strange nations under the sway of the British sceptre, and sown the seeds of a great civilisation. To do this, he had made unstinting sacrifice of leisure, ease, comfort, health, and the dear love of wedded life, and he carried home with him, in a shattered frame and a torn heart, in the wreck of a manhood at its very prime, mortal wounds nobly received in a great and heroic encounter.

Great always is the interest which attaches to the question of succession; greatest of all when such a ruler as Dalhousie retires from the scene. Who was to take the place of this great and successful states-

1856. man? Who was to carry out to its final issue the grand policy which he had so brilliantly inaugurated? This was the question in all men's mouths as the old year passed away and the new year dawned upon India; in some sort a remarkable year, for was it not the centenary of the great disaster of the Black Hole which had brought Clive's avenging army to Bengal? Ever at such times is there much talk of the expected advent of some member of the English Cabinet, some successful Colonial Governor, or some great Lord little experienced in statesmanship, of high lineage and dilapidated fortune. And so now there was the wonted high tide of speculation and conjecture, wild guesses and moonshine rumours of all kinds, from dim possibilities to gigantic nonsenses, until at last there came authentic tidings to India that the choice had fallen on Her Majesty's Postmaster-General, one of the younger members of Lord Palmerston's Cabinet.

Antecedents of Lord Canning. Scarcely within bounds of possibility was it, that, in the midst of so great an epidemic of faith in Lord Dalhousie, England could send forth a statesman to succeed him, whom her Anglo-Indian sons would not receive with ominous head-shakings, denoting grave doubts and anxious misgivings. Another great man, it was said, was needed to understand, to appreciate, to maintain the policy of the hero whom they so glorified. But they knew little or nothing of Viscount Canning, except that he was the bearer of a great
1822. name. Thirty-four years before, all England had been talking about the acceptance of the Governor-Generalship by this man's father. There were a

few, then, who, looking at the matter solely from 1856.
an Indian point of view, exulted in the thought that one who had done such good service at the Board of Control, and whose abilities were known to be of the very highest order, was about to devote some of the best years of his life to the government of our great Eastern empire. There was another and a baser few, who, festering with jealousies, and animosities, and dishonourable fears, joyed most of all that they should see his face no more for years, or perhaps for ever. But the bulk of the English people deplored his approaching departure from among them, because they felt that the country had need of his services, and could ill bear the loss of such a man. And it was a relief to them when the sad close of Lord Castlereagh's career brought George Canning back from the visit, which was to have been his farewell, to Liverpool, to take his place again in the great Council of the nation.

Great, also, was the relief to George Canning himself—great for many reasons; the greatest, perhaps, of all, that he was very happy in his family. In the first year of the century he had married a lady, endowed with a considerable share of the world's wealth, but with more of that better wealth which the world cannot give; the daughter and co-heiress of an old general officer named Scott. No man could have been happier in his domestic life; and domestic happiness is domestic virtue. Blind to the attractions of that Society in which he was so pre-eminently formed to shine, he found measureless delight in the companionship of his wife and children. And as an Indian life is more or less a life of separation, it was now a joy to him to think that the brief

1856. vision of Government House, Calcutta, had been replaced by the returning realities of the English fireside.*

Gloucester Lodge, 1822. At this time the great statesman had a son in his tenth year, at school with Mr. Carmalt, of Putney, on the banks of the Thames. He was the third son born to George Canning;† born during what was perhaps the happiest period of his father's life, his residence at Gloucester Lodge. This was the boy's birthplace. Lying between Brompton and Kensington, it was at that time almost in the country. There was not, perhaps, a pleasanter place near Town. It had a strange, memorable history, too, and it was among the notabilities of suburban London. In the days of Ranelagh, it had been, under the name of the Florida Gardens, a lesser rival to that fashionable haunt; and from this state, after an interval of desertion and decay, it had developed into a royal residence.‡ The Duchess of Gloucester bought the 1807. Gardens, built there a handsome Italian villa, lived and died there, and, passing away, bequeathed her interest in the estate to the Princess Sophia, who sold it to Mr. Canning. And there, in this pleasant umbrageous retreat, on the 14th of December, 1812, was born the third son of George Canning, who, in due course, was christened Charles John.

The Putney School. In 1822, as I have said, when George Canning

* "The unsullied purity of Mr. Canning's domestic life," says his last and pleasantest biographer, "and his love of domestic pleasures (for after his marriage he seldom extended his intercourse with general society beyond those occasions which his station rendered unavoidable), were rewarded by as much virtue and devotion as ever graced the home of an English statesman."—*Bell's Life of Canning.*

† At this time Charles was the second surviving son. The eldest, George Charles, born in April, 1801, died in March, 1820. The second brother was in the navy.

‡ See Bell's Life of Canning, chapter x., which contains an animated sketch of the early history of Gloucester Lodge, and of the social and domestic environments of the great statesman's residence there.

woke from his brief dream of Indian vice-regal power to take the seals of the Foreign Office, this boy Charles was under the scholastic care of Mr. Carmalt, of Putney. In those days his establishment enjoyed a great reputation. It was one of the largest and best private schools in the neighbourhood of London, perhaps in the whole kingdom, and as the sons of our highest noblemen mingled there with those of our middle-class gentry, not a bad half-way house to the microcosm of Eton or Harrow. The impression which Charles Canning made upon the minds of his schoolfellows was, on the whole, a favourable one. He was not a boy of brilliant parts, or of any large popularity; but he was remembered long afterwards as one who, in a quiet, unostentatious way, made it manifest to ordinary observers that there was, in schoolboy language, "something in him." One, whose letter is now before me, and who was with him for nearly two years in the same room at the Putney school, remembered, after a lapse of more than a third part of a century, the admiration with which he then regarded young Canning's "youthful indications of talent, and amiable and attractive manners." 1856.

Two years after George Canning's surrender of the Governor-Generalship, his son Charles left Mr. Carmalt's and went to Eton. Eton was very proud of the father's great reputation, and eager to embrace the son; for, verily, George Canning had been an Etonian of Etonians, and had done as much, as a scholar and a wit, to make Eton flourish, as any man of his age. It was, perhaps, therefore, in a spirit of pure gratitude and veneration, and with no "hope of future favours," that worthy Provost Goodall, than whom perhaps no man ever had a keener appreciation both Eton

1856. of scholarship and of wit, on intimation made to him that George Canning wished his son to be entered as an oppidan, sent Mr. Chapman, one of the masters of the school,* who had been selected as the boy's tutor, to examine him at Gloucester Lodge. These examinations, which determine the place in the school which the boy is to take, are commonly held in the tutor's house at Eton, not beneath the parental roof. But the Minister's son was examined in his father's library and in his father's presence at Gloucester Lodge; a double trial, it may be thought, of the young student's nerve, and not provocative of a successful display of scholarship. But it was successful.† Charles Canning was declared to be fit for the fourth form, and on the 4th of September, 1824, he commenced his career. It is on record that he was "sent up for good" for his proficiency in Latin verse. It is on record, also, if the recording minister at Eton does not kindly blot out such traces of boyish error, that he was also sent up for bad; in more correct Etonian phraseology, "in the bill," marked for the flogging block. And it is traditional that the avenging hand of Head-master Keate was sometimes stayed by a tender reluctance to apply the birch to the person of Secretary Canning's son. On the whole, perhaps, it is historically true that, at Eton, he had no very marked reputation of any kind. He was good-looking, and a gentleman, which goes for something; but I do not know that he was a great rower,

* Afterwards Bishop of Colombo; now retired.

† I am indebted for this incident to Sir Robert Phillimore, Queen's Advocate. The memorandum from which it is taken adds: "The well-known description of the storm in the first Æneid, 'Interea magno misceri murmure pontum,' &c., was the passage chosen for the trial of his proficiency, and the Bishop now remembers the anxiety with which the father watched the essay of his son, and the smile of approval which greeted his reading of the rather difficult transition, 'Quos ego — sed motos,' &c., and the final 'Not so bad,' which followed at the close of the whole translation."

a great cricketer, or a great swimmer, or was in any sense an athlete of the first water and the admiration of his companions; and, scholastically, it is remembered of him that he had "a reputation rather for intelligence, accuracy, and painstaking, than for refined scholarship, or any remarkable powers of composition." 1856.

But on passing away from Eton, the stature of his mind was soon greatly enlarged. At the close of 1827, having risen to the Upper division of the fifth form, he received the parting gifts of his schoolfellows; and soon afterwards became the private pupil of the Rev. John Shore, a nephew of Sir John Shore, Governor-General of India, and known to a later generation as Lord Teignmouth. This worthy Christian gentleman and ripe scholar lived, but without Church preferment, at Potton, a quiet little market-town in Bedfordshire, receiving pupils there of the better sort. Among the inmates of his house was the grandson of the first Lord Harris, with whom Charles Canning entered into bonds of friendship, riveted at Oxford, strengthened in public life at home, and again by strange coincidence in India, and broken only by death. Here, doubtless, he made great progress in scholarship. Perhaps the death of his father, and the after-honours which were conferred on the family, and, more than all, the subsequent calamitous end of his elder brother,* awakened within him a sense of the responsibilities of his position, and roused him to new exertions. Though born the third in succession of George Canning's sons, he was now the eldest, the only one. He and his sister alone survived. He was now the heir to a peerage, sufficiently, though not splendidly, en- August 8, 1827.

* William Pitt Canning, then a Captain in the Royal Navy, was drowned while bathing at Madeira, in September, 1828.

1856. dowed, and there was a public career before him. He applied himself to his books.*

Oxford. His next step was to the University. In December, 1828, he was entered on the roll as a Student of Christ Church, Oxford, as his father had been entered just forty years before. Among the foremost of his fellow-students were Mr. Gladstone, Mr. Bruce, and Mr. Robert Phillimore,† all of whom lived to take parts, more or less prominent, in public affairs. Among other members of the same distinguished house, at that time, was the young Lord Lincoln, heir to the Dukedom of Newcastle, and the representative of the great Scotch House of Ramsay, ennobled by the Earldom of Dalhousie. But the most intimate of all his associates was the present Lord De Tabley, with whom he lived in the closest bonds of friendship to the latest day of his life. By him, and a few other chosen companions, he was dearly loved and much respected; but neither achieving nor seeking extensive popularity among his cotemporaries, he was regarded by the outer University world as a man of a reserved and distant manner, and of a somewhat cold and unimpulsive temperament. The few in the inner circle knew that he was not cold; knew that he had a true loving heart, very loyal and constant in its affections; knew that in the society of his familiar friends he had a pleasant, a genial, and sometimes a playful manner, that he had a fine scholarly taste, a fund of quiet humour, a keen appreciation of character, and that he was all in all a delightful companion. They had great hope, too, of his future career, though he did not seem to be ambi-

* It need scarcely be indicated that the widow of George Canning, on his death, was created a Viscountess, with remainder to his eldest son.

† The present (1864) Chancellor of the Exchequer; the late Lord Elgin, Governor-General of India; and the present Queen's Advocate.

tious; nay, rather, it appeared to those who closely observed him, that he was haunted and held back by the thought of his father's renown, and a diffidence of his own capacity to maintain the glories of the name. But, although he did not care to take part in the proceedings of debating societies, and, apparently, took small interest in the politics of the great world, he was anxious that at least his University career should do no dishonour to his lineage, and that if he could not be a great statesman, he might not stain the scholarly reputation enjoyed by two generations of Cannings before him. He strove, therefore, and with good results, to perfect himself in the classic languages; and even more assiduous were his endeavours to obtain a mastery over his own language. At an early age he acquired a thoroughly good English style; not resonant or pretentious; not splintery or smart; but pure, fluent, transparent, with the meaning ever visible beneath it, as pebbles beneath the clearest stream. 1856.

His efforts bore good fruit. In 1831, he wrote a Latin Prize Poem, on the "Captivity of Caractacus;" and recited it in the great hall of Christ Church, standing beneath his father's picture.* And in the

* I am indebted for this to Sir Robert Phillimore. I give the incident in his own words: "In the year 1831, he won the Christ Church prize for Latin verse. The subject was 'Caractacus Captivus Romam ingreditur.' The verses were, as usual, recited in the hall. It was a remarkable scene. In that magnificent banqueting-room are hung the portraits of students who have reflected honour upon the House which reared them by the distinctions which they have won in after life. Underneath the portrait of George Canning, the recollection of whose brilliant career and untimely end was still fresh in the memory of men, stood the son, in the prime of youth, recalling by his eminently handsome countenance the noble features of the portrait, while repeating the classical prize poem, which would have gladdened his father's heart. Generally speaking, the resident members of Christ Church alone compose the audience when the prize poem is recited. But on this occasion there was a stranger present—the old faithful friend of Mr. Canning, his staunch political adherent through life—Mr. Sturges Bourne. He had travelled from London for the purpose of witnessing the first considerable achievement of the younger Canning."—*MS. Memorandum.*

1856 Easter term of 1833 he took his degree, with high honours: a first class in Classics, and a second in Mathematics. He was then in his twenty-first year; and Parliament would soon be open to him. But he was in no hurry to enter upon the realities of public life. He was diffident of his oratorical powers; he was constitutionally shy; and it did not appear to him that the House of Commons was a theatre in which he was ever likely to make a successful appearance. Moreover, he had other work in hand at that time; other yearnings to keep down any young ambitions that might be mounting within him. Love and courtship filled up a sweet interlude in his life, as they do in the lives of most men whose story is worth telling; and, in due course, they bore the rich fruit of happy wedlock. On the 5th of September, 1835, the Honourable Charles John Canning espoused the Honourable Charlotte Stuart, eldest daughter of Lord Stuart De Rothesay; a lady of a serene and gentle beauty, and many rare gifts of mind.

But, after a year of wedded life, he was prevailed upon to enter Parliament; and in August, 1836, he was returned for Warwick. In that month, however, Parliament was prorogued; and on its reassembling at the commencement of the following year he was content to be a silent member. His opportunities, indeed, were very few, for his whole career in the House of Commons extended over a period of little more than six weeks. During the month of February and the early part of March he attended in his place with praiseworthy regularity.* But, on the 15th of the latter month, his mother, Viscountess Canning, died; and, on the 24th of April, he took his seat in the House of Lords.

* His name is to be found in all the principal division lists. He voted sometimes against Lord Melbourne's Government, but more frequently with it.

For nearly twenty years he sate in that House, taking no very prominent part in the debates, but doing his duty in a quiet, unostentatious way, and gradually making for himself a reputation as a conscientious, painstaking young statesman, who might some day do good service to his country and honour to his great name. His political opinions, which were shared by most of his distinguished cotemporaries at Christ Church, were characterised by that chastened liberalism which had found its chief exponent in Sir Robert Peel; and when, in 1841, that great Parliamentary leader was invited to form a Ministry, Lord Canning, Lord Lincoln, and Mr. Gladstone were offered, and accepted, official seats. The seals of the Foreign Office had been placed in the hands of Lord Aberdeen. He had a high opinion of, and a personal regard for, Lord Canning, and there was no one whom the veteran statesman wished so much to associate with himself in office as George Canning's son. About the same time another distinguished member of the House of Lords was also moved by a strong desire to have the benefit of the young statesman's official co-operation and personal companionship. This was Lord Ellenborough, who, on the formation of the Peel Ministry, had been appointed President of the Board of Control, but who had subsequently been selected to succeed Lord Auckland as Governor-General of India. He offered to take Canning with him in the capacity of Private Secretary. 1836-56.

Creditable as this offer was to the discernment of Lord Ellenborough, and made in perfect sincerity, it was one little likely to be accepted by a man of high social position, good political prospects, and a sufficient supply of the world's wealth. Lord Canning

1836-56. elected to remain in England, and entered official life as Under-Secretary of State for Foreign Affairs. He liked his work; he did it well; and he had the entire confidence of his chief. But he did not take an active part in the debates and discussions of the House of Lords. The presence, in the same Chamber, of the Chief of his Department relieved him from the responsibility of ministerial explanations and replies, and his constitutional reserve forbade all unnecessary displays. It was not, indeed, until the Session of 1846 found him in the office of Chief Commissioner of Woods and Forests, that he took any prominent part in the business of the House. If the position which he then held afforded no opportunity for the development of his powers either as an orator or a debater, it kept him continually in Parliamentary harness, and the training was of service to him. It lasted, however, but a little time. At the end of June, 1846, Sir Robert Peel and his colleagues resigned; and a Whig Cabinet was formed under the leadership of Lord John Russell.

Lord Canning was then "in opposition;" but, in heart, he was a Liberal, and willing to support liberal measures, without reference to the distinctions of party. When, therefore, in May, 1848, Lord Lansdowne moved the second reading of the Jewish Disabilities Bill, Lord Canning was the first to speak in support of it. He answered Lord Ellenborough, who had moved the amendment, and he voted against all his old colleagues then in the Upper House, with the exception of Lord Hardinge. But in 1850 he supported, in a speech displaying an entire mastery of the subject, the resolution of Lord Derby condemnatory of the Foreign Policy of Lord Palmerston; and he spoke against the Ecclesiastical Titles Bill, introduced by Lord John Russell. So little, indeed, was he considered to be pledged to any party, that when the Russell Cabinet resigned in the spring of 1851, and Lord Derby was invited to form an administration, the great Conservative leader saw no reason why he should not invite Canning to become a member of it. The offer then made was a tempting one, for it was the offer of a seat in the Cabinet second in importance only to that of the First Minister. To the son of George Canning it was especially tempting, for it was the offer of the seals of the Foreign Office. In that office the father had built up his reputation, and the son had already laid the foundation of an honourable career of statesmanship. It was the department which, above all others, Lord Canning best knew and most desired. He had served a long apprenticeship in it, and if his humility suggested any doubts of his capacity to direct its affairs, they must have been removed by the manner in which he was invited to take their direction. 1836-56.

The offer now made to him was made through his old official chief, Lord Aberdeen, who pressed him to accept it. But there were many grave considerations which caused him to hesitate. He had sat for some years on the same ministerial bench with Lord Derby, but the latter had separated himself from his party, and the cause of the disruption was the liberal commercial policy of Sir Robert Peel, in favour of which Canning had freely declared his opinions. He had condemned the foreign policy of the Whig party; but, on the other hand, there were matters of home government, in which his liberality was far in advance of the opinions of Lord Derby and his colleagues; and, on the whole, he felt that he could not honestly and consistently support the Administration

1836-56. which he was invited to enter. He judged rightly, and in such a case he judged wisely. Lord Derby failed to construct a Ministry, and the Whigs resumed office for another year. This was the turning-point of Lord Canning's career; and it is impossible to say how different might have been the story which I am now about to write, if these overtures had been accepted.

In the following year, Lord Derby again endeavoured, and with better success, to form a Ministry, but its career was of brief duration. In November, its place was filled by an Administration under the premiership of Lord Aberdeen, composed of the leading members of the Governments both of Sir Robert Peel and Lord John Russell. In this Coalition Ministry Lord Canning held the office of Postmaster-General. Though held by many a distinguished man, the post was not one to satisfy the desires of an ambitious one. But he was not disappointed or discouraged. He knew the difficulties which lay in the path of his leader,* and he addressed himself cheerfully and assiduously to his work, with a steadfast resolution to elevate the importance of the appointment he held, by doing in it the largest possible amount of public good. In this office he had first an opportunity of displaying that high conscientious courage which bears up and steers right on, in spite of the penalties and mortifications of temporary unpopularity. What was wrong he endeavoured to set right; and knowing how much depended on the personal exertions of individual men, he strove, even

* In a "coalition ministry" there is necessarily an exceptional number of claimants for the higher offices with seats in the Cabinet. In the arrangements then made the seals of the Foreign Office fell, in the first instance, to Lord John Russell.

at the expense of certain very clamorous vested interests, to obtain the utmost possible amount of competency for the performance of all the higher departmental duties. During his administration of the Post-office many important reforms were instituted, and much progress made in good work already commenced. So effectually, indeed, had he mastered all the complicated details of the department, that when the Coalition Ministry was dissolved and a new Government formed under Lord Palmerston, the public interests required that there should be no change at the Post-office; so Lord Canning was reappointed to his old office, but with further acknowledgment of his good services in the shape of a seat in the Cabinet. But it was not ordered that he should hold the office much longer. There was more stirring work in store for him. His old friend and cotemporary, Lord Dalhousie, was coming home from India, and it was necessary that a new Governor-General should be appointed in his place. Practically the selection, in such cases, was made by the Imperial Government, but constitutionally the appointment emanated from the East India Company. The President of the Board of Control and the Chairman of the Court of Directors commonly took counsel together, when the Cabinet had chosen their man; and then the nomination was formally submitted to the Court. There is always, in such cases, much internal doubt and conflict among those with whom the selection rests, and much speculation and discussion in the outer world. It was believed in this instance, that some member of the Ministry would be appointed; but people said in England, as they said in India, that it would be no easy thing to find a fit successor for Lord Dalhousie; and when at last it transpired 1836-56.

1855-56. that the choice had fallen on Lord Canning, men shook their heads and asked each other whether there was anything great about him but his name. In Parliament the propriety of the appointment was questioned by some noisy speakers, and there was a general feeling in society that the appointment was rather a mistake. But those who knew Lord Canning—those especially who had worked with him—knew that it was no mistake. They knew that there was the stuff in him of which great administrators are made.

Appointment to the Governor-Generalship, 1855.

On the first day of August a Court of Directors was held at the India House, and Lord Canning was introduced to take the accustomed oath. On the evening of that day the Company gave, in honour of their new servant, one of those magnificent entertainments at which it was their wont to bid God-speed to those who were going forth to do their work. Those banquets were great facts and great opportunities. It was discovered soon afterwards that the expenditure upon them was a profligate waste of the public money. But the Government of a great empire, spending nothing upon the splendid foppery of a Court, was justified in thinking that, without offence, it might thus do honour to its more distinguished servants, and that, not the turtle and the venison, but the hospitality and the courtesy of the Directors, thus publicly bestowed upon the men who had done their work well in civil or military life, would find ample recompense in increased loyalty and devotion, and more energetic service. Many a gallant soldier and many a wise administrator carried back with him to India the big card of the East India Company inviting him to dinner at the London Tavern, and religiously preserved it as one of the

most cherished records of an honourable career. 1855-56.
There were many, too, who hoarded among their dearest recollections the memory of the evening when they saw, perhaps for the first and the last time, England's greatest statesmen and warriors, and heard them gravely discourse on the marvel and the miracle of our Indian Empire. Nor was it a small thing that a man selected to govern a magnificent dependency beyond the seas, should thus, in the presence of his old and his new masters, and many of his coadjutors in the great work before him, publicly accept his commission, and declare to the people in the West and in the East the principles which were to regulate his conduct and to shape his career. The words uttered on these occasions rose far above the ordinary convivial level of after-dinner speeches. There was a gravity and solemnity in them, appreciated not merely by those who heard them spoken, but by thousands also, to whom the Press conveyed them, in the country which they most concerned; and on the minds of the more intelligent Natives the fact of this grand ceremonial of departure made a deep impression, and elevated in their imaginations the dignity of the coming ruler.

Seldom or never had this ceremonial assumed a more imposing character than that which celebrated the appointment of Lord Canning to the Governor-Generalship of India. In the great Banqueting Hall of the London Tavern were assembled on that 1st of August many members of the Cabinet, including among them some of Canning's dearest friends; others besides of his old companions and fellow-students; and all the most distinguished of the servants of the Company at that time in the country. Mr. Elliot Macnaghten, Chairman of the East India Company,

1855-56. presided, and after dinner proposed the accustomed toasts. It was natural and right that, when doing honour to the newly-appointed Governor-General, the speaker should pay a fitting tribute to the distinguished statesman who was then bringing his work to a close; it was natural and graceful that tribute should be paid also to the worth of the elder Canning, who had done India good service at home, and had been selected to hold the great office abroad which his son was proceeding to fill; but there was something to a comparatively untried man perilous in such associations, and the younger Canning, with instinctive modesty, shrunk from the invidious suggestion. Perhaps there were some present who drew comparisons, unfavourable to the son, between the early careers of the two Cannings, which had entitled them to this great distinction; but when the younger stood up to speak, every one was struck—the many judging by busts and pictures, and the few recalling the living likeness of George Canning—by his great resemblance to his father. The singularly handsome face, the intellectual countenance, and, above all, the noble "Canning brow," like a block of white marble, bespoke no common capacity for empire, and gave emphatic force to the words he uttered. He said, after the usual expression of thanks for the kind words spoken, and the kind reception accorded to them, that the kindness which he had received had not created any delusion in his mind, for whether he contemplated the magnitude of the task that awaited him, or the great achievements of the distinguished men who had preceded him, he was painfully sensible that the labourer was unequal to the great work that had been entrusted to his hands. He was not ashamed to confess that there were times when he was tempted to shrink from the responsibility that awaited him. But this feeling, he added, was not inconsistent with his determination to devote all the energies of his mind, every hour, nay, every minute of his time, every thought and every inspiration, to the discharge of the duties which he had that day accepted from the hands of the Company. There were, however, other considerations, which had greatly reassured and encouraged him: "You have," he said, turning to the Chairman, "assured me, this day, of what you rightly describe as the generous confidence and co-operation of the Court of Directors. I thank you for that assurance, and I rely on it implicitly, for I know that the body of which you are the head are, wherever they bestow their confidence, no niggards in supporting those who honestly and faithfully serve them." And then, not perhaps without a knowledge of what, more than a quarter of a century before, his father had said on a similar occasion,* he added, "I feel that I can also rely on the cordial support and sympathy of my noble friend at the head of the Government, and of all those colleagues with whom I have had the proud satisfaction of serving as a Minister of the Crown, but, above all, I delight in the co-operation—for on that I must daily and hourly rely—of those two admirable bodies, the Civil Service and the Army of India. I hardly know whether there is any feature of our Government, any portion of our institutions, upon which Englishmen may look with more honest exultation than those two noble

1855-56.

* The occasion alluded to was the farewell banquet given by the East India Company to Sir John Malcolm, on his appointment to the government of Bombay. Then it was that George Canning said: "There cannot be found in the history of Europe the existence of any monarchy which, within a given time, has produced so many men of the first talents, in civil and military life, as India has first trained for herself, and then given to their native country."

1855-56. branches of our Public Service. The men of those branches have done much for the advancement of India, and have sent forth from their ranks men who were efficient in war and peace, in numbers of which any monarchy in Europe might be proud, and who have rescued their countrymen from charges formerly, and not unjustly, levelled against them of dealing sometimes too harshly with those whom they were bound to succour and protect. Sir, it is the possession of such men which enables you to exhibit a spectacle unequalled in the world's history—that of a hundred and fifty millions of people submitting in peace and contentment, in a country teeming with wealth, to the government of strangers and aliens."

Then, after a few more words on the high character of the Services, and a brief declaration of the fact that he assumed office "without a single promise or pledge to any expectant," he proceeded with increased gravity and solemnity of utterance, almost, indeed, as one under the spell of prophecy: "I know not what course events may take. I hope and pray that we may not reach the extremity of war. I wish for a peaceful time of office, but I cannot forget that in our Indian Empire that greatest of all blessings depends upon a greater variety of chances and a more precarious tenure than in any other quarter of the globe. We must not forget that in the sky of India, serene as it is, a small cloud may arise, at first no bigger than a man's hand, but which, growing larger and larger, may at last threaten to burst, and overwhelm us with ruin. What has happened once may happen again. The disturbing causes have diminished certainly, but they are not dispelled. We have still discontented and heterogeneous peoples united under our sway; we have still neighbours before whom we cannot altogether lay aside our watchfulness; and we have a frontier configuration that renders it possible that in any quarter, at any moment, causes of collision may arise. Besides, so intricate are our relations with some subsidiary states, that I doubt whether in an empire so vast and so situated it is in the power of the wisest Government, the most peaceful and the most forbearing, to command peace. But if we cannot command, we can at least deserve it, by taking care that honour, good faith, and fair dealing are on our side; and then if, in spite of us, it should become necessary to strike a blow, we can strike with a clear conscience. With blows so dealt the struggle must be short and the issue not doubtful. But I gladly dismiss from my mind apprehensions that may not be realised, and joyfully recognise a large arena of peaceful usefulness, in which I hope for your kind assistance and co-operation." 1855-56.

Equally surprised were the few then present, who were familiar with Lord Canning's parliamentary utterances, and the many, who had never heard him speak, but had been told that he was "no orator;" for the speech which they now heard from his lips was all that such a speech ought to have been. It was impressive rather than impassioned; slowly spoken, with a deliberate gravity, every sentence making itself felt, and every word making itself heard in the farthest corners of that great Banqueting Hall. There were few present in whose estimation the speaker had not risen before he resumed his seat; few present who did not, years afterwards, remember with strong emotion that picture of the little cloud rising in an unexpected quarter, and in time obscuring the firmament and overshadowing the land. Some, perhaps, thought also of another speech, then

1855-56. delivered by a more practised speaker; for the First Minister of the Crown, on that August evening, let fall some memorable words. It was only in common course that he should speak of the qualifications of his colleague for the high office to which he had been appointed; only in common course that he should express his gratitude to the Company who so materially lightened the cares of the Sovereign and her Ministers. But when Lord Palmerston dwelt on "the significant fact that, whereas of old all civilisation came from India, through Egypt, now we, who were then barbarians, were carrying back civilisation and enlightenment to the parent source," and added, "perhaps it might be our lot to confer on the countless millions of India a higher and a holier gift than any real human knowledge; but that must be left to the hands of time and the gradual improvement of the people," he supplemented Lord Canning's prophecy, though he knew it not, and pointed to the quarter from which the little cloud was to arise.

But although Lord Canning had been sworn in at the India House, and had stood before the magnates of the land as Governor-General elect, he was still a member of the Cabinet and her Majesty's Postmaster-General. Parliament was prorogued on the 14th of August, and in accordance with that wise official usage, which recognises the necessity of holidays no less for statesmen than for schoolboys, the Queen's Ministers dispersed themselves over the country, and Lord Canning went to Scotland. It had been settled that he should receive from the hands of Lord Dalhousie the reins of Indian Government on the 1st of February, 1856, and his arrangements, involving a short sojourn in Egypt, and visits to Ceylon, Bombay, and Madras, had been made with a view to his arrival at Calcutta on that day. But at Dalhousie's own request, his resignation was subsequently deferred to the 1st of March. When this request was first made to him, Canning thought that the intention of the change was simply to allow the old Governor-General more time not only to consummate the annexation of Oude, but to confront the first difficulties of the revolution; and it appeared to him, thinking this, that the postponement might be interpreted alike to his own and to his predecessor's disadvantage. It might have been said that the new Governor-General shrank from encountering the dangers of the position, or that the measure was so distasteful to him, on the score of its injustice, that he could not bring himself to put his hand to the work Both assumptions would have been utterly erroneous. The question of the Annexation of Oude had been a Cabinet question, and as a member of the Cabinet, Lord Canning had given his assent to the policy, which, after much discussion in Leadenhall and in Downing-street, found final expression in the Court's despatch of the 19th of November. The policy itself had been already determined, although the precise terms of the instructions to be sent to the Government of India were still under consideration, when Dalhousie's proposal reached him; and he was willing to accept all the responsibilities of the measure. The proposed delay, therefore, did not at first sight please him; but when, from a later letter, he learnt that Dalhousie required a few more weeks of office, not for special, but for general purposes; that he needed time to gather up the ends of a large number of administrative details, the case was altered, and he assented, with the concurrence of the Court of Directors, to the change.* 1855-56.

* "As long," he wrote to the Chairman, "as it turned upon Oude

1855-56. A few days afterwards, Lord Canning turned his face again towards the South, to superintend the final arrangements for his departure, and to take leave of his friends. Thus the month of October and the greater part of November were passed; but not without some study of Indian questions, some useful training for the great work upon which he was about to enter. On the 21st of November he went by command to Windsor, accompanied by Lady Canning, who was among her Majesty's cherished friends, and on the 23rd returned to London, after taking final leave of the Queen. Another day or two, and he had commenced his overland journey to the East. From the French capital he wrote, on the last day of November: "I intended to leave Paris this afternoon, but I received notice in the morning that the Emperor wished to see me to-morrow, so that it will be Tuesday morning (December 4th) before we embark at Marseilles. We still hope to reach Alexandria on the 10th." He arrived there, however, not before the 12th, and after a day's halt pushed on to Cairo, where he was received and entertained magnificently by orders of the Pacha, who was at that time absent from his capital.

The party consisted of Lord and Lady Canning, his nephew Lord Hubert de Burgh,* Captain Bou-

alone, I felt that there was some difficulty in making the change proposed by Lord Dalhousie, and some risk of its intention being misrepresented to the disadvantage of both of us. But it is now clear that for other reasons, apart from Oude, and for the general winding up of the work on his hands, it will be a great help to him to have a month more time. These are his very words to me; and I cannot hesitate, so far as I am concerned, to do that which will be agreeable and convenient to him, and probably advantageous to the public interests. I hope, therefore, that you will feel no difficulty in complying with Lord Dalhousie's wish, by putting off my succession until the day he names."—*Lord Canning to Mr. Macnaghten, September* 20, 1855.—*MS. Correspondence.*

* Afterwards Lord Hubert Canning.

verie, A.D.C., and Dr. Leckie. There was abundant 1855-56
time for an exploration of the wonders of Egypt, and, as the fine climate of the country invited a protracted sojourn there, it was arranged that some weeks should be spent in pleasant and profitable excursions, and that they should embark at Suez about the middle of the month of January. "The Pacha was in Upper Egypt until to-day," wrote Lord Canning to Mr. Macnaghten, on the 17th of December, "when he returned to this neighbourhood. I am to see him to-morrow, and on the following day we set out on our expedition up the Nile. Thanks to a steamer, which the Pacha lends us, we shall be able to accomplish all we wish, and to embark on the *Feroze* immediately upon its arrival at Suez, which, according to a letter from Lord Dalhousie, that met me at Alexandria, will not be until close upon the 12th of January. . . . The magnificence, not to say extravagance, of our reception here far exceeds anything that I had expected. I shall need to be very profuse of my thanks to the Pacha to-morrow."

It would be pleasant to follow Lord Canning and his family on their river-voyage, the grateful experiences of which he has himself recorded, but these personal incidents have no connexion with the stern story before me, and the temptation, therefore, to enlarge upon them must be resisted. The programme of his movements given in the above letter to the Chairman of the Company, was realised with but little departure from the original design. The Governor-General elect halted at Aden, where, under the guidance of Brigadier Coghlan*—an officer of the Company's Artillery, one of those excellent

* Afterwards Sir William Coghlan, K.C.B.

1856. public servants who, partly in a military, partly in a diplomatic capacity, represent great interests and undertake great responsibilities in the East—Lord Canning made his first acquaintance with the Sepoy Army of India. From Aden he steamed to Bombay, where he arrived on the 28th of January, 1856, and first planted his foot on Indian soil. "I found," he wrote to Mr. Macnaghten on the 2nd of February, "that Lord Dalhousie had given orders that I should be received with the full honours of Governor-General in possession; and of course I did nothing to check or escape from the demonstrations with which we were met, though I did not desire or expect them. I have been unceasingly busy for two-thirds of every twenty-four hours since our arrival; and by the 5th or 6th, I hope to have seen nearly all that calls for ocular inspection in the city and its neighbourhood. We shall then embark for Madras; for I have given up all thoughts of stopping at Ceylon, unless to coal, and hope to arrive there on the 14th or 15th. I cannot sufficiently congratulate myself on having come round by this Presidency. It has shown me much that I should not easily have learnt otherwise." It was a disappointment to him that he had not time to visit Ceylon, for his old Eton tutor, Chapman, had developed into Bishop of Colombo, and there would have been a grand old Etonian pleasure, on both sides, in talking over old times. But there was consolation in the thought that his friend Lord Harris, his fellow-pupil in the Bedfordshire market-town, was Governor of Madras. In that presidency he spent a few pleasant days, sojourning at Guindy, and then on the 25th of February set out to face the realities of Indian Government, and steamed up the Bay of Bengal.

On the last day of February, Lord Canning disembarked at Calcutta; and, proceeding to Government House, at once took his oaths of office and his seat in Council. It is the custom in such cases. No time is left for any question to arise as to who is Governor-General of India. So brief did the whole operation appear to him, that he wrote home that he had been sworn in and installed "within five minutes after touching land." As his dignities and responsibilities commenced at once, so did his work. At the end of his first week of office, he wrote that such had been the pressure of public business, that he had found time only for "one look out of doors" since he arrived. During that first week Lord Dalhousie tarried in Calcutta, and the past and future of the Government of India were discussed with interest, the depths of which were stirred by varying circumstances, between those earnest-minded men; the one all readiness to teach, the other all eagerness to learn. Dull and prosaic as its details often appear to Englishmen at a distance, it is difficult to describe the living interest with which statesmen in India of all classes, from the highest to the lowest, perpetually regard their work. February 29, 1856.

No man ever undertook the office of Governor-General of India under the impression that it would be a sinecure. But it is scarcely less true that no man, whatever opinion he may have formed in England, ever entered upon its duties without discovering that he had greatly underrated the extent of its labours. The current of work is so strong and so continuous; so many waters meet together to swell the stream; that at first even a strong man trying to breast it may feel that he is in danger of being overwhelmed. Time lessens the difficulty; but at the First days of Government.

1856. outset, the multiplicity of unfamiliar details distracts and bewilders even the sharpest wit and the clearest brain; and the first result is apt to be a chaos. Box after box is placed upon the Governor-General's table; and each box is crammed with papers rugged with the names of strange men and stranger places, and references to unknown events and incomprehensible states of society. By some means or other, he must master the antecedents of every case that comes before him for decision; and there are often very intricate cases purposely left for his decision, that he may not be embarrassed by the judgments of his predecessor. Week after week goes by and little impression is made upon this pile of work. "Another fortnight is gone," wrote Lord Canning towards the end of March, "and I am beginning to gather up by slow degrees the threads of business, as it passes before me; but it is severe work to have to give so much time to the bygones of almost every question that comes up; and some weeks more must pass before I shall feel myself abreast of current events." There was a strong conscientiousness within the new Governor-General which would not suffer him to pass anything lightly over, and he endeavoured to understand all that came before him even at the risk of some inconvenient delays.

So he did not rush at his work; but quietly confronted it, and was in no haste to impress people with a sense of the profundity of his wisdom and the greatness of his self-reliance. He knew that he had much to learn, and he adopted the best means of learning it; for he invited all the chief agents of his Government, scattered over the country, especially those who were representing British interests at the Native Courts, to correspond confidentially with him on matters relating to their respective charges; an invitation which gave to every man thus addressed full liberty to declare his sentiments and to expound his views. And thus he escaped the danger on the one hand of surrendering his own judgment, by succumbing to the influence of some two or three public functionaries immediately attached to the Executive Government, and, on the other, of the over-confident exercise of a dominant self-will rejecting all external aids, and refusing to walk by other men's experiences. He knew that there was no royal road to a knowledge of India; and he was well content that the first year of his administration should be unostentatiously devoted to the great duty of learning his work. 1856.

There were able men, too, at his elbow to assist him to a correct knowledge of facts, and to the formation of sound opinions. The Supreme Council consisted at that time of General John Low, Mr. Dorin, Mr. John Peter Grant, and Mr. Barnes Peacock. Of the first I can say little in this place that has not been already said. The only charge laid against him by the assailants of the Government was, that he was well stricken in years. But, although one who had fought beside Malcolm at Mehidpore, and then not in his first youth, must have lost some of the physical energy that animated him in his prime, his intellect was unimpaired. Ceasing to be a man of action, he had subsided gracefully into the condition of a councillor, the Nestor of the Political Service, a veteran without a stain. No man had so large an acquaintance with the Native Courts of India; no man knew the temper of the people better than John Low. He could see with their eyes, and speak with their tongues, and read with their understandings. And, therefore, he looked with some dis- The Council. General Low.

1856. may at the wide-spread Englishism of the Dalhousie school, and sorrowfully regarded the gradual dying out of the principles in which he had been nurtured and trained, and to which, heedless of their unpopularity, he clung with honest resolution to the last. Dalhousie had too often disregarded his counsel; but he had always respected the man. And now Canning equally admired the personal character of his colleague, but was not equally minded to laugh his principles to scorn.

Mr. Dorin. Of the two Bengal civilians who sat in that Council, it may be said that the one owed his position there apparently to chance, the other to his unquestionable abilities. Mr. Dorin was not a man of great parts; he was not a man of high character. If he had any official reputation, it was in the capacity of a financier; and finance was at that time the weakest point of our Government. He had limited acquaintance with the country, and but small knowledge of the people. He had no earnestness; no enthusiasm; no energy. He had a genius for making himself comfortable, and he had no superfluous activities of head or heart to mar his success in that particular direction. He had supported the policy of Lord Dalhousie, and had recorded in his time a number of minutes expressing in two emphatic words, which saved trouble and gained favour, his concurrence with the most noble the Governor-General; and now if the new ruler was not likely to find in him a very serviceable colleague, there was no greater chance of his being found a troublesome one.

John Peter Grant. In John Grant the Governor-General might have found both. He was many years younger than his brother civilian, but he had done infinitely more work. In him, with an indolent sleepy manner was

strangely combined extraordinary activity of mind. 1856.
He was one of the ablest public servants in the country. With some hereditary claim to distinction, he had been marked out from the very commencement of his career, no less by a favourable concurrence of external circumstances than by his own inherent qualifications, for the highest official success. No young civilian in his novitiate ever carried upon him so clearly and unmistakably the stamp of the embryo Councillor, as John Grant. In some respects this was a misfortune to him. His course was too easy. He had found his way; he had not been compelled to make it. He had not been jostled by the crowd; he had seen little or none of the rough work of Indian administration or Indian diplomacy. It had been his lot, as it had been his choice, to spend the greater part of his official life in close connexion with the Head-Quarters of the Government; and, therefore, his opportunities of independent action had been few; his personal acquaintance with the country and the people was not extensive; and his work had been chiefly upon paper. But as a member of a powerful bureaucracy his value was conspicuous. Quick in the mastery of facts, clear and precise in their analytical arrangement, and gifted with more than common powers of expression, he was admirably fitted to discharge the duties of the Secretariat. He was a dead hand at a report; and if Government were perplexed by any difficult questions, involving a tangled mass of disordered financial accounts, or a great conflict of authority mystifying the truth, he was the man of all others to unravel the intricate or to elucidate the obscure. Comparatively young in years, but ripe in bureaucratic experience, he entered the Supreme Council towards the close of Lord Dalhousie's administration. But he had sat long enough

1856. at the Board to establish his independence. He expressed his opinions freely and fearlessly; and his minutes, when minute-writing was in vogue, were commonly the best State papers recorded by the Government of the day. Closely reasoned, forcibly expressed, with here and there touches of quiet humour or subdued sarcasm, they cut through any sophistries put forth by his colleagues, with sharp incisive logic, and clearly stated the points at issue without disguises and evasions. On the whole, he was a man of large and liberal views, the natural manifestations of which were, perhaps, somewhat straitened by an acquired official reserve; and no one questioned the honesty of his intentions or the integrity of his life.

Barnes Peacock.

Mr. Barnes Peacock was the fourth, and, as is commonly called, the "Law Member" of Council. An English lawyer, appointed to aid the great work of Indian legislation, he was a member of the Executive rather by sufferance than by right. In a limited sense, he was supposed to represent the popular element in the Council. There was no very violent conflict of class-interests in those days. But so far as such division existed at all, he was regarded as the exponent of the views of the non-official Englishman and of the Europeanised Natives of the large towns, whose interests are bound up with our own. For the institution of the Company he was believed to have no respect, and for the exclusive system of Government by the Company's servants no toleration. He had a clear head, an acute understanding, but by no means a large mind. Assiduous in the work of law-making, he was the very soul of the Legislative Council; and had he confined his efforts to the work of moulding into draft-acts the ideas of other men, he would have been an invaluable public servant. But he sometimes went beyond this; and, when he did so, he commonly went wrong. For knowing little of the people of India, and having only thoroughly English notions of philanthropic reforms and legislative beneficences, he would have taught the people better manners with a rapidity for which they were not prepared, if he had unrestrainedly followed out his own ideas of social improvement. Indeed, he had already threatened to limit the polygamies of the Natives of India, and, doubtless, had a draft-act for the purpose on the legislative anvil, when circumstances arrested his career of reform. But, although it was in the legislative department that his especial strength lay, he did not confine himself to it. He grappled manfully with all the varied details of the general administration. There were times when his legal penetration was of service in the disentanglement of knotty questions of executive government, and he sometimes recorded minutes distinguished by no common powers of special pleading. But, on the whole, this laborious addiction to business was an encumbrance and an embarrassment to the Ministry; and Lord Canning had soon reason to complain of the conscientious excesses of his colleague. A general disinclination to take anything for granted impeded the progress of business; and the Governor-General, not without a feeling of admiration for a defect that had its root in honesty of purpose, endeavoured, and with good success, to wean the law member from his habit of mastering details which he was not expected to understand, and keeping back business which it was desirable to dispose of, whilst he was working up the past history of a Native State, or calculating grain- 1856.

1856. bags in a commissariat account. There must have been some inward promptings of self-knowledge in Canning's own mind to assure him that this laborious conscientiousness was a part of his own nature; but he felt, at the same time, that his larger scope of responsibility demanded from him a larger scope of action, and that what was right in the Governor-General was not therefore right in his departmental colleague.

Such were the fellow-labourers with whom Lord Canning was now about to prosecute the work of Government. On the whole, the Council was not badly constituted for ordinary purposes of administration in quiet times. It contained, indeed, many of the essential elements of a good Board. What it most wanted was military knowledge; for General Low, though an old soldier of the Madras Army, had seen more of the Court than of the Camp; and it was rather in the diplomacies of the Native States than in the conduct of warlike operations, or in the details of military administration, that he had earned, by hard service, the right to be accepted as an authority.* It was a constitutional fiction that, in an Indian Council, the necessary amount of military knowledge was supplied in the person of the Commander-in-Chief, who had a seat in it. The seat, though legally occupied, was for the most part practically empty, for duty might not, and inclination did not, keep the military chief at the Head-Quarters of the Civil Government. But it happened that, when Lord Canning arrived in India, he found General Anson in Calcutta. And it was a pleasure to him to see in the Indian capital a face that had been familiar to him in the English.

* Shortly after Lord Canning's arrival, General Low went to England, but returned at the commencement of the cold weather (1856-57).

The appointment of the Honourable George Anson to the chief command of the Indian Army took by surprise the English communities in the three Presidencies, who had seen his name only in the Racing Calendar, or in other records of the Turf. But there was one thing at least to be said in his favour: he was not an old man. It was not in the nature of things, after a long European peace, that good service should be found in the officers of the Queen's Army unaccompanied by the weight of years. But the scandal of imbecility had risen to such a height, the military world had grown so sick of infirmity in high places—of the blind, the lame, the deaf, the obesely plethoric—that they were prepared to welcome almost any one who could sit a horse, who could see from one end to the other of a regiment in line, and hear the report of a nine-pounder at a distance of a hundred yards. There was nothing to be said against George Anson on this score. He could hear and see; he could ride and walk. He was of a light spare figure, well framed for active exercise; and his aspect was that of a man who could "stand the climate." But with all men who first brave that climate in the maturity of life, there is a risk and an uncertainty; and appearances belied Anson's capabilities of resistance. During the hot weather and rainy season of 1856, the heats and damps of Bengal tried him severely; and Lord Canning more than once wrote home that his military colleague was reduced to a skeleton, and had lost all his bodily strength and all his buoyancy of spirit. But, at the same time, he spoke of the Chief as one who had many excellent points, both as an officer and as a man. The precise limits of authority vested in the chief civil and military functionaries are so ill defined, that, when the powers of both are combined in one individual, it is

1856.
General Anson.

1856. a mercy if he does not quarrel with himself. When they are divided, as is commonly the case, a conflict of authority is inevitable. And so at this time, the Governor-General and the Commander-in-Chief soon came into official collision; but it never grew into personal strife between Lord Canning and General Anson. The public prints hinted that there was a rupture between them; and the same story travelled homewards and penetrated Cannon-row. But the Civilian wrote, that though there had been some special points of difference between them, the temper of the Soldier was so charming, and he was so thoroughly a gentleman, that it was quite impossible to quarrel with him. The inevitable antagonism of official interests could not weaken the ties of personal regard; and when Anson, in the month of September, left Calcutta on a tour of military inspection in the Upper Provinces, he carried with him no kindlier wishes than those which attended him warm from the heart of the Governor-General.*

* What Lord Canning wrote about General Anson is so honourable to both, that it is quite a pleasure to quote it. "We get on admirably together," wrote the Governor-General in June. "His temper is charming, and I know no one whom I should not be sorry to see substituted for him." And again, in October: "I am not surprised at the report you mention that Anson and I do not get on well together, because such a rumour was current in Calcutta two or three months ago, and even found its way into the newspapers. I believe it originated in a difference between us on two points; one (of much interest to the Indian Army), the power of the Commander-in-Chief to withhold applications for furlough, transmitted through him to the Governor-General in Council; the other, an authority to exercise something very like a veto upon the Governor-General's selections of officers for civil and political service. Upon both of which I found it necessary to disallow his pretensions. But neither these disagreements, nor the reports to which they gave rise, have for a moment caused any misunderstanding or reserve between us. It would be very difficult to quarrel with any one so imperturbably good tempered, and so thoroughly a gentleman."—*MS. Correspondence.*

CHAPTER II.

LORD CANNING'S FIRST YEAR—THE OUDE COMMISSION—WAJID ALI AND THE EMBASSY TO ENGLAND—THE PERSIAN WAR—THE QUESTION OF COMMAND—JAMES OUTRAM—CENTRAL-ASIAN POLICY—DOST MAHOMED—JOHN LAWRENCE AND HERBERT EDWARDES AT PESHAWUR—HENRY LAWRENCE IN LUCKNOW.

WITH these colleagues in the Council Chamber, and with a staff of able, well-trained secretaries, of whom I shall speak hereafter, in the several Departments, the new Governor-General found the burden of his work, though it pressed heavily upon him, in no way galling or dispiriting. There are always small vexations and embarrassments; incidental details, that will not run smoothly in the administrative groove, but grind and grate and have a stubborn obstructiveness about them. But the great sum-total of the business before him wore an aspect cheerful and encouraging. There was tranquillity in India. Outwardly, it seemed that Lord Dalhousie had left only a heritage of Peace. Even in Oude, just emerging from a revolution, there were external signs of general quietude; of contentment, or at least of submission; and of the satisfactory progress of the administration. But a new administrator was wanted. Outram had done his work. He had been selected to fill the office of Resident, and no man could have more be-

1856.

The Administration of Oude.

1856. comingly represented British interests at a corrupt and profligate Court. In that capacity it had fallen to his lot to accomplish ministerially the revolution which had been decreed by the British Government. But it was work that sickened him; for although he believed that it was the duty of the Paramount State to rescue Oude from the anarchy by which it had so long been rent, he was one whose political predilections were in favour of the maintenance of the Native States, and he knew that much wrong had been done to the Princes and Chiefs of India under the plea of promoting the interests of the people. When the Proclamation converted Oude into a British province, the Resident became Chief Commissioner, and the superintendence of the administration was the work that then devolved upon him. But it was work that Outram was not now destined to perform. His health had broken down; the hot season was coming on apace; and a voyage to England had been urgently pressed upon him by his medical advisers. So he sought permission to lay down the Portfolio for a while, and asked the Governor-General to appoint an officer to act for him in his absence.

Question of succession.

It would have been comparatively easy to find a successor suited to the work, if the appointment to be disposed of had been a permanent one. But Lord Canning had to find a man able to conduct the administration at its most difficult stage, and yet willing to forsake other important work for the brief tenure of another's office. Outram said that there was one man in whom both the ability and the will were to be found. That man was Henry Ricketts, a Bengal civilian of high repute, whose appointment was pressed upon Lord Canning as the best that could be made. But Ricketts was wanted for other work.

The authorities at home were clamouring for a reduction of expenditure; and as retrenchment, public or private, commonly begins in the wrong place, a revision of official salaries was to be one of the first efforts of our economy. So Mr. Ricketts had been specially appointed to furnish a Report on the best means of extracting from the officers of Government the same amount of good public service for a less amount of public money. Lord Canning shook his head doubtfully at the experiment; but Cannon-row was urgent, and nothing was to be suffered to interrupt the labours of the man who was to suggest the means of increasing the financial prosperity of the Company by sapping out the energies of those upon whom that prosperity mainly depended. 1856.

Whilst Outram and the Governor-General were corresponding about this arrangement, another plan for the temporary administration of Oude was suggesting itself; but it never became more than a suggestion. Ever since the dissolution of the Lahore Board, Sir Henry Lawrence had held office as chief of the Political Agency in Rajpootana. It was a post of honour and responsibility; but there was not in the work to be done enough to satisfy so ardent and so active a mind, and he had longed, during that great struggle before Sebastopol, which he had watched with eager interest from the beginning, to show, when all the departments were breaking down, what a rough and-ready Indian Political might do to help an army floundering miserably in a strange land. But this field of adventure was closed against him. Peace was proclaimed: and Henry Lawrence, who had studied well the history and the institutions of Oude, and who had advocated the assumption of the government, but not the annexation of the pro-

1856. vince or the absorption of its revenues, thought that he might do some good by superintending the administration during the first year of our tenure. There were many interests to be dealt with in that conjuncture, which required a strong but a gentle hand to accommodate them to the great revolution that had been accomplished, and he felt some apprehension lest civilian-government, harsh and precise, should forthwith begin to systematise, in utter disregard of the institutions and the usages of the country, and should strike at once for a flourishing balance-sheet. It was too little the fashion to sympathise with the fallen fortunes of men ruined by the dominant influence of the White Race. In the chivalrous benevolence of the out-going Commissioner, Henry Lawrence had full confidence. The great-hearted compassion which Outram had shown for the Ameers of Scinde, proclaimed the mercy and the justice of the man. But a civilian of the new school from the Regulation Provinces might bring with him a colder heart and a sharper practice, and might overbear all ancient rights and privileges in pursuit of the favourite theory of the Dead Level. Anxious to avert this, which he believed would be a calamity alike to the people of Oude and to his own government, Henry Lawrence offered to serve, during the transition-period, in Outram's place; and the first misfortune that befel the ministry of Lord Canning was that the letter, conveying the proposal, arrived a little too late. A Commissioner had already been appointed.

The New Commissioner.

The choice had fallen on Mr. Coverley Jackson, a civilian from the North-West Provinces, an expert revenue-officer, held in high esteem as a man of ability, but more than suspected of some infirmity of temper. Aware of this notorious failing, but not deeming it sufficient to disqualify one otherwise so well fitted for the post, Lord Canning accompanied his offer of the appointment with a few words of caution, frank but kindly, and Jackson in the same spirit received the admonition, assuring the Governor-General that it would be his earnest endeavour to conciliate the good feelings of all who might be officially connected with him, so far as might be consistent with the claims of the public service and the maintenance of the authority entrusted to him. But he did not accomplish this; and there is slight evidence that he resolutely attempted it. It was an untoward occurrence that the man next in authority, and the one with whom the circumstances of the province brought him most frequently into official communication, was as little able to control his temper as Jackson himself. Mr. Martin Gubbins, of the Bengal Civil Service, was the Financial Commissioner. Upon him devolved the immediate superintendence of the revenue administration of our new territory, whilst Mr. Ommaney, of the same service, superintended the department of Justice. A man of rare intelligence and sagacity, eager and energetic, Martin Gubbins would have been a first-rate public servant, if his utility had not been marred by a contentious spirit. His angularities of temper were continually bringing him into collision with others, and his pertinacious self-assertion would not suffer him, when once entangled in a controversy, ever to detach himself from it. Of all men in the service he was the one least likely to work harmoniously with the Chief Commissioner. So it happened that, in a very short time, they were in a state of violent antagonism. Whether, in the first instance, Jackson

1856.

Jackson and Gubbins.

1856. overstrained his authority, and unwisely and unkindly expressed his displeasure in language calculated to excite irritation and resentment, or whether Gubbins was the first to display an insubordinate spirit, and to provoke the censure of his chief by the attempted usurpation of his powers, it is of little importance now to inquire. The sharp contention that grew up between them was soon made known to the Governor-General, who deplored and endeavoured to arrest it. How wisely and calmly he conveyed to the Commissioner an expression, less of his displeasure than of his regret, his correspondence pleasantly illustrated.* But no kindly counsel from Government House could smoothe down the asperities of Jackson's temper. As time advanced, the feud between him and Gubbins grew more bitter and more irreconcilable. In India, a paper war once commenced lasts out many a military campaign. There is something so exciting, so absorbing in it, that even the best public servants sometimes forget the public interests whilst they are wasting their time and expending their energies in personal conflicts and criminations. Had Coverley Jackson taken half as much pains to see that the pledges of the British Government were fulfilled, and the annexation of Oude rendered as little ruinous

* Take, for example, the following: "Judging by my own experience, I should say that in dealing with public servants who have incurred blame, everything is to be gained by telling them their faults in unmistakable language, plainly and nakedly; but that one's purpose (their amendment) is rather defeated than otherwise by the use of terms that sting them, or amplify their offences to them unnecessarily—even though all be done within the strict limits of truth and fact. I believe that if a man has at bottom a sense of his duty, and is possessed of the feelings and temper of a gentleman, the more simply his error is put before him, and the more plain and quiet the reproof, the better chance there is of his correcting himself readily and willingly, and that if we wish to get work done hereafter out of some one whom it is necessary to rebuke, we ought to give him as little excuse as possible (he will too often find it where it is not given) for feeling irritated against ourselves." —*Lord Canning to Mr. Coverley Jackson, July* 7, 1856.—*MS. Correspondence.*

as possible to all the chief people of the province, as he did to convict his subordinates of official misdemeanours, it would have been better both for his own character and for the character of the nation. But whilst Jackson and Gubbins were in keen contention with each other, covering reams of paper with their charges and counter-charges and their vehement self-assertions, the generous nature of the Governor-General was grieved by complaints and remonstrances from the King, who declared, or suffered it to be declared for him, that the English officers in Lucknow were inflicting grievous wrongs and indignities upon him and upon his Family, seizing or destroying his property, and humiliating the members and dependents of his House. 1856.

It has been shown that Wajid Ali, when he saw that all hope of saving his dominions from the great white hand that had been laid upon them had utterly gone from him, had talked about travelling to England and laying his sorrows at the foot of the Throne. But, in truth, travelling to England, or to any other place, was a thing rather to be whined about than to be done, by one so destitute of all activities, physical and mental, and it was almost certain that he would hitch somewhere; not improbably at the first stage. And so he did. Halting not far from Lucknow, the King awaited the on-coming of his minister, Ali Nuckee Khan, a man not wanting in activities of any kind, who had been detained at the capital to aid in the "transfer of the Government," out of which he had been ousted. But after a while King and Minister, and other regal appendages, male and female, moved on towards Calcutta —the first stages by land; then afterwards taking the river-steamer, at a time of year when there is ever a

Movements of the ex-King.

1856. scant supply of water for such travelling, they were constrained to go "round by the Sunderbunds," and make a long and by no means a pleasant voyage to the English capital; of which necessity Lord Canning shrewdly observed that it would give his Majesty such a foretaste of life on board as would inevitably drive out of him any lingering thought of the passage across the black water to England.

And so it was. The King arrived at Calcutta when the month of May had burnt itself half out, and was soon domiciled in a house on the river-side, which had erst been the suburban villa of an English Chief-Justice. It was enough for him to see the steamers smoking past him sea-wards; and to keep steadily before him the conviction that for a man of his tastes and habits, to take no account of his girth, Garden-Reach was a more recommendable place than the Bay of Bengal, the Red Sea, or the Mediterranean. But still the pilgrimage to the foot of the Throne was to be undertaken, not by but for the last of the Oude Kings. Without any sacrifice of his personal ease, or any abandonment of the delights of the Zenana, he might enter a vicarious appearance at St. James's by sending the chief members of his family—the nearest of his kindred, in each stage and relation, before, beside, and after him—his mother, his brother, and his son, with agents and ministers, black and white, to plead against the seizure of his dominions.

The Oude Mission.

There was one of the royal party with some substance of masculine vigour still left as God had given it; and that one was not the Heir-Apparent, or the so-called General, or a born manhood of any kind, but the Queen-Mother, who set the example of going across the dreary waste of black water and level sand straight to the feet of the Queen of England. And

they went, not scantily attended either, those three, 1856
like thieves in the night, embarking secretly in the darkness, and taking Government House by surprise with the report of the accomplished fact of their departure. Not that Government House would have opposed any obstacle to their going in broad daylight, with drums beating and flags flying; but that the steam-company, with an eye to business, thought it better to make a secret of it; such fellow-travellers, according to European notions, not increasing the comforts of the voyage. As to the Governor-General, all he could say was, "Let them go;" pitying the East India Company, thus compelled to receive such troublesome visitors, but claiming for them kindly and courteous treatment at the hands of the magnates of Leadenhall. And so those representatives of the exploded kingship of Oude went westward, with vague but extensive ideas of a recovery past looking for on this side of eternity, buoyed up and encouraged by men who well knew the hopelessness of the endeavour. The "case" was miserably mismanaged. There was much internal strife, and scarcely an attempt to strike out against the common foe. The so-called "Mission" went to pieces and rotted piecemeal. Not merely waste of treasure was there, but waste of life. The Queen-Mother and the Prince-General died, and were buried in the great cemetery of Père la Chaise. The Heir-Apparent, money-bound and helpless, threw himself upon the mercy of the enemy, borrowed from them half a lakh of rupees, and was carried homewards, somewhat dazed and bewildered as to the upshot or no upshot of the whole affair, but with a prevailing sense of escape and relief that it was all over. And the rest of the luckless embassy went at last, leaving behind

1856. them some scum of official trouble and mishap, and some legal perplexities not readily soluble by any "perfection of human reason" known in our English courts.

Grievances of the ex-King. Meanwhile, in the name of the King himself, ministerial activities had not been wanting in India to make substantial grievance, not so much of the thing done (for that was left to the "Mission") as of the manner of doing it, which had not been all right. In the Humanities, wherein is included the great art of letting down easily, good to be learnt alike by Men and by Governments, we had not taken first-class honours. Not without some reddenings of shame is it to be recorded that the wrongs inflicted upon the Princes of India in the shape of territorial dispossessions and titular extinctions had been sometimes supplemented by lesser wrongs, more grievous to bear upon the one side and less to be justified on the other. For there is some dignity in great wrong, doing or suffering; and a persuasion, in one case, not without sincerity at the bottom, that wrong is right. But look at the matter in what light we may, it can be nothing but miserable wrong to make these dispossessions and extinctions, which may be for the national good, the forerunners of personal distresses and humiliations to individuals thus dispossessed and extinguished. Yet men and, redder shame still, feeble Zenana-bred women had brought this charge against the strong Government of the British, before the kingdom of Oude was marked for extinction; and now again the same complaint of supplemental cruelties and indignities, more galling than the one great wrong itself, went up from Wajid Ali, or was uttered in his name. It was charged against us that our officers had turned the stately palaces of Lucknow into stalls and kennels, that delicate women, the daughters or the companions of Kings, had been sent adrift, homeless and helpless, that treasure-houses had been violently broken open and despoiled, that the private property of the royal family had been sent to the hammer, and that other vile things had been done very humiliating to the King's people, but far more disgraceful to our own. 1856.

Not only so disgraceful, but so injurious to us, so great a blunder, indeed, would such conduct have been, that all who had any hope of the restoration of the Oude monarchy must have devoutly wished the story to be true. There were those who had such hope. How could it be hopeless, when it was remembered that the Sepoy Army of the Company was full of men whose homes were in Oude; when it was believed that the great flood of English rule was sweeping away all existing interests, and destroying all the influential classes alike in the great towns and in the rural districts? The ministers and courtiers of the King of Oude were at large in Calcutta and the neighbourhood, and might journey whithersoever they pleased. Vast fields of intrigue were open before them. The times were propitious. It was plain that there was a feeling of inquietude in the native mind, and that fear had engendered discontent. It was certain that the British Government were weak, for the country was stripped of European troops. The good day might yet come. Meanwhile, it might be something to spread abroad, truly or falsely, a story to the effect that the English, adding insult to injury, had cruelly humiliated all the members of the Oude family left behind in Lucknow.

In these stories of official cruelty Canning had small faith. But the honour of his Government demanded that they should be inquired into and contradicted, and he urged the Chief Commissioner at

1856. once to investigate and report upon the charges put forth by the creatures of the King. But Jackson, full of his own wrongs, failed to see the importance of the task assigned to him, and his answers were unsatisfactory and apparently evasive. Privately as well as publicly he was urged by the Governor-General to address himself seriously to the work of effacing from the nation the dishonour with which the dependents of the old Court of Lucknow had endeavoured to besmear the British name. But the result was not what Lord Canning had sought, not what he had expected. So at last, bitterly grieved and disappointed by the manner in which his representative had dealt with a subject, at once of so delicate and so important a nature, the Governor-General thus becomingly poured forth his indig-

October 19, 1856. nation: "I will not conceal from you," he wrote to Mr. Jackson, "my disappointment at the manner in which from first to last you have treated this matter. Instead of enabling the Government to answer distinctly and categorically every complaint which the King has preferred, you have passed over unnoticed some upon which you must have known that the Government were without materials for reply. Upon placing your answers, now that all have been received, side by side with the King's letters, I find myself quite unable to say whether any buildings such as he describes have been pulled down, and if so, why?—although one building, the Jelwa Khana, had been especially mentioned to the King, as in course of demolition—whether dogs or horses have been quartered in the Chutter Munzil, and especially whether a stoppage of the allowances to the King's descendants has been threatened, a statement to this effect being pointedly made in the King's letter of the 14th of September You tell me that you have

delayed your answers in order that they may be more 1856.
complete. I can hardly think, therefore, that these matters have escaped you, and yet I do not know how otherwise to account for their being passed by. Be this as it may, the result of your course of proceeding is that the Governor-General is placed in an unbecoming, not to say humiliating position towards the King of Oude. The King brings complaints, which, whether true or false, are plain enough against the officers of Government, and the Governor-General, after assuring the King that as soon as reference shall have been made to the Chief Commissioner, satisfactory explanation shall be given, and relying, as he has a right to do, that that officer will obey his instructions and do his duty, finds himself altogether mistaken, and defeated upon points which, however unworthy of notice they may appear to the Chief Commissioner at Lucknow, cannot be slurred over by the Government in Calcutta. It matters nothing that these charges are instigated by disreputable hangers-on of the King, or that they are wholly or partly untrue, or even impossible. There they are in black and white, and they must be answered. It is surprising to me that you should have failed to appreciate the necessity."

And it was surprising; but Coverley Jackson, at that time, could scarcely appreciate any necessity save that of riding roughshod over Gubbins and Ommaney, and keeping them down to the right subordinate level. How far these charges of cruel indifference to the feelings of the Oude family were true, to what extent the dependents of the late King were wronged and humiliated, and the nobles of the land despoiled and depressed; how, indeed, the revolution affected all existing interests, are subjects reserved for future inquiry. It would have been well if the Chief Commis-

1856. sioner had done as much to mollify these poor people as to exasperate his own colleagues. But the temper of the man was to the last degree arbitrary and exacting, and Lord Canning, though with admirable patience and moderation he strove to control the excesses of his agent, could not hold them in check. Pointing to the great exemplar of John Lawrence, the Oude administration having been constructed on the Punjabee model, he showed that the reins of government might be held with a firm and vigorous hand by one not grasping at all departmental authority. But these kindly teachings were in vain. The old strife continued. Striking with one hand at Gubbins, and with the other at Ommaney, the Chief Commissioner was continually in an attitude of offence; and the administration was likely to be wrecked altogether upon the lee-shore of these internal contentions. So, at last, the Governor-General was forced upon the conviction that he had selected the wrong man to preside in Oude, and that the sooner he could be removed from it the better for the province.

The readiest means of effecting this, without any public scandal or any recorded reproach injurious to Jackson's career, was by the restoration of James Outram to the post which the civilian had been holding for him. Very unfit, doubtless, was the "officiating Chief Commissioner" for that post; but he had done good service to the State, he had some commendable points of character, and even at the bottom of his proved incapacity for this particular office there might be nothing worse than a distempered zeal. So Lord Canning, in the exercise of what is called a "sound discretion," as well as in obedience to the dictates of a kind heart, sought to accomplish the end in view by a return to the *status ante* in the natural order of things, rather than by any violent supersession of his unfortunate nominee. It was doubly a source, therefore, of satisfaction to him to learn that Outram, whose shattered health at the time of his departure in the spring had excited sad forebodings in the mind of the Governor-General, now in the autumn declared himself convalescent and about to return to his work. But the work, the very thought of which had breathed into the veins of the soldier-statesman new health, and revived all his prostrate activities, was not administrative business in Oude. It was altogether work of another kind and in another place, far enough away from the scene of all his former endeavours; work the account of which must be prefaced by some historical explanations. 1856.

The rupture with Persia.

Scarcely had Lord Canning taken his place in Government House, when the question of a war with Persia began to assume portentous dimensions. Truly, it was not his concern. Ever since the days when, nearly half a century before, there had been a strange mad scramble for diplomatic supremacy in Persia between the delegates of the Governor-General and of the Court of St. James's, the position of the Government of India towards our Persian Mission and our Persian policy had been very indistinctly defined. The financial responsibility of the Company had been at all times assumed, and the executive assistance of the Indian Government had been called for, when our relations with that perfidious Court had been beset with difficulties beyond the reach of diplomatic address. But the political control had been vested in the Imperial Government, as represented by the Foreign Office;* and the officers of the Mission had been

* Except during a brief interval; that is, between the years 1826 and 1835, when the King's Government delegated partially the management of affairs to the Governor-General, only to resume it wholly again.

1856. nominated by the Crown. Affairs were still in this state when Lord Canning assumed the Government of India, and found that Great Britain was rapidly drifting into a war with Persia, which it would be his duty to direct, and the resources for which must be supplied from the country under his charge.

Herat. The difficulties, which now seemed to render war inevitable, were chronic difficulties, which were fast precipitating an acute attack of disease. They were an after-growth of the great convulsion of 1838, which had culminated in the war in Afghanistan. We had tried to forget that hated country; but there was a Nemesis that forbade oblivion. It was an article of our political faith that Herat must be an independent principality, and we clung to it as if the very salvation of our Indian Empire depended on the maintenance of this doctrine. But there was nothing in the whole range of Eastern politics so certain to engender continual tribulation, and at last to compel us to apostatise in despair. The independence of Herat was a shadowy idea; it never could be a substantial reality. With an Army of Occupation in Afghanistan, and with British officers freely disbursing British gold at the "gate of India," we had for a while maintained the outward independence of the principality under Shah Kamran of the Suddozye House of Caubul; but even then the minister, Yar Mahomed, was continually declaring that his heart was with Iran, and threatening to throw himself into the arms of the Persian King. When the British Army had evacuated Afghanistan, the bold, unscrupulous minister, having soon relieved himself of the nominal sovereignty of the Suddozye, began to rule the country on his own account. And he ruled it well: that is, he ruled it with vigour; and for some ten years, by astute diplomacy, the soul of

which was a system of small concessions to Persia, 1852.
which soothed her pride and averted great demands, he governed the principality in peace, and maintained its nominal integrity. But his son, Syud Mahomed, who succeeded him, had none of the essentials of a great ruler. Plentifully endowed with his father's wickedness, he lacked all his father's vigour. Treacherous and unscrupulous, but feeble in the extreme, he was ready, on the first appearance of danger, to become a creature of the Persian Court. Persia eagerly seized the opportunity; and again England appeared upon the scene.

In the course of 1852, a Persian Army marched upon Herat. Not, indeed, in open defiance; not with any avowed object of conquest; but nominally, as a powerful ally, to perform an office of friendship. On the death of Yar Mahomed the affairs of the principality had fallen into confusion, and the Persian Army went forth with the benevolent design of restoring them to order and prosperity. But the mask was soon thrown aside. The real object of the expedition proclaimed itself. Herat was declared to be an appendage of the Persian monarchy. This was not to be borne. To maintain the independence of Herat, England a few years before had been prepared to send her legions to the gates of the city. And now Persia was destroying it by a trick. So, fortified by instructions from Downing-street, the British minister resisted the outrage. On pain of an entire forfeiture of the friendship of Great Britain, the Persian Government were called upon to withdraw their army, and to enter into a solemn covenant binding them to recognise and respect the independence of Herat. There were then the usual displays of trickery and evasiveness; but overawed at last by the resolute bearing of

1853. the British minister, the required pledge was given, and Persia bound herself to acknowledge the independence which she was so eager to crush. But she was sorely disturbed and irritated by our interference with her schemes of ambition; and thenceforth the British Mission became an object of dislike and suspicion at Teheran; and a rupture between the two Courts was only a question of time.

The war in the Crimea delayed—it did not avert—the inevitable crisis. The genius of Persia had then free scope for exercise, and turned to the best account its opportunities of double-dealing. Waiting the sentence of the great Judge of Battles, she coquetted both with Russia and with the Allies, and was ready to sell her good offices to the stronger party, or in a time of uncertainty to the higher bidder. But when the war ceased, her importance was gone; she had not been able to turn her position to account during the day of strife, and when peace dawned again upon Europe, she tried in vain to be admitted to the great international Council, which made the work of reconciliation complete. Disappointed and offended, perhaps, not thinking much of our boasted victory, for Russia had been successful in Asiatic Turkey, and Persia knew less about Sebastopol than about Kars, she could see no profit in the English alliance. The minister who then directed her affairs had no feeling of affection for the British representative at her Court. A strong personal prejudice, therefore, came in to aggravate the national antipathy; and before the end of 1855, the Mission had been so grievously insulted that Mr. Murray hauled down the British Flag, and set his face towards the Turkish frontier.

1855. Into the details of this affair it is unnecessary to enter. Another event occurred about the same time.

A rebellion broke out in Herat. Syud Mahomed was killed. In his place was installed a member of the old Suddozye House, a nephew of Shah Kamran, Yusoof Khan by name, who had no peculiar qualifications for empire, but who could not be worse than the man whom he had supplanted. A revolution of this kind is so much in the common course of Afghan history, that we need not seek to account for it by any other than internal causes. But it was said that it had been fomented by Persian intrigue; and it is certain that the Government of the Shah were eager to profit by the crisis. The times were propitious. There was in Central Asia at that time one great man, whose movements were regarded at the Persian Court with alarm not altogether feigned, though sometimes exaggerated for a purpose. Ever since the British had set the seal on their confession of gigantic failure in Afghanistan by restoring Dost Mahomed to empire, the energies and activities of the old Ameer had expended themselves on the consolidation of his former dominions; and now he was hot to extend them to the westward. It was not merely an impulse of ambition. In part, at least, it was an instinct of self-preservation. The pretensions of Persia were not limited, and her encroachments were not likely to be confined, to the principality of Herat. Already she had established a dominant influence in Candahar, and did not scruple to talk about her rights of dominion. It was impossible for Dost Mahomed to regard this with unconcern. That Persia had views of extended influence, if not of actual conquest, in Afghanistan was certain. She had proposed to the Ameer himself to reduce the whole country to the condition of a protected State. The time had now come for him to put forth a mighty hand and a 1855.

1855. stretched-out arm for the maintenance of the independence of Afghanistan. Kohun-dil-Khan, his half-brother, the Chief of Candahar, died in the autumn of 1855. Dost Mahomed had never trusted him; and his son was not to be trusted. So the Ameer, who had no love for half-measures, annexed Candahar to the kingdom of Caubul; and the Persian Government believed, or pretended to believe, that he included Herat itself in his scheme of conquest.

He had at that time no such design. But it was a favourite trick of Persia to justify her own acts of aggression by a reference to some alleged danger and the necessity of self-preservation. So, seeing in the internal state of Herat an encouraging opportunity, and in the movements of Dost Mahomed a plausible pretext for evading their obligations, the Government of the Shah tore the convention of 1853 into shreds,
1856. and again marched an army upon Herat. But it met with no welcome there. Alarmed by the movements of the Caubul Ameer, and threatened with a counter-revolution at home, the nominal ruler of Herat had turned towards the Persians for assistance, but when he found that the chief people of the place were opposed to such an alliance, and that a strong national Sooneeism prevailed among them, he hoisted British colours and invited Dost Mahomed to come to his aid. The characteristic bad faith of the Suddozye Princes was conspicuous in this wretched man. His own people could not trust him. The Persians were investing the place, and it was feared that Yusoof Khan would betray the city into their hands. It was easy, therefore, to raise a party against him. So Eesa Khan, the Deputy or Lieutenant-Governor of the place, caused him to be seized, and sent him a prisoner into the enemy's camp, with a letter declaring that he was of

no use in Herat, and that the Persians might do with him as they liked. 1856.

To this point events had progressed when Lord Canning was called upon to address himself seriously to the consideration of the troubled politics of Central Asia. To the new Governor-General these complications were a source of no common anxiety, for he could see clearly that England was drifting into war, and that, however little he might have to do with it in its origin and conception, its execution would be entrusted to him. There was a bitter flavour about the whole affair that was distasteful in the extreme to the Governor-General. "My hope of an accommodation," he wrote to the President in August, "has almost died out, and I contemplate the prospect of the inglorious and costly operations which lie before us with more disgust than I can express."* He had gone out, as others had gone before him, with an avowed and a sincere desire for peace; but warned by their cruel disappointments, he had laid fast hold in India of the resolution which he had formed in England, and he was not by any adverse or any alluring circumstances to be driven or enticed into unnecessary war. "Do not," he said, "be afraid of my being unduly hasty to punish Persia. Unless the Shah should steam up the Hooghly, with Murray swinging at his yard-arm, I hope that we shall be able to keep the peace until your instructions arrive."† And he was anxious to avoid, not only aggressive measures from the side of India, but any diplomatic entanglements that might at some future time be a cause of perplexity to his Government. The politics of Central Asia he regarded with extreme aversion. Remember-

* Lord Canning to Mr. Vernon Smith, August 8, 1856.—*MS.*

† The same to the same, April 22, 1856.—*MS.*

1856. ing the fearful lessons of the Past, he determined not, of his own free will, to send a single man into Afghanistan; and he resisted the promptings of Ministers at home, when it was suggested to him somewhat prematurely that seasonable donatives might convert Dost Mahomed into an effective ally, willing and ready to apply a blister from the side of Candahar.
August, 1856. And when, at a later period, instructions came from England to supply the Ameer with arms and money and authority was given to the Governor-General to send a British Mission to Herat, he shrunk from acting upon the latter suggestion. "I do not purpose," he wrote, "to use the permission to send British officers to Herat. We know much too little of things there to justify this step, which would for certain be full of risk. The place is hard pressed by famine as well as by the enemy. Our officers could take with them no relief nor any promise of it, for we are not going to march to Herat ourselves, and we cannot afford to promise on the faith of the Ameer's performances."

But unwilling as was Lord Canning to adopt the measures, to which reference was made in these letters, he could not maintain this policy of non-interference in Afghanistan after the Home Government had determined upon the declaration of war against Persia. The year had scarcely dawned, when such an upshot began to be discussed as something of no very remote reality, and before Parliament had broken up and her Majesty's Ministers had dispersed for the autumn, the equipment of an expedition to the Persian Gulf had been decreed. The orders from Home were that all preparations should be made for the despatch of a military and naval expedition from

1856.

Bombay to the Persian Gulf; but that pending the progress of some further diplomacies in Europe, which might end in concessions, no actual start should be made. It was not until the end of September that her Majesty's Government, through the legal channel of the Secret Committee of the Court of Directors of the East India Company, sent out final instructions for the sailing of the expedition and the commencement of the war.* On the evening of the last day of October, these instructions reached the Governor-General in Calcutta, and on the following morning—day of evil omen, for eighteen years before it had delivered itself of the sad Afghan manifesto—a proclamation of war was issued. On the same day it was sent to Lord Elphinstone at Bombay, and the General in command was charged with instructions respecting the conduct of the expedition, and ordered straightway to begin.

November 1st.

The question of command.

The question of the command of the expedition had been one, which Lord Canning by no means found it easy to solve. Many names had been suggested to him, and among them that of General Windham—"Windham of the Redan"—who had performed feats of gallantry in the Crimea, and was ready for hard service in any part of the world.

* The orders were, under date July 22, 1856, that measures were to be "immediately taken at Bombay for the preparation of an expedition sufficiently powerful to occupy the island of Karrack in the Persian Gulf, and the district of Bushire on the mainland; but the expedition is not to sail until further orders shall have been received from this country." On the 26th of September the Secret Committee forwarded to Lord Canning copies of Lord Clarendon's instructions to the British Consuls in Persia to withdraw from that country, and of a letter addressed by his Lordship to the Commissioners for the Affairs of India, "requiring that the expedition, which will have been prepared, under instructions of the 22nd of July, shall, as soon as it can be completed, proceed to its destination in the Persian Gulf."

1856 But Lord Canning, whilst thoroughly appreciating Windham's gallant services in the field, and knowing well that his appointment would be "popular in England," saw that there were strong reasons against it. "In a mixed force of Queen's and Company's troops," he said, "it is of great importance that there should be a willing and earnest co-operation of all subordinate officers with the Commander, and it is more difficult to obtain this for a stranger than for one who is known. The Commander should have some acquaintance with the Indian Army, if he has to lead a large force of it into an unknown and difficult country. He should know something of its constitution, temper, and details—of what it can and what it can not do. This would not be the case with Windham, fresh landed from England." And it is not to be doubted that he was right. If the force had been on a larger scale, the Commander-in-Chief himself might perhaps have been placed at its head; but Lord Canning, with the highest possible opinion of General Anson's fine temper, of the assiduity with which he had addressed himself to the business of his high office, and the ability with which he had mastered its details, had still some misgivings with respect to his prejudices, and doubted whether he had not formed certain conclusions unjust to the Company's Army.

On the whole, it was better, in any circumstances, that an Indian officer should command; and Lord Canning was resolute that such should be the arrangement. But he had been somewhat perplexed at first as to the choice to be made, and he had consulted Sir John Lawrence, as the man of all others who, not being by profession a soldier, had the finest soldierly instincts and the keenest appreciation of the essential qualities demanded for the command of such an expedition. What the great Punjabee administrator said in reply was an utterance of good sense and good feeling, the fulness of which, however, was not then as discernible as it now is, viewed by the light of intervening history. About the answer to be given there was no doubt; but clearly there was some difficulty. For the man whom of all men in India he held to be best fitted for the work in hand was his own brother, Sir Henry Lawrence; and if he could go, accompanied by Colonel Sydney Cotton, all would be well. "Cotton," wrote John Lawrence to the Governor-General, "is one of the best officers I have seen in India. He is a thorough soldier, loves his profession, and has considerable administrative talent. Of all the officers I have noted, with one exception, Sydney Cotton is the best." But his experiences, great as they were, had not lain in the line of diplomatic action, and, if it were necessary, as Lawrence believed, to unite the political and the military authority in the same person, Cotton, good soldier as he was, might clearly lack some of the essential qualifications for the double office. So John Lawrence proceeded to say: "The man whom I would name for the command of such an expedition is my brother Henry. I can assure your lordship that I am not in the slightest degree biased in his favour. He has seen a good deal of service, having been in the first Burmese war, in the second Afghan war, and in both the Sutlej campaigns. He is not an officer of much practical knowledge, except in his own branch (the Artillery), and he is not fond of details. But, on the other hand, he has great natural ability, immense force of character, is very popular in his service, has large political acumen, and much administrative ability. I do not think that there is a military man

1856.

Henry Lawrence.

1856. in India who is his equal in these points. He is also in possession of his full vigour, both of mind and body, and there is not a good soldier of the Bengal Army, in the Punjab or perhaps in Upper India, but would volunteer to serve under him. With him as the Commander, and Sydney Cotton as the Second-in-Command, the arrangement would be complete. Cotton is master of all technical details of every arm of the service, and devotes his entire energies and thoughts to the welfare of his soldiers."

All this might have been misunderstood; and a little man, in such a case, would perhaps have hesitated to recommend his brother; but John Lawrence knew that the advice was good, and that he was incapable of offering it if it had not been. "If I know myself," he wrote, "I would revolt against such conduct." But though strong in the conviction that of all men living Henry Lawrence was the best suited to the work in hand, he was loud in his praise of other good officers, and had various plans to recommend, any one of which might have a successful issue. If Sydney Cotton were sent in command, it would be well to associate with him such an officer as Herbert Edwardes, in the character of political adviser. "But, in such matters," said John Lawrence, "unity in council and action is of the highest importance, and a commander who unites the military and political functions is most desirable. If your lordship does not take my brother, and Outram is available, I would be inclined to recommend him. I never met this officer; but he has a high reputation." And John Jacob, as having much military ability and considerable political experience, was a man not to be overlooked in the account of available capacity for such an enterprise.

But not only in Calcutta and in the Punjab was this question of the command of the expedition being considered. It was well pondered at Bombay and in England, taking a shape eventually to overrule all other decisions. The expedition was to sail from Bombay, and all the arrangements for its organisation and equipment were proceeding there. Lord Elphinstone was Governor of that Presidency. Twenty years before he had been Governor of Madras. At that time he was young, and not so serious and sedate as some people thought the head of a Government ought to be. "We want a Governor," it was said, somewhat bitterly, "and they send us a Guardsman; we want a statesman, and they send us a dancer." But he had ripened into what these people wanted, and now with a higher sense of the responsibilities of office, with a keener pleasure in his work, and a statesmanlike assiduity, for which the companions of his youth had not given him credit, he was, a second time, administering the affairs of an Indian Presidency, and busying himself with our external relations. The troops to be despatched, in the first instance, to the Persian Gulf were mainly Bombay troops, and it seemed fitting that the choice of a Commander should be made from the Bombay Army. If under stress of circumstance the war should assume more important dimensions, and the military force be proportionably extended, another selection might be made. But meanwhile, Elphinstone was requested to name some officer attached to his own Presidency, in whom the troops of all arms would have common confidence. So he named General Stalker, not without a pang of regret that he could not select Colonel Hancock—Hancock, the Adjutant-General of the Bombay Army—whom ill health was driving to Eng-

1856.

Lord Elphinstone.

1856. land. Stalker was the senior of the available officers, so there were no heart-burnings from supersession; he had seen much service, he was experienced in command, and it was believed that the appointment would be both a popular and a safe one. "I hear favourable accounts of his good sense and temper," said Lord Canning; "and that is what is wanted for the service before him, which will require more of patient and enduring than of brilliant qualities."

James Outram. So General Stalker was appointed to the command of the expedition to the Persian Gulf. But whilst these and other arrangements were being made in India, in the belief that ere long they would be merged into others of a more comprehensive character, the question of the chief command was being solved in England in a manner hardly anticipated by the Governor-General. In the month of May he had taken leave of Sir James Outram, with painful misgivings raised in his mind by the sight of the General's shattered frame and feeble bearing. He had suspected that the mischief was far greater than Outram himself acknowledged or believed, and thought that years must elapse before he would be fit again for active service. And so thought all his friends in England. He appeared among them as the wreck only of the strong man who had left them a short time before; and they grieved to see the too visible signs of weakness and suffering which every look and gesture afforded. The summer faded into autumn; but there was little change for the better apparent in his outer aspect, when suddenly they were startled by the announcement that he was about forthwith to proceed to the Persian Gulf and take command of the expedition.

Nobody knew, nobody knows, how it happened

that suddenly in this conjuncture, James Outram shook off the incumbrances of disease, rose up from the prostration of the sick-room, and stood erect, active, robust before the world with the harness of war on his back. It was the autumnal season, when men scatter and disperse themselves in strange places, and elude in a vagrant life the rumours of the distant world; so there were many friends who, having left him at the summer's close a feeble invalid, were struck with a strange surprise when, returned or returning homewards, they were met by the news that Outram had gone or was going to Persia to take command of the invading force. The wonder soon gave place to delight; for they knew that though he was moved by strong ambitions, there was ever within him a sense of duty still stronger, and that on no account would he jeopardise the interests of the State by taking upon himself responsibilities which he had not full assurance in his inmost self of his ample competence to discharge. And so it was. The sound of the distant strife had rekindled all his smouldering energies. There was work to be done, and he felt that he could do it. On the pleasant Brighton esplanade, sauntering alone meditative, or perhaps in the stimulating companionship of a stalwart friend and high functionary, the Chairman of the Court of Directors of the East India Company, Master of Masters, new hopes were wafted upon him with the sea-breezes, and his step grew firmer, his carriage more erect, as with strong assurance of support from Leadenhall-street, he resolved to tender his services to her Majesty's Government for employment in Persia with a joint military and diplomatic command.

1856.

Colonel Sykes.

This was at the beginning of the last week of October. On the 26th he wrote to Lord Canning

1856. that he purposed returning to India by the mail of the 20th of December, "having perfectly recovered from the illness which drove him home." And he added, "In the supposition that I may be more usefully employed with the army about to proceed to Persia than necessary to your lordship in Oude, where everything is progressing so satisfactorily, I have offered my services to the President (of the Board of Control), should it be deemed advisable to entrust to me diplomatic powers in conjunction with the military command, and I believe that, should your lordship be disposed so to employ me, the home authorities would not object. In that case your lordship's commands would meet me at Aden, whence I would at once proceed to Bombay."*

This letter reached Calcutta on the 2nd December. By the outgoing mail of the 8th, Lord Canning wrote to Outram at Aden, rejoicing in his complete recovery, "on every account, public and private," but questioning the policy of the Persian appointment. The expedition, he said, was not likely to increase in magnitude; it was not probable that there would be any operations beyond the seaboard during the winter, or that any diplomatic action would be taken to call for the employment of a high political functionary; if, indeed, overtures were to be made, they would most probably be addressed through some friendly power to London; there would be little scope, therefore, for his services with the Persian expedition, and it would be better, therefore, that he should return to his old appointment. "Oude is completely tranquil," wrote Lord Canning, "and generally prospering. Nevertheless,

* So full was Outram at this time of the thought of his departure in December, and so eager for the advent of the happy day of release, that he dated this letter "December" instead of October.

I shall be very glad to see you resume your command there." The fact was that the Administration was by this time plunged into such a hopeless condition of internecine strife, that the Governor-General could in no way see any outlet of escape from the perplexities besetting him except by the removal of Chief-Commissioner Jackson; and now here was the opportunity, for which he had been waiting, to accomplish this end in an easy natural manner, without any official scandal, or the infliction of any personal pain. 1856.

But it was not to be so accomplished. Before the end of November the question of Outram's command of the Persian expedition had been fully discussed in the English Cabinet. Downing-street had laid fast hold of the idea, and pronounced its full satisfaction with it. Her Majesty the Queen had stamped the commission with the seal of her approbation, and the public voice, with one accord, had proclaimed that a good thing had been done, and that the right man would soon be in the right place. That it was thus virtually settled, past recal, went out, under the President's hand by the mail of the 26th of November, and greeted Lord Canning with the new year. In official language, however, of Court of Directors, or Secret Committee thereof, it took the shape not of an announcement of a thing done, but of a recommendation that it should be done; for it was substantially an interference with the prerogative of the Governor-General, and was to be softened down so as in no wise to give offence. But Lord Canning was not a man, in such a case, to raise a question of privilege, or, assured that it was, actually or presumedly, for the official good, to shoot out any porcupine-quills from his wounded official dignity. He took the interference

1856. in good part; thanked the Chairman for the delicacy with which it had been communicated, and promised to give Outram his best support. He had doubted, he said, whether Outram's health and strength would be sufficient to bear the burdens that would be imposed upon him. "But the Queen's Government," he continued, "and the Secret Committee have seen him in recovered health, and if they are satisfied that he is in a condition to undertake the labour and trial of such a command, without risk to the interest confided to him, I have no objection to make, nor any wish to shake myself clear of responsibility." And then, with a reference to a memorandum on the future conduct of the campaign which Outram had drawn up in England, the Governor-General added, "It is a pleasure to me to declare that I have been greatly struck by all that has proceeded from General Outram in regard to future operations in Persia. I think his plans excellent, prudent for the present, and capable of easy expansion hereafter, and the means which he proposes for carrying them out for the most part well suited. For everything that I have yet heard of his proposals he shall have my cordial support."

1857. Central-Asian Policy. Whilst the first division of the expeditionary force under Stalker was commencing operations with good success in the Persian Gulf, the new year found Outram at Bombay superintending the despatch of the second. But it was not only by these movements from the sea-board that an impression was now to be made on the fears of the Court of Teheran. Diplomacy was to do its work in the country which lay between India and Persia. Reluctant as he had been, in the earlier part of the year, to commit himself to any decided course of Central-Asian policy, Lord Canning now began to discern more clearly the benefits that might arise from a friendly alliance with the Ameer of Caubul. There was no longer any chance of a pacific solution of our difficulties. War had been proclaimed. Herat had fallen. Dost Mahomed had put forth plentiful indications of a strong desire for an English alliance; and the English Government at home appeared to be not unwilling to meet his wishes. That some action must now be taken in that direction was certain. Already had arms and money been sent into Afghanistan; but with no specific undertaking on the one side or the other, and it appeared desirable to put the matter now upon a more secure and a more dignified footing than that of temporary shifts and expedients. But there were great diversities of opinion as to the shape which should be taken by British action in the Afghan countries. Lord Canning had always had at least one clear conception about the matter; that it was better to do little than to do much, and wise not to do that little a day sooner than was needed. The terrible lessons which had been burnt into us fifteen years before had lost none of their significance. The warning voice was still sounding in our ears; the saving hand was still beckoning us away from those gloomy passes. It could never again enter into our imaginations to conceive the idea of turning back the tide of Russo-Persian invasion by making war against the national will and the substantive Government of the Afghans. But the monitions of the Past did not stop there. They cautioned us against ever sending a single British regiment across the Afghan frontier. Neither the Princes nor the People of Afghanistan were to be trusted, if the memories of their wrongs were to be reawakened within them by the presence of that which had done them such grievous harm.

1856.

1856. So, although among the schemes which were discussed, and in some military quarters advocated, was the project of an auxiliary British force, acting in close alliance with the Afghans, it was never for a moment seriously entertained in the Council Chamber. But to assail Persia in some measure from that side, whilst we were operating upon the sea-board; to recover Herat, and, at the same time, to occupy some of the littoral provinces of the Persian Empire; was doubtless to put enormous pressure upon the Shah, to hold him, as it were, in a vice, helpless and agonised, and to extort from him all that we might want. This, peradventure, might be done, by continuing to send British bayonets into Afghanistan, but without, as of old, British valour to wield them; so many thousands of stands of arms, not so many thousands of soldiers; and British money, lakhs upon lakhs, but no British hands to dispense it. In a word, if we could manage successfully to subsidise Dost Mahomed, and hold him, by the bonds of self-interest, to a friendly covenant, whereby, whilst aiding us he would aid himself, we might bring the war much more rapidly to a conclusion than if no such alliance were formed.

Dost Mahomed. But there were strong doubts of the good faith of Dost Mahomed. The wily old Ameer, it was said, was waiting upon the shore of circumstance, willing to sail in the same boat with us, if tide and stream should be in our favour and a fair wind setting in for success. For some time, there had been going on between the Governor-General of India and the Ruler of Caubul certain passages of diplomatic coquetry, which had resulted rather in a promise of a close alliance, a kind of indefinite betrothal, than in the actual accomplishment of the fact. We had condoned the offence committed by the Ameer at the close of the last war in the Punjab, when he had sent some of his best troops, in the uniforms of our own slaughtered soldiers, to aid the Sikhs in their efforts to expel us; and whilst Dalhousie was still the ruler of India, an engagement of general amity had been negotiated by John Lawrence on the one side, and Hyder Khan on the other, between the English and the Afghans. It was probably intended, with a forecast of the coming rupture with Persia, that this should in time be expanded into a more definite treaty with Dost Mahomed; and more than two years before the occasion actually arose, the subsidising of the Ameer loomed in the distance.* It was an old idea. Mr. Henry Ellis had entertained it; Sir John M'Neill had entertained it;† and if Lord Auckland's Secretaries had allowed him to entertain it, it is probable that the events of which I am about to write would never have afforded me a subject of History. In an hour of miserable infatuation, we had played the perilous game of King-making, and had forced an unpopular pageant upon

1849.

March 30, 1855.

* It was talked of, indeed, before the compact of 1855, but did not form a part of it. In 1854 (June 19), Sir Henry Lawrence wrote to the author: "I fancy that we shall have some sort of Treaty with Dost Mahomed, unless Lord Dalhousie overreach himself by too great anxiety and by agreeing to pay him a subsidy. If Persia attack Afghanistan, the help we should give the latter should be by attacking Persia from the Gulf. We should not send a rupee or a man into Afghanistan. We should express readiness to forgive and forget, to cry quits in Afghan matters, and pledge ourselves to live as good neighbours in future; but there ought to be no interference beyond the passes, and no backing of one party or another."

† One passage in Sir John M'Neill's early correspondence I cannot help quoting. There is rare prescience in it: "Dost Mahomed Khan, with a little aid from us, could be put in possession of both Candahar and Herat. I anxiously hope that aid will not be withheld. A loan of money would probably enable him to do this, and would give us a great hold upon him. . . . Until Dost Mahomed or some other Afghan shall have got both Candahar and Herat into his hands, our position here must continue to be a false one."

1856. a reluctant people. Now, after bitter experience, we were reverting to the first conception of our diplomatists; but mild as comparatively the interference was, it was held by some great authorities to be wiser to leave Afghanistan and the Afghans altogether alone. In spite of the present benefit to be derived from applying in that quarter a blister to the side of Persia, it might be better to suffer the old Ameer to make the most of the crisis after his own fashion. He would not fight our battles for us without substantial help; but he might fight his own, and there could be no time, for the extension of his dominion to Herat, so opportune as that which saw Persia entangled in a war with England. But Dost Mahomed had too clear a knowledge of the English, and Afghan cupidity was too strong within him, to suffer this gratuitous co-operation. He knew that, if he waited, we should purchase his aid; so he magnified the difficulties of the march to Herat, talked of the deficiency of his resources, and otherwise pretended that he lacked strength for a successful enterprise without continuous pecuniary aid from the English. Whether, having received such assistance from us, he would render effectual service in return for it, seemed to some of our Indian statesmen extremely doubtful, for there was the lowest possible estimate in their minds of Afghan truth and Afghan honour. There was the fear that the old Ameer would set an extravagant price on his services, and that by disappointing his expectations, if not scouting his pretensions, we might inopportunely excite his animosities against us. Some, indeed, thought that he looked eagerly to the conjuncture as one that might help him to realise his old day-dream, the recovery of Peshawur. There was, in truth, no lack of sagacity in these anticipations; but, perhaps, at the bottom of them there lay too deep a distrust of the personal character of the Ameer. He had, in all candour it must be admitted, too much reason to doubt the good faith of the English. He could fathom the depths of our selfishness as well as we could fathom the depths of his guile. In truth, there were causes of mutual suspicion; and little good was likely to come from the distant fencing of diplomatic correspondence. So at last it was resolved to test the sincerity of the Ameer by inviting him to a conference on the frontier. 1856.

At that time, Herbert Edwardes, he of whose glorious youthful impulses I have spoken in the first chapter of this work, was Commissioner of Peshawur. He had grown, by good-service brevet, rather than by the slow process of regimental promotion, from Lieutenant to Lieutenant-Colonel. His career had been a prosperous one, and its prosperity was well deserved. The great reputation which he had gained as an ambitious subaltern, brought down upon him at one time a shower of small jealousies and detractions. He had been feasted and flattered in England, and there were some who, doubtless, with a certain self-consciousness of what would be likely to flow from such adulations, said that his head was turned, and that he had been overrated. But one, the noble helpmate of a truly noble man, wrote to me at this time, as one, however, not doubting, for I had like faith, that Herbert Edwardes was one of Nature's true nobility, and that surely I should live to know it. It was right. Under the Lawrences, Henry and John, both of whom he dearly loved, he grew to be one of the main pillars of the Punjabee Administration; and now he was in charge of that part of the

Herbert Edwardes.

Honoria Lawrence.

1856. old dominions of Runjit Singh which lay beyond the Indus; the Proconsulate of Peshawur. Planted thus upon the frontier of Afghanistan, it was one of his special duties to watch the progress of events in that country, and duly to report upon them to the higher authorities. Of direct diplomatic action there had been little or none; but no one knew what a day might produce, and it was ever therefore among the responsibilities of the Peshawur Commissioner to be well versed in the politics of Caubul, and prepared, in any conjuncture, to counsel the course to be taken by the British Government.

For some time there had been much to observe and much to report, and now a conjuncture had arisen, which seemed to require from us that we should act. Persia was doing all that could be done to enlist the sympathies of Central Asia on her side, even in the far off regions of Bokhara and Kokund, by sending abroad, as a proof of the dangers of English friendship, copies of the pro-Christian Firman of the Sultan, which had been issued at the close of the Russian war. It was fortunate, therefore, that at this time the political animosities of the Afghans were strongly excited against the Persians, for, perhaps, under such pressure, the chronic sectarian jealousies which kept the two nations apart might for a while have been merged in a common religious hatred of the Feringhees. A very little done, or left undone on our part, to offend the old Ameer, might have lost to us for ever the only serviceable Mahomedan alliance that could have availed us in such a crisis. To no man was the value of this alliance so apparent as to Herbert Edwardes; no man pressed its importance so earnestly upon the Governor-General. He believed that Dost Mahomed would respond

with pleasure to an invitation to meet on the 1857.
frontier of the two States a representative of the British Government, and to discuss the terms of a friendly alliance; and he recommended that this invitation should be sent to him. Reluctant as Lord Canning had been in the earlier part of the year to commit himself to any decided course of Afghan policy, he now before the close of it, in the altered circumstances that had arisen, yielded to this suggestion, and afterwards, with that frankness which sat so becomingly upon him, gracefully acknowledged its wisdom, and thanked the suggester.

So Dost Mahomed was invited to a conference at Peshawur. He was, if willing to meet the representatives of the British Government, to discuss personally with them the terms of the alliance. Either Sir John Lawrence, accompanied by Colonel Edwardes, or Colonel Edwardes alone, as might be determined between them, was to meet the old Ameer on the frontier, to feel his pulse, and to prescribe accordingly. It would have been a great opportunity for the younger man; but Edwardes, to whom the decision was left by Lawrence, for ever giving the lie to all that had been charged against him on the score of vanity and self-assertion, strongly urged that the Mission should be headed by his beloved Chief. Lawrence much doubting, however, whether the Ameer would come, and little expecting a successful issue if he should come, lauded the magnanimity of his more sanguine friend, and prepared himself with all the earnestness of his nature to prove the groundlessness of his own anticipations of failure.

They were groundless. The Ameer accepted the invitation, marched down with two of his sons, some of his chosen counsellors, and a body of picked troops,

January 1, 1857 to the frontier; and on the first day of the new year received in the Khybur Pass the first visit of the British Commissioners. It was with no common interest that Lawrence, Edwardes, Sydney Cotton, and the other English officers who accompanied them, looked into the face of the old Ameer, whose white beard and venerable aspect had, fifteen years before, been so familiar to the eyes of the dwellers in Calcutta, and who in his fallen fortunes, half-prisoner and half-guest, had been a not unworthy object of our sympathies. When, nearly half a century before, the representatives of the British Government had been received almost on the same spot by Shah Soojah, they had found the Caubul ruler arrayed in gorgeous apparel, his whole person a blaze of jewellery, with the Koh-i-noor outshining it all; but the English gentlemen now saw before them only a hale old man, very simply attired in a garment of the coarse camel-hair of the country. They found him full of energy, full of sagacity; courteous and friendly in his outer manner; glad to welcome them to his camp. It was only a visit of ceremony; repaid, two days later, by the Ameer, who was received in the grand English style near Peshawur. Our troops formed a street more than a mile long, and after the Durbar marched past the Ameer and his host in review order. More than seven thousand British fighting men were assembled there, and among them were three complete European regiments, whose steady discipline, and solidity, and fine soldierly bearing, made a strong impression on the minds of the Afghan visitors, from the aged Ameer himself to the youngest trooper of his escort.

The formal interviews thus accomplished, the serious business of the conference commenced on the

5th of January. The Ameer had pitched his Camp at Jumrood, and there Lawrence and Edwardes visited him, accompanied by Major Lumsden of the Guides. Dost Mahomed, his sons standing behind him, and a few chosen Sirdars on his left, opened the discussions with a long exposition of the recent struggles in Herat, and of the policy which he had himself pursued. He had entertained no schemes of conquest embracing that principality. The movements which the Persians had thus pretended to interpret were directed only towards Candahar. But he frankly avowed his eager longing to recover Herat; and, please God and the English, he would take it from the Persians. Swearing by Allah and the Prophet that, from that time, he would be our friend, let all the world be against him, he declared, as his enthusiasm kindled, that let the English but make a diversion in the Persian Gulf and supply him with money and with arms, he would mine the walls of Herat, blow up the towers, and take the place at the point of the sword; or raise such a flame in the surrounding country as fairly to burn the Persians out of it. The Toorcomans and the Usbegs would rise at his bidding, and join against a common foe. 1857

From that distant-frontier post, on the very outskirts of our empire, the telegraphic wires ran right up to the vice-regal capital, and the Governor-General and the Chief Commissioner were corresponding by the "lightning post" between Calcutta and Peshawur. So it happened that whilst John Lawrence and Dost Mahomed were in conference, a horseman galloped up with a message from the former, despatched on the preceding day. In it Lord Canning told Lawrence that a reinforcement of five thousand men would be sent as quickly as possible to the Persian

1857 Gulf; and that amongst the conditions of Peace with Persia would be a stipulation that she should withdraw her troops from Herat, and renounce for ever her pretensions to interfere with Afghanistan. The significant words, "You may make use of this," were included in the message. But the time had not then come for the best use to be made of it; so John Lawrence, reserving the rest for more opportune disclosure, announced only that the reinforcements were about to be despatched to the Gulf. It was his design, at that first meeting, to elicit the views and intentions of the Ameer rather than to disclose those of his own Government.* So, making no promises of any kind, he indicated the difficulties that seemed to lie in the way of the Afghan ruler, and asked for a recital of the means and resources, by which they were to be overcome, already at his disposal, and the extent of the aid which he would require from the English. But this was too momentous a question to be answered, without much thought and calculation; so the Ameer, seeking time for deliberation, said that he would unfold his views fully at the next meeting; and so the conference broke up for the day.

January 7, 1857. On the 7th, Dost Mahomed, attended by a few chosen counsellors, visited the British Camp, and the conferences were renewed in the Chief Commissioner's tent. Pursuing the old process of drawing-out, John Lawrence, at the outset, reminded the Ameer of his

* This course, though doubtless the one that would have suggested itself to John Lawrence's unaided judgment, was expressly dictated by Lord Canning, who had written on the 2nd of December to the Chief Commissioner, saying, "It is not certain that our object will continue the same as the Ameer's; neither is it certain to what extent the Ameer can contribute towards it, even whilst it continues the same. For these reasons, it is necessary first that we should know what he can do; and next, that we should come to a clear understanding as to the conditions upon which he shall receive aid in doing it. The meeting ought to clear up the first point at once."—*MS. Correspondence.*

promise to state fully his views and intentions; but it required some resolution and perseverance to keep the old Afghan to this point, and it was not without difficulty that the promised revelation was extorted from him. At last he explained that, owing to the state of the season, he could not commence his march on Herat until after the expiration of a period of two months; grass and young grain would then be springing up, and with the aid of some not very elaborate commissariat arrangements, he would be able to find provisions for his troops; that he proposed to march one column from Balkh and another from Candahar. The muster-roll of his troops showed some thirty-five thousand men and sixty guns. These, he said, should be raised to fifty thousand men with a hundred guns; four-fifths of the men and nearly the whole of the guns should, he said, be moved upon Herat. "But," he added, "if you say take more troops, I will take more; if you say less will suffice, I will take less. I have given you my own opinion, but you Sahibs know Persia best." But when pressed for a statement of the amount of aid he would require, he said, that on the morrow morning his son, Azim Jah, would wait upon the English gentlemen with all the required information in a digested form, in order that they might judge for themselves. 1857.

So the conference broke up; and on the following day the Ameer's sons, accompanied by a few of his ministers, waited upon John Lawrence, and laid before him a detailed statement of the finances of Afghanistan, and of the military resources of the empire; together with an estimate of the aid that would be required from the English to enable the Afghans to drive the Persians out of Herat, and to hold their own against all comers. The aid that was

1857. thus sought amounted in money to sixty-four lakhs of rupees a year, whilst the war lasted, and in munitions to more than fifty guns, eight thousand stands of small arms, and ammunition at discretion. It was more than the English Government were likely to be willing to give, but not more than appeared really to be wanted. The largeness of the demand, however, suggested the idea of a less extensive enterprise; and so Lawrence asked what would be required to enable the Afghans, abandoning all aggressive movements, to hold their own, without danger of encroachments from the westward. The question was not a welcome one. The Afghans were hot for an advance on Herat. If they were to sit down within their own dominions, the Persians would assuredly occupy Furrah. It was for the English, of course, to decide upon the course to be pursued, but it was more in accordance with the genius and temper of the Afghans to take vigorous action in advance. Still, however, John Lawrence pressed for a statement of the requirements of the Afghans if a strictly defensive policy were maintained. The Sirdars could give no answer without consulting the Ameer, so the conference broke up; and next day they returned with the statement that, in addition to what had already been supplied, four thousand muskets would be required, and money to pay eight thousand regular troops; one-half to be employed in the Candahar country, and the other half in Balkh. But still they were eager for the larger enterprise; and one of them whispered to Edwardes that the enmity between the Afghans and the Persians was not merely an affair of this world, for that Sheeahs and Soonees must always hate each other in the world to come. There was nothing more now to be said. The Afghans, on their part, had made known their wishes; and all the English gentlemen could say in reply was, that they would at once communicate with their Government. 1857.

So the telegraphic wires were again set in motion, and the substance of what had passed at the two last meetings was communicated to the Governor-General at Calcutta. Then there was doubt in the Council Chamber. Would it be better to await detailed reports from Peshawur by post, or at once to send telegraphic instructions to Sir John Lawrence? The former course was determined upon, and a message to that effect despatched to Peshawur. Lawrence had sent in detailed reports of the meetings, and had added to the last an expression of his own views as to what should be done. He recommended that assistance on the larger scale, for the siege of Herat, should not be given to Dost Mahomed, but that we should give him the four thousand muskets that he required, and an annual subsidy of twelve lakhs of rupees, so long as England and Persia might be at war with each other. But it did not seem to him to be wise to await the slow process of correspondence by letter. The Ameer was eager to depart; and some time must be necessarily occupied in the negotiation of a formal agreement. So Lawrence telegraphed the substance of his recommendation to Calcutta, urged that nothing would be gained by awaiting his more detailed reports, and asked permission to communicate to the Ameer the proposal which he thought it best to make. To this a message was promptly returned, saying: "You may tell the Ameer that the terms are agreed to. Four thousand stand of arms and twelve lakhs a year, whilst England is at war with Persia. You will proceed to arrange the articles of agreement and report them by telegraph."

1857. This message was despatched on the 13th of January. On the following morning Lawrence and Edwardes proceeded to Dost Mahomed's camp, and unfolded to him the views and intentions of the British Government. With less appearance of disappointment than had been expected, the Ameer assented to the abandonment of the expedition to Herat, and accepted the modified proposal of the English. But the despatch of a party of British officers to Caubul, which was to form part of the agreement, appeared to be distasteful to him. When active offensive warfare against Persia had been contemplated, he cherished the thought of their presence with his troops; but now the state of affairs was altered. The point, however, was one not to be yielded. If the British were to give the subsidy, they were entitled to see it rightly appropriated. Then the Ameer lowered his tone, and said that he was ready to do what was expedient; and finally he agreed to all that was proposed. But next day, when his son Azim Khan, accompanied by other chiefs, visited, according to agreement, the English Commissioners, to settle the precise terms of agreement, the question of the Mission to Caubul was reopened. It was urged that the appearance of British officers at the Afghan capital might compromise the Ameer either with his own people or with his English friends. There would be danger in their path at Caubul; but at Candahar, threatened by the Persians, their presence would be better understood, and they might abide in perfect security. Nearly fifteen years had passed since our retributive Army had set its mark upon the Afghan capital; but still the hatred which our usurpation had engendered was fresh in the minds of the people, and Dost Mahomed knew that

there were those in Caubul whom he could not trust 1857.
within reach of an English throat. It was a sad thought; and Lawrence could not but ask how the alliance between the two nations could ever strike deep root when in one country such suspicions and animosities were never suffered to sleep. What the English wanted was not a temporary alliance dictated by an emergency of self-interest, but an enduring friendship based upon mutual confidence and respect. But Dost Mahomed knew the Afghans well, and little wisdom would there have been in disregarding a warning which every Englishman's heart must have told him was an utterance of the voice of truth. So it was resolved that, although we should claim, and duly record, our right to send British officers to Caubul, as to other parts of Afghanistan, yet that practically the Mission should, in the first instance, proceed only to Candahar. It was better than that our officers should be smuggled into the capital, surrounded by the Ameer's troops, virtually prisoners under the name of protected guests. There was, at all events, some definite meaning in their proceeding to the more western city, for it was a better point from which to observe the movements of the Persians. But what route were they to take? It was the Ameer's wish that the Mission should proceed by way of the Bolan Pass; but this, although the route by which Shah Soojah and the Army of the Indus had marched into Afghanistan, was said to be entering the country by a back door. It was, therefore, finally determined that the Mission should proceed by way of the Paiwar Pass,* an unexplored

* "It was deemed advisable that the Mission should journey to Candahar by the route of the Paiwar Pass, a road that had never before been traversed by Europeans, and was consequently unknown ground, and full of interest to the British in a military point of view, as being one

1857. road, to Candahar; and that Major Henry Lumsden, of the Guide corps, an officer of great courage and capacity, versed in the politics of Afghanistan, who had been marked from the first for the conduct of this enterprise, should be placed at its head. His brother, Lieutenant Peter Lumsden, was to accompany him, and Mr. Henry Bellew was selected to take medical charge of the Mission; a post of more importance than it appears to be in an official gazette, for in such diplomacies as these the Medicine-chest and the Lancet are often more serviceable than the Portfolio and the Pen.

On the 26th of January, the Articles of Agreement, having by the aid of the telegraph been approved by the Government at Calcutta, were ready for seal and signature; and a meeting for the conclusion of the compact was held in Dost Mahomed's tent. In attendance on the Ameer were his son Azim Khan and several of his chief counsellors, whilst Lawrence, Edwardes, and Lumsden appeared on behalf of the English. Written in Persian and in English, the articles of agreement were read aloud in Durbar. By these the Ameer engaged to maintain a force of eighteen thousand men; to allow British officers to be stationed at Caubul, Candahar, or Balkh, or wherever Afghan troops might be posted; to receive a Wakeel at Caubul, and to send one to Calcutta; and to communicate to the Government of India any overtures that he might receive from Persia and from the Allies of Persia during the war. On their part, the English undertook, during the continuance of hostilities, to pay to the Ameer a monthly subsidy of a lakh of rupees, to send him

of the approaches by which an invading force from the West might enter and attack their Indian Empire."—*Bellew's Journal of a Political Mission to Afghanistan in* 1857.

four thousand stands of arms, and, as if the wrong 1857
done had been all against us, to forget and forgive the past. It was explained that the British officers would in the first instance proceed to Candahar; and with this assurance the Ameer was satisfied. So the Articles of Agreement were signed and sealed. Then came some discussion and some interchange of compliments. A message from the Governor-General had been received by telegraph, desiring Sir John Lawrence to express to Dost Mahomed "the satisfaction which he had derived from his frank dealing, and from the clear understanding on which affairs had been placed," together with the best wishes for his health and long life, and a word of regret that he had not himself been able to meet the Ameer. The message was now delivered and received with manifest gratification. It would have delighted him, he said, to meet Lord Canning, but he could not expect his Lordship to take so long a journey to see him. He had known two Governor-Generals, Lord Auckland and Lord Ellenborough, who had been kind to him in old times; he remembered also with gratitude the kindness of two other English gentlemen, Mr. Wilberforce Bird and Mr. Thoby Prinsep,* who had paid him much attention in Calcutta. "And now," he said, in conclusion, "I have made an alliance with the British Government, and come what may, I will keep it till death." And the promise thus given was never broken. He was true to the English alliance to the last.

On the following day a Durbar was held in the Camp of the British Commissioner, and the chief officers of the Ameer's suite attended to take their leave of the English gentlemen. Dost Mahomed had January 27 1857.

* Then members of the Supreme Council of India.

1857. excused himself on the plea of age and infirmity. The visit to Peshawur, with its attendant anxieties and excitements, had visibly affected the Ameer's health. The hale old man, who, three or four weeks before, had spent hours in the saddle, and seemed to be full of health and energy, had lost much of his bodily vigour and his elasticity of spirit. A sharp attack of gout had prostrated him; and he seemed to be growing impatient under his protracted detention in Camp. So the conclusion of the Terms of Agreement was a manifest relief to him; and it was with no common satisfaction that, on the day following the Farewell Durbar, he set his face towards Jellalabad, carrying with him, in bills on Caubul, a lakh of rupees and some costly presents from the British Government.*

Nor was the gratification experienced at this time confined to the Ameer's camp. Lawrence and Edwardes were well pleased to think that all had gone off so smoothly; that the friendship of the Afghans had been secured at no very extravagant cost; and that, on the whole, although Dost Mahomed had not obtained all that he had asked, he had taken his departure tolerably well satisfied with the favourable issue of the meeting. Lord Canning, too, was more than well satisfied with the manner in which the negotiations had been conducted, and with the apparent result. He was one not stinting in free outspoken expressions of praise and gratitude to those who did good service to his Government; and, both

* The only present made by the Afghan ruler to his allies consisted of a batch of wretched horses, all of which, John Lawrence wrote, were spavined or worn out. The whole were sold for not more than 100*l*. Perhaps Dost Mahomed, remembering the "pins and needles" brought by Burnes, which had caused so much disappointment some twenty years before at Caubul, did not expect, on this occasion, to be the recipient of anything more valuable.

in public and private letters, he cordially thanked the Commissioners, even before their work was done, for the admirable judgment and good tact which they had displayed at the conferences; giving an especial word of thanks to Edwardes as the original suggester of the meeting,* and, it might have been added, the originator of the new policy which had more recently been observed towards the Afghans. To Major Lumsden he wrote, at the same time, a letter of kindly encouragement and good advice, cordially approving the selection, "not only from his trust in Sir John Lawrence's judgment on such matters, but from everything that the Governor-General had been able to hear of Lumsden from those who knew him." He knew the power of such words; as a statesman he felt assured that they would bear good fruit; but as a man he uttered them from the kindness of his heart. 1857.

So Dost Mahomed set his face towards Caubul, and Sir John Lawrence, after a month of administrative journeying about the province, returned to Lahore. It need be no subject of surprise if the latter, as he went about his work, thinking of all that had been done at Peshawur, sometimes asked himself, What good? and wished that the monthly lakh of rupees to be expended on the Afghan Army were available

* "I must ask you," wrote Lord Canning to Colonel Edwardes on the 19th of January, "to accept my best thanks for the part you have taken in the recent negotiations, and for their satisfactory issue. I feel the more bound to do this, because the first suggestion of a meeting came from you; and so far as I can judge from the reports as yet received, and from the tone of the discussion shown in them, I believe that the suggestion has proved a very wise and useful one. It would be a good thing if all diplomatic conferences were conducted so satisfactorily, and set forth as lucidly as these have been." All this was well deserved; for the policy was emphatically Edwardes's policy; he had been the first to recommend, in Lord Dalhousie's time, that we should try the effect of trusting the Afghans, and his recommendations had resulted in the general compact of 1855.

1857. for the improvement of the province under his charge; for he had never liked the project from the beginning. He had no faith in Dost Mahomed. He had detected him in at least one palpable falsehood, and the detection had excited in the Ameer no sense of shame, but rather a feeling of admiration at the clever incredulity of the Feringhees. The expulsion of the Persians from Herat, or even the raising of the Turcoman tribes, was, in Lawrence's opinion, so far beyond the power of the Ameer, that he believed, on the other hand, that the Persians would have little difficulty in seizing Candahar. This belief in the weakness of Dost Mahomed was based upon a somewhat exaggerated estimate of the disunion among the chief people of the country. But even if the Ameer had the power, Lawrence could not believe that he had the will to serve the British; and he doubted, therefore, whether the subsidy would produce any tangible results. As to the question of the future of Herat, it had never even approached a solution. Dost Mahomed had been assured that the evacuation of the place by the Persians would be an essential condition of peace; but he had not been able to offer, without manifest doubt and hesitation, any suggestion as to the best means of providing for its future government. In truth, there was a lack of available capacity in the direction in which it was most natural that we should look for a new ruler. When the Ameer was asked if there was any member of Yar Mahomed's family to whom the government could be entrusted, he replied that there was a brother of Syud Mahomed, but that, if possible, he was a greater reprobate and a greater fool than that unlucky chief. Syud Mahomed, however, had left a son, a boy of some ten years, in whose name a competent Wuzeer might administer the affairs of the principality; but a competent Wuzeer was not to be found more readily than a competent Prince. The future of Herat was, therefore, left to the development of the Chapter of Accidents. In the mean while, Lord Canning, though he had slowly come to this point, believed that the subsidising of the Ameer was not a bad stroke of policy. It bound the Afghan ruler by strong ties of self-interest to remain faithful to the British Government. Even neutrality was great gain at a time when Persia was doing her best to raise a fervour of religious hatred against the English throughout all the countries of Central Asia. The very knowledge, indeed, of the fact that Dost Mahomed had gone down to Peshawur to negotiate a closer alliance with the British, must have had a moral effect at Teheran by no means conducive to an increased confidence in the Shah's powers of resistance. Altogether, it was not an inefficacious, whilst comparatively it was an inexpensive, mode of pressing upon Persia from the side of Afghanistan. But whilst he went thus far, Lord Canning was resolute to go no farther. He had made up his mind that the independence of Herat could be written only on sand; that the waves of circumstance from one direction or another must utterly efface it after a while; and that it would be wiser to abandon an effort that was so fraught with tribulation, and so sure to result in failure. Certain he was that nothing would ever induce him to send a single regiment into Afghanistan to maintain the integrity of a petty state, which Nature seemed to have intended to be a part of Persia or a part of Afghanistan, and which, as in a

1857.

1857. national and religious sense it assuredly belonged to the latter, was certain, if left to itself, eventually to fall into the right hands.*

The question of the Oude Commissionership.

Whilst thus, in this first month of the new year, Lord Canning was eagerly watching the progress of his foreign policy, he was grappling with the great difficulty which beset his internal administration. The question of the Persian command had been settled; but it unsettled, by its solution, that other question of the Oude Commissionership. It was clearer than ever that Jackson must be removed; but it was no longer possible that his tenure of office should come to a natural end and peacefully die out. It was necessary to lay violent hands upon it, and bring it to an ignominious close. The necessity was painful to Lord Canning; but the interests of the State demanded it, and the Governor-General, in such a case, properly overrode the man. Therefore, as Outram could not quietly resume his old seat, another officer was to be found to take the place of Commissioner Jackson. Ample admissions were there of zeal and ability, of assiduous devotion to public business, of much good work well done in the province; but the tone and temper of the man, his contentious spirit, his insolent treatment of his colleagues, were past bear-

* Dost Mahomed and his counsellors, during the conferences at Peshawur, frequently asserted that Persia had, on this as on a former occasion, been instigated and aided by Russia to occupy Herat. I can discern no evidence of this. Prince Gortschakoff assured Lord Granville at Moscow that the Russian minister at Teheran had urged the Persian Government to evacuate Herat, and so to place themselves in a better position to demand from others a like observance of treaty obligations. It may be noted here, that the Ameer told Lawrence at Peshawur that he would show him the letter which the unfortunate Russian diplomatist, Viktevitch, had carried with him to Caubul from the Government of the Czar. But he did not produce it after all.

ing; and communication to that effect, with notice of appointment of a successor, was made to him in due course. 1857.

The choice was an admirable one. It has been said that in the spring of 1856, Sir Henry Lawrence had offered his services to the Governor-General, to officiate as Chief Commissioner of Oude, in Outram's absence, and that the first disaster that befel Lord Canning was that the offer was received too late.* When Henry Lawrence found that it was so, he saw at once the weak point of the arrangement, and an idea struck him that if whilst the civil administration of the province was placed in Jackson's hands, he himself were vested with political and military authority in Oude, all objects might be advantageously secured. It was but a passing thought, a fleeting suggestion; but it found expression in a letter addressed to the Governor-General, who said, "Two Consuls and Two Tribunes have worked well enough in old times, as we all know; but Two Commissioners at Lucknow would have been at a dead lock within a month I could not have delayed for a day the sending of a Third." A truth not to be disputed. So Henry Lawrence had fallen back upon his duties among those intractable Rajpoots; grieving over their degeneracy, striving mightily, but with no great success, to evolve something of good out of their transition-state, and at last admitting that the peace and security we had given them had not yet much improved the race. All through the year he had gone on, in his old earnest, unstinting way, doing what he could, through divers channels of beneficence, alike for the Ancient Houses and the national Chivalries, whereof History and Tradition had given such grand accounts.

* *Ante*, page 398.

1857. But often had he turned aside from the thought of the Princes and the people by whom he was surrounded to consider the general condition of our empire in the East, and most of all our Military System, wherein he discerned some rottenness, which needed to be arrested lest the entire edifice should some day become nothing but a prostrate ruin.

But as the new year approached, certain promptings of failing health inwardly admonished him that it would be well to turn his face towards England for a while; and he had just communicated his wishes upon this score to the Governor-General, when there sprung up a great need for his services on a new and more hopeful field of action. So the answer that went back contained the expression of a hope that he would reconsider his determination to go home and accept the Chief Commissionership of Oude. "There is no person in whose hands I would so gladly
January 19. and confidently place the charge," wrote Lord Canning, "and my only scruple in offering it to you is, that I am proposing that which will interfere with the immediate recruiting of your health. But I will not for this refrain from executing my intention to do so, which was formed many days before I received your letter." And truly a most wise intention; formed without any doubts and misgivings upon his part, for he knew the real character of the man; but not without some counsel against it, given in perfect honesty and good faith by one honest and faithful to the core, but under a false impression, an error afterwards frankly admitted. Had the counsellors been many, and all of the same singleness and sincerity, and the same ripe experience, they could not have turned Lord Canning from his good purpose, or shaken his conviction that he was right.

The invitation reached Henry Lawrence at Neemuch. It came to him, weak and dispirited as he was, with all the renovating influence of a breath of his native air. It was to him what the distant sound of the Persian war had been to James Outram. It made the blood course less languidly through his veins. With such work as lay before him in Oude, he could not be an invalid. The head-shakings of the medical profession were nothing, if the practitioners learned in physical symptoms took no account of the action of the mind. It was the spirit, not the flesh, that required rousing. Two great clouds, coming from opposite directions, had overshadowed his life, blighting both his honourable ambitions and his domestic affections; a heavy disappointment followed by a cruel loss. The black-edged paper on which he wrote still spoke of the latter; a certain sadness of tone in all his allusions to his public life told how fresh were the wounds of the former. "Annoyances try me much more than work," he now wrote to Lord Canning. "Work does not oppress me." He could work at his desk, he said, for twelve or fifteen hours at a time. He had just made a tour of Guzrat, riding thirty or forty miles a day, sometimes being in the saddle from morning to night, or from night to morning. "But," he added, "ever since I was so cavalierly elbowed out of the Punjab, I have fretted even to the injury of my health. Your lordship's handsome letter has quite relieved my mind on that point; so I repeat that if, on this explanation, you think fit to send me to Oude, I am quite ready, and can be there within twenty days of receiving your telegraphic reply." 1857.

The substance of this letter was telegraphed to Calcutta, and it brought back a telegraphic answer.

1857. The convictions on both sides were so strong in favour of the arrangement that it was not likely to break down under any conditions or reservations on either part; and so it was settled that Henry Lawrence should be Chief Commissioner of Oude. "I am in great hopes," wrote Lord Canning, "that the task being so thoroughly congenial to you, it will sit more lightly upon you than, measured by its labour alone, might be expected; and as to my support, you shall have it heartily. The field before you is a noble one, full of interest and of opportunities for good; and I look forward with the greatest confidence to the results of your exertions in it." So Henry Lawrence prepared himself to proceed to Lucknow, and was soon on his way thither by easy stages; for it was not desired that he should assume office before the middle of the following month. Halting at Bhurtpore, where he took counsel with the Political agent and the Engineer officer, and did much to give a right direction to their energies, he proceeded thence to Agra, which was then the seat of the Lieutenant-Governorship of the North-Western Provinces. It was vividly remembered afterwards by one old friend with whom he held sweet communion at that time, that though his thoughts were pregnant with many grave matters begotten of the great Condition-of-India Question, and though he conversed of many things and many men, there was nothing that seemed to press more heavily on his mind than an anxious, uncertain feeling with respect to the state of the Sepoy Army. There were few civilians in the service who knew the Native soldier so well as this friend; and as they talked over certain manifest signs and symptoms, and narrated what they had seen and heard, each saw plainly that there was a painful sense of coming danger in the other's mind. For twelve years Henry Lawrence had been publicly discoursing of the defects of our Indian military system, and emphatically indicating the dangers which might some day overtake the State in the most terrible of all shapes, an outburst of the Native Soldiery;* and he now playfully told his friend, but with more of sadness than of pleasantry in his speech, that the time was not far distant when the Sepoys would hold him and the Lieutenant-Governor and other "big Brahmins," as hostages in the Fort of Agra, until all their demands were granted. 1857.

Still thinking much of this, and mindful that in the province to which he was proceeding he would stand on vantage-ground for the clear discernment of the real causes of the malady, Henry Lawrence passed on to Lucknow. And before day had broken on the 20th of March, he had been received, at the Residency, by the man whom he had come to supplant. There must have been pain and embarrassment on both sides in such a meeting. But before he had broken his fast, the new Commissioner sat down and wrote a letter to Lord Canning, saying that he had had two hours' friendly conversation with Mr. Jackson, who had received him altogether "like a gentleman." He had found a long and encouraging letter from the Governor-General awaiting him on his arrival; and now he emphatically replied, "With your lordship's cordial support I

* See Lawrence's Essays, reprinted from the *Calcutta Review*: "How unmindful we have been that what occurred in the city of Caubul may some day occur at Delhi, Meerut, or Bareilly" (page 51). Again: "What the European officers *have* repeatedly done (*i.e.* mutinied) may surely be expected from Natives. We shall be unwise to wait for such occasion. *Come it will, unless anticipated.* A Clive may not be then at hand." The emphatic italics are Lawrence's. Other passages to the same effect might be cited.

1857. have no fear of success." His spirit rose as he thought of the work before him. What that work was, what he found done and what he found undone in the province, when he assumed charge of his new office, will be told in a subsequent page of this story.

*** No better opportunity than this may be afforded for a note on the opinions of Sir Henry Lawrence with respect to the maintenance of the Native States of India. Having said elsewhere that he was on principle opposed to the "Annexation Policy," I recently elicited the following reply from a distinguished writer in the *Edinburgh Review*: "A writer so well informed as Mr. Kaye need not have thus held on to the skirts of a popular delusion. The course which Sir Henry Lawrence favoured in respect to Oude, by whatever name it may be called, is plain enough. It is a course which, if submitted to the 'Law Officers of the Crown,' as a question of international law, would, probably, receive from these authorities some name harsher than 'annexation.'" To this I think it right to reply, that as any opinion which I may have formed of the sentiments, on this or any other subject, of Sir Henry Lawrence, has been derived either from oral communication with him or from his letters to myself, I ought not to be charged with "hanging on to the skirts of a popular delusion." That those sentiments were what I have represented them to be, I have numerous proofs in his own handwriting. A single extract, however, from his correspondence will suffice for all purposes. Writing to me from Mount Aboo on the 16th of July, 1856, with reference to the office under the Home Government of India which had recently been conferred on me, he said: "The appointment must be one of the pleasantest, unless, indeed, you feel as I do, that Government is going too fast, and that we are losing our good name among the Native States. I confess that I do not like the present system, and that I would gladly give up salary to change to a purely civil or military berth. When I read the tirades of the *Friend of India*, I half think myself (with many better men, including Elphinstone, Munro, and Clerk) a fool. The doctrine now is that it is wicked not to knock down and plunder every Native prince. My views are exactly what they were when I wrote the articles for you on the Mahrattas and on Oude. My paper on Oude would serve as a guide to present doings in all points save the disposal of the surplus revenue, which assuredly ought to be spent *in Oude*. Nor, indeed, do I think that we should materially lose, or fail to gain thereby. Is it nothing that we should make a garden of the nursery of our Sepoys, and open out the resources of a province bordering for a thousand miles on our old ones? . . . . . But I repeat, that my taste for politics is gone. There is no confidence left in the country; and one does not feel that the people about Government House care one straw about one's exertions on behalf of the Native States." Surely, the trumpet here gives no "uncertain sound."

CHAPTER III.

LORD CANNING AND THE NATIVE ARMY—THE CALL FOR "MORE OFFICERS" —DREAD OF THE BLACK WATER—THE GENERAL SERVICE ENLISTMENT ACT—ANXIETIES AND ALARMS—LORD CANNING AND THE MISSIONARY CAUSE—PROSELYTISING OFFICERS—POLITICAL INQUIETUDES—THE PROPHECY OF FIFTY-SEVEN.

THE anxieties which Henry Lawrence carried with him to Lucknow had then, for some weeks, been disquieting the mind of the Governor-General. The old year had died out, apparently leaving to its successor no greater troubles than those which were inseparable from the Persian war; but before the new year was many days old, there arose upon the horizon that little cloud no bigger than a man's hand, of which Lord Canning, at the great Farewell Banquet of the Company, had prophetically spoken. It might be little; it might be much. It might be blown away by a breath of wind; or it might expand into terrific dimensions, covering the whole heaven as with a pall. Anyhow, it had an angry threatening aspect; and the looker-on, being no alarmist, might well wish it away. The little cloud. January, 1857.

Memorable, and, doubtless, well remembered is it that, when Lord Dalhousie bade farewell to the cares Retrospect 1856.

1856. of Indian Government, he placed upon record an opinion that the condition of the Native soldiery left nothing to be desired. There was no reason why Lord Canning, at the outset of his career, should not take this assertion on trust; no reason why he should not hold to it for a while. He went out to India, prepossessed in favour of "the faithful Sepoy." He had, doubtless, read the noble picture which, nearly forty years before, his father had drawn of the fidelity of the Native soldiery of the Company, unshaken by threats, unallured by temptations.* There were no flutterings of disquiet apparent on the surface to raise anxious doubts and misgivings. But he had not long taken up the reins of Government, when the subject of the Native Army began to occupy his thoughts and to afford matter for much grave correspondence. The vast extension of territory which had made famous the career of Lord Dalhousie had not been followed by any corresponding extension of the Agency by which all this new country was to be administered. As so much more civil duty was to be

* As President of the Board of Control, George Canning had moved, in the House of Commons, the vote of thanks to Lord Hastings's Army for its service in the Second Mahratta war, and in the course of his speech had paid this fine tribute to the Native Army: "In doing justice," he said, "to the bravery of the Native troops, I must not overlook another virtue, their fidelity. Many of the Bombay Army had been recruited in the territories of the Peishwah; their property, their friends, their relatives, all that was valuable and dear to them, were still in that prince's power. Previously to the commencement of hostilities, the Peishwah had spared no pains to seduce and corrupt these troops; he abstained from no threats to force them from their allegiance, but his utmost arts were vain. The Native officers and soldiers came to the British Commanders with the proofs of these temptations in their hands, and renewed the pledges of their attachment. One man, a non-commissioned officer, brought to his captain the sum of 5000 rupees, which had been presented to him by the Peishwah in person, as an earnest of reward for desertion. The vengeance denounced by the Peishwah was not an unmeaning menace; it did, in many instances, fall heavily on the relatives of those who resisted his threats and his entreaties; but the effect was rather to exasperate than to repress their ardour in the service to which they had sworn to adhere."

done, it seemed, in strict logical sequence, that there was an increased demand for civil servants, and that this demand should have been supplied. But government by the Civil Service of the Company was costly; and to have called for increased agency of this kind would perhaps have supplied Leadenhall-street with an argument against the profitableness of annexation. Moreover, there was much rough work to be done in our newly-acquired provinces, for which, on the whole, perhaps, military administrators were better suited than civilians. So the military officer, as has before been said, was taken from his regimental duties to share in the civil administration of the country. Great had been, for this purpose, the drain upon the Native regiments, before the annexation of Oude. That event brought the ascendant evil to a climax; and Lord Canning wrote home that it had become necessary to add two officers to each Native Infantry regiment and four to the Europeans. "A request," he wrote, in the early part of April, "for an addition to the number of officers in each Infantry regiment—European and Native—goes home by this mail. Four for each European and two for each Native regiment are asked. The application comes singly and in a bald shape; because the necessity of an immediate increase is urgent, and because I have had no time to go into the complicated questions of our military wants generally." 1856.

"More officers."

There was, indeed, nothing more difficult to understand aright than these military questions; difficult to experienced statesmen: altogether embarrassing and bewildering to a Governor in his novitiate. Even this matter of "more officers," so smooth as it appeared to be on the surface, when you came to

1856. gauge it, was found to contain a deposit of doubt and conflict. It was held by some, who had studied well all the deteriorating influences of which so much has been said in these pages, that the cry for "more officers" was one to be responded to with caution; that, indeed, the Native Army had already too many officers; and that now to increase their number would be to increase one of the evils that had long been impairing its efficiency. That Lord Canning, fresh from England, should have taken the more popular view of this want of officers, was natural; and, indeed, it may be said that it was a plain common-sense view, not wanting in a certain kind of logic. It had become a proverb that the English officer was the Backbone of the Native regiment; and, assuredly, the administrative demands of our new provinces had left these Native regiments, according to the recognised reading, sadly enfeebled and incapacitated. All that he now sought to do was to restore them somewhat more nearly to their normal condition. The remedy seemed to lie on the surface, and straightway he exerted himself to supply it. But, the theory of the Backbone accepted, it was still possible that the vertebral column might be weakened by having too many joints; and therefore it was said by a few thoughtful and experienced men, emphatically by Sir George Clerk,* that there was more danger in giving our Native regiments too many English officers than in giving them too few; and for this reason, that being many they formed a society apart and kept aloof from their men, and became altogether in their ways of life too European. Doubts such as these, and from such a quarter, brought clearly to Lord Canning's mind the fact that

* Then Secretary to the Board of Control.

the Native Army question was a very difficult one; 1856.
that it was almost impossible, indeed, whilst avoiding one rock, to escape from steering upon another. But the call for more officers had been made; and, perhaps, with no want of wisdom. For, although there was profound truth in what was said about the evil of too much Englishism in the Native Army, the Regular Regiments of the Company had been formed upon the European model, and the principle of command by many officers was a vital part of the system. The Irregular system might have been better than the Regular, but a Regular Regiment denuded of its officers fulfilled the condition of neither. So the Home Government recognised the want of more officers, and responded to the appeal.

Evils of extended dominion.

Another, and still more important question, soon came up for solution. The specific evils, which resulted from the extension of our dominions, varied in accordance with the direction in which we had extended them. The acquisition of new territory on the south-eastern coast had caused but little political excitement in India; but the very circumstance to which we owed our exemption from evils of one kind was the immediate source of another class of evils. It has been said that the intervention of the black waters of the Bay of Bengal cut off the sovereigns of Burmah from the brotherhood of the Princes of the great continent of India, and made it a matter of small concern whether we gained battles or lost them in that part of the world.* But that very black water made it difficult for us to garrison the country which we had won. The new province of Pegu had been brought administratively under the Supreme Government of India, and in the first

Military defence of Pegu.

* *Ante*, pp. 67-68.

1856. arrangements made for its military defence, the regiments planted there had been drawn from the Bengal Army. But the great bulk of that Army eschewed Foreign service.* It was not part of the conditions, under which they had enlisted, that they should cross the seas. The Sepoy, on taking service, swore that he would never forsake or abandon his colours, and that he would march whithersoever he was directed, whether within or beyond the territories of the Company. Out of the seventy-four regiments composing the Native Infantry of the Bengal Army, six only were recruited for general service. When more Native troops had been required to take part in operations beyond the seas, it had been customary to call for volunteers from the limited-service regiments. There had been often a free response to this invitation, and the volunteer corps had done their duty well upon Foreign service. In the old times, indeed, before the new organisation, they had in this respect shown signal devotion; they had gone willingly to remote places beyond the seas and cheerfully endured all the miseries and privations of long and boisterous voyages. In one year, seven thousand Bengal Sepoys had volunteered for service against the French in the Mauritius and in Java; and had served for many years in those islands with unvarying fidelity and good conduct.† But, even in those days, they had

Volunteer corps.

1811.

* "The natives of India have, generally speaking, a rooted dislike to the sea; and when we consider the great privations and hardships to which Hindoos of high caste are subject on a long voyage, during which some of them, from prejudices of caste, subsist solely on parched grain, we feel less surprised at the occasional mutinies, which have been caused by orders for their embarkation, than at the zeal and attachment they have often shown upon such trying occasions."—*Sir John Malcolm in the Quarterly Review*, vol. xviii. p. 399.

† The battalions thus formed were the basis of the six general-service regiments, in the later organisation, of which mention is made in the text.

been at times capricious; and their caprices, as time 1856.
advanced and their devotion to their officers diminished, had grown more frequent and more embarrassing.* The mutiny and massacre at Barrackpore had risen out of the demands of the first Burmese war, and the second war in those transmarine regions had raised up a new crop of difficulties of the old type.

A few sentences will tell all that need be told of this last story: The Native troops employed in the
conquest of Pegu were either Madras troops or the 1852.
general-service regiments of the Bengal Army. But reinforcements were needed, and so a call was to be
made for volunteers. The Thirty-eighth Native Regiment was then at the Presidency. The Thirty-eighth.
It had served long and fought gallantly in Afghanistan, and it was believed that it would follow its officers to any part of the world. But when the day of trial came, the result was a bitter disappointment. The Sepoys were asked whether they would embark for Rangoon to take part in the war, or for Arracan, there to relieve a general-service regiment, which in that case would be sent on to Burmah. Their reply was, that they were willing to march anywhere, but that they would not volunteer to cross the seas. Perfectly respectful in their language, they were firm in their refusal. Doubt and suspicion had taken possession of their minds. How it happened I do not know, but a belief was afterwards engendered among them, that the English Government had a foul design to entrap them, and that if they commenced the march to the banks of the Irrawaddy, they would at a con-

* Sir John Malcolm, writing in 1817-18, says, that all the mutinies in the Bengal Army up to that time had arisen from the blunders of their commanding officers, or from orders given to go beyond the seas. See article, above quoted, in *Quarterly Review*.

1856. venient point be taken to the sea-board and forcibly compelled to embark. Lord Dalhousie, taking, therefore, the prudent rather than the vigorous view of the situation, and availing himself of the advanced state of the season as a plea for the adoption of the feebler of the two courses before him, yielded to these first symptoms of danger, and decreed that the Thirty-eighth should be sent neither to Rangoon nor to Arracan, but to the nearer and more inland station of Dacca. And so nothing more was heard for a time of the disaffection of the Bengal Army.

The Court of Directors of the East India Company, when this business was reported to them, saw clearly that it had become difficult to carry on the concerns of their vastly extended empire with one-half of their Army, and that the more important half, bound to render them only a restricted obedience; so they wrote out to the Governor-General that they hoped soon to be put in possession of the "sentiments of his Government on the expediency of adopting such a change in the terms of future enlistments as might eventually relieve them from similar embarrassments." But no action was taken during the remaining years of Lord Dalhousie's administration, and Lord Canning found, on his accession, that still but a twelfth part of the Bengal Army was available for service beyond the seas. What then was to be done, when reliefs were required for Pegu? Even if the old professional ardour of the Sepoy had been restored, the occasion was scarcely one on which the Government could have called for volunteers. The formation of volunteer regiments had been confined to periods of actual warfare; and now that we required them merely to garrison our acquisitions in time of peace, the difficulty that confronted

October 20, 1852.

Reliefs for Pegu.

Lord Canning was one not readily to be overcome. 1856.
He found at this time that of the six general-service regiments three were then in Pegu. They had embarked on a specific understanding that they should not be called upon to serve there for more than three years, and, in the rainy season of 1856, two of the three regiments were in their third year of transmarine service. In the early part of the following year, therefore, a relief would be necessary; but not one of the other three regiments could be despatched; for they had all returned only a year or two before from service in the same part of the country. It was clear, therefore, that the Bengal Army could not provide the means of despatching the required reliefs by water transport to Pegu.

So a question arose as to whether the relieving regiments might not, according to their bond, be marched to the Burmese coast. It was a circuitous and toilsome journey, but it had been done, under pressure of like difficulty, thirty years before, and might yet be done again. But although the improvement of the communications between the Hooghly and the Irrawaddy was then being urged forward by the Government, there was still a break on the line from Chittagong to Akyab, of which our Engineers could not give a sufficiently encouraging account to satisfy the Governor-General that the relieving regiments could be sent by land in the ensuing cold season. "A part of the road," said Lord Canning, "could not be made passable for wheels by that time without the addition of eight thousand labourers to those already employed. If the use of wheeled carriages were abandoned, there would still remain encamping ground to be cleared on many parts of it; the jungle, which is already choking the tract, to be

1856. removed; preparation to be made for halting the men on the march; wells to be dug, or water to be stored, where none has yet been found and stations and storehouses provided. Simple operations enough in themselves, but which in this case would have to be begun and completed, on two hundred miles of road, between the beginning of December, before which no work on that coast can be attempted, and February, when the troops must begin to pass over the ground, the supply of labour, as well as its quality, being very little trustworthy." "Obstacles of this kind," continued the Governor-General, "have been overcome again and again by the Sepoys of Bengal in their marches, whenever it has been necessary to do so; but I am of opinion that it will be better in the present instance to seek some other solution of the difficulty. And I believe that the one most available is a recourse to the Madras Army."

Demands on the Madras Army.

And why not? The Madras, or, as it was once called, the Coast Army, was enlisted for general service. Posted in the Southern Peninsula, and to a great extent along the sea-board, it was as readily available for service on the other side of the Bay as the Army in Lower Bengal. If the duty were unpalatable, it could not, when diffused over fifty regiments, press very heavily upon any individual soldier. Besides, service of this kind had some compensations of its own, and was not altogether to be regarded as a grievance.* So it was thought that the

* It must not be supposed, however, that the Madras Army had always cheerfully accepted this necessity for going upon foreign service. On several occasions they had broken into mutiny on the eve of embarkation. Once, towards the close of the last century, they had risen upon their European officers, when about to embark at Vizagapatam, and shot all but one or two, who had contrived to escape on board the ship which was waiting to receive the regiment. In a former chapter I have given some later instances, and others might have been cited. But there are some noble examples on record of another kind,

garrison of Pegu might, for a time at least, be drawn 1856.
from the Madras Army. But ready as the solution appeared to be, it was found that here also there was some hard, gritty, insoluble matter at the bottom of the scheme. The Madras Government, though not unwilling to send troops to Pegu, as a temporary arrangement, protested against being called upon to supply a permanent garrison to that part of our dominions. Such an arrangement would bring round to every regiment a tour of service beyond the sea once in every nine years, instead of once in twelve years; it would render service in the Madras Army unpopular; make recruiting difficult among the better class of Natives whom it was desired to enlist; and, inasmuch as every regiment lost much of its morale on Foreign service, and took two or three years to recover what was lost, the efficiency of the Madras Army would be permanently deteriorated.

So Lord Canning turned his thoughts in another

and one adduced by Sir John Malcolm, in the article above quoted, deserves to be recorded here, if only as an illustration of the influence for good of a trusted commanding officer. Speaking of the services of the Twenty-second Madras Regiment, he says: "This fine corps was commanded by Lieutenant-Colonel James Oram, an officer not more distinguished for his personal zeal and gallantry than for a thorough knowledge of the men under his command, whose temper he had completely preserved, at the same time that he had imparted to them the highest perfection in their dress and discipline. When he proposed to his corps on parade to volunteer for Manilla, they only requested to know whether Colonel Oram would go with them? The answer was, 'He would.' 'Will he stay with us?' was the second question. The reply was in the affirmative; the whole corps exclaimed, 'To Europe! —to Europe!' And the alacrity and spirit with which they subsequently embarked, showed that they would as readily have gone to the shores of the Atlantic as to an island of the Eastern Ocean. Not a man of the corps deserted, from the period they volunteered for service until they embarked; and such was the contagion of their enthusiasm, that several Sepoys who were missing from one of the battalions in garrison at Madras, were found, when the expedition returned, to have deserted to join the Twenty-second under Colonel Oram. We state this anecdote," adds Sir John Malcolm, "with a full impression of the importance of the lesson it conveys. It is through their affections alone that such a class of men can well be commanded."

1856.

The General Enlistment Act.

direction. Madras troops might be sent for the nonce to Pegu, but the permanent defence of that outlying province across the Bay must, it appeared to him, be provided for by drawing, in some way, upon the Bengal Army. There was then lying, unresponded to, among the Records of the Military Department, that despatch of the Court of Directors in which the Government of India had been urged to devise the means of relieving themselves from all such embarrassments by a change in the terms of future enlistments. After much inward thought and much consultation with others, he determined, therefore, to institute such a radical change in the constitution of the Bengal Army as four years before had been indicated by the Home Government. The reform which he contemplated was to have only a prospective effect. It was to touch no existing interests; but to be applied prospectively to all who might enlist into the military service of the State. Thenceforth every recruit was to engage himself for general service. There might be an alteration in the form of the oath, or it might simply be left to the European officer to explain to every recruit that he had been enlisted for general service. Such had been the custom with respect to the six general-service regiments of the Bengal Army, and it had been found to answer every requirement. An explanatory order might be issued by the Governor-General in Council, and then the military authorities might follow up, in their own way, the blow struck at the niceties of the old system. The Governor-General argued, with irresistible force, that every Government should be master of its own Army. He was, however, at that time, fresh from England; and he might be forgiven for not knowing how the Government could best make itself the master of such an Army as that with which he was then dealing. But he would have had no legitimate claim to forgiveness if he had failed to take counsel with those among his constitutional advisers who had spent all their adult lives in India, and who were presumedly familiar with the feelings and opinions of the people. He did take counsel with them; and they urged him to pursue this course. He who, of all the Councillors, best knew the Native character, was then in England; but the ablest man amongst them argued that there was no place like Calcutta for shipping off a large military force, and that the Bay of Bengal had become an Indian Lake. It does not seem that there was any one at Lord Canning's elbow to tell him that, whatsoever might be the facilities of transport, the Bay of Bengal would still be the black water, the salt water, in the thoughts of the people from whom our recruits were to be drawn; still regarded with mysterious awe, and recoiled from with unconquerable aversion.

1856.

General Low.

Mr. J. P. Grant.

So, on the 25th of July, 1856, a general order was issued by the Government of India, declaring that, thenceforth, they would not accept the service of any Native recruit who would not, "at the time of his enlistment, distinctly undertake to serve beyond the sea, whether within the territories of the Company or beyond them." In what light Lord Canning regarded this important change, with what arguments he supported the measures, may be gathered from his correspondence. "You will see," he wrote to the President of the India Board, "that a General Order has been published putting an end to the long-established, but most impolitic, embarrassing, and senseless practice of enlisting the Native

August 9, 1856.

1856. Army of Bengal for limited service only; the sole exceptions being six regiments of Native Infantry, which are recruited on the condition of serving anywhere, and the Artillery. It is marvellous that this should have continued so long, and that the Government of India should have tolerated, again and again, having to beg for volunteers, when other Governments, including those of Madras and Bombay, would have ordered their soldiers on their duty. It is the more surprising, because no one can allege any reason for conceding this unreasonable immunity to the Bengal Sepoy. The difficulties of Caste furnish none whatever, for the Bombay Army is recruited in great part from the same classes and districts as that of Bengal; and even in the latter the best Brahmin in the ranks does not scruple to set aside his prejudices, whenever it suits him to do so. There seems to have been a dim apprehension that there might be risk in meddling with the fundamental conditions upon which the bargain between the Army and the Government has hitherto rested, and there are some few alarmists on the present occasion, but I have seen no reason to fear that the order will cause any bad feeling in the Bengal Army. As it touches no existing rights, it could only do so by exciting apprehensions that something more remains behind; and, probably, this may prove to be the case, for whenever I can propose a reduction in the numbers of the Bengal Regiments, I shall endeavour to do so upon terms that will give a preference of remaining in the ranks to such men as may be willing to accept general service. But this is no part of, and is not necessarily connected with the present change; moreover, as yet

November 8, 1856. it is only in my own breast." And again, a few months later, he wrote, with still greater confidence:

"There is no fear of feelings of Caste being excited 1856.
by the new enlistment regulations in the Bengal Army. No one will come under it otherwise than voluntarily; and the fact that a vast number of the recruits who join the Bombay regiments come from the same country, and are of the same caste, and in every respect of the same condition with the bulk of the Army in Bengal, proves that they do not, on first entering the service, hold very closely to Caste privileges. You are aware that the Bombay Army is enlisted for general service without exception. The only apprehension I have ever had (and that has vanished) is, that the Sepoys already enlisted on the old terms might suspect that it was a first step towards breaking faith with them, and that on the first necessity they might be compelled to cross the sea. But there has been no sign of any such false alarm on their part."

No signs truly apparent at Government House; but many and great in the Native villages, and much talk in the Lines and Bazaars. It was hardly right even to say that there was no interference with existing interests. For the interest of the Sepoy in the Bengal Army was an hereditary interest. If the British Government did not at once assume the right to send him across the sea, it seemed certain that his sons would be sent. There was an end, indeed, of the exclusive privileges which the Bengal Sepoy had so long enjoyed; the service never could be hereafter what it had been of old; and all the old pride, therefore, with which the veteran had thought of his boys succeeding him was now suddenly extinguished. Besides, the effect, he said, would be, that high-caste men would shrink from entering the service, and that, therefore, the vacant places of his brethren

1856. would be filled by men with whom he could have no feeling of comradeship. And this was no imaginary fear. No sooner had the order made its way through the Provinces, than it became patent to all engaged in the work of enlistment that the same high-caste men as had before been readily recruited were no longer pressing forward to enter the British service.* As it was believed that we had too many Brahmins and Rajpoots in the Bengal Army, this in itself might have been no great evil. But it was of all things the least likely that such an order should pass into general circulation without being ignorantly misunderstood by some, and designedly misinterpreted by others.

Enlistment of Sikhs.

So it was soon said that the English gentlemen were trying to rid themselves of their old high-caste Sepoys, and that soon the profession which had been followed, with honourable pride, by generation after generation of old soldier-families would not be open to them. And this belief was greatly strengthened by a rumour which went forth about the same time, to the effect that Government had determined on enlisting thirty thousand more Sikhs. The conquest of the Punjab had placed at our disposal the services of a warlike race, always eager to wear the uniform of a successful ruler, for in their eyes success was plunder. Less dainty in the choice of their battle-

* Take, in proof of this, the following extract from a letter written by Sir Henry Lawrence to Lord Canning, on the 1st of May, 1857: "The General Service Enlistment Oath is most distasteful, keeps many out of the service, and frightens the old Sepoys, who imagine that the oaths of the young recruits affect the whole regiment. One of the best captains of the 13th Native Infantry, in this place, said to me last week that he had clearly ascertained this fact: Mr. E. A. Reade, of the Sudder Board, who was for years collector of Goruckpore, had the General Service Order given to him as a reason last year, when on his tour, by Rajpoots, for not entering the service. The salt water, he told me, was the universal answer." —*MS. Correspondence.*

fields, and not less brave or robust in battle, they were the very kind of mercenaries that we wanted to give new bone and sinew to the body of our Native Army. Whether there were or were not, at this time, a tendency to over-work this new and promising recruiting-ground, it is certain that the old race of Sepoys believed that we were designedly working it to their injury and their overthrow. They gave ready credence, therefore, to exaggerated reports of Sikh enlistments, and, coupling them with the New General Service Order, leapt to the conclusion that the English had done with the old Bengal Army, and were about to substitute for it another that would go anywhere and do anything, like coolies and pariahs. 1856.

Effects of the General Enlistment Order.

Moreover, there were not wanting those who were eager to persuade the Sepoys of the Bengal Army that this new Act was another insidious attempt to destroy the Caste of the people, and to make men of all creeds do the bidding of the English, by merging all into the one faith of the Feringhee. It was another link in the great chain of evidence which had been artfully employed to convict the British Government of the charge of aiming at the compulsory conversion of the people. The season was most propitious. The coming of Lord Canning had, by some strange process of association which I find it impossible to trace, been identified with certain alleged instructions from England, emanating from the Queen herself in Council, for the Christianisation, by fair means or by foul, of the great mass of the people; and now one of the first acts of his Government was to issue an order making it compulsory on the Sepoy to take to the transport vessel, to cross the black water, and to serve in strange parts of the world, far away, per-

1856. haps, from all the emblems and observances of his religion, among a people sacrilegious and unclean.

Apprehensions and alarms. The native mind was, at this time, in a most sensitive state, and easily wrought upon by suspicious appearances. What these appearances were, has, in some measure, been shown in former chapters of this narrative. Even the Railway and the Electric Telegraph had been accounted as blows struck at the religions of the country. Nor was this purely a creation of the Native mind, an unaided conception of the Priests or the People; for the missionaries themselves had pleaded the recent material progress of the English as an argument in favour of the adoption by the inhabitants of India of one universal religion. "The time appears to have come," they said in an Address which was extensively circulated in Bengal during the closing years of Lord Dalhousie's administration, "when earnest consideration should be given to the question, whether or not all men should embrace the same system of religion. Railways, Steam-vessels, and the Electric Telegraph are rapidly uniting all the nations of the earth. The more they are brought together, the more certain does the conclusion become that all have the same wants, the same anxieties, and the same sorrows;" and so on, with manifest endeavour to prove that European civilisation was the forerunner of an inevitable absorption of all other faiths into the one faith of the White Ruler. This had gone forth, an egregious Christian manifesto, not wanting in fundamental truth, or in certain abstract proprieties of argument and diction, to "Educated Natives," especially to respectable Mahomedans in Government employment, some of the leading Native functionaries of Bengal. What might truly be the purport of it,

and whence it came, was not very clear at first, but 1856.
ere long it came to be accepted as a direct emanation from Government, intended to invite the people to apostatise from the religions of their fathers. And such was the excitement that Commissioner Tayler, of the great Patna division, wherein some disquietudes had before arisen, mainly of the Mahomedan type, reported to Lieutenant-Governor Halliday that intelligent natives, especially the better class of Moslems, were "impressed with a full belief that Government were immediately about to attempt the forcible conversion of its subjects." It was added, that "a correspondence on this head had for some time been going on between native gentlemen in various parts of the Lower Provinces;" and Lieutenant-Governor Halliday saw so clearly that this was no impalpable mare's-nest, no idle scum of an alarmist brain, that he forthwith issued a sedative Proclamation; which sedative proclamation was speedily answered anonymously, but beyond doubt by an "intelligent native," or conclave of "intelligent natives," clearly showing by the inevitable logic of facts that if this notion of a war against the religions of India had laid hold of the national mind, the Government had by their own measures given encouragement to the dangerous belief.

Very obstinate, indeed, and hard to be removed, was this belief; so hard, that the very efforts made to efface it might only fix more ineffaceably the damaging impression on the native mind. For if the wondering multitude did not think, there were a crafty few ready to teach them, that if Government designed, by foul means, to destroy the caste of the people and the religions of the country, they would not hesitate to make the issuing of a lying proclama-

1856. tion a part of the process. The conviction that it was the deliberate design of the British Government, by force or fraud, to attain this great object, was growing stronger and stronger every month, when Lord Canning arrived in India, and at once became, all unwittingly, a special object of suspicion and alarm. The lies which attended, perhaps preceded, his advent, caused all his movements to be narrowly watched; and it began soon to be bruited abroad that he had subscribed largely to missionary societies, and that Lady Canning, who was known to be in the especial confidence of the Queen, was intent on making great personal exertions for the conversion of the women of the country.

Lord Canning and the Religious Societies.

But there was no truth in all this. The Governor-General had done no more than other Governors-General had done before him. He had sent a donation to the Bible Society, a society for the translation of the Scriptures into the Oriental languages, and the circulation of these new versions among the people. But the translation of the Scriptures had been carried on more than half a century before, in the College of Fort William, under the especial patronage of Lord Wellesley; and Lord Wellesley's successor, during whose reign the Calcutta Bible Society was established, headed the list with a large subscription. Lord Hastings, Lord William Bentinck, and Sir Charles Metcalfe, had all contributed to the funds of the society. But Lord Canning had also given a donation to the Baptist College at Serampore. What then? It had been established in 1818, under the auspices of Lord Hastings, whose name had been published as the "First Patron" of the Institution, and it had received the support of subsequent Governors-General without question or comment. Besides these donations, he had made a contribution to the support of the excellent school of the Free Church Mission, under the management of Dr. Duff, as Lord Dalhousie had done before him. "I admit," he said, "that the Head of the Government in India ought to abstain from acts which may have the appearance of an exercise of power, authority, solicitation, or persuasion towards inducing natives to change their religion. But if it is contended that a school like this, thoroughly catholic and liberal, open to students of every creed, doing violence to none, and so conducted as to disarm hostility and jealousy (the number of the Hindoo and Mussulman scholars shows this), is not to have countenance and support from the Governor-General because it is managed by missionaries, I join issue on that point. I am not prepared to act upon that doctrine." 1856.

And what had Lady Canning done? She had taken a true womanly interest in the education of native female children. She had visited the female schools of Calcutta in a quiet, unobtrusive way; but once only in each case, save with a notable exception in favour of the Bethune Institution, which had been taken by Lord Dalhousie under the special care of the Government.* In this Lady Canning had taken some observable interest. But as the Managing Committee of the school was composed of high-caste Hindoo gentlemen, there was assuredly no apparent necessity for restraining her womanly instincts and shrinking into apathy and indolence, as one regardless of the happiness and the dignity of her sex. Whatsoever may have been the zeal for the conversion of the Heathen that pervaded Government House, there were no indiscreet manifestations of it. There are times, how-

* *Ante*, page 187.

1856. ever, when no discretion can wholly arrest the growth of dangerous lies. A very little thing, in a season of excitement, will invest a colourable falsehood with the brightest hues of truth, and carry conviction to the dazzled understanding of an ignorant people. The sight of Lady Canning's carriage at the gates of the Bethune school may have added, therefore, Heaven only knows, some fresh tints to the picture of a caste-destroying Government, which active-minded emissaries of evil were so eager to hang up in the public places of the land.

Progress of social reform.

It was not much; perhaps, indeed, it was simply nothing. But just at that time there was a movement, urged on by John Grant and Barnes Peacock, in the purest spirit of benevolence, for the rescue of the women of India from the degradation in which they were sunk. It happened—truly, it happened, for it was wholly an accident—that one of the first measures, outwardly, of Lord Canning's Government was the formal passing of the bill "to remove all legal obstacles to the marriage of Hindoo widows," which had been introduced, discussed, and virtually carried, during the administration of his predecessor.* And this done, there was much said and written about the restraints that were to be imposed on Hindoo polygamy; and every day the appearance of a Draft Act, formidable in the extreme to Brahminism, was looked for, with doubt and aversion, by the old orthodox Hindoos. For they saw that in this, as in the matter of Re-Marriage, some of their more free-thinking countrymen, mostly of the younger generation, moved by the teachings of the English, or by some hope of gain, were beseeching Government to relieve the nation from what they called the reproach of Ku-

* *Ante*, page 190.

linism. And, at such a time, Orthodoxy, staggering under blows given, and shrinking from blows to come, looked aghast even at such small manifestations as the visits of the wife of the Governor-General to the Bethune female school. It was clear that the English, with their overpowering love of rule, were about now to regulate in India, after their own fashion, the relations of the two sexes to each other.* 1856.

Lord Canning found this movement afoot; he in no wise instituted it. He found that Lord Dalhousie, after an experience of many years, believed these social reforms to be practicable and safe; he found that the ablest member of his Council, who had spent all his adult life in India, was with all his heart and soul eager for their promotion, and with all the activity of his intellect promoting them. As to this movement against Hindoo polygamy, which was intended to prune down the evil, not wholly to eradicate it, there was something, to his European understanding, grotesque in the notion of a Christian Legislature recognising certain forms of polygamy, and addressing itself only to the abuses of the system, as though to Christian eyes it were not altogether an abuse. But he could see plainly enough that only by admitting such a compromise could the good thing be done at all; and seeing also the necessity of proceeding warily with such a delicate operation, he was not disposed, in the first instance, to do more than to feel the pulse of the people. It would be wise to delay

* Sir Henry Lawrence clearly discerned the danger of this, and in an article in the *Calcutta Review*, written in 1856, pointed it out: "Of late years," he wrote, "the wheels of Government have been moving very fast. Many native prejudices have been shocked. Natives are now threatened with the abolition of polygamy. It would not be difficult to twist this into an attack on Hindooism. At any rate, the faster the vessel glides, the more need of caution, of watching the weather, the rocks, and the shoals."

1856. actual legislation until public opinion should have been more unmistakably evoked.*

In the personal action of Lord Canning during this year of his novitiate, in the promotion either of the religious conversion or the social reformation of the people, I can see no traces of intemperate zeal. But it is not to be questioned that just at this time there was a combination of many untoward circumstances to strengthen the belief, which had been growing for some years, that the English Government were bent upon bringing, by fair means or by foul, all the nations of India under the single yoke of the White Man's faith. Nor is it less certain that at such a time the order for the enlistment of Native troops for general service appeared to their unaided comprehensions, and was designedly declared by others, to be a part of the scheme. There were those, indeed, who

* Lord Canning's opinions are so clearly expressed in the following passage, that it is right that his words should be given: "It will, no doubt, be a little staggering to find ourselves drawing up a law by which, although a horrible abuse of polygamy will be checked, a very liberal amount of it will be sanctioned, and which must recognise as justifying it reasons which we believe to be no justification whatever. It may be said that we shall only be enforcing Hindoo law, and that we are constantly doing this in many ways which abstractedly we should not approve. But I do not know that we have any examples of laws of our own making and wording, by which anything so contrary to our convictions of right and wrong as the taking of a second wife, for the reasons allowed by Menu (or at least for eight of them out of ten), is declared lawful. This, however, is a matter of appearance and feeling rather than of substance. Practically, a monstrous horror would be put an end to, and we might keep ourselves straight even in appearance by making it very clear in the preamble that the act is passed at the desire of the Hindoos to rescue their own law and custom from a great abuse, and that in no respect is it proposed to substitute English law for the laws of that people. . . . . Upon the whole, I come, without hesitation, to the conclusion that the movement ought to be encouraged to our utmost, and that the existence and strength of it ought to be made generally known. The presentation of the petitions to the Legislative Council, and their publication, will effect this. How soon the introduction of a bill should follow, or how much time should be given to seeing whether serious opposition is evoked, I should like to talk over with you some day, as also the scope of the bill."—*Lord Canning to Mr. J. P. Grant, June* 20, 1856. *MS. Correspondence.*

saw, or professed to see, in this matter, the very root of our cherished desire for the conversion of the people. It was said that we wished to bring them all to our own faith in order that we might find them willing to do our bidding in all parts of the world, that they might shrink from no kind of work by sea or by land, and even fight our battles in Europe; for it was plain that England had sad lack of fighting men, or she would not have drawn upon India for them during the Crimean war. In the art of what is called "putting two and two together," there were many intelligent natives by no means deficient, and deeper and deeper the great suspicion struck root in the popular mind. 1856.

There was another ugly symptom, too, at this time, which greatly, in some particular quarters, strengthened this impression of coming danger among the Sepoys of the Bengal Army. There were among the European officers of that army many earnest-minded, zealous Christians; men whose hearts were wrung by the sight of the vast mass of heathendom around them, and who especially deplored the darkness which brooded over their companions in arms, their children in the service of the State, the Sepoys who looked up to and obeyed them. Some, in their conscientious prudence, grieved in silence, and rendered unto Cæsar the homage of a wise forbearance. Others, conscientiously imprudent, believed that it was their duty to render unto God the just tribute of an apostolic activity. It was the creed of these last that all men were alike to them, as having souls to be saved, and that no external circumstances affected their own inalienable right to do their great Master's work. If under the pressure of these convictions they had changed the red coat for the black,

1856. and the sword for the shepherd's crook, they would have fairly earned the admiration of all good men. But holding fast to the wages of the State, they went about with the order-book in one hand and the Bible in the other; and thus they did a great and grievous wrong to the Government they professed to serve. To what extent this missionary zeal pervaded our English officers, it is not easy, with much precision, to declare. But there were some of whose missionary zeal there is now no remnant of a doubt—some who confessed, nay, openly gloried in their proselytising endeavours. One officer, who in 1857 was commandant of a regiment of Infantry, said vauntingly in that year: "I beg to state that during the last twenty years and upwards, I have been in the habit of speaking to natives of all classes, Sepoys and others, making no distinction, since there is no respect of persons with God, on the subject of our religion, in the highways, cities, bazaars, and villages—not in the Lines and regimental Bazaars. I have done this from a conviction that every converted Christian is expected, or rather commanded, by the Scriptures to make known the glad tidings of salvation to his lost fellow-creatures, Our Saviour having offered himself up as a sacrifice for the sins of the whole world, by which alone salvation can be secured. He has directed that this salvation should be freely offered to all without exception." Again, in another letter, he wrote: "As to the question whether I have endeavoured to convert Sepoys and others to Christianity, I would humbly reply that this has been my object, and I conceive is the aim and end of every Christian who speaks the word of God to another—merely that the Lord would make him the happy instrument of converting his neighbour to God, or, in other words, of rescuing him from eternal destruction." "On matters connected with religion," he added, "I feel myself called upon to act in two capacities—'to render unto Cæsar (or the Government) the things that are Cæsar's, and to render unto God the things that are God's.' Temporal matters and spiritual matters are thus kept clearly under their respective heads. When speaking, therefore, to a native on the subject of religion, I am then acting in the capacity of a Christian soldier under the authority of my heavenly superior; whereas in temporal matters I act as a general officer, under the authority and order of my earthly superior."* Reading this, one does not know whether more to admire the Christian courage of the writer or to marvel at the strange moral blindness which would not suffer him to see that he could not serve both God and Mammon; that ignoring the known wishes and instructions of his temporal master, he could not do his duty to his spiritual Lord; and that if in such a case the two services were antagonistic to each other, it was his part, as a Christian, to divest himself of his purchased allegiance to the less worthy Government, and to serve the Other and the Higher without hindrance and without reproach. He was not bound to continue to follow such a calling, but whilst following it he was bound to do his duty in that state of life to which it had pleased God to call him. 1856.

Whilst all these disturbing influences were at work, and on many accounts most actively in the neighbourhood of Calcutta, there came from afar, across the North-Western frontier, a current of political agitation, which was met by other streams of

* Lieutenant-Colonel Wheler to Government, April 15, 1857.—*Printed Papers.*

1856. native origin, turgid also with troublous rumours. The Persian Government, in best of times given to treachery and trickery, even under the fairest outside show of friendship, were not likely in such a conjuncture as had arisen at the end of 1856, to let slip any available means of damaging an enemy. Holding fast to the maxim that "All is fair in war," they endeavoured, not unwisely after their kind, to raise manifold excitements on our Northern frontier, and somehow to "create a diversion." There might be some inflammable materials strewn about, to which a firebrand skilfully applied, or even a spark dropped seemingly haphazard, might produce the desired result of combustion. Truly it was worth a trial. In spite of Sectarian differences something perhaps might be done by an appeal to the common faith of the followers of the Prophet. The King of Delhi, though not much as a substantial fact, was a great and potential name; there was some vitality in the traditions which were attached to it and the associations by which it was surrounded. The Mogul himself was a Soonee, and the people of Delhi and its surroundings were mostly Soonees, and there was doubtless a difficulty in this, but not one that might not be surmounted. So Persia sent forth her emissaries noiselessly to the gates of the Imperial City, perhaps with no very clear conception of what was to be done, but with a general commission to do mischief to the English. Mahomedans of all sects might be invited to lay aside their doctrinal differences for a while and to unite against a common enemy. There might be great promises of the restoration of a magnificent Mahomedan Empire; and, as the least result of the scattering of such seed, the minds of the people might be unsettled, and something might come of it in good time. A Proclamation was therefore prepared, and in due course it found its way to the walls of Delhi, and even displayed itself on the Jumma Musjid, or Great Mosque. There were stories, too, in circulation to the effect that the war on the shores of the Persian Gulf was going cruelly against us. It was bruited abroad, also, that though the English thought that they had secured the friendship of Dost Mahomed, the Ameer was really the friend and vassal of Persia, and that the amity he had outwardly evinced towards them was only a pretext for beguiling them to surrender Peshawur to the Afghans. 1856.

It was believed in Upper India that this was to be done; and it was reported also about the same time that the English intended to compensate themselves for this concession by annexing the whole of Rajpootana. This last story was not one of merely native acceptance. It had been set forth prominently in some of the Anglo-Indian newspapers, and unhappily there had been nothing in our past treatment of the Native States of India to cause it to be disbelieved. In the North-Western regions of India disturbing rumours commonly assume a political colour, whilst lower down in Bengal and Behar, their complexion is more frequently of a religious cast. The rumour of the coming absorption of these ancient Hindoo principalities into the great new Empire of the British was well contrived, not only to excite the anxieties and resentments of the Rajpoot races, but to generate further political mistrust throughout all the remaining states of the country. It was so mischievous a report that, when it reached England and obtained further currency in our journals, even the Court of Directors of the East India

1856. Company, the most reticent of all political bodies, broke, as I have before said, through their habitual reserve, and authoritatively contradicted it.

Seldom is it that the English themselves discern the effects of these disquieting rumours upon the minds of the people. In ordinary official language, at this time, all was quiet in Upper India. But ever and anon some friendly Mahomedan or Hindoo spoke of certain significant symptoms of the unrest which was not visible to the English eye;* and vague reports of some coming danger which no one could define, reached our functionaries in the North-West; and some at last began to awaken slowly to the conviction that there were evil influences at work to unsettle the national mind. The new year dawned, and there was something suggestive in the number of the year. In 1757 the English had established their dominion in India by the conquest of

* The old Afghan chief, Jan Fishan Khan, who had followed our fortunes and received a pension from the British Government, told Mr. Greathed, Commissioner at Cawnpore, in February, 1857, that these rumours had produced a very bad effect. A private note from that officer to Mr. Colvin, the Lieutenant-Governor, is worthy of citation in this place: "Jan Fishan Khan paid me a visit a few days ago with the special object of communicating his apprehensions on the present state of political affairs in India. He brought several members of his family, evidently to be witnesses of the interview, and prefaced his address with a recitation of the fruitless warnings he had given Sir Wm. MacNaghten of the course affairs were taking in Cabul. His fears for our safety rested on his belief that we intended to give up Peshawur to Dost Mahomed, and to annex Rajpootana. He said our maxim should be, 'Prevention better than cure,' and that, with enemies at the gate, we should take care to keep the inmates of the house our friends. He appeared quite relieved to receive my assurance that there was no probability of either of the apprehended events coming to pass. It would hardly have been worth while to mention this incident, but that we so rarely receive any indication of the political gossip of the day among the native community; and we may feel quite sure that Jan Fishan was actuated by fears for our welfare, and not by hopes of our overthrow, when he gave credence to the reports. I am afraid the frequent reports of annexation in Rajpootana have agitated the public mind and bred distrust among the Rajpoots. It is a pity so many years have elapsed since a Governor-General had an opportunity of personally assuring them of their political safety."

Bengal. For a hundred years they had now, by the progressive action of continued encroachments, been spreading their paramount rule over the whole country; and there were prophecies, said to be of ancient date, which foretold the downfal of the English power at the end of this century of supremacy. Ever in times of popular excitement are strange prophecies afloat in the social atmosphere. Whether they are revivals of old predictions, or new inventions designed to meet the requirements of the moment, it is often difficult even to conjecture.* But whether old or new, whether uttered in good faith or fraudulently manufactured, they seldom failed to make an impression on the credulous minds of the people. Coming upon them not as the growth of human intelligence, but as the mysterious revelations of an unseen power, they excited hopes and aspirations, perhaps more vital and cogent from their very vagueness. The religious element mingled largely with the political, and the aliment which nourished the fanaticism of believers fed also their ambition and their cupidity. In the particular prophecy of which men at this time were talking there was at least something tangible, for it was a fact that the first century of British rule was fast coming to an end. This in itself was sufficient to administer largely to the superstition and credulity of the people, and it was certain, too, that the prediction based upon it was not now heard for the first time. Lightly heeded, when long years were to intervene before its 1856.

* It is certain, however, that the most preposterous claims to antiquity are sometimes advanced on their behalf. For example, it was gravely stated in a leading Calcutta journal, that a prophecy had been discovered, a thousand years old, pointing to the downfal of the English at this time; in other words, that our destruction had been predicted many hundred years before we had ever been seen in the country, or ever heard of by the people.

1856. possible realisation, now that the date of the prediction had arrived, it took solemn and significant shape in the memories of men, and the very excitement that it engendered helped in time to bring about its fulfilment.*

* Whether the prophecy was of Hindoo or Mahomedan origin is still a moot question. The following, from a memorandum furnished to me by Mr. E. A. Reade, throws some light on the subject and will be read with no little interest :—"I do not think I ever met one man in a hundred that did not give the Mahomedans credit for this prediction. I fully believe that the notion of change after a century of tenure was general, and I can testify with others to have heard of the prediction at least a quarter of a century previously. But call it a prediction or supersitition, the credit of it must, I think, be given to the Hindoos. If we take the Hejra calendar, 1757 A.D. corresponds with 1171 Hejra; 1857 A.D. with 1274 Hejra. Whereas by the luni-solar year of the Sumbut, 1757 A.D. is 1814 Sumbut, and 1857 A.D. 1914 Sumbut. I remember on my remarking to a chowvey Brahmin, whose loyalty was conspicuous throughout the period (he was afterwards killed in action with the rebels), soon after the battle of Oct. 11, 1857, that the Sumbut 1915 was passing away without the fulfilment of the centenary prophecy, that he replied with some anxiety, there was yet a remainder of the year, *i. e.* till March 20, 1858; and before that time, in 1832, the Subadar, a Tewaree, of a cavalry regiment, in his farewell to a brother of mine leaving the service in that year, coolly telling him that in another twenty-five years the Company's Raj would be at an end, and the *Hindoo* Raj restored. It certainly does not much matter, but I think it is the safe view to accept the tradition as of Hindoo rather than Mahomedan origin."

CHAPTER IV.

THE NEW RIFLED MUSKET—THE STORY OF THE GREASED CARTRIDGES—DUM-DUM AND BARRACKPORE—EXCITEMENT IN THE NATIVE REGIMENTS—EVENTS AT BERHAMPORE—MUTINY OF THE NINETEENTH REGIMENT—CONDUCT OF COLONEL MITCHELL.

Jan., 1857.

The storm rising.

THE new year dawned upon India with a fair promise of continued tranquillity. But it was only a few weeks old when the storm began to arise. It is in the cold weather that the British officer sees most of the Sepoy, and best understands his temper. Company drills, and regimental parades, and brigade exercises, are continually bringing him face to face with his men, and he roams about Cantonments as he cannot roam in the midst of the summer heats and autumnal deluges. But this winter of 1856-57 had nearly passed away, and he had seen no indications of anything to disturb his settled faith in the fidelity of the native soldier. There was outward serenity everywhere, and apparent cheerfulness and content, when suddenly a cloud arose in an unexpected quarter; and a tremendous danger, dimly seen at first, began to expand into gigantic proportions.

For years the enemies of the English, all who had been alarmed by our encroachments, all who had suffered by our usurpations, all who had been shorn

1857. by our intervention of privileges and perquisites which they had once enjoyed, and who saw before them a still deeper degradation and a more absolute ruin, had been seeking just such an opportunity as now rose up suddenly before them. They had looked for it in one direction; they had looked for it in another; and more than once they thought that they had found it. They thought that they had found something, of which advantage might be taken to persuade the Native soldiery that their Christian masters purposed to defile their caste and to destroy their religion. But the false steps, which we had hitherto taken, had not been false enough to serve the purposes of those who had sought to destroy the British Government by means of a general revolt of the Native Army. For half a century there had been nothing of a sufficiently palpable and comprehensive character to alarm the whole Sepoy Army, Mahomedan and Hindoo. But now, suddenly, a story of most terrific import found its way into circulation. It was stated that Government had manufactured cartridges, greased with animal fat, for the use of the Native Army; and the statement was not a lie.

Brown Bess. The old infantry musket, the venerable Brown Bess of the British soldier, had been condemned as a relic of barbarism, and it was wisely determined, in the Indian as in the English Army, to supersede it by the issue of an improved description of fire-arm, with grooved bores, after the fashion of a rifle. As a ball from these new rifled muskets reached the enemy at a much greater distance than the ammunition of the old weapon, the Sepoy rejoiced in the advantage which would thus be conferred upon him in battle, and lauded the Government for what he regarded as

1857.

a sign both of the wisdom of his rulers and of their solicitude for his welfare. And when it was learnt that depôts had been established at three great military stations for the instruction of the Sepoy in the use of the new weapon, there was great talk in the Lines about the wonderful European musket that was to keep all comers at a distance. But, unhappily, these rifled barrels could not be loaded without the lubrication of the cartridge. And the voice of joy and praise was suddenly changed into a wild cry of grief and despair when it was bruited abroad that the cartridge, the end of which was to be bitten off by the Sepoy, was greased with the fat of the detested swine of the Mahomedan, or the venerated cow of the Hindoo.

Story of the greased cartridges.

How the truth first transpired has been often told. Eight miles from Calcutta lies the military station of Dum-Dum. For many years it had been the head-quarters of the Bengal Artillery. There all the many distinguished officers of that distinguished corps had learnt the rudiments of their profession, and many had spent there the happiest years of their lives. But it was suddenly discovered that it was not suited to the purpose for which it was designed. The head-quarters of the Artillery were removed to Meerut. The red coat displaced the blue. The barracks and the mess-house, and the officers' bungalows, were given up to other occupants; and buildings, which from their very birth had held nothing but the appliances of ordnance, were degraded into manufactories and storehouses of small-arm ammunition. Thus, by a mutation of fortune, when the Enfield Rifle began to supersede Brown Bess, Dum-Dum became one of three Cantonments at which the Government established Schools of Musketry for instruction in the use

1857. of the improved rifled weapon. Now, it happened that, one day in January, a low-caste Lascar, or magazine-man, meeting a high-caste Sepoy in the Cantonment, asked him for a drink of water from his lotah. The Brahmin at once replied with an objection on the score of caste, and was tauntingly told that caste was nothing, that high-caste and low-caste would soon be all the same, as cartridges smeared with beef-fat and hog's-lard were being made for the Sepoys at the depôts, and would soon be in general use throughout the army.*

The Brahmin carried this story to his comrades, and it was soon known to every Sepoy at the depôt. A shudder ran through the Lines. Each man to whom the story was told caught the great fear from his neighbour, and trembled at the thought of the pollution that lay before him. The contamination was to be brought to his very lips; it was not merely to be touched, it was to be eaten and absorbed into his very being. It was so terrible a thing, that, if the most malignant enemies of the British Government had sat in conclave for years, and brought an excess of devilish ingenuity to bear upon the invention of a scheme framed with the design of alarming the Sepoy mind from one end of India to the other, they could not have devised a lie better suited to the purpose. But now the English themselves had placed in the hands of their enemies, not a fiction, but a fact of tremendous significance, to be turned against them as a deadly instrument of destruction. It was the very thing that had been so long sought, and up to this time sought in vain. It required no explanation. It

* No greased cartridges had been issued at Dum-Dum. The Sepoys in the musketry school there were only in the rudiments of their rifle-education, and had not come yet to need the application of the grease.

needed no ingenious gloss to make the full force of the thing itself patent to the multitude. It was not a suggestion, an inference, a probability; but a demonstrative fact, so complete in its naked truth, that no exaggeration could have helped it. Like the case of the leathern head-dresses, which had convulsed Southern India half a century before, it appealed to the strongest feelings both of the Mahomedan and the Hindoo, but though similar in kind, it was incomparably more offensive in degree; more insulting, more appalling, more disgusting. 1857

We know so little of Native Indian society beyond its merest externals, the colour of the people's skins, the form of their garments, the outer aspects of their houses, that History, whilst it states broad results, can often only surmise causes But there are some surmises which have little less than the force of gospel. We feel what we cannot see, and have faith in what we cannot prove. It is a fact, that there is a certain description of news, which travels in India, from one station to another, with a rapidity almost electric. Before the days of the "lightning post," there was sometimes intelligence in the Bazaars of the Native dealers and the Lines of the Native soldiers, especially if the news imported something disastrous to the British, days before it reached, in any official shape, the high functionaries of Government.* We cannot trace the progress of these evil-tidings. The Natives of India have an expressive saying, that "it is in the air." It often happened that an uneasy feel-

* The news of the first outbreak and massacre at Caubul, in 1841, and also of the subsequent destruction of the British Army in the Pass, reached Calcutta through the Bazaars of Meerut and Kurnal some days before they found their way to Government House from any official quarter; and the mutiny at Barrackpore was known by the Sepoys of the British force proceeding to Burmah before it reached the military and political chiefs by special express. See *ante*, p. 269.

1857. ing—an impression that something had happened, though they "could not discern the shape thereof"—pervaded men's minds, in obscure anticipation of the news that was travelling towards them in all its tangible proportions. All along the line of road, from town to town, from village to village, were thousands to whom the feet of those who brought the glad tidings were beautiful and welcome. The British magistrate, returning from his evening ride, was perhaps met on the road near the Bazaar by a venerable Native on an ambling pony—a Native respectable of aspect, with white beard and whiter garments, who salaamed to the English gentleman as he passed, and went on his way freighted with intelligence refreshing to the souls of those to whom it was to be communicated, to be used with judgment and sent on with despatch. This was but one of many costumes worn by the messenger of evil. In whatsoever shape he passed, there was nothing outwardly to distinguish him. Next morning there was a sensation in the Bazaar, and a vague excitement in the Sepoys' Lines. But when rumours of disaster reached the houses of the chief English officers, they were commonly discredited. Their own letters were silent on the subject. It was not likely to be true, they said, as they had heard nothing about it. But it was true; and the news had travelled another hundred miles whilst the white gentlemen, with bland scepticism, were shaking their heads over the lies of the Bazaar.

It is difficult, in most cases, to surmise the agency to whose interested efforts is to be attributed this rapid circulation of evil tidings. But when the fact of the greased cartridges became known, there were two great motive powers, close at hand, to give an immediate impulse to the promulgation of the story.

The political and the religious animosities, excited by the recent measures of the English, were lying in wait for an opportunity to vent themselves in action. It happened at this time, that the enmities which we had most recently provoked had their head-quarters in Calcutta. It happened, also, that these enmities had their root partly in Hindooism, partly in Mahomedanism. There was the great Brahminical Institution, the Doorma Soobha of Calcutta, whose special function it was to preserve Hindooism pure and simple in all its ancestral integrity, and, therefore, to resist the invasions and encroachments of the English, by which it was continually threatened. There were bygone injuries to revenge, and there were coming dangers to repel. On the other side, there was the deposed king-ship of Oude, with all its perilous surroundings. Sunk in slothfulness and self-indulgence, with little real care for anything beyond the enjoyment of the moment, Wajid Ali himself may have neither done nor suggested anything, in this crisis, to turn to hostile account the fact of the greased cartridges. But there were those about him with keener eyes, and stronger wills, and more resolute activities, who were not likely to suffer such an opportunity to escape. It needed no such special agencies to propagate a story, which would have travelled, in ordinary course of accidental tale-bearing, to the different stations in the neighbourhood of the capital. But it was expedient in the eyes of our enemies that it should at once be invested with all its terrors, and the desired effect wrought upon the Sepoy's mind, before any one could be induced, by timely official explanation, to believe that the outrage was an accident, an oversight, a mistake. So, from the beginning, the story went forth that the English, in prosecution of a

1857. long-cherished design, and under instructions from the Queen in Council, had greased the Sepoys' cartridges with the fat of pigs and cows, for the express purpose of defiling both Mahomedans and Hindoos.

On the banks of the Hooghly River, sixteen miles from Calcutta by land, is the great military station of Barrackpore. It was the head-quarters of the Presidency division of the Army. There was assembled the largest body of Native troops cantoned in that part of India. There, on the green slopes of the river, stood, in a well-wooded park, the country-seat of the Governor-General. Both in its social and its military aspects it was the foremost Cantonment of Bengal. As the sun declined on the opposite bank, burnishing the stream with gold, and throwing into dark relief the heavy masses of the native boats, the park roads were alive with the equipages of the English residents. There visitors from Calcutta, escaping for a while from the white glare and the dust-laden atmosphere of the metropolis, consorted with the families of the military officers; and the neighbouring villas of Titaghur sent forth their retired inmates to join the throng of "eaters of the evening air." There the young bride, for it was a rare place for honeymoons, emerging from her seclusion, often looked out upon the world for the first time in her new state. There many a young ensign, scarcely less hopeful and less exultant, wore for the first time the bridal garments of his profession, and backed the capering Arab that had consumed a large part of his worldly wealth. It was a pleasant, a gay, a hospitable station; and there was not in all India a Cantonment so largely known and frequented by the English. There was scarcely an officer of the Bengal Army to whom the name of Barrackpore did not suggest some familiar associations, whilst to numbers of the non-military classes, whose occupations tied them to the capital, it was, for long years, perhaps throughout the whole of their money-getting career, the extreme point to which their travels extended. 1857.

At Barrackpore, in the early part of 1857, were stationed four Native Infantry regiments. There were the Second Grenadiers* and the Forty-third, two of the "beautiful regiments" which had helped General Nott to hold Candahar against all comers, and had afterwards gained new laurels in desperate conflict with the Mahrattas and Sikhs. There was the Thirty-fourth, an ill-omened number, for a few years before it had been struck out of the Army List for mutiny,† and a new regiment had been raised to fill the dishonourable gap. There also was the Seventieth, which had rendered good service in the second Sikh war. Three of these regiments had been recently stationed in the Punjab, or on its frontier, and the Thirty-fourth had just come down from Lucknow. This last regiment was commanded by Colonel S. G. Wheler, who had but recently been posted to it from another corps; the Forty-third was under Colonel J. D. Kennedy, whose tenure of command had also been brief; whilst the Seventieth and the wing of the Second were commanded by officers who had graduated in those regiments, and were therefore well known to the men. The station was commanded by Brigadier Charles Grant; and the General of Division was that brave soldier and distinguished officer, John Hearsey, of whose services I have already spoken in a previous chapter of this work.‡

* A wing of this regiment was at Raneegunge.

† *Ante*, p. 298.

‡ See Book II.—Account of the Mutiny in the Punjab.

1857. On the 28th of January, Hearsey reported officially to the Adjutant-General's office that an ill-feeling was "said to subsist in the minds of the Sepoys of the regiments at Barrackpore." "A report," he said, "has been spread by some designing persons, most likely Brahmins, or agents of the religious Hindoo party in Calcutta (I believe it is called the 'Dharma Sobha'), that the Sepoys are to be forced to embrace the Christian faith." "Perhaps," he added, "those Hindoos who are opposed to the marriage of widows in Calcutta* are using underhand means to thwart Government in abolishing the restraints lately removed by law for the marriage of widows, and conceive if they can make a party of the ignorant classes in the ranks of the army believe their religion or religious prejudices are eventually to be abolished by force, and by force they are all to be made Christians, and thus, by shaking their faith in Government, lose the confidence of their officers by inducing Sepoys to commit offences (such as incendiarism), so difficult to put a stop to or prove, they will gain their object." The story of the greased cartridges was by this time in every mouth. There was not a Sepoy in the Lines of Barrackpore who was not familiar with it. There were few who did not believe that it was a deliberate plot, on the part of the English, designed to break down the caste of the Native soldier. And many were persuaded that there was an ultimate design to bring all men, along a common road of pollution, to the unclean faith of the beef-devouring, swine-eating Feringhee, who had conquered their country and now yearned to extirpate the creeds of their countrymen.

There was a time, perhaps, when the Sepoy would

* The General, doubtless, meant to say, "those Hindoos in Calcutta who are opposed to the marriage of widows."

have carried the story to his commanding officer, and sought an explanation of it. Such confidences had ceased to be a part of the relations between them. But it was not the less manifest that the Native soldiery at Barrackpore were boiling over with bitter discontent. They had accepted not only the fact as it came to them from Dum-Dum, but the accompanying lies which had been launched from Calcutta; and they soon began, after the fashion of their kind, to make a public display of their wrath. It is their wont in such cases to symbolise the inner fires that are consuming them by acts of material incendiarism. No sooner is the Sepoy troubled in his mind, and bent on resistance, than he begins covertly in the night to set fire to some of the public buildings of the place. Whether this is an ebullition of childish anger—an outburst of irrepressible feeling in men not yet ripe for more reasonable action; or whether it be intended as a signal, whether the fires are beacon-fires lit up to warn others to be stirring, they are seldom or never wanting in such conjunctures as this. A few days after the story of the greased cartridges first transpired at Dum-Dum, the telegraph station at Barrackpore was burnt down. Then, night after night, followed other fires. Burning arrows were shot into the thatched roofs of officers' bungalows. It was a trick learnt from the Sonthals, among whom the Second Grenadiers had served; and the fact that similar fires, brought about by the same means, were breaking out at Raneegunge, more than a hundred miles away, stamped their complicity in the crime, for one wing of the regiment was stationed there. These incendiary fires were soon followed by nocturnal meetings. Men met each other with muffled faces, and discussed, in excited language, the intole-

1857.

1857. rable outrage which the British Government had deliberately committed upon them. It is probable that they were not all Sepoys who attended these nightly musters. It is probable that they were not all Sepoys who signed the letters that went forth from the post-offices of Calcutta and Barrackpore, calling upon the soldiery at all the principal stations of the Bengal Army to resist the sacrilegious encroachments of the English. All that is clearly known is, that the meetings were held, that the letters were sent; and Cantonment after Cantonment fermented with the story of the greased cartridges.

The mutiny at Berhampore.

A hundred miles from Barrackpore, to the northward, on the banks of the river, lies the military station of Berhampore. It was one well suited, by its position, for the development of the desired results. For only a few miles beyond it lay the city of Moorshedabad, the home of the Newab Nazim of Bengal, the representative of the line of Soubahdars, who, under the Imperial Government, had once ruled that great province. It was known that the Newab, who, though stripped of his ancestral power, lived in a palace with great wealth and titular dignity and the surroundings of a Court, was rankling under a sense of indignities put upon him by the British Government, and that there were thousands in the city who would have risen at the signal of one who, weak himself, was yet strong in the prestige of a great name. At Berhampore, there were no European troops; there were none anywhere near to it. A regiment of Native Infantry, the Nineteenth, was stationed there, with a corps of Irregular Cavalry, and a battery of post guns manned by native gunners. It was not difficult to see that if these troops were to rise against their English officers, and the people of Moorshedabad were to fraternise with them, in the name of the Newab, all Bengal would soon be in a blaze. No thoughts of this kind disturbed the minds of our people, but the truth was very patent to the understandings of their enemies. 1857.

It happened, too, unfortunately at this time, that the routine-action of the British Government favoured the growth of the evil; for when the excitement was great at Barrackpore, detachments went forth on duty from the most disaffected regiments of all to spread by personal intercourse the great contagion of alarm. Firstly, a guard from the Thirty-fourth went upwards in charge of stud-horses; and then, a week later, another detachment from this regiment marched in the same direction with a party of European convalescents. At Berhampore they were to be relieved by men from the regiment there, and then to return to their own head-quarters; so that they had an opportunity of communicating all that was going on at Barrackpore to their comrades of the Nineteenth, of learning their sentiments and designs, and carrying back to their own station, far more clearly and unmistakably than could any correspondence by letter, tidings of the state of feeling among the troops at Berhampore, and the extent to which they were prepared to resist the outrage of the greased cartridges.

When the men of the Thirty-fourth reached Berhampore, their comrades of the Nineteenth received them open-armed and open-mouthed. They were old associates, for, not long before, they had been stationed together at Lucknow; and now the Nineteenth asked eagerly what strange story was this that they had heard from Barrackpore about the greasing of the cartridges. It was not then a new story in the Lines

1857 of Berhampore, but was already two weeks old.* It had been carried as quickly as the post or special messenger could carry it from the one station to the other, and it was soon afterwards in every man's mouth. But it had wrought no immediate effect upon the outer bearing of the Sepoys of the Nineteenth. The story was carried to the commanding officer, who gave an assuring reply, saying that, if there were any doubts in their minds, the men might see for themselves the grease applied to their cartridges; and so for a while the excitement was allayed. But when the men of the Thirty-fourth went up from Barrackpore and spoke of the feeling there—spoke of the general belief among the Sepoys at the Presidency that the Government deliberately designed to defile them, and of the intended resistance to this foul and fraudulent outrage—the Nineteenth listened to them as to men speaking with high authority, for they came from the very seat of Government, and were not likely to err. So they took in the story as it was told to them with a comprehensive faith, and were soon in that state of excitement and alarm which is so often the prelude of dangerous revolt.

On the day after the arrival of the detachment from Barrackpore, a parade of the Nineteenth was
Feb. 27. ordered for the following morning. It was an ordinary parade, "accidental," meaning nothing. But it was a parade "with blank ammunition," and a meaning was found. There were in the morning no ap-

* The first detachment of the Thirty-fourth reached Berhampore on the 18th of February, the second on the 25th. Colonel Mitchell, writing on February 16, says, that about a fortnight before a Brahmin Pay-Havildar had asked him, "What is this story that everybody is talking about, that Government intend to make the Native Army use cow's fat and pig's fat with the ammunition for their new rifles?" It must have reached Berhampore, therefore, either by the post or by Cossid (messenger) at the very beginning of the month of February.

parent signs of disaffection, but, before the evening had passed away, Adjutant M'Andrew carried to the quarters of Colonel Mitchell a disquieting report, to the effect that there was great excitement in the Lines; that when their percussion-caps had been served out to them for the morning's parade, the men had refused to take them, and that they had given as the ground of their refusal the strong suspicion they entertained that the cartridges had been defiled. It was the custom not to distribute the cartridges among the men before the morning of parade; but the general supply for the regiment had been served out from the magazine, and, before being stored away for the night, had been seen by some of the Sepoys of the corps. Now, it happened that the paper of which the cartridges were made was, to the outward eye, of two different kinds, and, as the men had heard that fresh supplies of ammunition had been received from Calcutta in the course of the month, they leapt at once to the conviction that new cartridges of the dreaded kind had been purposely mixed up with the old, and the panic that had been growing upon them culminated in this belief.* 1857.

Upon receipt of this intelligence, Mitchell at once started for the Lines, and summoned his native officers to meet him in the front of the Quarter-Guard. In such a conjuncture, a calm but resolute demeanour, a few words of kindly explanation and of solemn warning, as from one not speaking for himself but for a benignant and a powerful Government, might have done much to convince those Native officers, and through them the Sepoys of the regi-

* The fact, however, was, that there were no cartridges among the stores recently received from Calcutta, which consisted mainly of powder in barrels.

1857. ment, that they had laid hold of a dangerous delusion. But Mitchell spoke as one under the excitement of anger, and he threatened rather than he warned. He said that the cartridges had been made up, a year before, by the regiment that had preceded them in cantonments, that there was no reason for their alarm, and that if, after this explanation, they should refuse to take their ammunition, the regiment would be sent to Burmah or to China, where the men would die,* and that the severest punishment would overtake every man known to have actively resisted the orders of his Government. So the Native officers went their way, with no new confidence derived from the words that had fallen from their Colonel, but, on the other hand, strengthened in all their old convictions of imminent danger to their caste and their religion. He would not have spoken so angrily, they argued, if mischief had not been intended. They looked upon the irritation he displayed as a proof that his sinister designs had been inopportunely discovered.†

Such was the logic of their fears. Colonel Mitchell went to his home; but as he drove thither through the darkness of the night, with the Adjutant beside him, he felt that there was danger in the air, and that

* After reading all the evidence that I can find throwing light upon this scene at the Quarter-Guard, I am forced upon the conviction that Colonel Mitchell did use some such words as these. Lord Canning was, however, under an erroneous impression when he wrote in his minute of May 13, "The inconsiderate threat, that if the men did not receive their cartridges he would take them to Burmah or to China, where they would die, which is not denied by Lieutenant-Colonel Mitchell," &c. &c.; for Mitchell had denied it on the 18th of March, saying, "I certainly did not make use of the expression above quoted."—*Lieutenant-Colonel Mitchell to Assistant-Adjutant-General. Published Papers.*

† "He gave this order so angrily, that we were convinced that the cartridges were greased, otherwise he would not have spoken so."—*Petition of the Native Officers of the Nineteenth Regiment. Published Papers.*

something must be done to meet it. But what could be done? There were no white troops at Berhampore, and the Nineteenth Regiment composed the bulk of the black soldiery. But there were a regiment of Irregular Cavalry and a detachment of Native Artillery, with guns, posted at the station, and, as these dwelt apart from the Infantry, they might not be tainted by the same disease. Weaker in numbers, as compared with the Infantry, they had a countervailing strength in their guns and horses. A few rounds of grape, and a charge of Cavalry with drawn sabres, might destroy a regiment of Foot beyond all further hope of resistance. Mitchell might not have thought that things would come to this pass; it was his object to overawe, and, by overawing, to prevent the crisis. But, whatsoever his thoughts at that time, he issued his orders that the Cavalry and Artillery should be prepared to attend the morning parade. 1857.

In India, men retire early to their rest, for they seldom outsleep the dawn. It was little past the hour of ten, therefore, when Mitchell, just having betaken himself to his couch, heavy with thought of the morrow's work, was startled by the sound of a strange commotion from the direction of the Lines. There was a beating of drums, and there were shoutings from many voices, and a confused uproar, the meaning of which it was impossible to misinterpret. Plainly the Regiment had risen. Ever since the Colonel's interview with the Native officers the excitement had increased. It had transpired that the Cavalry and Artillery had been ordered out. Suspicions of foul play then grew into assured convictions, and the Regiment felt, to a man, that the greased cartridges were to be forced upon them at the

1857. muzzle of our guns. A great panic had taken hold of them, and it required but little to rouse them, in an impulse of self-preservation, to resist the premeditated outrage. How the signal was first given is not clear; it seldom is clear in such cases. A very little would have done it. There was a common feeling of some great danger, approaching through the darkness of the night. Some raised a cry of "Fire!"; some, again, said that the Cavalry were galloping down upon them; others thought that they heard in the distance the clatter of the Artillery gun-wheels. Then some one sounded the alarm, and there was a general rush to the bells-of-arms. Men seized their muskets, took forcible possession of the dreaded ammunition stored for the morning parade, and loaded their pieces in a bewilderment of uncertainty and fear.

Mitchell knew that the Regiment had risen, but he did not know that it was Terror, rather than Revolt, that stirred them; and so hastily dressing himself, he hurried off to bring down upon his men the very danger the premature fear of which had generated all this excitement in the Lines. Before any report of the tumult had reached him from European or from Native officers, he had made his way to the quarters of the Cavalry Commandant, and ordered him at once to have his troops in the saddle. Then like orders were given for the Artillery guns, with all serviceable ammunition, to be brought down to the Infantry Lines. There was a considerable space to be traversed, and the extreme darkness of the night rendered the service difficult. But, after a while, the Nineteenth heard the din of the approaching danger, and this time with the fleshly ear; saw the light of gleaming torches which was guiding it on to their destruction. But they stood there, not ripe for action, irresolute, panic-struck, as men waiting their doom. There were many loaded muskets in their hands, but not one was fired. 1857.

It was past midnight when Mitchell, having gathered his European officers from their beds, came down with the guns to the parade-ground, where Alexander and his troopers had already arrived. The Infantry, in undress, but armed and belted, were drawn up in line, vaguely expectant of something to come, but in no mood to provoke instant collision. A very little, at such a time, would have precipitated it, for the excitement of fear, in such circumstances, is more to be dreaded than the bitterest resentments, and even if the European officers had then moved forward in a body, the movement would have been exaggerated by the darkness into a hostile advance, and the Nineteenth, under an impulse of self-preservation, would have fired upon them. What Mitchell did, therefore, in the unfortunate conjuncture that had arisen, was the best thing that could be done. He loaded the guns, closed the Cavalry upon them, and sent the Adjutant forward with instructions to have the call sounded for an assembly of the Native officers. The summons was obeyed. Again the Native officers stood before their Colonel, and again there fell from his lips words that sounded in their ears as words of anger. What those words were, it is now impossible to record with any certainty of their truth. The Native officers believed that he said he would blow every mutineer from a gun, although he should die for it himself. They besought him not to be angry and violent, and urged that the men were ignorant and suspicious; that they were impelled only by their fears; that believing the Cavalry and Artillery had been brought down to destroy them, they were wild

1857. with excitement and incapable of reasoning, but that if the Colonel would send back the troopers and the guns, the men of the Regiment would soon lay down their arms and return to their duty.

Then a great difficulty arose, which, in the darkness and confusion of that February night, might have perplexed a calmer brain than Mitchell's. That the Nineteenth were rather panic-struck than mutinous, was certain. It was plain, too, that a mistake had been committed in bringing down the Cavalry and guns to overawe the Regiment. It would have been wiser, in the first instance, to have used them only for protective purposes, holding them in readiness the while to act on the offensive in case of necessity. But, as they had been brought down to the Infantry Lines, it was difficult to withdraw them, until the Nineteenth had given in their submission. The men, however, required, as a condition of their submission, that which Mitchell naturally desired should be regarded only as a consequence of it. Clinging fast to the belief that violence was intended, they would not have obeyed the order to lay down their arms; and Mitchell could not be certain that the Native troopers and gunners would fall upon their comrades at the word of command. There was a dilemma, indeed, from which it was difficult, if not impossible, to escape with safety and with honour. As men are wont to do in such extremities, he caught at a compromise. He would withdraw the guns and the Cavalry, he said, but he would hold a general parade in the morning; he commanded the station, and could order out all branches of the service. But the Native officers besought him not to do this, for the Sepoys, in such a case, would believe only that the violence intended to be done upon them was deferred for a few hours.

So he consented at last to what they asked; the Cavalry and the guns were withdrawn, and the general parade for the morning was countermanded. Whether the Sepoys of the Nineteenth had shown signs of penitence before this concession was made, and had or had not begun to lay down their arms, is a point of history enveloped in doubt. But it would seem that the Native officers told Colonel Mitchell that the men were lodging their arms, and that he trusted to their honour. The real signal for their submission was the retrocession of the torches. When the Sepoys saw the lights disappearing from the parade-ground, they knew that they were safe. 1857.

On the following morning the Regiment fell in, for parade, without a symptom of insubordination. The excitement of the hour had expended itself; and they looked back upon their conduct with regret, and looked forward to its consequences with alarm. Though moved by nothing worse than idle fear, they had rebelled against their officers and the State. Assured of their contrition, and believing in their fidelity, the former might perhaps have forgiven them; but it was not probable that the State would forgive. A Court of Inquiry was assembled, and during many days the evidence of European and Native officers was taken respecting the circumstances and causes of the outbreak; but the men, though clearly demonstrating their apprehensions by sleeping round the bells-of-arms, continued to discharge their duties without any new ebullitions; and there was no appearance of any hostile combinations, by which the mutiny of a regiment might have been converted into the rebellion of a province. Under the guidance of Colonel George Macgregor, the Newab Nazim of Bengal threw the weight of his influence into the

1857. scales on the side of order and peace; and whatsoever might have been stirring in the hearts of the Mussulman population of Moorshedabad, in the absence of any signal from their chief, they remained outwardly quiescent

CHAPTER V.

CAUSES OF DELAYED ACTION—THE GOVERNMENT AND THE DEPARTMENTS—INVESTIGATION OF THE CARTRIDGE QUESTION—PROGRESS OF DISAFFECTION AT BARRACKPORE—THE STORY OF MUNGUL PANDY—MUTINY OF THE THIRTY-FOURTH—DISBANDMENT OF THE NINETEENTH.

In all countries, and under all forms of government, the dangers which threaten the State, starting in the darkness, make headway towards success before they are clearly discerned by the rulers of the land. Often so much of time and space is gained, that the slow and complex action of authority cannot overtake the mischief and intercept its further progress. The peculiarities of our Anglo-Indian Empire converted a probability into a certainty. Differences of race, differences of language, differences of religion, differences of customs, all indeed that could make a great antagonism of sympathies and of interests, severed the rulers and the ruled as with a veil of ignorance and obscurity. We could not see or hear with our own senses what was going on, and there was seldom any one to tell us. When by some accident the truth at last transpired, generally in some of the lower strata of the official soil, much time was lost before it could make its way

1857. upwards to the outer surface of that authority whence action, which could no longer be preventive, emanated in some shape of attempted suppression. The great safeguard of sedition was to be found in the slow processes of departmental correspondence necessitated by a system of excessive centralisation. When prompt and effectual action was demanded, Routine called for pens and paper A letter was written where a blow ought to have been struck, and the letter went, not to one who could act, but was passed on to another stage of helplessness, and then on to another, through all gradations, from the subaltern's bungalow to the Government House.

The direction of the military affairs of our Indian Empire was supposed to be confided to the Commander-in-Chief. But there was a general power of control in the Governor-General that made the trust little more than nominal. So little were the limits of authority prescribed by law, or even by usage, that, it has already been observed, there was often a conflict between the Civil and the Military Chiefs, which in time ripened into a public scandal, or subsided into a courteous compromise, according to the particular temper of the litigants. Sensible of his power, the Governor-General was naturally anxious to leave all purely military matters in the hands of the Commander-in-Chief; but in India it was hard to say what were "purely military" matters, when once the question emerged out of the circle of administrative detail. As harmonious action was constitutionally promoted by the bestowal upon the Commander-in-Chief of a seat in Council, there would have been little practical inconvenience in the division of authority if the Civil and the Military Chiefs had always been in the same place. But it often happened that the Governor-General, with his

official machinery of the Military Secretary's office, 1857.
was at one end of the country, and the Commander-in-Chief, with the Adjutant-General of the Army, at the other. And so it happened in the early part of 1857. Lord Canning was at Calcutta. General Anson was officially in the Upper Provinces; personally he was somewhere in Lower Bengal.* The Adjutant-General was at Meerut. The Adjutant-General's office was in Calcutta. The Inspector-General of Ordnance was in Fort William. All these authorities had something to do with the business of the greased cartridges, and it was a necessity that out of a system which combined a dispersed agency with a centralised authority, there should have arisen some injurious delay.

But the delay, thus doubly inevitable, arose rather in this instance from the multiplicity of official agencies, than from the distance at which they were removed from each other. On the 22nd of January, Lieutenant Wright, who commanded the detachment of the Seventieth Sepoys at Dum-Dum, reported to the commanding officer of the musketry depôt the story of the greased cartridges, and the excitement it had produced. Major Bontein, on the following day, reported it to the commanding officer at Dum-Dum, who forthwith passed it on to the General commanding the Presidency division at Barrackpore. On the same day, General Hearsey forwarded the correspondence to the Deputy-Adjutant-General, who remained in charge of the office at Calcutta in the absence of his chief. But though thus acting in accordance with military regulations, he took the precaution to

* Just at this time General Anson was coming down to Calcutta to superintend the embarkation of his wife for England. He must have been actually in Calcutta when the Sepoys were in the first throes of their discontent; but it does not appear that the subject of the greased cartridges then attracted his attention.

1857. add that he forwarded the correspondence "for immediate submission to the Government of India, through its Military Secretary," and suggested that the Sepoys at the Rifle depôt should be permitted to grease their own cartridges. General Hearsey's letter must have reached the Adjutant-General's office on the 24th of January; perhaps not till after office hours. The following day was the Sabbath. The letter of "immediate transmission" was dated, therefore, on the 26th.* On the following day, the Government of India, through its Military Secretary, addressed a letter to the Adjutant-General's office sanctioning Hearsey's suggestion. On the 28th, the General received the official sanction, and at once directed the concession to be made known to all the regiments in Barrackpore. But it was too late. On the previous day, a significant question had been put by a Native officer on parade, as to whether any orders had been received. The reply was necessarily in the negative. Had it not been for the intervention of the Adjutant-General's office, General Hearsey might have received his reply four days before. Whilst we were corresponding, our enemies were acting; and so the lie went ahead of us apace.

Onward and onward it went, making its way throughout Upper India with significant embellishments, aided by the enemies of the British Government, whilst that Government looked at the matter in its naked reality, divested of all the outer crust of lies which it had thus acquired. Confident of their own good intentions, the English chiefs saw only an accident, an oversight, to be easily rectified and explained. There did not seem to be anything dangerously irre-

* It is right that this should be borne in mind. In all cases of alleged official delays the almanack of the year should be consulted, that account may be taken of a *dies non*.

parable in it. But it was, doubtless, right that they 1857
should probe the matter to its very depths, and do all that could be done to allay the inquietude in the Sepoy's mind. It was hardly to be expected that the Governor-General, who at that time had been less than a year in India, should see at once all the difficulties of the position. But he had men of large experience at his elbow; and it was wise to confide in them. In such an emergency as had then arisen, the Military Secretary to the Government of India was the functionary whose especial duty it was to inform and advise the Governor-General. That office was represented by Colonel Richard Birch, an officer of the Company's Army, who had served for many years at the head of the Judge Advocate's department, and was greatly esteemed as an able, clear-headed man of business, of unstained reputation in private life. Lord Dalhousie, no mean judge of character, had selected him for this important office, and Lord Canning soon recognised the wisdom of the choice. The Military Secretary had no independent authority, but in such a conjuncture as this much might be done to aid and accelerate the movements of Government; and had he then sate down idly and waited the result, or had he suffered any time to be lost whilst feebly meditating action, a heavy weight of blame would have descended upon him, past all hope of removal. But when he heard that the detachments at Dum-Dum were in a state of excitement, his first thought was to ascertain the truth or the falsehood of the alleged cause of alarm; so he went at once to the Chief of the Ordnance Department to learn what had been done.

At that time, the post of Inspector-General of Ordnance was held by Colonel Augustus Abbott, an Artillery officer of high repute, who had earned a name in history as one of the "Illustrious Garrison of Jellalabad." His first impression was, that some greased cartridges had been issued to the Depôt at Dum-Dum; and it was admitted that no inquiries had been made into the natural history of the lubricating material. But he was relieved from all anxiety on this score by a visit from Major Bontein, the Instructor, who asked Abbott to show him a greased cartridge. The fact was, that though large numbers had been manufactured, none had ever been issued to the Native troops at Dum-Dum or any other station in the Presidency Division.* The discovery, it was thought, had been made in time to prevent the dangerous consequences which might have resulted from the oversight. It would be easy to cease altogether from the use of the obnoxious fat; easy to tell the Sepoys that they might grease the cartridges after their own fashion. The uneasiness, it was believed, would soon pass away, under the influence of soothing explanations. It was plain, however, that what had happened at Dum-Dum might happen at the other military stations, where schools of musketry had been established and the new rifles were being brought into use. The regiments there would assuredly soon hear the alarm-note pealing upwards from Bengal. But though some time had been lost, the "lightning post" might still overtake the letters or messages of the Sepoys before they could reach Umballah and Sealkote.

So Birch, having thus clearly ascertained the real fact of the greased cartridges, went at once to the Governor-General, and asked his permission to take

* It should be stated that much of the laboratory work of the Arsenal of Fort William was actually carried on at Dum-Dum; but that the ammunition manufactured there was always sent to the Arsenal and issued thence to the troops.

immediate steps to re-assure the minds of the Sepoys at all the Musketry Depôts. The permission was granted, and orders were forthwith sent to Dum-Dum; whilst the Electric Telegraph was set at work to instruct the Adjutant-General of the Army, at Meerut, to issue all cartridges free from grease, and to allow the Sepoys to apply with their own hands whatever suitable mixture they might prefer. For, at Meerut, a large manufacture of greased cartridges was going on, without any fear of the results.* At the same time he telegraphed to the commanding officers of the Rifle Depôts at Umballah and Sealkote, not to use any of the greased cartridges that might have been issued for service with the new rifles. It was recommended, at the same time, by Birch and Abbott, that a General Order should be published by the Commander-in-Chief, setting forth that no greased cartridges would be issued to the Sepoy troops, but that every man would be permitted to lubricate his own ammunition with any materials suitable to the purpose. But plain as all this seemed to be, and apparently unobjectionable, an objection was found at Meerut to the course proposed in Calcutta; and the Adjutant-General, when he received his message, telegraphed back to the Military Secretary that Native troops had been using greased cartridges "for some years," and the grease had been composed of mutton-fat. "Will not," it was asked, "your instructions make the Sepoys suspicious about what hitherto they have not hesitated to handle?" Further orders were requested; and, on the 29th of January, a message went from Calcutta to the Head-

1857. January 27.

* Materials for 100,000 cartridges, with implements of manufacture and pattern cartridges, were sent from the Calcutta Arsenal to Meerut in October, 1856. These were for the use of the Sixtieth Rifles.

1857. Quarters of the Army, stating that the existing practice of greasing cartridges might be continued, if the materials were of mutton-fat and wax.*

Prompt measures having thus been taken to prevent the issue of greased cartridges prepared in Calcutta or Meerut to any Native troops—and with such success that from first to last no such cartridges ever were issued to them†—the authorities, perhaps a little perplexed by this sudden explosion in a season of all-prevailing quiet, began to inquire how it had all happened. Not without some difficulty, for there were apparent contradictions in the statements that reached them, the whole history of the greased cartridges was at last disentangled. It was this. In 1853, the authorities in England sent out to India some boxes of greased cartridges. The lubricating material was of different kinds; but tallow entered largely into the composition of it all. It was sent out, not for service, but for experiment, in order that the effect of the climate upon the cartridges thus greased might be ascertained. But it did not wholly escape our high military functionaries in India, that these greased cartridges, if care were not taken to exclude all obnoxious materials from their composition, could not be served out to Native troops without risk of serious danger. Colonel Henry Tucker was, at that time, Adjutant-General of the Bengal Army, and he

* See the telegrams published in the papers laid before Parliament. I merely state the fact that such messages were sent. But I have found it impossible to reconcile the assertion of the Adjutant-General, that cartridges smeared with mutton-fat had been in use, with the actual facts of the case, as given in the following pages on the very highest authority. I am assured that the only grease used with the ammunition of the old two-grooved rifles was a mixture of wax and oil applied to the "patch."

† This was officially declared by Government, and in perfect good faith. I believe, however, that some greased cartridges were served out to a Goorkha regiment, at their own request.

obtained the permission of the Commander-in-Chief to sound a note of warning on the subject. There was in those days even a greater complication of military authority than when Lord Canning presided over the Government. There was an institution called the Military Board, composed of certain ex-officio members, one special salaried member, and a Secretary who did the greater part of the work. The trite adage that "Boards are Screens" was verified in this instance, if in no other, for responsibility was effectually obscured. It fell within the range of the Board's multifarious functions to direct the experiments which were to be made with the greased cartridges; so Colonel Tucker, in due official course, addressed a letter to the Secretary to the Military Board on the subject of these experiments, adding, "I am at the same time to communicate the Commander-in-Chief's opinion, that, unless it be known that the grease employed in these cartridges is not of a nature to offend or interfere with the prejudices of caste, it will be expedient not to issue them for test to Native corps, but to European soldiers only to be carried in pouch." But it does not seem that this warning had any effect upon the Military Board.* The ammunition to be tested was served out to Native Guards at Fort William, Cawnpore, and Ran-

1857.

December 1853.

* Colonel Tucker afterwards said in a public journal, "I do not presume to say with whom specifically the blame of this most culpable neglect may rest. Only investigation can settle that point; but I conceive that either the Military Secretary or the officer presiding in chief over the Ordnance Department in Calcutta, is, one or both, the party implicated." Investigation proves that both officers were blameless. The routine in those days was for the Commander-in-Chief to address the Military Board, and for the Military Board to address the Governor-General. In this case, however, the correspondence never went further than the Military Board; and it was not until after the mutiny had broken out, and Colonel (then Major-General) Tucker had publicly referred to his neglected warnings, that the Military Secretary had any knowledge of the correspondence of 1853.

1857. goon, who carried it in their pouches, and handed it from man to man every time that the guard was relieved. After being thus tested for many months, the cartridges were reported upon by Committees of European officers drawn from Native Infantry Regiments, and eventually sent back to England with these reports. No objection was ever made by the Sepoys to the handling of the cartridges, and none were ever started by their regimental officers or by the Committees.

The Sixtieth (Queen's) Rifles were at this time serving in India, but the weapon which they used was that known as the two-grooved rifle; and the ammunition consisted of a cartridge of powder only, and, separate from this cartridge, a ball covered with a "patch" of fine cloth, which was smeared with a mixture of wax and oil. When rifle-companies were raised in some of the Native regiments, this two-grooved rifle was served out to them with the ammunition above described, and no kind of objection was ever raised to its use.* The grease was known to be harmless, and the paper of the cartridge was never suspected. But, in 1856, these two-grooved rifles were condemned, and new Enfield rifles issued to the Sixtieth, and also to some of the Company's European Infantry. The ammunition then, in the first instance, supplied to them, consisted of the residue of the greased cartridges sent from England for experiment; and whilst these were being used up, others of the same description, in accordance with orders from England, were being made up by the Ordnance Departments at Calcutta, at Dum-Dum, and at Meerut. The mixture of wax and oil, though it answered the purpose of lubrication at the

* See orders of 1847, given at p. 655 *Addendum.*

time of use, was not applicable to bundled cartridges, 1857.
because its greasing properties soon disappeared. So the cartridges manufactured for the Enfield rifles were to be smeared with a mixture of stearine and tallow. The Ordnance Department then indented for tallow, without any specification of the nature of the animal fat composing it;* and, although no hog's-lard was supplied, there is no question that some beef-fat was used in the composition of the tallow. This was, doubtless, an oversight, for it would have been easy to enter into a contract for the supply of sheep and goats' fat, to which there would not have been the same objections; but it would seem that the Ordnance authorities had before them the fact that they were making ammunition, primarily for the use of the Sixtieth Rifles, in accordance with instructions that had been received from England.

It was true, then, that cartridges smeared with obnoxious grease had been in course of manufacture both at Fort William and at the Head-Quarters of Artillery at Meerut. It was true that, in October, 1856, large numbers of balled cartridges had been sent up the country by steamer for the use of the

* It was a part of a contract for "Petty Stores," to be supplied to the Arsenal of Fort William for two years, from the 15th of August, 1856, entered into by Gungadhur Banerjea and Co. The article is described in the contract as "Grease, Tallow;" and it was to be supplied at the rate of two annas (or threepence) a pound. From the Records of the Inspector-General's office, it appears that after the contract, dated 16th of August, 1856, was concluded, Grease and Tallow were indented for separately at various times. In an indent on the Contractor, dated September, 1856, the following entries appear:

Grease . . .	For ammunition purposes.
Tallow of the purest kind. . . .	For greasing composition for Minié rifle ammunition.

In subsequent indents the article is sometimes called "Grease," and sometimes "Tallow"—"Required for Arsenal purposes." A circular was issued to the Department, dated January 29th, 1857, directing that, when applying tallow to articles which Native soldiers are required to handle, only the tallow of sheep or goats is to be employed, that of swine or cows being most carefully excluded.

Musketry Depôts at Umballah and Sealkote.* But it was not true that any had been issued to the Sepoy regiments; for the time had not yet come for the detachments at the Musketry Depôts to use any kind of ammunition. These detachments had received the Enfield rifle; but they were merely learning its use; learning the construction and the properties of the new weapon; learning to take it to pieces and to put it together again; learning the mode of taking sight and aim at different distances—processes which occupied many weeks, and delayed the season of target practice. Meanwhile, the old two-grooved rifles were in full service with the rifle-companies; and cartridges, as above described, with detached balls greased with oil and wax, were in constant use for practice-drill.† To these cartridges the Commander-in-Chief referred, when he telegraphed to Calcutta that greased cartridges had been long in use without exciting any alarm. It was thought at Head-Quarters that if attention were once called to the matter of the greased cartridges, every Sepoy who had used the old "patches" would be filled with alarm.

But whether this surmise were right or whether it were wrong, it is certain that the minds of the Sepoys, first in one station, then in another, were already becoming overwhelmed by the great fear. The lie had gone a-head of the truth. It is doubtful whether any orders or proclamations could have ar-

* The numbers were 22,500 for the Umballah Depôt, and 14,000 for the Sealkote Depôt, sent on the 23rd of October to Delhi, *viâ* Allahabad, by steamer.

† It may be advantageous to caution the non-professional reader against confounding the rifle-companies here spoken of with the detachments at the Rifle Depôts. The former were with their regiments, using the old two-grooved muskets; the latter were detached from their regiments, learning the use of the Enfield rifle in the schools of musketry at Dum-Dum, Umballah, and Sealkote.

rested the feeling of alarm, which was rushing, with the force of an electric current, from cantonment to cantonment, and turning the hearts of the soldiery against us. It was plain that a very dangerous delusion had taken possession of them, and it was right that everything reasonable should have been done to expel it. But the Sepoys, at a very early stage, were past all reasoning. It was not grease, animal grease, alone that disturbed them. Grease of an obnoxious kind, for long years, had been applied by Native hands to the wheels of gun-carriages and waggons, and not even a murmur of discontent had been heard. At Calcutta and at Meerut the greased cartridges had been made up by Natives, and, at the latter place, even Brahmin boys had been employed in their manufacture. So it was thought that the objection might be confined to the biting-off of the end of the cartridge. It was true that the grease was applied to the part farthest from that which touched the lips of the soldier; but in a hot climate grease is rapidly absorbed, and there was a not unreasonable apprehension that it would insidiously spread itself from one end to the other of the cartridge. So, on the recommendation of Major Bontein, a change was introduced into the system of Rifle drill, by which the process of pinching off by the hand was substituted for biting off by the teeth. This was right, as far as it went; but it could not go far. The Sepoy was not satisfied. He argued that he had been accustomed always to bite-off the end of the cartridge, nd that the force of this strong habit would often bring it unwittingly to his lips, especially in the excitement of active service. There are times, doubtless, when both the Hindoo and the Mahomedan have an elastic conscience. But there are 1857.

1857. seasons also when both are obdurate and unyielding. It might have been easy to persuade the Sepoys that the British Government desired to place the matter entirely in their own hands, and to leave them to grease their cartridges and to use them after their own fashion; but too many vague doubts and suspicions had been raised in past times, and too much was being poisonously instilled into them in the present, to suffer even a remnant of confidence to cling to them in this conjuncture. To beat them back at one point was only to make them take up their ground more tenaciously at another.

Barrackpore, February, 1857. "We have at Barrackpore," wrote General Hearsey in February, "been dwelling upon a mine ready for explosion. I have been watching the feeling of the Sepoys here for some time. Their minds have been misled by some designing scoundrels, who have managed to make them believe that their religious prejudices, their caste, is to be interfered with by Government—that they are to be 'forced to become Christians.'" But day after day passed, and though it was manifest that there was an uneasy feeling in all the regiments, and especially in the Second and Thirty-fourth, there were no overt acts of insubordination. Their commanding officers had explained to them that Government had no such designs as were imputed to them; but even when the Sepoys were assured that no greased cartridges would ever be issued to them, and that they might themselves lubricate their ammunition with wax and oil, so deeply rooted were the misgivings that had taken possession of their minds, that they began to suspect that animal grease had been used in the composition of the cartridge-paper, and that the English were only abandoning one trick to fall back upon another. There was a glazed surface on the paper, which gave it a greasy aspect, and favoured the growth of the suspicion; and when it was burnt, it flared "with a fizzing noise, and smelt as if there was grease in it." So the suspicion soon grew into a certainty, and the fears of the Sepoy waxed stronger and stronger every day. 1857.

This was especially apparent in the Second Grenadiers; so a Court of Inquiry was held to investigate the matter. The paper was examined in Court, and the Sepoys were called upon to state their objections. This they did, with an obstinate adherence to their belief that grease had been used in its composition. When asked how this suspicion could be removed from their minds, they answered that they could not remove it—that there were no means of removing it, except by substituting another kind of paper. So Government resolved to submit the obnoxious paper to a chemical test, and the Chemical Examiner reported, after due investigation, that it had not been greased or treated with any greasy or oily matter during or since its manufacture; that by operating on a large quantity of paper he had been able to extract as much oil as could be discovered by the use of a higher power of the microscope, but that the grease was no more than might be contracted from the hands of the workmen who had packed it.* But there was little satisfaction even in this, for so obstinate was the conviction that the English designed to pollute the Sepoys, that a belief was gaining ground among them that the paper was little more than "bladder." The stiffness and transparency of it favoured this suspicion, and they could not rid themselves of the impression that it was an animal substance which

* Dr. M'Namara to the Inspector-General of Ordnance, Feb. 11, 1857. *Published papers.*

1857. they were called upon to use. This was a far greater difficulty than the other, for it affected not merely the Rifle Depôts, but the whole Native Army; and there was no possibility of grappling with it except by ceasing altogether from musketry drill. If the fear had been only a fear of the fat of cows and swine, it might have been removed by the substitution of one grease for another; or if the external application of any kind of animal grease were objected to, oil and wax might be employed in its place; or if the touching of the unclean thing with the lips were the grievance, the end of the greased cartridge might be pinched off by the hand, and that objection removed. But to this fear of the paper used in all the cartridges issued to the Army, greased or dry, there was practically no antidote that would not have been both an admission and a concession, very dangerous for Government to make. It remained only that the English officer should persuade the Sepoy that he was wrong.

There could hardly, in such a crisis, have been a better man in command of the Division than General Hearsey; for he was one who steered wisely a middle course between the troubled waters of alarm and the dead calms of a placid sense of security. He had a large-hearted sympathy with the Sepoys in their affliction. He understood them thoroughly. He saw that they were labouring under a great fear; and he was not one, in such a case, to think that the "black fellows" had no right to suspect the designs of their white masters. He saw clearly what a tremendous significance, in the eyes both of Mahomedans and Hindoos, there was in this incident of the greased cartridges, and he could not wonder at the mingled feeling of terror and resentment that it had excited.

It was a case that in his opinion required kindly treatment and delicate handling; and he thought that much might be done by considerate explanations to restore confidence to their minds. So, on the afternoon of Monday, the 9th of February, he paraded the Brigade, and in a loud, manly voice, using good vernacular Hindostanee, addressed the assembled regiments. Earnestly and emphatically he explained to them that they had laid hold of a foolish and a dangerous delusion; that neither the Government which they served, nor the officers who commanded them, had ever thought for a moment of interfering with their religious usages or depriving them of their caste; and that it was but an idle absurdity to believe that they could by any means be forced to be Christians. He told them "that the English were Christians of the book—Protestants; that they admitted no proselytes but those who, being adults, could read and fully understand the precepts laid down therein; that if they came and threw themselves down at our feet, imploring to be made Book Christians, it could not be done; they could not be baptised until they had been examined in the truths of the book, and proved themselves fully conversant with them, and then they must, of their own good will and accord, desire to become Christians before they could be made so." He then asked them if they understood him; they nodded their assent, and it appeared both to the English and to the Native officers that the Sepoys were well pleased with what they had heard, and that a heaviness had passed away from their minds.*

1857.

But the good effect of this address was but tran- March, 1857.

* General Hearsey to the Secretary to Government, Feb. 11, 1857. —*Published papers.*

1857. sitory; for when the troops at Barrackpore heard what had been done by their comrades of the Nineteenth, there was great excitement among them, great anxiety to know the result. It was plain that the game had commenced in earnest, and that they might soon be called upon to take a part in it. But it would be well first to see what move would be made by the Government; what punishment would be inflicted upon the mutinous regiment at Berhampore. Days passed, and days grew into weeks, but still the Government appeared to be inactive. The Nineteenth were quietly performing their duties, as if nothing had happened. In the excited imaginations of the Sepoys there was something ominous in this quietude. They dimly apprehended the truth, and the obscurity of their conceptions caused them marvellously to exaggerate it. They believed that an overwhelming European force, with Cavalry and Artillery, would come suddenly upon them and destroy them.*

Their fears were exaggerated; but they were not wholly baseless. When the tidings of the mutiny at Berhampore reached Calcutta, the Governor-General saw at once that a great danger had been providentially escaped; but with the sense of present relief came also a solemn sense of the magnitude of the crisis. The little cloud was growing larger—growing darker. Here was an act of overt mutiny, and from the very cause of all the perilous excitement at Barrackpore. The time had now come for the Govern-

* Take in illustration the following from the Barrackpore correspondence of the day: "The Drill Naick of my regiment came to me two days ago (March 8), and said the report in the Lines was, that there were five thousand Europeans assembled by the Government at Howrah—that they had arrived in two ships, and were to come up here during the Hoolee (festival)—that the men had not slept the previous night in consequence of this report."—*Major Matthews to Brigadier Grant.—MS. Correspondence.*

ment to do something to assert its authority, and to strike terror into the minds of the soldiery. But what was to be done? It was easy to decree the disbandment of the Nineteenth, but it was not easy to accomplish it. There was but one European regiment along the whole line of country from Calcutta to Dinapore, and one other at the latter place, with a large extent of country to protect. Only in the presence of an overawing European force could a thousand armed Sepoys be suddenly consigned to penury and disgrace, and neither of these regiments could be moved to Berhampore without dangerously laying bare other parts of the lower provinces. For a while, therefore, the stern resolution of Government was shrouded from the guilty regiment. But the punishment was slowly overtaking them, though they knew it not. A week after the commission of their offence, Colonel Mitchell had received his orders to bring down the Nineteenth to Barrackpore to be disbanded, and the spacious passenger-vessel *Bentinck* was steaming across the Bay of Bengal, charged with a commission to bring back with all possible haste the Eighty-fourth British regiment from Rangoon. The English officers at Barrackpore, even Hearsey himself, knew nothing of this, and laughed at the credulity of the Sepoys, who believed, on the faith of their own news from Calcutta, that this step had been taken by the Government. But it soon became apparent that the Native soldiery were better informed than the Division Staff, for on the 20th of March there was great rejoicing among the English residents in Calcutta and the neighbourhood at the thought that the *Bentinck* had returned, and that succours had arrived.

1857.

H. M.'s 53rd.

H. M.'s. 10th Foot.

In the mean while a state of sullen quietude ob- March, 1857.

March, 1857 tained at Barrackpore. Still clinging to the belief that the Government, detected in their first design to apply the grease of cows and pigs to the new rifle cartridges, had purposely employed those materials in the manufacture of the cartridge-paper, the Sepoys went about their work under a prevailing sense of an impending danger and the aggravation of a great wrong.* It is probable that their fears were stronger than their discontents. They believed that their lives, and what was dearer to them even than their lives, were in peril, and they saw no means of escape except by obtaining the mastery over those who threatened to bring down such terrible calamities upon them. To what extent this idea of overpowering the Government had taken possession of the minds of the soldiery, and how far it was ever shaped into a definite scheme of action by those who were moved against us by religious or political animosities, can only be dimly conjectured. There was a belief in Calcutta that a general rising of the Native troops had been fixed for a particular night in March. It happened that, at this time, the Maharajah Scindiah, the greatest of the remaining Mahratta Princes, was on a visit to the English capital. No one then charged, no one has since charged him, or his sagacious minister, Dinkur Rao, with any complicity in a plot hostile to the English. They were gratified by the kind and hospitable reception which had been extended to them by the Governor-General and all the chief people of the Presidency, and were pleased with everything they saw. But it happened that

* So great was their uneasiness, and so strong were their suspicions, that it was believed that Colonel Wheler, who at that time went daily into Calcutta to attend a general court-martial, of which he was president, was in close consultation with the Governor-General respecting the forcible or fraudulent conversion of the Sepoys.

the Mahratta Prince invited all the principal English March, 1857.
gentlemen and ladies in Calcutta to a grand entertainment on the 10th of March. The fête was to have been given at the Botanical Gardens on the opposite bank of the Hooghly river. It is said, that when the English were thus occupied with the pleasure of the moment, and the vigilance of the chief officers of Government was temporarily diverted, the Sepoys, stimulated by the agents of the King of Oude, were to have risen as one man, to have seized the Fort and all the chief buildings of Calcutta, and proclaimed war against the Feringhee. That the idea of such a rising found entrance into the active brains of some enemies of the British can hardly be doubted; but there is no proof that it ever took practical shape as an organised conspiracy, which would have had the result I have indicated if nothing had occurred to frustrate the plot. But a circumstance did occur, which some still regard as a special interposition of Providence for the deliverance of our people. Most unexpectedly, in the dry season of the year, there was a heavy storm of rain —one of those mighty tropical down-pourings which render all out-of-doors recreation wholly an impossibility. So the great entertainment, which the Maharajah of Gwalior was then to have given to the English society of Calcutta, was postponed to a more auspicious moment, and the evening of the 10th of March passed over as quietly as its predecessors.

Of this combination of the Native troops at the Presidency there were, indeed, no visible signs. Outwardly it appeared that only the Second Grenadiers were implicated in treasonable schemes. "The Forty-

March, 1857. third," wrote Lord Canning to the Commander-in-Chief, "have refused to join in a dinner or feast to which the Second invited them; and some of the Seventieth have given up a Jemadar of the Second, who came into their Lines and tried to persuade the men not to bite the cartridges when the time for using them should come, and to deter them from finishing their huts, saying that there would soon be a great stir at Barrackpore, and that their huts would be burnt down."* Another sign of this apparent isolation of the Second Grenadiers was afforded by an incident that occurred in Calcutta. The Native Guards for the Fort and for the public buildings in the city were furnished by the regiments at Barrackpore. On the evening of the 10th of March a detachment of the Second was in the Fort, and a Soubahdar's guard from the Thirty-fourth was posted over the Calcutta Mint. In the course of the evening, two Sepoys from the Second presented themselves at the guard-house and sought out the Soubahdar. He was reading an order book by the light of a lamp when the men appeared before him. One of them then represented that they had come from the Fort; that the Calcutta Militia were to join the Fort-Guards at midnight; that the Governor-General was going up to Barrackpore with all the Artillery from Dum-Dum; and that if the Soubahdar would march his guard into the Fort and join their comrades there, they might rise successfully against the Government.†

* March 15, 1857.—*MS. Correspondence.* The Second and Forty-third had served together at Candahar, and were old friends. The proposed dinner was to be given during the Hooley festival, and the officers commanding the two regiments had agreed that there was no harm in their men dining together. The refusal of the Forty-third was not intelligible to them.

† Lord Canning to General Anson, March 12, 1857.—*MS. Correspondence.*

This last was rather implied than expressed; but the March, 1857. meaning of the men was sufficiently clear; so the Soubahdar ordered them to be arrested. Next morning he sent them prisoners into Fort William; and, a few days afterwards, they were tried by a Native Court-martial, found guilty, and sentenced to imprisonment for fourteen years.

This was a significant incident, but it was one, also, which might be turned to some account; so Hearsey determined not to lose the opportunity. His former speech to the Barrackpore troops had not accomplished all that was desired; but it had at least been partially successful, and he believed that something might now be done by another address to the Brigade. So he suggested to the Governor-General the expediency of such a course. On the 14th of March they talked the matter over at Government House, and Lord Canning assented to the proposal. But before the day had worn out, some misgivings assailed him, as to whether the General might not be carried away, by the strength of his feelings and the fluency of his speech, to say a little too much; so after Hearsey had returned to Barrackpore, Lord Canning sent a letter after him, recapitulating the results of the morning conversation, "in order to prevent all mistakes." This letter reached Hearsey soon after sunrise on the following morning (it was Sunday), and he at once replied to it, promising to take the greatest care not to exceed his instructions. On the next day the Native officers, who had been warned as members of the Court-martial ordered to assemble for the trial of the Sepoys of the Second, were to leave Barrackpore for Calcutta; and the General thought it advisable not to address the Brigade until after their de-

March, 1857. parture.* So the order went forth for a general parade of the troops at Barrackpore on the morning of Tuesday, the 17th of March.

There was no little tact requisite, in such a conjuncture, for the exact apportionment of the several parts of the speech that was to be delivered. The main object of it was to warn the troops against designing persons, who were endeavouring to seduce them from their allegiance; but it was desirable, also, to endeavour to pacify and reassure them, for it was plain that they were overridden by a great terror, born of the belief that the Government had sent for European troops of all arms with the intent of exterminating the Brigade. In order thus to remove the dangerous delusion which had taken possession of them, it was necessary to speak of the designs of the Government towards the mutinous Nineteenth—to show that retribution was sure to overtake all whose guilt had been proved, but that there was no thought of harming those who had committed no overt acts of rebellion. But it was not easy in such a case to avoid saying either too much or too little. "I am afraid," wrote Lord Canning to the General, "that, however brief your observations on that regiment (and they should, I think, be very brief), you will find it a nice matter to steer between exciting undue alarm and raising hopes which may be disappointed. But I feel sure that you will master the difficulty, and I leave the task in your hands with perfect confidence of the re-

* "I cannot address the Brigade until Tuesday morning, as the Native commissioned officers, who are to be members of the General Court-martial to be convened at Calcutta for the trial of the Sepoys of the Second Grenadiers must go from hence before I do so. If they heard my address to the men on parade, it might bias them in their judgment."—*General Hearsey to Lord Canning, March 15, 1857.—MS. Correspondence.*

sult."* He was thinking mainly of the effect to be produced upon the minds of the Sepoys of the Nineteenth. He did not wish that the decision of Government should be announced before the time of carrying it into effect; but Hearsey saw plainly that it was better for the general pacification of the Brigade that the haze through which the intentions of Government appeared to the soldiery in such exaggerated dimensions should be dispersed. "For if the men of this Brigade," he wrote to Lord Canning, "know beforehand what is to take place, their minds will be made easy, and they will be disabused of the false rumours now spread about that it is the intention of the Government to attack and destroy them by European troops and Artillery."† March, 1857

It was truly a great thing, at that time, to remove from the minds of the Barrackpore regiments the great terror that held possession of them; but the Nineteenth had not then commenced its march from Berhampore, and it is always a hazardous operation to move a regiment, with sentence of disbandment proclaimed against it, to the place of execution. These considerations pressed heavily on Hearsey's mind, when, on the morning of the 17th of March, he rode out to the parade-ground, and saw the Brigade drawn up before him. There was much, however, when he prepared to address them, of which there could be no doubt. Most of all was it necessary to warn them of the evil-minded and designing men who were leading them astray; so he began by telling them to beware of such men, who were endeavouring to take the

* Lord Canning to General Hearsey, March 14, 1857.—*MS. Correspondence.*

† General Hearsey to Lord Canning, March 15, 1857.—*MS. Correspondence.*

March. 1857. bread from the mouths of good Sepoys by making them the instruments of their schemes of sedition; then he spoke of the discontent still prevailing among them with respect to the cartridge-paper, in which they had never ceased to believe that animal fat had been used. Then he began to explain to them, and wisely, too, as he would explain to children, that the glazed appearance of the paper was produced by the starch employed in its composition, and that the very best paper used by the Princes of the land had the same smooth surface and shiny appearance. In proof of this, he produced, from a bag of golden tissue, a letter he had received, whilst serving in the Punjab, from the Maharajah Gholab Sing of Cashmere, and, giving it to the Native officers, told them to open it and to show it to their men, that they might see that it was even more glossy than the paper which they suspected. Having done this, he asked them if they thought that a Dogra Brahmin or Rajpoot, ever zealous in the protection of kine, would use paper made as they suspected, and, after further illustrations of the absurdity of their suspicions, told them, that if they did not then believe him, they should go to Serhampore and see the paper made for themselves. Then approaching the more dangerous subject of the Nineteenth, who had been led into open mutiny by a belief in the falsehood of the defiled paper, he said that the investigation of their conduct had been laid before him as General of the Division, and that he had forwarded it to Government, who were exceedingly angry, and would, in his opinion, order him to disband the regiment. That if he received orders to that effect, all the troops within two marches of the place—Infantry, Cavalry, and Artillery, European and Native—would be assembled at Barrackpore to witness the disbandment, and that "the ceremony of striking the name and number of the regiment from the list of the Army would be carried out in exactly the same manner as the old Thirty-fourth Regiment were disbanded at Meerut." "I inform you of this beforehand," added the General, "because your enemies are trying to make you believe that European troops with Cavalry and Artillery will be sent here suddenly to attack you; these, and such lies, are fabricated and rumoured amongst you to cause trouble. But no European or other troops will come to Barrackpore without my orders, and I will give you all timely intelligence of their coming." Then he told them that nothing had been proved against them, and that therefore they had nothing to fear; that all their complaints would be listened to by their officers; that their caste and religious prejudices were safe under his protection, and that any one who attempted to interfere with them would meet with the severest punishment. March, 1857.

Having thus concluded, Hearsey deployed the Brigade, opened out the ranks to double distance, and rode through them, stopping to notice the men who wore medals on their breasts, and asking them, with kindly interest, for what special services they had been rewarded. The regiments were then dismissed, and went quietly to their Lines, pondering all that they heard from their General. What they had heard was, perhaps, a little more than the Governor-General had intended them to hear; and Lord Canning, though he much admired and much trusted the fine old officer, had not been wholly free from alarm lest Hearsey should be carried away by his feelings, and give vent to more than he had authority for declaring. But, he added, "it will be nothing

March, 1857. very mischievous even if he should do so." And he was right. Hearsey had intimated that Government would disband the Nineteenth, and in this he exceeded his instructions. But it is not certain that the Governor-General lamented the excess. He regarded the disbandment of the Nineteenth as a necessary, but "an odious business;" and, perhaps, in his inmost heart he was not sorry that he had thus escaped the painful, and to a generous mind the humiliating alternative of concealing from the regiment the doom in store for it, until he was strong enough to execute the sentence.* Indeed, he wrote to the Commander-in-Chief, saying, "The Nineteenth are marching down steadily, and will reach Barrackpore on the morning of the 31st. They do not know for certain that disbandment is to be their punishment, and, upon the whole, I think it was better not to tell them. But I admit that there were two sides to that question." The safer course on one side, and the manlier course on the other; and between these two the ruler and the man might well have oscillated. That there was danger in the knowledge, is not to be doubted. Hearsey had sought, by the partial revelations that he had made, to soothe the troubled spirit of the Barrackpore Brigade; but it soon became doubtful whether the knowledge they had gained would not excite within them more dangerous feelings than those which he had endeavoured to allay. "The regiments at Barrackpore, however, know it," wrote Lord Canning, "or, at least, fully expect it, and to-day it is confidently said in the Bazaars that the Second Grenadiers and the Thirty-fourth intend to protect the Nineteenth, and to join them in resist-

* Compare Book II., page 297 *et seq.*; Considerations on the subject of disbandment.

ing. This is leading to alarms and suggestions on all sides. Colonel Abbott, of Ishapore, advises the putting a gag upon the Native Press for a time. Major Bontein recommends bringing the Nineteenth to Calcutta instead of Barrackpore, and dealing with them under the guns of the Fort, where they will have no sympathisers within reach. Even Atkinson suggests that Dum-Dum would be better than Barrackpore. I am not in any way moved from my first intention, and nothing but the opinion of General Hearsey, who has to execute the orders, that a change of plan or place should be made, would dispose me to do so. I do not think that he will give any such opinion, and I hope that he will not." March, 1857

No such opinion was given; but it was plain to Hearsey, as the month of March wore to a close, that the hopes which he had once entertained of the speedy subsidence of the alarm which had taken possession of the Sepoys were doomed to be disappointed. For when the troops at Barrackpore knew that the Nineteenth were to be disbanded, and that an English regiment had been brought across the black water to execute the punishment, they believed, more firmly than they had believed at the beginning of the month, that other white regiments were coming, and that the Government would force them to use the obnoxious cartridges, or treat them like their comrades that were marching down from Berhampore to be disgraced. So the great terror that was driving them into rebellion grew stronger and stronger, and as from mouth to mouth passed the significant words, "Gora-logue aya"—"the Europeans have come"—their excited imaginations beheld vessel after vessel pouring forth its legions of English fighting-men, under a foregone design to

March, 1857. force them all to apostatise at the point of the bayonet.

Mitchell had started with his doomed corps on the 20th of March, and was expected to reach Barrackpore at the end of the month. The behaviour of the men of the Nineteenth, ever since the outburst that had irretrievably committed them, had been orderly and respectful, and they were marching steadily down to the Presidency, obedient to their English officers. On the 30th, they were at Barasut, eight miles from Barrackpore, awaiting the orders of Government, when news reached Mitchell to the effect that the troops at the latter station were in a fever of excitement, and that on the day before an officer had been cut down on parade.

The story of Mungul Pandy.

The story was too true. On the 29th of March—it was a Sunday afternoon—there was more than common excitement in the Lines of the Thirty-fourth, for it was said that the Europeans had arrived. Fifty men of the Fifty-third had come by water from Calcutta, and were disembarking at the river-side. The apprehensions of the Sepoys exaggerated this arrival, and it was believed that the cantonment would soon be swarming with English soldiers. On one man especially this impression had fixed itself so strongly, that, inflamed as he was by *bang*, which is to the Sepoy what strong drink is to the European soldier, he was no longer master of himself. He was a young man, named Mungul Pandy, a man of good character, but of an excitable disposition, and seemingly with some religious enthusiasm wrought upon by the story of the greased cartridges. He had heard of the arrival of the detachment of Europeans, and he believed that the dreaded hour had come; that the caste of the Sepoys was about to be destroyed. So, putting on his accoutrements and seizing his musket, he went out from his hut, and, calling upon his comrades to follow him, if they did not wish to bite the cartridges and become infidels, he took post in front of the Quarter-Guard, and ordered a bugler to sound the assembly. The order was not obeyed; but, with an insolent and threatening manner, Mungul Pandy continued to stride up and down, and when the European sergeant-major went out, fired his piece at him, and missed. March, 1857.

All this time the Native officer and men of the Thirty-fourth on duty at the Quarter-Guard saw what was going on, but did not move to arrest the drugged fanatic who was so plainly bent upon mischief. But hastening to the Adjutant's house, a Native corporal reported what had occurred, and Lieutenant Baugh, without a moment of unnecessary delay, buckled on his sword, loaded his pistols, mounted his horse, and galloped down to the Quarter-Guard. He had just tightened rein, when Mungul Pandy, hidden by the station gun in front of the Guard, took aim and fired at the Adjutant; but, missing him, wounded his charger, and brought both horse and rider to the ground. Baugh then, disentangling himself, took one of his pistols from the holsters and fired at the Sepoy. The shot did not take effect, so he drew his sword and closed with the man, who also had drawn his tulwar, and then there was a sharp hand-to-hand conflict, in which the odds were against the Sepoy, for the sergeant-major came up and took part in the affray. But Mungul Pandy was a desperate man, and the strokes of his tulwar fell heavily upon his assailants; and he might, perhaps, have despatched them both, if a Mahomedan Sepoy, of the Grenadier Company, named

March, 1857. Sheikh Pultoo, had not seized the mutineer and averted his blows.

All this passed at the distance of a few yards only from the Quarter-Guard of the Thirty-fourth, where a Jemadar and twenty men were on duty. The sound of the firing had brought many others from the Lines, and Sepoys in uniform and out of uniform crowded around in a state of tumultuous excitement. But with the exception of this Sheikh Pultoo, no man moved to assist his officer; no man moved to arrest the criminal. Nor was their guilt only the guilt of inaction. Some of the Sepoys of the Guard struck the wounded officers on the ground with the butt-ends of their muskets, and one fired his piece at them; and when Sheikh Pultoo called upon them to arrest the mutineer, they abused him, and said that if he did not release Mungul Pandy, they would shoot him. But he held the desperate fanatic until Baugh and the sergeant-major had escaped, and doubtless to his fidelity they owed their lives.

Meanwhile, tidings of the tumult had reached the quarters of General Hearsey. An orderly rushed into the portico of his house and told him that the Brigade had risen. His two sons, officers of the Sepoy Army, were with him; and now the three, having ordered their horses to be saddled and brought round, put on their uniform and accoutrements and prepared at once to proceed to the scene of action. It seemed so probable that all the regiments had turned out in a frenzy of alarm, that, whilst the horses were being saddled, Hearsey wrote hasty notes, to be despatched in case of need to the officers commanding the Europeans at Chinsurah and Dum-Dum, calling upon them to march down at once to his assistance. He had just sealed them, when first the Adjutant of the

Forty-third, smeared with the blood of the wounded officers, and then the Commandant of the Regiment, came up to report, in detail, what had happened. The story then told him was a strange one; for it seemed not that the Brigade, but that a single Sepoy had risen, and was setting the State at defiance. It is hard to say whether the surprise or the indignation of the gallant veteran were greater, when he asked whether there was no one to shoot or to secure the madman. But it was plain that no time was to be lost. So, mounting their horses, Hearsey and his sons galloped down to the parade-ground, and saw for themselves what was passing. March, 1857.

There was a great crowd of Sepoys, mostly unarmed and undressed, and there were several European officers, some mounted and some on foot; much confusion and some consternation, but apparently no action. Mungul Pandy, still master of the situation, was pacing up and down, in front of the Quarter-Guard, calling upon his comrades in vehement tones, and with excited action, to follow his example, as the Europeans were coming down upon them, and to die bravely for their religion. But the crowd of Sepoys, though none remembered at that moment that they were servants of the State, none came forward to support discipline and authority, were not ripe for open mutiny; and when Mungul Pandy reviled them as cowards, who had first excited and then deserted him, they hung irresolutely back, clustering together like sheep, and wondering what would happen next. The arrival of the General solved the question. As soon as he saw Mungul Pandy in front of the Quarter-Guard, he rode towards it, accompanied by his sons and by his Division-Staff, Major Ross, and when an officer cried out to him to take care, as the mutineer's

March, 1857. musket was loaded, answered, "Damn his musket," and rode on to do his duty.

Little inclination was there on the part of the Jemadar and the men of the Guard to obey the General's orders; but the manner of Hearsey at that moment was the manner of a man not to be denied; and supported by his sons, each of the gallant Three with his hand upon his revolver, there was instant death in disobedience. So the Jemadar and the Guard, thus overawed, followed Hearsey and his sons to the place where Mungul Pandy was striding about menacingly with his musket in his hand. As they approached the mutineer, John Hearsey cried out, "Father, he is taking aim at you." "If I fall, John," said the General, "rush upon him and put him to death." But Mungul Pandy did not fire upon Hearsey; he turned his weapon upon himself. He saw that the game was up; and so, placing the butt of his musket on the ground, and the muzzle of the piece to his breast, he discharged it by the pressure of his foot, and fell burnt and wounded to the ground.

As he lay there convulsed and shivering, with his blood-stained sword beneath him, the officers thought that he was dying. But medical assistance came promptly, the wound was examined and found to be only superficial, so the wounded man was carried to the Hospital; and then Hearsey rode among the Sepoys, telling them, as he had often told them before, that their alarms were groundless, that the Government had no thought of interfering with their religion, and that he saw with regret how lamentably they had failed in their duty, in not arresting or shooting down a man who had thus shown himself to be a rebel and a murderer. They answered that he was a madman, intoxicated to frenzy by bang.

"And if so," said Hearsey, "why not have shot him down as you would have shot a mad elephant or a mad dog, if he resisted you." Some answered that he had a loaded musket. "What!" replied the General, "are you afraid of a loaded musket?" They were silent; and he dismissed them with scorn. It was plain that they had ceased to be soldiers. March, 1857.

Hearsey returned to his quarters that Sabbath evening, heavy with thought of the work before him. He had received his orders to execute the sentence that had been passed on the Nineteenth Regiment. That sentence had now been publicly proclaimed in a general order to the whole Army. On Tuesday morning, in the presence of all the troops, European and Native, at the Presidency, the Berhampore mutineers were to be turned adrift on the world, destitute and degraded; and it was not to be doubted that they would carry with them the sympathies of their comrades in all parts of the country. That there was prospective danger in this was certain, for every disbanded Sepoy might have become an emissary of evil; but there was a great and present danger, far too formidable in itself to suffer thoughts of the future to prevail; for it was probable that the Nineteenth would resist their sentence, and that all the Native troops at the Presidency would aid them in their resistance. Some thought that the Barrackpore Brigade would anticipate the event, and that on Monday there would be a general rising of the Sepoys, and that the officers and their families would be butchered by the mutineers. The first blood had been shed. Mungul Pandy was only the fugleman. So many of the English ladies in Barrackpore left the cantonment and sought safety for a while in Calcutta. But there was no place at that time more secure than that

March, 1857. which they had quitted; and they found that the inmates of the asylum they had sought were as much alarmed as themselves.

It has been said that, halted at Barasut on the 30th of March, the Nineteenth learnt what had happened on the preceding evening. The Thirty-fourth had sent out their emissaries to meet their old friends and comrades of Lucknow, to prompt them to resistance, and to promise to cast in their own lot with their brethren and to die for their religion. And this, too, it is said, with murderous suggestions of a general massacre of the white officers. But the Nineteenth shook their heads at the tempters. They had expressed their sorrow for what had happened, and they had implored that they might be suffered to prove their loyalty by going on service to any part of the world. They had never at heart been mutinous, and they would not now rise against the Government whose salt they had eaten and whose uniform they had worn. But the bonds of a great sympathy restrained them from denouncing their comrades, so they suffered in silence the tempters to return to their own Lines.

March 31, 1857.

Disbandment of the Nineteenth.

As the morning dawned upon them, obedient to orders, they commenced the last march that they were ever to make as soldiers. Heavy-hearted, penitent, and with the remains of a great fear still clinging to them, they went to their doom. A mile from Barrackpore, Hearsey met them with his final orders, and placing himself in front of the column, rode back with them to the parade-ground which was to be the scene of their disbandment. There all the available troops in the Presidency division, European and Native, were drawn up to receive them. Steadily they marched on to the ground which had been marked out for them, and found themselves face to face with the guns. If there had been any thought of resistance, it would have passed away at the first sight of that imposing array of white troops and the two field-batteries which confronted them. But they had never thought of anything but submission. Obedient, therefore, to the word of command, up to the last moment of their military existence, they listened in silence to the General's brief preliminary address, in silence to the General Order of Government announcing the sentence of disbandment; without a murmur, opened their ranks, piled their arms at the word of command as though they had been on a common parade, and then hung their belts upon their bayonets. The colours of the regiment were then brought to the front, and laid upon a rest composed of a little pile of crossed muskets. It was an anxious moment, for though the Nineteenth were penitent and submissive, the temper of some of the other regiments, and especially of the Thirty-fourth, was not to be trusted; and for a while it was believed that the men, who two days before had thrown off the mask, were prepared to fire upon their officers. The rumour ran that many of the Sepoys of that guilty regiment were on parade with loaded muskets, and Hearsey was advised to prove them by ordering the regiment to spring ramrods. But he wisely rejected the advice, saying that all was going well, and that he would not mar the effect of the peaceable disbandment of the regiment by a movement that might excite a collision. He was right. The work that he had in hand was quietly completed. The men of the Nineteenth were marched to a distance from their arms, and the pay that was due to them brought out for disbursement. They had now ceased to be soldiers; but there was no March, 1857.

March, 1857. further degradation in store for them. Hearsey addressed them in tones of kindness, saying that though the Government had decreed their summary dismissal, their uniforms would not be stripped from their backs, and that as a reward for their penitence and good conduct on the march from Berhampore, they would be provided at the public cost with carriage to convey them to their homes. This kindness made a deep impression upon them. Many of them lifted up their voices, bewailing their fate and loudly declaring that they would revenge themselves upon the Thirty-fourth, who had tempted them to their undoing. One man, apparently spokesman for his comrades, said, "Give us back our arms for ten minutes before we go; and leave us alone with the Thirty-fourth to settle our account with them."*

Whilst the men of what had once been the Nineteenth were being paid, Hearsey addressed the other Native regiments on parade, very much as he had addressed them before; but urging upon them the consideration of the fact that the Nineteenth, in which there were four hundred Brahmins and a hundred and fifty Rajpoots, had been sent to their homes, and were at liberty to visit what shrines they pleased, and to worship where their fathers had worshipped before them, as a proof that the report which had been

* Lord Canning's reasons for sparing them the deeper degradation are thus given in a letter to General Anson: "I sent you a copy of the General Order yesterday. I have determined to omit the words which require that the men shall be deprived 'of the uniform which they have dishonoured.' Heavy as has been their crime—none heavier—it is not a mean or abject one: such as refusing to march to a post of danger; and the substance of their punishment is severe enough without being made to gall and rankle. It was for this reason that I did not originally prescribe that the number of the regiment should be removed from the Army List, or that the men should be turned out of cantonment ignominiously, as was done in the case of the Thirty-fourth thirteen years ago. The abstaining from stripping their uniforms from them will be a further relaxation in the same spirit."—*MS. Correspondence.*

circulated of the intention of Government to interfere with their religion was nothing but a base falsehood. The men listened attentively to what was said; and when the time came for their dismissal, they went quietly to their lines. It was nearly nine o'clock before the men of the old Nineteenth had been paid up; and, under an European escort, were marched out of Barrackpore. As they moved off, they cheered the fine old soldier, whose duty it had been to disband them, and wished him a long and a happy life; and he went to his house with a heart stirred to its very depths with a compassionate sorrow, feeling doubtless that it was the saddest morning's work he had ever done, but thanking God that it had been done so peacefully and with such perfect success. March, 1857.

CHAPTER VI.

THE MONTH OF APRIL—PROGRESS OF ALARM—THE PANIC AT UMBALLAH—GENERAL ANSON'S ADDRESS — EVENTS AT MEERUT — THE BONE-DUST FLOUR—THE STORY OF THE CHUPATTIES—INTRIGUES OF THE NANA SAHIB—AFFAIRS AT LUCKNOW.

Barrackpore. April, 1857.

NOT less thankful was Lord Canning, when tidings were brought to him at Calcutta that all had passed off quietly at Barrackpore. He had sent one of his Aides-de-camp, Captain Baring, to witness the disbandment of the Nineteenth, and to bring back to him, with all possible despatch, intelligence of the events of the morning. And now that good news had come, he telegraphed it at once to the Commander-in-Chief, and made it known throughout the city, to the intense relief of many frightened residents, who had anticipated a general rising of the Native troops, and the massacre of all the European inhabitants. For the moment, at least, the danger had passed; and a little breathing-time was permitted to Government. Now that the disbandment of the Nineteenth had been effected, and the men were going quietly to their homes, there was leisure to think of the far greater crime of the Thirty-fourth. The case of Mungul Pandy, who had cut down his officer, was one to raise no questionings. Nor, indeed, could there be much doubt about the Jemadar of the

Guard, who had suffered such an outrage to be committed before his eyes. The former was tried by Court-martial on the 6th of April, and sentenced to be hanged; and, on the 10th and 11th, the latter was tried, and sentenced to the same ignominious death. On the 8th, Mungul Pandy paid the penalty of his crime on the gallows, in the presence of all the troops, at Barrackpore. But although without loss of time the Jemadar was condemned to be hanged, the execution lagged behind the sentence in a manner that must have greatly marred the effect of the example. A legal difficulty arose, which, for a while, held retribution in restraint,* and the men of the Brigade began to think that Government lacked the resolution to inflict condign punishment on the offender. April, 1857.

Nor was this the only apparent symptom of irresolution. The Thirty-fourth had been more guilty than the Nineteenth; but punishment had not overtaken it. The men still went about with their arms in their hands; and there was scarcely a European in Barrackpore who believed that he was safe from their violence. As officers returned at night from their regimental messes, they thought that their own Sepoys would fall upon them in the darkness, and social intercourse after nightfall between the ladies

* "The execution of a Native officer of his rank," wrote Lord Canning to the President of the Board of Control, "convicted by his brother officers, will have a most wholesome effect. Such a thing is quite unprecedented. There has been a delay between the sentence and the execution which has vexed me, as it may give an appearance of hesitation to the proceedings of Government, which would be mischievous, and which never has existed for a moment. The delay was caused by the Commander-in-Chief not having given authority to General Hearsey, in his warrant, to carry out sentences against any but non-commissioned officers, and by an opinion utterly erroneous of the Judge Advocate, who is with the Commander-in-Chief, that the authority could not be given. Hence nearly a week was lost, and with it something of the sharpness of the example."—*MS. Correspondence of Lord Canning.*

April, 1857. of the station was suspended.* All this was known and deplored; but it was felt, upon the other hand, that if there were evil in delay, there was evil also in any appearance of haste.† Mindful that the disaffection in the Sepoy regiments had its root in fear, and believing that any undue severity would increase their irritation, the Governor-General caused all the circumstances of the excitement of the Thirty-fourth to be sifted to the bottom, and hoped thereby to elicit information which might guide him to a right understanding of the matter. The regiment once disbanded, there would be no hope of further revelations. So all through the month of April their doom was unpronounced. Courts of Inquiry were being held for the purpose of ascertaining the general temper of the regiment. It appeared that for some time there had been a want of loyalty and good feeling in the Thirty-fourth; that Native officers and Sepoys had been disrespectful in their manner towards their English officers; and altogether there had been such a lack of discipline, that the officers, when questioned, said that if the regiment had been or-

* It does not appear that any outrages were actually committed; but one night a Sepoy appeared suddenly in a threatening attitude before a young officer, as he was on his way home, upon which, being a stalwart and brave fellow, the English subaltern knocked him down.

† A little later the Governor-General wrote: "The mutinous spirit is not quelled here, and I feel no confidence of being able to eradicate it very speedily, although the outbreaks may be repressed easily. The spirit of disaffection, or rather of mistrust, for it is more that, has spread further than I thought six weeks ago, but widely rather than deeply, and it requires very wary walking. A hasty measure of retribution, betraying animosity, or an unjust act of severity, would confirm, instead of allaying, the temper which is abroad. It is not possible to say with confidence what the causes are; but with the common herd there is a sincere fear for their caste, and a conviction that this has been in danger from the cartridges and other causes. This feeling is played upon by others from outside, and, to some extent, with political objects. But, upon the whole, political animosity does not go for much in the present movement, and certainly does not actuate the Sepoys in the mass."—*Lord Canning to Lord Elphinstone, May 6, 1857.—MS. Correspondence.*

dered on service they would have had little faith in the fidelity of the great bulk of the soldiery. And at last an opinion was recorded to the effect that "the Sikhs and Mussulmans of the Thirty-fourth Regiment of Native Infantry were trustworthy soldiers of the State, but that the Hindoos generally of that corps were not to be trusted." So the Government took into deliberate consideration the disbandment of the regiment, with the exception of those officers and soldiers who had been absent from Barrackpore at the time of the outrage of the 29th of March, or who had at any time made practical demonstration of their loyalty and fidelity to the State.* April, 1857.

But before judgment was pronounced and sentence executed, there had been much in other parts of the country to disturb the mind of the Governor-General. He was a man of a hopeful nature, and a courageous heart that never suffered him to exaggerate the dangers of the Future, or to look gloomily at the situation of the Present; but it was plain that the little cloud which had arisen at the end of January, was now, in the early part of April, rapidly spreading itself over the entire firmament. Already the sound of the thunder had been heard from distant stations beneath the shadow of the Himalayahs,

* Three companies of the Thirty-fourth had been on detachment duty at Chittagong. No suspicion of disloyalty had attached to them, and when they heard of what had passed at Barrackpore, they sent in a memorial, saying that they had heard with extreme regret of the disgraceful conduct of Mungul Pandy and the Guard; that they well knew that the Government would not interfere with their religion; and that they would remain "faithful for ever." If they were sincere, their sincerity must be regarded as an additional proof of the external agency that was, I believe, at the beginning of 1857, employed to corrupt the Sepoys at the Presidency. It is a circumstance also to be noticed, that the very Soubahdar of the Mint-Guard, who had arrested the Sepoys of the Second Grenadiers, was accused, in the course of the inquiry into the conduct and temper of the Thirty-fourth, of being a prime mover of sedition.

April, 1857. and it was little likely that, throughout the intervening country, there was a single cantonment by which the alarm had not been caught—a single Native regiment in which the new rifle and the greased cartridges were not subjects of excited discussion.

Retrospect of events at Umballah. March, 1857. The Head-quarters of the Army were at that time at Umballah, at the foot of the great hills, a thousand miles from Calcutta. There General Anson, having returned from his hasty visit to Calcutta, was meditating a speedy retreat to Simlah, when the unquiet spirit in the Native regiments forced itself upon his attention. This station was one of the Depôts of Instruction, at which the use of the new rifle was taught to representative men from the different regiments in that part of the country. These men were picked soldiers, of more than common aptitude and intelligence, under some of the best Native officers in the service. The explanations of their instructors seemed to have disarmed their suspicions, and they attended their instruction parades without any sign of dissatisfaction. They had not advanced so far in their drill as to require to use the cartridges; and, indeed, the new ammunition had not yet been received from Meerut. But the Commander-in-Chief believed that the men were satisfied, until a circumstance occurred which loudly proclaimed, and ought to have struck home to him the conviction, that the great fear which had taken possession of men's minds was too deeply seated to be eradicated by any single measure of the Government, and too widely spread to be removed by any local orders. What solace was there in the assurance that no cartridges lubricated with the obnoxious grease had been, or ever would be, issued to them, if the cartridge-paper used by them were unclean? and even if their own minds were cleansed of all foul suspicions, what did this avail, so long as their comrades in the several regiments to which they belonged believed them to be defiled, and were, therefore, casting them out from the brotherhood? March, 1857. Umballah.

The Thirty-sixth Regiment formed the escort of the Commander-in-Chief. There was a detachment from it in the Rifle Depôt; and it happened that one day, at the end of the third week of March, two non-commissioned officers from this detachment visited the regimental camp, and were publicly taunted by a Soubahdar with having become Christians. They carried back this story to the Depôt, and one of them, when he told it to Lieutenant Martineau, the Instructor, cried like a child in his presence, said that he was an outcast, and that the men of his regiment had refused to eat with him. A man of more than common quickness of intelligence and depth of thought, Martineau saw at once the terrible significance of this, and he pushed his inquiries further among the men of the Depôt. The result left no doubt upon his mind, that in every detachment there was the same strong feeling of terror, lest having used the new greased cartridges, or having been suspected of using them, they should become outcasts from their regiments, and shunned by their brethren on returning to their own villages. This was no mere fancy. Already had the detachments found their intercourse with their regiments suspended. They had written letters to their distant comrades and received no answers; and now they asked, not without a great show of reason, "If a Soubahdar in the Commander-in-Chief's camp, and on duty as his personal escort, can taunt us with loss of caste, what kind of reception shall we meet on our

March, 1857. Umballah.

return to our own corps? No reward that Government can offer us is any equivalent for being regarded as outcasts by our own comrades." Plainly, then, it was Martineau's duty to communicate all that he knew to the Commander-in-Chief, and being his duty, he was not a man to shrink from doing it. So he wrote at once to the Assistant-Adjutant-General, Septimus Becher, and told his story—privately in the first instance, but afterwards, at Becher's suggestion, in an official letter. But already had the Commander-in-Chief learnt also from other sources the feeling of consternation that was pervading the minds of the men of the Depôt. On the 19th of March the Soubahdar had insulted the men of the detachment; on the 20th, Martineau wrote his first letter to Anson's Staff; on the morning of the 23rd the Commander-in-Chief was to inspect the Rifle Depôt; and on the previous evening a report reached him that the men of the detachments wished to speak to him, through their delegates, on parade. He determined, therefore, to take the initiative, and to address them. So, after the Inspection parade, he formed the detachments into a hollow square, and calling the Native officers to the front, within a short distance of his Staff, began his oration to the troops. He had not the advantage, which Hearsey enjoyed, of being able to address them fluently in their own language. But, if his discourse was therefore less impressive, it was not less clear; for calling Martineau to his aid, Anson paused at the end of each brief sentence, heard it translated into Hindostanee, and asked if the men understood its import. It was thus that he spoke to them:

Address of the Commander-in-Chief.

"The Commander-in-Chief is desirous of taking this opportunity of addressing a few words to the

Native officers assembled at this Depôt, which has been formed for the instruction of the Army in the use of the new Rifle. The Native officers have been selected for this duty on account of their superior intelligence upon all matters connected with the service to which they belong. The Commander-in-Chief feels satisfied, therefore, that they will exercise that intelligence, and employ the influence which their positions warrant him in supposing they possess, for the good of the men who are placed under their authority, and for the advantage of the Army generally. In no way can this be more beneficially proved than in disabusing their minds of any mistaken notion which they may have been led to entertain respecting the intentions and orders of the Government whom they have engaged to serve. The introduction of a better arm has rendered it necessary to adopt a different system of loading it, and an improved description of cartridge. The Commander-in-Chief finds that, on account of the appearance of the paper used for the cartridges, and of the material with which they are made up according to the patterns sent from England, objections have been raised to their use by Sepoys of various Religions and Castes, and that endeavours have been made to induce them to believe that it is the express object of the Government to subvert their Religion and to subject them to the loss of Caste on which they set so high a value. March, 1857. Umballah.

"A moment's calm reflection must convince every one how utterly groundless and how impossible it is that there can be the slightest shadow of truth in such a suspicion. In what manner or degree could the Government gain by such a proceeding? Can any one explain what could be the object of it? The

March, 1857. Umballah. Commander-in-Chief is sure that all will allow that nothing has ever occurred to justify a suspicion that the Government ever wished to coerce the Natives of India in matters of Religion, or to interfere unnecessarily with their Customs, or even with the ceremonies which belong to their different Castes.

"The Commander-in-Chief regrets to hear that there have been instances in the Army of the disbelief of the Sepoys in the assurances of their officers that they would not be required to use cartridges which were made of materials to which they could reasonably object, and that they have acted in a manner which must destroy all confidence in them as soldiers, whose first duty is obedience to the Government whom they serve, and to their superiors. The Government will know how to deal with such instances of insubordination, and the Commander-in-Chief does not hesitate to say that they should be visited with the severest punishment.

"But the object of the Commander-in-Chief is not to threaten, and he hopes that it is unnecessary even to point out to those whose breasts are decorated with proofs of gallantry and good service, what is their duty. He wishes simply to assure them, on the honour of a soldier like themselves, that it has never been, and never will be, the policy of the Government of this great country to coerce either those serving in the Army or the Natives of India in their religious feelings, or to interfere with the customs of their Castes. He trusts to the Native officers who are present here to make this known to their respective regiments, and to exert themselves in allaying the fears of those who may have been momentarily seduced from their duty by evil-disposed persons. He is satisfied that they will do everything in their power to prevent the shame which must fall upon all who are faithless to the colours under which they have sworn allegiance to the Government, and that they will prove themselves deserving of the high character which they have always hitherto maintained in this Army."

March, 1857. Umballah.

The Native officers in front, who alone, perhaps, were enabled by their position to hear the address of the Chief, listened attentively and with a respectful demeanour to what was said; and when the parade was over, they expressed to Martineau, through the medium of three of their body acting as spokesmen, their high sense of the honour that had been done to them by the condescension of His Excellency in addressing them on parade. But they urged upon him that, although they did not themselves attribute to the Government any of the evil designs referred to in that address, it was true that for one man who disbelieved the story, there were ten thousand who believed it; that it was universally credited, not only in their regiments, but everywhere in their native villages; and that, therefore, although the men of the detachments were ready to a man to use the cartridge when ordered, they desired to represent, for the paternal consideration of the Commander-in-Chief, the social consequences to themselves of military obedience. They would become outcasts for ever, shunned by their comrades, and discarded by their families, and would thus suffer for their obedience the most terrible punishment that could be inflicted upon them upon this side of the grave.* Martineau promised to repre-

* Lieutenant Martineau to Captain Septimus Becher. The writer adds: "Their being selected as men of intelligence and fidelity thus becomes to them the most fatal curse: they will obey the orders of their

March, 1857. Umballah.

sent all this to the Commander-in-Chief; and he did so in an official letter, through the legitimate channel of the Adjutant-General's office. The matter was weighing heavily upon Anson's mind. He saw clearly what the difficulty was. "I have no doubt," he wrote on that day to the Governor-General, "that individually they (the men of the detachments) are content, and that their own minds will be set at rest; but it is the manner in which they will be received by their comrades, when they regain their regiments, that weighs upon my mind." But what was to be done? To remove from their minds all fear of the greased cartridges was only to drive them upon an equal fear of the greased paper, which it was still more difficult to remove.* He had thought at one time of breaking up the Depôt, and sending back the detachments to their regiments, on the ground of the advanced state of the season; but this would only,

military superiors, and socially perish through their instinct of obedience. That their views are not exaggerated, some knowledge of the native character, and of the temper of the Native mind (non-military as well as military) at this present moment, tend to convince me. The Asiatic mind is periodically prone to fits of religious panic; in this state, reasoning that would satisfy us is utterly thrown away upon them; their imaginations run riot on preconceived views, and often the more absurd they are, the more tenaciously do they cling to them. We are now passing through one of these paroxysms, which we might safely disregard were not unfortunately the military element mixed up in it. What the exciting causes are that at this present moment are operating on the Native mind, to an universal extent throughout these provinces, I cannot discover; no Native can or will offer any explanation, but I am disposed to regard the greased cartridges, alleged to be smeared with cows' and pigs' fat, more as the medium than as the original cause of this widespread feeling of distrust that is spreading dissatisfaction to our rule, and tending to alienate the fidelity of the Native Army."

* "I am not so much surprised," wrote General Anson to Lord Canning on the 23rd of March, "at their objections to the cartridges, having seen them. I had no idea they contained, or rather are smeared with, such a quantity of grease, which looks exactly like fat. After ramming down the ball, the muzzle of the musket is covered with it. This, however, will, I imagine, not be the case with those prepared according to the late instructions. But there are now misgivings about the *paper*, and I think it so desirable that they should be assured that no animal grease is used in its manufacture, that a special report shall be made

he argued on reflection, be a cowardly staving-off of the question, so he determined merely to direct that the drill instruction should not proceed to the point of firing until a special report should have been received from Meerut on the subject of the suspected paper.

March, 1857. Umballah.

To Lord Canning, it appeared that any postponement of the target practice of the drill detachments would be a mistake. It would be a concession to unreasonable fears, which would look like an admission that there was reason in them; so, having first telegraphed to Umballah the substance of his letter, he wrote to General Anson, saying: "I gather that you are not decidedly in favour of this course, and certainly I am much opposed to it myself. The men, it seems, have no objection of their own to use the cartridges, but dread the taunts of their comrades after they have rejoined. These taunts will be founded, not on their having handled unclean grease, for against that the whole Army has been protected for many weeks past by the late orders, but upon suspicions respecting the paper. Now, although in the matter of grease the Government was in some degree in the wrong (not having taken all the precaution that might have been taken to exclude objectionable ingredients), in

April 4, 1857.

to me on that head from Meerut, and until I receive an answer, and am satisfied that no objectionable material is used, no firing at the depôts by the Sepoys will take place. It would be easy to dismiss the detachments to their regiments without any practice, on the ground that the hot weather is so advanced, and that very little progress could be made, but I do not think that would be advisable. The question having been raised, must be settled. It would only be deferred till another year, and I trust that the measures taken by the Government when the objection was first made, and the example of the punishment of the Nineteenth Native Infantry, and of the other delinquents of the Seventieth, now being tried by a general court-martial, will have the effect we desire." [It is probable that General Anson here referred to the trial of the men of the Second Grenadiers.] —*MS. Correspondence.*

April, 1857. Umballah.

the matter of paper it is entirely in the right. There is nothing offensive to the Caste of the Sepoys in the paper; they have no pretence for saying so. The contrary has been proved; and if we give way upon this point I do not see where we can take our stand. It may be, as you hope, that the detachments at Umballah, being well-conditioned men, would not consider a compliance with their request as a giving way on the part of the Government, or as a victory on their own part. But I fear it would be so with their comrades in the regiments. When the detachments return to their Head-quarters, they would give an account of the concession they had obtained, which would inevitably, and not unreasonably, lead to the suspicion that the Government is doubtful of the right of its own case. It could hardly be otherwise; and if so, we should have increased our difficulties for hereafter—for I have no faith in this question dying away of itself during the idleness of the hot season, unless it is grappled with at once. I would, therefore, make the men proceed to use the cartridges at practice. It will be no violence to their own consciences, for they are satisfied that the paper is harmless; and it will, in my opinion, much more effectually pave the way towards bringing their several regiments to reason, whether the objections thereto felt are sincere or not, than any postponement. Moreover, I do not think that we can quite consistently take any other course after what has passed with the Nineteenth Regiment; for, though the climax of their crime was taking up arms, the refusal of the cartridges has been declared to be the beginning of the offence. Neither do I like the thought of countenancing consultations and references between the men of a regiment upon matters in which they have nothing to do but to obey; and I fear that postponement would look like an acquiescence in such references." So it was determined that there should be no cowardly postponement of the evil day, and the detachments in the Musketry Schools were ordered to proceed, under the new regulations, to the end of their course of instruction.* April, 1857. Umballah.

Whilst this letter was making its way to the foot of the Hills, General Anson, whose health had been severely tried, and who had long been looking anxiously towards the cool, fresh slopes of the Himalayahs, betook himself hopefully to Simlah. That paradise of invalids, he wrote to the Governor-General, was "looking beautiful, and the climate now quite perfect." "I heartily wish," he added, "that you were here to benefit by it." But it was not a time for the enjoyment of Himalayan delights. At both ends of that long line of a thousand miles between the great Presidency town and the foot of the Hills there was that which, as the month advanced, must have sorely disquieted the minds of the civil and military chiefs. There was the great difficulty of the Thirty-fourth to disturb both the Governor-General and the Commander-in-Chief; and as time advanced, there came from other parts of the country tidings which, if they did not help them to fathom causes, brought more plainly before them the probable consequences of this great panic in the

* The orders issued from the Adjutant-General's office, in consequence of this decision, were, that the detachments should proceed to target practice, that they should choose and apply their own grease, and that they should pinch or tear off the end of the cartridge with their fingers. In the event of the men hesitating to use the cartridges, their officers were to reason with them, calmly in the first instance, and if the Depôt, after such an appeal to them, were to refuse to use the cartridges, more stringent measures were to be resorted to for the enforcement of discipline.—*See Letter from Adjutant-General to General Hearsey, in the Appendix.*

April, 1857. Umballah,

Sepoy Army. Those significant fires, which had preluded the outbreak at Barrackpore, were breaking out at other stations. At Umballah especially, in the middle of the month of April, they had become frequent and alarming. The detachments in the Musketry Schools were now proceeding steadily with their target practice. They dipped their own cartridges into a mixture of beeswax and ghee, and seemed to be fully convinced and assured that no foul play was intended against them. But they did not escape the taunts of their comrades; and the nightly fires indicated the general excitement among the Native soldiery. The European barracks, the commissariat store-houses, the hospital, and the huts in the Lines, night after night, burst out into mysterious conflagration. It was the belief at Head-Quarters that these fires, made easy by the dry thatched roofs of the buildings, were the work partly of the Sepoys of the regiments stationed there, and partly of those attached to the Musketry Depôt. The former still looked askance at the latter, believing that they had been bought over by promises of promotion to use the obnoxious cartridges, and, as a mark of their indignation, set fire to the huts of the apostates in their absence at drill. Upon this the men of the Musketry School retaliated, by firing the Lines of the regimental Sepoys.* But the Courts of Inquiry which were held to investigate the circumstances of these incendiary fires failed to elicit any positive information; for no one was willing to give

* "The night before last a fire-ball was found ignited in the hut of a Sepoy of the Fifth Native Infantry. The hut was empty, as the man is attached to the School of Musketry, and lives with them. On the following night the Lines of the Sixtieth Native Infantry were fired, and five huts, with all the men's property, destroyed. This was clearly an act of retaliation, for incendiaries do not destroy themselves."—*General Barnard to Lord Canning. April* 24, 1857.—*MS. Correspondence.*

evidence, and nothing was done to put pressure upon witnesses to reveal the knowledge which they possessed. April, 1857. Umballah.

Sir Henry Barnard.

At this time Sir Henry Barnard, an officer of good repute, who had served with distinction in the Crimea, commanded the Sirhind Division of the Army, in which Umballah was one of the chief stations. He was a man of high courage and activity, eager for service, and though he had not been many months in the country, he had begun to complain of the dreadful listlessness of Indian life, and the absence of that constant work and responsibility which, he said, had become a necessity to him. "Cannot you find some tough job to put me to? I will serve you faithfully." Thus he wrote to Lord Canning in the last week of April, seeing nothing before him at that time but a retreat to Simlah "when the burning mania is over." Little thought he then of the tough job in store for him—a job too tough for his steel, good as was the temper of it. The Commander-in-Chief wrote from Simlah that Barnard was learning his work. "It will take him some time," said Anson, "to understand the Native character and system." And no reproach to him either;* for nothing was more beyond the ordinary comprehension of men, trained in schools of European warfare, than Sepoy character in its normal state, except its aberrations and eccentricities. Anson had been two years in India; but he confessed that what was passing at Umballah sorely puzzled him. "Strange," he wrote to Lord Canning, "that the incendiaries should never be detected. Every one is on the alert

* That Sir Henry Barnard thought much and wrote very sensibly of the Sepoy Army, the defects of our Indian military system, and the causes of the prevailing disaffection, I have ample evidence in letters before me.

April, 1857. Umballah.

there; but still no clue to trace the offenders." And, again, at the end of the month, "We have not been able to detect any of the incendiaries at Umballah. This appears to me extraordinary; but it shows how close the combination is among the miscreants who have recourse to this mode of revenging what they conceive to be their wrongs, and how great the dread of retaliation to any one who would dare to become an informer." It showed, too, how little power we had of penetrating beneath the surface, and how great was the mistrust of the English throughout all classes of the Native soldiery. Let what might be the hatred and dissension among themselves, a common feeling still stronger closed their hearts and sealed their lips against their English officers.

Events at Meerut.

Day after day this fact became more and more apparent. To the most observant of our people it seemed at first that, although the ministers and dependents of the deposed Mahomedan ruler of Oude might have been insidiously employed in the corruption of our Native soldiery, the alarm, and therefore the discontent among the Sepoys, was for the most part an emanation of Hindooism. The inquiries into the state of the Thirty-fourth Regiment at Barrackpore had resulted in a belief that the Mahomedan and Sikh soldiers were true to their salt; and so strong was the impression that only the Hindoos of the disbanded Nineteenth were really disaffected, that, after the dispersion of the regiment, it was believed that the whole history of the mutiny, which had ruined them, might be gathered from the Mussulman Sepoys. But, although a sagacious civil officer was put upon their track, and every effort was made to elicit the desired information, the attempt was altogether a failure. Whether these first impressions were right or wrong, whether the mutiny was, in its origin and inception, a Hindoo or a Mahomedan movement, will hereafter be a subject of inquiry. But, before the end of the month of April, it must have been apparent to Lord Canning that nothing was to be hoped from that antagonism of the Asiatic races, which had ever been regarded as the main element of our strength and safety. Mahomedans and Hindoos were plainly united against us. April, 1857. Meerut.

From an unexpected quarter there soon came proof of this union. As the new Enfield rifle had been the outward and visible cause of the great fear that had arisen in the minds of the soldiery, it was natural that the anxieties of the Government should, in the first instance, have been confined to the Native Infantry. In the Infantry Regiments a very large majority of the men were Hindoos; whilst in the Cavalry the Mahomedan element was proportionately much stronger.* But now there came from Meerut strange news to the effect that a Cavalry regiment had revolted.

To this station many unquiet thoughts had been directed; for it was one of the largest and most important in the whole range of our Indian territories. There, troops of all arms, both European and Native, were assembled. There, the Head-Quarters of the Bengal Artillery were established. There, the Ordnance Commissariat were diligently employed, in the Expense Magazine, on the manufacture of greased cartridges. There, the English Riflemen of the Sixtieth, not without some feelings of disgust, were using the unsavory things. More than once there had

* As a rule, the Mahomedans were better horsemen and more adroit swordsmen than the Hindoos, and therefore they made more serviceable troopers. It is stated, however, that in the Third Regiment of Regular Cavalry, which led off the dance of death at Meerut, there were an unusual number of Brahmins.

April, 1857. Meerut.

been reports that the Sepoys had risen at Meerut, and that the Europeans had been let loose against them. With vague but eager expectancy the Native regiments at all the large stations in Upper India were looking in that direction, as for a signal which they knew would soon be discerned. Men asked each other what was the news from Meerut, and looked into the Native newspapers for the suggestive heading; for it was the cradle of all sorts of strange and disturbing stories. In this month of April its crowded Lines and busy Bazaars were stirred by indefinite apprehensions of something coming. Every day the excitement increased, for every day some new story, intended to confirm the popular belief in the base designs of the English, found its way into circulation. The emissary of evil, who, in some shape or other, was stalking across the country, was at Meerut in the guise of a wandering Fakeer, or religious mendicant, riding on an elephant, with many followers. That he was greatly disturbing the minds of men was certain; so the Police authorities ordered him to depart. He moved; but it was believed that he went no farther than the Lines of one of the Native regiments.*

In no place was the story of the greased cartridges discussed with greater eagerness than at Meerut; in

* Compare following passage in the Meerut Narrative of Mr. Williams, Commissioner First Division: "All the rumours by which the minds of the Native soldiers were prepared for revolt, were industriously disseminated at Meerut, especially those regarding the use of polluting grease in the preparation of the new cartridges, and the mixture of ground bones in flour, by which, it was said, Government desired to destroy the religion of the people. One of the many emissaries who were moving about the country appeared at Meerut in April, ostensibly as a fakeer, riding on an elephant with followers, and having with him horses and native carriages. The frequent visits of the men of the Native regiments to him attracted attention, and he was ordered, through the police, to leave the place; he apparently complied, but, it is said, he stayed some time in the Lines of the 20th Native Infantry —*Unpublished Records.*

no place was there a more disturbing belief that this was a part of a great scheme for the defilement of the people. It was of little use to declare to them that not a single soldier would ever be required to use a cartridge greased by any one but himself, for the greasing of the cartridges was in their estimation only one of many fraudulent devices, and every one believed that the dry cartridges contained the obnoxious fat. So, in the beginning of the fourth week of April, the excitement, which for many weeks had been growing stronger and stronger, broke out into an act of open mutiny. The troopers of the Third Cavalry were the first to resist the orders of their officers. They had no new weapons; no new ammunition. The only change introduced into their practice was that which substituted the pinching or tearing off, for the biting off, the end of the cartridges which they used with their carbines. This change in the drill was to be explained to them on a parade of the skirmishers of the regiment, which was to be held on the morning of the 24th of April. On the preceding evening a report ran through cantonments that the troopers would refuse to touch the cartridges. The parade was held, and of ninety men, to whom the ammunition was to have been served out, only five obeyed the orders of their officers. In vain Colonel Carmichael Smyth explained to them that the change had been introduced from a kindly regard for their own scruples. They were dogged and obdurate, and would not touch the cartridges. So the parade was dismissed, and the eighty-five troopers of the Third were ordered for Court-martial.

April, 1857. Meerut.

All this made it manifest to Lord Canning that the worst suspicions were deeply rooted in the Sepoy Army; and though he at all times maintained a

The story of the ground bones.

April, 1857. calm and cheerful demeanour, he thought much and anxiously of the signs and symptoms of the troubled spirit that was abroad. There were many indications that these suspicions were not confined to the military classes, but were disquieting also the general community. Not only in Meerut, but also in many other parts of the country, there was a belief that the English designed to defile both Hindoos and Mahomedans, by polluting with unclean matter the daily food of the people. It has been shown that a suspicion of a similar character was abroad at the time of the Mutiny at Vellore.* Now the disturbing rumour, cunningly circulated, took many portentous shapes. It was said that the officers of the British Government, under command from the Company and the Queen, had mixed ground bones with the flour and the salt sold in the Bazaars; that they had adulterated all the ghee† with animal fat; that bones had been burnt with the common sugar of the country; and that not only bone-dust flour, but the flesh of cows and pigs, had been thrown into the wells to pollute the drinking water of the people. Of this great imaginary scheme of contamination the matter of the greased cartridges was but a part, especially addressed to one class of the community. All classes, it was believed, were to be defiled at the same time; and the story ran that the "burra sahibs," or great English lords, had commanded all the princes, nobles, landholders, merchants, and cultivators of the land, to feed together upon English bread.

Of these preposterous fables, the one which made the strongest impression on the public mind was the

* *Ante*, page 248. It was then said that the English had mixed the blood of cows and pigs with all the newly manufactured salt.

† This is the ordinary grease used for cooking purposes throughout India.

story of the bone-dust flour. That it was current in March at Barrackpore is certain.* In the early part of April, a circumstance occurred which proved that the panic had then spread to the Upper Provinces. It happened that flour having risen to an exceptionally high price at Cawnpore, certain dealers at Meerut chartered a number of Government boats to carry a large supply down the canal to the former place. When the first instalment arrived, and was offered for sale at a price considerably below that which had previously ruled in the Bazaars, it found a ready market; but before the remainder reached Cawnpore, a story had been circulated to the effect that the grain had been ground in the canal mills, under European supervision, and that the dust of cows' bones had been mixed up with it, with the intention of destroying the caste of all who should eat it. Such a story as this, circulated in the Lines and the Military Bazaars of Cawnpore, at once stopped the sale of the Meerut flour. Not a Sepoy would touch it, not a person of any kind would purchase it, cheap as was the price at which it was obtainable in comparison with all the other supplies in the market. Rapidly spread the alarm from one station to another, and as tidings came of the arrival of imaginary boat-loads or camel-loads of flour and bone-dust, men threw away the bread that they were eating, and be- April, 1857.

* It was brought to the notice of General Hearsey by a native anonymous letter, picked up at the gate of Major Matthews, who commanded the Forty-third. The Major sent it to Hearsey's staff, describing it as "sad trash;" and Hearsey, in forwarding it to the Military Secretary, expressed regret that the contemptible production had not been burnt as soon as it was found. But History rejoices in the preservation of such contemptible productions. I have given it entire in the Appendix. There are many such in my possession, but this is the earliest in date, and gives the most comprehensive account of the rumours circulated by our enemies.

April, 1857. lieved themselves already defiled.* Whether, as some said, this was a trick of the Cawnpore grain merchants to keep up the price of flour, or whether the story had been set afloat under the same influences as those which had given so false a colouring to the accident of the greased cartridges, and had associated with all the other wild fictions of which I have spoken, cannot with certainty be declared. But, whatsoever the origin of the fable, it sunk deeply into men's minds, and fixed there more ineradicably than ever their belief in the stern resolution of the Government to destroy the caste of the people by fraudulently bringing, in one way or other, the unclean thing to their lips.

The story of the chupatties.

It fixed, too, more firmly than before in the mind of Lord Canning, the belief that a great fear was spreading itself among the people, and that there was more danger in such a feeling than in a great hatred. Thinking of this, he thought also of another strange story that had come to him from the North-West, and which even the most experienced men about him were incompetent to explain. From village to village, brought by one messenger and sent onward by another, passed a mysterious token in the shape of one of those flat cakes made from flour and water, and forming the common bread of the people, which, in their language, are called Chupatties. All that was known about it was, that a messenger appeared, gave the cake to the head man of one village, and requested him to despatch it onward to the next; and

* Colonel Baird Smith to Mr. Colvin—Mr. Martin Gubbins to the same. "Once alarmed," wrote the latter, "they drink in the greatest follies. Bone-dust attah alarm has taken hold of men's minds at several of our stations, and Sepoys, private servants, Zemindars attending Court, have flung away their roti (bread) on hearing that five camel-loads of bone-dust attah had reached the station."—*MS. Correspondence.*

that, in this way, it travelled from place to place; no one refusing, no one doubting, few even questioning, in blind obedience to a necessity felt rather than understood. After a while, this practice became known to the functionaries of the English Government, who thought much of it, or thought little of it, according to their individual dispositions, and interpreted it, in divers ways, according to the light that was in them.* The greater number looked upon it as a signal of warning and preparation, designed to tell the people that something great and portentous was about to happen, and to prompt them to be ready for the crisis. One great authority wrote to the Governor-General that he had been told that the chupatty was the symbol of men's food, and that its circulation was intended to alarm and to influence men's minds by indicating to them that their means of subsistence would be taken from them, and to tell them, therefore, to hold together. Others, laughing to scorn this notion of the fiery cross, saw in it only a common superstition of the country. It was said that it was no unwonted thing for a Hindoo, in whose family sickness had broken out, to institute this transmission of chupatties, in the belief that it would carry off the disease; or for a community, when the cholera or other pestilence was raging, to betake themselves to a similar practice. Then, again, it was believed by others that the cakes had been sent abroad by enemies of the British Government, for the purpose of attaching to their circulation another dangerous fiction, to the effect April, 1857.

* Mr. Ford, Collector of Goorgaon, first brought it to the notice of the Lieutenant-Governor of the North-Western Provinces, Mr. Colvin, who issued circular orders on the subject to all the local officers in charge of districts.

April, 1857. that there was bone-dust in them, and that the English had resorted to this supplementary method of defiling the people. Some, too, surmised that, by a device sometimes used for other purposes,* seditious letters were in this manner forwarded from village to village, read by the village chief, again crusted over with flour, and sent on in the shape of a chupatty, to be broken by the next recipient. But whatsoever the real history of the movement, it had doubtless the effect of producing and keeping alive much popular excitement in the districts through which the cakes were transmitted; and it may be said that its action was too widely diffused, and that it lasted for too long a time, to admit of a very ready adoption of the theory that it was of an accidental character, the growth only of domestic, or even of municipal, anxieties.† Some saw in it much meaning; some saw none. Time has thrown no new

* In this manner communication was sometimes held with the inmates of our gaols. See the "Revelations of an Orderly," by Paunchkowree Khan: "Suppose a prisoner is confined under the bayonet of Sepoys, he must be permitted to eat bread. The preparer of food is bribed, and a short note is put into a chupatty, or a sentence is written on a plate, and when the bread is taken up the prisoner reads what is written."

† The circulation of the chupatties commenced at the beginning of the year. "The year 1857," writes Captain Keatinge, "opened in Nimar by a general distribution of small cakes, which were passed on from village to village. The same, I am aware, has occurred all over Northern India, and has been spoken of as having been a signal for the disturbances which took place later in the year. At the time they appeared in Nimar, they were everywhere brought from the direction of Indore. That city was at the time afflicted with a severe visitation of cholera, and numbers of inhabitants died daily. It was at that time understood by the people in Nimar, and is still believed, that the cakes of wheat were despatched from Indore after the performance over them of incantations that would ensure the pestilence accompanying them. The cakes did not come straight from North to South, for they were received at Bujengghur, more than half way between Indore and Gwalior, on the 9th of February, but had been distributed at Mundlaiser on the 12th of January. This habit of passing on holy and unholy things is not unknown at Nimar. When small-pox breaks out in a village, a goat is procured, a cocoa-nut tied to its neck, and it is taken by the chowkeedar to the first village on the road to Mundatta; it is not allowed to enter the town, but is

light upon it. Opinions still widely differ. And all that History can record with any certainty is, that the bearers of these strange missives went from place to place, and that ever as they went new excitements were engendered, and vague expectations were raised. April, 1857.

Political intrigues.

That in all this there was something more than mere military disaffection was manifest to Lord Canning; but neither he nor his confidential advisers could clearly discern what it was. He had a general conception that evil-minded men, with strong resentments to be gratified by the ruin of the British Government, were sending forth their emissaries; but, with the exception of the ministers of the dethroned King of Oude, whom he had suspected from the first,*

taken by a villager to the next hamlet, and so passed on without rest to its destination." This last is the scripturally recorded scape-goat. With respect to the chupatties, consult also the report of Major Erskine, Commissioner of the Saugor and Nerbudda territories: "So far back as January, 1857," he writes, "small wheaten cakes (chupatties) were passed in a most mysterious manner from village to village in most of the districts, and, although all took it as a signal that something was coming, nobody in the division, I believe, knew what it portended, or whence it came, and it appeared to have been little thought about except that in the money-market of Saugor it is said to have had some slight effect in bill transactions. I reported the matter to Government at the time, but even now it is a matter of doubt if the signal was understood by *any one*, or if it referred to the coming rebellion, though such is now the general opinion." I have thrown together in the Appendix some further facts and fancies illustrative of this interesting subject of inquiry.

* In my mind there is no doubt of the activity, at this time, of the Oude people at Garden Reach. The Sepoys at Barrackpore were induced to believe that, if they broke away from the English harness, they would obtain more lucrative service under the restored kingship of Oude. I have before me some letters, original and translated, of a Jemadar of the Thirty-fourth Regiment, which contain numerous allusions to the Future of the King's service. Take the following: "The Second Grenadiers said, in the beginning of April, 'We will go to our homes sooner than bite the blank ammunition.' The regiments were unanimous in joining the King of Oude." "The Soubahdars of the Quarter-Guard said, 'We have sided with the King of Oude, but nothing has come of it.'" "Ramshaee Lalla said, 'It would have been well for us.'" This also has its significance: "Soubahdar Muddeh Khan, Sirdar Khan, and Ramshaee Lalla said, 'The Feringhee Beteechoots' (a vile term of opprobrium) 'are unequalled in their want of faith. The King of Lucknow put down his arms, and the

April, 1857. he could not individualise his suspicions. How was he to know, how was any Englishman, shut up all day long in his house, and having no more living intercourse with the people than if they were clay figures, to know what was passing beneath the surface of Native society? If anything were learnt at that time to throw light upon the sources of the great events that were to happen, it was by merest accident, and the full force of the revelation was rarely discernible at the time. It was remembered afterwards that, in the early part of this year, one man, a Mahratta by race, a Brahmin by caste, of whom something has already been recorded in this narrative, was displaying, in his movements, an unwonted activity, which created surprise, but scarcely aroused suspicion. This man was Dundoo Punt, commonly known as the Nana Sahib, of Bhitoor—the adopted son of the Peishwah, Badjee Rao. He was not given to distant journeyings; indeed, he was seldom seen beyond the limits of his own estate. But in the early months of 1857, having visited Calpee, he made a journey to Delhi, and, a little later in the year, paid a visit to Lucknow. It was in the middle of April that he started on this last journey. On the 17th of that month, Mr. Morland, then one of the Agra Judges, who shortly after the Peishwah's death had been Commissioner at Bhitoor, and who had endeavoured to rescue from resumption a part of his pension, paid a visit to the Nana at that

Government have given him no allowance. We advised the King to put down his arms. The treachery of the Government is unrivalled.'" Colonel Wheler said that the writer of these letters appeared to be "affected in the head." It will be remembered that the Native officer who reported the coming massacre of Vellore was also said to be mad. General Hearsey, sending on the correspondence to Government, said that there was "much method in his supposed madness;" and added, that "much important information on the whole cause and subject of this *supposed* Cartridge Mutiny might be elicited from him."—*MS. Correspondence.*

place. The wily Mussulman Agent, Azim-oollah Khan, who had pleaded his cause in England, was with Dundoo Punt when the English gentleman was announced, and they talked freely together, as friends talk, no suspicion on the one side, and no appearance of anything unwonted on the other. All was outwardly smooth and smiling. The Mahratta was as profuse as ever in his expressions of respect and esteem; and when Morland took his departure, the brother of Dundoo Punt told him that the Nana purposed to return the visit of the Sahib next day at Cawnpore. The next day happened to be Sunday, and Morland was anxious, therefore, to decline the visit; but the Nana Sahib went to Cawnpore, and again sent Baba Bhut to the English gentleman to propose an interview. What he wished to say to the man who had been kind to him will now never be known, for Morland declined the meeting, on the plea that it was the Sabbath, and expressed regret that the Nana Sahib should have made the journey to no purpose. To this the Brahmin replied, that his brother was on his way to Lucknow to visit one of the Newabs. There was something in all this strange and surprising. An English nobleman, in the course of three or four months, might visit all the chief cities of Europe without any one taking heed of the occurrence. But the nobility of India are little given to travelling; and the Nana Sahib had rarely gone beyond the limits of Bhitoor.* April, 1857.

* A different statement has, I know, been made and commonly accepted. It is the belief that the Nana Sahib was frequently to be seen at Cawnpore, riding or driving on the Mall, and mixing freely with the European residents of the place. But the truth is, he eschewed Cawnpore, for the reason which induced his adoptive father, Badjee Rao, to eschew it, namely, that a salute was not given to him on entering the cantonment. The person generally known in Cawnpore as the "Nana" was not Dundoo Punt, but Nana Nerain Rao, the eldest son of the ex-Peishwah's chief adviser and manager, the Sou-

April, 1857. That, within so short a time, he should make these three journeys, was a fact to excite speculation but he was held to be a quiet, inoffensive person, good natured, perhaps somewhat dull, and manifestly not of that kind of humanity of which conspirators are made, so no political significance was attached to the fact. What likelihood was there, at that time, that such a man as Dundoo Punt, heavy and seemingly impassive, who had for some years quietly accepted his position, and during that time done many acts of kindness and hospitality to the English gentlemen, should suddenly become a plotter against the State? Had any one then said that it behoved the Government to mark the movements of that man, he would have been laughed to scorn as an alarmist. We never know in India how many are the waiters and the watchers; we never know at what moment our enemies, sluggish in their hatreds as in all else, may exact the payment of old scores which we have thought were long ago forgotten.

So Dundoo Punt, Nana Sahib, passed on, about some business known to himself, utterly unknown to European functionaries, to Calpee, on the banks of the Jumna, to the great imperial city of Delhi, and to Lucknow, the capital of Oude. In the last of these places, when the Nana arrived, Henry Lawrence was diligently, with his whole good heart, striving to make right all that had gone wrong during the time of his predecessor. But again the handwriting on the wall traced those fatal words, "Too late." If he had but gone to Lucknow when he had first offered to go, how different would all have been! It was on the 18th of April that the Nana Sahib started on his journey to Lucknow. On

bahdar Ramchunder Punt, who, after his master's death, resided at Cawnpore, and was on terms of social familiarity with many of the principal European residents.

that day Henry Lawrence wrote a long letter to the Governor-General, telling him that he had discerned signs of dangerous coalitions between the regular Sepoy regiments, the Irregulars taken into our service from the old Oude Army, and the men of the Police battalions; symptoms also of intrigues on foot among some of the chief people of the city. There were many elements of trouble; and now they were beginning to develop themselves in a manner significant of a general outburst of popular discontent. "This city," wrote Henry Lawrence on that 18th of April, "is said to contain some six or seven hundred thousand souls, and does certainly contain many thousands (twenty thousand, I was told yesterday) of disbanded soldiers, and of hungry, nay starving, dependents of the late Government. This very morning a clod was thrown at Mr. Ommaney (the Judicial Commissioner), and another struck Major Anderson (Chief Engineer) whilst in a buggy with myself. . . . . The improvements in the city here go on very fast—too fast and too roughly. Much discontent has been caused by demolition of buildings, and still more by threats of further similar measures; also regarding the seizure of religious and other edifices, and plots of ground, as Huzool or Government property. I have visited many of these places and pacified parties, and prohibited any seizure or demolition without competent authority. The Revenue measures, though not as sweeping as represented by the writer whose letter your Lordship sent me, have been unsatisfactory. The Talookhdars have, I fear, been hardly dealt with; at least, in the Fyzabad division some have lost half their villages, some have lost all." Such stated here, in the hurried outline of a letter from the spot, to be dwelt upon more

April, 1857. Lucknow.

April, 1857. Lucknow.

in detail hereafter, was the condition of affairs which, in the third week of April, the Nana Sahib found in Lucknow. He could have scarcely wished for any better materials from which to erect an edifice of rebellion.

By this Dundoo Punt, Nana Sahib—by all who were festering with resentments against the English and malignantly biding their time, the annexation of Oude had been welcomed as a material aid to the success of their machinations. It was no sudden thought, born of the accident of the greased cartridges, that took the disappointed Brahmin and his Mahomedan friend to Lucknow in the spring of this year of trouble. For months, for years indeed, ever since the failure of the mission to England had been apparent, they had been quietly spreading their network of intrigue all over the country. From one native Court to another native Court, from one extremity to another of the great continent of India, the agents of the Nana Sahib had passed with overtures and invitations, discreetly, perhaps mysteriously, worded, to Princes and Chiefs of different races and religions, but most hopefully of all to the Mahrattas. At the three great Mahratta families, the families of the Rajah of Sattarah, of the Peishwah, of the Boonsla, Lord Dalhousie had struck deadly blows. In the Southern Mahratta country, indeed, it seemed that Princes and Nobles were alike ripe for rebellion. It was a significant fact that the agents of the great Sattarah and Poona families had been doing their master's work in England about the same time, that both had returned to India rank rebels, and that the first year of Lord Canning's administration found Rungo-Bapojee as active for evil in the South as Azim-oollah was in the North; both able and unscrupulous men, and hating the English with a deadlier hatred for the very kindness that had been shown to them. But it was not until the crown had been set upon the annexations of Lord Dalhousie by the seizure of Oude, that the Nana Sahib and his accomplices saw much prospect of success. That event was the turning-point of their career of intrigue. What had before been difficult was now made easy by this last act of English usurpation. Not only were the ministers of the King of Oude tampering with the troops at the Presidency, and sowing dangerous lies broad-cast over the length and breadth of the land, but such was the impression made by the last of our annexations, that men asked each other who was safe, and what use was there in fidelity, when so faithful a friend and ally as the King of Oude was stripped of his dominions by the Government whom he had aided in its need. It is said that Princes and Chiefs, who had held back, then came forward, and that the Nana Sahib began to receive answers to his appeals.* But whatsoever may have been its effect in

April, 1857. Lucknow.

* By those who systematically reject Native evidence, all this may be regarded as nothing but unsubstantial surmise. But there is nothing in my mind more clearly substantiated than the complicity of the Nana Sahib in wide-spread intrigues before the outbreak of the mutiny. The concurrent testimony of witnesses examined in parts of the country widely distant from each other takes this story altogether out of the regions of the conjectural. I speak only of the broad fact itself. With regard to the statement in the text, that the machinations of the Nana Sahib were much assisted by the annexation of Oude, I give the following, *quantum valeat*, from the evidence of a Native emissary detained and examined in Mysore, in January, 1858. After giving a list of numerous princes and chiefs whom the Nana had addressed, this man said: "The Nana wrote at intervals, two or three months previous to the annexation of Oude. But at first he got no answers. Nobody had any hope. After the annexation he wrote still more, and then the Soukars of Lucknow joined in his views. Maun Singh, who is the Chief of the Poorbeah, or Poordusee, joined. Then the Sepoys began to make *tajwiz* (plans) among themselves, and the Lucknow Soukars supported them. Until Oude was annexed, Nana Sahib did not get answers from any one; but when that occurred, many began to take courage and to answer him. The plot among the Sepoys first took place—the discontent about the

April, 1857. remote places, it cannot be questioned that in the condition of Oude itself after annexation there was that which must have gladdened the heart of every plotter against the State. Such men as Dundoo Punt and Azim-oollah Khan could not pass through the streets of Lucknow without clearly seeing what was coming. What they saw and what they heard, indeed, pleased them so greatly, that they assumed a bold and swaggering demeanour, which attracted the attention of the English functionaries to whom they were introduced. For they made no secret of their visit; but went about openly in the public streets, with numerous attendants, and even sought the presence of the Commissioner. The Nana said that he had come only to see the sights of Lucknow; so Henry Lawrence received him kindly, and ordered every attention to be shown to him by the authorities of the city. But his sojourn in Lucknow was brief, and his departure sudden. He went without taking leave of the English functionaries, saying that business required his presence at Cawnpore.

greased cartridges. Then answers began to pour in. Golab Singh, of Jummoo, was the first to send an answer. He said that he was ready with men, money, and arms, and he sent money to Nana Sahib, through one of the Lucknow Soukars." The former part of this statement may be readily accepted; the latter must be received with caution. Further extracts from this man's evidence will be found in the Appendix.

CHAPTER VII.

THE MONTH OF MAY—GENERAL SURVEY OF AFFAIRS—STATE OF FEELING AT THE RIFLE DEPÔTS—THE RISING STORM IN OUDE—THE REVOLT AT MEERUT—THE SEIZURE OF DELHI—MEASURES OF LORD CANNING—THE CALL FOR SUCCOURS.

THE month of May, with its fiery heat and glare, and its arid dust-charged winds, found Lord Canning in Calcutta watching eagerly, but hopefully, the progress of events, and the signs and symptoms of the excitement engendered in men's minds by the great lie which had been so insidiously propagated among them. From the multitude of conflicting statements and opinions which reached him from different quarters, it was difficult to extract the truth; but taking a comprehensive view of all that was manifest to him, from the plains of Bengal to the hills of the Himalayah, he could not discern in those first days of May that the clouds were gathering around him denser and blacker than before. If there were any change, indeed, it was rather a change for the brighter and the better. At Barrackpore there had been no more overt acts of mutiny. The Native regiments were doing their duty, sullenly perhaps, but still quietly. At Dum-Dum the detachments in the Rifle depôt, under the new system of drill, were proceeding to ball practice without any visible signs of discontent. It was hoped, indeed, that the troops in

May, 1857.

May, 1857. the immediate neighbourhood of Calcutta were yielding to the explanations and assurances which had been given to them, and slowly returning to reason. At the Rifle depôts also in the Upper Country the drill was quietly proceeding. At Sealkote, the detachments from the Native regiments in the Punjab, Regular and Irregular, were firing the new pieces without a murmur. Sir John Lawrence went to that station, at the beginning of the month, "to see the new School of Musketry, as well as to judge with respect to the feeling among the Sepoys;" and he wrote to Lord Canning that all were "highly pleased with the new musket, and quite ready to adopt it. They already perceive how great an advantage it will give them in mountain warfare." The officers assured him that no bad feeling had been shown, and he himself "could perceive no hesitation or reluctance on the part of any of the Sepoys."* From Umballah, General Barnard wrote on the first day of the month, that he had reported to Head-Quarters that so far from any insubordinate feeling existing at that place, he had reason to be satisfied with the patience, zeal, and activity that the men had shown on the severe night-picket work necessitated by the incendiary fires. "I have no reason," he added, "to accuse the Sepoy of causing these fires—no overt act has been elicited, and no instance of insubordination has occurred. The musket practice has been resumed with apparent good will and zeal. I have frequently attended it myself, and I will answer for it that no ill feeling exists in these detachments."†

Thus it was that, in the first days of May, there

* Sir John Lawrence to Lord Canning, May 4, 1857.—*MS. Correspondence.*

† Sir H. Barnard to Lord Canning, May 1, 1857.—*MS. Correspondence.*

was apparent to the eyes of the Governor-General something like a lull; and it seemed that at the Rifle depôts, which were the great central points of danger, the difficulty had been tided over. From Meerut, too, no fresh tidings of disturbance came. The men of the Third Cavalry were being tried by Court-martial; and it did not appear that any of their comrades were about to follow their insubordinate example. There were circumstances that rendered it probable that the motives which had driven these men into mutiny were altogether of an exceptional character. So Lord Canning, in the early part of this month of May, was able to direct his thoughts to all parts of the country, and to fix them on many topics of Indian government and administration, as calmly and as philosophically as in the quietest of times. He was corresponding with Lord Elphinstone on the subject of the Treaty with Persia and the Expenses of the War; with Lieutenant-Governor Colvin on Education Grants and Female Schools, and the Delhi Succession—little thinking how that last question would soon settle itself; with Major Davidson, the Resident at Hyderabad, about the recognition of a successor to the Nizam (his Highness being nigh unto death from a surfeit of prawns); with Sir Richmond Shakespear, Resident at Baroda, on the Finances of the Guicowar; and with Colonel Durand, the Governor-General's Agent at Indore, about the large amount of Native deposits in the Residency Treasury. Indeed, the current business of Government was but little interrupted. There was no fear in Government House. May, 1857

But, although at this time the Governor-General was cheerful and hopeful, and believed that the clouds of trouble would soon, by God's providence,

[M]ay, 1857. be dispersed, he had some especial causes of anxiety. The dawn of the month of May found the Thirty-fourth Regiment at Barrackpore, still awaiting its sentence. The Jemadar of the Quarter-Guard, Issuree Pandy, had been hanged on the 22nd of April, in the presence of all the troops, at Barrackpore. He had confessed his guilt on the scaffold, and with his last breath had exhorted his comrades to be warned by his example.* It was believed that this public execution of a commissioned officer would have a salutary effect upon the whole Native Army. But the punishment of one man, though that punishment were death, could not wipe out the offence of the regiment, or vindicate the authority of the Government. The great defect of Lord Canning, as a ruler in troubled times, was an excess of conscientiousness. The processes by which he arrived at a resolution were slow, because at every stage some scruple of honesty arose to impede and obstruct his conclusions. On the score both of justice and of policy he doubted whether the prompt disbandment of the Thirty-fourth would be right. It was certain that some companies were true to their colours, and he did not clearly see that all the rest were faithless. He had caused a searching inquiry to be made into the condition of the regiment, and he had hoped, up to the end of the third week of April, that all the require-

* There were many erroneous versions at the time of Issuree Pandy's speech from the scaffold. The words which he uttered, literally translated, were these: "Listen, Behaudur Sepoys. In such a manner do not let any one act! I have behaved in such a rascally way to the Government, that I am about to receive my just punishment. Therefore, let no Behaudur Sepoy behave in this wretched manner, or he may receive the same punishment." This is given on the authority of Colonel Mitchell of the Nineteenth, who brought the prisoner from the Quarter-Guard of the Fifty-third to the foot of the gallows, and whose own impressions were confirmed by the three orderlies who accompanied him.

ments of the case might be satisfied by the dismissal of some of the more patent offenders. But the weight of military authority was strongly in favour of disbandment. General Hearsey, at Barrackpore, was fully convinced that no measure short of this would produce the desired effect; and General Anson wrote earnestly from Simlah urging the expediency of such a course. The whole question was fully and anxiously discussed in Council; and at last, on the 30th of April, Lord Canning recorded a minute declaratory of his opinion that no penalty less general than disbandment "would meet the exigencies of the case, or be effectual as an example." But even then there were doubts with respect to the men who were to be exempted from punishment, and not until the 4th of May was the discussion exhausted and the order given for the disbandment of the regiment.*

May, 1857

Disbandment of the Thirty-fourth.

Two days afterwards, in the presence of all the troops at Barrackpore, of the detachments from Dum-Dum, and of the Eighty-fourth (Queen's) from Chinsurah, the seven companies of the Thirty-fourth, who had witnessed the great outrage of the 29th of March, were drawn up, before the sun had risen, to receive their sentence. There was to be no mitigation of their punishment, as in the case of the Nineteenth; so when they laid down their arms, the uniforms which they had disgraced were stripped from their backs, and they were marched out of cantonments under an escort of Europeans. And thus a second time the number of the guilty Thirty-fourth was erased from the Army List; and five hundred more

* It is especially to be noted that a question arose as to whether the Jemadar of the Mint-Guard, who had apprehended the men of the Second Grenadiers (*ante*, page 530), should be exempted, as a faithful servant, or, on account of later revelations, condemned as a traitor. The decision was ultimately in his favour.

May, 1857. desperate men, principally Brahmins and Rajpoots, were cast adrift upon the world to work out their own schemes of vengeance.

Oude. In the quarter to which a large number of them made their way as the Nineteenth had made their way before them—in Oude, the signs of approaching trouble increased. To no place, from one end of India to another, did the mind of the Governor-General, in this conjuncture, turn, with more painful interest, than to this newly-annexed province, the nursery of the Bengal Army. Henry Lawrence's letters to the Governor-General were wholly silent on the subject of the Nana's visit to Lucknow. But they spoke of much that pressed heavily on his mind. Recognising so many causes of popular discontent in Oude, and knowing well how large a portion of the Native Army was drawn from that province, he could not, at such a time, regard without much anxiety the demeanour of the Sepoys around him. There was one regiment at Lucknow, whose conduct, although it had been betrayed into no overt act of insubordination, was of a suspicious, almost of a threatening, character, and it seemed desirable that it should be removed from the province. There was no doubt that some of the chief people of the city were tampering with its allegiance; and much danger might therefore be averted if it could be removed to another station beyond the limits of the province. The suggestion was made, and Canning responded to it, giving full authority to Henry Lawrence to move the tainted regiment to Meerut. "Let the Commander-in-Chief know," wrote the Governor-General, "if you find it necessary to send it away; but do not wait for any further authority. . . . . If you have regiments that are really untrustworthy, there must be no delicacy in the matter." But before the letter sanctioning his proposal had arrived, Henry Lawrence had thought long and deeply about the results of such a measure; and on the 1st of May he wrote to Lord Canning, saying: "Unquestionably we should feel better without the Forty-eighth, but I do not feel confident that the feeling in the other regiments is materially better; and there is little doubt that the Forty-eighth would not be improved by a move, which is an important point of consideration in the present general condition of the Army." He was right; the removal of a single regiment could not benefit Oude, but it might do injury elsewhere by tainting other parts of the Army. May, 1857. Oude.

That other components of the Oude force were equally disaffected was presently apparent. On the 2nd of May, Captain Carnegie, who was Magistrate of the city of Lucknow, and who had the superintendence of the Police—a man, described by his immediate superior as "prudent and active, though so quiet in manner, and implicitly to be relied upon"—reported to Henry Lawrence that there had been a strong demonstration against the cartridges in the Seventh Regiment of Oude Irregulars. At first he was fain to believe that the story might be exaggerated; but there was soon undeniable evidence that it was only too true. The regiment, which had been in the King's service, was posted at a distance of some seven miles from Lucknow. A fortnight before, the recruits of the regiment had commenced practice with ball-cartridge, and had done their duty without any manifestations of discontent. But by the end of the month it was clear that the great fear, which was travelling about the country, had taken possession of their minds, and that they were on the very verge of revolt. Whether they had been wrought upon by Mutiny in the Oude Irregulars.

May, 1857. Oude. emissaries from the city, or whether any of the disbanded men of the Nineteenth had, by this time, found their way to Lucknow, is matter only of conjecture;* but as the month of May dawned upon them, they were ripe for rebellion—not only themselves prepared to resist, but eager to incite others to resistance. They had written a letter to the men of the Forty-eighth, urging them to rise for their religion; and no soothing explanations from their officers could induce them to shake off the mistrust which had fastened upon them. On the second day of the month the Brigadier rode out with his Staff to the Lines of the Seventh, and found them "as obstinate as possible with regard to the cartridges."† Returning at nightfall to Lucknow, he wrote at once to Lawrence, telling him the state of the regiment, and adding, "I think myself that this affair has
May 3. been a long time brewing." The next morning‡ brought with it no consolation. The Seventh were in a worse state than before. They had been sullen and obstinate on the preceding day. Now in a state

* It has been stated that both the Nineteenth and Thirty-fourth were stationed at Lucknow at the time of annexation; and it was believed that they were there first infected with rebellion. Henry Lawrence wrote that he had ascertained that in the Nineteenth there must have been nearly seven hundred Oude men. By this time, they had mostly found their way back to their native province.

† The official report said that the regiment "refused to bite the cartridges when ordered by its own officers, and again by the Brigadier." How it happened that, after the change introduced into the drill, the Sepoys at Lucknow were ordered to bite the cartridge at all, it is impossible to say. This did not escape Lord Canning, who, in a minute written on the 10th of May, said: "It appears that the revised instructions for the platoon exercise, by which the biting of the cartridge is dispensed with, had not come into operation at Lucknow. Explanation of this should be asked." But the time for explanation was past. It was ascertained, however, that the new drill instructions were sent to the Oude Irregular force in the middle of April.

‡ So difficult is the attainment of perfect accuracy in an historical narrative, that even Mr. Gubbins, whose work on the Mutinies of Oude is the best and safest authority extant, says that these events, which he witnessed himself, happened on Sunday, the 10th of May

of feverish excitement, violent, desperate, they assumed a menacing attitude, and talked openly of murdering their officers. It was obvious that a crisis was approaching, and that no time was to be lost; so Henry Lawrence, when he heard that the regiment was in this defiant and dangerous state, determined at once to disarm, and, if resisted, to destroy it. On that evening he moved up an overwhelming force of all arms to the parade-ground of the Seventh. The day was far spent when he commenced the march. "It was a ticklish matter," he wrote to Mr. Colvin, "taking the Forty-eighth down on Sunday night; but I thought that they were safer in our company than behind in cantonments. We had to pass for two miles through the city; indeed, Her Majesty's Thirty-second had four miles of it. I therefore hesitated as to moving after; but the moon was in its third quarter; and the first blow is everything. So off we started; and concentrated from four points, accomplishing the seven miles in about three hours."*

May, 1857. Ætat. 51.

The moon had risen, bright in an unclouded sky, on that Sabbath evening, when Henry Lawrence, accompanied by his Staff, appeared with the Brigade before the Lines of the Seventh. The regiment was drawn up on parade, in a state of vague uncertainty and bewilderment, not knowing what would come of this strange nocturnal assembly. But when they saw the Europeans, the Cavalry and the guns, taking ground in their front and on their flanks, the Native regiments being so placed as to destroy all hope of their aiding their comrades, the mutineers knew that their game was up, and that there would be death in

* Sir Henry Lawrence to Mr. Colvin, Lucknow, May 6, 1857.—*MS. Correspondence.*

May, 1857. Oude.

further resistance. What might then have happened if the course of events had not been determined by an accident, cannot be distinctly declared. The mutinous regiment had obeyed the word of command, and some of the men had expressed contrition; but it happened that, by some mistake, an artilleryman lighted a port-fire. The guns were pointed towards the mutineers, and though Lawrence and his Staff were posted between them and the Artillery, and would probably have been swept away by the first round, the Sepoys of the guilty regiment believed that the battery was about to open upon them. A panic then seized the Seventh. First one man, then another, broke away from his comrades and fled, throwing down his arms as he went in the overwhelming consternation of the moment; and presently great gaps appeared in the Line, and only a remnant of the regiment was left to obey the orders of the English officer. To these men, whilst the Cavalry went in pursuit of the fugitives, Henry Lawrence rode up; and as they broke into exclamations of "Jye Coompanee Behaudur Ko!"—"Victory to the great Lord Company!"—ordered them to lay down their arms, and to strip off their accoutrements. They obeyed without hesitation; and, an hour after midnight, the Brigade had returned to Lucknow, carrying with it all the arms of the Seventh, and escorting, under guards of the same force, the men who had so lately borne them. In the critical state of the other Native regiments, it was not thought wise to divide the Europeans.

Next day Henry Lawrence wrote to the Governor-General, saying, "The *coup* is stated to have had great effect in the city. But people go so far as to tell me that the Forty-eighth last night abused the

Seventh for running away, and said, that if they had stood, the Forty-eighth would not have fired. I don't believe one quarter of these reports." But, although there is always, in seasons of great popular excitement, a vast amount of exaggeration afloat, and Henry Lawrence, therefore, received with caution the stories that were brought to him, he was not one to disregard the signs of the times, and to close his eyes to the dangers that were surrounding him. As time advanced, these signs increased in significance. Some fifty of the ringleaders of the Seventh Irregulars had been seized and confined, and a Court of Inquiry had been assembled to investigate the causes of the outbreak in that regiment. But little or nothing had been elicited. As at Umballah, and other places, the mouths of the Sepoys were sealed. They might contend among themselves, but in their reticence, when the English sought to probe their discontents, they acted as one man. Words were not forthcoming, but there was one form of expression, well known to the Native soldiery in times of trouble, to which they betook themselves, as they had before betaken themselves elsewhere, and thus gave utterance to the strong feelings within them. On the 7th of May, the Lines of the Forty-eighth were burnt down. The fire commenced in the hut of the Soubahdar who had given up the seditious letter addressed by the Seventh Irregulars to the men of his regiment. There could be no doubt that it was the work of an incendiary. On the following day, Lawrence visited the scene of the conflagration, and found the men outwardly civil and respectful in their demeanour, but heavy and downcast at the thought of their loss of property. It was not easy to read the state of feeling which then existed in the Oude Army, so vague and varied was it;

May, 1857.
Oude.

May, 1857. Oude.

but if any man could have rightly discerned it, Henry Lawrence was that man. For he had free intercourse with those who were most likely to be its exponents, and had the gift, so rare among our countrymen, of inspiring confidence in the breasts of the people. After much communing with others and with himself, he came to the conclusion that the strongest feeling that held possession of the Sepoy's mind was a great fear, that this fear had long been growing upon him, and that it had only culminated in his belief in the story of the greased cartridges.*

Of one of these conversations a record has been left in Lawrence's handwriting. It is so significant of the great fear that was then dominating the Army, that I give the passage as it stands. "I had a conversation," he wrote to Lord Canning, on the 9th of May, "with a Jemadar of the Oude Artillery for more than an hour, and was startled by the dogged persistence of the man, a Brahmin of about forty years of age, of excellent character, in the belief that for ten years past Government has been engaged in measures for the forcible, or rather fraudulent conversion of all the Natives. His argument was, that as such was the case, and that as we had made our way through India, won Bhurtpore, Lahore, &c., by fraud, so might it be possible that we mixed bone-dust with the grain sold to the Hindoos. When I told him of our power in Europe, how the Russian war had quadrupled our Army in a year, and in another it could, if necessary, have been interminably increased,

* One of the earliest indications of this alarm appeared at Lucknow, when an Assistant-Surgeon in the Hospital of the Forty-eighth inadvertently put a phial of medicine to his lips to test it. This was seen by the Sepoys, and was believed to be a deliberate scheme to pollute them. Soon afterwards the house of the doctor was burnt to the ground by the Sepoys of his regiment.

and that in the same way, in six months, any required number of Europeans could be brought to India, and that, therefore, we are not at the mercy of the Sepoys, he replied that he knew that we had plenty of men and money, but that Europeans are expensive, and that, therefore, we wished to take Hindoos to sea to conquer the world for us. On my remarking that the Sepoy, though a good soldier on shore is a bad one at sea, by reason of his poor food, 'That is just it,' was the rejoinder. 'You want us all to eat what you like that we may be stronger, and go everywhere.' He often repeated, 'I tell you what everybody says.' But when I replied, 'Fools and traitors may say so, but honest and sensible men cannot think so,' he would not say that he himself did or did not believe, but said, 'I tell you they are like sheep; the leading one tumbles down, and all the rest roll over him.' Such a man is very dangerous. He has his full faculties, is a Brahmin, has served us twenty years, knows our strength and our weakness, and hates us thoroughly. It may be that he is only more honest than his neighbours, but he is not the less dangerous. On one only point did he give us credit. I told him that in the year 1846, I had rescued a hundred and fifty Native children, left by our army in Caubul, and that instead of making them Christians, I had restored them to their relations and friends. 'Yes,' he replied, 'I remember well. I was at Lahore.' On the other hand, he told me of our making Christians of children purchased during famines. I have spoken to many others, of all ranks, during the last fortnight; most give us credit for good intentions; but here is a soldier of our own, selected for promotion over the heads of others, holding opinions that must make him at heart a

May, 1857.

May, 1857. traitor." On the same day he wrote, in a similar strain, to Mr. Colvin, concluding with a significant hint to look well after the safety of the Forts in Upper India.*

If these letters from the Chief Commissioner of Oude had been read when written, they might have suggested grave thoughts of impending danger; but when they reached their destinations, they came only as commentaries upon the past, faint and feeble as seen by the glaring light of terrible realities. The Governor-General and his colleagues in the Supreme Council were discussing the conduct of the mutinous Oude regiment, and the measure of punishment which should be meted out to it. On the 10th of May Lord Canning and Mr. Dorin recorded minutes on the subject. The Governor-General declared for disbandment. Roused to a vigorous expression of opinion by this last manifestation of a growing evil, the senior member of Council wrote—and wrote well —"The sooner this epidemic of mutiny is put a stop to the better. Mild measures won't do it. A severe example is wanted. . . . . . I am convinced that timely severity will be leniency in the long run." On the same day, General Low recorded a minute, in which he expressed an opinion that "probably the main body of the regiment, in refusing to bite the cartridge, did so refuse, not from any feeling of disloyalty or disaffection towards the Government or their officers, but from an unfeigned and sincere dread that the act of biting them would involve a serious injury to their caste." On the 11th, Mr.

* In the letter to Mr. Colvin, Sir Henry Lawrence says that the Jemadar "went over all our anti-Hindoo acts of the last ten years, including Gaol-Messing, the General-Service Oath, &c., and did not conceal not only that he and all others saw no absurdity in the *ground-bones atta* belief, but that he considered we were quite up to such a dodge.'—*MS. Correspondence.*

Grant and Mr. Peacock placed on record their opinions, that it might be better to wait for fuller information before issuing the final orders of Government. On the 12th, the office-boxes were again passing from house to house; but with the papers then circulated, there went one, small in size, scanty in words, but, although perhaps scarcely appreciated at the time, of tremendous significance. "It is to be hoped," wrote Mr. Dorin, "that the news from Meerut (in the telegraphic message from Agra in this box) is not true." But it was true; yet, with all its terrors, only a small part of the truth. May, 1857.

The outbreak at Meerut. May 10, 1857.

The little paper, then, on that 12th of May, travelling from house to house in the office-box, was a telegraphic message from Lieutenant-Governor Colvin, announcing to Lord Canning that the great military station of Meerut was in a blaze, that the Cavalry had risen in a body, and that every European they had met had been slain by the insurgents. There was something terribly significant in the very form of this message. The Government at Agra had received no official tidings of the events that had occurred at Meerut. But a lady at the former place, who had been about to pay a visit to her friends at Meerut, had received a message from her niece, who was sister of the postmaster there, warning her not to attempt the journey, as the Cavalry had risen.*

* The following were the words of the message: "*May* 11, 1857.—Last night, at nine o'clock, a telegraph message was received here by a lady from her niece, sister of the postmaster at Meerut, to the following effect: 'The Cavalry have risen, setting fire to their own houses and several officers' houses, besides having killed and wounded all European officers and soldiers they could find near the Lines. If aunt intends starting to-morrow evening, please detain her from doing so, as the van has been prevented from leaving the station.' No later message has been received, and the communication by telegram has been interrupted; how, not known. Any intelligence which may reach will be sent on immediately."—*Published Correspondence. Parliamentary Papers.*

May, 1857. This was the last message despatched. Before the authorities could send intelligence of what had happened, the telegraph-wires were cut by the insurgents.

The week of telegrams.

The news, therefore, which now reached Agra, and was thence communicated to Calcutta, was of a vague, fragmentary character. Scattered facts welled up from uncertain sources, and were passed on from one station to another, suggestive rather than expressive, always indicating something more terrible in the background than the truth actually revealed. Not till some time afterwards was the whole truth apparent to the Governor-General, and therefore not now do I fill up the outlines of the story. The week that followed the 12th of May was a week of telegrams. The electric wires were continually flashing pregnant messages from North to South, and from South to North. That the Sepoys at Meerut had risen, was certain from the first. Then news came that they held some part of the road between Meerut and Delhi. Then, little by little, it transpired that the Meerut mutineers had made their way in a body to the Imperial City, and that the Delhi regiments had fraternised with them. A message from Agra, despatched on the 14th, stated, on the authority of a letter from the King of Delhi, that the town and fort and his own person were in possession of the insurgents; and it was added that Fraser, the Commissioner, and many other English gentlemen and ladies, had been murdered. Then, at last, it became apparent that the King himself had cast in his lot with the insurgents, that the rebel standard had been hoisted in the palace of the Mogul, that Englishmen and Englishwomen had been ruthlessly massacred in the streets of the city, and that the mutiny of a few regiments, by thus concentring at Delhi, was beginning to simulate a national rebellion. May, 1857

Never since, a century before, the foundation of our great Indian Empire had been laid by the conquest of Bengal, had such tidings as these been brought to the council-chamber of the English ruler. The little cloud no bigger than a man's hand, which had risen in the first month of the new year, and had been growing in its density and darkness until it had overshadowed the heavens, was now discharging its tempestuous terrors upon us. There was little before the eyes of Lord Canning but the one naked fact of the junction of the Meerut and Delhi troops, and the proclamation of the restored empire of the Mogul. With a feeling of wondering anxiety he awaited, all through that terrible week in May, the details which seemed as though they would never come, and the explanations of all that seemed so inexplicable to him. Most of all, he marvelled what our people had been doing, or not doing in this conjuncture, that such a post as Delhi, scarcely equalled in military, wholly unequalled in political importance, should thus in an hour have been wrested from their grasp. It seemed incredible that with a regiment of British Cavalry at Meerut, and the largest body of Artillery in the country gathered there at its head-quarters, such a catastrophe as this should have occurred. Was there no one, he asked, to do with the Carabineers and the Horse Artillery what Gillespie, half a century before had done, with his Dragoons and galloper-guns? But if such were the result in places where our English officers had Cavalry and Artillery to aid them, how would it fare with them at stations where no such help was to be had? There was no hope now that the conflagration would not spread from

May, 1857. cantonment to cantonment; no hope now that the whole country would not soon be in a blaze.

Measures of Lord Canning.

So Canning arose, and with his still, calm face, confronted the dire calamity. A braver heart than his never beat in a human breast. Happy was it for the nation that in him, to whom its honour was confided in that conjuncture, there was a resolute manhood of the finest, most enduring temper. Many thoughts pressed upon him, but dominant over all was a strong sense of the paramount duty of maintaining before all men a serene aspect and a confident demeanour. There was great work to be done, nothing less than the salvation of an empire; and with a solemn sense of his responsibility, he girded himself up for the conflict, knowing in how great a measure the deliverance of his countrymen depended, under God's good providence, upon their faith in his constancy and courage. He saw clearly that there was a tremendous danger, and he knew that the resources immediately at his command were wholly insufficient to enable him to cope with it; but even those who were nearest to his person never saw him quail for a moment, as he calculated the means and appliances of defence that could at once be brought into action, and those which might be summoned from a distance.

It was no time for lamentation; else he might have lamented that India, by a series of adverse circumstances, had been so stripped of European troops that now the whole country, with the exception of the frontier province of the Punjab, was lying naked and defenceless, without means of raising any barriers of resistance against the flood of rebellion that was pouring over Hindostan. He had lifted up his voice against the system, which placed it in the power of England, by giving to India either too much or too little of its manhood, to sacrifice the interests of the dependency.* He had resisted, only a little time before, an attempt to carry off some of the few English regiments at his disposal, to take a part in certain military operations against the Government of China, with which India had no concern. It had cost him much to send so many regiments to Persia; but that was a call to which he had been bound to respond, and happily now the emergency was past. All that he had said by way of warning had been more than verified by the event; but it was a time for looking forward, not for looking back, so he began to reckon up his available succours, and forthwith to summon them to the capital. May, 1857.

In the midst of all his tribulation there were some sources of unspeakable comfort. Whilst the clouds were thickening above him, before the great outburst, he had learnt with joy and gratitude that the war with Persia had been brought to a close. Outram had done his work rapidly and well. I cannot now pause to speak of his successes. What he did on the shores of the Persian Gulf must be narrated in another place. It is enough to say that Persia, alarmed by our demonstrations on the coast, and anticipating an advance into the interior of the country, thought that negotiation was better than war, acceded to our demands, and concluded, at Paris, a treaty with the British Government. The expedition which had gone

* "The interests of India," he wrote on April 22nd, "do not always make themselves heard in England, when other important matters are uppermost; and I am opposed to putting into the hands of the Government at home an increased power to diminish our main strength here for the purpose of meeting exigencies elsewhere. Such a diminution was made in 1854 by withholding two regiments which have not yet been given, although six regiments have been sent out of India to Persia."—*MS. Correspondence of Lord Canning.*

May, 1857. forth from Bombay, was, therefore, returning to that Presidency; and a word from the Governor-General would summon it, as fast as steam could bring it, to his aid. This was his first thought, when the seizure of Delhi confirmed all his worst apprehensions of the perilous want of European troops. Then, from these Persian succours, he turned with joy and gratitude not less profound, to the thought that English troops were speeding to China; that the arrogance and insolence of the Chinese Government having provoked our chastisement, an expedition had been fitted out under the conduct of a civil and a military chief, and was then, perhaps, at the very point of its journey at which it might most readily be wrested from its original purpose, and diverted into another and more necessitous channel. Rightly taking the measure of the two exigencies, and never doubting for a moment what the great interests of the nation demanded in that conjuncture, he presently determined to call these troops to his aid. The chastisement of China could wait; the salvation of India could not;* and so he resolved, even at the risk of frustrating the cherished designs of the Government in England, to call upon Elgin and Ashburnham to suspend their operations, and to send him the present help that he so much needed. It

* I did not think, when I wrote these words, that I had done more than express the natural feeling in Lord Canning's breast at that time; but I have since found that he gave utterance almost to the very words: "I have sent an officer," he wrote to the Commander-in-Chief, "to Galle by the mail to meet Ashburnham, and I hope Elgin, with an earnest request for the first use of the regiments bound to China, if they can be stopped at Singapore. Yeh may wait; but Bengal, with its stretch of seven hundred and fifty miles from Barrackpore to Agra, guarded by nothing but the 10th Queen's, cannot wait, if the flame should spread. And who shall say that it will not? No precaution against such a contingency can be too great."—*MS. Correspondence of Lord Canning.*

was a great responsibility, but he took it without a moment's hesitation on himself; and he thanked God, from the very depths of his heart, that by a providential dispensation this succour, in the very crisis of his necessities, had been placed within his reach. May, 1857

There were thus, in the peculiar circumstances of the moment, some sources of consolation, some good promise of relief over and above that which was to be sought in the normal condition of the empire under his charge. But it would take time to gather up the strength of these Persian and Chinese expeditions, and there were some available European troops more nearly at hand. It was another happy accident that at this time the Eighty-fourth Regiment, which had been summoned from Pegu in March, was still in the neighbourhood of Calcutta. The long-delayed disbandment of the guilty companies of the Thirty-fourth had not been carried into effect before the 6th of May; and the regiment had been detained until after the execution of the sentence. It seemed then that there was no further necessity for its presence in Bengal, but the arrangements for its return to Pegu were still incomplete, when the disastrous tidings from Upper India came to dissipate all thought of its departure. From the quarter whence it had come another English regiment might be drawn. The Thirty-fifth was stationed partly at Rangoon, partly at Moulmein; and a steamer was despatched to gather up the detachments and to bring them with all speed to Calcutta. At the same time, the telegraph carried to Madras a requisition to hold the Forty-third Foot and the Madras Fusiliers ready for immediate embarkation; and a trusted officer was sent on board the mail-steamer to Ceylon, with

May, 1857. an urgent request to the Governor to send him all the European troops he could spare.

Whilst thus every effort was strained to bring European troops from the southern and eastern coasts, the Governor-General was intent also on the organisation of measures for the concentration of the strength already at his disposal upon the points most exposed to danger. With this object, every available river-steamer was taken up for the conveyance of troops to the Upper Provinces, and the quicker but more limited means of locomotion afforded by wheeled carriages was resorted to for the conveyance of small detachments into the interior. But it was not, in the crisis of this first peril, from the South, but from the North, that the stream of conquest was to be poured down upon the great centre of rebellion. It was not to be doubted that General Anson, whom the news of the rising at Meerut and the seizure of Delhi must have reached at Simlah as soon as it reached Lord Canning at Calcutta, was doing all that could be done to despatch troops to the seat of the revolt. The telegraph, therefore, expressed only the confidence of Government that the Commander-in-Chief was bringing down to the plains the European regiments on the hills. But the main reliance of the Governor-General in this extremity was upon the military resources of the Punjab. Though all the rest of the empire was denuded of European troops, there was no lack of this material strength in the great frontier province conquered from the Sikhs. Moreover, it was believed that the Sikhs themselves would be eager to follow their English commanders to the siege and pillage of the renowned city of the Moguls. So, whilst a message went to Kurrachee, in Scinde, directing the Commissioner to send an English regiment to the Punjab to replace any that it might be found necessary to despatch from that province to the Lower Provinces, another went to Mr. Colvin, at Agra, saying, "Send word as quickly as possible to Sir John Lawrence that he is to send down such of the Punjab regiments and European regiments as he can safely spare. Every exertion must be made to regain Delhi. Every hour is of importance. General Hewitt has been ordered to press this on the Commander-in-Chief. If you find it necessary, you may apply, in the Governor-General's name, to the Rajah of Pateeala and the Rajah of Jheend for troops." And he added, with that union of kindliness and sagacity which made him at all times liberal of his encouragement to his Lieutenants, "I thank you sincerely for what you have so admirably done, and for your stout heart."* The praise, too, was well deserved. Colvin, at that time, had done all that could be done to help others at a distance, and to maintain the confidence of those around him, and he had strenuously exerted himself to forward to the Governor-General, by telegraph and by letter, all the tidings that had made their way to Agra.† "I have fairly taken upon myself," he wrote to Lord Canning on the 15th of May, "the position of Commander-in-Chief here. The arrangements are now on the point of completion, and our position may be regarded as safe. There has been a thorough co-operation and the most excellent May, 1857.

* In a letter to Mr. Vernon Smith of about the same date, Lord Canning says: "South of Delhi, Colvin at Agra is engaged in keeping the roads quiet, collecting troops from Gwalior (Scindiah has come forward loyally), and encouraging his own native garrison to fidelity. He is confident of keeping them straight, and he deserves to succeed. His courage and judgment are beyond praise."—*MS. Correspondence of Lord Canning.*

† The importance of this service, at a time when communication both by Post and Telegraph was so greatly interrupted, can hardly be over-estimated. The Commander-in-Chief's letters of the 14th and 16th of May did not reach Calcutta before the 7th of June.

May, 1857. spirit amongst us. Scindiah and Bhurtpore will be heartily with us against the new dynasty of the House of Timour. I shall rouse the Rajpoot States to arrest the flight of the mutineers westward, when they are driven out of Delhi. The horrible murders, you will see, have been chiefly by Mahomedan troopers of the Third Cavalry. There must be a fit and fearful expiation for such atrocities."

But for this fit and fearful expiation Lord Canning knew too well that the time had not yet come. The struggle now was for bare life. For this he had done all that could be done, with the scanty means at his own disposal. "The two points to which I am straining," he wrote to the Indian Minister at home, "are the hastening of the expulsion of the rebels from Delhi, and the collection of Europeans here to be pushed up the country." But not a day was to be lost in summoning that ulterior aid, by which not only was the safety of the empire to be secured, but the honour of the nation vindicated by the infliction of just retribution upon our enemies. The succours from Bombay he was sure to obtain; and there was something exhilarating in the thought, at a time when India had need of all her heroes, that Outram would come with them. How different would it have been if those regiments had been still engaged in the Persian Gulf! But he could not calculate with the same amount of certainty upon the succours from the Eastern seas; he could not be certain that Lord Elgin would respond to his appeal. All that he could do was to throw the whole earnestness of his nature into that appeal, and to take upon himself the full responsibility of the diversion. So he wrote officially, as the Governor-General of India, to Lord Elgin, and he wrote privately to him as an

Arrest of the China expedition.

old companion and friend. In the public letter, after setting forth in emphatic language the dangers by which our empire in India was surrounded, he continued: "I place the matter briefly before your Lordship; but I hope clearly enough to enable you to come to a ready decision. I will add, that I am anxious to bear the whole responsibility of all the consequences of turning aside the troops from China to India. But I beg your Lordship to believe that, in saying this, I am not influenced by any thought that whatever may be the course for which your Lordship's wise judgment shall decide, you will need any help from me in vindicating it to her Majesty's Government." May, 1857.

More earnest and emphatic still was his private letter; not a word of it should be omitted: "My dear Elgin,—I wish I could give you a more cheerful and acceptable greeting than you will find in the letter by which this is accompanied. As it is, you will not bless me for it, but the case which I have before me here is clear and strong. Our hold of Bengal and the Upper Provinces depends upon the turn of a word—a look. An indiscreet act or irritating phrase from a foolish commanding officer at the head of a mutinous or disaffected company, may, whilst the present condition of things at Delhi lasts, lead to a general rising of the Native troops in the Lower Provinces, where we have no European strength, and where an army in rebellion would have everything its own way for weeks and months to come. We have seen within the last few days what that way would be. I cannot shut my eyes to the danger, or to the urgent necessity under which I lie, to collect every European that can carry arms and aid to the Government of India in the event of such May 19, 1857.

May, 1857. a crisis. I do not want aid to put down the Meerut and Delhi rebels; that will be done easily, as soon as the European troops can converge upon Delhi, but not sooner. Meanwhile, every hour of delay—unavoidable delay—is an encouragement to the disaffected troops in other parts; and if any one of the unwatched regiments on this side of Agra should take heart and give the word, there is not a fort, or cantonment, or station in the plains of the Ganges that would not be in their hands in a fortnight. It would be exactly the same in Oude. No help that you could give me would make us safe against this, because it cannot arrive in time. The critical moments are now, and for the next ten or twelve days to come. If we pass through them without a spread of the outbreak, I believe all will go well. If we do not, the consequences will be so frightful, that any neglect to obtain any possible accession of strength whereby to shorten the duration of the reign of terror which will ensue, would be a crime. If you send me troops, they shall not be kept one hour longer than is absolutely needed. If you come with them yourself, you shall be most heartily welcome."

MS. Correspondence.

With this letter went another to General Ashburnham, who commanded the troops of the China expedition; and the steamer, which carried the bearer of these important missives to Galle, bore also letters from the Governor-General to the Chairman of the Court of Directors and the President of the Board of Control, calling upon them immediately to send out reinforcements from England. "Now let me beg your attention and support," he wrote to Mr. Mangles, "to a proposal which goes to you by the mail for the immediate raising of three European regiments for Bengal. No sane man will doubt that much of increase to our European force is wanted, and that the want should be supplied with as little delay as possible is obvious from the present exposure of our weak points. I do not ask for an augmentation to the established number of Queen's troops, because for permanent purposes I much prefer an addition to the Company's Army; and for the exigencies of the moment no reinforcement, except that of the China regiments, would avail. But I do beg that you will move the Government to make up the complement of Queen's troops, irrespectively of those which now or hereafter may come to us from China. Do not let the supply of the missing regiments depend upon the turn of affairs in China, but let the gap be filled up at once."* In the same strain he wrote to Mr. Vernon Smith, looking rather to any aid that might be sent him from England, as a means of preventing the recurrence of like disasters in the future, than of combating those which had already arisen. May, 1857

Whilst the first efforts of the Governor-General were thus directed towards the pressing duty of extinguishing, by sheer animal strength, the fires that had been kindled in Upper India, he was endeavouring also to prevent by moral means the flames from spreading to parts of the country not yet in a blaze. It was plain that a great fear, born of a terrible misapprehension, was driving the soldiery to madness. Might not something, then, be done—might not some authoritative declaration be put forth by Government, solemn and irresistible in its denials of the imputed treachery, to pacify men's minds, and to cast out from them the foul suspicions which were turning loyal soldiers into rebels and murderers? It Moral force appeals.

* Lord Canning to Mr. Mangles, May 19, 1857.—*MS. Correspondence.*

May, 1857. was true that they had been told this before by the Governor-General, by the Commander-in-Chief, by Generals of Division, and Regimental Commandants; but these appeals had been of local character and limited influence, and it was thought that something might yet be done by a general Proclamation addressed to the whole Army, and distributed throughout the country. It was not doubted, that whatsoever might have been the external agencies employed to keep alive this perilous excitement, there was at the bottom of it, in the breasts of the Sepoys, a deeply-rooted fear for the sanctity of their religion and the purity of their caste. If they could once be persuaded to believe that the British Government had never meditated any injury or offence to the religious or social prejudices of the people, there might be a return to quietude and to reason. It was wise, at least, to make one more trial. So a Proclamation was issued, setting forth that the Governor-General knew that endeavours had been made to persuade Hindoos and Mussulmans, both soldiers and civil subjects, that their religion was openly as well as secretly threatened by acts of the Government, who were believed to be seeking by various ways to entrap them into loss of caste for purposes of their own; but that they had never yet deceived their subjects, and they now, therefore, called upon all men to refuse their belief to the seditious lies of designing traitors, who were leading good men to their ruin. Translated into the vernacular, this Proclamation was sent to the military authorities to be distributed among the soldiery in all parts of the country, whilst the words of it were telegraphed to the Lieutenant-Governor at Agra, with emphatic instructions to "disseminate it in every town, village, bazaar, and serai." "It is for the people as well as for the troops." It was yet hoped that it might bear the good fruit of a return to order and tranquillity.* May, 1857.

At the same time, it appeared to the Governor-General to be in the highest degree important to arm the military authorities with new powers both for the prompt reward of good and loyal soldiers, and the prompt punishment of mutineers. The first might be done by a simple order of the Government. The latter required the interposition of the Legislature. So an act was passed to facilitate the trial and punish- May 16. ment of offences against the articles of war for the Native Army, by which commanding officers of Divisions, Brigades, and Stations, were authorised to assemble general and other Courts-martial, and to proceed to carry sentence into effect without reference to Head-Quarters. In such an emergency as had then arisen, Centralisation could not stand its ground. So whilst increased power was thus given to commanding officers to overawe rebellion, increased power to encourage loyalty and good conduct was delegated to them and to certain high civil and political functionaries. They were empowered to promote Native soldiers and non-commissioned officers on the scene of their good deeds, and to confer upon

* It has been often said that this Proclamation, which will be found in the Appendix, ought to have been issued at an earlier period. Colonel Birch advised the Governor-General, when the excited state of the Native soldiery first became apparent, to issue a proclamation of this kind, and Lord Canning afterwards frankly expressed his regret that he had not taken the advice of his military secretary. On turning back to page 243, the reader will perceive that a similar delay in issuing a sedative proclamation occurred in 1806, after the mutiny in the Madras Army. It is, however, very doubtful whether such manifestoes have any effect upon the Native mind, when once any popular belief of the intentions of Government has taken fast hold of it. I have already observed, that those who entertain a conviction that the Government have formed a deliberate design to trick the people out of their religion, are not likely to find any difficulty in believing that the issue of a lying proclamation is a part of the plot.

May, 1857. them the "Order of Merit,"* "in order that the reward for eminent gallantry, loyalty, and good conduct might be prompt, and might be conferred on the soldier in the sight of his comrades." But no proclamations and general orders—nothing that the Legislature could decree or the Executive Government publish—no words that men could utter, in that extremity, could avail to arrest the fury of the storm that was bursting over their head. It was too late for words, for none would hear. It was left to the English only to strike.

General Order, May 19.

Thus Canning did all that could be done, and waited for the issue—waited, fearfully and hopefully, for tidings of new disasters in one direction, and of coming succours from another. As he thus waited and watched, and pondered new details of the great rising, which every day added something to the clearness and completeness of the story, there were times when he felt in his inmost heart that there were no better resources than a few brave hearts and a few strong heads upon whose courage and coolness he could rely. It must be said, sorrowfully, and I would fain not say it, but History admits of no such reservations, that Lord Canning felt bitterly that, with some few honourable exceptions, the English officers at the Presidency were not giving him the moral support which, in such a crisis, would have been so grateful and refreshing to him, and for which truly he had a right to look. It is impossible to describe his mortification. Where he had hoped to see strength he saw only weakness. Men whom he thought to see sustaining and encouraging others by

* Authority in this latter respect was confined to the Lieutenant-Governor of Bengal and the North-Western Provinces, and to the Chief Commissioners in Oude and the Punjab.

their own resolute bearing and their cheerfulness of speech, went about from place to place infecting their friends with their own despondency, and chilling the hearts which they should have warmed by their example. Such a spectacle as this was even more painful than the tidings of disaster and death which came huddling in from all parts of the country. No one knew better, and no one more freely acknowledged that the men of whom he complained were "brave enough with swords by their sides." They would have faced death for their country's good with the courage of heroes and the constancy of martyrs; but strong as they would have been in deeds, they were weak in words, and they went about as prophets of evil, giving free utterance to all their gloomiest anticipations, and thus spreading through all the strata of English society at the capital the alarm which a more confident demeanour in the upper places might have arrested. And so strong was Lord Canning's sense of the evil that had arisen, and that might arise from this want of reserve, that he wrote specially to the authorities in England to receive with caution the stories that were likely to be sent home in the private letters which the mail was about to carry from Calcutta. May, 1857.

But the shame with which he beheld the failure of some of his countrymen at Calcutta, made him turn with the greater pride and the greater confidence towards those who were nobly seconding his efforts from a distance. The Governors of Madras and of Bombay, Harris and Elphinstone, had responded to his appeals, and without any selfish thoughts of their own wants, any heed of dangerous contingencies at home, were sending him the succours he so much needed; and he was profoundly grateful for their Harris and Elphinstone.

May, 1857. aid. The promptitude with which they responded to the call for help was something almost marvellous. The electric telegraph might fail us in some parts, but in others it did its work well. On the 18th of May, Canning knew that the Madras Fusiliers were already embarking, and had thanked Harris by telegraph for his "great expedition." On the 22nd he learnt that the first instalment of the troops from Persia had reached Bombay, and that a steamer had already started for Calcutta with a wing of the Sixty-fourth Queen's. The fire-ship was doing its work as well as the lightning-post.

The Lawrences. But although there was to the Governor-General great consolation in the thought that he would lack no material or moral support that Harris and Elphinstone could give him, it was, in a conjuncture so imminent, to the individual characters of men actually confronting the dangers which threatened the empire, that he looked with the most eager anxiety. And there were no points to which he turned his eyes with a keener interest than to those two great provinces, the history of the annexation of which I have written in the early part of this book, the great provinces of the Punjab and of Oude. It was from Oude that so large a part of the Bengal Army had been drawn; it was in Oude, the last of our acquisitions, that the animosities and resentments born of the great revolution we had accomplished were festering most freshly; it was in Oude that we had to contend with the reviving energies of a dynasty scarcely yet extinct, and an aristocracy in the first throes of its humiliation. All this Lord Canning distinctly saw. It was in the Punjab that all external dangers were to be encountered; it was from the Punjab that Delhi was to be recovered. There was consolation in the thought that only a few months before the good offices of Dost Mahomed had been purchased in the manner most likely to secure his neutrality. But death might, any day, remove the old Ameer from the scene; there would, in such a case, be internal convulsions, out of which would probably arise an invasion of our frontier by one contending faction or another: and, therefore, much as troops were needed below, a still greater danger might be incurred by weakening the force on the frontier. In other parts of the country there might be merely a military mutiny; but in Oude and the Punjab the Government was threatened with the horrors of a popular rebellion, and the embarrassments of a foreign war. May, 1857

But if there were much trouble and anxiety in these thoughts, they had their attendant consolations. Let what might happen in Oude and the Punjab, the Lawrences were there. The Governor-General had abundant faith in them both; faith in their courage, their constancy, their capacity for command; but, most of all, he trusted them because they coveted responsibility. It is only from an innate sense of strength that this desire proceeds; only in obedience to the unerring voice of Nature that strong men press forward to grasp what weak men shrink from possessing. Knowing this, when, on the 16th of May, Henry Lawrence telegraphed to the Governor-General, "Give me plenary military power in Oude; I will not use it unnecessarily," not a moment was lost in flashing back the encouraging answer, "You have full military powers. The Governor-General will support you in everything that you think necessary."

With John Lawrence it was less easy to commu-

May, 1857. nicate. A short time before the outbreak of the mutiny, the Chief Commissioner of the Punjab, whose health had been sorely tried by incessant work, had proposed to the Governor-General to occupy a part of the approaching hot weather in a tour through Cashmere, but Lord Canning, on political grounds, had discouraged the proposal; for Gholab Singh lay dying, and it was believed that such a visit to the dominions of the Maharajah would be associated in men's minds with some ulterior project of their annexation. John Lawrence, therefore, had happily not gone to Cashmere. When the news of the outbreak at Meerut reached the Punjab he was, on his way to the Murree Hills, at Rawul-Pindee; and thence, having first telegraphed to them both, he wrote, on the 13th of May, to the Governor-General and the Commander-in-Chief. Nine days afterwards Lord Canning received the missive which had been addressed to him, together with a copy of the Commissioner's earnest appeal to Anson to be up and doing. In the former, Lawrence urged upon the Governor-General the expediency of raising for immediate service a large body of Sikh Irregulars. "Our European force in India," he wrote,, "is so small, that it may gradually be worn down and destroyed. It is of the highest importance, therefore, that we should increase our Irregular troops. . . . In the event of an emergency, I should like to have power to raise as far as one thousand Horse; I will not do this unless absolutely necessary." Five days before this letter had reached Calcutta, Lord Canning had telegraphed his consent to the proposal, adding, "You will be supported in every measure that you think necessary for safety." He was unstinting in his expressions of confidence to those who deserved it.

Those were days when the best men stood upon the least ceremony, and if they had a suggestion to offer to Government, offered it with the full assurance that they were doing their duty, and would not be charged with presumption. So General Hearsey, when he learnt the news that had come from Meerut and Delhi, had written to the Military Secretary to urge the Government to call for troops from Madras and Bombay and the Persian Gulf, and to arrest the China expedition. So Henry Lawrence had telegraphed to the Governor-General to get every available European "from China, Ceylon, and elsewhere, also all the Goorkhas from the Hills." So Patrick Grant, the Commander-in-Chief at Madras, had telegraphed to him to send a swift steamer at once to intercept the China expedition;* and John Lawrence had sent a message setting forth these and May, 1857.

* There has been some discussion, I believe, respecting the quarter whence the suggestion to intercept the China troops first emanated. I can see no reason to think that Lord Canning required any prompting. But if the question is to be solved by reference to a priority of recorded date, it is, firstly, to General Hearsey, and secondly to Sir Henry Lawrence, that the merit is to be assigned. On the 15th of May, General Hearsey wrote to Colonel Birch, saying: "Send steamers to meet and bring the European troops now on their way to China (Hong-Kong) to Calcutta. Do not delay doing this." On the 16th of May, Henry Lawrence telegraphed to Lord Canning: "Get every European you can from China, Ceylon, and elsewhere." On the 17th, Sir Patrick Grant sent his message, more detailed and emphatic: "I most earnestly recommend the despatch to Singapore of the swiftest steamer obtainable, with an earnest request to Lord Elgin to forward on to you the whole of the troops intended for China. Whether China is coerced now, or months hence, is of no moment. The moral effect of such a force being brought to the spot would be incalculable, and be regarded as something miraculous and supernatural." At what precise moment Lord Canning first determined to arrest the China expedition, is not apparent on the face of the records; but on the 18th he telegraphed to Agra: "I hope to catch the regiments on their way to China." During the week immediately following the outbreak at Meerut, Lord Canning scarcely resorted to the post-office at all. The only letter that I can find is one to General Anson, dated the 15th, in which he does not mention the intended arrest of the China troops; but at that time he had received no detailed account of events at Meerut and Delhi, and scarcely knew the extent of the evil with which he had to contend.

May, 1857 other means of meeting the crisis. For all these suggestions Lord Canning was grateful; but it was with much satisfaction, perhaps with some pride, that when the detailed plans of the Chief Commissioner of the Punjab were laid before him, he sent back a message, through the Lieutenant-Governor of Agra, saying, "Every precaution which your message suggests has been taken long ago."

Then, every effort made, and every precaution taken to save alike the Christian people and the great empire committed to his care, there was an interval of reflection; and, with a feeling of solemn wonder, Canning dwelt upon the causes of all this tremendous excitement, and asked himself whether it could be only a military mutiny that he was combating. It did not seem as though the origin of such a commotion were to be found only in the unaided instincts of the soldiery. It might be that the activities then discernible were purely military activities, but it did not follow that external influences had not been at work to produce the state of mind that was developing such terrible results. There were even then some dawning apprehensions that, with the best possible intentions, grave mistakes might have been committed in past years, and that the tree of benignant error was now bearing bitter fruit. He thought over all that had been done by his great predecessor; the countries that had been annexed to the British Empire, the powerful interests that had suffered so grievously by our domination, the manifold encroachments, material and moral, of English muscle and English mind. Not at first did he perceive all that was afterwards made clear to him, for at the time of which I am now writing there were many breaks in the great chain of postal and telegraphic communication, and it was not easy to form a right conception of the actual situation of affairs in the Upper Provinces. But he soon ceased to speak of the mutiny, and called it a "rebellion"—a "revolt." Early in the year, he had felt disposed to attach some importance to the idea of political causes, but, as he wrote on more than one occasion, "not much."* Now his uncertainty upon this point began to disappear, and he wrote to the Indian Minister at home that he had not a doubt that the rebellion had been fomented "by Brahmins on religious pretences, and by others for political motives."† He saw, indeed, that for some years preceding the outbreak the English in India, moved by the strong faith that was in them, had striven, with a somewhat intemperate zeal, to assimilate all things to their own modes of thought, and that the Old Man had risen against the New, and resented his ceaseless innovations. To this pass had the self-assertions of the national character brought us. The Indian Empire was in flames. But, with a proud and noble confidence, Canning felt that this great national character which had raised the conflagration would, by God's blessing, ere long trample it out. Even those whose despondency had so pained him would, he knew, when called upon to act, belie the weakness of their words by the bravery of their deeds. Looking into the future, he saw the fire spreading; he saw the heathen raging furiously against him, and a great army, trained in our own May, 1857.

* See note, *ante*, page 550.

† Writing also to the Chairman of the Court of Directors (Mr. Ross Mangles), Lord Canning said: "I have learnt unmistakably that the apprehension of some attempt upon Caste is growing stronger, or at least is more sedulously spread. Mr. Colvin has found the same; and a proclamation, which goes to you herewith, has been issued with a view of arresting the evil. But political animosity goes for something among the causes, though it is not, in my opinion, a chief one."—May 19, 1857.—*MS. Correspondence.*

May, 1857. schools of warfare, turning against us the lessons we had taught them, stimulated by the Priesthood, encouraged, perhaps aided, by the nobles of the land, and with all the resources of the country at their command; but seeing this, he saw also something beyond, grand in the distance; he saw the manhood of England going out to meet it.

APPENDIX.

CIVIL PRIVILEGES OF THE SEPOYS

[THE following is the memorandum to which reference is made at page 256 :]

"By the regulations in force for the administration of Civil Justice, the Courts were prohibited from corresponding by letter with parties in suits before them, or from receiving pleadings or other applications in such cases except from the parties or their authorised representatives. All causes were required to be heard in the order in which they stood on the file of the Court, and the laws which required the use of stamped paper in judicial proceedings were very strict, and for a length of time of universal application.

"In all these respects a great change was made in the year 1816 in favour of the Bengal Sepoy.

"The regulation passed in that year made no change in respect of claims originating in loans granted by a Native officer or Sepoy, or in pecuniary transactions of a commercial nature; but in all other respects the position of the Native soldier, as a party to a suit in a Court of Civil Justice, was materially improved.

"If a Native soldier was desirous of instituting a suit in any Court, he had only to inform his commanding officer of his intention, and to execute a deed authorising any member of his family to appear and act for him. This document was to be sent by post by the commanding officer to the Judge of the Court having jurisdiction in the matter, who was then required to take the necessary steps for giving information to the party appointed to act for the applicant, and to afford every facility for carrying on the cause. In like manner, if the Sepoy was the defendant in a case, the usual notice was to be served upon him through his commanding officer, and similar facilities were to be afforded to him in defending as in prosecuting a case. If the Sepoy himself obtained furlough for the purpose of instituting or defending a suit, he carried with him a letter from his commanding officer to the Judge, who was then required to hear the case without reference to its order on the file, and to pass judgment in it with as little delay as possible.

"No stamps were to be required, and if judgment went against the Sepoy, and any land or rent property belonging to him was attached in execution of the judgment, the Court was required to postpone the sale of it for such period as might appear reasonable for the purpose of affording the Native soldier an opportunity of discharging the amount adjudged against him.

"In like manner, if any estate belonging to a Native soldier became liable to sale for the recovery of an arrear of revenue, information of the same was to be given to him through his commanding officer, and every indulgence was to be shown to him before the last step of selling the estate was taken.

"By the same regulation, the sub-treasurer at the Presidency, the collectors of land revenue, and the several paymasters in the Presidency of Fort William, including the paymasters serving beyond the territories of the East India Company, were authorised to grant bills payable at sight without deduction of any kind, and at the usual rate of exchange, on any other treasury, for any sums which might be paid into their respective treasuries on account of Native officers or soldiers, who might be desirous of remitting money from one part of the country to another."—*MS. Memorandum.*

CASTE AND RACE IN THE SEPOY ARMY.

[The following statements, referred to at page 330, are taken from the Appendix to the Report of the Royal Commission on the organisation of the Indian Army. It will be observed that the Bengal reports relate only to the remnant of the Sepoy Army after the mutiny :]

EXTRACTS from the Official Return showing the Number, Caste, and Country of the Native Officers and Soldiers of each Regiment, Regular and Irregular, of each Presidency, confined to Regiments borne on the Returns of each Army respectively; so far as can be stated from the Records in this House.—East India House, Sept. 1858.

BENGAL.

NATIVE INFANTRY, 7 Regiments, viz.: 21st, 31st, 47th, 65th, 66th, 70th, and 73rd.

NATIVE OFFICERS.		NON-COMMISSIONED, RANK AND FILE.	
Caste.		*Caste.*	
Mahomedans	25	Mahomedans	1,170
Brahmins	52	Brahmins	1,878
Rajpoots	39	Rajpoots	2,637
Hindus of inferior description	23	Hindus of Inferior description	2,057
		Sikhs and Punjaubees	54
	139		7,796

IRREGULAR AND LOCAL INFANTRY, 12 Regiments, viz.: Regiment of Khelat-i-Ghilzie, Regiment of Ferozepore, Regiment of Loodianah, Simoor Battalion, Kemaon Battalion, Nusseree Battalion, Hill Rangers, Assam Light Infantry Battalion, Mhairwarrah Battalion, Sylhet Light Infantry Battalion, Arracan Battalion, and Shekhawattee Battalion.

NATIVE OFFICERS.		NON-COMMISSIONED, RANK AND FILE.	
Caste.		*Caste.*	
Mahomedans	38	Mahomedans	1,185
Brahmins	23	Brahmins	849
Rajpoots	59	Rajpoots	2,711
Hindus of inferior description	43	Hindus of inferior description	2,247
Sikhs	17	Sikhs	1,309
Hill men	16	Hill men	1,112
Mughs	6	Mughs	705
Burmese	1	Burmese	6
Munniporees	1	Munniporees	167
		Jhats	48
	204		10,339

MADRAS.

NATIVE CAVALRY, 7 Regiments.

NATIVE OFFICERS.

Caste.	
Mahomedans	68
Mahrattas	6
Rajpoots	3
Indo-Britons	0
	77

Country.	
Central Carnatic, Madras, Vellore, &c.	64
Southern Carnatic, Trichinopoly	7
Mysore	3
Tanjore, Madura, and Tinnevelly	1
Ceded districts	2
	77

NON-COMMISSIONED RANK AND FILE.

Caste.	
Christians	32
Mahomedans	1,956
Rajpoots	90
Mahrattas	300
Other castes	2
Indo-Britons	159
	2,539

Country.	
Hindoostan	22
Northern Circars	67
Central Carnatic, Madras, Vellore, &c.	1,841
Southern Carnatic, Trichinopoly	205
Baramahal	48
Ceded districts	54
Mysore	212
Tanjore, Madura, and Tinnevelly	90
	2,539

NATIVE INFANTRY, 52 Regiments.

NATIVE OFFICERS.

Caste.	
Christians	4
Mahomedans	584
Brahmins and Rajpoots	83
Mahrattas	12
Telingas (Gentoo)	242
Tamil	97
Other castes	8
Indo-Britons	0
	1,030

Country.	
Hindoostan	51
Northern Circars	317
Central Carnatic, Madras, Vellore, &c.	239
Southern Carnatic, Trichinopoly	177
Carried forward	784

NON-COMMISSIONED, RANK AND FILE.

Caste.	
Christians	1,853
Mahomedans	15,272
Brahmins and Rajpoots	1,922
Mahrattas	385
Telingas (Gentoo)	15,371
Tamil	4,275
Other castes	1,616
Indo-Britons	1,011
	41,705

Country.	
Hindoostan	1,938
Northern Circars	16,938
Central Carnatic, Madras, Vellore, &c.	8,841
Southern Carnatic, Trichinopoly	4,760
Carried forward	32,477

Country.	
Brought forward...	784
Baramahal	29
Ceded districts	32
Mysore	59
Tanjore, Madura, and Tinnevelly	119
Deccan and Mahratta	7
	1,030

Country.	
Brought forward...	32,477
Baramahal	1,022
Ceded districts	1,705
Mysore	2,698
Tanjore, Madura, and Tinnevelly	3,617
Canara, Moulmein, Jaulnah, and Belgaum	28
Deccan and Mahratta	99
Portugal	1
Other parts	58
	41,705

BOMBAY.

NATIVE CAVALRY, 3 Regiments.

NATIVE OFFICERS.

Caste.	
Christians	1
Mahomedans	12
Brahmins and Rajpoots	9
Mahrattas	1
Telingas (Gentoo)	0
Tamil	0
Other castes	12
Indo-Britons	1
	36

NON-COMMISSIONED, RANK AND FILE.

Caste.	
Christians	66
Mahomedans	459
Brahmins and Rajpoots	252
Mahrattas	118
Telingas (Gentoo)	0
Tamil	0
Other castes	508
Indo-Britons	22
	1,425

Country.	
Hindoostan	29
Northern Circars	1
Central Carnatic, Madras, Vellore, &c.	2
Southern Carnatic, Trichinopoly	0
Deccan	2
Concan	1
Mysore	0
Tanjore, Madura, and Tinnevelly	0
Bombay	1
	36

Country.	
Hindoostan	1,073
Northern Circars	21
Central, Carnatic, Madras, Vellore, &c.	30
Southern Carnatic, Trichinopoly	0
Deccan	125
Concan	114
Mysore	0
Tanjore, Madura, and Tinnevelly	0
Guzerat	14
Persia	1
Lisbon	4
Africa	2
Bombay	4
Punjab and Scinde	21
Cabool and Affghanistan	15
Europe	1
	1,425

NATIVE INFANTRY, 29 Regiments.

NATIVE OFFICERS.

Caste.	
Christians	5
Mahomedans	111
Brahmins and Rajpoots	188
Mahrattas	116
Telingas (Gentoo)	6
Tamil	1
Jews	3
Other castes	130
Indo-Britons	0
Purwarrees	3
	563

Country.	
Hindoostan	268
Northern Circars	7
Central Carnatic, Madras, Vellore, &c.	37
Southern Carnatic, Trichinopoly	13
Deccan	57
Concan	173
Mysore	4
Tanjore, Madura, and Tinnevelly	0
Guzerat	4
	563

NON-COMMISSIONED, RANK AND FILE.

Caste.	
Christians	270
Mahomedans	2,048
Brahmins and Rajpoots	6,421
Mahrattas	7,980
Telingas (Gentoo)	107
Tamil	55
Jews	12
Other castes	7,728
Indo-Britons	22
Purwarrees	170
Mochees	29
Sikhs	28
	24,870

Country.	
Hindoostan	11,089
Northern Circars	135
Central Carnatic, Madras, Vellore, &c.	412
Southern Carnatic, Trichinopoly	203
Deccan	1,820
Concan	10,878
Mysore	36
Tanjore, Madura, and Tinnevelly	33
Mysore and Punjab	28
Guzerat	80
Scinde, Punjab, and Rajpootana	155
Europe	1
	24,870

General Return showing the Races and Castes of which the Native Army was composed on April 1, 1858.

CORPS.	European Commissioned Officers.	European Non-Commissioned Officers.	Native Commissioned & Non-Commissioned Officers, and Rank and File.	Number of each Race and Caste. Christians.	Mussulmans.	Brahmins.	Rajpoots.	Hindoos of inferior descriptions.	Seikhs.	Punjabees.	Hindoostanees.	Cis-Sutledge.	Trans-Sutledge.	Hill Stations of Nepaul.	Huzara Tribes.	Affghans.	Goorkhas.	Hill Men.	Mhairs.	Mhairats.	Bheels.	Morgeeahs, Grass-eeans, and other predatory tribes.	Total.
Artillery	6	4	2,241	...	552	77	88	445	...	...	...	...	...	...	...	...	...	...	...	...	...	...	1,169
Light Cavalry	26	3	1,259	25	624	344	231	35	...	...	...	...	...	...	...	...	...	...	...	...	...	...	1,259
Infantry, Regular ..	248	47	21,928	486	3,590	6205	6,404	4326	135	192	...	...	...	...	...	...	590	...	...	...	...	...	21,928
Infantry, Irregular.	240	29	42,715	20	1,853	1532	2,911	3821	3504	15,286	896	2270	2867	358	23	32	271	3677	566	915	803	223	41,828
Cavalry, Irregular..	94	...	10,703	41	3,831	350	549	181	833	2,401	1219	167	467	19	...	105	29	2	...	...	...	...	10,194
Artillery, Irregular.	10	6	998	...	.....	...	...	...	...	495	38	15	5	...	...	...	...	...	...	...	...	...	553
Sebundy Sappers & Miners	1	2	209	...	2	18	179	10	...	...	...	...	...	...	...	...	...	...	...	...	...	...	209
Total......	625	91	80,053	572	10,452	8526	10,362	8818	4472	18,374	2153	2452	3339	377	23	137	890	3679	566	915	803	223	77,133
N.B.—Aggregate of Corps the Races of which are not shown in this Return..................																							2,920
Grand Total.........																							80,053

Adjutant-General's Office, Head-Quarters,
Allahabad, August 13, 1858.

(Signed) W. Mayhew, Lieut.-Col.,
Adjutant-General of the Army.

COMPOSITION OF THE INDIAN ARMY.—[Page 341.]

RETURN showing the Numbers of the Troops, Regular and Irregular, which were serving in the three Presidencies immediately before the Mutiny.

—	Royal Troops.		East India Company's Troops.												Total.
				Artillery.			Native Cavalry.		Infantry.						
	Cavalry, 4 Regts.	Infantry, 22 Regts.	Engineers and Sappers.	Horse, 5 Brigades.	European Foot 12 Battalions.	Native Foot, 6 Battalions.	Regular, 21 Regiments.	Irregular, 33 Regiments.	European, 9 Regiments.	Native Regular, 155 Regiments.	Native Irregular, 45 Regiments.	Veterans.	Medical Establishment.	Warrant Officers.	
Officers	115	693	251	119	231	138	284	106	335	2,769	152	163	814	...	6,170
European non-commissioned officers, rank and file	2571	20,884	110	2029	4390	37	60	...	8103	259	59	...	...	...	38,502
European veterans	...	...	...	...	...	...	...	...	...	...	...	465	...	...	465
Native commissioned, non-commissioned, rank and file	...	...	3043	659	...	3517	9532	20,941	...	149,832	35,215	3613	...	...	226,352
Gun lascars	...	...	...	449	1658	343	...	...	...	...	...	...	...	...	2,450
Ordnance drivers	...	...	...	...	1489	848	...	...	...	...	...	...	...	...	2,337
Apothecaries and stewards	...	...	...	...	...	...	...	...	...	...	...	...	434	...	434
Native doctors	...	...	...	...	...	...	...	...	...	...	...	...	651	...	651
Warrant officers (Ordnance, &c.)	...	...	...	...	...	...	...	...	...	...	...	...	...	385	385
	2686	21,577	3404	3256	7768	4883	9876	21,047	8438	152,860	35,426	4241	1899	385	277,746
Totals	24,263		3404	15,907			30,923		196,724			4241	1899	385	277,746

Indian Army Commission.

Total Europeans—Officers 6,170
" " Men 39,352
" Natives 232,224

277,746

R. B. WOOD,
Colonel and Secretary.

[In Chapter I., Book III., some extracts are given from an interesting memorandum furnished by Sir Robert Phillimore, which is now given in its integrity.]

MEMORIALS OF THE EARLY LIFE OF EARL CANNING. BY SIR ROBERT PHILLIMORE, QUEEN'S ADVOCATE.

"WHEN young Canning was eleven years old, his father took the usual steps for procuring his admission to Eton, the scene on which his own brilliant talents had given the first promise of that future excellence which they afterwards so fully realised. Mr. (afterwards Bishop) Chapman went, at the request of the Provost, Dr. Goodall, in 1824, to Gloucester Lodge, and in the presence of the great statesman examined his boy, in order that there might be no doubt as to his fitness to be placed in the upper school. The well-known description of the storm in the First Æneid, 'Interea magno misceri murmure pontum,' &c., was the passage chosen for the trial of his proficiency; and the Bishop now remembers the anxiety with which the father watched the essay of his son, and the smile of approval which greeted his rendering of the rather difficult transition, 'Quos ego sed motos,' &c., and the final 'not so bad,' which followed at the close of the whole translation

"Young Canning was entered on the 4th September, 1824, at the house of Mr. Chapman. According to the records of the school, he was 'plus vice simplici,' sent up 'for good,' the only distinction at that time attainable at Eton. His reputation, however, at school was rather for intelligence, accuracy, and painstaking than for refined scholarship, or any remarkable powers of composition. The interval between Eton and Oxford was passed with a private tutor, the Reverend Thomas Shore, a nephew of Lord Teignmouth, who resided at Potton, Bedfordshire, but who discharged no public functions as a clergyman at that place. It is probable that he derived great benefit from the tuition of Mr. Shore. While under the care of this gentleman he formed an intimate friendship with the eldest son of the late Lord Harris (afterwards a contemporary at Christ Church), which continued without intermission to the last hour of his life. By a singular turn of fortune, Earl Canning became Governor-General of India while his friend Lord Harris was Governor of Madras. Upon the death of Mr. Canning in 1827, Mrs. Canning was created a Viscountess, with remainder to her son. It was, nevertheless, wisely determined not to send young Canning to Oxford as the son of a nobleman, but to obtain for him a studentship of Christ Church, and thereby to place him in exactly the same position at the University which his father had formerly occupied. It appears that he was nominated by Dr. Pett, the old friend and tutor of his father, and one of the canons of Christ Church, as a student on the roll which was made up December 24, 1827; but he was actually made a student by the Dean in filling up a roll dated December 20, 1828, 'in return for Dr. Pett's nomination' having been given up (a practice not unfrequent at that time) to the Dean 'in the last roll.'

"Mr. Gladstone, Lord Elgin (then Mr. Bruce), Mr. Henry Denison (a distinguished scholar), and Sir Robert Phillimore, were, among others, brother students with him; and in the number of his contemporaries at Christ Church, who afterwards became his colleagues in public life, were Lord Dalhousie and the Duke of Newcastle. He lived chiefly with a few intimate friends, among whom was Lord De Tabley, one of his executors. To them his naturally happy and cheerful temperament, his keen perception of character, his fund of quiet humour, his accomplishments as a scholar, and, above all, his loyal and affectionate heart, made him a delightful companion. He was not generally popular, and to those without his own immediate circle his manners were shy and reserved. He took at that time no particular interest in politics, and whether from a feeling that his father's great name imposed upon him an arduous responsibility, or from extreme sensitiveness to failure, did not then appear desirous to embark upon that stormy ocean of public life on which he afterwards so gallantly sailed and so nobly died.

"Those who heard his speech at the banquet given to him by the India House previous to his departure as Governor-General, know that he could, when strongly urged, put forth oratorical powers of a high order; but at Oxford, as in after-life, he showed no natural aptitude or inclination for speaking in public. His fastidious accuracy of language, his sensitive and proud nature, and a certain physical difficulty, as well, perhaps, as the ever-present recollection of his father's unrivalled success as a parliamentary chieftain, combined to dissuade him from often attempting this particular path to distinction. But at Christ Church he acquired, or matured that command of pure English, and that excellent style which in every letter or even note which he wrote excited just admiration.

"In the year 1831 he won the Christ Church prize for Latin verse. The subject was 'Caractacus captivus Romam ingreditur.' The verses were as usual recited in the hall. It was a remarkable scene. In that magnificent banqueting-room are hung the portraits of students who have reflected honour upon the House which reared them, by the distinctions which they have won in after-life.

"Underneath the portrait of George Canning, the recollection of whose brilliant career and untimely end was still fresh in the memory of men, stood the son in the prime of youth, recalling, by his eminently handsome countenance, the noble features of the portrait, while repeating the classical prize poem which would have gladdened his father's heart. Generally speaking, the resident members of Christ Church alone compose the audience when the prize is recited, but on this occasion there was one stranger present—the old, faithful friend of Mr. Canning, his staunch political adherent through life, Mr. Sturges Bourne. He had travelled from London for the express purpose of witnessing the first considerable achievement of the younger Canning.

"He closed his career at the University with distinguished success, obtaining, in Easter Term, 1833, a first-class in classical and a second-class in mathematical honours. He took the degree of B.A. in the same year, but never proceeded to the degree of M.A."—*MS. Memorandum.*

FINAL ORDERS TO THE MUSKETRY SCHOOLS.

[The following is the letter referred to at page 561—note:]

The Adjutant-General of the Army to Major-General Hearsey.

"Adjutant-General's Office, Simlah, April 13, 1857.

"SIR,—Referring to the telegraph message from this office dated the 23rd ultimo (and your acknowledgments of the 25th idem), communicating the Commander-in-Chief's orders to postpone the target practice of the Native soldiers at the Rifle Depôt at Dum-Dum, pending further instructions from this Department, I am now desired to request you will be good enough to inform the officer commanding at Dum-Dum, and through him the Depot authorities concerned, that the course of instruction is to be completed by the Native details, and that their target practice is to be commenced as soon as practicable after the Government General Order disbanding the Nineteenth Regiment of Native Infantry has been read to the troops at the station, including the detachments of Native regiments at the Depôt.

"2. The grease for the cartridge is to be any unobjectionable mixture which may be suited for the purpose, to be provided by selected parties comprising all castes concerned, and is to be applied by the men themselves.

"3. The paper of which the cartridges are constructed having been proved by chemical test, and otherwise, to be perfectly free from grease, and in all respects unobjectionable; and all possible grounds for objection in regard to the biting of the cartridge, and the nature of the grease to be used, having been removed, it is not anticipated that the men will hesitate to perform the target practice; but, in the event of any such unexpected result, the Commander-in-Chief desires that their officers may be instructed to reason calmly with them, pointing out the utter groundlessness for any objection to the use of the cartridges now that biting the end has been dispensed with, and the provision and application of the necessary greasing material has been left to themselves; and, further, to assure them that any one who shall molest or taunt them on return to their corps, shall be visited with severe punishment.

"4. The officer commanding the Depôt will be held responsible that the above directions respecting the greasing mixture, and those recently issued in regard to the new mode of loading, are strictly observed.

"5. If, notwithstanding all these precautions and considerate measures, any disinclination to use the cartridges shall be manifested, the parties demurring are to be warned calmly and patiently, but firmly, that a persistence in such unjustifiable conduct will be viewed as disobedience of orders and insubordination, and treated accordingly, and in the event of any individuals after such warning obstinately refusing to fire, the officer commanding at Dum-Dum will at once place such parties in arrest or confinement, according to the rank of the offenders, and cause them to be tried by Court-Martial.

"6. If, however, the entire Depôt shall combinedly refuse to fire, which is very improbable, the Commander-in-Chief, under such circumstances, empowers you to place all the Native officers in arrest pending his Excellency's further orders, which you will immediately apply for; to deprive the non-commissioned officers and Sepoys of their arms and accoutrements, and to pay them up and summarily discharge them on the spot, excepting, of course, any ringleaders in these latter grades or parties whose refusal may be accompanied by insolence or insubordination, who are to be placed under arrest or confinement, in view of their being arraigned before a District or General Court-Martial, as the case may require.

"7. This communication is to be considered purely confidential, and his Excellency relies implicitly on your carrying out the instructions it contains with the utmost caution and discretion.

"I have the honour to be, Sir,
"Your most obedient servant,
"C. CHESTER, Col.
"*Adjt.-Gen. of the Army.*"

—*MS. Records.*

THE CHUPATTIES.

[It is stated at page 571 that Mr. Ford, Magistrate and Collector of Goorgaon, was the first to call the attention of the Government of the North-Western Provinces to this subject. His letter, addressed, in official course, to the Commissioner of Delhi, is appended :]

"Goorgaon Magistracy, February 19, 1857.

"SIR,—I have the honour to inform you that a signal has passed through numbers of the villages of this district, the purport of which has not yet transpired.

"The Chowkeydars of the villages bordering on those belonging to Mutra have received small baked cakes of atta, with orders to distribute them generally through this district.

"A Chowkeydar, upon receiving one of these cakes, has had five or six more prepared, and thus they have passed from village to village; so quickly has the order been executed, that village after village has been served with this notice.

"This day, cakes of this description have arrived and been distributed in the villages about Goorgaon, and an idea has been industriously circulated that Government has given the order. "W. FORD, Magistrate.

"To Simon Fraser, Esq.,
"Commissioner, Delhi."

[In the course of the trial of the King of Delhi great pains were taken to extract from the witnesses, both European and Native, some explanation of the "Chupatty mystery;" but nothing satisfactory was elicited. The following opinions, however, were recorded :]

From the Evidence of Jat Mall, News-writer to the Lieutenant-Governor.

"*Q.* Did you ever hear of the circulation of chupatties about the country some months before the outbreak; and if so, what was supposed to be the meaning of this?

A. Yes, I did hear of the circumstance. Some people said that it was a propitiatory observance to avert some impending calamity; others, that they were circulated by the Government to signify that the population throughout the country would be compelled to use the same food as the Christians, and thus be deprived of their religion; while others, again, said that the chupatties were circulated to make it known that Government was determined to force Christianity on the country by interfering with their food, and intimation of it was thus given that they might be prepared to resist the attempt.

Q. Is sending such articles about the country a custom among the Hindoos or Mussulmans; and would the meaning be at once understood without any accompanying explanation?

A. No, it is not by any means a custom; I am fifty years old, and never heard of such a thing before.

Q. Did you ever hear that any message was sent with the chupatties?

A. No; I never heard of any.

Q. Were these chupatties chiefly circulated by Mahomedans or Hindoos?

A. They were circulated indiscriminately, without reference to either religion, among the peasantry of the country."

From the Evidence of Sir Theophilus Metcalfe.

"*Q.* Can you give the Court any information about the chupatties which were circulated from village to village some months before the outbreak; and has it been ascertained how they originated, or what was the purport of their being circulated?

A. There is nothing but conjecture regarding them, but the first suggestion made by the Natives in reference to them was, that they were thus sent about in connexion with some sickness that prevailed; but this was clearly an error, as I took the trouble of ascertaining that these chupatties were never sent into any Native States, but were confined always to Government villages; they were spread through only five villages of the Delhi territory, when they were immediately stopped by authority, and they never proceeded farther up-country.

I sent for the men who had brought them from the district of Bolundshuhr, and their apology for circulating them was that they believed it to be done by order of the English Government, that they had received them elsewhere, and had but forwarded them on. I believe that the meaning of the chupatties was not understood in the Delhi district; but originally they were to be taken to all those who partook of one kind of food, connecting a body of men together in contradistinction to those who lived differently and had different customs. I think these chupatties originated at Lucknow, and were, no doubt, meant to sound a note of alarm and preparation, giving warning to the people to stand by one another on any danger menacing them."

From the Evidence of Chuni, News-writer.

"*Q.* Do you recollect the circumstance of chupatties being circulated from village to village?

A. Yes, I remember hearing of it before the outbreak.

Q. Was the subject discussed in the Native newspapers; and if so, what was considered the meaning of it?

A. Yes, it was alluded to, and it was supposed to portend some coming disturbance, and was, moreover, understood as implying an invitation to the whole population of the country to unite for some secret object afterwards to be disclosed.

Q. Do you know whence these chupatties originated, or to what quarter general opinion among the Natives attributed them?

A. I have no knowledge as to where they were first started, but it was generally supposed that they came from Kurnaul and Paneeput."

From the Evidence of Captain Martineau.

"*Q.* Had you any conversation with these men (*i. e.* with the men assembled at Umballah for musketry instruction) relative to some chupatties that were circulated to different villages in these districts before the outbreak?

A. Yes, I had frequent conversations with various Sepoys on this subject. I asked them what they understood in reference to them, and by whom they supposed that they were circulated; they described them to me as being in size and shape like ship biscuits, and believed them to have been distributed by order of Government through the medium of their servants for the purpose of intimating to the people of Hindoostan that they should all be compelled to eat the same food, and that was considered as a token that they should likewise be compelled to embrace one faith, or, as they termed it, 'One food and one faith.'

Q. As far as you could understand, was this idea generally prevalent among all the Sepoys of the various detachments at the Depôt?

A. It was prevalent, as far as I could judge, among all the Sepoys of every regiment that furnished a detachment to the Depôt at Umballah.

Q. Was there any report of the Government having mixed ground bones with flour for the purpose of having it distributed to the Sepoys, and so destroying their caste?

A. Yes, I heard of this in the month of March. It was told me that all the flour retailed from the Government Depôts for the supply of troops on the march was so adulterated.

Q. Do you think the Sepoys generally firmly believed this?

A. I have seen correspondence from various men, which the Sepoys of the Depôt voluntarily placed in my hands, the writers of which, themselves Sepoys, evidently believed that such was the case.

Q. Did the Sepoys ever speak to you about any other cause of complaint, or points on which they sought information?

A. Their complaint, or rather fear, was this: they apprehended that Government was going forcibly to deprive them of their caste.

Q. Did any of them ever speak about Government interference regarding the re-marriage of Hindoo widows?

A. Yes, they alluded to that as an invasion of their social rights."

From the Statement of Hakim Ahsan Ullah, Confidential Physician to the King of Delhi.

"Nobody can tell what was the object of the distribution of the chupatties. It is not known who first projected the plan. All the people in the palace wondered what it could mean. I had no conversation with the King on the subject; but others talked in his presence about it, wondering what could be the object.

"I consider that the chupatty affair probably originated with the Native troops, and the distribution first commenced in Oude. I also wondered what it was, but considered that it implied something.

"I consider that the distribution of the chupatties first began in Oude.

"It was the opinion of some that the Native troops had designed these chupattles as emblematical of some particular object. Others believed that there was some charm attached to them, inasmuch as they were distributed unknown all over the country, and without it being known who first originated the idea, and whence they were first sent out. People also believed that these chupatties were the invention of some adept in the secret arts, in order to preserve unpolluted the religion of the country, which, it was reported, the Government had proposed to themselves to subvert in two years."

[The following extracts from published works bear upon the subject of inquiry. In the first, the preceding statement that the circulation of the chupatties commenced in Oude, is corroborated:]

"Some time in February, 1857, a curious occurrence took place. It began on the confines of Oude. A Chowkeydar ran up to another village with two chupatties. He ordered his fellow-official to make ten more, and give two to each of the five nearest village Chowkeydars with the same instructions. In a few hours the whole country was in a stir, from Chowkeydars flying about with these cakes. The signal spread in all directions with wonderful celerity. The magistrates tried to stop it, but, in spite of all they could do, it passed along to the borders of the Punjab. There is reason to believe that this was originated by some intriguers of the old Court of Lucknow. Its import has not been satisfactorily explained, and was probably not understood by many who helped it along. But the same thing occurred in Behar and about Jhansi in connexion with the discontent caused by the new income-tax. It has been stated by a Native authority, published by Mr. Russell of the *Times* (see *Friend of India*, March 10, 1859), that the first circulation of the chupatties was made at the suggestion of a learned and holy pundit, who told Rajah Madhoo Singh that the people would rise in rebellion if it were done, and that the person in whose name the cakes were sent would rule all India. This, however, is very doubtful."—*Siege of Delhi, by an Officer who served there.*

"That remarkable and still unexplained passage through Oude, and elsewhere, of the chupatty symbol, occurred early in 1857, and, from the first movement of its advent into Oude, spread with such amazing rapidity, that it was calculated ten days more than sufficed for every village Chowkeydar in Oude to have received the little bread-cake, and made and passed on similar little bread-cakes to every village Chowkeydar within the ordinary radius of his travels. The Natives generally may have viewed this sign-manual flying through their villages—so common a method amongst men in the early stages of civilisation to warn all for either peace or war—as a forerunner of some universal popular outbreak, but by whom or with what class the standard of rebellion would be raised certainly was not generally known."—*Narrative of the Mutinies in Oude, compiled from Authentic Records, by Captain G. Hutchinson, Military Secretary to the Chief Commissioner, Oude.*

"In the North-West Provinces it was discovered that chupatties were being circulated throughout the country in a somewhat mysterious manner.* The fact was duly reported from various quarters; inquiries were ordered to be set on foot, but nothing further could be traced as to their origin or object, and they were suffered to travel on from village to village with little let or hindrance. Some fifty years before a similar appearance in Central India had perplexed the authorities,† but no solution of the mystery had been gained, and as nothing had then resulted from it, the hope was grasped at that in the present instance also, if not meaningless, it might prove equally harmless: it might be some superstitious spell against disease, for cholera had ravaged several districts during the previous autumn, or against some impending calamity, for the whole country teemed with forebodings of coming trouble. At all events, the idea was scouted of its having any political meaning; and far-seeing old Indians, who dared to look gravely on the 'chupatty mystery,' were denounced as croakers."—*The Punjab and Delhi in* 1857, *by the Rev. T. Cave-Browne, Chaplain of the Punjab Moveable Column.*

"The leaders and promoters of this great rebellion, whoever they may have been, knew well the inflammable condition, from these causes, of the rural society in the North-Western Provinces, and they therefore sent among them the chupatties, as a kind of fiery cross, to call them to action. The cakes

* One district officer, who saw a chupatty-laden messenger arrive in a village, and observed him breaking his cake into pieces and distributing them among the men of the village, asked what it meant; he was told that there was an old custom in Hindoostan, that when their *malik*, or chief, required any service from his people, he adopted this mode to prepare them for receiving his orders, and every one who partook of the chupatties was held pledged to obey the order whenever it might come, and whatever it might be. "What was the nature of the order in the present case?" he asked. The answer, accompanied by a suspicious smile, was, "We don't know yet."

† Mr. Browne, in his very interesting and trustworthy work, quotes, as his authority for this, "Kaye's Life of Metcalfe;" but I have no recollection of the statement, and I have caused a diligent search to be made through the work, but with no success. I remember, however, to have read in the papers of Sir John Malcolm a statement to the effect that, at a time of political excitement, I believe just before the mutiny of the Coast Army in 1806, there had been a mysterious circulation of sugar. There was also, in 1818, a very perplexing distribution of cocoanuts in Central India; but it subsequently appeared to have been the result of a mere accident.—J. W. K.

passed with the most amazing rapidity over the length and breadth of the land. Where they came from originally, it is impossible to say, but I believe Barrackpore was the starting-point, where large masses of mutinous Sepoys were congregated. The chupatties entered my district from the adjoining one of Shajehanpoor, a village watchman of that place giving to the watchman of the nearest Budaon village two of the cakes, with an injunction to make six fresh ones, retain two for his own, and give the others to the watchman of the next village, who would follow the same course, and continue the manufacture and distribution. I truly believe that the rural population of all classes, among whom these cakes spread, were as ignorant as I was myself of their real object; but it was clear they were a secret sign to be on the alert, and the minds of the people were through them kept watchful and excited. As soon as the disturbances broke out at Meerut and Delhi, the cakes explained themselves, and the people at once perceived what was expected of them."—*Personal Adventures during the Indian Rebellion in Rohilcund, Futtehghur, and Oude, by William Edwards, Esq., B.C.S., Judge of Benares, and late Magistrate and Collector of Budaon, in Rohilcund.*

[Compare also the statement at page 647.]

THE BONE-DUST STORY.

[The following translations from Native letters and papers show how general was the belief among the Sepoys in all parts of the country that the Government had mixed ground bones with the flour, and purposed to compel or to delude them to eat it:]

Translation of an Anonymous Petition sent, in March, 1857, to Major Matthews, commanding the 43rd Regiment at Barrackpore.

"The representation of the whole station is this, that we will not give up our religion. We serve for honour and religion; if we lose our religion, the Hindoo and Mahomedan religions will be destroyed. If we live, what shall we do? You are the masters of the country. The Lord Sahib has given orders, which he has received from the Company, to all commanding officers to destroy the religion of the country. We know this, as all things are being bought up by Government. The officers in the Salt Department mix up bones with the salt. The officer in charge of the ghee mixes up fat with it; this is well known. These are two matters. The third is this: that the Sahib in charge of the sugar burns up bones and mixes them in the syrup the sugar is made of; this is well known—all know it. The fourth is this: that in the country the Burra Sahibs have ordered the Rajahs, Thakurs, Zemindars, Mahajans, and Ryots, all to eat together, and English bread has been sent to them; this is well known. And this is another affair, that throughout the country the wives of respectable men, in fact, all classes of Hindoos, on becoming widows, are to be married again; this is known. Therefore we consider ourselves as killed. You all obey the orders of the Company, which we all know. But a king, or any other one who acts unjustly, does not remain.

"With reference to the Sepoys, they are your servants; but, to destroy their caste, a council assembled and decided to give them muskets and cartridges made up with greased paper to bite; this is also evident. We wish to represent this to the General, that we do not approve of the new musket and cartridge; the Sepoys cannot use them. You are the masters of the country; if you will give us all our discharge we will go away. The Native officers, Soubahdars, Jemadars, are all good in the whole Brigade, except two, whose faces are like pigs: the Soubahdar Major of the 70th Regiment, who is a Christian, and Thakur Misser, Jemadar of the 43rd Regiment Light Infantry.

"Whoever gets this letter must read it to the Major as it is written. If he is a Hindoo and does not, his crime will be equal to the slaughter of a lakh of cows; and if a Mussulman, as though he had eaten pig; and if a European, must read it to the Native officers, and if he does not, his going to church will be of no use, and be a crime. Thakur Misser has lost his religion. Chattrees are not to respect him. Brahmins are not to salute or bless him. If they do, their crime will be equal to the slaughter of a lakh of cows. He is the son of a Chumar. The Brahmin who hears this is not to feed him; if he does, his crime will be equal to the murdering of a lakh of Brahmins or cows.

"May this letter be given to Major Matthews. Any one who gets it is to give it, if he does not, and is a Hindoo, his crime will be as the slaughter of a lakh of cows; and if a Mussulman, as if he had eaten pig; and if he is an officer he must give it."

Translation of a Letter from Inayut-Oolah Goolaothee, of Boolundshuhr, to his Brother Fyzool Hussan, Extra Assistant, Rawul Pindee.

". . . . . . The reason of my letters not reaching you is this: that on the 12th of Ramyan, in Meerut '*Khas*,' such a fight occurred between the Native and European troops on a point of religion as cannot be described. The foundation of the quarrel was this: that thousands of maunds of atta was taken into every ressalah and regiment; and with this atta was mixed the ground bones of the cow and pig; and the cartridges were also made with the fat of the cow and pig. The shopkeepers in the city were ordered to purchase "atta" from Government and sell it in all the villages. It was ordered by beat of drum that atta be not ground in any village, and that in every district all the mills should be confiscated to Government. It was also ordered that ten maunds of atta be thrown into every well, kuchcha or pukka, in every village and town. The troops at every station with one accord said, that if the troops at Meerut should receive the atta and cartridges, they would receive them without objection. A few European officers assembled at Meerut, and having collected the officers of the pultun and ressalah, ordered them to take the atta from the Government and to bite the cartridges with the mouth. A few Sirdars objected to do so; but two, one a Hindoo and the other a Mussulman, bit the cartridge with the mouth. A reward of one hundred rupees was immediately paid to both. The rest said that they would consult each other during the night, and intimate the result the next morning. There were about eighty-four men. They were instantly sent to jail in irons. One among them, a Syud, who was fasting, struck his head on the ground and died. About two hours before sunset the troops girded up their loins and killed all the European soldiers and officers that were present. Only the Commissioner and the District Officer escaped. The rest of the principal Europeans were killed—women nor even children, all that were Europeans, escaped. Afterwards they went to the jail. There was a sentry at the gate, whom they asked to open it. The sentry refused, upon which a Sowar, who was a Syud, advanced, and, with the name of God in his mouth, forced open the gate with a kick. They then collected blacksmiths from the city, and, taking them to the jail, unfettered several thousand prisoners. Both the jails were broken through. Then they went to and sacked the treasury. This state of things continued for two days. The people of the city of Meerut also joined them, as also the Syuds of Ubdoollapoor, a village near Meerut. The whole of the cantonment was fired; not a single bungalow escaped. The 'Dewanee Duftur' was also burnt. On the third day they went away to Delhi; small bodies of them also scattered themselves in different districts. Three days afterwards the troops at Umballah burnt that cantonment and went away to Delhi. The Native troops at Roorkee also fired that station, and went over to Meerut. The residue of the European troops, being joined by others, demanded their arms from the Native soldiery, but they refused. The European troops surrounded them with guns. In a single volley forty of the Natives were killed, but the latter in their turn sent sixty-five Gorahs to hell by a single volley of their muskets. The Native troops then took their way to Delhi. A few went to the village of Ubdoollapoor, the Syuds of which place gave them refuge and consolation. But secretly they sent a man and informed the Commissioner, who proceeded with ten guns to Ubdoollapoor, and cut off the road to Meerut and Delhi. Then the scoundrels (Syuds of Ubdoollapoor) informed the refugees that they had given them shelter, but that Government troops had arrived.

The poor fellows then fled, but in their flight about fifteen or twenty were killed and several wounded; but they also killed about forty men, and then went to Delhi. In short, from all sides the Native troops assembled at Delhi and desired the King to ascend the throne. His Majesty refused; but the Sepoys said: 'Do you ascend the throne, else we shall cut off your head and bury your body underneath the throne, and place one from among ourselves on the throne.' They then placed Shahzadah Jewan Bukht on the throne. They then fired the Tuhseel stations at Ghazeeabad, Mooradnuggur, Mooradabad, and Cawnpore, &c., and Thanas of the Badsha were located there. One month's pay has been distributed to the troops by the King. The King also wrote to the English, telling them that their troops, having been dissatisfied with them, had come over to the King and to take them away. The English replied, that the King himself should send them back. A Moulavee from Meerut and another from some other place have gone over to Delhi with about six thousand men to make religious war. The Royal mandates were issued to the different Rajahs to wait upon the King. It is said that the Rajah of Bullubgurh has waited upon his Majesty with his troops; and it is also said that the King has raised new troops, and has fixed the pay of the Foot soldier at twelve rupees, and that of the Sowar at thirty rupees, per mensem. I have sent a man to Delhi to ascertain the course of events there; when he comes back the real state of things will be known. Traffic has ceased in several districts. The Jats and Goojurs have commenced plundering, and news arrives daily of the plundering of villages here and there. A revolution has occurred in the whole country. . . . ."

"News from Meerut"—Translated from the "Soobah Sadik," published at Madras.

"The same newspaper* tells us that in the Patan Bélé Camp, at Meerut, the same cartridges arrived, on account of which the Barrackpore officers had earned a reputation, on

* The *Jami-Jamshid* of Meerut.

the 18th or 19th of the current month; and the flour-boxes, which had been publicly stated to contain hogs' bones mixed up in them, also came. The order was that the men of the regiment should purchase the flour. On this account no one ate food, and refused to take the flour or the cartridges. Though it is not right to suspect the Sirkars—as they have nothing to do with religion—yet in this business there is no doubt that, in the wisdom of Government, they have suddenly withdrawn from kindly feeling towards the hearts of their subjects. It is very lamentable. The sky kisses the earth from grief."

THE NANA SAHIB AND AZIM-OOLLAH KHAN

[The visit of the Nana Sahib to Lucknow, in April, 1857, referred to at page 576, is thus described by Mr. Martin Gubbins in his history of the Mutinies in Oude:]

"I must here mention a visit which was made to Lucknow, in April, by the Nana of Bithoor, whose subsequent treachery and atrocities have given him a pre-eminence in infamy. He came over on pretence of seeing the sights at Lucknow, accompanied by his younger brother and a numerous retinue, bringing letters of introduction from a former Judge of Cawnpore to Captain Hayes and to myself. He visited me, and his manner was arrogant and presuming. To make a show of dignity and importance, he brought six or seven followers with him into the room, for whom chairs were demanded. One of these men was his notorious agent, Azim-oollah. His younger brother was more pleasing in appearance and demeanour. The Nana was introduced by me to Sir Henry Lawrence, who received him kindly, and ordered the authorities of the city to show him every attention. I subsequently met him parading through Lucknow with a retinue more than usually large. He had promised before leaving Lucknow to make his final call on the Wednesday. On the Monday, we received a message from him that urgent business required his attendance at Cawnpore, and he left Lucknow accordingly. At the time his conduct excited little attention; but it was otherwise when affairs had assumed the aspect which they did at Cawnpore by the 20th of May. His demeanour at Lucknow and sudden departure to Cawnpore appeared exceedingly suspicious, and I brought it to the notice of Sir Henry Lawrence. The Chief Commissioner concurred in my suspicions, and by his authority I addressed Sir Hugh Wheeler, cautioning him against the Nana, and stating Sir Henry's belief that he was not to be depended on. The warning was unhappily disregarded, and, on the 22nd of May, a message was received stating that 'two guns and three hundred men, cavalry and infantry, furnished by the Maharajah of Bithoor, came in this morning.'"

[At pages 579-80 (note) there is an extract from the evidence of a Native emissary, taken by the Hon. H. B. Devereux, Judicial Commissioner of Mysore. This man, Seetaram Bawa by name, was very distinct and emphatic in his declaration that the Nana Sahib had been, for some time before the outbreak, stirring up this revolt against the English. The following further passages from this man's evidence, whether or not accepted as truth, will be read with interest:]

"Then Bajee Rao died at Bithoor. He left a widow and an adopted son named Nana Sahib, who was always a worthless and not very clever fellow, and never would have been anything but for the tuition of his Gooroo, Dassa Bawa (said to have come from a place called Kalee Dhar, beyond Kangra, this side of Jummoo). Three years ago, or perhaps a month less, Nana Sahib gave the Gooroo, Dassa Bawa, a sunnud, granting a five-lakh jaghir and five nachatras,* because Dassa Bawa had told him that he would become as powerful as the Peishwah had once been; and the sunnud was to take effect when he came into power. Dassa Bawa then made a Hunooman horoscope of eight angles. Nana then, after seven days of prayer, went to sleep on the horoscope, and Hunooman having revealed to him that he would be victorious, he felt that the truth of the prediction had been confirmed, and at once presented Dassa Bawa with twenty-

* Kettle-drums—marks of dignity.

five thousand rupees' worth of jewels. Dassa Bawa then went to Nepaul, &c. Dassa Bawa is the person who has helped and advised the Nana throughout. The Nana gives him much money. . . ."

"*Q.* How and when were the Sepoys induced to join in the revolt?

A. Not before the annexation of Oude, but before the affair of the greased cartridges, which was a mere pretext. After that, Maun Singh sent four or five Poorbeahs to every regiment in the service of the Company, and by their means all communications took place. Even down at the French Rocks there were men. They were able to enlist in the cause the Poorbeahs, Hindostanees, and many Mussulmans, but in no instance did they attempt to gain over the Tamil or Telegoo Sepoys, or other Hindoos of this side of India, for they knew it would be useless. They eat differently, and do not intermarry. The Hindoos of the South have no sympathy with those of the North, whereas the Mahomedans are united in feeling throughout India. If a Hindoo is glad, nobody but his own nearest people will sympathise; but if a Mussulman is glad, all Mussulmans rejoice.

Q. Explain what the plan of attack really was.

A. A night was to have been fixed on which, without risking anything, the whole of the European officers were to have been killed, and the treasuries plundered. The magazines were to have been taken possession of when possible, or else blown up. But it was never intended to injure women or children. *Nearly all* were of one mind in the different regiments. It is not the Brahmins and great men that have destroyed helpless children, women with child, and poor women. [He spoke this with great excitement.] It was the intention to destroy your men, but it was villagers and savages who destroyed your women and children, such as Maun Singh and his Poorbeahs. Nana Sahib, though always a worthless fellow, and nothing without Dassa Bawa, could never have ordered the massacre of the women and children. Had they no mothers or sisters! Had they no heart for them! I heard of what happened with sorrow. We object to your raj. All men have peace and freedom under it—such freedom as we never enjoyed before—but we sorrow for our caste. I am speaking of Brahmins. Brahmins love good food and ease. The Company does not give it (muft) gratis, and we wish for a return of that which will enable us to obtain it, or rather place matters in such a position that we can obtain it. We feel the pressure of your rule in this respect. Nana Sahib wrote both to Gholab Singh and to Russia, and he got an answer from Russia. In that answer he was told that no assistance could be given him unless he could take and could hold Delhi; but that, if he could succeed in that, then assistance would be given him to drive us from Calcutta. The letter was sent to Jummoo, and forwarded on from thence by the hands of the people who bring almonds and fruit. The country beyond Jummoo is said to be pure Mussulman, but I do not know anything about it. First, Gholab Singh joined, and as soon as the union of the Mussulmans and Hindoos was settled, several letters were sent to Russia.

Q. Can you explain anything about the chupatty cakes which were passed over India before the insurrection?

A. The cakes in question were a jadoo or charm, which originated with Dassa Bawa, who told Nana Sahib that he would make a jadoo, and, as far as these magic cakes should be carried, so far should the people be on his side. He then took the reed of the lotus, or rumul, called mukhana, and made an idol of it. He then reduced the idol to very small pills, and, having made an immense number of cakes, he put a pillet in each, and, as far as the cakes were carried, so far would the people determine to throw off the Company's raj. None came as far as this country.

Q. What made Nana Sahib originate this conspiracy?

A. The Company Sirkar placed all the treasure of his father under attachment, and he wanted to gain possession of it. The people about him urged him—the opportunity offered, and he took advantage of it.

Q. How do you know all this?

A. Every person, particularly every Brahmin, is well acquainted with all this, and the fact of these letters having been written. Why, every Baboo in Calcutta knew of it."—*MS. Records.*

[Many readers will smile at the statement that the Nana Sahib was in correspondence with Russia, and received an answer to his overtures. But, it is by no means improbable that Azim-oollah Khan entered into communication with some Russian officers, responsible or irresponsible, and it is certain that at the time of the Crimean war nothing could have better served the interests of Russia than a revolt in India. That Azim-oollah visited the Crimea, we know upon the best possible authority—that of Mr. Russell, who has given, in his "Diary in India," the following interesting account of his meeting with the Nana's agent in the trenches before Sebastopol:]

"Whilst I am writing about it, I may as well relate an incident in connexion with one of the Nana's chief advisers, which I mentioned to the Governor-General, who appeared much struck with it. After the repulse of the allies in their assault on Sebastopol, 18th June, an event closely followed by the death of Lord Raglan and a cessation of any operations, except such as were connected with a renewed assault upon the place, I went down for a few days to Constantinople, and, whilst stopping at Misseri's Hotel, saw, on several occasions, a handsome slim young man, of dark-olive complexion, dressed in an Oriental costume which was new to me, and covered with rings and finery. He spoke French and English, dined at the *table d'hôte*, and, as far as I could make out, was an Indian Prince, who was on his way back from the prosecution of an unsuccessful claim against the East India Company in London. He had made the acquaintance of Mr. Doyne, who was going out to the Crimea as the superintendent of Sir Joseph Paxton's Army Works Corps, and by that gentleman he was introduced to me one fine summer's evening, as we were smoking on the roof of the hotel. I did not remember his name, but I recollect that he expressed great anxiety about a passage to the Crimea, 'as,' said he, 'I want to see this famous city, and those great Roostums—the Russians—who have beaten French and English together.'

Indeed, he added that he was going to Calcutta, when the news of the defeat of June 18th reached him at Malta, and he was so excited by it that he resolved to go to Constantinople, and endeavour thence to get a passage to Balaklava. In the course of conversation he boasted a good deal of his success in London society, and used the names of people of rank very freely, which, combined with the tone of his remarks, induced me to regard him with suspicion, mingled, I confess, with dislike. He not only mentioned his *bonnes fortunes*, but expressed a very decided opinion that unless women were restrained, as they were in the East, 'like moths in candlelight, they will fly and get burned.' I never saw or heard anything more of him till some weeks afterwards, when a gentleman rode up to my hut at Cathcart's Hill, and sent me in a note from Mr. Doyne, asking me to assist his friend Azim-oollah Khan in visiting the trenches, and on going out I recognised the Indian Prince. I had his horse put up, and walked to the General's hut to get a pass for him. The sun was within an hour of setting, and the Russian batteries had just opened, as was their custom, to welcome our reliefs and working-parties, so that shot came bounding up towards the hill where our friend was standing, and a shell burst in the air at apparently near proximity to his post. Some delay took place ere I could get the pass, and when I went with it I found Azim-oollah had retreated inside the cemetery, and was looking with marked interest at the fire of the Russian guns. I told him what he was to do, and regretted my inability to accompany him, as I was going out to dinner at a mess in the Light Division. 'Oh,' said he, 'this is a beautiful place to see from; I can see everything, and, as it is late, I will ask you to come some other day, and will watch here till it is time to go home.' He said, laughingly, 'I think you will never take that strong place;' and in reply to me, when I asked him to come to dine with me at my friend's, where I was sure he would be welcome, he said, with a kind of sneer, 'Thank you, but recollect I am a good Mahomedan!' 'But,' said I, 'you dined at Misseri's?' 'Oh, yes: I was joking. I am not such a fool as to believe in these foolish things. I am of no religion.' When I came home that night I found he was asleep in my camp-bed, and my servant told me he had enjoyed my stores very freely. In the morning he was up and off, ere I was awake. On my table I found a piece of paper—'Azim-oollah Khan presents his compliments to Russell, Esquire, and begs to thank him most truly for his kind attentions, for which I am most obliged.'

"This fellow, as we all know, was the Nana's secretary, and chief adviser in the massacres at Cawnpore. Now, is it not curious enough that he should have felt such an interest to see, with his own eyes, how matters were going on in the Crimea? It would not be strange in a European to evince such curiosity; but in an Asiatic, of the non-military caste, it certainly is. He saw the British army in a state of some depression, and he formed, as I have since heard, a very unfavourable opinion of its *morale* and *physique*, in comparison with that of the French. Let us remember, that soon after his arrival in India he accompanied Nana Sahib to Lucknow, where they remained some time, and are thought by those who recollect their tone and demeanour, to have exhibited considerable insolence and *hauteur* towards the Europeans they met. Afterwards the worthy couple, on the pretence of a pilgrimage to the hills—a Hindoo and Mussulman joined in a holy excursion!—visited the military stations all along the main trunk-road, and went as far as Umballah. It has been suggested that their object in going to Simlah was to tamper with the Goorkha regiment stationed in the hills; but that, finding on their arrival at Umballah a portion of the regiment were in cantonments, they were unable to effect their purpose with these men, and desisted from their proposed journey on the plea of the cold weather. That the Nana's demeanour towards us should have undergone a change at this time is not at all wonderful; for he had learned the irrevocable determination of the authorities to refuse what he—and, let me add, the majority of the millions of Hindoos who knew the circumstances—considered to be his just rights as adopted heir of the ex-Peishwah of the Mahrattas. When the great villany was planned is not now ascertainable; but it must be remarked, as a piece of evidence in some degree adverse to the supposition that Nana Sahib had successfully tampered with the troops at Cawnpore, that the latter did not evince any design of making him their leader, nor did they hold any communication with him on their revolt, and that they were all marching off for Delhi when he and his creatures went to their camp, and by his representations, promises, and actual disbursements, induced them to go back and assault Wheeler in his feeble entrenchments."

[The statement in the above, that the Nana Sahib visited Umballah in the spring of 1857, is new. Azim-oollah Khan was certainly there: for Captain Martineau, who had previously made acquaintance with him on board a steamer, on his return to India, met him at that station in the early part of the year, but was not aware that he accompanied the Nana.]

NATIVE VERSION OF THE BEGINNING OF THE MUTINY.

[The subjoined letter, the original of which fell into the hands of the Punjabee officials, is, on many accounts, curious and interesting. It is important, too, as showing how general was the belief that the whole army was to "take time" from the Meerut Brigade. The statement in this letter may be advantageously compared with what is said on the same subject in the letter at page 641:]

From Nund Singh, Umritsur, to Sirdar Nehal Singh, Rawul Pindee.

"June 10, 1857.

AFTER COMPLIMENTS,—"You wrote to me to ascertain the true circumstances connected with the cartridges. I have made inquiries from different sources. The fact is this:

"Near Calcutta, five coss distant from it, there is a place called Achanuk.* There is a Government cantonment at that place. At that place a Hindostanee was drawing water out of a well. A 'Chumar' came in and asked the Hindostanee

* Barrackpore.

to give him water to drink. The Hindostanee told him that he had better go to some other place to drink water.

"'How,' said the Hindostanee, 'can I give you water to drink? You are a "Chumar."'*

"Upon this words were exchanged between them. The Chumar said:

"'You do not give me water to drink, and affect to be so religious; and the fat of the cow and pig which I prepare with my own hands you will bite off with your teeth.'

"These and similar words having been exchanged between them, they came to blows. The other people, who had heard the talk about the 'fat,' rescued the 'Chumar,' and made inquiries from him in a conciliatory manner.

"Then two men went along with him to that place,† which was a little removed from the cantonment. There they saw with their own eyes about fifty or sixty Chumars working and putting on the fat of both the animals on the cartridges. They returned from thence homewards, and described all to the Soubahdars and other officers.

"It was agreed between them that they should remain silent at the time, but refuse to receive the cartridges when they should be given to them.

"'It would then be proper to remonstrate. Let them (the Government) be doing whatever they like in private. What business have we to murmur?'

"For this reason, for some time nothing broke out. About two or one and a half months afterwards the regiment was ordered to receive these cartridges, (and it was explained to them) that, in the first place, the greased cartridges easily went down into the musket; and, secondly, they prevented the musket from being affected by the damp. But as the men already knew (all about them), they refused to receive them. The European officers at that place (Barrackpore) were very hot-tempered; therefore, in consequence of this refusal a quarrel soon sprung up. Immediately the European troops were brought out, and surrounded the regiment. The latter were ordered to give up their arms. They replied:

* The lowest class among the Hindoos, who work in leather.

† The place where cartridges were said to be made.

Give us our pay and take away the arms.' The regiments were then made to put down their arms, and they having received their pay each went away to their home. All the Sepoys in this country, at Kurnaul, Meerut, &c., were some way or other related (to those of the disbanded regiments). (The men of the latter) wrote to the former, telling them what had occurred, and stated 'that we have on this account quitted the service, and have seen all with our own eyes. We have written this to you for your information. If you should receive these cartridges, intermarriage, and eating and drinking in common shall cease between yourselves and us.'

"When, at Dinapore, the cartridges were distributed by the English, they were refused; the men stated that 'Meerut is the principal cantonment. Distribute the cartridges there first of all, and we will take them afterwards.'

"The distribution of the cartridges having been ordered at Meerut, and the men having been already acquainted with the circumstances connected with them, refused to receive them. But a company which was sent for to receive the cartridges, not having obeyed the order, were placed in confinement by the European officers. Intelligence of this having reached the rest of the troops, all attacked the jail, and set at liberty the men of the company, and also the other prisoners. The disturbance then grew high.

"At the very first, when the regiment at Achanuk (Barrackpore) was disbanded, a requisition was made to England for twenty more European regiments. But these did not sail in steamers, but are coming in other ships which sail with the force of the wind.

"The truth appears to be, that the report of the fat being used is not altogether untrue; much is commonly made of a little thing, but it cannot be that anything can be produced from nothing. Is ever a tree produced without the seed? It cannot be. And now that orders have been read to all the regiments to the effect that these cartridges will not be served out, and shall either be cut up or flooded, consider that the very circumstance of such an order having been read, annihilates the belief that there was nothing wrong in these cartridges.

"You are wise yourself; the real foundation of this disturbance is what I have described. But all things are known to God only, who is omniscient."—*MS. Records.*

THE MAY PROCLAMATION.

[The following is the proclamation referred to at page 608:]

"Fort William, Home Department, May 16, 1857.

"*Proclamation.*

"The Governor-General of India in Council has warned the Army of Bengal, that the tales by which the men of certain Regiments have been led to suspect that offence to their Religion or injury to their Caste is meditated by the Government of India, are malicious falsehoods.

"The Governor-General in Council has learnt that this suspicion continues to be propagated by designing and evil-minded men, not only in the Army, but amongst other classes of the people.

"He knows that endeavours are made to persuade Hindoos and Mussulmans, Soldiers and Civil Subjects, that their religion is threatened secretly, as well as openly, by the acts of the Government, and that the Government is seeking in various ways to entrap them into a loss of Caste for purposes of its own.

"Some have been already deceived and led astray by these tales.

"Once more, then, the Governor-General in Council warns all classes against the deceptions that are practised on them.

"The Government of India has invariably treated the religious feelings of all its subjects with careful respect. The Governor-General in Council has declared that it will never cease to do so. He now repeats that declaration, and he emphatically proclaims that the Government of India entertains no design to interfere with their Religion or Caste, and that nothing has been, or will be done by the Government to affect the free exercise of the observances of Religion or Caste by every class of the people.

"The Government of India has never deceived its subjects, therefore the Governor-General in Council now calls upon them to refuse their belief to seditious lies.

"This notice is addressed to those who hitherto, by habitual loyalty and orderly conduct, have shown their attachment to the Government, and a well-founded faith in its protection and justice.

"The Governor-General in Council enjoins all such persons to pause before they listen to false guides and traitors who would lead them into danger and disgrace.

"By Order of the Governor-General of India in Council,

"CECIL BEADON,

"Secretary to the Government of India."

ADDENDUM.

AMMUNITION FOR TWO-GROOVED RIFLES.

AFTER the statement at pages 516-18, respecting the composition of the greasing materials used with the old two-grooved rifles, was in type, I succeeded in tracing the original orders on the subject, drawn up by the Military Board in 1847. The following is the material part of the Board's Memorandum, approved by the Commander-in-Chief and the Governor-General:

"1st. The ammunition of two-grooved rifles is to be prepared as blank cartridge of three drachms of musketry powder, in blue paper, made up in bundles of ten.

"2nd. The balls to be put up, five in a string, in small cloth bags, with a greased patch of fine cloth—a portion carried in a ball-bag attached to the girdle on the right side, and the remainder in pouch.

"3rd. Patches to be made of calico or long cloth, and issued ready greased from magazines; a portion of greasing composition will also be issued with the patches for the purpose of renewal when required, and instructions for its preparation forwarded to magazine officers by the Military Board."

[The following were the instructions issued in accordance with this Memorandum :]

"The mode of preparing the grease and applying it to the cloth to be as follows:—To three pints of country linseed oil, add one-fourth of a pound of beeswax, which mix by melting the wax in a ladle, pouring the oil in and allowing it to remain on the fire until the composition is thoroughly melted. The cloth is then to be dipped in it until every part is saturated, and held by one corner until the mixture ceases to run, after which it is to be laid out as smooth as possible on a clean spot to cool. The above quantity of composition will answer for three yards of long cloth, from which 1200 patches can be made."

[These instructions were approved by the Governor-General (Lord Hardinge), in a letter from the Military Secretary to the Adjutant-General, dated April 6, 1847. I can trace no subsequent order cancelling the above; and as I am assured by the officer who held the post of Inspector-General of Ordnance during the administration of Lord Dalhousie and Lord Canning that this composition continued in use up to 1857, I cannot doubt that the impression at head-quarters that the "patches" were greased with mutton fat was altogether a mistake.]

END OF VOL. I.

A HISTORY OF THE GREAT REVOLT

A HISTORY OF THE GREAT REVOLT

(In Three Volumes)
Volume II

JOHN WILLIAM KAYE

A History of The Great Revolt

ISBN: 81-212-0194-2 (Set)
ISBN: 81-212-0196-9 (Vol. 2)

Reprinted in 2011 in India by
Gyan Publishing House
23, Main Ansari Road, Daryaganj,
New Delhi - 110002
Phone : 23282060, 23261060
Fax : (011) 23285914
e-mail : books@gyanbooks.com
gyanbook@vsnl.com
website : gyanbooks.com

Printed at : G. Print Process, Delhi

CONTENTS OF VOL II.

BOOK IV.—THE RISING IN THE NORTH-WEST.

CHAPTER I.

THE DELHI HISTORY.

CHAPTER II.

THE OUTBREAK AT MEERUT.

CHAPTER III.

THE SEIZURE OF DELHI.

CHAPTER IV.

CALCUTTA IN MAY.

PAGE

CHAPTER V.

LAST DAYS OF GENERAL ANSON.

CHAPTER VI.

THE MARCH UPON DELHI.

BOOK V.—PROGRESS OF REBELLION IN UPPER INDIA.

CHAPTER I.

BENARES AND ALLAHABAD.

CHAPTER II.

CAWNPORE.

CHAPTER III.

THE MARCH TO CAWNPORE.

CHAPTER IV.

RE-OCCUPATION OF CAWNPORE.

BOOK VI.—THE PUNJAB AND DELHI.

CHAPTER I.

FIRST CONFLICTS IN THE PUNJAB.

CHAPTER II.

PESHAWUR AND RAWUL-PINDEE.

CHAPTER III.

PROGRESS OF EVENTS IN THE PUNJAB.

CHAPTER IV.

DELHI—FIRST WEEKS OF THE SIEGE.

CHAPTER V.

PROGRESS OF THE SIEGE.

CHAPTER VI.

THE LAST SUCCOURS FROM THE PUNJAB.

PREFACE TO VOL. II.

WHEN the first volume of this book was published, I had little expectation that the second would be so long in course of completion, as the result has shown it to have been. In truth, I had not measured aright the extent of the work before me. But when I came to take account of the wealth of my materials, and to reflect upon the means of converting them into history, I saw clearly that the task I had undertaken was a more arduous and perplexing one than I had originally supposed.

It is not difficult to make the reader understand my perplexities; and I hope that, understanding, he will sympathise with them. The events to be narrated covered a large area of space but were compressed within a small period of time. Chronologically they moved along parallel lines, but locally they were divergent and distracting. The question was how it was best to deal historically with all these synchronous incidents. To have written according to date, with some approach to fidelity of detail, a number of separate narratives, each illustrative of a particular day, or of a particular week, would have been easy to the writer, and would in some sort have represented the character of the crisis, one of the most distinguishing features of which was derived from the confusion and distraction engendered by the multiplicity of simultaneous outbursts in different parts of the country. This mode of treatment, however, though it might accurately reflect the situation, was not likely to gratify the reader. The multiplicity of personal and local names rapidly succeeding each other would have bewildered him, and no distinct impression would have been left upon his mind. But though the nature of the subject utterly forbade all thought of unity of place and unity of action, with reference to the scope of the entire work, there was a certain unification of the several parts which was practicable, and which suggested what might be called an episodical treatment of the subject, with such connecting links, or such a general framework or setting, as historical truth might permit. And, in fact, different parts of the country were so cut off from each other when mutiny and rebellion were at their height, that each series of operations for the suppression of local revolt had a separate and distinct character. Certainly, in the earlier stages of the War, there was no general design—little co-operation or cohesion. Every man did what was best in his eyes to meet with vigour and sagacity an unexpected crisis. The cutting of our telegraph-wires and the interruption of our posts were among the first hostile efforts of the insurgents in all parts of the country. Joint action on a large scale was thus rendered impossible, and at the commencement of the War it would scarcely have been desirable. For our people had to deal promptly with urgent symptoms, and references and consultations would have been fatal to success.

Thus circumstanced with respect to the component parts of this History, I could not easily determine to what particular events it would be best to give priority of narration. One thing soon became unpleasantly apparent to me. I had made a mistake in forecasting the plan of the entire work, in an "Advertisement" prefixed to the First Volume. It was impossible to write adequately, in this instalment of my book, of all the operations which I had originally intended to record. With materials of such great interest before me, it would have been unwise to starve the narrative; so I thought it best to make confession of error, and to expunge my too-hasty promises from subsequent editions of the work. In pursuance of this revised scheme, I was compelled to put aside much that I had written for this Second Volume, and though this has necessarily retarded its publication, it has placed me so much in advance with the work to be accomplished, that I hope to be able to produce the next volume after a much shorter interval of time.

The selection made for this volume from the chapters which I had written may not perhaps be the best, but it is at least sufficiently intelligible. After describing the earlier incidents of the mutiny, as at Meerut and Delhi, at Benares and Allahabad, and at different stations in the Punjab, I have narrated, up to a certain point, those two great series of operations—the one expedition starting from Bengal with troops drawn from the Littoral, the other from the North-Western Frontier, with forces derived from the Hill Stations and the Punjab —which were consummated in the capture of Delhi and the first relief of Lucknow In the one I have traced the movements of Neill and Havelock, under the direction of Lord Canning, and in the other of Anson, Barnard, Wilson, and Nicholson, with the aid and inspiration of Sir John Lawrence. It is by thus following the fortunes of individuals that we may best arrive at a just conception of the general action of the whole. For it was by the energies of individual men, acting mostly on their own responsibility, that little by little rebellion was trodden down, and the supremacy of the English firmly re-established. It will be seen that I have adhered very closely to pure narrative. The volume, indeed, is a volume of fact, not of controversy and speculation, and as it relates to the earlier scenes of the great struggle for Empire, it is mostly an account of military revolt and its suppression.

Dealing with the large mass of facts, which are reproduced in the chapters now published, and in those which, though written, I have been compelled to reserve for future publication, I have consulted and collated vast piles of contemporary correspondence, and entered largely into communication, by personal intercourse or by letter, with men who have been individually connected with the events described. For every page published in this volume some ten pages have been written and compiled in aid of the narrative; and if I have failed in the one great object of my ambition, to tell the truth, without exaggeration on the one hand or reservation on the other, it has not been for want of earnest and laborious inquiry or of conscientious endeavour to turn my opportunities to the best account, and to lay before the public an honest exposition of the historical facts as they have been unfolded before me.

Still it is probable that the accuracy of some of the details in this volume, especially those of personal incident, may be questioned, perhaps contradicted, notwithstanding, I was about to say, all the care that I have taken to investigate them, but I believe that I should rather say "by reason of that very care." Such questionings or contradictions should not be too readily accepted; for, although the authority of the questioner may be good, there may be still better authority on the other side. I have often had to choose between very conflicting statements; and I have sometimes found my informants to be wrong, though apparently with the best opportunities of being right, and have been compelled to reject, as convincing proof, even the overwhelming assertion, "But, I was there." Men who are personally engaged in stirring events are often too much occupied to know what is going on beyond the little spot of ground which holds them at the time, and often from this restricted stand-point they see through a glass darkly. It is hard to disbelieve a man of honour when he tells you what he himself did, but every writer, long engaged in historical inquiry, has had before him instances in which men, after even a brief lapse of time, have confounded in their minds the thought of doing, or the intent to do, a certain thing, with the fact of having actually done it. Indeed, in the commonest affairs of daily life, we often find the intent mistaken for the act in the retrospect.

The case of Captain Rosser's alleged offer to take a Squadron of Dragoons and a Troop of Horse Artillery to Delhi on the night of the 10th of May (illustrated in the Appendix) may be regarded as an instance of this confusion. I could cite other instances. One will suffice:—A military officer of high rank, of stainless honour, with a great historical reputation, invited me some years ago to meet him, for the express purpose of making to me a most important statement, with reference to one of the most interesting episodes of the Sepoy War. The statement was a very striking one; and I was referred, in confirmation of it, to another officer, who has since become illustrious in our national history. Immediately on leaving my informant, I wrote down as nearly as possible his very words. It was not until after his death that I was able orally to consult the friend to whom he had referred me, as being personally cognisant of the alleged fact—the only witness, indeed, of the scene described. The answer was that he had heard the story before, but that nothing of the kind had ever happened. The asserted incident was one, as I ventured to tell the man who had described it to me at the time, that did not cast additional lustre on his reputation; and it would have been obvious, even if he had rejoiced in a less unblemished reputation, that it was not for self-glorification, but in obedience to an irrepressible desire to declare the truth, that he told me what afterwards appeared to be not an accomplished fact, but an intention unfulfilled. Experiences of this kind render the historical inquirer very sceptical even of information supposed to be on "the best possible authority." Truly, it is very disheartening to find that the nearer one approaches the fountain-head of truth, the further off we may find ourselves from it.*

* It may be mentioned here (though not directly in confirmation of the above) as a curious illustration of the difficulty of discerning between truth and error, that the only statement seriously impugned in a former work of history by the author of this book, was the only one which he had made as the result of his own personal knowledge—the only fact which he had witnessed with his own eyes.

But, notwithstanding such discouraging instances of the difficulty of extracting the truth, even from the testimony of truthful men, who have been actors in the scenes to be described, I cannot but admit the general value of such testimony to the writer of contemporary history. And, indeed, there need be some advantages in writing of events still fresh in the memory of men to compensate for its manifest disadvantages. These disadvantages, however, ought always to be felt by the writer rather than by the reader. It has been often said to me, in reply to my inquiries, "Yes, it is perfectly true. But these men are still living, and the truth cannot be told." To this my answer has been: "To the Historian all men are dead." If a writer of contemporary history is not prepared to treat the living and the dead alike—to speak as freely and as truthfully of the former as of the latter, with no more reservation in the one case than in the other—he has altogether mistaken his vocation, and should look for a subject in prehistoric times. There are some actors in the scenes here described of whom I do not know whether they be living or whether they be dead. Some have passed away from the sphere of worldly exploits whilst this volume has been slowly taking shape beneath my pen. But if this has in any way influenced the character of my writing, it has only been by imparting increased tenderness to my judgment of men, who can no longer defend themselves or explain their conduct to the world. Even this offence, if it be one against historical truth, I am not conscious of having actually committed.

I have but a few more words to say, but because I say them last it must not be thought that I feel them least. I am painfully sensible that in this narrative

I have failed to do justice to the courage and constancy of many brave men, whose good deeds deserved special illustration in this narrative, and would have received it, but for the exigencies of time and space, which have forbidden an ampler record. This, perhaps, may be more apparent in other volumes than in this. But, whatever may be the omissions in this respect, I do not think that they will be attributed to any want of appreciation of the gallantry and fortitude of my countrymen in doing and in suffering. No one could rejoice more in the privilege of illustrating their heroic deeds than the author ot these volumes. It is one of the best compensations of historical labour to be suffered to write of exploits reflecting so much honour upon the character of the nation.

J. W. K.

Penge—Midsummer, 1870.

HISTORY OF THE SEPOY WAR.

BOOK IV.—THE RISING IN THE NORTH-WEST.

[MAY, 1857.]

CHAPTER I.

IMPORTANCE OF THE SEIZURE OF DELHI—MORAL INFLUENCES—POSITION OF THE DELHI FAMILY—EARLY HISTORY—SUCCESSIVE DEGRADATIONS—THE QUESTION OF SUCCESSION—INTRIGUES OF ZEENUT-MEHAL—DEATH OF PRINCE FAKIR-OOD-DEEN—RENEWED INTRIGUES—VIEWS OF LORD CANNING—STATE OF MAHOMEDAN FEELING AT DELHI—THE NATIVE PRESS CORRESPONDENCE WITH PERSIA—THE PROCLAMATION—TEMPER OF THE SOLDIERY.

Lord Canning and the Delhi Question.

IT was a work of time at Calcutta to elicit all the details of the sad story briefly outlined in the preceding chapter. But the great fact was patent to Lord Canning that the English had been driven out of Delhi, and that, for a time, in that great centre of Mahomedanism, the dynasty of the Mogul Family was restored. The tremendous political significance of this revolution could not be misunderstood by the most obtuse, or glossed over by the most sanguine. The Emperors of Delhi had long ceased to exercise any substantial authority over the people whom they

1804–57. had once governed. For fifty years the Master of the Delhi Palace had been, in the estimation of the English, merely a pageant and a show. But the pageantry, the show, the name, had never ceased to be living influences in the minds of the princes and people of India. Up to a comparatively recent period all the coin of India had borne the superscription of the Mogul; and the chiefs of India, whether Mahomedan or Hindoo, had still continued to regard the sanction given to their successions by that shadow of royalty, as something more assuring than any recognition which could come from the substance of the British Government. If the Empire of Delhi had passed into a tradition, the tradition was still an honoured one. It had sunk deeply into the memories of the people.

Doubtful, before, of the strength of these influences, Lord Canning now began to suspect that he had been misinformed. In the preceding year, he had mastered the whole Delhi history, and he knew full well the peculiar circumstances which at that period made it so perilous that the Imperial Family should be appealed to in aid of the national cause. He saw before him, in all their length and breadth, the incidents of family intrigue, which imparted a vigorous individuality to the hostility of the Mogul. He knew that the chief inmates of the palace had never been in a mood of mind so little likely to resist the temptations now offered to them. He knew that the old King himself, and his favourite wife who ruled him, had been for some time cherishing animosities and resentments which rendered it but too likely that on the first encouraging occasion they would break into open hostility against the usurping Englishman, who had vaulted into the seat of the Mogul, reduced him to a suppliant, and thwarted him in all the most cherished wishes of his heart. 1804—57.

The Delhi story—Shah Allum.

With as much brevity as may suffice to make the position clear, the Delhi story must be told. The old King, Behaudur Shah, whose sovereignty had been proclaimed, was the second in descent from the Emperor Shah Allum, whom, blind, helpless, and miserable, the English had rescued from the gripe of the Mahrattas,* when at the dawn of the nineteenth century the armies of Lake and Wellesley broke up their powerful confederacy, and scattered the last hopes of the French. Shah Allum was the great-grandson of Aurungzebe, the tenth successor in a direct line from Timour, the great founder of the dynasty of the Moguls. Even in the depths of his misery and humiliation, he was regarded by the most magnificent of English viceroys as a mighty potentate, whom it was a privilege to protect, and sacrilege to think of supplanting. The "great game" of Lord Wellesley embraced nothing so stupendous as the usurpation of the Imperial throne. Perhaps it was, as his brother Arthur and John Malcolm declared, and as younger men suspected and hinted, that the Governor-General, worn out by the oppositions and restrictions of the Leadenhall-street Government, and broken in health by the climate of Calcutta, had lost his old daring and cast aside his pristine ambition. Perhaps it was believed by him and by his associates in the Council

1804.

* Lord Lake's first interview with him is thus officially described in the records of the day: "In the magnificent palace built by Shah Jehan the Commander-in-Chief was ushered into the royal presence, and found the unfortunate and venerable Emperor, oppressed by the accumulated calamities of old age and degraded authority, extreme poverty and loss of sight, seated under a small tattered canopy, the remnant of his royal state, with every external appearance of the misery of his condition."

1804—5. Chamber that it would be sounder policy, tending more to our own grandeur in the end, to gather gradual strength from this protective connexion with the Emperor, before endeavouring to walk in the pleasant paths of imperialism. But in either case, he recoiled from the thought of its being suspected in England, that he wished to place the East India Company, substantively or vicariously, on the throne of the Moguls. "It has never," he wrote to the Secret Committee of the Court of Directors, June 2, 1805, "been in the contemplation of this Government to derive from the charge of protecting and supporting his Majesty the privilege of employing the Royal Prerogative as an instrument of establishing any control or ascendancy over the States and Chieftains of India, or of asserting on the part of his Majesty any of the claims which, in his capacity of Emperor of Hindostan, his Majesty may be considered to possess upon the provinces originally composing the Mogul Empire. The benefits which the Governor-General in Council expected to derive from placing the King of Delhi and the Royal Family under the protection of the British Government, are to be traced in the statement contained in our despatch to your Honourable Committee of the 13th of July, 1804,* relative to the evils and embarrassments to which the British power might have been exposed by the prosecution of claims and pretensions

* The objects are thus enumerated in the despatch to which reference is made: "The deliverance of the Emperor Shah Allum from the control of the French power established in the North-West quarter of Hindostan, by which the Government of France has been deprived of a powerful instrument in the eventual prosecution of its hostile designs against the British Government in India, and the British Government has obtained a favourable opportunity of conciliating the confidence and securing the applause of surrounding states by providing a safe and tranquil asylum for the declining age of that venerable and unfortunate monarch, and a suitable maintenance for his numerous and distressed family."—*July* 13, 1804.

on the part of the Mahrattas, or of the French, in the name and under the authority of his Majesty Shah Allum, if the person and family of that unhappy monarch had continued under the custody and control of those powers, and especially of the French." 1804—5.

It must have taxed the ingenuity of Lord Wellesley, even with the experienced guidance and assistance of Sir George Barlow and Mr. Edmonstone, to design a scheme for the continuance or restoration of the Empire on a small scale—a scheme whereby Shah Allum might become more than a pensioner, a pageant, and a puppet, and yet less than the substance of a sovereign. He was to be a King and yet no King—a something and yet nothing—a reality and a sham at the same time. It was a solace to us, in the "great game," to know that we "held the King;" but it was a puzzle to us how to play the card. It was, indeed, a great political paradox, which Lord Wellesley's Government was called upon to institute; and he did the best that could be done, in the circumstances in which he was placed, to reconcile not only the House of Timour, but the people who still clung reverentially to the great Mahomedan dynasty, to the state of things which had arisen out of those circumstances. It was determined that a certain amount of that dignity, which is derived from territorial dominion, should still be attached to the person of the Emperor; that within certain limits he should still be the fountain of justice; and that (negatively) within those limits the power of life or death should be in his hands. And in addition to the revenues of the districts thus reserved as an appanage of the Throne, he and his family were to receive stipendiary allowances amounting to more than a hundred thousand pounds a year.

1804—5. Thus the Emperor of all the Indies—the Great Mogul, traditionally the grandest sovereign in the Universe—became, whilst still indued with the purple and the gold of imperial state, and rejoicing in the appearance of territorial dominion, virtually a pensioner of a Company of Merchants. The situation was one which conferred many advantages on the British Government in India, but it was not without its dangers. Even in the depths of his misery and degradation, the King's name was a pillar of strength; the rags of royalty were reverenced by the people. And Lord Wellesley saw clearly that if the ancestral State of the Mogul were perpetuated—if he were left to reside in the Palace of Shah Jehan, with all the accompaniments of his former grandeur around him, in the midst of a Mahomedan population still loyal to the House of Timour—there might some day be an attempt to reconstruct the ruined monarchy in the person of one of Shah Allum's successors, which might cause us grievous annoyance. So it was proposed that Monghyr should become the residence of the Imperial Family. But the old King shuddered at the thought of removal, and the shudder ran through his family, from the oldest to the youngest, male and female, relatives and dependants. Not, therefore, to inflict any further pain or humiliation upon them, Lord Wellesley consented that they should abide in the Delhi Palace. At some future time their removal might be effected without any cruel divulsions, any of those strainings and crackings of the heartstrings, which must attend the exodus of Princes born in the purple, with the memory of actual sovereignty still fresh within them.

1806. Akbar Shah. In December, 1806, Shah Allum died, and was succeeded by his son, Akbar Shah. It happened that the English officer, who at that time represented the British Government at Delhi, was a courtier of the old school, whose inveterate politeness of speech and manner had ample scope for exercise at the ex-imperial Court Mr. Seton would have died rather than hurt the feelings of the humblest denizen of the Palace. In the caricatures of the period he was represented saluting Satan with a low bow, and hoping that his Majesty was well and prosperous. Associated, at this time, in a subordinate capacity with Mr. Seton, but much trusted, and consulted by him with the deference shown to an equal in age and position, was young Charles Metcalfe, who, although little more than a boy, saw clearly the store of future trouble which the British Government was laying up for itself by not curbing the pretensions of the now effete Mogul. "I do not conform," he wrote, "to the policy of Seton's mode of managing the Royal Family. It is by a submission of manner and conduct, carried on, in my opinion, far beyond the respect and attention which can be either prescribed by forms or dictated by a humane consideration for the fallen fortunes of a once illustrious family. It destroys entirely the dignity which ought to be attached to him who represents the British Government, and who in reality is to govern at Delhi; and it raises (I have perceived the effect disclosing itself with rapidity) ideas of imperial powe and sway which ought to be put to sleep for ever. As it is evident that we do not mean to restore imperial power to the King, we ought not to pursue a conduct calculated to make him aspire to it. Let us treat him with the respect due to his situation; let us make him comfortable in respect to circumstances, and give him all the means, as far as possible, of 1806.

1806–37. being happy; but, unless we mean to re-establish his power, let us not encourage him to dream of it." No grey-haired politician could have written anything wiser than this; and when, after the lapse of a few years, the writer himself became "Resident" at Delhi, and had the supreme direction of affairs, all his boyish impressions were confirmed. He was brought face to face with a state of things offensive alike to reason and to humanity; but neither he nor his successors in the Residency could do more than recommend one measure after another which might gradually mitigate the evils which stood out so obtrusively before them.

Time passed; and the English in India, secure in their great possessions, dreading no external enemy, and feeling strong within them the power to tread down any danger which might arise on Indian soil, advanced with a firmer step and a bolder presence. They no longer recoiled from the thought of Empire. What had appeared at the commencement of the century to be perilous presumption, now seemed to be merely the inevitable accident of our position. The "great game" had been imperfectly played out in Lord Wellesley's time; and ten years afterwards Lord Hastings saw before him the results of that settlement where nothing was settled, and resolved to assert the supremacy of the British Government over all the potentates of India. Times were changed both at home and abroad, and our feelings had changed with them. The Company had not quite forgotten that it had been established on a "pure mercantile bottom." But the successes of our arms in Europe had given us confidence in ourselves as a great military nation; and, though the Directors in Leadenhall-street, true to their old traditions, might still array themselves against all projects for the extension of our military and political power in the East, it was felt that the people of England would applaud the bolder policy, if it were only successful. From that time England became arbiter of the fate of all the Princes of India. There was no longer any reluctance to assert our position as the paramount power. It was a necessary part of the scheme then to put down the fiction of the Delhi Empire. The word Empire was, thenceforth, to be associated only with the British power in the East; and the mock-majesty, which we had once thought it serviceable to us to maintain, was now, as soon as possible, to be dismissed as inconvenient lumber. 1806—37.

It might be narrated how, during a period of thirty years, the sun of royalty, little by little, was shorn of its beams—how first one Governor-General and then another resisted the proud pretensions of the Mogul, and lopped off some of the ceremonial obeisances which had so long maintained the inflated dignity of the House of Timour.* All these humiliations rankled in the minds of the inmates of the Palace; but they were among the necessities of the continually advancing supremacy of the English. It may be questioned whether a single man, to whose opinion any weight of authority can fairly be attached, has ever doubted the wisdom of these excisions. And humanity might well pause to consider whether more might not yet be done to mitigate that great evil of rotting royalty which had so long polluted the atmosphere of Delhi. That gigantic Palace, almost a city in itself, had long been the

* It was not until 1835, that the current coin of India ceased to bear the superscription of the Mogul emperors, and the "Company's rupee" was substituted for it.

1806–37. home of manifold abominations; and a Christian Government had suffered, and was still suffering, generation after generation of abandoned men and degraded women, born in that vast sty of refuge, to be a curse to others and to themselves. In subdued official language, it was said of these wretched members of a Royal House, that they were "independent of all law, immersed in idleness and profligacy, and indifferent to public opinion."* It might have been said, without a transgression of the truth, that the recesses of the Palace were familiar with the commission of every crime known in the East, and that Heaven alone could take account of that tremendous catalogue of iniquities.

1837. Behaudur Shah. On the evening of the 28th of September, 1837, Akbar Shah died, at the age of eighty-two. He had intrigued some years before to set aside the succession of the Heir-Apparent in behalf of a favourite son; but he had failed.† And now Prince Aboo Zuffer, in the official language of the day, "ascended the throne, assuming the title of Abool Mozuffer Surajoodeen Mahomed Behaudur Shah Padshah-i-Gazee." It is sufficient that he should be known here by the name of Behaudur Shah. He was then far advanced in age; but he was of a long-lived family, and his three-score years had not pressed heavily upon him. He was supposed to be a quiet, inert man, fond of poetry, a poetaster himself; and not at all addicted, by nature, to political intrigue. If he had any prominent characteristic it was avarice. He had not long succeeded to the title

* Sometimes, however, great crimes were punished. Prince Hyder Shekoh, for example, was executed for the murder of his wife.

† Indeed, he had made two separate efforts, in favour first of one son, then of another. The first endeavour was attended with some eventful circumstances which might have led to violence and bloodshed.

before he began to press for an addition to the royal stipend, which had in some sort been promised to Akbar Shah. The Lieutenant-Governor was unwilling to recommend such a waste of the public money; but the Governor-General, equally believing it to be wasteful, said that, although as a new question he would have negatived it, the promise having been given it ought to be fulfilled—but upon the original conditions. These conditions were, that the King should execute a formal renunciation of all further claims upon the British Government; but Behaudur Shah did as his father had done before him. He refused to subscribe to the proposed conditions, and continued to cherish a belief that, by sending an agent to England, he might obtain what he sought without any embarrassing restrictions.

1837.

Sir Charles Metcalfe.

Lord Auckland.

Akbar Shah had employed as his representative the celebrated Brahmin, Rammohun Roy, and ever still regarding himself as the fountain of honour, had conferred on his envoy the title of Rajah. English society recognised it, as it would have recognised a still higher title, assumed by a Khitmudgar; but the authorities refused their official recognition to the Rajahship, though they paid becoming respect to the character of the man, who was striving to enlighten the Gentiles, as a social and religious reformer. As the envoy of the Mogul he accomplished nothing; and Behaudur Shah found that the "case" was much in the same state as it had been when Rammohun Roy left India on the business of the late King. But he had still faith in the efficacy of mission to England, especially if conducted by a Englishman. So when he heard that an eloquent lecturer, who had gained a great reputation in the Western world by his earnest advocacy of the rights

Rammohun Roy.

George Thompson.

1843 of the coloured races, had come to India, Behaudur Shah invited him to Delhi, and was eager to enlist his services. He had many supposed wrongs to be redressed. Lord Ellenborough had given the finishing stroke to the system of nuzzur-giving, or tributary present-making, to the King, by prohibiting even such offerings by the Resident.* Thus had passed away almost the last vestige of that recognition, by the British Government, of the imperial dignity of the House of Timour; and although money-compensation had been freely given for the loss, the change rankled in the mind of the King. But the Company had already refused to grant any increase of stipend to the Royal Family until the prescribed conditions had been accepted;† and Mr. George Thompson had no more power than Rammohun Roy to cause a relaxation of the decision. And in truth, there was no sufficient reason why the stipend should be increased. A lakh of rupees a month was sufficient, on a broad basis of generosity, even for that multitudinous family; and it would have been profligate to throw away more money on the mock-royalty of Delhi, when it might be so much better bestowed.‡

There was, indeed, no ground of complaint against

* Nuzzurs had formerly been presented by the Governor-General and the Commander-in-Chief—by the latter, it would seem, as recently as 1837, on the accession of Shah Behaudur.—See Letter of the Government of India, May 23, 1838. And in the cold season of 1842–3 Lord Ellenborough's secretaries presented nuzzurs to the King, without any intimation to the Governor-General; who, on learning what they had done, was surprised and indignant in the extreme, and put a stop to the nuzzur-giving for ever. Mr. William Edwards, one of the secretaries concerned, has given an interesting account of the affair, which will be found in the Appendix.

† Letter of the Court of Directors, Feb. 11, 1846: "It being impossible for us to waive this condition (of executing a formal renunciation of all further claims) the King must be considered as having declined the offered benefit."

‡ In addition to this monthly lakh of rupees, paid in money, Behaudur Shah continued to enjoy the proceeds of some crown lands, and also of some ground-rents in the city.—See evidence of Mr. Sanders at the King's trial: "He was in receipt of a stipend of one lakh of rupees per

the British Government; and, perhaps, the King would have subsided into a state, if not of absolute content, of submissive quietude, if it had not been for that activity of Zenana intrigue, which no Oriental sovereign, with nothing to do but to live, can ever hope to resist. He had married a young wife, who had borne him a son, and who had become a favourite, potential for good or evil. As often it has happened, from the time of the patriarchs downwards, this son of his old age also became a favourite; and the King was easily wrought upon by Queen Zeenut-Mehal to endeavour to set aside the succession of the heir-apparent in favour of the boy-prince. The unjust supercession, which his father had endeavoured to perpetrate against him, might now some day be put in force by himself, for the gratification of his favourite. But it was necessary in such a case to walk warily. Any rash hasty action might be followed by a failure which could never be repaired. In any case, it would be better to wait until the child, Jewan Bukht, were a few years older, and he could be extolled as a youth of promise. Meanwhile the great Chapter of Accidents might contain something in their favour. So hanging on to the skirts of Circumstance, he watched for the coming of an opportunity. And ere long the opportunity came—bringing with it more than had been looked for, and not all to the satisfaction of the royal expectants.

1843—9. Zenana intrigue.

The story may be briefly told. In 1849, Prince

1849. The story of the succession.

mensem, of which ninety-nine thousand were paid at Delhi, and one thousand at Lucknow, to the members of the family there. He was also in receipt of revenue to the amount of a lakh and a half from the crown lands in the neighbourhood of Delhi. He also received a considerable sum from the ground-rents of houses and tenants in the city of Delhi."

1849. Dara Bukht, the Heir-Apparent, died. At this time the King, Behaudur Shah, had numbered more than seventy years. In natural course his death could be no very remote contingency. The question of succession, therefore, pressed heavily on the mind of the Governor-General. Lord Dalhousie was not a man to regard with much favour the mock sovereignty of the Mogul. Others before him, with greater tenderness for ancient dynastic traditions, had groaned over the long continuance of a state of things at which reason and truth revolted; and the extinction of the titular dignity of the Kings of Delhi, after the death of Behaudur Shah, had been urged upon the Government of the East India Company.* But the proposal stirred up divisions in the Council Chamber of Leadenhall, which resulted in delayed action. The usual expedient of waiting for further advices from India was resorted to, and so Lord Dalhousie found the question unsettled. The death of Prince Dara Bukht afforded an opportunity for its settlement, which a Governor-General of Dalhousie's temperament was not likely to neglect. The next in succession, according to Mahomedan law, was Prince Fakir-ood-deen, a man thirty years of age, reputed to be of quick parts, fond of European society, and tolerant of the British Government. And the Governor-General saw both in the character of the man and the circumstances of his position that which might favour and

* Writing on the 1st of August, 1844, the Court of Directors observed: "The Governor-General has given directions to the Agent that, in the event of the demise of the King of Delhi, no step whatever shall be taken which can be construed into a recognition of the descent of that title to a successor without specific authority from the Governor-General. If in these instructions the abolition of the title is contemplated, we cannot give it our sanction until we have heard further from you on the subject, and have had time to consider the purport and the grounds of the recommendation which may be offered."

facilitate the changes which he wisely desired to introduce. 1849

It was manifestly the duty of the British Government not to perpetuate a state of things which had nothing but tradition to gloss over its offensive deformity But the operation that had become necessary was not one to be performed violently and abruptly, without regard to times and seasons. Feeling sure that the opportunity could not be far distant, Lord Dalhousie had been contented to wait. It had now come. Prince Dara Bukht was the last of the Delhi Princes who had been "born in the purple." He had been reared and he had ripened in the expectation of succeeding to the Kingship of Delhi; and there might have been some hardship, if not a constructive breach of faith, in destroying the hopes of a lifetime at the very point of fruition. But Prince Fakir-ood-deen had been born a pensioner. He had no recollection of "the time when the King of Delhi still sat on the throne and was recognised as the paramount potentate in India." It could, therefore, be no injustice to him to admit his accession to the chiefship of the family upon other conditions than those which had been recognised in the case of his father; whilst it was, in the opinion of the Governor-General, sound policy, on the other hand, to sweep away all the privileges and prerogatives which had kept alive this great pretentious mock-royalty in the heart of our Empire.

Lord Dalhousie's measures.

The evils to be removed were many; but two among them were more glaring than the rest. The perpetuation of the kingly title was a great sore. Lord Dalhousie did not overrate its magnitude. Perhaps, indeed, he scarcely took in its true proportions For he wrote that the Princes of India and

1849. its people, whatever they might once have been, had become "entirely indifferent to the condition of the King or his position."* And he added: "The British Government has become indeed and in truth the paramount Sovereign in India. It is not expedient that there should be, even in name, a rival in the person of a Sovereign whose ancestors once held the paramountcy we now possess. His existence could never really endanger us, I admit; although the intrigues of which he might, and not unfrequently has been made the nucleus, might incommode and vex us." I have said before that Lord Dalhousie "could not understand the tenacity with which the natives of India cling to their old traditions—could not sympathise with the veneration which they felt for their ancient dynasties."† Time might have weakened the veneration felt for the House of Delhi, but had not, assuredly, effaced it. There was still sufficient vitality in it to engender, under favouring circumstances, something more than discomfort and vexation. But Lord Dalhousie erred only in thus under-estimating the proportions of the evil which he now desired to remove. He was not, on that account, less impressed with the fact that it would be grievous impolicy on the part of the British Government to suffer the kingly title, on the death of Behaudur Shah, to pass to another generation.

The other evil thing of which I have spoken was the maintenance of the Palace as a royal residence. Regarded in the aspect of morality and humanity, as already observed, it was an abomination of the worst kind. But, more clearly even than this, Lord Dalhousie discerned the political and military disadvantages of the existing state of things, by

* Minute, February 10, 1849. † *Ante*, vol. i. p. 356.

which, what was in reality a great fortress in the hands of a possible enemy, was suffered to command the chief arsenal of Upper India. "Here," wrote the Governor-General, "we have a strong fortress in the heart of one of the principal cities of our Empire, and in entire command of the chief magazine of the Upper Provinces—which lies so exposed, both to assault and to the dangers arising from the carelessness of the people dwelling around it—that it is a matter of surprise that no accident has yet occurred to it. Its dangerous position has been frequently remarked upon, and many schemes have been prepared for its improvement and defence; but the only eligible one is the transfer of the stores into the Palace, which would then be kept by us as a British post, capable of maintaining itself against any hostile manœuvre, instead of being, as it now is, the source of positive danger, and perhaps not unfrequently the focus of intrigues against our power."* 1849.

There was undoubted wisdom in this. To remove

* It does not appear, however, that Lord Dalhousie laid any stress upon the fact that no European troops were posted in Delhi. Nor, indeed, did Sir Charles Napier, who at this time was Commander-in-Chief of the British army in India. He saw clearly that the military situation was a false one, and he wrote much about the defence of the city, but without drawing any distinction between European and Native troops. In both cases the anticipated danger was from a rising of the people, not of the soldiery. With respect to the situation of the magazine, Sir Charles Napier wrote to the Governor-General (Lahore, Dec. 15, 1849), saying: "As regards the magazine, the objections to it are as follows: 1st. It is placed in a very populous part of the city, and its explosion would be very horrible in its effects as regards the destruction of life. 2nd. It would destroy the magnificent Palace of Delhi. 3rd. The loss of Government property would also be very great, especially if my views of the importance of Delhi, given in my report, be acted upon; namely, that it and Dinapore should be two great magazines for the Bengal Presidency. 4th. It is without defence beyond what the guard of fifty men offer, and its gates are so weak that a mob could push them in. I therefore think a powder magazine should be built in a safe place. There is a strong castle three or four miles from the town which would answer well, but I fear the repairs would be too expensive; more so, perhaps, than what would be more efficacious, viz., to build a magazine in a suitable position near the city."

1849. the Delhi Family from the Palace, and to abolish all their Alsatian privileges, upon the death of Behaudur Shah, could have been no very difficult work. But to Lord Dalhousie it appeared that this part of the duty which lay before him should be accomplished with the least possible delay. He conceived that there would be no necessity to wait for the demise of the titular sovereign, as in all probability the King might be persuaded to vacate the Palace, if sufficient inducement were held out to him. He argued that, as the Kings of Delhi had possessed a convenient and favourite country residence at the Kootab, some twelve miles to the south of Delhi, and that as the place was held in great veneration, generally and particularly, as the burial-place of a noted Mahomedan saint and of some of the ancestors of Behaudur Shah, his Majesty and the Royal Family were not likely to object to their removal, and, if they did object, it was to be considered whether pressure might not be put upon them, and their consent obtained by the extreme measure of withholding the royal stipend. But the representative of a long line of Kings might not unreasonably have demurred to the expulsion of his Family from the old home of his fathers, and it demanded no great exercise of imagination to comprehend the position.

Views of th Home Government.

When this exposition of Lord Dalhousie's views was laid before the Court of Directors of the East India Company, the subject was debated with much interest in Leadenhall-street.* Already had the strong mind of the Governor-General begun to influence the councils of the Home Government of India. There were one or two able and active members of

* Sir Archibald Galloway, who had taken part in the defence of Delhi at the commencement of the century, was Chairman of the East India Company.

the Court who believed implicitly in him, and were resolute to support everything that he did. There was another section of the Court, which had no special faith in Lord Dalhousie, but which, upon system, supported the action of the local Governments, as the least troublesome means of disposing of difficult questions. But there was a third and powerful party—powerful in intellect, more powerful still in its unflinching honesty and candour, and its inalienable sense of justice—and this party prevailed. The result was that the majority agreed to despatch instructions to India, negativing the proposals of the Governor-General. But when the draft went from Leadenhall-street to Cannon-row, it met with determined opposition from the Board of Control, over which at that time Sir John Hobhouse presided.* It was contended that the British Government were not pledged to continue to Shah Allum's successors the privileges accorded to him, and that the Court had not proved that the proposals of the Governor-General were either unjust or impolitic. Then arose one of those sharp conflicts between the Court and the Board which in the old days of the Double Government sometimes broke in upon the monotony of their councils. The Court rejoined that the proposals were those of the Governor-General alone, that the concurrence of his Council had not been obtained, that the contemplated measures were ungenerous and unwise,† and that it would give grievous offence to the

1849.

Conflict between the Court and the Board.

* Mr. James Wilson and the Hon. John Eliot were then Secretaries to the Board.

† "The question," they said, "is not one of supremacy. The supremacy of the British power is beyond dispute. The sovereignty of Delhi is a title utterly powerless for injury, but respected by Mahomedans as an ancient honour of their name, and their good feelings are conciliated to the British Government by

1849. Mahomedan population of the country. They were prepared to sanction persuasive means to obtain the evacuation of the Palace, but they most strongly objected to compulsion. The Board then replied that it was not necessary in such a case to obtain the consent of the Members of Council, and that if they had felt any alarm as to the results of the proposed measure, they would have communicated their apprehensions to the Court (which, however, was a mistaken impression)—that there was no sort of obligation to continue to the successors of Shah Allum what Lord Wellesley had granted to him—that it was a question only of policy, and that as to the effect of the proposed measure on the minds of the Mahomedans, the local ruler was a better judge than the Directors at home (and this, perhaps, was another mistake); but when the Indian minister added: "The chance of danger to the British Empire from the head of the House of Timour may be infinitely small; but if a Mahomedan should ever think that he required such a rallying-point for the purpose of infusing into those of his own faith spirit and bitterness in an attack on Christian supremacy, he would surely find that a Prince already endowed with the regal title, and possessed of a royal residence, was a more efficient instrument in his hands than one placed in the less conspicuous position contemplated by Lord Dalhousie and his advisers," he spoke wisely and presciently On receipt of this letter, the Court again

the respect it shows for that ancient honour. The entire indifference of the Princes and the people of India to the condition or position of the King is alleged; but the Court cannot think it possible that any people can ever become indifferent to the memory of its former greatness. The traditional deference with which that memory is regarded is altogether distinct from any hopes of its renewal But it is a feeling which it is impolitic to wound. From mere hopelessness of resistance it may not immediately show itself, but may remain latent till other causes of public danger may bring it into action."

returned to the conflict, urging that they felt so deeply the importance of the subject that they could not refrain from making a further appeal to the Board. They combated what had been said about the implied concurrence of the Council, and the argument against the claims of the Delhi Family based upon the action of Lord Wellesley, and then they proceeded to speak again of the feelings of the Mahomedan population. "The amount of disaffection," they said, "in the Mahomedan population, which the particular measure, if carried into effect, may produce, is a matter of opinion on which the means do not exist of pronouncing confidently. The evil may prove less than the Court apprehend, or it may be far greater than they would venture to predict. But of this they are convinced, that even on the most favourable supposition, the measure would be considered throughout India as evidence of the commencement of a great change in our policy." "The Court," it was added, "cannot contemplate without serious uneasiness the consequences which may arise from such an impression, should it go forth generally throughout India—firmly believing that such an act would produce a distrust which many years of an opposite policy would be insufficient to remove." Then, having again entreated most earnestly the Board's reconsideration of their decision, they concluded by saying, that if they failed, they would "still have discharged their duty to themselves, by disclaiming all responsibility for a measure which they regarded as unjust towards the individual family, gratuitously offensive to an important portion of our Indian subjects, and calculated to produce an effect on the reputation and influence of the British Government both in India and elsewhere, such as

1849.

1849. they would deeply deplore." But the last appeal fell on stony ground. The Board were obdurate. They deplored the difference of opinion, accepted the disclaimer, and, on the last day of the year, directed, "according to the powers vested in them by the law," a despatch to be sent to India in the form settled by the Board. So instructions were sent out to India, signed ministerially by certain members of the Court, totally opposed to what, as a body, they believed to be consistent with policy and justice.

December 31, 1849.

Summary of the argument.

On full consideration of this correspondence, conducted as it was, on both sides, with no common ability, it is difficult to resist the conviction that both were right and both were wrong—right in what they asserted, wrong in what they denied. It was, in truth, but a choice of evils that lay before the double Government; but each half of it erred in denying the existence of the dangers asserted by the other. Much, of course, on both sides was conjecture or speculation, to be tested by the great touchstone of the Future; and it depended on the more rapid or the more tardy ripening of events on the one side or the other to demonstrate the greater sagacity of the Court or the Board. If there should be no popular excitement before the death of Behaudur Shah, to make the King of Delhi, in his great palatial stronghold, a rallying-point for a disaffected people, that event, followed by the abolition of the title and the removal of the Family from the Palace, might prove the soundness of the Court's arguments, by evoking a Mahomedan outbreak; but, if there should be a Mahomedan, or any other popular outbreak, during the lifetime of Behaudur Shah, it might be shown, by the alacrity of the people to rally round the old imperial throne, and to proclaim again the sovereignty of the House of Timour, that the apprehensions of the Board had not been misplaced, and that the danger on which they had enlarged was a real one. There was equal force at the time in the arguments of both, but there was that in the womb of the Future which was destined to give the victory to the Board. 1849.

1850. Measures deferred.

Lord Dalhousie received the instructions bearing the official signatures of the Court in the early spring of 1850;* but he had before learnt in what a hot-bed of contention the despatch was being reared, and when it came, he wisely hesitated to act upon its contents. It is to his honour that, on full consideration, he deferred to the opinions expressed by the majority of the Court, and by others not in the Court, whose opinions were entitled to equal respect. "The Honourable Court," he said, "have conveyed to the Governor-General in Council full authority to carry these measures into effect But I have, for some time past, been made aware through different channels, that the measures I have thus proposed regard-

* Some powerful protests were recorded by members of the Court—among others by Mr. Tucker, then nearly eighty years of age. In this paper he said: "That they (the Delhi family) can be induced voluntarily to abandon their palace, I cannot, for one moment, believe. The attachment of the natives generally to the seats of their ancestors, however humble, is well known to all those who know anything of the people of India; but in this case there are peculiar circumstances, the cherished associations of glory, the memory of past grandeur, which must render the Palace of Delhi the object of attachment and veneration to the fallen family. . . . . If the object is to be accomplished, it must be by the exertion of military force, or intimidation disgraceful to any Government, and calculated to bring odium on the British name." "I have the highest respect," he said, "for the talents, the great acquirements, and the public spirit of Lord Dalhousie; but I must think that an individual, who has only communicated with the people of India through an interpreter, cannot have acquired a very intimate knowledge of the character, habits, feelings, and prejudices of the people." The veteran director erred, however, in making light of the strength of Delhi as a fortified city. "It is not," he said, "a fortress of any strength. . . . . It has been repeatedly entered and sacked by undisciplined hordes." "There is, in fact," he continued, "no ground for assuming that Delhi can become a military post of importance, especially now that we have advanced our frontier to the banks of the Indus."

1850. ing the throne of Delhi, have not met with the concurrence of authorities in England whose long experience and knowledge of Indian affairs entitle their opinions to great weight, and that many there regard the tendency of these proposed measures with anxiety, if not with alarm." He added that, with unfeigned deference to the opinions thus expressed, he still held the same views as before; but that, although his convictions remained as strong as ever, he did not consider the measures themselves to be of such immediate urgency as to justify his carrying them into effect, "contrary to declared opinions of undoubted weight and authority, or in a manner calculated to create uneasiness and doubt." He was willing, therefore, to suspend action, and, in the mean while, to invite the opinions of his Council, which had not been before recorded.

Palace intrigues.

Whilst the main questions thus indicated were under consideration, another difficulty of a personal character arose. The King protested against the succession of Fakir-ood-deen. Stimulated by his favourite wife, Zeenut-Mehal, he pleaded earnestly for her son, then a boy of eleven. One objection which he raised to the succession of his eldest surviving son was a curious one. He said that it was a tradition of his House, since the time of Timour, that no one was to sit on the throne who had been in any way mutilated; Fakir-ood-deen had been circumcised, and, therefore, he was disqualified.* The objection was

* The statement was an exaggerated one—as all the Mogul Emperors, up to the time of Hoomayoon, were circumcised. After the accession of this prince, for reasons given in a very interesting note, at the end of the volume, furnished by my learned friend, Moulavee Syud Ahmed, C.S.I., the rite was discontinued, generally, in the family. But for certain physical reasons, an exception was made, with respect to Fakir-ood-deen, and Zenut-Mehal seized upon the pretext.

urged with much vehemence, and, it was added, that Fakir-ood-deen was a man of bad character. The immediate effect of these representations was that Lord Dalhousie determined for a while to suspend official action with respect to the question of succession, and to see what circumstances might develop in his favour. 1850.

Opinions of the Council.

In the mean time he invited the opinions of his colleagues in the Supreme Council. It consisted, at that time, of Sir Frederick Currie, Sir John Littler, an old Company's officer of good repute, and Mr. John Lowis, a Bengal civilian, blameless in all official and personal relations, one of the lights of the Service, steady but not brilliant. The first shrewdly observed that we might leave the choice of a successor until the King's death, which could not be very remote, and that we might then easily make terms with, or impose conditions upon, the accepted candidate, for the evacuation of the Palace. The General looked doubtfully at the whole proposal. He believed that the Mahomedan population of India still regarded with reverence the old Mogul Family, and would be incensed by its humiliation. He counselled, therefore, caution and delay, and in the end persuasion, not compulsion. But John Lowis laughed all this to scorn. He did not believe that the Mahomedans of India cared anything about Delhi, or anything about the King; and if they did care, that, he said, was an additional reason why the title should be abolished, and the Palace vacated, with the least possible delay.*

* "But, if these fears are not groundless, surely they afford a positive reason for taking the proposed step, because the result anticipated, as it appears to me, can arise only if the Mahomedans (no doubt the most restless and discontented of our subjects) have continued to look upon the representatives of the House of Timour as their natural head, and to

1850. The result of these deliberations was that a despatch was sent to England, recommending that affairs should remain unchanged during the lifetime of the present King—that the Prince Fakir-ood-deen should be acknowledged as successor to the royal title, but that advantage should be taken of the pretensions of a rival claimant to the titular dignity, to obtain the desired concessions from the acknowledged Head of the Family—that inducements should be held out to him to leave the Palace and to reside in the Kootab, and that, if necessary, this advantage should be purchased by the grant of an additional stipend.

Agreement with the Heir-Apparent.

To all the recommendations of the Governor-General—so far as they concern this history—the Home Government yielded their consent. Permission was then granted to the Delhi Agent to make known to Prince Fakir-ood-deen, at a confidential interview, what were the intentions and wishes of the British Government. A meeting, therefore, took place between the Prince and Sir Thomas Metcalfe; and the former expressed himself, according to official reports, prepared to accede to the wishes of the Government, "if invested with the title of King, and permitted to assume the externals of royalty." An agreement was then drawn up, signed, sealed, and witnessed, and the work was done. It was, doubtless, pleasant to the authorities to think that the heir had acceded willingly to all the demands made upon him. But the fact is that he consented to them with intense disgust, and that throughout the Palace there were great consternation and excitement, and that no one

count upon the Palace of Delhi as a rallying point in the event of any outbreak amongst them. If it be so, it is surely sound policy, on the first favourable opportunity, to remove the head, and to put the projected rallying point into safe hands."

was more vexed than the mother of the rival claimant, 1850.
Queen Zeenut-Mehal.

I must pass hastily over the next two or three 1856.
years, during which the animosities of the Queen Death of
Zeenut-Mehal, and of her son, Jewan Bakht, con- Fakir-ood-deen.
tinued to fester under the irritations of a great disappointment. And ere long they were aggravated by the thought of a new grievance; for the King had endeavoured in vain to induce the British Government to pledge itself to make to his favourites, after his death, the same payments as he had settled upon them during his life. The intrigues which, if successful, would have secured to them so much at the expense of others, altogether failed. But the King lived on—lived to survive the heir whose succession was so distasteful to him. On the 10th of July, 1856, Prince Fakir-ood-deen suddenly died. It was more than suspected that he had been poisoned. He was seized with deadly sickness and vomiting, after partaking of a dish of curry. Extreme prostration and debility ensued, and although the King's physician, Ahsan-oollah, was called in, he could or would do nothing to restore the dying Prince; and in a little time there were lamentations in the Heir-Apparent's house, and tidings were conveyed to the Palace that Fakir-ood-deen was dead.*

How that night was spent in the apartments of

* The Palace Diary of the day says: "Having felt hungry, the Prince imagined that an empty stomach promoted bile, and partook of some bread with curry gravy, when immediately the vomitings increased, which produced great debility. Every remedy to afford relief proved ineffectual, and H.R.H. rapidly sunk. Meerza Elahee Buksh sent for Hakim Assan-oolah to prescribe. The Hakim administered a clyster, which, however, did no good. At six o'clock, the Heir-Apparent was in a moribund state, and immediately after the noise of lamentation was heard in the direction of the Heir-Apparent's residence, and news was brought to the Palace of H.R.H.'s demise. His Majesty expressed his sorrow. The Newab Zeenut-Mehal Begum condoled with his Majesty."

1856. Queen Zeenut-Mehal can only be conjectured. Judged by its results, it must nave been a night of stirring intrigue and excited activity. For when, on the following day, Sir Thomas Metcalfe waited on the King, his Majesty put into the hands of the Agent a paper containing a renewed expression of his desire to see the succession of Jewan Bakht recognised by the British Government. Enclosed was a document purporting to convey a request from others of the King's sons, that the offspring of Zeenut-Mehal, being endowed with "wisdom, merit, learning, and good manners," should take the place of the Heir-Apparent. Eight of the royal princes attached their seals to this address. But the eldest of the survivors —Meerza Korash by name—next day presented a memorial of his own, in which he set forth that his brethren had been induced to sign the paper by promises of increased money-allowances from the King, if they consented, and deprivation of income if they refused. An effort also was made to bribe Meerza Korash into acquiescence. He professed all filial loyalty to the King; declared his willingness to accede, as Heir-Apparent, to such terms as the King might suggest; but when he found that his father, instigated by the Queen Zeenut-Mehal, was bent on setting him aside altogether, he felt that there was nothing left for him but an appeal to the British Government. "As in this view," he wrote to the British Agent, "my ruin and birthright are involved, I deem it proper to represent my case, hoping that in your report due regard will be had to all the above circumstances. Besides being senior, I have accomplished a pilgrimage to Mecca, and have learned by heart the Koran; and my further attainments can be tested in an interview."

By this time Lord Canning had succeeded to the Governor-Generalship, and a new Council sate beside him. . The whole question of the Delhi succession, therefore, was considered and debated by men uninfluenced by any foregone expressions of opinion. In truth, the question was not a difficult one. The course which Lord Dalhousie meant to pursue was apparently the wisest course; although he had erred in believing that the Mahomedans of Upper India had no lingering affection for the sovereignty of the House of Delhi; and not less in supposing that the removal of the King and the Royal Family from the Palace in the city would not be painful and humiliating to them. But, with laudable forbearance, he had yielded to the opinions of others, even with the commission in his hands to execute his original designs. Lord Canning, therefore, found the Delhi question unsettled and undetermined in many of the most essential points. Bringing a new eye to the contemplation of the great danger and the great abomination of the Delhi Palace, he saw both, perhaps, even in larger dimensions than they had presented to the eye of his predecessor. He did not, therefore, hesitate to adopt as his own the views which Lord Dalhousie had recorded with respect to the removal of the Family on the death of Behaudur Shah. "It is as desirable as ever," he wrote, "that the Palace of Delhi—which is, in fact, the citadel of a large fortified town, and urgently required for military purposes—should be in the hands of the Government of the country, and that the pernicious privilege of exemption from the law, which is conceded to the Crown connexions and dependants of the King now congregated there, should, in the interests of morality and good government, cease." It was scarcely possible,

1856.

Views of Lord Canning:

1856 indeed, that much difference of opinion could obtain among statesmen with respect to the political and military expediency of placing this great fortified building, which dominated the city of Delhi, in the secure possession of British troops; nor could there be any doubt in the mind of a Christian man that, in the interests of humanity, we were bound to pull down all those screens and fences which had so long shut out the abominations of the Palace from the light of day, and excluded from its murky recesses the saving processes of the law.

But the extinction of the titular sovereignty was still an open question. Lord Canning had spent only a few months in India, and those few months had been passed in Calcutta. He had no personal knowledge of the feelings of the princes or people of Upper India; but he read in the minutes of preceding members of the Government that the traditions of the House of Timour had become faint in men's minds, if they had not been wholly effaced; and he argued that if there was force in this when written, there must be greater force after a lapse of years, as there was an inevitable tendency in time to obliterate such memories "The reasons," he said, "which induced a change of purpose in 1850 are not fully on record;* but whatever they may have been, the course of time has assuredly strengthened the arguments by which the first intentions were supported, and possibly has removed the objection to it." He further argued that as much had already been done to strip the mock majesty of Delhi of the purple and gold with which it had once been be-

* That is, not on record in India. The reasons are fully stated above; but Lord Canning apparently did not know that the "Court's despatch" was really not their despatch at all.

dizened—that as first one privilege and then another, which had pampered the pride of the descendants of Timour, had been torn from them, there could be little difficulty in putting the finishing stroke to the work by abolishing the kingly title on the death of Behaudur Shah. "The presents," he said, "which were at one time offered to the King by the Governor-General and Commander-in-Chief have been discontinued. The privilege of a coinage carrying his mark is now denied to him. The Governor-General's seal no longer bears a device of vassalage; and even the Native chiefs have been prohibited from using one. It has been determined that these appearances of subordination and dependence could not be kept up consistently with a due respect for the real and solid power of the British Government, and the same may be said of the title of King of Delhi, with the fiction of paramount sovereignty which attaches to it. . . . To recognise the title of King, and a claim to the external marks of royalty in a new person, would be an act purely voluntary on the part of the Government of India, and quite uncalled for. Moreover, it would not be accepted as a grace or favour by any but the individual himself. But," added the Governor-General, "whatever be the degree of rank inherited, the heir whom in right and consistency the Government must recognise, is the eldest surviving son of the King, Prince Mirza Mahomed Korash, who has no claims from early reminiscences to see the unreal dignity of his House sustained for another generation in his own person."

1856

The policy to be observed having thus been determined, the Governor-General, with the full concurrence of his Council, proceeded to issue definite in-

1856. structions for the guidance of his Agent. The substance of them is thus stated:

"1. Should it be necessary to send a reply to the King's letter, the Agent must inform his Majesty that the Governor-General cannot sanction the recognition of Mirza Jewan Bakht as successor.

"2. Mirza Mahomed Korash must not be led to expect that his recognition will take place on the same terms as Fakir-ood-deen's, and that during the King's lifetime no communication is to be made, either to his Majesty, or to any other member of the family, touching the succession.

"3. On the King's demise, Prince Mirza Mahomed Korash should be informed that Government recognise him as the head of the family upon the same conditions as those accorded to Prince Mirza Fakir-ood-deen, excepting that, instead of the title of King, he should be designated and have the title of Shahzada, and that this communication should be made to him not in the way of writing, negotiation, or bargaining, which it is not the intention of the Governor-General in Council to admit, but as the declaration of the mature and fixed determination of the Government of India.

"4. A report to be made of the number of the privileged residents in the Palace; to how many the privilege would extend, if the sons and grandsons, but no more distant relatives of any former King were admitted to it.

"5. The sum of fifteen thousand rupees per mensem from the family stipend to be fixed as the future assignment of the heir of the family."

Intrigues of Zeenut-Mehal.

Such, as represented by official documents—such

as they were then known to Lord Canning—were the state and prospects of the Delhi Family at the close of the year 1856. But there was something besides reserved for later revelation to the English ruler, which may be recorded in this place. The King, stricken in years, would have been well content to end his days in quietude and peace. But the restless intriguing spirit of the Queen Zeenut-Mehal would not suffer the aged monarch to drowse out the remainder of his days. She never ceased to cling to the hope that she might still live to see the recognition of her son as King of Delhi, and she never ceased to intrigue, at home and abroad, by the light of that pole-star of her ambition. One impediment had been removed by death. Another might be removed in the same way. And if the British Government would not favour the claims of Jewan Bakht, other powerful Governments might be induced to hold out to him a helping hand. It was stated afterwards that the King had never resented the determination to exclude the Delhi Family from the Palace, as the exclusion would not affect himself, and he had no care for the interests of his successor.* But it has been shown that Queen Zeenut-Mehal was loud in her lamentations when it was known that Fakir-ood-deen had surrendered this ancient privilege; for although she hated the recognised heir, she knew that he was not immortal; and changes of Government, moreover, might beget changes of opinion. There was still hope of the succession of Jewan Bakht so long as the old King lived; and therefore she desired to maintain all the privileges of the Kingship unimpaired to the last possible moment of doubt and expectancy. 1856.

* Evidence of Assan-oolah, on the trial of the King of Delhi.

1857. Meanwhile, the youth in whom all these hopes centred, was growing up with a bitter hatred of the English in his heart. The wisdom, the learning, the good manners of the Heir-expectant were evinced by the pertinacity with which he was continually spitting his venom at the English. He did not hesitate to say, even in the presence of British subjects, that "in a short time he would have all the English under his feet."* But his courage was not equal to his bitterness; for if he were asked what he meant by such language, he would answer that he meant nothing. He was "only in sport." He had been for years past imbibing this venom in the Zenana, under the traitorous tuition of his mother, and he was ever anxious to spit it out, especially in the presence of women.

To what extent the intrigues thus matured in the Queen's apartments may, by the help of her agents, have been made to ramify beyond the Palace walls, it is not easy to conjecture. There is no proof that in or about Delhi the question of succession was regarded with any interest by the people. It little mattered to them whether one Prince or another were recognised as the head of the Family and the recipient of the lion's share of the pension. If attempts were made to excite the popular feeling to

* See the evidence of Mrs. Fleming, an English sergeant's wife, who thus recites an incident which occurred on the occasion of a visit paid by her to the Queen Zeenut-Mehal: "I was sitting down with his sister-in-law, and Jawan Bakht was standing by with his wife. My own daughter, Mrs. Scully, was also present. I was talking with Jawan Bakht's sister-in-law, when Mrs. Scully said to me, 'Mother, do you hear what this young rascal is saying? He is telling me that in a short time he will have all the infidel English under his feet, and after that he will kill the Hindus.' Hearing this I turned round to Jawan Bakht, and asked him, 'What is that you are saying?' He replied that he was only joking. I said if what you threaten were to be the case, your head would be taken off first. He told me that the Persians were coming to Delhi, and that when they did so, we, that is, myself and daughter, should go to him, and he would save us. After this he left us. I think this must have occurred about the middle of April, 1857."

manifest itself on the side of Jewan Bakht, they were clearly a failure. But there is at least some reason to think that the emissaries of the Palace had been assiduous in their efforts to stir into a blaze the smouldering fires of Mahomedan zeal, and to excite vague hopes of some great Avatar from the North-West, which would restore the fallen fortunes of the House of Delhi, and give again to the Mahomedans of India the wealth and honour of which they had been deprived by the usurpation of the English. 1857.

State of feeling in Delhi.

So it happened that as the new year advanced there was unwonted excitement among the Mahomedans of Delhi. The Native newspapers teemed with vague hints of a something coming, that was to produce great changes, resulting in the subversion of the power of the English. Exaggerated stories of the Persian war, and most mendacious statements of reverses sustained by the English, were freely circulated and volubly discussed. At one time it was said that the Persians had come down to Attock, and at another that they were in full march through the Bolan Pass. Then it was alleged that the real history of the war was, that the Shah of Persia had for five generations been accumulating munitions of war and heaping up treasure for the purpose of conquering India, and that the time had now come for action. Russia, it was said, had placed its immense resources freely at the disposal of the Shah. A thoroughly appointed army of nearly half a million of men, with immense supplies of military stores, had been sent to the aid of Persia; and if the regular military forces of the Czar were not sufficient, a large contingent of Russian police would be sent to reinforce them. There were eager speculations, too, as to the course that would be adopted by the French and the Ottoman Govern-

1857. ments. "Most people," it was declared in a Native newspaper, rejoicing in the name of the "Authentic News," "say that the King of France and the Emperor of Turkey will both side with the Persians." And it was added that the Russians were the real cause of the war; for, "using the Persians as a cloak, they intend to consummate their own designs by the conquest of Hindostan." Other writers affirmed that although Dost Mahomed, Ameer of Caubul, pretended to be the friend of the English, and took their money and their arms, he was prepared to turn both against the infidels and to cast in his lot with Persia. Alike in the Bazaars and in the Lines—in the shops of the money-changers and in the vestibules of the Palace—these stories excited vague sensations of wonder and of awe, which were strengthened by the circulation of the prophecy, which took different shapes, but pointed in all to the same result, that when the English had ruled in India for a hundred years they would be driven out, and a Native dynasty restored.*

* See the following, written by Sir James Outram in January, 1858: "What amazing statements and opinions one hears both in India and in England. What can be more ridiculous than the cry that the rebellion was caused by the annexation of Oude, or that it was solely a military mutiny?" [This, it should be observed, is addressed to Mr. Mangles.] "Our soldiers have deserted their standards and fought against us, but rebellion did not originate with the Sepoys. The rebellion was set on foot by the Mahomedans, and that long before we rescued Oude from her oppressors. It has been ascertained that prior to that Mussulman fanatics traversed the land, reminding the faithful that it had been foretold in prophecy that a foreign nation would rule in India a hundred years, after which the true believers would regain their ascendancy. When the century elapsed, the Mussulmans did their best to establish the truth of their prophet's declaration, and induced the Hindoo Sepoys, ever, as you know, the most credulous and silly of mankind, to raise the green standard, and forswear their allegiance, on the ground that we had determined to make the whole of India involuntary converts to Christianity." As to the text of the prediction, a native newspaper, citing it as the prophecy of the "revered saint Shah Mamat-oollah," puts it in these words, the original of which are in verse: "After the fire-worshippers and Christians shall have held sway over the whole of

That the King was intriguing with the Shah of Persia was reported in the month of March to the Lieutenant-Governor of the North-Western Provinces by a Native correspondent, who added: "In the Palace, but more especially in the portion of it constituting the personal apartments of the King, the subject of conversation, night and day, is the early arrival of the Persians.* Hassan Askari† has, moreover, impressed the King with the belief that he has learned, through a divine revelation, that the dominion of the King of Persia will to a certainty extend to Delhi, or rather over the whole of Hindustan, and that the splendour of the sovereignty of Delhi will again revive, as the sovereign of Persia will bestow the crown upon the King. Throughout the Palace, but particularly to the King, this belief has been the cause of great rejoicing, so much so, that prayers are offered and vows are made, whilst, at the same time, Hassan Askari has entered upon the daily performance, at an hour and a half before sunset, of a course of propitiatory ceremonies to expedite the arrival of the Persians and the expulsion of the Christians." 1857. Warnings.

This warning was of course disregarded. A rooted confidence in our own strength and security, and a haughty contempt for the machinations of others, was at that time a condition of English statesmanship. It was the rule—and I fear that it is still the rule—in such a case to discern only the exaggerations and

Hindostan for a hundred years, and when injustice and oppression shall prevail in their Government, an Arab prince shall be born, who will ride forth triumphantly to slay them."

* It was stated, however, in evidence on the King's trial, that the war with Persia had excited very little interest in the Palace. Assanoolah, the King's physician, said, that the native newspapers, coming into the Palace, reported the progress of the war, but that "the King never seemed to evince any marked interest one way or the other."

† This man was a Mahomedan Priest of the Hereditary Priesthood, who dwelt near the Delhi Gate of the Palace, and was ever active in encouraging intrigues with Persia.

1857. absurdities with which such statements are crusted over. The British officer to whom such revelations are made sees at a glance all that is preposterous and impossible in them; and he dismisses them as mere follies. He will not suffer himself to see that there may be grave and significant truths beneath the outer crust of wild exaggeration. When, therefore, Lieutenant-Governor Colvin received the letter announcing that the King of Delhi was intriguing with the Shah of Persia, and that the latter would ere long restore the monarchy of the Mogul, he laughed the absurdity to scorn, and pigeon-holed it among the curiosities of his administration. He did not consider that the simple fact of such a belief being rife in Delhi and the neighbourhood was something not to be disregarded. It in reality very little mattered whether the King of Delhi and the Shah of Persia were or were not in communication with each other, so long as the Mahomedans of Upper India believed that they were. It is the state of feeling engendered by such a belief, not the fact itself, that is really significant and important. But there is nothing in which English statesmanship in India fails more egregiously than in this incapacity to discern, or unwillingness to recognise, the prevailing sentiments of the people by whom our statesmen are surrounded. The letter sent to the Lieutenant-Governor of the North-Western Provinces was produced, at a later period, as strong evidence of the guilt of the King of Delhi; but the recorded history of this document is, that it was "found among the papers of the late Mr. Colvin."

Intrigues with Persia.

The story of the correspondence between the King of Delhi and the Shah of Persia was not a mere fable. Authentic record of such transactions is rarely to be obtained, and history must, therefore, fall back upon evidence which may not be altogether conclusive. The facts, however, appear to be these.* The power of Mahomedanism is greatly weakened by sectarian divisions. A Soonee hates a Sheeah, or a Sheeah hates a Soonee, almost as much as either hates a Christian. The King of Delhi was a Soonee, whilst the King of Oude and the Shah of Persia were Sheeahs. Now, it happened that whilst Behaudur Shah was in great tribulation because he could not persuade the English Government to gratify the cherished wishes of his favourite wife, he was minded to become a Sheeah. There were some members of his family settled in Oude, who were also of this persuasion. Whether by invitation, or whether of his own motion, is not very apparent, but one of them, the King's nephew, Meerza Hyder by name, accompanied by a brother, visited his Majesty at Delhi, and carried back on his return tidings that the great change had been effected, and that the Mogul sought to be admitted within the pale of the Sheeah religion. This man was known in the Delhi Palace as one rejoicing in intrigue. It could not have been difficult to persuade the old King that the fact of his conversion might be turned to good account, and that if nothing else would come of it, it would make the Shah of Persia and the King of Oude more willing to assist him in the troubles and perplexities by which he was surrounded. It is probable that he had no very clear notion of what might come of such an alliance—no very strong hope that it would end in the overthrow of the English—but he was readily persuaded to address letters to the King of Persia, 1857.

* They are mainly derived from the evidence of Assan-oolah, the King's physician, of all the witnesses on the trial of Behaudur Shah the most accurate and trustworthy. I see no reason to question his statements.

1857. and to despatch them secretly by confidential agents. And this was done before the emissaries from Lucknow had taken their departure. There is a suspicion also that he sent letters to Russia; but, if he did, in all probability they never reached their destination. There was, however, from that time a vague belief in the Palace that both the Persians and the Russians were coming to the deliverance of the King, and that ere long he would again be surrounded by all the splendour that irradiated the Mogul throne in the meridian of its glory.

These intrigues, whatever their importance, were well known in Delhi in the early months of 1857; and the impression which they produced on the minds of the people was strengthened by the sight of a proclamation which was posted on the Jumma Musjeed in the middle of the month of March. This proclamation, purporting to have been issued by the King of Persia, set forth that a Persian army was coming to release India from the grasp of the English, and that it behoved all true Mahomedans to gird up their loins resolutely, and to fight against the unbelievers.* The name of Mahomed Sadik was attached to it; but none knew who he was. In outward appearance it was but an insignificant affair; though it bore rude illustrations representing a sword and a shield, it does

* It is well known that a copy of a proclamation addressed to Mahomedans generally, urging a war of extermination against the English, was found in the tent of the Persian prince at Mohumrah, after the engagement which took place there in the spring of 1857. There was no special reference in this document to the restoration of the Delhi sovereignty; it called upon "the old and the young, the small and the great, the wise and the ignorant, the ryot and the sepoy, all without exception to arise in defence of the orthodox faith of the Prophet." Afterwards it was frankly acknowledged by the Persian Government that they had attempted to create a diversion against us in India—such expedients being all fair in war.

not appear to have produced any great excitement in Delhi, and the attention which it attracted was short-lived, for the paper, after the lapse of a few hours, was torn down by order of the magistrate. But the Native newspapers published the substance of the proclamation, accompanying it with vague and mysterious hints, or with obscure comments, obviously intended, in some instances, to be read in a contrary sense. There was in these effusions hostility to the British Government—but hostility driven by fear to walk warily. Ambiguous, enigmatical language suited the occasion. It was stated that a communication had been addressed to the magistrate, informing him that in the course of a few weeks Cashmere would be taken; the intent being, it is said, to signify that the Cashmere Gate of Delhi would be in the hands of the enemies of the British Government. There was plainly a very excited state of public feeling about Delhi. The excitement was, doubtless, fomented by some inmates of the Palace; and the King's Guards conversed with the Sepoys of the Company, and the talk was still of a something coming. But Behaudur Shah, in the spring of 1857, was never roused to energetic action. Much was done in his name of which he knew nothing, and much besides which he weakly suffered. And as, in that month of May, news came from Meerut that there was great excitement among the soldiery, and some of the Native officers at Delhi were summoned to take part in the great on-coming trial, those who sat at the King's door talked freely about the revolt of the Native 1857

* See evidence of Sir Theophilus Metcalfe. It was stated, however, in the Native papers, that the proclamation was posted up in the streets and lanes of the city.

1857. army, and in the vestibules of the Palace it was proclaimed that the dynasty of the Moguls would soon be restored, and that all the high offices of State would be held by the people of the country.*

* Mokund Lal, the King's secretary, said: "I don't know whether any direct proposals came to the prisoner, but the King's personal attendants, sitting about the entrance to his private apartments, used to converse among themselves, and say that very soon, almost immediately, the army would revolt and come to the palace, when the Government of the King would be re-established, and all the old servants would be greatly promoted and advanced in position and emoluments."

CHAPTER II.

STATE OF THE THIRD CAVALRY—THE COURT OF INQUIRY—THE COURT-MARTIAL—IMPRISONMENT OF THE EIGHTY-FIVE—THE TENTH OF MAY—RELEASE OF THE PRISONERS—GENERAL REVOLT OF THE SEPOYS—INACTIVITY OF THE EUROPEAN TROOPS—ESCAPE OF THE MUTINEERS—QUESTION OF RESPONSIBILITY CONSIDERED.

WHILST the vague feeling of excitement above described was gathering strength and consistency at Delhi, and the "something coming" appeared to be approaching nearer and nearer, events were developing themselves in the great military station of Meerut, thirty miles distant, which were destined to precipitate a more momentous crisis in the imperial city than had been anticipated by the inmates of the Palace. The Native troops at that great Head-Quarters station were smouldering into rebellion, and the Sepoy War was about to commence. The brief telegraphic story already recorded,* when it expanded into detailed proportions, took this disastrous shape.

The Third Regiment of Native Cavalry was commanded by Colonel Carmichael Smyth. He had graduated in the regiment, and had seen some service with it, but he had never earned the entire confidence of officers or men. He was not wanting

Colonel Smyth and the Third Cavalry.

April—May. 1857.

* *Ante*, vol. i. p. 595.

April, 1857.

in intelligence or in zeal, but he lacked temper and discretion, and the unquestionable honesty of his nature was of that querulous, irritable cast which makes a man often uncharitable and always unpopular. He had a quick eye for blots of every kind; and, being much addicted to newspaper-writing, seldom failed to make them known to the public. Nobody knew better than Colonel Smyth that the Bengal Army was hovering on the brink of mutiny. He had, in the earlier part of the year, visited the great fair at Hurdwar, where the disaffection of the Nineteenth Regiment had been freely discussed. He had afterwards gone to Mussooree, where he learnt from day to day what was passing at Umballah, and he was so impressed by what he heard respecting the general state of the Sepoy regiments and their readiness for revolt, that he had written to the Commander-in-Chief to inform him of the dangerous state of the Army. But when the general order went forth that the men were no longer to bite the cartridges, Colonel Smyth thought that the opportunity was one of which he should avail himself to allay the excitement in his own regiment, and he therefore held the parade of the 24th of April, with results which have been already described.*

General Hewitt.

Not so thought the officer commanding the Meerut division of the Army. General Hewitt was an old Company's officer, who had risen to high rank by the slow process of regimental and army promotion, and who in quiet times might have drowsed through the years of his employment on the Staff without manifesting any remarkable incapacity for command. The burden of nearly seventy years was aggravated by

* *Ante*, vol. i. p. 567.

the obesity of his frame and the inertness of his habits. But he was a kind-hearted, hospitable man, liked by all, and by some respected. It was his desire to keep things quiet, and, if possible, to make them pleasant. He lamented, therefore, that Colonel Smyth had made that crucial experiment upon the fidelity of his regiment which had resulted in open mutiny. "Oh! why did you have a parade?" he said to the Colonel. "My division has kept quiet, and if you had only waited another month or so, all would have blown over."

April, 1857.

The Court of Inquiry.

It was necessary, however, after what had occurred, in an official point of view to do something. So he ordered a Native Court of Inquiry to be assembled. The Court was composed of six members, four of whom were Native officers of the Infantry and two Native officers of the Cavalry. The witnesses examined, including those who had manufactured and served out the cartridges, said that there was nothing objectionable in them—nothing that could offend the religious scruples of Hindoo or Mahomedan—nothing that in any way differed from the composition of the cartridges which the Sepoys had been using for years. The oldest troopers in the regiment, Hindoo and Mahomedan, were examined; but they could give no satisfactory account of the causes of alarm and disaffection in the regiment. They could only say that a general impression of impurity existed. One Mussulman trooper, with much insolence of manner, blustered out, "I have doubts about the cartridges. They may look exactly like the old ones, but how do I know that pig's fat has not been smeared over them?" But the next witness who was examined—a Hindoo—took one of the cartridges into his hand and handled it freely, to show

April, 1857. that in his eyes there was nothing offensive in the new ammunition. Altogether, the Court of Inquiry elicited nothing. It dealt with material facts, which were well known before. But it was not the palpable, but the impalpable—a vague and voiceless idea—that had driven the regiment to mutiny. That which the troopers dreaded was not pollution, but opinion. They were troubled, not by any fear of desecration to their faith or of injury to their caste, but by the thought of what their comrades would say of them. In a military sense, in an official sense, all this was unreasonable in the extreme; but every man felt in his inmost heart more than he could explain in intelligible words, and the shadow of a great fear was upon him, more terrible for its indistinctness.

The proceedings of the Court of Inquiry were sent to Head-Quarters; and whilst the orders of the Commander-in-Chief were awaited, the Eighty-five were dismissed from duty, and ordered to abide in their Lines. There was, then, for a little space, a fever of expectancy. What meetings, and conspiracies, and oath-takings there may have been in the Sepoys' quarter during that long week of waiting, can be only dimly conjectured; but one form of expression, in which their feelings declared themselves, was patent to all. It was written in characters of fire, and blazed out of the darkness of the night. From the verandahs of their houses the European officers saw these significant illuminations, and knew what they portended. The burnings had commenced on the evening preceding the fatal parade of the 24th of April, when an empty hospital had been fired.* Then followed a more expressive conflagration. The house of a Sepoy named Bridge-Mohun Singh, who

* Colonel Smyth says it was a horse-hospital.

had been the first to practise the new mode of using the cartridges, was burnt down. This man (the son of a pig-keeper), who had been dismissed from an Infantry regiment and imprisoned for theft, had enlisted under a new name in the Third Cavalry, and had managed so to ingratiate himself with the Commanding Officer, that he was seldom absent from the Colonel's bungalow. To the whole regiment, and especially to its high-caste men, this was an offence and an abomination, and nothing could more clearly indicate the feeling in the Lines of the Third than the fact that this man's house was burnt down by the troopers of his own regiment. May, 1857

In the bungalows also of the European residents, during this first week of May, there was much excitement and discussion. There was plainly a very disagreeable entanglement of events out of which it was not easy to see the way, and people said freely that it ought never to have arisen. But speculation with respect to the Future was even more busy than censure with respect to the Past. What, it was asked, would be the issue of the reference to Head-Quarters? The more general belief was, that orders would come for the dismissal of the recusant troopers; but even this, it was thought, would be a harsh measure, that might drive others, by force of sympathy, to rebellion. It was an interval which might have been turned by our English officers to good account in soothing the feelings of their men, and explaining everything that was of a doubtful or suspicious character. Some, indeed, did strive, with a wise foreknowledge of the coming danger, to accomplish this good object; but others believed that all was right, that there was no likelihood of their regiments being driven either by their fears or their

May, 1857.

resentments to revolt against the Law; and they drowsed on placidly in the conviction that it was but an accidental ebullition, provoked by the mismanagement of an indiscreet Commanding Officer, and that the general temper of the Native troops at Meerut was all that could be desired.

The Court-Martial.

In the first week of May the instructions so eagerly looked for were received from the Head-Quarters of the Army. The fiat of General Anson had gone forth from Simlah. A Native General Court-Martial was to be assembled at Meerut for the trial of the Eighty-five. The prisoners were then confined in an empty hospital, and a guard of their own regiment was placed over them. The tribunal before which they were to be brought up for trial was composed of fifteen Native officers, of whom six were Mahomedans and nine were Hindoos. Ten of these members were furnished by the regiments at Meerut—Artillery, Cavalry, and Infantry; five came from the Infantry regiments at Delhi. On the 6th of May the Court commenced its sittings,* and continued its proceedings on the two following days. The examination of Colonel Smyth and the other witnesses for the prosecution elicited no new facts, and, indeed, the whole case of military disobedience was so clear, that the trial, though it was protracted during three days, was little more than a grim formality. Every man felt that his condemnation was certain, and sullenly abided the issue. The prisoners could put forth no defence which either Law or Discipline could accept.

* The charge was, "For having at Meerut, on the 24th of April, 1857, severally and individually disobeyed the lawful command of their superior officer, Brevet-Colonel G. M. C. Smyth, commanding the Third Regiment of Light Cavalry, by not having taken the cartridges tendered to each of them individually for use that day on parade, when ordered by Colonel Smyth to take the said cartridges."

But when the Havildar Muttadeen Singh pleaded, on behalf of himself and comrades, that they suspected some foul design because their Commandant took so much pains to convince them that it was all right, and to induce them to fire the cartridges, there was something not altogether irrational or illogical in the argument. If there was nothing in the ammunition different from that which they had always used, why, it was asked, should the proceedings of the Colonel have been so different?* But in effect the defence of the prisoners was little more than a confession, and the Court, by a vote of fourteen members against one, found the Eighty-five guilty, and sentenced them to imprisonment and hard labour for ten years. But with this there went forth a recommendation to "favourable consideration on account of the good character which the prisoners had hitherto borne, as testified to by their Commanding Officer, and on account of their having been misled by vague reports regarding the cartridges."

1857. May.

The sentence confirmed.

The proceedings went up, in due course, to the General commanding the Division, and Hewitt approved and confirmed the sentence. "I would willingly attend," he remarked, "to the recommendation of the Court, if I could find anything in the conduct of the prisoners that would warrant me in so doing. Their former good character has been blasted by pre-

* The same difficulty suggested itself to the Court. Colonel Smyth was asked, "Why did you tell the men that they would have to fire, instead of merely ordering them to do so?" Colonel Smyth's answer was: "The parade was in orders the day before, and entered in the order-book as usual, and each man was ordered to receive three cartridges. I wished to show them the new way of loading without putting the cartridges to the mouth, and attended the parade for that purpose. When I came on parade, the Adjutant informed me that the men had not taken their cartridges, and it was on that account I ordered the Havildar-Major to take a cartridge and load and fire before them; and it was then, also, that I said, that when the whole Army hear of this way of loading they would be much pleased, and exclaim, 'Wah! wah!'"

1857. May.

sent misbehaviour, and their having allowed themselves to be influenced by vague reports instead of attending to the advice and obeying the orders of their European superiors, is the gist of the offence for which they have been condemned. It appears from these proceedings that these misguided men, after consultation together on the night of the 23rd of April, 1857, came to the resolution of refusing their cartridges. Having so far forgotten their duty as soldiers, their next step was to send word to their troop captains that they would not take their cartridges unless the whole of the troops in the station would do so likewise. Some of them even had the insolence to desire that firing parades might be deferred till the agitation about cartridges among the Native troops had come to a close. In this state of insubordination they appeared on parade on the morning of the 24th, and there consummated the crime for which they are now about to suffer, by repeatedly refusing cartridges that had been made as usual in their regimental magazine, when assured, too, by Colonel Smyth that the cartridges had no grease on them—that they were old ones, and exactly similar to what had been in use in the regiment for thirty or forty years. Even now they attempt to justify so gross an outrage upon discipline by alleging that they had doubts of the cartridges. There has been no acknowledgment of error—no expression of regret—no pleading for mercy." "To the majority of the prisoners," therefore, it was added, "no portion of the sentence will be remitted. I observe, however, that some of them are very young, and I am willing to make allowance for their having been misled by their more experienced comrades, and under these circumstances I remit one half of the sentence passed upon the following men, who have not been more than five years in the service." And then followed the names of eleven young troopers, whose term of imprisonment was commuted to five years. The sentence was to be carried into effect at daybreak on the 9th of May. 1857 May

The morning dawned, lowering and gusty, and the troops of the Meerut Brigade were drawn up on the ground of the Sixtieth Rifles to see the prisoners formally dismissed to their doom. The Third Cavalry had received their orders to attend unmounted. The European troops and the Artillery, with their field-guns, were so disposed as to threaten instant death to the Sepoys on the first symptom of resistance. Under a guard of Rifles and Carabineers, the Eighty-five were then brought forward, clad in their regimental uniforms—soldiers still; and then the sentence was read aloud, which was to convert soldiers into felons. Their accoutrements were taken from them, and their uniforms were stripped from their backs. Then the armourers and the smiths came forward with their shackles and their tools, and soon, in the presence of that great concourse of their old comrades, the Eighty-five stood, with the outward symbols of their dire disgrace fastened upon them. It was a piteous spectacle, and many there were moved with a great compassion, when they saw the despairing gestures of those wretched men, among whom were some of the very flower of the regiment—soldiers who had served the British Government in trying circumstances and in strange places, and who had never before wavered in their allegiance. Lifting up their hands and lifting up their voices, the prisoners implored the General to have mercy upon them, and not to consign them to so ignominious a doom. May 9. Execution of the sentence.

1857. May. Then, seeing that there was no other hope, they turned to their comrades and reproached them for quietly suffering this disgrace to descend upon them. There was not a Sepoy present who did not feel the rising indignation in his throat. But in the presence of those loaded field-guns and those grooved rifles, and the glittering sabres of the Dragoons, there could not be a thought of striking. The prisoners were marched off to their cells, to be placed under the custody of a guard of their own countrymen; the parade was dismissed; and the Sepoys, Cavalry and Infantry, went, silent and stern, to their work, to talk over the incidents of that mournful morning parade.*

It was Saturday. So far as English eyes could see or English brains could understand, the day passed quietly over. The troop-captains of the Third Cavalry visited the prisoners in the gaol, which was situated at a distance of about two miles from the cantonment, to be for the last time the channel of communication between them and the outer world. It was their duty to adjust the balances of the Sepoys' pay, and they were anxious, in the kindness of their hearts, to arrange the settlements of the prisoners' debts, and to carry any messages which the men might desire to send to the families from whom they had been sundered. And whilst this was going on in the gaol, wild reports were flying about the Bazaars, and there was a great fear in the Lines, for it was

* Lord Canning's commentary on these proceedings may be given here: "The rivetting of the men's fetters on parade, occupying, as it did, several hours, in the presence of many who were already ill-disposed, and many who believed in the cartridge fable, must have stung the brigade to the quick. The consignment of the eighty-five prisoners, after such a ceremony, to the gaol, with no other than a native guard over them, was, considering the nature of their offence, and the known temper of a part of the Army, a folly that is inconceivable."—*Letter to Mr. Vernon Smith, June* 5, 1857. *MS. Correspondence.*

said that the Europeans were about to take possession of the magazines, and that the two thousand fetters, of which Rumour had spoken before, were now ready, and that the work of the morning was only an experiment and a beginning. But the shades of evening fell upon Meerut, and the English residents, after their accustomed ride, met each other at dinner, and talked cheerfully and confidently of the Past and the Future. At one dinner-table, where the Commissioner and his wife and the Colonel of the Eleventh Sepoys were present, a rumour was mentioned to the effect that the walls had been placarded with a Mahomedan proclamation calling upon the people to rise against the English. But the general feeling was one of indignant disbelief, and each man went to his home and laid his head upon his pillow as tranquilly as though from one end of Meerut to another there had been no bitter resentments to be gratified, in the breasts of any but the manacled, harmless, helpless prisoners in the great gaol.

The Meerut Cantonment

I must pause here, a little space, for the better explanation of what follows, to speak of the great Cantonment of Meerut. This military station was one of the most extensive in India. It covered an area of some five miles in circumference, the space being divided by a great mall or esplanade, along which ran a deep nullah, or ditch, cutting the station into two separate parallelograms, the one containing the European and the other the Native force. The European Lines were on the northern quarter of Meerut, the Artillery Barracks being to the right, the Dragoons to the left, and the Rifles in the centre. Between the barracks of the two last stood the station church; a great plain or parade-ground stretching out still further to the northward. The Sepoy Lines

1857. May. lay to the south of the cantonment, and between what may be called the European and Native quarters, there was an intervening space covered with shops and houses, surrounded by gardens and trees Still further to the southward lay the city. The officers of the European regiments and Artillery occupied bungalows along the northern line, whilst the Sepoy officers dwelt chiefly near their own men. The Brigadier's house was on the right, not far from the Artillery Barracks and Mess-House. The General's residence was nearer to the Native Lines. The most noticeable features of the whole, and those which it is most important to bear in mind in the perusal of what follows, are the division of the great cantonment into two parts, the distance of the European barracks from the Native Lines, and the probability therefore of much that was passing in the latter being wholly unknown to the occupants of the former.

Sunday, May 10. The fierce May sun rose on the Sabbath morning, and the English residents prepared themselves to attend the ministrations of their religion in the station church. There was, indeed, a lull; but the signs of it, afterwards noted, clearly presaged that there was something in the air. In the European barracks it appeared that there was a general desertion of the Native servants, whose business it was to administer to the wants of the white soldiery, and in the bungalows of the officers there was a disposition on the part of their domestics, especially of those who had been hired at Meerut, to absent themselves from their masters' houses. But these things were observable at the time only as accidental circumstances of little significance, and the morning service was performed and the mid-day heats were lounged through, as in times of ordinary security. Severed from the great mass of the people, the English could see nothing of an unwonted character on that Sunday afternoon; but in the Lines of the Native soldiery, in the populous Bazaars, and even in the surrounding villages there were signs of a great commotion. The very children could see that something was about to happen. Men of all kinds were arming themselves. The dangerous classes were in a state of unwonted excitement and activity. Many people of bad character had come in from the adjacent hamlets, and even from more remote places, as though they discerned the prospect of a great harvest. Among the mixed population of the Lines and the Bazaars were men agitated by emotions of the most varied character. Hatred of the English, desire for revenge, religious enthusiasm, thirst for plunder, were all at work within them; but paramount over all was a nameless fear; for, ever as the day advanced, the report gained strength that the English soldiery, armed to the teeth, would soon be let loose amongst them; that every Sepoy before nightfall would have fetters on his wrists; that the People would be given up to massacre, and the Bazaars to plunder.

1857. May 10.

The sun went down and the time came for evening service, and the English chaplains prepared themselves for their ministrations. One has narrated how, when he was about to start with his wife for the station church, the Native nurse warned them that there was danger, and besought her mistress to remain at home. The woman said that there would be a fight with the Sepoys, but the Chaplain listened incredulously to the statement, and taking his wife and children with him, entered his carriage, and was driven to church.* In the church-compound he met

* See the Chaplain's (Mr. Rotton's) Narrative. He left his wife and children in a place of safety on the way to church.

1857. May 10.

his colleague and other Christian people with a look of anxious inquiry on their pale, scared faces. It was plain that the warning by which it was endeavoured to stay his progress was something more than an utterance of vague suspicion or senseless fear. Sounds and sights had greeted the church-goers on their way which could not be misinterpreted. The unwonted rattling of musketry on that Sabbath evening, the assembly-call of the buglers, the hurrying to and fro of armed men on the road, the panic-struck looks of the unarmed, the columns of smoke that were rising against the fast-darkening sky, all told the same story. The Native troops at Meerut had revolted.

Outbreak of he Sepoys.

It will never be known with certainty whence arose the first promptings to that open and outrageous rebellion of which these sounds and sights were the signs. What meetings and conspiracies there may have been in the Lines—whether there was any organised scheme for the release of the prisoners, the burning of cantonments, and the murder of all the Christian officers, can be only dimly conjectured. The probabilities are at variance with the assumption that the Native troops at Meerut deliberately launched themselves into an enterprise of so apparently desperate a character. With a large body of English troops—Horse, Foot, and Artillery—to confront them in the hour of mutiny, what reasonable hopes could there be of escape from swift and crushing retribution? They knew the temper and the power of English soldiers too well to trust to a contingency of inaction of which the Past afforded no example. There was not a station in India at which an outbreak of Native troops could appear to be so hopeless an experiment as in that great military cantonment which had become the Head-Quarters of the finest

Artillery Regiment in the world. But this very feeling of our overpowering strength at Meerut may have driven the Sepoys into the great panic of despair, out of which came the spasm of madness which produced such unexpected results on that Sabbath night. There had been for some days an ominous report, of which I have already spoken, to the effect that the Europeans were about to fall suddenly on the Sepoy regiments, to disarm them, and to put every man of them in chains. In fear and trembling they were looking for a confirmation of this rumour in every movement of the English troops. When, therefore, the Sixtieth Rifles were assembling for church parade, the Sepoys believed that the dreaded hour had arrived. The Third Cavalry were naturally the most excited of all. Eighty-five of their fellow-soldiers were groaning in prison. Sorrow, shame, and indignation were strong within them for their comrades' sake, and terror for their own. They had been taunted by the courtesans of the Bazaar, who asked if they were men to suffer their comrades to wear such anklets of iron;* and they believed that what they had seen on the day before was but a foreshadowing of a greater cruelty to come. So, whilst the European soldiers were preparing themselves for church parade, the Native troopers were mounting their horses and pricking forward towards the great gaol.

1857. May 10.

Then it became miserably apparent that a fatal error had been committed. There were no European

Rescue of the prisoners.

* This is stated very distinctly by Mr. J. C. Wilson (an excellent authority) in his interesting Moradabad Report. "And now," he writes, "the frail one's taunts were heard far and wide, and the rest of the regiment was assailed with words like these: 'Your brethren have been ornamented with these anklets and incarcerated; and for what? Because they would not swerve from their creed; and you, cowards as you are, sit still indifferent to your fate. If you have an atom of manhood in you, go and release them.'"

1857. May 10. soldiers posted to protect the prison-house in which were the condemned malefactors of the Sepoy Army The prisoners had been given over to the "civil power," and an additional guard, drawn from the Twentieth Sepoy Regiment, had been placed over the gaol. The troopers knew what was the temper of that regiment. They had no fear for the result, so they pushed on, some in uniform, man and horse fully accoutred, some in their stable dresses with only watering rein and horse-cloth on their chargers, but all armed with sabre and with pistol. Soon under the walls of the gaol—soon busy at their work—they met with, as they expected, no opposition. The rescue began at once. Loosening the masonry around the gratings of the cells in which their comrades were confined, they wrenched out the iron bars and helped the prisoners through the apertures A Native smith struck off their chains, and once again free men, the Eighty-five mounted behind their deliverers, and rode back to the Lines. The troopers of the Third Cavalry at that time had no other work in hand but the rescue of their comrades. The other prisoners in the gaol were not released, the buildings were not fired, and the European gaoler and his family were left unmolested.*

* There are conflicting statements on the subject of the release of the prisoners in the new gaol. Dr. O'Callaghan ("Scattered Chapters on the Indian Mutiny") asserts, that not only the eighty-five, but all the other prisoners had been released by the infantry guard before the cavalry arrived. When the troopers arrived, he says, "After their rapid and furious gallop at the gaol, they found their comrades already released and emerging from incarceration, and the general crowd of felons also rushing rapidly forth to join in the fire, pillage, and slaughter." But Mr. Commissioner Williams, in his very circumstantial official report, says that the troopers "dug out of the wall the gratings of some of the windows of the ward in which the eighty-five mutineers were confined, and took their comrades away, the guard of the Twentieth accompanying, and the armed guard of the gaol soon followed. None of the other convicts, in number about eight hundred, were released by the cavalry troopers, nor was any injury done by them to the buildings." But he adds,

Meanwhile, the Infantry regiments had broken into open revolt. The Sepoys of the Eleventh and the Twentieth were in a state of wild excitement. Maddened by their fears—expecting every moment that the Europeans would be upon them—believing that there was one great design in our hearts to manacle the whole of them, and, perhaps, to send them as convicts across the black water, they thought that the time had come for them to strike for their liberties, for their lives, for their religions. So it happened that when the excitement in the Lines was made known to some of our English officers, and they went down, as duty bade them, to endeavour to allay it, they found that the men whom they had once regarded as docile children had been[1] suddenly turned into furious assailants. Among those who, on that Sunday evening, rode down to the Sepoys' Lines was Colonel Finnis, who commanded the Eleventh. A good soldier, beloved by officers and by men, he had the old traditionary faith in the Sepoys which it became those, who had served with them and knew their good qualities, to cherish. Strong in the belief of the loyalty of his regiment, Finnis, with other officers of his corps, went into the midst of them to remonstrate and to dissuade. He was speaking to his men, when a soldier of the Twentieth discharged his musket and wounded the Colonel's horse. Presently another musket was discharged into his body. The ball entered at his back; he fell from his horse, and a volley was fired into him. He died, "riddled with bullets." Thus the Sepoys of the Twentieth had slain the Colonel of the Eleventh Regiment, and the

1857. May 10.

Revolt of the Infantry.

Death of Colonel Finnis.

"About three hundred or four hundred Sepoys released the convicts from the old gaol, which is between the city and the Native lines, and which contained about seven hundred and twenty prisoners altogether."

1857. May 10.

bullets of the former had been scattered in the ranks of the latter. For a little space the two regiments looked at each other; but there was no doubt of the issue. The Eleventh broke into open revolt, and fraternised with their comrades of the Twentieth.

Progress of the Revolt.

The whole of the Native Regiments at Meerut had now revolted. The Sepoys of the Infantry and the troopers of the Cavalry had made common cause against us. Hindoos and Mahomedans were stirred by one impulse to slaughter the Feringhees, man, woman, and child. So as the sun went down the massacre went on, and our people, who were returning from the unaccomplished evening service, or, ignorant of the excitement and the danger, were starting for the wonted evening ride or drive, were fiercely assailed by the infuriated soldiery, and shot down or sabred as they sate their horses or leaned back in their carriages to enjoy the coolness of the air. Wheresoever a stray English soldier was to be found, he was murdered without remorse. The Bazaars and the neighbouring villages were pouring forth their gangs of plunderers and incendiaries. From every street and alley, and from the noisome suburbs, they streamed forth, like wild beasts from their lairs, scenting the prey.* The prisoners in the gaols were

* "Cities, like forests, have their dens, in which everything that is most wicked and formidable conceals itself. The only difference is that what hides itself thus in cities is ferocious, unclean, and little—that is to say, ugly; what conceals itself in the forests is ferocious, savage, and grand—that is to say, beautiful. Den for den, those of the beasts are preferable to those of men, and caverns are better than hiding-places."—*Victor Hugo.* Mr. Commissioner Williams, in his official report above quoted, says that the towns-people had armed themselves and were ready for the onslaught before the Sepoys had commenced the carnage. "Before a shot had been fired, the inhabitants of the Sudder Bazaar went out armed with swords, spears, and clubs, any weapon they could lay hands on, collected in crowds in every lane and alley, and at every outlet of the Bazaars; and the residents of the wretched hamlets, which had been allowed to spring up all round it and between it and the city, were to be seen similarly armed, pouring out to share in what they evidently knew was going to happen."

let loose, and the police became their comrades in crime. But so little concert and arrangement was there, that some detachments on guard-duty, posted in the European quarter of the great straggling cantonment, appear to have remained faithful to their English masters after their fellow-soldiers had broken out into open revolt. Indeed, whilst in one part of the cantonment the Sepoys were butchering their officers, in another they were saluting them as they passed, as though nothing had happened.* Even at the Treasury, with all its manifest temptations, the Guard stood staunchly to its duty, and at a later hour made over the charge in all its integrity to the Europeans sent to defend it. Not a rupee had been touched by the Sepoys. And when the rabble from the city swarmed upon it, they found it covered by a guard of Riflemen.

1857. May 10.

But, in the midst of all this great tribulation, there was, in the hearts of our Christian people, a strength of confidence which calmed and comforted them; for they said to each other, or they said to themselves, "The Europeans will soon be upon them." There were two regiments of Sepoy Infantry at Meerut, and a regiment of Sepoy Cavalry. But the English mustered a battalion of Riflemen, a regiment of Dragoons armed with carbines, and a large force of European Artillery, with all the accessories of Head-Quarters.†

* I do not mean to signify that the Sepoys in the European quarter of the cantonment were uniformly quiescent at this time; for I am informed that the Guard at Brigadier Wilson's house fired at some officers who were passing, before they broke away. But there was obviously no general concert.

† History, however, must not exaggerate the actual strength of this European force. There were some deteriorating circumstances, of which account must be taken. A considerable number of the Carabineers could not ride, and there were no horses for them if they could. Not more than half of the regiment (five hundred strong) were mounted. Many of the European gunners, too, were young recruits, imperfectly acquainted with artillery drill. There were only two field-batteries fully equipped.

1857. May 10

There was not an Englishwoman in the cantonment—the model cantonment of India—who, remembering the presence of this splendid body of White soldiers, had any other thought, at the first semblance of open mutiny, than that there must be a sad massacre of the Native troops. With a regiment of British Dragoons and a few Galloper guns, Gillespie, half a century before, had crushed the mutiny of Vellore, and saved the Southern Peninsula from universal revolt and rebellion.* He struck decisively because he struck at once. And no one now doubted that a blow struck with promptitude and vigour on this Sabbath evening would save Meerut, and check the nascent activities of revolt in the adjacent country. But by God's providence, for whatsoever purpose designed, this first great revolt of the Sepoys was suffered, unchecked, unpunished, to make headway in a clear field, and to carry everything before it. The great confidence of the Christian people was miserably misplaced. They looked for a deliverance that never came. In some parts of the great cantonment they were abandoned to fire and slaughter as hopelessly as though there had not been a single English soldier in that great Head-Quarters of the Meerut Division.

[I]naction of [th]e Euro[p]eans.

The story of this great failure is not easily told, and the attempt to tell it cannot be made without sadness. Many narratives of the events of that night have been written; and each writer has told, with graphic distinctness of detail, what he himself saw and heard; but the confusion of those few critical hours is fully represented by the confusedness of the entire story; and it is difficult to impart unity and consistency to

* See *ante*, vol. i. pages 230—232.

a scene, made up of scattered effects, bewildering and distracting. What was wanted in that conjuncture was the one man to impart to our British manhood the promptitude and unity of action which would have crushed the mutiny and saved the place—perhaps the country: and that one man did not rise in the hour of our tribulation. 1857. May 10.

Conduct of Colonel Smyth.

There were three officers at Meerut whose bearing in that critical hour the historian is especially bound to investigate. They were, the officer commanding the Third Cavalry, the Brigadier commanding the Station, and the General commanding the Division. All three were resident in Meerut. It is not to be questioned that when a regiment breaks into mutiny, the place of the commanding officer, for life or for death, is in the midst of it. Not until all hope has gone can there be any excuse for his departure. As the captain of a blazing vessel at sea is ever the last to leave the quarter-deck and to let himself down the side of his ship, so the commandant of a regiment in the fire of revolt should cling to it as long as the semblance of a regiment remains, and the safety of others can be aided by his presence. When, therefore, intelligence reached Colonel Smyth that the troopers of his regiment had broken into mutiny, it was his duty to proceed at once to the Cavalry Lines. But he did not go near the Lines.* He went to the

* "Most of the officers of the Third Light Cavalry at once proceeded to the lines of their regiment, arming hastily, and ordering their horses to follow; but I have never been able to discover that the officer commanding the corps repaired to his post, or was seen in the lines amongst the men, during the whole of that eventful evening and night; and it would appear that Colonel Smyth was so fortunate as to make an early escape into the protection of the European military quarter."—*O'Callaghan. Scattered Chapters on the Indian Mutiny.* It should be stated, however, that Colonel Smyth was Field-Officer of the week—a fact upon which he himself has laid considerable stress, as though, in his estimation, it exempted him from all special regard for his own particular regiment.

1857. May 10.

Commissioner's house. He went to the General's; and he went to the Brigadier's.' He went everywhere but to his Regiment. From the moment that the troopers broke out into revolt they saw no more of their Colonel. He spent the night with the Head-Quarters of the Division, where the rifles and the carbines and the field-guns were collected, and never had the least conception all the time of what had become of his men.* But they were not all past hope. That something might have been done to save at least a portion of the regiment we know. Captain Craigie, at the first sound of the tumult, mustered his troop, ordered them to accoutre themselves as for a parade, and when they had mounted, galloped down to the gaol, accompanied by his subaltern, Melville Clarke. They were too late to prevent the rescue of the prisoners; but not to set a grand example. Craigie and Clarke kept their men together, and brought them back, with unbroken discipline, to the parade-ground of the regiment. And during that night many acts of heroic fidelity were written down to the honour of Craigie's troop. They had faith in their Captain. And it has been truly recorded of Craigie and Clarke, that "these gallant Englishmen handled the troop as if mutiny were a crime unknown to their men."*

Captain Craigie.

* Colonel Smyth has published his own account of his proceedings on the evening of the 10th of May: "I went," he says, "first to Mr. Greathed's, gave information to the servants, as Mr. G. was out. . . . . I then went on to the General's, and heard that he had just left the house in his carriage; so I galloped on to the Brigadier's. . . . . I went on to the Artillery parade, and found the Brigadier already on the ground; and I accompanied him with the troops to the other end of the cantonments, and remained with him all night, and accompanied him again the next morning with Cavalry, Infantry, and Artillery through the cantonments, and went with the Artillery and Cavalry on the right of the Delhi road," &c. &c.

† Official Report of Mr. Commissioner Williams. The writer states that "Lieutenant Clarke rode out from the head of the troop, and ran his sword through a trooper of the regiment who was insulting an European lady, and Captain Craigie gave the wretch his finishing stroke."

The station was commanded by Colonel Archdale Wilson, Brigadier of Artillery. He was a man of a spare and wiry frame, of active athletic habits, who had ever borne a good character in the splendid regiment to the command of which he had then risen. For some years, when the Head-Quarters of the Artillery had been at Dum-Dum, in the vicinity of Calcutta, he had been Adjutant-General of the regiment, and was thoroughly acquainted with all its details. But he had not seen much active service since his youth, and had never had any grave responsibilities cast upon him. His training had been too purely of a professional character to generate any great capacity for taking in a situation of such magnitude as that which he was now suddenly called upon to confront. But he was not a man, in such a crisis as had then arisen, to look idly on, or to shrink from a forward movement. What he did at the outset was what it became him to do. It was about half-past six when Brigade-Major Whish drove into the Brigadier's compound, and told him that the Native troops had broken into mutiny. Instantly Wilson ordered his horse to be saddled and brought round, and having sent orders to the Artillery and Carabineers to join him there, he galloped to the parade-ground of the Rifles, and finding them on the point of marching for church, directed their Colonel to dismiss the parade, and to reassemble them as quickly as possible with their arms. This was promptly effected; but there was some delay in supplying the regiment with balled cartridge. The Dragoons had not yet come up. It has been stated that the Colonel had suffered the regiment to be mustered as for an ordinary parade;* and the slow process of roll-call had been going on

1857. May 10.

Brigadier Wilson.

* This Colonel Custance has contradicted.—See Appendix.

1857. May 10. whilst the last hour of daylight was passing away, and the enemy were slaughtering our people with impunity.

Movements of the Europeans. Meanwhile, General Hewitt had appeared on parade, and the Artillery had been brought up to the ground. When Colonel Jones reported that the Rifles were ready for action, Wilson, with the General's sanction, detached one company to the Collector's cutcherry to protect the treasure, and another for the protection of the barracks. Taking the other companies, with the Artillery, he marched down upon the Native Infantry Lines, where he expected to find the main body of the mutineers assembled. On or near the parade-ground he was joined by the Carabineers, who had lost their way.* There was now a force ready for action which might have destroyed all the Sepoys in Meerut, if they could have been brought into action with the white soldiers—if, indeed, our people could only have seen the enemy for a little space of time. But the shades of night had now fallen upon the scene. And when, near the Native Infantry huts, the English troops were deployed into line and swept the whole space where it was expected that the mutineers would have been found, not a man was to be seen, either in the Infantry Lines or on the parade-ground; and none knew whither they were gone. But near the Cavalry Lines a few troopers were seen, and the Rifles opened fire upon them. The mutineers fled into a wood or copse at the rear of their huts, and the guns were then unlimbered, and a few harmless rounds of grape fired into the obscurity of the night.

It was plain now that the mutineers were dispersed. The question was, What were they doing?

* Brigadier Wilson did not see the Carabineers until the whole body of troops were returning to the European Lines.

To Wilson it seemed that the mutineers had moved round to the European quarter of the Cantonment; and he therefore recommended the General to move back the brigade for its protection. To this Hewitt, glad to be advised, assented; and the troops set their faces homewards. By this time the moon had risen, and the blazing bungalows of the English officers lit up the scene with a lurid glare. But our troops met only a few unarmed plunderers. The mutineers were not to be seen. What, then, was to be done? It has been often stated that one officer at least answered the question as it ought to have been answered. Captain Rosser, of the Carabineers (so the story runs), offered to lead a squadron of his regiment and some Horse Artillery guns in pursuit of the enemy along the Delhi road. But the statement has been authoritatively contradicted.* It is only certain that the enemy escaped; and that, with the exception of some pickets which were planted on the bridges across the nullah which ran between the European Cantonment and the Native Lines and Sudder Bazaar, the whole of Hewitt's force bivouacked for the night on the European parade-ground.

1857. May 10—11.

And the night was a night of horror such as History has rarely recorded. The brief twilight of the Indian summer had soon passed; and the darkness which fell upon the scene brought out, with terrible distinctness, the blazing work of the incendiary. Everywhere, from the European quarters, from the bungalows of the English officers, from the mess-houses and other public buildings, from the residences of the unofficial Christian community, the flames were seen to rise, many-shaped and many-coloured,

May 10—11. Terrors of the night.

* See Appendix for an inquiry into the truth of this story.

1857. May 10—11. lighting up the heavy columns of smoke which were suspended in the still sultry air. And ever, as the conflagration spread, and the sight became more portentous, the sounds of the great fiery destruction, the crackling and the crashing of the burning and falling timbers, the roar of the flames, and the shrieks of the horses scorched to death in their stables, mingled with the shouts and yells of the mutineers and the rattling of the musketry which proclaimed the great Christian carnage. The scared inhabitants of the burning buildings—the women and children and non-combatants—sought safety in the gardens and out-houses, whither they were often tracked by the insurgents, and shot down or cut to pieces. Some fled in the darkness, and found asylums in such places as had escaped the fury of the incendiaries. Some were rescued by Native servants or soldiers, faithful among the faithless, who, in memory of past kindnesses, strove to save the lives of their white masters at the peril of their own.

Escape of the Commissioner.

Among those who were thus saved were Hervey Greathed, the Commissioner, and his wife. Warned of the approaching danger, first by an officer of the Third Cavalry, and then by a pensioned Afghan chief, he had taken his wife, and some other English-women who had sought safety with him, to the terraced roof of his house; but the insurgents, after driving off his guard, applied the firebrand to the lower part of the building, plundered the rooms, and then surrounded the place. With the flames raging beneath him, and the enemy raging around him, his position was one of deadly peril. And Greathed and his companions must have perished miserably but for the fidelity of one of those Native servants upon whom so much depended in the crisis which was then threatening our people. With rare presence of mind and fertility of resource he simulated intense sympathy with the rebels. He told them that it was bootless to search the house, as his master had escaped from it, but that, if they would follow him to a little distance, they would find the Feringhees hiding themselves behind a haystack. Fully confiding in the truth of his story, they suffered themselves to be led away from the house; and its inmates descended safely into an empty garden just as the upper rooms were about to "fall in with a tremendous crash."* 1857. May 10—11

Incidents of the night.

There were others far less happy on that disastrous Sunday evening. Wives, left without protection whilst their husbands were striving to do their duty in the Lines, were savagely cut to pieces in their burning homes; and little children were massacred beneath the eyes of their mothers. Then delicate English ladies, girt about with fiery danger, death on every side, turned, with a large-hearted sympathy, their thoughts towards their suffering fellow-countrywomen, and tried to rescue them from the threatened doom. In adjacent bungalows were two ladies, wives of officers of the Brigade. One was under special protection, for her husband had endeared himself to the men of his troop by his unfailing kindness and consideration for them. The other, wife of the Adjutant of the Eleventh Regiment, had but recently come from England, and was strange to all the environments of her situation. The more experienced Englishwoman, seeing the danger of her position, and hearing the shrieks which issued from her house, was moved with a great compassion, and sent her servants

Mrs. Craigie

Mrs. Chambers.

* Mrs. Greathed's Narrative. See also note in Appendix for some account of the gallant and devoted conduct of Syud Meer Khan, an Afghan pensioner resident at Meerut.

1857. May 10—11. to rescue the affrighted creature from the fury of her assailants. But when, after some delay, they entered her house, they found her covered with wounds, lying dead upon the floor. Then the insurgents, having done their bloody work, raged furiously against the adjacent bungalow, and were only driven from their purpose by the fidelity of some of Craigie's troopers, who were ready to save the wife of their Captain at the risk of their own lives. In the course of the night, after doing good service, Craigie returned, in fear and trembling, to his household gods, thinking to find them shattered and desecrated; but, by the exceeding mercy of God, safe himself, he found them safe, and soon had matured measures for their escape. Wrapping up the ladies in dark-coloured horse-cloths to conceal their white garments in the glare of the burning station, he led them from the house, and hiding under trees, or in a ruined temple, they passed the night in sleepless horror. Often the voices of bands of mutineers or plunderers in the compound smote upon their ears; but there were help and protection in the presence of a few of Craigie's troopers, who hovered about the place, and in some of his own body-servants, who were equally true to their master. In the early morning the enemy had cleared off, and there was a prospect of escape. So they returned sadly to their dearly-loved home, collected a few cherished articles and some necessary clothing, and went forth from their Paradise with the flaming sword behind them, never again to return. And the leave-takings of that sorrow-laden night were the first of many cruel divulsions, which tore happy families from their homes and sent them forth into the wide world, houseless wanderers and fugitives, with a savage and remorseless enemy yelling behind them in their track.

Many other episodes of pathetic interest might here be related illustrative of the horrors of that night, if historical necessity did not forbid such amplitude of detailed recital. The sweepings of the gaols and the scum of the Bazaars—all the rogues and ruffians of Meerut, convicted and unconvicted, and the robber-tribes of the neighbouring villages—were loose in the Cantonment, plundering and destroying wherever an English bungalow was to be gutted and burnt. The Sepoys had left the work, which they had commenced, to men who found it truly a congenial task. Day dawned; and those who survived the night saw how thoroughly the work had been done. As they crept from their hiding-places and sought safety in the public buildings protected by the Europeans, they saw, in the mangled corpses which lay by the wayside, in the blackened ruins of the houses which skirted the roads, and in the masses of unmovable property, thrown out of the dwelling-places of the English, and smashed into fragments apparently by blows from heavy clubs, ghastly evidences of the fury of their enemies.* But with the morning light a great quietude had fallen upon the scene. The Sepoys had departed. The ruffians of the gaols and the Bazaars and the Goojur villages had slunk back into their homes. There was little more to be done—nothing more that could be done in the face of the broad day—by these despicable marauders. So our people gathered new heart; and as the sun rose, they thought that our time had come.

1857. May 11.

* "The inveterate animosity with which the work of destruction was carried out may be judged of by the fact that houses built entirely of masonry, with nothing inflammable except the doors and the beams, which for a considerable height from the ground supported the roofs, formed of cement, resting on kiln-burnt bricks, were as effectually destroyed as the thatched bungalows. Property which the miscreants could not carry off was thrown out and smashed into fragments, evidently pounded with heavy clubs."—*Report of Commissioner Williams.*

1857. May 11. The day after.

But the Meerut Brigade did nothing more in the clear morning light than it had done in the shadow of the darkness. The English troops, with the English leaders, rose from the bivouac; and it dawned upon them that more than two thousand mutineers had made their way to Delhi. Even then, if the Carabineers and the Horse Artillery had been let loose, they might, before noon, have reached the imperial city and held mutiny in check. But contemporary annals record only that the European troops, Horse, Foot, and Artillery, went out for a reconnaissance "on the right of the Delhi road." Not a man was despatched to the place which was the great centre of political intrigue and political danger—which was the great palatial home of the last representative of the House of Timour, and which held a large body of Native troops, and the great magazine of Upper India, unprotected by even a detachment of Europeans. Nor less surprising was it, that, with all these shameful proofs of the great crimes which had been committed, the rising indignation in the breasts of our English leaders did not impel them to inflict terrible retribution upon other criminals. The Bazaars on that Monday morning must have been full of the plundered property of our people, and of many dreadful proofs and signs of complicity in the great crime of the preceding night. Retribution might have fallen on many of the murderers red-handed; but not a regiment was let loose upon the guilty quarter. The murdered bodies were collected and laid out in the Theatre, where a mimic tragedy was to have been performed that evening; and the slayers of women and children, and the desecrators of our homesteads, were suffered to enjoy unmolested the fruits of their work;*

* "It is a marvellous thing that, with the dreadful proof of the night's work in every direction, though groups of savages were actually

whilst the Meerut Brigade, Horse, Foot, and Artillery, marched about Cantonments, and looked at the Delhi road along which the mutineers had made good their escape.* 1857. May 11

What might have been done by our people to overtake the guilty actors in the tragedy of that Sunday night, and to strike awe into the hearts of all who were minded to follow in the same track, may be gathered from an individual example, the record of which lies before me. It has been narrated how Mrs. Chambers, wife of the Adjutant of the Eleventh, was foully murdered in her bungalow. One of her husband's friends, Lieutenant Möller of the same regiment, obtained soon afterwards what appeared to be good evidence that a certain butcher of the Great Bazaar was the assassin. On this he started in his buggy for the Bazaar, tracked out the guilty man, seized him, and carried him back to Cantonments with a loaded pistol at his head. A drum-head court-martial was assembled, and whilst Chambers lay in convulsions in an adjoining room, the wretch was tried, found guilty, and sentenced to be hanged. And in a little while his lifeless body was swinging from the branch of a mango-tree.† There may, at this time, have been other examples of individual courage and resolution of the same stern character, as there were afterwards in all parts of the disturbed country; but the arm of authority was not uplifted to strike, and the multitude of criminals escaped.

seen gloating over the mangled and mutilated remains of the victims, the column did not take immediate vengeance on the Sudder Bazaar and its environs, crowded as the whole place was with wretches hardly concealing their fiendish satisfaction, and when there were probably few houses from which plundered property might not have been recovered. But the men were restrained; the bodies were collected and placed in the theatre, in which a dramatic tragedy would have been enacted, but for the real and awful one which occurred the night before."—*Report of Commissioner Williams.*

* See statement of Colonel Smyth, quoted *ante*, page 64, note.

† This was on the 14th of May.

1857. May 11. Indeed, wheresoever a number of Englishmen are gathered together there will surely be deeds of gallantry, many and great, though they may be obliterated by the hand of death or lost in the confusion of the hour. And Meerut saw many acts of personal bravery done by our people which will never perhaps find sufficient record.* Nor should it be forgotten that many noble instances of gratitude and generosity, or it might perhaps have been only of common humanity, were apparent in the conduct of the Natives, who, whilst their brethren were striking, put forth their hands to save, and risked their own lives to protect those of the people whose only crime it was that they had white faces.†

* "The firm bearing of the Deputy-Assistant Commissary-General, who stood by his office till his house was in flames, and a young officer rushed in with his lower jaw shattered by a musket-ball, and it was evident that the mutinous guard would abstain no longer; the gallant resistance of the Executive Engineer, Grand Trunk Road; the courage with which at least one woman attacked and wounded her assailants—these and many other instances of the fortitude with which our countrymen and countrywomen met the unexpected onslaught, deserve notice, but cannot be detailed in such a narrative."—*Report of Mr. Commissioner Williams. Unpublished Correspondence.*

† "Two Sepoys of the Eleventh Native Infantry most carefully escorted two ladies, with children, to the Dragoon Barracks. A Mahomedan in the city sheltered two Christian families, when the act was not only a singular deviation from the general conduct of his sect, but one full of danger to himself. A female servant and washerman succeeded in saving the young children of a lady, whom also they were attempting to save veiled in Native clothes, when a ruffian drew open the veil, saw the pale face, and cut the poor mother to pieces."—*Ibid.*

CHAPTER III

THE MEERUT MUTINEERS AT DELHI—EVENTS AT THE PALACE—PROGRESS OF INSURRECTION—STATE OF THE BRITISH CANTONMENT—MUTINY OF THE DELHI REGIMENTS—THE EXPLOSION OF THE MAGAZINE—ESCAPE OF THE BRITISH OFFICERS—MASSACRE OF THE PRISONERS.

1857. May 11. The ride to Delhi.

WHILST the Meerut Brigade were bivouacking on the great parade-ground, the troopers of the Third Cavalry, scarcely drawing rein on the way, were pricking on, in hot haste, all through the moonlit night for Delhi. And the foot regiments were toiling on laboriously behind them, making rapid progress under the impulse of a great fear. It is hard to believe that on that Sabbath evening a single Native soldier had discharged his piece without a belief, in his inmost heart, that he was going straight to martyrdom. A paroxysm of suicidal insanity was upon them. They were in a great passion of the Present, and were reckless of the Future. But the sound of the carbines and the rifles and the roar of the guns, with their deadly showers of grape and canister, must have been ringing in their ears, and they must have felt that they were lost hopelessly. And now, as they speeded onwards in the broad moonlight, they must have listened for the noise of the pursuing Dragoons, and must have felt, in their panic flight, that the Europeans would soon be upon them. But hour after hour passed, and there was no sound of pursuit; and soon after break of day they saw the waters of the

1857. May 11. Jumna glittering in the morning sun, and the great City of Refuge rose encouragingly before them. Before eight o'clock, the foremost troopers had crossed the river by the bridge of boats, had cut down the toll-keeper, had fired the toll-house, had slain a solitary Englishman who was returning to Delhi across the bridge; and under the windows of the King's Palace they were now clamouring for admittance, calling upon his Majesty for help, and declaring that they had killed the English at Meerut and had come to fight for the Faith.

At the Palace.

Hearing their cry, the King summoned to his presence Captain Douglas, the Commandant of the Palace Guards. In the Hall of Audience, supporting his tottering limbs with a staff, the aged monarch met the English Captain. Douglas said that he would descend and speak to the troopers; but the King implored him not to go, lest his life should be sacrificed, and laying hold of one of his hands, whilst Ahsan-oollah, the King's physician, took the other, imperatively forbade him to go down to the gate. Then Douglas went out on a balcony and told the troopers to depart, as their presence was an annoyance to the King. He might as well have spoken to the winds. Baffled at one point, they made good their entrance at another. It was in vain to tell them to close the gates, there were so many; and the guards were not to be trusted. It happened that the Thirty-eighth Sepoy Regiment was then on duty in the city—that regiment which had successfully defied the Government when it had been designed to send it across the Black Water.* Already they were prepared to cast in their lot with the mutineers. The Calcutta Gate was the nearest to the bridge of boats; but when this was closed, the

* See *ante*, vol. i. pages 461, 462.

troopers made their way along the road that runs between the palace walls and the river to the Rajghat Gate, which was opened to them by the Mahomedans of the Thauba-Bazaar, and they clattered into the town. 1857. May 11.

Progress of the Insurrection.

Then ensued a scene of confusion which it is difficult to describe. Cutting down every European they could find, and setting fire to their houses, they doubled back towards the Calcutta Gate, where they learnt that Commissioner Fraser, Douglas of the Palace Guards, and other leading Englishmen would be found. As they rode on, with the cry of "Deen-Deen!" they were followed by an excited Mahomedan rabble. The citizens closed their shops in amazement and terror, and from one end of Delhi to the other, as the news ran along the streets, there was sore bewilderment and perplexity, and everybody looked for the coming of the pursuing Englishmen, and feared that they would inflict a terrible retribution upon the city that had harboured the guilty fugitives. But no English regiments were coming to the rescue. And these maddened Native troopers, with such vile followers as they could gather up in the streets of Delhi, were now masters of the city. They knew that throughout all the Sepoy regiments in Cantonments there was not a man who would pull a trigger, or draw a sword, or light a port-fire in defence of his English officer. Without a fear, therefore, they rushed on, scenting the English blood, eager for the larger game, and ever proclaiming as they went glory to the Padishah and death to the Feringhees.

Whilst the Meerut mutineers were coming up from the further end of the long line of palace buildings, Commissioner Fraser at the other end was vainly endeavouring to secure the loyalty of the Sepoy Guards.

1857. May 11. Captain Douglas also had gone forth on the same vain errand. But it was soon clear that they were powerless. The troopers came upon them, and the Thirty-eighth, heedless of Fraser's appeals, fraternised with the new comers. Words now were nothing; authority was nothing. In the face of that surging multitude, increasing in numbers and in fury every moment, the English gentlemen felt that they carried their lives in their hands. When the leading troopers galloped up, Fraser and Douglas were in a buggy together; but seeing the danger that beset them, they descended and made for the gate of the civil guard-house, or police-station, where other Englishmen joined them. Taking a musket from one of the guards, Fraser shot the foremost of the troopers dead, and those who followed, seeing their comrade drop, fell back a little space; but the multitude behind pressed on, and it was soon apparent that safety was to be found only in flight. Fraser then re-entered his buggy and drove for the Lahore Gate of the Palace, whilst Douglas flung himself into the ditch of the Fort, and though severely injured by the fall, thus sheltered from the fire of the enemy, crept towards the Palace Gate. Some Chuprassies of the Palace Guard, who had followed him, lifted him up, almost powerless from the injuries he had received, and one of them took the Captain on his shoulders and carried him into the Palace. Presently Fraser and Hutchinson, the Collector, who had been wounded at the commencement of the affray, arrived also at the Palace.*

* All this is necessarily given upon Native evidence, adduced at the trials of the King of Delhi and Moghul Beg. In some respects the statements are contradictory. One witness says that Mr. Hutchinson accompanied Captain Douglas; another that he arrived with Mr. Fraser. A third says, that as soon as Captain Douglas was able to speak, he ordered his Chuprassies to search for Mr. Hutchinson and bring him into the Palace.

In the apartments occupied by Captain Douglas, there were then residing, as his guests, Mr. Jennings, the English Chaplain, Miss Jennings, his daughter, and a young lady named Clifford, a friend of the latter. Mr. Jennings had from an early hour of the morning been watching through a telescope the advance of the Meerut mutineers, and he knew that there was mischief in the wind. Hearing a noise, he went below, and found that Captain Douglas had just been brought in and placed on a stone-seat in a lower court. Under his directions, Douglas and Hutchinson were carried by some of the Palace Guards up the staircase to the apartments over the gateway,* whilst Fraser remained below, endeavouring to allay the excitement. Standing at the foot of the stairs, with a sword in his hand, the last-named was addressing a noisy crowd, when a man named Moghul Beg, an orderly of the Palace Guards, rushed upon him and clove his cheek to the bone.† The others followed up the attack, cutting at him with their swords, and presently Simon Fraser, Commissioner, lay a corpse at the foot of the stairs.

1857. May 11. Murder of Mr. Fraser.

Meanwhile, in the upper rooms, Douglas and Hutchinson were lying in grievous pain, and the Jennings family were ministering to them. The excited crowd, having murdered the Commissioner, now rushed up the staircase eager for the blood of the other English gentlemen. An attempt was made to

Murder of the Jenningses.

* Some statements are to the effect that Mr. Jennings and Mr. Hutchinson carried Douglas up-stairs.

† Here, again, there is discordant evidence. On the trial of the King, it was more than once stated that the first blow was struck by one Hadjee, a lapidary or seal-engraver, who (according to one witness) "inflicted a deep and mortal wound on the right side of his neck." But at the trial of Moghul Beg, five years afterwards (1862), it was stated by one Buktawuss Sing that he "saw the prisoner inflict the first wound which was on Mr. Fraser's face." Another witness, Kishun Singh, also stated, "I saw the prisoner strike the first blow." See further statements in the Appendix.

1857. May 11. close the doors at the head of the staircases, but the murderous gang forced their way upwards, streamed into the rooms where Douglas, Hutchinson, Jennings, and the innocent young Englishwomen were listening with dismay to the tumult below, and, before a prayer could be lifted up, had massacred them with exultant ferocity. It was quickly done. A brief and bloody murder, terrible to contemplate, then stained the Delhi Palace; but no circumstances of shameful outrage aggravated the horror of the deed.*

There was then a scene of fearful uproar and confusion, which filled the old King with bewilderment and terror. The murderers, with their blood-stained swords in their hands, went about boasting of their crimes, and calling upon others to follow their example. The court-yards and the corridors of the Palace were swarming with the mutineers of the Third Cavalry and of the Thirty-eighth, and soon the Meerut Infantry Regiments† began to swell the dangerous crowd, whilst an excited Mahomedan rabble mingled with the Sepoys and the Palace Guards. The troopers stabled their horses in the courts of the Palace. The foot-men, weary with the long night march, turned the Hall of Audience into a barrack, and littered down on the floor. Guards were posted all about the Palace. And the wretched, helpless King found that his royal dwelling-house was in military occupation.

* It was stated, and for some time believed, that the English ladies had been dragged before the King, and either murdered in his presence or by his orders, and some highly dramatic incidents have been published illustrative of this complicity of the Mogul in the first murders. But there is not the least foundation for these stories. On the other hand, it is on evidence that Captain Douglas, shortly before his death, sent a message to the King, requesting him to send palanquins to remove the ladies to the Queen's apartments, and that he did so—but too late.

† There is considerable diversity of statement relating to the hour at which the Meerut Infantry Regiments arrived.

Whilst these events were passing within the precincts of the Palace, in the quarter of the city most inhabited by the English residents the work of carnage and destruction was proceeding apace. It is not easy to fix the precise hour at which each particular incident in the dreadful catalogue of crime and suffering occurred. But it seems to have been under the meridian sun that the principal unofficial Englishmen in Delhi fell victims to the fury of the enemy. About noon the Delhi Bank was attacked and plundered, and all its chief servants, after a brave resistance, massacred. Mr. Beresford, the manager of the Bank, took refuge with his wife and family on the roof of one of the outbuildings. And there, for some time, they stood at bay, he with a sword in his hand, ready to strike, whilst his courageous helpmate was armed with a spear. Thus, with resolute bravery, they defended the gorge of the staircase, until the assailants, seeing no hope of clearing the passage, retired to scale the walls in the rear of the house. The attack was then renewed, but still the little party on the roof made gallant resistance. It is related by an eye-witness that one man fell dead beneath the lady's spear. But to resist was but to protract the pains of death. They were overpowered and killed, and the Bank was gutted from floor to roof. The Delhi Press establishment shared the same fate. The Christian compositors had gathered there, in pursuance of their craft; and never, perhaps, since the first dawn of printing, had work been done, sadder and grimmer than this—for it was theirs to record in type that the hand of death was upon them. The telegraph had brought in the early morning tidings that the Meerut mutineers were hastening to Delhi, and would soon be at the city gates. Some

1857. May 11.

The Delhi Bank.

The Delhi Press.

1857. May 11. must have felt then that they were composing their own death-warrants. The little slips of printed paper—Delhi Gazette "Extras"—went forth, and the printers remained to meet the crisis, which they had just announced. About mid-day a crowd of insurgents rushed into the office, killed all the Christian compositors, who could not effect their escape, and with clubs and poles destroyed the house and its contents, taking away all the type that they could carry, to turn to another and a deadlier use. Everywhere the Christian people were butchered, their property was plundered or destroyed, and then their houses were fired.* The Church was an especial object of the fury of the insurgents. They gloated over the desecration of all that was held in reverence by our Christian people. They tore down and shattered the monumental slabs on the walls; they seized the sacramental plate; then they ascended to the belfry, rang a peal in derision, and, loosening or cutting the ropes, let the bells fall with a crash on the stones below.

Events in Cantonments. Meanwhile, there was great excitement in the British Cantonments, where the Sepoy regiments of the Company were posted. Our military force was cantoned on a Ridge overlooking the great city, at a distance of about two miles from it. There had during the preceding week been no symptoms of inquietude

* "Private houses were entered by troopers (their horses being held at the gates of the gardens), who said they did not come for *loot* but *life*, and when they were disappointed in their greed for European life, they let in the budmashes of the city, who, in the space of half an hour, cleared out the best-regulated houses from punkah to floor-cloth. They then either set fire to the house, or, if it were not of an inflammable nature, they pulled out the doors and window-frames, &c., in some cases the beams from the roofs."—*Mr. Wagentreiber's Narrative.*

among them. Some Native officers from the Delhi regiments had been sitting on the great Meerut Court-Martial; but how far they sympathised with the prisoners cannot be confidently declared. It would have been strange, however, if what had happened at Barrackpore and Berhampore had not been discussed at Meerut, and if the Native officers had not carried back with them that uneasy feeling of the something coming which was rapidly spreading from station to station. It is certain, however, that on the afternoon of the Christian Sabbath, which saw at Meerut the first great baptism of blood, a carriage arrived in the Delhi Cantonments full of Natives, who, though not in regimental uniform, were known to be Sepoys from Meerut.* What was said or done in the Lines on that evening and during the ensuing night can only be conjectured. But the following morning found every regiment ripe for revolt.

1857. May 11.

At the early sunrise parade of that day all the troops in the Delhi Cantonments—the Thirty-eighth, the Fifty-fourth, and Seventy-fourth Regiments, with the Native Artillery—were assembled to hear the proceedings of the Court-Martial on Issuree Pandy, the Barrackpore Jemadar,† read aloud; and as they were read, there arose from the assembled Sepoys a murmur of disapprobation. There was nothing beyond this; but some officers in Cantonments, who had been eagerly watching the signs of the times, felt that a crisis was approaching. At the early breakfast, however, where our officers met each other, after morning parade, at mess-houses or private bungalows, there was the wonted amount of light-hearted conversation and careless laughter. And when they separated, and

* See evidence of Captain Tytler at the trial of the King of Delhi.

† Issuree Pandy had been hanged on April 22nd.—*Ante* vol. i. p. 584.

1857. May 11. each man went to his home to bathe and dress, and prepare for the larger breakfast and the business or the pleasure of the morning, it was not thought that the day would differ from other days. But before the work of the toilet was at an end, our people were startled by the tidings that the Native Cavalry from Meerut were forcing their way into the city. Native servants and Sepoy orderlies carried the news to their officers, and every man hurried on his clothes, feeling that there was work before him. But even then the prevailing idea was that there had been an escape from gaol; no more. No one thought that there was danger to an Empire. If, it was said, the troops at Meerut had mutinied, the strong body of Europeans there—the Rifles, the Carabineers, and the white Artillery—would surely have been upon their track. It was not possible that more than a few fugitives could ever reach Delhi.

Colonel Ripley and the Fifty-fourth.

So argued our officers on the Delhi Ridge, as they listened to the bugle-call and buckled on their swords. The Fifty-fourth were ordered out for service, and two of De Tessier's guns were to accompany them to the city. It was necessarily a work of time to get the field-pieces ready for action; so Ripley, leaving two companies to escort the Artillery, marched down to the nearest gate. This was the Cashmere Gate. A little way on the other side of it was the Main-guard, at which some men of the Thirty-eighth were posted. They had already in their hearts cast in their lot with the mutineers, and when Ripley appeared with the Fifty-fourth, the time for action had come, and they threw off then the last remnant of disguise. The troopers of the Third Cavalry, with the insurgent rabble from the town, were surging onwards towards the gate. The Fifty-fourth, who had brought down their pieces unloaded, now received the order to load; and meanwhile, Captain Wallace, acting as field-officer of the day, who had taken command of the Main-guard, ordered the Thirty-eighth to fire upon the mutineers. To this they responded only with insulting sneers. Not a man brought his musket to the "present." 1857. May 11.

This was the turning-point of the great disaster. The Fifty-fourth were scarcely less faithless than their comrades. They fired in the air, and some, perhaps, fired upon their officers.* After shooting two of the insurgents, Ripley was cut down, and near him fell also the lifeless bodies of Smith and Burrowes, Edwards and Waterfield. When the two companies in the rear approached the Cashmere Gate with the guns, they met Captain Wallace riding in hot haste towards them; he begged them, for mercy's sake, to hurry on, as the troopers were shooting down our officers. Soon they had ghastly evidence of this dismal truth, for the mangled body of their Colonel was being brought out, "literally hacked to pieces." Paterson then ordered his men to load, and pushed on with all speed to the gate. But the report of the approach of the guns had already awed the mutineers, and when they passed the gate, our officers found no trace of the enemy whom they had come to attack, except in the receding figures of a few troopers, who were scampering towards the city. But they found most miserable traces of the preceding conflict, in the dead bodies of their comrades, which were scattered about the place. These were now brought in to the Main-guard, before which the guns had been planted,

* There seems to be some doubt about the conduct of the Fifty-fourth in this first collision. It is stated, however, that Colonel Ripley declared that his own men had bayoneted him

1857. May 11. and the two companies of the Fifty-fourth posted as a garrison. And there they remained hour after hour, gaining no assured intelligence of the movements of the rebels, and ever cheerful in the thought that aid from Meerut, with its strong European force, must certainly be close at hand.

Major Abbott and the Seventy-fourth.

Meanwhile, Captain Wallace had been directed by Major Paterson to bring up the Seventy-fourth Regiment, with two more guns. Major Abbott, on gaining intelligence of the defection of the Thirty-eighth, and the doubtful conduct of the Fifty-fourth, mounted his horse, hastened to the Lines of his regiment, and addressed his men. He told them that the time had come for them to prove that they were true and loyal soldiers; and he called for volunteers to accompany him down to the Cashmere Gate. There was not a man there who did not come to the front; and when the order was given to load, they obeyed it with befitting alacrity. Then they marched down, with two more guns, under Lieutenant Aislabie, and about mid-day were welcomed by Paterson and his party at the Main-guard. The force at this post had now been strengthened by the return of some Sepoys of the Fifty-fourth, who had gone off in the confusion, and, having roamed about for some time in a state of bewilderment and panic, had at last turned back to the point from which they had started, hanging on to the skirts of circumstance, wondering what would be the result, and waiting to see whether a retributive force from Meerut was sweeping into the City of the Mogul.

At the Main-guard.

Time passed, and the slant shadows thrown by the descending sun were falling upon the Main-guard. Yet still no authentic intelligence of what was passing in the city reached our expectant officers, except that which was conveyed to them by European fugitives who sought safety there from other parts of the city. Scared and bewildered they had come in, each with some story of an escape from death, providential — almost miraculous. But there was little room for rejoicing, as it seemed to them that they had been saved from old dangers only to encounter new. At the Main-guard they were surrounded by Sepoys, waiting only a fitting opportunity to disencumber themselves of the last remnant of their outward fidelity. At any moment they might break out into open revolt, and shoot down the Europeans of both sexes congregated in the enclosure. It was a time of intense anxiety It was evident that the insurrection was raging in the city. There was a confused roar, presaging a great tumult, and smoke and fire were seen ascending from the European quarter. 1857. May 11.

Then there was, at intervals, a sound of Artillery, the meaning of which was not correctly known, and then a tremendous explosion, which shook the Main-guard to its very foundation. Looking to the quarter whence the noise proceeded, they saw a heavy column of smoke obscuring the sky; and there was no doubt in men's minds that the great Magazine had exploded —whether by accident or design could only be conjectured. But whilst the party in the Guard-house were speculating on the event, two European officers joined them, one of whom was so blackened with smoke that it was difficult to discern his features. They were Artillery subalterns, who had just escaped from the great explosion. The story which it was theirs to tell is one which will never be forgotten.

The great Delhi Magazine, with all its vast supplies of munitions of war, was in the city at no great Explosion of the Magazine

1857. May 11. distance from the Palace. It was in charge of Lieutenant George Willoughby, of the Bengal Artillery, with whom were associated Lieutenants Forrest and Raynor, officers of the Ordnance Commissariat Department, and six European Conductors and Commissariat Sergeants. All the rest of the establishment was Native. Early morning work is a condition of Anglo-Indian life, and Willoughby was at the Magazine superintending the accustomed duties of his department, and little dreaming what the day would bring forth, when Forrest came in accompanied by the magistrate, Sir Theophilus Metcalfe, and informed him that the Meerut mutineers were streaming across the river. It was Metcalfe's object to obtain from the Magazine a couple of guns wherewith to defend the Bridge. But it was soon apparent that the time for such defence had passed. The troopers had crossed the river, and had found ingress at the Palace Gate. A brave and resolute man, who, ever in the midst of danger, seemed almost to bear a charmed life, Metcalfe then went about other work, and Willoughby braced himself up for the defence of the Magazine. He knew how much depended on its safety. He knew that not only the mutinous soldiery, but the dangerous classes of Delhi, would pour down upon the Magazine, some eager to seize its accumulated munitions of war, others greedy only for plunder. If, he thought, he could hold out but a little while, the white regiments at Meerut would soon come to his aid, and a strong guard of English Riflemen with guns manned by European artillerymen, would make the Magazine secure against all comers. It was soon plain that the Native establishment of the Magazine was not to be trusted. But there were nine resolute Englishmen who calmly prepared themselves to face the tremendous odds which threatened them, and, if the sacrifice were required, to die beneath the ruins of the Magazine. Cheered by the thought of the approaching succour from Meerut, these brave men began their work. The outer gates were closed and barricaded. Guns were then brought out, loaded with double charges of grape, and posted within the gates. One of the Nine, with port-fire in hand, stood ready to discharge the contents of the six-pounders full upon the advancing enemy if they should find their way into the enclosure. These arrangements completed, a train was laid from the powder-magazine, and on a given signal from Willoughby, if further defence should be hopeless, a match was to be applied to it, and the Magazine blown into the air. 1857. May 11.

Whilst in this attitude of defence, a summons to surrender came to them in the name of the King. It was treated with contemptuous silence. Again and again messengers came from the Palace saying that his Majesty had ordered the gates to be opened, and the stores given up to the Army. If not, ladders would be sent, and the Magazine would be carried by escalade. Unmoved by these menaces, Willoughby and Forrest answered nothing, but looked to their defences; and presently it was plain that the scaling-ladders had arrived. The enemy were swarming over the walls. At this point all the Natives in the Magazine, the gun-lascars, the artificers and others whose defection had been expected, threw off their disguise, and, ascending some sloping sheds, joined the enemy on the other side

The time for vigorous action had now arrived. As the enemy streamed over the walls, round after round of murderous grape-shot from our guns, delivered with all the coolness and steadiness of a practice-

1857. May 11. parade, riddled the advancing multitudes; but still they poured on, keeping up a heavy fire of musketry from the walls.* Yet hoping almost against hope to hear the longed-for sound of the coming help from Meerut, the devoted Englishmen held their ground until their available ammunition was expended. Then further defence was impossible; they could not leave the guns to bring up shot from the Magazine, and there were none to help them. Meanwhile, the mutineers were forcing their way at other unprotected points into the great enclosure, and it was plain that the Nine—two among them wounded, though not disabled, for the strong will kept them at their posts—could no longer hold the great storehouse from the grasp of the enemy. So the signal was given. Conductor Scully fired the train. In a few seconds there was a tremendous explosion. The Magazine had been blown into the air.

Not one of that gallant band expected to escape with his life. But four of the Nine, in the confusion which ensued, though at first stunned and bewildered, shattered and bruised, made good their retreat from the ruins. Willoughby and Forrest, it has been seen, escaped to the Main-guard. Raynor and Buckley took a different direction, and eventually reached Meerut. Scully and his gallant comrades were never seen alive again. But the lives thus nobly sacrificed were dearly paid for by the enemy. Hundreds perished in that great explosion; and others at a distance were struck down by the fragments of the building, or by bullets flung from the cartridges ignited in store. But it was not possible that by any such explosion as this the immense material resources

* The assailants appear to have been principally Sepoys of the Eleventh and Twentieth Regiments from Meerut.

of the great Delhi Magazine should be so destroyed as to be unserviceable to the enemy. The effect of the heroic deed, which has given to those devoted Nine a cherished place in History, can never be exactly computed. But the grandeur of the conception is not to be measured by its results. From one end of India to another it filled men's minds with enthusiastic admiration; and when news reached England that a young Artillery officer named Willoughby had blown up the Delhi Magazine, there was a burst of applause that came from the deep heart of the nation. It was the first of many intrepid acts which have made us proud of our countrymen in India, but its brilliancy has never been eclipsed. 1857. May 11.

In the British Cantonment on the Ridge a column of white smoke was seen to arise from the city, and presently the sound of the explosion was heard. It was then four o'clock. Brigadier Graves and the officers under him had been exerting themselves to keep together such of the troops as had not marched down to the Delhi City, ever hoping that the Europeans from Meerut would soon come to their relief, and wondering why they were so long in making their appearance. It seemed strange, but it was possible, that the extent of the danger was not apprehended by General Hewitt; strange that it should be necessary to send for succours to Meerut, and yet, as the day advanced and no help came, it clearly had become necessary to appeal for the aid which ought to have been freely and promptly sent. Then one brave man stepped forward and offered to carry a letter to the General at Meerut. This was Doctor Batson, the Surgeon of the Seventy-fourth Regiment. The gallant Progress of mutiny in Cantonments.

1857. May 11. offer was accepted. The letter was written, and placed in Batson's hands. He took leave of his wife and children, whom he might never see again, disguised himself as a Fakeer, and set forth on his perilous journey. But well as he played his part, and able as he was to speak the language of the country as fluently as his own, he had not proceeded far before his disguise was penetrated; the colour of his eyes had betrayed him. He was fired upon by the Sepoys, robbed and stripped by the villagers, and finally cast adrift, to wander about naked and hungry, weary and footsore, passing through every kind of peril, and enduring every kind of pain

All day long the Sepoys in the Cantonment had been hovering upon the brink of open mutiny. They had committed no acts of violence against their officers, but, like their comrades at the Main-guard, though held back by the fear of the white regiments that were expected from Meerut, they were festering with the bitterness of national hatred, and eager to strike. The ladies and children had been gathered up and sheltered in a place known as the Flagstaff Tower.* There two of De Tessier's guns were posted, but the Native gunners were not to be trusted, and besides the officers, there were only nineteen Euro-

* This Flagstaff Tower became afterwards very celebrated in the history of the siege of Delhi. On that 11th of May it was little better than a "Black Hole." The scene within the tower is thus described by an eye-witness: "Here we found a large number of ladies and children collected in a round room some eighteen feet in diameter. Servants, male and female, were huddled together with them; many ladies were in a fainting condition from extreme heat and nervous excitement, and all wore that expression of anxiety so near akin to despair. Here were widows mourning their husbands' murder, sisters weeping over the report of a brother's death, and some there were whose husbands were still on duty in the midst of the disaffected Sepoys, of whose fate they were as yet ignorant. It was a Black Hole in miniature, with all but the last horrible features of that dreadful prison, and I was glad even to stand in the sun to catch a breath of fresh air." —*Mr. Wagentreiber's Narrative.*

peans, or Christians, in the Cantonment. It was felt that at any moment a crisis might arrive, when nothing but a sudden flight could save the lives of this little handful of our people. The explosion of the Magazine seems to have brought on the inevitable moment, when the last links that bound the Native soldiery to their European officers were to be broken. 1857. May 11.

Events at the Main-guard.

At the Main-guard in the City, as in the Cantonment on the Ridge, the same process was going on in the light of the setting sun. The disaffection of the Delhi regiments had ripened into general mutiny. The last restraints were flung aside under an assumed conviction that the Europeans from Meerut were not coming to avenge their slaughtered brethren. The great national cause was swelling into portentous external dimensions under the inflations of the King and Princes, and others of stronger lungs than their own. Everywhere it had been noised about from early morning that the King was on the side of the mutineers, and that to fight against the English was to fight for the King—to fight for the restoration of the Mogul throne—to fight for the religion of the Prophet. And as the day advanced, there were more unmistakable signs that this was neither an invention nor a delusion. The inmates of the Palace, timid, feeble, effete as they were, had plainly risen against the dominant Christian power. The yoke of the Feringhees was to be cast off. The time had come when all the great offices of State would again be filled by the people of the East—by Mahomedans and Hindoos, under the restored dynasty of the Moguls. And whilst many were inspired by these sentiments, many also were moved by a great lust of plunder; and as the sun neared the horizon, and still there

1857. May 11. were no signs of the avenging Englishmen on the road from Meerut, massacre and spoliation were safe and easy, and all the scum of Delhi, therefore, was seen upon the surface of the rebellion.

To hold out any longer against such overwhelming odds was now wholly impossible. At the Main-guard the massacre of our people was commenced by a volley from the Thirty-eighth, delivered with terrible effect into the midst of them. Gordon, the field-officer of the day, fell from his horse with a musket-ball in his body, and died without a groan. Smith and Reveley of the Seventy-fourth, were shot dead.* That any Christian person escaped amidst the shower of musketry that was poured upon them seemed to be a miraculous deliverance. There was now nothing left to the survivors but to seek safety in flight. There was but one means of escape, and that a perilous, almost a hopeless, one. There was an embrasure in the bastion skirting the court-yard of the Main-guard, through which egress might be obtained, and by dropping down into the ditch—a fall of some thirty feet—and ascending the opposite scarp, the slope of the glacis might be gained, beyond which there was some jungle, which might afford cover to the fugitives till nightfall. Young and active officers, not crippled by wounds, might accomplish this; but the despairing cries of some Englishwomen from the inner rooms of the Guard-house, reminded them that they could not think wholly of themselves. To remain in the Guard was to court death. The mutineers were not only firing upon our people with their muskets, but pointing their guns at us. The only hope left was a

* "The latter (Reveley) had a loaded gun in his hand; he quietly raised himself up with a dying effort, and discharging both barrels into a knot of Sepoys below, the next moment expired."—*Lieutenant Vibart's Narrative.*

1857. May 11

descent into the ditch, but even that was more like despair. So the women were brought to the embrasure, and whilst in terror and confusion they were discussing the possibility of the descent, a round-shot passed over their heads, and they felt that there was not a moment to be lost. The officers then fastened their belts together, and thus aided, whilst some dropped into the ditch to receive the women, others helped them from above to descend. At last, not without much difficulty, aggravated by the terror of the poor creatures who were being rescued, the whole were lowered into the ditch; and then came the still more difficult task of ascending the opposite bank. The steepness of the ascent and the instability of the soil made their footing so insecure, that again and again they were foiled in the attempt to reach the summit. The earth gave way beneath them, and helping men and helpless women rolled back to the bottom of the ditch amidst a shower of crumbling earth. Despair, however, gave them superhuman energy, and at last the whole of our little party had surmounted the outer slope of the ditch, and were safe upon the crest of the glacis. Then they made their way into the jungle which skirted it, and pushed on, some in the direction of the Cantonments, and some in the direction of Metcalfe House.

Escape from Cantonments

Meanwhile, in the British Cantonment on the Ridge our people had been reduced to the same extremity of despair. The Sepoys had turned upon them and now held possession of the guns. It was no longer possible to defend the place or to keep together even the few Native soldiers who were inclined to remain faithful, under the influence of old

1857. May 11. habits and personal attachments. Two circumstances, however, were in favour of the English in Canton ments. One was, that the Sepoys at a distance from the Palace and the City were less acquainted with the extent to which the Royal Family and the Mahomedan citizens of Delhi were aiding and supporting the mutineers. The other was, that our officers, being at their homes, had facilities of conveyance—horses, and carriages, and carts—wherewith to carry off their families to Meerut or Kurnaul, with some provisions for the journey, and perhaps some of the remnant of their household gods. When first they moved off, there was a slight show or pretence of the Sepoys going with them. They fell in to the word of command, and, for a little space, accompanied the departing Englishmen; but soon the columns were broken up, the Sepoys streamed into the Bazaars, and all semblance of discipline was abandoned. Three or four officers, who had remained with them, tried to rally their men in vain. The Sepoys implored them to escape before the rabble from the city burst upon the Cantonment. Already, indeed, the English carriages had been lighted upon their way by the blaze of our burning bungalows. If the officers who were the last to quit the Cantonment could rescue the regimental colours, it was the most that they could hope to accomplish.*

The flight from Delhi. So, forth from the Cantonment and forth from the City went our fugitive people. Many narratives of deep and painful interest have been written, descriptive of the sufferings which they endured, and the dangers which they encountered. It has been nar-

* The last to quit the Cantonment were, apparently, Colonel Knyvett of the Thirty-eighth, Lieutenant Gambier, Captain Peile, and Captain Holland.

rated how they hid themselves now in the jungle, 1857.
now in the ruins of uninhabited buildings; how they May 11—12.
tore off their epaulettes or other bright appendages of their uniform lest they should attract notice by glittering in the moonlight or the sunshine; how they crouched like hares in form, or hid themselves in gaps and hollows; how they were tracked and despoiled by robbers; how they were lured into seemingly friendly villages and then foully maltreated; how they waded through or swam rivers, carrying the women and children across as best they could; how they were beaten and stripped, and sent on their way under the fierce unclouded sun of the Indian summer, without clothing and without food; how they often laid themselves down at night weary, exhausted, and in sore pain, crouching close to each other for warmth, expecting, almost hoping that death would come at once to relieve them from their sufferings; how delicate women and young children struggled on, sometimes separated from their husbands or fathers, but ever finding consolation and support in the kindly and chivalrous ministrations of English gentlemen.* Some made good their way to Meerut, some to Kurnaul, some to Umballah. Others perished miserably on the road, and a few, unable to proceed, were left behind by their companions. This was the sorest trial of all that befel the fugitives. It went to the hearts of these brave men to abandon any of their fellow-sufferers who could not longer share their flight. But there was no help for it. So, once or twice, after vain endeavours to carry the helpless one to a place of safety, it was found that,

* And nobly the women played their parts, and not always as the weaker vessels. One published narrative relates how two ladies—Mrs. Wood and Mrs. Peile—saved a wounded officer, the husband of the former, who could not have moved onward without their support.

1857. May 11—12. with the enemy on their track, death to the Many must follow further efforts to save the One, and so the wretched creature was left behind to die.*

But truth would not be satisfied if it were not narrated here that many compassionate and kindly acts on the part of the Natives of the country relieved the darkness of the great picture of national crime. Many of the fugitives were succoured by people in the rural districts through which they passed, and sent on their way in safety. In this good work men of all classes, from great landholders to humble sweepers took part, and endangered their own lives by saving those of the hapless Christians.†

May 11—16. Massacre of Prisoners. Whilst these remnants of our British officers, with their wives and children, were thus miserably escaping from Delhi, there were others of our country people, or co-religionists, who were in pitiable captivity there, awaiting death in a stifling dungeon. These were, for the most part, European or Eurasian inhabitants of the Darao-gunj, or English quarter of Delhi, engaged in commerce or trade. On the morning of the 11th of May, many of these people, hearing that the mutineers were crossing the bridge, gathered themselves in one of the "largest and strongest houses" occupied by our Christian people, and there barricaded themselves. These, however, and others, burnt or dragged out of their houses, escaped death only to

* See Lieutenant Vibart's Narrative.

† Mr. Williams, in his official report, gives a list—but not a complete one—of the Natives who succoured the Delhi fugitives. See also narrative of the escape of Captain T. W. Holland: "There being no milk in the village, one Pultoo sweeper, or others of his family, used daily to take the trouble to go to procure some from adjacent villages." Again: "I remained with Jumnadass (a Brahmin) six days. He gave me the best part of his house to live in, and the best food he could," &c. &c.

be carried prisoners to the Palace, where they were 1857. confined in an underground apartment, without May 11—16. windows, and only one door, so that little either of air or light ever entered the dreary dwelling. There nearly fifty Christian people—men, women, and children—were huddled together, scantily fed, constantly threatened and insulted by the Sepoys and Palace-guards, but bearing up bravely beneath the burden of their sorrows. After four or five days of this suffering, a servant of the King asked one of the ladies in the dungeon how, if they were restored to power, the English would treat the Natives; and the answer was, "Just as you have treated our husbands and children." On the following day they were led May 16. forth to die. The Palace-guards came to the prison-door and told them to come forth, as they were to be taken to a better residence. Sorely mistrusting their guards, they crowded out of the dungeon. A rope was thrown round them, encircling the party so that none could escape. Then they were taken to a court-yard—the appointed shambles—where great crowds of people were gathered together to witness the massacre of the Christians. As they stood there cursing the Feringhees and throwing up their jubilant cries, the work of slaughter commenced. It is not easy to tell the story with an assured belief in its truth. It seems, however, that the Nemesis of the Third Cavalry was there; that some of the troopers fired with carbine or pistol at the prisoners, but by mischance struck one of the King's retainers. Then there began a carnage at the sabre's edge. It is hard to say how it was done. Whether many or whether few swordsmen fell upon the Christians is uncertain.* But, in

* One statement is to the effect that a hundred or a hundred and fifty men fell upon them with their swords; and another is, that two

1857. May 16. a brief space of time, fifty Christian people—men, women, and children—were remorselessly slain.* A sweeper, who had helped to dispose of the corpses, bore witness that there were only five or six men among them. The bodies were heaped up on a cart, borne to the banks of the Jumna, and thrown into the river.

So there was not, after that 16th of May, a single European left in Delhi, either in the Cantonment or in the City. The British had no longer any footing in the capital of the Mogul. We had been swept out by the great besom of destruction, and Behaudur Shah reigned in our place. Since the days of Suraj-ood-dowlah and the Black Hole, no such calamity had ever overtaken our people, and never since we first set foot on Indian soil any such dire disgrace. That a number of Christian people should be thus foully massacred was a great sorrow, but that nothing should be done to avenge the blood of our slaughtered countrymen was a far greater shame. The sorrow was at Delhi; the shame was at Meerut. The little band of Englishmen suddenly brought face to face with mutiny in the Lines, insurrection in the City, and revolution in the great teeming Palace of Delhi; who found, as their enemies on that May morning, six mutinous Sepoy Regiments, a hostile Mahomedan population, and the retainers of the old Mogul dynasty, with the King's name as the watchword, and the Princes as the leaders of the many-sided revolt, could not have done much more than they did to stem the tide that was rushing upon them. It was not possible that they should hold out for more

swordsmen did the entire butchery by themselves.

* A woman (Mrs. Aldwell) with three children, escaped by feigning Mahomedanism.

than one dreadful day with such a power arrayed against them. Their doom had been sealed in the early morning. When the hoofs of the foremost troop-horse rung upon the bridge across the Jumna, the death-knell of the British was sounded. From morn to noon, from noon to sunset, still our people were sustained by a strong faith in the manhood of their countrymen, who, at a little distance, had Horse, and Foot, and a great strength of Artillery to bring to their succour. But when the sun went down, and there was no sign at Delhi of the approach of the Dragoons or the Galloper guns, they saw that they were deserted, and what could they do but fly? 1857. May.

But did the responsibility of this grievous inaction rest with General Hewitt or with Brigadier Wilson? The General has asserted that, as the command of the station was in the hands of the Brigadier, the movement of the troops depended upon him. But when a General Officer, commanding a division of the Army, thus shifts the responsibility on to the shoulders of a subordinate, he virtually seals his own condemnation. When, at a later period, Wilson was called upon by the supreme military authorities for a full explanation of the causes of the inaction of the European troops on the night of the 10th of May, and reference was made to what Hewitt had stated, the former wrote in reply, "I would beg to refer to the Regulations of the Bengal Army, Section XVII., which will show what little authority over the troops is given to the Brigadier commanding a station which is the Head-Quarters of a Division, and that I could not have exercised any distinct command, the Major-General being present on the occasion. As Brigadier, Question of responsibility.

1857. May.

I only exercised the executive command of the troops under the orders of the Major-General." "I may or may not," he added, "have been wrong in offering the opinion I did to the Major-General. I acted to the best of my judgment at the time, and from the uncertainty regarding the direction taken by the fugitives, I still believe I was right. Had the Brigade blindly followed in the hope of finding the fugitives, and the remaining portion of the Cantonment been thereby sacrificed, with all our sick, women and children, and valuable stores, the outcry against those in command at Meerut would have been still greater than it has been."

Causes of Failure.

This, in part, is the explanation of that first great failure, which so perplexed and astounded all who heard of it, and which led to great and disastrous results hereafter to be recorded. The military commanders at Meerut believed that it was their first duty to protect life and property in the Cantonment. The mutinous Sepoys, aided by the escaped convicts, and by ruffians and robbers from the bazaars and villages, had butchered men, women, and children, had burned and gutted the houses of the white people in the Native quarter of the Cantonment, and it was believed that, if due precautions were not taken, the other great half of military Meerut would share the same fate, that the Treasury would be plundered, and that the magazines would fall into the enemy's hands. To Wilson it was natural that the safety of the Cantonment should be his first care; but Hewitt commanded the whole Meerut Division, including the great station of Delhi, with its immense magazine, and not a single European soldier to guard its profusion of military stores. It needed no breadth of vision, no forecast to discern the tremendous danger which lay at the distance only of a night's march from Meerut—danger not local, but national; danger no less portentous in its political than in its military aspects. But not an effort was made to intercept the fatal flood of mutiny that was streaming into Delhi. General Hewitt ignored the fact that the whole of the Meerut Division was under his military charge, and thinking only of the safety of the place in which he himself resided, he stood upon the defensive for many days, whilst the rebels of the Lines, of the Gaols, and the Bazaars, were rejoicing in the work that they had done with impunity equal to their success. 1857. May.

But the judgment of the historian would be but a partial—an imperfect—judgment, if it were to stop here. There is something more to be said. Beneath these personal errors, there lay the errors of a vicious system and a false policy. To bring this great charge against one Commander of a Division or another Commander of a Division, against one Commander-in-Chief or another Commander-in-Chief, against one Governor-General or another Governor-General, against this Department or against that Department, would be a mistake and an injustice. It was not this or that man that wanted wisdom. The evil lay broad and deep in the national character. The arrogance of the Englishman, which covered him ever with a great delusion, forbidding him to see danger when danger was surrounding him, and rendering it impossible in his eyes that any disaster should overtake so great and powerful a country, was the principal source of this great failure at Meerut. We were ever lapping and lulling ourselves in a false security. We had warnings, many and significant; but we brushed them away with a movement of impatience and contempt. There is a cant phrase, which, be-

1857. May cause it is cant, it may be beneath the dignity of History to cite; but no other words in the English language, counted by scores or by hundreds, can so express the prevailing faith of the Englishman at that time, as those two well-known words, "*All serene.*" Whatever clouds might lower—whatever tempests might threaten—still it was "All serene." It was held to be unbecoming an Englishman to be prepared for a storm. To speak of ugly signs or portents—to hint that there might be coming perils which it would be well to arm ourselves to encounter—was to be scouted as a feeble and dangerous alarmist. What had happened at Barrackpore and Berhampore might well have aroused our people to cautious action. We had before seen storms burst suddenly upon us to our utter discomfiture and destruction; but we were not to be warned or instructed by them. When Henry Lawrence wrote, "How unmindful have we been that what occurred in the city of Caubul may some day occur at Delhi, Meerut, or Bareilly,"* no one heeded the prophetic saying any more than if he had prophesied the immediate coming of the day of judgment. Everything, therefore, at Meerut, in spite of plain and patent symptoms of an approaching outbreak, was in a state of utter unpreparedness for action. There were troopers without horses, troopers that could not ride—artillerymen without guns, and artillerymen who did not know a mortar from a howitzer, or the difference between round-shot and grape. This was not the fault of General Hewitt or Brigadier Wilson; it was the fault of the system—the policy. The prevailing idea, and one for which there was good war-

* See *ante*, vol. i. p. 453.

rant, was, that the Government desired that things should be kept quiet. Even to have a battery of artillery equipped for immediate service was held to be a dangerous movement, that might excite alarm, and, perhaps, precipitate a crisis, which otherwise might be indefinitely delayed. When an officer of Artillery commanding one of the Meerut batteries sought permission, a few days before the outbreak, to load his ammunition-waggons, that he might be ready, in case of accident, for prompt service, he was told that such a step would excite suspicion among the Natives, and that therefore it could not be sanctioned. And this may have been right. The wrong consisted in having allowed things to drift into such a state, that what ought to have been the rule was regarded as something altogether abnormal and exceptional, and as such, a cause of special alarm. The policy was to believe, or to pretend to believe, that our lines had been cast in pleasant places; and the system, therefore, was never to be prepared for an emergency—never to be ready to move, and never to know what to do. In pursuance of this system the Commander-in-Chief was in the great play-ground of Simlah, and the Chiefs of Departments were encouraging him in the belief that the cloud "would soon blow over." So officers of all ranks in the great Divisions of the Army in the North-West—in the Sirhind, in the Meerut, in the Cawnpore Divisions—did, according to the pattern of Head-Quarters, and according to their instincts as Englishmen; and, therefore, when the storm burst, we were all naked, defenceless, and forlorn, and knew not how to encounter its fury.

1857. May.

It has been contended that a prompt movement in pursuit of the mutineers might not have been suc-

1857. May. cessful. And it is right that all circumstances of difficulty should be fully taken into account. Rebellion developed itself under the cover of the night. The mutineers dispersed themselves here and there, and our people knew not whither to follow them.

Question of pursuit considered.

The Cavalry, however, must have taken to the road, and where the Native troopers could go, our Dragoons might have pursued them; but the former had a long start, and it is said that, as they would have been the first to enter Delhi, they would have destroyed the bridge across the Jumna; and that even if our Cavalry and Horse Artillery had made their way into the City, they would have found themselves entangled in streets swarming with an armed rabble, stimulating and aiding the hostile Sepoy Regiments who had been prepared to welcome, and to cast in their lot with their comrades from Meerut. But it is to be observed, upon the other hand, that if the troopers of the Third Cavalry, who were the first to enter Delhi, had cut off the communication with Meerut, by destroying the bridge, they would have shut out large numbers of their own people, who were pouring, or rather dribbling, into Delhi all through the day. If the Meerut troops had arrived on the banks of the Jumna in a serried mass, under a capable commander, they would, when the whole had passed over, have destroyed the bridge, to cut off the pursuit of the enemy from Meerut. But straggling in at intervals, under no recognised chiefs, this was not to be expected; and if it had been done, a great part of the Meerut Infantry Regiments must have fallen into the hands of the pursuing Englishmen, and been destroyed by the grape-shot or sabres within sight of the Palace windows.

But the mere military argument in such a case

does not dispose of the historical question; for it was from the moral no less than from the material effects of the pursuit that advantage was to be derived. The sight of a single white face above the crest of a parapet has ere now put a garrison to flight. And it may not unreasonably be assumed that, if on that Monday morning a few English Dragoons had been seen approaching the Jumna, it would have been believed that a large body of white troops were behind them, and rebellion, which was precipitated by our inactivity, would then have been suspended by the fear of the coming retribution. Unless the Dragoons and Horse Artillery had headed the Sepoys, which was not indeed to be expected, the first sudden rush into Delhi must have occasioned wild confusion, and many lives must have been sacrificed to the fury of the troopers and the rabble of abettors. But the disaster would have been but limited—the defeat but temporary. It is doubtful whether, if the avenging Englishmen had, that morning, appeared under the walls of Delhi, the Sepoy Regiments stationed there would have broken into rebellion; and it is well nigh certain, that in the presence of the British troops the Royal Family of Delhi would not have dared to proclaim themselves on the side of the mutineers. All through the hours of the morning there was doubt and hesitation both in the Cantonments and in the Palace; and it was not until the sun was going down that it became manifest that Delhi was in the throes of a great revolution. Emboldened and encouraged by what seemed to be the sudden prostration of the English, our enemies saw that their time had come, whilst our friends lost confidence in our power and our fortune, and feared to declare themselves on our side. Better in that case for the English soldiers to

1857. May. come to Delhi to be beaten than not to come at all. It was the want of effort at such a moment that did us such grievous harm. For from one station to another the news spread that the Sepoys had conquered the English at Meerut, and proclaimed the Mogul Emperor at Delhi. The first great blow had been struck at the Feringhees, and ever from place to place the rumour ran that they had been paralysed by it.*

Alleged conspiracy for a general rising. There is another question to which, fitly here, a few sentences may be devoted. It has been said that, in looking at this great history of the Sepoy War as a whole, we shall not take just account of it, unless we consider that, inasmuch as there had been a conspiracy throughout the Bengal Native Army for a general rising of the Sepoys all over the country on a given day, the sudden outbreak at Meerut, which caused a premature development of the plot, and put the English on their guard before the appointed hour, was the salvation of the British Empire in India. Colonel Carmichael Smyth was ever assured in his own mind that, by evolving the crisis in the Third Cavalry Regiment, he had saved the Empire. It was his boast, and he desired that it should be made known to all men, that he might have the full credit of the act. And I am bound to say that there is high testimony in support of the belief thus confidently expressed. Mr. Cracroft Wilson, who was selected by the Supreme Government to fill the post of Special Commissioner, after the suppression of rebellion, with a view to the punishment of the guilty and the reward of the deserving, has placed

* There is an expressive Hindostanee word in very common currency among both Europeans and Natives on the Bengal side of India —"*lachar*," or helpless. It was currently said that the English were *lachar*.

upon record his full belief in this story of a general 1857
conspiracy for a simultaneous rising. "Carefully Ma
collating," he has written, "oral information with facts as they occurred, I am convinced that Sunday, 31st of May, 1857, was the day fixed for mutiny to commence throughout the Bengal Army; that there were committees of about three members in each regiment which conducted the duties, if I may so speak, of the mutiny; that the Sepoys, as a body, knew nothing of the plans arranged; and that the only compact entered into by regiments, as a body, was, that their particular regiments would do as the other regiments did. The committee conducted the correspondence and arranged the plan of operations, viz., that on the 31st of May parties should be told off to murder all European functionaries, most of whom would be engaged at church; seize the treasure, which would then be augmented by the first instalment of the rubbie harvest; and release the prisoners, of which an army existed in the North-Western Provinces alone of upwards of twenty-five thousand men. The regiments in Delhi and its immediate vicinity were instructed to seize the magazine and fortifications. . . . From this combined and simultaneous massacre on the 31st of May, 1857, we were, humanly speaking, saved by Lieutenant-Colonel Smyth commanding the Third Regiment of Bengal Light Cavalry, and the frail ones of the Bazaar.*

The mine had been prepared, and the train had been laid, but it was not intended to light the slow match for another three weeks. The spark, which fell from female lips, ignited it at once, and the night of the 10th of May, 1857, saw the com-

* *Ante*, Chapter II.

1857. May. mencement of a tragedy never before witnessed since India passed under British sway."*

This is strong testimony, and from a strong man —one not prone to violent assumptions or strange conjectures, who had unusual opportunities of investigating the truth, and much discernment and discrimination to turn those opportunities to account. But the proofs of this general combination for a simultaneous rising of the Native troops are not so numerous or so convincing as to warrant the acceptance of the story as a demonstrative fact. It is certain, however, that if this sudden rising in all parts of the country had found the English unprepared, but few of our people would have escaped the swift destruction. It would then have been the hard task of the British nation to reconquer India, or else to suffer our Eastern Empire to pass into an ignominious tradition. But whether designed or not designed by man, God's mercy forbade its accomplishment; and in a few hours after this first great explosion, the Electric Telegraph was carrying the evil tidings to all parts of the country. The note of warning was sounded across the whole length and breadth of the land; and wherever an Englishman was stationed there was the stern preparation of defence.

* Mr. J. C. Wilson's Moradabad Narrative (Official), Dec. 24, 1858.

CHAPTER IV.

EFFORTS OF LORD CANNING—STATE OF PUBLIC FEELING IN CALCUTTA—APPREHENSIONS AND ALARMS—BEARING OF THE GOVERNOR-GENERAL—CORRESPONDENCE WITH THE COMMANDER-IN-CHIEF—THE FIRST MOVEMENT TOWARDS DELHI—THE VOLUNTEER QUESTION—FIRST ARRIVAL OF SUCCOURS—APPEARANCE OF COLONEL NEILL.

WHILST little by little the details recited in the preceding chapter were making themselves known to Lord Canning in Calcutta, the Governor-General, calmly confronting the dangers and difficulties before him, was straining every nerve to repair the first great disaster, and to protect those defenceless tracts of country in which new rebellions were most likely to assert themselves. "The part of the country," he wrote to the President of the India Board, "which gives me most anxiety is the line which stretches through the length of Bengal from Barrackpore close by to Agra in the North-Western Provinces. In that length of seven hundred and fifty miles, there is one European Regiment at Dinapore, and that is all. Benares has a Sikh Regiment, but no Europeans; Allahabad the same; not reckoning a hundred European invalids, who were sent there a few days ago. At one of these places the Native Regiment is a suspected one, and at either the temptation to seize the Fort or the Trea- 1857. May.

1857. May 10. sury will be very great, if they hear that Delhi continues in the hands of mutinous regiments. Therefore, the two points to which I am straining are the hastening of the expulsion of the rebels from Delhi, and the collection of the Europeans here to be pushed up the country." What he did, in the early part of May, for the gathering of troops from a distance, has been told in the first volume of this History. The results of those initial efforts rapidly developed themselves; but what seems to be swift despatch, in tranquil times, is weary waiting, when the issues of life or death may depend upon the loss or gain of an hour.

Calcutta in the month of May.

Meanwhile, in the great vice-regal capital of India there was much tribulation. For there were gathered together large numbers of Christian people, men, women, and children. But numbers did not seem to impart to them either strength or courage. A vast majority of those Christian inhabitants were men who had been habituated, through long years, to peace and security. There was not in the whole world, perhaps, a more tranquil, self-possessed city, than Calcutta had ever been during a period of nearly a century. Even the local tumults, to which all great towns are more or less periodically subject, had been absent from the "City of Palaces." The worst disturbances had resulted from the excitability of stray sailors from the merchant-ships overmuch refreshed in the punch-houses of the Dhurrumtollah or the Chitpore Bazaar. And the Natives of the country generally had been regarded as a harmless, servile, obsequious race of men, to be reviled, perhaps beaten at discretion, by the haughty and intolerant Englishman. That Englishman, as seen in Calcutta, was, for the most part, of the non-official type; experienced in the ways of commerce, active, enterprising, intelligent, but with little knowledge of the Native character save in its trading aspects, and little given to concern himself about intricate questions of Indian policy. The name of "Ditcher" had been given to him, as one who seldom or never passed beyond the boundary of the Mahratta ditch. The railway had done something to diminish this inclusiveness; but still many of the European residents of Calcutta knew little of the great world beyond, and were prone, therefore, to attach undue importance to the busy commercial capital in which they were buying and selling, and were holding their household gods. Their idea of India much resembled the Chinese map-maker's idea of the world. The City of Palaces, like the Celestial Empire, covered, in their minds, nearly the whole of the sheet.

1857. May. The non-official Englishman.

It was not strange that men of this class, unaccustomed to great excitements, little used to strenuous action of any kind, and in many instances, perhaps, wholly unskilled in the use of offensive weapons, should have been stunned and bewildered by the tidings from the North-West, and what seemed to them the probabilities of a recurrence of similar tragedies in Bengal. Nor was it strange that they should have looked eagerly to the Government to put forth all its available resources to protect them against the dangers which their excited imaginations beheld rapidly approaching. The very confidence which they had before felt in their security, and their general contempt for the subject races, now rendered the reaction which had set in all the more exaggerated and overwhelming. The panic in May has, perhaps, been

1857. May. overstated in the recital. But stories are still current of Christian families betaking themselves for safety to the ships in the river, or securing themselves within the ramparts of the Fort, and of men staining their manhood by hiding themselves in dark places. But these manifestations of unmanly fear were principally among the Eurasians and Portuguese, or what are described as the "lower order of European shopkeepers." That some people left their homes in the suburbs, that some took their passages to England, that many bought guns and revolvers, and lay down to rest full-dressed and full armed, is not to be questioned.* And it is certain that the prevailing feeling was that the Governor-General failed to appreciate the magnitude of the danger—that nothing could rouse him from the lethargy indicated by his still face of marble and his tranquil demeanour—and that, in a word, he was not equal to the occasion.

It would be unjust to say that the apprehensions of the Calcutta community were altogether unreasoning and unreasonable, for there were many sources of alarm at this time. Foremost of all there was the great dread of the Sepoys, who, a little while before trusted guardians of our lives and properties, had suddenly grown into murderers and despoilers. There was but little space between Barrackpore and Calcutta. A night's march might have brought the

* I wish it to be borne in mind that this refers entirely to the state of things in May. A far more unmistakable panic, of which some account will hereafter be given, arose in the middle of June. But even of the former month a contemporary journalist wrote: "Men went about with revolvers in their carriages, and trained their bearers to load quickly and fire low. The ships and steamers in the rivers have been crowded with families seeking refuge from the attack, which was nightly expected, and everywhere a sense of insecurity prevailed, which was natural enough when the character of the danger apprehended is taken into consideration."—*Friend of India, May* 28.

whole brigade into the capital, to overpower the European guards, to seize the Fort, and to massacre the Christian inhabitants. Then there was in the immediate suburbs of Calcutta, along the river-bank, the great, reeking, overflowing sewer of the Oude household—the exiled King, his astute Prime Minister, and his multitude of dependents, all restless in intrigue, and eager to inflict measureless retribution upon the nation that had degraded and despoiled them. And then again there was a vague fear, dominant over all, that the vast and varied populations of the Native suburbs and bazaars would rise against the white people, release the prisoners in the gaols, and gorge themselves with the plunder of the great commercial capital of India. All these were at least possibilities. What had been done at Meerut and Delhi might be acted over again at Calcutta on a larger scale and with more terrible effect. 1857. May.

Bearing of Lord Canning.

After a lapse of years we may speak lightly of these dangers, and say that Lord Canning discerned the true state of things, whilst others saw them darkly through the glass of their fears. But the difference, perhaps, was rather that of outward bearing than of inward appreciation of the position of affairs. It is hard to say how much depends, in such a crisis, upon the calm and confident demeanour of the head of the Government. Day after day passed, and the Governor-General sat there, firm as a rock, waiting for fresh tidings of disaster, and doing all that human agency could do to succour our distressed people and to tread down the insolence of the enemy. The great English community of Calcutta thought that he did not see the magnitude of the danger, because he did not tremble for the fate of the capital. He did not know what it was to tremble,

1857. May. and some said that he did not know what it was to feel. But though he wore a calm face, in no man's mind was there a clearer sense of the magnitude of the crisis,* and in no man's heart was there a deeper pity. He pitied those at a distance, who were really girt about with peril, and whose despairing cries for help, in the shape of English troops, nearly broke his heart. But he pitied most of all, with a contemptuous pity, those who exaggerated the dangers around them, who could not conceal their fears, and who would fain have induced him to treat Calcutta as though it were the whole Indian Empire. If there were any impassiveness, any obduracy in him, it was simply that he could not bring himself to think much about the place in which he was living, whilst there were other places begirt with more imminent peril. He forgot himself, with the self-negation of a noble nature, and, forgetting himself, he may for a while have forgotten those immediately around him. And so it happened that the fears of many Englishmen in Calcutta were mixed with strong resentments, and they began to hate the Governor-General who could not bring himself to think that the Indian Empire was included within the circuit of the Mahratta ditch.

As the month of May advanced, the panic increased. It has been shown, in measured terms, what the Go-

* Lord Canning's correspondence abounds with proofs of this. Take the following from a characteristic letter to Bishop Wilson, which clearly shows that he did not underrate the danger, although he was confident of the national ability to surmount it: "The sky is very black, and as yet the signs of a clearing are faint. But reason and common sense are on our side from the very beginning. The course of the Government has been guided by justice and temper. I do not know that any one measure of precaution and strength, which human foresight can indicate, has been neglected. There are stout hearts and clear heads at the chief posts of danger—Agra, Lucknow, and Benares. For the rest, the issue is in higher hands than ours. I am very confident of complete success."

vernor-General thought of these manifestations of a great terror.* In later letters he spoke out in more emphatic language, and contemporary records of a less exalted character seem to support his assertions. Perhaps his eagerness to encourage others, by showing that he had no fear for the Presidency, carried him into an excess of outward indifference. Certainly, he did not seem to appreciate, in the first instance, an offer made by the British inhabitants to enrol themselves into a volunteer corps for the protection of the great City of Palaces. Many public bodies came forward at this time with protestations of unswerving loyalty and free offers of service. The Trades Association, the Masonic Lodges, the Native Christian Community, and side by side with our own compatriots and fellow-subjects, the representatives of the great French and American nations, sympathising with us in our distress. Such offers were worthy and honourable, and entitled to all gratitude from our rulers. Those communities desired to be armed and disciplined and organised after the manner of soldiers. Lord Canning told them in reply that they might enrol themselves as special constables. And it was thought that there was a touch of contempt in the very nature of the answer.

1857. May. Volunteer offers.

But, although Lord Canning believed that there was a "groundless panic," he had no design to reject contemptuously those offers of assistance. His desire was to display no outward symptom of alarm or mistrust. He was supreme ruler, not of a class or of a community, but of all classes and communities. He saw clearly that the great fear had possessed every quarter of the city and its suburbs, and was agitating

* *Ante*, vol. i. pp. 610, 611.

1857. May

the breasts of all the varied populations inhabiting them, and he knew that what might tranquillise and subdue in one direction might alarm and irritate in another. At no period of our history were the Natives of India in so great a paroxysm of fear. They shuddered to think that they might lose their caste—shuddered to think that they might lose their lives. All sorts of strange reports were afloat among the people, and the English were eager that Lord Canning should contradict them by public proclamation. "One of the last reports rife in the Bazaar," he wrote on the 20th of May, "is, that I have ordered beef to be thrown into the tanks, to pollute the caste of all Hindoos who bathe there, and that on the Queen's birthday all the grain-shops are to be closed, in order to drive the people to eat unclean food. Men, who ought to have heads on their shoulders, are gravely asking that each fable should be contradicted by proclamation as it arises, and are arming themselves with revolvers because this is not done. I have already taken the only step that I consider advisable, in the sense of a refutation of these and like rumours, and patience, firmness, and I hope a speedy return of the deluded to common sense, will do the rest." And clearly recognising all these conflicting fears and suspicions, he walked steadily but warily between them, assailed on all sides by cries for special help, but knowing well that the safety of all depended upon the strength and constancy of his resistance.

Celebration of the Queen's Birthday. May 25.

The Queen's birthday was celebrated in Calcutta after the wonted fashion. A grand ball was given at Government House.* It was the desire of Lord Canning, above all things, that nothing should be done to betray any want of confidence in the general

* The 24th of May fell on Sunday. The celebration was, therefore, on the 25th.

loyalty of the people. He had been besought to exchange his own personal guard of Natives for one composed of Europeans, but this he had refused to do. And the sweet face of Lady Canning was to be seen, evening after evening, calm and smiling, as she took her wonted drive on the Course or in the open suburbs of Calcutta. And now that it was represented that it might be expedient to omit the usual feu-de-joie fired in the Queen's honour, the suggestion was rejected; but in order that there might be no misapprehension as to the ammunition used on the occasion, a guard of Sepoys was sent to bring some of the old unsuspected cartridges out of the regimental stores at Barrackpore. The ball in the evening was well attended; but some absented themselves, believing that the congregation under one roof of all the leading members of the English community would suggest a fitting occasion for an attack on Government House.* There was not, indeed, a ruffle even upon the surface; although the day was likely to be one of more than usual excitement, for it was the great Mahomedan festival of the Eed, and it was thought in many places besides Calcutta that a Mussulman rising might be anticipated. After this there was some little return of confidence. But any accidental circumstance, such as the explosion of a few festal fireworks, was sufficient to throw many into a paroxysm of alarm.†

1857. May.

* "Two young ladies refused to go at the last moment, and sat up with a small bag prepared for flight, till their father returned from the ball and reassured them." . . . . . "Miss —— has hired two sailors to sit up in her house of a night; but they got tipsy, and frightened her more than imaginary enemies."—*Journal of a Lady, MS.*

† "A few nights ago woke up at two o'clock by what sounded like guns firing. Many thought the Alipore gaol had been broken open. Many gentlemen armed themselves, and got carriages ready for the ladies to fly to the Fort. On going into the verandah I was thankful to see a great display of fireworks going up, which was the cause of all the noise. It was the marriage of one of the Mysore princes."—*Ibid.*

1857. May. [T]he first [m]ovement on [D]elhi.

All this time, Lord Canning, aided by those immediately around him, was doing all that could be done for the successful attainment of the great ends to which he had addressed himself from the commencement—the recovery of Delhi and the protection of the Gangetic provinces. But it was not easy in the existing dearth of troops to accomplish both of these objects with the desired despatch; and it is not strange, therefore, that some difference of opinion prevailed among the advisers of Lord Canning as to the policy which, in these straitened circumstances, it was more expedient to adopt. It is believed that the Civil members of the Supreme Council, seeing how large a portion of our available military strength would be locked up under the walls of Delhi, and how, in the meanwhile, large breadths of country would be exposed to the fury of the enemy, advised that the attack on the great city of the Mogul should be delayed for a while, in order to employ the European troops in Upper India upon the general defence of the country. Sir John Low was of a different opinion; and he drew up a minute on the subject, full of sound arguments in favour of an immediate effort to recover the lost position. But the Governor-General had already come to that conclusion. Indeed, he had never doubted, for a day, that let what might happen elsewhere, it was his first duty to wrest the imperial city from the hands of the insurgents. He saw plainly that the fall of Delhi had imparted a political, a national significance to a movement, which otherwise might have been, regarded as little more than a local outbreak. It had, indeed, converted for a while a mutiny into a revolution; and the Governor-General felt, therefore, that to strike at Delhi, was to strike at the very heart of the danger—that to deliver a deadly blow at that point would be to cause an immediate collapse of the vital powers of rebellion from one end of the country to the other. 1857. May

So he at once issued his orders for the striking of that blow; and day after day the telegraph wires carried to the Commander-in-Chief briefly emphatic orders to make short work of Delhi. Though the Lower Provinces were all but bare of European troops there was some wealth of English regiments upon the slopes of the Northern Hills, where the Head-Quarters of the Army were then planted; and Lord Canning, with something of the impetuosity of the civilian, which is prone to overlook military difficulties, believed that those regiments might be gathered up at once and poured down with resistless force upon Delhi. Severed by nearly a thousand miles from the point of attack, he felt that he himself could do but little. But he had faith in the Commander-in-Chief—faith in the Lieutenant-Governor of the North-West Provinces—faith in the great Commissioner of the Punjab; and in the first letter which he wrote to England, after the outbreak at Meerut, he said: "As to expediting the crushing of the Delhi rebels, I work at some disadvantage at a distance of nine hundred miles; but the forces are converging upon the point as rapidly as the season will admit, and I am confident that with Colvin's aid and example, every man will be inspirited to do his utmost. I have made the Commander-in-Chief aware of the vast importance to the Lower Provinces that an end should be made of the work quickly. Time is everything. Delhi once crushed, and a terrible example made, we shall have no more difficulties." To what extent the realised facts fulfilled his sanguine anticipations, will presently be made apparent.

Meanwhile, the Governor-General was anxiously

1857. May. Movement of troops from below.

turning to good account the first-fruits of his initial measures for the collection of European troops, and trying to succour those defenceless posts at which the enemy were most likely to strike. The difficulties and perplexities which beset him were great. He had only two European regiments in the neighbourhood of the capital—the Fifty-third Foot, whose Head-Quarters were in Fort William, and the Eighty-fourth, who had been brought round from Rangoon in March, and who had since been stationed at Chinsurah, on the banks of the Hooghly, above Barrackpore. He would fain have sent upwards a part of the little strength thus gathered at the Presidency; but those two regiments were all that belonged to him for the defence of Lower Bengal. There was not another English regiment nearer than Dinapore, four hundred miles distant from Calcutta. And there, in the immediate neighbourhood of the capital, were many points which it was of extreme importance to defend. There was Fort William, with its great Arsenal; there was the Gun-manufactory at Cossipore, a few miles higher up the river; there was the Powder-manufactory at Ishapore, some twelve miles beyond, and there was the Artillery School of Instruction at Dum-Dum, with all its varied appliances for the manufacture of ordnance stores. A little way beyond Chowringhee, the fashionable suburb of the City of Palaces, lay the great gaol of Alipore, crowded with malefactors, many of the worst class; and hard by were the Government clothing godowns, or stores, from which the uniforms and accoutrements of the army were drawn. Then in different parts of the city were the Calcuttà Mint and the Treasury and the Banks, all groaning with coin—so that there was nothing wanting that could have supplied an insurgent army with all the munitions and equipments of war, and enabled them to take the field against us with the unfailing cement of high pay to keep them together. 1857. May.

Conduct of Government considered.

Wise after the event, public writers have said that if Lord Canning, in the third week of the month of May, had accepted the first offer of the European inhabitants to enrol themselves into a volunteer corps—that if he had disbanded the Sepoy Regiments at Barrackpore, and ordered the disbandment of those at Dinapore—events which were subsequently rendered necessary—a large portion of the European force in Bengal might have been set free and pushed up by rail and road to the points which were most beset with danger, and that great disasters which subsequently befel us might thus have been averted.* There are, doubtless, many things which, in that month of May, would have been done differently, and might have been done better, if the future had been clearly revealed to those who had the conduct of affairs. But we must judge men according

* The two ablest of the early writers, the author of the "Red Pamphlet," and Mr. Meade in his "Sepoy Revolt," dwell very emphatically on this point. The former says: "An enrolment on a large scale at this time would have enabled the Governor-General to dispense with the services of one European regiment at least; but so bent was he on ignoring the danger, that he not only declined the offers of the Trades' Association, the Masonic Fraternity, the Native converts, the Americans, and the French inhabitants and others, but he declined them in terms calculated to deaden rather than to excite a feeling of loyalty." Mr. Meade says: "A thousand English volunteer infantry, four hundred cavalry, and fifteen hundred sailors were at the disposal of the Government a week after the revolt became known. . . . Whilst the volunteers were learning how to load and fire, and the merchant seamen were being instructed in the use of artillery, Government might have placed from the terminus (at Raneegunge) to Cawnpore a line of stations for horses and bullocks, guarded, if necessary, by posts of armed men. . . . . Had Government only consented to do just a fortnight beforehand what they were coerced to do on the 14th of June, they might have had on the first day of that month a force of two thousand Europeans at Raneegunge, fully equipped with guns and stores."

1857. May. to the light of the day which shone upon them, not the light of the morrow, which had not yet broken when they were called upon to act. Illumined by this morrow's light, we now know that it might have been better if the Barrackpore and Dinapore regiments had been disarmed in the middle of May; but the former were then protesting their loyalty, and offering to fight against the rebels, and the latter were still believed in by General Lloyd, who commanded the Division.* The temper of the troops, in all parts of the country, seemed at that time to depend upon the fate of Delhi, and more experienced Indian statesmen than Lord Canning believed that Delhi would soon be crushed. And, whilst it was deemed expedient to keep the Bengal Native Army together so long as any hope survived, it was, at that time, in Bengal, held to be impossible to disarm all the Native regiments. Disarming, said Lord Canning, is "a very effective measure, where practicable, but in Bengal, where we have, spread over from Barrackpore to Cawnpore, fifteen Native regiments to one European, simply impossible. A very different game has to be played here."†

Moreover, in the neighbourhood both of Calcutta and of Dinapore, there were other dangers than those arising from the armed Sepoy regiments. In the latter there was the excited Mahomedan population of Patna, of which I shall speak hereafter; and in the former there were the many local perils, of which I

* As late as the 2nd of June, General Lloyd wrote to Lord Canning, saying: "Although no one can now feel full confidence in the loyalty of Native troops generally, yet I believe that the regiments here will remain quiet, unless some great temptation or excitement should assail them, in which case I fear they could not be relied upon. The thing required to keep them steady is a blow quickly struck at Delhi."—*MS. Correspondence.*

† Lord Canning to Mr, Vernon Smith, June 5, 1857.—*MS. Correspondence.*

have already spoken. And it was at least doubtful whether an undisciplined body of sailors and civilians, even with a few staff-officers to keep them together, would have supplied the place of a regular regiment of Europeans. Lord Canning, knowing well the constitution of the European community of Calcutta, did not think, from the very nature of their interests and their occupations, that they could form a defensive body on which any reliance could be placed. Where the treasure of men is there will their hearts be also; and, in many instances, if possible, their hands. It was hardly to be expected that, if there had been any sudden alarm—if the signal had been sounded, and every man's services needed in a critical emergency, many would not have thought rather of their wives and children than of the public safety, and some, perhaps, more of their own material property than of that of the State.* Doubtless there were brave and patriotic spirits among them who would have gone gladly to the front; but Lord Canning, perhaps, did not err in thinking that the majority of members of the non-military community were too much encumbered by their worldly affairs to make efficient soldiers, either for the performance of ordinary duties or the confronting of imminent peril. That they could have formed a substitute for regular soldiers was improbable, though they would have been a serviceable supplement to them.

1857. May.

If, then, the volunteers had been enrolled when the first offer of service was made to Lord Canning,

* It is very vividly in my recollection that, on the famous 10th of April, 1848, when there was a vague expectation that London would be sacked by the Chartists, and immense numbers of special constables had been sworn in, I asked one of the most experienced men in the district in which I lived how many of those sworn in would turn out on the given signal (it was to be the ringing of the church bell), and I was told "not ten per cent."

1857. May. he could not have done more than he did to send succours up the country. Nor did it, at the time, seem to him that the danger was so imminent on the Gangetic provinces as to demand that Bengal should be stripped, even for a few weeks, of her only reliable defences. It was just during that particular interval between the receipt of intelligence of the Meerut outbreak and the arrival of the first reinforcements from beyond the seas, that the accounts from the upper country were least alarming. There was, apparently, a suspension of rebellious activity. The telegraphic messages received from the principal stations were all of an assuring character. On the 19th and 20th the report from Benares was, "All perfectly quiet," "troops steady." On the 19th Sir Henry Lawrence telegraphed from Lucknow, "All very well in city, cantonments, and country." Sir Hugh Wheeler, at Cawnpore, on the same day, sent a kindred message, "All quiet here, the excitement somewhat less." From Allahabad, on the same day, the tidings were, "Troops quiet and well behaved;" and the Lieutenant-Governor of the North-West Provinces at Agra assured the Governor-General that "Things were looking cheerful." "There may," it was added, "be some delay in the actual advance on Delhi. It is generally felt, however, that it must soon fall, and the flame has not spread." The following days brought intelligence of the same satisfactory complexion, the only evil tidings being those which spoke of mutiny at Aligurh, and that was quickly followed by the announcement from Agra that a strong expedition had been organised for the recapture of the place.

There was little, therefore, that Lord Canning could do in the earlier weeks of May to succour the

North-Western Provinces, and judged by the light of the day no pressing necessity to incur, for that purpose, great risks in the neighbourhood of the capital. What little he could do with safety he did. He ordered up a detachment of the Eighty-fourth to Benares, and he suggested to General Lloyd, at Dinapore, that he might, perhaps, send a company or two of the Tenth to the same point. These first movements might save a few lives, and might give a general impression of action on our part, the importance of which was great at such a time. But it was to the reinforcements coming from beyond the seas that he eagerly looked for substantive aid. He had written on the 19th to the Indian Minister in England, saying: "Towards this object the steps taken are as follows—The Madras Fusiliers are on their way, and will be here on the 21st or 22nd. A regiment has been sent for from Rangoon, and will arrive in the course of next week. Two regiments at least with some Artillery (perhaps three regiments), will come round from Bombay as soon as they arrive from Persia. They are all on their way. Another regiment from Kurrachee is ordered up the Indus to Ferozepore, as a stand-by, if John Lawrence should want help. An officer goes to-day to Ceylon to procure from Sir Henry Ward every soldier he can spare. I have asked for at least five hundred Europeans, but will accept Malays in place of or besides them. The same officer carries letters to Elgin and Ashburnham, begging that the regiments destined for China may be turned first to India. . . . . This is all that I can do at present to collect European strength, except the withdrawal of one more regiment from Pegu, which, when a steamer is available, will take place." And now,

1857. May.

1857. May.

before the end of the month, he learnt that the Madras Fusiliers were in the river. Such was his confidence, that when succours began to arrive, he felt, however small they might be in proportion to his needs, that the tide was beginning to turn in his favour. After a fortnight of enforced inaction, there was something invigorating in the thought that he was now beginning to hold palpably in his hands the means of rendering substantial aid to his defenceless countrymen. And he knew, moreover, that the moral effect of the arrival of a single European regiment would be greater than the material assistance, for it would soon be noised abroad that the English were coming from beyond the seas to avenge their slaughtered brethren, and Rumour would be sure to magnify the extent of the arrival.*

Colonel Neill and the Madras Fusiliers.

Still, in itself the gain was very great; for the vessels which were working up the Hooghly were bringing not only a well-seasoned, well-disciplined regiment, in fine fighting order, but a chief who had within him all the elements of a great soldier. The First Madras European Regiment was commanded by Colonel James George Neill. It was one of those few English regiments which, enlisted for the service of the East India Company, and maintained exclusively on the Indian establishment, bore on their banners the memorials of a series of victories from

* I am aware that a contrary statement has been made. It has been asserted that the Government took pains rather to conceal than to make known the arrival of reinforcements at Calcutta. Especially by disguising the names of the vessels in which the troops were coming up the river. If the *Alethea*, for example, were coming up, she was telegraphed, it was said, as the *Sarah Sands*. Assuming the fact to be as stated, we may readily understand the object of the concealment. It might have been sound policy not to make known the coming of the troops until they were landed and fit for service. If there had been any combination for a rising, the moment seized would probably have been when it was known that our reinforcements were at the Sandheads. But I am assured, on the highest authority, that the story is not true.

the earliest days of our conquests in India. It had just returned from the Persian Gulf, when Neill, fresh from Crimean service,* found to his delight that he was to be appointed to command the regiment with which he had served during the greater part of his adult life. He had gone down to see the regiment disembark, and he had written in his journal that they were "a very fine healthy body of men, fully equal to any regiment he had ever seen." This was on the 20th of April, and he little then knew how soon he would be called upon to test their efficiency in the field. Three or four weeks afterwards, news came that Upper India was in a blaze, and the tidings were quickly followed by a summons for the regiment to take ship for Bengal. Then Neill rejoiced exceedingly to think of the lessons he had learnt in the Crimea, and the experience he had gained there; and he felt, to use his own words, "fully equal to any extent of professional employment or responsibility which could ever devolve upon him."

1857. May.

Born in the month of May, 1810, at a short distance from the chief town of Ayrshire, in Scotland, James Neill had entered the Indian service in his seventeenth year, and was, therefore, when summoned to take active part in the Sepoy War, a man of forty-seven years of age, and a soldier of thirty years' standing. Of a strong physical constitution, of active athletic habits, he shrunk from no work, and he was overcome by no fatigue. There were few men in the whole range of the Indian Army better qualified by nature and by training to engage in the stirring events of such a campaign as was

* He had been Second-in-Command, under Sir Robert Vivian, of the Anglo-Turkish Contingent.

1857. May. opening out before him. He was a God-fearing Scotchman, with something in him of the old Covenanter type. He was gentle and tender as a woman in his domestic relations, chivalrous and self-denying in all the actions of his life, and so careful, as a commander, of all under his charge, that he would have yielded his tent, or given up his meals to any one more needing them than himself. But towards the enemies of our nation and the persecutors of our race he was as hard and as fiery as flint; and he was not one to be tolerant of the shortcomings of our own people, wanting in courage or capacity, or in any way failing in their manliness. He knew, when he embarked for Bengal, that there was stern work before him; and he brooded over the future so intently, that the earnestness and resolution within him spoke out ever from his countenance, and it was plain to those around him that, once in front of the enemy, he would smite them with an unsparing hand, and never cease from his work until he should witness its full completion, or be arrested by the stroke of death.

May 23. On the 23rd of May Colonel Neill was off Calcutta with the leading wing of his regiment, and soon the whole corps had disembarked. But it was easier to bring troops into port along the great highway of the ocean, than to despatch them with the required rapidity into the interior of the country. Every possible provision, however, had been made and was still being made to push forward the reinforcements by river and by road. Every available horse and bullock along the line had been purchased by Government; every carriage and cart secured for the conveyance of the troops up the country.* The river

* "A steady stream of reinforcements is now being poured into Benares. Every horse and bullock that can be bought on the road is engaged,

steamers were carrying their precious freights of humanity, but too slowly for our needs, in that dry season, and the railway was to be brought into requisition to transport others to the scene of action. It was by the latter route that the bulk of Neill's regiment, in all nine hundred strong, were to be despatched towards Benares.* It might have been supposed that, at such a time, every Christian man in Calcutta would have put forth all his strength to perfect and to expedite the appointed work, eager to contribute by all means within his power to the rescue of imperilled Christendom. Especially was it to be looked for that all holding such authority as might enable them to accelerate the despatch of troops to our threatened, perhaps beleaguered posts, would strain every nerve to accomplish effectually this good work. But on the platform of the Calcutta terminus, on the river side, opposite to Howrah, all such natural zeal as this seemed to be basely wanting. There was no alacrity in helping the troops to start on their holy duty; and soon apathy and inaction grew into open opposition. When the second party of a hundred men was to be despatched, stress of weather delayed their arrival, from the flats in the river, at the platform or landing-stage, near which the train was waiting for them, under the orders of the Supreme

1857. May.

and the dawk establishments have been increased to the utmost. The men who go by horse-dawk reach Benares in five days; those by bullock in ten. The former conveyance can take only from eighteen to twenty-four a day; the latter a hundred. Some are gone up by steamers. These will be sixteen days on the journey."—*Lord Canning to Sir H. Wheeler, May* 26. *MS.*

* "I landed and saw the Military Secretary and the Deputy-Quartermaster-General, and made all arrangements to start off the men I had brought up by steamers to Benares. However, next day there was a change. Only a hundred and thirty men went up the country by steamer, and the rest I am starting off by the train."—*Private Letter of Col. Neill.* The rail then only went as far as Raneegunge.

1857. May. Government. But as the Fusiliers came alongside and were landing, in the darkness of the early night, without an effort of help from the railway people, the station-master cried out that they were late, and that the train would not wait for them a moment. Against this Neill remonstrated, but the official, growing more peremptory in his tone and insolent in his manner, threatened at once to start the train. Other functionaries then came forward, and addressed him in the same threatening strain. One said that the Colonel might command his regiment, but that he did not command the railway, and that the train should be despatched without him. On this, Neill telling them that they were traitors and rebels, and that it was fortunate for them that he had not to deal with them, placed a guard over the engineer and stoker, and told them to stir at their peril. A few weeks later, in parts of the country more distant from the central authority, such traitors as these would, perhaps, have been hanged.

The train started, some ten minutes after its appointed time, with its precious burden of Fusiliers; and the tidings of what Neill had done soon reached Lord Canning. It was not in the brave heart of the Governor-General to refuse its meed of admiration to such an act. Even official Calcutta, though a little startled in its proprieties, commended, after a time, the Madras Colonel, whilst at all the stations above, when the story was known, people said that the right man was on his way to help them, and looked eagerly for the coming succours.

Legislative enactments. And never, in a season of trouble, was there a more timely arrival; for the lull of which I have spoken now seemed to be at an end. As the month of May burnt itself out, the tidings which came from the country above were more distressing and more alarming. It was plain that the North-West Provinces, from one end to the other, were fast blazing into rebellion—plain that we were destined to see worse things than any we had yet witnessed—and that the whole strength of the British nation must be put forth to grapple with the gigantic danger. If there had been any hope before, that the rebellion would die out, or be paralysed by the infliction of swift retribution on Delhi, it had now ceased to animate the breasts of Lord Canning and his colleagues. They now saw that it was necessary to the salvation of the English power in India, not only that our people should be everywhere let loose upon the enemy, but that they should be armed with exceptional powers suited to, and justified by the crisis. A reign of lawlessness had commenced; but for a while the avenging hand of the English Government had been restrained by the trammels of the written law. It was time now to cease from the unequal conflict. The English were few; their enemies were many. The many had appealed to the law of brute force; and the few were justified in accepting the challenge. The time for the observance of municipal formalities—of niceties of criminal procedure—of precise balancings of evidence and detailed fulness of record—had clearly now passed away. A terrible necessity had forced itself upon the rulers of the land. In the great death-struggle which had come upon us, the written law had been violated upon the one side, and it was now to be suspended upon the other. The savage had arisen against us, and it had become our work to fight the savage with his own

1857. May.

1857. May. weapons. So the law-makers stood up and shook themselves loose from the trammels of the law. On the 30th of May, the Legislative Council passed an Act which swept away the old time-honoured seats of justice, wheresoever Rebellion was disporting itself, and placed the power of life and death in the hands of the executive officer, whatsoever his rank, his age, or his wisdom. The Act, after declaring that all persons owing allegiance to the British Government, who should rebel or wage war, or attempt to do so, against the Queen or Government of the East Indies, or instigate or abet such persons, should be liable to the punishment of death, transportation, or imprisonment, gave the Executive Government of any Presidency or Place power to proclaim any district as in a state of rebellion, and to issue a Commission forthwith for the trial of all persons charged with offences against the State, or murder, arson, robbery, or other heinous crime against person or property—the Commissioner or Commissioners so appointed were empowered to hold a Court in any part of the said district, and without the attendance or *futwah* of a law officer, or the assistance of assessors, to pass upon every person convicted before the Court of any of the above-mentioned crimes the punishment of death, or transportation, or imprisonment; "and the judgment of such Court," it was added, "shall be final and conclusive, and the said Court shall not be subordinate to the Sudder Court."* This gave immense power to individual Englishmen. But it armed only the civil authorities; so an order was passed by the Governor-General in Council authorising the senior

* The Act, which received the assent of the Governor-General, and thus passed into law on the 8th of June, is given entire in the Appendix.

military officer, of whatsoever rank, at any military station in the Bengal Presidency, to appoint General Courts-Martial, either European or Native, or mixed, of not less than five members, and "to confirm and carry into effect, immediately or otherwise, any sentence of such Court-Martial." 1857. May 11.

With the new month came in further reinforcements from beyond the seas, and something like confidence was re-established in the Christian communities of Calcutta; for although rebellion was spreading itself all over Upper India, the continual stream of English troops that was beginning to pour into the capital seemed to give security to its inmates. The regiments released from service in the Persian Gulf, were now making their appearance on the banks of the Hooghly. The Sixty-fourth arrived on the 3rd of June, and soon afterwards the Thirty-fifth came in from Moulmein. And then the kilted Highlanders of the Seventy-eighth, also from Persia, were seen ascending the ghauts of Calcutta, with their red beards and their bare knees—an unaccustomed sight to the natives of Bengal, in whose eyes they appeared to be half women and half beasts. Others followed, and every effort was made to expedite their despatch to the upper country. At Raneegunge, to which point the railway ran from the neighbourhood of Calcutta, an experienced officer was making arrangements to send on detachments by horse-dawk and bullock-dawk to Benares; but the resources of the State were miserably inadequate to the necessities of the crisis, and prompt movement by land, therefore, on a large scale was wholly impossible. The journey to Benares could be accomplished in five days; but

June. More reinforcements.

1857. June. it was officially reported to Lord Canning that only from eighteen to twenty-four men a day could thus be forwarded by horsed carriages. By the 4th of June, it was computed that, by these means of conveyance, ninety men with their officers would have reached Benares; by the 8th, eighty-eight more; and by the 12th, another batch of eighty-eight. The bullock-carriages, which afforded slower means of progression, but which could carry larger numbers, might, it was calculated, convey the troops onward at the rate of a hundred men a day.* So, on the 10th of June, Lord Canning was able to write to Mr. Colvin, saying: "The Europeans are still sent up steadily at the rate of a hundred and twenty men a day, and henceforward they will not be stopped either at Benares or Allahabad, but be passed on to Cawnpore. My object is to place at Sir Hugh Wheeler's disposal a force with which he can leave his intrenchments at Cawnpore, and show himself at Lucknow or elsewhere. He will best know where when the time arrives. To this end, I call upon you to give your aid by furthering by every means in your power the despatch southwards of a portion of the European force which has marched upon Delhi." It had not yet dawned upon the Government that Delhi was not to be "made short work of" by the force that had come down from the North to attack it. And there were many others of large experience all over the country who believed that there was no power of resistance in the place to withstand the first assaults even of such an English army as Anson was gathering up and equipping for service. What that force was, and what its efforts, I have now to relate.

* Mr. Cecil Beadon to Lord Canning, May 26.—*MS. Correspondence.*

CHAPTER V.

GENERAL ANSON AT UMBALLAH—FIRST MOVEMENT OF TROOPS—THE MILITARY DEPARTMENTS—DIFFICULTY OF MOVEMENT—THE PANIC ON THE HILLS—THE SIEGE-TRAIN—REMONSTRANCES AGAINST DELAY—VIEWS OF LORD CANNING AND SIR JOHN LAWRENCE—GOOD WORK OF THE CIVILIANS—CONDUCT OF THE SIKH CHIEFS—THE MARCH TO KURNAUL—DEATH OF GENERAL ANSON—SUCCESSION OF SIR HENRY BARNARD.

May 12. At Head-Quarters.

DISQUIETED by reports of the uneasy nervous state of the regiments at Head-Quarters, but little apprehending the approach of any gigantic danger, General Anson was recreating himself on the heights of Simlah, when, on the 12th of May, young Barnard rode in from Umballah bearing a letter from his father. It informed the Commander-in-Chief that a strange incoherent telegraphic message had been received at the latter place from Delhi. But it was plain that the Meerut Sepoys had revolted. An hour afterwards, another message was brought to Anson, confirming the first tidings of revolt. Confused though it was, it indicated still more clearly than its predecessor, that the Native Cavalry prisoners at Meerut had escaped from gaol, that the Sepoys thence had joined the Delhi mutineers, and that there had been at both places a massacre of Europeans.*

* The first telegram, as given in a letter from Anson to Lord Canning, ran thus: "We must leave office. All the bungalows are on fire—burning down by the Sepoys of Meerut. They came in this morning. We are

1857. May 12. When this intelligence reached the Commander-in-Chief, he did not at once take in its full significance; nor, indeed, did men of far greater Indian experience—the Head-Quarters Staff, by whom he was surrounded—perceive the dire purport of it. But he discerned at once that something must be done. He saw that the city of Delhi and the lives of all the Europeans were at the mercy of the insurgents; and that it was incumbent upon him to send down all the white troops that could be despatched from the Hills, to succour our imperilled people, if the flames of rebellion should spread. So he sent an Aide-de-camp to Kussowlee, on that day, with orders for the Seventy-fifth Foot to march to Umballah;* and, at the same time, the Company's European regiments at Dugshai and Sobathoo were directed to hold themselves in readiness to march at a moment's notice. But he did not put himself in motion. He wrote to Lord Canning, saying that he anxiously awaited further reports, and that if they were not favourable he should "at once proceed down to Umballah." He had scarcely despatched this letter, when a third telegraphic message was received, from which he learnt more distinctly what had happened at Meerut on the preceding Sunday. Next morning, he wrote again to Lord Canning, still saying that his

off. Mr. C. Todd is dead, I think. He went out this morning, and has not yet returned. We learnt that nine Europeans are killed." This was received at three P.M. The second message, received at four, said: "Cantonments in a state of siege. Mutineers from Meerut—Third Light Cavalry—numbers not known—said to be a hundred and fifty men. Cut off communication with Meerut. Taken possession of the Bridge of Boats. Fifty-fourth Native Infantry sent against them, but would not act. Several officers killed and wounded. City in a state of considerable excitement. Troops sent down, but nothing known yet. Information will be forwarded."

* Captain Barnard had, on his way to Simlah, warned the Seventy-fifth to be ready to march on the arrival of orders from Head-Quarters.

own movements would depend upon the information 1857. May 13.
he received. But he was beginning to discern more clearly the magnitude of the danger, and he ordered the two Fusilier regiments to move down to Umballah,* and the Sirmoor battalion† to proceed from Dhera to Meerut. From the first he appears to have perceived clearly that the most pressing danger which threatened us was the loss of our Magazines. He felt that the great Magazine at Delhi, with its rich supplies of arms and ordnance stores, and implements of all kinds, must already be in possession of the mutineers, and he lost no time in taking measures to secure our other great military store-houses, by sending European troops for their defence. "I have sent express," he wrote to Lord Canning on the 13th, "to desire that the Fort at Ferozepore may be secured by the Sixty-first Foot, and the Fort at Govindghur by the Eighty-first. Two companies of the Eighth from Jullundhur to Phillour." The importance of securing the latter place could scarcely, indeed, be over-estimated.‡ How it was accomplished by the authorities of the Punjab will hereafter be told. In this place it need only be recorded that thence was it that the siege-train was to be drawn which was to open the way for our re-entrance into Delhi, or to perform any other

* Major G. O. Jacob, of the First European Regiment, who happened to be at Simlah, rode down to Dugshai during the night, and warned the regiment early in the morning.

† A corps of brave and faithful Goorkahs, whose good services will be hereafter detailed.

‡ Mr. Cave-Browne says: "A report did float about the Punjab, the truth of which we have never heard denied, that one member of the Staff suggested that all European troops should concentrate on Phillour, and, taking boat down the Sutlej, make for England as fast as possible; another, however—one who, alas! fell among the earliest victims of the rebellion—suggested that the Phillour Fort, with its large magazine, might be made available for a very different purpose. Hence the idea of a siege-train." This last was Colonel Chester, Adjutant-General of the Army.

1857. May. service that circumstances might demand from it in the operations to be now undertaken. An Artillery officer was despatched thither with all speed to make the necessary arrangements;* and the Goorkah Regiment, known as the Nusseree Battalion, and then believed to be loyal to the core, was ordered down from Jutogh, near Simlah, to form, with a detachment of the Ninth Irregular Cavalry, an escort for the train from Phillour to Umballah. This was not more than any soldier of a few years' experience would have done; but as it was an important, though an obvious movement, and tended much to our subsequent success, it should be held in remembrance by all who say that in this conjuncture Anson did less.†

May 14. First movements of General Anson. Before the day was spent, the Commander-in-Chief had made up his mind that he must quit Simlah. "I am just off for Umballah," he wrote to Lord Canning, at eight o'clock on the morning of the 14th. . . . "This is a most disastrous business," he added, "and it is not possible to see what will be the result. They say the King of Delhi is at the bottom of it. I doubt it; but I have no doubt that he has taken advantage of the opportunity, and is assisting the insurgents. . . . If the mutineers, having possession of the city, make their stand behind the walls, we shall want a good force and artillery. This must be collected at Kurnaul, as it would not be wise, I think, to divide the force we shall have and send part from Meerut on the opposite side of the river. But I hope to hear something which will enable me to

* Captain Worthington, who was on sick-leave at Simlah at the time.

† The author of the "History of the Siege of Delhi," says: "On the 16th Sir John Lawrence telegraphed to Jullundhur to secure the Fort of Phillour. Two marches to the south, and commanding the bridge over the Sutlej, it contained the only magazine that could now furnish us with a siege-train," &c. &c. But it is clear that General Anson had sent instructions to this effect three days before.

decide what is best to be done when I get to Umballah." 1857. May 15.

He reached that place on the morning of the 15th, and many sinister reports met him there. It was plain that the Native regiments in the Punjab were in a state of open or suppressed mutiny, and, therefore, that he could not expect immediate assistance from that province. "We are terribly short of artillery ammunition," he wrote. "The two companies of Reserve Artillery I asked for from Lahore and Loodhianah cannot, of course, now be given, and we have no means of using the siege-train. All the European troops within reach will be here on the 17th. If we move upon Delhi, I think it must be from Kurnaul. It is extraordinary how little we know of what is going on in other parts of the country—nothing whatever from Agra, Cawnpore, Oudh, &c." On the following day, he wrote again to Lord Canning, saying: "I have been doing my best to organise the Force here, ready for a move; but tents and carriages are not ready, and they are indispensable. We are also deficient in ammunition, which we are expecting from Phillour. I hope we shall be in a state to move shortly, if required. But we have no heavy guns for Delhi, if we are to attack the mutineers there. We must not fritter away or sacrifice the Europeans we have, unless for some great necessity."

Many troubles and perplexities then beset him. It has been already shown that the Native regiments at Umballah were in a state of smouldering mutiny, kept only from bursting into a blaze by the contiguity of European troops.* The incendiary work, The Umballah Regiments.

* *Ante*, book iii. chapter v.

1857. May 11. which, in the preceding month, had so mystified the Commander-in-Chief and the General of Division, had by this time explained itself. It was clear that the Sepoys were ripe for revolt. With the strong European force now gathered at Umballah, Anson might have reduced them to impotence in an hour. To the vigorous understanding of Sir John Lawrence nothing was clearer than that the true policy, in that conjuncture, was to disarm the Native regiments at Umballah before advancing upon Delhi; and he impressed this necessity upon Anson by telegraph and by post from Rawul-Pindee, but the Commander-in-Chief refused to sanction the measure.* It seemed to be an easy escape out of some difficulties which beset his position at Umballah. He had the wolf by the ears. He could not with safety carry the regiments with him, and he could not leave them behind. But he was met with remonstrances from officers on the spot, who protested that some pledges had been given to the Sepoys which could not honourably be broken, though in truth the Sepoys themselves had practically violated the compact, and there would have been no breach of faith in turning their treachery against themselves. It was, however, resolved to appeal only to their good feelings, and so they were left with arms in their hands to use them on a future day foully against us in return for our forbearance.†

* See Punjab Report of May 25, 1858: "The Chief Commissioner conceived that the first step was to disarm these regiments whom it was equally dangerous either to leave at Umballah or to take to Delhi. This course the Chief Commissioner lost no time in urging, but when the Commander-in-Chief took the matter in hand, the local military authorities pointed out that they had pledged themselves not to disarm the Sepoys. It was in vain urged per contra that the compact had been no sooner made than it was broken by the Sepoys themselves. There was not, indeed, the shadow of a reasonable hope that these men would prove faithful."

† It should not be omitted altogether from the narrative that on the 19th the Commander-in-Chief issued another address to the Native Army, in the shape of a General

1857. May.

Mutiny of the Nusseree Battalion.

Another source of anxiety was this. Before the week had passed, news came to Umballah that the Goorkahs of the Nusseree Battalion, from no sympathy with the regular army, but from some personal causes of disaffection, had broken into revolt just when their services were wanted, had refused to march to Phillour, had plundered the Commander-in-Chief's baggage, and threatened to attack Simlah. Then there came a great cry of terror from the pleasant places which Anson had just quitted, and in which, only a few days before, the voice of joy and gladness had been resonant in a hundred happy homes. It was the season when our English ladies, some with their husbands, some without them, were escaping from the hot winds of the Northern Provinces and disporting themselves, in all the flush of renovated health and strength and new-born elasticity, under the cheering influence of the mountain breezes on the slopes of the Himalayahs. It might well have been regarded, in the first instance, as a happy circumstance that so many of our countrywomen were away from the military cantonments, in which mutiny and murder had so hideously displayed themselves; but when it was known that these joyous playgrounds were being stripped of their defences, and that if danger were to threaten the homes of our

The panic on the Hills.

Order, in which, after adverting to the general uneasiness of the Sepoys and to his former efforts to allay it, he said: "His Excellency has determined that the new rifle-cartridge, and every new cartridge, shall be discontinued, and that in future balled ammunition shall be made up by each regiment for its own use by a proper establishment entertained for this purpose. The Commander-in-Chief solemnly assures the Army that no interference with their castes or religions was ever contemplated, and as solemnly he pledges his word and honour that none shall ever be exercised. He announces this to the Native Army in the full confidence that all will now perform their duty free from anxiety and care, and be prepared to stand and shed the last drop of their blood, as they have formerly done, by the side of the British troops, and in defence of the country." Such words in season might be good, but the season had long since passed.

1857. May. people there would be nothing but God's mercy to protect them, a feeling of insecurity and alarm arose, which needed but little to aggravate it into a great panic. When, therefore, tidings came that the Nusseree Battalion, at a distance of some three or four miles from Simlah, had risen in rebellion, there was general consternation. It was rumoured that the officers and their families at Jutogh had been murdered, and that the Goorkahs were marching on Simlah intent on slaughter and spoliation. Then, for the greater part of two long days, many tasted the bitterness of death. The agony of terror swept our English families out of their holiday-homes, as with the besom of coming destruction; and in wild confusion men, women, and children streamed down towards the plains, or huddled together at the point esteemed to be best capable of defence.* Never, at any time or in any place, have the consummate gallantry of Englishmen and the heroic endurance of Englishwomen been more nobly—more beautifully—manifested than in the great conflict for supremacy of which I am writing. But the incidents of those two days on the Hills are not to be regarded with national pride. The strong instinct of self-preservation was dominant over all. Men forgot their manhood in what seemed to be a struggle for life;† and it is not strange, therefore, that delicate ladies with little children clinging to them, should have abandoned themselves uncontrolledly to their fears.

* This was the Bank. See Cave-Brown's "Punjab and Delhi in 1857," which contains an animated account of the two days' panic on the Hills. The writer says that at the Bank were congregated some four hundred of our Christian people, "of whom above a hundred were able-bodied men."

† Mr. Cave-Browne describes "ladies toiling along on foot, vainly trying to persuade, entreat, threaten the bearers to hurry on with their *jampans*, on which were their helpless children, while men were outbidding each other, and *outbidding ladies*, to secure bearers for their baggage."

But the panic was a groundless panic. The Nusseree Battalion, though grossly insubordinate, was not intent on the murder of our people. The Goorkahs had grievances, real or supposed, to be redressed, and when certain concessions had been made to them, they returned to their allegiance, and afterwards became good soldiers.* And not without some feeling of shame our people went back to their deserted homes and found everything just as it had been left. Those, whose excited imaginations had seen blazing houses and household wrecks, re-entered their dwelling-places to see with their fleshly eyes the unfinished letter on the desk and the embroidery on the work-table undisturbed by marauding hands. Even the trinkets of the ladies were as if they had never been out of the safest custody. But confidence, which is ever "a plant of slow growth," is slowest when once trampled or cut down; and it was long before our English families at the hill-stations recovered the serenity they had lost. Every officer fit for service was called to join his regiment, and the European soldiery were too much needed in the field to allow any force to be left for the protection of the tender congregation of women and children on the slopes of the great hills.† 1857 May

Preparation of the Siege Train.

The Commander-in-Chief had, indeed, other things to consider than these social alarms. The defection of the Nusseree Battalion was a source of perplexity

* It is said that one of their principal causes of complaint was the fact that they had been ordered to march down to the plains, and that no arrangements had been made for the protection of their families in their absence. They were also in arrears of pay.

† Mr. Cave-Browne relates that as the Commander-in-Chief was riding out of Simlah, Mr. Mayne, the Chaplain, informed him that the station was in great danger from the number of "budmashes" in the Bazaars, and asked that some Europeans might be sent up for its protection. The General said that he could not spare any. "What, then, are the ladies to do?" asked the Chaplain. "The best they can," was the answer.

1857. May. upon other grounds, as it was hard to say how the siege-train could be escorted safely to Umballah. It was of the highest importance, at this time, that the European troops should be exposed as little as possible to the blazing heats of the summer sun. It was the sultriest season of the year, and cholera was already threatening our camp. The regiment of hardy Goorkahs, of whose loyalty there had been no previous doubt, were just the men for the work; and now their services were lost to us for awhile. There was nothing, therefore, left but a resort to Hindostanee troops of doubtful fidelity, or to a contingent force supplied by a friendly Native chief. Meanwhile there was great activity in the Magazine of Phillour. Day and night our troops, under Lieutenant Griffith, Commissary of Ordnance, toiled on incessantly to prepare the siege-train and to supply ammunition of all kinds for the advancing army. A day, even an hour, lost, might have been fatal; for the Sutlej was rising, and the bridge of boats, by which the train was to cross the river, might have been swept away before our preparations were complete.

The Departments. But there were worse perplexities even than these. The elaborate organisation of the army which Anson commanded was found to be a burden and an encumbrance. The Chiefs of all the Staff-departments of the Army were at his elbow. They were necessarily men of large experience, selected for their approved ability and extensive knowledge; and it was right that he should consult them. But Departments are ever slow to move—ever encumbered with a sense of responsibility, which presses upon them with the destructive force of paralysis. These Indian Military Departments were the best possible Departments in time of peace. They had immense masses of correspondence written up and endorsed with the most praiseworthy punctuality and precision. They were always prepared with a precedent; always ready to check an irregularity, and to chastise an over-zealous public servant not moving in the strictest grooves of Routine. It was, indeed, their especial function to suppress what they regarded as the superfluous activities of individual men; and individual men never did great things until they got fairly out of the reach of the Departments. They were nominally War Departments. There would have been no need of such Departments if war had been abolished from off the face of the land. But it was the speciality of these War Departments that they were never prepared for war. Surrounded as we were, within and without, with hostile populations, and living in a chronic state of danger from a multiplicity of causes, we yet were fully prepared for almost anything in the world but fighting. Without long delay we could place ourselves in neither a defensive nor an offensive attitude. We could "stand fast" as well as any nation in the world, but there was never any facility of moving. As soon as ever there came a necessity for action, it was found that action was impossible. The Adjutant-General, the Quartermaster-General, the Commissary-General, the Chief of the Army Medical Department, each had his own special reason to give why the "thing" was "impossible." No ammunition—no carriages—no hospital stores—no doolies for the sick and wounded. Each head of a Department, indeed, had his own particular protest to fling in the face of the Commander-in-Chief. *Nunquam paratus* was his motto. It was the custom of Departments. It was the rule of the Service. No

1857. May.

1857. May. one was at all ashamed of it. It had come down by official inheritance from one to the other, and the Chief of the Department merely walked in the pleasant paths which, years before, as a Deputy Assistant, he had trodden under some defunct Chief of pious memory. In a word, it was the system. Every now and then, some seer like Henry Lawrence rose up to protest against it. And when, in the plain language of common sense, the truth was laid bare to the public, some cried, "How true!" but the many smiled incredulously, and denounced the writer as an alarmist. And so General Anson, having found things in that normal state of unpreparedness in which his predecessors had delighted, had followed in their footsteps, nothing doubting, until suddenly brought face to face with a dire necessity, he found that everything was in its wrong place. The storm-signals were up, but the life-boat was in the church steeple, and no one could find the keys of the church.*

It was not strange, therefore, that Anson felt it would not be prudent, with the means then at his disposal, to risk "an enterprise on Delhi." "It becomes now a matter for your consideration," he wrote to Sir John Lawrence on the 17th, "whether it would be prudent to risk the small European force we have here in an enterprise on Delhi. I think not. It is wholly, in my opinion, insufficient for the purpose. The walls could, of course, be

* On the 18th of May General Barnard wrote from Umballah, saying: "And now that they [the European regiments] are collected, without tents, without ammunition, the men have not twenty rounds apiece. Two troops of Horse Artillery, twelve guns, but no reserve ammunition, and their waggons at Loodianah—seven days' off! Commissariat without sufficient transport at hand. This is the boasted Indian Army, and this is the force with which the civilians would have us go to Delhi."—Compare also letter quoted in the text, page 165.

battered down with heavy guns. The entrance might be opened, and little resistance offered. But so few men in a great city, with such narrow streets, and an immense armed population, who knew every turn and corner of them, would, it appears to me, be in a very dangerous position, and if six or seven hundred were disabled, what would remain? Could we hold it with the whole country around against us? Could we either stay in or out of it? My own view of the state of things now is, that by carefully collecting our resources, having got rid of the bad materials which we cannot trust, and having supplied their places with others of a better sort, it would not be very long before we could proceed without a chance of failure, in whatever direction we might please. Your telegraphic message informing me of the measures which you have taken to raise fresh troops confirms me in this opinion. I must add, also, that this is now the opinion of all here whom I have consulted upon it—the Major-General and Brigadier, the Adjutant-General, Quarter-master-General, and Commissary-General. The latter has, however, offered a positive impediment to it, in the impossibility of providing what would be necessary for such an advance under from sixteen to twenty days. I thought it could have been done in less; but that was before I had seen Colonel Thomson. Indeed, it is very little more than forty-eight hours since I came here, and every turn produces something which may alter a previous opinion."*

1857. May.

* The views of General Anson at this time are thus stated in an unpublished memoir by Colonel Baird Smith, from which other quotations will be made: "It is generally understood that the course which recommended itself most to his mind was one strongly opposed to the popular instinct at the moment. Recognising, as all conversant with military affairs could not fail to do, that strategically considered the position of a weak force at Delhi must be, if not utterly false, yet of extreme

1857. May. Correspondence with Lord Canning.

But these doubts were but of brief duration. Let Adjutants-General, and Quarter-masters-General, and Commissaries-General suggest what difficulties they might, there were other powers, to North and South, in whose sight all delay, in such a crisis, was an offence and an abomination. Lord Canning, from Calcutta, and Sir John Lawrence, from the Punjab, flashed to the Head-Quarters of the Army emphatic messages, urging Anson to move on Delhi, with such force as he could gather; and followed up their eager telegrams with letters scarcely less eager. The Governor-General, to whom Anson had not communicated the views which he had expressed in the preceding letter to the Chief Commissioner of the Punjab, was overjoyed by the thought that there was so much activity at Head-Quarters. Encouraged by the earlier letters of the Military Chief, and still more by a message he had received from Mr. Colvin, at Agra, Canning wrote on the 17th to Anson, saying that he learnt the good news "with intense pleasure." "For," he added, "I doubted whether you would be able to collect so strong a body of troops in the time. I cannot doubt that it will now prove amply sufficient, and I am very grateful to you for enabling me to feel confident on this point. An unsuccessful demonstration against Delhi, or even any appearance of delay in proceeding to act, when once our force is on the spot, would have a most injurious effect—I mean in Bengal generally. Every station

danger, he is believed to have advocated the withdrawal of the small and isolated detachments on the Doab, and the concentration of the whole available British force between the Sutlej and the Jumna, there to await the arrival of reinforcements by the line of the Indus, and, while permitting the fire of revolt to burn as fiercely as it might within the limits indicated, to check its spread beyond them on the northward, and ultimately to proceed to quench it with means that would make the issue certain."—*Unpublished Memoir by Colonel Baird Smith. MS* and cantonment is in a state of excitement, and anything in the nature of a check would give confidence to the disaffected regiments, which might lead to something worse than the horrors of Delhi. Allahabad, Benares, Oudh (except Lucknow, which I believe to be safe), and a host of places of less importance where Native troops are alone, will continue to be a source of much anxiety until Delhi is disposed of. It is for this that I have telegraphed to you to make as short work as possible of the rebels, who have cooped themselves up there, and whom you cannot crush too remorselessly. I should rejoice to hear that there had been no holding our men, and that the vengeance had been terrible." 1857. May.

Correspondence with Sir John Lawrence.

Whilst Lord Canning was thus expressing his gratitude to Anson, Sir John Lawrence, who was nearer the scene of action, and in closer communication with the Commander-in-Chief, knowing better what were the prevailing counsels at Head-Quarters, was urgent in his remonstrances against delay. He knew the temper of the people well; and nothing was clearer to the eye of his experience than that, in the conjuncture which had arisen, it was necessary above all things to maintain an appearance of successful activity. Any semblance of paralysis at such a time must, he knew, be fatal to us. At such periods the Natives of India wait and watch. It is in conformity with the genius of a people, equally timid and superstitious, to be worshippers of success. John Lawrence knew well that if at any time the English in India should betray symptoms of irresolution in the face of danger, thousands and tens of thousands, believing that the day of our supremacy is past, would first fall away from, and then rise against their masters. But we had reached an epoch in the

1857. May. History of our great Indian Empire at which the impression of our coming fall was stronger than it had ever been before, and there were those who, on the first sign of weakness in our camp, would have pointed exultingly to the beginning of the end. It was not a time, indeed, to calculate military means and resources, or to regard strategical principles in the conduct of our armies; but simply to move and strike—to move somewhere and to strike some one. And it was to this necessity of prompt and vigorous action that the counsels of John Lawrence ever pointed—not to any particular line of procedure to be dictated to the Military Chief. "I do not myself," he wrote to Anson, on the 21st of May, "think that the country anywhere is against us—certainly not from here to within a few miles of Delhi. I served for nearly thirteen years in Delhi, and know the people well. My belief is, that with good management on the part of the Civil officers, it would open its gates on the approach of our troops. It seems incredible to conceive that the mutineers can hold and defend it. Still, I admit that on military principles, in the present state of affairs, it may not be expedient to advance on Delhi; certainly not until the Meerut force is prepared to act, which it can only be when set free. Once relieve Meerut, and give confidence to the country, no difficulty regarding carriage can occur. By good arrangements the owners will come forward, but in any case it can be collected. From Meerut you will be able to form a sound judgment on the course to be followed. If the country lower down be disturbed, and the Sepoys have mutinied, I conceive it would be a paramount duty to march that way, relieve each place, and disarm or destroy the mutineers. If, on the other hand, all were safe, it would be a question whether you should consolidate your resources there, or march on Delhi. I think it must be allowed that our European troops are not placed at this or that station simply to hold it, but to be ready to move wherever they may be required. Salubrious and centrical points for their location were selected; but so long as we maintain our prestige and keep the country quiet, it cannot signify how many cantonments we abandon. But this we cannot do, if we allow two or three Native corps to checkmate large bodies of Europeans. It will then be a mere question of time, by slow degrees, but of a certainty the Native troops must destroy us. We are doing all we can to strengthen ourselves, and to reinforce you, either by direct or indirect means.* But can your Excellency suppose for one moment that the Irregular troops will remain staunch, if they see our European soldiers cooped up in their cantonments, tamely awaiting the progress of events. Your Excellency remarks that we must carefully collect our resources but what are these resources, but our European soldiers, our guns, and our matériel: these are all ready at hand, and only require to be handled wisely and vigorously to produce great results. We have money also, and the control of the country. But if disaffection spread, insurrection will follow, and we shall then neither be able to collect the revenue, nor procure supplies." "Pray," he continued, "only reflect on the whole history of India. Where have we failed, when we acted vigorously? Where have we succeeded, when guided by timid counsels? Clive, with twelve hundred, fought at Plassey in

1857. May.

* This is to be understood as referring to the measures taken in the Punjab.

1857. May. opposition to the advice of his leading officers, beat forty thousand men, and conquered Bengal. Monson retreated from the Chumbul, and before he gained Agra, his army was disorganised and partially annihilated. Look at the Caubul catastrophe. It might have been averted by resolute and bold action. The Irregulars of the Army, the Kuzzilbashes, in short our friends, of whom we had many, only left us when they found we were not true to ourselves. How can it be supposed that strangers and mercenaries will sacrifice everything for us? There is a point up to which they will stand by us, for they know that we have always been eventually successful, and that we are good masters; but go beyond this point, and every man will look to his immediate benefit, his present safety. The Punjab Irregulars are marching down in the highest spirits, proud to be trusted, and eager to show their superiority over the Regular troops—ready to fight, shoulder to shoulder, with the Europeans. But if, on their arrival, they find the Europeans behind breastworks, they will begin to think that the game is up. Recollect that all this time, while we are halting, the emissaries of the mutineers are writing to, and visiting, every cantonment. . . . I cannot comprehend what the Commissariat can mean by requiring from sixteen to twenty days to procure provisions. I am persuaded that all you can require to take with you must be procurable in two or three. We have had an extraordinary good harvest, and supplies must be abundant between Umballah and Meerut. The greater portion of the country is well cultivated. We are sending our troops in every direction without difficulty, through tracts which are comparatively desert. Our true policy is to trust the Maharajah of Putteeala,

and Rajah of Jheend, and the country generally, for 1857.
they have shown evidence of being on our side, but May.
utterly to distrust the regular Sepoys. I would spare no expense to carry every European soldier—at any rate, to carry every other one. By alternately marching and riding, their strength and spirits will be maintained. We are pushing on the Guides, the Fourth Sikhs, the First and Fourth Punjab regiments of Infantry, from different parts of the Punjab, in this way. If there is an officer in the Punjab whom your Excellency would wish to have at your side, pray don't hesitate to apply for him. There is a young officer now at Head-Quarters, who, though young in years, has seen much service, and proved himself an excellent soldier. I allude to Captain Norman, of the Adjutant-General's office. Sir Colin Campbell had the highest opinion of his judgment; and when he left Peshawur it was considered a public loss."

Of the exceeding force and cogency of this no doubt can be entertained. It was the right language for the crisis—rough, ready, and straight to the point. The great Punjab Commissioner, with his loins girt about, eager for the encounter, impatient to strike, was not in a mood to make gentle allowances or to weigh nice phrases of courteous discourse. But, in what he wrote, he intended to convey no reproaches to the Military Chief. It was simply the irrepressible enthusiasm of a nature, impatient of departmental dallyings and regulation restraints, and in its own utter freedom from all fear of responsibility not quite tolerant of the weakness of those who, held back by a fear of failure, shrink from encountering heroic risks. It was not that he mistrusted the man Anson, but that he mistrusted all the cum-

1857. May. brous machinery of the Head-Quarters Departments, which never had been found ripe for sudden action—never had improvised an expedition or precipitated an enterprise, ever since Departments were created—though, in truth, he could not see that in the machinery itself there was anything to unfit it for prompt action. "I should greatly regret," he wrote two days afterwards, "if any message or letter of mine should annoy you. I have written warmly and strongly in favour of an advance, because I felt assured that such was the true policy. However much we may be taken by surprise, our military organisation admits of prompt action. The country is almost sure to be with us, if it were only that we save them from trouble; and this will more especially be the case in an affair like the present, when we have really to contend only with our own troops, with whom the people can have no sympathy." The Commissariat, in such a case, is ever the chief stumbling-block; and the impediments thrown up are those of which military men take the most, and civilians the least, account. Anson was told at Umballah that they were insuperable. But John Lawrence, at Rawul-Pindee, could not recognise the force of the obstructive argument. "I cannot comprehend," he wrote to Anson, "why Colonel Thomson requires so much supplies. To carry so much food with the troops is to encumber the column and waste our money. To guard against accidents, three or four days' supplies should be taken, but no more. My belief is, that ten thousand troops might march all over the North-West, and, provided they paid for what they required, no difficulty in obtaining supplies would be experienced." It is plain, too, that at this time the Delhi difficulty was, in the Punjab, held to be a light one, for Lawrence added: "I still think that no real resistance at Delhi will be attempted; but, of course, we must first get the Meerut force in order, and, in moving against Delhi, go prepared to fight. My impression is, that, on the approach of our troops, the mutineers will either disperse, or the people of the city rise and open their gates."* 1857. May.

Final orders of the Civil Government.

Whether General Anson ever recognised the fact that the conjuncture was one in which all rules of warfare must bow their necks to stern political necessity, is not very apparent; but if he still maintained his opinions as a soldier, he knew well that it was his duty to yield his judgment to the authority of the supreme Civil power; and when he received an emphatic enunciation of the views of the Governor-General, he prepared to march down upon Delhi. "I regret," he wrote to the Governor-General on the 23rd of May, "that it has not been possible to move sooner upon Delhi. The force is so small that it must not be frittered away. You say in your telegraphic message that Delhi must be recovered, 'but [the operations] to be undertaken by a strong British force.' There is not this in the country. We have collected all within reach. I venture to say that not an hour has been lost, and that the movement of the troops from Umballah will have been accomplished in a space of time which was not considered possible on my arrival here." And he concluded his letter by

* In a previous letter (May 21) Lawrence had written: "At Delhi the Sepoys have murdered their officers and taken our guns, but even there they did not stand. No number of them can face a moderate body of Europeans fairly handled. Of late years, even when fighting under our own banners in a good cause, with European officers at their head, and English comrades at their side, they have seldom done anything; as mutineers they cannot fight—they will burn, destroy, and massacre, but not fight."

1857. May. saying: "I should be glad to know whether you consider the Force with which I propose to attack Delhi sufficient—and, namely, 'a strong British

May 23. Force.'" He had by this time clearly calculated his available strength for the great enterprise before him —and it was this, as detailed in a letter which he wrote to General Hewitt at Meerut: "The force from Umballah consists of the Ninth Lancers, one squadron of the Fourth Lancers, Her Majesty's Seventy-fifth Foot, First European Regiment, Second European Regiment, Sixtieth Native Infantry, two troops of Horse Artillery. They are formed into two small brigades. Brigadier Halifax commands the first Brigadier Jones the second brigade. Four companies of the First Fusiliers, one squadron of Ninth Lancers, two guns, Horse Artillery, were moved to Kurnaul on the 17th, and arrived on the 20th. Six companies of the First Fusiliers followed on the 21st. Her Majesty's Seventy-fifth Foot and Sixtieth Regiment of Native Infantry marched on the 22nd. One squadron Ninth Lancers and four guns will march on the 24th or 25th. The above will be at Kurnaul on the 28th. The Second Europeans, third troop third brigade of Horse Artillery will probably follow on the 26th. The whole will be at Kurnaul on the 30th. I propose then to advance with the column towards Delhi on the 1st, and be opposite to Baghput on the 5th. At this place I should wish to be joined by the force from Meerut. To reach it four days may be calculated on." "A small siege-train," he added, "has left Loodianah, and is expected here on the 26th. It will require eleven days to get it to Delhi. It may join us at Baghput on or about the 6th, the day after that I have named for the junction of your force. I depend on your supplying at least one hundred and twenty Artillerymen to work it. You will bring, besides, according to statement received, two squadrons of Carabineers, a wing of the Sixtieth Rifles, one light field battery, one troop of Horse Artillery, and any Sappers you can depend upon, and of course the non-commissioned European officers belonging to them." 1857. May.

Whilst Anson was writing this from Umballah, Lord Canning was telegraphing a message to him, through the Lieutenant-Governor of Agra, announcing the reinforcements which were expected at Calcutta, and adding that everything depended "upon disposing speedily of Delhi, and making a terrible example. No amount of severity can be too great. I will support you in any degree of it." There was nothing uncertain in this sound. But it is clear that the Governor-General, in his eagerness to strike a sudden and a heavy blow at the enemy, very much underrated the military difficulties with which Anson was called upon to contend, and believed overmuch in the facile execution of the impossible; for, on the 31st of May, he telegraphed again to the Commander-in-Chief, saying: "I have heard to-day that you do not expect to be before Delhi till the 9th (June). In the mean time Cawnpore and Lucknow are severely pressed, and the country between Delhi and Cawnpore is passing into the hands of the rebels. It is of the utmost importance to prevent this, and to relieve Cawnpore. But rapid action will do it. Your force of Artillery will enable you to dispose of Delhi with certainty. I therefore beg that you will detach one European Infantry regiment and a small force of European Cavalry to the south of Delhi, without keeping them for operations there, so that Aligurh may be recovered and Cawnpore relieved immediately. It is

1857. May. impossible to overrate the importance of showing European troops between Delhi and Cawnpore, Lucknow and Allahabad, depend upon it."

It is easy to conceive what would have been the perplexity in General Anson's mind, if he had received these instructions. The recovery of Delhi seemed to be an enterprise beyond the reach of the slender means at his disposal; but he was expected also to operate in the country beyond, and in the straits of his weakness to display strength on an extensive field of action. The Army was already on its way to Delhi. For whilst the Military Departments were protesting their inability to move the Army, the Civilians at Umballah—officially the Commissioner of the Cis-Sutlej States, and the Deputy Commissioner of the district, individually Mr. George Barnes and Mr. Douglas Forsyth—were putting forth their strength, moving all the agents beneath them, and employing the influence which their position had given them among the people to accomplish promptly and effectually the great object now to be attained. It little mattered if, at such a time, the ordinary Civil business were temporarily suspended. It behoved, at such a moment, every man to be more or less a soldier. So the Civil officers, not only at Umballah, but all around it, in the important country between the Jumna and the Sutlej, went to work right manfully in aid of the military authorities; collected carts, collected cattle, collected coolies, and brought together and stored in Umballah large supplies of grain for the army.* And this, too, in the

* Mr. Barnes, in his official report, has recorded that, "As soon as it was seen by the Commander-in-Chief that an onward movement should be made, a sudden difficulty arose in the want of carriages. The Deputy Commissary-General having officially declared his inability to meet the wants of the army, the Civil Authorities were called upon to supply

face of difficulties and impediments which would have dismayed and obstructed less earnest workmen; for ever, after the fashion of their kind, Natives of all classes stood aloof, waiting and watching the issue of events; from the capitalist to the coolie all shrunk alike from rendering active assistance to those whose power might be swept away in a day. 1857. May 11.

Protected Sikh Chiefs.

There were other important services, which at this time the Civil officers rendered to their country; doing, indeed, that without which all else would have been in vain. In the country between the Jumna and the Sutlej were the great chiefs of what were known as the "Protected Sikh States." These states, at the commencement of the century, we had rescued by our interference from the grasp of Runjeet Singh, and ever since the time when the Rajah of Puteealah placed in the hands of young Charles Metcalfe the keys of his fort, and said that all he possessed was at the service of the British Government, those chiefs, secure in the possession of their rights, had been true to the English alliance. They had survived the ruin of the old Sikh Empire, and were grateful to us for the protection which we had afforded and the independence which we had preserved. There are seasons in the lives of all nations, when faith is weak and temptation is strong, and, for a little space, the Cis-Sutlej chiefs, when the clouds of our first trouble were lowering over us, may have been beset with doubts and perplexities and fears of siding with the weaker party. Their hesitation, however, was short-lived.

the demand. At Umballah there has ever been a difficulty to furnish cattle of any kind, the carts being of a very inferior description; however, such as they were, they had to be pressed into service, and in the course of a week, after the utmost exertions, five hundred carts, two thousand camels, and two thousand coolies were made over to the Commissariat Department; thirty thousand maunds of grain were likewise collected and stored for the Army in the town of Umballah."

1857. May. The excellent tact of Douglas Forsyth, who took upon himself the responsibility of calling upon the Maharajah of Puteealah for assistance, smoothed down the apprehensions of that chief, and he took his course manfully and consistently, never swerving from the straight path of his duty. The chiefs of Jheend and Nabha followed his example, and were equally true to the British alliance.* It was of the utmost importance, at that time, that the road from Umballah to Kurnaul should be kept open; for it was to the latter place—once a flourishing military cantonment, but at the time of which I am writing deserted and decayed—that the troops from Umballah were now marching; and there the fugitives from Delhi had mostly assembled, and something of an attempt had been made to re-establish the shattered edifice of British authority upon a fragment of the ruins of Delhi.† Above all, to hold Kurnaul was to keep open the communications between Umballah and Meerut, and so to facilitate the junction of the forces from those two points. Happily for us, in this juncture the Newab of Kurnaul, a Mahomedan

* See Mr. Barnes's report. "The first object was to provide for the safety of the Grand Trunk Road and the two stations of Thanesur and Loodhianah, which were without reliable troops. I accordingly directed the Rajah of Jheend to proceed to Kurnaul with all his available force. The Maharajah of Puteealah, at my request, sent a detachment of all arms, and three guns, under his brother, to Thanesur on the Grand Trunk Road between Umballah and Kurnaul. The Rajah of Nabha and the Newab of Malair Kotela were requested to march with their men to Loodhianah, and the Rajah of Fureedpore was desired to place himself under the orders of the Deputy Commissioner of Ferozepore. Thus all points of the main line of road were secured, and the Rajah of Jheend was also instructed to collect supplies and carriages for the field force, to protect the station of Kurnaul," &c. It should be added that Sir John Lawrence had telegraphed on the 13th to "get the Maharajah of Puteealah to send one regiment to Thanesur and another to Loodhianah." The policy from the first was to trust the great Cis-Sutlej Chiefs. See also note in the Appendix.

† Brigadier Graves and Mr. Le Bas, who had effected their escape from Delhi, were the representatives of the military and civil authority.

nobleman and land-owner of large influence in that part of the country, threw the weight of his personal power into the scales on our side.* This, doubtless, was great help to us; and when the Jheend Rajah sent down his troops to Kurnaul, the danger of a general rising of the mixed population of that part of the country had passed away. The Contingent arrived on the night of the 18th, and on the following morning the first detachment of Europeans marched into the cantonment.* Meanwhile, the Puteealah Rajah was occupying Thanesur, on the great high road between Umballah and Kurnaul, and thus the communication between these two important points was fully secured. 1857. May.

At the distance of a few miles from the station of Kurnaul lies the town of Paniput, a place famous in Indian annals; for there, on the neighbouring plain, had great armies contended, and thrice with tremendous carnage the destinies of India had been decided on its battle-fields. At this point the bulk of the Jheend Contingent was now posted, and as fresh detachments of the army from Umballah marched into Kurnaul, the advanced guard pushed on to Paniput, where it was presently joined by the rear companies of the Fusiliers, two more squadrons of the Lancer regiment, and four guns. The Europeans, weakened though they were by the burning heats of May, were eager for the conflict, and already there had grown up amongst them that intense hatred of the

* Mr. Raikes states, in his "Notes on the Revolt," that "When we had no military force near Kurnaul, and all men watched anxiously the conduct of each local chief, the Newab of Kurnaul went to Mr. Le Bas and addressed him to the following effect: 'Sir, I have spent a sleepless night in meditating on the state of affairs; I have decided to throw in my lot with yours. My sword, my purse, and my followers are at your disposal.'"

† This advanced detachment consisted of four companies of the First Fusiliers, two Horse Artillery guns, and a squadron of the Ninth Lancers.

1857. May. Native races which afterwards bore such bitter fruit, for even then they were beginning to see before them evidences of the destroying hand of the Insurgent.

May 27. Death of General Anson. With the last of the European regiments General Anson left Umballah, on the 25th of May; and, on the 26th, he was lying at Kurnaul, helpless and hopeless, on the bed of death, in the mortal agonies of the great pest of the country. On the following day, Sir Henry Barnard arrived in Camp, a little after midnight, just in time, as he said, to receive the dying farewell of his chief. Anson was all but gone; but he recognised his friend, and, in a faint voice, articulated: "Barnard, I leave you the command. You will say how anxious I have been to do my duty. I cannot recover. May success attend you. God bless you. Good-bye."* And another hour had not spent itself before General George Anson had passed beyond the reach of all human praise or censure. The great responsibility thrown upon the Chief-Commander had filled him with mental anxiety, which had increased the depressing influences of over-fatigue and exposure to the climate in the most trying season of the year. He had evinced much tender consideration for the health of his men, and he was one of the first to be struck down by the fiery blasts of the Indian summer. He was a brave soldier and an honest gentleman; and another brave soldier and honest gentleman, whilst the corpse lay unburied in the next room, wrote a letter, saying: "I solemnly declare to you on my character as an officer, who, at all events, came to this country with the prestige of recent service with him, that not an hour has been lost in getting the

* Letter of Sir H. Barnard to Sir Charles Yorke, May 27, 1857. "This," he adds, "was at half-past one A.M. on the 27th; at 2.15 he breathed his last." Cholera was the immediate cause of his death.

small force now advanced as far as Paniput, and I hope to keep pushing on, as fast as I can get them up, on Delhi. The day I heard of the disaster at Delhi—which at Umballah preceded any account from Meerut—I immediately despatched my son, who rode to Simlah during the night to warn the Commander-in-Chief, and bring him down. He has himself detailed all his movements to you, and I cannot but entertain hope, had he lived, you would have taken a different view of his conduct, and not attributed any want of energy to him. Whatever might have been accomplished by an immediate rush from Meerut could not be expected from Umballah. The European troops were all in the Hills. Nothing but three regiments of Native troops and some Artillery Europeans were at the latter place; and when the regiments on the Hills were assembled, the General was met by protests against his advance by the leading Staff and Medical Officers of his Army. The Commissariat declared their utter inability to move the troops; the medical men represented theirs to provide the requisite attendants and bearers. Still matters went on. Troops were moved as fast as could be done, and arrangements made to meet the difficulty of bearers. Ammunition had to be procured from Phillour, for the men had not twenty rounds in their pouches, and none in store; and the Artillery were inefficient, as their reserve waggons were all at Loodhianah. It is only this day that I expect the necessary supply of ammunition to arrive at Umballah. I have determined (I say *I*, for poor Anson could only recognise me and hand me over the command when I arrived last night) not to wait for the siege-train."*

1857. May.

* Sir Henry Barnard to Sir John Lawrence, May 27, 1857. MS.

1857. May. General Barnard in command.

Thus passed away from the scene one of its chief actors, just as the curtain had risen on the great drama of British action. With what success Anson might have played his distinguished part can now be only conjectured. There are those who believe that alike in wisdom and integrity he far outshone all his colleagues in the Supreme Council, and that when the crisis arrived he took in the situation and measured the work to be done with an accuracy and precision which none beside, soldier or civilian, brought to bear upon the opening incidents of the War.* Little time was allowed to him to recover from the first shock of the storm before it overwhelmed and destroyed him. But it would be unjust to estimate what he did, or what he was capable of doing, by the measuring-rod of those who, during that eventful fortnight, believed that the recovery of Delhi was to be accomplished by the prompt movement of a small and imperfectly equipped British force. It is not in contemporary utterances that we are to look for a just verdict. We must put aside all thought, indeed, of what even the wisest and the strongest said in the first paroxysm of perplexity, when all men looked to the Chief of the Army to do what then seemed to be easy, and found that it was not done. How difficult it really was will presently appear. And though the result of a sudden

* See the statements of the author of the "Red Pamphlet:" "It was a common practice to sneer at General Anson as a mere Horse-Guards' General, as one who had gained his honours at Newmarket. But it is nevertheless a fact that this Horse-Guards' General, by dint of application and perseverance, made himself so thoroughly a master of his profession, that, when the mutiny broke out, he drew up a plan of operations, which his successor, a Crimean General, carried out in all its details, rejecting as crude and ridiculous the suggestions sent up by the collective wisdom of Calcutta." History may not unwillingly accept this; but when it is said that General Anson, "when brought, in both the Councils"—that is, the Executive and Legislative Councils—"face to face with men who had made legislation for India the study of their lives, distanced them all," one cannot help being somewhat startled by the boldness of the assertion.

1857. May 11.

blow struck at Delhi might have been successful, it is impossible, with our later knowledge of subsequent events to guide us, not to believe that in the month of May the risk of failure was greater than the fair prospect of success. And we may be sure that if Anson had flung himself headlong upon the stronghold of the enemy and failed, he would have been stigmatised as a rash and incapable general, ignorant of the first principles of war.

Summing up of Lord Canning.

Perhaps the judgment of Lord Canning on these initial delays and their causes may be accepted as sound and just. "The protracted delay," he wrote, "has been caused, as far as I can gather from private letters from General Anson since I last wrote, by waiting for the siege-train, and by want of carriage for the Europeans. As regards the siege-train, I believe it to have been an unwise delay. We shall crush Delhi more easily, of course; but I do not believe that we should have been exposed to any reverse for want of a siege-train, and the time lost has cost us dear indeed. As to the carriage and Commissariat, it is impossible, in the absence of all information, to say how far the delay was avoidable and blamable. It would have been madness to move a European force at this season with any deficiency of carriage (with cholera, too, amongst them), but I greatly doubt whether General Anson was well served in this matter of carriage. From many letters from Head-Quarters which have been before me, I am satisfied that, with the exception of one young officer,* there was not a man on the Army Staff who gave due thought to the political dangers of delay and to

* It need scarcely be said that the officer here indicated was Captain, now (1869) Colonel Norman, who has abundantly justified all the high opinions of his character then entertained.

1857 May. the perils which hung over us elsewhere as long as no move was made upon Delhi. With the Staff, the Medical Staff especially, arguing the necessity of completeness, and none of them apparently conscious of the immense value of time, it is very probable that time was lost. On this subject you will see a letter from Sir John Lawrence to the Commander-in-Chief. It is very earnest and practical, like all that comes from him, and I wish with all my heart that he had been nearer to Head-Quarters. His counsels and his thorough knowledge of the country would have been invaluable. You must bear in mind, however, in regard to his estimate of the time which should have been sufficient to put the army in motion, that a great change was made in the Commissariat three years ago, when the Transport establishments were given up, and it was determined to trust henceforward to hiring beasts for the occasion. We are now making the first experiment of this change. Economically, it was a prudent one, and in times of ordinary war might work well; but I shall be surprised if General Anson were not greatly impeded by it. Could it have been foreseen that our next operations would be against our own regiments and subjects, no sane man would have recommended it."

From the death-bed of General Anson Sir Henry Barnard had received his instructions to take command of the Delhi Field Force. And taking that command, he cast up at once the difficulties of his position. He thought that if Anson's death had not been accelerated, his last moments had been embittered, by the reproaches of eager-minded civilians, who could not measure military difficulties as they are measured by soldiers; and he felt that, in the execution of his duty to his country, he might bring like censure upon himself. He was in a novel and wholly unanticipated position,* and he felt that he was expected to do what was impossible. But he went resolutely at the work before him; and flung himself into it with an amount of energy and activity which excited the admiration and surprise of much younger men. He determined, on the morning of the 27th, not to wait for the siege-train, but after exchanging some six-pounders for nine-pounders, to march on to Delhi, forming a junction on the way with the Meerut force under Brigadier Wilson. "So long as I exercise any power," he wrote to Lawrence on the day after Anson's death, "you may rest assured that every energy shall be devoted to the objects I have now in view, viz., concentrating all the force I can collect at Delhi, securing the bridge at Baghput, and securing our communication with Meerut. For those objects all is now in actual motion. The last column left Umballah last night, and the siege-train will follow under escort, provided by Mr. Barnes. I have noticed to the Commissariat that supplies will be required, and hope that, when within two days' march of Delhi, our presence may have the influence you anticipate, and you may soon hear of our being in possession of the place." On the 31st he wrote from Gurrounda: "I am preparing with the Commanding Engineer the plan of the position to take up

1857. May.

* "It is a novel position," he wrote to Sir John Lawrence, "for an officer to find himself placed in who comes to the country prepared to treat its army as his own; to make every allowance for the difference of constitution; to encourage its past good deeds and honourable name; to have 'side blows of reproof,' because he has not treated them with the utmost severity, and rather sought occasion to disgrace than endeavour to support them. That I have endeavoured to support them I fully admit, and, if a fault, I must bear the blame."—*MS. Correspondence.*

1857. May. when we reach Delhi, and hope that no let or hindrance will prevent our being ready to act upon the place by the 5th."

The force from Umballah was now in full march upon Delhi. The scorching heat of the summer, which was taking terrible effect upon the health of the European soldiery, forbade much marching in the daytime. The fierce sun beat down upon the closed tents of our people, and as they lay in weary sleep, or vainly courting it, there was stillness, almost as of death, in our camp. But with the coolness of evening Life returned. The lassitude was gone. Men emerged from their tents and were soon in all the bustle and preparation of the coming march. The clear starlit nights are said to have been "delicious."* But as the English soldier marched on beneath that great calm canopy of heaven, there was within him the turmoil and the bitterness of an avenging thirst for blood. It fared ill with those against whom charges were brought of inflicting injury upon fugitives from Delhi. Some villagers, believed to be thus guilty, were seized, tried, condemned, and executed amidst every possible indignity that could be put upon them by our soldiers under the approving smiles of their officers.† And ever as they marched on, there was an eager desire to find criminals and to execute judgment upon them; and it was not easy for the hands of authority to restrain the retributive impulses of our people.

* See the "History of the Siege of Delhi, by One who Served there," for a very animated account of the march.

† "The fierceness of the men increased every day, often venting itself on the camp-servants, many of whom ran away. The prisoners, during the few hours between their trial and execution, were unceasingly tormented by the soldiers. They pulled their hair, pricked them with their bayonets, and forced them to eat cow's flesh, while officers stood by approving."—*History of the Siege of Delhi, by One who Served there.*

The day of action was now not far distant; and all believed that it would be a day of signal retribution. "Most of the men," it has been said, "believed that one battle would decide the fate of the mutinous regiments. They would fight in the morning; they would drink their grog in Delhi at night."* Even the sick, in the hospital tents, sat up, declared that they were well, and with feeble voices implored to be discharged that they might be led against the hated enemy. But Barnard's force was weak, and impatient as were his troops to push forward, it was necessary that they should form a junction with Wilson's brigade, which was advancing from Meerut, on the other side of the river. What that brigade had done since the disastrous night of the 10th of May must now be briefly related.

1857. May.

* "The History of the Siege of Delhi, by One who Served there."

CHAPTER VI.

STATE OF MEERUT—THE SAPPERS AND MINERS—DEFENCE OF ROORKHEE—COLONEL BAIRD SMITH—MUTINY OF THE SAPPERS—MARCH OF WILSON'S BRIGADE—BATTLES OF THE HINDUN—JUNCTION WITH BARNARD—BATTLE OF BUDLEE-KA-SERAI—POSITION BEFORE DELHI.

1857. Meerut after the outbreak. May 12—27.

On the day after that dreadful night at Meerut, which witnessed the first horrors of the revolt, it was the effort of the authorities to concentrate all the surviving Europeans, and such property as could be saved, within the English quarter of the great Cantonment. All the outlying picquets and sentries were therefore recalled; and all who lived beyond the new line of defence were brought in and lodged in a capacious public building used as the Artillery School of Instruction, and known as the Dumdumma. There also the treasure was brought from the Collectorate, and safely guarded against the plunderers, who were roving about the place. For the predatory classes were now making high festival, the escaped convicts from the gaols, the Goojurs from the neighbouring villages, and all the vile scum and refuse of the bazaars were glorying in the great paralysis of authority which had made crime so easy and so profitable. From the Cantonment the great harvest of rapine stretched out into the surrounding district. There was no respect of persons, races, or creeds. All who had anything to lose and lacked strength to defend it, were ruthlessly despoiled by the marauders. Travellers were stopped on the highway; the mails were plundered; houses were forcibly entered and sacked, and sometimes all the inmates butchered.* And so entirely had all semblance of British authority disappeared, that it was believed that the English in Meerut had been slain to a man.† 1857. May.

Meanwhile, with the proverbial rapidity of evil tidings, news had travelled up from Delhi, which left no doubt of the total defeat of the English, the Proclamation of the Padishah, and the concentration of the rebel troops, who, it was believed, would soon return to Meerut with all the immense resources of the great Magazine at their command. And presently fugitives came in with the sad details of mutiny and massacre, and exciting narratives of their own providential escapes.‡ All this increased the

* Take the following illustration from the Official Report of Mr. Commissioner Williams: "Ramdyal, a prisoner confined in the Civil Gaol under a decree for arrears of rent, hastened to his village, Bhojpoor, during the night of the 10th, and the next day at daybreak collected a party and attacked a money-lender who had a decree against him, and murdered him and six of his household."

† See description of the state of Meerut after the outbreak given by Major G. W. Williams in his "Narrative of Events:" "I found the whole of the station south of the Nullah and Begum's Bridge abandoned, for here the storm that was to shake India to its basis first broke out, and the ravages there visible were, strange to say, not accomplished by bands of soldiery formidable from their arms and discipline, but by mobs of wretched rabble (hundreds of whom would have been instantaneously scattered by a few rounds of grape), and this in the face of an overwhelming European force. The General of Division, with several officers, inhabited one of the Horse Artillery barracks, whilst most of the residents occupied the Field Magazine, now universally known as the far-famed Dum-Dumma, an enclosed space of about two hundred yards square, with walls eight feet high, a ditch and four bastions at each corner. Thus strengthened, it was defensible against any number of rabble insurgents unprovided with heavy guns or mortars. So completely were the rest of the cantonments deserted, that many Natives believed that every European had been exterminated, and their power being unseen, unfelt, was readily supposed to have been subverted."

‡ Among those who escaped from Delhi, but perished on the way, was the gallant leader of the little party that defended the great Delhi Magazine. It is stated that Willoughby was murdered, with several companions, by the inhabitants of a village near the Hindun river.

1857. May. general consternation. It was plain now that there was wide-spread revolt. All Civil authority was practically suspended; so Martial Law was proclaimed in the joint names of General Hewitt and Mr. Greathed; and the first who tasted the ready justice of the improvised gallows was the butcher from the Bazaar, who had brutally murdered Mrs. Chambers in her house. But this seems to have been an isolated act of vigour, due rather to the energy of an individual than to the joint authority from which the edict had proceeded.*

The Sappers and Miners.

On the 16th an incident occurred which increased the general consternation. Sixty miles from Meerut, on the Ganges Canal, lies Roorkhee, the Head-Quarters of the Engineering science of the country. There the great Thomason College, with its famous workshops, was in all the bustle and animation of its varied mechanical industry. There was the centre of the Irrigation Department, whence issued the directing authority that controlled the great system of Canal Works which watered the thirsty land. There, too, was posted the regiment of Sappers and Miners—trained and educated native military Engineers under European officers. It was a great thriving bee-hive; and that month of May found the workers in all their wonted peaceful activity, with plans and projects suited to the atmosphere of quiet times, and no thought of coming danger to disturb the even tenor of daily life. "No community in the world," wrote one, who may be said to have been the chief of this prosperous colony, "could have been living in greater security of life and property," when

Baird Smith.

* *Ante*, page 73.

Major Fraser, who commanded the Sappers and Miners, received an express from the General at Meerut, ordering him to proceed by forced marches to that station, as the Sepoy regiments were in open revolt. When intelligence of this summons reached Colonel Baird Smith, he at once suggested that the regiment should be despatched by the route of the Ganges Canal. To this Fraser readily agreed; and within six hours boats were prepared sufficient for the conveyance of a thousand men. The regiment mustered only seven hundred and thirteen, who were equipped and ready for the journey, when another express came ordering two companies to stand fast at Roorkhee, for the protection of that place. So eventually some five hundred men set out, under Fraser, for Meerut. 1857. May.

Then came to Roorkhee the news of the Delhi massacre. And as the Sappers were moving down to Meerut, Baird Smith was making admirable arrangements for the defence of the great engineering depôt, in which he took such earnest and loving interest. Officially, he was Superintendent-General of Irrigation in the North-Western Provinces; a most useful functionary, great in all the arts of peace, and with a reputation which any man might be proud to possess. But the man of much science now grew at once into the man of war, and Roorkhee became a garrison under his command. Not an hour was lost.* The Defence of Roorkhee.

* "It was at daybreak that I received the first intimation of the Meerut mutiny and massacre. When I went to the porch of my house to mount my horse for a morning ride, I found Medlicott, our geological professor, sitting there, looking oppressed with some painful intelligence, and, on my asking what the matter was, he then told me that about an hour before, Fraser, the Commandant of the Sappers and Miners, had received an express from the General at Meerut, ordering him to proceed by forced marches to that place. I immediately suggested the Ganges Canal route instead of forced marches, which would have fatigued the men much, and made them unfit for service."—*MS. Correspondence of Colonel Baird Smith.*

1857. May. Those indeed were times when to lose an hour might be to lose everything; and Baird Smith knew that there was no emergency against which he might not be called upon to provide. Even the companies of Sappers, which had been left for the defence of Roorkhee, might soon become a source of infinite danger. It was soon settled that the workshops should become the citadel, to which women and children might be removed; and there, on the 16th of May, all these helpless ones, little less than a hundred* in number, were comfortably accommodated in the several rooms, whilst to each of our male people some fitting duty was assigned. Their number was not much greater than that of the women and children; and half of them were non-combatants, clerks attached to the establishment, and little accustomed to the use of arms. The trained soldiers were but about fifty† in number, with eight or ten good officers; and of these Baird Smith took the command, telling them off into different guards, and organising different departments, so that nothing was omitted or neglected that could add to the defence of the place.

The Sapper companies, suspected of disloyalty from the first, were placed under their officers in charge of the College buildings. Baird Smith had talked to some of their leading men, endeavouring to allay the obvious excitement among them by friendly explanations and assurances; and after that, he said, "I could do no more." The wretched story of the bone-dust flour was rife amongst them, and there was a vague fear, as in other places, of a meditated attack

* There were on the 28th of May fifty women and forty-three children, according to the Disposition List of the Roorkhee Garrison of that day.

† Baird Smith, in a letter dated May 30th, says that the trained soldiers were only about thirty, but the numbers given in the text is on the authority of the nominal roll of the garrison.

by the British, taking them by surprise, disarming, and then destroying them. In such a state of feeling every circumstance of an exceptional character is misinterpreted into an indication of offence, and when it was known to the Sappers at Roorkhee that the Sirmoor Battalion—a regiment of Goorkahs commanded by Major Charles Reid—was coming down from Dhera, on its way to Meerut,* a terrible suspicion took possession of them; they believed it was a hostile movement against themselves. When this became known to Baird Smith, he sent an express to Reid requesting him not to march upon Roorkhee, but to make straight for the Canal, and at once to embark in the boats that were waiting for him. Reid grasped the position at once, and acted upon the suggestion. Pretending that he had missed his way, he asked for a guide to lead him straight to the banks of the Canal, and so they marched on to the boats without increasing the general alarm. And, said Reid, Baird Smith "was right beyond doubt, and his good judgment and forethought may have been—indeed, I feel pretty sure was—the means of saving the place and the lives of the ladies and children."† 1857. May

Meanwhile, the main body of the Sappers, under Mutiny of the Sappers.

* Immediately on receiving intelligence of the state of affairs at Meerut, Baird Smith had written to Major Reid, warning him that his services would most probably be required at that place, and offering to provide boats for the regiment. A day or two afterwards the summons came from Head-Quarters.

† Major Reid has recorded that whilst he was embarking his Goorkahs—"almond-eyed Tartars," as Baird Smith described them—several men of the Sappers came from Meerut and entered into communication with them. "I took no notice at first," he adds, "but as soon as they moved on, I called up a couple of my men and asked them what the Sappers had said to them. One little fellow replied, 'They wanted to know if we were going over to Meerut to eat the ottah (flour) sent up especially for the Goorkahs by the Governor-General; that the ottah at Meerut was nothing but ground bullocks' bones.' 'And what was your reply?' I asked. 'I said,' was the answer, 'the regiment was going wherever it was ordered—we obey the bugle-call.'"

1857. May 15. Major Fraser, had marched into Meerut. Not without some feelings of suspicion and alarm, they had moved down the great Canal; but their behaviour had, on the whole, been orderly, and when, on the 15th, they arrived at their destination, there was no reason to doubt their fidelity. Brought, however, into the immediate presence of a large body of European troops, who had the blood of their slaughtered countrymen to avenge, they were in that excitable, inflammable state, which needs only a single spark to draw forth the latent fire. It soon fell. It seems that the Commandant had promised them that they should retain charge of their own ammunition. He had no intention of breaking faith with them; but he desired that, for greater security, it should be stored in a bomb-proof building, which had been placed at his disposal. If the object of this had been carefully explained to the men, they would probably have assented without a murmur. But when, on the day after their arrival, the ammunition was being conveyed to its destination, the Sepoys suspected treachery, resented the removal of the magazine, stopped the laden carts, and broke into open mutiny. An Afghan Sepoy fired his piece from behind the Commandant, and Fraser fell, shot through the back. Others fired at Adjutant Mansell, but missed him; and the Native non-commissioned officer who was in attendance on Fraser was killed in the affray. Having done this, the mutineers broke and fled, but their victory was but short-lived. A troop of the Carabineers and some Horse Artillery guns were let loose upon them. The greater number escaped; but some fifty of the fugitives were overtaken outside cantonments among the sand-hills, and were killed. And so the Sappers and Miners, as a regiment, ceased to exist. Two companies, however, which were at work in another part of Meerut, were disarmed and set to work on the fortification of the Dumdumma. 1857. May 15—24

Inactivity at Meerut.

After this, there was, for a time, a lull at Meerut. The destruction of the Sappers was, perhaps, regarded as a cause of congratulation and a source of confidence, and as the advancing month brought with it no new alarms, and it seemed that the mutineers were resolved to concentrate their strength at Delhi, and not to emerge thence—as people whose fighting powers were greater behind walls—things began gradually to assume a cheerful complexion, and the inmates of the Artillery School ceased to tremble as they talked of what was to come. But there was vexation in high places. The telegraph line between Meerut and Agra was sometimes, if not always open; and Lieutenant-Governor Colvin, who never could lose sight of the fact that there were a battalion of English Rifles, a regiment of English Dragoons, and two batteries of English Artillery at Meerut, was constantly urging them, for God's sake, to do something. Thinking, after a while, that it was quite useless to exhort General Hewitt to put forth any activity in such a case, Colvin addressed himself to Brigadier Wilson, thus virtually setting aside the General of Division. Nettled by this, Hewitt telegraphed to Agra respectfully to request that the Lieutenant-Governor would transmit through him orders to his subordinates when such a step could cause no delay. But the Lieutenant-Governor still continued to telegraph to the Brigadier, beseeching him to go out in force so as to keep open the main road and to prevent dangerous combinations of revolted troops throughout the Doab. "What plan," he had asked, "does

1857 May 15—24. Brigadier Wilson propose for making the Meerut force actively useful in checking an advance down the Doab? If the mutineers leave Delhi in force, it is plain that no wing of a corps, or even a single corps, could stay their march. Therefore a move in strength to Bolundshuhur seems to be the right one." And now the Agra authorities continued to urge these movements, but were met by protests that it would be inexpedient to divide the force. "The only plan," said Wilson, "is to concentrate our European force, and to attack Delhi. He had consulted," he said, "with all the European officers in the force, and they were unanimously of opinion that any movement of the force from Meerut would be highly imprudent without the orders of the Commander-in-Chief, as it might counteract any movement that he might be forming." "To move in full strength," he added, "would involve the abandonment of all the sick, women and children and [ ]." Then came the inevitable story that "the Commissariat report that they cannot supply carriage for a force of half the strength;" and yet it was, numerically, but a small force that would have taken the field.* So Colvin yielded the point, and no longer looked to Meerut for assistance.

It has been shown that, as one result of the inactivity of this beautiful force of all arms, a belief gained ground in the adjacent country that the English at Meerut had all been killed to a man. Although the surrounding villages were swarming with robber-clans, who had murdered our people and sacked our

* In this telegraphic message it is stated that the force consisted of—Rifles, 700; Carabineers, mounted, 380; dismounted, 100; Artillery recruits, undrilled, 364. As some portion of the efficient, and all the inefficient men would have been left in Meerut, the number for field-service would not have exceeded 1000.

1857. May 24. Death of Mr. Johnston.

houses, it was not until the 24th of May, two weeks after the great tragedy, that a small party of our Dragoons was sent out to chastise the inmates of one of these nests of plunderers. On that day, for the first time, the English magistrate, Mr. Johnston, obtained the assistance of troops to enable him to suppress the overflowing crime of the district. The village of Ikteeapore was then burnt, and the people learnt that English soldiers were still alive in Meerut. But the demonstration was an ill-fated one. For Johnstone, who had gone out with the troops, riding homewards in hot haste, when the work was done, eager to be again actively employed, was fearfully injured by the falling of his horse, and three days afterwards expired.

William Hodson.

But the Meerut Brigade had now done with inaction. The "orders of the Commander-in-Chief," for which it had been waiting, had arrived.* It had been supposed for some time that the road between Kurnaul and Meerut was closed; but in the camp of the Commander-in-Chief there was an officer, equal to any difficult work, who volunteered to carry despatches to the latter place, and to bring back the much-needed information of the state of Wilson's Brigade. This was Lieutenant William Hodson, a man of rare energy of character, who was then serving with the First (Company's) Fusiliers. He had been, years before, one of that little band of pioneers who, under Henry Lawrence, had cleared the way for the civilisation of the Punjab, and he had afterwards risen to the command of that famous Guide Corps, the institution of which had been one

* See *ante*, p. 158.

1857. May.

of the most cherished and the most successful projects of his accomplished chief. But, amidst a career of the brightest promise, a heavy cloud had gathered over him, and he had rejoined his old regiment as a subaltern, chafing under a sense of wrong, and eager to clear himself from what he declared to be unmerited imputations upon his character.* This gloom was upon him when General Anson, discerning his many fine qualities, offered him a place in the Department of the Quartermaster-General, and especially charged him with the intelligence branch of its duties, in prosecution of which he was to raise a body of a hundred horse and fifty foot.† This was at Umballah, to which place he had marched down with his regiment from Dugshai. He was soon actively at work. He hastened down to Kurnaul, and there picking up some horsemen of the Jheend Rajah's Contingent, rode into Meerut, a distance of seventy-six miles, delivered his despatches, took a bath, a break-

* It would not consort with the nature of this work to enter into an elaborate inquiry into the justice or injustice of the treatment to which Lieutenant Hodson was subjected by Lord Dalhousie's Government. It is right, however, to state that some misapprehension appears to prevail as to the alleged offence on account of which the Commandant of the Guides, who was also a Deputy-Commissioner in the Peshawur district, was remanded to his regiment. He was not removed from the command of the Guides in consequence of any irregularity in his accounts, but he was removed altogether from the Punjab on account of his treatment of an influential Eusofzye chief. It was the Court of Directors that decreed him to be unfit to hold any office of trust. And I must protest strongly against the charges brought by Lieutenant Hodson's fraternal biographer against certain high Punjabee officials, including Sir Herbert Edwardes, who has gone to his rest whilst this volume has been growing under my pen. It is impossible to believe that such men were influenced by feelings of envy, hatred, and all uncharitableness. Indeed, Mr. Hodson in no small measure furnishes his own refutation of such charges, when he says in one sentence that his brother was disliked becaused he was a protégé of Sir Henry Lawrence, and in another that Sir Herbert Edwardes was his chief opponent. Edwardes was the last man in India to be prejudiced against a favourite of Henry Lawrence.—*See a further note in the Appendix.*

† This order was subsequently extended to the raising of "an entire new regiment of Irregular Horse."

fast, and a little sleep, and then rode back with papers for the Commander-in-Chief. Meanwhile, the bulk of the Meerut Brigade was in the bustle of preparation for an advance, under Wilson, to join the column which was moving down from the hills to the attack of Delhi. Many then, who had chafed under the restraints of the past fortnight, took fresh heart, and panted with the excitement of coming action. In high spirits, the troops marched out of cantonments on the night of the 27th of May. The column consisted of two squadrons of the Carabineers; a wing of the Sixtieth Rifles; Scott's light field-battery; Tombs's troop of Horse Artillery; two eighteen-pounder guns, all manned by Europeans; with some Native Sappers and Irregular Horse. Brigadier Archdale Wilson commanded the force, and Mr. Hervey Greathed accompanied it as civil officer. And with them rode, at the head of an improvised body of Horse, Jan Fishan Khan, the Afghan chief, who, unlike most of his countrymen, thought that he was bound to do something in return for the British pension, which supported him and his house.* 1857. May 27.

The marches of the two first days were uneventful. No enemy appeared, and Greathed believed that the rebel force would not attempt to give us battle except before the walls of Delhi. But when, on the 30th of May, Wilson's force reached Ghazee-ood-deen Nuggur,† near the river Hindun, there were May 30. The battles on the Hindun.

* The feeling generally, at this time, and in some instances the conduct, of the Afghan pensioners, of whom there was quite a colony in Loodhianah, denoted the ingratitude of the race. See Mr. Ricketts's interesting Loodhianah Report, "Papers relating to the Mutiny in the Punjab, 1857."

† The position is thus described by Baird Smith in the unpublished fragment of history, to which I have above referred: "This town, of respectable size, and with some ancient traces of walls, stands on the left bank of the Hindun, about a mile from that river. A long causeway carries the Grand Trunk Road across the broad valley, within which the stream, shrunk during the scorching

1857. May 30. signs of a coming struggle. Flushed with success, and confident in their strength, the mutineers had left their stronghold, and had come on to give battle to the Meerut Brigade before its junction with the force from Umballah. They had planted some heavy guns on a ridge to the right of their position, and from this point they opened fire upon our people. Then the eighteen-pounders, under Light, and Scott's field battery, made vigorous answer, and under their cover the British Riflemen advanced, and moving along the causeway, came to close quarters with the enemy. For some time a stubborn conflict was maintained; but our Horse Artillery, under Henry Tombs, supported by the Carabineers, dashed to the right, crossed the Hindun, making light of its rugged bank and dangerous bed, and successfully turned the left flank of the enemy. Under the galling fire then poured in upon them the mutineers reeled and staggered, and presently broke. Some took refuge in a village, whence they were driven by our Riflemen, and soon the whole body of the enemy were in ignominious flight towards the walls of Delhi. Five of their guns fell into our hands, and they left many of their fighting men behind them. Our own loss would have been small, but for the explosion of an ammunition-waggon; not by an accident of warfare, but by an act of resolute and sacrificial courage on the part of one of the mutineers. A Sepoy of the Eleventh Regiment deliberately discharged his musket into the

heats of May to a mere rivulet, wanders in a channel of extreme tortuosity, fordable both by infantry and artillery, though, from the prevalence of quicksands, the process is not altogether free from risk of mishap. A suspension bridge spans the stream, and on the right bank the causeway is covered by a toll-house, capable, if need were, of some defence. Villages, furnishing considerable means of resistance in their mud-walled houses and narrow lanes are scattered at intervals along th road, and the ground in ridges o sensible magnitude on both banks but especially on the right."

midst of the combustibles just as a party of the Rifles, under Captain Andrews, were gallantly seizing the gun to which the cart belonged. The explosion cost the man his life; but Andrews and some of his followers were killed by it, and others were carried wounded from the scene.* It taught us that among the mutineers were some brave and desperate men, who were ready to court instant death for the sake of the national cause. Many acts of heroism of this kind brighten up the history of the war, and many more were, doubtless, performed, of which History has no record. 1857. May 30.

The mutineers fled in hot haste to Delhi, where they were reviled for their disgraceful failure, and sent back reinforced, to try whether Fortune would help them on another day. Stimulated by promises of large rewards to achieve a great success in honour of the restored monarchy, they again marched to the Hindun. That day was our Whit-Sunday There was no Church parade. But the morning was ushered in by the most solemn and beautiful of all our Church services—that of the Burial of the Dead. There was genuine sorrow for those who had fallen as they were laid in unconsecrated ground, "a babool tree and a milestone marking the spot."† Little space was then left for mournful reflections. It was soon known that the Sepoys were returning to the attack. About noon our bugles sounded the alarm. The enemy had taken up a position on the ridge to the right of the Hindun, about a mile from our advanced May 31.

* "The officers that night drank in solemn silence to the memory of the brave departed; and from the manner in which the toast was proposed by Dr. Innes, the surgeon of the regiment, and received by every officer and member of the mess, I am sure, from his gallantry and other estimable qualities, that the memory of poor Andrews' will be long and fondly cherished by them."—*The Chaplain's (Mr. Rotton's) Narrative.*

† Chaplain's Narrative.

1857. May 31. posts on the bridge. Pushing forward his guns, he opened a heavy fire upon Wilson's force. This was a signal for our advance. The Artillery were sent forward to reply to the enemy's fire—the Rifles, with two of Scott's guns, occupying the head of the bridge. The battle, which then raged for some two hours, was almost wholly an Artillery fight.* But Cavalry and Infantry were exposed both to the fire of the enemy, and to the more irresistible assaults of the sun. It was the last day of May, one of the hottest days of the year. The fiery blasts of the summer were aggravated by the heat thrown from the smouldering embers of the burnt villages. The thirst of our people was intolerable. Some were smitten down by sun-stroke; others fell exhausted by the way; and there is a suspicion that some were destroyed by water poisoned by the enemy.† But, in spite of all these depressing circumstances, Wilson's troops drove the enemy from their position. When the fire of the mutineers had somewhat slackened, the Brigadier ordered a general advance of his force, and the Sepoys recoiled before it. But although they felt that they could not hold their ground and continue the battle, they did not fly, shattered and broken, as on the preceding day. Having discharged into our advancing columns a tremendous shower of grape-shot, they limbered up their guns before the smoke had dispersed, and fell back in orderly array. Exhausted

* "The conduct of Tombs's troop yesterday was the admiration of every one; for a long time they were engaged on two sides with the enemy's artillery. Light then got his two eighteen-pounders down to the river-bank and drew off the fire upon himself, and paid it back with interest."—*Hervey Greathed's Letters.* Lieutenant Perkins, of the Horse Artillery, was killed by a shot from one of the enemy's guns.

† This is stated by Mr. Rotton, who says: "Some were sun-stricken, some slain, and a few, whose cruel thirst induced them to slake it with water provided by the enemy in vessels containing strong corrosive poison, were thus deprived of life."

by the cruel heat and suffering agonies of thirst, the English soldier could not improve his victory by giving chase to the retiring enemy. The mutineers carried off all their guns and stores, and made good their retreat to Delhi. But they had been thus twice beaten in fair fight by inferior numbers, and had nothing but their disgrace to carry back with them and to lay at the feet of their King. 1857. May 31.

In the English camp there was great rejoicing; and, as the news spread, all men were gladdened by the thought that the tide now seemed to have turned, and that retribution, which, though delayed, was certain, was now overtaking the enemies of our race and the murderers of our people. The old stern courage had been again asserted, and with the old results. Success had returned to our ranks; and there was special cause for congratulation in the fact that Wilson, with a portion only of the old Meerut Brigade, had been the first to inflict punishment on the rebels, and among them upon some of the very men who had prevailed against us so grievously a little time before. But the situation of the little force on the Hindun was not without its perils. It was doubtful whether our troops, exhausted as they were by the work that they had done under that fiery sky, could successfully sustain another attack, if, as was probable, the enemy should come out again from Delhi, and in increased numbers. But the month of June came in, bringing with it no fresh assaults, but June 1. a welcome reinforcement. The Goorkah regiment, nearly five hundred strong, having moved up from Bolundshuhur, marched into camp, under its gallant Commandant, Major Charles Reid. At first they were taken for a body of the enemy marching upon our rear. But no sooner were they identified than the

1857. June. British troops turned out and welcomed them with lusty cheers.*

Movements of Barnard's force. Meanwhile the Delhi Field Force, under Barnard, had marched down to Alipore, which lies at a distance of twelve miles from Delhi. It arrived there on the 5th of June, and was halted until the Meerut troops could come up from the Hindun. There had been some want of understanding between the commanders of the two forces as to the nature of the operations and the point of junction. It had been thought, at one time, that it would be strategically expedient to move upon Delhi from both banks of the Jumna; and after the battles of the Hindun, Wilson's force had halted for orders from the chief. Those orders were received on the 4th of June. That evening Wilson commenced his march, and soon after midnight on the morning of the 6th he crossed the Jumna at Baghput. The delay was a source of bitterness to the Umballah troops, who were furiously eager to fall upon the enemy. Fresh tidings of mutiny and murder had reached them, and the blood of officers and men alike was at fever heat. The impatience, however, was but short-lived. Wilson was now close at hand. And already the waiting was bearing good fruit. On the 6th the siege-train arrived.

June 6. Arrival of siege-train. Orders for the equipment of the train had been received on the 17th of May. On the morning of the 24th, the gates of the Fort were opened. The guns and waggons and the labouring bullocks were all ready. The Sepoys of the Third Regiment at Phil-

* "The whole force turned out and cheered the regiment into camp; but my poor little fellows were so dead beat they could not return the hearty cheers with which they were welcomed. 'Get something to eat sharp,' said the Brigadier, 'as we may have to turn out.' Exhausted as my men were, I certainly was not anxious for a fight, and was thankful the mutineers left us alone that day."—*Unpublished Memoir by Major C. Reid.*

lour had volunteered to escort the train;* and, with some troopers of the Ninth Irregular Cavalry, they now marched upon the Sutlej. The bridge was still passable, and the train crossed over. Two hours afterwards the boats, which spanned the river, had been swept away by the flooding waters. But, although the Sepoys of the Third Regiment, who had then the game in their hands, had suffered the train to cross the bridge, it was known that they were mutinous to the core.† So when the whole line of ordnance was secure on the other bank of the river, it was quietly explained to the Sepoys of the Third that their services were no longer needed. A Contingent of Horse and Foot had been furnished by the Rajah of Nabha, and it was now ready to relieve the men of the suspected regiments. Under this guard of auxiliaries, with which the detachment of Irregular Cavalry moved forward, the train laboured on to Umballah, which it reached on the 27th of May. But a new difficulty awaited it there; for, although the guns had arrived, they were useless for want of gunners. A weak company was, therefore, despatched from Ferozepore by bullock-train, to be afterwards strengthened by recruits from Meerut. Meanwhile, the position of the train was not without its surrounding dangers. The Nusseree Battalion, which had been guilty of such shameful defection in the

1857. June.

* The train consisted of eight eighteen-pounders, four eight-inch howitzers, twelve five-and-a-half-inch mortars, and four eight-inch mortars (*Norman*). The officer in charge of the train was Lieutenant Griffith. Major Kaye commanded the whole detachment.

† This is an instance of what has been called the "inexplicable inconsistency" of the Sepoys, who so often allowed their best opportunities to escape; but Mr. Ricketts sufficiently affords a clue to it when, in his interesting Loodhianah Report, he says that they were pledged in concert with others to a certain course of procedure, and that no temptation of immediate advantage could induce them to diverge from the programme. The later history of this corps will be found in Book VI

1857. June. hour of our need, had come into Umballah, and the Sepoys of the Fifth were striving to induce the Goorkahs to combine with them to seize the guns and to march to Delhi.* The plot, however, was frustrated, and the siege-train passed on safely to Head-Quarters.†

June 7. Junction with the Meerut force.

On the 7th of June, amidst hearty welcomings and warm congratulations, the Meerut contingent marched gaily into Alipore. At one o'clock on the following morning they commenced the march on Delhi, thirsting for the battle. Their scouts had told them that the enemy were strongly posted in front of the approaches to the city, resolute to contest the progress of the British Force. Never since the first English soldier loaded his piece or unsheathed his sword to smite the dark-faced, white-turbaned Moor or Gentoo—not even when Clive's army, a century before, landed in Bengal to inflict retribution on the perpetrators of the great crime of the Black Hole—had our people moved forward under the impulse of such an eager, burning desire to be amongst the murderers of their race, as on that early June morning, when Barnard's fighting men knew that the mutineers of Meerut and Delhi were within their reach. It had been ascertained that the enemy were strongly posted, Infantry and Cavalry, with thirty guns, about six miles from Delhi, at a place called Budlee-ka-Serai, where groups of old houses and walled gardens, once the country residences of some of the nobles of the Imperial Court, supplied positions capable of powerful resistance.‡ On this place marched Barnard, on the early morning of the 8th of June, along the

* The Fifth was afterwards disarmed in the presence of two companies of the Fusiliers.

† On a requisition from Major Kaye a detachment of Fusiliers was sent to join the escort. The artillerymen from Ferozepore joined at Kurnaul.

‡ Baird Smith.

Grand Trunk Road, with the river on one side and the Western Jumna Canal on the other, whilst Brigadier Hope Grant, with Cavalry and Horse Artillery, crossed the canal and moved down along its right bank with the object of taking the enemy in flank. 1857. June.

Day was just dawning when Barnard's columns came within fire of the Sepoy's guns. The dispositions which he had made for the attack were excellent, and they were not frustrated by any discovery of a mistaken estimate of the enemy's movements. He found the rebels where he expected to find them. Whilst Showers, with the First Brigade, was to attack upon the right, Graves, with the Second, was to lead his men against the enemy's position on the left; and Grant, on the first sound of the guns, was to recross the canal by the bridge in the rear of the rebel camp, and to take them in flank. The strength of the enemy was known to be in their Artillery. Four heavy guns, Money's Horse Artillery troop, and part of Scott's Battery, were sent in advance to silence their fire, but the guns of the mutineers were of heavier metal than our own, and it was not easy to make an impression on their batteries. For some time the Artillery had the fighting to themselves.* Officers and men were dropping at their guns, and for a little space it seemed doubtful whether they could hold their own. But the British Infantry now deployed into line; and the inspiring mandate to charge the guns went forth to the Seventy-fifth. Then Herbert led out his noble regiment with a ringing cheer, right up to the enemy's batteries, and

June 8. Battle of Budlee-ka-Serai.

* "Light, Kaye, and Fagan, with four heavy guns, bore the brunt for some time, until the brigade of infantry came up and got into line."—*Hervey Greathed's Letters.*—Major Kaye was in command.

1857. June 8. the Second Europeans followed in support. Nothing could resist the impetuous rush of these English soldiers; but the rebels stood well to their guns, and showed that there was some resolute spirits beneath those dusky skins, and that the lessons they had learnt in our camps and cantonments had not been thrown away. Many fought with the courage of desperation, and stood to be bayoneted at their guns. It was not a time for mercy; if it was sought, it was sternly refused.

Meanwhile the Second Brigade, under Graves, charged the enemy's position on the left, and, about the same time, Hope Grant, whose march had been delayed by the state of the roads along which he had advanced, appeared in the enemy's rear with his Cavalry and Horse Artillery. Thus the programme of the preceding day was acted out in all its parts, and the enemy, attacked on every side, had nothing left to them but retreat. At first, they seem to have fallen back in orderly array; but the Lancers, under Yule, fell upon them so fiercely, and the Horse Artillery guns, though impeded by the watercourses, opened so destructive a fire upon them, that they were soon in panic flight, shattered and hopeless. All the guns, and stores, and baggage which they had brought out from the great city were abandoned; and so our first fight before Delhi ended in an assuring victory.

But the day's work was not done. Barnard saw clearly that it was a great thing to make an impression on the enemy, not easily to be effaced, on the first day of the appearance of the Army of Retribution before the walls of Delhi. The sun had risen, and the fury of the June heats was at its height. Our men had marched through the night, they had fought a battle, they were worn and weary, and now the fierce sun was upon them, and there had been but little time to snatch any sustaining food, or to abate the thirst of the Indian summer; but the strong spirit within them overbore the weakness of the flesh, and there was no demand to be made upon them by their leader to which they were not prepared to respond. Barnard's soldierly experiences had taught him that even a force so broken as the advance of the enemy at Budlee-ka-Serai, might rally, and that they might have a strong reserve. He determined, therefore, to push onward, and not to slacken until he had swept the enemy back into Delhi, and had secured such a position for his force as would be an advantageous base for future operations. From Budlee-ka-Serai the road diverges into two branches, the one a continuation of the Grand Trunk leading to the suburb of Subzee-mundee, and the other leading to the old British Cantonments. Stretching in front of these two positions, and forming, as it were, the base of a triangle, of which the two roads were the sides, was a long rocky ridge overlooking the city. At the point of divergence, Barnard separated his force, and sending Wilson with one division along the former road, led the other himself down to the Ridge. There he found the enemy posted in some strength with heavy guns; but another dexterous flank movement turned their position, and, before they could change their line, the Sixtieth Rifles, the Second Europeans, and Money's Troop were sweeping along the Ridge; and soon Wilson, who had fought his way through the Subzee-mundee, and driven the enemy from their shelter there, appeared at the other end, and the rebels saw that all was lost. There was nothing left for them now but to seek safety behind the walls of

1857. June 8.

1857. June 8.

the city. From those walls their comrades, looking out towards the scene of action, could see the smoke and flame which pronounced that the Sepoys' Lines, in our old cantonments, were on fire. That day's fighting had deprived them of their shelter outside the walls, and given us the finest possible base for the conduct of our future operations against the city.*

Results of the battle.

So the victory of the 8th of June was complete, and it remained for us only to count what we had gained and what we had lost by that morning's fighting. The loss of the enemy is computed at three hundred and fifty men; and they had left in our hands twenty-six guns, with some serviceable ammunition, which we much wanted.† Our own loss was small, considering the dashing character of the work that had been done. Four officers and forty-seven men

* In these first operations, as in all others, as will subsequently appear, the Sirmoor Battalion did excellent service. Major Reid thus describes their conduct on the 8th: "About one o'clock P.M. we reached the Ridge, when I was directed by General Barnard to occupy Hindoo Rao's house, which is within twelve hundred yards of the Moree Bastion. Had just made ourselves comfortable, when the alarm was sounded. In ten minutes the mutineers were seen coming up towards Hindoo Rao's house in force. I went out with my own regiment and two companies of Rifles, and drove them back into the city. This, however, was not accomplished till five P.M., so that we were under arms for sixteen hours. Heat fearful. My little fellows behaved splendidly, and were cheered by every European regiment. It was the only Native regiment with the force, and I may say every eye was upon it. The General was anxious to see what the Goorkahs could do, and if we were to be trusted. They had (because it was a Native regiment) doubts about us; but I think they are now satisfied." It is true, as stated, that the Sirmoor Battalion was the only Native regiment engaged on our side; but there were other Native detachments. The Sappers from Meerut fought well, and were commended in Sir H. Barnard's despatch, as was also the Contingent of the Jheend Rajah. And Jan Fishan Khan, with his horsemen, did gallant service. Flushed with the excitement of the battle, the Afghan chief is said to have declared that another such day would make him a Christian.

† The statement in the text is given on the authority of Sir H. Barnard's official despatch. But the number of guns captured on the 8th of June is set down at *thirteen* in Major Norman's Narrative, Major Reid's Extracts from Letters and Notes, and in the "History of the Siege of Delhi, by an Officer who served there," &c. Norman has specified in detail the nature of the captured ordnance, and he is notable for his accuracy.

were killed in the encounters of that day, and a hundred and thirty-four men were wounded or missing. Among those who received their death-wounds at Budlee-ka-Serai was the chief of Sir Henry Barnard's Staff. Colonel Chester, Adjutant-General of the Army, was shot down, almost at the commencement of the action. As he lay there, in agony, with young Barnard, the General's son and aide-de-camp, vainly endeavouring to help him, he asked the young officer to raise his head, so that he might see the wound that was rending him; and, having seen it, he knew that he was dying. Telling Barnard that nothing could be done for him, he begged his young friend to leave him to his fate. Then presently the spirit passed away from his body: and, at sunset, all that was left of the Adjutant-General of the Army was laid in the grave. To the Commander of the Delhi Force this must have been a heavy loss, for Chester possessed all the knowledge and experience which Barnard lacked; and the Adjutant-General was a brave soldier and a man of sound judgment, and his advice, in any difficult conjuncture, would have been wisely received with respect.* But Chester had risen in the Department, and the time was coming when departmental experience and traditionary knowledge were to be stripped of their splendid vestments. And History, without any injurious reflection upon his character, may declare that the incident was not all evil that

1857. June 8.

* "Among the slain was unhappily Colonel Charles Chester, Adjutant-General of the Army, a brave and experienced soldier, whose loss thus early in the campaign was a grave and lamentable misfortune; for his sound judgment and ripe knowledge would have been precious in council as in action."—*Baird Smith's unpublished Memoir.* Two other officers of the Staff were killed, Captain C. W. Russell and Captain J. W. Delamain. The fourth officer who lost his life was Lieutenant Harrison of the Seventy-fifth; Colonel Herbert of that regiment was among the wounded.

1857. June 8. in due course brought Neville Chamberlain and John Nicholson down to Delhi.

But it is not by lists of killed and wounded, or returns of captured ordnance, that the value of the first victory before Delhi is to be estimated. It had given us an admirable base of operations—a commanding military position—open in the rear to the lines along which thenceforth our reinforcements and supplies, and all that we looked for to aid us in the coming struggle, were to be brought. And great as was this gain to us, in a military sense, the moral effect was scarcely less; for behind this ridge lay our old cantonments, from which a month before the English had fled for their lives. On the parade-ground the Head-Quarters of Barnard's Force were now encamped, and the familiar flag of the Feringhees was again to be seen from the houses of the Imperial City.

BOOK V.—PROGRESS OF REBELLION IN UPPER INDIA.

[MAY—JULY, 1857.]

CHAPTER I.

THE NORTH-WEST PROVINCES—STATE OF AFFAIRS AT BENARES—STATE OF THE CITY—THE OUTBREAK AT AZIMGURH—ARRIVAL OF GENERAL NEILL—DISARMING OF THE THIRTY-SEVENTH—THE MUTINY AT JAUNPORE—AFFAIRS AT ALLAHABAD—MUTINY OF THE SIXTH—APPEARANCE OF GENERAL NEILL—THE FORT SECURED—RETRIBUTORY MEASURES.

1857. May.

IT has been seen that whilst Lord Canning was eagerly exhorting the chiefs of the Army to move with all despatch upon Delhi, never doubting that a crushing blow would soon descend upon the guilty city, he was harassed by painful thoughts of the unprotected state of the country, along the whole great line of the Ganges to Allahabad and thence through the Doab to Agra. There was one English regiment at Dinapore; there was one English regiment at Agra; and besides these the whole strength of our fighting men consisted of a handful of white artillerymen and a few invalided soldiers of the Company's European Army. And, resting upon the broad waters of the Ganges, there was the great military cantonment of Cawnpore, with a large European population, a number of Sepoy regiments, and few, if any, white troops. To all these unprotected places on the banks of the Ganges and the Jumna, and the more inland stations dependent upon

1857. May. them, the most anxious thoughts of the Governor-General were now turned, and his most earnest efforts directed. If the Native soldiery, who were thickly strewn along these lines, not only in all the military cantonments, but in all the chief civil stations, guardians alike of the property of our Government and the lives of our people, had risen in that month of May, nothing short of the miraculous interposition of Providence could have saved us from swift destruction.

But in all that defenceless tract of country over which the apprehensions of the Governor-General were then ranging, and towards which he was then eagerly sending up reinforcements, rebellion was for a time in a state of suspension. Whether it was that a day had been fixed for a simultaneous rising of all the Sepoy regiments, or whether, without any such concerted arrangements, they were waiting to see what the English would do to avenge their brethren slaughtered at Meerut and Delhi, the Native soldiery at the stations below those places suffered day after day to pass without striking a blow. No tidings of fresh disaster from the great towns, or from the military cantonments dotting the Gangetic provinces, followed closely upon the news of the capture of the Imperial City. But everywhere the excitement was spreading, alike in the Lines and the Bazaars, and it was plain that many weeks would not elapse without a fresh development of trouble; more dreadful, perhaps, than the first growth, of which he already had before him the record.

ares. A little more than four hundred miles from Calcutta, in the direction of the north-west, lies the city of Benares. Situated on a steep sloping bank of the Ganges, which its buildings overhang, it is the most picturesque of the river-cities of Hindostan. Its countless temples, now beautiful and now grotesque, with the elaborate devices of sculptors of different ages and different schools; its spacious mosques with their tall minarets grand against the sky;* the richly carved balconies of its houses; its swarming marts and market-places, wealthy with the produce of many countries and the glories of its own looms; its noble ghauts, or flights of landing-stairs leading from the great thoroughfares to the river-brink, and ever crowded with bathers and drawers of the sacred water; the many-shaped vessels moored against the river-banks, and the stately stream flowing on for ever between them, render this great Hindu city, even as seen by the fleshly eye, a spectacle of unsurpassed interest. But the interest deepens painfully in the mind of the Christian traveller, who regards this swarming city, with all its slatternly beauty, as the favoured home of the great Brahminical superstition. It is a city given up to idolatry, with, in the estimation of millions of people, an odour of sanctity about it which draws pilgrims from all parts of India to worship at its shrines or to die at its ghauts. Modern learning might throw doubt upon the traditional antiquity of the place, but could not question the veneration in which it is held as the sacred city of the Hindoos, the cherished residence of the Pundits and the Priests.

1857. May.

But neither sacerdotal nor scholastic influences had softened the manners or tempered the feelings of the

* A recent writer states that it is computed that there are fourteen hundred and fifty-four temples and two hundred and seventy-two mosques in the city of Benares.—*See Sherring's "Sacred City of the Hindus."*

1857. May. people of Benares.* There had always been something more than the average amount of discontent and disaffection among the citizens; and now in the summer of 1857 this was increased by the high price of provisions—always believed to be one of the curses of British rule.† And there was another source of special danger. Some of the most disreputable members of the Delhi Family had been long resident at Benares, where they had assumed all the airs of the Imperial Family, and persistently endeavoured in secret to sow resentment in the city against the English. These wretched Mogul Princes, it was not doubted, would be well disposed, in such a conjuncture, to foment rebellion among the Sepoys; and it was scarcely less probable that the State prisoners—Sikhs, Mahrattas, Mahomedans, and others, who had been made to find an asylum in Benares, would find ample means of gratifying their love of intrigue in dangerous efforts against the power that had brought them to the dust.‡

* The population of Benares is estimated at about two hundred thousand, of which an unusually large proportion are Hindoos. The author of the "Red Pamphlet" computes the number at three hundred thousand, and Macaulay rhetorically amplifies it into "half a million." In May, 1857, Mr. Tucker, the Commissioner, writing to Lord Canning, speaks of "the huge, bigoted city of Benares, with a hundred and eighty thousand of the worst population in the country." This is probably rather under the number, but it is to be remembered that there is in Benares always an immense floating population of pilgrims from other provinces.

† "The city, always the most turbulent in India, was now the more dangerous from the severity with which the high price of corn pressed upon the poorer classes; the Poorbeah Sepoys, who had been more or less restless since the beginning of March, now publicly called on their gods to deliver them from the Feringhees, clubbed together to send messengers westward for intelligence, and, finally, sent away their Gooroo (priest), lest, as they said, in the troubles which were coming, he should suffer any hurt."—*Report of Mr. Taylor, Officiating Joint-Magistrate.*

‡ Major Charters Macpherson, who had been Governor-General's Agent at Benares, before the appointment was incorporated with the Commissionership, has thus described some of the leading features of the population of Benares: "These attenuated shadows of the regality of Delhi—these strong, noble, robust, and workman-like

1857 May. The Secrole Cantonment.

At a distance of about three miles, inland, from the city of Benares, is the suburb of Secrole. There was the English military cantonment—there were the Courts of Law and the great Gaol—the English Church and the English Cemetery—the Government College—the several Missionary Institutes—the Hospitals and Asylums—the Public Gardens, and the private residences of the European officers and their subordinates. The military force consisted of half a company of European Artillery and three Native regiments. These were the Thirty-seventh Regiment of Native Infantry, the Sikh Regiment of Loodhianah, and the Thirteenth Regiment of Irregular Cavalry—in all, some two thousand men, watched by some thirty English gunners. The force was commanded by Brigadier George Ponsonby.* He was an officer of the Native Cavalry, who fifteen years before, in the affair of Purwan-durrah—that charge, which was no charge, and which was at once so heroic and so dastardly—had covered himself with glory. The names of Fraser and Ponsonby, who flung themselves almost alone upon the horsemen of Dost Mahomed, will live as long as that great war is remembered, and will be enshrined in the calendar of our English heroes. In spite of those fifteen years, the incident was still fresh in men's minds in India, and there was confidence in the thought that Ponsonby commanded at Benares.

There other good soldiers also were assembled;

Sikh chiefs, whom my heart takes in straight; then the shroffs, merchant-zemindars, and bankers of four hundred years' standing, and insurance companies of Benares—the very essence, pride, and heart of Gangetic commerce, or rather half-heart, Mirzapore holding the other ventricle; then, also, its Pundit-dom in full strength yet, all this has passed before me most curiously."—*Memorials of an Indian Officer*.

* In the early part of May, Ponsonby had not taken command. Colonel Gordon then commanded the station.

1857. May. The civilians at Benares.

and civilians too, with the best courage of the soldier and more than his wonted wisdom. Mr. Henry Carre Tucker—one of a family famous alike for courage and for capacity—was Commissioner of Benares. Mr. Frederick Gubbins, who, some time before, as Magistrate, had acquired by a grand display of energy in a local crisis an immense ascendancy over the minds of the people, was now the Judge. Mr. Lind was the Magistrate of Benares. It is impossible to over-rate their exertions.* As soon as the fatal news arrived from Meerut and Delhi, they saw clearly the danger which beset them, and the work which lay before them, to preserve our old supremacy in such a place. The crisis was one which demanded that the civil and military authorities should take counsel together. Warned by the wholesale butcheries of Meerut and Delhi, they deemed it a point of essential urgency that there should be a common understanding as to the place of resort for women and children and non-combatants in the event of a sudden surprise or alarm. A council, therefore, was held; but it would seem that no definite plan of action was formed. On the following day two military officers called upon Mr. Lind, with a proposal that greatly startled him. One was Captain William Olpherts, commanding the Artillery, an officer of good repute, brave as a lion, but of uncertain temper, who had served under Williams of Kars, in the auxiliary operations connected with the Crimean War. The other was Captain Watson, of the En-

* "The magistrate and judge (Messrs. Lind and Gubbins) exerted themselves with great skill to maintain the peace of the city; now patrolling with parties of Sowars, now persuading Bunyahs to lower the price of corn, now listening to the tales of spies, who reported clearly the state of feeling in the city, and told the minds of the Sepoys far more truly than the officers in command."—*Mr. Taylor's Report.*

gineers. Their opinions were entitled to be received with respect; but when they suggested the propriety of an immediate retreat to the strong fortress of Chunar (eighteen miles distant from Benares), Mr. Lind resented the proposal, and said that nothing would induce him to leave his post. When his visitors had taken their departure, the Magistrate hastened to Mr. Gubbins, and, returning to his own house with the Judge, was presently joined by Mr. Tucker and by Colonel Gordon, who temporarily commanded the station. Olpherts and Watson had intimated that Gordon had approved the plan of retreat to Chunar; but when in answer to a question, which he put to Mr. Gubbins, the civilian said, "I will go on my knees to you not to leave Benares!" Gordon promptly answered, "I am glad to hear you say so. I was persuaded against my will." Mr. Tucker had never doubted that it was their duty to stand fast.* So it was resolved that no sign of anxiety should be made manifest, either to the soldiery or to the people; that every one should remain in his own home, as in quiet times, and that there should be no open display of arming, or any other symptom of distrust. But in the event of a sudden rising either of the soldiery or of the people, all the Christian residents not

1857. May.

* Mr. Taylor, however, in his official narrative, says: "They both (Lind and Gubbins) returned to Mr. Lind's house to discuss the best means of operation, and were soon joined by Mr. Tucker, the Commissioner, and Colonel Gordon. When the former alluded to the plan (the retreat to Chunar) in terms which seemed to imply he approved it, Mr. Lind condemned it most strongly," &c. &c. It is possible that for "former" we should read "latter." In a letter before me (May 19), addressed to Lord Canning, Mr. Tucker says: "One officer of high rank and much experience recommended that we should make a night march, and shut ourselves up in Chunar. Colonel Gordon, commanding the station, Mr. Gubbins, the judge, and Mr. Lind, the magistrate, unanimously agreed with me that to show any open distrust in this manner would cause a panic, the bazaars would be closed, and both the troops and the city would be up against us. We, therefore, determined to face the danger without moving a muscle."

1857. May.

engaged in suppressing it were to seek refuge in the Mint.

An interval of quiet.

And so the daily goings on of social life fell back again into the old groove; and some even found, in the prospect before them, causes of increased hopefulness and bountiful anticipations of a pleasure-laden future. Were there not European troops coming up from Dinapore and Calcutta, and would there not be gay doings at Benares? Those whose duty it was to know what was going on in the surrounding country, heard this careless talk with something of a shudder, but wisely refrained from saying anything to dash the cheerfulness of the talkers. "My game," wrote the Commissioner to the Governor-General, "is to keep people in good spirits; so I keep my bad news to myself, and circulate all the good." Meanwhile, he and his colleagues were doing all that could be done, without noise or excitement, to restore confidence alike to the soldiery and to the townspeople. It was no small thing to supply an antidote to the famine-prices which were then ruling in the markets of the city, and this might be done, so far at least as the evil bore upon the soldiery, without interfering with the privileges of the sellers. So the Commissioner guaranteed, on the part of Government, that for every rupee paid by the Sepoys for their *ottah*, a certain number of pounds, as in ordinary times, should be given, whilst the Judge and the Magistrate went about in the city endeavouring (and with good success) to convince the chief importers of grain that it would be sound policy in the end to keep down their prices to the normal rates.* These things had a good effect; but the

* "I guaranteed Ponsonby yesterday in issuing ottah to the troops at sixteen seers, and trust you will bear me out. It is ill talking to a hungry man. All the bazaars are open, but very naturally the grain-sellers are apprehensive, and raising their prices. Gubbins and Lind

utter weakness of the European force in Benares stared these brave and sagacious men in the face at every turn, and they felt that, under Providence, nothing could save them until the arrival of succour, except the calmness and confidence of their demeanour in the hour of danger. "So great is my confidence," wrote the Commissioner, "that I have not a single weapon, beyond a heavy-handled riding-whip, in my possession. In dealing with a parcel of children, which Sepoys and all Natives are, moral force goes a great way." And it should be noted here, as an encouraging symptom, that about this time all the Sikh Sirdars, then prisoners at Benares, offered their services to Mr. Tucker—and it was believed in good faith—to act as a body-guard to him, and to protect his house. 1857. May.

First arrival of reinforcements. May 24.

And the confidence thus felt—which in the breasts of some, at least, was a sustaining trust in the over-flowing mercy of God—was made manifest before all the people of Benares, by a practical illustration of a remarkable kind. On the 24th of May, a detachment of fourty-four men of the Eighty-fourth Queen's, who had been pushed up by the Governor-General by dawk, arrived from Chinsurah, near Calcutta. This reinforcement would have more than doubled the reliable military strength on which the security of the English at Benares was to depend. From every station along the great line of country between Delhi and Calcutta had come the despairing

have been in the city all the morning trying to show the principal importers the good policy of keeping down prices as much as possible."—*Mr. H. C. Tucker to Lord Canning, May* 23, 1857. "Through the exertions of Mr. Gubbins, assisted by Mr. Lind, and his influence with the wealthy merchants, the price of grain in the Bazaar has fallen from twelve or thirteen seers to fifteen seers (for the rupee). This is a great triumph of confidence, and has reassured the multitude wonderfully."—*The Same to the Same, May* 26, 1857.

1857. May 24. cry, "For God's sake send us Europeans!" And now that this help had come to the first of the great undefended stations—small, it is true, in numbers, but still at such a time an immense relief and reinforcement to the little band of Christian men, who were trusting in God, and maintaining a bold front before their fellows—they bethought themselves of others who were in greater need than themselves, and suffered the welcome detachment to pass on to Cawnpore; and that too at a time when they seemed to be in their greatest peril. For news had just come that the Seventeenth Regiment, at Azimgurh, some sixty miles distant, was on the verge, if not in the full stream, of open mutiny, and the Benares regiments seemed only to be waiting for a signal from their comrades in the neighbourhood. Still they thought more of others than of themselves. Sir Henry Lawrence had written earnestly to urge upon them the great need of Cawnpore, where General Wheeler was threatened by a dangerous enemy; and so Ponsonby and Tucker, taking counsel together, determined to let the succour which had been sent to them pass on to the relief of others. "Gordon," wrote the Commissioner, "thinks that we have run too great a risk in sending on at once the parties of the Eighty-fourth, whom you sent on to us by dawk; but Sir Henry Lawrence wrote to me so urgently to send every man who could be spared, that Ponsonby and I concurred in thinking that it was our duty to run some risk here, and stretch a point for the relief of Cawnpore. Besides, we argued that nothing could show better to the suspected Thirty-seventh Regiment than that when we had got Europeans from Calcutta, and placed our guns in safety, we did not care to detain, but sent them on straight to join the troops collecting above. This is a real mark of confidence in the Sepoys and in ourselves. Besides, it will do good at Allahabad, and along the road, to see Europeans moving up, party after party, so fast. So if anything does happen to Benares before other Europeans join, your lordship must excuse the despatch of these forty-four men as an error of judgment on the right side." Other Europeans had been expected from Dinapore, but scarcely had the men of the Eighty-fourth been pressed forward, when tidings came that the detachment of the Tenth from Dinapore, which had been proceeding upwards to the relief of Benares, had "stuck fast at Chapra." "So all hopes for the present," it was added, "from that quarter are gone." "Brave Brigadier Ponsonby," continued the Commissioner, "calls the failure of the Dinapore relief 'a slight contretemps, somewhat unpleasant, but it cannot be helped.' I am glad we did not know of it yesterday evening, as it might have prevented the despatch of the forty-four men to Cawnpore." But, next day, when further reinforcements arrived, they were all hurried onward to Cawnpore. "I had another telegram this morning," wrote Mr. Tucker to Lord Canning on the 27th, "from Sir Henry Lawrence, begging me to spare no expense in hurrying up European aid. We send up all the men we get from Calcutta. Thirty-eight more will go this evening. We do not keep one for ourselves." Even the detachment of the Tenth from Dinapore was to be sent on "the moment it arrives." "Your lordship may feel assured," added the Commissioner, "that nothing will be left undone to insure the quickest possible relief to Cawnpore. I have let Sir H. Wheeler know what we are doing to relieve him, as Hope is half the battle."

1857. May.

Diversities of English manhood.

Thus, already, was the great national courage of the English beginning to take many shapes. Whilst some, girding up their loins, were eager to anticipate danger and to strike at once, smiting everywhere, hip and thigh, like the grand remorseless heroes of the Old Testament, others were fain to oppose to the mass of rebellion that was surging upwards to the surface, the calm impassive fortitude of patient resolution, born of an abiding faith in God. Men of different temperaments and different convictions then wrought or waited according to the faith that was in them, with self-devotion beyond all praise. There was need of strenuous action in those days; but there was need also of that calm confidence which betrays no sign of misgiving, and the very quietude of which indicates a consciousness of strength. Restricted sympathy and narrow toleration are among the manifestations of our national character, not less than the broad many-sided courage of which I have spoken; and therefore it has happened that sometimes rash judgments have been passed by men incapable of understanding other evidences of bravery than those which their own would put forth in similar crises.* But it may be easier to go out to battle with death than quietly to await its coming. The energy that stimulates the one is less rare than the patience that inspires the other. But this quiet courage must be content to wait for quiet times to be estimated at its true worth.†

* Charles Dickens, in a notice of the Life of Walter Savage Landor, which I have read since the passage in the text was written, says that Landor's "animosities were chiefly referable to his singular inability to dissociate other people's ways of thinking from his own." But I am inclined to think that this inability so far from being singular, is the commonest thing in the world.

† How utterly free the Commissioner was from the least leaven of official jealousy, and how eager he was to do justice and to get justice done to his colleagues, may be seen

Henry Tucker was a Christian gentleman, in whom the high courage of our race took this latter form. He went about, fearless and confident, saying to himself, "The Lord is my rock, my fortress, and my deliverer; the God of my rock, in Him will I trust. He is my shield and the horn of my salvation; my high tower, and my refuge; my Saviour."* And in this abundant, overflowing confidence and resignation he seemed to despise all human means of defence, and almost to regard defensive efforts—"secondary means"—as a betrayal of want of faith in the Almighty. "Rather against Ponsonby's and my wish," he wrote to the Governor-General, "but by the advice of Messrs. Gubbins and Lind, and at the entreaty of the European residents, arms and ammunition have, this day, been issued out to all who required them. I hope that it will make their minds easy, and that they will rest quiet. I am so thankful we have no place of defence here. We have nowhere to run to, so must stand firm—and hitherto there has not been one particle of panic and confusion." And he said that if the enemy came he would go out to meet them with a bible in his hand, as David had gone out to meet Goliath with a pebble and a sling. He rode out in the most exposed places, evening after evening, with his daughter, as in quiet times; and when some one suggested to him that the

1857. May.

Henry Carre Tucker.

in the following extracts from letters written by him to Lord Canning: "Mr. F. Gubbins is a very superior man, and will make a model commissioner. I feel very thankful to have such a coadjutor here to make up for my own great deficiencies." And in another letter the Commissioner says: "Mr. Gubbins is carrying on the work in this district most energetically. Under the blessing of Providence, he has been the means of securing great peace and quiet in the city and neighbourhood." And again: "I hope your lordship will find time for a letter of *hearty* thanks to Mr. F. Gubbins for his beautiful police arrangements and general exertions, in which Mr. Lind has aided greatly."

* He wrote to Lord Canning that the 22nd chapter of Samuel II. (which contains these words) had been "their stand-by."

1857. May. hat which he wore, being of a peculiar character, would clearly indicate the Commissioner, and afford a mark for a rebel shot, he said that he was as safe in one head-dress as in another, and had no thought of a change.

Language and action of this kind might be regarded as mere imbecility. It is not strange, indeed, that a man of Mr. Tucker's character was described as an amiable enthusiast quite unequal to the occasion; for his courage was not of the popular type, and his character not intelligible to the multitude. But, even looked upon in the light of mere human wisdom, the course which was favoured by the Benares Commissioner had much, at that time, to recommend it. For as the absolute weakness of the European community, with only thirty effective soldiers to defend them, forbade any successful resort to arms, it was sound policy thus to preserve a quietude of demeanour, significant of confidence—confidence both in our own security and in the loyalty of those who surrounded and who might have crushed us in an hour.* In continual communication, not only with Lord Canning at Calcutta, but with the chiefs of all the great stations, as Dinapore, Cawnpore, Lucknow, and Agra, Henry Tucker knew what was being done in some quarters, and what was needed in others, to meet the difficulties of the crisis. He knew that help was coming from below; and that if rebellion were smouldering either in the Lines or in the City, the longer it could be left to smoulder,

* I do not wish it to be inferred from this that I think the serving out of arms and ammunition to the European residents was a mistake; but I can appreciate Mr. Tucker's motives, and understand his reasons for inscribing "Thorough" on his policy of inaction. It will be seen presently that Lord Canning, though he admired the calm confidence of Mr. Tucker, sided with Mr. Gubbins in this matter, and I do not doubt that he was right.

before bursting into a blaze, the better. The confiding policy was the temporising policy. Those who best knew the character of the Bengal Sepoy, knew that a vague fear, more impressive for its very vagueness, was driving thousands into rebellion; and that the best way to keep things quiet was to do nothing to excite or to alarm. And so the month of May wore on, and European reinforcements came from below; but, in spite of the great temptation to retain them, Tucker and Ponsonby had strength to send them onward to succour others. They knew that they were exposing themselves to the reproaches of their comrades; but they felt that they could bear even this. "You and I," wrote Ponsonby to the Commissioner, "can bear much in such a cause. To aid the distressed is not so very wicked."

1857 May.

Encouragement from Lord Canning.

The high bearing of the chief officers at Benares excited the admiration of the Governor-General. And in the midst of all his urgent duties—his pressing cares and anxieties—Lord Canning found, or made, time, to write letters of stirring encouragement to all, of whose good deeds he had ample assurance. Whether the well-doer were a General Officer, a Civil or Political Commissioner, or a young regimental subaltern, Lord Canning wrote to him, with his own hand, a letter of cordial thanks, full of frank kindliness, which braced up the recipient to new exertions and made him ever love the writer. He knew the effect at such a time of prompt recognition of good service, and he felt that such recognition, under the hand of secretaries, public or private, would lose half its influence for good. He had a wonderful grace of letter-writing; and there are

1857. May. many now who treasure up, as their most cherished possessions, the few expressive lines, warm from the heart, in which, amidst dangers and difficulties that might well have excused graver omissions, the Governor-General poured forth his gratitude to his subordinates for good aid of any kind—for wise counsel, for fertility of resource, for active heroism, or for patient courage.

Thus, on the 23rd of May, he wrote to Mr. Tucker: "Although it represents a most critical state of things at Benares, it satisfies me that the crisis is met with calm courage, based upon that which alone is the foundation of true courage, and that events as they arise will be dealt with temperately, firmly, and with sound judgment. You have, indeed, a precious stake upon the issue. I sympathise deeply with your family. If they need to be assured of it, I beg you to tell them that not an hour has been, or will be, lost in sending aid to Benares, and wherever else it may be most urgently required. . . . Come what may, do not fear any aspersions or misrepresentations. No one shall be ignorant how nobly the authority of our Government, and the honour and dignity of Englishmen, has been upheld at Benares."

May 30. And to Mr. Gubbins he wrote, a week afterwards, saying: "If I had more leisure for writing letters, I should not have left you so long without a word of thanks for your admirable and most judicious exertions. I know from Mr. Tucker's letters and messages, and also from other quarters, how much is due to you and to Mr. Lind, and I beg you both to believe that I am most grateful for it. You have all had a difficult game to play—if ever there was one; and your success has been hitherto complete. I pray that you may carry it through. You have done really good service in the Bazaars, in obtaining a reduction of the price of grain." And he then added, with reference to the difference of opinion which had prevailed respecting the arming of the Europeans, "I think you quite right in recommending that arms should not be refused to the Europeans, who desired them. Your self-confidence has been made quite plain by the calm front you have already shown to all danger; and I do not believe that any of the advantages thereby gained will be sacrificed by the adoption of a common-sense precaution, which does not necessarily imply mistrust of those more immediately around you, when, as is too surely the case, there is abundance of danger at a little distance."* 1857. May 30.

But although outwardly there was fair promise of continued tranquillity, as the month of May came to a close a crisis was, indeed, approaching. The birth of June was ushered in by the familiar work of the incendiary. A line of Sepoys' huts recently vacated was fired; and it was found that the wretched scum of Delhi royalty were in close communication with the incendiaries. Then news came that the Sepoy regiment at Azimgurh, sixty miles off, had revolted. This was the Seventeenth Regiment, under the command of Major Burroughs. It had been believed all along to be tainted, for it had been brigaded with the Nineteenth and Thirty-fourth, which had been ignominiously disbanded, and it was known that some of the men of the former were harboured in its Lines. Its insolence had been manifested unchecked, for Burroughs was not equal to the occasion; and, although the Magistrate, Horne, had himself addressed June, 1857. The mutiny at Azimgurh.

* MS. Correspondence of Lord Canning.

1857. May—June. the Sepoys, and otherwise striven to keep them true to their salt, the evil influences had prevailed, so that before the end of the month the men of the Seventeenth were ripe for revolt.* It happened that just at this critical moment they scented the spoil. The rattle of the rupees was heard in the distance. A treasure-escort was coming in from Goruckpore, under charge of a company of the Seventeenth Sepoys and some horsemen of the Thirteenth Irregular Cavalry, and this was to have been despatched, with the surplus treasure of Azimgurh, to Benares, under command of Lieutenant Palliser, who had been sent from the latter place with a detachment of the Thirteenth to escort it. Five lakhs of rupees had come from Goruckpore, and two lakhs were added to it at Azimgurh; seventy thousand pounds in the hard bright coin of the country, and this was now in the grasp of the Sepoys. The temptation was more than they could resist. So they rose and loudly declared that the treasure should not leave the station. This stern resolution, however, seems to have been lulled for a time, and on the evening of
June 3. the 3rd of June, the treasure-escort marched out from Azimgurh. It was felt, however, that the danger had not been escaped, and that at any moment the Sepoys might break into open rebellion. The officers and their wives were dining at the mess of the Seventeenth, when all their anxieties were confirmed by the well-known warning voice of the guns. It was plain that the firing was in the direction of the parade-ground. A beating of drums was soon heard; and no words were needed to express the assurance of

* On May 24, when some men impudently rejected extra cartridges which were served out to them, and afterwards violently assaulted a Native officer, Major Burroughs found himself too weak to punish.

all that the Sepoys had risen.* There was then a scene of confusion, which it is not easy accurately to describe. The ladies and non-combatants hurried off to the Cutcherry, which had been fortified by the Magistrate and his colleagues, and there barricaded themselves. Meanwhile the Sepoys, having shot their Quartermaster and their Quartermaster-Sergeant,† but, with the strange inconsistency of conduct which distinguished all their movements, having spared and, indeed, protected the rest of their officers, hurried after the treasure-escort to seize the coin on the road to Benares. And with them went the myrmidons of the Police-force, which Horne had made vast efforts to strengthen for the protection of the gaol, but which had displayed its zeal in the hour of our trouble by releasing the prisoners, and giving up the houses of the English to plunder and conflagration. 1857. June.

When they swarmed down upon him, all armed and accoutred and eager for the spoil, Palliser found that he was helpless. The troopers of the Thirteenth Irregulars were wavering. They were not so far gone in rebellion as to desire the death of their officers, but a strong national sympathy restrained them from acting against their countrymen. The officers, therefore, were saved. But the treasure was lost. The Sepoys of the Seventeenth‡ carried it back

* There were two post guns stationed at Azimgurh. These the mutineers seized at the commencement of the outbreak. They were afterwards taken into Oude.

† Lieutenant Hutchinson and Quartermaster-Sergeant Lewis.

‡ It is stated on the authority of Lieutenant Constable of the Seventeenth, that the Sepoys "behaved with romantic courtesy." "They formed a square round their officers, and said that they not only would not touch, but would protect them, only that there were some of the mutineers who had sworn the death of particular officers, and therefore they begged the whole party to take to their carriages and be off at once. 'But how are we to get our carriages?' said they, 'seeing that they are scattered all through the station.' 'Ah, we will fetch them,' said the Sepoys; and so they did, and gave the party an escort for ten miles out of the station on the

1857. June. to Azimgurh, whilst the Irregulars escorted their officers on to Benares. Meanwhile, the European residents of the former place had fled to Ghazeepore; and when the Sepoys returned to their old station, they found all European authority gone, and the official functionaries, civil and military, swept out of it to a man. So, flushed with success, they marched off to Fyzabad in military array, with all the pomp and panoply of war.

The crisis at Benares. June 4, 1857.

When news of these events reached Benares, crusted over in the first instance with some exaggerations, it was plain that the hour was approaching when tranquillity could no longer be maintained. But the vigorous activity of Gubbins and the calm composure of Tucker, holding rebellion in restraint whilst succours were far off, had already saved Benares; for now fresh reinforcements were at hand, and with them one who knew well how to turn them to account. After despatching his men, as has been already told,* by the railway to Raneegunge, Colonel Neill had made his way, by train and horse-dawk, to Benares with the utmost possible despatch, eager to avenge the blood of his slaughtered countrymen. And with this Madras Colonel came the first assertion of English manhood that had come from the South to the rescue of our people in the Gangetic provinces. Leading the way to future conquests, he came to strike and to destroy. He was one of those who wisely thought

Arrival of Neill.

road to Ghazeepore. It has been remarked that to complete the romance they ought to have offered the officers a month's pay out of the treasure they were plundering."—*Annals of the Indian Rebellion, Part IV.* This is somewhat inconsistent with the statement (*Red Pamphlet*) that the Sepoys of the Seventeenth implored the Irregulars to slay their officers, "appealing to religion, nationality, love of money, even offering 5000*l.* for each head." These inconsistencies, however, were fast becoming common phenomena.

* *Ante*, p. 132.

from the first, that to strike promptly and to strike vigorously would be to strike mercifully; and he went to the work before him with a stern resolution not to spare. Both from the North and from the South, at this time, the first great waves of the tide of conquest were beginning to set in towards the centres of the threatened provinces. From one end of the line of danger, Canning, and from the other, Lawrence, was sending forth his succours—neither under-estimating the magnitude of the peril, but both confident of the final result. It was the work of the latter, as will be told hereafter, to rescue Delhi, whilst the former was straining every effort to secure the safety of Benares, Allahabad, Agra, Cawnpore, Lucknow, and other lesser places dependent upon them. And now assistance had really come to the first of these places. A detachment of Madras Fusiliers was at Benares, and the men of the Tenth Foot, from Dinapore, whose arrival had been delayed by an accident, had also made their appearance. It was determined, therefore, that the Sepoys should be disarmed.

1857. June 4.

The question of disarming.

But a question then arose as to the hour of disarming. The first idea was, that the regiment should be paraded on the following morning, and that then the several companies, after an assuring explanation, should be called upon to lay down their arms. But there were those in Benares, to whom the thought of even an hour's delay was an offence and an abomination. When work of this kind is to be done, it should be done, they thought, promptly. Stimulated by the intelligence from Azimgurh, and suspecting what was in store for them, the Sepoys might rise before morning, and then all our councils and cautions would be vain. The chief command was in

1857. June 4. Ponsonby's hands, and it was for him to give the word for disarming. It appears that Colonel Gordon, who had ascertained that the more turbulent spirits of the city were in communication with the Sepoys, accompanied the Brigadier to the house of the Commissioner to consult with him. Tucker suggested that they should call on Gubbins; so they went to the Judge's residence, and there they received ample confirmation of the reports which Gordon had heard. Soon afterwards they met Colonel Neill, who was eager for immediate action;* and, after some dis-

* The circumstances conducing to this change of plan have been variously stated. Mr. Taylor, in his official report, already quoted, says: "It appears that as Brigadier Ponsonby was returning home after the Council, he met Colonel Neill, who recommended him to disarm the corps at once. Disregarding all other consideration, he hurried to the parade-ground." But in a letter before me, written by Brigadier Ponsonby in July, that officer states that, "On the 4th of June Lieutenant-Colonel Gordon, commanding the regiment of Loodhianah, called and informed me that he had reason to believe the men of the Thirty-seventh Native Infantry were entering into a conspiracy with some of the bad characters of the city, in view to the subversion of the British power in Benares. After some conversation on the subject, in which I ascertained from the Lieutenant-Colonel that he considered that he could rely on the fidelity of his own regiment, we agreed to go together to the Commissioner, Mr. Tucker, aud to acquaint him with what had been communicated. We proceeded to Mr. Tucker, and on broaching the subject of our visit, he proposed that we should go to Mr. F. Gubbins, who lived close at hand, and we did so. Mr. Gubbins, it appeared, had heard from his spies that which not only confirmed Colonel Gordon's report, but gave much more detailed information as to the secret proceedings of the men of the Thirty-seventh Native Infantry. Colonel Neill came in while Mr. Gubbins was speaking, and soon afterwards the Brigade-Major, Captain Dodgson, entered to report that the treasure, which was on its way from Azimgurh to Benares under a guard of fifty men of the Irregular Cavalry, had been plundered by the Seventeenth Native Infantry—the guard of the Irregulars having connived at the deed. It was immediately felt that this circumstance, occurring in such close proximity to Benares, rendered the adoption at once of some strong measures imperative, and Lieutenant-Colonel Gordon proposed the disarming of the Thirty-seventh Native Infantry, to which I acceded. There was some discussion as to whether this should be attempted at once, or at ten A.M. on the following day. Mr. Gubbins having expressed his opinion that emissaries from the Seventeenth Native Infantry would soon be in Benares, it was settled to disarm the Thirty-seventh at five o'clock, and it being now past four, it was also arranged to keep the measure as quiet as possible in order that the regiment might not be on its guard." Nothing can be more distinct than this. But Colonel

cussion, the Brigadier consented to hold a parade at 1857.
five o'clock, and at once to proceed to the work of June 4.
disarmament.

Then Ponsonby and Gordon went together to the house of the latter, where they found or were joined by Major Barrett of the Thirty-seventh. The Sepoy officer, after the manner of his kind, with that fond and affectionate confidence in his men, which was luring so many to destruction, solemnly protested against the measure, as one which would break their hearts. To this Ponsonby replied, that what he had learnt from Mr. Gubbins had left him no alternative, and that, therefore, it was Barrett's duty to warn the officers to be ready for the five o'clock parade. The Brigadier had ordered his horse to be brought to Gordon's house, and now the two mounted and rode to the parade-ground, to plan the best disposition of the troops. The horse which Ponsonby rode had not been ridden for a month. It was fresh and restive,

Neill, with equal distinctness, declares that Ponsonby and Gordon called upon him, and that he (Neill) recommended the afternoon parade. In his official despatch he says: "Brigadier Ponsonby consulted with me about taking the muskets from the Thirty-seventh, leaving them their side-arms. He proposed waiting until the following morning to do this. I urged its being done at once, to which he agreed, and *left my quarters* to make his arrangements." In his private journal, too, he records that, "The Brigadier *called on me* at three P.M. with Colonel Gordon of the Sikhs, informing me of the mutiny of the Seventeenth at Azimgurh . . . very undecided . . . . would put off everything until to-morrow. I speak out, and urge him to act at once, which he unwillingly agrees to . . . the Europeans to parade at five P.M. . . . the Thirty-seventh to be disarmed . . . the Irregulars and Sikhs said to be staunch to act with us." We have, therefore, before us three conflicting statements. Mr. Taylor says that Ponsonby met Neill as the former was going home from Gubbins's house. Ponsonby says that Neill came into Gubbins's house, when he (the Brigadier) and Gordon were there. And Neill says that the Brigadier and Gordon visited him in his own quarters. The matter is of little importance in itself; but the discrepancies cited afford an apt illustration of the difficulties which beset the path of a conscientious historian. On the whole, I am disposed to think that Neill, writing on the day of the events described, is more likely to be correct than Ponsonby, writing a month afterwards, or Taylor, collecting facts after the lapse of more than a year.

1857. June 4. and the motion of the animal, aided by the slant rays of the afternoon sun, soon began to affect him. Enfeebled as he was by previous illness, he became, in his own words, "most anxious and uneasy in mind and body." But, whilst Gordon was drawing up the Sikh regiment, he rode to the European Barracks, where he found Neill mustering the Europeans, and Olpherts getting ready his guns. The necessary orders were given; but the Brigadier felt that he was no longer equal to the responsibility of the work that lay before him.

And, in truth, it was difficult and dangerous work that then lay before the English commanders. The Native force was some two thousand strong. The Europeans hardly mustered two hundred and fifty.* Of the temper of the Sepoy regiment there was no doubt. The Irregulars had been tried on the road from Azimgurh, where they had betrayed the weakness of their fidelity, if they had not manifested the strength of their discontent.† But the Sikh regiment was believed to be faithful; and, if it were faithful, there could be no doubt of the result of that afternoon's parade. It is said that, as they were assembling for parade, they were in high spirits, and appeared to be eager to be led against the Hindostanees of the regular Army. Not merely in Benares,

* The official returns state—H.M.'s Tenth Regiment, one hundred and fifty men and three officers; Madras Fusiliers, sixty men and three officers; Artillery, thirty men and two officers.

† These regiments of Irregular Cavalry were differently constituted from those of the regular Sepoy Army. They had few European officers, and those only picked men, who had the greatest pride in their several corps, and seldom or never any desire to leave them. The troopers, who received high pay and found their own horses, were generally men of a better class, and the position of the Native officers was of a higher and more responsible character than in the regular Army. All these things were at first supposed to be favourable to the continuance of the fidelity of the Irregular Cavalry. But it was soon found that they were as incurably tainted as the rest.

but in all parts of the country, was it of the highest moment that the Sikh fighting men should be on our side; for it was believed that the fame of their loyalty would spread, on all sides, to the confines of our Empire, and that, throughout the Punjab itself, the renown of their achievements would stimulate others to do likewise. But everywhere so great a sensitiveness thrilled through the Native troops of all nationalities, that it was always possible that the weight of a feather in the balance might determine the out-turn of events on the side of loyalty or rebellion. 1857. June 4.

The disarming parade.

When the order for disarming had gone forth, Colonel Spottiswoode and his officers proceeded to the parade-ground of the Thirty-seventh, turned out the regiment, and ordered them to lodge their muskets in the bells-of-arms. There were about four hundred men on parade, the remainder, with the exception of one company at Chunar, being on detached duty in the station. To Spottiswoode it appeared that the men were generally well-disposed. There were no immediate signs of resistance. First the grenadier company, and then the other companies up to No. 6, quietly lodged their arms in obedience to the word of command. At this point a murmur arose, and some of the men were heard to say that they were betrayed—that the Europeans were coming to shoot them down when they were disarmed. Hearing this, Spottiswoode cried out that it was false, and appealed to the Native officers, who replied that he had always been a father to them. But a panic was now upon them, for they saw the white troops advancing. By word of command from Ponsonby the Europeans and the guns were moving forward towards the Sepoys' Lines. Opposite to the quarter-guard of the Thirty-seventh

1857. June 4. the Brigadier ordered the little force under Colonel Neill to be wheeled into line and halted. He then went forward and spoke to the Sepoys of the guard. He said that they were required to give up their arms, and that if they obeyed as good soldiers, no harm of any kind would befall them. As he spoke he laid his hand assuringly on the shoulder of one of the Sepoys, who said that they had committed no fault. To this Ponsonby replied in Hindostanee: "None; but it is necessary that you should do as you are ordered, as so many of your brethren have broken their oaths and murdered their officers, who never injured them." Whilst he was still speaking, some of the men shouted to their comrades on the right and left; a stray shot or two was fired from the second company, and presently the Sepoys rushed in a body to the bells-of-arms, seized their muskets, loaded and fired upon both their own officers and the Europeans. Going about the work before them in a systematic, professional manner, they sent some picked men and good marksmen to the front as skirmishers, who, kneeling down, whilst others handed loaded muskets to them, fired deliberately upon the Europeans from a distance of eighty or a hundred yards. Seven or eight men of the Tenth were shot down, and then the rest fell back in line with the rear of the guns. Meanwhile the officers of the Thirty-seventh, who had been providentially delivered from the fire of their men, were seeking safety with the guns; but Major Barrett, who had always protested against the disarming of the regiment, and now believed that it was foully used, cast in his lot with it, and would not move, until a party of Sepoys carried him off to a place of safety.

To the fire of the Sepoy musketeers the British Infantry now responded, and the guns were wheeled round to open upon the mutineers with irresistible grape. The English gunners were ready for immediate action. Anticipating resistance, Olpherts had ordered his men, when they moved from their Lines, to carry their cartridges and grape-shot in their hands.* The word of command given, the guns were served with almost magical rapidity; and the Thirty-seventh were in panic flight, with their faces turned towards the Lines. But from behind the cover of their huts they maintained a smart fire upon the Europeans; so Olpherts, loading his nine-pounders both with grape and round shot, sent more messengers of death after them, and drove them out of their sheltering homes. Throwing their arms and accoutrements behind them, and many of them huddling away clear out of Cantonments beyond the reach of the avenging guns, they made their way to the city, or dispersed themselves about the country, ready for future mischief and revenge. 1857. June 4.

Meanwhile, the detachment of Irregular Cavalry and Gordon's Sikhs had come on to parade. It was soon obvious what was the temper of the former. Their commander, Captain Guise,† had been killed by a Sepoy of the Thirty-seventh, and Dodgson, the Brigade-Major, was ordered to take his place. He had scarce taken command, when he was fired at by a trooper. Another attempted to cut him down. But the Sikhs appear to have had no foregone intention of turning against our people. Whether the object of the parade and the intentions of the British officers were ever sufficiently explained to them is not very

* Whether this was observed by the Sepoys I know not; but if it were, there can be no difficulty in accounting for their suspicion and alarm.

† One writer says that Guise's head was afterwards split open by his own troopers. He was shot on the rear of the Lines, as he was going to parade.

1857. June 4. apparent; but they seem to have been, in this juncture, doubtful and suspicious, and it needed but a spark to excite them into a blaze. The outburst of the Irregulars first caused them to waver. They did not know what it all portended; they could not discern friends from foes. At this critical moment, one of the Sikhs fired upon Colonel Gordon, whilst another of his men moved forward to his protection. In an instant the issue was determined. Olpherts was limbering up his guns, when Crump, of the Madras Artillery, who had joined him on parade and was acting as his subaltern, cried out that the Sikh regiment had mutinied. At once the word was given to unlimber, and at the same moment there was a cry that the Sikhs were about to charge. At this time they were shouting and yelling frantically, and firing in all directions—their bullets passing over and through the English battery. They were only eighty or a hundred yards from us on an open parade-ground; and at that time our Artillery were unsupported by the British Infantry, who had followed the mutineers of the Thirty-seventh Regiment into their Lines. It was not a moment for hesitation. The sudden rush of a furious multitude upon our guns, had we been unprepared for them, might have overwhelmed that half-battery with its thirty English gunners; and Benares might have been lost to us. So Olpherts, having ascertained that the officers of the Sikh corps had take refuge in his rear, brought round his guns and poured a shower of grape into the regiment. Upon this they made a rush upon the guns—a second and a third—but were driven back by the deadly showers from our field-pieces, and were soon in confused flight. And with them went the mutineers of the Irregular Cavalry; so the work was thoroughly done, and Olpherts remained in possession of the field. 1857. June 4

Neill in command.

Whilst these events were developing themselves on the parade-ground, the little power of endurance still left in the Brigadier was rapidly failing him, and before the afternoon's work was done he was incapable of further exertion. The slant rays of the declining sun, more trying than its meridian height, dazzled and sickened the old soldier. The pain and discomfort which he endured were so great that he was unable any longer to sit his horse. Having previously given orders to Colonel Spottiswoode to fire the Sepoys' Lines that none might find shelter in them, he made over the command to Colonel Neill, who eagerly took all further military responsibility on himself.* The victory of the Few over the Many was soon completed. Some who had sought shelter in the Lines were driven out and destroyed, whilst a few who succeeded in hiding themselves were burnt to death in their huts.†

* It is not easy to determine the exact period at which Ponsonby gave over the command to Neill. From the official report of the latter it would appear to have been done before the Sikhs broke into mutiny, but Ponsonby's own statement would fix the time at a later period. The account in the text is the official version of the transfer of command; but the fact, I believe, is that Neill, seeing Ponsonby on the ground, went up to him and said, "General, I assume command." So Neill's journal, and oral information of an officer who heard him say it.

† There is no passage in this history on which more care and labour have been expended than on the above narrative of the disarming at Benares on the 4th of June. In compiling it I have had before me several detailed statements made by officers present at the parade, including a full narrative written by Brigadier Ponsonby, and furnished to me by his widow, and the private journals and letters of Colonel Neill, as well as his official reports. Colonel Spottiswoode's statement is published in the Parliamentary Return relating to the regiments that have mutinied. There was also a very clearly written narrative by Ensign Tweedie (one of the young officers wounded by the fire of the Sikh regiment), printed in the newspapers of the day. Besides these, I have had the advantage of much personal conversation with one of the chief surviving actors in the scene described, and have received from him written answers to my questions on all doubtful points. I have a strong conviction, therefore, that the story cannot be more correctly told.

1857. June 4.

The military question considered.

All the circumstances of this parade of the 4th of June being fairly reviewed and impartially considered, it is not strange that some should think that it was grievously mismanaged. That this was the opinion of the highest authorities at the time is certain. Writing on the 6th of June to the Governor-General, the Benares Commissioner said, "I fear the business of disarming was very badly managed indeed. The Sepoys feel very sore at what they consider an attack on men, many of whom were unarmed at the time. This is not a point for a civilian to discuss, but the general opinion seems to be that the affair was much mismanaged." This opinion was shared by Lord Canning, who wrote, a fortnight afterwards to the President of the India Board, that the disarming "was done hurriedly and not judiciously." "A portion of a regiment of Sikhs," he added, "was drawn into resistance, who, had they been properly dealt with, would, I fully believe, have remained faithful." And, sixteen months afterwards, the civil functionary, on whom it devolved to write an official account of these transactions, deliberately recorded his belief, it may be assumed after full investigation, that the Sikhs were brought out not knowing what was to be done; that the whole affair was a surprise; that, as a corps, they were loyal, and "would have stood any test less rude.

The inference to be drawn from this is not so much that the business was done badly as that it was done hastily; or rather that it was done badly because it was done hastily The sudden resolution to disarm the Thirty-seventh on that Thursday afternoon left no time for explanations. If the whole of the black troops at Benares had been known to be steeped in sedition to the lips, and ready for an immediate outbreak, it would have been sound policy to surprise them, for only by such a course could our little handful of white soldiers hope to overthrow the multitude of the enemy. But whilst the regular Sepoys were only suspected, in whole or in part, of treacherous designs, and the intentions of the Irregulars were still doubtful, there had been nothing in the conduct of the Sikh regiment to cast a doubt upon its fidelity. It was an occasion, indeed, on which kindly explanations and assurances might have had the best effect. But there was no time for this. When it was tried with the Thirty-seventh, both by the Brigadier and by the Colonel, it was too late; for the Europeans were advancing, and the panic had commenced. And with the Sikhs it seems not to have been tried at all. It would, however, be scarcely just to cast the burden of blame on any individual officer. What was evil was the suddenness of the resolution to disarm and the haste of its execution. But this is said to have been a necessary evil. And whilst we know the worst that actually happened, we do not know the something worse that might have resulted from the postponement of the disarming parade. Even at the best, it is contended, if the Thirty-seventh had been quietly disarmed, it would have been sore embarrassment to us to watch all those disarmed Sepoys. It would, indeed, to a great extent have shut up our little European force, and, thus crippling its powers of action, have greatly diminished our strength. Moreover, it is contended that, in the crisis that had arisen, this stern example, these bloody instructions, had great effect throughout that part of the Gangetic provinces, and, indeed, through-

1857. June 4.

1857. June 4. out the whole of the country. It was made manifest that European military power was neither dead nor paralysed. There was a beginning of retribution. The white troops were coming up from beyond the seas. Though few in numbers at first, there were thousands behind them, and Upper India would soon be covered by our battalions. The moral effect of this, it was said, would be prodigious. The mailed hand of the English conqueror was coming down again crushingly upon the black races.

And even as regards the Sikh corps, it was said that a large proportion of the regiment—the regiment from Loodhianah—were not Sikhs, but Hindostanees; that they were the brethren of the regular Sepoys, and that they had come on to parade with their pieces loaded. This last fact is not conclusive against them. It may have been the result wholly of uncertainty and suspicion. But Olpherts, when he fired upon them, was fully assured that they had broken into open mutiny, and nothing ever afterwards tended to weaken his original conviction. That there was mutiny in the regiment—and mutiny of the worst kind—however limited it may have been, is certain; and if this were the first, it was far from being the last instance of a whole regiment being irrevocably compromised by the misconduct of a few Sepoys. An officer, with his guns loaded, in the presence of an overwhelming number of Native soldiers, cannot draw nice distinctions or disentangle the knot of conflicting probabilities. He must act at once. The safety of a station, perhaps of an Empire, may depend upon the prompt discharge of a shower of grape. And the nation in such an emergency will less readily forgive him for doing too little than for doing too much.

Complete as was the military success, the danger was not passed. The dispersion of a multitude of mutinous Sepoys might have been small gain to us in the presence of a rebellious population. If the malcontents of the city had risen at this time and made common cause with the dispersed soldiery and with their comrades under arms at the different guards, they might have overwhelmed our little gathering of Christian people. But the bountiful Providence, in which Commissioner Tucker had trusted, and which seemed to favour the brave efforts of Judge Gubbins, raised up for us friends in this awful crisis, and the fury of the many was mercifully restrained. It had been arranged that in the event of an outburst, all the Christian non-combatants should betake themselves to the Mint, which lay between the Cantonment and the city, as the building best suited to defensive purposes. The rattle of the musketry and the roar of the guns from the parade-ground proclaimed that the Sepoys had risen. There were then great alarm and confusion. Numbers of our people made for the Mint. The missionaries left Benares behind them, and set their faces towards Ramnuggur on their way to Chunar.* The civilians, some with their wives and families, sought refuge, in the first instance, in the Collector's Cutcherry, ascending to the roof of the building, where at least they were safe from capture.† But there was a great and reasonable fear that the Sikhs of the Treasury-guard,

1857. June 4—5 The night afterwards.

* There were some exceptions to the general exodus of the missionaries. Mr. Leupholt, of the Church Missionary Society, seems to have stood fast in the mission premises with his flock of Native Christians. This excellent man afterwards rendered good service to the British Government by exerting his influence, which was considerable in the neighbourhood, to obtain supplies for our European troops.

† The Commissioner was not of this party. He had gone to the Mint.

1857. June 4—5.

rendered furious by the slaughter of their countrymen, would seize the Government coin, and the crown jewels of their own exiled Queen, which were stored with it, and would then fire the building and attack our Christian people wheresoever they could be found.

Good services of Soorut Singh.

And that they would have struck heavily at us is not to be doubted, if one of their nation, a Sikh chief of good repute, had not come to our aid in the hour of our greatest need. This was the Sirdar Soorut Singh, who, after the second Sikh war, had been sent to reside at Benares, in honourable durance, and who had fully appreciated the generous treatment he had received from the English. He had unbounded confidence in Gubbins, and when the crisis arose, he manfully shouldered a double-barrelled gun and accompanied his English friend to the Cutcherry. Promptly and energetically he came forward to aid us, and by his explanations and persuasions softened down the anger of the Sikh soldiery, who might have been excused if they were burning to avenge the blood of their slaughtered comrades. Thus assured and admonished, they not only abstained from all acts of personal violence, but they quietly gave up the Government treasure and the Lahore jewels to the Europeans, to be conveyed to a place of safety.*

Pundit Gokool-Chund.

Nor was this noble-minded Sikh Sirdar the only friend who rose up to aid us in this conjuncture. Even from that great hot-bed of Hindooism, Brah-

* The place of safety was within the strong cells of the Artillery Congee-House, whither the treasure was taken, by the advice, I believe, of Captain Olpherts, who had always protested against the notion of making the same building available both as a refuge for the women and children and a storehouse for the treasure. Mr. Taylor, in his official narrative, says the treasure was taken to the magazine. In reward for the fidelity and forbearance of the Sikhs, the Commissioner next morning very properly distributed ten thousand rupees among them.

1857. June 4—5.

minism itself sent forth a staunch ally and potent deliverer to be a present help to us in our trouble. Pundit Gokool-Chund, a high-caste Brahmin, known to all, respected by all in Benares, flung all the weight of his influence into the scales in our favour. He was a servant of the Government—Nazir of the Judge's Court—and as such in constant intercourse with Gubbins. Had he been a Christian gentleman, he could not have striven, day and night, more ceaselessly and more successfully to succour our people. There was another, too, who put forth a protecting hand, and was earnest in his endeavours to allay the inquietude of the people. This was a wealthy and influential Hindoo noble—Rao Deonarain Singh—a loyal and devoted subject of the British Government, a man of high intelligence and enlightenment, liberal and humane. No words could exaggerate the importance of his services. Nor was the titular Rajah of Benares himself wanting in good offices to the English. On the night of that 4th of June, he succoured the missionary fugitives, and, from first to last, he placed all his resources at our disposal, and seemed honestly to wish well to our cause. Truly, it would have gone ill with our little handful of Christian people, if God had not raised up for us in our sorest need these staunch and powerful friends from among the multitude of the Heathen.*

Deonarain Singh.

The Rajah of Benares.

The prompt action of Soorut Sing saved the civilians at the Cutcherry. For many hours they remained there, anxious and uncertain, calculating the chances against them, but resolute to sell their lives at the highest price. But two hours after midnight a little party of English gentlemen, headed by

* See in Appendix a Memorandum on the Benares Rajahs.

1857. June 4—5. Gubbins, went forth in the broad moonlight to obtain the assistance of an European guard from the Mint to escort thither the fugitives at the Cutcherry. As they went, they were fired at by some Sepoys; but they returned, unharmed, with the guard, and safely conveyed their companions to the appointed place of refuge.* There the hours of morning darkness passed away in drear discomfort, and day dawned upon a scene of misery and confusion in the Mint. Officers and ladies, masters and servants, huddled together, for the most part on the roof, without much respect of persons or regard for proprieties of costume. The Europeans who had been sent for their protection bivouacked in the lower rooms, many of them utterly worn out with the exhausting labours of the day; whilst outside in the compound, or enclosure, was a strange collection of carriages, buggies, palanquins, horses, bullocks, sheep, goats, and packages of all sizes and all kinds brought in for the provisioning of the garrison.

June 5—9. State of the city. "The town is quite quiet," wrote Commissioner Tucker to Lord Canning on the following morning, "in the midst," as he said, "of the utmost noise and confusion of this crowded building," which made it difficult to write at all, and was altogether so distracting, that, though a man of grave speech, he described it as "such a Pandemonium, that it was impossible to think, write, or do anything in it." There had

* This incident is made still brighter by an act of heroism which it is a pleasure to record. It is thus officially narrated: "Messrs. Gubbins, Caulfield, and Demomet went in a buggy to the Mint, and Mr. Jenkinson, C.S., accompanied them on horseback. As the party was crossing the bridge, Mr. Jenkinson saw some ambushed Sepoys aiming at the party in the buggy. There was no time for warning or for hesitation, and he at once reined back his horse, covering with his own body his companions in danger. It were far easier to praise such an act than to praise it worthily, and I praise it best by not praising it at all."—*Mr. Taylor's Official Narrative.*

been an alarm in the course of the night of risings in the city; for the Mahomedans had hoisted the green flag, but nothing came of the demonstration. And days passed, but still there was quietude throughout Benares. All the circumstances of the "Sacred City of the Hindoos" being considered, it must be a source of wonder, not only that so little Christian blood was shed, but that there was so little resistance of any kind to the authority of the British Government.* "It is quite a miracle to me," wrote Commissioner Tucker to the Governor-General on the 9th of June, "how the city and station remain perfectly quiet. We all have to sleep at night in the Mint, but not a house or bungalow has been touched, and during the day everything goes on much as usual."† Wisely 1857. June 5—9

* Up to this time only one English officer (Captain Guise) had been killed, and four wounded—all on the parade of the 4th of June. The wounded officers were Captain Dodgson, and Ensigns Tweedie, Chapman, and Hayter. A letter from Captain Dodgson states that the last-named was "shot by the Sikhs when they turned round and fired upon us." Young Hayter was shot in both thighs, and had a third wound below the knee. The latter was so painful that the limb was amputated; but he sunk under his sufferings, and died a week or two afterwards. There is something so touching in the brief account of the poor young soldier's last days, in the letter above quoted from Captain Dodgson to Mr. Tucker, that I cannot refrain from giving the following extract from it. "He bore his wounds with the utmost fortitude, and when told that there was no hope of recovery, said he hoped he was prepared to die. . . . I used to read the Prayers for the Sick to him, and many of the Psalms of his own choosing. The last he selected was the fifty-first. He got his overland letters when I was with him, a few days before he died, and kissed them again and again, and asked me to read them to him, which I did, poor boy!"—*MS. Correspondence.*

† The following characteristic passage in the letter above quoted ought not to be withheld. "I do firmly believe," wrote Mr. Tucker, "that there is a special Divine influence at work on men's minds to keep them quiet. The few Europeans in the Mint and round the guns could do nothing to guard the Cantonment; but of all the three mutinous regiments not one seems to have thought of burning the station or plundering the houses of the residents. There is much prayer here, and I know that many prayers are offered up for us; and I fully believe that they are accepted at the Throne of Grace, and that this is the cause of the quiet we enjoy. Even with all the best possible arrangements that we can make, there is nothing to prevent the mutineers, who are hanging about, or the city rabble, from doing any mischief they please, but they do not attempt it."—*MS. Correspondence.*

1857. June 5—9. and vigorously was Gubbins now doing his work. He had sunk the judge in the magistrate. His court was closed, and he had taken the weight of the executive upon him. And now, partly by the fear, partly by the love he had inspired in the hearts of the people, he held them in restraint, and the great city lay hushed beneath his hand.

State of the rural districts.

But although there was extraordinary repose in the city, in the surrounding districts violence and anarchy arose with a suddenness that was quite astounding. It was not merely that the mutinous Sepoys, hanging about the adjacent villages, were inciting others to rebellion (this was to be expected), but a great movement from within was beginning to make itself felt upon the surface of rural society, and for a while all traces of British rule were rapidly disappearing from the face of the land. Into the real character and general significance of this movement I do not purpose here to inquire. The investigation is an extensive one, and must be deliberately undertaken. It is enough, in this place, to speak of immediate results. The dispersion of the Native soldiery on the 4th of June was followed almost immediately by disorder and rapine in the contiguous country A few days sufficed to sweep away law and order, and to produce a revolution of property, astonishing even to those who were best acquainted with the character and temper of the people. "I could not," wrote Mr. Tucker on the 13th, "have believed that the moment the hand of Government was removed there would have been so sudden a rising of landholders to plunder each other and people on the roads.* All the large landholders and auction-purchasers are paralysed

* "The Native idea now is," he added, "that British rule has slipped off, and that it is every man for himself."

and dispossessed, their agents being frequently murdered and their property destroyed."* To arrest this new danger, which threatened to become a gigantic one, overwhelming, irrepressible, our people had now to put forth all their strength. 1857. June 5—9.

On the 9th the Government of India caused Martial Law to be proclaimed in the divisions of Benares and Allahabad. On the same day, Mr. Tucker, not knowing that already the Legislature had provided the extraordinary powers which he sought†—nay, even more than he sought—wrote to the Governor-General, suggesting that he should place the Benares division "beyond the reach of Regulation Law, and give every civil officer, having the full power of magistrate, the power of life and death." "I would prefer this to Martial Law," he added, "as I do not think the greater proportion of the military can be intrusted with the power of life and death. The atrocious murders which have taken place have roused the English blood, and a very slight circumstance would cause Natives to be shot or hung. I would, therefore, much prefer retaining the powers in the hands of those who have been accustomed to weigh and to value evidence. No civilian is likely to order a man to be executed without really good cause."‡ June 9. Punitory enactments.

Time soon exploded the error contained in these last words. But the Benares Commissioner, though a little blinded by class prejudice, was right when he wrote about the hot English blood, which forbade the judgment of a cool brain. Already our military officers were hunting down criminals of all kinds, and hanging them up with as little compunction as

* See *ante*, vol. i. p. 157.

† The Act, of which a summary has been given (Book iv. chap. iv.), though passed on the 30th of May, did not receive the sanction of the Governor-General before the 8th of June.

‡ MS. Correspondence.

1857. June 9. though they had been pariah-dogs or jackals, or vermin of a baser kind. One contemporary writer has recorded that, on the morning after the disarming parade, the first thing he saw from the Mint was a "row of gallowses." A few days afterwards military courts or commissions were sitting daily, and sentencing old and young to be hanged with indiscriminate ferocity. These executions have been described as "Colonel Neill's hangings." But Neill left Benares four or five days after the outbreak, and it did not devolve on him to confirm the sentences, of which I have heard the strongest reprobation. On one occasion, some young boys, who, perhaps, in mere sport had flaunted rebel colours and gone about beating tom-toms, were tried and sentenced to death. One of the officers composing the court, a man unsparing before an enemy under arms, but compassionate, as all brave men are, towards the weak and helpless, went with tears in his eyes to the commanding officer, imploring him to remit the sentence passed against these juvenile offenders, but with little effect on the side of mercy.* And what was done with some show of formality, either of military or of criminal law, was as nothing, I fear, weighed against what was done without any formality at all. Volunteer hanging parties went out into the districts, and amateur executioners were not wanting to the occasion. One gentleman boasted of the numbers he had finished off quite "in an artistic manner," with mango-trees for gibbets and elephants for drops, the victims of this

* The general reader, however, must not calculate years in such a case as they would be calculated in Europe. What, estimated by years, is a boy in England is a man in India—a husband, a father, with all the full-grown passions of maturity—and an equal sense of personal independence and responsibility

wild justice being strung up, as though for pastime, in "the form of a figure of eight." 1857. June 9.

This, it is to be presumed, was the Martial Law, of which such graphic details have been given by contemporary writers, without a prevision of publicity.* But the Acts of the Legislative Council, under the strong hand of the Executive, fed the gallows with equal prodigality, though, I believe, with greater discrimination. It was a special immunity of this Benares mutiny that the prison-gates were not thrown open, and the city deluged with a flood of convicted crime. The inmates of the gaol remained in their appointed places. But even this had its attendant evils. For as crime increased, as increase it necessarily did; prison-room was wanted, and was not to be found. The great receptacle of the criminal classes was gorged to overflowing. The guilty could not be suffered wholly to escape. So the Gibbet disposed of the higher class of malefactors, and the Lash scored the backs of the lower, and sent them afloat again on the waves of tumult and disorder. But, severe as Gubbins was when the crisis was at its height, he restrained his hand when the worst had passed, and it had ceased to be an expedient of mercy to strike into the hearts of the people that terror, which diminishes crime and all its punitory consequences.

Meanwhile, other sources of anxiety were developing themselves in more remote places. One incident must be narrated here as immediately connected with the outbreak of the 4th of June. The story of the June. The mutiny at Jaunpore.

* See especially a letter, written by a private of the Seventy-eighth Highlanders, which was published in the *Times*, and quoted at some length by Mr. Montgomery Martin.

1857. June 8. Loodhianah regiment of Sikhs has not yet been fully told. There was a detachment of it at Jaunpore, a civil station, some forty miles from Benares. When news arrived on the 5th of June that the Thirty-seventh had revolted, and were pouring into the district, they made demonstrations of fidelity to their British officers; but when later tidings came that the head-quarters of their own regiment had been fired on by the Europeans, they rose at once in open mutiny. Lieutenant Mara, the officer commanding them, was shot down. Mr. Cuppage, joint-magistrate, on his way to the gaol, shared the same fate. The Treasury was plundered. And all surviving Europeans, after a humiliating surrender of their arms, were driven to seek safety in flight. British government was expunged, as it had been at Azimgurh, and its chief representatives were glad to find a hiding-place for themselves in quarters which, a little time before, their *fiat* could have swept away like summer dust. Then the station was given up to plunder; and the mutiny of a few Sikh mercenaries grew into a general insurrection of the people. The houses of the English were gutted and burnt. The soldiery, burdened with money-bags, having gone off towards Oude, the plunder of "the Treasury was completed by decrepit old women and wretched little boys, who had never seen a rupee in their lives."* And all over the district, the state of things, brought about by our settlement operations and our law courts, dis-

* Mr. Taylor's official narrative. The writer adds: "In the district not a semblance of authority was left to any one. Those who had lost their estates under our rule thought this a good time to regain them; those who had not, thought that they could make a little profit by plundering their weaker neighbours; the bolder spirits thought to secure more brilliant advantages by intercourse with the rebel powers in Oude." In no other district, Mr. Taylor observes, were "auction purchasers more numerous, old Zemindars more powerful, or the present landholders on worse terms among themselves."

1857. June.

appeared like the bursting of a bubble. The very presence of our fugitive people, though powerless and forlorn, was an offence and an abomination to the now-dominant class, who drove them from their sanctuary in the house of a friendly Rajah to take refuge in an indigo factory. And it became one of the Benares Commissioner's greatest cares to rescue Mr. Fane and his companions from the dangers which then beset them. Having discovered their abode, he sent out "a party of Europeans and volunteers to bring them into Benares."*

Despatch of troops upwards.

Troops were now coming up every day from below. Benares was safe. Other stations were to be saved. The best service that could be rendered to the State was the prompt despatch of reinforcements to the upper country—and most of all to Allahabad and Cawnpore. This service was intrusted to Mr. Archibald Pollock.† True to his great historical name, he threw himself into the work with an amount of energy and activity which bore the best fruits. Every kind of available conveyance was picked up and turned promptly to account in the furtherance of the eagerly looked-for Europeans, whose appearance was ever welcomed by our peril-girt people as a great deliverance. Nor was want of sufficient conveyance the only difficulty to be overcome. There was a want of provisions for Europeans, especially of flour and rum; and Mr. Tucker wrote eagerly to Lord Canning to send up commissariat stores of every kind for the soldiery, "as European necessaries are not to be had here in any quantity." He was

* Mr. Tucker to Lord Canning, June 9th. In this letter the fugitives are said to have consisted of sixteen men, five ladies, and eleven children.

† The youngest son of General Sir George Pollock. He was then joint-magistrate of Benares.

1857 June. very eager at this time to save the treasure in neighbouring civil stations along the main line, as Mirzapore and Ghazepore, and he sent parties of Europeans by steamer to bring it off in safety to Benares. It was, moreover, a great object to keep the white troops in motion, and thus to display European strength, first at one point, then at another, and by means of a few to make an appearance of many, as in a mimic theatre of war. At once to have recovered Azimgurh and Jaunpore, from which we had been so ignominiously expelled, would have been a great stroke; and the Commissioner wrote to Lord Canning, saying that if the Government would allow him to divert two hundred Europeans from the main line of operations, the magistrates and other civil officers might return to their posts, and British authority might be re-established. But troops could not be spared for the purpose, and it was left to another day and to other means, whereof due record will be made hereafter, to prove to the people of those districts that the English had not been swept out of the land. The narrative must now follow the upward line of the Ganges to the next great city of note.

Allahabad. About seventy miles beyond Benares, at the confluence of the Ganges and the Jumna, lies the city of Allahabad. It has none of that wealth of structural beauty which renders Benares so famous among the cities of the East. Its attractions are derived chiefly from its position, at the extreme point or promontory of the Doab, formed by the meeting of the waters. The broad rivers rushing down towards the sea, and mingling as they go their streams of varied colour and varied motion—the one of yellow-brown, thick and turbid, the other blue, clear, and sparkling* —the green banks between which they flow, the rich cultivation of the inner country dotted with groves and villages, make a landscape pleasant to the eye. But the town itself, principally situated on the Jumna, has little to command admiration. It has been called in derision by natives of Hindostan, "Fukeerabad," or the city of beggars; but the Fort, which towers above it, massive and sublime, with the strength of many ages in its solid masonry, imparts peculiar dignity to the place. Instinct with the historical traditions of the two elder dynasties, it had gathered new power from the hands of the English conqueror, and, garrisoned by English troops, might almost have defied the world. 1857. June.

It would be difficult to exaggerate the military importance of the situation at the junction of the two rivers, commanding, as it does, the great fluvial thoroughfare of Hindostan, and also the high road by land from the Upper to the Lower Provinces. Both in a strategical and political sense, its security had ever been of great moment; but the recent acquisition of Oude had rendered it still more essential that it should be safely in hand. In this powerful fortress of Allahabad was an arsenal stored with all the munitions of war, and an array of guns in position

* Historians and poets alike delight to describe the meeting of the waters. "The half-modernised fortress," says Trotter, "looks grandly down on the meeting of the clearer Jumna with the yellow waters of the broad Ganges" (*History of the British Empire in India*); Waterfield (*Indian Ballads*) sings of "the sisters blue and brown;" and again, "Where Yamuna leaps blue to Ganga's arms." And Bholonauth Chunder (*Travels of a Hindoo*), writing in prose, but scarcely less poetically, says: "The spot where the Sister Nuddees (Greek Nyades) meet makes a magnificent prospect. The Ganges has a turbid, muddy current—the Jumna, a sparkling stream. Each at first tries to keep itself distinct, till, happy to meet after a long parting, they run into each other's embrace, and, losing themselves in one, flow in a common stream. The Ganges strikes the fancy as more matronly of the two —the Jumna a gayer, youthful sister."

1857. commanding the approaches from the country below. And their possession by the enemy would have been a disaster beyond compare. Some time before, Sir James Outram had suggested to Lord Canning the expediency of adopting measures for the greater security of Allahabad, and had warned him of the, at least possible, danger of such a mischance befalling us.* I do not know whether these warnings were remembered — warnings afterwards repeated most emphatically by Sir Henry Lawrence; but there was no place to which Lord Canning turned his thoughts with greater anxiety and alarm—no place to which he was more eager to send relief in the shape of European troops.

Tidings of the great disaster at Meerut reached Allahabad on the 12th of May, and a few days afterwards came the story of the progress of the rebellion, and the restoration of the Mogul Emperors of Delhi. At the beginning of May, the force posted at Allahabad consisted of a single Sepoy regiment, the Sixth, under the command of Colonel Simpson, which had marched in from Jummalpore at the latter end of March, relieving the Eleventh, under Colonel Finnes. But on the 9th, a wing of the Ferozpore Regiment of Sikhs had arrived from Mirzapore; and ten days later two troops of Oude Irregular Horse came in, under orders from Sir Henry Lawrence, to place themselves under the civil authorities. Shortly afterwards sixty European invalids were brought in from Chunar. The bulk of the Native troops occupied their Lines in the Cantonment. which lay at a distance of two or three miles from the Fort between the two great rivers.

* "I myself am more shocked than surprised," he wrote from Baghdad to the Chairman of the East India Company, on first hearing of the outbreak, "for I have long dreaded something of the sort; and you may recollect I told you of the warning that I gave to Lord Canning when I was last at Calcutta, and suggested that measures should be adopted for the better security of Allahabad."—*June* 8, 1857. *MS.*

Detachments were posted in the Fort. The principal civil officers were Mr. Chester, the commissioner, and Mr. Court, the magistrate—both men of courage and resolution, not easily shaken or disturbed. They and the other civilians, as well as the military officers, dwelt in comfortable and pleasant garden-houses in the European station, without an anxious thought of the future to disturb them. 1857.

Colonel Simpson and the Sixth.

In the eyes of the commanding officer, and, indeed, of every Englishman who held a commission under him, the Sixth was true to the core, and was thoroughly to be trusted. It was one of those regiments in which the officers looked lovingly on their soldiers as on their children; cared for their comforts, promoted their amusements, and lived amongst them as comrades. They had done so much for their men, and seen so many indications of what at least simulated gratitude and affection, that it would have been to their discredit if they had mistrusted a regiment which had such good reason to be faithful to the English gentlemen who had treated them with the kindness of parents. But the civil officers, who had none of the associations and the sympathies which made the centurions of the Sixth Regiment ever willing to place their lives in the hands of the native soldiery, saw everywhere grounds of suspicion and causes of alarm. There was evidently a wide-spread feeling of mistrust both in the City and in the Cantonment.* All kinds of vague reports were in the

State of popular feeling.

* Mr. Willock, joint magistrate, says in his official report, "As each day passed some fresh rumour was circulated regarding the state of public feeling in the city. Agents of the rebel leaders were evidently busy poisoning the minds of the people. . . . The Bazaar was closed, and it was very evident that an outbreak in the city would follow an émeute of the soldiery. The men of the city warned the magistrate against the infidelity of the Sepoys, and the Sepoys cautioned their officers against the city people, protesting against the tales that had been circulated of their lukewarmness towards Government."

1857. air. Whether the disturbing faith had grown up spontaneously in the minds of the Natives, or whether the great lie had been maliciously propagated by active emissaries of evil, it was believed that a heavy blow was to be struck at the religion of the people.* At one time it was reported that the English had determined to serve out the greased cartridges on a given day, and that the regiment would be paraded on the glacis of the Fort, in a position commanded by our guns, and blown into the air if they disobeyed orders. Then it was said that the Sepoys had determined to prevent the treasure being moved into the Fort;† and again, that the Sikhs were conspiring with the Native Infantry for a joint attack upon the English. At the same time, the price of grain and of other kinds of food rose in the market, and the common feeling of disquietude was enhanced by the discontent occasioned by the dearness of provisions, which was always attributed to the agency of the English.

May 22. Conflicting projects. In this state of uncertainty, Colonel Simpson proposed to betake himself with his regiment to the Fort. This movement was strenuously opposed by Mr. Court, the magistrate, and the project was abandoned.

* I have remarked, and with much uniformity of observation, that these monstrous reports of "forcible conversion," or destruction of caste, were most rife where the Mahomedan population was the densest. Allahabad contained an unusual number of Mussulmans, whilst in Benares there was a great preponderance of Hindoos; but these reports appear to have been circulated more freely in the former than in the latter city.

† It was said that this ought to have opened the eyes of Colonel Simpson to the real state of his corps. But the fact is, that the circumstance referred to in the text was nothing more than an alleged conversation between a Native officer of the Irregular Cavalry and another of the Sixth. The former was said to have asked whether the Sixth would allow the treasure to be removed, and the latter to have answered, "Some of them would not until they had received their arrears of pay." "This," says Colonel Simpson, "was immediately reported to the Adjutant, who did not credit it. On the 23rd I made poor Plunkett and Stewart inquire into the business, and the latter reported to me there was no truth in it, as the Native officer and men of the Sixth guard denied the accusation."

On the same evening a council of the leading civil and military officers was held, and it was determined that the women and children only should be removed next morning into the Fort. But next morning, before daybreak, there was a change of plan. The order, which had decreed that "no (adult) male should be allowed to enter the Fort," was cancelled, in spite of Court's remonstrances, and two hours before noon "there was a regular flight to the Fort of men, women, and children, carrying with them all the property they could."* But later in the day the energy of the magistrate prevailed, and the non-military members of the community were enrolled into a volunteer guard, to patrol the city and station, accompanied by some mounted police. 1857. May 22.

As the month wore on to its close, appearances seemed rather to improve. Some apprehensions had been entertained lest the great Mahomedan festival of the *Eed*, which was to be celebrated on the 25th, should stir all the inflammatory materials gathered together in Allahabad into a blaze. The day, however, passed over without any disturbance; and at a parade held in the evening, two Sepoys, who, on the preceding day, had given up a couple of Mehwattees, charged with tampering with their fidelity, were May 25. Lip-loyalty.

* Official Report of Mr. Fendall Thompson, officiating magistrate. Colonel Simpson, in a narrative of events with which he has furnished me, says, "On the 23rd of May, the ladies, children, and non-military were ordered into the Fort for security, in consequence of the various reports received by the magistrate regarding the unsettled state of the city of Allahabad, aggravated by the high price of grain." It might be gathered from this that the magistrate had approved of the removal to the Fort of the non-military males, whereas the official report states that he had in reality protested against it. Colonel Simpson, however, says, in another memorandum, that "a notice to this effect" (*i.e.* the removal of "ladies, children, and non-military") "was circulated by the magistrate throughout the station, and regimentally by two of his sowars." Colonel Simpson says that it was signed both by himself and Court.

1857. May 25.

publicly promoted.* But this spasm of energy seems to have been designed only to throw dust into the eyes of the authorities. It is stated that, at the very same time, they were intriguing with the Oude Cavalry. Perhaps the arrest was designed to irritate the minds of the people of the city. If so, it was a successful movement; for it was soon noised abroad that a rescue would be attempted, and so the prisoners were removed to the Fort.

After this there were outward quietude and security, for although with the new month there arose increased excitement in the city, still more favourable appearances presented themselves in the cantonment. The Sepoys of the Sixth, seemingly not satisfied with the latent loyalty of quiescence, quickened into energy and enthusiasm, and demanded to be led against the rebels of Delhi. News of their noble offer was promptly telegraphed to Calcutta, and Lord Canning sent back by the wires a cordial expression of the thanks of Government. But to the civilians at least it was apparent that the danger was not passed, for every day the excitement became greater in the city.

News from Benares, June 4.

Affairs were in this state when news came from Benares that the Sepoys stationed there had risen in revolt, and that they had been dispersed by Neill's Europeans. The telegraph brought the first tidings to Simpson, who, as an initial measure of precaution, issued orders that the gates of the Fort should be closed night and day, and no one, of whatsoever

* Sir John Malcolm writes of the Mehwattees, that, "although usually reckoned Mahomedans, it is difficult to say whether they are Mahomedans or Hindoos; they partake of both religions, and are the most desperate rogues in India. They are turbulent, vindictive, cunning, cruel, robbers, murderers, and assassins—yet they are faithful, undaunted guards and servants to those whose nimuk (salt) they eat."—*Malwa Report*, p. 578, *note*.

colour or creed, admitted without a passport.* The next step was to guard the approaches to Allahabad. The road from Benares ran on the other side of the Ganges, which was crossed by a bridge of boats at a point nearly opposite to the Fort, to the suburb of Darao-gunj. It seemed to be so certain that the Benares mutineers would make for Allahabad, that, on a requisition of the Magistrate, a Company of the Sixth was sent, with two guns, to defend the bridge by which the passage of the river must have been made. At the same time, a detachment of the Oude Irregular Cavalry was posted on an open space between the bridge-head and the cantonment, so as to command all the approaches to the latter. And no one then seemed to doubt that those Native guards would defend the bridge and the station as staunchly and as truly as if the insurgents had been people of other races and other creeds.

1857. June 4.

It will, perhaps, never be known to the full satisfaction of the historical inquirer whether the Sixth Regiment was saturated with that deepest treachery which simulates fidelity for a time, in order that it may fall with more destructive force on its unsuspecting victim, or whether it had been, throughout the month of May, in that uncertain, wavering condition which up to the moment of the final outburst has no determined plan of operations. The officers of the regiment believed that the men were staunch to the core. Outwardly, there were no indications of

* "From this period (May 25) until the 4th of June more or less excitement prevailed in the city of Allahabad, and on that date the mutiny at Benares took place, and was reported to me by telegraphic wire. On the same evening I ordered the Fort Gates to be closed, day and night, and neither European nor Native was allowed ingress or egress without a pass, so as more particularly to guard against any tamperers from Benares or from the city of Allahabad."—*Memorandum by Colonel Simpson. MS.*

1857. June 6. hostility. But when news came that the Native regiments at Benares had risen, and that the Europeans had fallen upon them, the long-abiding vacillation rose into robust resolution, and the regiment sprung, as it were, in a moment upon its prey. Whether it was in a wild panic of fear, believing that Neill and the Europeans would soon be upon them, or whether in the belief that the time for action had now come, as they would probably soon be joined by the Sepoys from Benares, the evening of the 6th of June found them ripe for any deed of violence.

But even as the sun was setting on that day—the last sun that ever was to set upon this model regiment—there was unbroken faith in its fidelity. The warning voice, however, was not silent. The Adjutant of the Sixth received a letter from a non-commissioned officer of the regiment, telling him that the news from Benares had caused much excitement in the Lines. The Adjutant took the letter to the Colonel. But Simpson could not admit that anything was wrong. He added, however, that at the sunset parade, which was to be held for the promulgation of the thanks of the Governor-General to the regiment, the temper of the men would be clearly ascertained.

The Thanksgiving Parade. The parade was held. The thanks of the Governor-General were read. The Commissioner, who had attended at the request of the Colonel, addressed the regiment in Hindostanee, praising them for the loyalty they had evinced. The Sepoys appeared to be in the highest spirits; and they sent up a ringing cheer in response to the stirring words. When the parade was over, the officers, for the most part, rode or walked to the Mess. With Colonel Simpson rode Captain Plunkett—an officer of the Sixth, who had served for more than twenty years with the regiment. He spoke with delight of the pride he felt in its noble conduct, and his faith in its enduring fidelity. Thus conversing they rode to the Mess-house, where other officers had assembled, and were discussing the events of the day Among them was Captain Birch, the Fort-Adjutant, who besought the Colonel to recall the guns posted at the Bridge of Boats and to post them in the Fort, where they were more needed. To this, Simpson esteeming the Fort to be his first charge, and having been warned not to trust the Sikhs, of whom the garrison mainly consisted, gave his consent; and orders went forth for their recall.* 1857. June 6.

The last Mess-dinner of the Sixth.

There was a goodly gathering in the Mess-house, for the number of officers had been recently increased by the arrival of a party of young cadets, who had been ordered to do duty with the Sixth—mere boys, with the roses of England on their cheeks and the kisses of their mothers still fresh upon their lips. Without any sense of ills to come, old and young took their places at the dinner-table in perfect serenity of mind. There was at least one faithful regiment in the service! The civilians, equally assured, went to their houses and dined; and did as was their wont in the evening, wrapped themselves up in early slumber, or kept themselves awake with the excitement of cards. Some, indeed, who had slept in the Fort on the preceding night, were now again in their own homes. On no evening, perhaps, since the first startling news had come from Delhi and Meerut, had there been so little trepidation—so little excitement. But about nine o'clock the whole

* These warnings came from Sir Henry Lawrence at Lucknow and Sir Hugh Wheeler at Cawnpore. Simpson was advised not to trust the Sikhs, and to man the Fort with all the Europeans available at Allahabad.

1857. June 6. European community of Allahabad were startled by the sound of a bugle-call announcing the alarm. The Colonel had left the Mess, and was walking homewards, when the unexpected sound smote upon his ears and urged him onward to his house, where he called for his horse, mounted, and rode for the quarter-guard. Thither many other officers had repaired on the first sound of the bugle-notes. The truth was soon apparent to them. The faithful Sixth had revolted.

Revolt of the Regiment. The story was this: The detachment sent to defend the Bridge had been the first to rise, as it had been first to learn how the guns had been turned upon the Native troops at Benares, and whilst Simpson with his officers was dining comfortably at the Mess-house, the orders, which he had despatched for the withdrawal of the Artillery from Darao-gunj, had been sternly resisted. The Sepoy Guard, told off as an escort, rose against the Artillery-officer, Lieutenant Harward, and declared that the guns should be taken not to the Fort, but to the Cantonment; and the rest of the detachment turned out, armed and accoutred, to enforce the demand. True to the noble regiment to which he belonged, Harward hastened to the post of the Oude Irregulars, which lay between the Bridge-head and the Cantonment, to bring up succours to overawe the Sepoys and to save the guns. The Irregulars were commanded by Lieutenant Alexander—a young officer of the highest promise—who at once responded to Harward's call, and ordered out his men. Tardily and sulkily they pretended to obey. Whilst they were forming, a hastily-written note was despatched by Harward to the Fort. The sound of the guns, grating along the road to Cantonments, was distinctly heard; and the Irregulars, headed by Alexander and accompanied by Harward, whom the former had mounted on a spare horse, then rode out to intercept the mutineers. They soon came upon the party, under the broad light of the moon; but when the order was given to charge the guns, and the English officers dashed at them, only three troopers responded to the stirring summons. The rest fraternised with the enemy. Alexander, as he rode forward and was rising in his stirrups to strike, was shot through the heart, and Harward narrowly escaped with his life.* The mutineers, who had before sent out two of their party to warn their comrades, and had, it is stated, sent up signal rockets, now marched with the guns to the Lines, and when their colonel appeared on parade, the whole regiment was in the throes of rebellion. 1857. June 6.

It was then too late for the voice of authority to overawe or to persuade. Simpson saw that there was great excitement on the parade-ground. Some of his officers were commanding their men to fall in, but there was little appearance of obedience. And when he rode up to inquire why the guns had been brought on parade, two Sepoys of the Guard replied by firing upon him. Expostulation was vain. A volley of musketry responded to his words; and he saw that everywhere on the parade-ground the Sepoys were shooting down their officers. Seeing that there was no hope of saving the colours, he then rode to the left of the Lines, where some men of the Light Escape of Colonel Simpson.

* "During the night, the few Irregulars who had remained staunch came in, bringing with them the body of their officer, Lieutenant Alexander, who had been shot, as before related. His body bore witness to the mad cruelty of his enemies, for besides the shot in his breast, which killed him, there were sabre-cuts all over his head and face."—*Mr. Thompson's Report.*

1857. June 6. Company, in whom there still seemed to be a feeling of compunction, if not of regard for their chief, clustered, unarmed and unaccoutred, round his horse, and besought him to ride for his life to the Fort. Hoping still to save the Treasury, he rode, accompanied by Lieutenant Currie, in the direction of that building, but fired upon from all sides, he soon saw that the case was hopeless.* He had now well nigh run the gauntlet of danger, and though a ball had grazed his helmet, he had providentially escaped; but opposite the Mess-house, as he galloped towards the Fort, the Guard formed in line at the gate and fired upon him. A musket-ball took effect on his horse; but Simpson was still unhurt, save by a blow on the arm from a spent shot; and the last dying efforts of his charger landed him safely within the walls of the Fort, covered with the blood of the noble animal that had borne him.

Massacre of the Ensigns. Meanwhile, others less fortunate had fallen beneath the musketry of the mutineers. Currie, who had accompanied the Colonel to the Treasury, escaped the fire of the guards and sentries; Captain Gordon and Lieutenant Hicks escaped also, as did two of the cadets, to the Fort;† but Plunkett, with his score years of good service in the Sixth, Adjutant Steward, Quartermaster Hawes, and Ensigns Pringle and Munro were shot down on parade. Fort-Adjutant Birch and Lieutenant Innes of the Engineers were

* "As my duty was to save the Treasury, if possible, I proceeded in that direction, when I was immediately fired on by the whole guard of thirty-two men on one flank, with a night-picket of thirty men on the other. The detachment of the Third Oude Irregular Cavalry remained passive, and did not fire."—*Memorandum of Colonel Simpson. MS.*

† Hicks and the cadets (Pearson and Woodgate) were at the Daraogunj when the mutiny broke out. They were made prisoners and carried towards Cantonments, but, in their eagerness to join in the plunder of the Treasury, the Sepoys suffered them to depart, and afterwards they made good their escape by twice swimming across the river.

also killed, and eight of the unposted boy-ensigns 1857.
were murdered in cold blood by the insurgent June 6.
Sepoys.* The poor boys were leaving the Mess-house, when the brutal soldiery fell upon them. Seven were slaughtered on the ground; but one, a boy of sixteen, escaped with his wounds, and hid himself in a ravine. Having supported himself for some days, merely, it would seem, by water from a brook, he was discovered in his hiding-place, dragged before one of the insurgent leaders, and confined in a serai with a Native catechist. The faith of the convert was giving way to the sufferings which he endured, when Arthur Cheek, who had been scarcely a month in India, exhorted his companion to be steadfast in the faith. "Oh, my friend." he is reported to have said, "whatever may come to us, do not deny the Lord Jesus." He was rescued, but he was not saved. On the 16th of June the poor boy died in the Fort from exposure, exhaustion, and neglected wounds.†

It was fortunate that the bulk of our people were In the Fort.
shut up in the Fort, where no external perils could assail them. But there was danger within the walls. A company of the Sixth formed part of the garrison, and the temper of the Sikhs was doubtful. When the noise of firing was first heard it was believed that the Benares mutineers had arrived, and that the Sepoys of Allahabad were giving them a warm reception. But at a later hour the truth broke in upon them; and all doubt was removed by the appearance

* It has been commonly stated that these poor boys were killed whilst sitting at the Mess-table. I am assured, however, on the best authority that this is a mistake. Few incidents of the mutiny have excited greater horror than this, which is familiarly spoken of as the massacre of the "poor little griffins."

† See Mr. Owen's Journal. It has been erroneously stated elsewhere that he died in the hands of the enemy, on the day of Neill's arrival at Allahabad, the 11th of June.

1857. June 6. of the Commandant Simpson, smeared with the blood of his wounded charger. His first care was to order the Sepoys of the Sixth to be disarmed. This duty was entrusted to a detachment of the Sikh corps, under Lieutenant Brasyer—an officer who had won for himself a commission by his gallantry in the great battles of the Punjab, and who now proved his mastery over his men by forcing them to do a distasteful service. With the news that the Benares Sepoys of the Regular Army had been mown down by the white troops, came also tidings that Gordon's regiment had been riddled by our grape-shot. It was, therefore, fearfully probable that the offended nationality of the Sikhs at Allahabad would rise against their Christian masters, partly in revenge and partly in fear. Happily the treasure was outside the Fort. Had the design of bringing it within the walls not been abandoned, the love of loot and the thirst of blood would have prevailed together, and Allahabad might have been lost.

It was, in truth, a most critical moment. Had the men of the Sixth Regiment and the Sikhs then in the Fort made common cause with each other, the little Christian garrison could have made but feeble resistance against such odds. The Sepoys, who were posted, for purposes of defence, at the main-gate, had, on the first sound of firing in Cantonments, been ordered to load their pieces: so they were ready for immediate action. The Sikhs were drawn up fronting the main-gate, and before them were the guns, manned by the invalid Artillerymen from Chunar, in whom the energy of earlier days was revived by this unexpected demand upon them. And at a little distance, in overawing position, were posted little knots of European volunteers, armed

and loaded, ready on the first sign of resistance to 1857.
fire down from the ramparts upon the mutineers. June 6.
There is something very persuasive always in the lighting of port-fires, held in the steady hands of English Artillerymen. The Sepoys, charged to the brim with sedition, would fain have resisted the orders of the white men, but these arrangements thoroughly overawed them. They sullenly piled arms at the word of command, and were expelled from the Fort to join their comrades in rebellion.

The first danger was now surmounted. Those who knew best what was passing in the minds of the Native soldiery of all races, clearly saw the magnitude of the crisis. It is impossible to over-estimate the disastrous consequences that would have ensued from the seizure and occupation by the enemy of the Fortress of Allahabad, with all its mighty munitions of war. One officer, however, was prepared at any risk to prevent this catastrophe by precipitating another. Stimulated, perhaps, by the noble example set by Willoughby at Delhi, Russell, of the Artillery, laid trains of gunpowder from the magazines to a point, at which he stood during the disarming of the Sixth, near the loaded guns; and if mutiny had then been successful, he would have fired the trains and blown the magazines, with all the surrounding buildings, into the air.* The expulsion of the Hindostanee Sepoys, effected by Brasyer's cool courage and admirable management, averted for the moment this great calamity; and all that was left undone, did itself afterwards by the help of the national character of the Sikhs.

* I first read this anecdote in Mr. Clive Bayley's Official Report. Mr. Bayley has stated the fact on the authority of Mr. Court, the magistrate, whose testimony is not to be questioned.

1857. June 6. Rising in the City.

Such was the mutiny of the Sixth Regiment—in its purely military aspects one of the most remarkable in the whole history of the war, and, memorable in itself, still more memorable for its immediate popular results. For the great city rose in an instant. The suburbs caught the contagion of rebellion; far into the rural districts the pestilence spread, and order and authority lay prostrate and moribund. If a general rising of the people had been skilfully planned and deliberately matured, there could not, to all outward appearance, have been a more simultaneous or a more formidable insurrection. But, in truth, there was no concert, no cohesion. Every man struck for himself. In not one of the great cities of India was there a more varied population than in Allahabad. But there was a greater preponderance than is often seen of the Mahomedan element. And it was a perilous kind of Mahomedanism; for large numbers of the ancient dependents of decayed Mogul families were cherishing bitter memories of the past, and writhing under the universal domination of the English. The dangerous classes, indeed, were many, and they seem to have been ripe for revolt on the first sign of the rising of the soldiery. So, whilst the events above recorded were passing in the Fort, in the city and in the station were such tumult and confusion as had never been known before. All through the night of the 6th of June licence and rapine had full sway. The gaol was broken open, and the prisoners released. Vast numbers of convicted criminals, with the irons still rattling on their limbs, rushed forth, to the consternation of the peaceful inhabitants, to turn their newly-acquired liberty to account in the indulgence of all the worst passions of humanity. To the English station they made their way in large bodies, shouting and yelling as they went; and every European or Eurasian who crossed their path was mercilessly butchered on the spot. The houses of the Christian inhabitants were plundered; and the flames from our burning bungalows soon lit up the skies and proclaimed to many in the Fort that their pleasant homes would soon be only heaps of ashes. And there was a mighty pillage in the quarters of the Christian shopkeepers and the wharfs and warehouses of the steam companies. The railway-works were destroyed.* The telegraphic wires were torn down. All our people outside the Fort were ruthlessly put to death by the insurgents, and it has been said with every possible aggravation of cruelty. All the turbulent population of the great city turned out to glut their vengeance against the Feringhees, or to gratify their insatiate thirst for plunder. And with them went not only the Sepoys, who, a day before, had licked our hands, but the superannuated pensioners of the Company's Native Army, who, though feeble for action were blatant in council, and were earnest in their efforts to stimulate others to deeds of cowardice and cruelty.† Law and authority were, for a while, prostrate in the dust; whilst over the

1857. June 6.

* There seemed to be an especial rage against the Railway and the Telegraph. How far it was the growth of the superstitious feelings glanced at in the first volume of this work (pp. 190, *et seq.*), I do not venture to declare. There was apparently a great fear of the engines, for the insurgents brought the guns to bear upon them and battered them to pieces, some appearing to be afraid of approaching them as though they were living monsters.

† See the Red Pamphlet. The author states that he gives facts "from an undoubted source"—one who received them "from the lips of an eye-witness." "Houses were plundered and burnt," he says, "their inmates chopped to pieces, some roasted, almost all cruelly tortured, the children tossed on bayonets. Foremost in the commission of these atrocities were the pensioners. . . . . These men, unable from their infirmities to fight, were not thereby precluded from inflicting tortures of the most diabolical nature. They even took the lead in these villanies, and encouraged the Sepoys and others to follow their example."

1857. June 6. Cotwallee, or head-quarters of the city police, the green flag of the Prophet declared the supremacy of Mahomedan rule.

Nor was it only against the white-faced Europeans and the Christian people of the half-blood that the fury of the disaffected was at this time levelled. In some quarters of Allahabad were a large number of quiet settlers from the plains of Bengal, and many others drawn thither by the exigencies of their religion—peaceful pilgrims to the sacred Pryag. If to be a Bengallee were not at that time held in the North-Western Provinces to be the next thing to a Christian, it was at least known that he was an unwarlike, feeble personage, likely to have money in his possession, and small means of defending it. Upon these harmless people the "budmashes" fell heavily, and established a reign of terror among them. Their property was seized, their lives were threatened, and only spared by abject promises to disgorge the savings of a life, and to swear allegiance to the restored Government of the Mogul.*

June 7. To sack the Treasury was commonly the first thought of the insurgents, alike of military mutineers and criminals from the streets and bazaars. But the coin lay untouched during the night under a Sepoy guard, and the first impulses of personal greed were restrained by some feeling of nationality which had found entrance into their breasts, though only on the briefest tenure. It was agreed that the treasure

* "The Bengallees cowered in fear, and awaited within closed doors to have their throats cut. The women raised a dolorous cry at the near prospect of death. From massacring their officers, and plundering the Treasury, and letting open the gaol-birds, the Sepoys spread through the town to loot the inhabitants. Our friend, as well as his other neighbours, were soon eased of all their valuables, but were spared their lives on promise of allegiance to their (the Native) Government."—*Travels of a Hindoo, by Bholonauth Chunder.*

should be carried in its integrity by the regiment to Delhi, and laid, with their services, at the feet of the King. The spasm of self-devotion seems to have ended with the night. In the morning the Sepoys of the Sixth are said to have assembled on the parade-ground, and to have voted for the repudiation of this patriotic scheme. Soon after noon they went to the Treasury, opened its doors, and began to serve out the money-bags. Each Sepoy took as many rupees as he could carry, and when the whole had satisfied themselves, they left what remained to the predatory classes, convicted and unconvicted, of the city. Then there was very little more thought of the national cause, of Delhi, or of Behaudur Shah. As a regiment the Sixth disbanded itself, and each soldier, carrying his spoil, set out for his native village. But the spirit of rapine had been roused in all the adjacent country; and there were many who, in the absence of white-faced fugitives, were by no means reluctant to plunder the black. And it is suspected that very few of the Sepoys, carrying off an ample provision for the remainder of their lives, ever lived to spend the money in the ease and dignity of their native homes.*

1857. June 7.

Rebellion in the Districts.

It is supposed that many, escaping towards Oude, perished in the Gangetic villages not far from the city. For as at Benares, so at Allahabad, the peasantry rose at once under their old Talookhdars, who had been dispossessed by the action of our law-courts; and there was anarchy in the rural districts. The auction purchasers—absentee proprietors—dwelt principally in the city, and the ryots had no sympathy with them. For their own sakes they were eager but

* It is said that about thirty lakhs of rupees (about 300,000*l.*) were in the Allahabad Treasury, and that every Sepoy carried off three or four bags, each containing a thousand rupees (100*l.*)

1857. June 7.

feeble supporters of Government; all the muscle and sinew of the agricultural races were arrayed against us. Indeed, it soon became painfully apparent to the British authorities that the whole country was slipping away from them. For not only in the districts beyond the Ganges, but in those lying between the two rivers, the rural population had risen. The landowners there were principally Mahomedans, and ready to join any movement which threatened to drive the English from the land. It was there, too, in the Doab that Brahminism was most powerfully enthroned. The point where the Ganges and the Jumna meet, known as the Pryag, is one of peculiar sanctity in the estimation of Hindoos, and the Priesthood, therefore, were strong in numbers and in influence. The gathering of the pilgrims was a source of wealth to them, and they believed that if the supremacy of the English were overthrown their gains would be greater and their power on the ascendant. So these "Pryag-wallahs" stirred up the Hindoo population of the Doab; and soon there was scarcely a man of either faith who was not arrayed against us. But on the further bank of the Jumna affairs were more propitious. There were incidental risings, plunderings and burnings of villages, but more on the surface than on the Ganges or in the Doab. For it happened that some powerful Rajahs, whose interest it was to maintain order, either sided with the English or maintained a discreet neutrality whilst the tumult was at its worst, and rose up to aid us when the star of our fortune again began to ascend.*

The Rajahs of Manda, Ditrya, and Barra.

The Moulavee.

After the lapse of a few days, the first orgies of crime being over, and there being nothing more to plunder and little more to destroy, the universal

* See Mr. Fendall Thompson's Official Narrative.

rapine, with all its distractions and confusions and internecine conflicts, began to take a more consistent shape, and something like an organised rebellion arose in its place. There was a man known as the "Moulavee," around whom the insurgent population gathered, as he proclaimed the restored rule of the Emperor of Delhi. Whence he sprung few people at the time could say. But it was known at a later period that he came from one of the Mahomedan villages in the Doab, which had gone into rebellion. Making great pretensions to sanctity, and investing himself with the character of a prophet as well as of a ruler of men, he stimulated the dormant fanaticism of the people, and roused them to array themselves against the Feringhees. Establishing his head-quarters in the Chusroo Bagh—a spacious walled garden, in which were some tombs, held in high veneration—he simulated the possession of miraculous powers, by some obvious trickeries, which deluded his excited followers, and for awhile he was recognised as Governor of Allahabad. It little mattered who or what he was, so long as he was strong in his hatred of the English, and could induce the Mussulman population to believe that the Mahomedan dynasty would soon be restored. So for a little time he succeeded in setting up the likeness of a provisional government, and the name of the Moulavee was on the lips of all the followers of the Prophet. Telling them that the Book of Fate declared the speedy extinction of the white race in India, he urged his people, day after day, to attack the Fort; but, though they made sundry demonstrations, they kept at a discreet distance from our guns.*

1857. June 7.

* Some of the cotemporary accounts state that it was difficult to trace either the name or origin of the Moulavee, and my later investigations have not thrown muc[illegible] light upon the subject. From a [illegible] high civil authority, who had the [illegible]est opportunity of ascertaining [illegible] the history of

1857. June 7. Reinforcements from below.

But this state of things was not to be suffered much longer to endure. The man, who, by his timely energy, had saved Benares, was now pushing on for the rescue of Allahabad. The one true soldier that was needed to put forth a strong hand to smite down the growing rebellion in the Gangetic Provinces was hurrying upwards, with a little band of English fighting men, to show that the national manhood of the country had lost nothing of the might that had enabled it to establish the empire of the Few in the vast territories of the Many. Having sent forward an advanced party of the Fusiliers, under Lieutenant Arnold, and made over the command of Benares to

June 9.

Colonel Gordon, Neill left that place with another party of his regiment, and pressed on by horse-dawk to Allahabad. Arnold had reached the Bridge of Boats on the 7th, but he had been unable at once to cross, as the passage was held by the mutineers, and there had been some delay in sending a steamer to bring them across the river to the Fort. Their arrival did something to establish confidence in the garrison, but the news that Neill was coming did still more. The old high spirit of self-reliance had never waned; and it was still felt that a handful of European soldiers under a commander, with a clear head and a stout heart, might hold Allahabad against the whole world of mutiny and rebellion.

the man, I can learn only that "he was not known in the district before the mutiny," and was "said to be an emissary from Lucknow." The best account that I can find is that given by Mr. Willock in his official report. "At this time," he says, "the city and suburbs were held by a body of rebels under the now well-known Moulavee Lyakut Ali. This man, a weaver by caste, and by trade a schoolmaster, had gained some respect in his village by his excessive sanctity; and on the first spread of the rebellion, the Mahomedan Zemindars of Pergunnah Chail, ready to follow any leader, placed this man at their head, and marched to the city, proclaiming him Governor of the district in the name of the King of Delhi."

On the 11th of June Neill arrived. As he entered the gates of the Fort, the Sentry exclaimed, "Thank God, sir, you'll save us yet!" Lord Canning, who saw clearly that he had now at his disposal one of the men most wanted in such a crisis, had commissioned the electric wires to instruct the Colonel of the Madras Fusiliers to take command at Allahabad; and Neill had hastened upwards, under the burning heats of June, with a disregard for self, which well nigh cost him his life.* He had obtained entrance into the Fort, not without great personal risk; and only the indomitable will within him kept him from succumbing to the fierce rays of the noon-day sun. For some time after his arrival he could sustain himself only by continually lying down and drinking large quantities of champagne and water. But he never for a moment doubted his capacity to grapple successfully with the difficulties before him; whatsoever might be his physical prostration, he had no mental shortcomings, no deterring sense of responsibility to enervate and arrest him. "I had always the greatest confidence in myself," he wrote at this time to the partner of his life; "and although I felt almost dying from complete exhaustion, yet I kept up my heart." Whatever the conjuncture might be, it was the nature of the man to rise to the height of the occasion—"to scorn the consequence and to do the thing." He had long been looking for an opportunity, and, now that it had come, he was not one to succumb to the assaults of bodily weakness, and to

1857. June 11. Arrival of Neill.

* "I was quite done up by my dash from Benares, and getting into the Fort in that noonday heat. I was so exhausted for days, that I was obliged to lie down constantly. I could only sit up for a few minutes at a time, and when our attacks were going on, I was obliged to sit down in the batteries and give my orders and directions. . . For several days I drank champagne and water to keep me up."—*Letter from Colonel Neill to his Wife. MS. Correspondence.*

1857. June 11. halt with the goal before him. He was not a "Sepoy officer," and he had neither any credulity nor any tenderness to deter him from striking root-and-branch at the black soldiery who had betrayed us, and the people who were rising into rebellion on the ruins of the Native Army.

He took in the position of affairs at a glance. On his way from Benares, he had seen that the whole country on the banks of the Ganges was in a state of anarchy and confusion, and he knew that already the rising had become something more than a military mutiny.* At Allahabad, his first thought was, that it was a wonderful interposition of Providence that the Fortress was still in our hands. "How the place has not fallen," he wrote, "that is, not been taken by the Sikhs, is a wonder. They appear to be petted and made much of. The enemy are all around us; we are kept within the Fort. I shall settle that part of it ere long." And he did settle it. The Fort had been invested and menaced by the enemy. Neill's first impulse was to prove that the English could do more

June 12. Offensive operations. than defend themselves. On the morning after his arrival, he opened fire from the Fort guns on the village of Darao-gunj, which was held by a large body of insurgent rabble, and then sent forward to the attack detachments of Fusiliers and Sikhs, who cleared the village, burnt it, and regained possession of the bridge, which Neill afterwards repaired. A further detachment of a hundred men of the Fusiliers came up on that day, under the command of Major

* "June 10. The tone and bearing of the Native officials bad—evidently a good deal of plundering—villages burning in all directions—the country almost deserted—plundered by the Zemindars about. The revenues just about to be collected—the toll-house on road to Sydabad plundered—nearly destroyed—the body of the murdered man, an European, in the house; his daughter said to be taken off by a neighbouring Zemindar." —*Neill's Journal, MS.*

Stephenson, and passed over without interruption to the Fort. 1857. June 12—14.

Removal of the Sikhs from the Fort.

Neill now felt himself strong enough for any emergency. The first suggestion of this increased strength was the removal of the Sikhs from the Fort. In truth, they were fast demoralising our own people in the garrison. They had been going in and out revelling in the pillage, and the Volunteers had been by no means behind them in predatory activity, especially in the direction of the "six dozen cases" of strong drink. The stores of the European merchants and the go-downs of the river steam-companies, with all their undelivered consignments, had been plundered; and beer, wines, and spirits were as plentiful as water in the Fort. The Sikhs brought in large supplies of liquor of all kinds, drank what they could, and sold the rest to the Europeans. The finest champagnes of Clicquot and Perrier-Jouet, and the best brandies of Martel and Hennessey, were selling for sixpence a bottle. So a reign of intoxication commenced which, for a while, subverted all military authority, and made us as helpless as children. This was an enemy for which Neill was not prepared; but his clear brain soon discerned the means of meeting and subduing it. He directed the Commissariat Officers to purchase, at the prices asked by the Sikhs, all the liquor remaining in their hands, and to lodge it securely in the Government stores. This done, the removal of the Sikhs to quarters outside the Fort was comparatively easy; but it was not to be done by force. He had taken counsel with Brasyer and with the energetic Magistrate Court, and it had been determined that the characteristic greed of the Sikhs should still be stimulated by thoughts of the plunder of some of the rebel zemindarrees. So they were

1857. June 15.

persuaded to take up a position in some old Government buildings outside the Fort, commanded by the guns on its ramparts.

Attack on the Insurgents.

Having thus overcome the difficulties which lay in his path, Neill addressed himself earnestly to the work before him—the dispersal of the rebels and the restoration of order. On the 15th of June, having sent off the Christian women and children in a river steamer to Calcutta, he turned his available resources to the best account, and made an impression on the enemy, which greatly disheartened and enfeebled them. Having directed the guns of the Fort to open upon the villages or suburbs of Kydgunj and Moolegunj, he sent Harward, with a howitzer and a party of volunteer riflemen on board a steamer, to operate from the river, and marched a detachment of Fusiliers, Sikhs, and Irregular Cavalry upon the villages, with orders to scour them thoroughly and penetrate into the country beyond. The land party met with stalwart opposition, but the rush of the Sikhs was irresistible. They swept through the villages, and such was the terror that our demonstration on that day inspired, that when night fell, the Insurgent leaders sought safety in flight, and deserted the guns, which they had taken from us, and the prisoners whom they had captured at the commencement of the outbreak; and among them was young Cheek, of whose fate I have already spoken, and who was rescued only to die.*

The aspect of affairs now began rapidly to im-

* The Allahabad volunteers showed great spirit and pluck, erring, however, on the side of exuberance. Neill complained bitterly that upon this occasion they had impeded his operations by "firing upon a herd of bullocks, and other madness"—bullocks at that time being as valuable as European soldiers. "These gentlemen volunteers," he characteristically added, "behave so lawlessly and insubordinately, that I have threatened to shoot or hang a few if they do not improve."

prove. "On the 17th the Magistrate proceeded to the Cotwallee, and there restored his own authority and installed his own officers." "No resistance," it is added, "was offered, and the whole place seemed deserted."* A terrible rumour had been running through the streets of Allahabad. It had been reported that the English in the Fort were about to bombard the city. What was the origin of the story it is hard to say. It may have grown up, as other rumours grew up, in the hotbed of a people's fears; or it may have been propagated by those whose interest it was to sweep out the insurgents.† But from whatsoever source it sprung, it was almost magical in its effects. Nothing that the Moulavee and his lieutenants could do to reassure the minds of the people had availed to allay the panic and restrain the flight, and before nightfall, on the day of Neill's victory, according to the Moulavee's own story, "not a house was tenanted, and not a light was to be seen in the city." Lyakut Ali himself had escaped towards Cawnpore. 1857. June 17.

On the 18th, Neill marched out again with his whole force. Sending one detachment to attack the Pathan village of Derryabad and the Mehwattee villages of Syderbad and Russelpore, he led the main

* Report of Mr. Fendall Thompson.

† The following is the Moulavee's account of the evacuation. "Some evil-minded men," he said, "who had sided with 'the accursed ones,' urged that for a time the Fort would be a safe retreat, and that if they would remain in it a few days longer, they (the evil-minded Natives) would contrive to spread abroad in the city fearful reports that the English were preparing the Artillery of the Fort to destroy the city, and that before dawn they would begin bombarding it with shot and shell. To show the sincerity of their advice, these men, with their followers, set off, giving out to all that they had left their houses and property to God's protection, and were going to save themselves by flight. On hearing this fearful report, the people, notwithstanding my repeated injunctions, commenced a precipitate flight, with their families and goods."—*Perwannah addressed by the Moulavee Lyakut Ali, apparently to the King of Delhi.—Supplement to Allahabad Official Narrative.*

1857. June 18. body into the city, which he found deserted, and afterwards halted them in the now-desolated cantonment on the old parade-ground of the Sixth. The fighting was now over. The work had been done. The English were masters, not merely of the Fort, but of the recovered city, and the European station from which they had been driven scarcely two weeks before. And now there lay before them the great question—the most difficult, perhaps, which soldiers and statesmen ever have the responsibility of solving —whether, after such convulsions as have been illustrated in these pages, true righteousness and true wisdom consisted in extending the hand of mercy and aiming at conciliation, or in dealing out a stern and terrible retribution. Our soldiers and statesmen in June, 1857, at Allahabad, solved the question in practice by adopting the latter course.

Retribution. Over the whole history of the Sepoy War—over the whole length and breadth of the country which witnessed its manifold horrors—there is no darker cloud than that which gathered over Allahabad in this terrible summer. It is an early chapter of the chronicle of the great conflict of races which I am now writing; and though foul crimes had even then been committed by our enemies, they were light in comparison with what were to come, and the retribution also was light.* Perhaps, however, the English-

* It is to be observed, that at this time an impression was abroad that acts of barbarity had been committed, which were afterwards doubted, if not wholly disproved. I find the following in Neill's Journal, under date June 17, MS.: "A Sowar of Mr. Court's, named Syed Esau Ally, brought in for having joined the Moulavee and insurgents. Three witnesses saw him. He had served about twenty years. Direct his immediate execution by hanging. This is the sixth unfortunate wretch I have ordered for immediate death, a duty I never contemplated having

man had at this time a keener sense than afterwards possessed him of the humiliation which had been put upon his conquering race. Much of the anguish was in the novelty of the thing. The sting, though it struck deeper, was afterwards less severely felt, because the flesh had become indurated, and the nerves were more tensely strung. So it happened that whilst the first bitterness of our degradation—the degradation of fearing those whom we had taught to fear us—was still fresh upon our people, there came a sudden accession of stout English hearts and strong English hands, ready at once to punish and to awe. Martial Law had been proclaimed; those terrible Acts passed by the Legislative Council in May and June were in full operation; and soldiers and civilians alike were holding Bloody Assize, or slaying Natives without any assize at all, regardless of sex or age. Afterwards, the thirst for blood grew stronger still. It is on the records of our British Parliament, in papers sent home by the Governor-General of India in Council, that "the aged, women, and children, are sacrificed,

1857. June 18—30.

to perform. God grant I may have acted with justice. I know I have with severity, but under all the circumstances I trust for forgiveness. I have done all for the good of my country, to re-establish its prestige and power, and to put down this most barbarous, inhuman insurrection. The instances of refined cruelty, treachery, and the most brutal barbarity, are too numerous. One poor lady, Mrs. Macdonald, at Meerut, near her confinement, is brutally treated; has her nose, ears, hands, and breasts cut off, and at last has the child cut out of her. Mrs. Chambers, a beautiful young girl, only just come out married from home, at the same place, has her throat cut by a butcher. Miss Jennings and her father, a clergyman at Delhi, are both brutally murdered in the palace before the king, she, poor creature, subjected to the most unheard-of indignities and torture beforehand." I have already stated that Miss Jennings was murdered, not in the presence of the king, and that she was not outraged (*ante*, page 80). Mrs. Chambers was murdered, as is stated, by a butcher, and her murderer was hung (*ante*, page 69). I can find no evidence of the mutilations said to have been inflicted on Mrs. Macdonald. I have quoted this passage from Neill's Journal mainly to show that he had a strong religious sense of his responsibility, and that his executions were not as numerous as has been asserted.

1857. June 18—30. as well as those guilty of rebellion."* They were not deliberately hanged, but burnt to death in their villages—perhaps now and then accidentally shot. Englishmen did not hesitate to boast, or to record their boastings in writing, that they had "spared no one," and that "peppering away at niggers" was very pleasant pastime, "enjoyed amazingly."† And it has been stated, in a book patronised by high official authorities, that "for three months eight dead-carts daily went their rounds from sunrise to sunset to take down the corpses which hung at the cross-roads and market-places," and that "six thousand beings" had been thus "summarily disposed of and launched into eternity."‡

I merely state these things. There are some questions so stupendous that human weakness may well leave it to the Almighty Wisdom to decide them. There is a dreadful story to be told in another chapter. God only knows whether what has been told in this contributed to the results to be presently recorded. But there is one great lesson to be learnt from the tragedies of Benares and Allahabad. It is the great lesson of Universal Toleration. An Englishman is almost suffocated with indignation when he reads that Mrs. Chambers or Miss Jennings was hacked to death by a dusky ruffian; but in Native histories, or, history being wanting, in Native legends and traditions, it may be recorded against our people, that mothers and wives and children, with less familiar names, fell miserable victims to the first swoop of English

* Papers presented to Parliament, February 4, 1858, moved for by Mr. Vernon Smith, formerly President of the Board of Control, and signed H. D. Seymour.

† Ibid.

‡ "Travels of a Hindoo" (Bholonauth Chunder), edited by Mr. Talboys Wheeler. See note in the Appendix. I believe the statement in the text to be an exaggeration, but such exaggerations are very significant.

vengeance; and these stories may have as deep a pathos as any that rend our own hearts. It may be, too, that the plea of provocation, which invests the most sanguinary acts of the white man in this deadly struggle with the attributes of righteous retribution, is not wholly to be rejected when urged in extenuation of the worst deeds of those who have never known Christian teaching. 1857. June 18—30.

Preparations for an advance.

Whilst Neill was thus re-establishing British authority at Allahabad, he was depressed by the thought of the danger surrounding his countrymen at Cawnpore and Lucknow, and eager to equip a force with the utmost possible despatch for the relief of those important posts. Men were available for the purpose, but means were wanting. The scarcity of provisions suitable to the English soldier, concerning which Mr. Tucker had written to Lord Canning, and which the Governor-General was taking prompt measures to rectify, was one great impediment to the desired movement. There was, too, a want of carriage. Large numbers of Commissariat bullocks had been collected for the service of the Army, but, on the first burst of the rebellion, the insurgents had swept them away, and of all the losses we sustained this was, perhaps, the most grievous. Then, too, there was a want of tents. There was a want of well nigh everything required by British troops in the worst part of the Indian summer, when the intolerable heat might any day be followed by deluging rains, which would quickly turn the baked earth into a great morass.

It was no fault of the Commissariat at this time that the arrangements progressed so slowly. Captain

1857. June 18—30. Davidson, who was at the head of the department, did all that could be done to collect supplies and carriage; but the convulsions of the preceding fortnight had dispersed the people upon whom he would have relied for aid, and well nigh destroyed the resources of the place. Those who would have come forward as contractors at such a time, had fled in dismay—some from the violence of the insurgents, and some, in ignorant terror, from the anticipated retribution of the English—and many had returned to find themselves ruined. Property was destroyed. Industry was paralysed. The great incubus of fear pressed universally upon the trading classes. Whether more might have been done, at the commencement of the outbreak, to save the supplies then in hand—both the property of the Government and of private individuals—was not now the question. Davidson had to deal with things as they were, and it was not his fault that in the last week of June they did not wear a different complexion. Eager as Neill was to push forwards, he could not discern in this delayed departmental action any just ground of complaint. It was clear to him that the evil lay in the circumstances of his position, not in the incapacity of his agents.*

* It is right that Neill's opinion on this subject should be stated in his own words. Great blame was cast on the Commissariat by cotemporary journalists, especially by the editor of the *Friend of India*, who published an article with the stinging title, "How Cawnpore was lost." Upon this, Neill very generously wrote to Captain Davidson, saying: "The editor has certainly made a mistake in stating that your stores were outside. I understood that all we had was inside the Fort; and when I joined, and until the insurgents were cleared out of the place, the Commissariat were confined to the Fort entirely. The steamer Godowns had been gutted, the bazaar up to the walls of the Fort plundered, in the occupation of the enemy, your contractors driven away, and their property either plundered or not available for the service for some days after these insurgents had been driven away. It was no fault whatever of the Commissariat that it should have been reduced to the condition yours was, from being cut off from outside, and the dispersion of your people; but you had done all you could before the outbreak in

And soon a greater evil befel him; for whilst he was waiting for means to equip the relieving force, Cholera swept down upon his troops and struck them with terrific suddenness. The intense heat of the weather, the constant exposure, the want of wholesome food, and the abundance of stimulating liquors, combined to facilitate its pestilential approaches. On the 23rd of June the services of seventy men had been lost to the British Commander. "We buried twenty, three nights ago, at one funeral," wrote an officer of the Fusiliers, "and the shrieks of the dying were something awful. Two poor ladies who were living over the hospital died, I believe from fright." Then other very grievous wants afflicted our people. Whilst in this miserable condition, it was discovered that nearly everything that could diminish the miseries of the sick who were to be left behind, or enable the convalescent to move forward, was wanting to the British Commander. The reign of terror had done its sure work. Camp-followers of all kinds were "almost unprocurable." Whilst our invalids lay gasping in the stifling atmosphere of the improvised hospital, there were few or none to pull the punkah-ropes or to water the tatties. There were few dhoolies, and, as workmen were not to be obtained, none could be made; and if they had been made, there would have been no bearers to carry

1857. June 18—30 The outbreak of Cholera.

storing inside the Fort sufficient to make us independent for some time, had the insurgents kept hold of the city. In consequence of your being cut off from most of your people and resources outside, you were, in my opinion, at the time I arrived, disorganised, in so far as unable to equip a force or detachment to move. The exertions of yourself and officers, from my arrival until my departure from Allahabad, could not have been surpassed, and it surprised me you were so soon able to regain possession of the resources of the place, and enable me to move Renaud's detachment on the 30th." This was written on the 22nd of August. It may be added, that, two months before, Neill had written in his journal that great efforts were made to get in supplies and he had added, "Captain Davidson seems to be a most energetic man."—*MS. Corr.*

1857. June 18—30.

them.* For everywhere the terror-stricken Natives stood aloof from the chastising Englishmen. It was as though we had dried up the wells and destroyed the crops, from which we were to obtain our sustenance. Without the aid of the Natives we could do nothing; and yet we were doing our best to drive them far beyond the glimmer of our tents.

Renaud's advance.

And so the last day of June found Neill still at Allahabad. Not a single European soldier had been sent to succour Cawnpore. But on the afternoon of that day a detachment was to start under Major Renaud of the Madras Fusiliers. It consisted of four hundred European soldiers, three hundred Sikhs, one hundred troopers of Irregular Cavalry, and two guns. Renaud, a fine soldier, with his heart in his work, had received written instructions from Neill as to his course of action; and he had become the not unwilling recipient of orders to inflict a terrible retribution upon all suspected of guilty complicity in the foul designs of the enemy. But indiscriminate slaughter was no part of the commission. "Attack and destroy," wrote Neill, "all places en route close to the road occupied by the enemy, but touch no others; encourage the inhabitants to return, and instil confidence into all of the restoration of British authority." Certain guilty villages were marked out for destruction, and all the men inhabiting them were to be slaughtered. All Sepoys of mutinous regiments not giving a good account of themselves were to be hanged. The town of Futtehpore, which had re-

* Colonel Neill reported that "followers of all kinds are almost unprocurable; there are but few punkahs and no tatties; the men have, therefore, not the proper advantages of barrack accommodation for this hot season." It was discovered, too, that "there were but sixteen dhoolies available (although a considerable number of these was a primary requisite for the projected expedition), and all materials for making others were wanting, as well as workmen."

volted, was to be attacked, and the Pathan quarters destroyed, with all their inhabitants. "All heads of insurgents, particularly at Futtehpore, to be hanged. If the Deputy-Collector is taken, hang him, and have his head cut off and stuck up on one of the principal (Mahomedan) buildings of the town."* And whilst Renaud's column, with these terrible instructions, was to advance along the straight road to Cawnpore, Captain Spurgin, with another detachment, was to take a steamer up the Ganges to the same point, to co-operate with Renaud on his march, to anchor as near as possible to Wheeler's entrenchments, and to place the vessel at Sir Hugh's disposal for the rescue of the women and children, the sick and the wounded, of his distressed garrison. 1857. June 30.

* The significance of these instructions will be made more apparent in a future chapter, wherein the story of Futtehpore will be told.

*** It should have been observed, at page 259, with reference to the statement that "those terrible Acts passed by the Legislative Council in May and July were in full operation," that, in addition to the Act of May 30 (already recited), another was passed on June 6, extending the powers given in the former: "By Act No. XIV. of 1857, passed on the 6th of June, provision was made for the punishment of persons convicted of exciting mutiny or sedition in the army, the offender was rendered liable to the punishment of death and the forfeiture of all his property; and persons guilty of harbouring such offenders were made liable to heavy punishment. Power was also given to general courts-martial to try all persons, whether amenable to the Articles of War or not, charged with any offence punishable by this or the preceding Act; and the Supreme and Local executive governments were authorised to issue commissions in any district, for the trial by single commissioners, without the assistance of law officers or assessors, and with absolute and final power of judgment and execution, of any crime against the State, or any 'heinous offence' whatever; the term 'heinous offence' being declared to include every crime attended with great personal violence, or committed with the intention of forwarding the designs of those who are waging war against the State."—*Despatch of Government of India to Court of Directors, December* 11, 1857.

CHAPTER II.

ARRIVAL OF HAVELOCK AT ALLAHABAD—MEETING WITH NEILL—ADVANCE OF RENAUD—HAVELOCK'S BRIGADE—CAWNPORE—THE CITY—THE CANTONMENT—SIR HUGH WHEELER—DANGERS OF HIS POSITION—THE ENTRENCHMENTS—REVOLT OF THE NATIVE REGIMENTS—DOONDOO PUNT, "NANA SAHIB"—THE SIEGE—THE CAPITULATION—MASSACRE AT THE GHAUT—ESCAPE OF A SOLITARY BOAT—ITS ADVENTURES ON THE RIVER—HEROIC DEEDS OF THOMSON AND DELAFOSSE.

1857. June. ON that 30th of June—a day rendered memorable in the history of the revolt by a great event to be hereafter narrated—a new actor appeared on the scene at Allahabad. On that morning a soldier of high rank and high reputation arrived from Calcutta. His arrival would have been welcomed by all men, for good soldiers were sorely needed, but there was one adverse circumstance, which detracted from the general delight. The officer who had come up by dawk, with a special commission from Government to take command of the troops advancing to the relief of Cawnpore and Lucknow, thereby, in virtue of seniority, superseded Colonel Neill, in whom all men had a steadfast faith. Three days before the arrival of the officer who was to supersede him, he had written to the Governor-General, saying, "We are getting on well here, laying in grain and collecting carriage for Brigadier Havelock's Brigade." There might seem to be some taint of bitterness in these words. But Neill did not slacken in his exertions because the brigade, which he had hoped himself to command, was to be commanded by another. He had learnt some days before that it would not devolve upon him to rescue Sir Hugh Wheeler and his comrades, if already destruction had not descended upon them; but he had pushed forward his preparations for the advance with the utmost possible despatch, as though there had been no one coming, after he had borne so long the burden and heat of the day, to gather up the fruits of his toil, and to snatch from him the glory which he coveted. But recognising the chances of the service, to which every soldier must submit, he neither complained nor repined, but waited for his own time, feeling sure that it would come. 1857. June.

He was no common man who had now arrived to command the brigade. Colonel Henry Havelock was a veteran officer of the Queen's Army; but during his forty years of service he had done as much good Indian work, in camp and cantonment, as if he had been attached to one of the regiments of the Company in the old days, when officers did not live on furlough. He had fought in Burmah and in Afghanistan, and was familiar with nearly every great military station lying between those two extreme points. He had tested the temper of Mahratta armies in Central India, and of the old Sikh battalions in the zenith of their warlike pride. He was every inch a soldier. Military glory was the passion of his life. But he was a man of the middle classes, without powerful interest or wealthy connexions, having only his own merit to recommend him; and he had Havelock.

1857. June. risen slowly from subaltern to captain, from captain to field-officer, and now, at the age of sixty-two, he had never held an independent command; he had never been permitted to realise that great dream of his youth, that great ambition of his manhood—to head an army in the battle-field. For nearly half a century he had been sedulously studying his profession, reading every military memoir that he could obtain, English or Continental, and turning his matured knowledge to account by contributing from the wealth of his own personal experiences to the military history of his country. In a thorough, artistic knowledge of the principles of European warfare, no soldier in the country surpassed him. There was no disinclination anywhere to acknowledge this; but some thought that he was a theorist and a pedant, and doubted whether all his book-learning would profit him much amidst the stern realities of active service.

This mistrust was, perhaps, in some measure engendered by the fact that Henry Havelock was what in the light language of the camp was called a "saint." A man of strong religious convictions, he had married a daughter of the great Baptist Apostle, Dr. Marshman of Serampore. This alliance, which was one of unmixed happiness to him, was followed by his public acceptance of the tenets and formularies of the great and enlightened sect of Protestant Christianity in which his wife had been nurtured and reared. There was laughter and ridicule from the profane, but, perhaps, little surprise anywhere; for Havelock had ever been a God-fearing, self-denying man; somewhat rigid and austere; and having only Christian people to deal with, he had not hesitated to teach them to be good men as well as good soldiers. Even

in his first campaign, thirty years before the period 1857.
to which this History relates, the company which he June.
commanded was known as "Havelock's saints"—men who were never drunk and always ready for service. But the Christian zeal of Henry Havelock never overlaid his martial instincts. He was thoroughly persuaded in his own mind that war was righteous and carnage beautiful. And ever as years went on, and his hair grew white, and his features sharpened, and his small spare figure lost the elasticity, though never the erectness of his prime, he cherished the same strong desire to command an army in the field. He has often been likened to one of the Puritan warriors of the Great Rebellion, and it has been said that "a more simple-minded, upright, God-fearing soldier was not among Cromwell's Ironsides."*

He was Adjutant-General of Queen's troops in India, when, in the cold weather of 1856-57, he was selected by Sir James Outram to command a division of the Army then embarking for Persia; and, with the permission of the Commander-in-Chief, he proceeded to Bombay to join the force with the rank of Brigadier-General. Small opportunity of gaining distinction was permitted to him, for the war speedily collapsed, and the sword was returned to the scabbard. On the 5th of April, when Havelock was mustering his division for church service, Outram announced to him that a treaty of peace had been signed. Of all the bountiful illustrations of God's providence working in our behalf, which that eventful year witnessed, this was perhaps the most signal. It was a merciful deliverance beyond the power of words fully to express. Havelock did not then know its full significance; but in a little while he acknow-

* *Westminster Review*, quoted by Mr. Montgomery Martin.

1857. June.

ledged with thanksgiving the abundant goodness of God in thus setting free so many European regiments. Quitting Mohamrah on the 15th of May, he was at Bombay on the 29th. It had been his first thought to rejoin the Head-Quarters of the Army by a landward march, but, after consulting Lord Elphinstone and his Military Secretary, it appeared to him that the journey was not practicable; so he took ship for Galle, hoping there to catch a steamer for Calcutta. Off Cultura, in Ceylon, the vessel went aground at night, and was in infinite danger of going to pieces before assistance could come from shore. Mercifully delivered from the waves, he made his way to Galle, found a steamer there, which had been despatched for European troops, and embarked for Madras. There he found that Sir Patrick Grant, the Commander-in-Chief of that Presidency, had been summoned to Calcutta, and was waiting for the *Fire Queen* to convey him to the Hooghly.

Sir Patrick Grant.

It was of no small importance that Lord Canning should receive the advice and assistance of an experienced officer of the Bengal Army, acquainted with the character and the temper of the Native soldiery and versed in all military details. Sir Patrick Grant had been Adjutant-General of the Army of the chief Presidency; he had seen hard service in the field; and he was held in esteem both as a good soldier and as a ripe military administrator. When, therefore, tidings of General Anson's death reached Lord Canning,* he placed himself at once in commu-

* This was on the 3rd of June. The first intelligence came from Sir John Lawrence at Rawul Pindee. Writing to England on the following day, Lord Canning said: "It comes upon me as a sad and dispiriting blow in the midst of present troubles. But this is not a time to be depressed by any calamity, when every effort must be made to keep up the hearts of those around us. I assure you that they need it, though I am glad

nication with Grant. Having previously telegraphed to Madras, on the 6th of June the Governor-General wrote to him, saying, "My first impulse was to send for you to fill the place of acting Commander-in-Chief, and every day's deliberate consideration has confirmed it. I am satisfied that there is no man who can so well serve the State at this crisis as yourself, and I earnestly beg you to come to Calcutta as soon as you can. Should this not reach you in time to allow of your coming by the next packet, perhaps a sailing vessel could be taken up, by which time would be saved. But you will judge of this. I would have sent a steamer for you two days ago, but I have none here but the *Assaye*, and she must go to Rangoon for the Twenty-ninth as soon as she is coaled. The storm has not begun to clear yet, nor will it till Delhi falls." So Grant and Havelock, embarking together, steamed up the Bay to Calcutta, and arrived there on the 17th of June. It was a source of great personal happiness to the latter that he was accompanied by his son, then a subaltern of the Tenth Foot, in whom already were discernible all the instincts and capacities which combine to make a good soldier. 1857. June.

For a man eager for military service on an extended field of action, no time could be more propitious. Welcome, indeed, to Lord Canning was the advent of so tried and capable a soldier as Havelock; and Patrick Grant, who well knew his worth, was forward to recommend him for immediate employment. News had come that Benares had been saved; but the fate of Allahabad was still doubtful, and

to say that the panic which had seized the Calcutta world when the last mail left is, in a measure, suppressed. . . . I have telegraphed to Sir Patrick Grant to come to Calcutta immediately to assume the office of acting Commander-in-Chief."—*MS. Correspondence.*

1857. June. Cawnpore and Lucknow were girt around by deadly peril. It was the work of Government at this time, not only to push forward every available European soldier, but to take steps to turn those reinforcements to the best account by wise and skilful organisation. Havelock had already mapped out a plan of operations, the formation of a movable column, acting upwards from the Lower Provinces, being a part of it; and this column he was commissioned to command, with the rank of Brigadier-General. He was directed, "after quelling all disturbances at Allahabad, not to lose a moment in supporting Sir Henry Lawrence at Lucknow and Sir Hugh Wheeler at Cawnpore," and to "take prompt measures for dispersing and utterly destroying all mutineers and insurgents." The sovereign importance of swift action was earnestly impressed upon him, and it was added that the Commander-in-Chief, having "entire confidence in his well-known and often-proved high ability, vigour, and judgment," refrained from giving more definite instructions, and left him to shape his movements according to the circumstances that might develop themselves.*

The ambitious hopes of a life were now on the point of absolute fulfilment. He had an independent command; no one to control his movements in the field; no one to hamper his individual judgment. But with all his self-reliance, he rested, in his human weakness, more on the mighty arm of the God of Battles. "May God," he said, "give me wisdom to fulfil the expectations of Government, and to restore tranquillity in the disturbed districts." There were some circumstances against him. It was the worst season of the year for military operations. The alter-

* Marshman's Life of Havelock.

nations of scorching heat and drenching rain, which are the atmospherical necessities of an Indian July, were trying in the extreme to the European soldier. His force was to consist of four regiments of Infantry, with Cavalry and Artillery. Two of these regiments, the Sixty-fourth and the Seventy-eighth Highlanders, had belonged to his old Persian division; and this was a source of satisfaction to him. But he was sorely distressed when he thought of the want of horse, the want of guns, and the want of gunners, and the certain scarcity of carriage which would perplex him at Allahabad, where his force was to be formed, owing to the heavy loss of Commissariat cattle which had been sustained by us during the disorders of that place. Still, full of heart and hope, he took his leave of the Governor-General and the Commander-in-Chief, and turned his back on Calcutta, proceeding upwards by dawk, on the 25th of June. 1857. June.

And now, on the morning of the last day of the month, he was breakfasting with Neill at Allahabad. Much had these two fine soldiers to say to each other. Neill had to report what had been recently done at Allahabad. His instructions to Renaud and Spurgin were brought under review, and were cordially approved by Havelock. Nothing could have been better than the arrangements which had been made for the despatch of this vanguard of the relieving army, or more carefully considered than all the instructions which had been issued.* It was agreed Havelock and Neill.

* These instructions, the substance of which is given in the preceding chapters (and which were published verbatim in the Memoir of General Neill, in the "Lives of Indian Officers"), were highly commended by Sir Patrick Grant, who wrote: "Your instructions to Renaud and Spurgin are admirable, and provide for every possible present

1857. June. that Renaud should advance that evening, but that the steamer which was to carry Spurgin and his detachment should not steam out at once, as its progress would be more rapid than that of the marching column, whose advance it was intended to cover.

Advance of Renaud's Column.

So Renaud, leading the van of the relieving force, that after long delay was sent on to save our imperilled people at Cawnpore, pressed on, proud of his commission, and eager to do the bidding of his chief. It was a grand movement in advance—but, like many of our grand movements, the heart-breaking words "Too Late" were written in characters of darkest night across it. On they marched for three days, leaving everywhere behind them as they went traces of the retributory power of the English in desolated villages and corpses dangling from the branches of trees.* But on the 2nd or 3rd of July,† a Native spy, sent by Sir Henry Lawrence from Lucknow,

circumstances as well as all eventualities, and by them, and them only, Renaud should have been guided. I hope you were in time to prevent the withdrawing Spurgin's detachment from the steamer, and that the vessel has proceeded up the river according to your original intention. Sending her was an excellent measure, and I anticipate most favourable results from it, and she will be of incalculable value in collecting boats and assisting in making the passage of the river after the work to be done at Cawnpore is finished."—*MS. Correspondence.*

* I should be untrue to history if I did not record my belief that these retributory measures were distinguished by undue severity. William Russell, among whose many high qualities as a public writer truthfulness is conspicuous, records the following in his "Diary in India:" "In the course of a conversation to-day, an officer, who was attached to Renaud's column when it moved out in advance of Havelock's force, told me that the executions of Natives were indiscriminate to the last degree. . . In two days forty-two men were hanged on the roadside, and a batch of twelve men were executed because their faces were 'turned the wrong way' when they were met on the march. All the villages in his front were burnt when he halted. These 'severities' could not have been justified by the Cawnpore massacre, because they took place before that diabolical act. The officer in question remonstrated with Renaud, on the ground that, if he persisted in this course, he would empty the villages, and render it impossible to supply the army with provisions." This is confirmed by the account of the signs of retribution apparent to those who followed in the wake of Renaud's march.

† On the 3rd, Lieut. Chalmers rode into Allahabad with the news.

came into Renaud's camp, and announced that nothing could now be done for the relief of Cawnpore. Wheeler had capitulated, and all his people had been mercilessly destroyed. 1857. July 4.

This miserable intelligence was received with different emotions by Neill and Havelock. The former was long unwilling to believe that Cawnpore had fallen. He looked upon the story as an invention of the enemy intended to arrest the forward movement of the Force which the English were equipping for its relief. His wish was father to the thought; for, although he could not reproach himself for the delay that had occurred in the despatch of reinforcements to Wheeler's help—delays, which had the full sanction of the highest military authority in the country* —he could not, without reluctance, accept the fact that those delays had shattered all his hopes of succouring our distressed people, and had turned the relieving force into an army of retribution. But Havelock had full faith in the disastrous story. Two spies came into Allahabad. They spoke of what they had seen. Examined separately, they recited the same details; there were no contradictions or discrepancies in their evidence. They amply confirmed the reports which had reached Renaud's Camp, and had been sent in by him to Allahabad. Taking these

* Sir Patrick Grant had written to him more than once to urge him to be cautious, and not to strip Allahabad of troops or to send an insufficient force to Cawnpore. "You talk of an early advance towards Cawnpore, and I shall be right glad that you made a move in that direction; but I pray you to bear in mind that Allahabad is a point of the very greatest importance, the perfect security of which ought not to be neglected on any account." And again, on the following day: "Far be it from me to hamper you in any way—your energy, decision, and activity are admirable; but I must warn you to be cautious not to commit too small a force of Europeans towards Cawnpore. If Delhi has fallen, as we believe it has, the fugitives from it will all make for Cawnpore and Lucknow, and there will certainly be an immense gathering of scum of all sorts at those points."—*MS. Correspondence.*

1857. June. different views of the actual position of affairs in advance, the two soldiers differed with respect to the course to be pursued. Havelock despatched orders to Renaud to stand fast. But Neill was eager for him to push forward, and telegraphed to the Commander-in-Chief remonstrances against delay. Havelock argued that if Cawnpore had fallen, the troops that had besieged it would be released for action elsewhere, and would assuredly move down in immense numbers to intercept the advance of the column from Allahabad, and utterly to overwhelm it. But Neill, still thinking the report a *rusé* of the enemy, eagerly contended that all would be lost if we faltered at such a moment. Both were right in their several deductions. Time proved that Havelock was right as to the facts. Cawnpore had fallen, and the garrison had been destroyed almost to a man. How it happened—how for more than three weeks the little band of heroic Englishmen had stood their ground against the teeming multitude of the enemy, and how at last treachery had accomplished what could not be done by honest fighting, is now to be told. It is the saddest chapter in the whole history of the war—but, perhaps, the brightest. However feeble the recital, no Englishman can ever read it without the profoundest emotions both of pity and of pride.

The City of Cawnpore. The city or town of Cawnpore had nothing in or about it to make it famous in story. It had no venerable traditions, no ancient historical remains, no architectural attractions, to enable it to rank with Benares or Agra. Commercially it shone only as the city of the workers-in-leather. It was a great emporium for harness of all kinds, and for boots and shoes alike of the Asiatic and the European types of civilisation. If not better, these articles were cheaper than elsewhere, and few English officers passed through the place without supplying themselves with leather-ware. But life and motion were never wanting to the place, especially on the river-side, where many stirring signs of mercantile activity were ever to be seen. The broad waters of the Ganges, near the Great Ghaut, floated vessels of all sizes and all shapes, from the stately venetianed pinnace to the rude open "dinghy," or wherry; and there clustering about the landing-steps, busy with or idly watching the debarkation of produce and goods of varied kinds, or waiting for the ferry-boats that crossed and recrossed the Ganges, were to be seen a motley assemblage of people of different nations and different callings and different costumes; whilst a continual Babel of many voices rose from the excited crowd. In the streets of the town itself there was little to evoke remark. But, perhaps, among its sixty thousand inhabitants there may have been, owing to its contiguity to the borders of Oude, rather a greater strength than common of the "dangerous classes."

1857. May.

The Cantonment.

The station of Cawnpore was a large, straggling place, six or seven miles in extent. The British lines stretched along the southern bank of the Ganges, which about midway between the two extremities of the cantonment was spanned by a bridge of boats, leading from a point opposite the city to the Lucknow road on the other bank. There was nothing peculiar to Cawnpore in the fact that the private dwelling-houses and public offices of the English were scattered about in the most promiscuous manner, as though they had fallen from the skies or been projected by an earthquake. At the north-western extremity,

1857. May. lying between the road to Bithoor and the road to Delhi, were the principal houses of the civilians, the Treasury, the Gaol, and the Mission premises. These buildings lay beyond the lines of the military cantonment, in the extreme north-western corner of which was the Magazine. In the centre, between the city and the river, were the Church, the Assembly rooms, the Theatre, the Telegraph office, and other public edifices; whilst scattered about here and there, without any apparent system, were the principal military buildings, European and Native; the Native lines lying for the most part in the rear towards the south-eastern point of the cantonment. It was the essential condition of an English cantonment that it should straggle,—and there was not one more straggling than Cawnpore. But, on the whole, it was not a disagreeable, nor, indeed, an inconvenient place, although the distances to be travelled were great and the heat of the summer months was excessive. Even to the dust, which, except during the rainy season, was prodigious, the residents became accustomed after a little while; or, if they did not, they reconciled themselves to it by thinking that the station had many great social advantages, that it was well provided with means of amusement upon the most approved principles of western civilisation, and that "Europe goods" of all kinds were almost as plentiful as in Calcutta.

For during a long series of years Cawnpore had been one of the most important military stations in India. There were few officers either of the Queen's or the Company's Army who, during the period of their Eastern service, had not, at some time or other, done duty in that vast cantonment. But the extension of our Empire towards the Afghan frontier had greatly diminished its importance as a military position; and although the subsequent annexation of Oude had done something to restore the faded pretensions of the Cawnpore division, the station itself only suffered further decline. It was still the Head Quarters of the Division, and the commanding General resided there with the Division Staff. But there were no longer European Regiments, or even an European Regiment, in its barracks. A great strength of Native soldiery garrisoned the place, with some sixty European Artillerymen, and afterwards sixty men of Her Majesty's Eighty-fourth Regiment and a few Madras Fusiliers, whom Tucker and Ponsonby had sent on from Benares.* The First, the Fifty-third, and the Fifty-sixth Sepoy Regiments of Infantry were there, and the Second Regiment of Sepoy Cavalry—in all, about three thousand men. And it was computed that the aggregate population of the Cantonment, with its vast assemblage of camp-followers, was nearly equal to that of the Town. 1857. May.

Sir Hugh Wheeler.

The Cawnpore Division was then commanded by General Sir Hugh Wheeler. He was an old and a distinguished officer of the Company's Army. He had seen much good service in Afghanistan and in the Punjab, and had won his spurs under Gough in the second Sikh War, in command of a division of his army. No man knew the Sepoys better, and no man was more respected by them. But he had known them a little too long. Looking back through mor than half-a-century of good service, he could re-

* *Ante*, p. 211, Mowbray Thomson says that "the European force consisted of the officers attached to the Sepoy regiments; sixty men of the Eighty-fourth Regiment; seventy-four men of the Thirty-second, who were invalided; sixty-five men of the Madras Fusiliers, and fifty-nine men of the Company's Artillery—about three hundred combatants in all." Mr. Sherer, in his official narrative, computes the invalids of the Thirty-second at thirty.

1857 May. member how they fought in the good old days of Lake and Ouchterlony. There was nothing, indeed, to be said against him except that he bore the burden of more than seventy years. He bore it lightly, succumbing little to the pressure. Still it was there; and it was a necessity that he should have lost beneath it some measure at least of the vigour and energy of his prime. He was of short stature and of light weight; and to the last he was a good and active horseman. Accompanied by his daughters, he often went out in pursuit of a jackal, with a few imported hounds, which he kept for the purpose;* and there was still enough of the fire of the sportsman in the ashes of the veteran to suffer him, in the crisp air of the early morning, to enjoy the excitement of the chase.

But General Wheeler, though far advanced in years, had lost none of the clearness of his mental vision. He had not become blind to the failings of the Sepoy; he had not encased himself in that hard incredulity which forbade many to believe it possible that the Native soldier could ever be "untrue to his salt." Ever since the first symptoms of disquietude at Barrackpore and Berhampore had been manifested, he had watched narrowly the Sepoy regiments under his immediate command, looking for indications of a like temper among them.† And

* See Mowbray Thomson's narrative. The blood which ran in the veins of Wheeler's children was not that of the pure European race.

† "He had proved himself on so many occasions so fertile in resources, so ready to overcome difficulties, so prompt, active, and energetic, that he was thought the man of all others most competent to deal with an insurrection of this character —most fitted to unravel the web of mystery in which its origin was then clouded, and to open the minds of the Sepoys to the insensate folly of their proceedings. And if this had been a mere military outbreak, as some have imagined; if the dispossessed princes and people of the land, farmers, villagers, ryots, had not made common cause with the Sepoys, there is every reason to believe that but a portion of the Force would have revolted."—*Red Pamphlet.*

when news came of the revolt of the Native Regiments at Meerut and at Delhi, he saw clearly that it would demand the exercise of all his influence to prevent a similar explosion at Cawnpore. Then he lamented that hard necessity had stripped the station of European troops, in order that Oude and other newly-acquired territories might be defended. Annexation was doing its work. We had extended our Empire without increasing our Army; and so it happened that many of the most important stations between the new and the old capital of India were, saving a few English gunners, utterly without European troops. It would be difficult to conceive any position more dispiriting than Wheeler's in that fatal month of May. Lucknow had got the regiment, which might otherwise have been stationed at Cawnpore; and not only was the latter negatively, but positively, weakened by the arrangement, for all the human *impedimenta*, the women, the children, and the invalids of the Thirty-second Queen's, had been left at that place. And there were many besides these. Cawnpore abounded in excellent house accommodation, as well as in public buildings of all kinds; and not merely the wives and children of our civil and military functionaries, high and low, but the families also of European or Eurasian merchants and traders were gathered there in large numbers, and the grievous responsibility of protecting all these helpless ones then fell upon the aged General. His half-a-century of service had brought him no such work as this.

1857. May.

There was much then going on in the Lines of which, doubtless, the General knew nothing; but now and then, as the month of May advanced, unpleasant revelations were made to him through his officers. It did not appear that the Sepoys were disaffected or

State of the Soldiery.

1857. May. even discontented, but, as in other places of which I have spoken, a great fear was settling down upon our Native soldiery. The most extravagant stories were current among them. The Hindoo and Mahomedan troops on a given day were to be assembled upon an undermined parade-ground, and the whole of them blown into the air. This and other fables equally monstrous were freely circulated among the Sepoys and readily believed. Nothing could be more alarming to one well acquainted with the character of the Native soldier than the free acceptance of stories of this kind, which showed that the old bonds of confidence were utterly broken; and Sir Hugh Wheeler, therefore, plainly saw that the danger was one which it would be most difficult to arrest, for nothing is so intractable as a panic. For some days after the news from Meerut and Delhi had reached Cawnpore, he had hope that the public mind might be reassured; but this soon passed away. It was plain to him, as time wore on, that the excitement rather increased than diminished. And the peril which stared him in the face was not merely the peril of mutinous soldiery; he was threatened also by an insurgent population, which might have overwhelmed him. And it seemed to him in this emergency that the best means of defending the lives of the Christian communities and maintaining, though only on a narrow space, the authority of the Christian Government, until succours should throwing up some defensive works, within which the English might gather themselves together, and with the aid of their guns keep the enemy at a distance. Beyond this there was nothing that he could do; and it was not easy to determine how even this little was to be done.

Of all the defensible points in the Cantonment, it was held, in the first instance, that the Magazine in the north-western corner of the military lines was that best adapted, in the exigency which had arisen, for a defensive position. It almost rested on the river, and it was surrounded by walls of substantial masonry. But instead of this, Sir Hugh Wheeler selected a spot about six miles lower down to the south-east, at some distance from the river, and not far from the Sepoys' huts. There were quarters of some kind for our people within two long hospital barracks (one wholly of masonry, the other with a thatched roof)—single-storied buildings with verandahs running round them, and with the usual outhouses attached. This spot he began to entrench, to fortify with artillery, and to provision with supplies of different kinds. Orders went forth to the Commissariat, and their efforts were supplemented by the managers of the regimental messes, who freely sent in their stores of beer and wine, hermetically-sealed dainties, and other creature-comforts that might serve to mitigate the evils of the brief detention which was believed to be the worst that could befal us. But the aggregate amount of food was lamentably ill-proportioned to the exigencies of the occasion. The Native contractors failed, as they often do fail at such times, and the stores which they sent in fell short of the figures in the paper-indents. All else was of the same kind—weak, scanty, and insufficient. As to the so-called fortifications, they were so paltry that an English subaltern could have ridden over them on a cast-horse from the Company's Stud. The earthworks were little more than four feet high, and were not even bullet-proof at the crest. The apertures for the artillery exposed both our guns and our

1857. May. The Question of Defence.

1857. May. gunners, whilst an enemy in adjacent buildings might find cover on all sides. Not, however, from ignorance or negligence did this insufficiency arise. The last weeks of the dry season were upon us, and the earth was so hard that it was difficult to dig it, and so friable when dug that the necessary cohesion was almost unattainable.

It has often been said that Wheeler ought to have chosen the Magazine as the centre of his lines of defence, and that all the subsequent evil arose from the absence of this obvious precaution. The considerations which suggested themselves to the military critics were not absent from his own mind. But there was one paramount thought which over-ruled them. The first step towards the occupation of the Magazine would have been the withdrawal of the Sepoy guard; and to have attempted this would certainly have given the signal for an immediate rising. With the small European force at his disposal it would have been manifestly unwise to provoke a collision. If the first blow were to be struck by our own people, it would, he believed, have immediate results of a far more disastrous character than those which were likely to arise from a spontaneous revolt against British authority, detached from those feelings of animosity and resentment which might have been engendered by a first offensive movement on our part. It must be admitted that the spot selected for our refuge was, indeed, but a miserable place for the protection of a large body of Christian people against the thousands and tens of thousands that might surge up to destroy them. But it was not believed, at that time, that Wheeler and his followers would be called upon to face more than the passing danger of a rising of the "budmashes" of the city and the bazaars. All the information that reached him confirmed the belief that if the regiments should mutiny they would march off at once to Delhi. And he was in almost daily expectation of being recruited from below by reinforcements sent upwards from Calcutta. All that was needed, it then appeared to the General and to others, was a place of refuge, for a little space, during the confusion that would arise on the first outbreak of the military revolt, when, doubtless, there would be plunder and devastation. It was felt that the Sepoys had at that time no craving after European blood, and that their departure would enable Wheeler and his Europeans to march to Allahabad, taking all the Christian people with him.* 1857. May.

Whilst these precautions were being taken, the General sent an express to Lucknow, requesting Sir Henry Lawrence to lend him, for a while, a company or two of the Thirty-second Regiment, as he had reason to expect an immediate rising at Cawn- Help from Lucknow.

* However sound these reasons may have been, it is not to be questioned that the selection was a great misfortune. The Magazine position is thus described by General Neill, after visiting the place, on his first arrival at Cawnpore: "It is a walled defence, walled enclosure, proof against musketry, covering an area of three acres—ample room in it for all the garrison—close to the bank of the river; the houses close to it are all defensible, and they, with the Magazine, could have been held against any Native force, as having the large and [*obscure*] guns, with abundance of ammunition, neither the Nana nor the Natives would have come near them. They could have moved out and attacked them with the guns, and would have not only saved themselves but the city, to say nothing of a large arsenal and many thousand stand of arms, artillery tents, harness, &c. &c. General Wheeler ought to have gone there at once; no one could have prevented him; they might have saved everything they had almost, if they had. There is something awful in the number of catastrophes, which could have been avoided by a common degree of caution."—*MS. Correspondence*. It was not, however, want of caution, but perhaps over-caution, that caused Wheeler not to resort to the Magazine buildings. The distance between the Lines and the Magazine is to be taken into account; and some military authorities may differ from Neill's opinion, that no one could have prevented Wheeler from betaking himself, with his women, children, and invalids, to the Magazine.

1857 May. pore.* Little could Lawrence spare a single man from the troublous capital of Oude; but those were days when Christian gentlemen rose to noble heights of generosity and self-sacrifice; and Henry Lawrence, who, at any time, would have divided his cloak with another, or snatched the helmet with the last drop of water from his own lips, was not one to hesitate when such a demand was made upon him. He sent all that he could send—eighty-four men of the Thirty-second, Queen's—packed closely in such wheeled carriages as could be mustered. He sent also two detachments of the Oude Horse to keep open the road between Cawnpore and Agra, and render such other assistance as Irregular Horse well commanded can render, if only they be true to their leaders. A party of Oude Artillery accompanied them with two field guns, under Lieutenant Ashe—a young officer of rare promise, which was soon to ripen into heroic performance.†

Fletcher Hayes.

With these detachments went Captain Fletcher Hayes, Military Secretary to Sir Henry Lawrence—a man of great capacity and great courage; in the prime of his life and the height of his daring. He had graduated in one of our great English univer-

* It should be observed that Lucknow was within the Cawnpore Division of the Army, and therefore, in the normal state of affairs, Wheeler might have made any disposition of the troops under his command that seemed fit to him. But when the crisis arose, Sir Henry Lawrence had telegraphed to the Governor-General for "plenary military authority in Oude," and Lord Canning had gladly given him the powers he had sought (vol. i. page 616), writing to Wheeler at the same time a kindly explanation of the circumstances, which had reconciled the General to the change.

† The number of Europeans sent by Sir Henry Lawrence to Cawnpore has been variously stated. His Military Secretary, in a letter to Mr. Edmonstone, sets it down at fifty men and two officers. The Cavalry detachments were sent on by Sir Hugh Wheeler, and the officers were murdered; but Ashe and the guns remained, or returned, to take good part in the defence.

sities, and was an erudite scholar and an accomplished gentleman. He was now sent to Cawnpore to ascertain the real state of affairs there for the information of his Chief. So he mounted his horse and started with the Cavalry, giving up his carriage, in which he had at first intended to travel, to a party of European soldiers:—"For," he wrote, "as they represented three hundred rounds of balled ammunition ready at any moment for anybody, I thought that they were of far more importance than any number of military secretaries." All through the day, from dawn to some hours after sunset, they toiled on, suffering severely from the intense heat and the parching thirst. But they reached Cawnpore without disaster; and in a little while Hayes had taken in the situation and had flung himself into the work that lay before him, as if he had been one of the garrison himself.

1857. May.

And when English authority at Cawnpore appealed to Henry Lawrence for assistance, as though by some strange fatality it were doomed that aid should be sought, in the crisis which had arisen, from the two extremes of humanity, an appeal was made to our neighbour, the Rajah of Bithoor.

The Nana Sahib.

Doondoo Punt, Nana Sahib, after the visit to Lucknow, recorded in my first volume,* had returned to his home at Bithoor. He had, doubtless, clearly discerned the feeling in the Oudh capital—nay, throughout the whole province. He knew well that there was a great excitement—it might be of danger, it might be of fear—alive among the Sepoys

* *Ante*, vol. i. pp. 575—6.

1857. May. all over Upper India. He felt that he hated the English, and that his time had come. But all that was passing in the mind of the disappointed Mahratta was as a sealed book to the English. Of course the whole story of the disappointment was on record. Had it not gone from Calcutta to London—from London back to Calcutta; and from Calcutta again to Cawnpore? And did it not cover many sheets of foolscap? Military men might know little of the story which has been told in this book,* and to civilians a rejected memorial was so common a thing, that even to the best-informed of them there could have appeared to be no earthly reason why Doondoo Punt should not accept his position quietly, submissively, resignedly, after the fashion of his kind, and be ever after loyal to the Government that had rejected his claims. So when danger threatened them, it appeared to the authorities at Cawnpore that assistance might be obtained from the Nana Sahib. For although Lord Dalhousie and the Company had refused to increase his store, he had abundance of money and all that money could purchase, including horses and elephants and a large body of retainers—almost, indeed, a little army of his own. He had been in friendly intercourse with our officers up to this very time, and no one doubted that as he had the power, so also he had the will to be of substantial use to us in the hour of our trouble. It was one of those strange revenges, with which the stream of Time is laden. The "arbiter of others' fate" had suddenly become "a suppliant for his own;" and the representatives of the British Government were suing to one recently a suitor cast in our own high political courts. The madness of this was

* *Ante*, vol. i. pp. 98, *et seq.*

seen at Lucknow; but it was not seen at Cawnpore. So the alliance of the Nana Sahib was sought as an element of strength in our hour of trouble.* 1857. May.

It was in this wise: To secure the safety of the Government treasure was necessarily at such a time one of the main objects of both the military and the civil authorities. If it could be lodged within the entrenchments it would be out of the grasp of the soldiery, who, as our officers well knew, on the first open manifestation of revolt, would assuredly make for the Treasury and gorge themselves with the spoil. But when there was mention made of an intention to remove the coin, the Sepoys, by whom it was guarded, were outwardly all loyalty and devotion, and declared that it was safe in their hands. The reason of this was manifest; and Wheeler, anxious above all things not to precipitate a collision, shrunk from insisting upon a measure which would in all probability have been violently resisted. To counteract any danger from this source, it was considered a good stroke of policy to avail ourselves of the assistance of a party of the armed followers of the Nana Sahib, who had been in frequent intercourse with Mr. Hillersdon, the Collector, and who had smilingly assured that officer of his sympathy and friendship. The Treasury stood at a little distance from the Bithoor road, some miles away from the military lines; and very soon some two hundred of the retainers of the Nana, with a couple of guns, were posted at Newab-gunj, which commanded both the Treasury and the Magazine.†

* Mr. Martin Gubbins states that the General was distinctly warned not to trust the Nana Sahib. "Sir H. Lawrence," he says, "concurred in my suspicions, and by his authority I addressed Sir Hugh Wheeler, cautioning him against the Nana, and stating Sir Henry's belief that he was not to be depended upon."—*Mutinies in Oudh*, page 32.

† Some time afterwards, Tantia Topee gave the following account of

1857.
The Place of Refuge.
May 22.

This was on the 22nd of May. On the preceding day the reinforcements from Lucknow had arrived; and about the same time, on the suggestion of the General, the women and children and non-combatants had betaken themselves to the place of refuge within the improvised entrenchments. There was then a scene of frightful confusion, which one, who had just arrived from Lucknow, thus graphically described. "The General," wrote Fletcher Hayes in a private letter to Secretary Edmonstone, "was delighted to hear of the arrival of the Europeans, and soon from all sides, I heard of reports of all sorts and kinds which people kept bringing to the General until nearly one A.M., on the 22nd, when we retired to rest. At six A.M I went out to have a look at the various places, and since I have been in India never witnessed so frightful a scene of confusion, fright, and bad arrangement as the European barracks presented. Four guns were in position loaded, with European artillerymen in nightcaps and wide-awakes and side-arms on, hanging to the guns in groups—looking like melodramatic buccaneers. People of all kinds, of every colour, sect, and profession, were crowding into the barracks.

Mr. Hillersdon's negotiations with the Nana Sahib. I give it as the Native version of the transaction:—"In the month of May, 1857, the Collector of Cawnpore sent a note of the following purport to the Nana Sahib at Bithoor, viz. that he begged him (the Nana) to forward his wife and children to England. The Nana consented to do so, and four days afterwards the Collector wrote to him to bring his troops and guns with him from Bithoor to Cawnpore. I went with the Nana and about one hundred Sepoys and three hundred matchlock-men and two guns to the Collector's house at Cawnpore. The Collector was then in the entrenchments, and not in his house. He sent us word to remain, and we stopped at his house during the night. The Collector came in the morning and told the Nana to occupy his own house, which was in Cawnpore. We accordingly did so. We remained there four days, and the gentleman said it was fortunate we had come to his aid, as the Sepoys had become disobedient; and that he would apply to the General in our behalf. He did so, and the General wrote to Agra, whence a reply came that arrangements would be made for the pay of our men."—*MS. Records.*

Whilst I was there, buggies, palki-gharrees, vehicles of all sorts, drove up and discharged cargoes of writers, tradesmen, and a miscellaneous mob of every complexion, from white to tawny—all in terror of the imaginary foe; ladies sitting down at the rough mess-tables in the barracks, women suckling infants, ayahs and children in all directions, and—officers too! In short, as I have written to Sir Henry, I saw quite enough to convince me that if any insurrection took or takes place, we shall have no one to thank but ourselves, because we have now shown to the Natives how very easily we can become frightened, and when frightened utterly helpless. During that day (the 22nd) the shops in all the bazaars were shut, four or five times, and all day the General was worried to death by people running up to report improbable stories, which in ten minutes more were contradicted by others still more monstrous. All yesterday (23rd) the same thing went on; and I wish that you could see the European barracks and the chapel close to it—and their occupants. I believe that if anything will keep the Sepoys quiet, it will be, next to Providence, the great respect which they all have for General Wheeler, and for him alone. He has all his doors and windows open all night, and has never thought of moving or of allowing his family to move. Brigadier Jack, Parker, the cantonment magistrate, and Wiggins, the Judge Advocate-General, are, I believe, the only people who sleep in their houses."* 1857. May 22—23.

Temper of the Second Cavalry.

The chief source of immediate danger at this time was the temper of the Second Cavalry. The place in the Army List assigned to this regiment had, for some time, been a blank. It was the number of the regi-

* MS. Correspondence.

1857. May. ment which had disgraced itself at Purwandurrah, and had been ignominiously disbanded; and it was not until 1850, that the number had been restored to the List of the Bengal Army.* That the troopers were ripe for revolt was certain, for already they were quietly making arrangements to send away their families and their property, and soon they had nothing in their huts but their drinking-vessels. They stood, as it were, with their loins girt about for action, and Wheeler had more than once credible information that they were about immediately to strike. It was believed that, differing from the infantry regiments at Cawnpore, these cavalry Sepoys included in their programme the murder of their officers. There were many Mahomedans in the corps, and Mahomedan feeling was then strong in the place. There had been great gatherings at the mosques, in which the Mussulman Sepoys had taken a forward part, for the full discussion of the crisis. And it was thought, as had before been thought, in other places, that the festival of the Eed, on the 24th of May, would prove the appointed day for a great Mahomedan demonstration. But it passed over as quietly as any other day. There was the usual interchange of courtesies and compliments, as in quiet times, between the two races; and on one side, at least, there was much self-congratulation that the anniversary was well over.

Progress of mistrust.

But all this time, as the arrangements were proceeding apace for the security of our place of refuge, the general feeling of mistrust was fixing itself in the hearts of the soldiery. The principle of "trusting

* Another regiment (the Eleventh Light Cavalry) had been raised in the place of the Second; and the officers of the latter had been transferred to it bodily. Only one trooper of the Second had been re-enlisted — the Havildar-Major, Bhowany Singh, of whom more hereafter. The Eleventh was renumbered the Second, for its gallantry at Mooltan.

all in all or not at all" was in those days the only one to be worked out in action with any prospect of success. There was strength in striking the first blow with a heavy mailed hand. There was strength also in perfect quietude and composure. But in any middle course there was weakness; and whether in doing or in suffering, "to be weak is to be miserable." When, therefore, Wheeler began to throw up defences which could not defend him, and to betray his mistrust of the Sepoys, without having it in his power effectually to arrest the danger, of which such action indicated the dread, there was nothing but misery before him. Indeed, when our people were seen wildly leaving their homes and seeking safety either within our so-called entrenchments or in some strongly-built edifices in the neighbourhood, and the Sepoys beheld the English artillerymen placing guns in position, the end was certain, and the beginning of the end had come. Some regarded the movement as an indication of fear; some looked upon it as a menace. All regarded it as a proof of mistrust. Confidence was at an end; there was a deadly breach between the officer and the soldier. 1857. May.

But during that last week of May, whatever plots and perils might have been fermenting beneath the surface, outwardly everything was calm and reassuring. And the brave old General began to think that the worst was over, and that he would soon be able to assist Lawrence at Lucknow. On the 1st of June, he wrote to Lord Canning, saying, "I have this day sent eighty transport-train bullocks in relays at four stages for the purpose of bringing up Europeans from Allahabad; and in a few—a very few days, I shall consider Cawnpore safe—nay, that I may aid Lucknow, if need be." And he added, "I May 24—31. June 1

1857. June. have left my house and am residing day and night in my tent, pitched within our entrenched position, and I purpose continuing to do so until tranquillity is restored. The heat is dreadful. I think that the fever has abated; but the excitement and distrust are such that every act, however simple or honestly intended, is open to misapprehension and misrepresentation. My difficulties have been as much from the necessity of making others act with circumspection and prudence as from any disaffection on the part of the troops. In their present state, a single injudicious step might set the whole in a blaze. It is my good fortune in the present crisis, that I am well known to the whole Native Army as one who, although strict, has ever been just and considerate to them to the best of his ability, and that in a service of fifty-two years I have ever respected their rights and their prejudices. Pardon, my Lord, this apparent egotism. I state the fact solely as accounting for my success in preserving tranquillity at a place like Cawnpore. Indeed, the men themselves have said that my name amongst them had alone been the cause of their not following the example so excitingly set them."*

Help to Lucknow. And, indeed, this pleasurable anticipation of reciprocating Henry Lawrence's chivalrous generosity was not so much empty talk. Part of the detachment of the Eighty-Fourth, which had been sent from Benares,† was now passed on to Lucknow. And

* MS. Correspondence.

† See *ante*, page 289. They appear to have reached Cawnpore on the night of the 26th, or morning of the 27th of May. They were sent to Lucknow on the 3rd of June.—See Wheeler's telegram to Government. "Sir H. Lawrence having expressed some uneasiness, I have just sent him by post-carriages, out of my small force, two officers and fifty men of Her Majesty's Eighty-fourth Foot. Conveyance for more not available. This leaves me weak, but I trust to holding my own until more Europeans arrive."

as they crossed the Bridge of Boats and set their faces towards the Oudh capital, there was inward laughter and self-congratulation under many a dusky skin at the thought of what the English were doing. It was hard to say, in that conjuncture, at what particular point European manhood was most needed, but it is certain that in that entrenched position at Cawnpore it was weary work for those who kept watch and ward, day and night, with loaded guns, behind the low mud walls we had raised for our defence.* And bitter was the grief, a few days later, that a single white soldier had been suffered to leave Cawnpore. 1857. June.

Working of the plot.

For when the month of June came in, the revolt of the Native Brigade was merely a question of time —a question of precedence. It was to be; but it was not quite settled how it was to be—how it was to begin. There was not that perfect accord between the regiments out of which simultaneous action could arise. Some were eager to strike at once; some counselled delay.† The Cavalry troopers, always the most excitable and impetuous, were ready for the affray before their more slowly-moving comrades of

* "Last night I went the rounds of our positions with the General. The battery is divided in half, and placed east and west, commanding the principal approaches; we came upon one half battery without any challenge or the least exhibition of any alarm on the part of the gunners. I walked up and put my hand on one of the guns, and could have spiked all three with the greatest ease. . . . Some little time afterwards the officer in charge was found asleep, and was immediately put under arrest. . . Dempster, the Adjutant of the Artillery, was so worn out with watching at night and performing other duties, that, seeing he was so done up and could not look after both batteries, I said I would take one, and accordingly remained in charge till daybreak."—*Fletcher Hayes to Henry Lawrence. May* 26. *MS.*

† "The chief obstacle to a rise and insurrection of the Sepoys is, that they are undecided as to who should commence it. They have been wrangling among themselves for some days. An attempt was made by a Native officer to make the Cavalry seize their arms and turn out. He made a trumpeter take his trumpet and commence with the signal, but the trumpet was seized and snatched away by another Native officer. Last night there was an alarm, and the gunners stood to their guns, but everything passed over quietly."—*The Same to the Same. May* 26.

1857. June. the Infantry. But everywhere in the Lines and in the Bazaars the plot was working. And the plotters were not only in the Lines and the Bazaars. Out at Newab-gunj, where the retainers of the Bithoor Rajah were posted, and where the Rajah himself had fixed his quarters for a little while to do the bidding of his friends the Feringhees, were the germs of a cruel conspiracy. To Doondoo Punt and to the ministers, Hindoo and Mahomedan, who surrounded him, there could be no more grateful tidings than those which came from the Sepoy's quarters; and as they looked at the Treasury, the Magazine, and the Gaol, which lay so temptingly at hand, it seemed to them that the work was easy. Some of these retainers were in communication with the men of the Second Cavalry; and it is stated that arrangements were soon made for an interview between one of the Cavalry soubah-

Teeka Singh. dars, an active agent of sedition, and the Nana Sahib of Bithoor. It is not easy to extract from the mass of Native evidence—often second-hand reports derived from interested or prejudiced sources—the true history of all the secret meetings which have been described, and to feel in such a case the confidence which should never be absent from historical assertion.* But it is stated that during the first days of June there were frequent interviews between the

* The depositions taken down by Colonel Williams, Commissioner of Police, North-West Provinces, are very full, and they are of a highly interesting, and, in some respects, valuable character; but Colonel Williams himself admits that much must be received with caution, as being only hearsay evidence. Take, for example, the following from the evidence of Sheo Churren Das: "Three or four days before the troops broke out, Teeka Singh, Soubahdar of the Second Cavalry, began to have interviews with the Nana, and said to him on one occasion, 'You have come to take charge of the Magazine and Treasury of the English. We all, Hindoos and Mahomedans, have united for our religions, and the whole Bengal Army have become one in purpose. What do you say to it?' The Nana replied, 'I also am at the disposal of the Army.' *I heard this from the Sowars themselves.*"

chiefs of the rebellious Sepoys and the inmates of the Bithoor Palace; and that it was known to the soldiery before they broke into rebellion that the Nana was with them, and that all his resources would be thrown into the scale on the side of the nascent rebellion. 1857. June.

June 4. Outbreak of the Sepoys.

On the night of the 4th of June, the Second Cavalry and the First Infantry Regiment were ready for immediate action. The troopers had got to horse and the foot-men were equipping themselves. As ever, the former were the first to strike.* It was after the wonted fashion. There was a firing of pistols, with perhaps no definite object; then a conflagration which lit up the sky and told our people in the entrenchments that the game of destruction had commenced; and then a mad nocturnal ride to Newab-gunj, scenting the treasure and the stores in the Magazine. The First Regiment soon followed them. In vain their colonel, calling them his "baba-logue," his children, had implored them, in affectionate, parental tones, not to stain themselves by such wickedness. It was too late. The Sepoys did not wish to harm their officers, but they were bent on rebellion. They hurried after the Cavalry, setting their faces towards the north-west, where lay the Treasury, the Gaol, and the Magazine, with Delhi in the distance. Thither as they went they burnt, and

Colonel Ewart.

* A casual circumstance, of no great importance in itself, seems just at this time to have accelerated the crisis. It is thus summarised by Colonel Williams, in his synopsis of the evidence collected by him: "Again the unfortunate incident of a cashiered officer named Cox firing on a patrol of the Second Cavalry on the night of the 2nd of June, and his acquittal after trial on the following day, on the plea of being unconscious at the time from intoxication, caused much dissatisfaction, the mutinously-inclined Cavalry declaring openly that perhaps their fire-arms might be discharged by accident some day. The violent and insubordinate conduct of the troops, particularly of the Cavalry, though they still ostensibly took duty, caused many to take refuge in the entrenchments."

1857. June 4. plundered, and spread devastation along their line of march, but left the Christian people behind them as though not lusting for their blood.

Arrived in the neighbourhood of Newab-gunj, the Sepoys of the two regiments fraternised with the retainers of the Nana. The Treasury was sacked, the gates of the Gaol were thrown open and the prisoners released. The public offices were fired and the records burnt. The Magazine, with all its supplies of ammunition, and the priceless wealth of heavy artillery, fell into the hands of the mutineers.* The spoil was heaped upon elephants and on carts, which the troopers had brought from their Lines; and the one thought of the soldiery was a hurried march to the great imperial centre of the rebellion. But where were the two other regiments? The Sepoys at Newab-gunj had begun to doubt

* It is stated, and on very high authority, that Sir Hugh Wheeler and his Staff were ignorant of the contents of the Cawnpore Magazine. I find the following in a letter from General Neill, in which he gives the results of his inquiry into the "Story of Cawnpore." He had, at that time, been in communication with the only two surviving officers of the siege. "General Wheeler was then under the delusion that the Nana would assist him. All the mutineers went one march to Delhi. The Nana got them to return, and General Wheeler found himself surrounded, and guns firing upon him in every direction from our own Arsenal, of the existence of which guns General Wheeler and his staff were until then ignorant. It appears that a committee of officers, some time before, were sent down to examine the Arsenal, and to report what was in it. They came down in the usual easy-going style—only thought of tents and other trifles—happened not to be shown the gun-sheds, and did not enter the Magazine; in fact, forgot all about it, and reported that there was nothing in the 'Magazine,' as it was styled." The authority of such a man as General Neill must, in all cases, be respected, but it is hardly credible that the contents of the Magazine were unknown to the Artillery officers at Cawnpore, especially to the Ordnance Commissariat Department. Moreover, it is to be observed that the supposed ignorance is not consistent with the undoubted anxiety manifested by Wheeler and his chief officers to blow up the Magazine at the commencement of the outbreak. Arrangements had been made for this, but the feat could not be accomplished. Colonel Williams says: "The Assistant-Commissary, Mr. Riley, had been directed to blow up the Magazine, but was unfortunately prevented by the Sepoys on guard there."

whether their comrades were coming to join them.* 1857.
All through the hours of darkness and of dawn the Fifty-third and the Fifty-sixth gave no sign of comradeship. Their officers had spent the night with June 5.
them in their Lines, and from two in the morning till after sunrise the regiments had been on parade, every officer with his own company. Then they were dismissed; the men took off their uniforms, and prepared for their morning meal. The English officers went to the entrenchments or to their own bungalows. Then the latent fire of mutiny began to spread from man to man, from company to company. Some emissaries from the Second Cavalry had come in to tempt them. Their share of the spoil might be lost by delay. It might have been that no presence, no influence of English officers could then have kept the regiments true to their allegiance. The experiment was not tried, but another was substituted for it. Wheeler's entrenched position commanded the parade-ground, and a long far-reaching gun was brought to bear upon the Sepoys' Lines. They broke at the third discharge of the British cannon, and made their way in wild confusion to Newab-gunj. They broke, but not all; some, still true to their old masters, followed them into the entrenchments, and were faithful to the end of their lives.

The first march to Delhi.

It was still the game of the Cawnpore mutineers to make their way straight to Delhi, to join the regiments already assembled there, and to serve the cause of the King. And they gladly recognised the Nana Sahib as their leader. They had money and munitions of war and carriage for the march, and

* It seems that the Cavalry had broken into the Treasury and begun the work of appropriation before the Infantry arrived.

1857. June 5. they expected great things from the restored sovereignty of the Mogul. But Doondoo Punt, stimulated by those about him, and chiefly, it is thought, by the wily Mahomedan, Azimoollah, looked askance at the proposed centralisation of rebellion, and urged upon the Sepoy leaders that something better might be done. They had made one march to the imperial city, but halted at Kullianpore, whither the Nana had accompanied them. Then they began to listen to the voice of the charmer, and to waver in their resolution. The Bithoor people might be right. It might be better to march back to Cawnpore.*

Designs of the Nana Sahib. Wise in his generation, the Nana Sahib saw clearly the danger of an eclipse. To march to Delhi would be to place himself in a subordinate position—perhaps to deprive him of all substantive authority under the baneful influence of Mahomedan jealousy. The troops might desert him. The Emperor might repudiate him. In the neighbourhood of Cawnpore he would be supreme master of the situation. He knew well the weakness of the English. He knew

* This is the received version of what took place between the Bithoor people and the Sepoys. It is not, however, given with any certainty of its correctness. Tantia Topee afterwards endeavoured to make it appear that the Nana had acted under compulsion. The following is his evidence:—"Two days afterwards, the three regiments of Infantry and the Second Light Cavalry surrounded us, and imprisoned the Nana and myself in the Treasury, and plundered the Magazine and Treasury of everything they contained, leaving nothing in either. Of the treasure, the Sepoys made over two lacs and eleven thousand rupees to the Nana, keeping their own sentries over it. The Nana was also under charge of these sentries, and the Sepoys which were with us also joined the rebels. After this the whole army marched from that place, and the rebels took the Nana Sahib and myself and all our attendants along with them, and said, 'Come along to Delhi.' Having gone three coss from Cawnpore, the Nana said that as the day was far spent it was far better to halt there then, and to march on the following day. They agreed to this, and halted. In the morning the whole army told him (the Nana) to go with them towards Delhi. The Nana refused, and the army then said, 'Come with us to Cawnpore and fight there.' The Nana objected to this, but they would not attend to him. And so, taking him with them as a prisoner, they went towards Cawnpore, and fighting commenced there."

well that at Lucknow the danger which beset us was 1857.
such that no assistance could be looked for from June 5.
that quarter, and that from none of the large towns on the Ganges and the Jumna—as Benares, Allahabad, and Agra—had Wheeler any prospect of immediate relief. With four disciplined Native regiments and all his Bithoor retainers at his back—with guns and great stores of ammunition and treasure in abundance, what might he not do? If the range of his own imagination did not take in at once the grand idea of the restoration of the Peishwahship, there were those at his elbow to suggest the prospect of such a consummation. He had been told by Azimoollah that the power of the English in Europe was declining. He knew that we were weak in India—that vast breadths of country, over which Rebellion was running riot, lay stripped of European troops. Now, he felt, was the time to strike. The game was in his own hands. The ambition and the malice of the Mahratta might be gratified at one blow.

At Kullianpore, therefore, the Nana arrested the march of the mutineers to Delhi. It is not very clearly known what arguments and persuasions were used by him or his ministers to induce the mutinous regiments to turn back to Cawnpore. It is probable that, infirm of purpose, ductile, unstable, and wanting leaders with force of character to shape their plans, they were induced by promises of larger gain, to turn back to the place which they had quitted, and which lay, still with much wealth, at their mercy. Cawnpore had not been half gutted. And, perhaps, there were ties, of a better, or at least a tenderer kind, which lured some of the Sepoys, who were still men, back to their old haunts. In all such cases, it

1857. June 5. may be assumed that the mass of the soldiery huddle confusedly to their doom—objectless, rudderless, perplexed, and bewildered, not knowing what is to come. The blind impulse of the moment, perhaps a sudden contagion of fear, not the strength of a stedfast conviction, or a settled purpose, swept them along, like a flock of scared sheep on a dusty road.*

But there was no such want of purpose among those who swept the flock back to Cawnpore. There were teeming brains and strong wills and resolute activities among the people of the Bithoor Palace. It commonly happens that we know but little about the individual manhood which shapes events in the camps of our Native enemies. The chief actor is not always of the highest rank—he, in whose name the deeds, which make History, are done. And perhaps, we shall never know what foul promptings and instigations were the prologue of the great tragedy then about to be enacted. But from this time Doondoo Punt, Nana Sahib, stood forth in the eyes of men as our arch enemy; and with him were Balla Rao and Baba Bhut, his brothers; the Rao Sahib, his nephew; and Tantia Topee, who had been his playfellow in former days, and had grown into his counsellor and his guide. And ever by his side, linked to him by bonds of pitiless hatred for the English, the astute Mahomedan, Azimoollah, the sometime table-servant of an English master, who had pleaded the Nana's cause in England and made love to English ladies. He had played his game so well that no one had suspected him. Only a few days before the regiments had broken into rebellion, he had been in friendly and familiar intercourse with English officers,

* The Mutiny of the Bengal Army is still described by Natives of India as the "Sheeps' Mutiny."

veiling his hatred under the suavity of his manners and the levity of his speech. 1857.

June 6

The attack threatened.

But as day dawned on Saturday, the 6th of June,* Wheeler was startled by the receipt of a letter from the Nana Sahib, intimating that he was about to attack the entrenchments. The supposed departure of the Sepoys to Delhi had inspired the General and his companions with new hopes. It would be easy for them, they thought, in a little while, to drop down to Allahabad. But this pleasant dream was now rudely broken. The rebellious soldiery were returning to Cawnpore, strengthened in numbers by the retainers of the Nana, and still more invigorated by the identification with the rebel cause of men of influence and energy, able to keep together the scattered atoms of revolt, and to organise a great movement against the English. The blow fell heavily upon the brave old General; on soldiers and civilians; on officers and men; heavily upon all who clung to them for protection. There was not an hour to be lost. Forth went the mandate for all the English to concentrate themselves within the entrenchments. The women and children and non-combatants were already there—and those on duty in the garrison; but many of the Sepoy officers had slept or watched in the Sepoys' lines, and had gone thence to their own bungalows; and now they were summoned without a moment's pause or respite to the earthworks, with no time to snatch a hasty mouthful of food, to collect a change

* Captain Mowbray Thomson ("Story of Cawnpore") says that it was on Sunday the 7th, but Colonel Williams, who collated all the evidence on record, says it is proved that the mutineers returned to Cawnpore on the 6th. The Red Pamphlet gives the 6th as the date of the return of the troops to Cawnpore, and the 7th as the date of the receipt of the Nana's letter. This might explain the discrepancy; but Captain Thomson speaks of the two incidents as synchronous, and Mr. Trevelyan adopts this view.

1857. June 6. of clothes for the morrow, and scarcely to apparel themselves for the work of the day. Leaving their household gods, which they had hoped still to preserve, they obeyed, promptly but regretfully, the orders of their chief, and hurried into the entrenchments. Soon every one was at his post. It was a miserable place for defensive purposes, but such as it was, the best dispositions were made for its defence. And every man braced himself up for the work before him, with clenched teeth and a stern resolution to show what English manhood could do to prevail against the fearful odds to which it was opposed.

Approach of the Enemy.

And whilst our people were thus manning the several posts which had been marked out for the defence of our feeble earthworks, the enemy were surging onwards in confused numbers towards the entrenchments; but eager rather for plunder than for battle, they turned aside to gorge themselves with the spoil, in city and cantonment, which lay profusely at their mercy, and to murder all the defenceless Christian people who fell in their way.* The question of proprietorship disturbed them little. Not content with the pillage of the Feringhees, many enriched themselves at the expense of their own countrymen, and some at least straightway deserted the ranks of the rebel army and made their way to their own homes. But enough remained, after all defections, thoroughly to invest our position—and more, perhaps, than could be brought under effectual com-

* "An old gentleman, supposed to be a merchant, with his wife and two children, one a boy of sixteen, the other a little girl, on being found secreted in a house near the dawk-bungalow, were shot in front of it. ...ur office-writers, living in a house ...he bank of a canal . . . their house being set on fire, were obliged to abandon it, and were murdered as they fled. Another European (unknown) was shot by the troopers, who were indefatigable in their search after Christians."—*Col. Williams's Synopsis.*

mand and control. Organisation, however, was not wholly neglected. In the name of the Nana Sahib, promotions and appointments were made in the army of the Peishwah. The Soubahdar, Teeka Singh, who had been from the commencement the most active promoter of revolt, received the command of the cavalry, with the rank of General; whilst Jemadar Dulgunjun Singh and Soubahdar Gunga Deen were appointed to the command, as Colonels, of infantry regiments. The names of these dignitaries will suggest the fact that the chief commands were given to Hindoos. But whether, as has been supposed, this proceeded from the belief that "the boldest and most active of the mutineers were not Mussulmans, but Hindoos,"* or whether it were that the prejudices and predilections of the Mahratta Brahmin, who was recognised as the rebel leader, wrought strongly in favour of his co-religionists, can only be conjectured.

1857. June 6

The Attack commenced.

For some hours after the first alarm, the little garrison waited and waited; and there was no sound of the threatened attack. But about noon the booming of the cannon told that the enemy had commenced their operations. A round-shot from a nine-pounder came into our entrenchments, scaring and scattering a large party of ladies and children, who were gathered together outside the barracks. Then the bugle sounded; and our fighting men got to their posts, and prepared themselves for the unequal conflict. As the day advanced, shot after shot from the enemy's guns was poured in with increasing rapidity and deadliness of aim, and with the sound of every shot arose the screams of the women and the children. On that first day of the siege the

* See Mr. Trevelyan's interesting volume, "Cawnpore." The suggestion is contained in Colonel Williams's Synopsis of Evidence.

1857. June 6. unaccustomed horror tore down all barriers of self-restraint. But soon this human weakness, which vented itself in the shrill utterances of fear, passed away from these helpless ones; and in its place there was an unnatural stillness, more pathetic than the wailings of grief and the clamorous outbursts of terror.

June 6—27. The Siege. Then commenced a siege, the miseries of which to the besieged have never been exceeded in the history of the world. All the wonted terrors of a multitudinous enemy without, of a feeble garrison and scant shelter within, of the burden of women, and children, and sick people, with little to appease their wants or to allay their sufferings, were aggravated by the burning heat of the climate. The June sky was little less than a great canopy of fire; the summer breeze was as the blast of a furnace. To touch the barrel of a gun was to recoil as from red-hot iron. It was the season when European strength and energy are ever at their lowest point of depression; when military duty in its mildest form taxes the powers of Englishmen to the utmost, and English women can do little more than sustain life in a state of languid repose, in shaded apartments, with all appliances at command to moderate the temperature and to mitigate the suffering. But now, even under the fierce meridian sun, this little band of English fighting men were ever straining to sustain the strenuous activity of constant battle against fearful odds; whilst delicate women and fragile children were suddenly called to endure discomforts and privations, with all the superadded miseries peculiar to the country and the climate, which it would have been hard to battle with, in strong health, under their native skies. The morning and evening baths, the frequent changes of raiment, the constant ministrations of assiduous servants in the smallest things, which are the necessities of English life in India, were now suddenly lost to these helpless ones; and, to intensify the wretchedness, the privacy and seclusion so dear to them became only remembrances of the past. Even amidst the roar of the cannon and the rattle of the musketry, with death around them in many ghastly shapes, the loss of these privileges was amongst the heaviest of their trials, for it violated all the decencies and proprieties of life, and shocked the modesty of their womanly natures.

1857. June 6—27.

To the English soldier in India to be outmatched in numbers is scarcely a discouragement. Ever since, a century before, Clive had fought against heavy odds the great battle of Plassey, our English forces had ever been outnumbered in the field, and yet they had fought their way to empire. The overwhelming multitude of Sepoys which now encompassed our position at Cawnpore, were kept at bay by the little handful of English soldiers that now manned our feeble entrenchments. As men, all the mighty host of Hindoos and Mahomedans which the Nana Sahib sent against us were utterly contemptible in our eyes. Had the positions of the two nations been reversed, had the English been outside those paltry earthworks, one rush would have carried the place, and the whole garrison would have been put to the sword in an hour. There was nothing to keep the besiegers out of the entrenchments but the contrast between the indomitable pluck of the Few and the flaccid irresolution of the Many. The besiegers, who might have relieved each other every hour, who might have

1857. June 6—27.

bathed, and eaten, and smoked, and slept whilst their comrades were on duty, and sent any number of fresh troops to the assault, shrank from a close encounter with our weary people, overworked and underfed, ever labouring in the trenches, ever under fire, with the clothes rotting on their backs, and the grime from the guns caking on their hands and faces. But, poor and despicable as the enemy were, they were rich and royal in their possessions. They had an immense wealth of artillery. The Cawnpore Magazine had sent forth vast supplies of guns and ammunition.* And now the heavy ordnance of the Government was raking its servants with a destructiveness which soon diminished our numbers working in the trenches. The English artillerymen dropped at their guns, until one after another the places of our trained gunners were filled by volunteers and amateurs, with stout hearts but untutored eyes, and the lighter metal of their guns could make no adequate response to the heavy fire of their twenty-four-pounders. But, when the enemy neared our parapets, and sought further to molest us at close quarters, they met with such a reception as soon put them to panic flight.

Captain Moore.

In these encounters there was one man ever conspicuous—ever in the front of the battle—inspiring and animating all who served under him by his lustrous example. This was Captain Moore, of the Thirty-second—a soldier of a commanding presence, light-haired and blue-eyed, whom no toil could weary, no danger could daunt. Wounded at the commencement of the siege, he went about with his

* And in addition to the guns and stores taken from the Magazine, were other supplies of both found at the Ghaut, which were about to be despatched to Roorkhee.

arm in a sling; but the strong spirit within him 1857.
defied pain. Day and night he laboured on, now in June 6—27.
the trenches, now heading desperate sorties against the enemy, but even when he ceased to hope, he neither fainted nor failed. There was no greater heroism than this English captain's in all the war from first to last—no name more worthy than his to be recorded in the rolls of our English chivalry.

But though ever in the heroic annals of the siege this fair-haired captain must hold the foremost place as the Agamemnon of the defence, there were other heroic deeds than his worthy of distinguished record —other brave men whose names should find fitting mention in the page of history. There was Vibart, Major of the Second Cavalry, who held the Redan, slackening not, day or night, in his exertions, and though ever under the merciless fire of the enemy, active and robust to the last. There was Whiting, Captain of the Bengal Engineers, who commanded at the north-west point of the entrenchments, a man of stout heart and clear brain. There was Jenkins, Captain of the Second Cavalry, described as "one of the bravest and best of our party," who held one of our outposts beyond the trenches with unflinching gallantry, till a bullet through the jaws, from the musket of a Sepoy who was feigning death, brought his services to an agonising end. There was Mowbray-Thomson, Subaltern of the Fifty-sixth, who "had the miserable satisfaction" of avenging, on the spot, the death of his friend—a soldier ever to be found where danger was hottest, of whose deeds the world would have known more if any other pen than his had chronicled the events of the siege; now holding, with a few followers, a perilous outpost, now heading a desperate sortie against merciless odds, he

1857. June 6—27. exposed himself to death in every shape, but he seemed to bear a charmed life.* And there was his friend and comrade to the last, Delafosse of the Fifty-third, a young hero, equal to any feat of heroic daring. One day a shot from the enemy's battery had blown up a tumbril and set fire to the woodwork of the carriage, in the place where our ammunition was stored. It was clearly seen, both by the insurgents and by our own people, that if the fire were not extinguished there would soon be a most disastrous explosion. So the Sepoy batteries poured in a deadly stream of eighteen and twenty-four pound shot. But unmoved by these messengers of death, Delafosse went forth, threw himself down beneath the blazing carriage, tore off the burning wood with his hand, and throwing dry earth upon the fire, stifled it before it could spread. Then there was Sterling, the dead shot, who, perched up in a sort of crow's-nest on the barrack-wall, which Delafosse had improvised for him, picked off single Sepoys with unerring aim, and became a scourge to our assailants; and Jervis of the Engineers, who, with indomitable pride of race, refused to run from a black fellow, and was shot through the heart whilst walking across the open in stern composure, with the pingings of the hostile bullets, and the imploring cries of his comrades to save himself, sounding in his ears. There was Ashe, too, the stout gunner from Lucknow, who served his nine-pounders, to the admiration of the whole garrison and to the terror of the besiegers, with unfailing courage and constancy from day to day, pouring in round after round with astonishing rapidity,

* Mr. Trevelyan very felicitously says of him, "This officer did his best to lose a life which destiny seemed determined to preserve, in order that England might know how, in their exceeding distress, her sons had not been unmindful of their ancient honour."

and after each discharge leaping on to the heel of his gun, and, regardless of the danger of exposure, taking a new sight, and dealing out new death in the direction most disastrous to the enemy. And there were many other soldiers so good and true in the hour of our great national need, that History deplores its insufficiency to do full justice to the individual heroism of all the mighty defenders of those miserable works. 1857. June 6—27.

Nor were these great and glorious manifestations of the consummate bravery of our people confined to those who were combatants by profession. There were many in the entrenchments, not bred to arms, who started suddenly into stalwart soldiers. Among them were some railway engineers, potent to do and strong to endure, who flung themselves into the work of the defence with unstinting self-devotion, and made manifest to their assailants that they were men of the warrior caste, although they wore no uniforms on their backs. Conspicuous among them was Mr. Heberden, who was riddled with grape-shot, and lay for many days, face downwards, in extreme agony, which he bore with unmurmuring fortitude until death came to his relief.* And not the least heroic of that little band of heroes was the station-chaplain, Mr. Moncrieff, who went about ministering to the sick and the wounded, offering the consolations of religion to all who were passing away from the scene, and with that "access of unexpected strength" derived from prayer sustaining the toilers in the entrenchments, who turned aside for a little while from their ghastly work to listen to the sweet promises of the Gospel. Gallantry Civilians.

* Not until the close of the siege. "He was carried on a mattress down to the boats, where he died."

1857. June 6—27. Womanly endurance.

And never since war began, never "in the brave days of old," of which poets delight to sing, when women turned their hair into bow-strings, has the world seen nobler patience and fortitude than clothed the lives and shone forth in the deaths of the wives and daughters of the fighting-men of Cawnpore. No bow-strings were used in this defence; our arrows were of another kind. They went forth from the roaring mouths of our guns in the shape of round-shot and grape and canister. But when these missiles fell short, or by reason of the damage done to our pieces by the heavy artillery of the enemy, could not be used in the form from which they were issued from the expense-magazine, the gentlewomen of Cawnpore gave up some of the cherished components of their feminine attire to improvise the ammunition most needed.* It would take long to tell in detail all the stories of womanly self-devotion and patient endurance and calm courage waiting for the end. Among these heroines was Mrs. Moore, the true-hearted wife of the leader of the garrison. All the officers who fought under him had for her a tenderness equal to his own, and they "fitted up for her a little hut, made of bamboo and covered with canvas," where "she would sit for hours, bravely bearing the absence of her husband while he was gone on some perilous enterprise."† Many others, perhaps, suffered more. The pangs of child-birth came upon some in the midst of all this drear discomfort and painful publicity. Some saw their

* "In consequence of the irregularity of the bore of the guns, through the damage inflicted upon them by the enemy's shot, the canister could not be driven home; the women gave us their stockings, and having tapped the canisters, we charged them with the contents of the shot-cases—a species of cartridge probably never heard of before."—*Mowbray-Thomson's Narrative.*

† Mowbray-Thomson's Narrative.

children slowly die in their arms; some had them swept away from their breasts by the desolating fire of the enemy. There was no misery which humanity could endure that did not fall heavily upon our English women. It was the lot of many only to suffer. But those who were not prostrate, or in close attendance upon their nearest and dearest, moved about as sisters of charity, and were active in their ministrations. Nor was there wanting altogether the stalwart courage of the Amazon. It is related that the wife of a private of the Thirty-second, named Bridget Widdowson, stood sentry, sword in hand, for some time over a batch of prisoners tied together by a rope; and that the captives did not escape until the feminine guard had been relieved by one of the other sex.

1857. June 6—27.

The burning of the Barrack.

After the siege had lasted about a week a great calamity befel the garrison. In the two barracks of which I have spoken were gathered together all the feeble and infirm, the old and the sick, the women and the children. One of the buildings, it has been said, had a thatched roof, and whilst all sorts of projectiles and combustibles were flying about, its ignition could be only a question of time. Every effort had been made to cover the thatch with loose tiles or bricks, but the protection thus afforded was insufficient, and one evening the whole building was in a blaze. The scene that ensued was one of the most terrible in the entire history of the siege; for the sick and wounded who lay there, too feeble and helpless to save themselves, were in peril of being burnt to death. To their comrades it was a work of danger and difficulty to rescue them; for the enemy, rejoicing in their success, poured shot and shell in a continuous stream upon the burning pile, which guided their fire through

1857. June 6—27.

the darkness of the night. Two artillerymen only perished in the flames. But the destruction of the barrack was a heavy blow to the besieged. It deprived numbers of women and children of all shelter, and sent them out houseless to lie day after day and night after night upon the bare ground, without more shelter than could be afforded by strips of canvas and scraps of wine-chests, feeble defences against the climate, which were soon destroyed by the unceasing fire of the enemy. And there was a worse result even than this. The conflagration destroyed all the resources upon which our people had relied for the mitigation of the sufferings of the sick and wounded. All our hospital stores and surgical instruments were lost to us; and from that time Death and Pain had their way without anything to arrest the one or to soften the other.

There was another result of this conflagration, of which little or no notice has been taken by the chroniclers of the Siege. It has been narrated that a few faithful Sepoys cast in their lot with their white officers, and accompanied them within the entrenchments. It appears that they were told that they might find shelter in this barrack, and we may assume that they littered down in the verandahs. There was one old Native officer, the Soubahdar-Major of the Second Cavalry, who from the first had arrayed himself against the mutineers of his regiment, and had received the reward of his great loyalty to the English in the wounds which he carried off with him to the entrenchments. And this reward was soon supplemented by another. Death came to the brave old man whilst still clinging to his former masters. He was killed in the early part of the siege by a

Bhowany Singh.

shell.* The Fifty-third Regiment is stated to have sent ten Native officers, with Faithful Sepoys, into General Wheeler's camp. All the other regiments contributed their quota to the garrison, and there is evidence that during the first week of the siege they rendered some service to the English. But when the barrack was destroyed, there was no place for them. Provisions were already falling short, and although there was no reason to mistrust them, it was felt that they were rather an encumbrance than an assistance. So they were told that they might depart; and as, although there was danger beyond the entrenchments, there was greater danger within them, they not reluctantly perhaps turned their faces towards their homes. Some perished by the way; some succeeded in reaching their native villages; a few returned, after a time, to the British Camp, to detail their experiences of the early days of the siege.†

1857. June 6—27

Mortality in the Garrison.

Day after day passed, and ever as our little garrison

* This is the man of whom previous mention has been made (page 302) as the one Sepoy of the old disgraced Second Cavalry that had been re-enlisted. It is to be hoped that good provision has been made for the family of so brave a man and so faithful a servant.

† "The Major having gone to inquire of General Wheeler what we were to do, the latter came out and ordered us to occupy the hospital barracks; he said, 'In such a barrack we shall not manage to save our lives, as the round-shot will reach us from all sides.' . . . On the evening of the 9th or 10th, a hot round-shot fell on our barrack and set it on fire. On this we left it, and concealed ourselves for the night in a nullah not far distant." "We held the hospital barracks from the 5th to the 9th or 10th; we left because the house caught fire from the enemy's shot. I believe the shot was wrapped in some inflammable material, which catching the thatched roof, soon became a blaze."—(*Deposition of Bhola Khan, Sepoy Fifty-third Native Infantry.*) "The barracks caught fire about four o'clock P.M., on the 9th or 10th. The Major then told us he could do nothing for us, there being an order of General Wheeler prohibiting any Native from entering the entrenchment. He therefore recommended us to provide for our own safety. . . . The whole party then left the hospital barrack."—(*Deposition of Ram Buksh, Pay-Havildar, Fifty-third Native Infantry.*) The number of these Sepoys is supposed to have been about eighty or a hundred, with a considerable proportion of Native officers.

1857. June 6—27. waned weaker and weaker, the fire of the enemy grew hotter and hotter. With what terrible effect it told upon our suffering people in the entrenchments, on brave fighting men, on patient women, and on poor little children, has been narrated by one of the survivors with a simplicity of pathos which goes straight to the heart. Incidents, which in ordinary times would have been described with graphic minuteness of detail, have been told in a few words as events of such common occurrence, as scarcely to have excited a sensation in the garrison. If the "burra sahib," or great lord of the district, to whom a few weeks before all Natives would have crouched, were shot dead in an instant, or the commandant of a regiment, whose word had been law to a thousand armed men, were disabled by agonising wounds, it was the talk of the entrenchments for a quarter of an hour, and then a new tragedy brushed it away. In truth it did not much matter at what moment death came. Happiest those, perhaps, to whom it came soonest. Hillersdon, the Collector, who had negotiated the alliance with the Nana Sahib, fell a corpse at the feet of his young wife, with his entrails torn out by a round shot. A few days afterwards she was relieved from the ghastly memories of her bereavement by a merciful fall of masonry, which killed her. The General's son and aide-de-camp, Lieutenant Wheeler, was lying wounded in one of the barrack-rooms, when, in the presence of his whole family, father, mother, and sisters, a round shot boomed into the apartment, and carried off the young soldier's head. Another round shot struck up splinters into Major Lindsay's face, gashing and blinding him. He lingered on in darkness and in agony for some days, attended by his wife, when Death took him, and she soon followed. Colonel Williams, of the Fifty-sixth, being disabled by a wound early in the siege, died of apoplexy from sunstroke, leaving his wife and daughters in the entrenchments. The former, shot in the face and frightfully disfigured, lay for some days, tended by her wounded daughter, until death came to the suffering widow's relief. Colonel Ewart, of the First, who would have taken an active part in the defence if he had been spared, was disabled at an early period, but lingered through the siege, attended by his admirable wife, only to be brutally murdered at the end of it. Captain Halliday was shot dead carrying from the barracks to the entrenchments a little horse-soup, which he had begged for his famishing wife. Thus many of Wheeler's chief officers were rendered powerless for good by the unceasing fire of the enemy, whilst the old General himself issued orders from the shelter of the barracks, but was seldom capable of taking part in the active duties of the defence. In bitterness of spirit he saw his garrison diminishing every day before his eyes. There was a well a little way outside the entrenchments, which served as the general cemetery of the Christian people; and night after night the carnage of the day was carried to this universal mausoleum. And there were some who died hopelessly, though not in the flesh; for the horrors of the siege were greater than they could bear, and madness fell upon them, perhaps as a merciful dispensation.

1857. June 6—27

Chastisement of the enemy.

It is impossible to compute the aggregate of death which our people dealt back to the enemy in return for these visitations. It is known that in the space of three weeks the English consigned to the well two hundred and fifty of their party. The number of bodies buried by the insurgents or devoured by

1857. June 6—27. vultures and jackals, must have been counted, if ever counted at all, at this amount many times told. If hands were scarce in the entrenchments, muskets were not; and every man stood to his work with some spare pieces ready-loaded, which he fired with such rapidity that the enemy marvelled when they thought of what was supposed to be the number of our garrison. But it was not only from the entrenchments that death went forth to greet our assailants. Incidental allusion has been made to our outposts. There was a row of unfinished barracks at one corner of our position, which it was of immense importance to us to possess, in whole or in part, lest the enemy should hold them against us, and make sad havoc within our miserable earthworks. There were in all eight of these buildings. Two the English contrived to occupy, and between these two was a third, with the well attached in which we buried our dead, and which we saved from the grasp of the enemy. From the shelter which we thus held, and which must have given good command over two sides of our entrenched position, our people poured in a deadly fire on the insurgents, whenever they approached our works. Conspicuous among the defenders of these outposts, as has already been told, were Jenkins and Mowbray-Thomson; and to these good names should be added that of Lieutenant Glanville, of the Second Bengal Europeans, who held with sixteen men "Number Two" barrack, described as the key of our position, until he was incapacitated by a dangerous wound.* From the barracks, or carcasses of barracks, thus gallantly held, such punishment was inflicted upon the enemy, as even after a lapse of years could not be remembered by any one living to look back upon it

* He was succeeded in the command by Mowbray-Thomson.

without a shudder. Here was the hardest work, and hence came the greatest carnage.* Any adventurous Sepoy coming within the reach of our rifles or muskets, paid the penalty of his audacity, and never troubled us or disported himself any more. Sometimes, if a favourable opportunity presented itself, our little garrisons made bold sallies into the open, spiking the enemy's guns and cutting off all who fell in their way. It was not of much use; for whether guns were spiked or men were killed, there were so many of both in the background, that the loss was scarcely felt for a moment. Indeed, the ranks of the besiegers were recruited from time to time, as the siege went on, amongst others by the Sepoys from Azimgurh,† and the new hands were often found to be better than the old. To us, on the other hand, the loss of every man was a grievous calamity, for we waited and waited for succours that never came; and though sometimes our people were stimulated by the belief that firing was to be heard in the distance, intimating the approach of reinforcements, they were soon driven back again upon disappointment and despair.

1857. June 6—27.

The incidents of one day much resembled those of another, both in what was done and what was suffered. Few landmarks broke the uniformity of that great expanse of glorious disaster. One day, however, at Cawnpore, as in other places where the great struggle for empire was going on, differed from the rest; for it was the centenary of the battle of Plassey. On

June 23. Centenary of Plassey.

* "The orders given to us were not to surrender with our lives, and we did our best to obey them, though it was only by an amount of fatigue that in the retrospect now seems scarcely possible to have been a fact, and by the perpetration of such wholesale carnage that nothing could have justified but the instinct of self-preservation, and, I trust, the equally strong determination to shelter the women and children to the last moment."—*Mowbray-Thomson.*

† The Seventeenth Native Infantry.

1857. June 23. the previous night there had been signs of extraordinary activity in the enemy's ranks, and a meditated attack on our outposts had been thwarted by Moore's fertility of resource;* and as the morning of the 23rd dawned upon Cawnpore, the insurgents, stimulated to the utmost by the associations of the day, came out in full force of Horse, Foot, and Artillery, flushed with the thought of certain success, to attack both our outposts and our entrenchments. If the whole strength of the Nana's force was not brought forth to surround us on this memorable day, all its components were fully represented. And there was a stern resolution, in many cases strengthened by oaths on the Ganges-water or the Koran, to destroy the English or to die in the attempt. The excitement of all branches of the rebel-army was at its highest pitch. The impetuosity of the Cavalry far exceeded their discretion, for they galloped forward furiously within reach of our guns, and met with such a reception, that many horses were left riderless, and the troopers who escaped wheeled round and fled in fearful confusion. The Infantry, more cautious, improvised moving ramparts to shelter their skirmishers, by rolling before them as they advanced huge bales of cotton; but our guns were too well

* The following illustrative anecdote, told by Mowbray-Thomson, claims insertion in this place: "We saw the Pandies gathering to this position from all parts, and fearing that my little band would be altogether overpowered by numbers, I sent to Captain Moore for more men. The answer was not altogether unexpected. 'Not one could be spared!' Shortly afterwards, however, the gallant captain came across to me in company with Lieutenant Delafosse, and he said to me, 'Thomson, I think I shall try a new dodge; we are going out into the open, and I shall give the word of command as though our party were about to commence an attack.' Forthwith they sallied out, Moore with a sword, Delafosse with an empty musket. The captain vociferated the words, 'Number one to the front.' And hundreds of ammunition pouches rattled on the bayonet sheaths as our courageous foes vaulted out from the cover afforded by heaps of rubbish, and rushed into the safer quarters presented by the barrack walls."

served to suffer this device to be of much use to the enemy, for some well-directed shots from our batteries set fire to these defences, and the meditated assault was defeated before it had developed itself into action. The attack on the outer barracks was equally unsuccessful. The enemy swarmed beneath our walls, but were saluted with so hot a fire from Mowbray-Thomson and his companions, that, in a little time, the seventeen had laid one more than their number dead at the doorway of the barrack. The great assault of the Centenary of Plassey, which was to have humbled the Feringhees to the dust, and to have revenged the victory of Clive, was in the issue a disastrous failure. The enemy begged to be permitted to bury their dead; and the remains of their cotton-bales served to stop the gaps in the earthworks of the English. But there was a more deadly foe than this weak and disordered crowd of Hindoos and Mahomedans to be encountered by our distressed people; and the Nana Sahib saw another source of victory than that which lay in the number of his fighting men. 1857. June 23.

For hunger had begun to gnaw our little garrison. Food which in happier times would have been turned from with disgust, was seized with avidity and devoured with relish. To the flesh-pots of the besieged no carrion was unwelcome. A stray dog was turned into soup. An old horse, fit only for the knackers, was converted into savoury meat. And when glorious good fortune brought a Brahminee bull within the fire of our people, and with difficulty the carcase of the animal was hauled into the entrenchments, there was rejoicing as if a victory had been gained. But in that fiery month of June the agonies of thirst were even greater than the pangs of hunger. The well from which our scant supplies of water were Approaches of Famine.

1857. June. drawn was a favourite mark for the Sepoy gunners. It was a service of death to go to and fro with the bags and buckets which brought the priceless moisture to the lips of our famished people. Strong men and patient women thirsted in silence, but the moans of the wounded and the wailings of the children it was pitiable to hear. The bheesties, or professional water-carriers, were soon slain in the exercise of their calling, and then English soldiers addressed themselves to the hazardous work of ministering at the well. A brave-hearted civilian, John Mackillop, appointed himself captain of the well, and, after a week of this hazardous service, was shot down at his post. As he lay dying, his care was still for those in whose cause he had yielded up his life, and he besought, almost with his last breath, a stander-by to carry the precious fluid to the lady to whom it had been promised. And so as day by day our people were wasting under these dire penances of hunger and thirst, the hopes of the Nana grew higher and higher, and he knew that the end was approaching.

The Capitulation. June 25.

Three weeks had now nearly passed away since the investment had commenced—three weeks of such misery as few, since sorrow entered the world, have ever been condemned to suffer. No reinforcements had come to their assistance. The looked-for aid from below seemed now to be a grim delusion. Their numbers were fearfully reduced. Their guns were becoming unserviceable. Their ammunition was nearly expended; and starvation was staring them in the face. To hold their position much longer was impossible. To cut their way out of it, with all those

women and children, was equally impossible. The 1857. June 25.
shadow of a great despair was over them. When thus, as it were, at the last gasp, there came to them a message from the Nana Sahib, brought by the hands of a Christian woman. It was on a slip of paper in the handwriting of Azimoollah, and it was addressed "to the subjects of Her Most Gracious Majesty Queen Victoria." "All those who are in no way connected"—so the document ran—"with the acts of Lord Dalhousie, and are willing to lay down their arms, shall receive a safe passage to Allahabad."*

There was not a soldier in garrison who did not recoil from the thought of surrender—who would not have died with sword or musket in hand rather than lay down his arms at the feet of the treacherous Mahratta. Sir Hugh Wheeler lifted up his voice against capitulation. To the English General the bitterness of death was as nothing to the dishonour of abandoning his post. He had not yet given up the hope of relief from the lower country, and he mistrusted the Nana of Bithoor. The younger officers were all for fighting it out to the last; but Moore and Whiting, whom the General consulted in this conjuncture, reluctantly declared themselves in favour of capitulation. They had no thought for themselves. Had there been only men in the entrenchments, they would have counselled and clung to the nobler and the manlier course. But when they thought of the women and children, and of what might befall them in the hands of the enemy, they turned hopefully to

* There are contrary statements with respect to the identity of the messenger. Some say that it was Mrs. Greenaway, some Mrs. Jacobi. Mr. Trevelyan speaks of it as an "important point." But I cannot say that I think it is of much use to discuss, or of consequence to determine, the question.

1857. June 25. whatsoever promised deliverance from the horrors of the past and the greater horrors that might be in the future. There was, too, a great crowd of sick and wounded, who could not be abandoned, and yet who could not be carried off in the face of an opposing enemy. So the overtures of the Nana Sahib were not rejected; and the messenger carried back to the enemy's Camp an announcement that Wheeler and his chief officers were deliberating upon the offer that had been made to them.

June 26. Next morning (there was then an armistice) Azimoollah and Jowalla-Persaud presented themselves near our entrenchments, and Captain Moore and Whiting, accompanied by Mr. Roche, the Postmaster, went out with full powers to treat with the emissaries of the Nana. It was then proposed that the British should surrender their fortified position, their guns, and their treasure, and that they should march out with their arms and sixty rounds of ammunition in each man's pouch. On his part, the Nana was to afford them safe conduct to the river side, and sufficient carriage for the conveyance thither of the women and the children, the wounded and the sick. Boats were to be in readiness at the Ghaut to carry them down the Ganges, and supplies of flour (some added "sheep and goats also") were to be laid in for the sustenance of the party during the voyage to Allahabad. These proposals were committed to paper and given to Azimoollah, who laid them before his chief, and that afternoon a horseman from the rebel camp brought them back, saying that the Nana had agreed to them, and that our people were to evacuate the entrenchments on that very night.

Against this Wheeler protested; and the draft-treaty was returned with an intimation that it was impossible to march out until the morning. Then the enemy began to gasconade and to endeavour to intimidate our people. They might as well have threatened to move the Himalayahs. Doondoo Punt, Nana Sahib, sent word that he knew exactly the state of our defences, the condition of our guns, and the scarcity of our provisions; that he would open fire at once upon our wretched place of refuge, and that in a few days not a man would be alive. Whiting and Mowbray-Thomson went out to meet the Bithoor emissaries, and the former replied, as became a lion-hearted Englishman, that they might carry our entrenchments, if they could; that their soldiers had generally shown greater alacrity in retiring from than in advancing towards our fortifications, and that we had, at all events, abundance of powder in our magazine to blow up both armies together. This determined language had its effect. The Nana consented to wait till the morrow. And a gentleman named Todd, who had been his English tutor, carried the treaty to the Rajah's quarters, at the Savada Kotee, and obtained his signature to it. 1857. June 26.

The Nana is represented to have been very courteous to his old preceptor. It was the time, indeed, for serenity of manner and suavity of demeanour—nay, indeed, for kindly and compassionate utterances and mollifying assurances. So, also, when Jowalla-Persaud, with two others, went over as hostages to the British entrenchments, he blandly condoled with the British commander, expressed his sorrow that the old General should have suffered so much—that after half a century of service with the Sepoy Army of the Company they should turn against him at the close of his life. But God be praised, it was now all over—deliverance was

1857. June 26—27.

hand. Every care would be taken that the English gentlemen and their families should not be molested on their way to the river. And the companions of Jowalla-Persaud talked to others in the same polite and almost obsequious strain. That night our guns were made over to the enemy, and some of the old Golundauze of the Company were placed in charge of them.

The massacre at the Ghaut. June 27.

So forth from their entrenchments, in the early morning, went the remnant of our garrison, with the women and the children, who had outlived the horrors of the siege—gaunt and ghastly, in tattered garments, emaciated and enfeebled by want, worn by long suffering, some wounded and scarred with the indelible marks of the battle upon them. The river was distant only a mile from our starting-point. But to them it was a long and a wretched journey. The wounded were carried mostly in palanquins. The women and children went in rough native bullock-carriages or on the backs of elephants, whilst the able-bodied marched out on foot with but little semblance of martial array, Moore as ever in the van, and Vibart bringing up the rear of the funeral procession. The veteran Wheeler, with his wife and daughters, is said to have walked down to the boats.* With what faith and hope within him, the

* This is very distinctly stated by Mowbray-Thomson: "Poor old Sir Hugh Wheeler, his lady, and daughters, walked down to the boats." Other accounts, of a more circumstantial, but perhaps not more trustworthy character, indicate that the ladies were conveyed to the Ghaut on an elephant, and that the General himself went in a palanquin. This is the statement of Mr. Trevelyan, who very carefully collated all the evidence that has been produced. Colonel Williams, in his synopsis, says, "Hassim Khan, the rider of General Wheeler's elephant, after taking Lady Wheeler and her two daughters to the first boat on the line, returned for the General, whom meeting on the way mounted on a galloway, he likewise conveyed to the boats." The Christian wife of a musician of the Fifty-sixth regiment, named Bradshaw, says: "General Wheeler came last in a palkee (palanquin). They carried him into the

poor old man turned his face towards the Ghaut, He alone who reads the secrets of all hearts ever knew. But there were many in that woe-begone train who, although there was no sunshine on their faces, had glimmerings in their hearts of a peaceful future, and who were fain to carry with them as they went such of their household gods as they had saved from the great wreck, or little memorials of the past, relics, perhaps, of departed friends, to be treasured after long years in the old home beyond the seas. Little was all they could take with them, weighed against what they had left behind; parents, husbands, wives, brothers, sisters, children, friends. The beautiful had left their beauty, the young had left their youth, in those battered barracks; and even the children had old and wizened faces, which told that they had lived long years in the last miserable month. 1857. June 27.

The place of embarkation was known as the Suttee Choura Ghaut, so called from a ruined village hard by which bore that name. The road ran across a wooden bridge, painted white, which reminded a traveller, who afterwards visited the spot, "of a bit in a Surrey common."* Over this bridge they defiled down into a ravine, which led past the compounds of some of our English residences to the Ghaut on the river-side. Near the Ghaut was a Hindoo temple,†

water, near the boat. He said, 'Carry me a little further towards the boat;' but the Sowar said, 'No, get out here!' As the General got out of the palkee, head foremost, a Sowar gave him a cut with his sword in the neck, and he fell into the water. . . . My son was killed near him. I saw it, alas! alas!" Another statement is: "The General and some officers were on elephants—Mrs. Wheeler was in a palkee." The further the investigation is pursued, the greater the uncertainty that is left upon the mind. This is given as another instance of the difficulty of extracting the truth from a mass of conflicting evidence.

* Mr. Trevelyan: "Story of Cawnpore."

† "Small but in good repair, resembling nothing so much as those summer houses of a century back, which at the corners of old houses overhang Dutch canals and suburban English bye-ways."—*Trevelyan*.

1857. June 27. known as the Temple of Hurdeo, or the Fisherman's Temple, a structure of somewhat fanciful and not unpicturesque design. The incidents of this mile-march were not many. The Sepoys, as our wretched people huddled on towards the river, sometimes crowded round and talked to their old officers, uttering words of admiration or of compassion, which were not wholly feigned. But as everywhere the Sepoy stands out as a living inconsistency of the strangest kind, no one can read with surprise any story illustrating the malignant and cruel hatred that, at the same time, burned in the bosoms of some who had once served in our ranks. Among those who left the entrenchments on that June morning were Colonel and Mrs. Ewart, a brave and good man, with a wife every way worthy of him. He, sorely wounded, was carried on a bed or litter, and the lady walked anxiously beside him. But their progress was slow; they fell in the rear before they had reached the bridge, and some Sepoys of his own regiment—the First—seeing his helpless condition, thus severed from his countrymen, came up to him and taunted him. Ordering the litter to be placed on the ground, they mocked and mimicked him, saying, "Is not this a fine parade, Colonel; is not the regiment well dressed up?" Saying which, they fell upon him with their swords and killed him; and though some made profession of not slaying women, Mrs. Ewart was presently cut down, and lay a corpse beside the body of her husband.

That the boats were ready on the river-side had been ascertained by a Committee of our own people; and when the dreary procession reached the appointed place of embarkation, the uncouth vessels were seen a little way in the stream, in shallow water;

for it was the close of the dry season, and the river was at its lowest. The boats were the ordinary eight-oared budgerows of the country—ungainly structures with thatched roofs, looking at a distance like floating hay-stacks, and into these our people now began to crowd without order or method, even the women with children in their arms, with but little help from others, wading knee-deep in the water, and scrambling as they best could up the sides of the vessels. It was nine o'clock before the whole were embarked, and some, Heaven only knows, for their voices are sealed, may have breathed more freely as they awaited the friendly order to push off and to drop down the stream towards the great goal of ultimate deliverance. But there were those on the river banks—those even in the boats themselves—who had far other thoughts, far other expectations. Every boat that had been prepared for our people was intended to be a human slaughter-house. They had not gone down to the banks of a friendly river that was to float them to safety. They had been lured to the appointed shambles, there to be given up to cruel death.

1857. June 27.

So foul an act of treachery the world had never seen. Doondoo Punt, Nana Sahib, the adopted son of the last of the Peishwahs, had studied to some purpose the early history of his race. He knew how the founder of the Mahratta Empire—the head of the great family who had been the masters of the Peishwahs—had, under false pretext of friendly embrace, dug his wagnuck into the bowels of the Mahomedan envoy, and gained by foulest treachery what he could not gain by force. The wagnuck was now ready—the wagnuck of a thousand claws—in the hands of the man who aspired to be the founder of a

1857. June 27. new or renovated Mahratta Empire. Day after day, week after week, the English, with their little band of fighting men, had defied all the strength of this new confederacy, aided by the moral and material help of our lessons and our resources; and now the enemy, under the garb of a new-born friendship, was hiding the cruel weapon that was to destroy them. Everything was ready for the great carnage. Tantia Topee, who had been appointed master of the ceremonies, sat enthroned on a "chaboutree," or platform, of a Hindoo temple, and issued his orders to his dependents. Azimoollah, also, was there, and the brethren of the Nana, and Teekha Singh, the new Cavalry General, and others of the leading men of the Bithoor party. And many Zemindars from the districts, and merchants and lesser people from the city, are said to have gone forth and to have lined the river banks to see the exodus of the English; not knowing what was to come, and not all, perhaps, rejoicing in our humiliation. It looked like a great holiday-show. Scarcely is a more animated scene to be witnessed on the banks of the Thames on the day of our great national boat-race. And it was something even more than this, for there was a great military display. The soldiery had gone out in force —Horse, Foot, and Artillery; and the troopers sat their horses, with their faces turned towards the river, as though anxious for the sport to begin. And their patience was not long tried. The signal had been given, and the butchery was to commence.*

* As Tantia Topee is here stated to have been the foremost agent in this hellish work, it will interest the reader to see the master-butcher's own account of the butchery: "The Nana," he declared, "got a female who had been captured before to write a letter to General Wheeler to this effect: that the Sepoys would not obey his orders, and that, if he wished, he (the Nana) would get boats and convey him and those with him in the entrenchment as far as Allahabad. An answer came from

No sooner were our people on board the boats, than the foul design became apparent. The sound of a bugle was heard. The Native boatmen clambered over the sides of the vessels and sought the shore. Then a murderous fire of grapeshot and musket-balls was opened upon the wretched passengers from both banks of the river; and presently the thatch of the budgerows, cunningly ignited by hot cinders, burst into a blaze. There was then only a choice of cruel deaths for our dear Christian people. The men, or the foremost amongst them, strenuous in action to the last, leaped overboard, and strove, with shoulders to the hulls of the boats, to push them into mid-channel. But the bulk of the fleet remained immovable, and the conflagration was spreading. The sick and wounded were burnt to death, or more mercifully suffocated by the smoke; whilst the stronger

1857. June 27.

the General that he approved of this arrangement, and the same evening the General sent the Nana something over one lac of rupees, and authorised him to keep the amount. The following day I went and got ready forty boats, and having caused all the gentlemen, ladies, and children to get into the boats, I started them off to Allahabad. In the mean while, the whole army, artillery included, having got ready, arrived at the river Ganges. The Sepoys jumped into the water, and commenced a massacre of all the men, women, and children, and set the boats on fire. They destroyed thirty-nine boats; one, however, escaped as far as Kala Kunkur, but was there caught, and brought back to Cawnpore, and all on board of it destroyed. Four days after this the Nana said he was going to Bithoor, to keep the anniversary of his mother's death." This statement is at least partially true, and it might be suggested that the signal which Tantia Topee was seen to give was, according to his statement, a signal to start the boats. On this point, however, witnesses were examined and cross-examined with the same result. One said, "In my presence and hearing Tantia Topee sent for Teeka Sing, Soubahdar of Second Cavalry, known as a General, and gave him orders to rush into the water and spare none." Another said, "I was standing concealed in a corner, close to where Tantia Topee was seated, and I heard him tell Teeka Sing, a Soubahdar of the Second Cavalry, who was known as the General, to order the Sowars to go into the water and put an end to the Europeans, and accordingly they rushed into the river and murdered them." Other witnesses spoke distinctly to the same effect; one man adding, "All orders regarding the massacre, issued by the Nana, were carried into execution by Tantia Topee." I do not think that there can be the least doubt of the guilty activity of Tantia Topee in this foul deed.

1857. June 27. women, with children in their arms, took to the river, to be shot down in the water, to be sabred in the stream by the mounted troopers, who rode in after them, to be bayoneted on reaching land, or to be made captives, and reserved for a later and more cruel immolation. The fewest words are here the best. I should have little taste to tell the foul details of this foul slaughter, even if authentic particulars were before me. It is better that they should remain in the obscurity of an uncertain whole; enough that no aspect of Christian humanity, not the sight of the old General, who had nearly numbered his fourscore years, nor of the little babe still at its mother's breast, raised any feeling of compunction or of pity in these butchers on the river-side. It sufficed that there was Christian blood to be shed.

Whilst this terrible scene was being acted at the Ghaut, the Nana Sahib, having full faith in the malevolent activity of his lieutenants on the river-bank, was awaiting the issue in his tent on the cantonment plain. It is related of him that, unquiet in mind, he moved about, pacing hither and thither, in spite of the indolence of his habits and the obesity of his frame. After a while, tidings of the progress of the massacre were brought to him by a mounted trooper. What had been passing within him during those morning hours no human pen can reveal. Perhaps some slight spasm of remorse may have come upon him, or he may have thought that better use might be made of some of our people alive than dead. But whether moved by pity or by craft, he sent orders back by the messenger that no more women and children should be slain, but that not an Englishman was to be left alive. So the murderers, after butchering, or trying to butcher, the remnant of our fighting-men, stayed their hands and ceased from the slaughter; and a number of weaker victims, computed with probable accuracy at a hundred and twenty-five, some sorely wounded, some half-drowned, all dripping with the water of the Ganges and begrimed with its mud, were carried back in custody to Cawnpore, by the way they had come, envying, perhaps, those whose destiny had been already accomplished.

1857. June 27.

Escape of the Single Boat.

But among the men—survivors of the Cawnpore garrison—were some who battled bravely for their lives, and sold them dearly. Strong swimmers took to the river, but often sunk in the reddened water beneath the fire of their pursuers; whilst others, making towards the land lower down the stream, stood at bay on bank or islet, and made vain but gallant use of the cherished revolver in the last grim energies of death. There was nothing strange, perhaps, in the fact that the foremost heroes of the defence were the last even now to yield up their lives to the fury of the enemy. One boat held Moore and Vibart, Whiting and Mowbray-Thomson, Ashe, Delafosse, Bolton, and others, who had been conspicuous in the annals of that heroic defence. By some accident or oversight the thatch had escaped ignition. Lighter, too, than the rest, or perhaps more vigorously propelled by the shoulders of these strong men, it drifted down the stream; but Moore was shot through the heart in the act of propulsion, and Ashe and Bolton perished whilst engaged in the same work. The grape and round-shot from the Oude bank of the river ere long began to complete the massacre. The dying and the dead lay thickly together entangled in

1857. June 27. the bottom of the boat,* and for the living there was not a mouthful of food.

As the day waned it was clear that the activity of the enemy had not abated. That one drifting boat, on the dark waters of the Ganges, without boatmen, without oars, without a rudder, was not to be left alone with such sorry chance of escape; so a blazing budgerow was sent down the river after it, and burning arrows were discharged at its roof. Still, however, the boat was true to its occupants; and

June 28. with the new day, now grounding on sand-banks, now pushed off again into the stream, it made weary progress between the two hostile banks, every hour lighter, for every hour brought more messengers of death.† At sunset, a pursuing boat from Cawnpore with fifty or sixty armed Natives on board, came after our people, with orders to board and to destroy them. But the pursuers also grounded on a sand-bank; and then there was one of those last grand spasms of courage even in death which are seldom absent from the story of English heroism. Exhausted, famishing, sick and wounded, as they were, they would not wait to be attacked. A little party of officers and soldiers armed themselves to the teeth,

* "The horrors of the lingering hours of that day seemed as if they would never cease. We had no food in the boat, and had taken nothing before starting. The water of the Ganges was all that passed our lips, save prayers, and shrieks, and groans. The wounded and the dead were often entangled together in the bottom of the boat; to extricate the corpses was a work of extreme difficulty, though imperatively necessary from the dreaded consequences of the intense heat and the importance of lightening the boat as much as possible."—*Mowbray-Thomson.*

† "At two P.M. we stranded off Nuzuffgurh, and they opened upon us with musketry. Major Vibart had been shot through one arm on the preceding day; nevertheless, he got out, and whilst helping to push off the boat was shot through the other arm. Captain Athill Turner had both his legs smashed. Captain Whiting was killed. Lieutenant Quin was shot through the arm; Captain Seppings through the arm, and Mrs. Seppings through the thigh. Lieutenant Harrison was shot dead. . . . . Blenman, our bold spy, was shot in the groin."—*Mowbray-Thomson.*

and fell heavily upon the people who had come down 1857.
to destroy them. Very few of the pursuers returned June 28.
to tell the story of their pursuit. This was the last victory of the hero-martyrs of Cawnpore.* They took the enemy's boat, and found in it good stores of ammunition. They would rather have found a little food. Victors as they were, they returned to the cover of the boat only to wrestle with a more formidable enemy. For starvation was staring them in the face.

Sleep fell upon the survivors; and when they woke June 29.
the wind had risen, and the boat was drifting down the stream—in the darkness they knew not whither; and some even then had waking dreams of a coming deliverance. But with the first glimmer of the morning despair came upon them. The boat had been carried out of the main channel of the river into a creek or siding, where the enemy soon discerned it, and poured a shower of musket-balls upon its miserable inmates. Then Vibart, who lay helpless, with both arms shot through, issued his last orders. It was a forlorn hope. But whilst there was a sound arm among them, that could load and fire, or thrust with a bayonet, still the great game of the English was to go to the front and smite the enemy, as a race that seldom waited to be smitten. So Mowbray-Thomson and Delafosse, with a little band of European soldiers of the Thirty-second and the Eighty-fourth, landed to attack their assailants. The fierce energy of desperation drove them forward. Sepoys and villagers, armed and unarmed, surged around them, but they charged through the astounded mul-

* Mowbray-Thomson was one of these. Nothing can be more modest than this part of his narrative. "Instead of waiting for them to attack us, eighteen or twenty of us charged them, and few of their number escaped to tell the story."

1857. June 29. titude, and made their way back again through the crowd of blacks to the point from which they had started. Then they saw that the boat was gone. The fourteen were left upon the pitiless land, whilst their doomed companions floated down the pitiless water.

The last Stand.

There was one more stand to be made by Mowbray-Thomson and his comrades. As they retreated along the bank of the river, seeing after a while no chance of overtaking the boat, they made for a Hindoo temple, which had caught the eye of their leader, and defended the doorway with fixed bayonets. After a little time they stood behind a rampart of black and bloody corpses, and fired, with comparative security, over this bulwark of human flesh. A little putrid water found in the temple gave our people new strength, and they held the doorway so gallantly, and so destructively to the enemy, that there seemed to be no hope of expelling them by force of arms. So whilst word went back to Dundoo Punt, Nana Sahib, that the remnant of the English Army was not to be conquered, the assailants, huddling round the temple, brought leaves and faggots, which they piled up beneath the walls, and strove to burn out the little garrison. Then Providence came to their help in their sorest need. The wind blew smoke and fire away from the temple. But the malice of the enemy had a new device in store. They threw bags of powder on the burning embers. There was now nothing left for our people but flight. Precipitating themselves into the midst of the raging multitude, they fired a volley and then charged with the bayonet. Seven of the fourteen carried their lives with them, and little else, to the bank of the river. There they took to the stream; but presently two of the swimmers were shot through the head, whilst a third, well nigh exhausted, making for a sand-bank, had his skull battered in as soon as he landed. But the surviving four, being strong swimmers, and with heroic power in doing and in suffering, struck down the stream, and aided by the current, evaded their pursuers. Mowbray-Thomson and Delafosse, with privates Murphy and Sullivan, reached alive the territory of a friendly Oude Rajah, and survived to tell the story of Cawnpore. 1857. June 29.

Neglected Heroism.

Teeming as it does with records of heroic exploits, this narrative of the Sepoy War contains nothing that surpasses—perhaps nothing that can justly be compared with—this wonderful episode of the last struggles of the martyrs of Cawnpore. The grand national courage, of the manifold developments of which it is impossible to write without strong emotion, has no nobler illustration than that of the last stand of the remnant of the Cawnpore garrison. A year before, England had made tardy reparation of past neglect by instituting an Order of Valour. It bears a name which renders it personally dear to the recipients of this generation, and will be cherished in historical ages yet to come. It was right that of such an order there should be but one class. But if there had been many classes, Mowbray-Thomson and Delafosse, Murphy and Sullivan, would have earned the highest decoration of which the order could boast. But, I know not by what strange omission, by whose neglect, or by what accident for which no one is responsible, it happens that not one of these heroes has borne on his breast the Victoria Cross. Doubtless, they are the representatives of a gigantic disaster, not of a glorious victory. But the heroism of failure is often greater than the heroism of success. And since the time when, in the days of early Rome, the

1857. June

Three kept the Bridge, there have been none more worthy of all the honour that a sovereign or a nation can bestow on the doers of brave deeds, than those who held the temple on the banks of the Ganges, and fought their way through an armed multitude thirsting for their blood, until from village to village there ran the cry that the Englishmen could not be beaten.

Fate of the boat's company.

Whilst the gallant Four, thus mercifully saved by what, humanly regarded, had seemed to be a summons to certain destruction, the companions from whom they had been severed were losing all hope of deliverance. What befel them after they drifted away, leaving Mowbray-Thomson and his little band of resolute fighting-men on the shore, can never be accurately known in detail. But the boat was overtaken, and all its living cargo carried back to Cawnpore, and turned out upon the well-known landing-place, where a great assemblage of Sepoys was ready to receive them. Some eighty Christian people in all had been brought back, after three days of agony and terror on the dark waters of the Ganges, too merciless to overwhelm them.* From the river bank they were driven, a miserable herd of men, women, and children, to the old cantonment, to await the execution of the orders of the Nana. He went out himself to gloat upon their sufferings. The men were doomed to death at once. The women and children, with greater refinement of cruelty, were suffered to survive their husbands and their fathers, and reserved for a second death. One English lady clung to her husband, and

June 30.

* Eighty is the number given by Mr. Sherer after very careful inquiry and collation of evidence. They were brought back on carts, and arrived at the Ghaut on the 30th of June.

perished. The rest were torn away, whilst the muskets of the Sepoys were loaded for that fatal fusillade. Then an English officer, who throughout all the accidents of that river voyage had preserved a prayer-book of the Church of England, sought permission to read to his doomed comrades a few sentences of that beautiful liturgy, whose utterances are never so touchingly appropriate as amidst the sorest trials and troubles of life. Leave was granted. And with one arm in a sling, whilst with the other he held the precious volume before his eyes, Seppings proclaimed to that doomed congregation the great message of salvation; and even amidst the roar and rattle of the musketry the glad tidings were still ringing in their ears, as they passed away to another world. 1857. June 30.

Then the women and children were sent to swell the crowd of captives, which these conquerors of the hour were holding still in store as a final relish for their feast of slaughter. All who had not been burnt, or bayoneted, or sabred, or drowned in the great massacre of the boats on the 27th of June, had been swept up from the Ghaut and carried to the Savada House, a building which had figured in the history of the siege as, for a time, the head-quarters of the rebel leader. And now these newly-made widows and orphans were added to the shuddering herd of condemned innocents.

This done, Doondoo Punt, Nana Sahib, carrying with him an infinite satisfaction derived from the success of his machinations, went off to his palace at Bithoor. Next day, in all the pride and pomp of power, he was publicly proclaimed Peishwah. No formality, no ceremony was omitted, that could give dignity to the occasion. He took his seat upon the throne. The sacrament of the forehead-mark was

July 1. The Nana proclaimed Peishwah.

1857. July 1. duly performed. The cannon roared out its recognition of the new ruler. And when night fell, the darkness was dispersed by a general illumination, and showers of fireworks lit up the sky. But it was not long before, even in the first flush of triumph, heaviness fell upon the restored sovereignty of the Peishwah. He was, after all, only a miserable tool in the hands of others. And news soon reached him that, in his absence from Cawnpore, his influence was declining. The Mahomedan party was waxing strong. It had hitherto been overborne by the Hindoo power, probably more than all else for want of an efficient leader. But there was a Mahomedan nobleman, known as the Nunny Newab, who had taken a conspicuous, if not an active, part in the siege. At the commencement of the outbreak he had been made prisoner by the Nana Sahib, and his house had been plundered; but subsequently they had entered into a covenant of friendship, and a command had been given to the Newab. He directed or presided over one of the batteries planted at the Racquet Court, driving down to it in his carriage, and sitting on a chair, in costly attire, with a sword at his side and a telescope in his hand; and there was no battery that wrought us greater mischief than the Nunny Newab's. He had got together some cunning Native artificers, who experimentalised on red-hot shot and other combustibles, not without damage to the lives of those working in the batteries; and it was a projectile from one of his guns—described as a ball of resin—which set fire to the barrack in the entrenchments. The Nana was so delighted with this exploit that he sent the Newab a present of five thousand rupees, and the story ran, that in the administrative arrangements which were to follow the extirmination of the

English, he was to be Governor of Cawnpore. Among 1857. July.
the Mahomedans of the neighbourhood he was held in high estimation, and large numbers of followers attended him as he went down every day to his battery.

And now there was some talk of setting up the Newab as head of the new Government. If this had been done there would have been faction fights between Hindoos and Mahomedans, which would have weakened the power of the general enmity to the Christian races, and hastened the day of retribution. Then other disturbing rumours reached him. The English reinforcements were advancing from Allahabad—hot for revenge, eager for blood. The story ran that the white soldiers were hanging every Native who came in their way. It was plain that the time for strenuous action had come. A great fear was settling down upon the minds of the inhabitants of Cawnpore, who were leaving their homes in the city and seeking refuge in the villages; and the military classes, as is ever their wont at such times, were clamouring for donatives, and declaiming against the parsimony of the Nana. To send forth assuring and even boastful addresses alike to the citizen and to the soldier, was his first care in this month of July;* and it was necessary, without delay, to issue largesses in money, and in the alluring shape of those much-coveted gold bangles, the thought of which, ever since the commencement of the siege, had stimulated the activity of the Sepoys.

So the Peishwah of the hour was summoned back July 6.
to Cawnpore by the lieutenants whom he had left to govern in his absence. He established himself in an edifice, of goodly proportions, which had been built

* Some of these will be found in the Appendix.

1857. July 6. for an hotel by a Mahomedan capitalist; and here he held high carnival. The native gossips of the day related how, after the fashion of the East, he strove to drown the cares and anxieties which gathered round him, with music, and dancing, and buffoonery in public; and that he solaced himself, in more retired hours, with strong drink and the caresses of a famous courtesan. Day after day his scouts brought exaggerated stories of the advance of the English battalions; and he issued instructions to his officers to go out to meet them. He had put forth astounding proclamations to assure the people that the pride of the English had been humbled to the dust, and that their armies had been overwhelmed by more powerful nations, or, by God's providence, drowned in the sea. There was no lie which Doondoo Punt and his lieutenants had not put forth, in some shape or other, to assure the minds of the people and to make men believe that there was nothing now to be hoped or feared from the prostrate Feringhees. But ever, as the month of July wore on, news came from below that the English were advancing; and the Peishwah trembled as he heard, even in the midst of his revelries. There was, however, one more victory to be gained before the collapse of the new Mahratta power on the banks of the Ganges. And the Nana smiled as he thought that the game was all in his own hands.

The captives in the Beebee-ghur.

It was only a victory over a number of helpless women and children—a victory safe and easy. The English prisoners had been removed from the Savada Kotee to a small house, which had been built by an English officer for his native mistress (thence called the "Beebee-ghur"); but had more recently been the residence of a humble Eurasian clerk. There

was scanty accommodation in it for a single family. 1857. July 7—15.
In this wretched building were now penned, like sheep for the slaughter, more than two hundred women and children. For the number of the captives had by this time been increased by an addition from a distance. Whilst our Christian people at Cawnpore had been suffering what has been but dimly portrayed in the preceding pages, there had been a great crisis at Futtehgurh, the British military station adjacent to the city of Furruckabad, in the district of that name. It lies on the right bank of the Ganges, eighty miles above Cawnpore. In the first week of June, after nearly a month of extreme anxiety, it had become apparent that the lives of all the Europeans, and they were many, would be sacrificed if they continued to dwell at Futtehgurh. So, not knowing in the first week of June the true position of affairs at Cawnpore, a large number of our people took to their boats and drifted down to the great British cantonment, as to a place of refuge. The story of Futtehgurh must be told in another chapter of this narrative. It is enough that it should be related here that those who descended the river were attacked on the way, and that when one boat reached the neighbourhood of Cawnpore the Nana Sahib's people captured it, dragged out its unhappy inmates, and carried them, bound, to the feet of their master. Then there was a slaughter, in his presence, of all the men, three excepted; and the women and children were carried off to swell the miserable crowd in the "Beebee-ghur."

This new prison-house lay between the Native city and the river, under the shadow of the improvised palace of the Peishwah, within sound of the noisy music, and within sight of the torch-glare which sig-

1857. July 7—15. nalised his highness's nocturnal rejoicings.* Thus huddled together, fed upon the coarsest provender of the country, doled out to them by sweepers, their sufferings were intolerable. Cholera and diarrhœa broke out among them, and some were mercifully suffered to die.† If, in the agony and terror of this captivity, bereft of reason, any one of these sufferers anticipated, by action of her own, the day of doom, God will surely take merciful account of the offence. The horror of a fouler shame than had yet come upon them may have crazed more intellects than one. But there was in this no more than a phantom of the imagination. Our women were not dishonoured save that they were made to feel their servitude. They were taken out, two at a time, to grind corn for the Nana's household. An educated English gentle-

* The following minute description of the "Beebee-ghur" is from a private journal kept by Major Gordon of the Sixty-first: "It was a dismal kind of bungalow in a small compound near what used to be the Assembly Rooms. There was a narrow verandah running along nearly the whole of the front. At the two ends of it were bathing-rooms, opening both into the verandah and into side-rooms. Then came an inner entrance room, and then one about sixteen by sixteen, and then an open verandah as in front. At either side was a narrow room. . . . It was, in fact, two small houses, built on exactly the same plan, facing each other, and having a space enclosed between them."

† Mr. Trevelyan, referring to a diary kept by a Native doctor who visited the prisoners, says, "There is a touching little entry which deserves notice. In the column headed 'names' appears the words 'ek beebee' (one baby), under that marked 'disease' is written 'ap se,' of itself." As a "beebee" is not a baby, but a lady or woman, I attributed this error to the writer's brief residence in India, but I find the passage is taken from Mr. Sherer's official report, a document of the highest value. I must still, however, hold to the opinion that "ek beebee" means one lady, and I should have thought that the pathos of the "ap se" lay in its meaning that she killed herself, if it were not for a suspicion that in Sherer's report "beebee" is a misprint for "baba." I have not seen the original list, but it was translated by Major Gordon, who was on General Neill's Staff. This officer wrote down in his journal, at the time, most of the names. "From the 7th," he says, "to the morning of the 15th, twenty-eight people died; nine cholera; nine diarrhœa; one dysentery; three of wounds; one, an infant two days old; five, disease not mentioned. I could not make out all the names, but those of which I am sure are" . . and then a list is given, including, under date July 10, "A baby of two days old—of itself." This seems to be conclusive.

woman needed not even a week's residence in India to teach her the meaning of this. As they sat there on the ground, these Christian captives must have had some glimmering recollection of their biblical studies, and remembered how in the East the grinding of corn was ever regarded as a symbol of subjection—how, indeed, it was one of the crowning curses of the first great captivity on record.* When the wives of the English conquerors were set to grind corn in the court-yards of the Mahratta, the national humiliation was then and there complete—then, but only for a little while; there, but only on a little space. And the pathos of the picture is perfected when we see that these delicate ladies, with their faces to the grindstone, did not find the office so wholly distasteful, as it enabled them to carry back a little flour to the "Beebee-ghur" to feed their famishing children.

1857. July 7—15.

So here, just under the windows of the Nana Sahib, was a very weak, defenceless enemy, which might be attacked with impunity and vanquished with ease. But, with that other enemy, which was now advancing from Allahabad, and, as the story ran, destroying every one in their way, the issue of the contest was more doubtful. A great body of Horse and

* Some, perhaps, may have called to mind, in this hour of humiliation, the awful appropriateness of the forty-seventh chapter of Isaiah, and mostly of these solemn words:—"Come down and sit in the dust, O virgin daughter of Babylon, sit on the ground. . . . . . for thou shalt no more be called tender and delicate. Take the millstones and grind meal: uncover thy locks, make bare the leg, uncover the thigh, pass over the rivers. . . . . Thou saidst, 'I shall be a lady for ever,' so that thou didst not lay these things to thy heart, neither didst remember the latter end of it. Therefore, hear now this, thou that art given to pleasures, that dwellest carelessly, that sayest in thine heart, 'I am and none else beside me; I shall not sit as a widow, neither shall I know the loss of children. But these two things shall come to thee in a moment, in one day, the loss of children and widowhood. . . . Evil shall come upon thee; thou shalt not know from whence it riseth; and mischief shall fall upon thee; thou shalt not be able to put it off, and desolation shall come upon thee suddenly."

1857. July 7—15. Foot, with a formidable array of guns, had gone down to dispute the progress of the British; but, before the month of July was half spent, news came that they had been disastrously beaten. Havelock had taken the field in earnest. The hopes of his youth, the prayers of his manhood, had been accomplished; he had lived to command an army, to gain a victory, and to write a despatch in his own good name.

*** At the close of this chapter, I must express my obligations to the printed volumes of Captain Mowbray-Thomson and Mr. Otto Trevelyan. The reminiscences of the one writer and the investigations of the other have been equally serviceable to me. But to no one am I more indebted than to Colonel Williams for the invaluable mass of oral information which he has elicited and placed on record, and the admirable synopsis which accompanies it. From an immense pile of conflicting evidence, I believe that, guided by Colonel Williams, I have extracted the truth. There are still, however, some doubts and uncertainties as regards points of detail, especially in respect of the numbers both of the fighting men in the entrenchments and of the women and children in the "Beebee-ghur." The discrepancy with respect to the former may have arisen from the circumstance that in some lists the sick were computed, but not in others. Colonel Williams gives a nominal roll of European troops composing the English portion of the Cawnpore garrison who were killed between the 6th and 30th of June. In this we have the names of fifty-nine Artillery-men, seventy-nine men of the Thirty-second, forty-nine of the Eighty-fourth, and fifteen of the Madras Fusiliers—making in all two hundred and two, exclusive of officers. Mr. Sherer's numbers differ from these—his aggregate being a hundred and sixty-four. With regard to the women and children in the "Beebee-ghur," I think that Major Gordon's estimate is most probably correct. He says, after studying the list of prisoners, "It appears from this that two hundred and ten were left on the 11th, and as twelve died between that and the 15th, there must probably have been a hundred and ninety-seven when the massacre took place."

CHAPTER III.

GENERAL HAVELOCK AT ALLAHABAD — EQUIPMENT OF THE BRIGADE — ADVANCE TOWARDS CAWNPORE—JUNCTION WITH RENAUD—THE BATTLES OF FUTTEHPORE, AONG, AND CAWNPORE—THE MASSACRE OF THE WOMEN AND CHILDREN—RE-OCCUPATION OF CAWNPORE.

ASSURED of the miserable fact that Cawnpore had 1857.
fallen, General Havelock, having halted Renaud's July.
column at Lohanga, was eager to advance to join him and to push on for the recovery of the important position that we had lost, and the chastisement of the insolent enemy. He telegraphed to Sir Patrick Grant at Calcutta, saying: "We have lost Cawnpore, an important point on the great line of communication, and the place from which alone Lucknow can be succoured; for it would be hardly possible, at this season of the year, to operate on the cross-roads. My duty is, therefore, to endeavour to take Cawnpore, to the accomplishment of which I will bend every effort. I advance along the trunk-road as soon as I can unite fourteen hundred British Infantry to a battery of six well-equipped guns. Lieutenant-Colonel Neill, whose high qualities I cannot sufficiently praise, will follow with another column as soon as it is organised, and this fort is left in proper hands."*

* Marshman's Life of Havelock.

1857. July 4—7. Preparations for the March.

Havelock had hoped to commence his march on the 4th of July, but the impediments in the way of the complete equipment of his force were too numerous and too serious to admit of so early a movement. All the old difficulties, of which I have already spoken, were in his way, and it was not until the sun was dimly declining on the 7th that he could give the order to march. It was but a small force for the work before it. A thousand European Infantry soldiers, belonging to four different regiments, composed the bulk of Havelock's army. Some of these were seasoned soldiers, but some were raw recruits. Then there were a hundred and thirty of Brazier's Sikhs, a battery of six guns, and a little troop of Volunteer Cavalry, mustering only eighteen sabres, but in the hands of such men worth their number five times told. Among them were young officers, whose regiments had revolted,* and civilians whose cutcherries were closed; and as they rode out, badly mounted (for Palliser's Irregulars had taken the best horses), under their gallant leader, Captain Barrow of the Madras Cavalry, there was a large-hearted enthusiasm among them which made them feel equal to the encounter of any number of Native horsemen that could be brought against them. Nor should there be omission from the record of the fact that, when Havelock marched forth for the recovery of Cawnpore and the relief of Lucknow, he was accompanied by some of the best staff-officers with

* "New to the country, new to the service, unaccustomed to roughing it, brought up in every luxury, and led to believe that on their arrival in India they would have the same, these young officers (deprived of employment by the mutiny of their regiments) willingly threw themselves into the thick of the work, often without a tent or cover of any sort to shelter them from the rain or sun, with bad provisions and hard work. Side by side with the privates they took their turn of duty, and side by side with them they fought, were wounded, and some died."—*Quoted in Marshman's Life of Havelock. Author not stated.*

whom it has ever been the good fortune of a general to be associated. In Lieutenant-Colonel Fraser-Tytler and Captain Stuart Beatson he had a Quarter-Master General and an Adjutant-General of his brigade, selected by himself, not to be out-matched in efficiency by any officers of those departments. 1857. July 7—12.

March for Allahabad.

It was a dull, dreary afternoon when Havelock's Brigade marched out of Allahabad, and very soon the rain came down in torrents to damp the ardour of the advancing force. Neither on that day nor on the succeeding one was the progress rapid. Many of the men were unused to Indian marching, and numbers fell in the rear, weary, footsore, disabled. There was great discouragement in this; but as Havelock advanced, it became more and more apparent to him not only that Cawnpore had fallen, but that a large body of the enemy were advancing to meet him, and this rendered it not only expedient, but imperative, that no time should be lost in joining the advanced column. Neill, doubtful, as it has been seen, of the fall of Cawnpore, had telegraphed to Sir Patrick Grant, urging him to push on Renaud's column, and Renaud was moving forward into the clutches of the Nana's force; and though Havelock's knowledge of the inestimable value at such a time of English life and English health rendered him careful of his men, he now recognised a paramount emergency overruling these considerations, and sped onwards by forced marches to overtake his Lieutenant. And an hour after the midnight of the 11th—12th of July, in the broad light of an unclouded moon, his foremost details came up with Renaud's detachment. Before dawn the junction was completed. Renaud drew up his men along the side of the road; and as the Highlanders struck up the stirring strain of the

1857. "Campbells are coming," welcomed the new arrivals with ringing cheers. Then they marched on together, and about seven o'clock the whole force halted at Belindah, a spot some four miles from the city of Futtehpore.*

July 12. The Battle of Futtehpore.

The troops were weary and footsore, and Havelock was eager to give his men the rest and refreshment they so much needed. So arms were piled, and our soldiery were preparing for the morning meal, when their hungry hopes were disappointed by the unexpected arrival of a twenty-four-pound shot, which well-nigh reached the feet of the General. The truth was soon apparent. Colonel Tytler had gone forward with an escort to reconnoitre, and some spies, despatched by Lawrence from Lucknow, had brought him word that the enemy were at Futtehpore. There was no more thought of the breakfast. The battle was before them. The men stood to their arms and fell in at the word of command, and, forgetful of the long and weary night-march just ended, set their faces towards the camp of the enemy, and strode on, steady and stern, to meet them.

They soon met. For the enemy, thinking that they had come up with the advanced column only, under Major Renaud, swept forward with an insolent front, confident of victory. Conspicuous before all were the troopers of the Second Cavalry, who came on menacingly in an extended line, as though eager to

* *Calcutta Review*, vol. xxxii., Article, "Havelock's Indian Campaign," written by one who took part in it. This writer, a very able one, says, "We shall not soon forget the scene. . . . We well recollect how anxious Major Renaud was to capture Futtehpore before Havelock reached us, it having been reported to us that it was defended only by a few matchlock-men. This was probably correct at the time, but the Nana, with his large force, was marching down upon it, and had we advanced not a soul would have lived to tell the tale; but Providence preserved us from a fate which at that time would have been ruinous to our power in India."

enclose our little band in the toils of a swift destruction. So Havelock, as he wrote, unwilling "to be bearded, determined at once to bring on an action." Then the truth became miserably apparent to the enemy; and in an instant the light of proud defiance paled beneath the astounding disclosure. The weak detachment, that was to have been so easily overwhelmed, had suddenly grown, as though under the hand of Shiva the Destroyer, into a strong, well-equipped, well-handled force of all arms, advancing to the battle with a formidable line of guns in the centre. Flushed with the savage memories of the past, and eager for fresh slaughter, these bloodhounds of the Nana Sahib had rushed upon their prey only to find themselves brought face to face with death. Surprise, disappointment, fear, trod down even the brutal instincts within them, and the paralysis of a great reaction was upon them. The fight commenced. It was scarcely a battle; but it was a consummate victory. Our Enfield rifles and our guns would not permit a conflict. The service of the Artillery was superb. There had come upon the scene a new warrior, of whom India had before known nothing, but whose name from that day became terrible to our enemies. The improvised battery of which Havelock made such splendid use was commanded by Captain Maude of the Royal Artillery. He had come round from Ceylon, with a few gunners, but without guns; and he had gone at once to the front as one of the finest Artillerymen in the world. The best troops of the Nana Sahib, with a strength of Artillery exceeding our own, could make no stand against such a fire as was opened upon them.* Falling back upon the

1857. July 12.

* "The enemy's fire scarcely touched us," wrote Havelock; "ours for four hours allowed him no repose." "Twelve British soldie—

1857. July 12. town, with its many enclosures of walled gardens, they abandoned their guns one after another to our exhausted battalions; and after one vain rally of the rebel Horse, which solved the vexed question of the unworthiness of Palliser's Irregulars, gave up the contest in despair. Then Havelock again lamented his want of Cavalry; for he could not follow up, as he wished, his first brilliant success; and more of the rebel Sepoys escaped than was pleasing to the old soldier. But he had done his work well and was thankful; thankful to his troops for their gallant services; thankful to the Almighty Providence that had given him the victory; and proud of the great national character which was now so nobly reasserting itself.* It was the first heavy blow struck at the pride of the enemy in that part of the country. The glad tidings were received with exultant delight in every house and bungalow in the country. In due time England caught up the pæan; and the name of Havelock was written at the corners of our

were struck down by the sun and never rose again. But our fight was fought neither with musket nor bayonet nor sabre, but with Enfield rifles and cannon: so we lost no men." This probably means no Europeans; for Havelock's biographer, after quoting the General's despatch, says, with reference to the conduct of the Irregular Cavalry at this time, that "only twelve followed their commanding officer, Lieutenant Palliser, whose blind confidence in his men and gallant spirit carried him headlong into the midst of the enemy (at Futtehpore), without a glance behind to ascertain if he were supported. Here he was overpowered and knocked off his horse, and would inevitably have been cut to pieces had he not been rescued by the devoted gallantry of his Native Ressaldar, who sacrificed his own life in endeavouring to save that of his leader."

* See Havelock's Order of Thanks issued next day to the troops under his command, in which he attributes the victory, with a sort of Cromwellian many-sidedness, "to the fire of British Artillery, exceeding in rapidity and precision all that the Brigadier has ever witnessed in his not short career; to the power of the Enfield rifle in British hands; to British pluck, that great quality which has survived the vicissitudes of the hour and gained intensity from the crisis; and to the blessing of Almighty God on a most righteous cause—the cause of justice, humanity, truth, and good government in India."

streets, on the sides of our public conveyances, and on the sign-boards over our houses of public entertainment.* 1857. July 12.

The story of Futtehpore.

Futtehpore was given up to plunder. It was a guilty—a blood-stained city. A few weeks before it had risen in rebellion. And now the mark of a just retribution was to be set upon it. The story may be briefly told in this place. The Treasury-guard consisted of some sixty or seventy Sepoys of the Sixth Regiment. About the end of May, a large detachment of the Fifty-sixth, with some Sowars of the Second Cavalry—both of which regiments were then fast seething into rebellion at Cawnpore—arrived at Futtehpore with treasure from Banda, and passed on to Allahabad. What dark hints and suggestions may have passed between them can never be known. No great uneasiness was then felt by the European residents. The temper of the people did not seem to differ much from what it had been in more quiet times, and public business went on from day to day in the old groove without interruption.

The Chief Civil Officer at Futtehpore was Mr. Robert Tudor Tucker, the Judge. He was a brother of the Commissioner of Benares. There were some strong resemblances between them. Both were de-

* It appears from Tantia Topee's narrative, which on such a point as this may be trusted, that the Sepoys were anxious that the Nana should accompany them to Futtehpore. "The Nana refused," he said: "I and the Nana remained at Cawnpore, and sent Jowalla-Persaud, his agent, along with them to Futtehpore." Teeka Sing, the Second Cavalry General, accompanied him. The Allahabad Moulavee, also, appears to have been with the Nana's party at this time. One of the witnesses, whose depositions have been published by Colonel Williams, when asked, "Who commanded at the battle of Futtehpore?" answered, "I myself saw Teeka Singh, the General, and the Allahabad Moulavee, and Jowalla-Persaud, going off to command. Many others went—small fry of leaders."

1857. vout Christian men, earnestly and conscientiously treading the appointed path of official duty. People spoke of Henry Tucker as an enthusiast; but the enthusiasm of Robert Tucker had been roused to a still higher pitch by the intensity of his religious convictions, which, even from his schoolboy days up to the prime of his mature manhood, had been striking deeper and deeper root, in spite of all the discouragements and distractions of Eastern life. At the entrance to Futtehpore he had erected four pillars of stone, on two of which were engraved the Ten Commandments, in Persian and Hindee, and on the others, in the same characters, scriptural texts containing the essence of the Christian faith. There they stood, that he who ran might read, proclaiming to Hindoos and Mahomedans the cherished creed of the Feringhees; but no man defaced or insulted them. And the good Judge made no disguise of his efforts to convert the people; but still no man molested him. His kindness and liberality seem to have endeared him to all classes. They saw that he was just and gentle; merciful and self-denying; and that he taught lessons of love by the practice of his daily life. In very literal truth, he was what the Natives of India, often in exaggerated language, call a "poor man's provider." Wherever misery was to be found, his helping hand was present. The destitute and the sick were his children, in the absence of those endeared to him by the tenderest ties. For he was a husband and a father; but his family at this time were in England; and when the day of trouble came he rejoiced that he stood alone.

The storm burst on the 9th of June. The two great waves of rebellion, the one from Allahabad, the other from Cawnpore, met here with overwhelming force. Hindoos and Mahomedans rose against us; the latter, as ever, with the more cruel violence. The roving bands of Sepoys and Sowars and escaped gaol-birds, who were flooding the surrounding districts, wholly disorganised our police; and what was said to be a Mahomedan conspiracy was hatched in the very heart of the city. Then the dangerous classes seem to have bubbled up, and there were the usual orgies of crime. The Treasury was plundered. The prison-gates were broken open. The Record-office was burnt down. Other public offices were condemned to the same destruction. The Mission premises were attacked. And, when the European community gathered together in a barricaded house resolved that it would be utter madness to remain any longer at Futtehpore, for all authority was gone, all hope of maintaining any longer a semblance of Government utterly departed, they left the station by the light of blazing bungalows, and sallied forth to find themselves "amidst a perfect Jacquerie of the surrounding villages."* But they made their way across the Jumna to Banda, and were saved. 1857. June 9.

One Englishman stood fast. One Englishman could not be induced to quit his post, whatever might be the perils which environed him. As long as there was a pulse of life in his body, Robert Tucker believed that it was his duty to give it to the Government which he served. Throughout the day he had been most active in his endeavours to suppress crime and to restore order. Unlike his brother Henry. who had never fired a shot in his life, or carried a more formidable weapon than a riding-whip, the Futtehpore Judge armed himself, mounted his horse, and went out against the enemy, with a few horse-

* Mr. Sherer to Mr. Chester, June 19, 1857. MS.

1857. June 9. men at his back. He left some rebels dead in the streets, and carried back with him some wounds upon his person.* His countrymen, when they turned their backs on Futtehpore, left him in the Cutcherry, still hoping against hope that he might weather the storm; and believing that, if this by God's Providence were denied to him, it was his duty alike to God and Man to die at his post.

The issue was soon determined. What followed the departure of his countrymen is but obscurely known. Of the one patent, miserable fact, that Robert Tucker was killed, there was never a moment's doubt. The story ran that at the head of the Mahomedan conspiracy, or if not at its very heart, was a well-known Native functionary—Deputy-Magistrate by office—Hikmut-oollah by name. He had received great benefits from Mr. Tucker, who had full faith in the man; and for some time it was believed that Mussulman treachery and ingratitude had culminated in the crowning crime of this man's life. "Poor Tucker," wrote Mr. Sherer, the Magistrate of Futtehpore, to Commissioner Chester, "was shot by Hikmut-oollah's orders, he himself reading out the Koran whilst the guns were fired. A Native Christian, Joseph Manuel, a servant of mine, was present when this took place." But many still doubt, if they do not wholly discredit, much that has been said of Hikmut-oollah Khan. He might have saved his benefactor, but did not. Perhaps he went with the stream, not having courage to oppose it. The crime may have

* Mr. Clive Bayley, in his Allahabad report, says: "It is impossible not to admire, however much it might be regretted, the heroic devotion of the late Mr. Tucker; nor is it much a matter of wonder that his conduct and his personal prowess (Mr. Tucker was, I believe, more than once wounded early in the day) actually succeeded in preserving, for a few hours longer, some show of order."

been but negative. But History does not doubt that the Futtehpore Judge sold his life dearly on the roof of the Cutcherry. Resolutely and fiercely he stood at bay, loading and firing, loading and firing, until he had shot down many of his assailants. It is said that he was not overcome at last until the insurgents had fired the Cutcherry. And so the quiet Christian Judge, so meek and merciful in time of peace, giving unto Cæsar the things that were Cæsar's, rose in the hour of war to the noblest heights of heroic daring, and died for the Government that he had served. 1857. June 9.

There were some, however, even in that guilty city, who viewed with horror and indignation the murder of the good Judge. And as the ruffians were returning from the Cutcherry, rejoicing in their cruel work, two Hindoos met them, and openly reviled them for slaying so just and righteous a man. Had he not always been the friend of the poor? But the murderers were in no mood to be rebuked. Furious before, they were infuriated to a still higher pitch by these reproaches. So they fell upon the witnesses and slew them.

In Havelock's camp there was at this time one of the civil officers who had escaped, more than a month before, from Futtehpore. Mr. Sherer, the Magistrate, after many adventures, had made his way to Allahabad, and had thence marched upwards with the avenging army.* For five weeks anarchy and confusion had reigned throughout the district. The authority of the Nana Sahib had been nominally recog- The punishment of Futtehpore. July 12—13.

* Mr. Willock had gone on, as civil officer, with Renaud's detachment. He had been very active during the crisis at Allahabad, and both then and afterwards had proved himself, in conflict with the enemy, to be a gallant soldier.

1857. July 12—13.

nised, but in truth there was scarcely any semblance of Government. Every man stood up for himself, taking and keeping what he could. Along the line of Havelock's march, Sherer observed the significant symbols of a widespread desolation—telling afterwards the story of what he saw in one of the best of those admirable official narratives through which many of our foremost civilians have done so much for historical truth. "Many of the villages," he wrote, "had been burnt by the wayside, and human beings there were none to be seen. . . . The swamps on either side of the road; the blackened ruins of huts, now further defaced by weather-stains and mould; the utter absence of all sound that could indicate the presence of human life, or the employment of human industry, such sounds being usurped by the croaking of frogs, the shrill pipe of the cicala, and the under-hum of the thousand winged insects engendered by the damp and heat; the offensive smell of the neem-trees; the occasional taint in the air from suspended bodies, upon which, before our very eyes, the loathsome pig of the country was engaged in feasting;—all these things appealing to our different senses, combined to call up such images of desolation, and blackness, and woe, as few, I should think, who were present would ever forget."* And

* The other side of the picture should, in fairness, also be given. In the following we see some of the phenomena of the great revolt against civilisation which preceded the retribution whose manifestations are described in the text: "Day by day," says a writer in the *Calcutta Review*, "as we marched along, we had ample evidence of the certainty with which the Asiatic had determined to tear us out of the land, root and branch; the untiring malignity which had, not content with murder and mutilation, burned our bungalows and desecrated our churches only as an Asiatic can desecrate, we had witnessed, but we scarcely expected what we saw in passing along the road. There was satisfactory evidence that the genius of the revolt was to destroy everything that could possibly remind one of England or its civilisation. The telegraph wires were cut up, strewing the ground, and in some instances carried off, the

now in the city itself were silence and solitude scarcely less impressive and significant. The streets were deserted; but there were signs of recent habitation. In the shops and houses much wealth of plunder was left, which could not be removed in time by the affrighted owners beyond the reach of the despoilers. So now our soldiers, English and Sikhs, were let loose upon the place, and before the day was spent it had been sacked. Next morning, when the column moved on, the Sikhs were left behind, flushed with delight at the thought that to them had been entrusted the congenial task of setting fire to the town. 1857. July.

Battle at Aong. July 15.

On the 15th of July, Havelock, having on the preceding day dismounted and disarmed the Irregular Cavalry, whose treachery was undeniable, again came in front of the enemy. They had posted themselves in strength at the village of Aong, with something of an entrenchment in front, and on either flank some walled gardens, thickly studded with trees, which afforded serviceable shelter to their musketeers. But no superiority of numbers or of position could enable them to sustain the resistless rush of the English. Very soon they were seen in confused flight, strewing the ground as they fled with all the abandoned impedimenta of their camp—tents, stores, carriage, and munitions of war. But the cost of that morning's success was indeed heavy. For one of the best soldiers in the British camp was lost to it for ever. Major Renaud, who had charged at the head of the Madras Fusiliers—his beloved "Lambs"—was carried mortally wounded to the rear. Those who knew him best deplored him most; but the grief which

...graph posts were dug out, the bungalows burnt, and the poor unoffending milestones, so useful even to themselves, but still English, were defaced, and in many instances destroyed."

1857. July 15.

arose when it was afterwards known that he was dead was not confined to his old comrades of the Coast Army. He had already earned an Indian reputation.

Passage of the Pandoo-nuddee.

The day's work was not then over. A few miles beyond the village of Aong was a river to be crossed, known as the Pandoo-nuddee. It was but a streamlet in comparison with the Ganges, into which it flowed. But the July rains had already rendered it swollen and turbid; and if the bridge by which it was crossed had been destroyed by the enemy, Havelock's progress would have been most disastrously retarded. So, when his scouts told him that the enemy were rallying, and were about to blow up the bridge, he roused his men, exhausted as they were, and called upon them for a new effort. Nobly responding to the call, they pushed forward with unexpected rapidity. It was a two hours' march to the bridge-head under a fierce sun; but our weary people carried the energies of victory with them to the banks of the Pandoo-nuddee. The enemy, strengthened by reinforcements which had come in fresh from Cawnpore, under Bala Rao, the brother of the Nana, were entrenched on the other side with heavy guns, which raked the bridge. But Maude's battery was soon brought into action; and a favourable bend of the river enabling him so to plant his guns as to take the enemy in flank, he poured such a stream of Shrapnel into them that they were bewildered and paralysed, and, some say, broke their sponge-staffs in despair. They had undermined the bridge-head, and had hoped to blow the whole structure into the air before the English could cross the river. But there was not a cool head or a steady hand among them to do this work. And the Fusiliers, under Major Stephenson, with an expression on their stern faces not to be misunderstood, swept across the bridge, and put an end to all fear of its destruction. Then the rest of Havelock's force accomplished the passage of the river, and pushed on with their faces towards Cawnpore, weary and exhausted in body, but sustained by the thought of the coming retribution. 1857. July 15.

The last massacre.

They did not then know the worst. The crowning horror of the great tragedy of Cawnpore was yet to come. On the afternoon of that 15th of July, Doondoo Punt, Nana Sahib, learnt that Havelock's army had crossed the Pundoo-nuddee, and was in full march upon his capital. The messenger who brought the evil tidings was Bala Rao himself, with a wound in his shoulder, as proof that he had done his best. It might be that there was a coming end to the short-lived triumphs of the new Peishwah. What now was to be done? The chief advisers of the Nana Sahib were divided in opinion. They might make a stand at Bithoor, or form a junction with the rebel force at Futtehgurh, or go out to meet the enemy on the road to Cawnpore. The last course, after much confused discussion, was adopted, and arrangements were made to dispute Havelock's advance. The issue was very doubtful; but, as already said, the mighty conquerors of Cawnpore had one more victory to gain. They could slaughter the English prisoners. So, whether it were in rage, or in fear, or in the wantonness of bestial cruelty; whether it were believed that the English were advancing only to rescue the prisoners, and would turn back on hearing that they were dead; whether it were thought that as no tales can be told by the dead, the total annihilation of the captives would prevent the identification of the arch offenders on

1857. July 15. the day of retribution; whether the foul design had its birth in the depths of the Nana's black heart, or was prompted by one still blacker, the order went forth for the massacre of the women and children in the Beebee-ghur. The miserable herd of helpless victims huddled together in those narrow rooms were to be killed. What followed is best told in the fewest and simplest words. There were four or five men among the captives. These were brought forth and killed in the presence of the Nana Sahib. Then a party of Sepoys was told off, and instructed to shoot the women and children through the doors and windows of their prison-house. Some soldierly instincts seem to have survived in the breasts of these men. The task was too hideous for their performance. They fired at the ceilings of the chambers. The work of death, therefore, proceeded slowly, if at all. So some butchers were summoned from the bazaars—stout Mussulmans accustomed to slaughter; and two or three others, Hindoos, from the villages or from the Nana's guard, were also appointed executioners.* They went in, with swords or long

* Some obscurity surrounds this terrible incident, and perhaps it is better that it should be so. Colonel Williams, to whose investigations History is so much indebted, says with respect to the evidence before him, that, "on approaching the last and most terrible scene, all seem instinctively to shrink from confessing any knowledge of so foul and barbarous a crime as the indiscriminate slaughter of helpless women and innocent children. Evidence that seems clear and strong from the 15th of May to the 14th of July, suddenly ceases on the fatal day of the 15th of that month." The most reliable testimony was that of some half-caste drummers or band-boys. But the principal witness, whose narrative is the most detailed, and seemingly the most authentic of all (John Fitchett, drummer of the Sixth Native Infantry), who stated that he had been a prisoner with our people, was clearly convicted of a direct falsehood in this respect; and it is only where his evidence was supported by others that it is to be entirely trusted. It should be stated here that the male prisoners, shot to death on the 15th of July, were three of the principal fugitives from Futtehgurh, and two members of the Greenaway family. The Sepoy-Guards at the Beebee-ghur, who refused to slaughter the women and children, belonged to the Sixth Regiment from Allahabad. The Nana is stated to have been so incensed by their conduct that he threatened to blow them from guns.

knives, among the women and children, as among a flock of sheep, and with no more compunction, slashed them to death with the sharp steel. 1857. July 15—16.

And there the bodies lay, some only half-dead, all through the night. It was significantly related that the shrieks ceased, but not the groans. Next morning the dead and the dying were brought out, ghastly with their still gaping wounds, and thrown into an adjacent well. Some of the children were alive, almost unhurt; saved, doubtless, by their low stature, amidst the closely-packed masses of human flesh through which the butchers had drawn their blades; and now they were running about, scared and wonder-struck, beside the well. To toss these infantile enemies, alive or dead, into the improvised cemetery, already nearly choked-full, was a small matter that concerned but little those who did the Nana's bidding. But beyond this wholesale killing and burying, which sickened the whole Christian world, and roused English manhood in India to a pitch of national hatred that took years to allay, the atrocity was not pushed. The refinements of cruelty —the unutterable shame—with which, in some of the chronicles of the day, this hideous massacre was attended, were but fictions of an excited imagination, too readily believed without inquiry and circulated without thought. None were mutilated—none were dishonoured. There was nothing needed to aggravate the naked horror of the fact that some two hundred Christian women and children were hacked to death in the course of a few hours.*

* This is stated, in the most unqualified manner, by the official functionaries, who made the most diligent inquiries into all the circumstances of the massacres of June and July. Mr. Sherer and Mr. Thornhill, in their official reports, speak most distinctly in denial of the assertion that our women had been mutilated and dishonoured. Colonel Williams, than whom there can be no better authority, says that the most searching and earnest inquiries totally disprove the unfounded assertion, which was

1857. July 16. Battle of Cawnpore.

Then, this feat accomplished, the Nana Sahib and his allies prepared to make their last stand for the defence of Cawnpore and the Peishwahship. On the morning of the 16th, Doondoo Punt went out himself with some five thousand men—Horse, Foot, and Artillery—to dispute Havelock's advance. The position—some little distance to the south of Cawnpore—which he took up was well selected; and all through that July morning his lieutenants were disposing their troops and planting their guns. Meanwhile, Havelock and his men, unconscious of the great tragedy that, a few hours before, had been acted out to its close, were pushing on, under a burning sun, the fiercest that had yet shone upon their march. Exhausted as he was by the mid-day heats the English soldier toiled on, sustained by the thought that he might still rescue from destruction the two hundred women and children held in foul durance by the Nana. To faint or fail at such a time would have been, he thought, cowardice and crime. So weary and foot-sore, dizzy beneath the vertical rays of the meridian sun, and often tortured by parching thirst, he plodded along the baked road and panted for the coming encounter.

The hour of noon had passed before the English General learnt the true position of the enemy. It was plain that there was some military skill in the rebel camp, in whosesoever brain it might reside;

at first so frequently made and so currently believed, that personal indignity and dishonour had been offered to our poor suffering countrywomen. To this it may be added, that some of the administrators of the Mutiny Relief Fund in England took great pains to investigate certain alleged cases of mutilation, said to have been brought over from India, but failed to track down a single one. The most authentic case of mutilation with which I am acquainted is one that comes to me from Ireland, whilst I am writing this chapter. Some wild Irishmen went into the house of a Mr. Connor, and, taking him for another man, against whom they had a grudge, deliberately cut off his nose.

for the troops of the Nana Sahib were disposed in a manner which taxed all the power of the British Commander, who had been studying the art of war all his life. To Havelock's column advancing along the great high road from Allahabad—to the point where it diverges into two broad thoroughfares, on the right to the Cawnpore cantonment and on the left, the "great trunk," to Delhi—the Sepoy forces presented a formidable front. It was drawn up in the form of an arc, bisecting these two roads. Its left, almost resting upon the Ganges, had the advantage of some sloping ground, on which heavy guns were posted; whilst its right was strengthened by a walled village with a great grove of mango-trees, which afforded excellent shelter to the rebels. Here also heavy guns were posted. And on both sides were large masses of Infantry, with the Second Cavalry in the rear, towards the left centre, for it was thought that Havelock would advance along the Great Trunk Road. When all this was discerned, it was plain that to advance upon the enemy's front would be to court a great carnage of the troops, upon the care of which so much depended. Havelock's former victories had been gained mainly by the far-reaching power of the Enfield Rifles and the unerring precision of Maude's guns. But now he had to summon to his aid those lessons of warfare—both its rules and its exceptions—which he had been learning from his youth upwards; and they did not fail him in the hour of his need. He remembered "old Frederick at Leuthen," and debouching to the right, advanced in open column against the enemy's left flank The movement had its disadvantages, and had he been the paper-pedant, which some thought him, he might not have resorted to such a manœuvre. But its success

1857. July 13.

1857. July 16. proved the efficacy of the exception. He had fully explained the intended movement to his commanders. Standing in the midst of them, he had traced in the dust, with the point of his scabbard, the plan of operations, and had convinced himself that they thoroughly understood it. Then the order was given for the advance; and primed with good libations of malt liquor, they moved forward in column of subdivisions, the Fusiliers in front, along the high road, until they reached the point of divergence. Then the Volunteer Cavalry were ordered to move right on, so as to engage the attention of the enemy and simulate the advance of the entire force, whilst the Infantry and the guns, favoured by the well-wooded country, moved off unseen to the right. The feint succeeded admirably at first. The Cavalry drew upon themselves the enemy's fire. But presently an open space between the trees revealed Havelock's designs, and the Nana's guns opened upon our advancing columns, raking the Highlanders and Sixty-fourth, not without disastrous effect. But nothing shook the steadiness of the advance. That hardest lesson of all to the British soldier, to reserve his fire, had been learnt to perfection by these brave fellows. The last subdivision having emerged from the wood, they were rapidly wheeled into line, and, to the consternation of the enemy, moved forward with a resolute front and disconcerted the arrangements on which the Nana had prided himself so much and so confidently relied. But the native legions had strong faith in the efficacy of their guns, which outmatched our own in number and in weight of metal. At that time we could not make fitting response, for Maude's battery was struggling through ploughed fields, and his draft-cattle were sinking exhausted by the way; and even when they came up, these light field-pieces, worked as well as guns were ever worked, could but make slight impression on the heavy ordnance from the Cawnpore magazine. 1857. July 16.

For a little space, therefore, the Sepoys exulted in the preponderance of their Artillery-fire, and between the boomings of the guns were heard the joyous sounds of military bands, striking up our stirring national tunes, as taught by English band-masters, and, as though in mockery, selecting those with the greatest depth of English sentiment in them. It was a dire mistake. As he caught the familiar sounds of "Cheer, boys, cheers!" the face of the British soldier settled down into that stern, compressed look, when the rigid jaw tells how the teeth are clenched and the muscles strung, and the heart is hard as a stone. The battle now was to be won by the pluck of the English Infantry. It was not a number of "mere machines" that Havelock was urging forward, but so many individual men with great hearts in their bosoms, every one feeling as if he had a personal wrong to redress. The awful work of charging heavy guns, well served by experienced gunners, was now to be commenced; and the Highlanders, led by Colonel Hamilton, took the post of honour, and were the first to charge. The shrill sounds of the pibroch from the bagpipes in the rear seemed to send them all forward as with the force of a catapult. The rush of the kilted soldiers, with their fixed bayonets, cheering as they went, was what no Sepoy force could withstand. Strongly posted as the guns were in a walled village, village and guns were soon carried, and there was an end to the strength of the enemy's left.

The Sepoy troops fled in confusion—some alon

1857. July 16. the Cawnpore road, others towards the centre of their position, where a heavy howitzer was posted, behind which for a while they rallied. There was more work then for the British Infantry. A few minutes after their first grand rush they had gathered breath, and fallen again into orderly array. Then Havelock challenged them a second time with a few of those spirit-stirring words which, from the lips of a trusted general, are as strong drink to the weary soldier, and every man felt invigorated, and equal to any work before him. The Highlanders responded with a cheer, and, followed by the Sixty-fourth, flung themselves on the trenchant howitzer and the village which enclosed it, and again the burst was irresistible. The gun was captured, and the village was cleared.

For, just at this critical moment, the little body of Volunteer Cavalry, composed mainly of English officers, appeared upon the scene, flushed with a noble enthusiasm, resolute and dauntless, determined to show with their flashing sabres what they could do against any odds. Never was there a more heroic charge. It was the charge of but Eighteen. Captain Barrow led it. And among those who went into action was Captain Beatson, who had been struck down by cholera, and who was powerless to sit his horse; but, dying as he was, he could not consent to lose his chance of taking his part in the great act of retribution. So he placed himself upon a tumbril and was carried into action, and as dear life was passing away from him, his failing heart pulsed with great throbs of victory. The sabres of the Eighteen were less bright and sharp after they had encountered the enemy. When they drew rein, diminished in numbers—for horses and riders had been shot down—the Footmen of the British Army saluted them with a ringing cheer; and the General again and again cried, "Well done! I am proud to command you!" It was this body of "Gentlemen Volunteers," into which the "Bayard of the Indian Army"—James Outram—felt it, a month afterwards, a high privilege to enlist, when he might have commanded the whole of the force. 1857. July 16.

Whilst the Cavalry were thus covering themselves with glory, the Infantry swept on to the enemy's right, where two more guns were posted, and carried them with the irresistible ardour that takes no denial. But the enemy, having found fresh shelter in a wooded village, rallied with some show of vigour, and poured a heavy fire into our line. Weary and exhausted as our people were, they had lost none of the grand enthusiasm, which made every man a giant; and when the calm clear voice of the General was heard, inquiring who would take that village, the Highlanders bounded forward, as if they had newly come into action, and the rest responded with like alacrity to the appeal. Again the Sepoy host were swept out of their cover, and seemed to be in full retreat upon Cawnpore, as though the day were quite lost. But there was yet one more stand to be made. As gun after gun was captured by the rush of our Infantry, still it seemed ever that more guns were in reserve, far-reaching and well-served, to deal out death in our ranks. Baffled and beaten as he was, the Nana Sahib was resolute to make one more stand. He had a twenty-four pounder and two smaller guns planted upon the road to the Cawnpore cantonment, from which fresh troops had come pouring in to give new strength to the defence. It was the very crisis of the Peishwah's fate. Conscious of this, he threw all his individual energies into the work before him,

1857. July 16. and tried what personal encouragement could do to stimulate his troops. And he flashed his gaudy presence on his people in a last convulsion of courage and a last effort of resistance.

For there was at this moment a pause in our onward operations. The great tidal wave of British conquest seemed for a moment to be receding. Our gun-bullocks were utterly exhausted by the day's work, and could not bring our artillery to the front. Our Infantry soldiers, not less physically exhausted, though wonderfully sustained by the strong humanity within them, were lying down, partly to rest, partly to escape the tearing fire of the enemy. As they lay on the ground, they heard exultant noises in the enemy's camp. The clanging of the cymbals, the shrill blasts of the bugles, and the roll of the drums heard between the intervals of the artillery fire, told that there was unwonted excitement in the Sepoy ranks. It sounded like a boast and a menace; and it filled with fresh fury the breasts of our weary troops. Sights followed sounds rapidly. There was the bustle of a hostile advance. The Infantry were moving forward. The Cavalry were spreading themselves out as though to swoop down upon our little body of fighting men and to encompass them with swift destruction, whilst the guns continued to pour forth their round shot in an almost unintermittent stream. To the quick eye of the General it then appeared that there was not a moment to be lost. So he called upon his men to rise; and they leaped at once to their feet, stirred almost to madness by the taunts of the enemy. One more rush, and the victory, like those which had gone before, would be complete.

Then Havelock's eyes were gladdened by a sight which seemed to be a glorious response to all the dreams of his youth and all the prayers of his manhood. The Infantry prepared to advance right upon the death-dealing battery of the enemy, the Sixty-fourth Foot, led by Major Sterling, in front. At this moment the General's aide-de-camp—"the boy Harry"—wheeled his horse round to the centre of the leading regiment, and rode straight upon the muzzle of the twenty-four pounder, whose round shot had now been supplanted by grape, which was making deadly gaps in our advancing column. It was a moment of rapture to the white-haired veteran, compensating him for all disappointments and delays, for all unjust supersessions, for all professional discouragement, when he saw that last battery carried and knew that his son was safe. The work was well nigh done, when four guns of Maude's battery came up to complete it. A terrific fire was opened upon the beaten enemy, who were soon in confused flight; and, after such a day's fighting as might have tried to the utmost the powers of the best troops in the best of climates, they bivouacked at nightfall two miles from Cawnpore, every man too weary to need a pillow and too thirsty not to relish even a draught of dirty water. 1857. July 16.

They were then two miles from the cantonment, and next morning they marched on to occupy it. But ere they were under arms a dreadful story ran like a shudder along the line. They were too late to save: they had come only to avenge. Havelock's spies had brought in word that the captive women and children, whom they had hoped to rescue, had passed beyond the reach of human aid. The morning's news clouded the joy of yesterday's victory; and our men went on with heavy hearts to the scene of our recent national sorrows. The enemy had evacuated the place, leaving behind them only a body of horse to announce the July 17. Cawnpore re-occupied.

1857. July 17. exodus of the rebel force by blowing up the great magazine, the resources of which had constituted their strength, and given them six weeks of victory. As our advanced guard neared the Cawnpore cantonment, there was seen to rise from the earth an immense balloon-shaped cloud, and presently was heard a terrific explosion, which seemed to rend the ground beneath one's feet with the force of a gigantic earthquake. There was no mistaking such a proclamation; and as one man said to another, "There goes the magazine!" many, doubtless, thought how different it would have been if this exploit had not been left to our successors. By this one fatal omission all had been lost to us at Cawnpore.

But now the English flag was again hoisted, and Havelock, profoundly thankful to the Almighty disposer of events, who had given him the victory, put forth an eloquent, spirit-stirring "Order," in which the just meed of hearty commendation was given to the troops which had won his battles for him. "Soldiers," he said, "your General is satisfied, and more than satisfied, with you. He has never seen steadier or more devoted troops. Between the 7th and the 16th you have, under the Indian sun of July, marched a hundred and twenty-six miles and fought four actions." Such troops and such a General were worthy of each other. No troops fought better throughout the war, and none were ever better commanded. The last engagement, known as the Battle of Cawnpore, stamped Havelock's character as a military commander. The battle, as he wrote, "was won by God's blessing, *non vi sed arte*." It was one of those triumphs of mind over matter, "by which man conquers man." We had everything against us. Numbers some five times told; a far greater strength of artillery; a commanding position, with strong natural defences—all favoured the enemy; whilst a climate more deadly to the exotic soldier than grape and canister, and heavy, broken ground, over which our exhausted cattle could not drag their guns, so as to bring them into action when most wanted, fearfully diminished the fighting powers of our scanty force. Had Havelock, after the fashion of some rash and inexperienced commanders, attempted to carry the enemy's position in front, he would probably have lost half his men; but the dexterous flank movement, which so disconcerted the plans of the Nana Sahib, saved our own people from the wholesale carnage which would otherwise have descended upon them. There was not a life wasted. The indomitable pluck of the British Infantry was husbanded to the best purpose, and every man felt that confidence in his leader which makes each soldier worth a file. 1857. July 17.

But Havelock had only made a beginning, and he did well in reminding his followers that their work was only begun. Cawnpore was but the first stage of the career of victory which lay before them. "Your comrades at Lucknow," said the General in his order of thanks, "are in peril. Agra is besieged; Delhi is still the focus of mutiny and rebellion. You must make great sacrifices if you would obtain great results. Three cities have to be saved, two strong places to be disblockaded. Your General is confident that he can accomplish all these things, and restore this part of India to tranquillity, if you only second him with your efforts, and if your discipline is equal to your valour."

It might be thought that these "ifs" were not needed; that the English soldiers who had followed Havelock from Allahabad to Cawnpore, and had

1857. June 17—18. already so nobly seconded his efforts, had placed themselves beyond the reach of all such doubts and suspicions. But the General was a practised writer of despatches and general orders; for years he had been doing for others what he was now doing for himself. Few men knew better the use of words or was less likely to make a slip in any public manifesto. There was, in truth, no ingratitude and no inadvertence in this language of misgiving. There was only too much justice, and too deep a meaning in it. For, scarcely had the Force reached Cawnpore, when it was seen that the demoralisation of drunkenness was upon it. "Whilst I was winning a victory," said Havelock, "on the sixteenth, some of my men were plundering the Commissariat on the line of march." And once within reach of the streets and bazaars of Cawnpore, strong drink of all kinds, the plunder chiefly of our European shops and houses, was to be had in abundance by all who were pleased to take it. And that they did take it was not surprising. Even "Havelock's saints," if there had been a re-birth of them, would have been sorely tempted and tried by this upward march, by the heat, the hunger, the thirst, the fatigue; by the excitement of constant battle, by the thought of the intolerable wrong that had been inflicted on our people, and by the burden of the retribution which they carried with them. They had seen death in many shapes; and now they had brought in for burial the bodies of their comrades slain in the battle or stricken down by the pestilence. These evil influences—still more evil in their alternations, now of excitement, now of depression—drove the British soldiers to the brief solace of strong drink; and such a state of things arose, that Havelock now did what Neill had before done at Allahabad—he "ordered all the beer, wine, spirits, and every drinkable thing at Cawnpore, to be purchased by the Commissariat." "If it had remained," he said, reporting what he had done to the Commander-in-Chief, "it would have required half my force to keep it from being drunk up by the other half, and I should not have had a soldier in camp." 1857. July.

CHAPTER IV.

HAVELOCK AT CAWNPORE—STATE OF THE SOLDIERY—DISCOURAGING CIRCUMSTANCES—FLIGHT OF THE NANA—DESTRUCTION OF THE BITHOOR PALACE—ARRIVAL OF NEILL—HIS PUNISHMENT OF CRIMINALS—FIRST MOVEMENT TOWARDS LUCKNOW—GENERAL ASPECTS OF THE REBELLION.

1857. July. State of the Soldiery

THE English soldier is never a model of forbearance. When the blood is up and the drink is down he is very terrible to all who come across his path. Even in fair fight with a Christian enemy, there are times and seasons when the instincts of a brutal nature are stronger than the conscience and the reason of the man. The honourable resistance of brave men, fighting for their hearths and altars, has often roused the passions of our soldiery to such a height that they have spared neither sex nor age, yielded to no pity, and abstained from no crime. But never, since England had a standing army, have such provocations assailed our fighting-men as those which hardened the hearts of Havelock's battalions on their march to Cawnpore. The rage within them was not wholly an unrighteous rage, for at the bottom of it was an infinite compassion for the women and children who had been so foully wronged, and a just hatred and horror of the crime of the wrong-doers; and they did well to be angry. The Tragedy of Cawnpore excited an intense national hatred in the breasts of Englishmen in distant countries and after a long lapse of time; but here our soldiers were on the very scene of the butchery, the butchers were still red-handed, and the evidences of the slaughter were still fresh—visible to the eye, clear to the understanding, with a horrible suggestiveness even to the most obtuse. Our people went to the Entrenchments, and there they wondered and admired. They went to the Beebee-ghur, and there they shuddered and wept. To think of so much consummate bravery and of the end of it, was enough to madden even sober-minded men, and to stimulate them to acts of fearful retribution. 1857. July 16—18.

If, then, the first days of the re-occupation of Cawnpore had been stained by excesses on the part of our soldiery — far greater than any which are recorded against them—it would be the duty of the historian to speak lightly of their offences. Neither in the Cantonment nor in the Town was there any enemy, in the military sense of the word; for the once boastful army of the Nana was broken and dispersed, and none clearly knew whither it had gone. But those were days in which whole races were looked upon as enemies, and whole cities were declared to be guilty and blood-stained. And if Havelock's fighting-men, whilst the blood was still wet in the slaughter-house, had looked upon every Native found in the neighbourhood of that accursed spot as an adherent of the Nana, and struck at all with indiscriminate retribution, such sweeping punishment might now be looked back upon with less feeling of shame than upon much that was done, before and after, under less terrible provocation. As the record runs, it does not seem that the burden laid

1857. July 16—18.

upon Cawnpore was heavy in relation to its guilt.* Heaven knows what was in their hearts, or what might have been done, but for the strong restraining hand laid upon them by their Commander. That the citizens themselves expected chastisement is certain. For whilst a few, on our arrival at Cawnpore, came to our camp with propitiatory offerings of milk and vegetables, fruits and flowers, large numbers flocked panic-struck out of the town to hide themselves in the adjacent villages, or to seek safety on the Oude side of the river. Some were propelled by the knowledge of their guilt; some, scared by the tidings that had come from below, fled under the instinct of self-preservation. Meanwhile, our people were plundering in all directions, the Sikhs, as ever, showing an activity of zeal in this their favourite pursuit. It is probable that much of the property then seized underwent only a process of restoration, and came back to the nation at last to which it properly belonged. But this did not hallow it in Havelock's eyes. He set his face stedfastly against it, and issued an order in which he said, "The marauding in this camp exceeds the disorders which supervened on the short-lived triumph of the miscreant Nana Sahib. A Provost-Marshal has been appointed, with special instructions to hang up, in their uniform, all British soldiers that plunder. This shall not be an idle threat. Commanding officers have received the most distinct warnings on the subject."

Doubts and anxieties.

This was not cheerful work, but there was other

* Most exaggerated stories of this retributory carnage at Cawnpore were at one time in circulation. It was stated both in Anglo-Indian and in Continental journals that ten thousand of the inhabitants had been killed. This was a tremendous assertion, representing rather what might have been than what was. Some wished that it had been so, for vengeance' sake; others, that there might be a pretext for maligning the English.

perhaps still more depressing. The sick and wounded were to be visited. Cholera and dysentery were in his Camp. Two of the finest soldiers in the army lay dying—one stricken in the battle, the other by the pestilence. Human aid could do nothing for them. Then there was great doubt as to the position of the enemy. Strong as it was in courage, Havelock's column was very weak in numbers, and tidings came that the Army of the Nana Sahib was at Bithoor, mustering five thousand muskets and sabres, and forty-five guns. It was probable that the place had been strengthened by every possible means which the wealth of material in his hands could supply, and it was certain that our light artillery could make no impression on a stronghold so fortified and defended. It was not strange, therefore, that, in the lull which succeeded the re-occupation of Cawnpore, all these discouragements caused a feeling of depression almost amounting to despondency to sink for a little space into Havelock's mind.* But it presently passed away. For the good Providence which had battled so often for us was still on our side, and the dangers which he had dreaded were delusions.

1857. July 16—18. Renaud and Beatson.

In truth, he had already accomplished more than he had ventured to hope. He had beaten the enemy more thoroughly on the 16th than he knew at the time, and there was no present fear of the Nana bringing his broken battalions into the field against us. After the battle, the baffled Mahratta had taken

Flight of the Nana.

* "As he sat at dinner with his son on the evening of the 17th, his mind appeared, for the first and last time, to be affected with gloomy forebodings, as it dwelt upon the possible annihilation of his brave men in a fruitless attempt to accomplish what was beyond their strength. After remaining long in deep thought, his strong sense of duty, and his confidence in the justice of his cause, restored the buoyancy of his spirits, and he exclaimed, 'If the worst comes to the worst, we can but die with our swords in our hands.'"—*Marshman's Life of Havelock.*

1857. July 16—18. flight to Bithoor, attended by a few Sowars; and as he rode through Cawnpore, his horse flecked with foam, he might have met the public criers proclaiming that the Feringhees had been well nigh exterminated, and offering rewards for the heads of the few who were still left upon the face of the earth. But the lie had exploded, and his one thought at that moment was escape from the pursuing Englishman. Arrived at Bithoor, he saw clearly that the game was up. His followers were fast deserting him. Many, it is said, reproached him for his failure. All, we may be sure, clamoured for pay. His terror-stricken imagination pictured a vast avenging Army on his track; and the great instinct of self-preservation prompted him to gather up the women of his family, to embark by night on a boat to ascend the Ganges to Futtehgurh, and to give out that he was preparing himself for self-immolation. He was to consign himself to the sacred waters of the Ganges, which had been the grave of so many of his victims. There was to be a given signal, through the darkness of the early night, which was to mark the moment of the ex-Peishwah's suicidal immersion. But he had no thought of dying. The signal light was extinguished, and a cry arose from the religious mendicants who were assembled on the Cawnpore bank of the river, and who believed that the Nana was dead.* But, covered by the darkness, he emerged upon the Oude side of the Ganges, and his escape was safely accomplished.†

* Mr. Sherer, from whose report these particulars are taken, says: "The Gungapootras were waiting on the shore. About mid-stream the light was extinguished, and, with a yell that must have reached the boat, the mendicant Brahmins rushed up to the Palace and commenced plundering all that they could lay their hands on. The crafty Nana was disembarking in the darkness on the other side."

† His last act before leaving Bithoor was the murder of the only

Meanwhile, Havelock, thinking that a strong force of the enemy would probably soon march down upon his position, had moved the bulk of his little army to the north-western point of the cantonment, near Newab-gunj, to defend the line of the Great Trunk Road. Strategically, the movement was the result of an error; but, in another sense, it was grounded upon a too substantial fact, and had a wisdom of its own, apart from the manœuvres of the enemy. It took the troops far away from the temptations of the liquor-shops, and contributed greatly to the maintenance of that discipline which he had sorrowfully seen fading away. And whilst the military chief was thus taking measures for the protection of both races, the civil magistrate was proclaiming through the City the re-assertion of the British power and the re-establishment of the British law. At the Cotwalee, the people flocked around Sherer and his escort, and professed their delight at our reappearance amongst them. And there was probably much sincerity in these professions, on the part at least of the trading classes, who commonly lost more than they gained by these convulsions. Not only were the English and their followers good customers in quiet times, but the peaceful citizens had an interest in the maintenance of order and the upholding of the law, for with the predatory classes, who thrive in times of tumult and terror, there was little respect for colour or creed. The wolfish propensities of humanity were, in all such conjunctures, strongly developed, and as

1857. July 16—18.

July 18.

captive in his hands. This was a woman, named Carter, who had been taken prisoner, and who had survived the pangs and perils of childbirth in the Nana's Palace. The widows of the deceased ex-Peishwah had treated her with kindness: but when the Nana fled from Bithoor he ordered the woman and her infant to be put to death, and the guard faithfully obeyed him.

1857. at Allahabad so at Cawnpore, innocent industry cowered beneath the rampant rapacity of crime.

July 19. Destruction of the Bithoor Palace.

On the following day, it was determined that the actual position of affairs at Bithoor should be ascertained beyond all doubt. So a detachment was sent out under Major Stephenson, of the Madras Fusiliers, to beat up the quarters of the some-time Pretender to the Peishwahship, and to set our mark upon the place. The information which Havelock had received from his spies caused him rightly to think that it would not need the services of a strong force to do all that was required. The old home of the Nana had been abandoned. There was no enemy to be seen. So the Palace lay at the mercy of our soldiery —and it was soon despoiled and destroyed. There was much of the plunder of our dwelling-houses in its apartments—traces of our English civilisation everywhere in kid gloves and champagne, and books for hot-weather reading. But the Government treasure, to which the Nana had helped himself in such profusion, was not to be found, and the family jewels had either been carried off or hidden away, past all chance of immediate discovery. It was reserved for a later domiciliary visit to disclose some of the hiding places of the abandoned property.* But a considerable wealth of artillery was carried off by Major Stephenson on his return march to Cawnpore.

So, for the time at least, there was a clearance on that side of the river. The local influence of the Nana was gone. The last home of the Peishwahs

* A Native witness, who kept a diary of the incidents of this eventful summer—"a humble but loyal subject of the State, Nanuck-chund by name"—says that the treasure (coin) had been looted by the people before the English arrived. Mr. Sherer says that, in his opinion, the destruction of the Palace was a mistake, as it rendered more remote the prospect of discovering concealed treasure.

was a ruin. The only important member of his household who remained was the Nana Narain Rao, son of the Soubahdar Rumchunder Punt. This man had been well known to the English at Cawnpore, and had been by many of our people, with only a hazy knowledge of native individuality, mistaken for the other and greater Nana, the adopted son of the Peishwah, of whom he was in truth only a retainer.* Whether this man were one of those double-dyed traitors who hang on to the skirts of success and are driven backwards and forwards by every gust of fortune, or whether his sympathies had all along been with the English, it is hard to say; but it is stated that he had been imprisoned by the Nana, and it is certain that, after his master's flight, he made tenders of allegiance and offered his services to the British General.† He had been the first to send word

1857. July 19.

* See note on this subject, vol. i. page 575. I suspect that many who have talked of their acquaintance with the Nana, knew only Nana Narain Rao.

† The "humble but loyal subject of the State," whose evidence is cited in a previous note, was very anxious to convict Narain Rao of double treachery. He states, that "Nana Narain Rao conducted Nana Doondoo Punt to the other bank of the Ganges and returned to Bithoor. Those men went to him and reminded him that his father, Rumchunder Punt, had been a faithful servant and Soubahdar of the Nana, and he (Narain Rao) was bound to protect the property at Bithoor. But Narain Rao paid no attention. On the contrary, he gave out that the Nana's boat had capsized, and then presented himself at Bithoor. He declares that the Nana forcibly took him away; but he ran away, and came here. People say it is a great falsehood, and if this Nana (the Soubahdar's son) wished it, and was really attached to the British cause, he could easily get Nana Doondoo Punt captured."—In another entry in his journal, he says: "*July* 19. I was told to-day that, owing to the treachery of Nana Doondoo Punt, the Bara, &c., of Bithoor have been set on fire, and that the traitor Nana Narain Rao wishes to pass himself off as a well-wisher of the Government."—"*July* 20. It is just as I anticipated. Nana Narain Rao, son of the Soubahdar, wishes to pass himself off as a well-wisher of the Government; but there is a great crowd at this moment, and the Suhib-logue have no time to spare. It is also very difficult to find witnesses against him by summary inquiries, and I see no chance of filing a complaint against him before any officer." This man's evidence is not very trustworthy. He says that, on the 17th of July, he saw General Havelock and General Neill near the Cotwallee, at Cawnpore. But Neill did not arrive till three days afterwards.

1857. July 19. to Havelock that Bithoor had been evacuated by the Nana and his followers, and it was at least probable that some useful information might, at a later period, be derived from him. So he was kindly received, but not without some cautionary words.

Neill's departure from Allahabad.

In the meanwhile Colonel Neill was making his way up to Cawnpore. After the departure of Havelock, he had been actively employed in maturing his arrangements for the defence of Allahabad, and in endeavouring to collect troops from below. In this last respect he had made no great progress; for the unsettled state of affairs at Benares* made Colonel Gordon, who thought that the latter place was of the two in the greater danger, reluctant to diminish his military strength. But he had pushed forward his defensive measures with an elaborate completeness, which left nothing unconsidered, scarcely anything undone. And when he found that his duty summoned him to Cawnpore, to take a more active part in the coming campaign, he drew up an elaborate paper of instructions for the guidance of his successors, which he committed to the care of Captain Drummond Hay.† On the important subject of "Supplies" he wrote at some length. On the number and disposition of the troops he next commented. "By order of Government," he said, "this garrison

* "I look upon Benares as much more exposed than Allahabad, inasmuch as you have a regular fort, whereas our position as a military one is bad as bad can be without fortifications. A few hundred Europeans separated from the river by city containing half a million of inhabitants, and the country people already becoming more and more hostile every day, while we are at any time exposed to an invasion from Oude, *viâ* the unoccupied post of Jaunpore." — *Gordon to Neill. July* 11.

† Of H.M.'s Seventy-eighth, Colonel O'Brien had been appointed Neill's successor at Allahabad, but he did not arrive in time to receive charge directly from Neill.

is to be maintained at the strength of six hundred and forty-five Europeans. Of these I would not have more than three hundred and forty-five inside the Fort, seventy in the Musjid, a Company at the Railway Station near the Kooshen Gardens, a Company at Mr. Hodgson's house, and some in the Church in Cantonments. . . . The church would be occupied by soldiers as a barrack." Those were days when we could not afford to be nice in matters of this kind, and such desecrations were of ordinary occurrence. He wrote also of the state of the defences, pointing out all the weak points; of the Police; of the Arsenal and the Ordnance Stores; of the Intelligence Department; and under the head of "Hanging" he wrote, "I have always tried by general court-martial any prisoners connected with the garrison, the Provost hanging those so sentenced." Then, after precise instructions relating to the families of officers and soldiers, to the training of picked Infantry soldiers in the gun-drill, to repair the distressing deficiency of Artillerymen, and to the sanitary condition of barracks and other quarters for the soldiery, he proceeded to speak of the operations to be undertaken in the event of fresh manifestations of revolt. This section he headed "Defensive Operations;" but he characteristically added, "I prefer the offensive system." "If I had the power," he wrote, "I should never permit an enemy to enter the City. With a small force, in addition to a garrison sufficient to hold the Fort, the City, Cantonment and all between the two rivers, could be disputed for long against superior numbers. I would hold Kydgunge to the last, and if closely invested would cut down the trees within fire and gunshot of the Fort, knock down some garden walls near the Fort, and if the

1857. July 7—15

1857. July 7—15. enemy attempted to assault from the Papamow or Benares side, they could easily be prevented crossing the river. I prefer the offensive system, and always follow it when possible; make frequent sharp attacks, well planned and supported, using as much artillery, nine-pounders if possible, as I could muster. The general object is now to put down the parties moving about and plundering villages; Native troops (the Sikhs) answered well, and did good service. When Europeans are en route, they may be employed, but I would never send them out on purpose, except in cases of emergency. Powder-bags, to blow in doors, &c., are useful things to have in this village. Also rockets, when to be had, and persons who know the use of them."

July 15. All this done for the continued security of the important position which his energy had saved, Neill was eager to go to the front. The opportunity was before him. On the 15th of July he had received a telegraphic message from the Commander-in-Chief, containing laudatory recognition of Havelock's victory before Futtehpore, and of the general conduct of the operations intrusted to him. With this had come also an important addition: "But his (Havelock's) health is not strong, and the season is very trying; it is urgently necessary, therefore, that provision should be made for placing the command of the column in tried hands of known and assured efficiency, in whom perfect confidence can be placed, in case Havelock should become from any cause unfit for duty. You have been selected for the post, and accordingly you will proceed with every practicable expedition to join Havelock, making over the command of Allahabad to the next senior officer." The rank of Brigadier-General had been conferred on

Neill, and, thus stimulated by the feeling that he had the full confidence of Government, he started on the same evening for Cawnpore; and on the morning of the 20th he arrived there and reported himself to the Commander of the Force. "I had hardly seen General Havelock," he wrote afterwards in a letter to a friend, "before he said to me: 'Now, General Neill, let us understand each other; you have no power or authority here whilst I am here, and you are not to issue a single order.'"* 1857. July 20.

Neill at Cawnpore.

But it was arranged that whilst Havelock, being in chief command, should mature his arrangements for the crossing of the Ganges, Neill should remain in charge of Cawnpore. One of his first acts, after his arrival, was to inquire into all the circumstances of the recent massacres, and to do what he could to avenge them. There are deeds which it is better to suffer the actor to chronicle in his own words. In a letter before me, Colonel Neill, after describing events already recorded in this narrative, says: "The men were shot, the women and children were brought up to a little bungalow near the Assembly-rooms. The Futtehgurh fugitives, such as were saved, were brought in there too. I have sent a list of all, and their fate. Upwards of two hundred women and

* It should be stated, however, that as Neill entered in his journal at the time that he had been well received by Havelock, it may be assumed that there was no discourtesy in the manner in which this intimation was conveyed. See following passage: "Got into Cawnpore about seven A.M., Monday 20th . . . and am well received by General Havelock. Poor Captain Beatson, Adjutant-General, died of cholera, and [illegible] Eighty-fourth, died of his [illegible] saw Renaud, his left leg taken off, high up the thigh, looking very pale and ill. . . . Stephenson, with remainder of Fusiliers, gone out to Bithoor with Cavalry and Sikhs to destroy it. Cavalry with Barrow bring in guns in the forenoon. . . . General Havelock informs me he will leave me at Cawnpore in command during his absence. . . . Much plundering in the city by Sikhs, Sixty-fourth and Seventy-eighth; most disgraceful."

1857. July. children were brought into that house; many had been killed in the boats, many killed and died in the entrenchments; all who survived fever, dysentery, and cholera, in the confinement in that house, were barbarously murdered, after the receipt of the intelligence of Havelock's first victory—this by the Nana's order. They were badly fed and treated at first, but afterwards got more and clean clothing, and servants to wait on them. They were sent their evening meal on that fatal day, and after it these fiends rushed in and butchered them all; they were shot and hacked to pieces. The bodies of all who died there were thrown into the well of the house, all the murdered also. I saw that house when I first came in. Ladies' and children's bloody torn dresses and shoes were lying about, and locks of hair torn from their heads.* The floor of the one room they were all dragged into and killed was saturated with blood. One cannot control one's feelings. Who could be merciful to one concerned? Severity at the first is mercy in the end. I wish to show the Natives of India that the punishment inflicted by us for such deeds will be the heaviest, the most revolting to their feelings, and what they must ever remember.† I issued the following order, which, however objectionable in the

* Other narrators have described the scene in similar language. Major North says: "Tortured by the fierce thirst of revenge, and penetrated by the sense of their sufferings, strange wild feelings awoke within us. Vaunting, eager, maddened, we sped onward to the dreary house of martyrdom, where their blood was outpoured like water; the clotted gore lay ankle deep on the polluted floor, and also long tresses of silken hair, fragments of female wearing apparel, hats, books, children's toys, were scattered about in terrible confusion." The alleged inscriptions on the walls were malicious or silly forgeries.

† In another letter, Neill says: "My object is to inflict a fearful punishment for a revolting, cowardly, barbarous deed, and to strike terror into these rebels. . . . No one who has witnessed the scenes of murder, mutilation and massacre, can ever listen to the word 'mercy' as applied to these fiends."

estimation of some of our Brahminised infatuated elderly gentlemen, I think suited to the occasion, or rather to the present crisis: '25th July, 1857. The well in which are the remains of the poor women and children so brutally murdered by this miscreant, the Nana, will be filled up, and neatly and decently covered over to form their grave: a party of European soldiers will do so this evening, under the superintendence of an officer. The house in which they were butchered, and which is stained with their blood, will not be washed or cleaned by their countrymen; but Brigadier-General Neill has determined that every stain of that innocent blood shall be cleared up and wiped out, previous to their execution, by such of the miscreants as may be hereafter apprehended, who took an active part in the mutiny, to be selected according to their rank, caste, and degree of guilt. Each miscreant, after sentence of death is pronounced upon him, will be taken down to the house in question, under a guard, and will be forced into cleaning up a small portion of the blood-stains; the task will be made as revolting to his feelings as possible, and the Provost-Marshal will use the lash in forcing any one objecting to complete his task. After properly cleaning up his portion, the culprit is to be immediately hanged, and for this purpose a gallows will be erected close at hand.'—The first culprit was a Soubahdar of the Sixth Native Infantry, a fat brute, a very high Brahmin. The sweeper's brush was put into his hands by a sweeper, and he was ordered to set to work. He had about half a square foot to clean; he made some objection, when down came the lash, and he yelled again; he wiped it all up clean, and was then hung, and his remains buried in the public road. Some days after, others were brought

1857 July.

1857. July. in—one a Mahomedan officer of our civil court, a great rascal, and one of the leading men: he rather objected, was flogged, made to lick part of the blood with his tongue. No doubt this is strange law, but it suits the occasion well, and I hope I shall not be interfered with until the room is thoroughly cleansed in this way. . . . I will hold my own, with the blessing and help of God. I cannot help seeing that His finger is in all this—we have been false to ourselves so often."

This story has been told before,* and with comments of various shades of opinion. It is very safe and easy in quiet times, and in a Christian land, to condemn such acts as these with placid judicial severity, for the sentence of condemnation demands no thought, and is sure to evoke much sympathy. But we must re-live that month of July, and transport ourselves to the threshold of the Beebeeghur, rightly to estimate them. If ever, in the history of human strife, it were righteous to invest retribution with unknown terrors, it was whilst the blood of our innocents was still red in the slaughter-house. It was not that men, in ordinary conjunctures strong-headed and tender-hearted, lost the power of discerning between right and wrong in the face of the horrors that beset them, but that many of the wisest and best amongst our people, sternly composed in the midst of all excitements and bewilderments, deliberately harboured the conviction, that it was their duty to put mercy far away from them, and to visit exceptional wickedness with an exceptional severity of punishment. There was a remorseless logic in the arguments on which they built up this faith. It was contended that as there were different degrees of

* It was first published, soon after the event, in an Ayrshire journal.

murder, there should also be different degrees of death-punishment. Colonel John Nicholson, of whose heroic character and illustrious career it will hereafter be my privilege to write in detail, was eager to have a special Act passed, legalising in certain cases more cruel forms of execution—that is to say, death with torture. "Let us," he wrote to Colonel Edwardes, at the end of May, "propose a Bill for the flaying alive, impalement, or burning of the murderers of the women and children at Delhi. The idea of simply hanging the perpetrators of such atrocities is maddening. I wish that I were in that part of the world, that if necessary I might take the law into my own hands." Again, a few days later, vehemently urging this exceptional legislation: "You do not answer me about the Bill for a new kind of death for the murderers and dishonourers of our women.* I will propose it alone, if you will not help me. I will not, if I can help it, see fiends of that stamp let off with simple hanging." Edwardes, it seems, was naturally reluctant to argue the question with his energetic friend; but Nicholson could not rid himself of the thought that such acts of cruel retribution were justified in every sense, and he appealed to Holy Writ in support of the logical arguments which he adduced. Writing at a later period, he said, "As regards torturing the murderers of the women and children: If it be right otherwise, I do not think we should refrain from it, because it is a Native custom. We are told in the Bible that stripes shall be meted out according to faults, and if hanging is sufficient punishment for such wretches, it is too severe for ordinary mutineers. If I had

1857. July.

* This was the mistake of the day. There had been no dishonouring of our women, in the sense intended.

1857. July. them in my power to-day, and knew that I were to die to-morrow, I would inflict the most excruciating tortures I could think of on them with a perfectly easy conscience. Our English nature appears to me to be always in extremes. A few years ago men (frequently innocent) used to be tortured merely on suspicion. Now there is no punishment worse than hanging, which is a very easy death, for atrocities which could not be exceeded by fiends. We have different scales of punishment for different kinds of theft, assault, forgery, and other crimes—why not for murder?"

Kindred sentiments might be quoted from other sources. Even the wisest and best in those days, though some might have shrunk from the open advocacy of torture, were prone to think that instantaneous death to men, who perhaps gloried in it as an anticipatory dismissal to eternal beatitude, was but an inadequate requital for the enormous crimes that were committed against us. Christian piety, indeed, was not slow to rebuke those who, in that conjuncture, had any bowels of compassion, making them reluctant to smite heavily at the persecutors of our race. It was from one of the purest hearts and one of the soundest heads in all our Christian community that the following remonstrance issued. It was addressed to Henry Tucker, Commissioner of Benares: "I fear in your case your natural tenderness. But, consider that we have to crucify these affections as well as our lusts. The magistrate bears not the sword in vain. The Word of God gives no authority to the modern tenderness for human life which would save even the murderer. I believe that your duty now is to be firm and resolute, to execute the law rigorously in its extreme penalties, and to set your face as a flint against all concessions. It is necessary in all Eastern lands to establish a fear and awe of the Government. Then, and not till then, are its benefits appreciated. Previously, they are ascribed to weakness. We must be sternly, rigorously just against all treason, violence, and treachery, and hand down a tradition of our severity. Otherwise these troubles will recur." And even now, after the lapse of many years, there are few righteous men who will not readily accept this doctrine. What is dreadful in the record of retribution is, that some of our people regarded it not as a solemn duty or a terrible necessity, but as a devilish pastime, striking indiscriminately at the black races, and slaying without proof of individual guilt. That Neill was fully assured in his own mind that the men, on whom he had inflicted the terrible punishment, thus described in his own words, were among the actual perpetrators of the great crime which he was called upon to punish, cannot be questioned; and we must all devoutly hope that he was right.

1857. July.

Preparations for advance.

But the chastisement of the enemy was but a small part of the work which then lay before the English Generals. Their mission, indeed, was to save, not to destroy. Havelock had reminded his followers that the campaign was only begun—that Lucknow was in peril, Agra besieged, and Delhi still a focus of rebellion. And he had written to Neill, saying, "The instant you join me, I will, by the blessing of God, strike a blow that shall resound through India." He uttered these words in the flush of victory, when the excitement of battle had, perhaps, unhinged the habitual caution of the sagacious commander. And now that there was a lull in the operations of the

1857. war, the difficulties which lay before him presented themselves in their true proportions. But, although less sanguine and confident than before, he was not less determined to cross the river and to push on into Oude with the utmost possible despatch.

The defence of Cawnpore. July 19—23.

It was necessary, however, before all things, at that time to secure the position of the detachment that was to be left under the command of General Neill. Havelock could ill spare a single man from the little force with which he was to advance on Lucknow, and it was with reluctance that he consented to leave so large a number as three hundred men for the defence of Cawnpore. But with the terrible experience of the past before him, he felt that he could not do less. Uncertain as to the position of his late antagonists—apprehending the probability that, on his crossing the Ganges with the bulk of his force, a large body of the Nana's troops would double back on Cawnpore—Havelock had resolved from the first to select the most advantageous site for an entrenched camp, and before the arrival of Neill the entrenchments had been commenced. "At a little distance from the common ferry," says Havelock's biographer,* "there was an elevated plateau, about two hundred yards in length and a hundred in breadth, situated on the bank of the river. At the distance of about five hundred yards from it there was an island on the river, partly submerged in this season of the year. Between it and the Oude Bank were two smaller islands of alluvial land, thrown up by the action of the river, but covered with water two or three feet deep, and visible only from the reeds which spring up upon them. The General was of opinion that these islands might be turned to good account, if he was

* Marshman's Life of Havelock.

obliged to recross the river, while the entrenchment 1857.
on the right bank would effectually cover that opera- July 19—23.
tion. On this mound, accordingly, a field-work capable of accommodating and also of being defended by three hundred men was commenced on the 19th, and pushed on with extraordinary vigour."* The work was done by Native day-labourers chiefly from the city. The offer of good wages, paid regularly every evening, brought us the ready services of hundreds—nay, thousands of men, careless of what government or what race were in the ascendant, so long as they could eat, and smoke, and sleep, with certainty and without molestation. Disarmed and dismounted troopers of the Irregular Horse were also set to work at the trenches; and any skilled Europeans, willing to help, were retained, and their assistance paid for by the State.

So Neill found the works already in progress when he arrived, and they grew beneath the hands of the great swarm of labourers with surprising rapidity. His quick soldierly eye saw at once that there were some defects in the position; but he admitted that none better could have been selected. Whilst the workmen plied their shovels, our baggage was sent into the entrenchments, and the two Generals went about collecting the guns which were to defend the works in course of construction.† Then the sick were

* Mr. Sherer, in his official report, says: "General Neill was left with a garrison of less than two hundred men to hold Cawnpore." There can be no doubt, however, that the number stated by Mr. Marshman is the more correct. General Neill himself, writing on the 22nd, says: "I shall have nearly three hundred men of all kinds."

† See the following extracts from General Neill's Journal, which illustrate the narrative of these proceedings: "*Wednesday, 22nd.*—Heavy rain this morning—ride out to see entrenchment—don't like the ground about it, but suspect there is no better position. Have a long talk with the General about it. . . . Go with General to see the Arsenal; it is entirely destroyed; in a bad position. There are some brass dis-

1857. July 19—23.

Arrangements for crossing the River.

sent in, and every preparation made for sheltering and providing for the effective garrison. And whilst this was being done, arrangements were being made for the conveyance of the bulk of Havelock's force across the waters of the Ganges. The old bridge of boats had been, for all practical purposes, destroyed; and now the steamer, which had brought Spurgin and his party up from Allahabad, was employed in collecting boats; but it was a work of no small difficulty to obtain them. Boatmen, too, were wanting, for men of this class, conscious that they had aided and abetted the foul murder of our people, had prudently dispersed on our reappearance on the scene. But, after a while, some were induced to return to their craft, on a promise of indemnity for past offences. A number of them were enrolled into a corps, and organised on a fixed scale of payment.*

mounted guns there, also three large iron ones in carriages. These, with all the guns here, are being taken down to the entrenched position. . . . . . There is great plundering going on by the troops—most disgraceful—and on the part of Commandants, more particularly the Sixty-fourth; a disinclination to prevent their men misconducting themselves. I should have adopted very decided steps with all these regiments, and this force at first, but this has been neglected. All have taken to plundering, and the example set by officers has been very bad indeed; the plundering of the merchants and shopkeepers in the city by bands of soldiers and Sikhs has been most outrageous, and there has been no check to it. Orders here seem to be unattended to. Pistols and guns fired off in camp. Colonel Tytler informs me the want of attention to orders by Commandants of Corps and others is disgraceful, and I see it plainly. I suppose no orce ever marched with a set of so inferior commanding officers. I fear General Havelock will not get off in time he expected; the difficulties in crossing the Ganges are very great. *Thursday*, 23*rd*. — Agreeably to orders of yesterday, send all sick down to entrenchment, get baggage down, and start myself with Gordon and Bruce. . . . . Governor-General's proclamation giving rewards for capture of rebels and bringing back property, published and promulgated in the bazaars, and all about—get copies printed off. Heavy rain at night. The entrenched position has no strength — except with three times the men—but I will hold it."

* "See Tytler—arrange about a corps of boatmen. He sends me part of a note he has sent to General Havelock about my going with him. . . . . So I may be off soon—set my house in order, as it were. Arrange about what I shall take and what leave behind, &c. &c."—*General Neill's Journal, July* 25. *MS.*

1857 July.

State of affairs in Oude.

There were many, at that time, who, as they had believed that it was easy "to make short work of Delhi," believed also that the relief of Lucknow would be attended with no kind of difficulty. Even in Havelock's camp it seemed to some to be an easy task to make good the march to the Oude capital. The distance was not great, but it was not a question of distance. The whole of Oude was up in arms against us. It was no more than any sane man, acquainted with the circumstances that had attended and the events which had followed the annexation of the kingdom of Oude, must have involuntarily predicated. The passions of all the influential classes were roused, and their antagonism stimulated to the utmost, against us. The remnant of the old Court of Lucknow, the Soldiery, the Landed Aristocracy, were all arrayed against the power that had trodden them down into the dust. It was not strange, therefore, that before the end of June there had been mutiny and rebellion in nearly every station throughout the province. Moreover, it was the great nursery of the Sepoys of the Bengal Army. Every village held the homes and families of men who were fighting against us; and, therefore, bristled with our enemies. Our regular regiments had ripened rapidly in rebellion. For a little space Sir Henry Lawrence had believed that he might play off the Irregulars against the battalions of the Line.* But they

* At the end of May, Sir Henry Lawrence had written to Lord Canning, saying: "Hitherto the country has been quiet, and we have played the Irregulars against the Line regiments. But being constituted of the same materials, the taint is fast pervading them, and, in a few weeks, if not days, unless in the interim Delhi be captured, there will be one feeling throughout the army—a feeling that our prestige is gone—and that feeling will be more dangerous than any other. Religion, fear, hatred, one and all, have their influences; but there is still a reverence for the Company's Ikhbal. When it is gone, we shall have few friends, indeed."

1857. July. were composed of the same elements; and in Oude, as in other parts, this faith was soon stripped of all that had sustained it, and stood out as a naked delusion. The great "ikhbal" of the Company was fast waning, and even our friends forsook us, believing us to be weak. There was little hope, indeed, from any source but from the wisdom of our leaders and from the courage of our English fighting-men. Of all these conditions, so hostile to British supremacy in Oude, I shall write more fully in another part of this narrative. It is sufficient in this place to give a brief account of the results, which had developed themselves—results obstructive in the extreme to the advance of Havelock's army.

These results, as apparent at the end of June, were thus described by Mr. Gubbins* in a letter to Lord Canning: "Every corps at every station in the province has mutinied, and the districts now are in a state of anarchy. Talookhdars are forcibly resuming their former villages, and burning and slaying all who oppose them. Old feuds are again breaking out, and fighting, both with guns, musketry, &c., is going on in every quarter, more or less. The head Civil Authority having been forced in each instance to abandon his Sudder Station; his Thannahs and Tehseels have gone also, and there is no restraint on violence and anarchy. Did the mutineers pass through and away, civil officers might again go out, and order might again be restored; but they are *not* gone, and are hanging about the province, looking for an opportunity of attacking Lucknow. This I believe they will never obtain, and they are meanwhile melting daily away. The following is the present

* Martin Gubbins, Financial Commissioner of Oude—brother of Frederick Gubbins of Benares.

aspect of the stations of mutineers in the province: 1857. July.
"*Khyrabad Division* (Seetapoor, Mohumdi, and Mullaon).—Entirely abandoned. There was a terrible massacre of the Europeans of Shahjehanpoor and Mohumdie. Of the mutinous troops, the Forty-first Native Infantry and Tenth Oude Irregular Infantry have gone towards Delhi; and eleven hundred men, the remains of the Ninth Oude Irregular Infantry and Police Corps, are at Mehmoodabad, forty miles hence, trying to induce the Tolookhdars to join, and daily melting away.—*Lucknow Division* (Lucknow, Onao, Duriabad): Lucknow, and eight miles round it, is all that remains orderly in Oude. We hold two posts, the Residency and Muchee Bhowan, besides a miserable European force in cantonment. The Muchee Bhowan is imposing for the townspeople; but the Natives know, and our engineers have declared, it to be utterly untenable. Should, therefore, a siege be attempted, it will be blown up. The works at the Residency have been greatly strengthened, including my residence and others, and really a prolonged defence can be made. At Duriabad is the Fifth Oude Irregular Infantry in mutiny, but with numbers diminished. They have been joined by Fisher's Horse (Fifteenth), and the Eighth Oude Irregular Infantry from Sultanpore.—*Baraitch Division:* the Second and Third Oude Irregular Infantry, and Tulloh's Battery, and a hundred Horse, in mutiny, have not yet crossed the Gogra; are waiting.—*Fyzabad Division:* this was the most dangerous quarter; the Twenty-second Native Infantry, the Seventeenth from Azimgurh: the Sixth Oude Irregular Infantry, part of the Fifteenth Oude Cavalry, and Mill's Battery making up the mutineers there. This is dissipating somewhat—the Fifteenth

1857. July. Oude Horse having turned towards (as we believe) Cawnpore. Sultanpore abandoned and burnt; many Europeans killed. Salone: ditto; Europeans saved."

Such was the state of things that had grown up in Oude, whilst the English at Cawnpore had been engaged in that fatal struggle for existence which has been narrated in the preceding chapters. Notwithstanding all these reverses, there had been great confidence in the final issue, and, from one end of the country to the other, men felt that Sir Henry Lawrence was a tower of strength. But the month of June had closed in darkly and sadly upon the Lucknow garrison. On the last day of the month, the English had been disastrously defeated in battle at Chinhut. July had dawned upon the siege of Lucknow. And Havelock's victorious entrance into Cawnpore had been saddened by the news which met him —that one of the first victims of that siege had been Henry Lawrence himself. The General had known him well in old times. They had served together in Afghanistan; and were associated by bonds of mutual esteem and affection.* And none knew better than Havelock the loss which the country had sustained. But little time was left for the indulgence of personal or public sorrow. The first thoughts of the General were to be given to the living, not to the dead. It was plain to him that our beleaguered people in Lucknow were in deadly peril, and that all depended, under Providence, upon the rapidity with which he could make good his march to the Oude capital. He felt, too, that the work before him was not restricted to the relief of Lucknow. He did not,

* "Their acquaintance had commenced sixteen years before, amidst the embarrassments in Afghanistan, and it had gradually ripened into a sacred friendship, under the influence of that mutual appreciation and esteem by which great minds are attracted to each other."—*Marshman's Life of Havelock.*

1857. July.

at first, appreciate the full extent of the difficulties which beset his course, and, in the enthusiasm born of success, he thought that, having relieved Lucknow, he might either march to the reinforcement of the Army before Delhi, which was still holding out with undiminished effrontery, or he might operate effectually in other parts of the country, for the suppression of the mutiny and rebellion which in the North-Western Provinces had now become almost universal.

General condition of the country.

For from many parts of Upper India evil tidings had reached the Cawnpore commanders. Disaster had followed disaster with astounding rapidity. Almost every day brought a new story of mutiny and massacre—a new list of murdered men, women, and children. Some stories were more terrible, some lists were longer than others; but ever there was the same sad, but not inglorious, record of chivalrous action and heroic endurance on the part of the Few, and of cruelty and cowardice on the part of the Many. The gigantic horror of Cawnpore dwarfed all other calamities that had overtaken our people. But there were other crimes committed in that month of June light only when weighed against the burden of guilt borne by the butcher of Bithoor. In Jhansi —one of Lord Dalhousie's annexations by Right of Lapse*—there had been an insurrection headed by the Ranee, with a great destruction of English life. Nearly all Bundlekund was bristling up in arms against us. The troops of Scindiah and Holkar had mutinied and cast in their lot with the Poorbeahs of the Company's army; and many of our people had perished miserably in the territories of those princes, though as yet there were no signs of the hostility of the Durbars. Higher up in Rohilkund not only were the Sepoys in mutiny, murdering their officers, but

* See Volume I., pages 91—92.

1857. July. the country was in rebellion, and Mahomedan rule was proclaimed under the vice-royalty of Khan Behaudur Khan. Hansi and Hissar had seen their own tragedies; and there had been other episodes of the most painful interest to stir English hearts to their depths. In the Punjab, although it seemed that we were riding out the storm, strained to the utmost but not yielding to its blows, it was becoming plain that the Bengal regiments were breaking into revolt, and streaming down to swell the tide of rebellion at the great centre of Delhi. And ever as week followed week, though false rumours, too readily accepted, of the capture of the great imperial stronghold reached the lower country, only to sow the seeds of future disappointment, the Mogul capital was held by the mutinous troops that had proclaimed the supremacy of Behaudur Shah.

From Agra—then the seat of the Government of the North-Western Provinces—the tidings were not assuring. The great provincial capital, which all through the month of May had been held in security, though not without much doubt and anxiety, had in June been beleaguered by an enemy, which, in the shape of the mutinous regiments from Neemuch and Nusseerabad, had marched down to attack the second city in Hindostan. And whilst Lieutenant-Governor Colvin and all his Chief Officers had been shut up at Agra, the districts under his charge had been rolling away from him. That great triumph of British administration, so vaunted, so believed—the Settlement of the North-Western Provinces—had suddenly collapsed. For a time there was a great revolution of landed property, and almost all that the English had decreed had been down-trodden with a remorseless heel, as though what we had done and boasted had been purposely done in violent scorn of the genius and instincts of the people. Even the Supreme Government, in the first week of July, were constrained to admit that "the North-Western Provinces were for the moment lost."* However humiliating the fact may have been, it was a fact. Our latest administrative triumphs had crumbled away at our feet. 1857. July.

There was some comfort in the thought that the main bodies of the Madras and Bombay armies had not fallen away from their allegiance. But it was hard to say what any hour might bring forth. One Bombay regiment was rising; there were threatening movements in the Southern Mahratta Country, and more than a suspicion that the old adherents of the Rajahs of Sattarah were in league with the representatives of the Peishwahs. The Bombay services in the persons of Brigadier Le-Grand Jacob and Messrs. Rose and Seton-Karr were emulating the good deeds of their brethren in Bengal, and Lord Elphinstone was nobly vindicating the confidence which the British Government had reposed in him, by placing him, for a second time, at the head of an Indian presidency. It was not beyond the pale of probability that Western India would soon be in a blaze. Then, in the Deccan, there was the great Mahomedan State of Hyderabad, where the Nizam, guided and supported by his accomplished minister, Salar Jung, holding fast to the English alliance, still doubted whether they could much longer restrain their troops,

* "The Bengal Native Army was in mutiny; the North-Western Provinces were for the moment lost; the King of Delhi and our treacherous Sepoys were proclaiming a new empire; small bodies of gallant Englishmen were holding out in isolated stations against fearful odds; the revolt was still extending; and the hearts of all Englishmen in India were daily torn by accounts of the massacre, and worse than massacre, of their women and children."—*Government of India to Court of Directors, July* 4, 1857.

1857. July. if Delhi continued to defy the English Government and to baffle all the efforts of its armies. The great chiefs of Rajpóotana had as yet given no sign; but if Western India were to rise, the contagion might spread to them, and, in such circumstances, it would have been difficult to calculate the embarrassments of having a hostile country intersecting our communications between our leading positions on the East and on the West. Nepaul professed fidelity to her alliance, and was willing to lend us an auxiliary body of troops to operate upon Oude; but there were those who believed that on the first symptom of disaster, they would be eager to turn against us; and that, in any case, the enlistment of such allies would be a confession of weakness, which would inflict a severe moral injury on our Government. In whatsoever direction we turned our eyes there was not a gleam of comfort to be seen.

Crossing the river. July 25.

By the 25th of July, Havelock's little army had crossed the Ganges. It had been a work beset with difficulties; but the practical energy of Colonel Tytler had surmounted them. The whole were now on the Oude side of the river. The entire force consisted of about fifteen hundred men, with ten guns imperfectly equipped and inefficiently manned. There was, as before, a great dearth of Cavalry. Excellent as it was in all soldierly qualities, this little band of volunteer Horse mustered only sixty sabres. It was in truth a very weak Brigade, such as only the glorious audacity of the English could have conceived for a moment to be capable of accomplishing the work before it. The hopes of the Lucknow garrison had been raised by something like a promise of relief in the little space of five or six days.* But it was one that now seemed to be beyond the reach of fulfilment. And the wonder is not that the difficulties of the enterprise should have forced themselves upon Havelock's mind, in all their real magnitude, when he found himself across the Ganges, but that he should for a moment have made light of them. The week between the 21st and 28th of July had brought with it an amount of knowledge of the circumstances which surrounded him very fatal to the sanguine views which he had encouraged on his first arrival at Cawnpore. On the 28th he was at Mungalwur—it cannot be said encamped. That he might move as lightly and rapidly as possible, he had advanced without the impediment of tents. "Some," it has been narrated by an officer of the force, "were fortunate enough to get native huts; some managed to get native vaults, in which over-crowding was the rule; while the Sikh soldiers ingeniously rigged up thatched huts for themselves."† There was need, for the rain fell, day

1857. July 25—28.

* See the following extract from Mr. Martin Gubbns's "Mutinies in Oudh." On the 22nd or 23rd of July, the trusty spy Ungud arrived with tidings of Havelock's arrival at Cawnpore. "We had, it will be remembered," says the Financial Commissioner, "received no single iota of intelligence since the siege began; and now Ungud recounted to us the marvellous tale of a handful of men under Havelock having defeated the Nana in three engagements, and being actually at the moment master of Cawnpore. The news was astounding. We had all along been expecting that the Nana would cross the river and join the besieging force, if he had not actually done so already. I examined Ungud strictly, and came to the conclusion that the joyful and wondrous news was true."—"Many persons had entertained great doubt of the truth of Ungud's information. But their doubts were happily removed by his reappearance at my post on the night of the 25th of July; and this time he brought a letter. It was a reply by Colonel Fraser Tytler to the letter which Ungud had carried from me, and confirmed the intelligence which Ungud had previously given me. Colonel Tytler wrote that the General's force was sufficient to defeat the enemy, that the troops were then crossing the river, and that we might hope to meet in five or six days."

† *Calcutta Review*, vol. xxxii., Article, "Havelock's Indian Campaign."

1857. July 28. after day, in torrents, after the manner of an Indian July, and cholera had broken out in the force. There was nothing to cheer or to animate the leader but the one hope of saving the garrison of Lucknow. "I have this morning," wrote Havelock to Sir Patrick Grant, who had suggested that the enterprise was a hazardous one, "received a plan of Lucknow from Major Anderson, engineer in that garrison, and much valuable information in two memoranda, which escaped the enemy's outpost troops, and were partly written in Greek characters.* These communications, and much information orally derived from spies, convince me of the extreme delicacy and difficulty of any operation to relieve Colonel Inglis, now commanding in Lucknow. It shall be attempted, however, at every risk, and the result faithfully reported."†

The advance into Oude. July 29. So Havelock marched on—Cawnpore with its ghastly memories behind him; before him, at Lucknow, the great horror of a catastrophe still more tragic and overwhelming; around him everywhere a multitude of mutinous soldiers and an armed population, hostile to the core; and with him only the fearlessness of the Englishman to make headway against these terrific odds.

* These had been brought by Ungud, the spy, of whom mention has been made in a former note.

† Marshman's Life of Havelock.

BOOK VI.—THE PUNJAB AND DELHI.

[MAY—JULY, 1857.]

CHAPTER I.

GENERAL CONDITION OF THE PUNJAB—SOURCE OF DANGER—BRITISH RELATIONS WITH AFGHANISTAN—CAUSES OF CONFIDENCE—MONTGOMERY AT LAHORE—EVENTS AT MEEAN-MEER—SERVICES OF BRIGADIER CORBETT—DISARMING OF THE NATIVE REGIMENTS—RELIEF OF THE FORT OF LAHORE—EVENTS AT UMRITSUR AND GOVINDGHUR—THE MUTINIES AT FEROZEPORE AND PHILLOUR.

May, 1857.

State of the Punjab.

ALTHOUGH to Lord Canning it had appeared that the most formidable dangers which threatened the security of the Anglo-Indian Empire took shape in the lower countries, because those countries were almost wholly destitute of the defence of European troops, he saw far off, at the furthest extremity of our British dominions, other great perils scarcely less in degree, but of a widely different kind, and counteracted by more favourable conditions. In the lower provinces he feared the malice of the Native soldiery. In the Punjab he dreaded, most of all, the enmity of the people. Sepoy regiments were scattered all over the Sikh country; but the province was, indeed, the great European garrison of British India. The strength of English manhood may have been slight in relation to the actual defensive requirements of our frontier-province abutting upon the Afghan country, from which, even from remote periods, suc-

1857. May. ceeding dynasties had looked for the stream of foreign invasion—small, too, in comparison with the numerical power of the Native regiments, regular and irregular, which were posted in all parts of the Punjab. But even with the mysterious failure of Meerut before his eyes, the Governor-General was full of confidence when he counted up the European regiments on the frontier, and felt that they might overawe the Sepoys. Yet he could not help regarding with some disquieting apprehensions the state of the general population of the province. Little more than seven years had passed since the Empire of Runjeet Singh had been brought under the yoke of the English. The State had been overthrown by the soldiery. It was the license of its military bands that had unintentionally opened to us the gates of the country of the Five Rivers, and the same power, revived or reawakened, might now cast us out, and restore for a while the dynasty of the Singhs. Men of the most sanguine temperament, inflated well-nigh to bursting with national self-love, could hardly believe that the Sirdars of the Punjab, who had lost so much by the conquest of their country, had become wholly reconciled to British rule and eager to perpetuate it. The truth embodied in a few pregnant words by the greatest master of common sense that the world has ever seen—"So many overthrown estates, so many votes for troubles"—could not be ignored at such a time. Then there was that other great fount of danger—"disbanded soldiery"—which might send forth a sudden torrent to swell the great stream of trouble.* "Walled towns, stored arsenals and armories,

Bacon.

* The numbers, however, must not be exaggerated. The remains of the Punjabee Army, after the second Sikh war, probably did not exceed 26,000 men. Of these about 10,000 were Sikhs, 7000 Punjabee Mahomedans, 4000 hill Rajpoots, 4000 Hindostanees, and 1000 Goorkahs. About 4000 of these old soldiers were enlisted into the Punjab Irregular Force, and an equal number into the Military Police.

goodly races of horse, chariots of war, elephants, ordnance, artillery, and the like," wrote the same great master—"all this is but a sheep in lion's skin, except the breed and disposition of the people be stout and warlike." The breed and disposition of the Sikhs were stout and warlike. We could not regard with contempt the military prowess of the nation which had sent forth the men who, in the great battles of the Sutlej, had taxed to the utmost the skill and valour of Hardinge and Gough, with the best troops of the British Empire at their back, and had driven our Dragoons like sheep before them on the plain of Chillianwallah.

1857. May.

Nor was the only danger which threatened the position of the British in our great frontier province, that which glared upon us from the Punjab itself. Beyond the border were turbulent tribes, occupying the Afghan passes, whom it had been our policy now to bribe, now to awe, into submission. An irruption of these predatory hordes into the plain of Peshawur would have caused wide-spread confusion, in the midst of which bodies of Afghan Horse, led, perhaps, by one of the chiefs of the Barukzye family of Caubul, might have streamed down upon our position, and burying, as they had before done, all jealousies and animosities in the grave of a common purpose, might have allied themselves with the Sikhs, and swept the English out of the country. But thinking of this, Lord Canning thought also of the recent subsidiary treaty with Dost Mahomed, of the friendship that had been outwardly established between the two nations, and, above all, of the fact that the strongest feelings of self-interest dictated to the Ameer a course of neutrality at such a time, and that love of English money was stronger than hatred of the English race

1857. May. Thankfully and hopefully, he remembered the wise advice of Edwardes and the admirable diplomacy of Lawrence;* and he ceased to be troubled by the thought of an Afghan invasion, tremendous as would have been the disaster if it had come upon us at such a time.

There were some other circumstances, too, in our favour. The population of the Punjab was a mixed population. There were national and religious diversities, which forbade the union and concentration which give force even to the feeble. In other parts of our Empire there were diversities of faith, but long contact had rubbed off the angularities which kept them apart, and in the Hindooised Mahomedan, or the Mahomedanised Hindoo, might be seen something almost amounting to fusion. But there was a gulf between the Sikhs and the Mahomedans of the Punjab—between both and the people of Hindostan. The Sikhs learnt with no feeling of joy or sympathy that the King of Delhi had been proclaimed in his old capital, and that Mahomedanism was likely again to be dominant in Upper India. They called to mind exciting national prophecies, which said that the Sikhs would some day stream down to the sack of Delhi; and the old greed of plunder was revived strenuously within them. It might be better for them, at first, to cast in their lot with the Feringhees, whose hour would come sooner or later; it was too soon to strike then. There was some comfort in this thought. There was comfort, too, in the remembrance that the Punjab had been disarmed; that the warlike population of the conquered country no longer went about with swords at their sides, or had firelocks stored in their houses. In all such cases it is probable that the dis-

* *Ante*, vol. i. pp. 432, *et seq*.

armament is but partial; for whilst the searchings of authority are active, many implements of war are buried in the ground, or hidden in stacks or thatches, ready to be exhumed or extracted from their hiding-places, if necessity for their use should arise. Still the danger from that source—of many arms in the hands of men knowing how to use them—though not, perhaps, wholly removed, had been greatly diminished; and in numerous instances the sword had been turned into the ploughshare or the reaping-hook, and soldiers had settled down into the peaceful ways of agricultural life. That they felt the benefits of a strong and a just Government after the years of unrest which had followed the death of Runjeet Singh is not to be doubted; and their martial instincts might have been dying out under the subduing influences of a reign of order.

1857. May.

These circumstances were to be counted up in our favour; and there was one more to be added to the account. As the country below the Sutlej had been well-nigh swept of its military strength to garrison the Punjab, so also might it be said that the lower provinces had been drained of the best energies of the political and civil branches of the service to govern and to administer it. Lord Canning, ever hopeful and sanguine; and, manly himself, appreciating the power of individual manhood in others, looked confidently towards the country in which John Lawrence and his lieutenants stood vigilant and ready for action. Resolute that the Punjab should in all senses be a success, Lord Dalhousie had looked around him for men of good performance and of good promise, and the flower of the two services was planted there when he handed over the Government of India to his successor. There Robert Montgomery and Donald

1857. May.

Macleod, afterwards Chief Rulers of the Province, filled the places next in rank to the Chief Commissionership. There Thornton and Roberts, Barnes and Ricketts, of the one service—Edwardes and Nicholson, Becher and Lake, Taylor and James, of the other, and many other resolute and sagacious men, were teaching the people to respect and love them. There, too, was that famous Punjab Irregular Force raised by the Lawrences, and commanded by Neville Chamberlain, with picked officers under him—men such as Coke, Wilde, Daly, and others of the same stamp—a force of horse and foot, trained alike to activity and to endurance amidst the difficulties of a mountain frontier eight hundred miles in extent, and little likely, it was believed, to sympathise with the Poorbeah regiments of Hindostan. If anywhere throughout our Indian dominions confidence could be placed in the men whose lot it would be to grapple with the dangers rising up before them, it was in the "pet province" of Lord Dalhousie. No man knew better than Lord Canning how all might be lost by individual feebleness, or all might be won by individual strength. All had been lost at Meerut and Delhi; but he had abundant faith in Lawrence and in those who worked under him in the Punjab; and as days passed, and he learnt, somewhat slowly by reason of postal and telegraphic interruptions, the events which were developing themselves in that province, he felt more and more assuredly that his confidence was not misplaced. Of these events I now proceed to speak

Lawrence at Rawul-Pindee.

The summer heats had driven Sir John Lawrence from Lahore. The ceaseless labour of years had weakened a robust frame and impaired a naturally strong constitution. A visit to England had been recommended to him; but with that great love of his work, which was shared by all who worked under him in the Punjab, he was reluctant to leave the country so long as he could do his duty with manifest advantage to the State. But he had recognised the necessity of consenting to a compromise, and going out half-way to meet the urgency of the case.* There were cool and pleasant places within the range of the great province which he administered—places in which he might do his work, during the extreme heats of the summer weather, without the waste of strength, which could not be arrested at Lahore. So he had been wont, in the month of May, to repair to the refreshing slopes of the Murree Hills; and thither he was this year bound, when the first tidings of the disastrous events at Meerut and Delhi were brought by telegraph to the Punjab. Then he stood fast at Rawul-Pindee, a spot from which he could observe well all that was passing in the Punjab, and looking down, as it were, from an eminence on the varied scene below, could issue mandates to his lieutenants all over the country, and make his presiding genius felt beyond the limits of the province he governed. 1857. May.

Next in authority to the Chief Commissioner was the Judicial Commissioner. Mr. Robert Montgomery was a Bengal civilian of thirty years' standing in the service. A member of a good Irish Protestant family, he had been taught and disciplined in early youth at that school which had imparted the rudiments of education to the Lawrences. There, on May 11—12. Montgomery at Lahore.

* On the 13th of May, Sir John Lawrence, in a letter to Colonel Edwardes, wrote: "I have been very unwell and unable to write. The night before last I put some aconite on my temple. It is a deadly poison. In the night it worked into my eye, and I was nearly blinded."

1857. May. the banks of the Foyle, these young contemporaries had become familiar with the stirring watch-words of Derry: "No surrender!" There, if they did not acquire much classic lore, they laid broad and deep the foundations of a manly character. Hardy, robust, and well-disciplined, they went forth into the world by different paths; but time brought the Derry boys again together to sit beside each other on the same Bench, and to learn the same great lessons. When the Lahore Board of Administration was dissolved, Henry and John Lawrence and Robert Montgomery were its members. On the institution of the new administrative system, under the Chief Commissionership of John Lawrence, Mr. Montgomery became Judicial Commissioner.* There were some characteristic differences between him and his chief; but they lay mainly on the surface. An unmistakable benevolence of aspect, and a rare gentleness of manner, might have led some to suppose that he was one made to shine only in quiet times and in happy circumstances. But the genial smile and the kindly voice, which won all hearts, denoted not the absence of that resolute will and that stern courage which spoke out so plainly in the look and bearing of the Chief Commissioner. It only needed a great occasion to show that he could be hard as a rock and cruel as steel to resist the oppressions of the proud, and to smite the persecutors of our race. And those who knew him best said of him that it was a fortunate

* During the existence of the Lahore Board of Administration, Montgomery, who was a civilian of the Thomasonian school, who had graduated in the North-Western Provinces, concurred in the opinions and supported the views of John more frequently than those of Henry Lawrence; but, at a later period, his measures both in Oude and the Punjab indicated his mature acceptance of the principles and policy of the latter. In no one have the Native aristocracy found a more generous advocate than in Sir Robert Montgomery.

circumstance that they had then at Lahore, as chiet director of affairs, one who was a man of impulse, with whom to think was to act, and whose very defects, including a want of caution and circumspection, were of a kind to be essentially serviceable in such a conjuncture. 1857. May.

State of the troops at Meean-Meer.

The hour of the great crisis found Mr. Montgomery at the civil station of Anarkullee, situated at the distance of a mile from the Punjabee capital. In the city of Lahore itself there was a mixed population, numbering nearly a hundred thousand, the most numerous classes being Sikhs and Mahomedans, many of them born soldiers. The Fort, which was within the walls of the city, was garrisoned by a company of an European regiment, some details of European Artillery, and half a regiment of Sepoys. These detachments for garrison duty were relieved at fixed intervals, and returned to the Cantonment of Meean-Meer, six miles from Lahore, where the great bulk of our military force was posted. At that station were three regiments of Native Infantry and a regiment of Native Cavalry, watched by the Eighty-first Foot and two troops of European Horse Artillery. Two of the Sepoy regiments were among the most distinguished in the service. The Sixteenth Grenadiers was one of the "beautiful regiments" which had fought under Nott against the Afghans of Candahar, and the Twenty-sixth had done so well under Pollock, that Lord Ellenborough had made it a Light Infantry corps. The other Native regiments were the Forty-ninth Infantry and the Eighth Cavalry. Roughly computed, it may be said that the Native troops outnumbered the Europeans as four to one.

On Monday, the 11th of May, it was known at Lahore that the Meerut regiments had revolted. On Ma-

1857. May 12. the morning of the 12th came the still more exciting intelligence that Delhi was in the hands of the rebels. The tremendous significance of these tidings was not likely to be underrated by a man of Montgomery's intelligence and experience. But it did not bewilder him for a moment. He saw clearly that the safety of India depended at such a time on the salvation of the Punjab. The Punjab in the hands of the enemy, and all Upper India must be lost. It was certain that the great arsenal of Delhi had gone from us; it was impossible to exaggerate the helplessness of the English if the magazines of the Punjab and the adjacent territories were also to be wrested from them. Any success on the part of the Regular Sepoy regiments might stimulate all the Irregular battalions in the Punjab to revolt, and this might be followed by a rising of the people. But it was not equally clear how this gigantic evil was to be arrested. Understanding well the Native character, Montgomery knew that the Sepoy was not less likely to be driven into hostility by his fears than by his resentments. It might, therefore, be the safer course to keep things quiet, and to betray no symptom of suspicion. But, on the other hand, it was impossible to overrate the advantage of striking the first blow. The party that is first to be the party of action has a double chance of success.

But the general knowledge that there was a spirit of mutiny in the Bengal Army might not have induced the authorities at Lahore to take the initiative, and might not have justified them in doing it, if there had been no particular knowledge of local disaffection among the Punjabee troops. This knowledge, however, had been obtained. On a suggestion from Mr. Montgomery, Captain Richard Lawrence,

Chief of the Police and Thuggee Departments in the Punjab, had commissioned the head-writer of the Thuggee office, a Brahmin of Oude, to ascertain the feelings and intentions of the Lahore troops. A fitter agent could not have been employed, for his were both the country and the caste of the most influential of the Poorbeah Sepoys. He did his work loyally and well. Scrupulous as he was, on the score of caste, as any Brahmin in the service, he had no sympathy with the treacherous machinations of men who were eating the salt of the British Government, and were under the kindly care of its officers; and he brought back to Richard Lawrence, after brief but satisfying inquiry, tidings that the regiments at Meean-Meer were ripe for revolt. "Sahib," said the faithful Brahmin, "they are full of *fissad**—they are up to *this* in it;" and he laid his hand upon his throat. It was plain that they were only waiting for information from the countries below to break into open mutiny.

1857. May 12.

The Council at Anarkullee.

In this conjuncture Montgomery took counsel with his colleagues—the chief civilians and staff-officers at Anarkullee, who assembled in the house of Macpherson, the Military Secretary. They were Mr. Donald Macleod, Mr. Egerton, Colonel Ommaney, Mr. Roberts, Captains Macpherson, Richard Lawrence, and Waterloo Hutchinson. There was an animated discussion. Macpherson had already talked the matter over with Robert Montgomery, and they had agreed that it would be expedient to deprive the Sepoys of their ammunition. It was now suggested by the former that this should be done—that the ammunition should be lodged in store, and that the regiments should be told that, as they had obviously much

* Sedition.

1857. May 12. anxiety with respect to the greased cartridges, it was the order of the Government that all ground of alarm should be removed for the present by leaving them without any ammunition at all. On this Richard Lawrence said, "I would disarm them altogether;" to which Macpherson replied that it was scarcely probable that the military authorities would consent to such a measure. After some further discussion, Montgomery determined that he and Macpherson should drive over to the military station and propose to the Brigadier, at any rate, to deprive the Native regiments of their ammunition. In ordinary course of affairs, the Chief Commissioner would have been consulted. But there was an interruption of the telegraphic communication between Lahore and Rawul-Pindee; so the responsibility of deciding upon immediate action rested with Montgomery, and he cheerfully undertook it.

Brigadier Corbett. The station of Meean-Meer was then in military charge of Brigadier Stuart Corbett, an officer of the Indian Army, who had served the Company for nearly forty years, but had lost but little of the bodily and none of the mental vigour of his prime; and it was a happy circumstance that he had none of that incapacity to grasp strange incidents and new situations—none of that timid shrinking from responsibility—which is so often evinced by feeble minds, trammelled by the associations of long years of convention and routine. A happy circumstance, indeed, that to such a man Montgomery now communicated the alarming tidings which had been received from Meerut and Delhi. Corbett saw at once that there was a pressing necessity for prompt and vigorous action; and though, at first, knowing well the feelings of the officers under his command, he could not embrace the bold project of disarming the troops, he did not hesitate to adopt the proposal to render the Native regiments comparatively harmless by the seizure of their ammunition. But, as the day advanced, he began to doubt whether the precautionary measures on which they had resolved in the morning would suffice for such an emergency. So he wrote to Macpherson in brief decided language, more emphatic than official, saying that he would "go the whole hog" and disarm the troops altogether. And Montgomery readily consented to the proposal.* 1857 May 12.

The Station ball.

It was a bold measure, and to be accomplished only by secrecy and suddenness. But neither Mont-

* It has been stated, and upon authority commonly trustworthy—that of Mr. Cave-Browne, in his very valuable work, "The Punjab and Delhi in 1857"—that it was the consideration of a more pressing local danger that caused the extreme measure of disarming the troops to be agreed upon. It is said that intelligence had been received to the effect that the Sepoy regiments had conspired to seize the fort of Lahore. It was garrisoned, as above related, by some European Infantry and Artillery, and a wing of a Native regiment. During the first half of the month of May, the Twenty-sixth were on garrison duty; but on the 15th of the month they were to be relieved by the Forty-ninth. And it was agreed that the wing marching out and the wing marching in—more than a thousand men in all—should turn upon the Europeans and slay them; and then, at a given signal to be seen from a distance, the Sepoys at Meean-Meer should rise, massacre their officers, seize the guns, fire the Cantonments, and release all the prisoners in the gaol. Nor was the rising to be confined to Meean-Meer. It was believed that at Umritsur, at Ferozepore, at Phillour, and Jullundhur the Sepoy regiments were alike prepared to break into rebellion, and that everywhere their first measure would be the seizure of our magazines. The authority for this story was a Sikh police-officer – said to be a man of more than ordinary intelligence, and of undoubted loyalty to the British Government—who had communicated it to Richard Lawrence. But after a very searching inquiry into the events of that morning at Meean-Meer, I have been compelled to discard the whole story, so far at least as concerns its alleged effect upon the minds of Montgomery and Corbett, and the consequent disarming of the troops. Mr. Browne says that God's mercy in permitting the timely discovery of this plot "alone saved hundreds from the snare laid for them." But there are grave doubts as to the existence of the plot, and it was not even talked of until *after* the measure of disarming the troops had been agreed upon. What Richard Lawrence, Captain of Police, really ascertained, at Montgomery's suggestion, was that which is stated in the text. And it is the belief both of Montgomery and Richard Lawrence, as now before me under their own hands, that no new information of any kind caused Corbett to adopt the bolder course.

1857. May 12—13. gomery nor Corbett doubted for a moment that a single white regiment, with a good complement of European Artillery, resolutely commanded and skilfully handled, could overawe the Native Brigade, and force them to lay down their arms. A general parade was, therefore, ordered for the following morning. There was nothing in it to invite suspicion. Everything went on as usual in Cantonments. A ball was that evening to be given by the officers of the station to Colonel Renny and the officers of the Eighty-first Foot. All suggestions as to its postponement were wisely set aside. Nothing was to be done to excite suspicion. The Sepoys of Meean-Meer, and their brethren of all classes, were to see that the English were feasting and dancing in total unconcern, as ever conscious of their strength and confident in their security. So the rooms of the Artillery Mess-House were lighted up at the appointed time; and hosts and guests assembled as though bent only on the enjoyment of the hour. A few there knew what was coming in the morning, and others had a vague impression of an impending danger—an approaching crisis—that might turn that gaily decorated ball-room into a grim battle-field. Some vague reports passed from one to another about the muster of which they had read in the order-book; and the more suspicious were well pleased to think that they could lay their hands upon their swords in a moment. The greater number neither knew nor suspected, but grumbled, saying that it was an inconsiderate and unkindly thing at best to order a general parade for the morning after a ball. And so they danced on into the small hours of the morning, and saw their wives and daughters home, as though there were nothing to disturb the smooth surface of ordinary events. The

Native sentries posted here and there in Cantonments saw nothing in the movements of the English to indicate anxiety or mistrust. If the Sepoys had, as was alleged, really planned the destruction of the English at Meean-Meer, they must have rejoiced in the thought that their victims, utterly regardless of their doom, were going blindfold to the shambles.

1857. May 12—13.

May 13. The disarming parade.

But when the hours of morning-darkness were past, and day had dawned upon Meean-Meer, other thoughts than these took possession of the Sepoy mind. The Brigade assembled on the parade-ground. There was nothing peculiar in the appearance of that assembly, except that Montgomery, Roberts, and others of the chief civil officers from Anarkullee, were to be seen mounted on the ground.* Every soldier obeyed the orders that were issued to him. The regiments were drawn up in line of contiguous columns. The Artillery and Eighty-first (not numbering more than two hundred and fifty men) were on the right, the Native Cavalry on the left, and the Infantry regiments in the centre; the white men appearing as a mere dot beside the long line of the blacks. At the head of each regiment was read aloud the Government order disbanding the mutinous Thirty-fourth at Barrackpore. These formal proceedings over, the serious business of the morning commenced. The Native regiments were ordered to change front to the rear, and at the same time the Eighty-first also changed front, so as to face the Sepoys; the Artillery, then in the rear, loading their guns unseen by the Native regiment. When this manœuvre, which seemed whilst in execution to be only a part of the Brigade exercise of the morning.

* They had ridden over from Anarkullee in the morning. It appears that they were not at the ball.

1857. May. had been accomplished, a staff officer, Lieutenant Mocatta, Adjutant of the Twenty-sixth Regiment, who could speak the Native languages fluently and correctly, was ordered forward by the Brigadier to read his address to the Sepoys. He did it well, in a clear loud voice, explaining to them that now, a mutinous spirit having evinced itself in other regiments, and brought many good soldiers to certain destruction, it was better that the distinguished regiments at Meean-Meer, which had done so much good service to the State, should place themselves beyond the reach of temptation by surrendering all means of offence; so they were ordered to—"Pile arms."

Whilst this address was being delivered to the Sepoys, the Eighty-first fell back by subdivisions between the guns; and when the word was given to pile arms, the Native regiments found themselves face to face with a long line of Artillery, and a row of lighted portfires in the hands of the English gunners. At the same time the voice of Colonel Renny rung out clearly with the command, "Eighty-first, load!" and then there was the rattle of the ramrods, which told that there was death in every piece. For a minute the Grenadiers had hesitated to obey the order; but thus confronted, they saw that to resist would be to court instant destruction; so they sullenly resigned themselves to their fate, and piled their muskets to the word of command, whilst the Cavalry unclasped their belts and laid their sabres on the ground. The Eighty-first then came forward and removed the arms, for which a large number of carts were waiting near the parade-grounds, and the Sepoys went baffled and harmless to their Lines.* It was a

* The arms were taken under a guard of the Eighty-first to the Lahore Fort.

great design executed with consummate skill; and if by a first blow a battle was ever won, the battle of the Punjab was fought and won that morning by Montgomery, Corbett, and Renny. 1857. May 13.

Seizure of the Fort of Lahore.

But this bloodless victory at Meean-Meer was not the whole of that morning's work. Whilst the parade was being held, three companies of the Eighty-first were marching to Lahore to secure the Fort. A wing of the Twenty-sixth Sepoys was on garrison duty there. It was yet wanting two days of the completion of their tour of duty; and unless they wondered why none of their officers were dancing at Meean-Meer, there was nothing to create suspicion that there was anything unwonted in the air. But when suddenly, a little while after sunrise, news came that the Europeans were marching on the Fort, they saw at once that whatever plots were to have been acted out on the 15th, they had been discovered, and that the game was altogether lost. Colonel Smith, with his three companies, marched into the Fort. The Sepoys were ordered to lay down their arms. Resistance was hopeless, and they obeyed to a man. The companies of the Eighty-first were then told off to their various duties, and the Sepoys were marched to Meean-Meer, crest-fallen and dispirited, there to learn the history of the eventful parade of the morning. They found the place bristling with the bayonets only of the white men. European picquets and sentries were posted everywhere. Arrangements were being made to secure the safety of the women and children in the English barracks, and messengers were speeding to different parts of the country to warn our countrymen of the danger with which they were threatened.

1857. May 13. Govindghur and Umritsur.

To secure the safety of one point, although that one point were the great capital of the Punjab, had not been, on that 12th of May, the sole object of Montgomery's exertions. With a strong European Brigade, Horse, Foot, and Artillery, the authorities at Meerut had refused to divide their force, and had looked only to the safety of the station. But at Lahore, with only one regiment of English Infantry and a few English gunners, in the face of a still larger body of Native troops, Montgomery took a comprehensive view of all surrounding dangers, and turned the scanty means at his disposal to larger account than most men would have deemed possible. But it was his good fortune to find in the military chief a kindred spirit, and to meet with ready response to all his suggestions. If at that time there had been, on the part of the military, any ominous shakings of heads and feeble wringings of hands, all would have been lost. But to Corbett and Renny nothing seemed impossible. With the perilous work before them of disarming the Meean-Meer troops, they had sent off three companies of their one white regiment to Lahore; but the crisis was one which demanded even further sacrifice of immediate strength. It was certain that there was much to be done with small means; but it is in such daring and such doing that greatness consists. Another company of the Eighty-first was despatched in Native carriages, hastily collected, to afford succour to another place which seemed to be girt with danger.

The fortress of Govindghur, which lies some thirty miles from Lahore, is the military stronghold of the great city of Umritsur, the spiritual capital of the Punjab—a city invested in the minds of the Sikh people with the holiest associations. In no place throughout the Punjab was the influence of the priesthood so powerful; in no place had the spirit of nationality so largely survived the subjugation of the people. There the Sikh inhabitants were more likely to rise than in any part of the country; and to that centre, more than to any other point, were the Sikhs likely to turn their eyes for a given signal of general insurrection. From the first moment, Montgomery had recognised the paramount importance of securing the Fort and overawing the city. On the morning of the 12th, with the Delhi telegrams before him, he had written to Mr. Cooper, Deputy Commissioner, advising him of what had happened below, telling him that at Lahore they might have to fight for their lives, and urging upon him the immediate necessity of "caring for Govindghur." "I would advise," he said, "every precaution being adopted beforehand, so as to be ready in case of a row. You shall have the best information of all that is going on, and the more quietly we move the better. Do not alarm the Sepoys by any previous acts, but keep the strictest watch on them; and the feelings of the city should be ascertained by every source at your command. Open communication with Jullundhur, and find out what is going on there. My advice is to be fully alive and awake, and prepared for the worst, without creating any alarm by any open act. If the troops should rise, you have the Fort to go to, and can defend yourselves." And these stirring words were addressed to a lieutenant worthy of his chief. Mr. Cooper was not a man to be appalled by any danger; and under him again there was another civil officer, Mr. Macnaghten, Assistant Commissioner, equally ripe for any hazardous enterprise that might fall in the way of his duty.

1857 May 11.

Cool and collected, and fertile in resources and ex-

1857. May. pedients, these two now bethought themselves of turning to the best account every possible circumstance that was in their favour. The report at Umritsur was that the disarmed Sepoys from Meean-Meer were coming in a body to help the regiments at the former place to seize upon Govindghur. The fortress was garrisoned mainly by Sepoy troops. The only Europeans were the gunners of a weak company of Artillery. There was, however, in the Cantonment a horse-battery, under Captain Waddy, manned by white soldiers, and this was now removed into the Fort. Cooper, with a party of Irregular horsemen and some faithful Sikhs, took post opposite the Fort gates, whilst Macnaghten went out on the Lahore road to raise a body of villagers to intercept the advance of the rebel Sepoys. The agricultural communities were known to be on our side. They were in a state of unexampled prosperity. There had been one of the richest harvests known for years. Many of the peasantry were hardy Ját cultivators, with no sympathetic leanings towards the Sepoys from Hindostan. They promptly responded to the call, and arming themselves with whatsoever weapons they could seize—perhaps only the implements of their calling—went forth to form a living barrier against the wave of insurrection which, it was believed, was pouring in from Lahore. But safety, not danger, was on the road. About midnight, a noise as of a coming multitude was heard. Macnaghten mustered his villagers, and formed across the highway a sturdy rampart of carts, behind which they awaited the approach of the enemy. But they found themselves face to face with a most welcome arrival of friends. It was the company of the Eighty-first, under Chichester, that had been sent to the relief of Govindghur.

Before daylight the relief had been accomplished, and the fortress was safe. 1857. May.

So, for the time, by the exertions of Montgomery and Corbett, and those who worked under them, the two great cities of Lahore and Umritsur were placed beyond the reach of immediate danger. By prompt and unexpected movements on the part of British authority, the revolt of the Sepoys had been paralysed in the very hour of its birth, and on the spots most favourable to its vigorous development. But there were other places, at no great distance, which, although of far less political importance, suggested grave doubts and anxieties to our chiefs; and Montgomery, therefore, on the same day sent expresses to all the principal civil officers in the Punjab, bearing copies of a confidential circular letter, in which they were informed of what had taken place, and warned to be in readiness to act promptly and vigorously in the event of an emergency, but to maintain outward calmness and quietude in the face of danger—to be fully alive to the magnitude of the crisis, but to betray no symptom of alarm or excitement. Instructions were issued for the safe custody of the Treasuries, for the strengthening of the Sikh Police, and for the detention of all Sepoy letters; and it ended with the assuring words: "I have full reliance on your zeal and discretion." Ferozepore.

There were two places, especially, which it was most important to secure, on account of the military resources they contained. At Ferozepore and Phillour were large quantities of munitions of war, with but few European troops to defend the magazines against the too probable assaults of the Sepoys. At the

1857. May 13. The Forty-fifth and the Fifty-seventh.

former place were an arsenal and a magazine of considerable dimensions—the largest in that part of India. Two regiments of Native Infantry and a regiment of Native Cavalry were posted there, and the temper at least of one of the regiments was more than suspected. Appearances, however, were less formidable than at Meean-Meer, for the European strength was greater in proportion to the Sepoy force. The Sixty-first Queen's was cantoned at Ferozepore, and there also were two companies of European Artillery. The station was commanded by Brigadier Innes, an old Sepoy officer of good repute; but he laboured at that time under the disadvantage of being a stranger. He had arrived to take command of the brigade only on the morning of the 11th. On the following night news came from Lahore that the Sepoys in Meerut and Delhi had risen, and the Brigadier was informed that the Native troops at Lahore were to be disarmed on the following day. On the 13th the Brigadier, anxious to discern for himself the bearing of his men, held a morning parade. Their demeanour was not encouraging. If there were nothing openly defiant in their manner, there was an absence of that easy, careless, unoccupied look which characterises the Sepoy in quiet times. It was plain that something was coming.

The parade dismissed, Brigadier Innes called a Council of War. The members summoned were the principal political officers, the Commandants of the several regiments, and the Commissary of Ordnance. There was no attempt to obscure the fact that the temper of the Sepoys was most suspicious, and that the safety of the station depended on prompt and vigorous action. Instantly to disarm the Native regiments in a body was not held to be a measure that could be attempted without danger; why is not very clear. So it was determined to divide them—a poor half-measure, which could scarcely be crowned with success—and to disarm them separately on the morrow. But the morrow of vigorous action never comes. The man for a crisis is he who knows no morrow, but is resolute to strike to-day. The regiments were paraded separately, and marched off to different camping-grounds at a distance from their Lines. The Fifty-seventh quietly obeyed orders, and bivouacked on their allotted space for the night. The Forty-fifth, who were marched through the great Bazaar, lost there the little loyalty that was left in them; for among the buyers and the sellers were scatterers of sedition, and sparks flew about everywhere to bring on a great explosion. It happened, too, that as they went the Sepoys caught sight of the European soldiery, and, believing that a hostile movement was intended, raised a cry that there was treachery abroad, and numbers of them fell out, loaded their muskets, and made a rush for the magazine. The rest marched on to their camping-ground. 1857. May 13.

The outer defences of the magazine were in a state to favour the ingress of the mutineers. The ditch was filled up, and the walls were in ruins; so the Sepoys of the Forty-fifth were soon within the so-called intrenchments. But the magazine itself was less assailable, for it was protected by a high wall, and the only entrance was defended by a guard of Redmond's Europeans. The Sepoys within did their best to assist their comrades with scaling-ladders;* but the English soldiery were more than a match for the

* Brigadier Innes says that the Sepoys of the Forty-fifth "made a rush at the intrenchments with scaling-ladders, which must have been previously prepared."

1857. May 13—14. mutineers within and without. The former were seized and disarmed; the latter were driven back, but not before Redmond himself had been wounded. The magazine was thus saved, and three more companies of the Sixty-first having been thrown into it, its security was established. But to save the magazine was in effect to sacrifice the Cantonment. With so small a body of European troops, it was impossible to defend one part without exposing another. The very division of the Sepoys, which had been thought an element of strength, was in result only a source of difficulty and danger. The remaining companies of the Sixty-first, menaced on both sides, could do little or nothing to save the Cantonment. For the great Bazaar poured fourth its multitudes to plunder and destroy. The bungalows of the European officers, the mess-houses, the churches, Protestant and Catholic, were sacked and fired. The night was a night of terror; but the families of the English officers were safe in the barracks of the Sixty-first, and the fury of the assailants did not fall on our defenceless people.

Meanwhile the Fifty-seventh had remained inactive on their camping-ground, and when morning dawned it was found that there had been but few deserters. The Brigadier, therefore, declared that he would regard them as loyal soldiers, if they would lay down their arms in the European Lines. The Light Company marched in with apparent willingness; but as the others were following, they saw a movement of the Sixty-first, directed against some men of the Forty-fifth, who had been tampering with their more loyal comrades, and believing that the Light Company had been trapped, they broke in dismay and fled across the plain. After some time the efforts of their officers to dispel the fear which had seized them were successful, and they were brought back again to their camping-ground. Little by little, as the day advanced, confidence was restored; and before nightfall they had been marched to the European barracks, and had surrendered their arms and the colours of their regiment. But the Sepoys of the Forty-fifth were still roaming about the station, defiant and ripe for mischief; and in the morning there was a report that the mutineers intended to seize the regimental magazines. To remove the ammunition into the general magazine was impossible; so the Brigadier determined to destroy it. Two loud explosions were presently heard, and it was known that the magazines of the Forty-fifth and Fifty-seventh had been blown into the air. 1857. May 13—14.

There was now nothing left for the Forty-fifth but flight. Their comrades were disarmed. Their ammunition was destroyed. The Europeans were now comparatively free to act, and the troopers of the Tenth Cavalry had not yet drawn a sabre against their officers. The chances, therefore, were all against the Sepoys; so they took their colours, and turned their faces towards Delhi. And then, for the first time, a spasm of energy seized upon the Brigadier. Some companies of the Sixty-first, with two guns of the horse-battery, went in pursuit, and then two squadrons of the Tenth Cavalry took up the work of the tired footmen, and with Major Marsden, the Deputy Commissioner—a dashing officer and a bold rider—drove them some twelve miles from Ferozepore, and scattered them over the country, till they threw away their arms and colours, and hid themselves in villages or crouched in the jungle. Some were taken prisoners by their pursuers, some were given up by the villagers; but it is believed that some also suc-

1857. May 13—14. ceeded in joining the Sepoy force within the walls of Delhi.

The great magazine of Ferozepore had been saved; but there was no lustre in the achievement. The British had nothing on which to congratulate themselves but the bare fact. The fact was one of large proportions, for the loss of such supplies of ordnance stores and their gain to the enemy would have weakened our means of offence, and made the work of reconquest far slower and more difficult.* But when we think of what Corbett had done with his one weak regiment at Meean-Meer against a far larger body of Sepoys, we marvel and are mortified as we dwell upon the record of events at Ferozepore. The Sixty-first, supported by the Artillery, could have done what the Eighty-first had been doing, and might have saved the Cantonment. But Innes, shrinking from responsibility, resorted to half-measures, and accomplished only a half-success. We must not, however, judge him too severely. He did at least as much as most Native Infantry officers, accustomed only to the routine of quiet times, the harness of the regulations, and the supremacy of the Adjutant-General's office, would have done, and indeed afterwards did, when suddenly brought face to face with a great and trying emergency. Perhaps it is less strange that he only half succeeded, than that he did not fail outright.

Phillour. There was yet another place of great military im-

* Mr. Cave-Browne says: "Thus, although the Cantonment had to some extent been sacrificed, there was the consolation of knowing the magazine was saved. Had it fallen into the hands of the mutineers, with its piles of shot and shells, its pits of gunpowder, and its well-stored armoury, Delhi had not been re-won under four times four months."

portance, the seizure of which was supposed to form part of the first great group of measures designed for the subversion of British authority in the Punjab, and which it was, therefore, of the utmost moment to secure. This was the Fort of Phillour, lying between Jullundhur and Loodhianah, on the great high road to Delhi. It had been described as the "key of the Punjab;" but, like other keys of the same kind, it was by no means in safe keeping. A considerable arsenal was planted there, but there were no European troops to protect it. When the day's work was done, and the Ordnance Commissariat officers had gone to their homes, there was not a white face to be seen in the Fort. The Sepoys of the Third Infantry garrisoned the place and occupied the adjacent Cantonment. At a distance of some twenty-four miles was the military station of Jullundhur, where the Eighth Queen's were posted, with two Native Infantry regiments, a regiment of Native Cavalry, and a proportionate force of Artillery. The Infantry regiments —the Thirty-sixth and the Sixty-first—were known to be tainted. They had been in recent contact with corps which had already broken into rebellion. That these Jullundhur regiments had, in concert with the Third, plotted the seizure of the Fort of Phillour, with its guns and stores, was believed, if it was not proved to be a fact; and only prompt action could avert the threatened disaster. The work to be done was very much the same work as had been so successfully accomplished at Meean-Meer, and with the same means. The European regiment and the Artillery might have disarmed the Sepoys and secured the Fort of Phillour. 1857. May.

The brigade was under the command of Brigadier Johnstone, a Queen's officer of the regulation pattern.

1857. May 11—12. He was absent from Jullundhur when news came of the great events at Meerut and Delhi, and Colonel Hartley, of the Eighth Queen's, was in temporary command of the force. On the 11th, the first vague tidings of disaster were passing along the telegraph wires through Jullundhur to Lahore. No action was taken on that day; the story might be exaggerated; it might, therefore, be better to "wait for further information." Next day all doubt was removed, and Colonel Hartley took counsel with the chief civil and military officers at the station. It was plain to every one that, as an essential measure of security, Phillour must be occupied by European troops. It was agreed, therefore, that a detachment of the Eighth should be sent off secretly under cover of the night. Other measures of precaution were to be taken. The guns, duly covered by European detachments, were to be posted so as to sweep the parade-grounds of the Native troops, and the gunners were to be always at their posts. Europeans from Olphert's* troop of Horse Artillery were to act as Cavalry and patrol the station. The ladies and children were placed either in the Royal Barracks or in the Artillery schoolroom and library. Every officer in the Cantonment was constantly alert, day and night, in case of the anticipated surprise; and as it was expected that the Native Cavalry troopers would make a rush upon the guns, heaps of stones were scattered about so as to impede the advance of the horsemen, and to throw them into confusion whilst our grape-shot was acting upon them. But with these defensive measures our action ceased. If there was any thought of striking the arms from the hands of the Native soldiery it was

* Henry Olpherts of the Bengal Artillery—cousin of William Olpherts of the same corps, then serving at Benares.—*Ante*, p. 82, &c.

speedily abandoned. The reason given is, that in the neighbourhood of Jullundhur were several smaller stations occupied only by Sepoy troops, and that if the regiments there had been disarmed, their comrades at Hosheyapore, Kangra, Noorpoor, and Phillour would have risen against their defenceless officers at those places, and would have streamed down upon Jullundhur, recovered the arms of the regiments there, and set the whole country in a blaze. 1857. May 12.

Meanwhile, at Phillour, on the 12th of May, the Artillery Subaltern Griffith, who, as an Assistant Commissary of Ordnance, was in charge of the magazine, was doing all that resolute manhood could do to protect the precious charge confided to him. Intelligence of the outbreak had been brought by an officer of the Telegraph Department, who came laden with help in the shape of the necessary apparatus to place the interior of the Fort in direct communication with Jullundhur. In the course of a few hours this was done, and a message came right into Griffith's private office-room, informing him that succours were on their way. Hopefully, cheerfully, the Artillery Subaltern then, with a little handful of Europeans attached to the magazine, addressed himself to the work of holding the Fort during the critical hours of the darkness. At sunset the gates were closed. A gun was brought down to the gateway, and all through the night the little party of Englishmen kept guard, relieving each other with ready portfire, and keeping watch from the ramparts to catch the first sound of any commotion in Cantonments which might indicate that the Sepoys had risen. But all was quiet in the station, and all was quiet within the Fort. The Sepoys of the Third were not yet ready. The appointed hour of revolt had not come. So the

1857. May. night passed, and the day dawned; but ere the dawn had come the looked-for deliverance was at hand. A hundred and fifty men of the Eighth Foot, two Horse Artillery guns, and a party of Punjabee Horse, appeared under the walls of the Fort. The gate was thrown open. The relieving force marched in; and, to the dismay of the Sepoys, European sentries were posted everywhere in their place, and the arsenal of Phillour was saved. It was truly a good night's work; for the Fort might have become the rallying-place of all the mutinous regiments in that part of the country, and it was preserved, as has been already shown, to be of immense importance to us in our subsequent retributory operations.*

* See *ante*, pp. 188, 189, for the story of the equipment of the siege train and its march from Phillour.

CHAPTER II.

PESHAWUR—INTERNAL AND EXTERNAL DANGERS—THE CIVIL AND MILITARY AUTHORITIES—EDWARDES—NICHOLSON—COTTON—CHAMBERLAIN—THE COUNCIL AT PESHAWUR—ARRANGEMENTS FOR A MOVABLE COLUMN—SIR JOHN LAWRENCE AT RAWUL-PINDEE—DESPATCH OF TROOPS TO DELHI—THE MARCH OF THE GUIDE CORPS.

BUT the place to which, of all the military stations in the Punjab, the thoughts of men were turned at this time with the deepest interest, was the frontier-post of Peshawur. There, in May, 1857, was a strong defensive force of all arms—the Native troops greatly outnumbering the Europeans. There were two regiments of Queen's troops, with Artillery, horse and foot, the whole, perhaps, amounting to little more than two thousand men, whilst the Native troops might be counted up at nearly four times the number. In the neighbourhood, at Nowshera and Hote-Murdan, were other components of the brigade, planted in the Peshawur Valley. At the former place were the Twenty-seventh Foot, nearly a thousand strong, and at the latter was the famous Guide Corps, under Captain Daly, which, though recruited in the country, was believed to be as staunch as if every soldier were an English yeoman. Counting up all the components of the brigade in the valley, it may be said, in round

Peshawur, May, 1857.

1857. May. numbers, that there were two thousand five hundred Europeans and ten thousand Natives, and that only a tithe of the latter could be trusted by their English officers.

External dangers. These were heavy odds against us; but they did not constitute the main sources of danger. If the British troops were free to act against the mutinous Sepoys, there could be little doubt that, well handled, they could dispose of all comers. But beyond the frontier, as I have already briefly said,* were other great and imminent perils. If the Afghan tribes occupying the passes beyond Peshawur—the Afredis, the Eusofzyes, the Mohmunds, and other wild clans, whom we had been endeavouring to reclaim from their lawless habits, and not wholly without success—had been incited, partly in the interests of the faith and partly in the interests of plunder, to pour down upon us a great mass of humanity, predatory and fanatic, we might have been simply overwhelmed by the irruption. Our English manhood could not have sustained the burden of the double calamity, if the internal and external enemy had risen against us at the same time.

And the external enemy, which might in such a crisis have risen against us, was not merely a gathering of these barbarous mountain tribes. Beyond the passes were the Afghans of Caubul and Candahar. The friendship of Dost Mahomed had been purchased by our British gold, but he had never ceased to deplore the dismemberment of his empire by the Sikhs; he had never ceased to hanker after the recovery of the Peshawur Valley, now part of a British province by the intelligible right of conquest. For this he had already risked much—for this he might risk much

* *Ante*, page 404, with reference to Lord Canning's previsions.

more. This eager longing after Peshawur has been described as the madness of a life. It might, at such a time as this, be stronger than the teachings of experience—stronger than the dictates of sagacity—stronger even than the great national avarice which was burning within him. It was difficult to feel any confidence in his forbearance at such a time. A well-developed mutiny of the Sepoy troops in the Peshawur Valley would afford such an opportunity as might never arise again in the history of the nation. The formidable British force which guarded the frontier would then be as a chained giant, powerless to resist a foreign invasion. If then the Ameer were to raise the green standard and to call upon the chiefs and people of Afghanistan, in the name of the great prophet, to pour down upon the Feringhees, who in days past had so humiliated them—who had rooted up their vines and destroyed their orchards, and set their mark upon the capital city of their empire—all the great chiefs and the leading tribes would have gathered around him, and a great flood of Mahomedanism would have poured upon us, swollen, perhaps, by more distant streams. It was difficult to say, at such a time, what might not be written down in the great Book of the Future. A very little thing might turn the tide against us and overwhelm us. The natural feeling, therefore, amongst our people was one of perilous insecurity; and the Natives of India asked each other, then and afterwards, with significant earnestness of inquiry, "What news from Peshawur?"*

1857. May.

* Mr. Cave-Browne gives the following suggestive anecdote in his narrative. The incident occurred when he was at Umritsur, in the middle of June: "One of the most influential of the Sikh Sirdars was paying his usual visit of courtesy to the head civilian of the station. In the course of conversation, the latest news from Camp (Delhi) was exultingly mentioned, when the Sikh, seeming to pay little heed to what

1857. May. Political charge of Peshawur.

At this time the political charge of Peshawur was in the hands of two of the most remarkable men to be found among the younger officers of the Indian Army. Both had been reared under the Lawrences; and in that mixed service known in India as "political employment," which at one time demands the exercise of the highest energies of the military officer and, at another, of the finest qualities of the civil administrator, had ripened into soldier-statesmen of the best kind. Of Herbert Edwardes I have already spoken.* He was Commissioner at Peshawur. John Nicholson was his lieutenant, or deputy-commissioner, They were close friends, full of love and admiration of each other. If either had greater love or admiration for another friend at a distance, that other friend was Henry Lawrence, whom both revered and strove to imitate, walking not unworthily in the footsteps of their great exemplar.

John Nicholson.

The son of a physician in Dublin, who died at the commencement of a professional career in which were the germs of a great success, John Nicholson had entered the Company's service as a cadet of Infantry on the Bengal establishment at the age of sixteen. He was still a boy when the chances of service sent him with his regiment—the Twenty-seventh—into Afghanistan; and when in that dreary, sorrow-laden winter of 1841 the national spirit of the tribes rose against the intrusion of the English, young Nicholson, after much good promise of the finest soldierly qua-

was generally received with so much joy, asked: 'What news from Peshawur?' 'Excellent; all quiet there,' he was told. 'That,' said he, 'is the best news you can give me!' 'Why do you always ask so anxiously about Peshawur?' the civilian said. The Sirdar did not at once reply, but, with much significance of manner, took up the end of his scarf and began rolling it up from the corner between his finger and thumb. 'If Peshawur goes, the whole Punjab will be rolled up in rebellion like this.'"

* Vol. i., page 26, *et seq.*

lities, became a prisoner at Ghuznee and afterwards a captive in the hands of Akbar Khan. Rescued by General Pollock, he returned to the provinces of India, and when again the peace of India was broken by the incursion of the Sikh army, John Nicholson, after a brief period of service in the Commissariat Department, was, on the recommendation of Henry Lawrence, who had taken note of his fine soldierly qualities, appointed by Lord Hardinge to instruct and discipline the Infantry regiments of Golab Singh, the new ruler of Cashmere. He was afterwards appointed an assistant to Lawrence, who was then Resident at Lahore, and became permanently attached to the Political Service. From that time John Nicholson, independent of military rank, was released from the trammels of his youth. He saw his opportunity before him, and he bided his time. His desires were towards military action, and in due course that which he had longed for came; the Sikh chiefs were rising against the military occupation and political interference of the English, and John Nicholson soon found that he had work to do in the field. He did it with a cool head and a stout heart, and, although his freedom of speech sometimes gave offence to his seniors, he made it clear to those under whom he served that he was a man to be trusted. The great conflict for the supremacy of the Punjab came; Nicholson was in the midst of it—at Chillianwallah, at Guzerat, and in the front of Gilbert's pursuit of the Afghan auxiliaries. And when the country became a British province Sir Henry Lawrence enlisted his services into the commission, and, toiling on for years on the outskirts of civilisation, he manifested an extraordinary aptitude for the coercion and the government of barbarous

1857. May.

1857. May. tribes. After this service in Bunnoo, where the wild people deified him, he had for a little space thought of leaving the Punjab and serving under his old master in Oude, or of taking part in the Persian war as a commander of Irregulars. But the cloud which seemed to overshadow his prospects soon passed away, and in the spring of 1857 he was, as I have before said, at Peshawur as the lieutenant of his friend Herbert Edwardes, or in other and more official words, Deputy Commissioner of the division. Only a little time before, Edwardes, being on a brief visit to Calcutta, had said to Lord Canning, "You may rely upon this—that if ever there is a desperate deed to be done in India, John Nicholson is the man to do it." And now the truth of these friendly but prophetic words was about to be realised. The hour had come and the man was present.

At this time John Nicholson was in his thirty-sixth year. Of lofty stature, of a handsome open countenance, with strong decision of character stamped upon it, he carried with him a noble presence, which commanded general observation, and among the Natives excited awe. His manner was not genial. Some said it was cold; it was certainly reserved; and the first impressions which he made on men's minds were often unfavourable. His words were few; and there was a directness and authoritativeness about them which made strangers think that he was dogmatical: perhaps, overbearing. But those manifestations were not the growth of an arrogant self-conceit, but of great conscientiousness and self-reliance. For he thought much before he spoke, and what he said was but the utterance of a strong conviction which had taken shape, not hastily, in his mind; and he was not one to suppress what he felt to be the truth, or to mince nice phrases of expression. Still it would be flattery to deny, or to obscure the fact, that he had at one time little control over a naturally fiery temper, and that, as he grew older, he brought it with difficulty under subjection. There could have been nothing better for one of Nicholson's temperament than constant intercourse with such a man as Herbert Edwardes; and he now gratefully acknowledged in his heart that his character was ripening under these good influences, and that, please God, much that was crude and imperfect in it might soon disappear.* 1857. Ma

Sydney Cotton.

It was another happy circumstance at that time that the Brigade was commanded by an officer altogether of the right stamp. Brigadier Sydney Cotton—a true soldier, and one of a family of soldiers—commanded the troops in the Peshawur Valley. He had seen service in many parts of the world. Owing no extraneous advantages to his family connexions, he had ever been one of those hard-working, unshrinking, conscientious military officers, who do not serve the State less ungrudgingly because it has been ungrateful to them, but who, rising by slow gradation, never have an opportunity of going to the front and showing of what stuff they are made, until age has enfeebled their powers. Of his forty-seven years of service in the Royal Army the greater number had been passed in India. But he was of a constitution well adapted to sustain the assaults of the

* In 1849, Sir Henry Lawrence wrote to him: "Let me advise you as a friend to curb your temper, and bear and forbear with Natives and Europeans, and you will soon be as distinguished a civilian as you are a soldier. Don't think it is necessary to say all you think to every one. The world would be one mass of tumult if we all gave candid opinions of each other. I admire you sincerely as much as any man can do, but say thus much as a general warning." In writing this, Lawrence wrote as one conscious of the same natural infirmity in himself. He had manfully struggled against, and in a great measure overcome it.

1857. May. climate, and his threescore years had taken from him little of the vigour and activity of his prime. Of good stature, but of a spare, light frame, he had all the external attributes of a good soldier, and there were few men in the whole range of the service who were more familiar with the duties of his profession in all its grades. Constant intercourse with the British soldier, in the Barrack and in the Camp, had not only made him thoroughly acquainted with his habits and feelings, but had developed within him a tender and tolerant affection for, a generous sympathy with, all who worked under him. Few commanding officers had been more careful of the common soldier than Sydney Cotton, or had more thoroughly earned his confidence. He was known and acknowledged to be one of the best regimental officers in the Army. No opportunity until now had been afforded to him of testing the higher qualities, which enable a man to face large responsibilities, and to combat great difficulties and dangers with a serene front. But the latent power was in him; the opportunity had now come, and he was equal to it. Edwardes and Nicholson had confidence in the Brigadier; and although, like many of his class, he had an habitual contempt for civilians and soldier-civilians, he could not help thanking God, in the depths of his heart, that circumstances had now rendered him the fellow-labourer, in a great cause, of two soldiers, of whom any army in the world might be proud—two soldiers, though vested with civil authority, as eager to take the field and to share its dangers, as though they had never left the camp.

First tidings of the outbreak. These three men were at Peshawur, when, on the 12th of May, news reached them to the effect that one of the greatest military stations in Upper India was in a blaze, and that the European regiments were on the defensive. Edwardes, who had an assured faith in the good results of the Afghan policy, which he had so successfully advocated, had little apprehension that Peshawur would be lost to the Empire. "As to this place," he wrote to Sir John Lawrence, "it will be the last to go; and not go at all, if the intermediate country be occupied by a good field-force engaged in making stern examples. The celebrated Sixty-fourth Native Infantry is here;* and the report in the station is, that the Native regiments here are prepared to follow whatever lead is set them by the Twenty-first Native Infantry, which, *cæteris paribus*, is a good one." But he did not, although not fearing for Peshawur, under-estimate the magnitude of the crisis. He knew that a great struggle was approaching, and that the energies of the British nation must be strained to the utmost. He knew that, in the Punjab, there would be much strife and contention, and that every Englishman in the province would have to put forth all his strength. He was a man ever ripe for action, and he had in John Nicholson a meet companion. "I have not heard yet," he wrote in the letter above quoted to the Chief Commissioner, "whether you are at Pindee or Murree; but as we have received here telegraphic news of the 10th of May from Meerut that the Native troops were in open mutiny, and the Europeans on the defensive only, I write a line to tell you that Nicholson and I are of opinion that a strong movable column of reliable troops (Europeans and Irregulars) should take the field in the Punjab at once—perhaps at Lahore would be best, so as to get between the

1857. May.

* See, for an account of a previous mutiny of this regiment, *ante*, vol. i., pages 281—289.

1857. May 12. stations which *have* mutinied and those that have *not*; and move on the first station that stirs next; and bring the matter, without further delay, to the bayonet. This disaffection will never be talked down now. It must be put down—and the sooner blood be let the less of it will suffice. Nicholson desires me to tell you that he would be ready to take command of them, and I need not add the pleasure it would give me to do the same. We are both at your disposal, remember; and if this business goes, as it soon will, to a question of personal influence and exertion, either of us could raise a serviceable body out of the Derajat in a short time." And he added in a postscript, "Whatever you do about a movable force, do it at once. There is no time to be lost in getting to the struggle which is to settle the matter."

Neville Chamberlain.

There was then at no great distance from Peshawur another man, whose counsel and assistance were eagerly desired in this conjuncture. It was felt that the presence of Neville Chamberlain was needed to complete that little confederacy of heroes, on the wisdom and courage of whom the safety of the frontier, under Providence, mainly depended. Brigadier Chamberlain at this time commanded the Punjab Irregular Force. He was in the prime of his life and the fulness of his active manhood. Of a fair stature, of a light but sinewy frame, he had every physical qualification that could make a dashing leader of Irregular Horse. And in early youth, he had acquired a reputation as an intrepid and eager soldier, who was ever in the front where danger was to be faced and glory was to be gained. On the battle-fields of Afghanistan and the Punjab, he had shown what was the temper of his steel, and he had carried off more honourable wounds in hand-to-hand encounter with the enemy than any of his contemporaries in the service. It was said, indeed, that his great fault as a soldier was, that he exposed himself too recklessly to danger. But with this irrepressible military enthusiasm, which had well-nigh cost him his life, he had a large fund of sound common sense, was wise in council, and had military knowledge far beyond that of the bold swordsman who heads against heavy odds a charge of Horse. And with all these fine qualities he combined a charming modesty of demeanour—a general quietude and simplicity of character, which not only forbade all kinds of self-assertion, but even shrunk from the commendations of others. He had been selected, as the fittest man in the Army, to command the Punjab Irregular Force, of which I have before spoken,* and which had already won immense confidence in the Punjab, and no little reputation in more distant parts of India. Next to the European regiments, this was the most reliable portion of the military force in the Punjab—indeed, the only other reliable part of the great Army planted there for the defence of the frontier. It was of extreme importance at this time that Chamberlain and Cotton should be in communication as to the best means of co-operating, especially with respect to the proposed Movable Column; and so Edwardes wrote to him, asking him to ride over to Peshawur and to take counsel with him and the chief military authorities—a measure of which they entirely approved. Chamberlain at once responded to the summons, and hastened over to Peshawur. 1857. May 12.

So, on the 13th of May, an hour or two after his arrival, a Council of War was held at the house of General Reed. The members present were the The Peshawur Council. May 13.

* *Ante*, page 422.

1857. May 13. General, the Brigadier, Edwardes, Chamberlain, and Nicholson. Half an hour before their assembling, Edwardes had received a telegraphic message from John Lawrence approving the formation of the Movable Column, and announcing that the Native troops at Meean-Meer had that morning been disarmed. There was no division in the Council. The military and political authorities at Peshawur were moved by a common spirit, and acted as one man. It was agreed that in the conjuncture which had arisen, all civil and military power in the Punjab should be concentrated on one spot; that to this effect General Reed should assume the command of all the troops in the province, that he should join the Chief Commissioner at Rawul-Pindee, or at such place as might be the seat of the local government at the time, in order that he might be in constant intercourse with the Chief Commissioner, and harmonious action might thus be secured between the civil and military authorities. The real object of this did not lie on the surface. There was an occult meaning in it, which caused Edwardes and Nicholson to smile complacently at the Council-table, and to exchange many a joke in private. This concentration of the military authority of the Punjab in the person of General Reed—a worthy old officer, without very strong opinions of any kind—really transferred it to the hands of the political officers. It was a great thing not to be checked—not to be thwarted—not to be interfered with—not to have regulation, and routine, and all sorts of nervous fears and anxieties thrust upon them from a distance. It was desirable, however, that the semblance of military authority should be maintained throughout the land—that the rights of seniority should be outwardly respected—that every man should be in his own place, as upon parade, and that a General should at all times be a General, even though for purposes of action he should be merely a stock or a stone. The Natives of India watch these things shrewdly and observingly, and estimate, with rare sagacity, every indication of a failure of the wondrous union and discipline, which they look upon as the very root of our supremacy.* But, though it was at all times and in all places, desirable to keep up this show of a wonderful machinery, working wheel by wheel with perfect regularity of action, it was not always expedient to maintain the reality of it. There were times and conjunctures when the practical recognition of the authority of rank, which in the Indian army was only another name for age, might wisely be foregone; and such a crisis had now to be confronted. On the whole, it was a fortunate circumstance that just such a man as General Reed—a man not obstinate, not wedded to any opinions or foregone conclusions of his own, and yet not more cautious, irresolute, or fearful of responsibility than the majority of old soldiers who had never been called upon to face a momentous crisis—was then the senior officer in that part of

1857. May 13.

* In the first volume of this History I observed, with immediate reference to the dissensions between Lord Dalhousie and Sir Charles Napier, that these conflicts of authority were generally regarded, by the more intelligent Natives of India, as proofs of weakness in the British Government, and that some regarded them as precursors of our downfall. I have since read the following confirmation of this opinion in the Correspondence of the Duke of Wellington: "Of this I am certain," wrote the Duke to Lord Combermere, "that any public and continued difference between the Governor-General and the Commander-in-Chief is prejudicial to the public interests, and cannot be allowed to exist. It is prejudicial for this reason. It shakes the authority of Government to its very foundation; and while such differences continue, every little man, who takes part with either one or the other, becomes of importance. The interests of the party are the great object. Those of the public are laid aside and forgotten, and even injured with impunity."

1857. May 13.

the country; indeed, under the Commander-in-Chief, the senior officer of the Bengal Presidency. He had good sense of the most serviceable kind—the good sense to understand his own deficiencies, and to appreciate the fact that there were abler men than himself about him. So, whilst he was rising to the honourable position of military dictator of the Punjab, he wisely ceased to dictate. The time had come for the universal domination of Brains—John Lawrence, with Herbert Edwardes for his Wuzeer, then took the supreme direction of affairs, always consulting the chief military authorities, but quietly educating them, and flattering them with the belief that they dictated when they only obeyed.

The Movable Column.

The next resolution was that a Movable Column of reliable troops, as before suggested, should be organised, to take the field at once, under a competent commander, and to operate upon any point where rebellion might bristle up, or danger might threaten us in the Punjab. A suspected Sepoy garrison was to be removed from the Fort of Attock—an important position, which it was of immense moment to secure; and our communications were to be placed beyond the reach of danger by posting at the Attock ferry a Pathan guard under a tried and trusty Pathan leader. At the same time other changes in the disposition of the troops were to be made; the Native regiments being drawn into the posts at which they might least readily co-operate with each other, and most easily be overawed by the Europeans. At the same time, it was determined that Brigadier Chamberlain should proceed at once to Rawul-Pindee to take counsel with the Chief Commissioner; and that John Nicholson, if his services were not called for in a military capacity, should accompany the Movable

Column as its political officer. These proposals were telegraphed to Sir John Lawrence, and all but the last were cordially accepted. The Chief Commissioner thought that Nicholson's services were required at Peshawur, and in that particular juncture it was believed that the public service would suffer by his departure. Moreover, he had a faith, that had been bravely earned, in the general efficiency of his assistants all over the country. And he knew that it would not be wise to supersede local authority by a delegate from Head-Quarters. And never, perhaps, did John Lawrence exhibit his instinctive sagacity more clearly than in this first resolution to place every officer in the Punjab on his own particular stand-point of responsibility, and thus to evoke to the utmost all the power within him.

1857. May 13.

The details of the Movable Column were soon jotted down, but it was not so easy to settle the question of command. Cotton and Edwardes, Chamberlain and Nicholson, were all equally eager to place themselves at its head. It was to be determined only by superior authority; so General Reed made a reference to the Commander-in-Chief. Edwardes could not be spared from the frontier, where he was a tower of strength: the names of Cotton, Chamberlain, and Nicholson, were submitted to Head-Quarters. And the telegraph wires brought back the intimation that General Anson had selected Neville Chamberlain as the leader of the column.

The Rawul-Pindee Council. May 16.

On the 16th, General Reed and Brigadier Chamberlain joined the Chief Commissioner at Rawul-Pindee, and on that evening Colonel Edwardes received a telegraphic message summoning him to join the Head-Quarters Council. Making over his own particular charge to Nicholson, he proceeded at once

1857. May 16. to Pindee, and was soon in eager but confident discussion alike of the present and the future. The stern resolution and unflinching courage of John Lawrence were then lighted up by the radiant aspect of Herbert Edwardes, whose cheerfulness was so unfailing, and whose political wisdom so often glinted out in bright flashes of wit, that the Councils of War which were held during that gathering at Rawul-Pindee were said to be "great fun."* Never, perhaps, in the face of such enormous difficulty and danger, shaking the very foundations of a great empire, did men meet each other with brighter faces or more cheering words. It was an occasion on which the eventual success of our resistance depended, more than all else, upon the heart and hope of our great chiefs, on whose words all men hung, and in whose faces they looked for the assurance and encouragement which inspired and animated all beneath them. It was said of John Lawrence, at that time, that he was as calm and confident as if he had been contemplating only the most common-place events, and that Herbert Edwardes was in higher spirits, more natural and more unrestrained, than he

* It may be mentioned here that the capital story, repeated in so many contemporary memoirs, to the effect that Sir John Lawrence, being at the whist-table, answered a telegraphic message from General Anson with the words, "Clubs are trumps—not spades; when in doubt play a big one"—originated in a joke of Herbert Edwardes. The story always was one of doubtful authenticity, as it was less likely that Sir John Lawrence than that General Anson would be caught at the whist-table. The fact is, that Lawrence, Edwardes, Charles Nicholson, and one or two others were together, when a telegram from Mr. Barnes was received, stating that there was some talk at Umballah of intrenching, and not marching. Edwardes humorously suggested that a telegram should be despatched to "Major A. wherever he may be found," saying, "When in doubt play a trump—act up to your own principles"—the belief being that General Anson had written the well-known work on whist by "Major A." Charles Nicholson then suggested as an amendment the words, "Clubs are trumps, not spades." Lawrence consented, and the pregnant sentence was despatched to Mr. Barnes, who, doubtless, communicated it to General Anson.

had ever been known to be by men who had served with him in more quiet times. A great and ennobling faith was settling down in the breasts of our Punjabee chiefs. It had dawned upon them that it would be their work, not merely to save the Province, but to save the Empire. 1857. May 16.

History will take the measure of men's minds in accordance with the extent to which they looked upon this crisis, as a local or an imperial one, and directed their efforts to the suppression of the one or the other. Physically, it is known rarely to happen that men, who have a clear, steady sight to discern distinctly near objects, have that wide range of vision which enables them to comprehend what is observable in the distance; and the faculty which, either on a large or a small scale, enables a man to grasp moral objects, both immediate and remote, is equally rare. General Hewitt's small mind took in nothing beyond the idea that, as he lived at Meerut, it was his duty to save Meerut. But the great intellect of Sir John Lawrence grasped all the circumstances of the imperial danger, and held them in a vice. He had his own particular province in hand—carefully and minutely; no single post overlooked, no single point neglected. He knew what every man under him was doing, what every man was expected to do; there was nothing that happened, or that might happen, in the Punjab over which he did not exercise the closest vigilance; but the struggle for supremacy at his own doors never obscured the distant vision of the great imperial danger. He never domesticated his policy; he never localised his efforts. He never said to himself, "The Punjab is my especial charge. I will defend the Punjab. I have no responsibility beyond it." He would have weakened the Punjab to

1857. May. strengthen the Empire. He would, perhaps, have sacrificed the Punjab to save the Empire. In this, indeed, the strength of his character—his capacity for government on a grand scale—was evinced at the outset, and, as time advanced, it manifested itself in every stage of the great struggle more signally than before.*

It was felt in the Pindee Council that, "whatever gave rise to the mutiny, it had settled down into a struggle for empire, under Mahomedan guidance, with the Mogul capital for its centre.† From that time, this great centre of the Mogul capital was never beyond the range of John Lawrence's thoughts—never beyond the reach of his endeavours. Seen, as it were, through the telescope of long years of political experience, sweeping all intervening time and space, the great city of Delhi, which he knew so well, was brought close to his eyes; and he felt that he had a double duty. Much as he might think of Lahore, Umritsur, or Peshawur, he thought still more of Delhi. He felt as lesser men would not have felt, that it was his duty in that emergency to give back to the Empire, in time of intestine war, all that he could give from that abundance of military strength which had been planted in the province at a time when the defence of the frontier against external aggressions was held to be the first object of imperial importance. Knowing well the terrible scarcity of reliable troops in all the country below the Punjab, and the encouraging effect of the occupation of Delhi by the rebel troops, he resolved to pour down upon the imperial city every regiment

* A fuller account of Sir John Lawrence's internal policy is reserved for another chapter.

† These are the words of Colonel Edwardes in his Peshawur Military Report—a document of great interest and ability, and one most serviceable to the historian.

that he could send to its relief. From that time his was the directing mind which influenced for good all that was done from Upper India, working downwards to rescue our people from the toils of the enemy, and to assert our dominion under the walls of Delhi, where the great battle of supremacy was to be fought. 1857 May.

The march the Guide Corps.

And the first succour which he sent was the famous Guide Corps, which Henry Lawrence had designed ever to be ready for service—ever to be the first for action. It was at that time stationed at Hote-Murdan, under the command of Captain Henry Daly. On the morning of the 13th, two officers, who had gone over to Nowshera to attend a ball which had been given at that station, brought to Hote-Murdan tidings that the Fifty-fifth Regiment at the former place had received orders to relieve the Guide Corps at the latter. All was then excitement and conjecture. No man knew the reason of the movement; no man knew what had happened or what was coming. "No uproar," it was said, "along the line of frontier. No incursion to repress. No expedition to join." The story told, at six in the morning, was true; and two hours afterwards its truth was confirmed by the sight of the approaching regiment in the distance. About the same time an express came in from Peshawur, bringing orders for the Guide Corps to march at once to Nowshera. With the official orders came a private letter from Edwardes to Daly, which cast a terrible glare of light upon all that had before been obscure. "That you may better know how to act on the enclosed instruction to move to Nowshera, I write privately to tell you that telegraphic news of open mutiny among the Native troops at Meerut having reached

1857. May. us here to-day, we think a movable column should be assembled in the Punjab, and get between the stations that have gone wrong and those that have not, and put down further disaffection by force. It is obviously necessary to constitute such a column of reliable troops, and therefore it has been proposed to get the Guides and Her Majesty's Twenty-seventh Regiment together without delay as a part of the scheme." So Daly at once mustered his Guides, and before midnight they were at Nowshera. He had not long laid himself down to rest, when he was awakened by an express from Cotton ordering the Guides to move upon Attock. At gun-fire they recommenced their journey, and before noon, after a trying march, under a fierce sun, they reached their destination, scorched and dried, but full of spirit and ripe for action. "The Punjab," wrote the gallant leader of the Guides on that day, "is paying back India all she cost her, by sending troops stout and firm to her aid."

May 16. From Attock, after securing the Fort, and holding it until the arrival of a detachment sent from Kohat, Daly marched, two hours after midnight, on the morning of the 16th, in the light of the rising moon, which soon was obscured by a blinding dust-storm. When it cleared away, the air was fresh and pleasant, and the corps marched on, a distance of more than twenty miles, until, at eight o'clock, it bivouacked in a grove of peach and apricot trees, which enabled them to dispense with tents. At midnight, after a few hours of early slumber, the trumpet-call was again heard, and they resumed their march, in the cool morning air, through a beautiful country skirted by a range of verdant hills; and on the morning of the 18th they were at Rawul-Pindee.

There was nothing needed to stimulate a man of Daly's high enthusiasm, but it was refreshing and invigorating to be, even for a little while, in close and familiar intercouse with such men as Lawrence, Chamberlain, and Edwardes—and a fourth, Hugh James, then acting as Secretary to the Chief Commissioner, who had a noble spirit and a high intelligence worthy of the confidence of his great master. There is nothing more delightful than this attrition of ardent natures. Great men become greater by such sympathetic contact. It was a source of infinite rejoicing to Daly to learn that the Guides, which might have done great service as a part of the Movable Column in the Punjab, were honoured by being the first regiment selected to move down to the relief of Delhi. "The Guides, I believe," wrote Daly in his journal on the 18th of May, "are to march down and to show to the people Native troops willing and loyal. I shall rejoice at this, and march down with all my heart." And so they marched down—with a great enthusiasm stirring their gallant leader, and through him, all who followed; officers and men, moved by one common heroism of the best kind. "I am making, and I mean to make," wrote Daly on the 1st of June, "the best march that has been heard of in the land!" And nobly he fulfilled his promise. 1857. May 18.

At this time he had reached Loodhianah. In the early morning of the 4th the Guides were at Umballah, and on the 6th they were at Kurnaul. There they found Mr. Le Bas and Sir Theophilus Metcalfe, who had escaped from Delhi, and were eager to punish some neighbouring villages, which were believed to have harboured insurgents, and to be full of people bent upon the plunder of the Feringhees. Eager as Daly was to push on to Delhi, and reluctant June 1—4.

1857. June. to destroy wholesale, in retaliation for what might only be an offence of the few, he for some time resisted the retributory eagerness of the civilians, but at length yielded to their wishes, and sent the Guides forward to the attack. The villagers fled in dismay; some were killed on their retreat; others were made prisoners; and soon the blaze of their burning houses could be seen from many a distant mile. But the mercy of the Christian officer was shown towards the helpless and unoffending; Daly saved the women and the children, and helped them to remove the little property they possessed.

The delay was unfortunate. The unwelcome duty thus forced upon the Guide Corps deprived it of the coveted honour of taking part in the first attack upon the Delhi mutineers. Had not the civilians, in that great zeal for the desolation of villages, which distinguished many, perhaps too many of them, before the year was at an end, arrested Daly's onward march, he would have been present with his corps at the battle of Budlee-ka-serai. As it was, he marched into camp a day too late.* The battle had been fought, but the corps, by the march alone, had covered itself with glory, and it was received on its arrival by the Delhi Field Force with ringing cheers. There were now two Native regiments in the British camp whom all men trusted—the Goorkahs under Reid, and the Punjabee Guide Corps under Daly. And

June 9. The Guide Corps at Delhi.

* "The morning after the battle the Guides entered camp under the command of Captain Daly. They were already well known as one of the finest regiments in India. They were almost all of Afghan or Persian race, and consisted of three troops of cavalry, perhaps the best riders in our pay, and six companies of infantry armed with the rifle. They had marched in this, the hottest time of the year, from near Peshawur to Delhi, a distance of five hundred and eighty miles in twenty-two days. Their stately height and military bearing made all who saw them proud to have such aid. They came in as firm and light as if they had marched only a mile."—*History of the Siege of Delhi, by One who Served there.*

soon it will be seen how gallantly they proved the fidelity that was in them. Indeed, on the very day of their arrival, the Guides went out, fresh as if they had slept a long sleep, and loitered through a cool morning, to give the Delhi mutineers a taste of their temper. The enemy were not prepared, on the day after the battle, to risk another great engagement; but, intent on not suffering us to rest, they sent out parties of Horse and Foot to attack our advanced position. The Guides went gallantly to the front. The sabres of their horsemen were crossed with those of the troopers of the Third Cavalry; but not long could the rebels stand the onslaught. The failure of the attack would have been complete, if it had not cost us the life of one of our finest officers. Daly was unharmed, though struck by a spent shot, and his horse killed in the encounter; but his second in command, young Quintin Battye, who had charged at the head of the Guides' Cavalry, was carried mortally wounded from the field. The gallantry of his bearing throughout this fierce encounter had attracted the admiration of his chief; and Daly, when last he saw his lieutenant in action, had cried out with the irrepressible enthusiasm with which one brave man regards the bravery of another, "Gallant Battye! well done, brave Battye!" and soon afterwards a rebel came up within two yards of the English officer, and, after vainly endeavouring to bayonet him, discharged his piece into Battye's body. The deed was amply revenged. A Soubahdar of the Guide Corps cut the Sepoy down as he fired.*

1857. June.

* Soubahdar Merban Singh. This gallant soldier was a Goorkah, "one of those sent down by Sir Henry Lawrence" to join the Guide Corps. He fell in action, some days afterwards, at the head of the first company, which he commanded. "The men," wrote Daly to John Lawrence, "speak of him with tears and sobs." He had two brothers also killed in action.

1857. June. Death of Quintin Battye.

And as the young hero lay dying, in grievous pain, on that night which was to be his last, a remembrance of the pleasant Argos of his school days mingling with the pride of the soldier and the great love of country which sustained our people, he said, with a smile on his handsome face, to the chaplain who was ministering to him, "Dulce et decorum est pro patriâ mori;" and so ended his brief and honourable career.*

* See Chaplain's "Narrative of the Siege of Delhi."

CHAPTER III.

GENERAL POLICY OF SIR JOHN LAWRENCE—THE RAISING OF LOCAL LEVIES—EVENTS AT PESHAWUR—DISARMING OF THE NATIVE REGIMENTS—PUNISHMENT OF DESERTERS—MUTINY OF THE FIFTY-FIFTH—EXPEDITION TO HOTE-MURDAN—MUTINY OF THE SIXTY-FOURTH—THE OUTBREAK AT JULLUNDHUR.

May, 1857

Policy of Sir John Lawrence.

WHILST Daly's Guide Corps was making this splendid march, and the Punjab was contributing the first-fruits of its accumulated strength to the succour of the English Army at Delhi, events were ripening in the frontier province, and John Lawrence and his associates were laying fast hold of the crisis with a vigorous tenacity, as men knowing right well the sovereign importance of promptitude of action The Chief Commissioner, in earnest council with Edwardes and Chamberlain, had clearly marked out the policy which was now to be pursued for the preservation of the Punjab. When intelligence of the events at the capital, and especially of the disarming of the Native regiments at Meean-Meer, reached him, he had been at first somewhat startled by the boldness of the conception, and perhaps inclined to question the wisdom of the achievement. For John Lawrence, with all his immense energy and resolution, was a man cautious and circumspect, who never acted upon impulse. If he thought at the beginning that this open movement

1857. May. against the Sepoys on the part of the Sirkar—this vehement declaration of want of confidence in men who had as yet, within his own circle of administration, done nothing disloyal—was hastily to proclaim a war that it was not desirable to precipitate, there was substantial reason for the doubt.* But he very soon felt full assurance that what had been done had been done wisely and well. And from that time, sternly recognising the fact that the crisis had come, that there was nothing to be postponed, or coqueted with, or smoothed down, he flung himself into the work before him, full-brained and strong-armed, and grappled with it as, perhaps, no other man could have done. Then he, in his turn, startled others by the boldness of his conceptions. There were men equally shrewd and courageous at Lahore, who learnt with alarm that the Chief Commissioner was enlisting Sikhs and Afghans into the service of the State. But this policy was based upon a sound estimate of the antagonism between the Poorbeah Sepoys from Hindostan aad the Punjabee races, whether Sikhs or Mahomedans—a natural antagonism fostered and increased by the conduct of the former.† To replace

* See the following extract from a private letter addressed by Lawrence to Edwardes, in which the position of affairs is most accurately stated in a few words: "The misfortune of the present state of affairs is this,—Each step we take for our own security is a blow against the regular Sepoy. He feels this, and on his side takes a further step, and so we go on, until we disband or destroy them, or they mutiny and kill their officers."

† On the parts of the Sikhs and Punjabees there happily existed a considerable degree of antipathy, if not downright enmity, towards the Sepoys of the Native Corps of the Line. The latter had rendered themselves insufferable by assuming airs of superiority, and regarding the former with disdain, as being themselves more warlike and better soldiers. "We mar-ed (beat) Caubul, we mar-ed the Punjab," was the every-day boast of the Poorbeah Sepoy to the Sikh, whom he further stigmatised as a man of low caste. The bad feeling between the two races was still further fostered by the cold shoulder usually turned by the Poorbeahs to the Sikhs and Punjabees, whom they could not openly prevent enlisting into regiments of the Line

these Hindostanees, among whom it every day became more apparent that mutiny was spreading like a pestilence, by the mixed races of the province and the frontier, might be to substitute a new danger for the old; but the one was certain, the other merely conjectural. And there was good reason to believe that so long as we were capable of asserting our strength, the military classes of the Punjab would array themselves on our side, if only for the sake of gain. Among the Sikhs, Delhi was both an offence and a temptation. Old prophecies had foretold that the Imperial City of the Mogul would some day be given up to the plunder of the Khalsa. And it was not to be doubted that the destruction of the Hindostanee Army of the Company would tend, sooner or later, to assist them to recover the ascendancy they had lost. Sir John Lawrence saw this clearly enough; but he had to deal with an immediate necessity, and he had no need at such a time to take thought of the Future. So he asked the consent of the Governor-General to the raising of local levies, and this, sought and granted on a small scale, soon expanded into larger proportions, and Sir John Lawrence held in his hand an open commission to act according to his own judgment and discretion.*

1857. May.

This policy met with general favour among the chief political officers in the province, and there were few who did not press for permission to recruit in their own districts. But it was soon apparent that there was in some parts, especially on the frontier, overmuch of hesitation, resulting from want of confidence in our strength. Meanwhile other precau-

* I ought not to omit to state that, as many Sikhs had enlisted into the Sepoy regiments, an order went out to excerpt these men from the Hindostanee corps, and form them into separate battalions.

1857. May. tionary measures were being pressed forward with that promptitude and energy which always distinguished such operations in the Punjab. The Police were strengthened. The utmost vigilance was enforced upon them. The different passages of the Punjab Rivers—the fords and ferries—were watched and guarded; and every effort was to be made to intercept those emissaries of evil who, in the guise of wandering fakeers or other religious mendicants, were sowing the seeds of sedition broadcast over the country.* Then, again, great endeavours were made—and with wonderful success—to save the Government Treasure, the loss of which was not to be calculated by the number of rupees to be struck off our cash-balances. It was emphatically the sinews of war to the enemy. Wherever it was held, under Native guards, at outlying stations, it was removed to places of security and stored under the protection of European soldiers. And at the same time an order went forth—merciful in the end, but terrible in the hour of our need—to punish all offenders against the State with a deterring severity, which would strike a great fear into the hearts of the people. "There was no room then for mercy," it was said; "the public safety was a paramount consideration." The ordinary processes of the law were set aside, and authority was given to any two civil officers to erect themselves into a special commission to try criminals, and to execute upon them, when needed, the sentence of death At the same time, seeing that it was better to remove

* I have been told that the picture in the first volume of this History, of the wandering emissaries of sedition, who, in one disguise or another, traversed the country, was purely an effort of my imagination. As this opinion has been made public through an influential channel, I may note that the statement in the text is from Sir John Lawrence's official report, laid before Parliament.

the means of offence than to punish its commission, 1857. May.
he tried to clear the province of all that mass of disaffected non-military humanity from Hindostan,* which was either hanging on to the skirts of the Poorbeah Army, or had followed the Feringhees in the hour of success, moved by the great lust of gain to worship what they now reviled. And all these measures for the internal security of the province seemed to John Lawrence the more necessary, as he was straining every nerve to send down troops to Delhi, and thus was weakening his own defensive powers. For this reason, too, it seemed to him that we should act vigorously, and at once, against our declared enemies, taking the initiative whenever opportunity presented itself, and establishing a reputation for that confidence in our own resources, the belief in which by our adversaries is always a tower of strength. And already events were hurrying on to this desired point. One great opportunity was close at hand, and others were pressing on tumultuously behind.

On the 21st of May, Colonel Edwardes returned to Peshawur.† Little sunshine greeted him there. His colleagues, Cotton and Nicholson, had no cheerful intelligence to offer him. A great cloud was over Events at Peshawur.

* "The traitorous symptoms evinced and the intrigues set on foot by the non-military Hindostanees in the Punjab territories, rendered it necessary to remove large numbers of them. These people were employed to a considerable extent among the police and other subordinate civil establishments; and as camp-followers they swarmed in every Cantonment, and in the adjacent cities. Most of the lower class of employés were discharged, and numbers of camp-followers deported out of the province."—*Sir John Lawrence's Official Report.*

† The regular Hindostanee regiments at Peshawur consisted of the Fifth Cavalry and the Twenty-first, Twenty-fourth, Twenty-seventh, and Fifty-first Infantry regiments.

1857. May. the place. The Sepoy regiments had shown unmistakable signs of that feverishness which presages revolt. Cotton had divided his Hindostanee troops in such a manner as to render joint action more difficult; and he had placed Europeans, with guns, in their immediate vicinity, to be prepared for a sudden rising. From many parts of the country tidings of fresh mutinies had come in, and there was a general belief that the whole Native Army was rotten to the core. Intercepted letters showed that the excitement was not confined to those whose names were written on the muster-rolls of our regiments.* Nicholson, who, with his wonted energy, had been pushing forward the work of raising local levies, had found an uneasy feeling among the chiefs of the principal tribes, and a general unwillingness to enlist into the service of a Government which seemed to be in a state of decrepitude, if not of decay. "Men remembered Caubul," wrote Edwardes at a later period. "Not one hundred could be found to join such a desperate cause." It was clear, therefore, both to him and to Nicholson that it was necessary to sweep away the doubts and uncertainties which were keeping up this dangerous state of unrest, and to assert, vigorously and undeniably, the power of the English on the frontier.

May 21. On the night of the 21st, they had gone to rest in their clothes beneath the same roof, both assured that a few more hours would ripen their plans, when an express arrived informing them that the companies of the Fifty-fifth had mutinied at Nowshera, some

* "Thanesur Brahmins and Patna Mahomedans, Hindostanee fanatics in the Swat Valley, and turbulent outlaws in Gitanah, were calling upon the Sepoys to declare themselves. . . . . The whole disclosed such a picture of fanatic zeal and base treachery as made the very name of a Poorbeah Sepoy suspected and loathed."—*Cave-Browne.*

twenty-four miles distant from Peshawur, and that 1857.
there was no reliance to be placed on the Tenth May 21—22.
Regiment of Irregular Cavalry at the same place. The former regiment had been brigaded at Meerut and other stations with the Third Cavalry, and was regarded as a fugleman corps, whose every movement would be strictly followed by the regiments in the Punjab. It needed not any long-sustained conversation between Edwardes and Nicholson for both to arrive at the conclusion that the Native troops at Peshawur should be at once disarmed. So the Commissioner and Deputy-Commissioner of Peshawur went straightway to the Quarters of the Brigadier, and woke him up in the dead of the night. Starting from his sleep, Cotton saw beside him his two political associates, and, wondering what had brought them to his bed-side, prepared himself to listen. He was not a man in any emergency to be flustered, and he soon took in with a cool brain the whole state of the case. It would be necessary to send European troops from Peshawur to coerce the refractory regiment at Nowshera and Hote-Murdan, and the white troops at Cotton's disposal, already weakened by the requirements of the Movable Column and by summer sickness, could little afford a further draft from them, whilst the Hindostanee regiments were in armed force in the Cantonment. Moreover, it was plain that the tribes on the Frontier were eagerly watching events, and that the excitement was every day increasing. But there were two aspects in which this might be regarded, for thus to strip the Frontier of a large part of its defenders—to reduce the available force at the disposal of the British Government to a handful of European troops—might be to encourage the Afghans to stream through the Khybur

1857. May 22. Pass in an irresistible spasm of energy for the recovery of Peshawur. The risk of action was great, the risk of quiescence seemed also to be great. But to those three brave men, in midnight council assembled, it appeared that the bolder would be the better course; and so it was resolved that they should be the first to strike, and that four of the five Sepoy regiments should be disarmed at break of day * The responsibility of the blow would rest with Cotton. He did not hesitate to accept it.

Disarming of the Sepoy regiments.

There was no time to be lost. So he at once summoned the Commanding Officers of the Native regiments to his Quarters. Day broke before they were assembled. There, in the presence of Edwardes and Nicholson, Cotton told them what he had determined to do, and ordered them to parade their regiments with all possible despatch. Then there arose a storm of remonstrance. Protesting their entire confidence in the fidelity of their men, these Sepoy Commandants clamoured vehemently against the threatened disgrace of their regiments; and one declared his conviction that his corps would never submit to lay down its arms, but would rise against the order and resolutely attack the guns.† Cotton listened

* The Twenty-first Sepoy regiment was exempted from the operation of the disarming order. It was the senior regiment in the Cantonment, and as such, according to military etiquette and usage, the other battalions looked to it for an example. It had certainly not given a signal for insurrection, and whatever may have been the feelings with which it regarded the supremacy of the English, it had shown no active symptoms of disaffection. It was thought advisable, therefore, to spare it, the more especially as it was held to be "indispensable to keep one Native Infantry corps to carry on the duties of the station."

† "It was impossible not to sympathise with the soldierly feelings of Colonel Harrington and Major Shakespeare; but when Colonel Plumbe has implicit confidence in the Twenty-seventh Native Infantry to be unshaken by events in Hindostan, and had nothing to recommend but conciliation, whilst the Colonel of the Fifty-first, on the other hand, predicted that his men would attack the guns if called on to give up their muskets, hesitation was at an end."—*Edwardes's Report.*

attentively to all that was said, but the discussion proceeded after argument had been exhausted, and, after a while, Edwardes, thinking that time and words were being wasted, broke in with an emphatic sentence, to the effect "that the matter rested entirely with Brigadier Cotton." On this Cotton at once exclaimed: "Then the troops as originally determined will be disarmed." This silenced all further remonstrance. Not another word was said by way of argument. The regimental Commandants received their instructions and went forth to do the bidding of their chief. 1857. May 22.

It has been stated that the Peshawur Force had been wisely cut in two, as a precautionary measure, by Brigadier Cotton. It was now arranged that Edwardes should accompany Cotton to the right wing, whilst Nicholson went to the left with Colonel Galloway of the Seventieth Queen's, who stood next in seniority.* With the former were Her Majesty's Eighty-seventh Fusiliers, with the latter the Seventieth, both with detachments of Artillery to support them. It was a moment of intense anxiety. The Sepoy Commandants were parading their men, and the Queen's Regiments were lying in wait to attack them on the first sign of resistance. The suddenness of the movement took the Sepoys aback; they laid down their arms to the bidding of their own officers. And as the piles grew and grew, under the mournful process of humiliating surrender, a feeling of profound grief and shame took possession of their officers, and it is recorded that some of them cast their own swords and spurs upon the heaps of abandoned musketry and sabres in token of the strength of their

* Brigadier Cotton at this time commanded generally the Frontier force, whilst Colonel Galloway was Brigadier commanding the station.

1857. May 22. sympathy with the Sepoys, and their detestation of the authority which had degraded them.*

The arms surrendered, Brigadier Cotton addressed the regiments, praising them for the readiness with which they had obeyed orders; and they went to their Lines. Thus was the work done well and thoroughly—and without the shedding of a drop of blood. The effect upon the minds of the people was magical. They believed that we were strong because we were daring. The old aphorism, that "nothing succeeds like success," was here triumphantly verified. The tribes, who had held aloof whilst danger threatened us, and the issue was doubtful, now pressed forward eagerly to do homage to the audacity of the English. Without another halt of doubt, or tremor of hesitation, they came forward with their offers of service. "As we rode down to the disarming," said Herbert Edwardes, "a very few chiefs and yeomen of the country attended us, and I remember, judging from their faces, that they came to see which way the tide would turn. As we rode back friends were as thick as summer flies, and levies began from that moment to come in." Good reason, indeed, had Sir John Lawrence to write to the Peshawur Commissioner, with hearty commendation, saying: "I look on the disarming of the four corps at Peshawur as a master-stroke—one which will do much good to keep the peace throughout the Punjab. Commandants of Corps are under a delusion, and

* Colonel Edwardes's official report. "As the muskets and sabres of the once honoured corps were hurried unceremoniously into carts, it was said that here and there the spurs and swords of English officers fell sympathisingly upon the pile." General Cotton says that the conduct of some of the Sepoy office then, and afterwards, was of a highly insubordinate character, and that serious consequences to them would have ensued, "had it been prudent to exhibit such a division in the European element in the eyes of the Native troops and the people of the country."

whilst in this state their opinions are of little value. . . . We are doing well in every district—Becher famously."* 1857. May.

Punishment of Deserters.

But although the Native regiments at Peshawur had been disarmed, they had not been rendered altogether innocuous. Arms on that frontier, though for the most part of a ruder kind than our own, were abundant, and our disciplined Sepoys, fraternising with the border tribes, might have returned to do us grievous injury.† It was, perhaps, too much to expect that the entire body of Sepoys would remain quietly in their Lines; for if the active principle of rebellion were within them, they would be eager to cross the Frontier, and if they were under the pressure of a great panic, confused and bewildered by the blow which had fallen upon them, they would surely believe that it was the design of the English to destroy the soldiers whom they had disarmed. It was scarcely, therefore, to be hoped that at such a time there would be no desertions. But it was necessary at once to arrest these natural impulses to leave the Lines.‡ It was not a time for tenderness—for mercy—even for justice. A stern example was to be made of the first offenders. So the Police were put upon their track, and the tribes were encouraged to arrest the fugitives. Many were brought back, in the firm grip of their supposed friends and confederates—some of them after falling among thieves and being despoiled of all they possessed.

Those were the early days of our great trouble, and Regulation and Routine were still paramount amongst us. The technicalities of the Judge-Advocate had

* Major John Becher of the En- ers, Deputy-Commissioner of the ·eh Division of the Punjab.

† MS. Correspondence.

‡ The desertions were principally from the Fifty-first Regiment.

1857. May 28.

not been dispensed with, and the trial of these deserters, therefore, was conducted with all due ceremony and formality.* Colonel Galloway was President of the Court-Martial assembled by order of General Reed, and the first result was that the Soubahdar Major of the Fifty-first, found guilty of desertion, was sentenced to death; whilst a Havildar and a Sepoy were condemned to short terms of imprisonment. The leniency of these latter sentences provoked Cotton and Edwardes; but the public execution of a high Native officer might still have a good deterring effect. So on the evening of the 28th of May, what was called, in the demi-official language of the time, "an useful timber frame-work" was erected on the parade-ground, and a general parade was ordered for the following morning. "The Soubahdar Major of the Fifty-first was hanged this morning," wrote Edwardes to Nicholson on the 29th, "in presence of all the troops, who behaved well. I occupied the road in rear of Cantonments with Horse and Foot levies, in case the Fifty-first should refuse to attend the parade, as some people expected, in which case General Cotton would have put them to the bayonet."† But soon the "useful timber frame-work" thus called into requisition for the first time at Peshawur was put to larger uses, until the process of suspension became tedious, and convicted offenders were blown from the guns.

Destruction of the Fifty-fifth.

In the meanwhile retribution was overtaking the Fifty-fifth Regiment at Murdan. "An hour hence," wrote Edwardes on the day after the disarming at Peshawur, "a small force of three hundred European Infantry, about two hundred and fifty Cavalry (Native

* The Judge-Advocate said that drum-head courts-martial were "obsolete." It was not long before they were revivified into institutions the present.

† MS. Correspondence.

Irregulars), and eight guns, six of which are howitzers, will march from this Cantonment to the ferry at Dobundee, and thence proceed to-morrow night in one long march to the Fort of Murdan, for the purpose of disarming the Fifty-fifth Native Infantry, which is said to be in a state of mutiny." The expedition was commanded by Colonel Chute of the Seventieth Queen's,* and with it, as political officer, went Colonel John Nicholson, ever eager to be in the thick of the action. It has been already related that the Fifty-fifth had been ordered to relieve the Guide Corps at Hote-Murdan. It had proceeded thither from Nowshera, leaving two companies at the old station under Captain Cameron. There the Queen's Twenty-seventh (Enniskillens) had been stationed with Brougham's battery; but the former had been ordered to Rawul-Pindee, and the latter to Peshawur. And now, with the exception of a little handful of Europeans, who had been placed in charge of the sick and the women and children of the old European garrison, the place was left to the mercy of mutinous Native troops.† The situation was one of extreme danger. But it was manfully confronted by Lieutenant Davies of the Enniskillens, who, having placed his helpless charge in a convenient barrack, drew up his little body of staunch Englishmen, fully accoutred and ready for action, and prepared to meet his assailants. These signs of resistance were too much for the mutineers. Having fired a few random shots from a distance, they made off towards the river, intending to cross by the bridge of boats, and to join their comrades in 1857. May.

* Brigadier Cotton wished himself to go in command, but Edwardes persuaded him to remain at Peshawur, where his services were more needed.

† It should be stated that there was a detachment of the regiment posted on the Attock to guard the ferry at Khyrabad. These men were the first to mutiny.

1857. May 22—24. Hote-Murdan. But Taylor, of the Engineers, with characteristic readiness of resource, broke the bridge, by drawing out the boats in mid-channel, and only a few men made the passage of the river and joined their head-quarters in the course of the night. The rest returned to their Lines, and for a while remained sullen and inactive. But a summons came to them to march to Murdan, and on the night of the 22nd they went thither peaceably under Cameron's command.

They went to swell the tide of treason. There was no doubt of the treachery of the main body of the regiment, although with lip-loyalty it was still deceiving its officers, after the old fashion; and its Colonel, Henry Spottiswoode, who is described as "a devoted soldier, who lived for his regiment," protested that he had "implicit confidence" in his men, and implored Cotton not to act against them. So strong, indeed, was his trust, that even the warnings of some men of his own corps could not shake it. Two hundred Sikhs had been enlisted into the regiment since it had been stationed in the Punjab, and these men now offered, if separated from the rest, to fight the whole of the Hindostanee Sepoys. But Spottiswoode shook his head and declined the offer. He had faith in his children to the last. He would "stake his life on their staunchness;" and he did. On the night of the 24th, the advance of the force from Peshawur was suspected, if not known, by the Sepoys, and the Native officers went to the Colonel for an explanation. Spottiswoode knew the truth of the report but too well. He could answer nothing of an assuring kind, and the deputies went unsatisfied from his presence. Then his heart sunk within him. It was all over. The mutual confidence on which he had relied so much was gone for ever. He could not bear the thought of the future, so left alone in his room he blew out his brains.* 1857. May 25.

As day was breaking on the 25th, Chute's column, having been strengthened by a body of Punjab Infantry under Major Vaughan, came in sight of the Fort of Hote-Murdan. No sooner was their advance discerned from the walls than the Fifty-fifth rose in a body and rushed forth tumultuously, turning their faces towards the hills of Swat. Now that their Colonel was gone, they felt that there was no hope for them. So they went, taking with them their arms, their regimental colours, all the treasure they could seize, and all the ammunition that they could carry with them. Chute sent on a detachment of all arms of his little force, whilst he occupied the Fort with the remainder;† but the mutineers had a long start, and the country was such that our guns could not be brought within range of the fugitives. These things were in their favour. But there was one thing terribly against them. Nicholson was there. His foot in the stirrup, his sword by his side, and a few trusty horsemen behind him, all his old martial instincts, of which civil employment had long denied the gratification, grew strong within him again, and he swept down upon the flying Sepoys with a grand swoop, which nothing could escape or resist. It was said afterwards that the tramp of his war-horse was heard miles off. "Spottiswoode's light-hearted boys," Nicholson in pursuit.

* See an interesting note in Mr. Cave-Browne's book, vol. i., p. 170. Colonel Spottiswoode had served chiefly with the Twenty-first, and had been only for a few months in command of the Fifty-fifth.

† It should be stated that the officers of the Fifty-fifth, with about one hundred and twenty men, came out of the Fort and joined Chute's force. It was doubted whether they were more faithful than the rest. Colonel Edwardes (Official Report) says that they were brought over by the threats and persuasions of their officers.

1857. May 24—26. he wrote to Edwardes on the 24th, "swear that they will die fighting. *Nous allons voir.*" And a day or two later he wrote to the same beloved correspondent saying, "The Fifty-fifth fought determinately, as men, who have no chance of escape but by their own exertions, always do." But the pursuing party killed about a hundred and twenty of the mutineers, captured abcut a hundred and fifty, with the regimental colours, and more than two hundred stands of arms.* The rest took refuge in the Loond-khoor hills. And many of those who fell on that day feil under Nicholson's own strong arm. Of those under him, none fought so well as his own Mounted Police. The men of the Irregular Cavalry only "pretended to act."† "I did not get home till 7 P.M. yesterday," he wrote to Edwardes on the 26th of May, "having been just twenty hours in the saddle, and in the sun the whole day. So you may fancy I was dead beat, and my horse too. He carried me over seventy miles."

If there had been any doubt before as to the man of men—the one, of all others, strong in action and swift in pursuit, by whom desperate work, such as Edwardes had spoken of in Calcutta, was to be done best, the question was now settled. All men saw in this the first of Nicholson's great exploits in

* Colonel Chute to Brigadier Cotton, Murdan, May 26.

† "There were some Irregulars, but they only pretended to act. Captain Law, who commanded a party of the Tenth Irregular Cavalry, got wounded in setting a vain example to his men, one of whom treacherously fired into the Fifth Punjab Infantry. The Fifth, under Major Vaughan, followed as close as infantry could do, and showed an admirable spirit throughout the day."—*Edwardes's Report.* Nicholson wrote that "the casualties in the Tenth Irregular Cavalry the other day were an excellent index of the state and value of the corps."—"These casualties were one European officer, wounded whilst trying to get his men to advance, one Sowar killed, not by the Fifty-fifth, but by Vaughan's men, into whom he treacherously fired."—*MS. Correspondence.*

1857. May.

the mutiny-war, the forerunner of many others of the same stamp. It was a fine thing at that time—nothing finer in the whole history of the War—to mark the enthusiasm with which men, all earnest in the great work before them, rejoiced in the successes of their brethren, and sent forth, one to another, pleasant pæans of encouragement. The chief officers of the Punjab were bound together not merely by the excitement of a common object; the bonds of a common affection were equally strong within them, and each was eager to express his admiration of the good deeds of another. There may have been good fellowship in other provinces, but in none was there such fellowship as this. Men of the stamp of Edwardes and Nicholson, Becher and Lake, James and M'Pherson—all having equal zeal for the public, but not all enjoying equal opportunities, or, perhaps, possessing equal powers, free from all jealousies, all rivalries—were strong in mutual admiration, and were as proud of the exploits of a comrade as of their own. This great raid of John Nicholson stirred the hearts of all men to their depth. Edwardes in letter after letter, in brief but emphatic sentences, had sent him those fine, frank, genial words of hearty commendation, which no man ever uttered more becomingly or more acceptably, and afterwards recorded officially that his friend "with a handful of horsemen hurled himself like a thunderbolt on the route of a thousand mutineers." And John Becher, all a-glow with admiration of the two Peshawur Commissioners, wrote to Edwardes, saying, "I rejoice to see you thus riding on the whirlwind and controlling the storm, and glad amidst the thunder-clouds. Your letter sounds like a clarion-blast full of vigour and self-reliance; and I am proud to see you and Nicholson in this grand

1857. May. storm, masters at your work; right glad that Nicholson did not leave. There was work for his war-horse, and he is in his element—the first who has struck a death-blow. And we may be proud of John Lawrence as a master-spirit in these times."*

June 2. A terrible example was now to be made of the mutineers of the Fifty-fifth. A hundred and twenty Sepoy prisoners were in the hands of the British. They were all liable to the punishment of death. It was not to be doubted that the time had come when the severity of the hour would be the humanity of all time. But these rebels, though taken fighting against their masters, and known to have had murder in their hearts, had not shed the blood of their officers, and there were some amongst them who in the tumult of the hour had been carried away by the multitude without any guilty intent. The voice of mercy, therefore, was lifted up. "I must say a few words for some of the Fifty-fifth prisoners," wrote Nicholson to Edwardes. "The officers of that regiment all concur in stating that the Sikhs were on their side to the last. I would, therefore, temper stern justice with mercy, and spare the Sikhs and young recruits. Blow away all the rest by all means, but spare boys scarcely out of their childhood, and men who were really loyal and respectful up to the moment when they allowed themselves to be carried away in a panic by the mass." And Sir John Lawrence wrote also in the same strain to the Commissioner of Peshawur. "In respect to the mutineers of the Fifty-fifth, they

* Nicholson himself was very anxious that too much credit should not be given to him for this exploit. It was stated in the public prints that he had commanded the expeditionary force from Peshawur, and that he had been twenty hours in pursuit of the enemy; and he requested that it might be explained with equal publicity that Colonel Chute commanded the force, and that he (Nicholson) had been twenty hours in the saddle, but not all that time in pursuit.

were taken fighting against us, and so far deserve little mercy. But, on full reflection, I would not put them all to death. I do not think that we should be justified in the eyes of the Almighty in doing so. A hundred and twenty men are a large number to put to death. Our object is to make an example to terrify others. I think this object would be effectually gained by destroying from a quarter to a third of them. I would select all those against whom anything bad can be shown—such as general bad character, turbulence, prominence in disaffection or in the fight, disrespectful demeanour to their officers during the few days before the 26th, and the like. If these did not make up the required number, I would then add to them the oldest soldiers. All these should be shot or blown away from guns, as may be most expedient. The rest I would divide into batches: some to be imprisoned ten years, some seven, some five, some three. I think that a sufficient example will then be made, and that these distinctions will do good, and not harm. The Sepoys will see that we punish to deter, and not for vengeance. Public sympathy will not be on the side of the sufferers. Otherwise, they will fight desperately to the last, as feeling certain that they must die."* 1857. June.

And in these opinions, equally politic and merciful, the military authorities concurred; indeed, there was at one time some talk of suffering those men of the Fifty-fifth, who had not actually committed themselves, to retain their arms, and even of rewarding the best of them. But subsequent investigation proved that the Hindostanees who had not left the Fort owed their immunity from actual crime rather to accident than to loyal design; so they were discharged without pay,

* MS. Correspondence.

1857. June 10. and sent beyond the Indus, whilst the Sikhs, who had made gallant offer of service, were left with their arms in their hands, and drafted into other regiments.

Then came the stern work of retribution. On the 3rd of June, twelve deserters of the Fifty-first had been hanged; and now on the 10th, the parade-ground of the Eighty-seventh Queen's, on which the gallows had been permanently erected, witnessed another scene of execution still more ghastly in its aspect. The fugitives from Hote-Murdan had all been sentenced to death. A hundred and twenty criminals had been condemned to be blown away from our guns. But the recommendations of the Chief Commissioner had tempered the severity of the sentence, and only one-third of the number had been marked for execution. Forty prisoners were brought out manacled and miserable to that dreadful punishment-parade. The whole garrison of Peshawur was drawn up, forming three sides of a square, to witness the consummation of the sentence. The fourth side was formed by a deadly array of guns. Thousands of outsiders had poured in from the surrounding country to be spectators of the tremendous ceremony—all curious, many doubtful, some perhaps malignantly eager for an outbreak, to be followed by the collapse of British ascendancy. The pieces of the Europeans were loaded. The officers, in addition to their regulation arms, had for the most part ready to their clutch what was now becoming an institution—the many-barreled revolver pistol. The issue was doubtful, and our people were prepared for the worst.

Under a salute from one of the batteries, the Brigadier-General appeared on parade. Having ridden along the fronts of the great human square, he ordered the sentence to be read. And this done, the grim ceremony commenced. The forty selected malefactors were executed at the mouth of the guns.* No man lifted a hand to save them. The Native troops on parade bore themselves with steadiness, as under a great awe, and when orders went forth for the whole to march past in review order, armed and unarmed alike were obedient to the word of command. To our newly-raised levies and to the curious on-lookers from the country, the whole spectacle was a marvel and a mystery. It was a wonderful display of moral force, and it made a deep and abiding impression. There was this great virtue in it, that however unintelligible the process by which so great a result had been achieved, it was easy to understand the fact itself. The English had conquered, and were masters of the position. Perhaps some of the most sagacious and astute of the spectators of that morning's work said to each other, or to themselves, as they turned their faces homeward, that the English had conquered because they were not afraid. The strength, indeed, imparted to our cause by the disarming-parade of the 24th of May had been multiplied ten-fold by the punishment-parade of the 10th of June. And it is hard to say how many lives—the lives of men of all races—were saved by the seeming severity of this early execution.

1857. June 10.

Among the rude people of the border the audacity thus displayed by the English in the face of pressing danger excited boundless admiration. They had no longer any misgivings with respect to the superiority

* It is a significant fact that neither Sir Herbert Edwardes, in his Official Peshawur Report, nor Sir Sydney Cotton in his published Narrative, says one word about this punishment-parade. And what these brave men, being eye-witnesses of the horror, shrunk from describing, I may well abstain from dwelling on in detail. There is no lack, however, of particulars, all ghastly and some grotesque, in the cotemporary letters before me.

1857. June 10. of a race that could do such great things, calmly and coolly, and with all the formality of an inspection-parade. The confidence in our power, which the disbandment of the Native regiments had done so much to revive, now struck deep root in the soil. Free offers of allegiance continued to come in from the tribes. Feeling now that the English were masters of the situation, their avarice was kindled, and every man who had a matchlock or a tulwar, or, better still, a horse to bring to the muster, came forward with his tender of service to the British officers at Peshawur. The difficulties and perplexities of the crisis could not obscure the humours of this strange recruiting. Herbert Edwardes, who was the life and soul of every movement at that time, has himself sketched its comic aspects with an almost Hogarthian fidelity of detail.* But this passed, whilst every week developed more strikingly its serious results. For, as the month of June advanced, and news came that the English had not retaken Delhi, and across the border went from mouth to mouth the rumour of the fiery crescent, there was increasing danger that Mussulman fanaticism might prevail over all else, and that a religious war once proclaimed, it would be impossible to control the great tide of Mahomedanism that would pour itself down from the North. If in that hour the English had been weak at Peshawur, they might have been overwhelmed. But much as those wild Moslems loved Mahomed, they loved money more, and when they saw that we were strong, they clung to us, as the wiser policy.

The end of the Fifty-fifth may be narrated here.

* See the Peshawur Mutiny Report, especially paragraph 66, which will be found entire in the Appendix.

Even more deplorable than the fate of these men, thus suddenly brought face to face with ignominious death, was the doom impending over their comrades, who had escaped from Nicholson's pursuing horsemen across the border into Swat. There they found the country rent by intestine feuds; almost, indeed, in the throes of a revolution. The temporal and spiritual chiefs—the Padshah and the Akhoond—were at strife with one another. The mutineers took themselves and their arms to the former, but he had no money to pay them, and our sleek, well-fed Hindostanees soon discovered that they had committed a grievous blunder. In a little while the body of their leader—the self-made shattered corpse of a white-bearded Soubahdar—was floating down the river under the walls of Nowshera, and his followers, disappointed and destitute, were turning their faces towards the country of the Rajah of Cashmere, sick of Mussulman fanaticism, and hoping to excite sympathy and obtain service under a Rajpoot government. These poor deluded Hindoos, who had abandoned pay, pension, peace, everything that was dear to them, under a blind besetting belief in the bigotry of their Christian masters, now found themselves breast-high in the bitter waters of Mahomedan persecution.* They had escaped the chimera of a greased cartridge to be despoiled of their sacred threads and circumcised. They had fled from a random rumour to confront a revolting reality. And now they were fain to go skulking along the border, taking their gaunt bodies and tattered garments to any place of refuge open to them, seeking rest, but finding none; for as they huddled

1857 June.

* Mr. Cave-Browne says that "many a sleek Brahmin was made a compulsory Mahomedan, doomed to servile offices in their musjids; others were sold for slaves. Rumour has it that one fat old Soubahdar was sold for four annas (sixpence)."

1857. June. along the Hazareh border, stumbling through rocky defiles, more inhospitable than their Mahomedan persecutors, John Becher raised the friendly clans to hunt them out like vermin. Then their misery was at its height. Hungry and naked and footsore, it was death to them to move, it was death to them to remain still. Another venerable Soubahdar set an example of suicide to his followers by shooting himself, declaring that it was better to die at once than to perish slowly by starvation. Becher himself has told with rare force of language how first one detachment then another was assisted by friendly Kohistanees and others, whose services he had most sagaciously enlisted, until the whole were either destroyed or brought prisoners into our camp.* Then came the last scene of all, in which the Gibbet and the Guns were the chief actors. On the very outskirts of civilisation, where only a few Englishmen were gathered together, the last of "Spottiswoode's light-hearted fellows" paid the penalty of their folly

* See Major Becher's published report—Punjab Mutiny Papers. In a private letter to Edwardes (July 1) he gives a graphic description of the flight of the Sepoys and the raising of the border clans. "After making a march," he said, "in the direction of Khagan, they turned back and went by the more difficult road through the Kohistan, along the Indus to Chilass, and with faces towards Ghiljet, or some other portion of Cashmere, as to the promised land of safety. One of their officers shot himself at the prospect; one or two have died already; several are very ill. They have no carriage and are rather hungry. . . . . The road is very difficult even for men of the country. They have no shelter, and I believe that very few can escape; besides which, the Maharajah Gholab Singh has moved a regiment to his Ghiljet frontier, and swears he will polish off every man he meets. He has also warned the Goojurs and people of the country to pay them off. I have had several messengers who have seen them. They are mostly Hindoos. Looking naked as they do, the women and children throw stones at them and cry, 'Out on you, black Kaffirs without decency!' And they were shocked by the habits which they witnessed in the early morning. The people of Pucklee and Hazara have come forth like spirits at my bidding. I have been deluged with clansmen, and our camp is very picturesque. . . . I have received satisfactory assurances from all our border chiefs. If the Syuds of Khagan had not, like good men and true, manned their front, I think the Sepoys would have tried an easier route; but then again they would have found men of Gholab Singh's ready at Mozufferabad."—*MS. Correspondence.*

or their crime. One party after another of the fugitives was brought in, tried by a military court and sentenced to death; and they were hung up, or blown away, on some commanding ground, to be a warning and a terror to others. Brave and sullen they went to their doom, asking only to die like soldiers at the cannon's mouth, not as dogs in the noose of the gibbet. Little less than two hundred men were executed at that time in the Hazareh country. "Thus, hunted down to the last like wild beasts, was consummated the miserable fate of the Fifty-fifth Regiment, and thus they afforded a salutary example to other mutinous regiments, by proving the far reach of our power, and that there was no refuge even beyond our border."* If any had not been thus hunted out, their fate was perhaps worse than that of the executed malefactors, for they were sold into slavery, and compelled to apostatise for their lives.

1857. June.

Alarms on the Frontier.

Elsewhere, however, were ominous symptoms upon the Frontier. Nicholson, since his great raid against the fugitives of the Fifty-fifth, had been still in the field, and he had frequently written to Edwardes that the Mussulman chiefs on the border were eagerly watching the progress of events, and encouraging the rebellion of our Native soldiery; who, at the same time, had been making overtures to them. There was, too, a notorious outlaw, named Ajoon Khan, who was believed to be intriguing with our troops at Abazye, a fortress on the banks of the Swat River, and Nicholson was eager to make a swoop upon him.†

* Major Becher's Report.

† This uneasy feeling on the frontier had been of long standing. See the following significant passage in Mr. Forsyth's Mutiny Report: "Of the causes which led to this

1857. May 26. "The game is becoming nicer and more complicated," he had written on the 26th of May from Murdan, "Ajoon Khan has come down to Prangar, and it is generally believed that he has done so at the instigation of our troops there. This does not seem improbable. There is no doubt that for some time past emissaries (mostly Moollahs) from the Hills had been going backwards and forwards between the Fifty-fifth Native Infantry here and certain parties in their own country." Four days

May 30. afterwards, he wrote from Omurzye, saying: "We are just starting for Abazye. I will let you know this evening whether I recommend the disarming of the Sixty-fourth Native Infantry. I am strongly inclined to believe that we should not merely disarm but disband that corps, and the Tenth Irregular Cavalry. There is no doubt that they have both been in communication with the Akhoond of Swat. . . . . If the disarming of both or either corps be determined upon, we can do it very well from here, without troubling the Peshawur troops. I believe we did not pitch into the Fifty-fifth one day too soon. That corps and the Sixty-fourth were all planning to go over to the Akhoond together. I have got a man who taunted my police on the line of march with siding with infidels in a religious war. May I hang him?"

rebellion it is not for me to speak, but I cannot refrain from recording one fact, which was not without significance. In August, 1856, a letter from the Akhoond of Swat, addressed to Futteh Khan, of Pindee Gheb, was brought to me at Rawul-Pindee. Among much other news, the writer stated that the Mahomedans of Lucknow had written to Dost Mahomed, informing him that Oude had been taken by the British, and that as they supposed that Hyderabad would follow, there would soon be no stronghold of Islam left in Hindostan, and unless some effort were made the cause of true believers would be lost. In the event of the Mahomedans of Oude entering on any plan, they wished to know what aid they might expect from the Dost. The sagacious reply to this observation was stated by the writer to be, 'What will be remains to be seen.'"

On the following day Nicholson wrote from Abazye, saying: "We arrived here all right yesterday, and found the Sixty-fourth looking very villainous, but of course perfectly quiet. They have been talking very disloyally both to the Ghilzyes" (men of the Khelat-i-Ghilzye Regiment) "and people of the country, and the former have ceased to associate with them. The latter have been rather hoping for a row, in the midst of which they may escape paying revenue." What he saw was quite enough to convince him that it would be well to do the work at once. Approval had come from Cotton, from Edwardes, and from Lawrence. So a detachment of Europeans, with some Punjabee details and some guns of Brougham's battery, the whole under that officer, were sent to disarm the companies at Shubkudder, and afterwards those at Michnee, whilst the force at Abazye was being dealt with by other components of Chute's column. The teeth of the Sixty-fourth were drawn without difficulty. But the annihilation of the Tenth Irregular Cavalry was reserved for another day. Nicholson recommended that no action should be taken against the Irregulars until tidings of the fall of Delhi should have reached the Punjab. He little thought how remote was this event at the beginning of June; that long months were yet to wear away in unsuccessful efforts to accomplish the great object for which the Punjab was pouring out so much of its military strength. And others were of the same sanguine temper all over the Province—fortunately, for this faith, strong though delusive, sustained them, and they worked with better heart and greater vigour for holding fast to the lie.

1857. June.

There was now no further service for Chute's column to perform. So it marched back to Peshawur,

1857. June 10. and Nicholson rode on in advance of it, to resume his political duties. On the 10th of June, Edwardes welcomed his friend and fellow-workman with warm congratulations on his success. "Nicholson came in from Abazye this morning," he wrote to Sir John Lawrence, "looking rather the worse for exposure; and we have been going over the batta question, &c., with the General, and have decided to say nothing about it till Delhi falls, and then to disarm the Tenth Irregular Cavalry, and exempt from the abolition of batta the Twenty-first Native Infantry, the Khelat-i-Ghilzye Regiment, and the Seventeenth and Eighteenth Irregular Cavalry, if they keep quiet." And in the same letter he wrote to the Chief Commissioner, saying, "What a terrible job is the going off of those three regiments from Jullundhur and Phillour towards Delhi!" It was a source of sore distress and dire aggravation to Edwardes and Nicholson that, whilst they had been doing so much for the defence of the province and the maintenance of the honour of the nation, others were throwing away every chance that came in their way, and by their weakness and indecision suffering the enemy to escape.

Mutiny at Jullundhur. For in other parts of the province there was not always that glorious audacity which secures success by never doubting its attainment. In the first week of June, the Sepoy regiments at Jullundhur, whom, as we have already seen, Brigadier Johnstone had not disarmed in May, were swelling with sedition and ripe for revolt. Major Edward Lake, who, in early youth, had shared with Herbert Edwardes the distinction of striking the first blow at the Mooltanee insurgents of '49, was Commissioner of the Jullundhur division. He had been absent on circuit when the events occurred which have been detailed in a previous chapter,* but before the end of the month he had returned to Head-Quarters, had closely observed the temper of the Sepoys, and had been convinced that they were only waiting an opportunity to break into open rebellion. He strongly counselled, therefore, the disarming of the regiments. But there was no Cotton at Jullundhur. The Sepoy commandants shook their heads after their wonted fashion; and the Brigadier, tossed hither and thither by wild conflicts of doubt, at last subsided into inaction. Events were left to develope themselves, and they did so with all possible advantage to the mutineers. On the night of the 7th of June, the Native battalions—two regiments of Foot and one of Horse—inaugurated a general rising by setting fire to the house of the Colonel of the Queen's regiment. In a little while the Lines were all astir with the sights and sounds of open mutiny; and the officers were making their way to the parade-grounds, whilst women and children, in wild excitement, were hurrying to the appointed place of refuge. It is not easy to describe the uproar and confusion which made the midnight hideous, nor to explain the reason why, in the presence of an European regiment and a troop of European Artillery, the insurgents were allowed to run riot in unrestrained revolt. The incidents of the rising were of the common type. They were not distinguished by any peculiar atrocities. It seems that there was a general understanding among the Sepoys that on a given day they should set their faces towards Delhi. As a body, they did not lust for the blood of

1857. June.

June 7.

* *Ante*, pp. 427-28.

1857. June 7. their officers; but in the excitement of the moment, murderous blows were dealt. Adjutant Bagshawe, of the Thirty-sixth Regiment—a gallant officer and a good man—was mortally wounded whilst endeavouring to rally a party of his Sepoys. The death-blow did not come from one of his own men, but from a trooper who "rode up and shot him." Other officers were wounded in the confusion of the hour; houses were burnt, and property was destroyed. But there were instances of fidelity and attachment on the part of the Sepoys; men came forward staunchly and devotedly to save the lives of their officers. And altogether there were the usual contradictions and anomalies, which, more or less all over the country, seemed to indicate the general half-heartedness of the Sepoy revolt.

It was obviously the intention of the Jullundhur Brigade to pick up the long-wavering regiment at Phillour, and then for the whole to march on to Delhi.* A trooper of the Cavalry galloped forward in advance of the rebel force to give the Third the earliest tidings of their approach. The conduct of the last-named corps appears to be inscrutable, except upon the hypothesis of a long-cherished design, and that patient, sturdy resistance of all immediate

* I find the following in the Punjab Mutiny Papers. It seems to leave little doubt with respect to the foregone design: "These intentions were by chance divulged by a wounded Havildar of the Third Native Infantry to an officer, who found him concealed at Homayoon's tomb, after the capture of Delhi. This information was given without any attempt at palliation or reserve. . . . . It was from the lips of a man who knew his end was near, and conveyed the impression of truth to its hearer; it is, moreover, borne out by known facts and circumstances. It was, strictly, that all the troops in the Jullunder Doab had agreed to rise simultaneously; a detachment from Jullunder was to go over to Hooshiarpore, to fetch away the Thirty-third Native Infantry, failing which the Thirty-third were to remain (and they did so); then their arrival at Phillour was to be the signal for the Third to join, when all were to proceed to Delhi, facing the river as best they could."—*Report of Mr. Ricketts.*

temptations, which seems in many instances to have distinguished the behaviour of men waiting for an appointed day and a given signal. The Third, that might have done us such grievous injury when the siege-train was in its grasp, now that the time had come, cast in its lot with the Jullundhur mutineers, and swept on towards the city of the King. It is one of the worst disgraces of the war that these Jullúndhur regiments were ever suffered to reach Phillour. There was no lack of men eager to pursue the mutineers; but the one word from the one responsible authority was not spoken until all orders might as well have been given to the winds. The mutineers had done their work and marched out of cantonments by one o'clock in the morning, and not until seven was the word given for the advance of the pursuing column. The extreme consideration of Brigadier Johnstone for his European troops was such that he waited until the fierce June sun had risen—waited until the commissariat was not ready—waited until the enemy had escaped.* The pursuers marched out and marched back again, never having seen the enemy at all.

1857. June 8.

The history of the so-called pursuit appears to be this. In the course of the day, there being a vague impression that Phillour might be in danger, Olpherts, with two of his guns, carrying a small party

* I give this on the authority of Brigadier Johnstone, who himself says: "The pursuit of the mutineers commenced before seven o'clock of the morning following the night of the outbreak. It could not have been undertaken earlier. The direction taken by the rebels was not ascertained till half-past three o'clock. Preparations had to be made in obtaining carriage for the infantry, providing rations, &c., perfecting the equipment for guns, horses, &c., and these, after the utmost despatch of officers, as ready and zealous as men could be, were found impossible to be completed at an earlier hour. The complaint of one writer I understand is, that the haste of departure in pursuit was so great, that the Infantry had to march without rations and other comforts, which is true," &c. &c.—*Letter to Lahore Chronicle.*

1857. June 8. of the Eighth Queen's on their carriages, and accompanied by the Second Punjab Cavalry, pushed on to that place, where they found that the officers of the Third had escaped into the Fort, and that the Sepoys were crossing the river at a ferry some four miles distant. After a while, the main body of the troops from Jullundhur came up, and then the question arose as to whether anything could be done. Those who would fain have done something, did not know what to do, and those who knew what should be done, were not minded to do it. No one from Jullundhur knew the way from Phillour to the Sutlej, and the Phillour officers, shut up in the Fort, sent out no one to guide them. So the result was that no one did anything, and the pursuing column bivouacked bravely for the night. It is understood that the highest military authorities were convinced that Brigadier Johnstone had done his duty nobly—but History and the Horse Guards are often at issue.

Ricketts and Thornton. Such, however, are the alternations of light and shadow in this narrative, that the narrator has never to tarry long without an example of that activity of British manliness which saved the Empire in this great convulsion. Whilst the Jullundhur Brigadier was thus earning the approbation of the highest military authorities, two junior civilians, acting only on their own impulses, were doing their best to cut off the march of the mutineers. One of these was a young gentleman named Thornton, who had been one of the first to enter the service by the open door of general competition, and who seemed to be bent on proving that the reproach levelled at the new order of civilians—that they were men of books, not men of action—was unfounded and unjust. He had ridden over from Loodhianah to Phillour to pay the regiment there, had learnt that the troops had risen, and had pushed on with all haste to the river-bank and cut away the bridge of boats. Hurrying then back to Loodhianah, he found that Mr. Ricketts, the Deputy-Commissioner, had received by telegraph information of the rising at Jullundhur, and was already making such preparations as he could for the security of that important post. Lying on the great high road from the Punjab to Hindostan, it was to be assumed that the mutineers would sweep through it, carrying destruction with them, on their route to the appointed goal of Delhi. Little was it that Ricketts could have done in any case, but that little was made less by the fact that the news of the Jullundhur rising reached the Sepoys at Loodhianah almost as soon as it had reached himself, and they were not less prompt in action. Those Sepoys were a detachment of the Third from Phillour. They were waiting for the signal and ready to strike. Their first movement was to seize the Fort and the Treasury. There were no European troops, so this was easily accomplished. The situation was one of infinite peril. The mutineers from Jullundhur and Phillour might be expected at any hour. But the Sutlej was still between them, and if Ricketts could guard the passages of the river only for a little space, the pursuing column might come upon the fugitives before they had crossed. Fortunately, the Fourth (Rothney's) Sikh Regiment had reached Loodhianah that morning after a long and weary march. Three companies, under Lieutenant Williams, were now told off for service, and the Rajah of Nabha was called upon for a Contingent. The chief sent detachments of Horse and Foot, with two six-pounder guns, and with these Ricketts went out to dispute the passage of the river.

1857. June.

1857. June 8. The first thing was to ascertain the exact position of the enemy. So Ricketts, crossing the river in a ferry-boat, walked along the opposite bank to Phillour, and there learnt that the insurgents, having been baulked by Thornton's destruction of the bridge, had made for a Ghaut, some four miles higher up, at a narrow bend of the stream, and were preparing for the passage of the Sutlej.* Possessed of this important information, the gallant civilian recrossed the river, rejoined the detachment, and, in concert with Lieutenant Williams, made his arrangements to check the advance of the mutinous regiments. Had Johnstone, with the Europeans, been in pursuit of the mutineers, the enemy would have been between two fires, and the bulk of them would have been destroyed. But the Brigadier made no sign; and so Ricketts and Williams had all the work and all the glory to themselves. It was ten o'clock at night when they came within sight of the Sepoy regiments. The road was bad, the sand deep, the ditches numerous. Their guides had misled and deserted them, and much good time had been lost. The main body of the enemy, some sixteen hundred in number,† had already crossed, and our little handful of Sikh troops now came suddenly upon them. Ricketts, who improvised himself into a Commandant of Artillery, took charge of the guns, and Williams directed the movements of the Cavalry and Infantry. The guns were at once unlimbered, but the horses of one of them took fright and fled, carrying the six-pounder with them.

* "At the Lussam Ferry, four miles above Phillour, the advanced guard of the mutineers managed to seize a boat that was on the Jullundhur side, and crossing over in numbers, took possession of the other side also."—*Mr. Barnes's Report.*

† "The greater part of three regiments of Infantry and one regiment of Cavalry, but without guns."

The other gun, a nine-pounder, was well served, and before the enemy knew that we were upon them, it delivered a round of grape with good effect, whilst at the same time Williams's Sikhs poured in two destructive volleys. The mutineers returned the fire, and then the Nabha troops turned their backs upon the scene and fled like a flock of sheep. For some time the unequal contest was nobly maintained. Round after round from the one gun was poured in so rapidly and so steadily, that practised ears in Johnstone's camp, on the other side of the river, thought that they discerned the utterances of two or three field-pieces; whilst at the same time the Sikhs, spreading themselves out so as not to be outflanked by superior numbers, poured in volley after volley with destructive effect. But gallant as were these efforts, they could not last. During well-nigh two hours they kept back the surging multitude of the enemy; but then the gun ammunition was expended. The cartridges of the Sikhs had been nearly fired away; Williams had fallen, shot through the lungs; and the midnight moon revealed, with dangerous distinctness, the position of our little band. There was nothing, therefore, left for Ricketts but to draw off his force and return to the British Cantonment.

1857. June 8—9.

Rising at Loodhianah. June 9.

Then the mutinous regiments, no longer obstructed or opposed, swept on to Loodhianah. About an hour before noon, on the 9th of June, they entered the city. The company in the Fort fraternised with them. The turbulent classes rose at once, scenting a rich harvest of rapine, and for a little while disorder and destruction were rampant in the place. There were some peculiar elements in the population of Loodhianah from which danger was ever likely to

1857. June 9. flash out in seasons of general excitement.* Large numbers of aliens were there. Foremost amongst these were the Caubul refugees—the miserable incapables of the Suddozye Family, with their swarms of dissolute retainers—all eating the bread of British compassion, but hating the hand that fed them. Then there was the great colony of Cashmere shawl-weavers, who, sheltered and protected as they never could have been elsewhere, followed their peaceful calling unmolested, and held their gains in the most perfect security. Both of these classes now rose against us with a vehemence proportioned to the benefits they had received. The Caubulees were "conspicuous in the outrages and plunder committed in the city;" and the Cashmerees were among the foremost in "plundering the Government stores, in pillaging the premises of the American Mission, in burning the churches and buildings, in destroying the printing presses, and in pointing out the residences of Government officials, or known well-wishers of Government, as objects of vengeance for the mutinous troops." Besides these, there were large numbers of Mahomedan Goojurs, who had been wrought up to a high state of fanaticism by the preachings of an energetic Moulavee, and who were eager to declare a *jehad* † against us. All these persons now welcomed the mutineers, and aided them in the work of spoliation. The prisoners in the gaol were released. Whatsoever belonged to Government—whatsoever belonged to Englishmen—was destroyed, if it could not be carried off; the quiet, trading communities were

* "It is filled with a dissolute, lawless, mixed population of Caubul pensioners, Cashmere shawl-workers, Goojurs, Bowreahs, and other predatory races. There is a fort without Europeans to guard it, a city without regular troops to restrain, a district traversed by roads in every direction . . . a river which for months in the year is a mere net-work of fordable creeks."

† Holy war.

compelled to contribute to the wants of the mutineers in money or in kind; grain and flour were carried off from the bunniahs' shops; and, wherever a horse or a mule could be found, the rebel hand was laid instantly upon it. It was too much to expect that these traders, how much soever they may have benefited by British rule and profited by the maintenance of order, should take any active steps to aid the authorities in such a crisis. The bankers secreted their money-bags, and the merchants locked up their wares, and every man did what he thought best for himself in the face of the general confusion. 1857. June 9.

Escape of the Mutineers.

And what was Johnstone doing all this time? Johnstone was playing out with admirable effect another act of the great tragedy of "Too Late." The Europeans had heard the firing of the preceding night, and had waited eagerly for the order to move, but no order came. Three hours after Ricketts's one gun had been silenced by want of ammunition, Henry Olpherts, with his splendid troop of Horse Artillery, and a party of the Eighth Foot, was suffered to go through the ceremony of taking command of the "advance" of the force that was to march to the rescue of Loodhianah and to the extermination of the Jullundhur mutineers. But no sooner were they ready to move than fresh misgivings assailed the mind of the Brigadier. It would not be "safe" to send forward such a force without adequate supports. In vain Ricketts sent expresses to Johnstone's Camp, urging him to send forward the Horse Artillery to his aid; but the day wore on, the succours never came, and the enemy rioted unchecked in Loodhianah until nightfall.* Then the insurgent regi-

* "In the mean time no troops arrived in pursuit. I sent twice, begging the Horse Artillery might advance, and they might have caused them (the mutineers) immense loss; but they could not be trusted to the

1857. June. ments made a forced march towards Delhi, and when at last our Europeans made their appearance at Loodhianah, pursuit was hopeless. The Jullundhur insurgents had escaped.

The evil, which had been thus done or suffered by our inertness, was small in comparison with the danger which had been escaped. It was the true policy of the enemy, at that time, to occupy Loodhianah. With the Fort in their possession—guns mounted and manned, the Government treasure in their hands, and the bulk of the population on their side—they might, for a while at least, have successfully defied us. To the British cause, the loss of this important city, lying on the great high road from the Punjab to Delhi, would, indeed, have been a heavy blow. It would have affected disastrously, perhaps ruinously, the future operations of the war, by deferring indefinitely the capture of Delhi. But instead of this, the mutinous regiments merely carried themselves off, by the least frequented routes, to the Great Head-Quarters of Rebellion, there to swell the already swollen numbers of the garrison, without increasing its actual strength.*

Fourth Sikhs or the small detachment of Punjab Cavalry, and had to wait for the European Infantry; and so this second great opportunity to destroy these mutineers was lost, and as they had four miles' start of the European Infantry, of course pursuit was hopeless that evening."—*Ricketts.*

* "I imagine their plan was temporarily to hold the Fort and City of Loodhianah, where they could command the Grand Trunk Road from the Punjab to Delhi, whence they could have spread disorganisation throughout Cis-Sutlej, and have shaken the Sikh States, and by cutting off supplies and placing troops in requisition to attack them, have made a most untoward diversion for our small force before Delhi; but their ammunition was expended; in their hurry in leaving Jullundhur they had carried off blank for balled ammunition, and so they had to hurry on by forced marches, avoiding any possibility of collision with our troops."—*Mr. Ricketts's Report.* The writer admits that this is for the most part conjecture, but he thinks that it is borne out by the fact that, if their ammunition had not failed them, the mutineers had the game in their own hands. I have had no opportunity of investigating the hypothesis that the Jullundhur regiments supplied themselves with blank cartridges by mistake.

It was now necessary to make a severe example of all who had been guilty of aiding and abetting the mutinous Sepoys, or who had taken advantage of the confusion which they had created. It was easy to bring the guilt home to the offenders, for plundered property was found in their possession; and now that English authority had reasserted itself in all its strength, witnesses flocked in from all sides, eager to give damnatory evidence against their fellow-citizens. More than twenty Cashmerees and others were promptly tried, and as promptly executed. The telegraphic wires brought from higher official quarters the necessary confirmation of the sentence of death, and on the evening of their trial the prisoners were hanged. Others detected in seditious correspondence shared the same fate. "It was by such measures as these," wrote the Commissioner of the Cis-Sutlej States, "that the peace was preserved; any vacillation or tender-heartedness would have been fatal, for rebellion would have spread in the province, and many valuable lives would have been lost in recovering our authority. So long as order was maintained here, our communications with the Punjab on the one hand, and the Delhi force on the other, were kept unimpaired; as it was, with daily convoys of treasure, ammunition, stores, and men passing down the road, I am happy to say that not a single accident occurred." 1857. June

The next step was to disarm the people of Loodhianah. Taking advantage of the presence of Coke's regiment, which afterwards made good its march to Delhi, Ricketts disarmed the town of Loodhianah. And in other parts of the Cis-Sutlej States the same process was carried on with the zeal, vigour, and success that distinguished all the efforts of the officers

1857. June—July. of the Punjabee Commission. But, doubtless, as on former occasions, of which I have spoken, there were many concealments, even in our own territories; and, moreover, the contiguity of the Protected Native States afforded opportunities of evading the search, to which the people on the border eagerly resorted. Mr. Barnes called upon the chiefs to adopt similar measures, and they formally complied; but he said that they were slow to move and suspicious of our intentions.* There was, in truth, a general feeling of mistrust; and it was presently ascertained that the people were not only concealing arms, but making large purchases of saltpetre and sulphur, and other components of gunpowder, for use in a day of danger. It was all in accordance with their genius and their temper, and it could excite no surprise in any reasonable mind. But it was necessary to grapple with these evils; so proclamation was made, rendering the carrying of arms a misdemeanor, and restrictions upon the sale and export of all kinds of ammunition and their components.†

Whilst preventive and precautionary measures of this kind were being pushed forward throughout the Punjab, there were unceasing efforts all along the great road to Delhi to furnish the means of transporting stores for the service of Barnard's army. In this most essential work civil and military officers worked manfully together; and although there were many difficulties to be overcome, the great thoroughfare

* Mr. Barnes's Cis-Sutlej Report.

† At this time communication between Calcutta and the Punjab was very slow and irregular, and tidings of the legislative enactments passed in Calcutta had not yet reached the Frontier Province. But Mr. Barnes, writing at a later period, observed, "That in the measures adopted for the trial and punishment of mutineers and heinous criminals, or for disarming the population, or checking the importation of military stores, we only anticipated the acts almost simultaneously passed at Calcutta by the wisdom of the Legislative Council."

was soon alive with carts and carriages and beasts of burden conveying downwards all that was most needed by the Army, and especially those vast supplies of ordnance ammunition which were required to make an impression on the walls of the city which we were besieging.* It is hard to say what might not have befallen us if, at this time, the road had not been kept open; but the loyalty of the great chiefs of the Protected Sikh States, and the energy and sagacity of Barnes and Ricketts, secured our communications, and never was the Delhi Field Force in any danger of the interception of its supplies.† 1857. June—July.

Thus was the Punjab aiding in many ways the great work of the recovery of Delhi and the suppression of the revolt. It was sending down material, and it was sending down masses of men. Nor was this all that it could do. The Punjab had become the Nursery of Heroes. And it was from the Punjab that now was to be drawn that wealth of individual energy upon which the destinies of nations so greatly

* To the activity of Captain Briggs, who organised a military transport train, and worked it with admirable success, we are mainly indebted for these good results. But we are a little too prone to forget such services as these, or, perhaps, we undervalue the importance of feeding an army and loading its guns.

† These services were afterwards becomingly acknowledged by General Wilson, who wrote to Sir John Lawrence, saying: "I beg to bring specially to your notice the very important services rendered by the Commissioner of the Cis-Sutlej States, Mr. G. C. Barnes, to whose good government, under yourself, may be partly attributed the preservation of peace in these districts, and to whose influence with the independent chiefs I am mainly indebted for the valuable aid of the Puteeala and Jheend Contingents, by means of which our communication with our rear has been kept open, and the safe escort of numerous convoys of stores and ammunition to the camp has been effected; and his most energetic assistant, Mr. G. H. Ricketts, the Deputy-Commissioner of Loodhianah, of whose unflagging exertions in procuring carriage, aiding the movements of troops, and forwarding supplies, and of his hearty co-operation with the magazine officer in the despatch of ammunition, I am deeply sensible, and cannot speak too highly."

1857. June. depend. Death had made its gaps in the Delhi Army. The death of General Anson sent General Reed down to the Head-Quarters of the Army as Senior Officer in the Presidency, and, therefore, Provisional Commander-in-Chief. Who then was to command the Frontier Force? For some little time there was a terror in the Peshawur Council lest Brigadier Johnstone, who had smoothed the way for the safe conduct of his Native troops to Delhi, should be appointed to the command of the division. It could not be permitted whilst Sydney Cotton was there. Little by little regulation was giving way to the exigencies of a great crisis; and when news came that the Adjutant-General of the Army had been killed in the battle of Budlee-ka-serai, there was a demand for the services of Neville Chamberlain as the fittest man in the country to be Chief of the Staff of the besieging Force. So Nicholson was "instinctively selected to take command of the Punjab Movable Column, with the rank of Brigadier-General,"* whilst Chamberlain proceeded downwards to join the Head-Quarters of the Army. What Barnard and his troops were doing it is now my duty to narrate.

* These words are in Colonel Edwardes's Official Report. The writer adds: "How common sense revenges itself on defective systems, when real danger assails a state! Had there been no struggle for life or death, when would Neville Chamberlain and John Nicholson, in the prime of their lives, with all their faculties of doing and enduring, have attained the rank of Brigadier-General? Why should we keep down in peace the men who must be put up in War?"

CHAPTER IV.

GENERAL BARNARD'S POSITION—IMPORTANCE OF THE CAPTURE OF DELHI—DELHI AND ITS ENVIRONS—QUESTION OF AN IMMEDIATE ASSAULT—COUNCILS OF WAR—ABANDONMENT OF THE NIGHT ATTACK—WAITING FOR REINFORCEMENTS—ENGAGEMENTS WITH THE ENEMY—THE CENTENARY OF PLASSEY—ARRIVAL OF NEVILLE CHAMBERLAIN AND BAIRD SMITH—DEATH OF GENERAL BARNARD.

June, 1857

The British position at Delhi.

THE Delhi Field Force having planted its Head-Quarters on the old site of the British Cantonments on the "Ridge," was now spreading itself out over the ground which it had conquered, in the manner best adapted to both offensive and defensive operations. Seldom has a finer position been occupied by a British Army; seldom has a more magnificent panorama turned for a while the soldier's thoughts from the stern realities of the battle. It was difficult not to admire the beauty of the scene even amidst the discomforts of the camp and the labours of the first encamping. The great city, with its stately mosques and minarets, lay grandly at our feet, one side resting upon the Jumna, and others forming a mighty mass of red walls standing out threateningly towards the position which we had occupied. And scattered all about beneath us were picturesque suburbs, and stately houses, walled gardens and verdant groves refreshing to the eye; whilst the blue waters of the flowing Jumna glittered in the light of

1857. June. the broad sun. It was not an hour for philosophical speculation or for the indulgence of any romantic sentiments concerning the decay of empires and the revolutions of dynasties; else was there much food for thought in the strange circumstances which had brought a British Army to besiege a city which, only a month before, had been regarded as securely our own as London or Liverpool, and to contend against a Sovereign who, within the same brief space of time, had been held in contempt as a harmless puppet. There was no room in the minds of our military chiefs for such thoughts as these. They contemplated the position on which they had encamped our Army with the keen eyes of practical soldiers, and looked around them from their commanding position upon the ground that was to be the scene of their future operations. And this was the result of the survey.

Roads and canals. Intersecting the old Cantonment towards the left-centre, and then following its front towards the right, was a road which joined the Grand Trunk from Kurnaul, beyond the extremity of the Ridge, and led down, through a mass of suburban gardens and ancient edifices, to the Caubul Gate of Delhi. Two other roads, also leading from Kurnaul, diverged through the Cantonment to different gates of the city. And scarcely less important to us than the roads were the canals which were cut through the country in the neighbourhood of our camp. In the rear of our encampment was a branch canal, known as the Nujufgurh Jheel Aqueduct, which carried the waters emptied into this lake to the stream of the Jumna. To the right rear of our position this great drain was intersected by the Western Jumna Canal, which passing through a bold excavation of the solid rock, flowed through the great suburbs of Delhi, and entering the city by a culvert under the walls, traversed the length of its main street and emptied itself into the river near the walls of the Imperial Palace. And it was a source of especial rejoicing to the British chiefs, firstly, that our position was open to the rear, and that there were good roads leading down to it, from which we could keep up a constant communication with the Punjab, now become our base of operations; and, secondly, that there was an abundant supply of water in the Nujufgurh Canal. It was the driest season of the year, and in common course the canal would have been empty. But the excessive rains of 1856 had so flooded and extended the area of the lake, that it had not ceased even in the month of June to emit an unfailing supply of pure good water to fill the aqueduct in the rear of our position*—water in which not only our people could freely bathe, but which they could drink with safety and with pleasure; and it is hard to say how much the salubrity of the camp was maintained by this providential dispensation. Nor was it merely in a sanitary point of view that this flow of water was so advantageous to the English, for in its mili-

1857. June.

* See remarks of Colonel Baird Smith on this subject (Unfinished Memoir): "By one of those remarkable coincidences of which so many occurred to favour the English cause as to suggest the idea of a special Providence in them, the rains of the year preceding the mutiny had been unprecedented in magnitude, and the whole basin had been gorged with water, the area covered exceeding a hundred square miles. . . . . From the enormous accumulation of water in the Jheel during 1856, this canal, ordinarily dry during the hot season, was filled with a deep, rapid stream of pure and wholesome water during the whole period of the siege. It is scarcely possible to over-estimate the value of such a provision both to the health and comfort of the troops, for without it the river, two miles distant, or the wells in Cantonment, all brackish and bad, must have been the sole sources of water supply for man and beast. Sanitary arrangements were facilitated, good drainage secured, abundant means of ablution and healthy aquatic exercises were provided, and the Jheel Canal was not merely a good defensible line for military operations, but a precious addition to the comfort and salubrity of the camp."

1857. June. tary aspects it was equally favourable to defensive purposes. And so there were comfort and encouragement in the contemplation of our position.

The Ridge. And a nearer inspection of the Ridge, though there were some countervailing circumstances to detract from the general satisfaction, had an assuring effect upon the British Leader and the Staff by whom he was surrounded. It had been, in part at least, the site of the old Delhi Cantonment. The left of this rocky chain rested upon the Jumna some three or four miles above Delhi, whilst the right extremity approached the Caubul Gate of the city at a distance of about a thousand yards. "Formed of a hard, compact, semi-crystalline quartz rock, disposed in layers, and presenting occasional natural cliffs on the city side,"* it extended along a line of rather more than two miles, at an elevation of from fifty to sixty feet above the general elevation of the city.† The natural soil was so hostile to cultivation that the general aspect of the Ridge was bare and rugged; and the same gritty, friable qualities of the earth rendered it especially ill-adapted to defensive purposes, for where no cohesive properties existed the construction of earth-works was almost impossible. On the left and centre of the Ridge, obliquely to the front of attack, the tents of the English were pitched a little to the rear of the ruins of their old houses, which effectually concealed us from the besieged. The extreme left of the Ridge was so far retired from the main position of the enemy as to be in little danger from his assaults, but our post on the ex-

* MS. Memoir by Colonel Baird Smith.

† Baird Smith says in the Memoir quoted above that its utmost height above the level of the city does not exceed eighty or ninety feet." In another memorandum he says that "the average command may be taken for practical purposes at about forty feet."

treme right "invited attack from the moment of occupation to the close of the operations."* 1857. June.

Hindoo Rao's house.

This position on the extreme right was surmounted by a somewhat extensive building of comparatively modern construction, known as Hindoo Rao's House. The former owner of this edifice was a Mahratta nobleman, who is said to have been nearly connected with the family of Scindiah. Political necessities had compelled his residence at a distance from Gwalior, and he had settled himself in the neighbourhood of Delhi, where he had earned a good reputation among all classes of the community. Of a robust manhood and a genial temperament, he was noted for his hospitality.† The house had been built and fitted up much after the fashion of an Anglo-Indian mansion of the better class. But on his death it had been left without an occupant, and on the arrival of Barnard's force it was found empty and deserted. It was a roomy and convenient edifice, with good approaches both from the Cantonment and the City; and, apart from the excellence of the situation, which strongly recommended it as an advanced post, it afforded good shelter and accommodation for a considerable body of troops.

The Flagstaff Tower.

Between the two extreme points of the Ridge were other important posts, destined to occupy conspicuous places in the history of the coming siege. Near the point at which the middle road of the three crossed the Ridge, was the Flagstaff Tower, of which mention has before been made; for thence was it that our people, on the fatal 11th of May, huddled together for transient safety, had looked forth despair-

* Baird Smith.

† "The old man was a well-known member of the local society—a keen sportsman, a liberal and hospitable gentleman, of frank, bluff manners, and genial temperament."—*Baird Smith's Unfinished Memoir.*

1857. June. ingly towards the city, from which the signal for massacre was to come.* A double-storied, circular building, it had a fine command of observation, comprehending the country lying between the Ridge the walls of the city, and was sufficiently strong to afford good shelter to troops. Further on to the right—about midway between the Flagstaff and

The Mosque. Hindoo Rao's house—was a ruined mosque "of the old Pathan type," which had also good walls of masonry, and was well suited for an outpost, as it afforded both shelter and accommodation to our men; and still further along the Ridge road, at a distance of some two hundred yards from our position on the extreme right, was an ancient Observa-

The Observatory. tory,† of somewhat irregular structure, ill-lighted and ill-ventilated, but still a serviceable building, as it afforded good support to the advanced position on our right, which was so long to bear the brunt of the affray. At these four points, Sir Henry Barnard, after the battle of Bud'ee-ka-Serai, established strong picquets, each supported by guns.

The Suburbs. The country around Delhi, which the roads and canal-cuttings above described intersected after passing the Ridge, was a varied mass of ruined and habitable houses, walled gardens, green woodlands, cultivated rice fields, and unhealthy swamps. Beyond Hindoo Rao's house to the rear was the beautiful suburb of Subzee-mundee (or the Green Market), lying along the Grand Trunk Road—a cluster of good houses and walled gardens, which afforded shelter to the enemy, and were, indeed, the very key of our position. And beyond this the plain was "covered with

* *Ante*, book iv., chap. iii. It is stated that a cart-load of dead bodies was found in it, supposed to be the bodies of officers of the Fifty-fourth.

† Built by the Rajpoot Astronomer, Rajah Jeit Singh.

dense gardens and thick groves, houses, and walled enclosures bordering upon the great canal." Beyond Subzee-mundee, on this line of the Grand Trunk Road, stretching towards the Caubul Gate of the city, were the villages of Kishen-gunj, Trevelyan-gunj, Pahari-poor, and Tallewarree. These villages were amongst the worst of the local evils opposed to us, for they were near enough to the walls of the city to cover the enemy as they emerged from their stronghold, and afforded them a sheltered approach as they advanced towards our position on the Ridge; whilst they were too far off from our posts to admit of our occupying them in force.* Looking out from the Ridge towards the centre and left of our encampment, the space before the city appeared to be less crowded. There were a few somewhat imposing buildings irregularly scattered about this expanse of country, among which that known as Metcalfe House was one of the most conspicuous. It stood on the banks of the river, in the midst of an extensive park, and was almost buried in thick foliage. Some substantial outbuildings in the park, with a mound of some altitude in their rear, seemed to recommend themselves as serviceable outposts for future occupation. Between the Metcalfe House and the city was an old summer-palace of the Delhi Emperors, known as the Koosya Bagh. It was then little more than one of the many memorials of the former grandeur of the Mogul sovereigns with which the new capital was surrounded; but the lofty gateways, the shaded cloisters and arcades, and the spacious court-yards, of which it was composed, showed, even in their decay,

1857. June.

* "They were all strong positions, and Kishen-gunj pre-eminently so, from its massive masonry enclosures and commanding site on the slope of the right flank of the Gorge."—*Baird Smith.*

1857. June. that it had once been a place of no common architectural beauty.* More remote from the river, and almost in a line with the Cashmere Gate of the city, was Ludlow Castle—a modern mansion of some importance, which had been the home of the late Commissioner, Simon Fraser, slaughtered in the Delhi Palace.† It was erected on the crest of a ridge sloping down towards the city walls, with the dry bed of a drainage canal at its base. And on the line of the Jumna, between the Koosya Bagh and the water-gate of the city, was a spacious modern building of the English official type, but surrounded by trees and shrubs, looking out from the windows of which it almost seemed that the city walls were overhanging the place.‡ These were the most noticeable edifices, which attracted the attention of our people on the Ridge, as posts, which in the coming operations might be turned to account, whilst in the intervening spaces it was seen that there were gardens and groves, sometimes intersected by deep ravines. These fine breadths of luxuriant foliage, seen from the higher ground, were pleasant to the eye of the English soldier; but it was too probable that they would prove to be as favourable to the operations of the enemy as damaging to our own.§

* "Its interior was in ruins, but sufficient indications of its design and structure remained to show it to have been one of the rich examples of florid architecture of the later Moguls, of which Delhi possesses so many beautiful illustrations; and the broad space, with its walls, was overgrown with orange-trees, and limes, and rose-bushes, and other shrubs, all growing in the wildest luxuriance."—*Baird Smith, Unpublished Memoir.*

† Mr. Russell, in his "Diary in India," speaks of Ludlow Castle as "a fine mansion, with turrets and clock-towers, something like a French château of the last century."

‡ Baird Smith.

§ "They offered innumerable facilities for occupation by armed men of any degree of discipline, and in truth so incompatible were its features generally with the action in mass of disciplined troops that the many combats of which it was the scene were rather trials of skill between small bodies or individuals than operations by mass."—*Baird Smith.* "The luxuriant foliage, though picturesque as a landscape-effect, concealed to a damaging ex-

And over these tracts of country the British Commander now looked at the great city itself, and surveyed the character of its defences. The circuit of its walls extended to some seven miles, two of which were covered by the side which ran parallel to the river, and were completely defended by it. The rest formed an irregular figure, partly facing obliquely the line of our position on the Ridge, and partly turned towards the country on the left. These landward walls, about twenty-four feet in height, consisted of a series of curtains of red masonry, terminating in small bastions, each capable of holding from nine to twelve guns. Around them ran a dry ditch, some twenty-five feet in breadth and somewhat less than twenty feet in depth, the counterscarp being an earthen slope of very easy descent, "much water-and-weather worn." There was something that might be called a glacis, but to the eye of a skilled engineer it was scarcely worthy of the name.* The entrances to the city through these substantial walls of masonry were numerous. A series of so-called gates—for the most part in the near neighbourhood of the several

1857. May 12. The City.

tent the movement of our enemies, who, creeping out of the Cashmere or Lahore Gates, would, under cover of trees and walls and houses, reach unperceived almost the foot of our position on the Ridge. It was thus that our engineers found it necessary to lop away branches and cut down trees and bushes, marring the beauty of the scene, but adding to our security."—*MS. Memorandum by an Officer of Artillery.*

* Baird Smith. The most recent writer on the subject of the material aspects of Delhi, quoting a professional description of the fortifications, says, "The 'original round towers formed into angular bastions,' the 'crenelated curtains,' and the fine glacis covering three-fourths or more of the height of the wall, are the additions and improvements of English engineers of the present century."—*Bholonauth Chunder—Travels of a Hindoo.* I rely, however, on Baird Smith's authority more confidently than on any other. [Since this was written I have read in Major Norman's "Narrative" that there was before Delhi "an admirable glacis covering the wall for a full third of its height." As this is a high authority I think it right to quote Baird Smith's words: "The glacis scarcely merits the name, as it is but a short slope, seventy or eighty feet in breadth, springing from the crest of the counterscarp, and provided with no special means of obstruction."]

1857. June. bastions—were to be seen at irregular intervals along the walls. They were abutments of heavy masonry, but not without some architectural pretensions, comprising handsome arched gateways, which were surmounted by towers, forming stations or look-out posts for the city guards. These gates were ten in number —one was on the river side of the city; another led down to the Bridge of Boats from the extreme corner of the King's Palace; and the rest were on the landward sides. The gates, known as the Cashmere Gate, the Moree Gate, and the Caubul Gate, were those most easily assailable from our position on the Ridge. Indeed, it was only on one side of the great walled city that the English Commander, looking down from his newly-erected camp, could hope to make an early impression. To invest so extensive a place with so small a force was an absolute impossibility. It was as much as we could do to invest this front—about one-seventh of the entire enceinte—leaving all the rest to the free egress and ingress of the enemy.

The Palace. The Palace, or, as it was sometimes called, the Fort of Delhi, was situated about the centre of the river-front of the city, one side almost overhanging the waters of the Jumna. The artist pronounced it to be "a noble mass of building of truly beautiful design, vast magnitude, and exquisite detail;" but to the eye of the scientific soldier it appeared to be capable of only very feeble resistance to the appliances of modern warfare. Its defences consisted chiefly of high walls and deep ditches, with "most imperfect arrangements for flanking or even direct fire."† And on the north-east side, partly resting on

* These gates were known respectively as the Raj-ghaut and the Calcutta Gates. By them the mutineers had entered on the 11th of May.

† Baird Smith.

the main stream of the Jumna, was the ancient Pathan Fort of Selimghur, separated from the Palace by a narrow stream of the river, which was crossed by a bridge of masonry. It was, for defensive purposes, an important out-work, which, manned with heavy guns, might play along the river-side as far as the Metcalfe House, and enfilade the approaches to the city in that direction. Such were the principal material objects which presented themselves to Barnard and his Staff, when their telescopes on that June morning swept the country which lay between the River and the Ridge. And as they estimated the worth of all these several posts for offensive or defensive purposes, they endeavoured to calculate also the numerical strength of the enemy within the walls. But there was little more than dim conjecture to guide them. It was assumed that the bulk of the Meerut and Delhi troops—five regiments of Infantry, one regiment of Cavalry, and a company of Native Artillery—were now within the walls of the city. And it was not less certain that the Sappers and Miners from Meerut, the head-quarters of the Aligurh Regiment, the bulk of the regiments from Ferozèpore, large detachments of Native Infantry from Muttra, and Irregulars from Hansi, Hissar, and Sirsa, had swollen the stream of insurrection within the circuit of Delhi. To these might be added the King's Guards, and, probably, large numbers of Native soldiers of all branches absent from their regiments on furlough, according to custom at that season of the year. And these trained soldiers, it was known, had at their command immense supplies of ordnance, arms, ammunition, and equipments, wanting none of the materials of warfare for a much larger force. To the General, who had served at Sebastopol, it appeared that the strength of Delhi thus garrisoned had been

1857. June.

1857 June. greatly underrated by those who believed that it was to be disposed of in a day.*

And against this great walled city thus garrisoned what had Barnard brought? Collectively it may be said that he had three thousand European soldiers and twenty-two field guns. This European force consisted of—

Her Majesty's Ninth Lancers. Two squadrons of the Carabineers. Six companies of Her Majesty's Sixtieth Rifles. Her Majesty's Seventy-fifth Foot. The First Bengal (Company's) Fusiliers. Six companies of Second Bengal (Company's) Fusiliers. Sixteen Horse Artillery guns, manned by Europeans. Six Horse Battery guns, also Europeans: with the Siege-train, the details of which have been already given.

Besides these there were two other bodies of reliable troops, as good as Europeans—the Goorkah battalion under Reid, and the Punjab Guide Corps under Daly. There were also a hundred and fifty men of the old regiment of Sappers and Miners, that had mutinied at Meerut, and who were still believed to be staunch. In Barnard's camp, also, were a regiment of Irregular Native Cavalry (the Ninth), and a portion of another (the Fourth), but the fidelity of both was doubtful.

June 9, 1857. General Barnard at Delhi. There were many then in all parts of India, especially among the more eager-minded civilians, who

* I have endeavoured in this description of Delhi to represent merely the appearances of the great city and the environs as they presented themselves to General Barnard and his Staff at the time of their first encamping on the Ridge. Other details will, from time to time, be given as the narrative proceeds. I have consulted a variety of authorities, but I am principally indebted to Colonel Baird Smith's unfinished Memoir of the Siege of Delhi. As this was written after he had been enabled to verify by subsequent inspection his impressions formed during the siege, I confidently accept the accuracy of his descriptions.

believed that to reach Delhi was to take it. Habituated to success, and ever prone to despise our enemies, it seemed to our people, in this conjuncture, to be a settled thing that the force moving on Delhi, by whomsoever commanded, should, in the language of the day, "dispose of it," and then proceed to finish the mutineers in other parts of the country. Even the cool brain of Lord Canning conceived this idea of the facility of the enterprise. It was thought that the Delhi Field Force might march into the city, make short work of the rebels, the King and Royal Family included; and then, leaving there a small British garrison, proceed to the relief of Lucknow, Cawnpore, or any other beleaguered position in that part of Hindostan. And this belief in the possible was so common, that it soon began to take in men's minds the shape of the actual; and before the month of June was half spent, it was said in all parts of the country that Delhi had been retaken, and that the star of our fortune was again on the ascendant.

1857. June.

Whether, as was said at the time, and is still confidently maintained by some, if, after the victory of Budlee-ka-Serai, Barnard had swept on and pursued the enemy into the city, he might have driven them out, after great slaughter, with the loss of all their munitions of war, must ever remain a mystery. It was not attempted. But it was no part of the General's plan to sit down before Delhi and to commence the tedious operations of a protracted siege. It was assuredly not his temper to magnify dangers and difficulties or to shrink from any enterprise that promised even a chance of success. It might be a hazardous undertaking; he felt, indeed, in his inmost heart, that it was. But he knew that his countrymen expected him to do it. He knew that

1857. June 11. anything like hesitation at such a moment would bring down upon him a storm of reproach. He knew, also, that if he failed in the perilous enterprise, he would be charged with rashness and incapacity. But this appeared to the fine old soldier to be the lesser evil of the two. Right or wrong, he was prepared to risk it.

Question of a *coup-de-main.* With such thoughts heavy within him, Barnard was by no means slow to accept the counsel of the young Engineer officers, who urged upon him the expediency of an immediate attack upon the city. Nothing was plainer, than that delay would weaken our chances of success; for not only was the numerical strength of the enemy increasing by fresh accessions of mutineers, making the city of the Mogul their central rallying-point, but there was strong probability that the material defences of the place would be strengthened—especially by the simple device of bricking up the gateways. That this had not been done on the 11th, the Engineers ascertained; and on that day they were prepared with the plan of a *coup-de-main*, which they laid before the General, urging him to attempt it on the following morning at break of day. "We find," they said in the Memorandum placed in Barnard's hands, "that the Caubul and Lahore Gates are not as yet bricked up—that the bridges in front of them are up to this time perfect—and that troops can approach from camp under cover to four hundred and nine hundred yards of these gates respectively. An entrance can also be effected close to the Caubul Gate by the channel through which the canal flows into the city. We recommend a simultaneous attempt to blow in the Lahore Gate by powder-bags, and such one of the two obstacles at the other point (namely, either the

Caubul Gate or the Canal grating close by it), as may be preferred on reconnaissance by the officers in charge of the explosion party." . . . "We are impressed with the necessity," they added, "of driving the enemy out of the City and into the Fort by the simultaneous advance of several columns, of which two shall pass along the ramparts right and left, taking possession of every bastion and capturing every gun, whilst the remainder, advancing towards the Palace by the principal streets of the city, will establish posts on the margin of the esplanade, which surrounds the Palace, communicating right and left with the heads of the adjoining columns. To this end we believe it essential that the attack should commence at the peep of dawn. We propose to effect the explosions at half-past three A.M.; intimation of success to be immediately followed by the advance of the columns detailed for each attack, which will be in readiness at the points hereafter indicated, half an hour before that time." 1857. June 11.

The report embodying this scheme was signed by four subaltern officers—by Wilberforce Greathed, by Maunsell and Chesney, of the Engineers, and Hodson, of the Intelligence Department, at a later period known as "Hodson, of Hodson's Horse."* The

* Hodson himself has thus referred to the matter in one of the letters published by his brother: "Yesterday I was ordered by the General to assist Greathed, and one or two more Engineers, in forming a project of attack, and how we would do to take Delhi. We drew up our scheme and gave it to the General, who highly approved, and will, I trust, carry it out; but how times must be changed when four subalterns are called upon to suggest a means of carrying so vitally important an enterprise as this, one on which the safety of the Empire depends. Wilberforce Greathed is the next Senior Engineer to Laughton, Chesney is Major of the Engineer Brigade, and Maunsell commands the Sappers. I was added because the General complimentarily told me that he had the utmost value for my opinion; and though I am known to counsel vigorous measures, it is equally well known I do not urge others to do what I would not be the first to do myself."

1857. June 12. scheme was accepted by Barnard, and orders were issued for its execution. Soon after midnight everything was ready. The troops selected for this enterprise were duly warned. Each Engineer officer had his appointed work. They were to assemble, under cover of the darkness of the night, between one and two o'clock, and to proceed noiselessly to the gates which were to have been blown in with powder-bags. But when the parade was held, an important part of the destined force was missing. A body of three hundred men of the First European Fusiliers was to have been brought up by Brigadier Graves; but at the appointed hour there was no sign of his appearance; and the column, thus weakened by their defection, was not strong enough to do the work before it. It was an intense disappointment to many eager spirits, who, on that June morning, believed that the stronghold of the enemy was within their grasp. But there seemed to be nothing left but the postponement of the enterprise; so, reluctantly, orders were given for the return of the storming party to their quarters. It is difficult not to believe that Brigadier Graves disobeyed orders. The excuse was that he misunderstood them, and the kind heart of Sir Henry Barnard inclined him to accept the excuse.*

Contemplated night attack.

* Graves was Brigadier of the day on duty. The orders conveyed to him were verbal orders, and he rode to Barnard's tent to ask for a confirmation of them. The story is thus told, and with every appearance of authority, by Mr. Cave-Browne: "Brigadier Graves was the field-officer of the day. About eleven o'clock that night he received verbal orders that the Europeans on picquet along the heights were to move off without being relieved for special duty; with a vague hint that a night-assault was in contemplation. On reaching the Flagstaff picquet we found the Native guards in the act of relief, and unable to believe that it was intended to leave that important position, with its two guns, in the charge of Natives only, he galloped down to the General's tent for further instructions. Here he heard that they were on the point of assaulting, and that every European infantry soldier was required. Now the Brigadier probably knew more of the actual strength of Delhi than any other soldier in the force;—he had commanded the brigade at

But the project of a surprise, though thus delayed, was not abandoned. Wilberforce Greathed went hopefully to work, revising his scheme, and never ceasing to urge at Head-Quarters the necessity of a night attack. The brief delay had at least one advantage. The moon was waning, and the cover of darkness was much needed for such an enterprise. Every day had made Barnard more and more sensible of the underrated strength of the great city which lay before him. But he still clung to the idea of a sudden rush, and either a grand success or a crippling failure. "The place is so strong," he wrote to Lord Canning on the 13th of June, "and my means so inadequate, that assault or regular approach were equally difficult —I may say impossible; and I have nothing left but to place all on the hazard of a die and attempt a *coup-de-main*, which I purpose to do. If successful, all will be well. But reverse will be fatal, for I can have no reserve on which to retire. But, assuredly, you all greatly under-estimated the difficulties of Delhi. They have twenty-four-pounders on every gate and flank bastion; and their practice is excellent —beats ours *five* to *one*. We have got six heavy guns in position, but do not silence theirs, and I

1857. June.

Revised scheme of assault.

June 13.

the time of the outbreak; and when asked his opinion as to the chance of success, he replied, 'You may certainly take the city by surprise, but whether you are strong enough to hold it is another matter.' This made the General falter in his plans. Some of the young officers who were to take a leading part now came in and found him wavering. The Brigadier's remark had so shaken his purpose that, in spite of entreaty and remonstrance, he withdrew the consent which, if truth be told, he had never very heartily given to the project, and the assault was abandoned. The Rifles, already under the walls, and the advancing columns were recalled into camp." Major Reid expresses his opinion that the Brigadier was "perfectly justified in having declined to allow his picquets to be withdrawn without written orders" (Reid himself had received written orders, which he obeyed), and declares that the mischance was a fortunate event. Major Norman says that "there are few who do not now feel that the accident which hindered this attempt was one of those happy interpositions in our behalf of which we had such numbers to be thankful for."

1857. June 14. really see nothing for it but a determined rush; and this, please God, you will hear of as successful."

About this time, Barnard had under consideration the revised scheme of Wilberforce Greathed for an attack on Delhi, "by means of simultaneous explosions of powder-bags at the Caubul and Lahore Gates, and of a charge against the Cashmere Gate, to be fired at such time as the attention of the defenders of that enclosure may be engaged by the first-mentioned operations." Maunsell and Hodson were to conduct one explosion party, and Greathed and M'Neill the other. On the sound of the bugle, the appointed storming parties were to advance and stream through the openings thus effected. Every precaution was taken in the event of failure at any point, and precise instructions laid down as to the course to be pursued by each column of attack on the occurrence of any possible contingency, and nothing was wanted to show, not only by written description, but also by plans and charts, what each detail of the force was to do after entrance had been effected.

Councils of war.

This project, signed by Wilberforce Greathed, was dated June 14. On the following day a Council of War was held, and the scheme was considered. It was summoned by General Reed, who on Anson's death had come down from Rawul-Pindee, to assume as senior officer in the Presidency the Provisional Command in Chief of the Army,* and it was held

* He had joined the army about the time of its arrival at Delhi; but he was prostrated by sickness, unable to mount a horse, and quite incompetent to take any active part in the prosecution of the siege. It was not before the 11th that he was enabled to sit up and write a letter to Sir John Lawrence. But from that time his health began to improve, and he did good service by keeping the Chief Commissioner informed of the state of affairs at Delhi. The letters which the General then wrote were full of interesting and important details, and are distinguished by much clear good sense.

in his tent. Sir Henry Barnard, Brigadier Wilson, 1857.
Hervey Greathed, and the chief Engineer officers, June 14.
were present. The old adage that a Council of War never fights was not falsified in this case. It was set forth very strongly that the project of the Engineers involved the employment of nearly the whole of the Delhi Field Force; that there would be no reserve to fall back upon in the event of failure; and that, in the event of success, the enemy, streaming out of Delhi, might attack our camp, seize our guns, and otherwise inflict grievous injury upon us. The military authorities were all in favour of delay, until such time as a reinforcement of at least a thousand men might arrive. The Civilian who appeared in Council as the representative of the Government of the North-Western Provinces was opposed to this delay. Very forcibly Hervey Greathed urged that Views of Hervey Greathed.
"the delay of a fortnight would disappoint expectations, protract the disorders with which the country is afflicted, increase the disaffection known to exist among the Mahomedan population in the Bombay Presidency, and cause distrust on the part of our Native allies;" but he added that he could not take upon himself to say that the delay would lead the Native States actually to throw off their allegiance to the British Government, or endanger the safety of Cawnpore and Oude, and of the country to the eastward. He assumed that British relations with the Native States were too close to be so easily dissolved, and that the concentration of English troops at Cawnpore would insure the safety of the districts to which allusion had been made. Wilberforce Greathed, ever ready for an immediate attack on the blood-stained city, pleaded that it would be easy to revise the scheme, so as to leave a larger reserve in

1857. June 16.

camp. And, finally, it was agreed to defer the decision to the following day.

The Council reassembled.

On the 16th of June, therefore, the Council again assembled. The military leaders had thought over the grave question before them. The feeling at the first consultation had been that, on political grounds, it would be desirable to attack the city immediately on the arrival of the first reinforcements. But even this much of forwardness waned on the evening of the 15th, and the Commandant of Artillery, who had been moved by Hervey Greathed's arguments at the first Council, had fallen back upon his military experience, and had recorded a Memorandum, which had in no small measure influenced Barnard.* For the General was a man too little self-reliant for his position—too prone to be swayed hither and thither by the gusts of other men's recorded or spoken opinions. When, therefore, on the 16th of June, the Council of War again met, and all the military members of Council, except Wilberforce Greathed, were opposed to immediate operations, his resolution yielded to the array of authority before him, and again he began

* Barnard recorded a note on the 15th, in which he said that circumstances were altered "by the fact that the Chief Officer of Artillery had represented that the means at his command were inadequate to silencing the enemy's guns on the walls, so necessary before any approach could be made," and that the "Chief Engineer represented that, as he had not the means of undertaking any necessary siege operations, the only practicable mode of attack rested on a *coup-de-main*, to effect which, and to occupy so large an area as the city of Delhi, required the employment of so much of the force under my command as to prevent my leaving a sufficient number to guard my camp, and enable me to sustain the position in the case of any reverse attending the attempt." But he added that political considerations of moment had been so strongly urged upon him, that, although reinforcements were shortly expected, and, in a military point of view, there could be no doubt that it would be expedient to wait for them, he must "submit to those intrusted with the political interests to determine whether to wait is less hazardous than to incur the risk of failure." He halted, indeed, between two opinions; but he added, "I am ready to organise the attack to-night, if deemed desirable."

to intrench himself behind military principles and precedents. 1857. June 16.

Opinion of Brigadier Wilson.

At that Council, on the 16th of June, Archdale Wilson put in, as the expression of his matured judgment on the subject, the paper which he had written on the day before, and which was now read aloud: "Taking into consideration the large extent of the town to be attacked," it said, "a full mile in breadth, nearly two miles in length from the Cashmere to the Delhi Gate, I must own that I dread success, on entering the town, almost as much as failure. Our small force, two thousand bayonets, will be lost in such an extent of town; and the insurgents have shown, by their constant and determined attacks upon our position, how well they can and will fight from behind cover, such as they will have in street-fighting in the city, when every man will almost be on a par with our Europeans. With the large number of heavy ordnance they have mounted on the walls (from thirty to forty pieces), we must also expect heavy loss during the assault of the gateways, as their grape-shot will command the ground from seven hundred or eight hundred yards round the walls. I gave my vote for the assault, on the arrival of our first reinforcements, solely on the political grounds set forth by Mr. Greathed, feeling, at the same time, that, as a military measure, it was a most desperate and unsafe one. It has, however, since struck me that, even in a political point of view, it would be wiser to hold our own position and wait for the reinforcements from Lahore, when we could insure success in our attack. So long as we hold this position we keep the whole of the insurgents in and round Delhi. On taking the city, they will naturally form into large bodies and go through the country,

1857. June 16. plundering in every direction. These bodies should be immediately followed by movable brigades, and cut up whenever come up with. It would be impossible, with the small force we now have, to leave a sufficient force for the protection of Delhi, and at the same time to send out such brigades as will be required. It appears to me a question of time only. The country all round, it is true, is in the hands of the insurgents and other plunderers, and must remain so until we can clear the country by our brigades. Mr. Greathed also contemplates the probability of the Native chiefs, who are now favourable to us, becoming lukewarm in our cause; but what have they yet done for us? The Gwalior and Bhurtpore forces have long ago left us to our resources; and, from what I hear, little is to be expected from the Jeypoor Contingent, until they are quite satisfied of our complete success over the insurgents."

Opinion of General Reed.

General Reed then declared his opinion at some length.* He said that "our success on the 8th had placed us in a favourable position, and one which we could hold for any time. It, therefore, became a question whether it would not be better to await the arrival of the strong reinforcements that were on their way to join us—the rear guard of which must have reached Loodhianah, so that by ordinary marches they ought all to be assembled here in fifteen days—than to risk an attack on the place at once, which would require every available bayonet of our force to effect, leaving no reserve, except Cavalry and heavy guns in position, thus risking the safety of our camp,

* The substance of what follows in the text was stated orally before the Council of the 15th. General Reed afterwards embodied it in a letter to Sir John Lawrence, and it was read out at the meeting on the following day.

stores, and magazines, which would be exposed to the incursion of many bodies of mutineers which we knew were encamped outside the walls of Delhi, and would take the opportunity of looting our camp, while our troops were attacking the city. There can be no question," he continued, "of the propriety of waiting, in a military point of view. In that all agree. We have, then, to look upon it in a political aspect, and to inquire whether, in that sense, so great a risk is to be run as an immediate assault would entail. There can be no doubt that expedition in terminating this state of affairs—which it is to be hoped that the capture of Delhi would accomplish—is a great consideration; but the possibility of failure, either total or partial, in that operation should be averted. This can only be done by having in hand such a force as will insure success. That force, it is believed, will be assembled here in the course of fifteen days. In the mean time, by holding this position, we keep the chief body of the mutineers concentrated in and about Delhi. They know they cannot dislodge us, and that strong reinforcements are on their way to join us, while they are prevented from dispersing and marauding the country, which would be the effect of a successful attack upon Delhi at any time. Now we have not the means of sending out detachments to pursue them; then we should have ample means, and movable columns would be organised without delay to drive out the mutineers, and re-establish order in the neighbouring places which have suffered. It is not apparent, therefore, that the delay contemplated can have an effect, politically, sufficiently injurious to warrant the certainty of great loss and risk of possible failure, than which nothing could be more disastrous in its consequences.

1857. June 16.

1857. June 16. We have suffered no diminution of prestige since we advanced on Delhi; all our objects have been accomplished, in spite of great obstacles, by the well-known redoubtable bravery of our troops, the mutineers driven from their strong positions, and their guns taken. Their sorties in force have since been repulsed with great loss to them, and in no one instance have they succeeded in gaining any, even the smallest, advantage. Their only effective defence lies in their walls, which, instead of being weak and unable to support the weight and resist the concussion of guns, are strong (recently repaired and strengthened by us), capable of sustaining a numerous and heavy artillery, with which all their bastions are mounted. As neither our time nor material would admit of a regular siege, an assault or storm can only be resorted to; but the success of this must *be insured.* A contrary event would endanger the Empire. Another reason has been alleged for an immediate attack—the approaching rains; but they are seldom heavy till the ensuing month, and the sickness does not ensue till the month after. Every precaution must, of course, be taken in cutting drains in camp previously, to carry off the water, for the wounded (there are, I am happy to say, few sick); there are good pucka buildings, Native hospitals, in the Lines which we occupy, so that no inconvenience need be expected as far as they are concerned, nor do I anticipate any for the Force. There has been no 'Chota Bursaut' yet, which generally precedes the regular rains, and is succeeded by some fine weather before these regularly set in. The necessity of having as large a force as can be made available is also apparent in the size of Delhi, the circumference of which is six or seven miles. Having accomplished a lodgment, a strong force would be required to clear the ramparts and occupy the town, in which they may expect to be opposed at every house and wall behind which an insurgent can find room, under which it is known they can defend themselves with vigour. All things considered," concluded the General, "it is my opinion that the military reasons for awaiting the arrival of a sufficient force to insure success far outweigh any political inconvenience that might arise, and which would all be remedied by certain success in the end." 1857. June 16.

The result of these decided expressions of opinion on the part of the principal military officers at Delhi was that again the project of a *coup-de-main* was abandoned. In the face of such opinions, Barnard did not consider that he would be justified in incurring the serious risks so emphatically dwelt upon by Wilson and Reid. The expression of his personal views is on record. Writing on the 18th to Sir John Lawrence, he said: "I confess that, urged on by the political adviser acting with me, I had consented to a *coup-de-main* which would have entailed all the above considerations; accident alone prevented it; it may be the interposition of Providence. From what I can hear, and from the opinion of others whom it became my duty to consult, I am convinced that success would have been as fatal as failure. A force of two thousand bayonets, spread over a city of the magnitude of Delhi, would have been lost as a military body, and, with the treachery that surrounds us, what would have become of my *matériel?* Be sure that I have been guided by military rule, and that it required moral courage to face the cry that will be raised against our inactivity Abandonment of the assault. June 18.

1857. June 18. before Delhi; I can but act for the best, and wait any favourable opportunity for striking the blow. The great point raised by Mr. Greathed was the security of the Doab, and the desirableness of sending troops to Aligurh from Delhi; but were I in the city now I could not do this. The Castle and Selimgurh yet remain before me, and to hold the city and attack these with a force under two thousand would prevent my detaching any there. The fact is, Delhi, bristling with lances, and garrisoned by men who, however contemptible in the open, have sagacity behind stone walls and some knowledge of the use of heavy ordnance—for hitherto they beat us in the precision of their fire—is not to be taken by the force from Umballah, with two troops of six-pounders; and its present strength has been greatly under-estimated. We have fought one action at Budlee-ka-Serai, where, so long as their guns remained to them, they appeared formidable. We have been subject to frequent attacks ever since, each made with some spirit, but repulsed with heavy loss, and having now the position taken up from which we must eventually reduce the place. It strikes me the best policy is to view it in its best light; it is a difficult task, and not to be accomplished without a sufficient force. Once in the town, the game is over if we can hold it, and immediately a force will be available for any purpose Mr. Colvin requires. Delay is vexatious, and losing men daily in these attacks is heart-breaking. I am well, but much harassed. I do assure you, the more I think of it, the more I rejoice in the hap-hazard experiment failing. It is some comfort to see that you agree; I hope others will now see I had more to do than to walk into Delhi."*

* To this letter Barnard added a postscript, saying: "We gave them

But Wiberforce Greathed still did not despair of turning the hearts of the military chiefs towards his schemes of energetic action. Before a week had passed, he had submitted to Barnard another memorandum, urging that since the date of the last Council the mutineers had been reinforced by the Nusserabad Brigade of two regiments and six guns, and the Jullundhur force of three regiments with one gun; that information had been received of the near approach to join the insurgents of the revolted Bareilly force, six regiments of Infantry with eight guns, and a regiment of Cavalry; and that, moreover, there were tidings of the Gwalior Contingent, of seven regiments of Infantry, three of Cavalry, and three batteries of Artillery, with a siege-train and magazine, having declared for the King of Delhi; and that in all human probability Agra would be besieged by the latter force—perhaps, indeed, already was in imminent peril. In such circumstances it had become a matter of infinite importance that a portion of the Delhi force should be detached to the relief of the former city. "But this is possible," he added, "only after Delhi is in our possession, and the mutineers' force dispersed. I respectfully submit, therefore, that a political necessity for pressing the attack of Delhi at

1857. June.

a great beating yesterday, with *heavy loss*. They had attempted to take up a position, seize [ ] and Kishen-gunj, and Trevelyan-gunj and Paharipoor; with two small columns under Major Tombs, B.A., and Major Reid, Sirmoor Battalion, we not only dislodged them, but drove them out of the serai above, and, in fact, drove all before us on this side of the Force. It has had a very chilling effect, we hear, and their spirits are much disturbed. But their fire from the north is as true as ever; so hot is it, that, until we approach ours nearer, we shall do no good; and such is the state of the service, that with all the bother of getting the siege-train, my commanding Artillery Officer can only man six guns, and my Engineer has not a sand-bag. It is really too distressing. I never contemplated making regular approaches, but I did expect my guns to silence those brought against me. But to do this they must be got nearer. Delay concentrates the insurgents."

1857. June. almost any risk has arisen, and upon this ground I venture to submit a project of immediate attack concurred in by the officers who were commissioned to prepare the first project." But Barnard was not to be induced to swerve from the resolution formed by the Council of War. So, again, the younger and more eager spirits of the British camp were disappointed; and our troops fell back upon their old daily business of repulsing the enemy's sorties.

Work in camp. There was indeed, whilst this great design of the *coup-de-main* was under consideration at Head-Quarters, no lack of work in camp, and no lack of excitement. There were real alarms and false alarms, and officers and men on the Ridge were compelled to be constantly on the alert. Greatly outmatched as we were in Artillery, we could make little or no impression upon the batteries of the enemy or the walls of Delhi, and were, in truth, except when our Horse Artillery guns were brought into close quarters, only wasting our ammunition. The Sepoys, who knew our habits but too well, were wont to come out against us in the midst of the fiercest mid-day heats. In the climate they had an ally, to which they felt that they could trust; and many of our best and bravest were struck down, or went about shivering with ague or confused by quinine. The days were very hot and the nights were unwontedly cold; and these severe alternations are ever trying in the extreme to the European constitution. But nothing could abate the elastic cheerfulness and hopeful spirit of our people. Some of our younger officers then ripened into heroism of the highest order, and all displayed a constant courage in action, and an enduring fortitude in suffering, unsurpassed in the military annals of any country or any time. Day by day sad tidings came in of new mutinies and new massacres, and ever and anon fresh reinforcements of rebel regiments marched into Delhi to the sound of band-instruments playing our well-known English tunes. But the dominant feeling ever was, as these regiments arrived, that it was better for our countrymen and our country that they should be in the doomed city of the Mogul than they should be scattered about the provinces, assailing weak garrisons or defenceless cantonments, for, please God, the Delhi Field Force could not only hold its own, but, on some not very remote day, make short work of the Delhi rebels. How that was best to be done there were eager discussions in camp, leading to small results and no convictions. It must be admitted that there were many who shook their heads at the project of the *coup-de-main*, of which Greathed and Hodson had been the eager authors and the persistent exponents. It was said that, although the Force might have made its way into Delhi, only a small part of it would have ever made its way out. And yet as weeks passed and no change came over the position of the Army before Delhi, men began to chafe under the restraints which had held them back. They felt that, in all parts of India, Englishmen were asking each other why Delhi was not taken; and it was painful to those gallant souls to think that their countrymen had expected of them that which they had not done.

1857. June.

Ever active among the active was Sir Henry Barnard. There was not an officer in camp, in the flower of his youth, who, all through this fiery month of June, worked day and night with such ceaseless energy as the Commander of the Delhi Field Force. He was not inured to the climate by long acquaintance with it. He had arrived in India at that very

1857. June. period of life at which the constitution can least reconcile itself to such extreme changes. But nothing could now induce him to spare himself. All day long he was abroad in the great glare of the summer sun, with the hot wind in his face; and it was often observed of him that he never slept. Men have ere now been carried safely through the most trying conjunctures by the possession of a power enjoyed by many of the world's greatest men—a power of sleeping and waking at will. But sleep had forsaken Barnard, and therefore the climate and the work were grievously assailing him. Not only was there strong within him, amidst all perplexities, an eager, dominant desire to do his duty to the country, for the sake of which he would at any moment have gone gladly to his death, but a tender concern for the welfare of all who were under his command, which kept him unceasingly in a state of unrest, passing from post to post by day and by night, now visiting a battery or directing a charge, and now gliding into an officer's hut, and seeing that he was sufficiently covered to resist the cold night air, as he lay asleep on his bed. He impressed all men with the belief that he was a good and gallant soldier, and the kindliest-hearted, truest gentleman who ever took a comrade by the hand.

But although he bore himself thus bravely before men, the inward care was wearing out his life. Never since War began, was General in command of an Army surrounded by so many discouragements and distresses. For in truth there was no possibility of disguising the fact that instead of besieging Delhi, he was himself the besieged. The inadequacy of his means of regular attack became every day more apparent. He had planted strong picquets with guns at some of

1857. June.

the principal outposts of which I have spoken; and the enemy were continually streaming out to attack them. At Hindoo Rao's house, at the Flagstaff Tower, and at the Observatory, detachments of Infantry, supported by heavy guns, were planted from the commencement of our operations. The Metcalfe House would also have been garrisoned from the beginning, but for its distance from our supports and the paucity of troops at our disposal. The occupation of these buildings by the enemy was among the first effects of their offensive activity. It is believed that there was a peculiar feeling of animosity against the Feringhees in connexion with this edifice. It was said to have been erected on land formerly the site of a Goojur village; and that the Goojurs had flown upon it, eager for its demolition and resolute to recover their ancient holdings, on the first outbreak of the mutiny.* And there is another story still more significant. The building was originally the tomb of one of the foster-brothers of the Emperor Akbar. It had been converted into a residence by an English civilian, who was murdered, and the act of profanation had been vainly appealed against to another civilian, who afterwards shared the same fate.† Whatsoever effect these circumstances may have had upon

The Metcalfe House.

* Cave-Browne's "Punjab and Delhi in 1857."

† Sir William Sleeman says: "The magnificent tomb of freestone covering the remains of a foster-brother of Akbar was long occupied as a dwelling-house by the late Mr. Blake, of the Bengal Civil Service, who was lately barbarously murdered at Jeypoor. To make room for his dining-tables, he removed the marble slab which covered the remains of the dead from the centre of the building against the urgent remonstrances of the people, and threw it carelessly on one side against the wall, where it now lies. The people appealed in vain, it is said, to Mr. Fraser, the Governor-General's representative, who was soon afterwards assassinated, and a good many attribute the death of both to this outrage upon the dead foster-brother of Akbar." Bholonauth Chunder, in his "Travels of a Hindoo," quotes this passage, and adds, "Rooms are let in the Metcalfe House for a rupee a day for each person." See "Addenda."

1857. June. the conduct of the insurgents, it is certain that they gutted the building and did their best to destroy it.*

June 11. It was a wreck when we returned to Delhi. A month had passed, and now the enemy were in force at the Metcalfe House, where they had established a formidable battery, which played upon the left of our position on the Ridge. On the morning of the 12th, the Sepoy mutineers came out to attack us both in front and rear. The ground between the Flagstaff Tower and the Metcalfe buildings favoured, by its ravines and shrubberies, the unseen approach of the enemy, who stole up within a short distance of our picquet at the former post, and before the English officer in command† could realise the position of affairs, had opened fire upon him within a range of some fifty yards. Our men replied promptly with the Enfield rifle, but Knox was shot dead by a Sepoy musketeer, and many of his men fell wounded beside him, whilst our artillerymen dropped at their guns. Meanwhile a party of mutineers had made their way to the rear of the British camp, and were pushing onward with desperate audacity into the very heart of it

* "They stripped the roof of all its massive and valuable timber, carried off all the doors and windows, everything which they could themselves bring into use or convert into money; they demolished the costly marble statues and the unnumbered small articles of *vertù*, and then, with consistent Goth-like ruthlessness, tore up and piled in the centres of the rooms the volumes of that far-famed library, believed to be without its equal in India, and then set fire to the building." — *Cave-Browne.*

† Captain Knox, of Her Majesty's Seventy-fifth. Mr. Cave-Browne says that he "seemed to imagine that the Sepoys were coming to lay down their arms, and refused to let the men fire." Mr. Rotton (Chaplain's Narrative) says that Captain Knox "only a moment before shot with his own hand one of the enemy, when his eye caught sight of a Sepoy levelling a musket at him: 'See,' said he to one of his men, 'that man pointing at me; take him down.' The words had hardly escaped his lips, when the fatal shot took effect on his person. He was on one knee when singled out as a mark by the mutineer; and I am told, that as soon as he received the shot, he rose regularly to 'attention,' and then fell and expired without word or groan."

before our people were aroused. There was danger, indeed, on both sides. But the English got to their arms in time to repulse the attack and to carry victory before them. The enemy turned and fled; and after them went swift retribution. Rifles, Fusiliers, and other infantry detachments, aided by Daly's gallant Guide Corps, pushed after them, and dealing death as they went, pursued the fugitives through the Metcalfe grounds up to the walls of the city. The lesson was not thrown away upon us. A strong picquet was, from that time, planted at the Metcalfe House, and communications with this advanced post were kept open with the Flagstaff Tower on the Ridge.* 1857. June 12.

Reid's Picquet.

On the same day an attack was made on the right of our position, on that famous post of Hindoo Rao's House, where Reid with his regiment of Goorkahs, two companies of the Rifles, Daly's Guides, two guns of Scott's Battery, and some heavy artillery, was destined to bear the brunt of the affray through weeks and months of incessant fighting. Exposed to the fire of the enemy's guns planted on the Cashmere, Moree, and other bastions, this picquet was seldom suffered to enjoy many hours of continuous rest.† On the morning of the 12th, under cover of the guns, the mutineers came out in two bodies towards our right flank, the one moving directly on

* "Thus throwing up, as it were, the left flank of our defences, and rendering it almost impossible for the enemy to pass round on that side."—*Norman.*

† Major Reid commanded all the posts on the right of the Ridge. He describes the disposition of his troops as follows: "My own regiment and one company of Rifles occupied the House, and one company of Rifles the Observatory, where a battery for three heavy guns was constructed on the night of the 9th to reply to the Cashmere bastion. The centre battery for three eighteen-pounders was close to the House, and the guns were all laid for the Moree bastion. The Guides I located in and behind the outhouses." Whenever the alarm was sounded, two more companies of the Rifles were sent up in support.

1857. June 12. the picquet at Hindoo Rao's house, the others pushing into the gardens of the Subzee-mundee.* Both attacks were repulsed, and with heavy loss to the enemy. But it was not without a disaster on our own side; for a detachment of Native Irregular Cavalry, on whose loyalty we had relied, went over to the enemy. And so sudden was the retrograde movement that the greater number of them escaped from the fire of our guns, which were turned upon them as soon as their treachery was disclosed.† Nor was this the only disheartening circumstance which, about this time, showed how little the Native soldiery generally believed that the Ikhbal of the Company was on the ascendant, even though we had recovered our old position before Delhi, and had beaten the enemy in three pitched battles. The officers of the Sixtieth Sepoy Regiment had come into Delhi without their men. This corps was under the command of a distinguished soldier, Colonel Thomas Seaton, who had made a name for himself, fifteen years before, as one of the illustrious garrison of Jellalabad. He had believed, as other Sepoy officers had believed, in his men, but they had broken into rebellion at Rohtuck, and had now gone to swell the tide of rebellion within the walls of Delhi. No sooner had they arrived than they went out against us and were amongst the most vehement of our assailants.

Mutiny of the Sixtieth.

June 13—17. Again and again—day after day—the enemy came

* "The first of these attacks was not serious, but the latter threatened the Mound picquet, and supports of all arms had to be moved up. The First Fusiliers, under Major Jacob, then advanced and drove the mutineers out of the gardens, killing a considerable number of them."—*Norman's Narrative.*

† Major Reid says that, "They went to the front just as if they were going to charge, but no sooner had they closed than, to my horror, I saw them mix up with the enemy and walk off with them. Immediately I saw this I ordered the guns to open upon them, but the wretches were too far off, and I don't think that more than half a dozen were killed."

out to attack our posts with an uniformity of failure of which it would be tedious to recite the details. On the 13th and 15th, they again flung themselves upon our position at Hindoo Rao's House, and, as ever, the Goorkahs and the Guides distinguished themselves by their unflinching gallantry.* On the afternoon of the 17th, we began to act on the offensive. The enemy were strongly posted in the suburbs of Kishen-gunj and Trevelyan-gunj, between our right and the city, and were erecting a battery on rising ground, which would have completely enfiladed the Ridge. So two columns were sent out to destroy their works. It was a dashing enterprise, and Barnard selected the right men for it. One column was intrusted to Reid, the other to Henry Tombs. The former moved from Hindoo Rao's house, the latter from the camp. Both were completely successful. After a gallant resistance by the Sappers and Miners of our old Army, who, after firing their muskets, drew their swords and flung themselves desperately upon us, the battery and magazine were destroyed, and the village in which they were planted was burnt. Large numbers of the enemy were killed and wounded, and their rout was complete. Our own loss was trifling. Tombs, always in the thick of the affray, had two horses shot under him,† and was himself slightly wounded. Captain Brown, of the First Fusiliers,

1857. June 13—17. Renewed attacks.

* It is said that some regiments newly arrived from Oude took part in these attacks. The Sixtieth was conspicuous in the action of the 13th. Major Reid writes, that they "marched up the Grand Trunk Road in columns of sections right in front, and led the attack headed by the Sirdar Behaudur of the regiment, who made himself very conspicuous, calling out to the men to keep their distance, as he intended to wheel to his left. They fought most desperately. The Sirdar Behaudur was killed by his orderly, Lall Singh. I took the riband of India from his breast and sent it to my wife."

† "Making," at this early stage, writes Major Norman, "five horses that from the commencement of the campaign up to that date had been shot under him."

1857. June 17. well-nigh received his death-wound. That evening General Barnard walked into the Artillery mess-tent, and with characteristic appreciation of gallantry lavished his well-merited praises upon Tombs.

Artillery practice of the enemy.

There was much, in all this, of the true type of English soldiership. But it was weary and disheartening work at the best. If we lost fewer men than the enemy, they had more to lose, more to spare, and their gaps could be more readily filled. Every victory cost us dearly. And we made no progress towards the great consummation of the capture of Delhi. Every day it became more apparent that we were grievously outmatched in Artillery.* Their guns could take our distance, but ours could not take theirs. They were of heavier metal and longer reach than our own, and sometimes worked with destructive precision. On one occasion (June 17) a round shot from a twenty-four-pounder was sent crashing into the portico of Hindoo Rao's house, and with such deadly effect that it killed an English officer† and eight men and wounded four others, including a second English subaltern. We could not silence these guns. A twenty-four-pounder had been taken from the enemy in battle, but we had no ammunition in store for a gun of such calibre, and were fain to pick up the shot which had been fired from the city walls. Whilst the ordnance-stores at our command were dwindling down to scarcity-point, so vast were

* At first our offensive operations were principally confined to shelling the city. "We annoy them excessively with our shells, some of which reach almost to the Palace." But afterwards, perhaps because it was thought that we thus afflicted the townspeople rather than the mutineers, this course was abandoned. "I told you a little while ago that we were firing into the town, but last night there was an order given to fire on the gateways only, not into the town."—*Journal of an Artillery Officer. June* 16.

† Lieutenant Wheatly of the Fifty-fourth Native Infantry, who was doing duty with the Sirmoor Battalion. Among the Goorkahs killed was Tecca Ram, "one of the best shots in the regiment, who had killed twenty-two tigers in the Dhoon."

the supplies in the city, that it little mattered to our assailants how many rounds they fired every hour of the day. The gallantry of the Artillery subaltern, Willoughby, had done but little to diminish the resources of the enemy. There were vast supplies of material wealth that could not be blown into the air. 1857. June.

The fire from the Moree bastion, especially, played always annoyingly and sometimes destructively on the Ridge. The Sepoy gunners seemed to take a delight, which was a mixture of humour and savagery, in watching the incidents of our camp, and sending in their shots just at a critical moment to disturb our operations, whether of a military or a social character. If one detachment were marching to the relief of another—if a solitary officer were proceeding to inspect a battery—if a line of cook-boys were toiling on with their caldrons on their heads for the sustenance of the Europeans on picquet, a round shot was sure to come booming towards them, and perhaps with fatal precision of aim. In time our people became accustomed to this exercise, and either avoided the exposure altogether, or kept themselves on the alert so as to anticipate the arrival of the deadly missile, and secure safety by throwing themselves upon the ground. The cook-boys, whose journeys—as men must eat—could not be arrested or postponed, became adepts in this work. They went adroitly down on their knees and deposited their burdens till the danger had passed. The water-carriers, too, were greatly exposed. And it is characteristic of the relations which at that time existed between the two races, that although these servile classes did their duty with all fidelity—and it would have fared ill with us indeed if they had failed us in the hour of need—not only was there little kindliness and sym-

1857. June. pathy extended towards them, but by some at least of the Englishmen in camp, these unarmed, harmless, miserable servitors were treated with most unmerited severity. There is something grotesque, but not less terrible for its grotesqueness, in the story that when the cook-boys thus deftly saved themselves from swift death, and secured also their precious burdens, the European soldiers would sometimes say, "It is well for you, my boys, that you have not spilt our dinners."*

June 18—19. Attack on our rear. On the 18th, two Sepoy regiments that had mutinied at Nusserabad streamed into Delhi, bringing with them six guns.† This welcome reinforcement raised the hopes of the mutineers, and they resolved, on the following day, to go out in force against the besiegers. They had so often failed to make an impression on our front, that this time it was their game to attack our position in the rear. So, passing the Subzee-mundee, they entered the gardens on our right, and, disappearing for a while, emerged by the side of the Nujufgurh Canal, to the dismay of the camel-drivers, whose animals were quietly browsing on the plain. The day was then so far spent that the expectation of an attack, which had been entertained in the morning, had passed away from our camp, and we were but ill-prepared to receive the enemy. Our Artillery were the first in action against them. Scott, Money, and Tombs brought their guns into play with marvellous rapidity;‡ but for a while they were unsup-

* I am writing of this now only with reference to the practice of the enemy in the city. I shall speak more fully hereafter of the treatment of the Natives in camp.

† This reinforcement consisted of the Fifteenth and Thirtieth Sepoy Regiments, the Second Company Seventh Battalion (Golundauze) Artillery, with No. 6 Horse Battery attached, and some men of the First Bombay Light Cavalry.

‡ The Field Artillery employed on this occasion consisted of three guns each of four different batteries, under Turner, Money, Tombs, and Scott. The battle was fought by them.

ported, and the enemy's fire, artillery and musketry, was heavy and well directed. The guns of the mutineers were the far-famed guns of the illustrious garrison of Jellalabad, known in history as Abbott's Battery—guns with the mural crown upon them in honour of their great achievements. The Infantry, too, of the Nusserabad Brigade were proving their title to be regarded as the very flower of the rebel army. So fierce and well directed was the fire of a party of musketeers under cover, that Tombs, seeing his men dropping at their guns, and unable to reach the sheltered enemy, doubted for a little space whether he could maintain himself against them. But in this crisis up rode Daly with a detachment of his Guides' Cavalry, and a word from the heroic artilleryman sent him forward with a few followers against the musketeers in the brushwood. The diversion was successful; but the gallant leader of the Guides returned severely wounded, and for a while his services were lost to the Force.*

1857. June 18. Waterloo Day.

Meanwhile, our Cavalry had been getting to horse, and Yule's Lancers were to be seen spurring into action. But the shades of evening were now falling upon the battle, and ere long it was difficult to distinguish friends from enemies. Yule's saddle was soon empty;† and Hope Grant, who commanded, well-nigh fell into the hands of the enemy, for his charger was

* The author of the "History of the Siege of Delhi" thus describes this incident: "A portion of the Guide Cavalry came up. 'Daly, if you do not charge,' said Tombs to their leader, 'my guns are taken.' Daly spurred into the bushes—scarcely a dozen of his men followed him. He returned with a bullet in his shoulder; but the momentary diversion saved the guns."

† The contemporary annalists of the siege do not relate in what manner Yule met his death, but his horse galloping riderless into camp seems to have conveyed the first news of his fall, and his body lying all night on the field, it may be assumed that he was killed in the confusion which arose when the brief twilight had closed upon the scene. It is distinctly stated that our own Artillery fired upon the Lancers.

1857. June 18—19. shot under him, and it was sore trouble to rescue him in the confusion and darkness of the moment. The engagement, scattered and discursive as were its incidents, is not one easily to be described. A confused narrative of that evening's fighting must be most descriptive of the chaos of the fight. Night fell upon a drawn battle, of which no one could count the issues, and, as our officers met together in their mess-tents, with not very cheerful countenances, they saw the camp-fires of the enemy blazing up in their rear. We had sustained some severe losses. That fine field-officer of the Lancers, Yule, had been killed; Daly, of the Guides, had been incapacitated for active work; Arthur Becher, Quartermaster-General of the Army, had been wounded; and we had left many men upon the field. The enemy had increased in numbers, and with numbers their daring had increased. It would have gone ill with us if the mutineers had succeeded in establishing themselves in our rear, and the strength of the rebel force within the walls had enabled them to renew their attacks on our front and on our flanks. They were welcoming fresh reinforcements every day, whilst our reinforcements, notwithstanding the ceaseless energies of the authorities above and below Delhi, were necessarily coming in but slowly. Perhaps at no period of the siege were circumstances more dispiriting to the besiegers.

There was little sound sleep in our camp that night, but with the first dawn of the morning, and the first breath of the morning air, there came a stern resolution upon our people not to cease from the battle until they had driven the exulting enemy from our rear. But it was scarcely needed that we should brace ourselves up for the encounter. The vehemence of the enemy was seldom of long duration.

It expended itself in fierce spasms, often, perhaps, the growth of vast druggings of *bang*, and was generally exhausted in the course of a few hours. On the morning of the 19th, therefore, our people saw but little of the desperate energy of the 18th. Soon after our camp turned out there was another scene of wild confusion. Nobody seemed to know what was the actual position of affairs, and many were quite unable in their bewilderment to distinguish between enemies and friends. The former had nearly all departed, and the few who remained were driven out with little trouble. One last spasm of energy manifested itself in a farewell discharge of round-shot from a Sepoy gun; but the worst that befel us was an amazing panic among the camp-followers beyond the canal, and a considerable expenditure of ammunition upon an imaginary foe.

1857. June 19.

June 20—21. A lull.

It always happened that after one of these storms of excitement there was a season of calm. To the irresistible voluptuousness of perfect repose the Sepoys ever surrendered themselves on the day after a great fight. The 20th and the 21st were, therefore, days of rest to our Force. The latter was our Sabbath, and early service was performed by Mr. Rotton in the mess-tent of the Second Fusiliers, and afterwards in other parts of the camp. There were many then amongst our people instant in prayer, for they felt that a great crisis was approaching. They may have laughed to scorn the old prophecy that on the centenary of the great battle of Plassey, which had laid Bengal at our feet, and had laid, too, broad and deep the foundations of our vast Anglo-Indian Empire, our empire would be finally extinguished. The self-reliance of the Englishman made light account of such vaticinations; but no one doubted that the superstition

1857. June 22. was strong in the minds of the Delhi garrison, and that the 23rd of June would be a great day, for good or for evil, in the History of the War. It was certain, indeed, that then one of those convulsive efforts, with which already our people were so well acquainted, would be made on a larger scale than ever had been made before. On such a day, warned by the thought of the prophecy which designing people had freely circulated in the Lines of all our rebel regiments, it could not be doubted that Hindoos and Mahomedans would unite with common confidence and common enmity against us, and that an unwonted amount of confidence and *bang* would hurl their regiments against us with unexampled fury and self-devotion, in full assurance of the re-establishment of Native rule from one end of India to the other. Our force had been growing weaker and weaker every day, whilst the rebel force had grown stronger and stronger. It was not, therefore, a very cheerful prospect which lay before the English when they thought of the issues of the morrow.

June 23. The Centenary of Plassey. Day had scarcely broken on the 23rd when our people learnt that their expectations were not unfounded. The enemy, in greater force than had ever menaced us before, streamed out of the Lahore Gate, and again moved by our right towards the rear of the British camp, But they encountered an unexpected difficulty, which disconcerted their plans. On the previous night our Sappers had demolished the bridges over the Nujufgurh Drain, by which the enemy had intended to cross their guns; and thus checked, they were compelled to confine their attacks to the right of our position. The effect of this was, that much of the day's fighting was among the houses of the Subzee-mundee, from which the enemy poured in a deadly fire on our troops. Again and again the British Infantry, with noble courage and resolution, bearing up against the heats of the fiercest sun that had yet assailed them, drove the Sepoys from their cover, and fought against heavy odds all through that long summer day. We had need of all our force in such a struggle, for never had we been more outmatched in numbers, and never had the enemy shown a sterner, more enduring courage. Fresh troops had joined us in the morning, but weary as they were after a long night's march, they were called into service, and nobly responded to the call.* The action of the 19th had been an Artillery action; this of the 23rd was fought by the Infantry, and it was the fighting that least suits the taste and temper of the English soldier. But the Sixtieth Rifles went gallantly to the attack, and the Goorkahs and Guides vied with them in sturdy, unflinching courage to the last. At noonday the battle was raging furiously in the Subzeemundee; and such were the fearful odds against us, that Reid, cool and confident as he was in the face of difficulty and danger, felt that, if not reinforced, it would strain him to the utmost to hold his own.† But his men fought on; and after a while the reinforcements which he had sent for came up, and then, though the contest was still an unequal one, the

1857. June.

* These reinforcements consisted of a company of the Seventy-fifth Foot, four companies of the Second Bengal Fusiliers, four European Horse Artillery guns and part of a Native troop, with some Punjabee Infantry and Cavalry—in all about 850 men.

† "The mutineers, about twelve o'clock, made a most desperate attack on the whole of my position. No men could have fought better. They charged the Rifles, the Guides, and my own men again and again, and at one time I thought I must have lost the day. The cannonade from the city, and the heavy guns which they had brought out, raged fast and furious, and completely enfiladed the whole of my position. Thousands were brought against my mere handful of men; but I knew the importance of my position, and was determined to do my utmost to hold it till reinforcements arrived."—*Reid's Letters and Notes.*

1857. June. chances of war were no longer desperately against us, and our stubborn courage prevailed against the multitude of the enemy. As the sun went down, the vigour of the enemy declined also, and at sunset the mutineers had lost heart, and found that the work was hopeless. Before nightfall the Subzee-mundee was our own, and the enemy had withdrawn their guns and retired to the city. It had been a long weary day of hard fighting beneath a destroying sun, and our troops were so spent and exhausted that they could not charge the rebel guns, or follow the retreating masses of the mutineers. It was one of those victories of which a few more repetitions would have turned our position into a graveyard, on which the enemy might have quietly encamped.

June 24. State of affairs in Camp. After this there was another lull, and there was again time for our chief people to take account of the circumstances of their position and to look the future in the face. The result of the fighting on the Centenary of Plassey was somewhat to abate the confidence of the enemy. There were no signs of the descent of that great Star of Fortune which had risen above us for a hundred years. Little now was to be gained by them from spiritual manifestations and encouragements. They had only to look to their material resources; but these were steadily increasing, as the stream of mutiny continued to swell and roll down in full current towards the great ocean of the imperial city. Nusserabad and Jullundhur had already discharged their turbid waters, and now Rohilkund was about to pour in its tributaries. All this was against us, for it was the custom of the enemy upon every new accession of strength to signalise the arrival of the reinforcements by sending them out to attack us. Thus the brunt of the fighting on the 19th had been borne by the Nusserabad force, and on the 23rd by the regiments from Jullundhur. It was felt, therefore, that on the arrival of the Rohilkund Brigade there would be again a sharp conflict, which, although the issue of the day's fighting could not be doubtful, would tend to the diminution of our strength, and to the exhaustion of our resources, and would place us no nearer to the final consummation for which our people so ardently longed.

1857. June.

Arrival of reinforcements.

On the other hand, however, it was a source of congratulation that our reinforcements were also arriving. Sir John Lawrence was doing his work well in the Punjab, and sending down both European and Sikh troops, and every available gun, to strengthen Barnard in his position before Delhi. The dimensions of the British camp were visibly expanding. The newly arrived troops were at first a little dispirited by the thought of the small progress that had been made by their comrades before Delhi; for the besiegers were found to be the besieged. But they soon took heart again, for the good spirits of the Delhi Field Force were contagious, and nothing finer had ever been seen than the buoyancy and the cheerfulness which they manifested in the midst of all sorts of trials and privations. Many old friends and comrades then met together in the mess-tents to talk over old times, and many new friendships were formed by men meeting as strangers, on that ever-memorable Ridge—friendships destined to last for a life. Hospitality and good-fellowship abounded everywhere. There was not an officer in camp who did not delight in the opportunity of sharing his last bottle of beer with a friend or a comrade. And from the old Crimean General down to the youngest subaltern in camp, all were alike chivalrous, patient, and self-denying.

1857. June.

Last days of General Barnard.

There was never any despondency among them. Vast divergencies of opinion prevailed in camp with respect to the great something that was to be done. Some of the younger, more eager, spirits panted for a rush upon Delhi. The Engineer subalterns—Greathed and his gallant brethren—never ceased to urge the expediency of a *coup-de-main*, and as the month of June wore to a close, Barnard again consented to the enterprise—doubtfully as to the issue, and altogether reluctantly, but with a dominant sense that there was nothing else to be done. He was very active at this time. No subaltern, in the flower of his youth, was more regardless of exposure and fatigue. Under the fierce June sun, never sparing himself, he was continually abroad, and night seldom found his anxious head upon the pillow. Sometimes he and his son laid themselves down together, with revolvers in their hands, but still the general notion in camp was that he "never slept." He was torn to pieces by conflicting counsels. But he wore outwardly a cheerful aspect, and ever resolute to do his best, he bore up manfully against the troubles which surrounded him. Even the feeling that, do what he might, his reputation would be assailed, did not, to outward appearance, very sorely distress him. All men placed in difficult conjunctures must be prepared to encounter reproach, and Barnard well knew it. But ever as time went on he won upon the hearts of the officers under his command by his kindliness and generosity. It was said that he kept open tent; he had a liberal table; and never had an officer in high command a keener sense of individual merit or a more open-hearted desire to bestow his personal commendations on all who had distinguished themselves by acts of gallantry. So, before the month of June was at an end, Sir

Henry Barnard had securely established himself in the affections of the Delhi Field Force. 1857. June 28.

But, as weeks passed away, and he saw that he was making no impression upon Delhi, the inward care that was weighing upon his very life grew heavier and heavier. He wrote many letters at this time both to public functionaries in India and to private friends in England, in which he set forth very clearly his difficulties and perplexities, and suggested that he had been, and was likely to be, misjudged. To Sir John Lawrence he wrote, on the 28th of June, a letter, in which he reviewed the Past and set forth the circumstances of the Present. "You have, of course," he said, "been well informed of our proceedings, which, from the commencement, have been a series of difficulties overcome by the determined courage and endurance of our troops, but not leading us to the desired termination. When first I took up this position, my Artillery were to silence the fire of the town from the Moree and Cashmere Gates, at *least*, and our heavy guns then brought into play to open our way into the city. So far from this, however, we have not silenced a single gun, and they return us to this day at least four to one. The Chief Artillery Officer admits the distance to be too great; but to get nearer we must look to our Engineers, who are only now commencing to collect some few materials, such as trenching tools, sand-bags, &c., of which they were destitute, and even now have not enough to aid me in strengthening any outpost. In the mean time, my force is being worn out by the constant and sanguinary combats they are exposed to—the attacks which require every soul in my camp to repel—for it is never certain where the enemy intend to strike their blow, and it is only by vigilance I can

1857. June 28. ascertain it, and having done so, withdraw troops from one place to strengthen the threatened one; and thus the men are hastened here and there, and exposed to the sun all day. To me it is wonderful how all have stood it. It is heart-breaking to engage them in these affairs, which always cost us some valuable lives. The Engineers had arranged a plan of approach on the Cashmere side; the difficulties that meet one here are the constant interruptions the operations would experience by the fire from the town, and more so by the more frequent renewal of these dangerous attacks. But a greater one was in store for me when, on inquiring into the means, the amount of siege ammunition was found to be so totally inadequate, that the Chief Engineer declared the project must be abandoned. There remains, therefore, but one alternative. My whole force will be here in a day or two, when our entire project will be matured. Disappointing as, I fear, our progress has been to you, the results of our exertions have been great; an immensely superior force has been on all occasions defeated with great loss, and I have reason to believe that the spirit of this mutineering multitude—contemptible in the open, but as good, if not better, than ourselves behind guns—is completely broken, and that the game is in our hands; for, by confining, or rather centralising the evil on Delhi, the heart of it will be crushed in that spot, and that 'delay,' so far from being detrimental, has been of essential use! But for the prestige, I would leave Delhi to its fate. Anarchy and disorder would soon destroy it; and the force now before it—the only one of Europeans you have in India set free—would be sufficient to re-establish the greater part of the country. To get into Delhi will greatly reduce this small force, and I feel much moral courage in even hinting at an object which I have no intention of carrying out—at all events, till after an attempt has been made. You may say, why engage in these constant combats? The reason simply is that, when attacked, we must defend ourselves; and that to secure our camp, our hospitals, our stores, &c., every living being has to be employed. The whole thing is too gigantic for the force brought against it. The gates of Delhi once shut, with the whole of your Native Army drilled, equipped, and organised within the walls, a regularly prepared force should have been employed, and the place invested. Much as I value the reduction of Delhi, and great as I see that the danger to my own reputation will be if we fail, still I would rather retire from it than risk this army! But, by God's blessing, all may be saved yet." And in this letter, having set forth the general state of the great question before him, he proceeded to speak of some of its personal bearings. "My position," he said, "is difficult; and not the less so for its undefined responsibilities, which must always be the case when a Commander-in-Chief is in the same field. But the valuable assistance which you have given me, in Brigadier-General Chamberlain, will henceforward greatly lighten my anxieties." 1857. June.

A few days before—on the 24th of June—Brigadier Chamberlain had arrived in Camp to take the post of Adjutant-General of the Army. His coming had been anticipated with the liveliest emotions of satisfaction. Some said that he would be worth a thousand men. Those who had ever encouraged the bolder and the more hazardous course of action rejoiced most of all, for they believed that his voice would be lifted up in June 24. Arrival of Brigadier-General Chamberlain.

1857. June.

favour of some dashing enterprise.* It was, doubtless, at that time great gain to have such a man at the elbow of the Commander.† A few months before officialism would have stood aghast at such a selection. Neville Chamberlain had little departmental experience. But the Departments, in that great crisis, were not in the highest honour. Not that they had failed—not that they had done any worse or any better than Departments are wont to do in great conjunctures; but that the Delhi Field Force did not want Departments, but men. There was no want of manliness in the general Staff, for already within the space of three weeks one departmental chief had been killed and another disabled. But it was felt that there were men in the country, cast in the true heroic mould, with a special genius for the work in hand. Some said, "Oh, if Henry Lawrence were but here!" others spoke of John Nicholson as the man for the crisis; and all rejoiced in the advent of Neville Chamberlain. There was another, too, whose name at that time was in the mouth of the general camp. It was known that Baird Smith had been summoned to direct the engineering department, which had been lamentably in want of an efficient chief. All these things were cheering to the heart of the Crimean General, for he mistrusted his own judgment, and he

* "Neville Chamberlain has arrived; of this we are all glad, as well as the General. Wilby's bold conceptions may now receive more consideration." — *Greathed's Letters.*— "Everything will be right, they used to say, when Chamberlain comes, and all took courage when they saw his stern pale face."—*History of the Siege of Delhi.*

† "You have sent me a sound, good auxiliary in Brigadier Chamberlain, who fully sees and admits the difficulties I have been placed in. He is favourable to the trial of getting into the place, and a reasonable hope of success may be entertained. I am willing to try, provided I can see my way to honourably secure my sick and wounded, and keeping open my supplies."—*Sir H. Barnard to Sir John Lawrence, July 1. MS. Correspondence.*

looked eagerly for counsellors in whom he could confide. 1857. July.

Baird Smith was at Roorkhee, leading an active, busy life, thinking much of the Army before Delhi, but never dreaming of taking part in the conflict, when, in the last week of June, news reached him that he was wanted there to take the place of the Chief Engineer, who had completely broken down. Having improvised, with irregular despatch, a body of some six hundred Pioneers, and loaded fifty or sixty carts with Engineer tools and stores, he started on the 29th of June, accompanied by Captains Robertson and Spring.* Pushing on by forced marches, he was within sixty miles of Delhi, when, on the morning of the 2nd of July, after a weary night-march, an express reached him with the stirring news that an assault on Delhi had been planned for the early dawn of the morrow, and that all were anxious for his presence. After an hour or two of sleep, he mounted again, and rode—or, as he said, "scrambled"—on; getting what he could to carry him—now a fresh horse, now an elephant, and again the coach-and-four of the Rajah of Jheend; and so, toiling all through the day and the night, he reached Delhi by three o'clock on the morning of the 3rd. Weary and worn out though he was, the prospect of the coming assault braced him up for the work in hand; but he had made the toilsome march for nothing. The projected attack was in abeyance, if it had not wholly collapsed.

Colonel Baird Smith.

It was the old story: that fatal indecision, which had been the bane of General Barnard, as leader of such an enterprise as this, had again, at the eleventh

Postponement of the Assault.

* The latter was going to join his regiment in the Punjab. On the morning of his arrival at Jhelum he was killed in an attack on the Native troops that had broken into mutiny in that place.

1857. July 3. hour, overthrown the bolder counsels which he had been persuaded to adopt. All the expected reinforcements had arrived, and he was stronger than he had ever been before.* The details of the assault had been arranged; the plans had been prepared; the troops had been told off for the attacking columns, though they had not yet been warned, and the project was kept a secret in Camp—when information reached him that the enemy were contemplating a grand attack upon our position by the agency of the rebel regiments recently arrived from Rohilkund. The time of early morning appointed for the assault—a little before daybreak—would have been propitious, for the hour before dawn was dark and cloudy, and our troops could have advanced unseen to the City walls. But now the opportunity was lost. The time was coming for "the moon and day to meet," and so all hope of our creeping up, unseen, beneath the shadow of the darkness, was passing away. What Barnard and others called the "Gamester's Throw," was not destined to be thrown by him.†

* The reinforcements which had joined our Camp from the Punjab between the 26th of June and 3rd of July were the Head-quarters of Her Majesty's Eighth Foot, released by the defection of the Jullundhur Brigade; the Head-quarters of Her Majesty's Sixty-first Foot; the First Regiment of Punjab Infantry (Coke's Rifles); a squadron of Punjab Cavalry; with two guns of European and two of Native Horse Artillery; some European Reserve Artillery, and some Sikh gunners. The want of artillerymen to work our guns had been severely felt, and Sir John Lawrence had done his best to supply them from all sources. The reinforcements detached above made up, according to Norman, our effective force to six thousand six hundred men of all arms.

† The causes of the abandonment of the enterprise were thus stated by Sir H. Barnard: "I had all prepared for the *gamester's throw* last night, when the arrival of the reinforcements of Coke's gave me all the available means I can expect. It was frustrated, first, by hearing that we were to be attacked in great force this morning at dawn of day, when to a certainty our Camp would be destroyed; and, secondly, on account of serious disaffection in (Charles) Nicholson's Regiment, all the Hindoos of which I have disarmed—and hung two of the Na-

The threatened attack on our position, said to have been fixed for the morning of the 3rd, was not then developed into a fact; but at night the Rohilkund Brigade*—some four thousand or five thousand strong, Horse, Foot, and Artillery—the Infantry in the scarlet uniforms of their old masters—went out, under cover of the darkness, and made their way towards Alipore, in rear of our Camp, with some vague intention of cutting off our communications by destroying a post we had established there, and of intercepting some convoys on their way to or from the Ridge.† A force under Major Coke, of the Punjab Irregular Army, who had arrived in Camp on the last day of June, was sent out to give battle to the mutineers. It was a compact, well-appointed column of Cavalry and Infantry, with some Horse Artillery guns; and the leader was held in repute for his achievements in border warfare. But the result was a disappointment. The ground was marshy; the progress was slow; and we were too late to do the work. Soon after daybreak on the 4th, our column came in sight of the Sepoy Regiments which were then returning from Alepore, and our guns were brought into action. But Coke had not taken

1857. July 4. The Bareilly Brigade.

tive officers. The Ninth Irregulars evinced evident sign of '*shake*,' and as they numbered some four hundred and fifty, it became a serious question to leave all these natives in my Camp, when all my own forces were employed elsewhere. Chamberlain admits that few men were ever placed in a more painfully responsible position. If I lose this small force, it will be felt all over the Punjab, and yet, if I do not take Delhi, the result will be equally disastrous. It will be a good deed when done!—and I will take care and do it, with every chance in my favour, in good will."—*Sir Henry Barnard to Sir John Lawrence, July 3, 1869. MS. Correspondence.*

* The Rohilkund, or Bareilly, Brigade marched in on the 1st and 2nd of July. It consisted of the Eighteenth, Twenty-eighth, Twenty-ninth, and Sixty-eighth Infantry Regiments; the Eighth Irregular Cavalry, No. 15 Horse Battery, and two 6-pounder post guns from Shahjehanpore.

† The enemy expected to find a convoy of wounded men going from our Camp to Umballah, and another with treasure and ammunition coming from Ferozepore. But he fortunately missed both of them.

1857. July. right account of the distance; our light field pieces made little impression upon the enemy, and our Infantry had not come up in time to take part in the engagement. The Sepoy General, Bukht Khan, was, however, in no mood to come to closer quarters with us, so he drew off his forces and set his face towards Delhi, leaving behind him his baggage, consisting mainly of the night's plunder—an ammunition waggon and some camel-loads of small-arm cartridges. But they carried off all their guns, and returned to garrison not much weaker than when they started. "The distance we had come from Camp," wrote General Reed to Sir John Lawrence, "and the deep state of the ground, prevented our guns and cavalry from pursuing. In fact, the horses were knocked up, and the guns could scarcely be moved, while the enemy, being on higher ground, managed to get away their guns."* But if we had gained no glory, the enemy had added another to their long list of failures. They had taken out some thousands of their best troops, and had only burnt a village, plundered a small isolated British post, and left the plunder behind them on the field. But, if our eyes had not been opened before to the danger of some day having our rearward communications with Kurnaul and the Punjab—all the upper country from which we drew our supplies and reinforcements—interrupted by a swarming enemy, who might attack us at all points

* *MS. Correspondence.*—The author of the "History of the Siege of Delhi," who was obviously with Coke's force, adds: "Our men returned completely exhausted by the heat. Indeed, many of the Sixty-first sank down beneath trees, and our elephants had to be sent from Camp to carry them in."—Hodson says that "our loss was about thirty or forty Europeans, and three of my Native officers temporarily disabled." Another writer (*MS. Journal*) says: "Our loss was one Irregular, who came from the Punjab with Coke, and an Artillery driver."

at the same time, so as to prevent us from effectively protecting our rear, this expedition of the Rohilkund force dispersed all the films that still obscured our vision. And our Engineer officers, therefore, were directed to adopt every possible measure to render the establishment of the enemy in our rear a feat of difficult, if not impossible, accomplishment; and the chief of these was the destruction of the bridges across the Nujufgurh Canal, except the one immediately in our rear, which we could always command and protect.

1857 July.

Very soon Baird Smith and Barnard were in close consultation. The General rejoiced greatly in the presence of his new adviser, and gave him his unstinted confidence. The arrival, indeed, of such a man as the accomplished Engineer, who knew every nook and crevice in Delhi, and who, before he had any expectation of being personally connected with the siege, had devised a plan of attack, was great gain to the besieging force; and Barnard, whose ignorance of Indian warfare and mistrust of his own judgment drove him to seek advice in all likeliest quarters, would gladly have leant most trustingly on Smith. But it was not decreed that he should trust in any one much longer. His life was now wearing to a close.

Death of General Barnard.

On the second day after Baird Smith's arrival in Camp, cholera fell heavily upon the General, and smote him down with even more than its wonted suddenness. General Reed had seen Barnard in the early morning, and observed nothing peculiar about him; but by ten o'clock on that Sunday morning a whisper was running through the camp that the Commander of the Delhi Field Force was dying.

July 5.

1857. July 5. He had been missed from his accustomed place at church-service; and, before many hours had passed, his broken-hearted son, who had ministered to him with all the tenderness of a woman, was standing beside his lifeless body. "Tell them," said the dying General, speaking of his family in England, almost with his last breath—"tell them that I die happy." Next day his remains were conveyed on a gun-carriage to their last resting-place. "The only difference," wrote the Chaplain who performed the burial-service, "between the General and a private soldier consisted in the length of the mournful train, which followed in solemn silence the mortal remains of the brave warrior."

From his death-bed he had sent a message to Baird Smith, saying that he trusted to him to give such an explanation of the circumstances in which he was placed as would save his reputation as a soldier. And, indeed, the same generosity of feeling as he had evinced in all his endeavours to brighten the character of his dead friend Anson was now displayed by others towards him; for all men spoke and wrote gently and kindly of Barnard, as of one against whom nothing was to be said except that circumstances were adverse to him. "I found him," wrote Baird Smith, "one of the most loveable men I had ever met—rigidly conscientious in every duty, a perfect gentleman in manner and feeling, a brave soldier, but unequal to the present crisis from an apparent want of confidence in himself and an inability to discriminate between the judgments of others."—"In him," wrote General Reed to Sir John Lawrence, "the service has lost a most energetic and indefatigable officer, and I fear his untimely end was in a great measure to be attributed to his fearless exposure of himself, not only to the fire of the enemy, but to the more deadly rays of the sun."—"He was a high-minded, excellent officer," said Mr. Commissioner Greathed; "and on European ground, in a European war, would have done the State good service; but he was too suddenly thrust into the most difficult active service in India that could be imagined, and found himself placed in command of an Army which General Anson had organised, and obliged to carry out operations which he would not himself have undertaken with the means at his command. With more knowledge of the relative merits of his troops and of the enemy, he would, I think, have achieved a great success."—"How he has carried on so long," wrote Neville Chamberlain, "is wonderful. All day in the sun, and the most part of the night either walking up and down the main street of the camp or visiting the batteries and posts. His constitution was such that he could not command sleep at the moments when he might have rested, and exhausted nature has given way. We all deeply lament his loss, for a kinder or more noble-minded officer never lived."

1857. July 5.

I need add nothing to these tributes from the foremost officers in the Camp. Only three months before Barnard had written to Lord Canning, saying: "Cannot you find some tough job to put to me? I will serve you faithfully."* The "tough job" had been found, and a single month of it had sufficed to lay him in his grave. But he had redeemed his promise. He had served the State faithfully to the last hour of his life.

* *Ante,* vol. i., page 563. Some further extracts from Barnard's Correspondence will be found in the Appendix.

1857. July. And here fitly closes the second part of this Story of the Siege of Delhi. It is the story of a succession of profitless episodes—desultory in narration as in fact; the story of a month's fighting with no results but loss of life, waste of material resources, and bitter disappointment in all the dwelling-places of the English in India, as week after week passed away, and every fresh report of the fall of Delhi was proved to be a mockery and a lie.

CHAPTER V.

GENERAL REED IN COMMAND—EXERTIONS OF BAIRD SMITH—INADEQUACY OF RESOURCES—QUESTION OF ASSAULT RENEWED—ENGAGEMENTS WITH THE ENEMY—HOPES OF THE ENGLISH—ASSAULT ABANDONED—DEPARTURE OF GENERAL REED—BRIGADIER WILSON IN COMMAND—HIS POSITION AND EFFORTS—SOCIAL ASPECTS OF THE CAMP—STATE OF THE DELHI GARRISON.

July, 1857.

Question of Materials for a Siege.

FROM the first hour of his appearance at Delhi, Baird Smith had begun to examine thoroughly the means and resources at his disposal. He had no great opinion of the power of the place to stand a siege, if the besiegers had adequate material for its prosecution. But never was a besieging army in worse plight for the conduct of great operations than the British Army before Delhi. The Chief Engineer found that his siege ordnance consisted of two 24-pounders, nine 18-pounders, six 8-inch mortars, and two or three 8-inch howitzers. The enemy were much stronger in Artillery. They could bring to any point open to attack from twenty-five to thirty guns, and ten or twelve mortars—all as well served as our own. But there was something even worse than this. If we had possessed more guns we could not have used them, for there was a deplorable want of ammunition. Baird Smith stood aghast at the discovery that the shot in store for the heavy guns was scarcely equal to the requirements of a day's siege, and there was no immediate prospect of the receipt of further supplies; whilst, on the other

1857. July.

hand, the enemy were furnished with the inexhaustible resources of the great Delhi Magazine. It was plain, therefore, that in this helpless state it would have been madness to commence siege operations, which must have been speedily abandoned from the exhaustion of our material supplies.

Question of Assault.

But the question still suggested itself: "Might not the place be carried by assault?" It was easier to answer this in the affirmative. "Here," he argued, "the relative forces are materially changed in value. We have a highly disciplined body under a single head, completely in hand, full of pluck, and anxious to attack, and with almost unlimited self-reliance. The enemy is without any head, not in hand at all, so far broken in spirit that he has never met us in battle—with any odds in his favour—without being beaten. It is very true that his numbers much exceed ours, and that in a town, in street-fighting, discipline is of less value than in the open battle-field. It is true, also, that assaults are proverbially precarious. Napoleon said of them, 'a dog or a goose may decide their issues.' The results of failure would be as terrible and depressing as those of success would be glorious and inspiriting."* All these things he deliberately considered; but, weighing the chances on either side, he came to the conclusion that "the probabilities of success were far greater than those of failure, and the reasons justifying an assault stronger than those which justified inaction." He therefore urged upon the General, in an official letter, the advantages of an assault by escalade, the gates which we desired to force being blown in by powder-bags. "And," he wrote, four months afterwards, "looking back now with the full advantages of actual ex-

* MS. Correspondence of Colonel Baird Smith.

perience, and with, I believe, very little disposition to maintain a foregone conclusion, because it was foregone, I think at this moment, if we had assaulted any time between the 4th and 14th of July, we should have carried the place." * 1857. July.

When the Engineer's letter reached the Head-Quarters of the Force, Sir Henry Barnard was dead, or dying.† The command was then assumed by General Reed. Since he had been in the Delhi Camp, with no immediate responsibility upon him, his health had improved; and although he still appeared to others, especially to men with the inexhaustible energies of Baird Smith, a feeble invalid, he believed himself to be equal to the work, and wrote that, "with the aid of the Almighty, he trusted to carry it to a successful issue." To this officer Baird Smith's plan of assault was submitted. He did not immediately reject it. On the 9th, he wrote to Sir John Lawrence, saying, "We still have the assault in contemplation, the details of which are not yet quite completed by the Engineers' Department under Baird Smith." But the delay, whether originating in the Engineers' Department, or in the councils of the General, was fatal to the scheme; and, as Baird Smith afterwards wrote, "the opportunity passed away, and the question of assault or no assault finally resolved itself into doing nothing by sheer

General Reed

* MS. Correspondence of Colonel Baird Smith.

† I have here again to notice the confusion of dates, of which I have spoken in a former note. Baird Smith, in a letter before me, says, "My letter recommending the measure went in on the 6th. I doubt if Sir Henry Barnard ever saw it, as he died a day or two afterwards." But Mr. Greathed, in a letter dated July 6, says that the remains of the General were buried at ten o'clock on that day; and Mr. Rotton (*Chaplain's Narrative*), who performed the funeral service, says most distinctly that Barnard died at three o'clock on Sunday afternoon, July 5. There is not the least doubt of the fact. Baird Smith's letter, therefore, was not sent in until after Barnard's death, unless he is wrong about the date of its despatch.

1857. July. force of circumstances." "Whatever is," he added, "being best, I am content with things as they are, and I am very far indeed from attaching the slightest blame to those who differed from me on the question of assaulting. They, doubtless, examined the probabilities as conscientiously as I did, but realised them differently, and came to a contrary conclusion. The difficulties were great enough, and the consequences grave enough, to require every man to form and to hold to his own opinion, and yet to promote toleration at differences—at any rate, that was my view of the case, right or wrong." And, truly, it was very right. For there is nothing, perhaps, which calls for more toleration than the solution of great military questions, when there are antagonistic arrays of difficulties to be considered. It has been said of other places than Delhi, which have stood protracted sieges, that they might have been carried by assault within the first hour of our appearance before them. It was said of Bhurtpore; it was said of Sebastopol; but neither Combermere nor Raglan thought that it was his duty to risk the chance of a failure by attempting it.

Action of July 9. The circumstances, the force of which was said by the Chief Engineer to have settled the momentous question of assault or no assault, were these. Whilst in the English Camp our people were considering the best means of attacking the enemy within the walls of Delhi, the enemy were making renewed attacks on the British Camp outside the walls; and every new attack reduced our scanty numbers. On the 9th of July they came out in force against us. Intelligence of their design reached General Reed in the morning, and he was in some measure prepared for them; but he scarcely expected a daring inroad of rebel Cavalry into our Camp.* But about ten o'clock,† through a mist of heavy rain, our English officers, on the "Mound" discerned their approach. Here, on a piece of elevated ground to the right rear of our Camp, was planted a battery of three heavy guns, with the usual Infantry Picquet. In addition to this a Cavalry Picquet was thrown out, somewhat in advance of the Mound, and this now consisted of a party of Carabineers, two Horse Artillery guns of Tombs's troop, and a detachment of the Ninth Irregular Cavalry, under a Native officer, which occupied the extreme point in advance.‡ Perplexed by

1857. July 9.

* "We had a sharp affair with the enemy yesterday. I had received a report in the morning that they were coming out in force on the right, and Major Reid applied for their usual reinforcement at Hindoo Rao's house, which was sent, and the rest of the troops held in readiness to turn out. About ten A.M. a party of insurgent Sowars made a most daring inroad to the rear of our right by a road leading to the Grand Trunk. These men were dressed exactly like the Ninth Irregulars, which led to the supposition that part of that regiment, which was on picquet on that flank, had mutinied; but it turned out that the greater part of them, at least, belonged to the Eighth Irregulars from Bareilly. About a hundred men of their people actually swept through the right of our camp by the rear, by the bridge adjoining the burial-ground."—*General Reed to Sir John Lawrence, July* 10, 1857. *MS.*

† It will have been seen that, in the preceding note, General Reed says that the enemy appeared about ten o'clock. Major Reid says, "the action commenced about seven o'clock." The latter may refer to the opening of the enemy's guns. Major Tombs says that, to the best of his recollection, it was about three P.M. when he first learnt that the troopers were entering our Camp. Cotemporary accounts often differ greatly with respect to the time of day.

‡ "The Mound was about halfway between the Ridge and the Canal, which protected the British rear. It was on the right rear flank of Camp, and overlooked the Subzee-mundee. Between the Mound and the Canal there were several clumps of trees, and the Canal-bank being also fringed with them, the view in that direction was confused and interrupted, and for this reason a Cavalry picquet was thrown out on the Canal-bank, somewhat in advance of the Mound, from which, however, the videttes of the Cavalry picquet were visible. . . . The guns and Carabineers were not stationed on the Mound, but at the foot of and on the right flank of it, so that facing to their proper front — the Subzee-mundee—the Mound was on their left hand and the Canal on their right. The ground on the right of the picquet was somewhat elevated, and on this the tents of the men were pitched and the Cavalry horses picqueted. The guns were, as it were, in a hollow, with the Mound on their left and the elevated ground on the right. To their front was a small breastwork, to which it was ordered that the guns should be run up and fought behind in case of an attack, and until the picquet could be reinforced."—*MS. Memorandum.*

1857. July. the appearance of the familiar uniform of the Irregular Cavalry of our own Picquets, our people at first thought that they had been driven in by the advance of the enemy; and so the guns, which might have opened upon them, were pointed harmlessly at the troopers.* But there was something much worse than this. The mistake of the British Artillery was followed by the disgrace of the British Cavalry As the Irregulars of the Eighth from Delhi swept on, the detachment of Carabineers, which formed a part of the Picquet, turned and fled. Stillman, who commanded them, remained alone at his post. The first error was soon discovered. Hills, who was in charge of the artillery—two horse-artillery guns—of the Picquet, saw presently that it was a hostile attack, and ordered out his guns for action. But the enemy were upon him; he had not time to open fire. In this emergency the dashing Artillery subaltern—a man of light weight and short stature, young in years, but with the coolness of a veteran and the courage of a giant—set spurs to his horse and rushed into the midst of the advancing troopers, cutting right and left at them with good effect, until two of them charged him at the same time, and by the shock of

* The actual assailants were troopers of the Eighth Irregular Cavalry, who had mutinied at Bareilly; but it was more than suspected that the men of the Ninth were cognisant of and favoured the attack. It has been seen (*Note, ante*, page 565) that General Barnard had been very doubtful of their fidelity. There had been many desertions from their ranks, but no signs of open mutiny. It may be stated here that after this affair of the 9th of July, the regiment was quietly moved out of Camp, apparently on duty. "On the 11th of July the Head-Quarters of the Regiment proceeded to Alipore, for the purpose of keeping open the communication with the rear. Large detachments were sent into the divisions of Saharunpore, Soneput, and Paneput. On the 21st of July, in consequence of a large desertion from the Soneput detachment, it was deemed advisable to march the regiment back towards the Punjab."—*Parliamentary Return of Regiments that have Mutinied.* A wing of the Ninth Irregular had accompanied the first siege-train to Delhi (*ante*, page 189), and the other (Head-Quarters) wing had joined our Camp on the 2nd of July.

the collision, both horse and rider were thrown violently to the ground. Regaining his feet after his assailants had passed on, he recovered his sword in time to renew the combat with three Sowars, two mounted and one on foot. The two first he cut down,* and then engaged the third, a young, active swordsman of good courage, who came fresh to the encounter, whilst Hills, scant of breath and shaken by his fall, had lost all his first strength, but none of his first courage. The heavy cloak, too, which he wore, as a protection against the rain, dragged at his throat, and well-nigh choked him. The chances were now fearfully against him. Twice he fired, but his pistol snapped, and then he cut at his opponent's shoulder. The blow did not take effect; and the trooper, watching his opportunity, clutched at the English subaltern's sword and wrested it from him. Hills then closed with his enemy, grappled him so that he could not strike out with the sabre, and smote him with clenched fist again and again on the face, until the Englishman slipped and fell to the ground. 1857. July 9.

The "Mound" was a favourite place of gathering in Camp. It commonly happened that many of our officers were to be seen there, watching the progress of events below, or discussing the operations of the siege. But the heavy rain of the 9th of July had driven our people to the shelter of their tents. Among others, Major Tombs was in the Artillery mess-tent—one of the cheeriest places in Camp—when a trooper of the Ninth Irregular Cavalry, in a state of high excitement, rode up and asked the way

* "The first I wounded and dropped him from his horse; the second charged me with a lance. I put it aside, and caught him an awful gash on the head and face. I thought I had killed him; apparently he must have clung to his horse, for he disappeared. The wounded man then came up, but got his skull split."—*Hills' Narrative.*

1857. July 9. to the General's quarters. In reply to a question from Tombs, he said that the enemy were showing in front of our picquets; but the man's words seemed but scantly to express all that was in him, so Tombs hurried to his own tent, took his sword and revolver, and ordering his horse to be brought after him, walked down to the Mound Picquet. As he approached the post, he saw the Carabineers drawn up, in mounted array, and our guns getting ready for action. In a minute there was a tremendous rush of Irregular Horse, the troopers brandishing their swords and vociferating lustily; and then there was to be seen the sad spectacle of our Dragoons broken and flying to the rear, whilst one of our guns went right-about, some of the horses mounted and some riderless, and galloped towards our Camp. Tombs was now in the midst of the enemy, who were striking at him from all sides, but with no effect. A man of a noble presence, tall, strong, of robust frame and handsome countenance, dark-haired, dark-bearded, and of swart complexion, he was, in all outward semblance, the model of a Feringhee warrior; and the heroic aspect truly expressed the heroic qualities of the man. There was no finer soldier in the Camp. Threading his way adroitly through the black horsemen, he ascended the Mound, and looking down into the hollow, where his two guns had been posted, he saw the remaining one overturned, the horses on the ground, struggling in their harness or dead, with some slain or wounded gunners beside them. Near the gun he saw the prostrate body of Hills, apparently entangled in his cloak, with a dismounted Sowar standing over him with drawn sword, about to administer the death-stroke. At this time Tombs was some thirty paces from his friend. He could not hope to reach the enemy in time to cut him down with the sabre, so resting his revolver on his left arm, he took steady aim at the trooper, who was turned full-breasted towards him, and shot him through the body. The blood oozed out through the white tunic of the wounded rebel, and, for a while at least, Hills was saved. 1857. July 9.

But the danger was not yet passed. Tombs helped his fallen subaltern to rise, and together they ascended the slope of the Mound. As they were watching the movements of the enemy, they saw a little way beneath them another dismounted Sowar, who was walking away with Hills' revolver in his hand. They made at once towards him. He was a young, strong, active trooper, who turned and attacked them with his sword, as one well skilled in the use of the weapon. His first blow aimed at Hills was parried. Then he struck at Tombs, who with like address guarded the cut. But the third blow, struck with despairing energy, as he sprung upon the younger of his opponents, broke down Hills' guard, and clove the skull to the brain. In a moment he had turned upon Tombs, who coolly parried the blow and drove his sword right through the trooper's body.*

* This narrative differs from some of the published versions of this incident, and, in one respect at least, from the account (quoted above) written by Hills himself, and printed at the time in the English journals. Hills says that the Sowar with whom he and Tombs had the second encounter was the very man who had attacked him in the first instance, and from whom his friend had saved him. "When we got down," he says, "I saw the very man Tombs had saved me from moving off with my pistol (he had only been wounded, and shammed dead). I told Tombs, and we went at him." But it is the assured belief of Tombs, who saw the first trooper fall, and the blood streaming from the man's chest over his white tunic, that their second antagonist was "another dismounted Sowar." *Cæteris paribus*, there would seem to be more reason to accept Tombs's version than that of his subaltern, as the circumstances of the former were more favourable to cool and accurate observation. And I would rather believe this version, as the one that best illustrates the

1857. July 9. Meanwhile, the Sowars, flushed with their first success, were sweeping onwards through our picquets, to the main street of our Camp. What could account for the rout of the Carabineers—what could explain the flight of the Horse Artillery?* The utmost confusion prevailed. Our people turned out in excited haste, not knowing what it all portended. The road which the rebel-troopers had taken led to the Artillery Lines. There was a Native troop of Horse Artillery there under Major Renny; and the Sowars called upon them to fraternise with their party, and to march back with them to Delhi. The loyal Natives sternly replied that they obeyed only their own officers. Near them was Henry Olpherts' European troop, unlimbered and ready for immediate action. The black troop was between them and the enemy; but the Native gunners called upon the white troopers to fire through their bodies. There was no need for this. The whole Camp was now astir. For a little while the Sowars had profited by the uncertainty and perplexity in our Camp. But

splendour of the achievement. If the same Sowar were the hero of both combats, he assuredly well earned by that morning's fighting the Behaudur-Shah Cross for personal bravery. I should not omit to add that it has been recorded that "Tombs's account of the affair of the 9th, when the enemy's Horse rode through our Camp, was torn up by Colonel Mackenzie. He had omitted to say a word about himself, so Mackenzie gave the General the true version."—*Greathed's Letters.* Both Tombs and Hills were deservedly rewarded with the Victoria Cross.

* It seems to have been a question among earlier writers whether the artillery on picquet duty did run away; but there can be no doubt of the fact. In a letter written from Camp on the same day, an artillery officer, describing what he saw, says: "A gun of the Horse Artillery, that had been on picquet on our right, had just retreated into Camp, into our main street, close to my tent." The statement of Major (Sir Henry) Tombs, as embodied in the text, is quite conclusive on the subject. With respect to the flight of the Carabineers, General Reed writes: "In the confusion, I am sorry to say a detachment of the Carabineers, who were escorting the guns, gave way, in spite of the endeavours of their officers to stop them. These men I propose to dismount as a disgrace to them. It would appear that they are composed mostly of recruits, and, being mounted on half-broken horses, do not know how to manage them."—*MS. Correspondence.*

their triumph was soon turned to defeat, and they fled back to Delhi, leaving many of these audacious rebels behind them, including the originator of the perilous exploit.* That so many of them escaped unscathed, returning by the way they had come, is not to be accounted for, except on the ground of surprise and confusion. Acts of individual gallantry are recorded—none more lustrous than those scored up to the honour of the brave artillerymen, Renny and Fagan.† But some dark clouds overshadowed the scene. It is related that in the absence of tangible enemies, some of our soldiery, who turned out on this occasion, butchered a number of unoffending camp-followers, servants, and others, who were huddling together, in vague alarm, near the Christian churchyard. No loyalty, no fidelity, no patient good service, on the part of these poor people, could extinguish for a moment the fierce hatred which possessed our white soldiers against all who wore the dusky livery of the East.

1857. July 9.

Affairs in the Subzee-mundee.

This bold incursion of Irregulars into our Camp did not supply all the day's fighting. All through the morning a brisk cannonade had been maintained by the enemy, and answered by our guns on the Right. It was soon apparent, however, that the

* "They were at first supposed to be the Ninth, but, being discovered, were charged by Brigadier Grant with his Lancers, and Captain Hodson with the Guides, who drove them out of Cantonments."—*General Reed to Sir John Lawrence. MS. Correspondence.* This, however, as regards Hodson's part in the expulsion of the enemy, is erroneous. Hodson started in pursuit with the Guides, mistook the enemy for our own people, and rode some three miles parallel to them, until they suddenly crossed a bridge and "galloped off to Delhi."—*See Greathed's and Hodson's Letters.*

† Renny is said to have shot several of the rebel troopers with his revolver. Fagan rushed out of his tent with only a pen in his hand, got together a few men, killed fifteen of the enemy, and returned with a sword and Minie rifle, of which he had "eased" a Ressaldar of the Irregulars. — *Norman's Narrative,—Greathed's Letters.—History of the Siege of Delhi.*

1857. July 9. rebel musketeers were as active as their gunners. A body of Sepoys had posted themselves in the suburb of the Subzee-mundee, where, screened and aided by houses and walled gardens, and other enclosures, they kept up a galling fire on our picquets. This could not be endured; so a column was formed to attack and dislodge them. It consisted of the Head-Quarters and two companies of the Sixtieth Rifles, detachments of the Eighth and Sixty-first Foot, and the Fourth Sikh Infantry, with the six guns of Major Scott's battery; whilst Major Reid was instructed to co-operate with them with such men as could be spared from the Main Picquet. Commanded by General Chamberlain, our column swept through the Subzee-mundee, and was soon in close conflict with the insurgents. Posted as they were, and often firing down upon us from some elevated structure, it was not easy to dislodge them. The fighting was of the kind most distasteful and most destructive to our British soldiery. But their stubborn courage prevailed at last. The work was done thoroughly;* but such thorough work always was done by us, at heavy cost to our ever-decreasing force. We could ill spare at that time a single fighting man; but the cotemporary historians relate that more than two hundred of our people were killed or disabled on that 9th of July.† And so the chances of a successful assault upon the city began to dwindle into a certainty of failure; and those who had urged it with

* "Eventually everything was effected that was desired, our success being greatly aided by the admirable and steady practice of Major Scott's battery under a heavy fire—eleven men being put 'hors de combat' out of its small complement."—*Norman.*

† The number stated is two hundred and twenty-three, including one officer killed and eight wounded. The officer killed was Captain Mountsteven, of the Eighth. There was heavy carnage in the enemy's ranks.

the greatest confidence, now had their misgivings.* 1857. July 9.
It is true that the carnage among the enemy had been far greater than in our ranks; but they had never been numerically stronger than at that time, and the heaps of dead which they left behind them diminished but little the vital resources of that enormous garrison.

Action of July 14.

And, a few days afterwards, this question of assault, as Baird Smith wrote, had finally "resolved itself into nothing by sheer force of circumstances;" for there was another hard fight, and another long list of casualties. On the 14th, the enemy again came out in force to the attack of our position on the Right. It was said that they had vowed to carry our batteries, and destroy that formidable picquet at Hindoo Rao's house, which had sent the message of death to so many of their comrades. Becher's spies had gained intelligence of the movement, and Reid had been warned of the coming onslaught. He was quite ready for them, and said, laughingly, that they had attacked him and been beaten nineteen times, and that he did not expect to be worsted on the twentieth. The attack commenced about eight o'clock in the morning. For some time our people stood on the defensive, keeping the mutineers at bay. Both forces were under cover, and little execution was done. But when the sun was going down, Neville Chamberlain saw that the time had come to resort to other measures. So despatching a letter to Reid, desiring him to be prepared to attack the enemy, and act in concert with him, he sent Showers with another column, consisting of detachments of the First Euro-

* See letters of Hervey Greathed. Writing on the 10th, he says: "It may now be prudent to defer the attack for a short time, for at this moment they (the enemy) may be considered in the plenitude of their force," &c. &c.

1857. July 14. peans, the 75th Queen's, Coke's Rifles, and Hodson's Horse, with six Horse Artillery guns under Turner and Money, to take them in flank. The walled gardens, and other places of shelter, in which the mutineers had posted themselves, were now to be cleared; and it was a fine thing to see our columns sweeping down upon the enemy, Reid's little Goorkahs setting up a ringing cheer, and every man panting eagerly for the affray. Then two of our great Punjabee warriors were to be seen ever in the thickest of the fight. Where danger threatened most, Chamberlain and Hodson were sure to be seen. The enemy were driven from point to point, in confused flight, clean out of their sheltering walls; and the more impetuous of their assailants pushed on after them along the main road, within the fire from the walls of Delhi. There was it that Chamberlain, fearlessly exposing himself, according to his wont, well-nigh met his death-wound. A party of the enemy, covered by a low wall, had made a stand, and were pouring in a destructive fire upon our advancing soldiery, which made them for a moment recoil, when the Adjutant-General, setting spurs to his horse, called upon the men to follow him, and cleared the enclosure. He was gallantly supported; but a musket-ball took effect upon him, and broke his left arm below the shoulder.* Our people were then so near the city walls that the pursuit became disastrous. For the enemy gathered fresh courage, and rallied before their defences, whilst the hot haste with which

* It was thought at first to be a gun-shot wound. A cotemporary letter says: "Chamberlain was brought in with a sorely shattered arm. His impression was that he had been struck by grape, which was being showered on them from the city walls. He bore his wound and his pain nobly, with a high cheerful courage, but getting out of the narrow dooley was too much for him, and as he leant on two or three people he stumbled forward and fell, almost on the shattered limb."

we had pushed on to chastise the mutineers was throwing confusion into our ranks. The management of the pursuing force was not equal to the gallantry of the pursuit. At one point we had driven the mutineers from their guns, but we were not prepared to take advantage of their desertion. Hodson's quick eye marked the opportunity, and he was eager to charge the battery. But the men, upon whom he called to aid him, were exhausted, and at the moment there was no response. It is always, in such straits, a question of moments. Seeing that there was hesitation, a Sepoy gunner applied the port-fire to a piece loaded with grape; and before the smoke had cleared away the guns had been limbered up, and the opportunity was lost for ever. 1857. July 14.

Again the old story was repeated. We had gained a profitless, perhaps, indeed, a dubious victory, at a loss of two hundred men, killed or disabled.* The finest soldier in the Camp, foremost in reputation, foremost ever in action, and all but first in official position, had been carried maimed and helpless to his tent. It was a sorry day's work that sent Neville Chamberlain, Adjutant-General of the Army, to the Sick List. It was a sorry week's work that had deprived our little force of the services of twenty-five officers and four hundred men. It had quite settled the question of the assault. With these diminished numbers, how could a sufficient force be left for the protection of our Camp? Even the most eager spirits now felt that it must be a hopeless effort. "There will be no assault on Delhi yet," wrote Hodson on the 16th; "our rulers will now less than ever decide on

* The author of the "History of the Siege of Delhi" says: "Seventeen men killed, and sixteen officers and a hundred and seventy-seven men wounded."

1857. July 16.

a bold course, and, truth to tell, the numbers of the enemy have so rapidly increased, and ours have been so little replenished in proportion, and our losses for a small army have been so severe, that it becomes a question whether now we have numbers sufficient to risk an assault. Would to Heaven it had been tried when I first pressed it!"

July 17. Resignation of General Reed.

On the 17th of July General Reed resigned the command of the Delhi Field Force. During his brief season of responsibility his health had broken down under the exertions and anxieties of his position, and it was useless any longer to struggle against his daily-increasing infirmities. So he made over the command of the Force to Brigadier Archdale Wilson, and betook himself to the quietude of the Himalayahs.* The selection of an officer who had done so well in the actions on the Hindun was the source of general satisfaction in the Camp.† There were few who did not see in the change good promise of increased energy and activity in the prosecution of the siege. But, in truth, we had reached a period of its history at which energy and activity could be displayed only in acts of defensive warfare.

Brigadier Wilson in command.

It is certain that when Brigadier-General Wilson took command of the Delhi Field Force, the circumstances which he was called upon to confront were of

* Hodson says that Wilson succeeded by virtue of seniority. The author of the "History of the Siege of Delhi" says, "he was not the Senior General in Camp." The senior officer in Camp, according to substantive rank, was Colonel Congreve, of H.M.'s Twenty-ninth, Quartermaster-General of Queen's troops. It is stated that he sent in a protest against his supercession and retired to Simlah. General Reed had anticipated the difficulty on the score of rank by making Wilson a Brigadier-General—an appointment afterwards confirmed by Government.

† See Greathed's Letters and the "History of the Siege of Delhi."

a most discouraging character. Two Commanders had been struck down by Death, and a third had been driven from Camp by its approaches. The Chiefs of the Staff—the Adjutant-General and Quarter-master-General—lay wounded in their tents. For more than five weeks the British troops before Delhi had been standing upon the defensive. Time after time, assaults upon the City had been projected, and had been deferred; and at last the bold experiment had been finally abandoned. During those five weeks the enemy had attacked us a score of times, and it had long been acknowledged that the British were the Besieged, not the Besiegers. It was impossible that all this should not have had its effect upon the discipline of the Delhi Field Force. It must be an eternal honour to that force, that the deteriorating effects of such a state of things were so slight; but, nevertheless, they were clearly discernible. The strength of the rebel garrison had been continually increasing; and though their loss was even heavier than our own, our numbers were so inferior, that in proportion to them our sufferings were greater. It was hard to say how much longer the endurance of our people would be proof against a constant succession of vexatious attacks on the part of the enemy, and profitless victories on our own. Our troops had grown weary of beating the enemy, without apparently weakening their resources, or diminishing their confidence, or lengthening the intervals between their attacks. It is not strange, therefore, that in the middle of this month of July the British Chief looked the difficulties of our position very gravely in the face, and that there were some doubts as to whether we could hold our own much longer with such fearful odds against us. But no such doubts ought to have

1857.
July 17.

1857. July 17.

been entertained for a moment. Our troops had been much harassed; they were diminished in numbers; they had seen a constant succession of stubborn encounters, which had conduced nothing to the final issue; and they were growing very weary of a state of things of which they could not see the end. But, if they had lost some of their discipline, they had lost none of their heart. They were impatient, but not desponding. They were equal to any demands that could have been made upon them, and would have resented the idea of retreat.

Question of retirement.

But ever since the commencement of the month the thought of a retrograde movement had been fixing itself in the minds even of men who had been at one time eager for the bolder course, which had been described as the "gamester's throw." Before the death of General Barnard, Hervey Greathed—though he had thrown in the weight of his authority as Chief Civil Officer at Delhi, into the scales on the side of vigorous action—had begun to discern the fact that there might be some advantages to the country generally in liberating the troops now pent up before the walls of the great city, and wasting their energies in the strenuous idleness of a disastrous defence.* They were much needed at other points where our people were girt around with danger, and a great moral effect might be produced by a succession of victories, such as the Delhi Field Force, under happier circumstances, might calculate on achieving. The time for assaulting had passed. Neville Chamberlain and Baird Smith, who were both

* "The determination to take Delhi by assault has been twice on the eve of execution, and I no longer feel confident that it will again be so far matured. And supposing I am right, the question will arise whether we should maintain our position, or raise the siege, and dispose of our forces as may best serve the public interests, until a second campaign be opened."—*Greathed to Lawrence, July 4. MS. Corres.*

1857. July 17.

by official position and native worth the moving principles of the besieging force, had given up all hope of succeeding in such an enterprise. Chamberlain, indeed, had begun to apprehend that, in their existing state of discipline, it might be hazardous in the extreme to entangle them in the streets of Delhi. There was nothing left for us, therefore, but to hold on until the arrival of reinforcements; and the question had arisen and had been freely discussed at Head-Quarters, whether, until we could appear before Delhi in greater strength, it would not, both on military and political grounds, be a wiser course to relax our hold, and employ our eager troops in other parts of the country. When Wilson assumed command, he found matters in this state. He did not originate the question of withdrawal.

Protests of Baird Smith.

What might have been his resolution, if left to his own unaided counsels, History can never declare. But the eager protests of Baird Smith soon swept away any doubts that the General might have entertained.* As soon as the Chief Engineer learnt that the proposal was likely to be laid before him, he resolved to anticipate the formal reference. On the first occasion of Wilson consulting him professionally, he threw all the earnestness of his nature into a great remonstrance against the project of withdrawal. He

* It was on the 17th of July, the first day of Wilson's command, that Baird Smith pressed upon him the duty of not relaxing his hold on Delhi. On the 18th the Brigadier-General wrote to Sir John Lawrence urging him to send further reinforcements immediately. The letter was in French, and it contained these words: "Je retiendrai cette position jusqu' à la fin. Car il est de la plus grande importance que l'ennemi soit empêché de quitter Delhi pour ravager le pays. Pour faire ceci il est absolument nécessaire que je sois renforcé de la plus grande force et aussi vite qu'il est possible. J'entends que ce renforcement ne peut venir du sud, et en conséquence je prie que vous m'enverrez du Punjab un Regiment Anglais complet et deux de Sikhs ou Punjabees. Si je ne suis pas bien vite renforcé je serai forcé de retirer à Kurnaul. Les conséquences de ce mouvement seraient désastreuses."—*MS. Corres.*

1857. July 17. told the General that to raise the siege would be fatal to our national interests. "It is our duty," he said, "to retain the grip which we now have upon Delhi, and to hold on like grim Death until the place is our own." He dwelt upon the many circumstances in our favour. Our communications with the Punjab were open. There was still there a considerable amount of available strength, which the increasing security of that great province would soon place at the disposal of the Delhi leader. The army was in good health, and it was well supplied. It was true that little had been done to strengthen the position of our besieging army, or to bring our guns to bear with more fatal effect upon the enemy's works. But he pledged himself to do what as yet had been undone. And then he urged the General to consider what would be the result of the withdrawal of the Force. "All India," he said, "would at once believe that we retreated because we were beaten, and in such circumstances an adverse impression of this kind was as disastrous as the severest defeat we could sustain. We must abandon, in such a case, our communications with the Punjab, and cease to act as a covering force to that province, from which all the reinforcements we could hope for must be drawn; we must again fight our way to Delhi against reinvigorated enemies, increased in numbers and spirits, and we must cease to perform the incalculably important function of check-mating the entire strength of the revolt, by drawing towards Delhi, as a great focus, all the mutinous regiments of all arms, and so preventing them from dispersing themselves over the country, and attacking and overpowering our defenceless posts." These arguments prevailed. Wilson listened, and was convinced. He thanked

Baird Smith for this frank statement of his views, said that he would hold on, and then called upon him, as Chief Engineer, to state what could be done to maintain our position before Delhi with the least possible loss, until such time as the Delhi Field Force could be so strengthened as to render the final assault upon Delhi secure in its results. Then Baird Smith stated what Wilson, as an experienced Artilleryman, had long felt, that our great want was a want of far-reaching guns, that we had been always beaten by the heavy metal and wide range of the enemy's Artillery; but that as soon as we could bring down a siege-train of sufficient magnitude and sufficient weight to silence the guns on the walls of Delhi, success would be certain. To all of this Wilson readily assented. He asked for a statement of the strength of ordnance which would be required for siege operations, which in due course was given; and at the same time the Chief Engineer undertook to have the work of his own department in a sufficient state of forwardness to give every possible advantage to the operations of the Artillery. "And from that time forward," said Baird Smith, in a letter written at a later period, "we were guided by these plans, and prepared busily for the resumption of active work on the arrival of the siege-train."

1857. July 17.

The first week of Wilson's command was enlivened by two more attempts on the part of the enemy to drive us from our advanced position; firstly, on the Right, and then on the Left. Our scouts in the city had obtained intelligence that the enemy purposed to proceed in force to the neighbourhood of Alipore,*

Further attacks on our position.

* Reinforcements had entered Delhi—mutineers from Jhansi, who, according to custom, were to try their luck on first arrival against the Feringhees.

1857. in our rear, to intercept an expected convoy on its way to our camp, and when they had thus drawn out a considerable part of our strength, to make a vehement attack upon our Right. The movement to
July 18. Alipore was never made, but, on the 18th of July, the enemy again betook themselves to the old work of harassing us from the shelter of the suburbs; so a detachment of Infantry and Artillery was sent out, under Colonel Jones of the Sixtieth Rifles, with the old result. What had come to be called "rat-hunting" went on for a while, and a number of British officers and men fell beneath the fire of the enemy.* But there was this time no attempt at pursuit. Colonel Jones, having driven the mutineers from their shelter, withdrew his own men carefully and skilfully, covering their retirement with his guns. It was the last of our many conflicts in the Subzee-mundee suburb. Our Engineer officers were already at work clearing away the cover—the garden-walls, the ruined houses, and the old serais, of which the enemy had made such good use from the commencement of the siege, and were connecting our advanced posts in that direction with the Main Picquet on the Ridge.

July 23. Perhaps it was in despair of making any impression upon our Right, that a few days afterwards, July 23rd, the enemy in considerable force streamed out of the Cashmere Gate, and endeavoured to establish themselves at Ludlow Castle, whence they opened a fire both on the Metcalfe Picquet and the Ridge. A column of British and Sikh Infantry, with guns from Turner's and Money's troops, was, therefore, sent out, under Brigadier Showers, to dislodge them. The

* Our loss was one officer and twelve men killed, and three officers (one mortally) and sixty-six men wounded.

work was soon accomplished. The enemy were in retreat to the city walls, but again the fatal inclination to press on in pursuit was irresistible, and our column was drawn on towards the city walls, and many of our best officers were carried wounded to the rear. Colonel Seaton, who had been appointed to officiate as Adjutant-General, was shot through the body. Turner and Money of the Artillery, and others, were wounded;* and Captain Law, who was serving with Coke's rifles, was killed. The loss of the enemy was not heavy, and they carried off all their guns. After this, orders went forth prohibiting the forward movements, which had always been attended with so much disaster. Our main losses had commonly been incurred after we had driven back the enemy towards the walls of their stronghold. This system of warfare had been too long permitted. Had the enemy's numbers been more limited, it would have been less necessary to restrain the natural impetuosity of our people to push on and to punish in pursuit; but scarcely any amount of carnage that we could inflict upon the mutineers was any substantive gain to ourselves. 1857. July 23.

And so the month of July came to an end and left Wilson in good spirits; for Sir John Lawrence, never slackening in his great work, had responded to the General's appeal by fresh promises of help, and he had cast away all thoughts of raising the siege. Writing on the 30th of July to Mr. Colvin, who had earnestly protested against the thought of withdrawing from Delhi, he said: "It is my firm determination to hold

* Mr. Cave-Browne says that Brigadier Showers was wounded, and compelled to give over the command to Colonel Jones. His name is not in the list given by Norman, and, therefore, it would seem that it was not officially returned. The wound must have been a very slight one, if any, for Showers was in action again on the 12th of August.

1857. July. my present position and to resist every attack to the last. The enemy are very numerous, and may possibly break through our entrenchments and overwhelm us. But this force will die at its post. Luckily, the enemy have no head and no method, and we hear dissensions are breaking out among them. Reinforcements are coming up under Nicholson. If we can hold on till they arrive, we shall be secure. I am making every possible arrangement to secure the safe defence of our position."

Unrecorded Heroism. And here I may fitly pause in this recital of military events—of engagement after engagement with the enemy, following each other in quick succession, all of the same type and all leading to the same results. The true story of the Siege of Delhi is not to be found in the bare record of these exploits. Many as were those gallant soldiers, whose active heroism it has been my privilege to illustrate in these pages, there were many more in the British Camp whose names have been unwritten, but whose gallantry, in doing and in suffering, was not less conspicuous. It was the fortune of some to be continually called to the front, to be specially thanked by commanding officers and named in official despatches, whilst others, day after day, week after week, month after month, laboured on, exposed to the fire of the enemy and to all the evil influences of camp-life in the worst season of the year, without praise, without encouragement, almost without notice. A signal instance of this presents itself in the circumstances of the two branches of the Artillery. The Light Batteries were always to the front, and the names of Scott, Turner, Money, Tombs, and others of the Horse Artillery or Horse

1857. July.

Batteries have repeatedly claimed admiring recognition; but of the Heavy Batteries, which, in their own way, were equally well served, scant mention has yet been made in this narrative of the siege.* The time for breaching operations had not yet come, and it was a dull and weary season for the Siege Artillery thus expending themselves in defensive efforts, outmatched in numbers, outmatched in weight of metal, outmatched in profuseness of ammunition. There was a scarcity of officers for duty in the batteries; there was a scarcity of gunners. Both had to be improvised and supplemented as best we could, so that men found themselves working at the guns who, a little while before, did not know a portfire from a sponge-staff. Stray Lancers, for whom there was not much cavalry-work in camp, were caught up and set to learn the gun-drill, and right good gunners they often made; whilst old Sikhs, who had learnt artillery practice under Runjit Singh's French officers, and

* The principal officers with the siege batteries were Colonel Garbett, Major James Brind, Major Murray Mackenzie, and Major Kaye. The last-named had come down to Delhi with the first siege-train. Major Brind joined soon afterwards, and took a leading part in the siege operations up to the hour of final success. Colonel Garbett, who arrived at a later period, was appointed Brigadier of Artillery, on Wilson's nomination to the chief command; but he was wounded on his way from one battery to another, and though the wound was little more than a graze, of which he took no notice at first, it became afterwards a most virulent sore, which compelled him to take to his bed, and subsequently to leave the camp. He ultimately died of fever. Major Mackenzie was struck by the splinter of a shell on the 30th of June, and though in this case, also, the wound did not appear to be a severe one, he was driven also to Simlah, where he died. [Mackenzie and Kaye had served together with the Native troop of Horse Artillery which ascended the Hindoo Koosh, and was engaged in the battle of Bamcean]. Major Gaiskill, who joined at a later period of the siege, succeeded Colonel Garbett in command of the Artillery. Among the younger officers distinguished during the siege were Captain Johnson, Assistant Adjutant-General of Artillery, who came down with Wilson from Meerut, and as chief staff-officer did excellent service, and Lieutenant Light, an active and energetic officer, always eager to go to the front, who was incapacitated by sickness about the middle of July, and unable to return to his duties. Griffith, Commissary of Ordnance, was driven from camp by cholera, and was succeeded by Captain Young.

1857. July.

had served the guns of the Kalsa at Sobraon and Chillianwallah, were recruited by John Lawrence, who never missed a chance of aiding the Delhi warriors, and sent down to man Wilson's batteries. But the time was now approaching when the real business of the Siege would commence in earnest, and the officers of the heavy batteries would contribute their share of good work towards the capture of the great city.

Incidents of the Siege.

Over and above the excitement of the frequent actions with the enemy, which always added the names of many brave men to the list of killed and wounded, there were sometimes lesser sensations to stir the heart of the Camp. On one occasion, an officer of good repute, whilst reconnoitring as a field-engineer, failed to give the parole with sufficient promptitude when challenged by one of our sentries, and was shot dead in the darkness of the night.* It often happened that officers on the look-out from exposed positions, or passing from post to post, or showing their heads above the breastworks of our batteries, became special marks for the rebel artillery-men, and narrowly escaped, if at all, with their lives.† Among the current Camp jokes was one to the effect that a soldier had made it matter of complaint that, since the Engineers had built up the parapets so high, a fellow at work in the batteries behind them could

* Captain Greensill, Her Majesty's Twenty-fourth Regiment.

† See following account of the bursting of a shell, which nearly deprived the Force of one of the best officers in it—Major Scott of the Artillery: "Major Scott had a very narrow escape from a shell yesterday; he was standing by his horse on the Ridge, looking through his glass, when a shell fell close by him and burst as it touched the ground. I saw his horse running off, and saw him on the ground, but he got up and walked on, and I saw him riding by just now, so I suppose he is not hurt. I was on the 'General's Mound' at the time, and the explosion drew my attention, and we heard afterwards who it was, and that a man of the Fusiliers had been wounded by a piece of the shell."—*Letters of Hervey Greathed.*

only get shot in the head. One officer is stated by the contemporary chroniclers of the Siege to have had such a fancy for exposing himself in the embrasures, that, in spite of repeated warnings from his comrades, he was killed one day at his dangerous post. 1857. July.

Cheerfulness of the Camp.

The general cheerfulness of our People, in spite of all dispiriting circumstances, was something upon which it is a pleasure to comment. Day after day our officers met each other with bright faces, laughed and joked, reciprocated kindly offices, and exchanged the news of the Camp or the tidings brought from a distance. There was ever alive amongst them a warmth of good-fellowship, which nothing could weaken or cool. To make a friendly visit to the tent of a wounded or sick officer was a part of every sound man's duty, which he was sure not to neglect. Such was the overflowing kindness shown to every man who was down, that if it had not been for the eager desire to be at work again that animated all, it would have been a privilege to be upon the sick-list. On fine evenings, when the sun was going down, the sick and wounded were brought out from the tents on their beds and litters, thus to taste the fresh air, to be exhilarated by the liveliness of the Camp, and to commune with their comrades. Officers and men alike enjoyed this change. There was one, however, the noblest sufferer of all, who would not permit himself to be thus brought out of the privacy of his tent, lest it should appear that he was parading his wounds.

Meanwhile, those, who were well, found great delight in the comradeship of their several Messes, and seemed to enjoy the rough Bohemianism which necessity had substituted for the polite amenities of the peaceful Cantonment. The rougher the ménage, the

1857. July. better the cheer. It has been recorded that in one notable instance, when tablecloths came into use, a good deal of the special jollity of the gathering was scared away by their introduction. It does not appear that at any time there was a scarcity of provisions. But many things, which had become almost necessities with our officers, fell short from time to time, and were painfully missed. Some were more fortunate, or had more forethought, than others; but what one Mess, or one man, missed, another was able to lend him. Sometimes the supplies of beer or wine were drunk out to the last bottle, and commonly each member of a Mess was put upon an allowance of drink;* sometimes the last cigar was smoked, and the generosity of a neighbour supplied the inconvenient want. There were no Sybarites among them, and even those who had been wont to fare sumptuously every day, were thankful for what they got, and laughed at the privations they were compelled to endure. Good clothes, too, after a while, became scarce in Camp. There was little regard for proprieties of costume, and men who had delighted to walk daintily in fine linen, went about in strange costumes of flannel, half civil half military in their attire, and were fain to possess themselves of the second-hand garments of their departed brethren. Even the chief civil officer in Camp, Hervey Greathed, was glad to get a pair of boots from his brother in the Engineers, and to buy the leavings of young Barnard's toilet when he quitted Camp after his father's death. And the Chaplain of the Force has told us how he was compelled to abandon all thought

* The greatest inconvenience of all was that no allowance was made for guests, and this limited hospitality. Stray arrivals in Camp were sometimes sore pressed for dinner, and compelled to fall back on Commissariat Beef.

of ministering in appropriate clerical vestments, and to go about clothed like a brigand. 1857. July.

And whilst our officers thus met each other with cheerful, sometimes radiant faces, the English soldier was quite jubilant. "I have been pleased," wrote one of the bravest and best of the Delhi warriors, "to observe the cheerful tone displayed at all times by our troops. I never saw British soldiers in camp so joyous. They walk and run about, in the afternoon and evening, when the rain and Pandy are at rest, as though they had nothing serious to do. Nor has it ever occurred to them that there was anything doubtful in the conflict." When off duty, the men amused themselves as in the most peaceful times, playing cricket and quoits, getting up pony races, and invigorating themselves with gymnastics. There was some talk of getting up rackets; but the old cantonment racket-court was in so exposed a situation that it was thought by no means an improbable contingency that the Enemy would take part in the sport, and with balls of a larger diameter than those proper to the game.

Drunkenness among the soldiery.

That the excitement of strong drink was much coveted by the soldiery in the English Camp need scarcely be set down in the narrative; but, on the whole, it may be recorded in their honour that few outrages were committed under its influence. The wet season had set in. The lowering skies, the drenching downfalls of rain, the constant damps, and all the wonted accompaniments of such weather, at a time when the activities of service rendered shelter impossible, not only had a depressing influence upon men's spirits, which rendered stimulants ever welcome to them, but had external results, in saturated clothes and boots oozing with water, that justified, if

1857. July.

they did not demand, a resort to such supposed correctives. There were some wise officers in Camp, who thought that still better precautions might be taken; and when fever and ague were prevalent among our people, bethought themselves of the value of quinine, as a prophylactic, and were minded to serve out a dose of it every morning to their men. An Artillery officer, of whom frequent mention has been made in this story of the Siege, when he found that his gunners demurred to imbibing the bitter draught, as no part of their military duty, told them that no one who refused to take it should ever have an extra dram; and so they swallowed the quinine for the sake of the rum which followed in the course of the day. And the result was, that scarcely a man of this Company was knocked over by the fever of the season.

Tidings from a distance.

During seasons of comparative quietude in Camp, news from the outer world was greedily sought and eagerly discussed. There was little or no communication with the country below, and so far as the present safety or future success of the Delhi Force was affected by operations in the lower country, there was little reason to concern themselves about those distant events, tidings of which commonly reached them crusted over with error, if not in the shape of substantial lies. Of the doings of the Governor-General and Commander-in-Chief they knew, and indeed cared, little or nothing.* Sir John Lawrence was their Governor-General—their Commander-in-Chief. They looked to the great Punjab Commissioner for the means of taking Delhi, and with these

* I have a letter before me, written by the Military Secretary to Government, from Council Chamber, Calcutta, from which it is plain that on the 26th of July, three weeks after General Barnard's death, Government were ignorant of that event.

means he was furnishing them with an energy of self-denial beyond all praise. But the great work which lay before our people on the Ridge, with all its toil and anxieties, its dangers and sufferings, did not so engross men's minds as to leave them no thought, no sympathy for their brethren who were girt with peril elsewhere. Most of all they sought news from Cawnpore and Lucknow, where Wheeler and Henry Lawrence, threatened by an overwhelming enemy, were looking anxiously for succours from below. False tidings of the relief of Lucknow were continually coming into Camp. It was said, time after time, that Wheeler was safe, sometimes with the addition that he was marching upon Delhi, and at others that the Sepoy regiments that had besieged him were bound for that place. At a later period it was reported (long before the first relief of Lucknow) that Havelock had fought a great battle with Maun Singh and defeated him, had entered the Oude capital, and that for three days the city had been given up to plunder and slaughter. From Calcutta, through some circuitous channel, there came a report that the French troops, forming part of the China expedition, were coming to help us; and it was rumoured in Camp that so great had been the excitement in London on the arrival there of news of the revolt, that the populace had burnt the India House, and hung the Directors up to the lamp-posts.

1857. July.

But tidings came at last, only too fatally true, that the garrison of Cawnpore, with all our women and children had been foully massacred, and that Sir Henry Lawrence was dead. It is hard to say whether the indignation excited by the one event or the sorrow born of the other were the stronger and more abiding feeling. There was not a man in Camp who did not

1857. July. grieve for the great and good commander of the Lucknow garrison; and there were many who, loving him as a father or a brother, shed such tears for him as they would have shed for the nearest and the dearest of their kin.* All felt that one of the Pillars of the State had fallen—perhaps the stoutest and the grandest of all—and that such a master in Israel was little likely to be seen again. In strong contrast to the tender feelings and pathetic utterances which this calamity called forth throughout the general camp, was the vehement exasperation which the news of the Cawnpore massacre elicited—the bitter hatred, the intense thirst of revenge. It was natural—it was commendable. Those stern soldiers "did well to be angry." No such foul act as this had ever stained the annals of British connexion with the East. The foul tragedy of the "Black Hole," which for a hundred years had been cited as the great horror of horrors, now paled beside the massacre of Cawnpore; for the victims of Surajah Dowlah's cruelty had been strong men. And ever as the atrocity was discussed in Camp, our people longed for tidings of the onward march of Havelock and Neill; and yearned for the coming of the day when the order would be given to them to set the mark of the avenger on the guilty city which had so long resisted and defied them.

Treatment of the Natives. It was not strange that, after this, the feeling of hatred against the coloured races, already strong in

* One officer touchingly records in his journal now before me: "I do indeed feel that I have lost a prop in the world." The same writer, a day or two afterwards says: "In these days of battle and death there is so much to excite the mind, that one is not long, by any possibility, in the same vein of thought, but I felt beaten down when this sad tale reached me. Reflection brings home to one the sad public loss which his death occasions. At any time India would mourn his fall, but now, when she so much needs his guidance and his wisdom, the death of the soldier-statesman fills all with grief, and this to the putting aside of personal feeling. He was a rare specimen of God's handiwork."—*MS. Journal.*

the British Camp, should have become more vehement and outspoken. It showed itself in many ways. We were everywhere surrounded by Natives. The typical Pandy, whose name was in every man's mouth, was the representative only of one of many phases of Native humanity, which were then ever present to us. It was one of the most curious characteristics of this Mutiny-war, that although the English were supposed to be fighting against the Native races, they were in reality sustained and supported by the Natives of the country, and could not have held their own for a day without the aid of those whom we hated as our national enemies. Not only were the coloured races fighting stoutly upon our side,* but thousands of non-combatants were sharing the dangers, without the glories, of the siege, and doing their appointed work with fidelity and alacrity, as though there had never been any rupture —any division of interests—any departure from the normal state of things, as it existed in quiet times. How utterly dependent upon Native Agency is the exotic European, though sprung from the working classes, and in his own country accustomed to the performance of the most menial and laborious duties, is known to all who have dwelt in India for a week. If the labour of the people had been utterly lost to us, our power must have suddenly collapsed. The last drop in the cup of domestic bitterness was the desertion of our Native household servants. But a Family could do better without this aid than a company of Infantry, a troop of Horse, or a battery of

1857. July.

* "In camp," wrote Wilberforce Greathed to Mr. Colvin (August 23, 1857), "there is a feeling of confidence in our Native troops. Guides, Goorkahs, Cokey's (Coke's Rifles), and Sikhs, are all popular, and, I think, all smart and useful."

1857. July. Artillery.* Without these Native attendants of various kinds, our people would have had no food and no drink. They could not have fed their horses, or served their guns, or removed their sick. Both public and private servants, with but few exceptions, remained true to their employers throughout the siege, and some displayed instances of rare personal devotion.† It little matters what was the source of this fidelity. It may have been that these people, accustomed to the domination of the English, satisfied to move in the old groove, and sure of their accustomed pay from month to month, never troubled themselves to regard the national aspects of the struggle, and, with characteristic hatred of change, clung, therefore, to their old employments. But, of whatsoever it was the growth, the fact was there; and I am afraid that it was not sufficiently appreciated by those who profited so largely by it. It has been shown how the cook-boys, carrying the coveted dinners to our picquets, were exposed to the merciless fire of the enemy, and how lightly their danger was regarded. This was but one of many signs of the little gratitude that was felt towards these service-

* The author of the "History of the Siege of Delhi," says: "There were ten Natives for every European in camp. In every troop of Artillery there were four times as many Natives as Europeans; in the Cavalry two men for every horse; without them the work could not go on."

† Take, for example, the following, illustrative of the good and gallant conduct of some of our Native Artillery drivers. It is from a letter addressed to the author: "When returning from this day's work, my guns brought up the rear, and I had to hold the mutineers in check, picking up any of our wounded and placing them on my limbers until they could be provided for. One of my Native drivers was shot through the leg and the bone broken below the knee. He was riding one of the leaders in the gun-team. I rode up and told him to stop the gun until I could dismount him; but he said, 'Kuch-purwan-neh (never mind), Sahib. I would sooner remain on my horse with my gun.' And he would have remained had I not insisted on dismounting him and placing him in a dooly. This was the sort of spirit many of my Natives showed throughout."—*MS. Correspondence.*

able auxiliaries. But there was more than this negative unkindliness. For many of our people in Camp, in return for the good services of the Natives, gave back only the words and blows of contumely and insult more readily even than in quiet times.* Those times were changed, but we were not changed with them. The sturdy iron of the national character was so inflexible that the heat of the furnace through which we were passing had not yet inclined it to bend. As arrogant, as intolerant, and as fearless as ever, we still closed our eyes to the fact that our lives lay in the hollow of the hand which we so despised. Even in the midst of disasters and humiliations, which would have softened and enfeebled others, our pride of race still upheld us, stern, hard, and immovable. 1857. July.

* The following statement is made by the author of the "Siege of Delhi:" "So many sanguinary fights and executions had brutalised our men, that they now regarded the life of a Native as of less value than that of the meanest of animals; nor had their officers endeavoured by precept or example to correct them. . . . . Men of humanity were shocked, and this made the most reckless reflect. . . . . The spirit of exasperation which existed against Natives at this time will scarcely be believed in Europe. Servants, a class of men who behaved, on the whole, throughout the mutiny with astonishing fidelity, were treated even by many of the officers with outrageous harshness. The men beat and ill-used them. In the batteries they would make the bheesties (water-carriers), to whom they showed more kindness than to the rest, sit out of the works to give them water. Many of the unfortunates were killed. The sick syces, grass-cutters, and dooly-bearers, many of whom were wounded in our service, lay for months on the ground, exposed to the sun by day and the cold at night; and it was with difficulty that one or two medical men could get, for those under their care, a few yards of canvas or a reed-hut under which they might huddle together. A general massacre of the inhabitants of Delhi, a large number of whom were known to wish us success, was openly proclaimed. Bloodthirsty boys might be heard recommending that all the Native orderlies, irregulars, and other 'poorbeahs' in our camp should be shot. These sentiments were not those of all, nor of the best and wisest; but few ventured to gainsay them." Although this is an anonymous work, the authorship is well known, and carries some weight of authority with it. I am bound, however, to say that some of my informants, to whom I have referred with especial reference to the alleged inhumanity of our people towards the Natives in camp, are disposed to doubt whether it manifested itself during the siege more strongly than before the mutiny. It is said to have been only the old normal state of things — unaltered, unrepressed.

1857. July. And in spite of all human calculations, and in defiance of all reason, the very obduracy and intolerance, which might have destroyed us in this conjuncture, were in effect the safeguard of the nation. That stubborn, unyielding self-reliance, that caused the noblest of our enemies to say that the English never knew when they were beaten, had caused the Indian races to believe that if a single white man were left in the country, he would regain the Empire for his race. And though it is impossible for those who sit deliberately in judgment upon such conduct towards a subject people not to condemn it, the fact remains that this assertion, this appearance of strength, *was* strength in the midst of our weakness.

Within the City. Meanwhile, within the walls of Delhi the national character was shaping events with equal force and distinctness. There were feebleness and irresolution and divided councils in high places, and elsewhere a great antagonism of interests, internecine strife, oppression, and misery not to be counted. Whilst the English were clinging together and moving as one man, the inmates of Delhi were dislocated and distracted. The Court, the Soldiery, the industrial inhabitants were in deadly feud the one with the other, and as the numbers of our enemies increased, their difficulties also increased. A state of things had indeed arisen very fatal to the continued supremacy of the King, the circumstances of which will be detailed in another chapter of this history.

CHAPTER VI.

QUESTION OF THE ABANDONMENT OF PESHAWUR—VIEWS OF SIR JOHN LAWRENCE, COLONEL EDWARDES, AND GENERAL NICHOLSON—FURTHER DISASTERS IN THE PUNJAB—JHELUM AND SEALKOTE—THE MOVABLE COLUMN AFFAIR OF THE TRIMMOO GHAUT—NICHOLSON AT DELHI—THE BATTLE OF NUJUFGHUR.

1857.
May—July.
The Question of Peshawur.

THE hope of the Army before Delhi in the noble efforts of Sir John Lawrence was not doomed to be disappointed. It has been seen how he responded to every call for reinforcements; how, as time went on, and the pride of the Mogul was still unbroken, the great Punjab Commissioner was little by little stripping his province of its most reliable troops, until it appeared to others that he was going too far in these sacrificial efforts. A great conflict of opinion, indeed, had arisen among the leading intelligences of the Punjab. To the chiefs of the great Peshawur Council it seemed that the maintenance of the integrity of the frontier was a paramount necessity, to which all other considerations should yield. Before the end of May Edwardes had written to the Chief Commissioner, saying: "Things seem to be settling down in Hindostan, and to be pretty safe throughout the Punjab, and I think that if you could in any way manage, it would only be prudent to throw some

1857. more strength upon this point. For Peshawur is a vital point, as it were, and if we conquer here we are safe everywhere, whereas disaster here would roll down the Punjab. It was absolutely necessary to disarm the regiments, and yet it recoils on us, for we want Native troops. . . . . We must husband our Europeans, and we do so. We carry them about on elephants and carts like children. If they want a post-chaise per man they must have it. Can you not think of any way to help us at this pinch? . . . You know on what a nest of devils we stand. Once let us take our foot up, and we shall be stung to death."*

But the eyes of the Chief Commissioner were turned in another direction, and far other thoughts were pressing on his mind. Peshawur seemed to him to be a source of infinite weakness to the whole Empire. Sir John Lawrence had ever held fast to the opinion that the recovery of Delhi was an object of such magnitude, that all else was dwarfed beside it; and in the stedfast pursuit of this object he was prepared even to abandon the Peshawur valley, leaving it in the hands of Dost Mahomed of Caubul in free and friendly cession, and retiring within the line of the Indus. For Peshawur was ever a great blister to our European Army, drawing thither to the frontier regiment upon regiment, and battery upon battery, whose presence could not be dispensed with so long as we held those dangerous breadths of country beyond the river. To release these regiments from the necessity of keeping watch and ward upon the border would have been immense gain to us at such a time. So Lawrence proposed, in the event of the weakness of our European Army threatening with failure the enterprise against Delhi, to invite the

* Colonel Edwardes to Sir John Lawrence, May 27.—*MS. Correspondence.*

Ameer of Caubul to Peshawur, to ask him, in pursuance of his alliance with the British Government, to occupy the valley with his troops, and finally to promise that, if he should remain true to us, the British Government would make over the coveted territory to him in perpetuity. 1857. June.

To this effect, therefore, Lawrence wrote to Edwardes, telling him to consult Nicholson and Cotton on the expediency of the projected movement. The letter was written on the 9th of June. His Secretary —Captain Hugo James, a man of great mental vigour, capable in action as in council, but who seems to have shared the common fate of Secretaries, of whom little more account is taken than of the pens they wield, and to have received far less than the credit which he deserved—was startled by the proposal, and recorded a memorandum against it. With characteristic frankness and candour John Lawrence sent it on to Peshawur, adding a note to it in the following words: "Here is James's view of the matter. All appears to depend upon the *if* in the third line. If we can hold the Punjaub, doubtless we should retain Peshawur. But I do not think that we could do so. Troops from England could not be in Calcutta before October, and up here before December or January. A retreating army which has not been beaten can command supplies. . . . . One thing appears to be most certain, which is, that if disaster occurs at Delhi, all the Native Regulars, and some of the Irregulars (perhaps many) will abandon us. We should, then, take time by the forelock."

Protest of Colonel Edwardes.

But there was nothing in this to convince the Peshawur Council. Nicholson had just returned from his first great raid, and he and Cotton concurred with Edwardes heartily in their opposition to

1857. June 11. the project: "We (Edwardes, Nicholson, and Sydney Cotton)," wrote Edwardes on June 11, "are unanimously of opinion that with God's help we can and will hold Peshawur, let the worst come to the worst, and it would be a fatal policy to abandon it and to retire across the Indus. It is the anchor of the Punjab, and if you take it up the whole ship will drift to sea. For keeping the mastery of the Punjab, there are only two obligatory points—the Peshawur valley and the Maunjha; all the rest are mere dependencies. Mooltan is valuable as the only practicable line of retreat to the sea; but if we hold on resolutely to Peshawur and the Maunjha, we shall never need to retreat. If you abandon Peshawur, you give up the Trans-Indus; and giving up the Trans-Indus, you give up the homes of the only other troops besides Europeans from whom you expect aid. . . . The loyalty of the Mooltanee Pathan border is a source of the greatest comfort to us now, but what a blow to them if we let the Afghans overrun the Derajat. And as to a friendly transfer of Peshawur to the Afghans, Dost Mahomed would not be a mortal Afghan—he would be an angel—if he did not assume our day to be gone to India, and follow after us as an enemy. . . . Europeans cannot retreat—Caubul would come again! . . . We believe that at Peshawur and Lahore we can ride out the gale, if it blow big guns, till the cold weather comes, and the English people send us a white army, in whom (to use the slang of the day) 'implicit confidence' can be placed." And again on the following day: "The more I think over your proposal to abandon Peshawur, the more fatal it seems, and I am convinced that whatever doubt may hang over our attempt to hold it, the attempt to give it up would be

June 20. certain ruin." Eight days afterwards he wrote again, still more earnestly: "I don't know anything in this war that has surprised me so much as the judgment you have now formed on this subject. It is useless to re-discuss it; but I earnestly hope you will never have cause to propose it to Government, and that if you do, Government may not consent, for I believe that the move would be more damaging than any other we could make. As to deliberately giving up the Trans-Indus, by choice as a boundary, on the score of expense, it surprises me more and more, for you and I have often considered this matter, and I always understood you to be convinced that the Indus is not a practicable boundary, and that it would take an army of twenty thousand men or more between Attock and Mooltan, and never be secure." 1857.

Reply of Sir John Lawrence.

To this the Chief Commissioner replied, earnestly setting forth the advantages of concentrating the British forces in the territories upon the hither side of the Indus: "Here we are," he wrote, "with three European regiments, a large artillery, and some of our best Native troops locked up across the Indus—troops who, if at Delhi, would decide the contest in a week. What have we got for all the rest of the Punjab? We have barely two thousand Europeans. I doubt if we have so many holding the posts of Philour, Govindghur, and Ferozepore, Lahore, and Mooltan. We have not a man more with a white face whom we can spare. We cannot concentrate more than we have now done, except by giving up Rawul-Pindee, and eventually Peshawur. Should the Sikhs rise, our condition on this side the Indus will be well-nigh desperate. With the Peshawur force on this side we should be irresistibly strong. There was no one thing which tended so much to the ruin of Napoleon in 1814 as the tenacity with which,

1857. June 22. after the disasters at Leipsic, he clung to the line of the Elbe, instead of falling back at once to that of the Rhine. He thus compromised all his garrisons beyond the Elbe, and when he was beaten in the field, these gradually had to surrender. But these troops would have given him the victory had they been at his side at Bautzen, and the other conflicts which preceded Leipsic."

June 25. On the evening of June 25, the Peshawur Commissioner received from Sir John Lawrence, at Rawul-Pindee, a message in the following words: "A severe action (at Delhi), apparently with little result, on the 23rd. Bareilly mutineers en route to Delhi. Gwalior Contingent have mutinied. Agent has left. If matters get worse, it is my decided opinion that the Peshawur arrangements should take effect. Our troops before Delhi must be reinforced, and that largely. They must hold their ground." On the receipt of this message, Edwardes, Cotton, and James* met together in Council and determined on another remonstrance against the project, which from the first hour of its enunciation had so much disturbed and alarmed them. The letters of the Chief Commissioner were sufficiently perplexing, but they suggested rather proposal and discussion than immediate action, whilst the brief, expressive sentences of the telegram indicated an intention to do the thing and at once. The language, indeed, was fast becoming the language of absolute instruction. There was no time to be lost. The chief military and the chief civil authority at Peshawur, therefore, put forth severally energetic written protests against what they believed to be so fatal a measure. "We have

* Captain James had by this time been appointed to succeed Colonel Nicholson as Deputy-Commissioner at Peshawur.

pushed our conquests," wrote General Cotton, "up to the very mouths of the Afghanistan passes, and at this very moment, by God's blessing, our strongest position in India is at the mouth of the Khyber. By our good rule we have engaged the affections (I may say) to a considerable extent of the border tribes, and in the hour of need they (who, not many years since, were our most bitter enemies), relying on our great name and power, have come forward to help us against the disaffection of the very troops with whom we had conquered the Sikhs, Punjabees, and others. A retrograde movement from Peshawur, believe me, would turn all these parties, now our friends, against us. The Punjab Irregular Force, Pathans, Sikhs, Punjabees, and such like, no longer respecting our power, will, in all likelihood, turn against us, and their most valuable services be lost to us for ever. My dear Sir John, our removal from Peshawur cannot fail to be disastrous, and cannot be effected without immediate confusion throughout the whole of this part of the country, and throughout the length and breadth of British India. Hence the measure will seriously injure the interests of our forces in all quarters, whilst the additional strength to be gained would be small, and, indeed, we could afford no timely aid. In handing over the Peshawur district to the Dost (a measure which we may pretend to be a mere matter of expediency and not of necessity), the Afghans will at once see our weakness, and will duly profit by the same against the common enemy. To this frontier, and to the present strength of our position on it, as well as to Calcutta at the opposite end of our territory, we must look for the recovery of our power throughout the intermediate kingdoms of the Bengal Presidency. Our great name is upheld

1857. June 26.

Opinions of General Cotton.

1857. June 26. on our frontier, whilst Calcutta and this seaboard, in the plenitude of power, with European reinforcements continually arriving, will afford eventually and more surely the necessary succour. At this very moment six or eight regiments of Europeans must be between Calcutta and Delhi, en route to the seat of war, and treble that amount will be eventually thrown in from home and elsewhere, and by such means must our supremacy be recovered. When could our troops reach the seat of war, and in what numbers and condition? These questions must be duly considered, and by them the loss, and gain of our removal from hence be balanced and determined on. I earnestly implore of you, my dear Sir John, to hold to our position on this frontier. The required succour must indeed be thrown in from Calcutta, not from this. When the reinforcements from above and below, at present in progress towards Delhi, have reached their destination, I feel confident that that city will again fall into our hands, and I am very much mistaken if disaffection does not then cease in all quarters, and our power being thus established, mutiny will gradually disappear throughout the land."

Opinion of Colonel Edwardes. On the same morning, Colonel Edwardes wrote, with like decision: "General Cotton, James, and myself are all of opinion that you should not go on throwing away your means in detail by meeting General Reed's. demands for reinforcements. Delhi is not India, and if General Reed cannot take it with eight thousand men, he will not take it with nine thousand or ten thousand. However important a point, it is only a point, and enough has been done for it. You will serve the Empire better by holding the Punjab than by sacrificing the Punjab and recovering Delhi. You will sacrifice the

Punjab, if you either withdraw General Cotton's force from Peshawur, or fritter away Nicholson's Movable Column, already too weak. Make a stand! 'Anchor, Hardy, anchor!' Tell General Reed he can have no more men from here, and must either get into Delhi with the men he has, or get reinforcements from below, or abandon the siege and fall back on the Sutlej, leaving Delhi and its dependencies to be reorganised in the cold weather. There are two policies open to you—to treat the Punjab as secondary to the North-West Provinces and go on giving and giving troops to General Reed till you break down in the Punjab, or to maintain the Punjab as your first duty and the most important point of the two, and to refuse to give General Reed any more troops than you can spare. We are decidedly and distinctly of the latter opinion. . . . . We consider that if you leave the Peshawur frontier, we shall not hold together for a month, but be demoralised and despised, and reduced to the condition of a flock of sheep. . . . If you hold the Punjab, you will facilitate the reconquest of India from the sea-board. We have only got to hold on three months. Do not try too much. We are outnumbered. Stick to what you can do. Let us hold the Punjab, *coute qui coute*, and not give up one European necessary to that duty. Whatever takes place in Central India, we shall stand in a firm and honourable attitude if we maintain the capitals on the sea and the frontiers here. Between the two it is all a family quarrel—an insurrection in our own house. If we let foreigners in from the frontier, the Empire is invaded. We may pretend to make friendly presents of provinces, but we cannot disguise that we have lost them by weakness. India has not yet recovered from our

1857.

1857. June 26. expulsion from Afghanistan. The world ignores our voluntary cession of it after Pollock's expedition, and knows well that we could not hold it. Do not repeat the policy, and give up the Trans-Indus. No words of mine can express my sense of the disgrace and ruin that it will bring upon us. It is abandoning the cause of England in the East. Don't yield an inch of frontier; gather up your resources, and restrict yourself to the defence of the Punjab. It is a practicable and a definite policy, and we will support you to the last. . . . If General Reed, with all the men you have sent him, cannot get into Delhi, let Delhi go. Decide on it at once. . . . Don't let yourself be sucked to death as General Reed is doing. He has his difficulties, and we have ours. You have made vast efforts for him, and no one can blame you for now securing your own promise. . . . The Empire's reconquest hangs on the Punjab."

Opinion of General Nicholson. Whilst Cotton and Edwardes were thus throwing all the earnestness of their natures into their letters to the Chief Commissioner, protesting against the abandonment of Peshawur, Nicholson, who was proceeding to take command of the Movable Column, visited Lawrence at Rawul-Pindee, and orally reiterated the arguments on which the three friends based their opposition to the retrograde movement. Lawrence, however, still clung to his opinion. "Admitting," he said, "which I do, that there is much force in the arguments adduced in favour of the maintenance of our hold on Peshawur, what are we to do when all the British troops which we can scrape together, exclusively of those at Peshawur, have been despatched to Delhi and still more be required?" "Rather than abandon Peshawur," answered Nicholson, "let us give up Murree and Rawul-

Pindee. Give up every place but Peshawur, Lahore, and Mooltan." To this Lawrence replied "that such a measure would isolate those three places, lock up a fine force in Peshawur, and expose us to destruction in detail." But nothing that Lawrence could urge shook Nicholson's deeply-grounded convictions. They parted. The soldier passed on to his appointed work. The statesman remained to ponder the eagerly enforced opinions of his chief advisers in the Punjab, whilst awaiting the decision of the Governor-General to watch the progress of events, and to do all in his power to avert the necessity, the apprehension of which had so much alarmed and perplexed him. 1857. June—July.

He had written to Lord Canning on the 10th of June, enclosing the letter which on the day before he had sent to Edwardes; but communication with Calcutta was at that time slow and uncertain in the extreme, and the brief telegraphic message which he had asked for in reply had not arrived in the third week of July. The momentous question was still unsolved. Neither had come the order, "Hold on to Peshawur to the last," nor the permission, "You may act as may appear expedient regarding Peshawur"—in one or the other of which forms he had requested that a telegraphic message might be sent to him. Events, as they were then developing themselves, seemed rather to strengthen the probability of the dreaded alternative being presented to us. He knew little of what was passing below Delhi, but there and in the Punjab itself were awkward symptoms of accumulated danger. The numbers of the enemy were increasing, and with numbers there was increased confidence within the great imperial stronghold. And regiment after regiment was falling away from its allegiance in the territories which John Lawrence

1857. July. governed; so that we appeared to be drifting closely and more closely upon the terrible alternative which he had so greatly dreaded. Still, therefore, he felt convinced that the advice which he had given was wise and salutary; and again he wrote to Lord Canning on the 24th of July, saying: "All these reinforcements ought to enable our army to maintain itself in its present position, and allow the mutineers to expend their power against our entrenchments. But should further aid be required from this quarter, our only resource would be to abandon Peshawur and Kohat, and to send the troops thus relieved on to Delhi. It seems to me vain to attempt to hold Lahore, and insanity to try to retain Peshawur, &c., if we are driven from Delhi. The Punjab will prove short work to the mutineers, when the Delhi Army is destroyed. . . . . . My policy would then be to bring the troops from across the Indus and send them to Delhi; in the mean time to send all our women and children down the rivers to Kurrachee, and then, accumulating every fighting man we have, to join the Army before Delhi or hold Lahore, as might appear expedient. Colonel Edwardes, General Cotton, and Nicholson are for maintaining our hold on Peshawur to the last. They argue that we could not retire in safety, and that the instant we attempted to make a retrograde movement all would be up against us. This I do not believe; but granting that insurrection would immediately ensue, I maintain that the force at Peshawur would make good its retreat. It contains more soldiers, more guns, more power, than that with which Pollock recovered Caubul after forcing the passage of the Khyber. Between Peshawur and the Indus are no defiles, but an open country; the only difficulty is the passage of the Indus, which, with Attock in our hands, ought not to be a work of danger. It is for your Lordship to decide what course we are to pursue. In the event of misfortune at Delhi, are we to leave that Army to its fate and endeavour to hold its own, or shall we, by a timely retirement from beyond the Indus, consolidate our resources in the Punjab, and maintain the struggle under the walls of Delhi. I pray that your Lordship will decide one way or the other. If we are left to decide the matter ourselves, time will be lost in vain discussions; and by the time we decide on the proper course to follow, it will prove too late to act effectually." 1857. July.

Whilst this appeal was slowly making its way to its destination, an answer to Lawrence's letter of the 10th of June was circuitously travelling up to the Punjab. It was dated July 15, and it said: "The outbreak at Indore on the 1st will no doubt have interrupted the dawk as well as the telegraph to Bombay. I therefore send a steamer to Madras with this letter and the despatches which accompany it; and I shall request Lord Harris to telegraph to Lord Elphinstone my answer to your question regarding Peshawur. It will be, 'Hold on to Peshawur to the last.' I should look with great alarm to the effect in Southern India of an abandonment of Peshawur at the present time, or at any time until our condition becomes more desperate or more secure." Thus, officially, was the momentous question settled by the "highest authority;" practically, indeed, it had settled itself before Lord Canning's letter was received. The contingency, which had been contemplated, never arrived; it was not left for the nation to discern the evil effects of either the retreat from Delhi or the abandonment of Peshawur. The question never went beyond the

July 15. Decision of Lord Canning.

1857. July. domain of discussion, and it is of little use now to speculate as to which movement would have been attended with the more disastrous results. But there would have been a grave omission from the pages of this history if there had been no mention of this discussion. For nothing is more significant of the magnitude of the dangers which threatened our Indian Empire in the Summer and Autumn of 1857, than the fact that at a time when the English held fast to the maxim, which Clive had enunciated nearly a century before, that "to stand still is danger, to recede is ruin," the strong spirit of Sir John Lawrence counselled the abandonment of the frontier-station of Peshawur and the adjacent territory to the Afghans, who, not long before, had been our enemies in the field. It must be admitted that, at the time, the weight of authority bore heavily against the proposal; and no man was more willing than Lawrence himself to acknowledge that a measure which met with strenuous opposition from such men as those who set their faces against it, was certainly a doubtful measure.* But time and maturity of reflection

* It ought always to be remembered that the strongest opponents of the measure were the chief Peshawur officers, whose tendency it naturally was to take a local view of the question. Lawrence, years afterwards, with characteristic frankness, wrote that "certainly, in having Herbert Edwardes, John Nicholson, and Sydney Cotton against me, it is clear that there was a great deal to be said on the other side." Indeed, their arguments, as to the danger of abandoning Peshawur, were altogether unanswerable. But so also were the arguments as to the danger of withdrawing the Delhi Field Force. And this danger Sir John Lawrence was more capable of estimating aright than the little confederacy of military and political officers on the frontier. On the other hand it is to be observed that Neville Chamberlain, who knew well how nearly the siege of Delhi had been raised, confessed after the capture of the place, that he concurred in the views, which Lawrence had declared some months before. It was his belief that to retreat from Delhi would have been absolute ruin. "We should have lost all our heavy guns and matériel; our Native troops and our camp-followers would have deserted us; and our British force would have been worn down and destroyed. The Delhi Force could not have made good its retreat on the Punjab, and, in such circumstances, the Punjabee Force could

did not affect his original convictions. He remained stedfast to his first opinion; and years have rather increased than diminished the number of adherents to the policy which he enunciated when the crisis was upon us. Our larger and more accurate knowledge of the state of affairs, that existed in the Summer of 1857, has taught us better to understand the arguments by which the Chief Commissioner justified a proposal, by which alone he conceived that in the last resort he could secure the salvation of the empire. Those arguments, as more clearly discerned by the later light of history, may be thus briefly summarised: 1857. July.

The Question reviewed.

No one knew so well as John Lawrence what, in the months of June and July, was stirring the hearts of the English leaders at Delhi, for to no one did they write so frequently, so fully and so freely, to declare their wants and to describe their prospects. He knew that the thought of raising the siege was present to them; for it was before him in letters, some of which are quoted in these pages. He knew that all depended upon the support which he could give the besieging force. He did not disguise from himself for a moment the fact that the abandonment

not have maintained itself at Lahore. It was doubtful whether, with all its available means it could have retreated on Mooltan." It must be remembered, too, that Lord Canning, who took a very unfavourable view of Sir John Lawrence's proposal, and attributed this policy to the failing health of the Chief Commissioner, had no accurate knowledge of the state of affairs at Delhi—between which place and Calcutta all communication was cut off, and the capture of which still seemed to be a proximate event of no sort of difficulty to the besieging Force. It should be added that the Lumsdens, who were at Candahar at the time, looking at the question from the stand-point of Afghan politics, sent an urgent missive in cipher, urging him to hold on to the last. "If Peshawur and Kohat," they said, "are given up at this moment, we shall have all Afghanistan down upon our backs, besides throwing open the gate of Afghanistan, the Khyber, for ever. . . . Don't give an inch of ground; but trust in Providence, fight it out, and recal us sharp to help you."—*MS.* [The extracts preceding are from unpublished letters.]

1857. July. of Peshawur would be an immense evil; but those were times in which there was often only a choice of evils, and it seemed to Lawrence that, in a large imperial sense, the retirement of the British Army from Delhi would be the greater evil of the two. He stood pledged to the policy of regaining that great centre of Mahomedanism, and crushing the rebellion rampant there in the name of the King; for he had himself earnestly and energetically, and with an overpowering force of argument, urged upon General Anson, at the commencement of the crisis, the paramount necessity of an immediate advance upon Delhi, at a time when the chiefs of the Army Staff were representing the thing to be impossible. He was bound, therefore, in honour to do all that lay in his power to bring it to a successful issue. The policy which he had so stoutly advocated in May seemed still in June and July to be the policy which the national safety imperatively demanded; nay, every succeeding day had rendered it more apparent to him that our inability to "dispose of" Delhi was creating everywhere an impression of our weakness, which was encouraging our enemies and enervating our friends. All eyes were turned towards that great city, and as weeks passed, and still it seemed that the English, who had gone to besiege had become the besieged, there was a growing mistrust as to the wisdom of holding fast to the English alliance, which would soon have rendered us a friendless and feeble few, to be easily mastered and destroyed. With this knowledge pressing hourly upon him, Sir John Lawrence, the more he thought, was the more convinced that, in the last extremity, if the paucity of British troops before Delhi should render its capture impossible, and necessitate the withdrawal of our Army, he would release the force posted in the Peshawur valley, and make over the territory to the Ameer of Caubul. 1857. July.

But it was never intended that this should be a precipitate movement, or that we should prematurely anticipate an extremity which might never arise. It was his design, in the first instance, to move all our women and children to the Lahore side of the Indus, so that our troops might retain their grip of the country unencumbered to the last moment, and then move lightly and rapidly across the river. The cession, it was felt, would be a source of unbounded delight to Dost Mahomed, and it was believed that though it might not secure the permanent fidelity and friendship of the Afghans, it would, for a time at least, hold them in the bonds of a flattered and self-satisfied durance, and afford us the security of the forbearance which we desired.

The Jhelum Mutiny.

It has been said that there were increasing signs of general unrest in the Punjab. The most portentous of these were the mutinies at Jhelum and Sealkote. The Jhelum cantonment lies on the bank of the river which bears that name. That the Fourteenth Sepoy Regiment posted there was on the brink of mutiny was well known. Sir John Lawrence, therefore, despatched a force thither to disarm them—a small compact force consisting of some companies of the Twenty-fourth Queen's, some Horse Artillery guns, under Lieutenant Henry Cookes, and a party of Lind's Mooltanee Horse, the whole under the command of Colonel Ellice, of the Twenty-fourth. The Chief Commissioner had prepared a plan of operations for taking the Sepoys by surprise; but the Colonel,

1857. July 7. thinking that he knew better than any civilian how to manage an affair of this kind, departed from Lawrence's views, and sketched out a plan of his own. There was, therefore, no surprise. When the Europeans were seen filing down the rising ground opposite the cantonment, the Sepoys knew what was coming.* Happening to be out on morning parade, they saw the English column advancing. Regardless of the orders and entreaties of their officers, they began at once to load their muskets. The officers saw that they had no longer any power over their men, and sought safety with the European troops. Then the Sepoys took up their main position in the quarter-guard. It was a strong brick building, with a battlemented roof, erected for purposes of defence by Sir Charles Napier, and afforded good cover to the insurgents, who threw out a party in advance to guard the approaches to it, whilst others took shelter in their Lines, the mud-huts of which had been loopholed in expectation of the crisis. Our people were full of courage and enthusiasm, and they flung themselves headlong upon the enemy. Lind's Mooltanees charged gallantly, but were met by a galling fire, which they could not resist. Cookes' guns opened, but within too near a range, and the musketry of the enemy did better execution than our own Artillery at so short a distance. The Sepoys fired from behind the cover of their mud-walls, and our grape was comparatively harmless. But now the British Infantry came up with their intrepid commander at their head, and advanced full upon the quarter-guard. The attack was a gallant and successful one; the quarter-guard

* Mr. Cooper ("Crisis in the Punjab") says Colonel Gerrard, full of confidence in his men, had "informed them of the object of the European arrival."

was carried, and the Sepoys then vacated their huts and fell back upon the empty lines of the Thirty-ninth, from which they were driven by the bursting of a well-directed shell to a village on the left of the cantonment. 1857. July 7.

By this time the noon-day sun was beating fiercely down upon our exhausted people. Colonel Ellice had been carried from the field dangerously wounded. Captain Spring had been shot dead,* and we had lost many men and many horses in the encounter. Our troops had been marching from the hour of midnight, and had been actively engaged since sunrise. Nature demanded rest; and it was sound discretion at such a time to pause in our offensive operations. It would have been well, perhaps, if the pause had been longer and the renewed operations more carefully matured. At four in the afternoon, when the heat was still great, an attack on the village was ordered. Colonel Gerrard, of the Fourteenth, took command of the Force that went out to destroy the mutinous regiment, in whose fidelity he had once trusted. The result was disastrous. Again the Sepoys had good cover, and we found ourselves entangled in streets, in which we suffered much, but could do little. The guns were brought up within too short a range, and the musketry of the enemy told with deadly effect upon the gunners. The Europeans, partly from fatigue, and partly, perhaps, from the stimulants which they had taken to reinvigorate themselves and the effect of the slant rays of the afternoon sun, are said to have "staggered" up to the village and to have been easily repulsed. The retreat was sounded,

* He had left Roorkhee, as previously stated, with Baird Smith, on the 29th of June (*ante*, page 563), and had only just joined his regiment when his career was thus closed on the battle-field.

1857. July 7. and our troops were withdrawn. Two guns were carried back, but a third, in spite of the gallant efforts of Lieutenant Battye, with a party of Mounted Police, fell into the hands of the enemy, and was turned against our retreating people.

July 8. Nothing more could be done on that evening. At dawn on the morrow the conflict was to be renewed. Both forces had bivouacked on the plain. But when day broke it was found that the mutineers had evacuated their position and fled. Many had been killed in the two engagements; some were drowned in the Jhelum; others fell into the hands of our Police, or were subsequently given up by the Cashmere authorities, in whose country they had sought refuge, and thus surrendered, they were blown away from our guns. Very few of them ultimately escaped; but the manner in which the affair was managed greatly incensed the Chief Commissioner. For, in plain words, with Horse, Foot, and Artillery, we were beaten by part of a regiment of Sepoys. If we had quietly surrounded the village and attacked it in the cool of the evening, it is probable that not a man would ever have escaped from Jhelum.

Mutiny at Sealkote. When tidings of the sharp resistance of the Fourteenth reached Sealkote, a still more disastrous state of things arose at that place. The station was commanded by Brigadier Frederick Brind, an Artillery officer of high repute—a man of lofty stature and large proportions, who had done good service in his time, and who was still amply endowed with physical and mental vigour. But seldom was man left by hard circumstances in a position which afforded so little scope for the display of his power. The cantonment had been stripped of European troops for the formation of the Movable Column, and there were nearly a thousand Native soldiers—Horse and Foot —all armed and ready for action.* In such circumstances a commanding officer has no choice to make—no discretion to exercise. He must appear to trust his men whether he does or not; for to betray suspicion is surely to precipitate an outbreak. So to all outward appearance Brind had full confidence in his men, and as time went on the quietude of their demeanour seemed to justify more than the pretence. But when, on the 8th of July, the Lines of Sealkote were all astir with the tidings that the Fourteenth at Jhelum had been in action with the white troops, who had attempted to disarm them, it was felt by our people that the beginning of the end had come. And there was another source of excitement on that evening, for a messenger had come from Delhi, bringing a summons from the King commanding them to join the Royal Army. The night was, therefore, one of preparation. On the morning of the 9th everything was ready.

1857. July 8.

Sealkote was a large, and had been an important military station. In quiet times European troops had been stationed there in large numbers, with the usual results. There were good barracks and commodious houses and pleasant gardens, and more than the wonted number of English gentlewomen and young children. There were a church and a chapel, and other indications of the progress of western civilisation. When, therefore, the storm burst, there was much that lay at the mercy of the enemy, and on our side no possible means of defence. Before the

* "Brigadier Brind protested against the European troops being entirely removed, and desired that two hundred and fifty should remain. In reply, he was requested to disarm. But, to the last, he shared in the belief (almost grevious) in the honour of the Sepoy."—*Cooper's Crisis in the Punjab.*

1857. July 6. sound of the morning-gun had been heard throughout the cantonment, and our people, according to their wont, had mounted their horses or entered their carriages, to proceed to their wonted duties, or to take the air before the sun was high above the horizon, the Sepoys had planted picquets all round the place, to prevent the escape of the Feringhees. And presently the din and uproar of rebellion announced to our people, just waking from their slumbers, that the Sepoys had risen. Our officers were soon mounted and on their way to the parade-ground. The truth was then only too apparent The troopers of the Ninth were already in their saddles, and the Forty-sixth were under arms. Our people were suddenly brought face to face with mutiny in its worst form. All circumstances and conditions were in the last degree unfavourable to the English. Sealkote was one of the great stations at which there had been a gathering of detachments from different regiments for the new rifle practice, and, therefore, great opportunities of conspiracy. It lay in proximity to the Jummoo territory of the Maharajah of Cashmere, who the Sepoys believed, and our authorities feared, would, in the hour of danger, forsake his alliance; and it was utterly without any defence of European troops. So when the hour came to strike, the confidence and audacity of the enemy had everything to foster and encourage them.

As ever, the Cavalry were foremost in the work of mutiny—foremost in their greed for blood. Mounted on good chargers, they could ride with rapidity from place to place, and follow the white men on horseback or in their carriages, and shoot them down as they rode. For weeks the outburst had been expected, and every English inhabitant of Sealkote had thought painfully over the coming crisis, and had calculated the best means of escape. The only place of safety for which they could make was the old Fort, once the stronghold of the Sikh Chief, Tej Singh, and to this, when they saw that nothing could be done to arrest the tide of rebellion, which was already at the flood, they endeavoured to make good their retreat. Some happily reached the Fort. Others perished on the way. A ball from the pistol of a mounted trooper entered the broad back of the Brigadier, and he was carried to the Fort only to die. The Superintending Surgeon, Graham, was shot dead in his buggy, as his daughter sat by his side.* Another medical officer of the same name was "killed in his carriage among his children." A Scotch missionary, named Hunter, on his way to the Fort in a carriage, with his wife and child, was attacked by some chuprassies of the gaol-guard, and all three were ruthlessly murdered. The Brigade-Major, Captain Bishop, was killed, in the presence of his family, under the very walls of the Fort. Some hid themselves during the day, and escaped discovery and death almost by a miracle. Some were preserved by their own men, and concealed till nightfall in the Lines. The officers of the Forty-sixth, who had remained with their men

1857. July 9.

* His daughter escaped. She was dragged to the Cavalry Guard, where she "found Colonel and Mrs. Lorne Campbell surrounded by a few faithful troopers, who conducted them in safety to the Fort."—There is a significant commentary on this incident in one of Herbert Edwardes's letters to John Lawrence: "These individual stories convey better notions than public despatches. In ordinary times India would have shuddered over 'Dr. Graham shot dead in his daughter's arms. Now, all we say is, 'What a wonderful escape Miss Graham has had!'" Habituated, after two months of mutiny and massacre, to horrors of this kind, the recital of them had ceased to create the intense sensations which they had once caused. And so, in this History, it will be observed, as it proceeds, that whilst the earlier tragedies, then novel and strange to the European mind, are dwelt upon in detail, some of the later ones are dismissed with the brevity of a telegraphic message. In this the narrative only reflects the varying temperature of the times.

1857. July 9. until the road between the Parade-ground and the Fort was closed by the enemy, rode off towards Gogranwallah, and reached that place, scorched and weary—but not hungry and athirst, for the villagers fed them on the way—after a mid-day journey of some forty miles. The personal incidents of that 9th of July at Sealkote would fill an interesting and exciting chapter. But there is nothing stranger in the story than the fact that two of our field officers—one, Colonel of a regiment—were invited to take command of the mutineers, and to lead them to Delhi, with a promise of high pay, and a significant pledge, not perhaps without a touch of irony in it, that they might always spend the hot weather on the Hills.

Whilst our people were seeking safety within the walls of the old Fort, and securing their position by strengthening its defences, the Sepoy mutineers were revelling in the work of spoliation with the congenial companionship of the criminal classes. The old story, so often already told, and still to be told again and again, was repeated here: the mutineers made for the Gaol, released the prisoners, plundered the Treasury, destroyed the Cutcherry with all its records, blew up the magazines, and gutted the houses of the Christian inhabitants. If there were any special circumstance about the Sealkote insurrection, it was that the household servants of our English officers, generally faithful, or at least neutral, on these occasions, took an active part against their old masters. That they knew what was coming seems to be proved by the fact that the Brigadier's sirdar-bearer, or chief body servant, an "old and favourite" domestic, took the caps off his master's pistols in the night, as they lay beside him while he slept.* And how thoroughly they cast in their lot with the soldiery is demonstrated with equal distinctness by the fact that they afterwards fought against us, the Brigadier's khansaman, or butler, taking an active part in operations which will be presently described. There seems to have been perfect cohesion between all classes of our enemies—the mutineers, the criminals from the gaols, the "Goojurs" from the neighbouring villages, and the servants from the houses and bungalows of the English. From sunrise to sunset the work went on bravely. Everything that could be carried off by our enemies was seized and appropriated; even the old station-gun, which morning and evening had proclaimed the hours of uprising and down-setting. And nearly everything belonging to us, that could not be carried off, was destroyed and defaced, except—a strange and unaccountable exception—the Church and Chapel, which the Christians had reared for the worshipping of the Christian's God. 1857. July 9.

Before nightfall, all this rabble had made off for the Ravee river, on their way to Delhi, rejoicing in

* This might be supposed to have arisen merely from the instinct of self-preservation if it had not been for the after-conduct of these domestics. It is certain that, in many parts of the country, the Native servants were in a state of deadly fear lest their enraged masters, seeking objects for their revenge, should turn upon them and kill them. There is an anecdote illustrative of this, almost too good to be an invention. It is said that a gentleman in Calcutta, observing one day a strange table-servant waiting at dinner, asked him who he was and how he came there. His answer was, "Hum budlee hain, sahib" ("I am a substitute"); and he explained that he had come to take the place temporarily of a member of the establishment who was sick—a common practice in Anglo-Indian domestic life. A few days afterwards the old servant returned to his work, looking very sleek and well; and when his master questioned him as to the cause of his absence, he naively replied that he had received secret information that, on a given day just passed, the sahib-logue intended to shoot all their Native servants, in the middle of dinner, and that, therefore, he had thought it prudent to send a "budlee" to be shot in his place.

1857. July 9—10. and excited by, their day's work. It was a delightful relief to the inmates of the decayed old Fort, who now thought that if the danger were not wholly past, at least the worst of it was over. It has been said that they "slept more soundly and fearlessly than they had slept for weeks before. The mine had exploded and they had escaped."* It is often so; the agony of suspense is greater than that of the dreaded reality. But there was one there to whom no such relief was to be given. The Brigadier lay dying. A true soldier to the last, he had, whilst the death-pangs were upon him, issued his orders for the defence of the Fort, and for what little else could be done in that extremity. But the ball from the trooper's pistol had done its work, and though Brind lingered through the night, he died before the sun had risen; and all felt that a brave man and a capable officer was lost to the country, which he had so well served.

Nicholson and the Movable Column. The triumph of the Sealkote Mutineers was but brief. Retribution followed closely on their victory. On the 22nd of June, Colonel John Nicholson, with the rank of Brigadier-General, had taken command of the Movable Column. That so young an officer should be appointed to such a command, in defiance of what were called the "claims" of many officers in the Division of longer standing and higher rank, was an innovation by no means grateful to the Departments or to the Seniority-mongers in the service, but it startled many with a pleasurable surprise, and to some it was a source of infinite rejoicing. Elderly men with elderly wives, who had never heard of such a thing before, affected to think that there was no great wisdom in the appointment,

* Cave-Browne's "Punjab and Delhi."

and showed their contempt by talking of Mister Nicholson. Of this the young General could afford to speak tenderly. "I fear," he wrote to Edwardes on the 17th of June, "that my nomination will give great offence to the senior Queen's officers, but I shall do all in my power to get on well with them. I feel so sorry for the disappointment they must experience, that I think I shall be able to put up with a great deal of coldness without taking offence." But among the younger officers of the Army, especially among those in the Movable Column, the selection was most popular. The exigencies of the General Staff having taken Chamberlain to Delhi, there was not a man in the Army whose selection would have been more welcome to those who meant work, and were resolute to do it. When Edwardes wrote to John Lawrence, saying, "You have been very vigorous in pushing down reinforcements, and those appointments of Chamberlain and Nicholson are worth armies in this crisis. . . . Amid the ruins of the Regular Army these two Irregular Pillars stand boldly up against the sky, and I hope the Tomnoddies will admire their architecture," he expressed the sentiments of all the bolder spirits in the Army, eager to be led, not by age and rank, but by lusty manhood in its prime, and who could see better hope for a glorious deliverance even in the rashness and audacity of youth than in the irresolution and inactivity of senile command. It was truly a great day for India, when it was decreed that Chamberlain should go down to Delhi and Nicholson place himself at the head of the Movable Column in the Punjab. 1857. June—July.

The force of which Brigadier-General Nicholson took command consisted of Her Majesty's Fifty-second Light Infantry; a troop of European Horse Artillery,

1857. June—July.

under Major Dawes, an excellent officer, who had done good service in the Afghan war; a Horse Battery, also European, under Major George Bourchier; the Thirty-third* and Thirty-fifth Sepoy Regiments; and a wing of the Ninth Cavalry. He joined the force at Jullundhur, and moved thence to Phillour, as though he had been marching down upon Delhi. Then some people shook their heads and wondered what he was doing in thus carrying down with him many hundreds of Sepoys, with rebellion in their hearts, only to swell the host of the enemy. What he was really doing was soon apparent. He was intent on disarming the Native regiments. But as this was to be best accomplished by secrecy and suddenness, he did not blazon his design about the Camp. But in good time, the necessary instructions were given. On the morning of the 25th of June, the Column was under the walls of the fort of Phillour. The guns were drawn up on the road and unlimbered, the Fifty-second taking post on both flanks. The Sepoy Regiments marched on, little dreaming of what was to come. Nicholson had given orders to the Police that, on the first sound of firing, the bridge across the river should be cut away, so as to prevent all chance of escape if the Sepoys should break and fly with their arms in their hands. Leaning over one of Bourchier's guns, he said to that officer, "If they bolt, you follow as hard as you can; the bridge will have been destroyed, and we shall have a second Sobraon on a small scale."† But the Sepoys did not bolt. In the presence of those guns, they felt that it would be madness to resist the

Disarming of the Thirty-third and Thirty-fifth Regiments.

* The Thirty-third, which had been stationed at Hooshyapoor, joined the column near Phillour.

† Bourchier's *Eight Months' Campaign.*

order; so they sullenly piled their arms at the word of command. 1857. July.

Having disarmed the two Infantry regiments, Nicholson determined to retrace his steps from Phillour, and to pitch his camp at Umritsur. On the 5th he was at that place, the central position of which recommended itself to him, as it enabled him to afford speedy aid, if required, either to Lahore or the Jullundhur Doab, while at the same time it overawed the Maunjha, and rendered hopeless any attempt to mutiny on the part of the Fifty-ninth Regiment stationed in the cantonment.* On the morning of the 7th, the stirring news of the mutiny of the Fourteenth at Jhelum reached his Camp, and he hoped hour after hour to be comforted by the tidings that Colonel Ellice had defeated and destroyed them. But the day passed, and the night also was spent, and still the wished-for intelligence did not come, but in its place were ominous tidings of disaster; so on the morning of the 9th, Nicholson, with reluctance which he frankly expressed,† proceeded to disarm the Fifty-ninth. There was a punishment parade that morning. A rebel or a deserter was to be executed, and all the troops, European and Native, were ordered out to witness the ceremony. The ground selected lay between the city and the fort, about a mile from the cantonment, and there the regiments and the guns were drawn up on parade, and the ghastly ceremony was duly performed. This done, the Sepoys of the Fifty-ninth, who only the

Disarming of the Fifty-ninth.

* Brigadier-General Nicholson to the Adjutant-General of the Army, July 19, 1857.

† "I feel bound to place on record my belief that both in conduct and feeling this regiment was quite an exceptional one. It had neither committed itself in any way, nor do I believe that up to the day it was disarmed it had any intention of committing itself; and I very deeply regret that even as a precautionary measure it should have become my duty to disarm it."—*Ibid.*

1857. July. day before had been complimented on their loyalty, were ordered to lay down their arms. Though surprised and bewildered by the command, they obeyed without a murmur; and though many men of the Regiment were not present on parade, and, therefore, a quantity of arms were still left in possession of the Sepoys, they testified the sincerity of their obedience by afterwards voluntarily surrendering them.

Thus were the teeth of another Native regiment quietly drawn, and the danger glaring at us from the ranks of our own Sepoys was greatly diminished. Elsewhere the same process, as Nicholson now learnt, was going on with more or less success. At Rawul-Pindee were the Fifty-eighth Regiment and two companies of the Fourteenth—the regiment which had fought so desperately at Jhelum. A letter from Sir John Lawrence announced that the business of disarming had been done, but in no very satisfactory manner. "We have disarmed," the Chief Commissioner wrote to Nicholson on the 7th, "the seven companies of the Fifty-eighth and the two companies of the Fourteenth. We had three guns and two hundred and forty Europeans, and were very nearly having a fight. The main body broke and bolted to their lines, and we did not fire on them. After about an hour's work, however, during which a good many loaded, we got all but about thirty to lay down their arms. The latter bolted, and about half were killed or taken by the Police Sowars. Miller was badly wounded a little above the right wrist; both bones were broken. He had a narrow escape. A Sepoy gave him a dig in the chest with his bayonet, but somehow or other the wound was slight." At the same time Edwardes was reporting the entire success of his arrangement for the disarming of the Sepoys of

Disarming of the Fifty-eighth.

the Twenty-fourth at Fort Mackeson.* By the help of Brougham's mountain guns and some detachments of the Punjab Irregular Force this was accomplished without a hindrance or a hitch; and the disarmed Sepoys were marched into Peshawur, escorted by Brougham's guns, whilst the Fort was garrisoned by some Mooltanee levies, horse and foot. Nothing could have been more adroitly managed than the whole affair. 1857. Disarming of the Twenty-fourth.

But tidings more exciting than these were to reach the ears of the Commander of the Movable Column. The telegraph wires brought news from Lahore that the Sepoys at Sealkote had risen, and that rapine and murder were abroad in the place; another half-hour, and the story was confirmed by a musician of the Forty-sixth, who had ridden in with a few blurred lines from Assistant-Commissioner M'Mahon, begging him to bring the Force to their aid.† Nicholson could now no longer hesitate about disarming the wing of the Ninth Cavalry attached to his column. He had hitherto abstained lest such an act should precipitate the rising at Sealkote, and now the wing at Movements of Nicholson's Column.

* "As day dawned, the two parties from north and south closed in upon the Fort, and threw a chain of horsemen round it, whilst Major Brougham drew up his guns so as to command the gateway. Major Shakespear, commanding the Twenty-fourth Regiment, and Lieutenant Hovenden, of the Engineers, then rode into the Fort, and ordered the Sepoys to parade outside. They were much surprised and confused, but made no resistance, and when ordered by Major Shakespear, piled their arms and gave up their belts and pouches in an orderly manner."—*Edwardes to Cotton, July* 8, 1857. *MS. Correspondence.*

† The note, the original of which is before me, is significant in its brevity: "The troops here are in open mutiny. Jail broke. Brigadier wounded. Bishop killed. Many have escaped to the Fort. Bring the Movable Column at once, if possible. 6½ A.M., 9th July." The name of the bearer of this chit ought not to be omitted. Mr. Cave-Browne says, "A young band-boy, named M'Douglas, of the Forty-sixth, had galloped off from the regimental parade-ground on a little tat (pony), and by dint of borrowing and seizing fresh ones in the villages as he passed through, he finished his ride of some eighty miles into Umritsur, and hastened to the General's quarters just as the mail-cart brought in the message from Lahore."

1857. July. that place was in the fulness of rebellion. Their arms and horses, therefore, were now to be taken from them. The troopers felt that resistance could only bring destruction upon them, so they quietly gave up all that made them soldiers; and then Nicholson prepared himself to march. As the day wore on, fresh tidings of the movements of the Sealkote mutineers reached him. It was obvious that they were marching down on Goordaspore, intent probably on stirring up the Second Irregular Cavalry stationed there, and, joined by them, on plundering the station. Thence Nicholson believed that they would make their way, by the route of Noorpore and Hooshyapore—at which places they might reinforce themselves with Horse and Foot*—to Jullundhur, and thence march, a strong body of mutineers, down to Delhi. To frustrate this expected movement was now the desire of the Commander of the Movable Column. He was forty miles from Goordaspore, and the Sepoys had two days' start of him. But Nicholson was born to overcome difficulties which would have beaten down other men. He determined on a forced march to Goordaspore, and went resolutely to work to accomplish it. The July sun blazed down upon his camp with a ferocity more appalling than the malice of the enemy. But even that was to be disregarded. Whatsoever the country could yield in the shape of carriages, horses, and ponies was at once enlisted into the service of the Column.†

The March to Goordaspore.

July 10.

* The Fourth Native Infantry was at Noorpore. The Sixteenth Irregular Cavalry at Hooshyapore.

† Great praise is due to the civil authorities for their activity in this conjuncture. Mr. Montgomery, in his official report, says: "To the commercial men of Umritsur and Lahore the metalled road offers special advantages, for it enables hundreds of native gigs or ekas to fly unceasingly between the two cities. On the day I allude to the district officers of both places were ordered to seize every eka, bylee, and pony that was to be seen, and to despatch them, under police guards, to General Nicholson's camp at Umritsur, on

All possible advantage was taken of the coolness of the night; but when morning came they were still some fifteen or sixteen miles from Goordaspore, with the prospect of a sultry march before them.* With all his care and labour, Nicholson had not, even with the aid of the troop-horses of the Ninth, been able to mount the whole of his force, and some weary foot-sore work was therefore a necessity of the conjuncture. So, many were struck down by the heat; yet, notwithstanding these discouraging circumstances, they pushed forward in excellent spirits, and even with a strong enjoyable sense of the humourous side of the service they were performing.† It was not until the evening of the 11th that the whole of the force was assembled at Goordaspore. There intelligence was received that the mutineers from Sealkote were then at Noorkote, some fifteen miles from the right hand of the Ravee. There were two courses then open to Nicholson. He might dispute the pas-

1857. July 11.

urgent public service. These vehicles, on their arrival there, were promptly loaded with British soldiers, and the force started at dusk for Goordaspore, which is at a distance of forty-four miles from Umritsur, reaching it at three P.M. of July 11. It was joined at Battala by Mr. Roberts, Commissioner, and Captain Perkins, Assistant-Commissioner at Umritsur."

* Colonel Bourchier ("Eight Months' Campaign") says that they made twenty-six miles in the night, and had then eighteen miles before them. But General Nicholson, in his official report, says that the entire distance was "over forty-one miles," some three miles less than Bourchier's computation.

† Colonel Bourchier, in his narrative, gives the following amusing account of the humours of the march: "Yet, under these circumstances, trying as they were, the spirit of fun was not extinct. The Artillery made extemporary awnings of branches of trees over their gun-carriages and waggons, giving them the appearance of carts 'got up' for a day at Hampstead; officers, crowned with wreaths of green leaves, were 'chaffed' by their comrades for adopting head-dresses à la Norma. Here might be seen a soldier on a rampant pony, desiring his companion, on a similar beast, to keep behind and be his 'edge de camp;' there a hero, mindful perhaps of Epping on Easter Monday, bellowing out his inquiries as to who had seen the fox (stag?) Privates, never intended for the mounted branch, here and there came to grief, and lay sprawling on mother-earth, while ever and anon some mighty Jehu in his *eka* dashed to the front at a pace a Roman charioteer would have envied."

1857. July 12. sage of the river, or he might draw them on towards him, by remaining inactive and keeping the enemy ignorant of his position. He determined on the latter course, and much to the perplexity of some and the dissatisfaction of others, remained quiescent at Goordaspore till nine o'clock on the following morning. Then he learnt that the enemy were crossing the river by a ford about nine miles distant, at a place known as the Trimmoo Ghaut; so he prepared at once to fling himself upon them.

The Trimmoo Ghaut affair. At noon he was in sight of his prey, about a mile from the river. The mutineers had crossed over with their baggage, and the grey jackets of the videttes of the Ninth Cavalry were first seen flitting about in our front, and then the Infantry were observed drawn up in line, their right resting on a serai and a dismantled mud fort, and their left on a small village and cluster of trees, with parties of Cavalry on each flank. Nicholson now made his dispositions for the attack. Eager to get his guns within short range of the enemy, he masked his advancing batteries with bodies of mounted Police, and moved on to within six hundred yards of the mutineers, when the Cavalry, excited to the utmost by the artificial stimulant of *bang*, rushed furiously to the encounter, some shouting, some gnashing their teeth. On this Nicholson unmasked one of his batteries, and the maskers went rapidly to the rear.* It was a moment of doubt and anxiety, especially with the Artillery commanders, whose Native drivers might have deserted them at a critical moment, for they had been acquainted at

* Nicholson himself speaks very gently and forbearingly of this rearward movement of the Police Ressalahs: "The Police," he says, "being no longer useful as maskers, and seeming undesirous of engaging, were ordered to the rear." Colonel Bourchier says that they ran away. "Away scampered the mounted levies back to Goordaspore."

Sealkote with the very Sepoys against whom they had now been brought. One half of the old Brigade was, indeed, fighting against the other. But the suspected men were as true to their salt in the Punjab as they were at Delhi.* The guns were brought into action without a hitch, and the enemy, though they fought steadily and well, and sent in a volley from the whole line with the precision of a parade, staggered beneath the fire of our batteries, upon which some of the men of the Forty-sixth flung themselves with heroic courage. The grape and shrapnel from our nine guns scattered death among the foremost of the mutineers; and presently the Enfield rifles of the Fifty-second began to give deadly proof that the smooth-bored muskets of the Sepoys were as playthings contending against them. Still there were some amongst them to be convinced only by the thrust of the bayonet. In truth, the enemy were terribly out matched. With all their gallantry in doing and their fortitude in enduring, what could "Brown Bess" and the old station-gun do against our batteries and our rifles? The battle was soon over. The mutineers fell back upon the river, and Nicholson, whose want of Cavalry was severely felt, did all he could in pursuit; but could not inflict much damage upon them. It is said, however, that they had already left "between three and four hundred killed and wounded on the field." And all their baggage fell into our hands—arms, ammunition, clothing, and other plundered property, public and private, the spoil of the Sealkote cantonment.

1857. July 12.

* Colonel Bourchier says: "I took the precaution to warn my European gunners to watch them. In the reply of my Farrier-Sergeant spoke the whole company: 'If they only attempt to run, sir, we'll cut off their heads.' But in this case, as in every other, my Native drivers nobly did their duty."

1857. July 12—16. There was nothing more to be done that day. The mid-day heat had completely exhausted our European fighting men, so, whilst a party of Punjab Infantry was left to guard the ford and protect the baggage, the Fifty-second and the Artillery were marched back to Goordaspore. But the day's fighting had resulted in a "conclusion where nothing is concluded," so conclusions were to be tried again. The Sepoy force was shattered, but not destroyed. Their fighting power was not yet gone. Perhaps the energy that sustained them was the energy of desperation; for to fall back was as perilous to them as to stand still. There was no security for them in any direction. They had not more than half the number that first marched down to the Ravee; but they were brave and resolute men, and, even with such fearful odds against them, they did not shrink from another conflict. The river had risen, and that which had been a ford had now become an island. The old station-gun which they had brought from Sealkote was their sole piece of artillery, and they had no gunners with their force; but the Brigadier's old "khansaman" had lived for too many years at Artillery stations not to have a shrewd conception of the manner of working a gun. And thus planted on the island in the middle of the Ravee, they thought that, for a time at least, they might defy us. The river had ceased to be fordable, and the civil authorities, as a precautionary measure, had sunk all the boats in the immediate neighbourhood. So, when Nicholson again advanced from Goordaspore, he could do little more in the first instance than take up a position out of reach of the enemy's one gun and send to a distance for some boats. At daybreak
July 16. on the morning of the 16th, the desired means of

transport had been obtained, and he was prepared to attack the enemy on their insular stronghold. The Infantry crossed over one extremity of the island, a mile and a quarter from the enemy's position, whilst the Artillery took post so as to cover the advance of the column and to play upon the hostile gun.* The Sepoys were taken by surprise. Not until a large part of the Fifty-second had formed upon the island did the mutineers know that we had even obtained a boat. The Assembly was then sounded; the black troops mustered in haste and moved round their gun to sweep our advancing column. But the piece had been elevated for service at a longer range, and in the hurry of the moment the amateur artillerymen had failed to depress the screw, which was old and rusty, and not easily to be worked; so the shot went harmlessly over the heads of our people. On went the British Infantry, with Nicholson at their head; and though some, stern and steadfast to the last, stood to be shot down or bayoneted at their gun, the rout soon became general. Many were killed on the island; many were drowned in the river; and a few who escaped were given up by the people of the surrounding villages. These were afterwards tried by Special Commissions, and paid the penalty of their crimes on the gibbet.

1857. July 16.

Nicholson at Lahore.

The Movable Column then marched back to Umritsur; and Nicholson hastened to Lahore, whither Sir John Lawrence had already proceeded from Rawul-Pindee. The General was there on the 21st of July; on the 22nd, the Chief Commissioner wrote, through his secretary, to the Commander of the

* Colonel Bourchier says that "to silence it at such a distance (twelve hundred yards), whilst it was nearly concealed by grass and an earthern breastwork, was almost impossible."

1857. July 22. Reinforcements for Delhi.

Delhi Force, that "the following troops were on their way to Delhi, or would immediately march:" "The Kumaon Battalion, about four hundred strong, which has passed Loodhianah, and ought to be at Delhi on the 4th or 5th of August; Her Majesty's Fifty-second from the Movable Column, now at Umritsur, six hundred bayonets; Mooltanee Horse, two hundred; and a nine-pounder battery. All these troops should be at Delhi by the 15th, and in an emergency might make double marches. General Nicholson will command the force." And then it was added: "The Chief Commissioner further proposes to despatch the troops marginally noted as quickly as possible, and all can be at Delhi by the end of August, some of them a good deal earlier. The Second Punjab Infantry and Wing of Her Majesty's Sixty-first ought to be there by the 15th proximo. The former is now on its way from Mooltan to Ferozepore, whence it will march on the arrival of the detachment of the Bombay Fusiliers, which left this place last night. The wing of the Belooch Battalion has not yet left Mooltan; but orders for its march have been despatched. The Fourth Punjab Regiment is at Peshawur, and will march in two or three days. It can hardly be at Delhi before the end of August. The Two Companies of Her Majesty's Eighth are holding Jullundhur and Phillour, and cannot be spared until relieved by a detachment of Her Majesty's Twenty-fourth, now on its way from Rawul-Pindee. Rothney's Sikhs are at Loodhianah, and will join Brigadier-General Nicholson *en route*. Lieutenant-Colonel Dawes's troop

Second Punjab Infantry	700
H.M.'s Sixty-first (a wing)	400
Wing of Belooch Battalion	400
Fourth Punjab Infantry	600
Two Companies of H.M.'s Eighth	200
Detachment of Fourth Sikhs	100
Dawes's Troop of H. A.	100
	2500

will be sent or not, as you may desire. It is believed that light guns are not required at Delhi. All these troops are of excellent quality, fully equal, if not superior, to any that the Insurgents can bring against them, and comprise a force of four thousand two hundred men." Thus was Lawrence, who did all things on the grand Titanic scale, still sending down his reinforcements by thousands to Delhi—thousands of Europeans and trustworthy Sikhs, with a young General, whose personal presence alone was worth a Brigade of Horse, Foot, and Artillery. 1857. July 22.

On the 24th of July, Nicholson returned to Camp. His arrival had been anxiously awaited, for doubt and uncertainty were in all men's minds. Speculation had been rife, and all sorts of rumours of the future movements of the force had been circulated among them. Few had ventured to hope that the order would be given to them to march down to Delhi; for the general feeling was that the Punjab had already been so stripped of European troops that it could not afford to divest itself of another regiment or another battery. But Nicholson had returned to the column with the joyous tidings that they were to set their faces towards the scene of the great struggle. "Our only fear," wrote an officer of the Force, "was that Delhi would fall before we could possibly arrive there." But all felt that if any one could take them down in time to participate in the crowning operations of the siege, Nicholson was the man to do it. He was not one to lose an hour. On the following day the column crossed the Beeas, moved down by forced marches to the Sutlej, and thence pushing on with all speed to the Jumna. At Bara, on the 3rd of August, Nicholson received a letter from General Wilson, saying, "The enemy have re-esta- July 24. The Column ordered to Delhi.

1857. August 6—7.

blished the bridge over the Nujufgurh Canal (which we had destroyed) and have established themselves in force there, with the intention of moving on Alipore and our communications to the rear. I, therefore, earnestly beg you to push forward with the utmost expedition in your power, both to drive these fellows from my rear, and to aid me in holding my position." On the 6th, Nicholson was at Umballah, whence he wrote, "I am just starting post for Delhi by General Wilson's desire. The column should be at Kurnaul the day after to-morrow, and I shall, perhaps, rejoin it at Paneeput."

Nicholson at Delhi.

On the following day he stood upon the Delhi Ridge looking down at the great city, taking in all the wonderful suggestiveness of the scene with that quiet, thoughtful, self-contained solemnity of mien, which distinguished him from all his cotemporaries. He had much then to think of in this little breathing-space—much of the past, much of the future. The time which had elapsed since his first appointment to the command of the Movable Column had not been without certain personal annoyances, which even in the midst of the stirring work around him he had not been wholly able to brush aside. It was scarcely possible that, in the position in which he was placed, a man of Nicholson's peculiar character should, on no occasion, give offence to higher authority. It was his nature to steer straight on to independent action; to "scorn the consequence and to do the thing." And so it happened that those above him thought that he was taking too much upon himself, and that he was grievously deficient in those references and explanations which Officialism, in ordinary times, not improperly demands. Even Sir John Lawrence, most emphatically a man of action, was somewhat disturbed by the fact that Nicholson had disarmed the Thirty-third and Thirty-fifth regiments without previously consulting the Chief-Commissioner, or very promptly explaining to him the "reason why." But afterwards, with the unfailing frankness which relieved all that was outwardly stern and harsh in his nature, he admitted that he "could not expect Nicholson, after knocking about in the sun all day, to write long yarns." "On such occasions," he added, "a line or two semi-officially will satisfy me, until I get your formal report; all I want to know is, what is done and the reason." But no sooner had this little difference with the Commissioner been smoothed down, than another and more serious one arose between the Commander of the Movable Column and the General commanding the Division. Nicholson had taken upon himself to move troops, under the command of the latter, without consulting him, and had been so severely rebuked, that he declared that nothing but the thought of the public inconvenience, which might result from such a step, restrained him from throwing up his appointment. These wounds were still fresh, when he reached Delhi and asked himself whether it were likely that, in the work which lay before him, he would be able wholly to avoid collisions with his fellow-workmen. He felt that much had been done of which he could not approve, and that much had been left undone which he would have earnestly counselled; and he knew that all this might come over again, and that his resolute freedom of speech and independence of action might bring forth much that would be painful to himself and embarrassing to others. But he had written a few days before to Sir John Lawrence, saying: "I might have preserved

1857. August 7.

1857. August 7. silence, but when in a great crisis an officer holds a strong opinion on any matters of consequence, I think he fails in his duty if he does not speak it out, at whatever risk of giving offence."* And now he was determined that, cost him what it might, he would suffer his convictions to declare themselves without restraint, regardless of everything but the good of the Empire.

His coming had been eagerly looked for in Camp. As day after day tidings of the rapid approach of the Movable Column, under Nicholson, were brought in, men began to see clearly before them the consummation of the final assault, and their hearts were gladdened by the prospect. The approach of this column was, indeed, as the promise of a great deliverance; and when it was whispered through the camp that Nicholson had already arrived, it was as a cordial to men's souls, for a great reputation had preceded him, and it was felt among our people that a mighty warrior had come among them, who was destined to lead our troops into Delhi, and to crush the power of the Mogul. His personal presence

* See the following extract from a letter written to Sir John Lawrence from Umballah, August 6. Lawrence had written to Nicholson, saying, half-seriously, half-jestingly, that he was incorrigible, and suggesting that he might do more good by carrying others with him than by running counter to them. To this Nicholson had replied: "I am very sorry to hear that General Gowan has taken offence again. I don't wish to ignore him or any other superior; I dislike offending any one, and, except on principle, would never have a disagreement. You write as if I were in the habit of giving offence. Now I cannot call to mind that since my return to India, upwards of five years and a half ago, I have had any misunderstandings, except with —— and ——. The former, I believe, is conscious that he did me wrong, and I trust the latter will eventually make the same admission. . . . I fear that I must have given offence to you, too, on the Rawul-Pindee question. I can truly say that I opposed my opinion to yours with great reluctance, and had the matter been one of less importance, I might have preserved silence; but when in a great crisis an officer holds a strong opinion on any matter of consequence, I think he fails in his duty if he does not speak it out, at whatever risk of giving offence."

did much to generate in men's minds the sublime idea of a Hero—a King of Men; of the Megistos who was to reign among them. He had come on in advance, by Wilson's request, to take counsel with him; and he was soon passing from picquet to picquet, taking in with a soldier's eye all the points of our position, and looking down critically upon the defences of the enemy. He did not at once make his way into the hearts of men, but he impressed all with a sense of power. On the evening of the 7th of August, on which day he arrived in Camp, he dined at the Head-Quarters Mess, and the silent solemnity of his demeanour was unpleasantly apparent to men whose habitual cheerfulness, when they met together for the social meal, had been one of the sustaining influences of Camp Life, during all that long dreary season of waiting and watching. Next morning, accompanied by Norman, he visited the great position at Hindoo Rao's house, which for two long months had borne the brunt of the enemy's attacks. Baird Smith at that time was in consultation with Reid.* The brave commander of the Picquet, who had done such good service, could not help inwardly resenting Nicholson's imperious manner. But when, after the visitor had passed on, Reid complained to

1857. August 7.

* The following description is from the "History of the Siege of Delhi:" "About this time a stranger of very striking appearance was remarked visiting all our picquets, examining everything, and making most searching inquiries about their strength and history. His attire gave no clue to his rank; it evidently never cost the owner a thought. Moreover, in those anxious times every one went as he pleased; perhaps no two officers were dressed alike. It was soon made out that this was General Nicholson, whose person was not yet known in Camp, and it was whispered, at the same time, that he was possessed of the most brilliant military genius. He was a man cast in a giant mould, with massive chest and powerful limbs, and an expression ardent and commanding, with a dash of roughness; features of stern beauty, a long black beard, and deep sonorous voice. There was something of immense strength, talent, and resolution in his whole gait and manner, and a power of ruling men on high occasions that no one could escape noticing."

1857. Aug. 7—12. his companion of Nicholson's haughty, overbearing style of address, the Chief Engineer answered, "Yes, but that wears off; you will like him better when you have seen more of him." And never were words of good omen more surely verified, for afterwards they became "the best friends"—bound together by an equal desire to do their duty to their country, and, if God willed it, to die the soldier's death.

Eager to be at his work, Nicholson made ready offer of his column to perform any service that might be required on its first arrival. He saw at once that there was something to be done. The enemy had established themselves at a place on the left of our position, known as Ludlow Castle, and had planted a battery there, from which they contrived greatly to harass our picquets, especially that known as the "Metcalfe Picquet;" and it was desirable in the extreme to dislodge them. This attack upon the enemy's new position Nicholson would have gladly undertaken. But the activity of the mutineers was so great, and their fire was so annoying, that it was found to be inexpedient to wait for the arrival of the Movable Column. The work was to be done at once, and Brigadier Showers, a right good soldier, always cool and collected in the midst of danger and difficulty, was commissioned to do it.

August 12. Affair of Ludlow Castle. Before daybreak on the morning of the 12th, Showers led down his men, along the Flag-staff Road, upon Ludlow Castle. Covered by the darkness, they marched quietly on, and took the enemy completely by surprise. A rattling fire of musketry roused them from their sleep, and numbers were shot down, scared and bewildered, before they could realise what was upon them. The Golundauze rushed confusedly to the battery; but our attack was so sudden and impetuous, that they could hardly fire a shot before the First Fusiliers were among them, bayoneting the brave fellows at their guns. Many, unable to work their pieces, drew their swords, and with their backs against the wall, sold their lives as dearly as they could. Masters of the battery, our men pushed on, in the grey dawn of the morning, following the mutineers into the houses, where they had endeavoured to find shelter, and shot them down like beasts in a cage. Some cried for mercy, and were answered with a laugh and a bayonet-thrust. By sunrise the work had been done. The enemy had been driven from Ludlow Castle, and four of their six guns had been taken. The victory, however, had been dearly purchased. The intrepid leader of the assailing party had fallen severely wounded; and Coke, who had led the Punjabees to the attack, had shared the same fate. It was in the confusion attending the fall of Showers that two of the enemy's guns were suffered to escape; and when Colonel Edward Greathed was afterwards sent to bring the force out of action, he did not know that these trophies of victory were to be recovered, or we may be sure that he would not have returned without them. Enough, however, had been gained to make the return to Camp a triumphal one. To secure the success of the surprise, the expedition had been rendered as secret as possible. When, therefore, the sound of the firing broke through the morning stillness the British Camp was aroused, and men wondered what was the meaning of it. The truth was soon apparent to them, and then numbers went out to meet the returning force, and welcomed them, as they came

1857. August 12.

1857. in with the captured guns, rejoicing exceedingly that so good a day's work had been done before the breaking of the morning's fast.*

Arrival of the Movable Column. August 14.

It may with truth, I think, be said, that at this point of the long and weary siege the great turning-point was attained. The siege-train, which was to remedy our deplorable want of heavy ordnance, was labouring down from Ferozepore; and on the 14th of August, Nicholson, who had ridden back to meet his column, marched into the Delhi Camp at the head of his men. It was a sight to stir the spirits of the whole Camp. Our people turned out joyously to welcome the arrival of the new comers; and the gladsome strains of our military bands floated down to the rebel city with a menace in every note. Braced with action, flushed with victory, Nicholson was eager for new exploits. And he did not wait long for an opportunity to demonstrate to the Delhi Force that they had not over-estimated the great qualities of the Punjabee warrior. The enemy had gained tidings of the approach of our siege-train from Ferozepore, and they had determined to send out a strong force to intercept it. No more welcome task could have been assigned to Nicholson than that of cutting this force to pieces. A well-chosen, well-equipped force of all arms was told off for this service, under his command; and, with full assurance of victory, he prepared himself for the encounter.

August 25. Battle of Nujufgurh.

In the early morning of the 25th of August, amidst heavy rain, the force marched out of Camp, and took the road to Nujufgurh, in which direction it was believed that the Bareilly and Neemuch Brigades

* Hervey Greathed says, that on this occasion we lost nineteen men killed, and ninety-four wounded. He adds: "Nobody would have supposed the force had suffered at all, from the jolly way in which they marched back, except for seeing the litters."

of the Rebel Force had moved on the preceding day. 1857
It was a toilsome, and, for some time, a dispiriting August 25.
march; for the road, little better than a bullock-track at best, was sometimes lost altogether in swamps and floods. At many points our gun-wheels sank in the mud up to their axles, and needed all the strength of the Artillerymen to extricate them from the slough. The Infantry, slipping and sliding on the slimy soil, could scarcely make good their footing, and toiled on laboriously, wet to the skin, and draggled with dirt; whilst the horses of the Cavalry struck up the mud blindingly into the troopers' faces; and the camels, ever so serviceably adroit on arid soil, sprawled hopelessly in the mire, and often fell with their burdens by the way. Many a lusty oath was sworn on that morning; but if temper was lost, hope and heart remained; and when, after a halt, and some renovation of exhausted nature, news came that they were upon the track of the enemy, and would soon be amongst them, the difficulties of the road diminished, or appeared to diminish, and they moved on with cheerful eagerness. The sun was sinking when our leading column espied the enemy, and at the same time came upon a stream, which the rains had flooded into the depth and dimension of a river. The mutineers were posted along the line of Nicholson's advance, to the left. Divided into three bodies, they occupied two villages and a serai in front of them—all protected by guns. As our troops passed the ford—the water even there breast-high—the enemy opened upon the British column with a shower of shot and shell from the serai. But advancing steadily under this fire, Nicholson took in the situation with his quick soldier's eye, forecast the action in his mind, and when his force had crossed the

1857. August 25. water, at once made his dispositions. The foremost point of attack, and the most perilous, was the serai. Against this Nicholson determined to fling the strength of his European troops, whilst he provided for the attack of the villages by other components of his force. Then, having ordered the Sixty-first and the Fusiliers to lie down, so as to be clear of the enemy's fire, he drew himself up in his stirrups, and addressed his men. He told the Sixty-first that they knew well what Sir Colin Campbell had said at Chilianwallah, and what he had again told the Highland Brigade before the battle of the Alma. "I have now," he said, "the same words to say to you, and to you, my friends of the Fusiliers. Hold your fire till you are within twenty or thirty yards of the enemy, then pour your volleys into them, give them a bayonet-charge, and the serai is yours." Then Tombs and Remington opened a smart fire on the serai; and up the Infantry sprang with a ringing cheer, and, sinking ankle-deep in the swampy ground, steadily advanced, Nicholson at their head, in the face of a shower of grape and musketry. Then holding back their fire—the hardest of all possible tasks—they carried the serai, and captured the guns.*

But the resistance was resolute, the conflict desperate. The heroism which was displayed by our people was emulated by the enemy. The Sepoys fought well, and sold their lives dearly. There was a sanguinary hand-to-hand encounter. Many of the gunners and the drivers were bayoneted, or cut down in the battery, and those who escaped limbered up and

* "Poor Gabbett of the 61st, a fine brave soldier, twenty yards in advance of his men, made a rush on one of the guns; his foot slipped, and he was bayoneted by a gigantic Pandy; but Captain Trench, of the 35th N.I., who was A.D.C. to General Nicholson (that moment rising from the ground, his horse having been shot under him), quickly avenged his death by bringing down the rebel with his revolver."—*Cave-Browne.*

made, in hot haste, for the bridge crossing the Nujufgurh Canal. But the attacking party pressed closely upon them. The swampy state of the ground was fatal to the retreat. The leading gun stuck fast in the morass, and impeded the advance of those in the rear. Then our pursuing force fell upon them, and before they had made good their retreat, captured thirteen guns and killed eight hundred of their fighting men.* 1857. August 25.

In the mean while, the Punjabees, having swept on to the attack of the village on the right, and gallantly cleared it, crossed over by the rear to do like service on the other village, against which a brisk fire of artillery had been directed; but here they met with a stubborn resistance. Lumsden, who led them to the attack, was shot down; and not until a party of the Sixty-first had been sent in support, were the despairing energies of the mutineers suppressed. Night had by this time fallen upon the scene. Nicholson was master of the Field, and the enemy were in panic-flight. But our circumstances were not cheering. Our baggage had not come up, and our people were compelled, hungry, weary, and soaked as they were, to bivouac in a morass, without food, or anything to console and sustain them, except the thought of the victory they had gained. Next morning, having collected their spoil, and blown up the Nujufgurh bridge, they commenced their march back to Delhi, carrying their trophies with them. It was ascertained afterwards that it was the Neemuch Brigade which Nicholson had thus routed. The Bareilly Brigade had not come up to take part in the action. It was a mortifying reflection to the

* The enemy had four guns at the serai, three at each of the villages, and three at the bridge over the canal.

1857. August 26. British leader that this information had not been communicated to him at an earlier period. "I do not exaggerate," he wrote afterwards to Sir John Lawrence, "when I say that had I had a decent political officer with me to get me a little information, I might have smashed the Bareilly Brigade at Palum, the next day. As it was, I had no information—not even a guide that I did not pick up for myself on the road; and had I obeyed my instructions, and gone to Behauder-gurh, the expedition would have been a fruitless one. I feel very thankful for my success; for had these two brigades succeeded in getting into our rear, they would undoubtedly have done much mischief."

The news of the victory, first conveyed to Delhi by young Low, Nicholson's aide-de-camp, who had ridden on in advance of the returning force, caused great rejoicing in Camp, and there was strong desire to give the victors an ovation as they marched in with their trophies. But Nicholson's men were weary and in sorry plight for any needless spectacular display, so they made all haste to their quarters, and as evening had closed in upon them before the whole force had arrived, the ovation would have been impossible, if they had been inclined to receive it. But there were hearty congratulations next day freely tendered to Nicholson, who had done his work right well, and secured the safe advance of the siege-train. It was believed, too, that he had weakened the enemy's force, not merely to the number of those who were killed and wounded in action, for the whole brigade was broken and dispersed, and many never again showed their faces in Delhi.* Since the battle of

* "According to all accounts, the Neemuch Brigade (the one I dealt with) only numbers six hundred men now. Many of those who fled would

Budlee-ka-serai on the 8th of June, the English at Delhi had gained no such victory as that which crowned the action at Nujufgurh. 1857. August 25.

Congratulations upon this brilliant achievement poured in from all sides; but from none came they with greater heartiness and sincerity than from Sir John Lawrence, who wrote to him, saying: "Though sorely pressed with work, I write a line to congratulate you on your success. I wish I had the power of knighting you on the spot. It should be done. I hope you destroyed no end of villanous Pandies."* To this Nicholson replied, August 30, 1857: "Many thanks for your kind letter of the 27th. I would much rather earn the good opinion of my friends than any kind of honorary distinction. I enclose, for your perusal, and Edwardes's, the rough draft of my report. The field was of such extent, that it was not easy to estimate the mutineers' loss. I think, moreover, that they suffered more severely from the fire of our Artillery, after they had bolted across the bridge, than they did on the actual battle-field. . . . . Except where poor Lumsden was killed, they made little attempt to stand. Most of the killed were Kotah Contingent men. We took the Neemuch troop of artillery complete, three light field battery guns, and four of the King's Own. I wish sincerely that they had had as many more, as, after their flank was turned, they could not have used them, and must have lost them all." August 30.

appear never to have returned to Delhi. Most of the officers with me in the action rated them at six, seven, and eight thousand men. My own idea is, that they were between three thousand and four thousand."—*Nicholson to Lawrence, August* 30, 1857.

* In this letter Lawrence writes: "Don't assault until you have given the mutineers all the powder and shot which the siege-train can spare, and then go in, and may God be with you all. I think if all the troops were warned not to disperse, it might have an effect upon them."

1857. August. After this there was quiet for a little space in Camp. All men were looking eagerly for the arrival of the siege-train, and for those last reinforcements which Lawrence was sending down from the Punjab. Reports were floating about to the effect that the Bareilly Brigade was going out again, under Bukht Khan, to make another effort to intercept our convoys; but if this design were ever entertained it was soon abandoned, for it never developed into even the semblance of a fact; and all again was composure. There was not a soldier in camp who did not then feel that the time of waiting and watching had well-nigh passed—that we should soon assume the offensive in earnest, with ample means to secure success. Delhi now seemed to be in our grasp, and the spirits of men rose with the thought of the coming triumph. Then was it that the mess-tents of our officers rang with the loudest laughter; then was it that our military bands sent up their gayest music; then was it that the inactivity of a disheartened enemy gave unaccustomed repose to the besieging force; then the healthy could enjoy their books or games, and the sick and wounded could be brought to the doors of their tents to inhale the pleasant evening air, or take in the marvellous beauty of the "view from the Ridge." For nearly three months the great city, with its wealth of ordnance, had defied the best courage and the best skill of the English nation. We had been beaten by the material resources of an enemy, whom, without such aids, we could have crushed in a day. But now, as our Engineers brought all the appliances of their craft to bear upon the strengthening and securing of our positions, as the space between our siege-works and the city-walls was narrowed by their efforts, and breaching-batteries were rising under their hands, no man doubted that 1857. the coming month would see Delhi prostrate at our August. feet, and the consummation of our hopes gloriously accomplished. Again the supremacy of the English race in India, obscured only for a little while, was to be re-asserted and re-established; and there was not a white man in camp who did not long, with a great hunger of the heart, for the day when the signal would be given, and it would be left for our English manhood to decide for itself whether any multitude of Natives of India, behind their walls of masonry, could deter our legions from a victorious entrance into the imperial city of the Mogul.

APPENDIX.

THE LAST NUZZUR TO THE KING OF DELHI.—Page 12.

[From Mr. William Edwards' "Reminiscences of a Bengal Civilian"—a work which contains much interesting and suggestive information relating to the rebellion in the North-West Provinces.]

"As soon as the camp arrived at Delhi, the Government durbar records were produced, in order that reference should be made to the etiquette followed as regarded the Emperor, on those previous rare occasions in which Governor-Generals had visited the imperial city. It was found that although the relative position of the Governor-General and the Emperor did not admit of their exchanging visits, yet that a deputation had been sent on the part of the Governor-General to ask after the health of his Majesty, and tender him a 'Nuzzur' of a certain amount of gold mohurs, which in reality amounted to an expression of submission and fealty on the part of the British Government to the Great Moghul, and an acknowledgment of holding our Indian possessions as his feudatory. As, however, this had been the usual practice, no question was raised as to its propriety; and therefore, without any previous intimation to the Governor-General of what was about to be done, Mr. Thomason and myself, accompanied by Colonel Broadfoot, proceeded to the palace on elephants, each being provided with a silk bag full of gold mohurs for presentation to the King. We were required to proceed without any shoes into the immediate presence—such having been in all ages in India the usual mark of respect on the part of an inferior on approaching a superior. On this occasion we compromised the matter by putting short worsted cashmere socks over our boots, and thus entered the hall of audience. On a curtain being drawn aside, we saw the old King, then apparently a very feeble old man above seventy years of age, seated on his throne, which was elevated so as to have the royal person, as he sat cross-legged, on a level with our faces. We made a low obeisance to the Emperor, and on approaching the throne, each in succession presented his bag of gold mohurs, and inquired after his Majesty's health and prosperity. I confess to a feeling of awe and solemnity passing over me as I stepped up and addressed this representative of a long line of kings and of a once powerful empire, and presented my Nuzzur to his Majesty's acceptance, which was remarkable as being the last that was ever offered on the part of a British subject to the imperial house of Timour. The King simply received it, and ordered us to be robed in dresses of honour, and to have turbans bound round our heads. This was done in due form; we made our obeisance to the King, and departed. We remounted our elephants, and were paraded through the chief streets of Delhi as "those whom the King delighted to honour." The ridiculous transformation we had all three undergone, clad in these robes of tinsel tissue, drove all feelings of solemnity and respect out of my mind. I contrived to get ahead of my party, and stripping off my own finery as I sat on the howdah, made my way to the Governor-General's tent, to beg his lordship to come and see the chief secretary and Colonel Broadfoot as they arrived in camp, and before dismounting from their elephants, as these two estimable gentlemen looked as if they had gone suddenly mad, and decked themselves out in a manner worthy of 'Madge Wildfire.' The Governor-General begged me to explain what we had been doing, and on my informing him, his lordship's indignation and surprise were extreme; and then, for the first time, I myself became alive to the impropriety of an act which, in reality, made Queen Victoria, in Eastern estimation at least, hold her Indian possessions as a mere feudatory and vassal of the imperial house of Delhi.

The Governor-General immediately issued instructions, forbidding the presentation in future to the King of any offerings by British subjects, and directed me to ascertain the average annual amount of gifts received by his Majesty for the past ten years, in order that an equivalent amount should be added to the royal stipend from the British treasury in future. The Governor-General's measure was without doubt right and politic. The misfortune was that it had not been adopted years before."

CAPTAIN ROSSER AND THE FLIGHT TO DELHI.—Page 67.

[THE following extracts from letters, addressed to the author, with reference to the statement referred to in the text, frequently made and never before, I believe, publicly contradicted, that the late Captain Rosser, of the Carabineers, had, on the 10th of May, proposed to take a squadron of his regiment and a troop of Horse Artillery, to cut off the flight of the mutineers to Delhi, afford a curious illustration of the difficulties which beset the path of the historical inquirer.]

Sir Archdale Wilson.

"It is certainly not true that Captain Rosser offered to take his squadron in pursuit of the mutineers bound for Delhi on the evening of the 10th of May, 1857—at least, to my knowledge—the first I ever heard of such a story being shown to me in some rough sheets of your History. Captain Rosser was a good and gallant officer, and may have made such an offer to his own immediate commanding officer, Colonel Custance, though I do not believe that any one of the force knew that evening that the mutineers had made for Delhi. I did not until the next morning."—*Dec.* 6, 1868.

Mr. Charles Raikes.

". . . . I had the good fortune to become well acquainted with Major Rosser during the voyage from India to Suez early in 1858. He told me in so many words what I asserted in my little work. It was not possible for me to doubt the statement of a man so modest, grave, and straightforward, of such high principle and solidity of character, and I, therefore, asserted as a fact what I believed and still believe to be true."—*Dec.* 17, 1868.

Colonel Custance.

"The late Major Rosser was a gallant and good officer, but he did not offer to take a detachment of Dragoons and Horse Artillery in pursuit of the mutineers escaping to Delhi on the 10th of May, 1857. Had he done so I must have known it, as I was his commanding officer."—*Dec.* 21, 1868.

[It was not thought necessary to pursue the inquiry any further. If the offer were not made by Captain Rosser to the commanding officer of his regiment or to the Brigadier commanding the station, it cannot have been made at all in any military—any public—sense, and certainly the proposal cannot have been officially recognised. But that, on the night of the 10th of May, Captain Rosser expressed his willingness to lead a mounted detachment to cut off the mutineers (though the offer may never have taken the regulation-shape), can hardly, I think, be questioned.]

SERVICES OF SYUD MEER KHAN.—Page 69.

"The Sirdar Behaudur, Syud Meer Khan Sahib, a pensioner receiving six hundred rupees a month, for aid rendered to the Caubul prisoners and good conduct in Afghanistan, who had, on hearing the disturbance, immediately joined the Commissioner, and offered to escort him to the European lines; but it was decided that there was no hope of the lady escaping through the crowd. He then went out to hold back the mob, and was shot through the thigh, and his horse mortally wounded. This fine Afghan was obliged to retire to the city. He came to the Dum-Dumma the next morning in spite of his wound, and was at the battles of the Hindun. When the mob attacked the house, the Commissioner and his wife, with

the wife of one of the residents of the station, retired to the roof; when asked where their master and mistress were, the servants said that they had gone to church: though drawn swords were put to his throat, the Jemadar, Gholab Singh, persisted in this statement, and the other servants were faithfully silent regarding their master's presence."—*Report of Mr. Commissioner Williams.*

THE MURDER OF MR. FRASER.—Page 79.

[The following is the evidence of Buktawuss, or Bukhtawar Singh, Chuprassy, as given at the trial of the King ot Delhi.]

"I was the servant on duty supervising the repairs of the Fort ditch, and was going with the account book for Captain Douglas' inspection. I was on my way, when a trooper came galloping up from the direction of the Calcutta Gate. The trooper had not reached the Palace Gate when I observed that Captain Douglas was standing there. I saw Captain Douglas speaking to the man; but before I reached the Palace Gate myself the trooper turned his horse and rode off. Captain Douglas told me to go up to his apartments, and said that he was going to the interior of the Palace and should return immediately. Captain Douglas did so, and I stayed at the gate, Makhan, Kishan Singh and others accompanied him. Captain Douglas had hardly gone when Mr. Fraser arrived in his buggy and inquired for him. Mr. Fraser alighted and walked on through the covered way up to the opening. He then said to me he was going to the Calcutta Gate, and that I was to tell Captain Douglas so on his return. I then myself proceeded in the direction of the King's apartments and met Captain Douglas returning in a state of excitement. I gave him Mr. Fraser's message. Captain Douglas went to the Lahore Gate of the Palace, and told the Native officer on guard there to close it, which was done. Captain Douglas at the same time gave orders that no crowd was to be allowed to assemble on the bridge leading into the

Palace. Just about this time an officer of the King's, styled a captain, also came there from the direction of the main street of Delhi. The gate had been closed and Captain Douglas' buggy was inside, so he directed me to ask this Native officer for his buggy that he might go in it as far as the Calcutta Gate, whither Captain Douglas proceeded in it, I occupying the seat behind. At the Calcutta Gate we found Mr. Fraser, Mr. Nixon, head clerk, and four or five other gentlemen. The gate was closed after a short time. Mr. Fraser and Captain Douglas got into the buggy together, and were returning to the Palace accompanied by the other gentlemen on horseback, but had not proceeded far when four or five troopers came galloping up at full speed from the direction of the Ellenborough Tank. About this time, there was a general cry that the troopers had come. On reaching the party of gentlemen, one of the troopers wounded Mr. Hutchinson in the arm with a pistol shot; the others also fired, but without effect. On this Mr. Fraser and Captain Douglas both got out of the buggy and went out of the way of the mutineers, and stood by the guard-room of the Constabulary Force at the gate: two more gentlemen joined them there. Mr. Fraser got a musket from the Constabulary Force, and shot one of the troopers. This checked the others, and they turned and fled. A great crowd had by this time collected, and Captain Douglas and another gentleman jumped into the Fort ditch, along which they came on to the Palace Gate, Mr. Fraser and others coming by the road; but there was such confusion at the time, I can't say how. Captain Douglas was in a fainting state from the injuries he had received from jumping into the ditch, and we accordingly laid him on a bed in the Kuliyat Khana. In a short time Mr. Jennings, the clergyman, came down, and at his suggestion Captain Douglas was taken up to the apartments above the gate, where he was placed on a bed, Mr. Jennings sending the servants away, and telling them not to crowd about the place. We then received an order to go for the King's physician, and Abdulla Chuprassy fetched him accordingly. The physician, Ahsan Ullah Khan, had just left, when we servants who were sitting there saw some five

Mahomedans, King's servants, coming along the covered way calling out, 'Din, din!' Just at this time Mr. Fraser happened to come down to the foot of the stairs, and these men immediately attacked him and killed him with their swords. While this was happening on the north side of the gate, a mixed crowd, armed with swords, bludgeons, &c., ran up the stairs on the south side, and gained the apartments above, those assembled on the north side joining them there."

THE CIS-SUTLEJ CHIEFS.—Page 162.

[The further note on the loyal bearing of the Cis-Sutlej chiefs will be given in volume iii.]

REMOVAL OF CAPTAIN HODSON FROM THE GUIDE CORPS.—Page 182.

[The following passage from a letter written to Hodson's biographer by the Military Secretary to the Punjab Commissioner, explains fully the circumstances referred to in the text. After speaking of the question of the regimental accounts and the action of the Court of Inquiry, the writer proceeds to say:]

"Still, in so far as the inquiry was concerned, Major H., had he survived, might perhaps have commanded the Guides to this day. His removal was entirely another affair. In addition to the command of the Guides, Lieutenant H. held the office of Accountant Commissioner in civil charge of Euzofyze. Lieutenant Godby, of the Guides, was severely wounded by an assassin at Murdan, the Guides Corps station in December, 1853. The assassin was cut to pieces on the spot by some men of the corps. His body was identified, but all efforts to discover the motives of the miscreant or his abettors proved fruitless. Lieutenant Hodson's suspicions, however, fell upon Kader Khan, the Mullik of Tooroo (four miles distant from Murdan), the most wealthy and influential chief in Euzofyze. He even further entertained the hope of being able to convict this Kader Khan of having caused the murder of the late Colonel Mackeson; but finally, and after a lengthened imprisonment of seven months in the Peshawur gaol, Kader Khan was arraigned by him in the Commissioner's Court on one charge only, viz. that of having instigated the attack upon Lieutenant Godby. The case completely broke down, and the trial ended in a full acquittal. Lieutenant Hodson's proceedings were strongly condemned by Lord Dalhousie, who directed his dismissal from civil employ, and that he should not retain command of the Guides, it being incompatible with the public interests that he should ever again hold any position of authority in the district of Euzofyze, and that his getting another command thereafter should depend upon the result of the Military Court of Inquiry. The inquiry had not, however, closed so far as to produce any result, when the Court of Directors took notice of the trial of Kader Khan of Tooroo, and in conveying their approval of the Governor-General's decision upon it, they added their 'desire' that Lieutenant Hodson should not 'again be entrusted with any command whatever.' "

THE PUNISHMENT OF ALLAHABAD.—Page 270.

[From the "Travels of a Hindoo," by Bholanauth-Chunder. Edited by a Government Secretary, and dedicated to the Governor-General of India.]

"They speak of it as a fearful epoch of unexampled atrocities on the one side, and of an unparalleled retaliation on the other. There were the Sepoys with the blood of murdered officers on their heads, and budmashes and bullies, and cut-throats and cut-purses, all acknowledging a fraternal tie, and holding a bloody carnival. But it was impossible that twenty uncongenial parties, divided by quarrels about caste, quarrels about religion, quarrels about power, and quarrels about plunder, could long act together in an undisturbed concert. Soon as batch after batch of Englishmen arrived to re-establish the Saxon rule, they were driven like chaff before the wind. Then followed a dreadful sequel—the horror of horrors. The martial law was an outlandish demon, the like of which had not been dreamt of in Oriental demonology. Rampant and ubiquitous, it stalked over the land devouring hundreds at a meal, and surpassed in devastation the rakhasi, or female carnival of Hindoo fables. It mattered little whom the red-coats killed; the innocent and the guilty, the loyal and the disloyal, the well-wisher and the traitor, were confounded in one promiscuous vengeance. To 'bag the nigger,' had become a favourite phrase of the military sportsmen of that day. 'Pea-fowls, partridges, and Pandies rose together, but the latter gave the best sport. Lancers ran a tilt at a wretch who had taken to the open for his covert.' In those bloody assizes, the bench, bar, and jury were none of them in a bland humour, but were bent on paying off scores by rudely administering justice with the rifle, sword, and halter, making up for one life by twenty. The first spring of the British Lion was terrible, its claws were indiscriminating.

"One's blood still runs cold to remember the soul-harrowing and blood-freezing scenes that were witnessed in those days. There were those who had especial reasons to have been anxious to show their rare qualifications in administering drum-head justice, scouring through the town and suburbs, they caught all on whom they could lay their hands, porter or pedlar, shopkeeper or artisan, and hurrying them on through a mock trial, made them dangle on the nearest tree. Near six thousand beings had been thus summarily disposed of and launched into eternity, their corpses hanging by twos and threes from branch and sign-post all over the town, speedily contributed to frighten down the country into submission and tranquillity. For three months did eight dead-carts daily go their rounds from sunrise to sunset, to take down the corpses which hung at the cross-roads and market-places, poisoning the air of the city, and to throw their loathsome burdens into the Ganges. Others, whose indignation had a more practical turn, sought to make capital out of those troublesome times. The martial law was a terrible Gorgon in their hands to turn men into stone, the wealthy and timid were threatened to be criminated, and they had to buy up their lives as best they could under the circumstances."

PROCLAMATIONS AND CORRESPONDENCE OF THE NANA SAHIB.

Page 351.

[The following extracts from the correspondence of Doondoo Punt, Nana Sahib, illustrate the means by which he endeavoured by a succession of boastful lies to stimulate the animosity and to sustain the courage of his followers. These papers were sent in by Nana Nerain Rao, of whom mention is made in the text, and placed in the hands of General Neill, who commissioned Major Gordon to translate them. The following is from the journal of that officer :]

"A relative of the Nana sent in a quantity of the Nana's property and ten of his horses from Bithoor this morning, and came himself and called on General Neill in the forenoon. He had been confined by the Nana. In the evening two boxes were brought in containing the whole of the Nana's correspondence, and his letter-book containing copies of all his orders, written in the Persian language. They have been made over to me, which is a rich treat; and I sat poring over these letters until eleven o'clock at night, and finished with the one in which he ordered the destruction of all Europeans who left in boats."

PROCLAMATION, DATED JULY 6TH.

"A traveller just arrived at Cawnpore from Calcutta, had heard that previous to the distribution of the cartridges, a council had been held for the purpose of depriving the Hindoostanees of their faith and religion. The members of the council came to the decision, since it was a matter affecting religion, it would be right to have seven or eight thousand European soldiers that fifty thousand Hindoostanees might be destroyed, and all (the rest) become Christians. This resolution was sent to Queen Victoria, and received her approval. Again another council was held, at which the English merchants assisted. It was here determined that the European force should be made equal to the Hindoostanee army (in numbers) so that when the contest took place there should be no fear of failure. When this representation (from the council) was read in England, thirty-five thousand soldiers were embarked in all haste and despatched to India, and the news of their departure has reached Calcutta. The Sahibs of Calcutta ordered the distribution of the cartridges with the especial object of making Christians of the Native army, so that when the army became Christians there would be no delay in making Christians of the ryots. These cartridges were rubbed over with the fat of pigs and cows. This fact has been asserted by Bengalees who were employed in the manufacture of the cartridges, and of those who related this, one has been executed and all the rest put into confinement. They (the Sahibs) made their arrangements here. This is the news from thence (Europe). The Turkish Ambassador wrote from London to the Sultan to inform him that thirty-five thousand men have been despatched to Hindoostan for the purpose of making Christians of the Hindoostanees. The Sultan of Room—may God perpetuate his sovereignty!—despatched a Firman to the Pasha of Egypt to this effect: 'You are an ally of Queen Victoria. But this is not the season for amity, inasmuch as my Ambassador writes that thirty-five thousand soldiers have been despatched to Hindoostan for the purpose of making Christians of the Native ryots and troops. Therefore, in this case, whilst a remedy is in my power, if I should be negligent, how shall I show my face to God? And this day (i.e. conjuncture) may some time or other be my own [meaning this may some day be his own case] since, if the English make the Hindoostanees Christians, they will make an attempt on my dominions.'

"When the Pasha of Egypt received this Firman, he, previous to the arrival of the (English) force, assembled and organised his troops at Alexandria, which is on the road to Hindoostan. The moment the soldiers (English) appeared, the Pasha's troops opened an artillery fire upon them from all sides, and destroyed and sunk their ships, so that not a single soldier escaped.

"When the English at Calcutta had issued their order for the distribution of the cartridges, and the disturbances had arisen, they anxiously looked out for the troops from London to aid them. But the Almighty, in his perfect omnipotence, had already disposed of these. When the news of the slaughter of the army from London became known, the

Governor-General was greatly afflicted and distressed, and *thumped his head.*

"Persian Quatrain.—In the beginning of the night he possessed the power over life and property.—In the morning his body was without a head, and his head without a crown.—In one revolution of the cœrulean sphere neither *Nadir* (Shah*) remained nor any sign of him.

"Issued from Painted Garden of the Peishwah."

"To Holas Sing, Cotwal of Cawnpore.

"You are hereby ordered to make known within your jurisdiction, that whoever may have in his possession any property plundered from the English, such as chairs and tables, china and metal dishes, arms, buggies, medical apparatus, horses, and wood, or railway officers' property, such as beams, iron, wire, jackets, coats and trousers, goats and sheep, must, within four days, produce such property. Should any one secrete such things, and they be found hereafter in his house when searched, he will be visited with condign chastisement. Should any person have in his house an Englishman or any children (baba logue), he must produce them, and will not be questioned; but any person concealing the above, will be blown into the path of destruction from the cannon's mouth.

"Dated 4th Zikad, or 24th June."

[The following appears to have been written after the massacre at the Ghaut.]

"To Rughoonath Sing, Bhowany Sing, &c.,

"Officers of the Regiment at Seetapoor (Forty-first N. I.), and Wahid Ali Khan, Naib Ressaldar, First Irregular Cavalry, at Sikandra.

"Greeting,—Your petition, presented by Meer Punah Ali, has been received. Its contents have become known to me. The report of your bravery and gallantry has given me great

* Play upon words—"Nadir," if I remember rightly, is the zenith.—*Translator.*

pleasure, 'much praise be yours, thus should you ever act, thus let men act.' Here (Cawnpore) this day 4th Zikad (27th June), the white faces have fought with us. The whole of them, by the grace of God, and the destroying fortune of the Jing, have entered hell. A salute in honour of this event has been fired as *usual.* It behoves you also to celebrate this victory with rejoicings and peals of artillery. Moreover, your request for permission to fight with the infidels has given me great satisfaction. In a few days, when order shall have been restored in this district, the victorious force which has now swelled to a large army, still daily increasing, will cross the Ganges, continue to hem in the infidels until the arrival of my camp. This event will take place shortly; and then display all your valour. Bear in mind that the people pertain to both faiths. They must be neither molested nor injured in any way. Have a care to protect them, collect supplies, and keep them in readiness.

"Dated 4th Zikad St. 1273, 27th June, 1857."

"To Holas Singh, Cotwal.

Whereas, by the grace of God and fortune of the king, all the English at Poona and in Punna have been slain and sent to hell, and five thousand English who were at Delhi have been put to the sword by the royal troops. The Government is now everywhere victorious; you are, therefore, ordered to proclaim these glad tidings in all cities and villages by beat of drum, that all may rejoice on hearing them. All cause for apprehension is now removed.

"Dated 8th Zikad, 1st July, 1857."

"To Baboo Rambuksh, Talooqdar, Dhondia Khera, Oude.

"Greeting.—Your petition dated 6th Zikad (29th June), reporting the slaughter of the English, and the deaths in battle of your brother Sudhainan Sing, with two officers, and also begging for my favour as a reward for your self-devotion, has been perused. You are hereby informed, that I also am grieved at your loss, but the will of God must be submitted to. Moreover, this event (the death of his brother) has happened in the cause of Government, and you will ever remain the object of my protection. Have no manner of fear, Government will certainly befriend you.

"Dated 10th Zikad, or 3rd July, 1857."

"*To Holas Sing, Cotwal.*

"Whereas sundry persons of the town, on hearing the report of European troops having marched from Allahabad, are abandoning their homes and seeking shelter in villages, you are hereby ordered to have proclaimed throughout the town that infantry, cavalry, and artillery have marched to repel the English. Wherever they may be met, at Futtehpore, Allahabad, or wherever they may be, the revenging force will thoroughly punish them. Let all remain without fear in their homes, and pursue their usual avocations.

"Dated 12th Zikad, or 5th July, 1857."

"*To the Officers of the Army.*

"I have been greatly pleased with your zeal, valour, and loyalty. Your labours are deserving of the highest praise. The organisation and scale of pay and rewards established here will have likewise to be established for you. Let your minds be at rest, all promises made will be fulfilled. Troops of all arms have this day crossed the Ganges *en route* to Lucknow; you will be aided in every possible way to slay the unbelieving Nazarines, and despatch them to hell. The greatest reliance is placed on your readiness and bravery to secure victory. On receipt of this order, certify to me, under your hand and seal, that you have learned its contents, and are ready to co-operate in the destruction of the infidels. Have no fears as regards ordnance stores. Any amount of ammunition and heavy guns is available. Shurf-ood-Dowlah and Ali Reza Beg, Cotwal of Lucknow, have been ordered to supply provisions. They will do so; but should they fail in this duty inform me, and a conspicuous example will be made of them. All of you display valour and fortitude. May victory speedily crown your efforts, thus shall I myself be at liberty to proceed towards Allahabad. There can be no hesitation on your part or on mine. After this rapid success, march to Allahabad and conquer there.

"Dated 14th Zikad, 7th July, 1857."

"To Kalkapershad, Canoongoe—Oude.

"Greeting.—Your petition has been received, stating that seven boats containing Europeans were going down the river from Cawnpore, and that two parties of your men who were at the spot joined the Government troops and fired on them so unremittingly that they proceeded, slaying the English the whole way, as far as the villages of Abdool Azeez, when the horse artillery and yourself in person joined the rest, and sank six of the boats, the seventh escaping through the force of the wind. You have performed a great deed, and I am highly pleased with your conduct. Persevere in your devotion to the Government cause. This order is sent you as a mark of favour. Your petition, with which a European was sent in, has also reached me. The European has been sent to hell, thus adding to my satisfaction.

"Dated 16th Zikad, or 9th July, 1857."

"To the Thanadar of Sirsoul.

"The victorious army of Government had marched towards Allahabad to oppose the Europeans, and it has now been reported that the latter have deceived the Government troops, attacked and scattered them. Some troops are said to remain there; you are, therefore, ordered to instruct the landholders in your jurisdiction and in Fuftehpore, that every brave man should join heart and hand to defend his faith, to put the Europeans to the sword, and send them to hell. Conciliate all ancient influential landholders, and persuade them to unite in the cause of their religion to slay and send to hell all the infidels. Moreover, tell them that Government will give every man his due, and that those who assist it shall be rewarded.

"Dated 20th Zikad, 13th July, 1857."

"*To the Bahadoors and Officers of Cavalry, Artillery, and Infantry at Lucknow.*

"Greeting.—A force of about one thousand British, with several guns, were marching towards Cawnpore from Allahabad. To arrest and slay these men an army was despatched. The British are advancing rapidly. On both sides men fall wounded or killed. The Europeans are now within seven koss of Cawnpore, and the field of battle is warmly contested. It is reported that Europeans are coming up the river in steamers, and strong defences have consequently been constructed without the town of Cawnpore. Here my troops are prepared, and at a distance the battle rages; you are, therefore, informed that the aforesaid British are opposite the district of Baiswara, on this bank of the river. It is very probable that they may attempt to cross the Ganges. You must, for this reason, send some troops into the Baiswara country to shut them in on that side. My force will press them from this direction, and by this combined action the slaughter of the infidels may be achieved, as is most desirable.

"Should these people not be destroyed, there can be no doubt they will press on to Delhi. Between Cawnpore and Delhi there is no one that could stand against them. We must without fail combine to destroy them root and branch.

"It is also said that the British may cross the Ganges; some English still remain in the Bailey Guard and maintain the fight, whereas here there is not a living English person left. Send troops immediately across the river, at Sheorajpore, to surround and cut up the Europeans.

"Dated 23rd Zikad, or 16th July, 1857."

[This is the last of the series. On that same evening Havelock's force encamped near Cawnpore, and whilst victory was being proclaimed by the Nana's order in the city, he himself was flying for his life, and his followers were being dispersed in all directions.]

RECRUITING AT PESHAWUR.—Page 492.

[The following is the paragraph in Colonel Edwardes's Mutiny Report, to which reference is made in the text. There is no contribution to the history of the great Crisis in the Punjab more valuable or more interesting than the document from which this extract is made:]

"Delhi was not to be recovered by a *coup de main.* The Hindoo Sepoys, having mutinied about a cartridge, had nothing to propose for an empire, and fell in of necessity with the only policy that was feasible at the moment, a Mahomedan King of Delhi; and certainly no other policy could have given such life to the coming struggle. Hitherto the question had been purely domestic between the English and their Hindoostanee army, a quarrel in which the Afghan tribes would merely desire to be on the conquering side. But a war between the Moslem and the Christian for empire must needs agitate every village in which there was a mosque and a moollah; and the city of Peshawur in particular, with its sixty thousand inhabitants, had always been a hotbed of intrigue. Humanly speaking, I consider that the border at this critical period was mainly kept under by the levying of a militia. Afghans are fanatical, but avarice is their ruling passion. Every idle vagrant, every professional robber, every truculent student in the mosques, at whose finger-ends fanaticism was beginning to tingle, found a market for his sword. The population of the Peshawur Valley had never been disarmed. Being liable to raids from their neighbours, they had been allowed to keep arms in their houses; though none but outside villagers might wear arms abroad. It was not difficult, therefore, to collect any number of armed footmen at a short notice. Good horses are not plentiful in this irrigated country; but the head men of every village have two or three hacks, and the enlistment of their farm servants on these rips, attached all the hamlets, one by one, to our cause, and got up quite a hearty feeling, such as certainly I never saw before among them. One can smile now at the scenes that took place morning and evening at the hours of enlistment. It was necessary to sustain the dignity of the Imperial

Government even in our distress. Long before the time crowds of candidates for employment thronged the gateways and overflowed into the garden, the jockeys of unconquerably vicious horses endeavouring to reduce them to a show of docility by galloping them furiously about till the critical moment of inspection came. At last, sick at heart from the receipt of a bad telegram from the provinces, but endeavouring to look happy, out I used to go, and face some hundreds of the chiefs and yeomen of the country, all eager to gather from the Commissioner Sahib's countenance how the 'King of Delhi' was getting on. Then the first horseman would be brought up. The beast perhaps would not move. The rider, the owner, and all the neighbours would assail him with whips, sticks, stones, and Pushtoo reproaches that might have moved a rock; but nothing would do till the attempt was given up, and the brute's head turned the other way, when he went off at a gallop amid roars of laughter from the Pathans, who have the keenest perception of both fun and vice. No. 2 would make a shift to come up, but every man and boy in the crowd could see that he was lame on two or three legs. Then the argument began, and leg by leg, blemish by blemish, the animal was proved by a multitude of witnesses (who had known him for very many years) to be perfectly sound; and so the enlistment went on from day to day, affording immense occupation, profit, and amusement to the people, and answering a great many good ends. Now and then an orderly of the Hindoostanee Irregular Cavalry, admirably armed and mounted, would pass the spot, and mark his opinion of the 'levies' by a contemptuous smile. But, nevertheless, he told his comrades in the lines that the country people were all with the English, and it was of no use to desert or to intrigue."

SIR HENRY BARNARD'S LAST LETTER TO THE GOVERNOR-GENERAL.—Page 569.

[The following letter was written to Lord Canning by Sir H. Barnard, three days before his death. He seems to have desired that, in the event of his demise, its contents should be made known to the world:]

"Camp above Delhi, July 2, 1857.

"MY DEAR LORD CANNING;—Ere this reaches you, the business here will have been settled; if successfully, well; if a failure, I shall like to leave behind me a brief record of the service of the little force.

"The work of reduction or re-occupation of Delhi was evidently greatly under-estimated. Delhi, when once its gates were shut, and its immense arsenal and magazine in the hands of insurgent troops, became a formidable operation to reduce. When added to this the passions of the people were roused, and the cry raised of a new 'Mogul dynasty,' it became as important as formidable.

"With means totally inadequate, this force was sent against it, reinforced by detachments from Meerut, who were to have provided sappers, gunners, and field implements; when all had formed a junction the force barely arrived at three thousand eight hundred. Meerut sent no gunners, and only a small number of sappers, and these unprovided. On the 8th June we started from Alipore, met the enemy at Budlie-ka-Serai, and from thence drove them from the height above Delhi. Here the Commanding Artilleryman and Chief Engineer proposed to commence the attack; batteries were planned and erected, but the distance was too great. After eight days, I found the side of the town which must be silenced before we got approaches quite as alive as ever. The Artilleryman admitted the distance too great, and the Engineer his inability to make batteries, having positively not a single sandbag! I was promised reinforcements, and for their arrival I determined to wait. They have arrived, and now comes the decisive moment, and I confess to you I never was so puzzled. The force I have amounts to about five thousand, and comprises almost all the Europeans in the Upper Provinces; quite enough, if free, to re-establish the country, but quite insufficient to storm Delhi, guard the camp, and keep open my communications with the rear for supplies, &c. If I succeed in the gambler's throw, well and good, but if I fail, the game is up, and all I can expect to be able to do would be to effect an honourable retreat, carrying off sick, wounded, and guns. To add to my distresses, dissatisfaction is proved to exist in the Native troops just arrived, and some have been detected in trying to tamper with the men of Coke's Corps. These fellows are to be hanged to-night; but the Ninth Irregular Cavalry and some of the Seikh Corps are known to be tainted, and would like an opportunity of doing us any mischief they could. Thus it is, with enemies without, traitors within, and a task before me I cannot in reason feel my force competent to undertake, I am called upon to decide. Much is said about the Native character and aptitude at turning tail, but where the treasure is I fear the heart will be found also, for all these miscreants are laden with plunder they will not abandon, and they know full well that every man's hand is against them. They dare not fly.

"My men are very tired; we have had since the action of Budlie-ka-Serai no less than ten affairs, seven of which employed my whole force, cavalry and infantry; in each we experienced heavy loss, but inflicted greater. The traitors are, or rather were, tired; they openly said it was no use fighting, and that unless assisted they would fly in four days. Yesterday brought them the Bareilly people, so we shall have our eleventh to-morrow. After that I think the game is over. The Gwaliors are not coming on, and we shall have defeated them all in turn. But to be useful I must enter the city, and this will, I am fearful, be a sanguinary affair, for it is clear the Sepoy knows well how to fight behind stone walls.

"I hope to hear of the head of the European columns coming up from Calcutta, and then matters will begin to look up again.

"Pray excuse this scrawl; it is written in a gale of wind. The rain has fallen for two days, but it is again fine.

Very truly yours,

"H. Barnard."

ADDENDA.

THE BENARES RAJAHS.

[The following extract, from an important paper furnished to me by a distinguished officer of the Bengal Civil Service, with large experience in the North-Western Provinces, should have been inserted in its proper place in the Appendix, with reference to page 231 of this narrative:]

"How, whence, or wherefore the notion of disloyalty attached to the Rajah of Benares and his predecessors was a mystery. It was something like an epidemic. Whatever others might have said and done, the present one had received a good English education, was pleasant and gentlemanly, liberal in the matter of public entertainments and contributions. Yet, somehow, he was not popular with officials, the cantonment, or the city. The only persons who seemed to commend him were the missionaries of Segra, who at least dwelt nearest to his ordinary residence at Ramnuggur.

"By slow degrees I got some enlightenment on the subject. When the administration of the Benares Province was made over to British officers, it was covenanted that the Rajah should retain a special jurisdiction over certain tracts called 'the family domains;' that a fixed sum should be given him for the maintenance of his own official establishment, and a fixed rent-charge on the whole province. Now the Collector of Benares, from whose treasury the disbursements were made, had a very weak establishment, and was always longing to supplement the deficiency from the Rajah's allowance. It was a constant source of contention—the two establishments, or a portion, were under the same roof, and assistance was often exacted. Unhappily, too, Mr. Thomason lent himself to a project for a compulsory cession. It appeared to me the public faith was pledged; the original covenant was brought up, its terms were clear; the perpetuity and unchangeableness absolutely expressed. In fine, the Court of Directors affirmed this judgment, and this question was ended. . . .

"When, after some years of better acquaintance, I was

about to leave Benares, I asked him to explain this still unsolved, mysterious adhesion of disloyalty to his predecessors and himself, and if he was aware of it. His answer was remarkable: 'It is so, it must be so, it always will be so, but I cannot as a point of honour explain the reason. You know as well as I do that the British Government made this Raj, and if that Government went down, where would the Raj be?'

"So we parted, and I left Benares no wiser on this point than when I came. At last, by the merest accident, I got the clue.

"In 1857, when we were immured in Agra Fort, and it was my duty to control every item of disbursement, an applicant for his pension was announced: 'The Rajah of Benares!' 'Who on earth are you?' 'The Rajah of Benares, Bulum Bahadur. Come for my pension of two thousand rupees per mensem.' I asked him to bring me all his papers; he had no hesitation, and was, in fact, abundantly communicative.

"Now, never once had the real Rajah of Benares given me the least hint of any such person's existence. Yet here was the grandson of the rebel Cheyt Sing, whose expulsion had been followed by the substitution of the present line, receiving a Government bounty conditionally, like Shimei of old, on his not crossing the boundary of the Agra district, and he had contrived to get copies of secret papers, from which it appeared that the Court of Directors, perhaps in alarm at Burke's vituperation, had of their own motion granted this allowance to the family of the deposed rebel. In reading these papers, it recurred to me that on one occasion, when I went to visit the famous fort of Bejegurh, Cheyt Sing's last stronghold, an elephant and palanquin were there at the foot of the hill, which moved off at my approach, and which did not return, when I sent a message to the party begging him not to consider my presence a hindrance. So I made a shot and taxed Bulum Bahadur with being that party. After much hesitation he allowed I was right, and was immensely relieved that we had both gone to the same place, seeing that his grandfather and mine (who was at the capture) had once been there, and Shimei's fate should not be his. After which,

Bulum Bahadur was full of intelligence. He, of course, was brimful of loyalty, while 'that other man,' as he called him, was head and chief in all the mutinies and local rebellions, and closely associated with the Nana. It was one of our amusements in the intelligence department, with which the Rajah of Benares was keeping up communication at great personal expense, and all the more valuable that we had no other, except *viâ* Bombay, to have B. B.'s grave reports of 'that other man's' defections.

"Not long afterwards came another accidental elucidation. The records of the Revenue Board had been gotten into the Fort and stowed anyhow in its recesses. When there was leisure for some arrangement, some papers turned up which had belonged to the old Benares Residency. Amongst them was some secret correspondence with Lord Cornwallis and this with others explained the mystery.

"The Benares Raj originated with Munsa Ram, a small landowner of Gungapoor. By the ability of Bulwunt Sing, and repeated cessions of the Nawaub Vizier, it extended to the whole province, and Bulwunt Sing fixed his hold of it by alliance with the English—a defection not forgiven nor forgotten by Oude.

"Bulwunt Sing was succeeded by Cheyt Sing, who quarrelled with his minister, Owsan Sing, the grandfather of Deenarayun Sing. The minister took part with Hastings, Cheyt Sing intrigued with Francis.

"Then followed Hastings's journey to Benares, the arrest of Cheyt Sing, his rescue, rebellion, defeat, and flight to Gwalior, and the selection of his successor. Hastings thought it due to Bulwunt Sing to choose his daughter's son, Maheep Narayun. Had he followed the usage and traditions of the tribe, he would have reverted to the next male line of Deyaram, of which Koonr Juggut Sing was the representative.

"That might have passed away into oblivion, on the admitted principle that if the paramount Government can depose, it can also choose; but, unfortunately, Maheep Narayun, jealous of Koonr Juggut Sing's greater popularity, basely endeavoured, and for the time succeeded, in implicating Koonr Juggut Sing in Vizier Alee's rebellion. He was deported to Calcutta, and, according to some accounts, died in gaol; to others, committed suicide. Ultimately, Government gave a pension to his family, and Baboo Futteh Narayun, a worthy, harmless old gentleman, his descendant, is still resident at Benares.

"When I next visited Benares, I told the Rajah the discoveries I had made. He was not a little astonished, but, after many throes, spoke out to this effect: 'Of course I knew all about Bulum Bahadur, his visit to Bejegurh, and his detestation of "that other man." But is he not the lineal male descendant of Bulwunt Sing? What am I that I should complain? I am an interloper according to the laws of the Boenhar tribe, and generally may pass, but we shall be interlopers still. By favour of the British Government we might get over this, but the memory of Koonr Juggut Sing's fate will never pass away. It can never leave the city of Benares, nor can the secession of Bulwunt Sing ever be forgotten in Lucknow. If you want me to be hanged as a traitor, you will get plenty of aid in those quarters.' 'But, surely,' I said, 'Baboo Futteh Narayun Sing would not lend himself to any such intrigue?' 'No, on no account,' he replied; but he pleasantly added: 'He is always incurring debts, and I, of course, shall pay them as hitherto.' 'Well,' I said, 'I hope you and Deenarayun Sing will be always good friends.' He smiled. 'Certainly; but, remember, Owsan Sing betrayed Cheyt Sing.'

"Of course nothing of this inner revelation of Native character had been made to Mr. Tucker or Mr. Gubbins, and it is not surprising that neither of them formed just estimates of the two leading men of Benares during the mutinies. Mr. Tucker was too apt to consider physical activity an element of loyalty, Mr. Gubbins was extreme in his likes and dislikes; the consequence was, where, as the result subsequently proved, both had done their duty, one was extravagantly commended, the other disparaged.

"Deenarayun Sing behaved nobly; but he had only a house in Benares, his landed estates were in another district out of harm's way. The other had an extensive district to protect; his treasures were plundered to the cry of 'The

Nawaubee!' and his measures for protection were regarded with suspicion.

"When the political atmosphere was clear, and George Edmonstone's cool judgment was available, the circumstances and the individuals were better considered. I can only give the general result, for I had quitted India before. The Rajah of Benares was promoted to the rank of Maha-Rajah, and his salute restored to its integrity. Deenarayun Sing was confirmed in the dignity of Rajah, and honoured with a seat in the Legislative Council, but the proposal of the local officers to confer on him a territory larger than many English counties was reduced to more reasonable proportions. Good old Futteh Narayun Sing, who did his best, also had a liberal grant assigned him."

CEREMONIAL USAGES OF THE DELHI FAMILY.

[The following is the interesting note referred to at page 24 :]

"21, Mecklenburgh-square, W.C., June 29, 1870.

"MY DEAR AND RESPECTED FRIEND,—I am in receipt of your favour of yesterday, and am glad to give you as much information as I can on the point in question.

"It is not the fact 'that since the time of Timour no member of the family, who had been in any manner mutilated, could sit upon the throne.' The best proof of which is, that all the Mogul Emperors, from Timour down to Humayun, were circumcised. The reason why the Mogul Emperors and Princes discontinued the rite of circumcision is as follows:

"About the time of the birth of the Emperor Akbar, his father, Humayun, being engaged in a war with Shere Shah, was compelled by the latter to fly from India and take refuge in Persia. History tells us that Humayun and Akbar were placed in such circumstances that the former could get no opportunity of having his son (Akbar) circumcised, and when Humayun recovered the throne of Delhi, his son was somewhat about twelve years of age, so that the proper time of circumcision had expired. In addition to this circumstance, the death of Humayun, which took place not more than about six months after his retaking Delhi, rendered the people indifferent as to the above rite not having been performed, as, in fact, Mahomedans do not consider it so important or indispensable a right as the Jews do.

"The intermarriages with the Hindoo princely families of India, a custom introduced by Akbar, caused the Imperial family to adopt many Hindoo customs and ceremonies, the consequence being that the male issue from the Hindoo princesses were, according to the Hindoo religion, not circumcised. After a few generations, this Hindoo custom became so prevalent in the Imperial family, that not a single member of the whole Mogul Dynasty was circumcised—a circumstance which produced a superstitious notion among the common people that the Royal family were not circumcised because mutilation was considered a bad omen.

"Prince Fukhroodin was circumcised on account of an affection . . . . . . ; but this circumstance could be no bar to his coming to the throne. Bahaudoor Shah was a mere puppet in the hands of his consort; and this latter, who opposed Fukhroodin being nominated heir-apparent, originated this merely nominal objection.

"Hoping that the information that I have been able to give on the point will be found satisfactory,

"Believe me, ever very truly yours,

"Syed Ahmed.

"J. W. Kaye, Esq."

POSTSCRIPT TO NEW EDITION.

THE CARABINEERS ON THE TENTH OF MAY.

It was stated in the first edition of this volume that the turning out of the Carabineers at Meerut on the 10th of May, 1857, was delayed by the slow process of a regimental roll-call. This Colonel Custance denied, and supported his denial with an overwhelming amount of documentary evidence. I therefore wrote him the subjoined letter, with permission to publish it:

Penge, Surrey, Dec. 20, 1870.

"Sir,—I am perfectly convinced, by the documentary evidence which you have afforded me (I should have been satisfied, indeed, with your own denial), that the statement at page 65 of the second volume of my 'History of the Sepoy War,' to the effect that on the 10th of May, at Meerut, there was a roll-call of the Carabineers (then under your command) before they moved out against the Sepoy mutineers, was based upon erroneous information. As the passage was written some years ago, I cannot, without a laborious search, which I have not yet had time to make, ascertain the authority or authorities on which the statement was made; but whatever the authority may have been, I regret that I should have been, however unintentionally, the means of giving publicity to a statement at variance with the fact. I need not add, that I wish to do all that lies in my power to correct the error in future issues of my History; and all the more willingly, as I have reason to believe that the story which I have published was commonly accepted as a fact before the appearance of my book. I may add to this that from a careful perusal and collation of the several documents which you have sent me, containing the evidence of officers and non-commissioned officers of your regiment, it appears that the Carabineers, when proceeding towards the Lines of the Native battalions, were countermarched, by order conveyed to you by a staff-officer, and marched towards the gaol, which lies, at a considerable distance, in a different direction. It seems that, on reaching the gaol, it was found that the prisoners had already escaped, so the Carabineers were marched back again towards the Native Lines. On their return, darkness having set in, they lost their way, although under the guidance of the staff-officer who had directed you to the gaol. That this was the real cause of the tardiness with which you reported your arrival on the general parade to the Brigadier is sufficiently plain from the evidence which you have afforded me. I have much pleasure in informing you that I am perfectly satisfied of the truth of these statements.

"You may make any use of this letter that you may wish.

"I am yours faithfully,

"J. W. KAYE.

"Major General Custance, C.B."

[After this had been published, I received another letter on the subject, which I also feel bound to publish; and I am the more willing to give it publicity, because the record is highly honourable to the splendid regiment (though in May, 1857, owing to accidental circumstances, it was not in the height of its splendour) which Colonel Custance then commanded. I thought when I last saw it, on the occasion of Lord Mayo's funeral, that such a regiment might have demolished at least half of the Native Cavalry of Bengal:]

"Junior U.S. Club, Pall Mall, London, Feb. 27, 1871.

"DEAR SIR,—On return home I have looked over my memoranda of Meerut and Delhi in 1857, and have carefully read the passage in your History to which Colonel Custance, of the Carabineers, takes objection. As I can personally vouch for certain points, I here state them.

The Carabineers turned out with extreme rapidity. I ought to know, for it was I who ordered a sergeant of the regiment from the bridge close to the parade of the mutineers to run to Colonel Custance himself, and I sent a rifleman also to the Brigade Office. This was the first intimation given, as the firing, in which Colonel Finnis and others were killed, was then proceeding. This sergeant afterwards told me that Colonel Custance had 'instantly ordered out his

A HISTORY OF
THE
GREAT REVOLT

A HISTORY OF THE GREAT REVOLT

(In Three Volumes)

Volume III

JOHN WILLIAM KAYE

GYAN

GYAN PUBLISHING HOUSE

New Delhi - 110002

A History of The Great Revolt

ISBN: 81-212-0194-2 (Set)
ISBN: 81-212-0197-7 (Vol. 3)

Reprinted in 2011 in India by
Gyan Publishing House
23, Main Ansari Road, Daryaganj,
New Delhi - 110002
Phone : 23282060, 23261060
Fax : (011) 23285914
e-mail : books@gyanbooks.com
gyanbook@vsnl.com
website : gyanbooks.com

Printed at : G. Print Process, Delhi

PREFACE.

In the autumn of last year, I hoped and believed that this volume of the History of the Sepoy War would be laid before the public in the course of the following month of November. But it was otherwise ordained. I was compelled to lay aside the pen, when I thought myself most capable of using it; and not until the dawn of the next summer was I permitted, or, indeed, able, to resume my work, with a feeling that I was equal to the task. Some had exhorted me to finish it any-how; others, to get some one to help me. I could only answer that I would rather not finish it at all, if I could not put my best powers of workmanship into it; and, whatever the toil and travail might be, write every line myself. So I waited patiently for the hour and the hour came. My old love of historical research came back upon me, and with it my power of sustained work.

Let no man deceive himself as to the nature of that work. There is no such thing as the easy writing of History. If it be not Truth it is not

History; and Truth lies very far below the surface. It is a long and laborious task to exhume it. Rapid production is a proof of the total absence of conscientious investigation. For History is not the growth of Inspiration, but of Evidence. It is scarcely reasonable, therefore, to complain of delay, when without delay, or in other words, protracted inquiry, there can be no approximation to the Truth. I cannot, therefore, apologise for that to which these volumes owe any little value that they may possess in the eyes of the present or a future generation.

As I went further into the depths of this strange story I found that the difficulties of narration, to which I had referred in my second volume, had greatly increased. Materials were superabundant. I cannot sufficiently express my gratitude to friends and strangers (strangers only, in the flesh) who provided me so freely with memorials of one of the most wonderful episodes in the history of the British nation. But the very wealth of these materials increased my difficulties. It is comparatively easy to describe a series of events. But I had not to do with events rising out of, or following each other in succession, but with a multitude of detached and almost contemporaneous incidents, the only connecting link being the universal fact that the Black man had risen against the White. As illustrative materials, some of them of the most interesting character, were showered upon me, it became increasingly difficult to deal with such a mass of details, without extending the dimensions of the work far beyond the limits that would be acceptable to the Public. I have endeavoured to give prominence to the most significant and suggestive events. I cannot hope that I have altogether succeeded; but I trust that I have not wholly failed. Doubtless, many an exciting adventure which would have stirred the heart of the reader, and many an act of personal gallantry, which it would have been a delight to me to narrate, has found no record in these pages. Nothing but the stern laws of necessity have compelled these omissions. It will be said, perhaps, that greater compression in some parts might have afforded larger space for amplification in others. But compression, though doubtless a virtue, is, like some other virtues, not always very interesting; and every man must write his books in his own way. It might have been better for me if I had not undertaken this work; but having undertaken it, I was bound to complete it, with all the power I had in me, at any cost of worldly fortune, or health, or even of life itself.

I have been told by one or two friends, to whom I have shown some passages of this volume, that they will "excite controversy and give pain." No one can be more unwilling than I am to cause unnecessary suffering. There is no greater literary crime than the infliction of pain, without thorough inquiry into the painful statements made and ample proof of their truth, except to stand by them after their falsehood has been made manifest. And, assuredly, it is pleasanter to praise than to blame. "But," I am told, "admitted that it is all true, it is injudicious to publish the truth, and there will be much controversy arising out of it." The Historian who shrinks from controversy has mistaken his vocation. I have told and I intend to tell the truth, so far as I can discern it, after laborious and conscientious inquiry, without any regard of persons. As I would speak of a stranger I would speak of a friend; and as I would speak of a friend, I would speak of a brother or of a son—of living and of dead alike. If a man is not prepared to do this, and to take the consequences, let him write novels and travels in the manner of Gulliver and leave History alone.

The present volume, like its predecessors, contains three books. The FIRST of these relates to affairs in Bengal and Behar, including some account of the excitement at Calcutta, of the rising in Shahabad, the mutiny at Dinapore, the defence and relief of Arrah—together with some notices of Lord Canning's defensive and suppressive measures and of the general policy observed by the Government in the earlier days of the rebellion. In the preparation of these chapters I have been much aided by the private correspondence of Lord Canning, by a mass of documents, printed and manuscript, lent to me by Mr. William Tayler, Commissioner of Patna, and by the simple, manly narratives of Sir Vincent Eyre. The SECOND (Book VIII.) contains a narrative of the several risings in the North-Western Provinces, the wide-spread subversion of British authority, the bearing of the principal Native Princes and Chiefs, and the defence of Agra up to the period of Mr. Colvin's death. My information with regard to these events is principally derived from Mr. E. A. Reade, Sir William Muir, who had charge of the Intelligence Department, Mr. Charles Raikes, Major Weller of the Engineers, and the Confidential Reports of the several civil and political officers whose narratives were called for by Government after the suppression of the insurrection. The THIRD part (Book IX.) is devoted, firstly, to affairs in Oude, the general state of the Provinces, the risings in the Districts, the siege and defence of Lucknow, the death of Sir Henry Lawrence, and subsequent events up to the time of the first relief of the Residency by Havelock and Outram; and secondly, to the final and victorious siege, assault, and capture of Delhi. These last chapters have caused a greater expenditure of time, labour, and thought, than any other part of the work. And I cannot be too grateful to those who have enabled me, in some measure, I hope, to overcome the difficulties of the task. Among these, I may mention the late Sir Archdale Wilson, the family of the late Colonel Baird Smith, Sir Neville Chamberlain, Colonel George Chesney, and Colonel Welby Greathed of the Engineers, Sir Edward Greathed, so highly distinguished in subsequent operations against the insurgents in the North-West, Sir Charles Reid, who held so long the Picket at Hindoo Rao's, and Sir Henry Daly, then of the Guides. Among artillerymen, from whom I have derived the most important assistance, are Sir James Brind, Sir Edwin Johnson, General E. W. Scott, and my brother, Lieutenant-General Edward Kaye. From such authorities as these I must have evolved a large measure of truth, amounting almost to perfect accuracy. But I wish the reader to understand that I have not pretended to write a MILITARY history of these or any other operations—that my narrative was not intended to bear "a stamp exclusive or professional," but to command the common interests and catholic sympathies of all classes of readers. It is, therefore, necessarily deficient in personal and statistical details, such as may be gathered from old Army Lists or the official reports of the day. And I have purposely abstained as much as possible from technical phraseology, though having had the advantage of a military education and having served my apprenticeship to the profession, such language would have come readily from my pen.

I had intended in this volume to have included some account of the first relief of Lucknow: and, indeed, the narrative of Havelock's operations were already in print; but not only did I find that the fulfilment of this design would have swollen the volume to an inconvenient bulk, but it appeared to me on reconsideration that it would be more advantageous to the entire work to embrace in one consecutive narrative the story of the campaign of Havelock and Outram and the final operations of Sir Colin Campbell. This will form a not unimportant part of the next volume, which will contain also, if I am suffered to complete it, some account of Delhi within the walls, of the Trial of the King and others implicated in the slaughter of our people, a history of the Central-Indian Campaign under Sir Hugh Rose, of later events in Agra and Rajpootana—of the risings in Western India, of affairs in the Deccan, and of the general pacification of the country; concluding with a chapter on the Fall of the East India Company, the proclamation of the Queen's Government throughout the country, the remedial policy of Lord Canning, and the manner in which our promises and pledges, given in the day of danger, have been, in the day of safety, fulfilled.

J. W. K.

Rose Hill, Forest Hill.

CONTENTS OF VOL. III.

BOOK VII.—BENGAL, BEHAR, AND THE NORTH-WEST PROVINCES.

CHAPTER I.

AT THE SEAT OF GOVERNMENT.

CHAPTER II.

THE INSURRECTION IN BEHAR.

CHAPTER III.

THE SIEGE OF ARRAH.

CHAPTER IV.

BEHAR AND BENGAL.

BOOK VIII.—MUTINY AND REBELLION IN THE NORTH-WEST PROVINCES.

CHAPTER I.

AGRA IN MAY.

CHAPTER II.

INSURRECTION IN THE DISTRICTS.

CHAPTER III.

BEARING OF THE NATIVE CHIEFS.

CHAPTER IV.

AGRA IN JUNE AND JULY.

CHAPTER V

AGRA IN AUGUST AND SEPTEMBER.

BOOK IX.—LUCKNOW AND DELHI.

CHAPTER I.

REBELLION IN OUDE.

CHAPTER II.

REVOLT IN THE DISTRICTS.

CHAPTER III.

LUCKNOW IN JUNE AND JULY.

CHAPTER IV.

THE SIEGE OF DELHI.

CHAPTER V.

CAPTURE OF DELHI.

ERRATA.

[*In First Edition of Vol. II.*]

Page 79, *note*, for "Buktawuss Sing" read "Buktawur Khan."

Page 88, lines 4 and 5, for "officers of the Bengal Artillery" read "officers of the Ordnance Commissariat Department."

Page 169, line 10, for eight-pounders" read "nine-pounders."

Page 187, line 5 from bottom, for "having moved down from Bolundshuhur" read "having moved up from Bolundshuhur."

Page 266, line 13, for "Moole-gunj" read "Mootee-gunj."

Page 376, line 12, for "stimulate" read "simulate."

Page 395, line 5, for "Kooshen Gardens" read "Khoosroo Gardens."

Page 397, *note*, for "short" read "shot."

Page 426, line 3 from bottom, for "Punjabee troops" read "troops in the Punjab."

Page 447, 6 lines from the bottom, for "Inniskillen Dragoons" read "Twenty-seventh Foot (Inniskillens)."

Page 667, Appendix (quotation), line 10 from bottom, for "Accountant Commissioner" read "Assistant Commissioner."

. . . For to think that an handful of people can, with the greatest courage and policy in the world, embrace too large extent of dominion, it may hold for a time, but it will fail suddenly. —*Bacon.*

. . . As for mercenary forces (which is the help in this case), all examples show that, whatsoever estate, or prince, doth rest upon them, he may spread his feathers for a time, but he will mew them soon after.—*Bacon.*

If there be fuel prepared, it is hard to tell whence the spark shall come that shall set it on fire. The matter of seditions is of two kinds, much poverty and much discontentment. It is certain, so many overthrown estates, so many votes for troubles. . . . The causes and motives for sedition are, innovations in religion, taxes, alteration of laws and customs, breaking of privileges, general oppression, advancement of unworthy persons, strangers, deaths, disbanded soldiers, factions grown desperate; and whatsoever in offending people joineth and knitteth them in a common cause.—*Bacon.*

HISTORY OF THE SEPOY WAR.

BOOK VII.—BENGAL, BEHAR, AND THE NORTH-WEST PROVINCES.

[JUNE—JULY, 1857.]

CHAPTER I.

STATE OF AFFAIRS IN CALCUTTA—ANXIETIES OF THE GOVERNOR-GENERAL—DESPATCH OF REINFORCEMENTS—RETRIBUTORY MEASURES—THE VOLUNTEER QUESTION—RESTRICTIONS ON THE INDIAN PRESS—DISARMING OF THE BARRACKPORE REGIMENTS—THE GREAT CALCUTTA PANIC—ARREST OF THE KING OF OUDE—SIR PATRICK GRANT—FINANCIAL DIFFICULTIES OF THE CRISIS.

1857. June.

The Governor General at Calcutta.

WHILST the incidents recorded in the preceding books were occurring—whilst Havelock and Neill were pushing on from the South to the relief of Cawnpore and Lucknow, and John Lawrence was pouring down from the North all his available military strength to the attack of Delhi—events were developing themselves, in many different parts of the country, which showed how wide-spread was the disaffection, and how momentous was the crisis, with which the head of the British Government was called upon to contend. To Lord Canning, who wisely continued to reside in the capital, the month of June was one of intense anxiety and vexation—anxiety

1857. June. for the fate of his countrymen in the Upper Provinces, vexation engendered by the attitude assumed by some influential classes of the European community at Calcutta, who grievously misunderstood his character, and continually condemned his conduct.

The lull which immediately followed the outbreaks at Meerut and Delhi had now been rudely disturbed. Every post was freighted with tidings of some new manifestation of the all-prevailing excitement in the Native Army of Bengal, and made more clear to him the enormous difficulties which now threatened the security of the Empire. The North-Western Provinces were in a blaze. Not only was the whole Native Army falling away from him, but the fabric of civil government was in many places crumbling to pieces. Whether this disorganisation were the result merely of the ravages of the soldiery, and the love of rapine natural at all times to the predatory classes, or whether the discontents of our trained fighting men were shared by the peaceful communities, and the country was ripe for civil rebellion no less than for military revolt, was not at that time apparent. But it was certain that the first efforts of the Government must be directed to the suppression of the mutinous activities of the Sepoy Army. And to the accomplishment of this, Lord Canning, never disguising from himself or from others the magnitude of the danger to be grappled with, had put forth all his personal strength, and evoked all the resources of the State.

That on the first receipt of intelligence of the capture of Delhi by the insurgent army, the Governor-General addressed himself, with the utmost promptitude and vigour, to the work of collecting troops from all available sources, has been shown in the first volume of this History. The looked-for succours were of two kinds: those already on the Indian establishment, which could be easily gathered up and brought speedily to the scene of action by his own authoritative word; and those which lay at a distance under the control of other authorities, and for which he could do no more than ask The first, it has been seen, soon began to pour in, and they were despatched to the Upper Provinces with all possible speed. That the Government were taken by surprise, that the available means of transport were inconsiderable, and that the Military Department at the Presidency was not strong during the first month of trouble, is not to be denied. But it is equally clear to me that Lord Canning neglected no means at his disposal to despatch European troops to the endangered provinces with all the speed which could be attained by the functionaries under him, who had never before been prepared for such an emergency, and were not likely now to be in an abnormal state of preparation. With what success these primal efforts were attended has been shown. Benares and Allahabad were saved by the succours sent upwards from Calcutta. But Cawnpore was lost; Lucknow was still in imminent danger; and the flames of rebellion were spreading all over North-Western India.

1857. June.

And there was a never-ceasing source of dire affliction to him in the thought that all he could do at such a time was but little and light, weighed against what needed to be done. "It is enough to break one's heart," he wrote in June, "to have to refuse the imploring prayers of the Europeans at out-stations for protection by English troops against the rising of the Sepoys in their neighbourhood, or against the savage marauders and mutineers who are

1857. June.

afoot. But to scatter our small force over the country would be to throw away every chance of a speedy success."

Efforts for the relief of Cawnpore.

Throughout the whole country, there was no place, the perilous environments of which had been regarded with profounder anxiety by Lord Canning, than the cantonment of Cawnpore. All his letters written in the month of June express the painful uneasiness with which he contemplated Wheeler's position, and the eagerness with which he sought to relieve him by succours both from below and from above. Benares and Allahabad being secured, he desired that all the reinforcements sent up from the southward should pass on to Cawnpore; and he wrote to Sir Henry Barnard, urging him to send down a regiment from the Delhi Field Force.* "Benares," he wrote in the middle of June, "has been made safe. So has Allahabad, I hope, but only just in time. Henceforward, the reinforcements will be pushed up still further—to Cawnpore; but the disorganised state of the country between Allahabad and Cawnpore may interpose delay; and both telegraph and dawk from any place north of Allahabad is now cut off from Calcutta. I cannot, therefore, speak so confidently of the time when help will reach Sir Hugh Wheeler. It may not be for four or five days, or even more.† This makes it all the more urgently necessary that you should push down an European force immediately. When it reaches the Cawnpore Division, it will, ac-

* It has been shown (vol. ii. p. 136) that he wrote at the same time to Mr. Colvin, desiring him to make every effort to despatch southwards all the troops that Barnard could spare.

† I have not the original of this letter before me; perhaps it does not exist. The passage is correctly transcribed from the copy, in the private secretary's handwriting, kept by Lord Canning. There is some reason, however, to suspect the word "days" is a clerical error for "weeks." If not, it is difficult to understand the context.

cording to the instructions which have been sent to you, pass under Sir Hugh Wheeler's command. And with him will rest the responsibility of relieving Lucknow and pacifying the country from Cawnpore downwards. It will be for you to judge what your own movements should be. All that I require is that an European force, as large an one as you can spare, shall be sent southwards with the least possible delay, and that it should not be detained an hour for the purpose of finishing off affairs at Delhi, after once the great blow has been struck." Whether this letter ever reached its destination is uncertain.* If it did, it must have been received with astonishment on the Delhi Ridge. And it was not merely in that direction that the expectations of the Governor-General were overleaping the stern realities of the position. The succours from Allahabad, by which first Cawnpore and then Lucknow were to be saved, were almost as remote contingencies as those summoned from the northward. This misconception resulted not from a want of sagacity, but from a want of information. The magnates of Calcutta were groping hopelessly in the dark. The difficulties of their position had been rendered still more difficult by the interruption of postal and telegraphic communication between Calcutta and many of the chief stations of Upper India. Nearly all the country above Allahabad was sealed to them. News from Agra, from Delhi from the Punjab, came in by many devious channels after long intervals, and was often little to be relied on when it came. Again and again news came that Delhi had fallen. Not only in Calcutta, but in Allahabad,

1857. June.

* It was drafted on the 10th of June, but was not despatched till the 21st. Lord Canning retained it, after a duplicate had been made, until that day, probably in uncertainty as to whether the accounts which reached him of the fall of Delhi were true or false.

1857. June.

Agra, Cawnpore, Lucknow, all our chief British posts, the cheering report came down only to disappoint and to mock our people; and in some places royal salutes were ostentatiously fired in honour of the auspicious event.

Lord Canning's correspondence.

In spite, however, of postal interruptions—often only delays—Lord Canning received many letters, at this time, from officers in responsible positions, who rightly took upon themselves, in total disregard of official proprieties, to write directly to the Governor-General; and from others, too, upon whom the crisis had conferred no such right, but who were eager to offer advice to the head of the Government. These letters were of very different kinds and characters. In many there was serviceable information of the best kind; in others, sound good sense, often too late to be of any service to the chief ruler, as it related to the causes of the revolt, not to its remedies. In some there was blatant folly. Military reformers and religious enthusiasts spoke out freely, and the Adjutant-General and Armageddon alternately figured in these volunteer despatches. Many, it may be supposed, counselled the most sanguinary retributory measures. All these letters Lord Canning attentively perused, and then handed them over to his Private Secretary, to be duly docketed and properly pigeon-holed. Often he answered them. When good service was done he was prompt to recognise it. Those who said that he was cold-hearted because he was cool and collected in danger, little knew the warmth which he threw into his more private correspondence. Sometimes this warmth took the shape of reprobation rather than of applause—reprobation of principles asserted, not approval of actions performed. But even in this repro-

1857. June.

bation there was generally some recognition of the zeal and loyalty of the man, though the counsel offered to him was of a kind altogether foreign to his own sentiments and opinions. Thus to one correspondent, who recommended that measures of a most vigorous (or otherwise sanguinary) character should be taken for the purpose of overawing the Native soldiery, he wrote: "You talk of the necessity of striking terror into the Sepoys. You are entirely and most dangerously wrong. The one difficulty, which of all others it is the most difficult to meet, is that the regiments which have not yet fallen away are mad with fear—fear for their caste and religion, fear of disgrace in the eyes of their comrades, fear that the European troops are being collected to crush and decimate them as well as their already guilty comrades. Your bloody, off-hand measures are not the cure for this sort of disease; and I warn you against going beyond the authority which Government has already given to you, and even that authority must be handled discreetly. Don't mistake violence for vigour." And these sentiments were shared by the wisest and most heroic of Lord Canning's Lieutenants. Sir Henry Lawrence, both by word and deed, strove to allay the fears of the timid, to encourage the loyalty of the wavering, and in all to reward the good rather than to punish the evil. Sir John Lawrence, in pure, intelligible vernacular, said that he believed it was "all funk" that was driving the soldiery into armed opposition to the Government, and that the greatest difficulty with which he had to contend, was that our measures of repression had a necessary tendency to prolong the crisis by increasing the general alarm. And Sir James Outram rebuked an officer who had recom-

1857. June. mended sanguinary measures of retaliation, by saying that he had always observed that men the most blood-thirsty in council were the least gallant and courageous in action. There were, doubtless, times and seasons in the development of this revolt, when the cruelty of the hour was the prescience of enlarged humanity—when, to strike remorselessly at all, taken red-handed, in the first flush of rampant crime, would be merciful to the thousands and tens of thousands who were waiting for the encouragement of a successful beginning to fling themselves into the troubled waters of rebellion. But this dire and deplorable necessity differed greatly from the vindictive eagerness which longed to be let loose, not only upon proved murderers and mutineers, but upon whole races of men guilty of the unpardonable offence of going about with dark skins over their lithe bodies.

And already, indeed, Lord Canning was beginning to fear that this intense national hatred was bearing bitter and poisonous fruit. The tidings which he received directly or indirectly from Benares and Allahabad filled him with apprehensions, lest the wild justice of the hour, which was running riot in the Gangetic Provinces, should become a reproach and a misery for years. He feared that the great powers which had been given both to soldiers and to civilians were already being abused; and yet he felt that he could not arrest the hand of authority without paralysing the energies of the very men to whom he most trusted to crush the rebellion which was destroying the lives of our people and threatening our national supremacy. There had been no feeble humanitarianism—no sentimental irresolution—in Canning's measures. It has been seen that, on the 30th of May, an Act had been passed sweeping away many of the old legal fences, and giving extraordinary powers to officers in the trial and execution of offenders; and now, on the 6th of June, another Act was passed extending these powers of life and death.* That the Governor-General should have watched the result of this exceptional legislation with anxious forebodings is not strange. But that the head of a Government, which had given what it rightly described as "enormous powers" to individual Englishmen, for the suppression of mutiny and rebellion by hanging the Natives of the country, with scarcely the formality even of an impromptu trial, should have been charged, as he was, with not appreciating the gravity of the position, is, rationally considered, one of the strangest facts in the whole history of the war. 1857. June.

The strangest things, however, are not always unaccountable. The self-esteem of the Calcutta citizens had been wounded; and egotism often affectionately adopts what reason contemptuously discards. Lord Canning had not accepted the first offer of the European community of Calcutta to enrol themselves into a Volunteer Corps for the protection of the City; and it was thought or said, therefore, that he could not see the dangers which beset our position. But even this ground of reproach was now to be removed. In the second week of June, the reconsideration of the question, which had been decided adversely in the preceding month, was urged upon Lord Canning by the ablest of his counsellors. Very earnestly, and with a great show of authority, Mr. Grant, on the 10th of June, pressed the Governor-General to recall his refusal. His memory grasped the fact that, three years before, the whole question of Volunteer Corps The Calcutta Volunteers.

* This is given in the Appendix.

1857. June. for the protection of the chief cities of India had been discussed and minuted upon by Lord Dalhousie's Government. That was the time of the Crimean War; and the Governor-General saw but too plainly that whenever English troops might be wanted for purposes of European warfare, little thought would be given to the requirements of the great Indian dependency. It had, therefore, been held worthy of consideration whether in all the large towns in which Europeans and Eurasians congregated in sufficient numbers to enrol themselves into Volunteer Corps of respectable strength, the movement might not wisely be encouraged by the State. And the views of the Government of the day had been received with favour by the East India Company. This weighty precedent being now exhumed, the papers recording it were put together and circulated after the wonted fashion, and with the papers, which thus brought up the Governor-General of yesterday to bear witness against the Governor-General of to-day, Mr. Grant despatched a note to Lord Canning, saying: "I entreat your Lordship to read so many of the papers in this box as I have put at the top of the bundle. It is not a quarter of an hour's reading. You will see that the general question of having a Volunteer Rifle Corps here, when the Europeans come forward, has been settled both by the recommendation of Lord Dalhousie's Government and the Court's decision thereon. Now, not only have these inhabitants come forward, but they are grumbling at their offer having been virtually declined. Certainly an emergency has occurred infinitely greater than was contemplated at the time by any member of Lord Dalhousie's Government."* And he added to this that it was highly

* In this letter Mr. Grant thus describes the situation with all its probabilities of danger. I do not think the language exaggerated. "I think

probable that if a Volunteer Corps were not raised in such a crisis as was then before them, the Home Government, after what had passed a few years before, would ask the "reason why." Lord Canning was not a man to be moved by any apprehensions of this kind; but the persuasive utterances of his colleague induced him to reconsider the whole question, and to reverse his former judgment. Perhaps he was not sorry to prove to the Christian community of Calcutta that they had erred in believing that he had rejected their former offer with studied contempt. In the middle of June, as in the middle of May, it was still his impression that a body of amateur soldiers, with other interests and other responsibilities, would not materially augment the military strength at his disposal, or enable him to release a single company of Regulars from the immediate defence of the capital.*

1857. June.

it is one thing to show alarm gratuitously and another thing to make all secure against bad weather, when the glass falls below stormy. In reality, as well as in appearance, we are very weak here, where we ought to be—and if we can't be, should at least appear to be—as strong as possible. We have as enemies three Native Infantry regiments and a half, of which one and a half are the very worst type we know; one, two, three (for no one knows) thousand armed men at Garden Reach, or available there at a moment; some hundred armed men of the Scinde Ameers at Dum-Dum; half the Mahomedan population; and all the blackguards of all sorts of a town of six hundred thousand people. Against these we have one and a half weak regiments, most of whom dare not leave the Fort. There is no reason to expect real help in real danger from the Native Police. The insurrection is regularly spreading down to us. Is this an emergency or not? My conviction is that even a street row at the capital would give us an awful shake—not only in Bengal, but in Bombay and Madras—at this moment."—*MS. Correspondence.*

* "Another sedative to the fears of Calcutta has been the acceptance of the offer of Volunteers. They resented being made special constables, and objected to act with the Police. They have now been enrolled as Volunteer Guards. Arms have been given to them, and their present duty is to patrol at night. After a little training they will make a very useful patrol guard, when needed; but I was not long in finding out that any duty which should take them away from their homes for any length of time—such, for instance, as garrisoning the Fort in place of European troops—would be strongly objected to by three-fourths of them. The truth is, that Calcutta does not furnish men idle enough and independent enough to be able to give themselves to that duty continuously."—*Lord Canning to Mr. Vernon Smith, June 19, 1857, MS. Correspondence.*

1857. June.

But he consented to the enrolment and the arming of the citizens, and he sent for Colonel Cavenagh, the Town-Major, and instructed him to make immediate arrangements for the organisation of the force, and to take the command of it himself.

And it is to the honour of the community that, notwithstanding what they considered to be a rebuff in the first instance, they again made offers of their services—not so numerously, not so enthusiastically, as in the month before, but still in sufficient force to constitute two serviceable bodies of Horse and Foot. Lawyers and merchants, covenanted and uncovenanted civilians, tradesmen and clerks of all kinds and degrees, turned out to drill in the worst seasons of the year, in scorching heat and in steamy damp; and we can take just account of what they did and suffered only by remembering the quiet, easy, monotonous lives from which many suddenly emerged into a forced and unnatural activity. One thing at least was certain—the enrolment of these volunteer bands had an assuring effect on the minds of the community at large. They seemed to start suddenly into life, as by a wave of the enchanter's wand. Cavenagh went about his work with promptitude and energy of the best kind, and although he was soon afterwards honourably relieved from the command, on account of the urgent pressure of other duties, it is hard to say how much the efficiency of the Volunteer Corps was due to his first efforts.

Restrictions on the Indian Press.

But that which of all causes of vexation vexed Lord Canning most in this month of June was the language of the Indian Press—the malignant outpourings of the Native and the unguarded utterances

of the European journals. That, for some time past, 1857.
the former had been overflowing with sedition was June.
certain; but the latter had always been loyal, if not to the local governments, at least to the Crown and the Nation. The Native newspapers, printed in Persian or Nagari characters, or sometimes only lithographed as rude fly-sheets, were generally supposed by the European communities to be of small circulation and smaller influence. But with a partially educated and a generally poor people, the influence of a published journal is out of all proportion to the number of copies printed. Not only did every impression of a Native newspaper pass through a number of hands, but each one of the numerous recipients read it aloud, or recited its contents to a still larger audience. And as every reader and every hearer was, in an extreme degree, credulous and suspicious, every lie uttered and printed was believed as gospel, and other lies were encrusted upon it. There were, doubtless, some exceptions, especially in Bengal; but the majority of Native journals were either intentionally hostile and false to the British Government, or they scattered abroad, with reckless prodigality, lying rumours, which were perhaps more dangerous in their insidiousness than the utterances of open sedition. Though generally disregarded, as I have said, by Englishmen in India, these manifestations of an unquiet spirit in the depths of Native society had attracted, during a long series of years, the attention of some shrewd observers; and it was sometimes prophetically said that the fidelity of the Native Army could not long survive the establishment of a Free Press. And it is not improbable that not one of those shrewd observers, from Sir Thomas Munro downwards, ever

1857. June. discovered half the mischief lurking beneath the ambiguously worded articles and enigmatical paragraphs of the Native journalists.*

The European journals, on the other hand, which were for the most part conducted by educated English gentlemen holding a good position in society, prided themselves on being intensely English. A large proportion of their readers, and a still larger proportion of the purchasers of these journals, were either "in the services," or members of the commercial communities of the large towns. That there was also a Native Public for these writings is true; but the English journalist and the Hindoo or Mahomedan reader were commonly brought together by the medium of translations in the Native papers. The classes, therefore, for which the English newspapers were edited were those most interested in the maintenance of good order and the supremacy of the British Government. But Anglo-Indian editors, whilst loyally fulfilling their duty to the Public and to the State, on the whole with praiseworthy conscientiousness, were not exempt from the besetting infirmity of their craft—an intense craving for news. The fault was not in the Journalist so much as in the Public. The journal that published a lying report one morning was held in greater esteem than the contemporary who contradicted it on the next. Anything was more acceptable than dulness; and to be cautious is always to be dull. And this not only with respect to facts, but also with respect to opinions. A critical conjuncture not only generates an extreme desire for news on the part of the public, but an ex-

* Sir Thomas Munro's famous minute has been often quoted, but this narrative would be incomplete without some more particular reference to it. I have, therefore, given some remarkable passages in the Appendix.

cessive tendency towards strong writing on the part of the public instructor. The excited journalist naturally throws out at such times the angry sparks of his peculiar national tendencies with a freedom which, however gratifying to himself, cannot be otherwise than embarrassing to the State. His patriotism is not to be doubted. He is English to the backbone. He will fight and die for his country. He will do all things for it—but one. He will not be reticent when he ought to be; he will not forego the privilege of saying just what he likes.

1857. June.

But there are times and seasons when even the honourable impulses of loyal journalists may wisely be held in restraint, and assuredly such a time had arrived in the month of June, 1857. In the official language of the day, "The Bengal Native Army was in mutiny; the North-Western Provinces were for the moment lost; the King of Delhi and our treacherous Sepoys were proclaiming a new empire; small bodies of gallant Englishmen were holding out for Government in isolated stations against fearful odds; the revolt was still extending; and the hearts of all Englishmen in India were daily torn by accounts of the massacre of their brethren, and the massacre, and worse than massacre, of their women and children."* In a word, there was a great crisis, and European journalism did not sufficiently take account of it—did not sufficiently consider that, whatever in ordinary times might be the uses of plain-speaking, a little reticence at such a season as this might be advantageous to the general interests of the Public and not dishonourable to public writers themselves.

It may be said, that when everybody else is excited,

* The Government of India to the Court of Directors, July 4, 1857.

1857. June. it is not to be expected that the journalist should be free from excitement—that if, in the midst of general tribulation and confusion, he maintains serenity of mind and moderation of speech, he is superior to the majority of his fellows. But it is not to be forgotten that he assumes a superiority—a superiority, on the strength of which he criticises and controverts the acts and opinions of the highest officers of the Government, even of the Government itself—and that he, above all others, therefore, is bound, as a self-appointed public teacher, to set an example to the community. The responsibility which he takes upon himself is great; and he must stand or fall as he proves himself worthy or unworthy to be invested with it. If an individual communicates important information to the enemy—if he spreads abroad false reports tending to endanger the interests of the State and to jeopardise the lives of his countrymen—if he inflames and alarms the minds of those whom his Government are striving to pacify and to reassure—every journal in the land forthwith denounces him as a pestilent spy, a dangerous agitator, and a public foe; and calls for condign punishment to be inflicted upon him. But the newspaper that does these things is not a single spy—a single agitator—a single foe; but a legion of spies, and agitators, and foes. Its emissaries spread themselves all over the country, and do their mischief in the most remote as in the nearest places. The treason is of the most dangerous kind, and none the less so because it is unintentional.

It seemed, therefore, to Lord Canning and his colleagues in the middle of the month of June, that the malignant hostility of the Native and the reckless unreserve of the European Press were evils which it was the duty of the State to arrest. When the Press was liberated, some twenty years before, it had been one of the most cogent arguments in favour of the liberation — one, indeed, which had disarmed the hostile and encouraged the wavering—that, in the event of a critical conjuncture of affairs calling for such a measure, the Government of the day might in the course of an hour reimpose such restraints as it might think fit upon the Press. That circumstances might arise to render the reimposition of such restraints a salutary measure, and that it would be not only justifiable, but commendable on the part of Government to exercise the power vested in it, was never questioned even by the most liberal contemporaries of Sir Charles Metcalfe. And those exceptional circumstances, calling for exceptional measures, were now present to the Governor-General and his counsellors. 1857. June.

The Legislative Council of Calcutta was then composed of the members of the Executive Government and others especially appointed thereto, including the Chief Justice and one of the Puisne Judges. The legislators who met the Governor-General on the 13th of June consisted of four covenanted civilians, one military officer, and three English lawyers. The English element, therefore, of which the Governor-General, who had been little more than a year in India, was a conspicuous part, was certainly not overborne by the "services." The Governor-General brought in the Bill and proposed its first reading, which was seconded by Mr. Dorin, as senior member of Council. Lord Canning made a brief and emphatic speech, taking the whole responsibility on himself; but Chief Justice Colvile frankly declared his willingness to share that responsibility with the head of the

1857. June. Executive Government. There was not a dissentient voice in Council. There was not, indeed, any reluctance or any reserve on the part of a single legislator in that assemblage. Even Sir Arthur Buller, a Liberal of Liberals, accorded his assent as freely as Mr. Dorin and Mr. Grant. And Mr. Peacock was equally convinced that the *salus populi—suprema lex* demanded the exercise of exceptional powers for the suppression of an exceptional evil. The Act was passed, placing for a year the whole Press of India under penal restraints. Thenceforth no printing-press, within that time, was to be kept without a license from Government—if so kept, in defiance of the law, it might be seized and confiscated; —and the Executive Government was vested with full power to suppress at will, by an announcement in the Government Gazette, any publication which might be considered injurious to the interests of the State.

June 13. Ever since the days of John Milton, Englishmen, in all parts of the world, have had a just reverence for the privilege of "unlicensed printing." It is not surprising, therefore, that the law passed on the 13th of June—No. XV. of 1857—excited a howl of indignation at the time, and by later writers has been severely condemned. It was forthwith christened the Gagging Act, and loaded with every term of reproach. The prompt cries of the daily papers were followed by the more deliberate execrations of the weeklies. It is unnecessary to examine in detail what was written under the influence of intense excitement, and would hardly now be justified by the writers themselves. But there is one statement, repeated in calmer moments, that may be noticed here. It has been said that by passing this Act Lord

Canning insulted the whole European community at a time when it was his special duty to conciliate them. But it is stated by the assailants of the Governor-General that the Company's civilians prompted the measure; so they were not insulted. It has been seen that the most eminent lawyers in Calcutta voted unhesitatingly in favour of the Bill; and it is not to be believed that they would have deliberately sanctioned a measure regarded as an offence to the whole legal profession. The sentiments of the merchants and traders are not equally apparent in the retrospect. But as they had a greater interest in the preservation of order and the protection of property, and were more largely connected with the Native inhabitants than any other class of Europeans, it must not be hastily assumed that a measure intended to allay public excitement and to moderate antipathies of race, was an abomination to the commercial community.* Moreover, to have drawn a distinction in such a case between the European and the Native Press would have been an insult to the loyal Native

1857. June.

* A letter before me, written a week after the Act was passed (by a high civil officer, one not likely to deviate from the truth), says: "I don't know what you will think of the Press Act, but no one ought to object to it who has not given a week to the study of the Indian newspapers. Sir Henry Lawrence tells us that the English Press has done us more harm in the Native mind than the Native Press, and that no paper has done us more harm than the *Friend of India*, which preaches the duty of spoliation in so many words, and almost in terms recommends forcible conversion, or the next thing to it. . . The sensible part of the European public approve of the Act. The good Native Press openly approves of it." The remarks of Sir Henry Lawrence, as contained in a letter to Lord Canning, were these: "Whatever may be the danger from the Native Press, I look on it that the papers published in our language are much the most dangerous. Disaffected Native editors need only translate as they do, with or without notes, or words of admiration or exclamations, editorials from the *Friend of India* (on the duty of annexing every Native State, on the imbecility, if not wickedness, of allowing a single Jagheer, and of preaching the Gospel, even by commanding officers), to raise alarm and hatred in the minds of all religionists, and all connected with Native principalities or Jagheers. And among the above will be found a large majority of the dangerous classes."

1857. June. inhabitants who were supporting the Government in all parts of India. I think that the highest praise that can be bestowed on Lord Canning is that he never lost sight of the fact that he was Governor-General of India —that India was a great country, inhabited by vast millions of people, of different races and different religions, and that although it was his duty to maintain by all just means the Empire which he had been commissioned to govern, it did not become him to keep prominently before the Natives of the country the fact that they were a conquered people—a subject race—bound by other laws and amenable to other conditions than those recognised by their white-faced conquerors.

But no man knew better than Lord Canning that distinctions, which he was himself disinclined to draw, would be drawn by others both in India and in England; and he wrote to the President of the Board of Control, saying: "Another step taken last week, and which will provoke angry comment at home, is the check put temporarily upon the Press. The papers which go to you show the grounds on which this has been done. As regards the Native Press, I shall be surprised if even in England there are two opinions as to the propriety of the measure. The mischief which such writings as these which I send to you do amongst the ignorant and childish, but excitable Sepoys, and the fanatical Mahomedans of every class, will be easily understood, especially when it is known that they are eagerly sought and listened to by the Native soldiers. I consider that this evil is one which cannot, in the present state of India, be allowed to continue without positive guiltiness on the part of the Government. Therefore, I have not hesitated to take the power of arresting it by the only means which will be summary and efficacious. As to the English Press, it has no claim to exemption. If it were read only by English readers, something might be urged in its defence. Such an article as appeared in the *Friend of India* four weeks ago, pointing out our temporary weakness and the opportunity which it affords to our enemies, might then be harmless enough. But the articles of the English newspapers are translated into the Native languages and read by all. Again, as regards the announcement of facts, where a very little trouble of inquiry would avoid error, this morning (June 19) the *Hurkaru* states that European troops have been sent to Berhampore to arrest the Nawab of Moorshedabad, who, with his principal officers, has been discovered, through papers which the Government have seized, to be deeply implicated in the rebellion. This is wantonly false. The Nawab has hitherto been perfectly faithful, but how long he may remain so, if this paragraph meets his eye, is very doubtful. Of its effect upon the bigoted Mahomedan population of Moorshedabad there can be no doubt. They are ripe for revolt, and have already tampered with the Sepoys at Berhampore, and unless the means which have been taken to prevent any copy of the newspaper reaching Moorshedabad shall be successful, the risk of a rising against the Europeans will be most imminent; for the post will arrive there two days before the troops, who have been sent for no other purpose than to protect the station."*

1857. June.

* The displeasure of the Government was naturally very much increased by the recollection of the fact that the Calcutta journalist was freely supplied with information from Government House, in the shape both of actual news and the verification or correction of current rumours. "He has," wrote Lord Canning, "all information of interest supplied to him daily by the Government, and all his questions receive immediate answers; and yet he puts in a paragraph for which there is not a shadow of

1857. June. Perhaps now that Time has allayed the popular excitement and moderated the rash judgments of men, the sober conclusions of most people resemble these. I am aware that they are mere commonplaces; but they are the commonplaces of common sense. That it is the duty of a Government, in the general interests of the community, at periods of great popular excitement, to obtain the sanction of the Legislature for the exercise of exceptional powers, has never been questioned. The Liberty of the Subject and the Liberty of the Press are blessings to which every Englishman holds fast as to an inalienable birthright. But there are times and seasons when the most constitutional of Governments impose restrictions on the former, by suspending the Habeas Corpus Act, and do so without reproach when the public safety seems to demand a temporary suspension of the ordinary laws of the land. It is necessary to the justification of such a measure only that the crisis should be one of extreme urgency, and that the violence of persons should be sufficient to demand such violent interference with their liberties. And the same with respect to liberty of speech. Now the urgency of the crisis in this case was unquestioned and unquestionable. The only consideration was, whether the unrestrained utterances of the Anglo-Indian Press had been such as to increase, or to threaten to increase, the danger which menaced the State and the lives of the Christian community? Lord Canning thought that they were. All the members of his Council thought that they were. The most eminent lawyers in Calcutta thought that

foundation, and has not the sense to see that he is perilling the lives of a whole community of unprotected Europeans. Such editors in such times as these, and in this country, need to be controlled, whether they be European or Native."

they were. The Governors of the other Presidencies thought that they were. Not because the attitude of the Press was hostile to the Government, for, indeed, the general tendency of the most influential portion of it was to support the British authorities—but because—notwithstanding the loyalty, which had never been suspected, which, indeed, was English to a fault—it had manifested signs of a dangerous want of caution, both in the dissemination of facts and the utterance of opinions tending to expose the weakness of the British Empire, to inflame the passions of the people of India, and to excite alarm among her Princes and Chiefs. 1857. June.

But it has been said that, although the circumstances were such as to justify the Government of the day in placing restrictions upon the liberty of the Press, as upon the liberty of the Subject, the same results might have been attained in a less offensive manner. In other words, a censorship might have been established. But a censorship is, at all times, an inconvenient and embarrassing affair, and, in times of great popular excitement, the difficulty is increased almost to the point of impossibility. For it is in such times that a Government has most need of the services of every one of its best officers; and it is only to one of its best officers that the work of a censorship can be safely intrusted. To take away any such officer from his normal duties to watch the imprudences of the Press, would have resembled the great evil which all men were bewailing at the time—the necessity of employing European regiments in keeping watch over suspected Sepoy battalions. "Better disarm them at once!" was the cry. But Lord Canning had another and still more incisive reason for rejecting the alternative of the censorship.

1857. June. If he had an officer whom he could spare for this difficult and delicate duty, he had not one to whom, he thought, he could safely intrust the performance of it. "I should have had to do it myself," he said afterwards to a gentleman who discussed the question with him; and this may be considered conclusive.

But it is not to be doubted that this and other measures, however little understood, increased Lord Canning's unpopularity with some classes of the European community. To say that he was indifferent to it would not be true. No man can be altogether indifferent to the opinions of his countrymen. But he bore up bravely against it. It is more than probable that a certain feeling of contempt, which he could not suppress, contributed to the strength of his endurance. Perhaps, he had formed too low an estimate of the courage and constancy of the men by whom he was surrounded, and that he was too prone to draw general conclusions unfavourable to his countrymen from a few isolated facts. This was, doubtless, in some degree at least, to be attributed to the peculiarities of his position. For the head of the Government often lacks information of what is passing beyond the walls of Government House, and knows little or nothing of the tone and temper of general society. Those who sought his presence—I do not speak of the official functionaries, who had daily access to him—commonly came, with much excitement of manner, to tell alarmist stories, which he did not believe, or to suggest defensive measures, which he could not approve; whilst of the calm, quiet courage of those who stood aloof he probably heard nothing. Even those who liked him least and reviled him most never asserted that he showed the slightest symptom of fear; and it must be admitted by the warmest of his admirers that he was not tolerant of those who did. It has been said, too, that his high personal courage, in which there was nothing boastful, sometimes led him into errors, which, though the errors of a noble nature, one may see reason to regret. This may not be wholly untrue. But the greater part of the charges brought against him—charges, which after ample circulation on the spot were sent home to friends in England, and by them published in the London newspapers, were based upon allegations absolutely, and in some instances ridiculously, false. Even Lady Canning, who was as little afraid as her lord, but who was full, to overflowing, of sympathy and compassion towards her distressed countrymen and countrywomen, did not escape the mendacious censoriousness of Calcutta. It was said of her that she had spoken of the "poor, dear Sepoys;" and, though no such words had ever passed her lips, the rumour ran from house to house and found its way to England, and the unpopularity which had gathered so thickly around Lord Canning began also to encompass his wife. And lies grew apace—how, no man knew; for every one believed, who uttered them.

1857. June.

Lull in Calcutta.

In the first week of June, and in the earlier part of the second, there appears to have been some subsidence of the excitement, the manifestations of which, in the latter part of the preceding month, had aroused such bitter feelings of indignation in the breast of Lord Canning; but ere the second week had expired, there was a renewal of the alarm, in a more exaggerated form, and for a little while a great fear of the armed Sepoys took absolute possession of large num-

1857. June. bers of Christian people. There had always been a loud cry for the disarming of the Native regiments in Bengal, to the extreme limits of that province up to the great military station of Dinapore, hard by the city of Patna, not seldom in a state of Mahomedan fermentation. Of this I shall speak presently; but first must be recorded the events which occurred at the Head-Quarters of the Presidency Division of the Army.

The Barrackpore regiments. Whilst the first reinforcements of European troops were pouring into the great Presidency town, at Barrackpore the Sepoys seemed to be recovering from the epidemic which had recently assailed them. On the 25th of May, the Seventieth Regiment of Native Infantry had made offer of their services to march against the rebels at Delhi. Struck by this evidence of loyalty, and eager by all means to encourage it, for he believed that many might yet be reclaimed by generous proofs of confidence on the part of Government, Lord Canning, without loss of time, had driven to Barrackpore, where the regiment was drawn up to receive him, and in a brief, stirring address thanked them for their offer, and said that they should march up the country. The example of the Seventieth was soon followed by the Forty-third, who requested also that their regiment "might be allowed to proceed against the mutinous regiments at Delhi." And in the first week of June all the corps at Barrackpore besought the Government to supply them with the new Enfield rifle. Outwardly it was wise to accept this movement as another proof that the Sepoys had cast out their old suspicions, and were prepared faithfully to serve the Government, whose salt they had so long eaten. But to comply with the request, if compliance were possible, might have been to strengthen the hands of our enemies by placing in them a new and formidable weapon, which ere long might be turned against us. Whether such were the hidden purpose of the request, or whether the regiments who, from the first, had been swayed backwards and forwards by varying gusts of confidence and fear, of loyalty and infidelity, were at that time sincere in their protestations, can never be satisfactorily determined.* There was, fortunately, no need that Government should unravel this knotty question. The difficulty was cut through at once by the opportune fact that there was no supply of Enfield rifles in store that could be served out to the three regiments. 1857. June.

And before another week had spent itself, the whole complexion of things was changed. Instead of thinking of marching the regiments to Delhi with Enfield rifles in their hands, the authorities were now busy with the thought of dispossessing them even of the old clumsy instrument known among British soldiers as "Brown Bess." On the night of Saturday, the 13th of June, an express arrived at Government House from General Hearsey, stating that the Sepoys at Barrackpore had conspired to rise in the course of the night, and that he had sent for the Seventy-eighth Highlanders, who were then at Chinsurah, to disarm the suspected regiments, if the measure were approved by Government. The sanction to the disarming was reluctantly given. General Hearsey had "shown such firmness and nerve before," that Lord

* The words of the Native officer of the Seventieth are worth quoting. "We have thought over the subject, and as we are now going up country, we beg that the new rifles, about which so much has been said in the army and all over the country, may be served out to us. By using them in its service, we hope to prove beyond a doubt our fidelity to Government; and we will explain to all we meet that there is nothing objectionable in them, otherwise why should we have taken them? Are we not as careful of our caste and religion as any of them?"

1857. June. Canning "could not resist the appeal." He was never satisfied that the measure was necessary. But he issued instructions with all promptitude, and that night one European regiment was marching up from Calcutta, and another was coming down from Chinsurah, to enforce the disarming.*

June 14. The regiments disarmed. The night passed quietly in the Lines, though anxiously in the English bungalows; and, perhaps, not without some efforts on the part of the worst-disposed of the Sepoys to excite their comrades to an immediate outbreak, this quietude was maintained. About five o'clock on the morning of the 14th the Highlanders marched into Barrackpore. Misled by a guide, they had gone out of their way; and when they made their appearance at Head-Quarters, weary and footsore, and in many instances only half dressed and accoutred—according to contemporary chroniclers, some without shoes and stockings, and some in their sleeping drawers—the time had passed for immediate action. The day was spent quietly, as the night had been, and when towards evening the Native regiments were suddenly warned for parade, and marched to the parade-ground, they found themselves face to face with a line of guns, and with a body of Europeans on each of their flanks. Then General Hearsey addressed them, tenderly and kindly, in his wonted

* A week afterwards he wrote to Mr. Vernon Smith, saying: "I am not now satisfied that there was any sufficient ground for a general disarming; and, although all Calcutta is delighted at it, I look forward with some apprehension to the effect which the measure will have at the several stations in Lower Bengal. I have always foreseen this danger in disarming at the Presidency. I shall rejoice if my fears prove groundless—but already several desertions have taken place since the disarming, and some of the men are making their way to Barrackpore with the news. The Forty-third, the best behaved regiment in Bengal, against which there has never been a breath of reproach, is completely panic-stricken, and the men are deserting one day and coming back the next, not knowing what to do with themselves, but confident that some further disgrace or injury is intended to them."—*MS. Correspondence.*

manner, and told them that it was the order of Government that they should lay down their arms, lest they should be incited by ill-disposed persons to acts of mutiny and rebellion. They obeyed, promptly and patiently, with the air of men who had been wrongfully treated rather than baffled in an iniquitous design. They were fearful and sorrowful, and many of their English officers were well-nigh heart-broken by what they considered the unjust punishment and humiliation of their men. Some asked that the Sepoys' arms might be restored, whilst the Sepoys themselves, believing that they would be massacred by the Europeans, deserted in large numbers, glad to escape even with their lives.

1857. June 14.

The Sepoy guards in Calcutta, at Fort William, and in the suburbs of the great city, were furnished from the regiments at Barrackpore. If the main bodies of the several battalions at the Head-Quarters of the Division were to be disarmed, it could not be otherwise than necessary to subject to similar treatment the offshoots on scattered duty elsewhere. Whilst, therefore, the disarming parade was being held at Barrackpore, the detachments at the Presidency were disarmed. It was effected without resistance. The work was easily done; and in the same quiet orderly manner the Sepoy guards at Dum-Dum were deprived of their arms by a party of the Fifty-third sent up for the purpose.

"Panic Sunday."

Meanwhile, on that 14th of June, there was great excitement in Calcutta. It was reported that the Sepoys at Barrackpore had risen in the night; and soon the rumour ran that they were in full march upon Calcutta. Then also went abroad the story, and ready credence grasped it, that the Oude people at Garden-Reach were to rise at the

1857. June 14. same time, and to join in the threatened massacre of the Christian people. So the hearts of many failed them through fear, and some, terror-stricken and bewildered, left their homes, seeking refuge wheresoever safety could be found. From an early hour in the morning a great shudder ran through the capital, and soon the confused activity of panic flight was apparent. The streets, in some parts of the city, were alive with vehicles. Conspicuous among them were those great long boxes on wheels, known as "palanquin carriages." Within might be seen the scared faces of Eurasians and Portuguese, men, women, and children; and without, piled up on the roofs, great bundles of bedding and wearing apparel, snatched up and thrown together in the agonised hurry of departure. Rare among these were carriages of a better class, in which the pale cheeks of the inmates told their pure European descent. Along the Mall on the water-side, or across the broad plain between the City and the Fort, the great stream is said to have poured itself. The places of refuge which offered the best security were the Fort and the River. Behind the ramparts of the one, or in the vessels moored on the other, a safe asylum might be found. So these fugitives are described as rushing to the gates of the Fort, or disgorging themselves at the different ghauts, calling excitedly for rowing-boats to carry them to the side of ship or steamer. There was a prevailing feeling that the enemy were on their track, and that swift destruction would overtake them if they did not find shelter within the earthworks of Fort William or the wooden walls of the shipping on the Hooghly.* Hard work had

* An informant, resident in Calcutta at the time, who describes the flight as "what might have been seen if a modern Herculaneum had been

Colonel Cavenagh to dispose of all these refugees—harder still to persuade them that all the wild stories with which they were full to bursting were nothing more than the figments of an excited imagination. But he contrived to dismiss them at last, and sent them back to their homes.* 1857. June 14.

It is recorded, too, by contemporary chroniclers and correspondents, how, in the securer parts of the city, other Christian people were garrisoning their houses and giving ingress to friends, who, living in remoter places, or in residences less capable of defence, sought shelter from the coming danger—how doors

evacuated in broad daylight on the approach of a visible eruption from a neighbouring volcano," says: "The whole line of the ghauts was crowded with fugitives, and those who could find no shelter in the ships took refuge within the Fort, of which the squares, the corridors, all the available space everywhere, indeed, were thronged by many, who passed the night in their carriages."—*MS. Memorandum.* [As some guarded statements in my second volume have been contradicted on the authority of Dr. Mouat, it is right that I should state that the writer of the above is Dr. Mouat himself.]

* Very contradictory accounts of the rush to the Fort having reached me, I think it right to record the evidence of the highest official authority on this point. Colonel Cavenagh, early on the morning of the 14th, had ridden to Government House to receive instructions from the Governor-General: "On my return home," he has recorded in his journal, "I found my house besieged by all sorts of people wishing to obtain shelter in the Fort, and all full of rumours of the worst description from Dum-Dum and Barrackpore. I endeavoured to reassure them to the best of my power; but I am sure that many left under the impression that I was misleading them. However, in time I pacified them and sent them away." This was written at the time. Subsequently, in reply to my inquiries for fuller information, Colonel Cavenagh wrote: "I took my ride in the evening to visit the different guards, and satisfy myself that my orders had been duly executed. I noticed that there were, comparatively speaking, few carriages on the Course, but did not observe any unusual number of vehicles in the Fort. Being Sunday, there may have been a few drawn up on the roads leading to the church, but none on the parade-grounds, for I am certain I should at once have ordered them off. In the forenoon, two ladies, perfect strangers to me, had asked for shelter. I told them that they were welcome to the use of my drawing-room, but that I thought they had better return home, upon which they departed. I believe that some of the officers in the garrison gave accommodation to friends, and I heard of one lady and gentleman coming during the night to the officer commanding the Main Guard, with whom, if I remember rightly, they were connected."

1857. June 14. and windows were fast closed; rifles and revolvers were loaded, and how some took down their hog-spears and placed them ready for the expected assault.* From the less fashionable outskirts, as Entally and the Circular Road, occupied mainly by the great world of clerkdom—the so-called "crannies," official and commercial, of Calcutta—the exodus is described as universal. The thoroughfares were as those of a city which had been smitten with a pestilence. Save by a few sturdy pensioners, who were to be seen unconcernedly smoking their pipes, the houses in that neighbourhood were wholly deserted. Many had been left with doors and windows open, at the mercy of any lawless citizens who might chance to covet their neighbours' goods.† A few active plunderers might have gathered a rich booty. But it seems as though even crime itself were bewildered and incapable on that Sunday afternoon; for not a house was entered for an unlawful purpose; not an outrage was committed in the streets.

There were others, who bore themselves bravely before their fellows, and, confident themselves, inspired confidence by their calm and resolute bearing. The ministrations of the Church were not neglected, and the pews were not empty, though many believed that our Christian temples would be the first points

* It has been stated (Red Pamphlet) that among the most panic-stricken were men highest in authority. "Those highest in office were the first to give the alarm. There were secretaries to Government running over to members of Council, loading their pistols, barricading the doors, sleeping on sofas; members of Council abandoning their houses with their families, and taking refuge on board ship; crowds of lesser celebrities, impelled by these examples, having hastily collected their valuables, were rushing to the Fort, only too happy to be allowed to sleep under the Fort guns." Compare note, p. 34.

† One informant (Dr. Mouat), who drove that evening through Entally, the Circular Road, &c. &c., tells me that "the very dogs and cats seemed to have vanished from the earth." He had never witnessed "a scene of such utter and absolute abandonment."

of attack for the furious raging of the heathen or the wild fanaticism of the followers of the Prophet.* It was on a Sunday that the great storm had first burst upon us; it was on a Sunday, three weeks afterwards, that, as many believed, a far more desolating storm was to have swept over the country; and now again it was on a Sunday that, in the excited imaginations of our people, their chief city was to be given up to the cruel vengeance of barbarous enemies. But these barbarous enemies were as much scared as our Christian people. A great panic was upon them. They were expecting that the European soldiers who had recently arrived from beyond the seas would be let loose upon the unarmed populace. And many shut themselves up in their houses, bolted and barred their doors and windows, and looked forth furtively with frightened faces when they heard the sounds of horses' hoofs or wheeled carriages in the streets. But nothing came of these wild alarms. The day, the evening, the night passed, and there was no shedding of blood, no disturbance of the peace. Never since Fear first entered the world had there been a more groundless and unreasonable panic. No demonstration was made by the Sepoys of the Presidency Division, and if any mischief had been designed by the Oude colony at Garden Reach, it never developed into action. The promptitude of Government strangled it in the womb.

1857. June 14.

It will be seen that, of the phenomena of this "Panic Sunday," I have written more doubtfully,

* Dr. Duff says, that "Almost all the ministers in Calcutta had expostulatory letters sent them, dissuading them from preaching in the forenoon, and protesting against their attempting to do so in the evening. And though, to their credit, no one, as far as I have heard, yielded to the pressure, the churches in the forenoon were half empty, and in the evening nearly empty altogether."

1857. June 14. after a lapse of years, than others whose knowledge of facts both time and place must have favoured. Contemporary chroniclers and correspondents who were in Calcutta, or the vicinity, on that 14th of June, have written, in graphic language, of the flight to the Fort and the Fleet; and others have narrated to me verbally some of the incidents of the great Christian exodus. But, on the other hand, men of high character and position have denied, with equal strength of assertion, the accuracy of these records and reminiscences of a reign of terror. After most diligent inquiry, I have come to the conclusion that the truth is to be found mid-way between the two extremes. That men of high official rank, whose first duty it was to set an example of confidence and constancy to the community, stained their manhood and disgraced their office by betraying the cowardice in their hearts, I have discovered no satisfactory evidence to convince an impartial historical inquirer.* But that there was no panic—no flight—no confusion; that there was little to distinguish the 14th of June from any other day; that the ordinary goings-on of social life moved in the accustomed groove; and that the outward signs of a great bewilderment were discernible only by the eye of imagination—are assertions equally remote from the truth. The excitement of the times drove men, otherwise honest and truthful, into excessive generalisation, and the shortcomings of a few were described as the failure of a whole community. On the other hand, after a

* It is to be borne in mind that even in ascertained cases of high functionaries having left their houses in the suburbs to dwell nearer the centre of business, the ostensible reason of the change was the inconvenience, at a time of frequent official references, of residing at so great a distance from Government House; and it would be uncharitable not to accept the ostensible reason as the real one.

lapse of years, there is a natural tendency to ignore what cannot be spoken of with pleasure or with pride, and broad denials take the place of broad assertions, equally to the obscuration of the truth.* 1857. June 14.

For some weeks the rumour had been gaining ground that the King of Oude, or more properly the people about him, had been tampering with the Native soldiery, and instigating them to rebellion. It was currently believed that the exiles of Garden Reach were, in fact, the prime movers of the insurrection which was bearing such bitter fruits. It was so inevitable that such reports should be in circulation, and so probable that the truth, in such a case, should be greatly exaggerated, at a time when everything was magnified or distorted, that Lord Canning was slow to credit all the stories which reached him, sometimes from notorious alarmists. But as the month of June advanced, it became more and more apparent that the reports, which came to his ears, were not wholly without the foundation of fact.† It June 15. Arrest of the King of Oude.

* It is a significant fact that, four days afterwards, the following graphic account was published as part of an editorial article (*Friend of India*, June 18, 1857), and I do not observe that it was contradicted: "Whilst the work of disarming was going on at Barrackpore, precisely the same process was being carried through at Calcutta, where it was rumoured that murder and mutiny were triumphant at the former place, and that a strong force of rebels was marching down upon the city from Delhi. The infection of terror raged through all classes. Chowringhee and Garden Reach were abandoned for the Fort and the vessels in the river. The shipping was crowded with visitors, and in houses which were selected as being least likely to be attacked, hundreds of people gladly huddled together, to share the peculiar comforts which the presence of crowds imparts on such occasions. The hotels were fortified; bands of sailors marched through the thoroughfares happy in the expectation of possible fighting and the certainty of grog. Every group of Natives was scanned with suspicion. . . . . Many years must elapse before the night of the 14th of June, 1857, will be forgotten in Calcutta."

† One incident in particular created a great sensation, in high places, at the time. A man had been caught tampering with a Sepoy

1857. June 15. was certain that people living within the great circle of the new Oude home on the banks of the Hooghly had endeavoured to corrupt the Sepoys in the Fort —and especially the sentries posted at its gates. Colonel Cavenagh, the Town-Major, had received repeated warnings from Mahomedan friends that mischief was brewing, that Mussulman Sepoys were frequently visiting the King's people at Garden Reach, and that some influential visitors from Oude, including the great Talookhdar, Maun Singh, had visited Calcutta, and held conferences with the King or his Minister.* Of his obese Majesty himself, it was generally said that he had not energy sufficient to take active part even in intrigue. But in his own indolent way, beguiled by large promises of restoration to his lost kingdom, he suffered the work to be done for him; and it went forward—with what de-

in the Fort, had been tried by court-martial, and had been sentenced to death. The trial took place on the 14th of June; and the man was to have been hanged on the following morning. But in the course of the night he managed to effect his escape.—*See Note in the Appendix.*

* The fact of this visit to the King of Oude, and of the subsequent correspondence with Maun Singh, was asserted very unreservedly by a Native informant of Colonel Cavenagh, Town-Major of Fort William. See following extracts from that officer's journal: "*May* 21. My old friend Amir Ali called. He stated positively that the King of Oude had carried on a correspondence with Rajah Maun Singh, who had addressed him in the first instance, calling for his sanction to a rising in his favour, and on this being refused on the plea of the King's relations being in our hands, was reminded by the Rajah of the fact of Akhbar Khan having secured the release of his father, Dost Mahomed, upon which a firman was prepared and despatched to Oude, authorising the movement proposed, provided he, the King, was not in any way compromised, and promising to remit three years' revenue to any one who should join his cause." . . . "*May* 27. Amir Ali called. He states that the letter from Rajah Maun Singh was despatched, though not by public dawk, to the address of Zemindar Mullyan Singh, and that the correspondence was carried on by cipher" (certain Persian letters being substituted for others of the same alphabet). "He asserts that Rajah Maun Singh has certainly reached Calcutta and been closeted with the King." Lord Canning did not then credit the story, and it was afterwards made clear that the Rajah was not in Calcutta at the end of May, being then under surveillance at Fyzabad. It is believed that he visited Calcutta earlier in the year. See *post*—Chapters on Oude.

vices we may never know, but certainly with such activity as would have rendered it wrong in Government any longer to neglect it. So the resolution was taken. The King of Oude, his chief minister (Ali Nuckee Khan), and one or two others of the principal people about him, were suddenly to be made prisoners on the morning of the 15th of June, and to be conveyed in custody to Fort William. 1857. June 15.

Mr. Edmondstone.

The performance of this duty was intrusted to Mr. George Edmonstone. Bearing a name of high repute in Indian history, he had well maintained his hereditary title to distinction. The energy and ability which had placed his father in the very foremost rank of a past generation of Indian statesmen, and which, indeed, in a great measure had made the reputation of the greatest of India's Governor-Generals, had descended to him unimpaired; and there was not one of all Lord Canning's immediate advisers whose counsel might be more safely trusted. Holding the office—the most honoured of all under the Governor-General in Council—of Political or Foreign Secretary, it devolved upon him to transact ministerially all the business of the Native States and Native Princes of India—chiefly by correspondence; but, in some instances, as in this, by more personal action. The mission on which he was now sent was a delicate and a painful one. Firm, but yet courteous in his bearing, he acquitted himself with excellent address, and did the work intrusted to him with all fidelity to the Government, and with as little offence as possible to the exiled monarch whom he was sent to arrest.

The colony at Garden Reach.

Accompanied by some officers of Lord Canning's staff, and escorted by a considerable body of European troops, with a supplementary force of police,

1857. June 15. Edmonstone arrived under the outer walls of the King's residence in the first dim light of the dawn. Having surrounded the premises, so as to render escape impossible, he entered the compound with a detachment of the Fifty-third under Colonel Powell. A strange sight greeted him there. In the garden-grounds of Wajid Ali's new home a great village, or a small town, had arisen. The area was thickly covered with Native houses—a great confused mass of thatched buildings, huddling one upon another, without a symptom of arrangement or design. This rendered the advance and the disposition of the troops difficult; but there was small need for military coercion of any kind. There was not a sign of resistance, not even of preparation. The strong hand of the British had descended suddenly and unexpectedly on the new Oude colony, and the most active members of that great Mussulman community were rousing themselves in the early morning to respond to nothing more formidable than the Azan, or Mahomedan call to prayer. The troops had been warned not to use their arms unless there were signs of armed resistance. One man only was put under fixed bayonets and gently coerced to show the way to the residence of the chief minister; for the seizure of Ali Nuckee Khan was the first step to be taken. After some delay the Nawab came forth, and was at once arrested, with two other principal members of the suite—Ahsun Hoossein Khan and his son. These last, together with Tikaet Rao, the Dewan of the Chief Begum, were sent under a guard on board the *Semiramis*, which had been steaming down the river to Garden Reach whilst the troops had been marching along the road.

Arrest of the King.

It was now Edmonstone's duty to obtain ingress

to the King's apartments. This was a work of some difficulty and delicacy, and only to be accomplished after further delays. For there was a general reluctance to convey the unwelcome message to his Majesty's ears; and Wajid Ali had to bathe and to attire himself before he could receive the English gentlemen. But the regal ablutions and the toilet having been duly performed, Edmonstone and his companions were admitted to the presence of the King. Seated on a couch, and surrounded by members of his suite, he welcomed the Government Secretary with a sickly smile, shook him by the hand, and courteously received the other English officers. When they were all seated, Edmonstone spoke. He said that intelligence had reached the Governor-General, which had satisfied his Lordship that emissaries using his Majesty's name had spread themselves in all directions over the British dominions, and had instigated many of the Native soldiers of the Army to swerve from their allegiance. "It is the wish of the Governor-General, therefore," he added, "that your Majesty should accompany me on my return to Calcutta." 1857. June 15.

Roused by this address into something at least resembling energy of manner and emphasis of speech, the King replied that he had not been guilty of the offence imputed to him, and that if he had done anything to tamper with the loyalty of the troops, he would be deserving of any punishment which the British Government might be pleased to inflict upon him. Edmonstone answered that he had no authority to discuss the question, and requested his Majesty to prepare for departure. A number of his courtiers clamoured for permission to accompany him. Liberal compliance was accorded to them; and ere long the unwieldy, tottering exile was leaning on the arm of

1857. June 15. the British Secretary, who escorted him to the outer door, where the Governor-General's carriage was waiting to receive them.

On their way to the Fort the firmness of the King broke down. He seemed suddenly to awaken to the misery and humiliation of his position. Bursting into tears, he spoke of the dignity of his ancestors, his own heavy fall and wretched condition as an exile and a suspect, and asked whether, if he had ever intended to array himself against the British Government, he would not have done so when he had twenty lakhs of men at his back. "But ask General Outram," he added, "if I did not quietly submit to his authority, and deliver up my kingdom into his hands." He then subsided into silence, almost into insensibility; but presently he burst again into tears, protested his innocence, and pointing to an amulet, on which some passages of the Koran were inscribed, and which hung from his neck, he said, "When I read in the *Hurkaru* newspaper that I was accused of tampering with the troops, I swore upon this that I would keep clear of all such machinations." To this Edmonstone could only reply that justice would be done, and every consideration shown to his Majesty, by the Government which he represented. The rest of the journey was accomplished in silence, and about eight o'clock the King of Oude was placed, with becoming courtesy and respect, in the hands of Colonel Cavenagh, the Town-Major, who was prepared to receive him.

Thus, on the morning of June 15th, Wajid Ali, Ali Nuckee Khan, and three other members of the King's suite, were conveyed, state prisoners, to Fort William. There quarters were provided for them in the building known as the Government House—an edifice appropriated to many uses, but seldom or never to the one for which it was originally designed. Although on a limited scale, the accommodation was not ill-suited to the purpose to which it was now to be put; for there was at least one large state apartment, with several smaller ones opening into it, and there was a dignity in the name which may have rubbed off some of the degradation of the captivity. It was the best place that could be found as the temporary home of his Majesty of Oude and the wily ministers who directed his political movements. But little or nothing was brought to light to implicate the King in the alleged conspiracies against the British Government. If there were damnatory evidence in letters or documents at Garden Reach, it was not discovered. The premises could not be searched without violating the sanctity of the female apartments; and this an English officer, save in extremest cases, is ever bound to respect.* 1857. June 15.

The disarming of the Sepoys and the captivity of

* This measure calls for neither justification nor explanation; but I may as well place upon record Lord Canning's brief statement of his reasons, as contained in a letter to the Indian Minister at home: "The King of Oude and four of his suite have been placed in Fort William. The immediate grounds of this will be found in the deposition of a Sepoy, who was twice tampered with by a Mahomedan, who described himself as coming from the King's people, and although no complicity in the act has been fixed upon the King or his chief courtiers, I deem it necessary for the safety of the State that it should for the present be put out of the power of any one to seduce the State's soldiers by speaking in the name of the King of Oude, and that his name should not be made a rallying-point for disaffected soldiers. I think this the more necessary, because I know that offers of enlistment were made a few weeks ago by a person in the King's service to another supposed to be seeking employment. Of the four who are in the Fort, Ali Nuckee Khan is the King's minister; Hoossein Khan is a notorious intriguer of the Court, of the worst repute from the time of Colonel Sleeman. Hassan Khan is his son; Tikaet Rao is a Hindoo, a Dewan or steward in the Queen's service. His character makes him an object of suspicion."—*Lord Canning to Mr. Vernon Smith, June 19, 1857.—MS. Records.*

1857. June. the King of Oude restored for a time tranquillity to Calcutta. To this result the activity of the Volunteer Guards greatly contributed. Any doubts which might at first have been entertained respecting the practical efficiency of these citizen-battalions, were soon removed by the zeal which they continuously manifested. It was not permitted to them, as to Havelock's volunteers, of whom I have already spoken, or Henry Lawrence's, of whom I shall speak presently, to flash their sabres in the faces of an overwhelming enemy; but night after night, amidst all the inclemencies of the rainy season, they were found at their posts, ready for any service which they might be called upon to perform. Some hundreds of Infantry were thus enrolled under Major Davies, with a proportionate number of Cavalry under Captain Turnbull, whilst Captain Dickens of the Artillery organised the Ordnance branch of the brigade. Major Strachey of the Engineers had succeeded Colonel Cavenagh in command of the entire force. And all did their work so well that it was not long before Lord Canning took occasion publicly to express his appreciation of their "zealous and excellent services."*

* See reply to Address of Calcutta inhabitants, petitioning for martial law throughout the Bengal Provinces. At a later period Lord Canning wrote with reference to the Volunteers: "It has received every encouragement from the Governor-General, from the day of its formation, and has done useful service in patrolling the town and giving confidence. It is not to be denied that the mutinies, which then declared themselves, have grown into a more formidable revolt than was anticipated; but at the time . . . whilst every preparation was made to meet the growth of the danger, whatever dimensions it might assume, the Governor-General felt it to be urgently necessary to check panic in places where no real danger existed, especially in Calcutta, where it could not fail to be mischievous, both politically and commercially. There is not a doubt that the exaggerated fears, which a great part of the Calcutta population have exhibited on at least three occasions during the progress of the mutinies, have led the Natives to doubt our self-reliance and our strength, whilst nothing of safety has been gained to ourselves thereby."

The centenary of Plassey came and went. In Calcutta, as in other parts of the country, apprehensions had been entertained that on that day there would be a formidable rising; and when it arrived there was something more than the wonted vigilance and preparation. But the most memorable incident connected with that 23rd of June, was the publication, two days afterwards, in the Serampore journal, of an article in celebration of that important anniversary—an article in which Mahomedan Princes were reviled as "cruel, sensual, intolerant, unfit to rule"—and Mahrattas and Sikhs were triumphed over with equal insolence of self-laudation—an article closing with the words, "the first centenary of Plassey was ushered in by the revolt of the Native Army; the second may be celebrated in Bengal by a respected Government and a Christian population." There was not much in the words. Such words had been often published before and smiled at complacently by the Government of the day. But there was much in the time of publication. The article was peculiarly calculated, in such a conjuncture, to irritate the minds of the people, for it might bear a meaning which perhaps the writer never intended to assign to it. Straightway, therefore, the Government "warned" the publisher of the *Friend of India*. This brought forth a rejoinder, headed "The First Warning," still less discreet than its predecessor. And the ablest journal in Bengal, which had always been regarded as a model of respectability and discretion, would have been suppressed, if some friends of the absent proprietors had not come forward to protect their interests, and guaranteed that the "officiating" editor should no longer have it in his power to

1857. June 23.

1857. June.

sacrifice their property by his want of temper and want of tact.*

Military precautions.

Meanwhile, every exertion was being made to expedite the movements and to secure the efficiency of the reinforcements despatched, or about to be despatched, to the North. The arrival of Sir Patrick Grant had infused new vigour into the military department of Government, and had afforded to the Governor-General himself most appreciable assistance and support.† The troops from the Coast and from the Persian Gulf had been despatched to the Upper Provinces before the end of the third week of June;‡ and now Lord Canning looked eagerly for the coming of the regiments which he had urged Lord Elgin and General Ashburnham to divert from the China Expedition. It was necessary to prepare for the arrival of these by providing all the necessary appliances of equipment and carriage; so orders were sent to

* I do not purpose to dwell any further upon the practical results of the passing of this law, which were, indeed, so slight, that it has been said of the Act that it was a "dead letter." It is right, however, thus to state, with respect to the *Friend of India*, which has always borne a high reputation, by no means confined to the place of its nativity, that the proprietors of the paper and the responsible editor were, at the time, absent from India, and that the literary management was then in the hands of a public writer of more ability than discretion, who has placed on record, in a permanent form, his impressions of the great events which were passing around him. ("Mead's Sepoy Revolt," published by Mr. Murray in 1857.) I have a conviction amounting to certainty, that if either of the absentees, to whom I have referred, had been in India in May and June, 1857, no such articles as those which brought temporary discredit on the *Friend of India* would ever have been written.

† Sir Patrick Grant arrived at Calcutta on the 17th of June.—Vol. ii. p. 281.

‡ "The European troops are being pushed up as quickly as possible. The whole of the Madras Fusiliers must now be at Allahabad, and the Eighty-fourth have passed beyond Benares, as also a portion of the Sixty-fourth. The last of the Seventy-eighth Highlanders leave by bullock-train to-morrow, the 20th, when the wing of the Thirty-seventh will be despatched. One European battery left by steam this morning, and another is preparing to follow. The detachment of the Royal Artillery will also be sent up by bullock-train."—*Memorandum of General Birch, June* 19.—The wing of the Thirty-seventh had come from Ceylon.

Madras to despatch immediately to Calcutta a large proportion of the clothing and camp-equipage that had been collected there, whilst the Bombay Government were called upon to procure from Bushire and other places "as large a supply of horses as possible for Cavalry and Artillery purposes." Efforts at the same time were made to communicate to Agra the instructions of Government that no exertion should be spared in the North-Western Provinces to collect carriage for the upward march of the troops. The miserable want of conveyance for the sick and wounded, which had so palpably presented itself to General Neill at Allahabad,* was being supplied as rapidly as possible by the artificers of Calcutta. If there had before been any short-comings, omissions, or delays, nothing now was neglected that could give completeness to the military organisation by which the succours received from beyond the seas were to be turned to the best account. Nothing escaped the practised eye of Sir Patrick Grant. His training had been of the right kind to qualify him for the apt performance of the work in hand. His coming, therefore, supplied what was most wanted to give strength to the administration, which had before been essentially wanting in military efficiency. Perhaps, if the General had been moved only by his own natural impulses, he would have proceeded at once to the seat of war to take an active part in the great struggle. But his better judgment taught him that in no place could he, at that time, be so serviceable to the State as at the seat of Government; and in this opinion Lord Canning and all the members of his Council concurred.† To the Governor-General it

1857. June.

* Vol. ii. p. 273.

† "I am of opinion that as soon as the course of events shall tend to allay the general disquiet, and to

1857. June.

appeared that his new colleague possessed most of the essential qualifications to be looked for in a man, to whom the chief command of the Indian Army, with the great after-work of reconstruction, might now be safely intrusted; and he wrote letters to the Home Government urging the permanent confirmation of the provisional appointment. He was afraid of the coming of a stiff-necked Horse Guards General; and dwelt emphatically on the importance, in such a juncture, of that knowledge and experience which can be acquired only by long years of residence in India and familiarity with its camps and cantonments.

Succours from England.

From the first, Lord Canning, though hoping to gather up troops enough from our outlying colonies, or from the great highway of the ocean, to break the neck of the first revolt, felt that there would be much after-work to be done, which would demand the aid of large reinforcements from England. On the 19th of May, he had written to the President of the India Board, saying: "From England what I ask is, that you should immediately send out the regiments which are due to the full complement of Queen's corps in India without making us wait for the issue of events in China; and that you will give support to the demand for three new European regiments to be added to the Company's Army in place of the six which have now erased themselves from the Army List. You will see that there will be no additional

show to what points our force should be mainly directed, with the view of crushing the heart of the rebellion, it will be proper that his Excellency should consider anew the question of his movements. His Excellency's experience and high authority will then, in all probability, be most usefully employed in the disturbed districts or their neighbourhood. For the present there will be the greatest advantage in his Excellency remaining at the seat of Government."—*Minute of Lord Canning, June 22, 1857.*

cost. I beg that you will grant me both these requests." But ere the first week of June was at an end, these moderate views had expanded under the expanded significance of the revolt. The magnitude of the work to be accomplished was now shown to be far greater than it had appeared some two or three weeks before. "Be the issue what it may," wrote Lord Canning to Mr. Vernon Smith on the 5th of June, "whether with the speedy fall of Delhi the rebellion at once collapses, or whether before this happens ravages extend and the Europeans are driven from the Central Provinces, and those parts hence to be recovered, I reckon that we shall require an additional force of twelve regiments of Infantry and one regiment of Dragoons. We must not conceal from ourselves that our Government must henceforth rest much more openly than heretofore upon military strength. There must be no arsenal, or strong places, such as Allahabad and Delhi; no fanatical stronghold, such as Benares; no large tract of rich, defenceless country, such as Lower Bengal, without a European regiment. No brigade of Native troops should be without one. A strong force, not less than eight regiments, should be always near the capital, ready to be directed to any point in the Bay of Bengal. Second and third-class arsenals and depôts must have a defence of Europeans. Europeans must be seen in Central India and Nagpore. We must for a time, and no short time, make our European strength visible and sensible to all India. Our power and name have had a rude shock, and nothing must be spared to make them firm again. Until this has been done, no confidence, political, social, or commercial, will be re-established. I have no hope that it can be done by anything short of ten regiments to be added

1857.
June.

1857. June. permanently, and at first I should greatly desire to have twelve." But, although he saw clearly the necessity, and thus urgently impressed upon the Home Government the duty, of immediately strengthening the European Force in India, he was careful not to make, under the influence of this pressure, such demands upon the military resources of Great Britain as might result in the infliction of a permanent burden upon India such as it would be difficult to bear up against on the restoration of peace. He saw clearly in the distance an immense strain upon the finances of the Indian Empire, and he was anxious not to increase it by any unnecessary military expenditure.*

Economical measures.

It was not, indeed, only the great trouble of the present that oppressed him. He was even then compelled, amidst all the distractions of the hour, to look the future of the Empire in the face. The mutiny—the rebellion—whatsoever it should prove to be, might be trodden down; but still it would leave behind it a great incubus of disorder and disaster, rendering the work of settled government difficult, for years to come. There was necessarily an enormous additional expenditure of money at a time when, in many parts of the country, the sources of revenue were being dried up by the fire of revolt; and how to meet all these extraordinary charges was a question of no very easy solution. The only certainty was, that it had become an absolute necessity to provide for the exigencies of the moment at any sacrifice of future efficiency and prosperity. There are seasons

* "I am very anxious," he wrote to Mr. Vernon Smith, "that we should not, under the present pressure, great as it is, rush into any superfluous expenditure for purposes of safety. The material progress of the country has at the best been pushed back many years, and every lakh unnecessarily spent upon military establishments will retard its advance." — *MS. Correspondence of Lord Canning, July* 3, 1857.

when nations, like individuals, must live from hand to mouth; when the struggle is for bare existence, and all principles of sound financial economy must yield to the exigencies of the crisis. It is a sore trial to a statesman to be compelled to cast away the means of large prospective gain in the pursuit of some necessary scheme of present retrenchment. And thus now was Lord Canning tried. He had to get money as he could; he had to save it as he could. To get it was not easy. That such a crisis as this must have greatly shaken the credit of the British Government was inevitable. The wonder is that it was so little shaken. "It is astonishing," wrote Lord Canning to Mr. Vernon Smith on the 3rd of July, "how little Government securities have suffered during the convulsion. Four-per-cent. paper at the beginning of June was at fourteen to fourteen and a half discount—an ordinary rate. About the 12th of June it reached its lowest depreciation—twenty to twenty-one discount. Since that it has been pretty steadily rising, and has got back to fifteen to fifteen and a half per cent. This does not look very bad." A five-per-cent. loan was then open. At this time the Governor-General reported that it had "stopped, or all but stopped, at close upon two millions sterling." It was obvious, therefore, that to meet the enormous military expenditure some extraordinary means must be resorted to, to raise the necessary finances. Whether to raise the money in India or in England was then the question. After much discussion, Lord Canning's Government determined that the wisest course would be to open a six-per-cent. loan in India, but to obtain the promise of the Court of Directors that they would be "prepared to help if need be, in order that it may be known here that we are not

1857. June—July.

1857. July. altogether at the mercy of the holders of money in this country." "I apprehend," added the Governor-General in his private letter to the President of the Board of Control, "that in order to be ready to help the Government in India, the East India Company must have recourse to Parliament for permission to borrow. At least I know not how any considerable sum can be forthcoming from the Court by any other means. Whether these means shall be had recourse to, you at home will decide. My belief is that we in India shall still be able to raise what we want (I put it at three crores) by offering six per cent.; but I am sure that the chances of being able to do so will be greatly increased if we have an assurance that in case of failure help will come from home."* Meanwhile, there was a pressing necessity to reduce the expenditure of the Government by every possible means, at any sacrifice of future advantages to the State.

So an order went forth for the immediate suspension of all the great reproductive public works, which

* What was actually done in Calcutta may be gathered from the following statement, which forms part of the comments of Lord Canning on the petition for his recall: "When the notifications of the 20th and 27th July were issued, the position of affairs was altogether changed. The mutiny had spread, the money market was daily becoming tighter, a falling off in the revenue had become certain, and on its thus being unquestionable that more favourable terms than five per cent. would be necessary to secure subscriptions to a loan, the arrangement for taking four, four and a half, and three and a half paper in part subscription to the five-per-cent. loan was resolved on, in preference to opening a six-per-cent. loan, chiefly out of consideration to the then holders of Government securities. That the credit of the Government was destroyed is proved not to be the case by the fact that cash subscriptions have been received since the 21st July to the amount of 97,81,390 rs., while the transfers have amounted to 96,09,710 rs., and this notwithstanding that the subscriptions in Calcutta have been greatly curtailed by the Bank of Bengal having, for a considerable period, refused any accommodation in the way of fresh loans. At the present date (9th November) the loan has reached three millions sterling."—It need not be added that loans were afterwards raised in London, on the security of the revenues of India.

would have added so much to the wealth of the Empire. How it pained him to do this may be gathered from his correspondence. Respecting what he had done, he wrote on the 3rd of July to the President of the India Board: "The stoppage of public works is made as absolute as possible. No new works of public improvement to be entered upon; many already in full swing to be abandoned, and nothing but the real necessities of the military and civil establishments to be provided for, and repairs. The Staff, too, will be reduced. This sounds prudent and economical. It is neither one nor the other. It is wasteful to the last degree—wasteful of money already expended—wasteful of much labour of organisation and discipline, and much dearly-bought experience; and, besides, disheartening to the invaluable Staff of officers who have been trained to the works, and humbling to the Government. But there is no choice for the present, at all events." 1857. July.

And still, as these cares pressed heavily upon him, there were trouble and vexation at his own door. For the Christian communities of the capital continued to clamour for much that his deliberate judgment told him it would be unwise and unjust to concede. As weeks passed, and every week brought a fresh catalogue of crimes committed against our Christian people by Natives of the country, Mahomedans and Hindoos—and not all, not nearly all by men who had once worn the uniform of the British Government—as many, many households in the capital were mourning the miserable deaths of their nearest and dearest—nay, as fugitives came in from the Upper Country with dreadful stories to relate, and the horrors which they truthfully recited were magnified in repetition, till there was not a con- Personal vexations.

1857. July. ceivable outrage which men or fiends could commit not laid to the charge of the black races—it was not strange that both fear and hatred should have grown stronger among our white people, and that there should have been a cry, ever increasing in strength, both for protection and for retribution. To have yielded to the cry would, at that time, have won the hearts of the Christian communities of Calcutta. But he could not sacrifice his sense of duty to any yearning after popularity; and though the imploring cries of his countrymen from all parts pained him deeply, and he grieved for the tribulation of the great English capital, he could not bring himself to concede all that they asked. So as week followed week, the Governor-General grew more and more distasteful to the European communities of Calcutta, until there began to be much eager talk about a Petition to the Home Government for his recall.

Instructions to the Executive.

He bore up bravely against it, never for a moment thinking of yielding to the clamour. Indeed, the louder it grew, the more convinced he was that it was his duty, in all ways and by all means, to resist it. For every day it became more and more sadly apparent, that in all parts of the country the resentments of the Englishman had been roused to such a pitch, that he was ready on every possible opportunity and occasion to take the law into his own hands, and to execute upon the Native races the wild justice of revenge. There was nothing in this to astonish Lord Canning, and he could not severely condemn it. But he knew only too painfully, to what, if not arrested, this must tend; and he bethought himself and invited the counsel of others as to the best means of arming the Executive with full power promptly to punish the guilty without placing in their hands authority to smite unsparingly at every Sepoy who might cross their path, and all suspected of abetting him. So, at the end of July a resolution of Government was passed, embodying instructions to officers in Bengal and the North-Western Provinces to draw lines of discrimination between, firstly, Sepoys of regiments which had not mutinied, not being found with arms in their possession; secondly, Sepoys, unarmed, being mutineers or deserters from regiments guilty of simple rebellion, but not charged with the murder of their officers or any other sanguinary crime; and thirdly, mutineers or deserters, found to belong to regiments guilty of the murder of their officers or other Europeans, or of having "committed any other sanguinary outrage." In the two former cases the prisoners were to be sent for trial by the military authorities; in the last they were to be tried by the civil power, and the sentence passed upon them to be carried out forthwith—with this reservation, however, that execution should be stayed, pending a reference to the Government, if the accused should furnish evidence of his not having been present with his regiment at the time of the commission of the crime, or that, if present, he had endeavoured to prevent it. It had become all the more imperative on Government to enforce the observation of these distinctions, since it had become known that in some instances Sepoys on leave from their regiments (it was the furlough season of the year) had been seized and executed when passing to and from their respective homes.

1857. July 31.

Having recorded these instructions with respect to military prisoners of all classes, the Government proceeded to define, but in less precise language, the

1857. July 31. course to be pursued by the civil authorities "in regard to acts of rebellion committed by persons not mutineers." "It is unquestionably necessary," said the Resolution, "in the first attempt to restore order in a district in which the civil authority has been entirely overthrown, to administer the law with such promptitude and severity as will strike terror into the minds of the evil-disposed among the people, and will induce them, by the fear of death, to abstain from plunder, to restore stolen property, and to return to peaceful occupations. But this object once in a great degree attained, the punishment of crimes should be regulated with discrimination. The continued administration of the law in its utmost severity, after the requisite impression has been made on the rebellious and disorderly, and after order has been partially restored, would have the effect of exasperating the people, and would probably induce them to band together in large numbers for the protection of their lives and with a view to retaliation—a result much to be deprecated. It would greatly add to the difficulties of settling the country hereafter, if a spirit of animosity against their rulers were engendered in the minds of the people, and if their feelings were embittered by the remembrance of needless bloodshed." The district officers were in this spirit exhorted, "without condoning any heinous offences," to encourage all persons to return to their usual occupations, and to "postpone as far as possible all inquiry into political offences until such time as the Government are in a position to deal with them in strength after thorough investigation." The wholesale burning of villages was especially deprecated, as tending morally to the general exasperation of the people, and practically to the prevention of their resumption of the cultivation of their fields—"a point,"

it was added, "at this season of vital importance, 1857. July 31.
inasmuch as if the lands remain much longer unsown, distress and even famine may be added to the other difficulties with which the Government will have to contend."

These instructions, the extreme moderation and plain practical good sense of which cannot at this distance of time be questioned, were not proclaimed or published, as was afterwards stated, but were sent, in the shape of confidential circulars, to the officers whom they concerned. A copy of them, however, was printed in a Calcutta paper. And the more violent section of the European inhabitants of the capital were roused to a high pitch of indignation by what they afterwards denounced as "indiscriminate forgiveness," though the avowed object and practical effect of the measure was to enforce a wholesome discrimination in the punishment of accused or suspected persons. "Lenity," it was added, "towards any portion of the conspirators is misplaced, impolitic, and iniquitous, and is calculated to excite contempt and invite attack on every side, by showing to the world the Government of India so powerless to punish mutiny, or so indifferent to the sufferings which have been endured by the victims of the rebellion, that it allows the blood of English and Christian subjects of Her Majesty to flow in torrents, and their wives, sisters, and daughters to be outraged and dishonoured without adequate retribution." It was forgotten that this adequate retribution, if it had been commendable and desirable, would, at the time when these orders were issued, have been impossible, from sheer lack of strength to execute it, and that the attempt would only have rendered greater the disproportion between the evil to be suppressed and the means of suppress-

1857. July. ing it. In fact, the retribution party were clamouring for that which would have aggravated their dangers and increased their fears, and that the policy which they advocated would, in its adoption, have been as fatal to the interests as damnatory to the character of the nation.

The sale of arms. Another source of discontent was this: a new element of danger was supposed to have been discovered in the fact that there had been a large importation of arms into Calcutta, and that the Natives of the capital and of the surrounding districts were purchasing them freely from shopkeepers not disinclined to make money by the crisis. In truth, the Natives of the country were more alarmed than the Christian inhabitants; and when they saw our people arming themselves everywhere, and knew that we were disarming their military compatriots, they began to suspect that we should, at no distant period, use our rifles and revolvers for other than defensive purposes. July 20. On the 20th of July, the subject was brought to the notice of Government by the Town-Major. About the same time, the Commandant of the Calcutta Militia, Major Herbert, sent in reports to the effect that an English firm had imported a large quantity of arms, which had been sold to a Native dealer, and that they were being freely bought in the bazaars. On the 22nd, the Grand Jury, in the Supreme Court of Calcutta, made a presentment recommending that all the Native population of the capital should be forthwith disarmed, and that the sale of arms and ammunition should be legally forbidden. And on the following day, a number of the Christian inhabitants appealed to the Government to disarm all the Natives in the place. To this reply was given, two days afterwards, that it was not intended to disarm any class of the residents of Calcutta or the neighbourhood—that sufficient precautions had been taken for the safety of the city; and that a General Arms Bill was under consideration.* 1857. July.

Confidence of Lord Canning.

This was not considered a satisfactory reply; but the sincerity with which it was given was beyond all question. For Lord Canning had up to this time refused to disarm his own body-guard—a body of picked Native soldiers, well armed and well mounted. He never went abroad without some of these troopers in attendance upon him. He was earnestly exhorted to disarm them; but he was reluctant, at this time, to consent to such a measure. Some said that it was "fool-hardy;" others argued that it was another proof that he did not understand the gravity of the position. But none could dispute that it testified his assured conviction that the general disarming of the people was uncalled for, and proved that he was not one to exhort others to manifestations of confidence of which he did not himself set a conspicuous example.

But in this disregard of his own personal safety Lord Canning may have erred. The persistent manner in which he long refused to change the Sepoy guard at Government House for one composed of European soldiers, is said, however commendable it might have been in a lesser man, to have been an indiscretion in the Governor-General. It was, doubtless, a noble example that he set. If he had dismissed his Sepoy guards at the commencement of our troubles, the news would have run, like an alarm-note, through all classes of the community, and there would have been a diminution of that confidence which it was so im-

* Confidential Memorandum by Lord Canning—unpublished.

1857. July. portant to maintain in every quarter where Christian people were assembled. So, although oftentimes urged not to trust himself any longer to the dangerous guardianship of men whose comrades had stained their hands with the blood of their officers, he continued to confide in them, and could not be induced to order Europeans to be posted at his doors. Secretaries and members of Council deplored this; but they could not bend him to their will. At last, Mr. Halliday. Mr. Halliday, Lieutenant-Governor of Bengal, who had come down to the Presidency from Darjeeling, so wrought upon the Governor-General by telling him that his duty to his country demanded that he should take every precaution to protect a life, which at such a time was of incalculable value, that he began reluctantly to yield, and to bethink himself of consenting to the change which had been so often vainly pressed upon him.

It was no easy task that Halliday had set himself, and it was not easily accomplished. Time did something to mitigate the difficulty, for the general disaffection of the Bengal Army was every week becoming more apparent. But the personal influence of the Lieutenant-Governor did more. Lord Canning said of him afterwards, that for many months he had been the "right hand of the Government." A man of commanding stature and altogether of a goodly presence, he looked like one born to command. He had all his life been a steady, robust workman, and he had brought to his work no small amount of natural ability and administrative sagacity of the most serviceable kind. His lot had been cast in the hitherto tranquil regions of Bengal. No opportunity of proving his powers in action had been afforded to him; but his sufficiency in council had won the confidence of successive Governments, and in all that related to the Lower Provinces there was no man whose experiences were of greater value. To Lord Canning, who, wisely or unwisely, had been chary of his confidences to those immediately about him, the arrival of Mr. Halliday had been extremely welcome, and from that time there was no member of the Government whom he so frequently consulted or whose opinions he so much respected. But still only by repeatedly urging upon the Governor-General that his life belonged to his country, and that he had no right to expose it to any unnecessary risks, could his Lieutenant induce him to allow the order to be issued for European guards to be posted at Government House. It was not, indeed, until the month of August had expired that the European Guard marched into the compound of Government House, under the immediate orders of the Lieutenant-Governor.*

1857. July.

In the mean while events were developing themselves in the country below Benares, which seemed in some measure to confirm the apprehensions of the European community at Calcutta, and which doubtless rendered the Governor-General's outward calmness of demeanour, which they so grievously misinterpreted, more offensive and irritating to them than before. It seemed as though the toils were closing around them—that Bengal itself would soon be in a blaze, and murder and pillage rampant in the capital—whilst the head of the Government was complacently closing his eyes to the surrounding danger. But no one saw it more clearly than Lord Canning. Writing at the beginning of August to the Indian

* This was either on the 31st of August or the 1st of September.

1857. July. Minister at home, he said: "For the moment everything must give way to the necessity of arresting rebellion or general disorder below Benares. If this is not done our slender remains of revenue will be in jeopardy, and every isolated regiment throughout these provinces will mutiny; for it is impossible to reach them with any European force strong enough to disarm them, without their having full warning of what is coming upon them." The events to which reference is here made must now be fully narrated.

CHAPTER II.

THE BENGAL PROVINCES — CHARACTER OF THE POPULATION — THE CRY FOR DISARMING — STATE OF THE DINAPORE REGIMENTS — CONDITION OF THE PATNA DIVISION — ARREST OF WAHABEES — GENERAL LLOYD'S HALF-MEASURE — MUTINY AT DINAPORE — DUNBAR'S EXPEDITION — THE DISASTROUS RETREAT — GALLANT EXPLOITS.

1857.

The Bengal Provinces.

THE India Bill of 1853 had placed the provinces of Bengal, Behar, and Orissa under a Lieutenant-Governor. They extended from the borders of the Madras Presidency on the south to the limits of the Nepaul country on the north. Of all our acquisitions in Upper India, they had been the longest under our rule; and the people had become, therefore, most habituated to our systems. A peaceful, pliant, plastic people, the genuine Bengalees were easily intimidated, easily subjected, easily moulded. They were, indeed, what the moist, relaxing climate had made them, a feeble, languid race of men. They did not recruit our armies; but they were adepts in trade. They could not fire a musket or handle a sabre; but they were the most litigious people in all the world. Whilst they schemed and trafficked with immense success, they did not hesitate to acknowledge, with self-condemning frankness, that, in the active business of fighting, they were cowards. They had, however, a passive kind of courage of their

1857. June. own. They had great powers of endurance. They could lie down to be crushed to death under the wheels of Juggernauth, or they could swing from a high pole with iron hooks in their backs. In the aggressive business of insurrection, such a people could be no proficients. Their idea of a popular revolt was a great assemblage of people, sitting on their haunches, hungry and silent, and defying the Government by sheer force of utter inaction and inexhaustible patience.

Such was the general character of the population. But there are no places in which there are not exceptional elements of violence—it may be of an indigenous, it may be of a foreign character. In Bengal were large numbers of immigrants from all parts of the East—some settled and some transitory. The Bazaars of Calcutta were swarming with them—with men of all races, from the flat-faced, close-shaven Chinaman to the aquiline, bearded Afghan. The predatory classes were not absent from Bengal. Budducks and Kechucks, and other professional robbers, plied their trade with audacious success. The Police was about the worst in the world—part and parcel often of the predatory organisation—and certain, in the event of an insurrection, to side with the insurgents as the more profitable course. Notwithstanding, therefore, the non-military character of the rural population, there was some reason to regard with dismay the rising of the Native troops in the Lower Provinces, where no European battalions were posted; whilst higher up in the circle of the Lieutenant-Governorship were people of different instincts and habits from those of the populations of Bengal and Orissa.

Here, indeed, were some sources of reasonable inquietude. To one of the chief of these the moneyed interests of Calcutta looked with intelligible anxiety. If the rich indigo districts of Behar were overrun by a mutinous soldiery, aided by the Budmashes of the country, what would become of all the money advanced upon the growing crops? This was a substantial ground of alarm to many of the merchants and agents of the capital, but the ruin which would have followed such incursions of rebels into the indigo districts would not have been confined to them. It would have been wide-spread and most disastrous. Now, the apprehension of disturbances in Behar was by no means the growth of the creative powers of an excited imagination. The Lieutenant-Governor had represented in June that there was danger to be apprehended from the return of mutinous Sepoys to their homes in Behar—for, although few Native soldiers were ever drawn from Lower Bengal, further up in Behar were races of a more warlike character—immigrants partly from higher latitudes. Then there was the great city of Patna, which had for long years been a not unreasonable source of suspicion and mistrust to the ruling authorities. Mahomedanism was strong and rampant at Patna; and it was the most active kind of Mahomedanism, for there we saw the followers of the Prophet in the rejuvenescence of Wahabeeism. Then there were three Sepoy regiments at Dinapore, and, although they were watched by Her Majesty's Tenth Foot, it was still probable that they might suddenly break into mutiny and escape, as others had escaped before them. The result of this might have been mischievous in the extreme. Already were there great alarm and excitement. Strange rumours agitated the people. Mr. Tayler, the Commissioner of

1857. June.

Alarm in the indigo districts.

The Seventh, Eighth, and Fortieth Regiments.

1857. June. Patna, had written to Mr. Secretary Beadon, saying: "The whole English community at Tirhoot have demanded protection, as they believe that the people will rise and the Nujeebs mutiny. All Buxar and Shahabad fled like sheep and flocked into Dinapore. . . . . Richardson, of Chuprah, writes that the whole country opposite his cutcherry on the Ghazepore Doab, and the people of all the districts to the west of Chuprah, are in open revolt." In this excited condition of the people, it was argued, if the Sepoys at Dinapore should rise and sweep down upon Patna, carrying off the treasure, looting the rich opium-godowns, and thence spreading desolation through the homes of the indigo farmers of Tirhoot, the contagion might spread lower and lower, Moorshedabad might rise, in spite of the steadfast loyalty of the Nawab Nazim, and the insurgents gathering strength as they went, might pour themselves down upon the capital. Why, then, not prevent a calamity of so probable a kind by disarming the Dinapore regiments? It was a feat of no difficult accomplishment. The Tenth Foot, aided by some of the reinforcements passing up the river, which might have been detained a little while for this special service, could have easily overawed the Sepoy battalions, and deprived them of all means of offence. But the Governor-General believed that there was still greater danger in disarming, and so the Sepoys were left with arms in their hands; and a regiment of Europeans, when every English soldier was worth his weight in gold, was kept at Dinapore to watch them. And there were many in Bengal, who, admiring and upholding the Governor-General, and condemning the popular clamour which had been raised against him as intemperate and imbecile, thought that he had erred in refusing, for so long a time, to disarm the regiments at Dinapore. 1857. June.

Arguments against disarming.

It is right, however, that the arguments with which the Governor-General sustained his declared reluctance to disarm the Dinapore Brigade should be recorded. If the question before him had related only to the measures best calculated for the protection of the indigo districts of Behar, the disarming of the regiments (its successful accomplishment assumed) might have been the stroke best tending towards the deliverance of those whose lives and properties there were in danger. But Lord Canning had not merely to consider what was locally or individually best, but what was generally most conducive to the interests of those under his charge. And he could not but perceive that, however safe it might be to disarm Native regiments in the neighbourhood of European troops, the result might be dangerous in the extreme to our people in other parts of the country, where Sepoys abounded and not a detachment of Europeans was to be seen. He was looking anxiously for the arrival of fresh reinforcements, when the game would be more in his own hands; but in the then destitute state of the Lower Provinces, it seemed to him and to the members of his Council to be sounder policy to temporise. It could not be wise, he thought, to precipitate a crisis, which he had not the power successfully to confront. All parts of Lower Bengal were dotted over with Sepoy detachments, waiting eagerly for news, perhaps for instructions, from Head-Quarters, and ready to break out into rebellion at an hour's notice. And it had been industriously circulated among them that disarming was only another name for destruction, and that when they had given up their muskets, they

1857. June. would either be shot down or sent as prisoners beyond the seas.

The intelligence, which Lord Canning had received from the General Officer commanding the Dinapore Division, tended to confirm him in the impression that an outbreak at that station was not to be expected.

The Dinapore regiments. On the 2nd of June, General Lloyd had written to the Governor-General, saying: "Although no one can now feel full confidence in the loyalty of the Native troops generally, yet I believe that the regiments here will remain quiet, unless some great temptation or excitement should assail them, in which case I fear that they could not be relied upon."* A few days afterwards it seemed that the hour of temptation had come; for news had arrived from Benares of the disarming of the regiments there, and what had followed, and all the exertions of the Dinapore officers were needed to allay the alarm, which is so often the precursor of revolt. This passed; but ere many days had lapsed, General Lloyd, in reply to a suggestion from Government, wrote to Lord Canning that the opium-godown at Patna was in a good state of defence, and that he did not believe that there was any danger of an attack upon it, as no treasure was kept there. But, he added, "the temptation to an outbreak consists in the presence in the Collector's cutcherry at Patna of

* Writing at the end of May, the commandant of one of the regiments—an excellent Sepoy officer—said: "I am very happy to inform you that the three Native regiments here display the best temper, and all duties are being regularly carried on—parades, drills, and target practice every morning. Not a murmur is heard about cartridges. All commanding officers and others are doing their best to keep matters right, and the real state of the case fully explained to the officers and men; and they are warned that the wild stories and lies purposely spread about by emissaries are only to alarm and disturb them. They have been told that if they can seize and give up any of these emissaries, they will be promoted and rewarded with a money present."

some twenty lakhs of rupees—money brought in 1857.
from Chuprah, and expected to arrive from Arrah, June.
under the escort of Captain Rattray's men, to-morrow morning.* The Treasury is under the charge of the Nujeebs, and a guard of Sikhs goes for its protection during the night. The money is to be sent to Calcutta by the first downward steamer. . . . I believe the worst feeling towards us prevails in Patna and in Behar generally—particularly among the Mahomedan population and the sect of Wahabees. As yet it is confined to words only; but a very little more excitement would cause it to show itself in deeds." The temptation, however, here anticipated had been resisted, and the Native regiments, all through the remaining weeks of June and the earlier part of the month of July, had gone about their accustomed duties without any outward manifestations of disloyalty. And General Lloyd had continued to report that he believed they would remain true to their salt, unless some fresh temptation should arise to elicit the momentary madness that had driven so many others to perdition.

It was not to be doubted, however, that, as time went on, there was, apart from these apprehensions of the sudden falling of a spark upon the combustible elements of Sepoy discontent, a not unreasonable cause of anxiety in the chronic state of fear into which the Native regiments had subsided, owing to reports industriously circulated among them that the river steamers passing upwards were crowded with large numbers of European troops, who would bring upon them swift destruction under cover of

* Rattray, with his Sikhs, reached Patna in the early morning of the 8th of June. Subsequent mention will be made of their excellent services.

1857. June. the darkness of the night. In vain their officers tried to reassure them. The panic grew. As had happened, and was yet to happen in other places, the strong instinct of self-preservation moved them to concert measures for their liberation from the toils which it was believed were closing around them. To allay these fears, orders were issued that each regiment should furnish a picket, to be posted at night in its Lines, ostensibly for the purpose of refusing ingress to mutineers or deserters from other regiments, and to seditious and intriguing persons of all kinds who might seek to corrupt them. This wise precaution was not without good results. It seemed for awhile to pacify the men. If it did not altogether restore confidence to them, it kept them quiet for awhile. And it was the desire of the General commanding to keep the Native regiments together at a time when the Government were straining every effort to send upwards, along the Grand Trunk Road, small detachments of Europeans in wheeled carriages; for an outbreak of the Native troops at Dinapore might have closed the road and delayed the advance of our reinforcements in the hour of our greatest need.

Excitement in the Patna Division. Meanwhile, irrespectively of all military disloyalty, there was increasing excitement in Behar. It has been shown in an earlier chapter that, some years before the general outbreak of mutiny in the ranks of the Bengal Army, there had been dangerous plots developed, if not originated, in Patna for the corruption of our Sepoy regiments, as the first step towards the subversion of British power in the East.* In no place were large and influential classes of the Native com-

* Vol. i., p. 304—309.

munity better prepared for a rising of the soldiery; and nowhere, when the crisis came, was there more of the excitement of ill-disguised sympathy. As a link between them there were the Police—the Nujeebs—a hybrid race, but a power in the State. The fusion of the three, whichsoever might be the prime mover of sedition, was dangerous in the extreme; and it was certain that an inert policy would not be a successful one. So already the civil authorities were striking heavy blows at incipient rebellion, and endeavouring to overawe the suspected classes by repressive measures, which engendered as much hatred as fear. 1857. June.

The chief civil officer of the division was Mr. William Tayler, of whom mention has already been made. A man of varied accomplishments and of an independent tone of thought and speech, he had studied the Native character, as only it can be rightly studied, with large-hearted toleration and catholicity of sentiment. Fully alive to the melancholy fact of the great gulf between the two races,* he had often dwelt, in his public correspondence, on the evils attending the self-imposed isolation of his countrymen, and the want of sympathy, and therefore the want of knowledge, in all that related to the feelings of the people, of a large majority of official and non-official William Tayler.

* Nothing can be better than the following, which I extracted some years ago from one of Mr. Tayler's official papers: "Separated as we necessarily are from the millions around us, by our habits and ideas, we are still further, and without the same necessity, isolated from their hearts by the utter absence of all individual feeling or sympathy. The great mass see or hear of functionary after functionary coming and going, and holding the destinies of the people in the hollow of their hands, but they seldom, perhaps never, know what it is to feel that the minds of their rulers have ever been directed to understand or sympathise with the great heart that is beating around them. The result is an utter absence of those ties between the governors and the governed, that unbought loyalty which is the strength of kings, and which, with all his faults, the Native of India is well capable of feeling."

1857. June. Englishmen in India. Nearly two years before the outbreak of the mutiny, he had reported to Government that, "owing to sundry causes, the minds of the people in these districts are at present in a very restless and disaffected state, and they have generally conceived the idea that there is an intention on the part of Government to commence and carry through a systematic interference with their religion, their caste, and their social customs." Utterances of this kind are never very palatable to Government; and Mr. Tayler was regarded in high places, if not actually as an alarmist, as a man who suffered his imagination to run away with him; and although it is impossible to govern well and wisely without it, nothing is more detestable to Government than imagination. So it happened that Mr. Tayler had fallen into disrepute with some above him, and had excited the resentments of some below him. He was a man of strong convictions, not chary of speech; and there was small chance at any time of a division under his charge subsiding into the drowsy, somnolent state which gives so little official trouble, and is therefore so greatly approved.

There was, a short time before the outburst of the revolt, one especial matter which had been a source of much conflict, and had resulted in the determination of the Lieutenant-Governor of Bengal to remove Mr. Tayler from the Patna Commissionership. It was a question of the establishment of an Industrial Institution, to be supported by the landholders of the several districts; and Mr. Halliday was of opinion that undue influence had been used to obtain the adhesion of the Zemindars to a scheme which they did not really approve. Into the merits of this question I do not purpose to enter. Mr. Tayler manfully declared that it appeared to him, after the storm of trouble had burst, to be so paltry a matter that it should be dismissed from the consideration of the local officers. But it is necessary to the right understanding of what follows that the general position of affairs, as thus described, should be known to the reader. It was an unfortunate circumstance that the Commissioner's authority should have been weakened by the notoriety of the displeasure of his Government. There were undoubtedly two parties in Patna; and a house divided against itself is always infirm. When hostile multitudes are swarming around us, nothing but the united action of such handfuls of Englishmen as we can muster to oppose them, can ever work out perfect deliverance. 1857. June.

Alarm in the districts.

The chief out-stations of the Patna Division were at Chuprah, Arrah, Mozufferpore, Gya, and Moteharee.* There resided the usual staff of administrators—judges, collectors, magistrates, and opium-agents—and under their charge were the gaols, and treasuries, and godowns, the repletion of which bespoke the activity wherewith they pursued their callings. The guardianship of these was intrusted to the Police. It would have been in favour of our people that no detachments of Sepoys were posted at these stations, if the Nujeebs had been trustworthy; but it was generally felt that their fidelity would not survive an outbreak of the soldiery, and they might, any day, following the suit of their military brethren, release the prisoners in the gaols, carry off the coin in the treasuries, and murder every Christian in the district. When, therefore, news came that Delhi

* The districts were Sarun, Shahabad, Tirhoot, Behar, and Chumparum. The civil head-quarters were at Patna, which gave its name also to a district.

1857. June. was in the hands of the insurgents, and no news came, after waiting awhile for it, that the English had recovered the city and crushed the short-lived power of the Mogul, there was considerable uneasiness in the minds of all the English inhabitants of Behar. At first, there was the comforting reflection to sustain them, that the Native gentry were on their side—that the influential Zemindars and others would place all their resources at the disposal of our people. This belief, however, soon passed away. It is curious to mark in the private or demi-official correspondence of the day, how, as time went on, the confidence entertained by our civil officers in the loyalty of the local gentry gradually waned and at last disappeared. The month of May had not come to a close before stories began to reach the Commissioner from different out-stations, showing how great was the mistrust that was beginning to overshadow the minds of our public functionaries. Just ten days after the outbreak at Meerut, one wrote to Mr. Tayler, saying: "A Bazaar report was abroad that the Persian Army was close to Lahore, and hourly expected, and that all was up with the British in India. This is enough to alarm the loyal, as well as to encourage the disaffected. There is another story that I heard privately, and some weight may be attached to it, namely, that Maun Singh, the outlaw of Oude, is in Nepaul, and has been down on our frontier making observations and arrangements; that he excited the sympathy of many in our provinces, and that our great Rajahs in those parts are not to be depended upon for a moment; that they encourage revolt, though not, perhaps, ready to join in it, unless an invading army should come. . . . . I know the Hutwah man has a *mooktear* at Lucknow. For what possible object? . . . . You may depend upon it that the cartridge question is all fudge. Some deeper scheme than that has been laid." Early in June, one of our magistrates wrote from Gya to the Secretary to the Bengal Government, saying: "I have reason to believe that the Mahomedans throughout this province are greatly disaffected; they are anxiously looking out for news from the North-West, exaggerating matters, and publishing *pro bono publico* all they hear. In Gya this feeling has shown itself to a great extent." And again, some days later: "My last mentioned state of feeling up to 11th. From that time the people have become much more disaffected. Reports were duly received that Budmashes and numbers of the Mahomedan population, in parties, were strolling about, poisoning the minds of their neighbours with wild stories of our reign having come to its conclusion, the massacre of the Europeans in the North-West, &c.; and in many other ways was the animus but too apparent, and excitement was thus shown to be at its highest pitch, bordering upon an outbreak. . . . . It is reported from several places in my jurisdiction that men are wandering about in the guise of Fakeers and tampering with the villagers." And on the same day, the chief civil officer of Chuprah wrote to the Commissioner: "There is no concealing the present condition of the Chuprah people, and it requires but the tidings of a disturbance at Dinapore to make the Mussulmans, aided by the Nujeebs, rise."*

1857. June.

* Another letter, written from Chuprah (May 25th), said: "I have, these last two days, been visited by numbers of the Natives, and I have been explaining the whole matter to them—impressing upon the wealthy men that the first thing the Sepoys did in Delhi was to loot every wealthy man. I also informed them that the regiments which were on their way to China would now probably pay Calcutta a visit, and that in a few days there would be a European force there sufficient to conquer the

1857. June. Alarm at Patna. At the chief station of Patna there was the greatest alarm of all. It was not unreasonably anticipated that if the Dinapore regiments should revolt, they would pour themselves upon Patna with a great destruction of property and of life. At the end of

June 7. the first week of June the chronic alarm of the Europeans culminated in an acute paroxysm of panic. A report had arrived from Dinapore that the Sepoys were expected to mutiny in the course of the night, Then our people asked what was to be done? Mr. Tayler, to whom all resorted for guidance in this emergency, counselled concentration in his own house. And in a little while the spacious residence of the Commissioner and his family was gorged to repletion.* The moon rose that night on a scene of strange bewilderment and confusion. Outside the house, a large body of Nujeebs, in their dark-green dresses, were drawn up under their English chief;† and a guard, from Holmes's Irregulars, warlike and picturesque, was mounted at the chief entrance.‡

whole of India over again." . . . . "There are some disaffected people at work, and I only wish that I could get hold of them. I have my eye upon one or two; but they seem to be raking up all the old causes of complaint. Twice to-day I have been asked why the Government wish to cut off the prisoners' hair and beards, and though I explained to them that the Mussulman's beard was only to be clipped, and that four fingers' breadth was to be left, they were not satisfied, and said, 'One day it will be four, the next two fingers, and then it will be cut off altogether.'"

* "My wife and myself were in a curricle when we received the news; we drove off at once to the houses of the nearest residents and informed them quietly of the plan decided upon, begging them to come over without delay, bag and baggage, to the rendezvous; messengers were at the same time despatched to warn the more distant residents. In less than an hour almost every man, woman, and child (excepting some few who lived close to the opium-godown and found refuge there) were hurrying helter-skelter to our house, followed by a heavy phalanx of beds, clothes, pillows, mattresses, and other domestic impedimenta."—*Tayler's Patna Crisis.*

† Major Nation—whence they came, in the language of the province, to be called the National Guard.

‡ The head-quarters of Holmes's regiment was at Segowlie. An account of this corps will be found in subsequent pages of the narrative.

Inside, our people, men, women, and children, were huddling together, some confident and some scared. The usual strong contrasts that a season of danger commonly evokes were strikingly developed by the crisis. Some looked to the locks of their guns or felt the edges of their swords; some resigned themselves tranquilly to their fate. Some groaned in spirit; some laughed regardless of their doom. And whilst some elders were examining the ladders which led to the roof of the house, and preparing themselves for a sudden ascent, young men and maidens, in the Commissioner's garden, could not resist a little moonlit flirtation, although it might be their last.* 1857. June.

But there was no need of the ladders—no use for the guns. As the night advanced, the danger seemed to thicken. Letters from Dinapore had been received by the Nujeebs, saying that the Sepoy regiments were all of one mind, that they were coming down upon Patna, and that if the Police battalions would join them, success would be assured. With the exception of a few troopers from Segowlie, the Nujeebs were the sole protection of our people. The gloom, therefore, grew darker and denser. But never were the scriptural words, "Heaviness may endure for a night, but joy cometh in the morning," more signally verified than in this Patna crisis. There was hourly expectation of the arrival of Captain Rattray's well-known and much-trusted regiment of Sikh Irregulars. The Commissioner had already sent urgent missives to Rattray to hasten his advance, and on that very

* "On the garden side, our daughters, with some other girls and the juveniles among the gentlemen, in spite of the hubbub and ignorant of the real danger, were enjoying the open walks and moonlit grass of the garden, and somewhat scandalised the more nervous portion of the assemblage by their laughter and merriment. My wife was, as is her wont, engaged in ministering to the comfort of all who had taken shelter in the house."—*Tayler's Patna Crisis.*

1857. June.

afternoon he had despatched fresh messengers, in the light-wheeled carriages of the country, to urge and to assist the rapid progress of the regiment. And when about the hour of dawn, Rattray himself, with his picturesque accoutrements, his high jack-boots, and his long sword, clanked into the Commissioner's house, and announced that his men were behind him, there was a general feeling of deliverance. But in fact there was no danger from which the European community of Patna were to be delivered. The Dinapore regiments did not rise; and next morning the strange assembly of people that had been gathered together in the Commissioner's house returned, safe and hopeful, to their several homes.

Repressive measures.

There was not a man in the country more disposed towards strenuous action than Mr. William Tayler. The instructions which he issued to his subordinates all through the months of June and July were of the most encouraging and assuring kind. He exhorted all men to put on a bold front, to maintain their posts, and to crush all incipient sedition with the strong arm of authority. It was in these words that he wrote to the chief civil officer of Tirhoot, and all his directions to others were in the same strain: "I don't think that you are in danger. The Sepoys, if they rose, would not go so far out of their way. Your own Budmashes, therefore, are all you have to fear. If you look sharp and raise your extra Police—keep your Sowars in hand—stir up your Darogah—tell that little Rajah to send you men in different parts to help you—keep a look-out at the ghauts, and at the same time quietly arrange for a place of rendezvous in case of real danger, where you may meet, all will go right. . . . . Make everybody show a good face—be plucky, and snub any fellows who are impudent. If any people talk sedition, threaten them with a rope, and keep a look-out on the Nujeebs. Try and form without any fuss a body of volunteers, mounted gentlemen, so that in case of any extremity they might all meet and pitch into any blackguards. If anything really bad were to happen, the branch volunteers should come into Patna and join the main body, and we would keep the province till assistance should come. These are only probabilities, so don't tell people they are anticipated. The word for Tirhoot just now is 'All serene.'"* And it was, doubtless, the true policy to betray no fear, but to be thoroughly awake to and prepared for all possibilities of surrounding danger. 1857. June 14.

I say it reluctantly—but I fear that it is to be said most truthfully—that all the Englishmen in the Patna Division were not of the same high courage as Mr. William Tayler himself. There had been sudden alarms and flights from some out-stations, and bewildered rushings into Dinapore. "Such a cowardly panic-struck set as have rushed in here yesterday and to-day I never saw," wrote General Lloyd to the Commissioner on the 9th of June. And the Commissioner himself had been compelled to rebuke some, who had shown too great an alacrity to leave their posts without sufficient reason for running away. But it must in all fairness be conceded, that there were some exceptional grounds of apprehension on the part of the European residents in Behar. Already, in general terms, has mention been made of these. The sources of danger were of two kinds—external and internal—military and civil. Not only

* M.S. Records.

1857. June.

was it clear that into the Patna Division would pour all the Sepoy deserters and refugees from the Lower Provinces, but that large numbers of the influential local gentry were disaffected to the core, and were watching the movements of the soldiery with grateful anticipations of a time of trouble to the English. The fact that Sepoys of nine different regiments were known to have fought against us in Shahabad, afterwards afforded substantial proof of the former. The plots which were actually discovered, and the treasonable correspondence which was intercepted at the time, left no doubt of the latter; and if any had remained, subsequent revelations would have thoroughly dispersed it. Apart from the indigenous sedition—the sedition of "fanaticism" as it has been called (for a sincere belief in other creeds than our own is always fanaticism in the Christian vocabulary)—there were foreign influences at work to stimulate the Mussulman inhabitants of Patna and the neighbourhood to rise, whenever a fitting opportunity should present itself, against the British Government. Foremost among these were the sinister influences that issued from Lucknow. The annexation of that country had sent to Patna a small Oude colony with all kinds of embittered resentments against the British Government, and there was an active correspondence continually going on between the Mahomedans of the two great cities; whilst in the districts intrigue was incessantly at work to weaken, and eventually to overthrow, the hateful power of the Feringhees.

Arrest of Waris Ali.

One incident deserves special narration. About the end of the third week of June, intelligence reached the authorities of Tirhoot that one of their Jemadars of Police, Waris Ali by name, said to have been of the blood-royal of Delhi, was in treasonable correspondence with some disaffected Mahomedans of Patna. The Magistrate, seeing at once the necessity of immediately arresting this man, who was at a police-station in the interior of the district, asked Mr. William Robertson, a young civilian of two or three years' standing, if he would undertake the work. Robertson, a fine, high-spirited youth, who seems at all times to have been cheery and confident, and ripe for action, accepted the offered duty with alacrity; and it was agreed that four Englishmen of the district should be selected to share the dangers and the honours of the enterprise. The gentlemen finally selected were Messrs. Urquhart, Baldwin, Holloway, and Pratt, indigo-planters of the neighbourhood, "all of them," as Mr. Robertson wrote, "steady, cool chaps, and yet fighting men." All arrangements made, this little party of five, well-mounted and well-armed, rode for Mr. Baldwin's factory, some three miles from the police-station, where they dined and matured their plans; and before daybreak started, in high spirits, for the Jemadar's quarters. Coming suddenly upon him, they found Waris Ali in the act of writing a treasonable letter to one Ali Kureem, a Mahomedan of wealth and influence, notoriously disaffected, who was then living upon the road between Patna and Gya. The culprit was seized with all his correspondence. He had evidently girded up his loins for immediate flight; and if William Robertson had swooped down upon him an hour later, the prey would have been lost. His horse—a remarkably fine one—stood saddled in the stable, with holsters at the pommel. Carts, already laden for a journey, with the draught cattle beside them, were standing in front of the house. Every article of furniture, down to the cook-

1857. June.

1857. June.

ing pots and pans, were heaped up ready for departure. There was no doubt of the man's guilt. Taken *flagrante delicto*, he resigned himself to his fate. He was carried a prisoner to the station, and soon afterwards he was hanged. It is said that at the foot of the gallows he cried aloud, "If there is any friend of the King of Delhi here, let him come and help me."

Flight of Ali Kureem.

The correspondence found in the house of Waris Ali clearly implicated Ali Kureem. It was sent to the Commissioner, who determined to apprehend this man. A party of Sikhs, with ten mounted troopers, under Captain Rattray, and accompanied by Mr. John M. Lowis, the Magistrate, were despatched to his house; but either warned of the movements of the English, or scared by the capture of his friend, Ali Kureem had placed himself on the back of an elephant and taken flight. What now was to be done? The answer was obvious. The troopers, with one of the English officers at their head, might have gone in pursuit and captured him. But in an evil hour, Mr. Lowis suffered himself to be persuaded by his Nazir, of whose treachery there was afterwards little doubt, not to take the horsemen with him. So he started in a wheeled carriage ill-suited to rapid travelling, and when Ali Kureem caught sight of his pursuers he astutely forsook the open road and struck across the fields, where the elephant made good progress but the ecka could not follow. On this, Lowis, still eager in the chase, left the carriage and followed on foot. But everything was against him. The sympathies of the people were clearly on the side of the fugitive.* They rendered the English officer no assistance; but

* Mr. Tayler ("The Patna Crisis") says: "The villages not only gave him no assistance, but actually removed a tattoo (pony) that he had secured."

on the other hand actively impeded the pursuit. So next day he returned, "wearied and disheartened," leaving his Native assistant to follow up the chase. But the heart of the Nazir was with the enemies of the Nazarene, and the fugitive escaped. A reward of five thousand rupees was afterwards offered for Ali Kureem's head. 1857. June.

Meanwhile a crisis was approaching in the city of Patna itself. Profoundly mistrustful of the population of that great city, especially of its Wahabee inhabitants, some of whom were men of wealth and influence, Commissioner Tayler had from the first endeavoured to overawe the disaffected by vigorous measures, only to be justified by the extremity of the danger to be combated. The practice which he pursued was described in the rough vernacular of the day, as "hanging right and left." There was some exaggeration in this; but the policy was, doubtless, one of intimidation, and the process of intimidation necessarily involved a somewhat slender regard for proofs. Of calm judicial investigation there could be none at such a time. To strike promptly was to strike successfully; and to be suspected was often to be condemned. Arrest followed arrest. A great panic arose among the Mahomedans of Patna. No one knew whose turn would come next, or what form the offensive movements of English authority would take. The Commissioner was equally courageous and adroit. Though he fought openly and struck boldly, he did not despise the aid of stratagem. One story, of the arrest of some of the principal Wahabee suspects, is worthy of narration. Excitement in the city.

There were three Moulavees in the city, believed to exercise, by means of their reputed saintliness, great influence over many of the townspeople. They Arrest of the Moulavees.

1857. June. were described by Mr. Tayler as "little, shrivelled, skin-dried men, of contemptible appearance and plain manners," but with "a large body of followers, who would sacrifice everything at their beck." There was reason to believe that these men were busily intriguing against us. So Tayler determined to arrest them. "I felt sure," he wrote afterwards, "that with their necks at my disposal, and their persons under the drawn sabres of the Sikhs, not one genuine Wahabee in the district dare stir a finger." It was obviously, however, a thing to be done as quietly as possible. A violent seizure of these holy men in the heart of the city might have precipitated an outbreak, which would have had inconvenient results. So the Commissioner bethought himself of a device whereby this danger might be avoided. He sent a Circular to all the most respectable Natives of the city inviting them to visit him on the following day, "for consultation on the state of affairs." At the appointed time they assembled in considerable numbers, and the three Moulavees were among them. When they were seated around Mr. Tayler's long dining-table, the Commissioner with his Civil Staff entered the room. With them also entered Major Nation, Chief of the Police, Captain Rattray, of the Sikh Regiment, and Soubahdar Hedayat Ali, of the same corps. The long swords of the two last in their steel scabbards clanked ominously on the floor, as they took their seats near the little Moulavees. The performance then commenced. There was some talk about the troubled times and the measures to be most expediently adopted for the safety and welfare of all classes of the community. When sufficient time had been given to the decencies of the sham, the Native gentlemen were formally dismissed; but, as the party was breaking up, the Moulavees were requested to remain, as the Commissioner had a few private words to say to them. 1857. June.

So the little shrivelled men, who had been sitting very uncomfortably during the conference, with their legs tucked up on Tayler Sahib's chairs, and who had clearly foreseen what was coming, resigned themselves to their fate. The Commissioner told them that he considered it his duty, in the interests of the public safety, to keep them under arrest until the coming of more quiet times. No resistance was attempted or thought of for a moment. There was not even a word of complaint. With the quiet dignity habitual to them, they courteously addressed the British Commissioner, saying, "Great is your Excellency's kindness—great your wisdom. What you order is best for your slaves. So shall our enemies be unable to bring false charges against us!" To this the Commissioner responded with equal courtesy. Then, "smiles and salutations" having been exchanged, the wretched men, bearing up bravely under their lot, were escorted to their palanquins, and under a guard of Sikhs conveyed to the Circuit-house, not without some apprehension of being hanged.

"To this day," wrote Mr. Tayler, a year afterwards, "I look at the detention of these men as one of the most successful strokes of policy which I was able to carry into execution." But it can hardly escape the consideration of any candid mind that what is thus regarded as a successful stroke of policy, when executed by Englishmen against Mahomedans, would, if Englishmen had been the victims of it, have been described by another name. To invite men to a friendly conference, and when actually the

1857. June. guests of a British officer, to seize their persons, is not only very like treachery, but is treachery itself. If these little shrivelled men had resisted, they would, perhaps, have been cut down; and if they had been, a Mahomedan historian would, doubtless, have described the successful policy of Commissioner Tayler in language similar to that in which I described the treacherous assassination of Sir William Macnaghten by Sirdar Mahomed Akbar Khan. The exigencies of a great crisis justify exceptional acts in the interests of the national safety; but I do not know any excuses that may be pleaded or arguments that may be advanced by a British officer in such a case, that might not, and doubtless have been pleaded and advanced, by Native chiefs in like circumstances, and freely echoed by the popular voice.

July 3. The rising in the city. But, whatsoever other successes this stroke of policy may have wrought, the tranquilisation of Patna was not one of them. Following closely upon the arrest of the Moulavees, an attempt was made to disarm the city of Patna. Like all attempts of the same kind, it was only partially successful. There was a limited surrender of offensive weapons; but many more were concealed. And the fanatical hatred of the Mahomedan population seems to have been increased by these acts. On the evening of the 3rd of July they rose. A large body of Mahomedans, bearing aloft the green flag, and summoning others to join them by the beating of drums, marched through the streets of the city and attacked the house of a Roman Catholic priest. The Sikhs were at once ordered out, and an express was sent to Dinapore for European troops. Meanwhile, Dr. Lyall, with praiseworthy but incautious zeal, had mounted his horse and ridden down to the scene of tumult, thinking by his influence to pacify the crowd. He had scarcely appeared on the scene when he was shot dead. But when Rattray with his men came down upon them, the victory of the mob was at an end. Hating with a bitter hatred these Mahomedans, they struck out with hearty goodwill. The rioters were soon dispersed, and quietude was restored to the city.

1857. July.

Execution of Peer Ali.

A number of the most notorious malcontents were arrested in the course of the next few days. Among these was one Peer Ali—a Mahomedan bookseller, whose professional acquaintance with the amenities of literature may have sharpened his intellect, though it had by no means mollified his manners. He was brave and unscrupulous, and he hated the English. He had been a long time plotting against us, now in communication with Delhi, now with Lucknow—mainly, indeed, with the latter city, of which he was a Native. When his house was searched much treasonable correspondence was found in it. One document said: "The state of affairs at Patna is as follows. Some respectable persons of the city are in prison, and the subjects are all weary and disgusted with the tyranny and oppression exercised by Government, whom they all curse. May God hear the prayers of the oppressed very soon!" It was generally said that this man had shot down Dr. Lyall with his own hand. He was tried and sentenced to death. Brought before the Commissioner and other English gentlemen, "heavily fettered, his soiled garments stained deeply with blood from a wound in his side," he was asked whether he had any information to give that might induce the Government to spare his life. With dignified composure, such as our own people did not always maintain under excit-

1857. July. ing circumstances, he confronted his questioners, and replied: "There are some cases in which it is good to save life—others in which it is better to lose it." He denounced the oppression of the English, especially of the Commissioner, and added, "You may hang me, or such as me, every day, but thousands will rise in my place, and your object will never be gained." After some further conversation, throughout which, except when he spoke of his children, he betrayed no emotion, Peer Ali was taken out to execution. He salaamed respectfully to the Commissioner, and went forth "unmoved and unconcerned." He was hanged. His house was razed to the ground, and his property was confiscated.

Arrest of Lootf Ali Khan.

But Peer Ali was not a rich man. And Commissioner Tayler was thoroughly convinced by "the fact that men had been kept for months on pay regularly distributed, under a conditional compact to come forward when called for," that "some wealthy party was at the bottom of the intrigues, that were shown to have been carried on for months." He had no difficulty in naming the man. There was one Lootf Ali Khan, a wealthy banker, against whom there was a strong suspicion by no means confined to the Commissioner. One of the men arrested and executed for the outrage which had resulted in the death of Dr. Lyall, was this man's Jemadar. He was known to have harboured a Sepoy of the Thirty-seventh Regiment that had revolted at Benares; and he was suspected of being in communication with Sepoy regiments, and to have supplied, for rebellious purposes, the money distributed by Peer Ali and others. When the Magistrate went to the banker's residence in the city, accom-

July 5.

panied by a guard of Sikhs under an English officer, to arrest him, Lootf Ali came forth, and being informed that he was to accompany the Magistrate to the Commissioner's house, blandly assented, and at once ordered his carriage to be brought round. After the manner of his tribe, the coachman was absent when he was called for; so Lootf Ali, having requested the English gentlemen to take their seats in the carriage, mounted the box and drove his captors to Mr. Tayler's door—a manner of arrest, perhaps, unprecedented in the annals of police.* The banker was formally tried by Mr. Farquharson, the Judge; but the evidence adduced was insufficient to convict him, and in due course he was released.† If the majority of English residents were not surprised, they were exasperated and alarmed by the acquittal.‡ 1857. July.

* As this statement has been questioned, upon high authority, I give the following confirmatory passage from Mr. Lowis's official report: "One of the chief events to be noted is the capture of Synd Lootf Ali Khan, a wealthy banker, whom I, at the request of the Commissioner, Mr. W. Tayler, arrested on the night of the 5th instant. I was accompanied by Lieutenant Campbell with a guard of Sikhs, who surrounded the house, but the precaution was needless, as there was no show of resistance or attempt at escape. He at once came out to meet me, and when informed that he had been summoned by the Commissioner, ordered his carriage, and, as the coachman was not forthcoming, got himself on the box, and drove us to Mr. Tayler's house."

† The Sepoy whom he had harboured was hanged—as well as (as stated in the text) Lootf Ali's servant, who was known to have taken an active part in the murder of Dr. Lyall.

‡ One letter before me, after stating what had been proved against Lootf Ali, says: "We" (the residents at Patna) "knew all this, which was afterwards proved upon his trial, and doubted not of his fate; but to our astonishment and mortification and disgrace, he was acquitted and borne away from court in triumph by his supporters. This was sufficiently alarming, one would suppose, to the supporters of order; but this was not the climax. A few days after his release, the man who, with hardly one exception, the Europeans of Patna and Dinapore considered a rebel of the blackest dye, was received with all the honours due to a highly faithful and meritorious subject by his late acquitting judge, in his then merely temporary position of Acting Commissioner. Could any act of a single man have alienated me from the allegiance due to our Government, this would have done it. I would rather we had been all driven from house and home by an open rebellion in Patna than that this moral victory should have been yielded."—*MS. Correspondence.*

1857. July. Stories were freely circulated to the effect that the great wealth of Lootf Ali had carried him triumphantly through the ordeal. It was said that large sums of money had been remitted to Calcutta for the purpose of working out his deliverance. That deliverance, when it came, was quite an ovation. The pæans of party were resonant from Calcutta to Dinapore. The great Mahomedan capitalist, who, a little time before, had been suspected of holding large numbers of armed men in his pay to exterminate the Nazarene, was now welcomed and consoled as a martyr to the prejudice of an individual. Received with favour by some of the Government officers, and invited to their houses—an act of toleration only too rare in official circles—he could afford to laugh at the malice of his enemies, and so he expanded into greater exuberance than before. As to the guilt or innocence of the man, it still remains a subject of controversy; but it is right that history should give him the benefit of the popular doubt, and, still more, the benefit of the judicial acquittal. It is to be remembered that in those days, not only in the Patna Division, but throughout the whole country, a strong anti-Mahomedan feeling pervaded the minds of the English communities; and that many fell under suspicion of complicity in treasonable designs upon evidence far more slender than that on which the Patna banker was arrested. If we cannot blame Judge Farquharson for acquitting him, it is equally certain that we must not condemn Commissioner Tayler for committing him.

After the anti-Mahomedan demonstrations above recorded, there was, as the month of July wore to a close, a season of comparative quietude at Patna; and outwardly the Sepoy regiments at Dinapore main-

1857. July.

tained the order and discipline habitual to them in the most tranquil times. But ever was flowing on an undercurrent of disaffection and intrigue in the towns and through the districts; and, as weeks passed, and still no tidings came of the recovery of Delhi—but instead of this intelligence so eagerly looked for and confidently expected by the English, fresh stories of defeat and disaster fatal to the British rule came huddling on each other—when it was known that Cawnpore had fallen, with a great massacre of Christian people, that Lucknow, the only spot in Oude still held by us, was beleaguered, that Agra was in peril, and nearly all parts of the North-Western Provinces in a great blaze of rebellion—when all these things were known, and many wild exaggerations were associated with these truthful reports in the mouths of the inhabitants of Behar, it became more and more apparent that the thoughts of the Native gentry were turning, with vague expectancy, to a coming time, when they would recover their ancient dignities and privileges; whilst men of less note were summing up the offences committed by the English against Mahomedans and Hindoos, and prophesying the approach of a day of retribution.

Mutiny of the Sepoy regiments.

In this excited state of the public mind, when all were watching with eager interest the movements of the soldiery at the Dinapore Head-Quarters, and still they gave no sign of open mutiny, the long-anticipated crisis was evolved in a most unexpected manner. The cry for the disarming of the Dinapore regiments had been resisted; but it had not been stilled. An advantageous opportunity for the successful accomplishment of this design was presented in the middle of July by the arrival at Calcutta of the Fifth Fusiliers, which was to be sent up at once to recruit General

1857. July. Havelock. The detention of this regiment would have been a great evil. But the Calcutta Government, urged onwards by the importunities of the commercial communities, consented to allow its stoppage for a little space at Dinapore, just, in the language of the day, "to polish off the Sepoys," in conjunction with its brethren of the Tenth, and then to pass on to its destination. So, on the 15th of July, Sir Patrick Grant wrote confidentially to General Lloyd, saying: "The first detachment of Her Majesty's Fifth Fusiliers left Chinsurah this morning on flats towed by steamers in progress towards Benares, and the remaining portions of the regiment will follow by the same means of transit to-morrow and Friday. If, when the regiment reaches Dinapore, you see reason to distrust the Native troops, and you entertain an opinion that it is desirable to disarm them, you are at liberty to disembark the Fifth Fusiliers to assist you in this object; but it is imperatively necessary that the detention of the regiment should be limited to the shortest possible period. If you decide on disarming, it should extend to all three regiments, and it should be carefully explained that it is merely a measure of precaution to save the well-disposed from being led to commit themselves by the evil machinations of designing scoundrels, some few of whom are always to be found in even the best regiment. If resistance to authority is exhibited, the most prompt and decided measures for its instant suppression should be adopted." Although these instructions were very clear, they left, to a certain extent, the responsibility in the hands of General Lloyd; and General Lloyd was one of those who shrunk from responsibility. And for some days after the receipt of this letter he was minded to do nothing.

But on the 24th of July, in an evil hour, General Lloyd, feebly halting between two opinions, bethought himself of a compromise. Still reluctant to disarm the regiments, yet unwilling to turn a deaf ear to the increasing implorations and remonstrances of the Europeans of Bengal, now at last, after long delay, supported by Government, he fell back upon the fatal folly of a half-measure. There was nothing to command success, in those days, that had not inscribed upon it the great watchword of "Thorough." But General Lloyd did not see clearly that to give to his men all his confidence or none—to do the thing all in all or not at all—was the only way to success. He shrunk from the decided act of taking away from his men their muskets and their pouches. But he thought that he might render their possession harmless by depriving the regiments of percussion-caps. So taking advantage of the arrival of two companies of the Thirty-seventh Foot on the 24th of July, he ordered a parade of the Europeans for the following morning, and directed arrangements to be made for carting away all the caps in the magazines.* 1857. July.

At the appointed time the parade was held. The European troops and the Artillery were drawn up in the great barrack-square; and two bullock carts were July 25.

* These companies had come round from Ceylon to Calcutta. Lord Canning had written urgently to Sir Henry Ward (sending his letter by Major Bazeley on a special steamer) to despatch the whole of the Thirty-seventh; but both the Governor and the Commander-in-Chief of the colony had demurred to the proposal thus to strip the island of all European defence. "I entirely agreed," wrote Sir Henry Ward, "with Major-General Lockyer's view that nothing would justify us in parting with the whole of the Thirty-seventh Regiment, and in thus placing the colony at the mercy of a regiment of Malays and Sepoys, who may, I think, be relied upon as against the Natives, if kept in check by a proper admixture of the European element, but who may also, though all now appears to be gained, be brought under those mysterious influences which have worked so fatally upon the Bengal Army."—*MS. Correspondence.*

1857. July 25. sent to the magazines to bring the percussion-caps to the English quarters. Between the magazines and the square were the Sepoy Lines—so the laden carts, which told the story of the present disgrace, and, perhaps, the coming destruction of the Native regiments, had to pass beneath their eyes. As they crossed the Lines, there was a great commotion among the Sepoys of the Seventh and Eighth Regiments; but the Fortieth appears to have been quiescent on the side of mutiny, if not active on that of "order and discipline."* The Seventh, who were being paraded for guard at the time, were the most tumultuous. They are said to have cried out for the murder of the Sahibs and the rescue of the ammunition. But their officers went among them and pacified them; and the danger for the moment was tided over.† The two cart-loads of percussion-caps were stored away under charge of the Europeans. The officers went home to their breakfasts, and the General issued some supplementary orders to his Staff, of such small importance he thought, as not to require that he should see them executed himself.

* General Lloyd says: "The Fortieth Native Infantry made a decided demonstration towards the cause of order and discipline, being ready to oppose any attempt to rescue the caps." Colonel Cumberlege, who commanded the Fortieth, says: "About six A.M. on the 25th of July, 1857, the Fortieth Regiment had just been dismissed from parade, when a cart containing percussion-caps for the three regiments, taken from the magazines, passed along the road in front of our parade-ground; an angry buzz of voices had arisen amongst the men in the lines on our right, and some of the men of the Seventh Regiment Native Infantry were rushing in a disturbed and excited manner, and some tried to make across the corner of our parade to intercept the carts. In this they were most decidedly opposed and turned back by the men of our grenadiers and right wing—our men meanwhile keeping perfectly quiet and orderly."—*Parliamentary Papers.*

† In the official statement of Brevet-Colonel Templer (*Parliamentary Papers*) there is no mention of these threats. The colonel says, "The Seventh Regiment under my command, for the first time showed a mutinous spirit to exist in some of the men on the morning of the 25th of July, 1857, by the regimental guards (at guard-mounting) dispersing, instead of obeying the orders of the officer of the day to wheel into column."

The supplementary orders related to the percussion-caps which were already in the possession of the Sepoys—those which had been served out to them for immediate use, together with the corresponding rounds of ball-cartridge. Had there been no signs of disaffection in the early morning, these few caps might have been left with the men, and fired away, in course of ordinary duty, without exciting suspicion; but the bearing of the Sepoys rendered it expedient that prompter action should be taken. So a parade was ordered at noon, at which it was to be explained by the Native officers to their several companies that the measure then ordered was "merely one of precaution to save the well-disposed from being led away to commit themselves by the evil machinations of designing scoundrels"*—and then the caps were to be collected. It was easier, however, to empty out the magazines than to take this little residue out of the clutches of an excited soldiery.

1857. July 25.

A little after the hour of noon the regimental parades were held. The soothing explanations were given. But when the time came for them to surrender their caps, the Seventh and Eighth Regiments broke out into open mutiny. Rushing towards the bells-of-arms they seized their muskets and fired at all the Europeans they could see. They took their regimental colours and their regimental treasure, and prepared themselves for flight. The Fortieth, however, hesitated. There was still some sense of duty left in them. The Native officers and non-commissioned officers, and some of the Sepoys, formed and marched into the square with their colours and treasure, intending to defend them; and it is possible that the whole regiment might have stood fast; but in a critical moment of doubt and perplexity

* Regimental Orders of the Seventh Native Infantry, July 25, 1857.

1857. July 25. some Europeans of the Tenth fired upon them from the roof of the Hospital, and panic completed what disaffection had only half done. So the three regiments went off together *en masse*—taking their arms and accoutrements, but not their uniforms, with them. And the Commander of the English forces put himself on board a steam-boat in the river.

How it happened that, at such a time, the General could have abandoned his proper post it is not easy to explain. He was old and infirm. He was grievously afflicted with the gout. He could not walk. He could not ride. But he could sit upon the deck of a steamer, and there dimly survey the operations on the shore. Perhaps the feeling of thorough helplessness reconciled him to a desertion which could not be regarded as otherwise than discreditable. Had he confessed his physical inability to cope with the crisis, and made over the command to the officer next in seniority, there would have been a far better result. But the crisis had arrived at Dinapore; and there was no responsible officer on the spot to confront it.*

* It is right that General Lloyd's own words should be quoted. The following is from a letter written to his brother and published in a London newspaper: "I had no horse in cantonments. My stable was two miles distant, and being unable at the time to walk far or much, I thought I should be most useful on board the steamer with guns and riflemen, in which I proceeded along the rear of the Native lines—the river being only two hundred yards, or thereabouts, distant from the right of the advancing column of guns and Europeans, and expecting to get some shots at the Sepoys on shore or escaping by the river. Considering that I had fully previously given instructions for the attack and pursuit of the Sepoys by the guns and Her Majesty's Tenth, under their respective commanding officers, I left it to them to follow up the mutineers by land." The letter from which this passage is quoted will be found complete in the Appendix. There is no incident detailed in this volume regarding which I have had more travail in elucidating the truth than this story of the Dinapore mutiny. I had been led to believe by previous published statements that General Lloyd went on board the steamer *before* the regiments had mutinied. His own statement, however, distinctly refutes this—whether to his advantage or not I leave the reader to determine. I confess that his apology appears to me to be altogether unsatisfactory.

1857. July 25. Flight of the Sepoys.

It had been supposed that in any emergency of this kind the European force at Dinapore would have been more than strong enough to turn a mutiny of the Native regiments into something like a massacre of insurgents. There was the Tenth Foot, less two companies; and there was a battery of Foot Artillery, but wanting some of its guns and gunners, which had been sent to Benares; and there were two companies of the Thirty-seventh Foot. The assembly was sounded in the barrack-square, and the English Infantry and Artillery were mustered under their commandants, Fenwick and Huyshe. But the Sepoys' power of flight was greater than our soldiers' power of pursuit. The state of the country was in favour of the Natives. The parade-grounds were mostly under water, and the country beyond was a great swamp. The Sepoys in their scanty undress, literally with their "loins girt about for flight," traversed easily the familiar morasses. But our Infantry floundered in them, and our Artillery stuck fast. Both fired when it was too late at "impossible distances,"* and the Sepoys made good their escape almost to a man. Full notice had been given to them, and they had wisely spent the morning in making their preparations for a triumphant exodus, whilst the Europeans made only a feeble effort at pursuit; and as they could not overtake the fugitives, set fire to their huts and halted for further orders. The General was missing. No one liked to take the responsibility upon himself; no one, perhaps, knew what was to be done. The emergency that had now come upon our people had been anticipated for months, and yet when it came no one seems to have had any conception of the way in which it was to be met.

* These are General Lloyd's words.

1857. July 25. It was not so with the Sepoys. Some few made the mistake of taking to the Ganges, where their boats were fired into and run down by the steamer, and some of their inmates shot or drowned. But the majority hastened to the river Soane, which skirts the south-east boundary of the district of Shahabad, dividing it, for some fifteen miles, from the Patna district, and emptying itself into the Ganges about ten miles south of Dinapore. It was the object of the mutineers to enter this district of Shahabad, from which it is said that the Dinapore regiments had been largely recruited.* On the banks of the river, they had it all to themselves. It was not without some trepidation that they looked at the waters swollen by a month's rain, and thought that it would go hard with them if the English should arouse themselves into aught approaching the activity of pursuit. But any apprehensions which they may have entertained were shown to be groundless. There was not a white man on their track. Everything, indeed, was in their favour. They had friends before them; and no enemies behind. All that they wanted was a little time; and the complacency of the military authorities at Dinapore afforded them even more than they required. So they crossed the river with as much ease and comfort as they could desire, some in boats and some by the public ferry; and then they set their faces towards Arrah, the official capital of Shahabad.

* Mr. Trevelyan, in his graphic account of the defence of Arrah, relates that "the men were all drawn from the notoriously turbulent district of Shahabad, of which Arrah is the official capital, and were united by the bond of an undefined allegiance to Kower Singh, who was recognised as chieftain by the Rajpoots or soldier-caste of that region." This, perhaps, may be a little too broadly stated; but it is not to be doubted that a large number of Rajpoot Sepoys were drawn from Shahabad. If the Dinapore regiments contained an exceptional number of these recruits, it was a grievous mistake to post them at Dinapore at all—still more grievous not to watch them more closely.

There was nothing there to oppose the insurgent Sepoys but the pluck of a few English civilians—public functionaries, indigo-planters, and railway engineers, and a handful of Sikh mercenaries, who might or might not be faithful to their employers. On the side of the Sepoys there was a friendly country, auxiliaries from other mutinous regiments flocking to meet them, and, more than all, that which had so often been wanting to give due effect to the efforts of the mutineers—a leader ready to place himself at their head. He was an old man. The burden of some fourscore years was upon him; but he had retained some remnant of the energy of his younger days. His name was Kower Singh. He was of Rajpoot stock; and he was, or he had once been, the owner of great estates. It was said that the revenue systems of the English, the tendencies of which were so much towards the Dead Level, had greatly impoverished him; but, if it were so, his influence in the district had survived his wealth, and he was still a power in Shahabad. The story ran that he had been for weeks past maturing his plans to cast in his lot with the rebellious Sepoys—that he had intrigued largely with the mutinous regiments of the Lower Provinces—and that he had even been in communication with the Nana Sahib. It is not easy to ascertain the exact amount of truth in these contemporary stories. The popular voice of the English at the time proclaimed him a miscreant. The usual strong colours, with which we are wont to daub our enemies, especially when they are successful, were freely used in our portraiture of this man. But there was afterwards, as often happens in such cases, a reaction of sentiment; and he grew into a veteran warrior; a hero and a deliverer;

1857. July. Kower Singh

1857. July. rising from a sick-bed, forgetful of his infirmities, regardless of the approaches of death; eager to redress the wrongs of his countrymen and to smite the persecutors of his race; arming himself for the strife and going forth to the battle.

But the truth lay midway between these two extremes; and the story of Kower Singh must be told in less ambitious language. A little while before the Dinapore revolt, the old Baboo had been held in high esteem for his loyalty by the Patna Commissioner. On the 14th of June, Mr. Tayler had written to Government, saying: "Many people have sent me letters, imputing disloyalty and disaffection to several Zemindars, especially Baboo Kower Singh. My personal friendship for him, and the attachment he has always shown me, enable me confidently to contradict the report." Again on July 8th: "Baboo Kower Singh would, I am sure, do anything he could; but he has now no means. He has written to me several times to express his loyalty and sympathy." It was, perhaps, true that he had no means for good; but he had immense means for evil, for the hearts of the people were against us. But his position was a critical one. The good opinion of Kower Singh entertained by the Commissioner was shared by the Magistrate of Shahabad, who wrote to the Government of Bengal, saying: "With regard to the Baboo, there have been, ever since the commencement of the present disturbances, reports, some of them tending to implicate him seriously. . . . I have no reason to believe them. The Commissioner has the highest opinion of his loyalty, and I see no reason to doubt it." But there were officers in other districts who knew, and who did not hesitate to report that there were many influential Zemindars watching the movements of Kower Singh, and prepared to follow his example. He was a man in such times to be narrowly watched; and so Commissioner Tayler wrote to him, inviting him to come into Patna (of course for the Baboo's own good), and sent an officer of the Commission to visit him and personally to observe the state of affairs. But the wily old Rajpoot, who knew that this was only a courteous mode of making him a prisoner, pleaded age and infirmity, and was not to be lured from his sheltered home in Jugdespore. He made, however, specious promises of attending to the Commissioner's wishes at some future period of restored health, knowing very well that something would happen in the interval to prevent their accomplishment. The old man was waiting and watching. He had "a case" of his own, about the issue of which he was anxious in the extreme; and it is possible that if this had gone well for him, he might not have desired to precipitate the convulsions which seemed to afford a shorter, if a more rugged way, out of the jungle of his difficulties. The embarrassed state of his affairs had, some time before, caused the intervention of Government. His estates were in liquidation, and it required the support of official authority to carry him successfully through the ordeal. At a critical moment, when Kower Singh was in doubt and perplexity as to the part he should play in the great historical drama which he saw clearly in the foreground of the future, an adverse decision was communicated to him. The support of Government was suddenly withdrawn. There was but one thing that could have kept the old Rajpoot free from the entanglements that surrounded him, and that one thing was such aid from Government as would have enabled him to end his days in

1857. July.

1857. July. quietude and peace, and to leave an honourable name behind him in the district. But instead of this, he was, like many others, driven to despair by that miserable want of imagination and lack of sympathy which characterised the action of our "Boards."* So as the saving hand of Government was not to be extended to him, he betook himself to the other way out of his difficulties; to the new and shorter road to the coveted release which lay through the troubles sweeping over the country.† There were many about him to counsel this course of action—many who, eager for rebellion themselves, turned for a leader to

* As some readers may wish to have a more specific account of this transaction, it may be briefly stated that Kower Singh had engaged to obtain an advance of money, to the extent of twenty lakhs of rupees, for the payment of his debts. There was to have been a gradual process of liquidation from the proceeds of his estates through the Collector of Shahabad. This loan had not been actually negotiated. But the capitalist had promised that the money was shortly forthcoming. There were some delays, as there commonly are when money is to be advanced—but in the meanwhile some smaller sums had been advanced by other parties, and some advantageous compromises had been arranged. Affairs were in this state when suddenly the Sudder Board of Revenue sent through the Patna Commissioner "a peremptory message to Kower Singh that unless he obtained the entire loan within a month (which was impossible) they would recommend the Government to withdraw all interference with his affairs and to abandon the management of his estates."

† This opinion was entertained by Mr. Wake, the local magistrate, who, writing to Government on the 19th of July, said: "He is nominally the owner of vast estates, whilst in reality he is a ruined man, and can hardly find money to pay the interest of his debts. As long, therefore, as law and order exist, his position cannot improve: take them away, and he well knows that he would become supreme in this district. I do not think he will ever openly oppose the Government as long as he thinks that Government will stand, but I do think that, should these districts be ever the scene of a serious outbreak, he may take it into his head that it is time to strike a blow for his own interests, and his feudal influence is such as to render him exceedingly dangerous in such an event. I am narrowly watching his conduct, and the Commissioner has sent for him to Patna to speak to him on the subject of the reports about him; he is said to be ill, and I dare say will object on that plea, but I have heard that he has stated that he will not go to Patna, and will resist if he is sent for. I hope soon to be able to speak with more certainty on the subject." The Bengal Government officially described him as "the ruined owner of vast estates, who would become supreme in the district on the occurrence of disorder, but who, so long as law and order prevailed, could barely find the means to pay the interest of his debts."

this venerable chief. So he consented to cast in his lot with them; and his name became great in Shahabad. When the Dinapore regiments revolted, the whole district rose, and the Jugdespore man fell naturally into the place of leader of the insurgents. 1857. July.

Whilst, in those last days of July, the old Rajpoot chief was up and doing, the old English General was thinking what was to be done. Under the powerful influence of Kower Singh, the insurgents had marched on Arrah, released all the prisoners in the Gaol, plundered the Treasury, and but for the wisdom and bravery of the European inhabitants (of which more will be said presently), would have butchered them all to a man. But Lloyd, though not so far stricken in years, could only think and think wrongly. It appears that his first idea was to assume the defensive and to intrench himself at Dinapore. He expected that the mutineers, having possessed themselves of Arrah and slain all the white men in the place, would return flushed with conquest, under the leadership of Kower Singh, and attack the great military station. But Commissioner Tayler, to whom the General referred the proposal, protested against such an exhibition of weakness, and urged the immediate despatch of a strong force into the Shahabad district to crush the insurrection, and, if not too late, to rescue our people.

General Lloyd and Mr. Tayler.

July 26.

This was on the 26th. All through the previous day there had been great excitement at Patna. The firing of the guns at Dinapore had been distinctly heard. The English residents had chuckled over the thought of the victory that our people were achieving, and had counted up the "butcher's bill." The

1857. July. slaughter of the mutineers was variously estimated at from five hundred to eight hundred men. But as the hours passed away, and the sound of the guns passed away too, doubt and anxiety began to take the place of the first expectation of a great carnage. Then a rumour came that the mutineers were escaping, and that the English soldiery could not follow them through the swamps which stretched out before them. Before nightfall there was a gathering of all our people at the Commissioner's house; and a little force was improvised, consisting of Sikhs and Nujeebs, and a few English gentlemen, which went out at night, in the hope of being able to cut off stragglers, and perhaps to intercept a diversion of the enemy towards Patna. But as the following day broke, news came which gave a new complexion to affairs. "Whilst it was yet scarcely daylight," wrote the Commissioner, "a note was brought to my bedside. By the imperfect light I could just distinguish the words, 'Major Holmes and his wife.' I felt at once what it was, and shall never forget the sensation of pain and horror with which I read the announcement of this gallant and chivalrous officer's murder. I immediately," added the writer," recalled our volunteer detachment." A new difficulty had come upon us from a most unexpected quarter.

Major Holmes and his regiment. At Segowlie was a regiment of Irregular Horse (the Twelfth), commanded by Major James Holmes, an officer made of the right heroic stuff. A man of an ardent temperament, eager, impulsive, and bold as a lion, he shrunk from no responsibility, and was ready, in the hour of difficulty, to assume authority, which he did not rightfully possess, and to trust for future indemnity to the generosity of his masters. As soon as the first developments of insurrection rendered it certain that our positions in Behar would be threatened, he placed himself in direct communication with Lord Canning, and expressed his opinions with a freedom rarely seen in similar correspondence. Like Commissioner Tayler, he was all for prompt action and vigorous repression. "If every one," he wrote on the 25th of May to the Governor-General, "is true to himself and to the Government, and does his duty with smiling cheerfulness, all things will go well. I have endeavoured to impress this on the civilians of the district. I have also pointed out the necessity of their informing the wealthy Natives and Zemindars that the chief object of the turbulent Sepoys is plunder, and that it is their interest to seize any mutinous person and hand him over for punishment." "It is absolutely necessary," he added, "to strike terror by putting such persons to death by military law, and this power should, I think, be granted. If any person already discharged for mutiny from the Army should make such attempt, I would act on my responsibility."* What Lord Canning replied to this has been already shown.† But notwithstanding this plain expression of the opinions of the supreme authority, the fiery commander of Irregulars took upon himself the responsibility of placing the entire districts of Tirhoot, Chuprah, and Chunparum, as well as Azimgurh and Goruckpore, under martial law. "As a single clear head," he wrote on the 19th of June, "is better than a dozen in these times, and as military law is better than civil in a turbulent country, I have assumed absolute military control from Goruckpore to Patna, and have placed under absolute

1857. July.

* MS. Correspondence.

† The letter quoted in the last chapter, p. 7, was addressed to Major Holmes.

1857. July. military rule all that country, including the districts of Sarun, Chunparum, and Tirhoot. The Governor-General having requested me to write to him direct, I do so daily, and have informed his lordship on this head." The Commissioner reported that Major Holmes had done this "with the knowledge and concurrence of the Governor-General." But this was a mistake—at least it was only half true. Major Holmes had written to the Governor-General, saying: "Hearing that some seditious letters and speeches have been coming into the district, I have thought it proper to order my patrolling parties to proclaim martial law over the districts of Goruckpore, Sehwan, Chunparum, and Tirhoot, and that I shall punish with instant death the following offences, namely:

"1. Openly bearing arms against the State.

"2. Seditious speaking, or exciting others to rebellion, or any expression of disaffection to the Government.

"3. Concealing rebels, or even hearing others talk treason, and not immediately reporting to the nearest authorities.

"4. Plundering—if caught *in flagrante delicto.*

"All this," he added, "may not be lawful; but I don't care for that. There are times when circumstances are above the law. I am determined to keep order in these districts, and I'll do it with a strong hand."* Nothing can be plainer than this—nothing more certain than that Holmes proclaimed martial law, with the subsequent knowledge of the Governor-General. But the Government promptly repudiated these unauthorised publications.†

* Major Holmes to Lord Canning, June 15, 1857.—*MS. Correspondence.* In a letter to Mr. Tayler, he wrote that it had been said that this hot-headed Major would not be content till he had strung up a high civilian.

† I cannot find the slightest trace in Lord Canning's correspondence of any sort of concurrence in

Major Holmes had full confidence in the fidelity of his men. He commanded a model regiment, supposed to be proof against all temptation. There was not a civil officer in the district who did not covet the protection of a few sabres from Holmes's Incorruptibles; and he freely scattered them about in little parties of fifty or thirty, never doubting that they were true to the core. "My parties now," he wrote to Lord Canning on the 14th of June, "patrol the whole country from Goruckpore and Azimgurh to Tirhoot, Chuprah, and Patna; and I believe that at the present not a word of sedition is spoken on the banks of the Ganges. I have proclaimed that I shall punish with instant death civilians as well as soldiers for one word of mutiny; and all know that I shall keep my word. In consequence all is quiet. Last night, at nine P.M., two unfortunate Sepoys of the Seventeenth,* mutineers, were sent into me from Sehwan. Within an hour I had hanged them both. I enclose copy of court-martial, that your lordship may understand how I act. It is vile, dirty, unsoldierly work; but at the present moment I should hang or shoot my own brother under similar circumstances. My party with the treasure have escaped with honour, for they retired by word of command from Captain Palliser, when overpowered by eight hundred Sepoys and gaol-birds, and three guns. They escorted the officers to Benares, and

1857. July.

Holmes's act; I presume, therefore, that he must have leaped hastily to the conclusion that silence gave consent. I believe that the Governor-General only wrote one letter to him—the one referred to above—in which he cautioned him against going beyond the authority already given to him. In that letter (May 30th) the Governor-General did not request Major Holmes to write to him directly. He merely in reply to that officer wrote, "I shall be glad to hear further from you, especially on matters within your own observation. I cannot undertake," he added, "to answer your letters, for I have no time for writing."—*MS. Correspondence.*

* This was the Azimgurh regiment. See *ante*, vol. ii. p. 213, *et seq.*

1857. July. returned to their post at Goruckpore in good order." And so letter after letter was written—now to the Governor-General, now to the Commissioner, all in the same confident strain—the fearless utterances of a strong, bold man, who believed that all things would yield to the force of his own resolute will.

But those were days when appearances were most delusive, and the most reasonable hopes were often doomed to bitter disappointment. One evening Major Holmes was taking his accustomed drive, accompanied by his wife. The lady had once been known as Dinah Sale, and afterwards as the wife of Sturt the Engineer.* She had survived the horrors of the retreat from Caubul, which had made her a widow, and had become the wife of another brave man, to confront greater dangers than those which she had escaped. Neither thought so at that moment; for they believed that, though all else might be false, Holmes's troopers were as true as steel. But suddenly the truth was revealed to them. A party of Sowars rode up and fell upon them with their sabres. The butchery was brief but effectual. I cannot give the details of it. But a little time after the murder, Mrs. Holmes's Native ayah (or tire-woman) went to the spot where the crime had been committed and saw the bodies of her master and mistress. The corpses of both were headless. The troopers, in whose devotion he had trusted to the last, had decapitated their late commander, and carried off his head as a trophy and a witness to their comrades. The lady's head lay still there; and the ayah bent reverently over it, lifted the streaming hair, rich and

* Daughter of Sir Robert Sale—distinguished in the Afghan and Sikh wars—and of the heroic Lady Sale, who gave us so vivid an account of the former in her published journal.

beautiful in its abundance, and cut it off, as a memorial to be cherished by those who had loved her.* Meanwhile, a party of troopers had completed the work thus begun by murdering the other Europeans at Segowlie. Dr. and Mrs. Garner were sitting in their bungalow when the Sowars rushed in upon them and cut them down, with one of their two children.† The other, a little girl, escaped from the house, and was rescued by a Native functionary. The house was then fired, and the bodies of the doctor's family were burnt. Mr. Bennett, the Deputy-Postmaster, also fell a victim to the fury of the troopers. The great body of the regiment broke out into open mutiny of the worst kind; but some scattered branches stood fast, and a detachment of them did good service under Captain Johnson in the subsequent operations in Oude. 1857. July.

In the mean time, what had been done at Dinapore to compensate for the first great failure? The mutinous Sepoys had been suffered to escape towards the most dangerous district of the whole great province of Behar. At first it was thought that their flight to Shahabad might be arrested by the difficulty of crossing the Soane, as what were called "precautions" had been taken to have all the available boats removed to the other side of the river. But though this wise project had been conceived, the right man had not been found to accomplish it; and so the surging insurrection met with no check, and the flood poured on uninterruptedly. On the 26th, a feeble and unsuccessful effort was made to send a detachment of riflemen on board a steam-boat after the fugitives; Proceedings at Dinapore.

* The bodies were afterwards carried into Matchuree by the police, as was also that of Mr. Bennett.

† Dr. Garner was, I believe, a relative of Major Holmes, whose name was James Garner Holmes.

1857. July 27. but it came back, having accomplished nothing.* Another effort was then made with equal want of success. On the 27th, a steamer with a detachment of the Thirty-seventh was again despatched towards the Soane, with intention to land our men at a point some nine miles from Arrah, and "to bring away the civilians there besieged." This vessel did not return to Dinapore, but it stuck fast upon a sand-bank, not without suspicion of foul play on the part of a Native pilot. General Lloyd would then have recalled the detachment. But against this the Commissioner had protested, and had urged, on the other hand, the expediency of despatching another steamer with a strong reinforcement to pick up the stranded vessel, and then for the united force to march upon Arrah. Another steamer had come in, most opportunely, from Allahabad. It was full of passengers escaping to Calcutta. That this vessel should be turned, for present purposes, into a troop-ship, and that the Dinapore Protestant Church should be converted into a great caravanserai during the employment of the vessel on this special duty, was then determined by the military authorities, and arrangements were made to give effect to the design.

The departure of this third body of English troops was to have taken place at daybreak on the 29th;

* The following is taken from General Lloyd's letter to his brother, to which reference has already been made: "It is, perhaps, to be regretted that some (English troops) were not sent that night or next morning, but only a small party in comparison to the strength of the mutineers could have been detached —no guns could have gone, and as the mutineers avoided the road and kept to the fields, where they could scarcely have been followed by a small party of Europeans, they would probably not have been of much use. However, as the readiest means of following them to prevent them crossing the Soane, I next day (the 26th) sent off some riflemen in a steamer up that river, expecting that at this season there would have been sufficient water—but unfortunately the steamer could not get up high enough, and returned in the evening without having effected anything."

but when the men of the Tenth had been marched down to the river-side, it was found that the steamer was full of sleeping passengers, and the captain was reluctant to disturb them.* Then it was discovered that the steamer could not take so large a number of men, as it was designed that she should also take in tow the boat that was stranded with the detachment of the Thirty-seventh.† So, one-half of the men of the Tenth were sent back to their barracks, and Colonel Fenwick, who was to have commanded, made over the charge to Captain Dunbar. A hundred and fifty Europeans were thus embarked; and with them went some seventy Sikhs under Lieutenant Ingleby—a spirited young officer of one of the revolted regiments, who had volunteered for this service. 1857. July 29.

And there were other volunteers. On the 29th, the Commissioner was at Dinapore supporting on

* Mr. Tayler's statement on this subject is too distinct and detailed not to be given in illustration of the narrative in the text: "Colonel Fenwick appealed to the General for authority to have the sleepers turned out, which was promptly given; the word was passed on to the non-commissioned officers, and from them to some of the privates. In another minute, it was discovered that the steamer could not tow her own flat as well as that of the *Horungutta*, which it was arranged she was to take on, and consequently only half the force told off could go. Colonel Fenwick retired in disgust, and the command was delegated to Captain Dunbar. From that moment all was confusion. No progress was made, no one took upon himself to disturb the happy sleepers. As Civil Commissioner, I had no authority in matters purely military, but I could not quite refrain from interference. I saw the man, apparently a sergeant, to whom the order for turning out the passengers was given, but who, after Colonel Fenwick's departure, had done nothing in the matter. I went up to him and suggested that if he would send three or four hard-hearted men to turn the passengers out, 'neck and crop,' if necessary, it would be a beneficial move, and they would never get off if he didn't; he had just said, 'All right, sir,' with much alacrity, and was telling off the men to set to work, when somebody called out to him, 'Hallo! you may knock off, you're not to go!' The man, a splendid specimen of a soldier, turned short off, muttering, and, with several others, went away in no good humour. *Several hours* elapsed before the final start was made, and the steamer did not get clear away till about half-past nine!"—*The Patna Crisis.*

† It should be explained to the English reader that what is commonly described as a "steamer" consists of a flat, or large pinnace, with good accommodation, towed by a steam-vessel.

1857. July 29. the spot his protests in favour of a forward movement.* Mr. M'Donell, the Magistrate of Chuprah and Mr. Ross Mangles, Assistant to the Patna Commissioner, went with him. Both were eager to accompany any force that might be despatched to the relief of Arrah. For such men there was great attraction in the enterprise; firstly, for love of a friend, who was in peril there; secondly, out of that strong love of action and adventure, that irrepressible ardour of generous youth, which will not suffer it to be quiescent when danger is to be faced and work to be done. With the means already at the disposal of the military authorities, and fresh reinforcements continually coming up the river, what could be looked for but a successful—a glorious crusade? But these well-founded expectations were most delusive. Human calculations were as nothing in this emergency. The energy, the sagacity, the fertility of resource, which Englishmen were now displaying in many parts of the country, were wanting at Dinapore, as they had before been wanting at Meerut. Not only did misfortune track our steps, but grievous incapacity obstructed us at every stage. How it happened that Dunbar was selected for the command of such an expedition it is not easy to conjecture. General Lloyd did not hesitate to declare his opinion that the leader of this expedition was chosen by his commanding officer on account of his incompetency.† He had been a regimental pay-

Mr. Wake.

* Mr. Tayler says that he went to Dinapore on the evening of the 29th, which must be a mistake, as he was obviously there on the morning of the 29th, when Dunbar's detachment embarked. The date should be the 28th.

† General Lloyd's letter will be found complete in the Appendix. I was guided to it, as to other very valuable references, by Mr. Montgomery Martin's work. It is observable, however, that that painstaking writer, by a clerical or typographical error, makes it appear that the General hinted that Colonel Fenwick was "*un*aware" of Dunbar's incompetence. The word is "aware."

master, and he had but scant knowledge of military operations in the field. But he took the work upon him readily as a brave man, and went forth to his doom. 1857. July 29.

Dunbar's expedition.

About half-past nine, the vessel put off amidst cheers from the river-bank. "The gallant appearance of the men," wrote one who watched their departure, "the eager countenances of the officers, the anticipation of certain success in the enterprise, gave the expedition a character of bright and buoyant hopefulness."* But a terrible sentence was written down against it. It appeared as though nothing prosperous could ever come out of Dinapore. At every stage there was mismanagement of the worst type. The men embarked hungry; and hungry they were suffered to remain. There was abundance on board, but neither food nor drink was served out to them; and when some hours after noon, having picked up the stranded vessel, and obtained the assistance of some roomy country boats,† they disembarked at the nearest point to Arrah, they went fasting and feeble on a service which demanded all the spirit and strength that could be imparted to them by generous internal stimulants. They had a long march before them, and nothing was to be obtained on the way.

It was about seven o'clock before the whole of the troops were landed. The early moon was shining brightly, and, aided by it, Dunbar made his military dispositions, and, having secured a guide, marched on with the Sikh detachment in front. At a distance of two or three miles from their destination, they came

* Tayler's "Patna Crisis."

† Mr. Trevelyan says: "It was the height of the rainy season, and much of the country was under water. Accordingly, on arriving nearly opposite Arrah, the troops left the steamer and embarked in some large boats, in which they followed the course of a nullah, which brought them some miles nearer their point."

1857. July 29. upon a bridge which seemed well suited for a halting-place. Here the leader of the expedition was recommended to serve out some rum and biscuits to the troops, and to bivouac for the night. But Dunbar determined to push on to Arrah. The moon was now waning, and, before midnight, darkness closed upon the advancing force. The Sikh skirmishers had been drawn in, and our people were moving forward, unsuspicious of the presence of an enemy, when, in the vicinity of a dense mango-grove, a tremendous fire was opened upon them. They were then marching on a raised causeway terribly exposed; whilst their assailants were concealed by their leafy shelter; so none knew how to return the fire. The white uniforms of the Europeans were seen through the darkness of the night, but the dusky Sepoys in undress, little short of nakedness, could not be discerned among the trees. It was plain now that our people had been drawn into an ambuscade. And it was a fatal one to our relieving force. Officers and men fell fast beneath the fire of the concealed enemy. One of the first to receive his death-wound was the commander of the expedition. If Dunbar had erred, he paid dearly for the error. He was never seen alive after this first discharge.

From the front of our column, from the right flank, from the left flank, came through the darkness, with fatal effect, the heavy shower of musket-balls. What the strength of the enemy was at that point it is hard to say.* But it was plain to our people that they were surrounded by a multitude of Sepoys,

* Some statements fix the number at two thousand—others at three thousand or even five thousand. It is obvious that if only the Dinapore regiments were there, the number could not much have exceeded the former amount. There were unquestionably, however, in Shahabad at this time many men from other revolted regiments, and many Sepoys on furlough.

and that their ranks were being rapidly thinned. 1857. July.
The sudden attack, followed by the fall of their leader, had thrown them into confusion, and, straggling as they were, they could not return the enemy's fire, in the darkness, without imminent risk of shooting down their own comrades. After a time, however, they rallied, and were got together by the bugle-call in an enclosed field, at some little distance from the grove, where they found shelter in a hollow,* and there they might have lain in comparative safety if our men could have been restrained from firing; but the occasional crack of our rifles revealed our position, and brought back bullets with destructive interest.† Thus the night passed miserably with our people, hungering for the dawn. But daylight brought no relief to their sufferings—no confidence to our afflicted people. There were those who counselled the prosecution of the march to Arrah; but a retrograde movement was determined upon, in utter despondency of heart.

The retreat.

A disastrous retreat was now to be commenced by the survivors of this luckless expedition. Fatigued and famished, and sore at heart, for the grievous necessity of leaving the wounded behind them was theirs, they set their faces again towards the river. That morning's march will never be forgotten by the few who live to think of it. As they went, it seemed to them that the enemy were ubiquitous—that they started up on every side; from copses and coverts of all kinds, from walled enclosures and mud villages, from hollows and ditches and the roofs of houses,

* Mr. Trevelyan describes it as an empty tank, which is confirmed by Mr. M'Donell, in a narrative published in the *Times*.

† "Young Anderson, a very nice young fellow of the Twenty-second Native Infantry, a volunteer, was standing up behind the hedge; he was shot through the head, and jumped up like a buck—of course killed on the spot." — *M'Donell's Narrative.*

1857. July. came with destructive activity the fire of the insurgents. Against it our people, if far less exhausted and dispirited, could have done little or nothing. For when they formed and fired, as they sometimes did, there was no enemy to be seen; the aim of our people was directed only towards the puffs of smoke which indicated the position whence the fire had come, and every rebel volley was followed by a rapid retirement of the enemy. But these efforts soon ceased. Our retreat became a rout. Men thought of little but their own lives. All things were against them but one. As our men dropped by the wayside, the ammunition of their assailants was running short. This was a great deliverance. But for it, scarcely a man would have escaped.

July 30. As it was, only a wretched remnant of the party that, flushed with the thought of victory, had left Dinapore on that July morning, returned to the nullah which they had crossed by the light of the rising moon. Happily the boats were still there, on the left bank, as we had left them. But the sight of them, presenting, as they seemed to do, the means of escape, extinguished the little discipline that was left in the retreating force. There was a scene of wild confusion—of crowding and huddling—at the ghaut, each man seeking his own safety, and, with a few bright exceptions, caring but little for his fellow-men. It was not strange, for the enemy were upon them—firing upon the fugitives from all sides, and striving hard to burn or to sink the boats. In this they were only too successful. Some of our people were shot; some were burnt; some were drowned. The commands and entreaties of their officers were of no avail. Many threw away their arms and accoutrements—some stripped themselves to the skin, and flung themselves into the water. It is stated that the last man to leave the shore was Lieutenant Ingelby, who had volunteered to lead the Sikhs to Arrah. He stepped into a burning boat, as it was putting off, and ere it was half-way across the stream, the flames had so spread that all on board were compelled to take to the water. Ingelby was struck on the neck by a musket-ball and went down; but rising again to the surface, he threw up his arms, cried aloud, "Good-bye, Grenadiers!" and sunk—never to be seen alive again. 1857. July 30.

Those, who reached the opposite bank of the nullah, were now safe. The steamer and flat were soon gained; and back the diminished party went to the cantonment of Dinapore. Our people there had looked anxiously for their coming—eager to welcome the victors and to congratulate the rescued—never doubting that there would be a great ovation; and now as the vessel appeared in sight, the inmates of the Barracks went out, men and women, to the river-side, straining eyes and ears to catch a sight of the crowded deck and the sound of triumphant exultation proclaiming the success of the expedition. But not a shout was heard as she steamed on; and there was little sign of life on board. All indeed was ominously quiet. People asked each other what it meant. But when the vessel came-to beside the Hospital, there was no need for further questioning. The silence was the silence of disaster and death. The whole sad story was soon known; and then there was such a wail from the women as those who heard it can never cease to remember. Some beat their breasts and tore their hair in the wild excitement of their grief, and called down the judgment of God on the authors of this great calamity. It is said that if General Lloyd had appeared amongst them at that

1857. July 30.

moment, they would have torn him to pieces. Of the four hundred men who had gone out on the day before, full of health and hope, one-half had been left behind to gorge the vultures and the jackals, and of those who returned only about fifty were unwounded.*

Heroic exploits.

But disastrous as was the retreat, it was not all disgraceful. There will always be acts of individual heroism when Englishmen go out to battle. It may be a soldier, or it may be a civilian, in whom the irrepressible warrior-instinct manifests itself in some act of conspicuous gallantry and devotion—but it is sure never to be wanting. In those days well-nigh every man was more or less a soldier; and there were few better soldiers than the members of the Bengal Civil Establishment. The traditions of the old Indian Service gave them a pride in their profession, and they held that nothing was incompatible with its duties that tended to maintain the honour and security of the Anglo-Indian Empire. Accustomed, in most instances, from boyhood upwards, to the use of fire-arms, with firm seats in the saddle, and often mighty hunters of the boar and the tiger, rejoicing in the perilous excitement of such sport, these men, especially in the earlier stages of their career, were well braced up for vigorous action, and had little to learn to fit them for the front of the battle. From the days when Charles Metcalfe headed the attack at Deeg, and Mountstuart Elphinstone rode side by side with the Wellington of the future at Assaye, the Indian Civil Service had been fertile in heroes. But never before the convulsions of 1857 had the martial energies of our civilians been so

* The official return says: 2 captains, 2 lieutenants, 3 ensigns, 3 sergeants, 10 corporals, 3 drummers, 112 privates killed; 1 lieutenant, 2 ensigns, 3 sergeants, 3 corporals, 2 drummers, and 49 privates wounded.

largely reduced; never had the pen so often been laid aside for the sword or the rifle. It has been already shown in these volumes how George Ricketts fought the Nabha guns on the bank of the Sutlej, how John Mackillop kept the well at Cawnpore, and how other soldierly deeds were done by men whose cutcherries were closed and whose judgment-seats were empty. And many more such stories will be told as the narrative proceeds. Two at least lighten up the record of the retreat from Arrah. They have been told before and better than I can tell them. But this History would be incomplete without the recital. 1857. July 30.

I have said that with Dunbar's relieving force went Mr. M'Donell and Mr. Ross Mangles, of the Civil Service. They did excellent service on the way. The local knowledge of the former enabled him to act as a guide, and the rifles of both were in constant requisition. In the first attack on our columns, Mangles had been stunned by a musket-ball, but he soon recovered himself, and was helping the surgeon who accompanied the force to bind up the wounds of his comrades, or carrying water to them in their agony. When morning dawned he shouldered his piece and stepped on with the rest towards the nullah, resolute to sell his life dearly. In the flower of his youth, a man of a fine presence, with a long stride and a firm hand on his two-barrel, our men looked to him, in the morning light, as to one who, though without official command, had natural right to be obeyed; and he did much good service as he went by his animating influence upon others and by his own personal prowess.* Though by reason of

* Mr. Trevelyan says that "he succeeded in keeping together a small knot of men, who supplied him with a succession of loaded muskets. As he was a noted shikaree, a dead hand at bear and antelope, the Sepoys thought proper to keep their distance."

1857. July 30. his stature a conspicuous mark for the enemy, and "though dozens of poor fellows," as he wrote afterwards, "were knocked over close to him," by the blessing of God he escaped unharmed. He escaped to do a noble deed. A soldier of the Thirty-seventh, who had been struck down and was left helpless on the ground, where he would presently have been murdered by the Sepoys, implored the young civilian not to desert him. So amidst a destructive fire of musketry, Ross Mangles the Younger halted and knelt down, bound up the man's wounds, hoisted him on his back, and strode on with his burden. He had fasted for twenty-four hours; he had watched for forty-eight; but notwithstanding this want of food and rest, he declared afterwards that he had "never felt so strong in his life." And well was it that the invigorating sense of a great duty so sustained him. For the man whom he bore was as big as himself, and the enemy were close upon his track. Compelled, now and then, to lay his burden down, he stood over the wounded man, and if opportunity offered, turned the interval of rest to account by taking a shot at the insurgents. And the good God watched over this deed of mercy and love; for young Mangles carried the wounded soldier, over rough and swampy ground, for a space of six miles, till he reached the nullah; and then swimming out and holding up the helpless man in the water, he reached a boat, laid his charge safely in it, and soon had the delight of seeing him in good hands at the hospital of Dinapore, with leisure to thank God and his preserver for his almost miraculous deliverance.*

* The man's name was Richard Taylor. He was not dismissed from hospital till the 19th of November, and he was then invalided and sent to England. This story has a remarkable sequel. It was the first deed of the kind that eventually solved the question as to whether

Differing in kind, but not in degree, from this heroic exploit, was another act of daring self-devotion done by Mr. M'Donell, of the same service. It was in no small measure owing to his representations and to his offer to act as a guide to the relieving force, for he knew the country well, that General Lloyd consented to send the European detachment into Shahabad. Always in the front, always in the thick of the battle, he did excellent service, as I have said before, on the march. Many a mutineer sunk beneath the fire of his rifle. He was beside Dunbar when he fell, and was sprinkled with the life-blood of the luckless leader. Wounded himself, he still fought on gallantly during the retreat, and reached the 1857. July 30.

civilians could share with their military brethren the honour of the Victoria Cross. Those were days when, in the all-prevailing excitement, heroic acts were often overlooked at the time. And it was not until the lapse of more than a year that official notice was taken of this honourable incident; and then it was brought to the attention of Lord Canning by Sir James Outram. Both were men, who, courageous themselves, had a keen appreciation of courage in others, and never neglected an opportunity of recording their admiring approval. It was not before the summer of 1858 that Outram was made acquainted with the exploit above narrated. It had been his first thought to recommend young Mangles for the Victoria Cross. But meanwhile another gallant deed, done by an uncovenanted civilian in Oude (hereafter to be recorded), had been recommended for this reward, and the decision was that members of the military and naval services alone were entitled to this distinction. Believing this to be final, the Governor-General, on receipt of Outram's letter, wrote a letter to the Home Government, forwarding it for their information, and emphatically indorsing its contents. The letter adds, "The modesty which has allowed the event to remain unknown to those in authority until after the lapse of a twelvemonth it was brought to light by the journal of a surgeon recording the gratitude of the wounded soldier, is not the least remarkable feature in the story." Lord Canning wrote also to the younger Mangles saying, "It is a satisfaction to me to tell you with what pleasure I have done this; but the pleasure would have been greater if (as ought to have been the case) my official letter could have been addressed to your father." Mr. Ross Mangles the Elder had vacated the Chair of the Court of Directors in April, 1858, and had been succeeded by Sir Frederick Currie. The whole question of the claim of civilians to the Victoria Cross was afterwards with reference to this and the Oude case (Mr. Kavanagh's) finally decided in favour of the claim of soldier-civilians—and I feel that there was not a soldier in the service who did not rejoice in the withdrawal of the invidious distinction.

1857. July 30. nullah with a stiffened limb, but with no abatement of vigorous courage. There, having done his best to assist others more helpless than himself, he entered the last of the boats; and deliverance seemed to be at hand. But the insurgents had taken away the oars and had lashed the rudder, and though the breeze was favourable for the escape of our people, the current carried the boat back to the river-bank, and fast and furious came the shower of musket-balls from the pieces of the enemy. The boats were the large covered boats—the "floating haystacks"—of the country, which afforded excellent shelter to those who huddled together beneath the clumsy thatch. There were thirty-five European soldiers on board the boat; and M'Donell, seeing the difficulty and danger which the impossibility of steering the vessel brought upon them, called upon the men to cut the lashings of the rudder. But no man stirred. So M'Donell went out from the shelter, and climbing on to the roof of the boat, perched himself on the rudder and cut the lashings, amidst a very storm of bullets from the contiguous bank. It was truly a providential deliverance that he escaped instant death. Coolly and steadily he went about his perilous work, and though some balls passed through his hat, not one did him any harm. Thus the rudder was loosened, the boat answered to the helm, and by M'Donell's gallant act the crew were saved from certain destruction. The good deed was not forgotten. It afterwards earned for the noble-hearted civilian the crowning glory of the Victoria Cross.*

* The following is the official account of the exploit as given by Captain J. W. Medhurst, of the Sixtieth Rifles, previously of the Tenth Foot: "On the ill-fated expedition retiring from Arrah on the morning of the 30th July, 1857, and on arriving at the village and stream of Bherara, as is well known, the men, exhausted and dispirited, broke

Nor was heroism of this best kind confined to our officers in high position, whose exploits are ever sure to find chroniclers, whilst the doings of humbler men are often obscured at the time, or afterwards forgotten. In the ranks of our luckless army, beaten as they were, driven back disastrously to their boats, by an enemy whom a little while before they had despised, were some stout-hearted English soldiers, who, in the midst of that confused flight for life, could think of the sufferings of their wounded comrades, and pause to aid them amidst the thickest fire of the enemy. Among the officers shot down during the retreat was Ensign Erskine, of the Tenth Foot, a good soldier, who had risen from the ranks. As he lay there in his helplessness, to be bayoneted or brained by the Sepoys, two men of the Tenth espied him and carried him off, thus encumbering themselves at the risk of their own lives. Erskine died, but one at least of these true noblemen survived to receive the honour for which some of the greatest 1857. July 30.

and made for the only six large country boats moored close to the right bank. After assisting some wounded men into the furthest boat, and being myself pulled in, I saw that Mr. M'Donell, who was one of our number, was exerting himself with a sergeant to move the boat into the stream. It being discovered that the boat was bound to the bank, one or two men jumped out and loosened the rope, and the boat moved. Assisted by the less exhausted of my party, I was keeping up a fire of Enfields on the enemy, whose musketry was very galling. Whilst so employed, I heard Mr. M'Donell call out for a knife to cut away some rope which bound the rudder to the right, causing the lumbering boat to veer round into the right shore again, and for a time causing it to stick fast. On looking round I saw him seated on the stern extremity of the boat in full view of the enemy, and quite exposed to their fire. He cut away the mentioned rope, and guiding the rudder himself, a fortunate breeze carried our boat across the stream, grounding at about ten yards from the left bank, whereby all those who were alive were enabled to jump out and reach the steamer in safety. The number of men thus saved was about thirty-five; and during the passage across three men were shot dead, one was mortally, and two or three slightly, wounded. I may safely assert that it was owing to Mr. M'Donell's presence of mind, and at his personal risk, that our boat got across on that day."

1857. July 30. captains of the age would have willingly surrendered their crosses and collars. For this and other subsequent acts of valour, Dennis Dempsey, of the Tenth Foot, was decorated with the Victoria Cross.*

One more episode of this Dinapore mutiny must be narrated. I wish that it were as honourable to the national character as those which have preceded it in the record. It happened that amidst the almost general defection of the Native troops at Dinapore, a few Sepoys of the Fortieth Regiment were found true to their colours. When their comrades had deserted they remained at their post—doubtless believing that their loyalty would be respected. But it appears that the fact of their fidelity—the truth that these few men had remained "faithful among the faithless"—sufficed not to countervail the other patent fact that these people had dark skins. So, when this little residue of loyal Sepoys, having been burnt out of their huts, were gathered together beneath a tent, or some other temporary shelter, it befel that under cover of the night a party of European soldiers rushed suddenly upon them with fixed bayonets and thrust out among them, striving to kill as many as they could. What the actual result was in killed and wounded it is not easy to ascertain. From authority which it would

* The following is the official record of the cumulative services which obtained for Dennis Dempsey the Victoria Cross: "Private Dennis Dempsey, Tenth Regiment: for having, at Lucknow, on the 14th of March, 1858, carried a powder-bag through a burning village with great coolness and gallantry, for the purpose of mining a passage in rear of the enemy's position. This he did exposed to a very heavy fire from the enemy behind loopholed walls, and to an almost still greater danger from the sparks which flew in every direction from the blazing houses. Also for having been the first man who entered the village of Jugdespore on the 12th of August, 1857, under a most galling fire. Private Dempsey was likewise one of those who helped to carry Ensign Erskine, of the Tenth Regiment, in the retreat from Arrah in July, 1857." The chronological arrangement of these incidents favours the supposition that, in the mind of the compiler, History should be read backwards.

be almost presumption to question, I learn that none were killed by the onslaught. Bayonet-wounds are seldom mortal. But this matters not. The intent to kill was palpable; and it was a brutal and dastardly act. By reason of their own inactivity, or the ineptitude of their officers, these British soldiers, having suffered our enemies to escape, disgraced their uniform and stained their manhood by quietly bayoneting our sleeping friends, because they were of the same colour as the people who had baffled them.* 1857. July 30.

* I have been informed, since the above passage was written, that the men of the Tenth were not moved to this act solely by their resentment at the thought that the mutineers had escaped. They had a personal wrong to revenge, for not long before some men of the regiment, having come upon a party of Sepoys sitting in consultation one night, under cover of the darkness, had been brutally assaulted by their Native comrades, and I believe that one of the Europeans was killed. This may not give a much fairer complexion to the story; but it imparts a more intelligible meaning to the act.

CHAPTER III.

THE ENGLISH AT ARRAH—FORTIFICATION OF BOYLE'S HOUSE—APPEARANCE OF THE MUTINEERS—PROSECUTION OF THE SIEGE—GALLANT DEFENCE BY THE GARRISON—MAJOR VINCENT EYRE—IMPROVISATION OF A FIELD FORCE—DEFEAT OF THE ENEMY—RELIEF OF ARRAH—FLIGHT OF KOWER SINGH—DESTRUCTION OF JUGDESPORE.

1857. July. The English at Arrah.

MEANWHILE the little party of English residents at Arrah was holding out, against tremendous odds, with a stern resolution worthy of Sparta in her prime. Anything more hopeless, on the face of the enterprise, than an attempt to defend a house or a cluster of houses against some two thousand Sepoys and a multitude of armed insurgents, perhaps four times the number of the disciplined soldiery, could not well be conceived. The almost absolute certainty of destruction was such that a retreat under cover of the night would not have been discreditable. Reason suggested it. Nay, indeed, such was the value of European life at that time, that what are called the "claims of the public service" were all in favour of what seemed to be the safer course. But the European residents at Arrah had other thoughts of their duty to the State. There were about a dozen Englishmen, official and non-official, and three or four other Christians of different races. Already the women and children had been sent away to places of comparative safety, and some few of the male sex had departed in expectation of a coming crisis in Shahabad. So what was left was of the best stuff of muscular Christianity, and there was nothing of a feebler kind to cling to its skirts and encumber it. Still it was so very little in bulk, and so weak in physical power of resistance, that self-preservation would have been impossible, but for a happy circumstance which amplified and strengthened the little garrison in the hour of its need. Commissioner Tayler had despatched to Arrah a party of fifty Sikhs, of whose fidelity he had no doubt. At such a time, indeed, the Grunth was the next best thing to the Bible. There were fifty good fighting men cherishing no sympathy with Poorbeahs of any kind, and plenty of honest pluck under English leaders to make a vigorous defence against any odds. So it was resolved that there should be no flight, but that the issue should depend upon the arbitrament of hard fighting.

1857. July.

The centre of defence had been wisely chosen. The works of the East Indian Railway were then in course of construction, and at the head of the staff so employed in the neighbourhood of Arrah was Mr. Vicars Boyle, a gentleman who with the best knowledge of the civil engineer combined some acquaintance with military science, especially in the serviceable branch of fortification. The premises which Boyle occupied contained two houses.* The smaller one—a two-storied building with a flat roof—appeared to him to be best suited for purposes of de-

Fortification of Boyle's house.

* In the old days of English hospitality in India it was a common practice to erect within the "compound," or premises of the general dwelling-house, a smaller supplementary building, to be used as a guest-house. In this instance the principal apartment had been used, before Mr. Boyle's time, as a billiard-room.

1857. July.

fence; and he had been for some time, in contemplation of the storm which had now burst, fortifying and provisioning this structure. If they could hold out for a few days—or it might be only a few hours—against a sudden incursion of mutinous Sepoys aided by the Budmashes of the place, all would be well: for who could doubt that relief would speedily arrive from Dinapore. So Boyle set to work and brought in stores of flour, grain, biscuits, beer, and other provender that would not spoil by keeping in that July weather—with water enough to supply seventy men for a fortnight. He got together, too, as much ammunition as he could find; and by building up the lower parts of the house, sufficient loopholes being left, and ranging sand-bags on the roof, he not only provided shelter for our people, but the means of operating freely against an enemy outside the walls of his little fortress. Nor was this all. Seeing that use might be made by the insurgents of the other and larger house in the compound, some fifty yards off, he had razed its front parapet, which would have afforded shelter to our assailants and aided their means of attack. When, therefore, news came that the Dinapore regiments had broken into rebellion and were streaming down upon Arrah, these wise precautions and preparations had determined the Government officers not to desert their post, but to hold out within the improvised fortifications so long as a pulse of life should beat in their bodies. So they gathered themselves together in the "chota ghur" in Mr. Boyle's compound, and braced themselves up to give a warm reception to the insurgents.

Commencement of the attack.

On the 27th of July, the bulk of the Dinapore mutineers, after doing, on the way, as much damage

as they could to all that belonged to the white men, 1857. July.
poured into Arrah, and did according to the authorised Sepoy programme—they plundered the Treasury and released the prisoners in the Gaol. Having thus recruited themselves with the sinews of war and the rough material of murder, they made for Boyle's little fortress, the inmates of which seemed to them like so many rats in a cage. But marching up with a bold front, and maintaining a smart fire, as they advanced, they met with such a welcome from the British garrison as to check their confidence for a while, and make them think that it would suit them better to fight behind walls or trees. As the foremost men fell beneath the fire of our rifles or muskets from the loopholed walls or from the well-sheltered roof of the small house, the military order in which the insurgents had advanced was broken up, and they dissolved into scattered groups, looking lovingly towards the big house or the trees which studded the compound. And soon they had disposed themselves in this safer manner, eschewing the open, and taking up their head-quarters in or about Boyle's house. But it happened that the smaller house had a command of fire over the larger, and whenever one of the mutineers exposed himself for a moment, it was fortunate for him if a bullet, from behind the sandbags on the roof, did not put an end to his temerity.

It has been shown that there was not an English military officer in the garrison; but never was a most unequal defence more gallantly or more skilfully conducted. Herwald Wake, the Magistrate, took command of the Sikhs, and they had confidence in their leader, as he now had confidence in them. And yet their fidelity was sorely tried. Since the

1857. July. annexation of the Punjab to our British-Indian Empire, there had been a considerable enlistment of Sikhs into many of our Sepoy battalions, and in the Dinapore regiments were some who had cast in their lot with the Hindostanees. These men were now used as decoys. They called upon their comrades to join them; they offered large sums of money—readily payable from the spoil of the Treasury—to each Sikh soldier who would desert the English; but the answer returned went from the muzzles of our rifles and carbines, and was more eloquent than the best of words.

Prosecution of the siege. This hope having now departed from the besiegers, they bethought themselves of new devices. Our little fortress with its seventy fighting men might be treated like a wasp's nest: the garrison might be smoked into torpor and death. So under cover of the night our assailants brought together a large quantity of combustibles, such as straw, and fagots, and bamboos, and heaped them up under our walls. Next morning these inflammable materials were ignited, and on the burning pile were thrown all the chillies—the raw material of cayenne pepper—that could be culled from the gardens of Arrah, where they were growing abundantly in aid of the savoury dishes of both races. The pungency of the smoke so raised was distressing to the besieged, and in time they might have been suffocated by it; but, not for the first time in our national history, a providential wind arose and frustrated the knavish tricks of our opponents. The peppery smoke was swept away, before it had grievously affected our garrison; and the only tangible result of the attempt was that the remains of an adventurous insurgent, who had been active in the creation of the bonfire that was to have smoked our garrison to death, were found charred and calcined amidst its ashes. A bullet from our little fortress had penetrated the pile and killed the stoker in the midst of his work. 1857. July.

Another device was tried. It was not a dainty one. The Sepoys may have heard of the use of stink-pots. But it was not easy to make them, and they thought that they could produce the same results in a simpler manner. The horses of Herwald Wake and Vicars Boyle and others were at the mercy of the enemy, if their masters were not; and it occurred to the Sepoys that the English warriors might be subdued by their own steeds. So they shot the Arabs where they stood, hastily picketed, and left their carcasses to rot under the walls of our fortress.* It was calculated that the delicate sensibilities of the Sahib-logue could not hold out against the effluvium of the putrefying horseflesh, supplemented by a few corpses of Sepoys, who might more materially aid the siege in death than in life. It was, indeed, a very heavy trial of their powers of endurance. Unfortunately, those useful scavengers, the vultures and the jackals, who would soon have left only bleached skeletons, as studies of comparative anatomy for Dr. Hally, one of the garrison, were scared away by the incessant firing from our rifles and carbines and fowling-pieces, and compelled to glut themselves on such carrion as they could find at a distance. But again a favouring breeze sprung up, and swept the foul stench away from the defenders. And they fought on none the worse for any of these devices.

The next tactical experiment was this. The sturdy

* The horses were shot at the commencement of the siege, after our first brush with the enemy.

1857. July. veteran, Kower Singh, had dug up a couple of guns of small calibre. To what extent the soil of India was fertile with root-crops of this kind it is difficult to ascertain; but it is certain that, in many parts of the country, arms of various kinds were hidden underground, to be exhumed when occasion might require them. So the old Rajpoot brought these buried treasures to the surface. It was said afterwards, as a complaint against the Governor-General, who had been slow to pass the Act restricting the sale of arms, that these guns had been bought in Calcutta. The truth of the matter is as I have stated it. It is plain, indeed, that if, with malice prepense, there had been a purchase of guns at the great Presidency city, it would not have escaped the sagacity of Kower Singh that guns are not of much use without ammunition. But it happened at Arrah that the old Rajpoot having dug up the guns, was sorely perplexed by want of the means of loading them. Only a very few round shot could be found, and these were soon exhausted. But the Natives of India are an ingenious people. Having occupied Mr. Boyle's house, they were not slow in turning its contents to account. They had thrown up a battery in the compound, constructed out of the most substantial bits of furniture to be found in the sitting-rooms and bedrooms of the Engineer, and behind this they had sheltered themselves whilst working their guns. But the happiest thought of all was the discovery of implements of offensive warfare in these articles of domestic utility. Whatever metal could be found on Boyle's furniture was promptly converted into ammunition; and it was no small source of merriment to him to find that the enemy were firing into his fortress the castors of his wife's piano and his own easy-chair. But although the assailants did the best that they could with their guns—soon to be supplied with more suitable ammunition—and tried their effect from different points, including the roof of the big house, they could not bombard our people out of the fortress. 1857. July.

But there was an enemy more formidable than the Sepoy battalions—more formidable than Kower Singh and his followers. That enemy was Time. As days passed and still no relief came, it was impossible altogether to suppress the thought that the prospects of the besieged were gloomy. They fought on stoutly as before; and they talked cheerfully to one another; but as they saw both their water and their ammunition running short, and there were no tidings of the looked-for succours, even the bravest felt the gnawings of inward care. They had heard the firing on the night and morning of Dunbar's disaster, and had rightly divined that the first attempt at relief had failed. Speculation had been afterwards turned into certainty by the arrival of a wounded Sikh soldier, who had contrived to crawl to the walls of our fortress, and being received within them, told the sad story of the repulse of our relieving force. It seemed scarcely possible that they would be left to their fate; but no one could say what greater exigencies elsewhere might prevent the timely assistance which alone could save them.* Aid might come—but too late. All they could look to with any certainty was their own audacious self-reliance—their magnificent fertility of resource. If ball-cartridges were scarce, could they not be manufactured? If water failed them, could they not sink a well? So

* It should be stated that the garrison had determined, in the event of succours not arriving before the exhaustion of their provisions, to make their way to some ford on the river Soane. But this a correspondent describes to me as "a forlorn chance."

1857. July. some took to casting bullets, and some to boring the earth for water. And soon the eyes of the Sikhs were gladdened with the sight of the welcome supplies. If every bullet had its billet, there would have been cartridges enough of home manufacture to erase the Dinapore regiments altogether; and there was good water at a depth of eighteen feet from the surface, dug down from a chamber beneath the house, to last out any possible length of siege. The digging, too, had double uses. Earth was wanted almost as much as water, for our defences were growing weaker under the fire of the enemy, and the soil thus excavated was very serviceable for earthworks. But there was still another difficulty to be encountered. Boyle had provisioned the garrison with grain of all kinds. But Englishmen cannot work day and night, for any length of time, upon rice and chupatties. The want of the accustomed animal food soon began to be severely felt. But how were the needed supplies of butcher's meat to be provided? Some sheep were still browsing about in the compound, wondering why they did not get their wonted allowances of grain to fatten them. But it would have been certain death to our people to have gone out to capture the animals, except under cover of the night, when the enemy might not be on the alert. So a nocturnal sortie was determined upon in aid of our empty flesh-pots. The sally was as successful as could have been desired. Four sheep, not much the worse for recent limitation to pure pasturage, were brought in amidst great rejoicing. Contemporary history is silent as to the manner in which, in the absence of butcherly experiences, the live animals were converted into joints; but we may be sure that this difficulty was gallantly overcome like the rest, and that the roast mutton was none the worse for the absence of any professional dissection of the carcass. 1857. July.

But the most formidable peril of all that threatened the lives of the garrison was this. Having tried every other means of expelling the English and their allies from their little fortress, the enemy bethought themselves of mining operations. There were signs of this, too significant to be neglected. So again Boyle's engineering knowledge was brought vigorously into work to frustrate the designs of the assailants. If the enemy could mine, the besieged could countermine. Rapidly and successfully the work proceeded to its completion; and it was felt that the safety of the fortress was secured. It was subsequently proved that the suspected danger was not imaginary. The enemy's mine "had reached our foundations, and a canvas tube, filled with gunpowder, was lying handy to blow us up."*

And thus a week passed. The second Sunday came round. From their look-out places the defenders could see, on that morning, that there was unusual excitement among the people of Arrah. Something evidently had happened, or was going to happen, which might for good or for evil have an important influence on the fate of the garrison. There was unwonted commotion in the vicinity of the town, "whence crowds of people were hurrying with carts, elephants, camels, and horses, laden with plunder."† The fire of the enemy was not silent, but it had somewhat slackened, and but few of the besiegers were to be seen. Then as the day ad- August 2.

* Report of Mr. H. C. Wake. The writer, however, adds: "I do not think they would have succeeded, for their powder was bad, and another stroke of their pickaxe would have broken into our countermine."

† Account of the Siege of Arrah, written to illustrate Mr. Tayler's picture.

1857. August 2. vanced, the ears of the garrison were strained to catch what seemed to be the sound of a distant cannonade, and they asked each other what was its meaning. It might be the sound of a coming deliverance, or it might be a portent of greater danger. They listened and listened; they watched and watched; and, as the day advanced, all outward interpretations seemed to be in favour of the besieged. It was plain that the enemy were drawing off—that they had other work in hand; that the guns which had been heard were the guns of a relieving force, and that the Sepoy regiments had gone out to meet it. Before the sun had set the siege was

August 3. at an end. Next morning they welcomed their deliverers.

Major Vincent Eyre. How the deliverance came to pass must now be told. There was in the Company's Army an officer named Vincent Eyre. He was a Brevet-Major of Bengal Artillery in the prime of his life; but, though as a subaltern he had come out of the disastrous war in Afghanistan with a good reputation, both as a soldier and as a military historian, and had subsequently been selected to organise and to command the Artillery of the new Gwalior Contingent, the fortunes of the service had given him nothing better in 1857, on his return from a visit to England on sick furlough, than a company of European gunners with a horse field battery of six guns. With this he had been sent into the obscurity of British Burmah at the beginning of the year; but the convulsions in Upper India called him and his battery away from the outlying province, and he arrived off Calcutta in the midst of the great panic of the 14th of June, and at once took the measure of the crisis. It was plain that there was work for him to do, and he was eager to do it. Intelligence of fresh disasters, each more grievous than the last, was coming in every day. There was no military station at which Eyre, with his sixty European gunners and his Light Field Battery, would not have been a valuable accession to our strength; but it was hard, amidst so many imploring cries for help, to determine to which first to respond. On the 10th of July the battery was embarked on a river-flat, and was being tugged up the Ganges on its way to Allahabad.

1857. July 10-25.

Eyre improvises a field force.

On the evening of the 25th of July the steamer was off Dinapore. That very evening had witnessed the mutiny and the flight of Lloyd's regiments. So Eyre landed at once, and offered his services to the General, who accepted the loan of three guns for the night. But next morning they were re-embarked, and the Artillery company went on its way up the river, with instructions, if occasion should require, to succour the station of Ghazepore. Between Dinapore and Ghazepore lies the town of Buxar, near which the Company had one of their breeding-studs for horses, with an extensive establishment, but neither any Sepoy regiments nor any European troops. There Eyre learnt that the Dinapore mutineers had crossed the Soane, and had marched upon Arrah, where the lives of all the European residents were in imminent danger. So he at once determined to rescue them. A company of Artillery alone could not accomplish this. He resolved, therefore, to steam on to Ghazepore, and to borrow or barter a handful of European Infantry. At the latter place was a Native Infantry regiment, watched by only a hundred men of the Seventy-eighth Highlanders. It was not strange

1857. July. that there should be some reluctance to part from any of these; for Ghazepore was one of the places on the river that was most in danger. Although the bulk of the coin in the Treasury had been removed, there was great wealth of opium in the Company's godowns, and a great temptation, therefore, to a rising of the Sepoys. But a couple of well-manned guns, with an Artillery officer to command them, might be considered to contribute as much to the safety of the place as twenty-five foot soldiers. So a bargain was effected. Eyre landed his only subaltern, with two guns, and the right complement of gunners, and took on board with him his little party of Highlanders, ripe and ready for the work before them. He then turned back to Buxar, where he had left some high-spirited officers, as eager as himself to go to the relief of Arrah, who had promised to beat up for volunteers, and to do all that they could to help him. But the Captain of the steamer had his duty to perform as well as the Commander of the Artillery, and that duty was to go forward, not to go backward. There was a heavy penalty payable to Government for every day's delay, and his destination was Allahabad. Eyre, however, was not a man to shrink from responsibility of any kind, so he took upon himself to hold the Captain and his employers harmless; and on his arrival at Buxar, put the guarantee in official documentary shape. There, to his delight, he found that a detachment of Her Majesty's Fifth Fusiliers—a hundred and sixty strong—had arrived during his absence. They were under the command of Captain L'Estrange. To him Eyre at once made requisition; and again was met with the question of responsibility. There are many men more afraid of the Government which they serve than of the Enemy whom they are sent to encounter. Eyre was not one of them. He addressed, therefore, a public letter to Captain L'Estrange, ordering him to place the detachment of Fusiliers at his disposal, and to make ready for a march upon Arrah. This done, he had to provide draught cattle for his guns. He had necessarily left the horses of his battery at Burmah; and now he had to fall back upon the old rejected beasts of burden, and to take bullocks from the plough to flounder on with his field-pieces. His ammunition-boxes and his commissariat stores he placed on a number of country carts; and by the evening of the 30th of July he was fully equipped for the march. 1857. July.

The twenty-five Highlanders borrowed from Ghazepore having been ordered to return to that station, where they were much needed, Eyre's force consisted of a hundred and fifty men of the Fifth Fusiliers, fourteen mounted Volunteers, and thirty-four Artillerymen, with three guns—in all, two hundred fighting men, wanting two. Captain Hastings, whose acquaintance Eyre had made on his first visit to Buxar, and who had helped him to beat up for volunteers,* was appointed staff officer of the force. At five o'clock on the evening of the 30th of July, the little party set out in high spirits, never doubting the issue. Being one of those men who are by nature inclined "just to scorn the consequence and just to do the thing," Eyre reported to Divisional General Lloyd what he was going to do, and straightway proceeded to do it, leaving the sanction of higher authority to follow after him, or not to come at all, as the case might be.

* Eyre says in a family letter: "The Honourable Captain Hastings (as fine a fellow as e er breathed) entered enthusiastically into my plans, as likewise did Lieutenant Jackson in charge of the stud."

1857. July—Aug. The march to Arrah.

After five or six weeks of heavy rain, the country between Buxar and Arrah was not likely to be very favourable to the passage of gun-carriages and heavy-laden carts. The bullocks, too, resented the new kind of work that had been imposed upon them, and were not easily persuaded, or stimulated practically, to recognise the necessity of prompt movement. Still Eyre contrived to make progress; and after a two days' march he came in front of the enemy. On the second day he had learnt the disaster that had overtaken Dunbar's relieving force. This had increased his eagerness to reach his destination and to release our beleaguered people. It was plain to him now that Providence had assigned this good work to him, and, despite the odds against him, he never doubted its successful accomplishment.

August 2.

In the early dawn of Sunday, the 2nd of August, he had just commenced his third morning's march, when the familiar notes of the "assembly," as sounded by our buglers in the Company's Cantonments, came from a wood in his front; and soon his two hundred English fighting men were in the presence of thousands of the enemy. It was plain that they were extending themselves on both sides, so as to outflank and to surround us. So Eyre drew up his force and offered them battle. There were three things now in our favour to counterbalance the immense disparity of numbers; we had Artillery, the enemy had none; our Infantry were armed with Enfield rifles, whilst the insurgents had only Brown Bess; and we had a Commander equally skilful and intrepid. The well-directed fire of the guns soon disconcerted the insurgents; and the skirmishers of the Fifth Fusiliers, pressing forward, sent such messages of death to them, with unerring aim from long distances, that the Sepoys were not minded to advance. Profiting by this, Eyre concentrated his fire upon their centre, and on the grand old principle of *aut viam inveniam aut faciam*, cleared the way and marched through them with all his baggage. Having extricated himself from the wood, he pushed forward towards the village of Beebee-gunj, which lay on his road to Arrah. But there the enemy had destroyed the bridge, by which alone he could pass a deep stream, intersecting his route; so he was compelled to make a flank movement, which brought him clear of the nullah and on to the works of the unfinished railway on the direct line to Arrah. Meanwhile, the Sepoy regiments were marching down on the opposite side of the stream, eager to intercept his further advance, whilst Kower Singh, with a large body of armed retainers, was following his track. It was plain now that another battle, and a harder one than the first, was inevitable before the end of morning prayer in our churches. 1857. August.

The line of railway gained, Eyre drew up his force, and the fight speedily commenced. Awed by the foretaste they had had in the morning of our Enfield rifles and our field-guns, the enemy again sought shelter in a wood, from which they poured a galling fire on our people. Our want of numbers was now severely felt. There was a general want of fighting men to contend with the multitude of the enemy, and there was a special want, almost as great, which rendered the service of a single man, in that conjuncture, well-nigh as important as a company of fusiliers. Eyre had left his only Artillery subaltern at Ghazepore, and was compelled, therefore, himself to direct the fire of his guns when he would fain have been directing the general operations of his force. More than once the forward movements of the Infantry had left the guns without support; and the

1857. August 2. Sepoys, seeing their opportunity, had made a rush upon the battery, but had been driven back by showers of grape. Another charge made in greater force, and the guns might, perhaps, be lost to us. The Infantry were fighting stoutly and steadily, but they could not make an impression on those vastly superior numbers, aided by the advantage of their position. The staff officer, Hastings, indeed, had brought word that the Fusiliers were giving way. The moment was a critical one. Nothing now was so likely to save us as the arbitrament of the cold steel. So Eyre issued orders for a bayonet-charge. With the utmost alacrity, Hastings carried back the order to the Commander of the Infantry; but not immediately finding L'Estrange, who was in another part of the field, and seeing that there was no time to be lost, he "collected every available man," placed himself at their head, and issued the stirring order to charge. L'Estrange, meanwhile, had come up with another body of Fusiliers, and the whole, sending up as they went a right good English cheer, cleared the stream, which at this point had tapered down to the breadth of a few feet, and charged the surprised and panic-stricken multitude of Sepoys. It was nothing that they had our numbers twenty times told. They turned and fled in confusion before the British bayoneteers; whilst Eyre poured in his grape, round after round, upon the flying masses. The rout was complete. They never rallied. And the road to Arrah was left as clear as though there had been no mutiny at Dinapore—no revolt in Behar.*

* Among the foremost in the charge under L'Estrange was Arthur Scott, then a young Captain in the same regiment, who had recently been under hot fire in the capture of the Redan at Sebastopol. I am told that he said that this day's work was far the more trying of the two.

So they marched on along the line of the railway until, as the shades of evening were falling upon them, they came upon a rapid stream—another branch of the Beenas nullah—over which Eyre could not cross his guns. It was necessary, therefore, after some fashion or other, to improvise a bridge for the occasion. It was a fortunate circumstance that the railway works supplied abundance of bricks. To span the stream with a bridge of masonry in a single night was an effort beyond the reach of human power. But by casting large numbers of bricks into the nullah they so narrowed the extent of water to be passed, that by the help of the country carts, which they had brought with them, they formed a wooden bridge, across which the guns and the baggage were conveyed in safety; and on the morning of the 3rd of August they entered Arrah and marched upon Boyle's little house. The rapture of the moment, when Vincent Eyre learnt that he was in time to save the heroic garrison, must have been more than enough to compensate him for all the sufferings of his long captivity in Afghanistan. And it would be hard to say, when that little band of warriors, drawn from the two great services, met each other on that Monday morning, unshaven and unwashed, with the marks of battle on their faces, who were the prouder of the two—the Deliverers or the Delivered.

1857. August 3. Relief of Arrah.

At Arrah, Eyre halted for a little space. He had need to recruit the strength of his weary force; and he had some accounts to settle with mutineers and rebels, otherwise than on the field of battle. A merciful, humane man, Vincent Eyre was not one to delight in "indiscriminate hangings;" but there were

Eyre's march on Jugdespore.

1857. August. stern duties to be executed within the pale of righteous retribution; there were proved culprits to be executed, and there were populations to be disarmed. A week was spent in this work and in the better equipment of his troops; and then Eyre, reinforced by two hundred men of the Tenth Foot from Dinapore, and a hundred of Rattray's Sikhs, prepared himself again to take the field against the rebels of Behar. With him went Herwald Wake, at the head of the fifty Sikhs who had formed the bulk of the old Arrah garrison;* whilst others of the European defenders enrolled themselves as troopers in Jackson's Volunteer Horse.

Kower Singh had taken up his position in the neighbourhood of Jugdespore, where he owned an ancestral castle or mansion, of large dimensions and considerable strength. Within its walls he had stored up vast quantities of grain, the collection of which had grievously afflicted the people, and he had brought together munitions of war on a scale sufficient to enable him to stand a protracted siege. It might well have been asked, "Who would have thought that the old man had so much blood in him?" He had obviously made great preparations for a campaign; and there had flocked to his standard not only the Sepoys of the revolted regiments, but men who were on furlough from other corps, and even the old pensioners, who were living on the bounty of the Company, in Behar. It was shown by the accoutrements found upon the field that men of no less than nine regiments had fought against Eyre at Beebee-gunj. And this was the feeble, sick old man, who when

* There was glorious compensation in this, for Wake, before the siege, had distrusted the Sikhs, and begged that none might be sent to Arrah.

William Tayler had invited him to Patna, could not stir from his couch. This was the friendly "Baboo" whose fidelity, in the fulness of our national self-complacency, had not been questioned or suspected, and who might have arrayed himself on our side if he had been better treated. 1857. August.

On the afternoon of the 11th of August, Eyre's force commenced its march to Jugdespore. On the following morning they found themselves before a "formidable jungle," covering the approaches to the town. The enemy were drawn up near the village of Dulloor—the Sepoy battalions being on the right and Kower Singh's Irregular levies on the left, but so sheltered by broken ground and dense jungle as to be scarcely discernible by our people as they advanced. But the fire of our skirmishers presently revealing their position, a shower of grape was poured in upon them from our nine-pounders; and then the enemy, after some temporary confusion, began to shift their line to the right. On this the men of the Tenth Foot, maddened by recollections of the past, became almost ungovernable in their eagerness to fling themselves on the insurgents. It would not have been wise to restrain such impetuosity, so the word was given to charge; and on they went, headed by Captain Patterson, with a ringing cheer, hoping that the enemy would stand the shock of the attack. But when our people, showing such a front as to portend that, notwithstanding the fewness of our numbers, there could be nothing but death and destruction in the impact, were within some sixty yards of the enemy, the Sepoys turned and fled, some seeking safety in the jungle, some the shelter of the walls of Dulloor. And thither the Tenth pushed on and pursued them. August 11. The fight at Jugdespore.

1857. August 11.

Meanwhile, Kower Singh's levies had been closing in upon the right flank of Eyre's force, and L'Estrange's Infantry, with Wake's Sikhs and the Volunteers, were gallantly holding them in check. Happily, the howitzer had been left with this part of the British column, and, directed by Staff-Sergeant Melville, it opened upon the rebels with destructive effect. The result was that ere the fighting had lasted more than an hour, both the Sepoys and the Irregulars were in full retreat upon Jugdespore, pursued by Patterson and L'Estrange. Two of the enemy's guns fell into our hands during the pursuit; and an hour after noon, the British force had entered the stronghold of Kower Singh. The town was almost deserted, and of the rebel Rajah himself no tidings could be learnt. But on the following day it was known that Kower Singh had deserted his stronghold, just before Eyre's arrival under its walls, and had sought refuge in the jungle. There, at a distance of some seven miles from Jugdespore, he had an umbrageous retreat, to which, it was reported, he had betaken himself; so L'Estrange was sent to beat up his quarters. But whilst the old Rajpoot knew every path and winding of the jungle, and could rapidly make his way through it, the English officer, having no such knowledge, was comparatively slow of movement; and ere he reached the place of refuge, Kower Singh had fled onwards to Sasseram, with the remnant of the Fortieth Regiment. So L'Estrange destroyed the evacuated asylum, and marched back to Jugdespore.

Destruction of Jugdespore.

Having found good quarters for his force in the commodious residence of Kower Singh, Eyre halted them there for a little while, determined to leave no shelter for the enemy after his departure from it. He undermined all the chief buildings, and whilst the work was going on, he distributed among the villagers the large supplies of grain that had been stored up in the Rajah's mansion,* and destroyed all the munitions of war that he could not take away with him. On the 15th of August everything was ready for the explosion. About mid-day the force marched out of the Jugdespore quarters, and soon afterwards the mines were sprung. All the principal buildings within Kower Singh's premises were soon heaps of blackened ruins; and a Hindoo temple, on the Rajah's estate, shared the fate of the other edifices. 1857. August.

The destruction of the temple excited some adverse comment. Major Eyre was censured for this act of severity by the Commander-in-Chief of the Army.† But it is probable that the case was not understood at Head-Quarters. The temple which Eyre destroyed was not an ancient fane, held in veneration for ages by the people of the surrounding country. It was little more than what we are wont to describe as a "hobby" or "folly"—an edifice recently built, at considerable cost, by Kower Singh himself. It was, indeed, a sort of private chapel, or pantheon, by the

* In Major Eyre's statement, as taken down by Mr. Gubbins at Lucknow, it appears that "Kower Singh had collected within his walls *stores of grain sufficient to have subsisted* 20,000 *men for six months*." I thought that there must be some exaggeration in this. But Sir Vincent Eyre has assured me that this was the calculation made at the time by the Commissariat officers and civil officials: "Supposing each man to consume one pound of rice per diem, the total supply for six months for 20,000 men would be 45,000 maunds. The surrounding villages complained that Kower Singh had seized all their stores of grain to hoard up at Jugdespore, and the quantity found seemed to justify their complaint."

† No such censure was ever transmitted to Major Eyre by his superiors; but Sir Colin Campbell, while expressing his satisfaction to the Governor-General at Major Eyre's military proceedings, hesitated to extend his praise to so unusual an act as the destruction of a temple. Lord Canning, with a fuller knowledge of the circumstances, approved of it.

1857. August. erection of which—at least as Eyre believed—the old Rajpoot sought to glorify himself rather than the deities which he had idolised there. The distinction thus drawn must not be denied its just weight. It is one thing to destroy an ancient religious edifice, in which generations after generations have worshipped, and another to demolish a modern fane, reared, in ostentation, by a living individual. Kower Singh was, doubtless, grievously pained and shocked by the demolition of his cherished temple; but the feelings of the peaceful inhabitants of the country were not outraged by it, as they would have been by the destruction of a popular shrine.*

The destruction of Kower Singh's stronghold was in effect the termination of Eyre's short and brilliant campaign. He marched on the 16th in pursuit of the enemy towards Sasseram; but he received on the way instructions to return to Arrah—his force being required for other and more urgent service. But already in that fortnight he had done such work as fairly to secure for him a place among the foremost soldiers of the war. He had rescued from certain destruction our beleaguered people. He had broken, at least for a time, the neck of the rebellion in Behar. He had dispersed the Sepoy mutineers, and shown, brilliantly and unmistakably, that there was still a robust vitality in the British Army, and that the sun of the Company's "*ikhbal*" had not set for ever in disaster and disgrace. He had restored

* Since the words in the text were written I have chanced upon the following passage in a private letter from Sir Vincent Eyre to Mr. Tayler: "It was curious to see how the Hindoos in my camp seemed rather to delight than otherwise in the sacrilege of its destruction. I suppose the fact is that they care as a rule only for public fanes such as Juggernauth, and are indifferent as to the fate of private ones, built like this one for self-glorification. I regarded the act at the time as necessary to injure Kower Singh's prestige, and I think it had that effect."

tranquillity and confidence to the British residents in districts where before there had been excitement and alarm. And over and above these local influences, there was the great fact that these successes opened out our communications, by road and river, with the capital, which otherwise would have been disastrously closed. These were the results palpable at the moment of victory. It was left for time to develop the full benefits of Eyre's noble exploits. What those who followed him in the track of victory owed to his audacity will appear as the narrative proceeds.* 1857. August.

* I must acknowledge my obligations, at the close of this chapter, to an excellent article on Sir Vincent Eyre's operations, in the *Calcutta Review*, vol. xliv., which has, since these pages were printed, been acknowledged by Colonel Malleson, and republished in his "Recreations of an Indian Official." I am also indebted to a narrative written by Mr. Martin Gubbins, from Eyre's dictation, and published at the end of the history of the "Mutinies in Oudh." Sir Vincent Eyre's private and public correspondence have enabled me to verify these printed statements.

CHAPTER IV

MR. TAYLER'S WITHDRAWAL ORDER—STATE OF AFFAIRS AT GYA—RETREAT TO PATNA—RETURN OF MR. MONEY—THE MARCH TO CALCUTTA—GOVERNMENT CENSURE OF MR. TAYLER—THE QUESTION DISCUSSED—ARRIVAL OF SIR JAMES OUTRAM—APPOINTMENTS OF MR. GRANT AND MR. SAMUELLS.

1857. July. Mr. Tayler's withdrawal order.

THERE is no part of this vast comprehensive history, in which the lights and shadows do not alternate. Whilst all men were rejoicing in this assertion of British pluck, a cloud came over the prevailing joy; for tidings ran through the country that elsewhere there had been a great collapse. To the astonishment of most men, it became known that William Tayler, the Patna Commissioner, on learning that Dunbar's expedition had failed, had issued an order instructing the few remaining civil officers at the out-stations to withdraw their establishments to Patna. To do this, it was said, was to abandon much Government property, to leave the gaols at the mercy of the populace, to sacrifice the good name of the British Government, and to give an impetus to rebellion in Behar, that it might take long months to suppress. That Commissioner Tayler, who had in the months of June and July restrained the fugitive propensities of men under his control, should have commanded a precipitate flight to the Civil Head-Quarters, was something strange and incredible; but it was a fact. Mr. Tayler believed that there was no hope for Arrah, and that as the fall of this important station would be the forerunner of other similar disasters, there was nothing left for him but to save the lives of the Christian people in the districts. So he resolved to direct the chief officers at Mozufferpore and Gya to withdraw their establishments to Patna, where the Chuprah officers, having abandoned the station on learning that Holmes's regiment had mutinied at Segowlie, had already sought safety. In this resolution, he recorded a Minute, stating fully his reasons for the step; and then he sent a copy of it to the Bengal Government, with a brief recital, in the form of an official letter, of the motives which had actuated him.*

1857. July.

July 31.

When this order reached Mozufferpore, the head-quarters of the Tirhoot district, there had already been some discussion as to the expediency of withdrawal, and some difference of opinion had prevailed among the chief civil officers respecting it. Mr. Forbes, the Judge, had written to Mr. Tayler on the 29th, declaring that the station was in extreme danger, and that unless some better protection could be afforded to them, the officials, "with due regard to

Mozufferpore.

* The following is the text of Mr. Tayler's letter: "Separated as Englishmen are, and scattered in small numbers over several districts, with no sufficient protection whatever, we can now expect nothing but murder and disaster. Concentration for a time, therefore, appears an imperative necessity, and is the only means of recovering our position. I have therefore authorised all the officials of the districts to come in to Patna. Those of Chuprah have been in for some days; they made an attempt to return to Doorigunge yesterday, but returned when they heard of the defeat of our force. I trust the Government will approve of the measures taken; whatever be the temporary confusion caused by this measure, the object appears to me to justify it. I have hitherto endeavoured to encourage all public officers to stand fast, but I now consider that their so doing only increases the danger to all."

1857. July. their own safety," could "not reasonably be expected to wait before quitting the station;" but Mr. Lautour, the Magistrate, had "attempted to persuade the residents to remain" at their post. The non-official residents of Tirhoot had, on the same 29th of July, written to General Lloyd, saying, that "owing to what had recently taken place at Dinapore and Segowlie, the district was in the greatest danger"—that, on the outbreak of any active disturbance, the "whole district would rise," and imploring the General to send a few European soldiers for their protection, or at least a sufficient number to escort their families into Dinapore. In this state of almost general alarm, the orders of the Commissioner were received and acted upon without hesitation. But, in this instance, the anticipated results were not realised. The people did not rise. The Treasury was not plundered; the inmates of the Gaol were not released; the houses of the Europeans were not burnt. Perfect quietude, however, did not prevail. There was a detachment of Holmes's Irregulars at Mozufferpore, and when the European gentlemen departed, they broke out into open mutiny. If the Nujeebs had then joined them, the station would have been sacrificed and the district would have been overrun by Budmashes. But the Nujeebs stood up staunchly against the Irregulars, and defended the public buildings; so the troopers, being repulsed in their attempts upon the Government property, consoled themselves with the plunder of some private houses, and made off in search of further mischief. When, soon afterwards, Mr. Lautour returned to Mozufferpore, he found that his own residence had been despoiled, but that the station was quiet, and the people ready to welcome the re-establishment of Government authority, if it could be said ever to have been effaced. So the episode of Mozufferpore took but a minor place in history; not so the story of Gya. 1857. July.

The city of Gya, the chief civil station of the Behar district, lay at a distance of fifty-five miles from Patna, and two hundred and sixty-five miles from Calcutta. It was a place of considerable antiquity, instinct with historical associations, and a favoured home of Brahminical superstitions.* In the month of July, 1857, the two chief British officers stationed there were Mr. Trotter, the Judge, and Mr. Alonzo Money, the Magistrate of Behar. There had, ever since the commencement of the convulsions in Upper India, been indications in the district of an unquiet spirit, pervading more or less all classes of the community, and strongest perhaps among the Hindoo Zemindars. In the city itself the Brahmins had been busy, industriously disseminating the fiction, so rife in all parts of the country, of the mixture of the bones or blood of swine and oxen with the *atta*, or flour, in the bazaars. It seemed to be one of their principal objects to corrupt the Sikh soldiery who were posted there, and to win them over to the rebel cause by these infamous fabrications. When it was found that this was of no avail, they ostracised the Sikhs, de- Gya.

* Mr. Edward Thornton, to whose "Gazetteer of India" every writer on Indian subjects is much indebted, says that "the town consists of two parts, one the residence of the priests and the population connected with them; the other, the quarters of the great bulk of the population. This last was much enlarged by Law, and thence denominated Sahib-gunj." In a note Mr. Thornton says: "Law commanded the French force in this part of India from 1757 to 1761." But I suspect that the Sahib thus commemorated was Mr. Thomas Law—a genuine Englishman—who presided for many years over the Company's establishments at Gya, in the latter part of the last century. He has been described (perhaps in imitation of the famous description of Boyle) as "the Father of the Permanent Settlement and the brother of Lord Ellenborough." He was uncle of the second Lord Ellenborough, formerly Governor-General of India, who died in December, 1871.

1857. July. claring them to be Christians, and refusing to smoke from the same hookah with them. It became necessary to suppress these machinations with a strong hand; so a carpenter, against whom there was proof of having attempted to corrupt two Sikh soldiers, was
July 22. hanged in the most public manner before all the troops and the police in the place. And the example had a salutary effect in the city.*

But still the Gya Magistrate felt that he was surrounded by enemies only waiting the signal to rise. Writing on the 24th of July, he said: "There are rumours of hostile preparations on the part of Kower Singh in Arrah. Though he belongs not to my district, I have taken steps to ascertain the truth. A rise on his part would be felt here. A messenger from him three days ago went to the Deo Rajah in this district, and came on to Moodenarain Singh. For myself, I believe that half the people in the district would rise against us, were they not afraid. I hear constantly of ryots being instructed by their Zemindars to hold themselves in readiness." And in another letter he said: "If Kower Singh goes, half Behar would follow." Strange rumours were afloat of hostile movements on the part of other great landholders. Moodenarain Singh was reported to have exhumed numbers of buried guns, to have enlisted and armed a large body of retainers, and to have put his castle in a state of defence; and it was added that the Rajah of Benares had been in communication with the great Zemindar. There was nothing improbable in this; but when it was stated that this was a hostile conspiracy against the British Raj, there was a violent

* "The punishment," wrote Mr. Money, "appeared to have a great effect. One or two executions, I believe, strike terror and do good. But I hope not to have many. I am confident that the daily repetition of such scenes (where the people are against us) hardens and aggravates."

presumption not justified by ascertained facts. The Rajah of Benares had not swerved from his allegiance to the British Government, and it may be fairly conjectured that any movement upon his part was against the insurgents.* 1857. July.

When news reached Mr. Money that the Dinapore regiments had revolted, he bethought himself of active measures of defence. "The mutiny at Dinapore," he wrote to the Bengal Government, "has thrown Gya into a ferment. There is nothing, however, to be apprehended from the townspeople. They are surrounded by a new and strong police, and have a wholesome dread of the forty-five English and one hundred Sikhs. The present causes of apprehension are two: the inroad of any large number of Dinapore mutineers, or the approach of the Monghyr and Deoghur Fifth Irregulars, who are sure to rise, I imagine. . . . If the mutineers, or any portion of them, come this way, they will either remain in the district and be joined by disaffected Zemindars, or they will make for Gya. There are plenty of Zemindars who would join them if they once got the upper hand; but there are none, I think, who will hazard life and property before that. The following is our plan of operations: any body of the mutineers under three hundred or three hundred and fifty, are to be met about two miles from the town; forty-five English, one hundred Sikhs, and forty Nujeebs, besides four or five residents, will oppose them. I shall put the Nujeebs between the Sikhs and the English, so they July 28.

* See *ante*, vol. ii. page 231; and the Memorandum by Mr. E. A. Reade in Appendix to same volume. The information respecting Moodenarain Singh and his guns was communicated to Mr. Tayler, who wrote to Money on the subject. Money was eager to go out against the Zemindar and beat up his quarters, but he admitted that the facts did not justify the inference of treason, and the issue proved that he was correct.

1857. July 31. must be staunch or be cut to pieces. The mutineers would be dejected and tired after a long march, and I have no doubt of giving them a good thrashing. If they come in large numbers, I shall place the treasure in a pucka house, which is being provisioned, and we will defend it with the same numbers as above." The man who wrote this must have had the right stuff in him; he was sure not to be wanting when the hour of danger should come.

Affairs were in this state when, news of Dunbar's disaster having reached Patna, Mr. Tayler issued the orders of which I have above spoken. How those orders were received at Gya cannot be better told than in the words of the Magistrate himself. "On the 31st of July," wrote Mr. Alonzo Money, not long afterwards, "I was sitting in my room, talking to the Soubahdar of the Nujeebs, when a letter marked 'urgent' and 'express' was put into my hands. I opened it. It was from the Commissioner. It contained an electric telegraph message from the Government and an order for me. The message spoke of the defeat of Dunbar's party at Arrah, and continued: 'Everything must now be sacrificed to holding the country and the occupation of a central position.' The order decided me and the other civil authorities to come with all our force to Patna, making our arrangements as promptly and quickly as possible. It contained an injunction to remove the treasure, if doing so endangered not personal safety. 'What does the Commissioner Sahib say?' asked the Soubahdar. I made some excuse, and after a minute or two sent him off. I then despatched a circular round the station, and within an hour every one was present. It was agreed that we should start at five that evening. . . . . At six we started." They went, leaving everything behind them—seven or eight lakhs of rupees in the Treasury, and a gaol gorged with criminals. They went, leaving the station and all that it contained under charge of the Darogah and the Soubahdar of the Nujeebs, and set their faces towards Patna, in obedience to the orders they had received. But the orders were that they should not abandon the treasure unless their lives were endangered by the attempt to remove it, and there were those at Gya who thought that they might have safely remained to complete their measures for the safe custody of the coin. 1857. July—Aug.

But they had not ridden more than two or three miles, when Alonzo Money fell into conversation with a gentleman of the Uncovenanted Service, named Hollings. He was an officer attached to the Opium Agency, and he had no duty demanding his return to Gya. But he felt acutely the degradation of this sudden abandonment of the station. Mr. Money was moved by kindred feelings. So these two brave men determined to return to Gya and see what could be done to save the property of the Government, and to lessen the discredit of this precipitate retreat. Whilst, therefore, the rest went on to Patna, Money and Hollings went back to the station which they had so lately quitted. They found things nearly as they had left them. The treasure remained intact; the Gaol held fast its prisoners. Up to this time the Nujeebs had faithfully fulfilled their trust.* The

* On the 1st of August Mr. Money wrote to the Government of Bengal: "The abandonment of the Government property and almost certain giving up of the district and town to anarchy and plunder was repugnant to me. I felt that I could personally be of very little use at Dinapore. At Gya I might preserve order. Mr. Hollings was also anxious to return. We rode back together, having gone about three miles from the town. All was quiet. We went first to the Gaol; and I called out the Nujeebs and addressed them. They all professed loyalty. We then

1857. August 4. return of the Magistrate seemed to give confidence to the people. Many of the most respectable inhabitants waited on Mr. Money, and welcomed him back with expressions of joy. But when, as a measure of precaution not unwise in itself, he burnt the Government stamped paper, the first feelings of confidence subsided, and presently the Nujeebs rose against us.

It was now plain that the position of these gallant Englishmen was one of no common difficulty and danger. Not only was there, so far as their information then extended, a prospect of being visited by the Dinapore mutineers and the insurgent rabble under Kower Singh, but they were threatened more imminently by an incursion of mutineers from Hazarabaugh, where the Native troops had revolted. The first step, therefore, to be taken was to recall the detachment of Her Majesty's Sixty-fourth, which had left Gya just before the European exodus; and, this done, the treasure was to be secured. Every effort was made to collect carriage for the transport of the coin; and on the 4th of August the convoy was ready to depart. But in what direction was it to proceed? The order (it has been shown) which Money had received, was that he should convey the treasure to Patna, if it could be done without endangering European life. And this was the course which, in the first instance, he had resolved to pursue. But when false rumours came from Dinapore that a body of mutineers was marching upon Gya, and that martial law had been proclaimed in all the Behar districts, there seemed to be little hope of so small a party, heavily encumbered, reaching Patna in safety.* It

rode to the Treasury, and there again I addressed the Nujeebs. We had been absent three hours from the town (for the stoppages had been numerous), and I was glad to find all quiet."

* "The next day (August 3rd) brought a letter to Captain Thomp-

was determined, therefore, at a council of civil and military officers that the better course would be to take the Grand Trunk Road to Calcutta—a far longer but a safer journey. So the treasure-party moved out from Gya, under command of Captain Thompson, and Money prepared to join them. He was rescuing a few of his household gods from the certain wreck which would follow his departure, when a noise of shouting and yelling was heard, which needed not the explanation of a servant who presently ran in to announce that the Gaol was broken into and the prisoners loose. It was added that already they were streaming down upon the Magistrate's house. No time was then to be lost. His horse stood ready saddled in the stable. Nothing could be saved but life. So Money mounted, and rode with all speed to join the convoy.*

1857. August 4.

That night our little party was attacked by a mixed crowd of gaol-birds and gaolers. The escaped prisoners and the Nujeebs, who should have forbidden

son, written by an officer at Dinapore of his own corps. It contained these words in pencil: 'For God's sake look out. The Eighth Native Infantry mutineers have marched upon Gya, they say, with one gun.' The news of martial law proclaimed in all the Behar districts reached us the same morning. I called another council, and told Captain Thompson he was now the principal authority in the district. I gave him my opinion that, encumbered with treasure, we were too weak to run the risk of meeting so large a body of mutineers, and recommended falling back on the Grand Trunk Road. All coincided in the view of the case."—*Mr. Alonzo Money to Secretary to Bengal Government.*

* "I had been busy all day (August 4th) with the carriage of the troops, the loading of the treasure, &c., and having seen the convoy started safe out of Gya, I returned to my own house to save a few things of value. I was shutting down a small portmanteau, when I heard shouts and yells, and a servant ran in saying the Gaol was loose and the prisoners near. I had just time to get to the stable and mount my horse, which fortunately was saddled. A minute's delay would have prevented my escape. I got away, but with the loss of everything. I have not even a change of clothes. However, I have, I trust, saved the Government property. If I succeed in conveying it safely to Calcutta, I shall feel quite satisfied."—*Alonzo Money to Secretary to Bengal Government.*

1857. August 4—5. their escape, had made the expected combination; and now, with the Government arms in their hands, they came down to seize the treasure. It was not to be expected that such a temptation would be resisted. So, although it was a night-attack, it was not a surprise. Thompson's men were ready for them, and they gave the would-be plunderers such a reception that they were soon in a state of hopeless panic, some of them shot down, and the rest glad to carry their lives back with them to Gya. Of course it was an easy victory over such a rabble. From that time Money, with the treasure he had saved, escorted by the detachment of the Sixty-fourth, went on his way, uninterrupted and unmolested; and in the middle of August he rode into Calcutta, and delivered over to Government the large amount of treasure which he had rescued from the clutches of the insurgents. And among the exploits of the War, scored down to the credit of the Bengal Civil Service, there are few which at the time excited more enthusiasm than this. The Governor-General and his colleagues commended the conduct of Alonzo Money, and sent him back to Gya with enlarged responsibilities and increased emoluments. Mr. Hollings also had substantial reasons for being convinced that his conduct was approved by the higher authorities. To Money Lord Canning wrote on the 5th of August: "I should reproach myself if I lost a day in expressing to you, not my approval only, but my admiration of the manly and wise course which you chose for yourself. Happen what may at Gya, you have done your duty nobly in the face of heavy discouragement, guided by sound sense and a stout heart, and without a superstitious fear of responsibility. You and Mr. Hollings have acted in a manner to secure to you both the respect of all who know the circumstances in which you were placed." This was written before it was known that Money had made good his march to Calcutta and saved the treasure. The commendation was afterwards repeated, and the Governor-General, announcing to him his promotion, wrote: "I am heartily glad that there is an opportunity of enabling you to carry with you an unmistakable mark of the approval and confidence of the Government."* 1857. August.

But whilst Authority was thus extolling and rewarding Alonzo Money's exploit, a great storm of official disapprobation was overtaking Commissioner Tayler. The Government of Bengal, with a little more haste, perhaps, than was decorous in such a case, pronounced the conduct of the Commissioner to have been disgraceful, and forthwith dismissed him ignominiously from his post. "It appears from a letter just received from Mr. Tayler," wrote Lieutenant-Governor Halliday, on the 5th of August, "that whilst apparently under the influence of a panic, he has ordered the officials at all the stations in his division to abandon their posts and to fall back on Dinapore. Had it not been for the spirited and judicious conduct of Mr. A. Money, the Collector and Magistrate of Behar, who, in spite of his orders, and with only Mr. Hollings to bear him company, determined on remaining at Gya even after all the other residents and troops had left the place, this act of Mr. Tayler's would have entailed at that station alone the certain loss of eight lakhs of rupees in the Treasury, besides other public and private property, the release of many hundreds of determined convicts from the Gaol, and the risk of the whole town and Mr. Tayler's dismissal.

MS. Correspondence.

1857. August. district being thrown into anarchy and confusion. What has happened elsewhere is unknown; but there is the strongest probability everywhere of disaster arising from this unhappy measure. Under these circumstances, I have determined at once to remove Mr. Tayler from his appointment of Commissioner of Patna."* It is patent on the surface of this paragraph, that when the Lieutenant-Governor dismissed Mr. Tayler, he was imperfectly acquainted with the facts of the case. But the historical inaccuracies which it contains were caught up in London; and an eminent public writer,† whose name carried, and rightly carried with it, immense weight in all discussions relating to India, indorsed these errors, and they were disseminated by the leading journal of Europe. Mr. William Tayler was a man pugnacious to the backbone; one who never could be brought to understand the great truth contained in the aphorism that "speech is silver; silence is gold;" and such a flood of controversy arose, as would have sufficed to drown not only the patience, but the reason, of any man not endowed with large powers of endurance, who might be condemned to breast it. No incident of the Sepoy War has elicited such an ocean of words. The great Whig Chancellor who wrote that India is a country in which "eloquence evaporates in scores of paragraphs," might have added "and energy also." Mr. Tayler's mode of battle was to fight upon his stumps and to slay the slain; so the storm of controversy, which his removal from Patna excited, has scarcely been stilled
1873. up to the present time; and the usual effect has been produced by the conflict. There is still an anta-

* Parliamentary Papers.

† Sir Charles Trevelyan—"Letters of Indophilus," originally published in the *Times* newspaper.

gonism of opinion. And it is probable that if Mr. Tayler had written less, he would have been more appreciated and more applauded. 18: Aug

On the whole, it appears to me, on mature consideration, that the orders issued by Mr. Tayler were not of such a character as to merit the condemnation which Government passed upon them. It is not to be questioned that up to the time of the mutiny of the Dinapore regiments, the whole bearing of the Patna Commissioner was manly to a point of manliness not often excelled in those troubled times. He had exhorted all his countrymen to cling steadfastly to their posts. He had rebuked those who had betrayed their fears by deserting their stations. His measures had been bold; his conduct had been courageous; his policy had been severely repressive. If he had erred, assuredly his errors had not leaned to the side of weakness. He was one of the last men in the service to strike his colours, save under the compulsion of a great necessity. But when the Dinapore regiments broke into rebellion—when the European troops, on whom he had relied, proved themselves to be incapable of repressing mutiny on the spot, or overtaking it with swift retribution—when it was known that thousands of insurgent Sepoys were overrunning the country, and that the country, in the language of the day, was "up"—that some of the chief members of the territorial aristocracy had risen against the domination of the English, and that the predatory classes, including swarms of released convicts from the gaols, were waging deadly war against property and life—when he saw that all these things were against us, and there seemed to be no hope left that the scattered handfuls of Englishmen at the out-stations could escape utter

7. destruction, he deemed it his duty to revoke the
ust. orders which he had issued in more auspicious times, and to call into Patna such of our English establishments as had not already been swept away by the rebellion or escaped without official recall. In doing this he generously took upon himself the responsibility of withdrawal, and absolved all the officers under him from any blame which might descend upon them for deserting their stations without the sanction of superior authority. It was not doubted that if there had been any reasonable ground of hope that these little assemblies of Englishmen could hold their own, that they could save their lives and the property of Government by defending their posts, it would have been better that the effort should be made. But their destruction would have been a greater calamity to the State than their surrender. It was impossible to overvalue the worth of European life at that time, and the deaths of so many Englishmen would have been a greater triumph and a greater encouragement to the enemy than their flight. It was the hour of our greatest darkness and our sorest need. We know now how Wake and Boyle and Colvin and their comrades in the "little house" held the enemy in check, and how Vincent Eyre taught both the Sepoy mutineers and the Shahabad insurgents that there was still terrible vitality in our English troops. Of this William Tayler knew nothing. But he had palpably before him the fact of Dunbar's disaster, and he believed that nothing could save the little garrison at Arrah. The probabilities at the time were that the Dinapore regiments, with Kower Singh and his followers, having done their work in that direction, would move, flushed with conquest and gorged with plunder, upon Gya

and other stations, carrying destruction with them wheresoever they might go. What the Commissioner then did was what had been done and what was being done by other authorities, civil and military, in other parts of the country; it was held to be sound policy to draw in our scattered outposts to some central point of safety where the enemy might be defied. In this I can perceive no appearance of panic. If Tayler had not acted thus, and evil had befallen the Christian people under his charge, he would have been condemned with a far severer condemnation for so fatal an omission. 1857. August.

But events so greatly in favour of the nation were all against the Patna Commissioner. Eyre's triumph was Tayler's disgrace. The apprehensions of the latter were not realised. So it would have been better, in the issue, if the withdrawal order had been held in abeyance. Still if the order were an error—the error of one not a prophet—I can hardly think that in itself it merited the official punishment which it brought down upon the Commissioner—a punishment which involved the total non-recognition by the Crown of all the previous services which he had conferred on the country in the earlier stages of the rebellion in Behar. But the Bengal Government was not at that time in a temper to overlook any failure on the part of Mr. William Tayler. He had given dire offence to his superiors by his "high-handed" mode of conducting the duties of his office. Not only was it his wont to do his work in his own way without consulting any one—to do it first and to write to Government afterwards; but sometimes, in the hurry and crush of overwhelming business, he did it without reporting it at all; and this irritated superior authority. The same thing was being done

1857. August. on a larger scale elsewhere; but Patna was comparatively near to Calcutta, and Calcutta had not yet released itself from the coils of the Red Tape. Those were days when men — the best of our men—the men, indeed, who saved the country, thought more of doing than of writing. But Bureaucracy was still fain to assert that there could be no duty on the part of a public functionary more urgent than that of reporting his proceedings to Government. It is not too much to say that if this duty had been generally recognised we should have lost India. But, although at such a time great toleration should have been shown towards the errors of men called upon to act promptly, in sudden emergencies, with imperfect information before them, Mr. Tayler's conduct was stigmatised by his Government, and he was summarily removed from his office. All appeals against this decision were fruitless. The Governor-General, the Court of Directors, the Crown Government, all recorded adverse decisions; and Mr. Tayler withdrew from the service of the State. But I cannot, after full consideration of all the circumstances of the case, resist the conviction that if there was not, in this instance, a miscarriage of justice, there was a lack of that generous disposition to overlook occasional errors of judgment committed by men who had done good service in critical conjunctures, which is a distinguishing characteristic of Indian Government. Happily such instances as these are few—if, indeed, there be any other of a like character; or there might be a fear that, warned by the fate of William Tayler, if a great storm should again overtake us, the masters of our vessels might be found sitting quietly in their cabins, with their pens in their hands, minuting and recording, asking leave to save the ship after the most approved fashion, and trying to still the troubled waters with the oil of official correspondence. 1857—1865.

The Wahabees.

But the story of Mr. Tayler's disgrace would be incomplete, if one special reason alleged for his condemnation were not noticed and examined. It was said at the time that the Wahabee conspiracies of which he spoke were phantoms of his imagination. Time sets all things right—whether by illustrating truth or by unmasking imposture. The Commissioner of Patna was said to have ill-treated innocent Wahabee gentlemen. It is hard for a man who has been stripped of fame and fortune to wait patiently, during long years, for his vindication. Mr. Tayler did not wait patiently; but he waited long, and the vindication came. It was patent in rebellions and wars; in secret plots and open assassinations. It was pronounced by high courts and solemn tribunals. It was proved that there was a network of Wahabee conspiracy all over the land, and that "the centre of this truly bitter and formidable conspiracy was Patna."*

This ought to have been no unknown history in Calcutta, at the time of the events of which I have written; for in the Government archives were two minutes of that great minute-writer Lord Dalhousie, in which his sagacity was shown by exposing the

* Sir Herbert Edwardes to Mr. Tayler. "The Bengal Government," wrote this most able of public officers, and most upright of judges, "was determined not to believe in the Wahabee conspiracy, and punished you for your vigour. Time has done you justice, shown that you were right, and hanged or transported the enemies whom you suspected and disarmed." It may be observed here that Mr. Otto Trevelyan, in his admirable historical chapter "Cawnpore," sneers at that "favourite bugbear of the Calcutta alarmists," "the city of Patna," and says that after Mr. Tayler's removal "Patna was as quiet as Madras." Later experiences of life have doubtless satisfied this brilliant young writer that the places in which conspiracies are quietly hatched are not those which see their violent developments.

1857—1865. dangerous character of the Wahabee combinations even then existing. But the new doctrine of 1857 was, that the Wahabees were the least dangerous communities in the country—and at Patna especially to be encouraged. But not long afterwards it was apparent to the whole of India that the Patna Propagandists were fomenting frontier wars; that they were sending forth missionaries to preach destruction to the infidel; and that they had in the city a cunningly contrived asylum, in the penetralia of which were secret chambers and passages alike for concealment and escape.* It would be foreign to the purpose and design of this history to narrate the incidents of the frontier wars provoked by rebel colonies deriving their strength from the great forcing-house of Patna. It is enough to state that a famous trial was held at Umballah in 1864, and another at Patna in 1865. The first was presided over by Sir Herbert Edwardes, before whom eleven prisoners were brought charged with "attempting to wage war and abetting the waging of war against the Queen." Five of these prisoners were residents of Patna. The arch-offender was one Yahiya Ali, "high priest of Patna." Sir Herbert Edwardes said of him: "It is proved against the prisoner that he has been the mainspring of the great treason which this trial has laid bare. He has been the religious preacher, spreading from his mosque at Patna, under

The Umballah trials

* See Mr. William Hunter's most interesting volume on the "Indian Mussulmans:" "They (the Wahabees) converted the Patna Propaganda into a caravanserai for rebels and traitors. They surrounded it with a labyrinth of walls and outhouses, with one enclosure leading into another by side-doors and little secret courts in out-of-the-way corners. The early caliphs had threatened to resist the magistrate's warrant by force of arms, but their successors found a less dangerous defence in a network of passages, chambers, and outlets. When the Government at length took proceedings against this nest of conspirators, it found it necessary to procure a plan of the buildings, just as if it were dealing with a fortified town."

the most solemn sanctity, the hateful principles of the Crescentade. He has enlisted subordinate agents to collect money and preach the Moslem Jehad. He has deluded hundreds and thousands of his countrymen into treason and rebellion. He has plunged the Government of British India, by his intrigues, into a frontier war, which has cost hundreds of lives. He is a highly-educated man, who can plead no excuse of ignorance. What he has done, he has done with forethought, resolution, and the bitterest treason." This man was sentenced to death, with two others. But the Judicial Commissioner, Mr. A. Roberts, a man of rare attainments, whose early death was greatly deplored, observed, when reviewing the proceedings, "The particular treason of which these prisoners have been convicted is no new thing, but has been going on uninterruptedly for the last forty years, although the Government has had full cognisance of its existence. Ever since Syed Ahmed appeared on the Peshawur border in 1823-24, and proclaimed a religious war primarily against the Sikhs, but also in fact against the British Government, whose allegiance he threw off, a continuous stream of men and money, supplied by an extensive and well-organised system, having its centre at Patna, has been flowing up from Bengal and Hindostan to the fanatic colony across the border.* Influential 1857

* Mr. Hunter gives, as an eye-witness, the following graphic account of a Wahabee missionary—which I am doubly willing to quote, because a very experienced and well-informed reviewer laughed at the generic description given, in a former volume, of the grey-bearded emissary and his pony: "Generally speaking the Wahabee missionary has little to fear from the magistrates of the districts through which he passes; and, indeed, his favourite preaching-ground is the open space thronged with suitors outside the magistrate's court. The first preacher whose acquaintance I made was encamped in the avenue of the Commissioner's Circuit House. It was only an old man talking to a group of Mussulmans under a pepal-tree. Close by an undersized reddish

57. members of the family to which the prisoners Yahiya Ali and Abdool Ruhmeen belong, have from time to time, up to the year 1862, gone forth from Patna, and passing through the British provinces, have almost openly joined the hostile band. Those who have remained behind have been active, as Yahiya Ali is proved to have been, in furnishing their brethren with men and money." He, therefore, recommended the commutation of the punishment to transportation for life, and confiscation of property.

But the work of retribution was not then complete. There was yet another arch-conspirator to be brought to the judgment-seat. This was the Moulavee Ahmed-oollah, of Patna—brother of the above-mentioned Yahiya Ali. He was one of the three Wahabee Moulavees whom Commissioner Tayler had arrested in his dining-room in June, 1857—and was their spokesman on that occasion.* After Tayler's degradation, Moulavee Ahmed-oollah was fondled by the Government officials of Bengal. He might have been seen shaking hands at Belvedere with the Lieutenant-Governor, in the presence of the Viceroy. It was said that the inoffensive Wahabee gentlemen, whom Tayler had arrested, were mere "book-men;"† and for awhile they laughed among themselves at the pleasant credulity of the English. But when Captain Parsons, in 1864, swept up a number of these Wahabee martyrs, and carried them off to Umballah to

pony with a large head fixed on a lanky neck, was trying to switch off the flies from a saddle-gall by means of a very ragged tail. . . . The old man had a fresh complexion and a long white beard."

* *Ante*, page 83. I wish the reader who refers to this passage to bear in mind, that I objected therein only to the manner of arresting the Moulavees.

† There could not have been, for exculpatory uses, a more unfortunate designation than that of "book-men," for the most desperate of the Patna rebels, Peer Ali, was a bookseller (*ante*, page 85), and one of the chief agents of the Patna conspiracy of 1845, as described in my first volume, was a "wandering bookseller."—See book ii. chapter iv.

be tried for their lives, on charges of high treason, the position of Ahmed-oollah—the official pluralist, high in honour, drawing the money of the State—did not seem to be quite so secure.* It was doubtful whether the good fortune, which had compassed him for so many years and enabled him to laugh at his enemies, would much longer sustain him in prosperity. Parsons came down to Patna, and for two months was helping the Magistrate, Ravenshaw, to hunt out evidence against the harmless "book-man." Nothing could be clearer or more convincing than the fact that he had aided and abetted the making of war against Her Majesty the Queen. He was tried at Patna, before Mr. Ainslie, the Sessions Judge, and convicted mainly upon the evidence of one of his fellow-conspirators, who had been tried and sentenced at Umballah. The Sessions Judge awarded the punishment of death; but the High Court commuted it to transportation for life and confiscation of property. So the honoured guest and favoured friend of the Patna Commissioner and the Lieutenant-Governor of Bengal was sent to the Andamans, where he had the satisfaction of seeing the Viceroy of India assassinated by a brother-convict. 1857.

* "He was appointed member of a committee under Act XX. of 1856, on the 15th of October, 1862, and again under Government Orders No. 2577, of 21st September, 1860, he was appointed Deputy Collector and Income Tax Assessor on a salary of two hundred and fifty rupees per month. He had also been appointed a member of the Patna Committee of Public Instruction, so that he was in office during the greater part of the time this treason was being carried on, and the business of the Committee on Treason at Sadikpore was carried on simultaneously with his employment as Deputy Collector."—*Report of Mr. G. F. Cockburn, Commissioner of Patna.* In the same report the Commissioner writes with respect to the arrest of the Moulavees by Mr. Tayler, that "his information appears to have been correct, though the propriety of the arrests was called in question at the time." "Subsequent to the mutinies," it is added, "these Patna Moulavees redoubled their exertions, and brought about the frontier war in the latter end of 1863."—*Published Correspondence.*

1857. Views of Lord Canning. It has been shown that the events recorded in the preceding chapters made a strong impression on Lord Canning's mind, and that for awhile even the recovery of Delhi seemed to be of less importance to the State than the restoration of tranquillity to Behar. It was becoming clearer and clearer to him every day, that there was something more to be grappled with than a mutiny of the Bengal Sepoys, and that it would demand all the best energies of England's foremost soldiers and statesmen to prevent the flames from spreading in every direction, or rather—for it was hard to say where the conflagration raged not—to tread them out in one place whilst they were gathering strength in another. The crowning difficulty was this, that the very measures which seemed to be best calculated to overawe and to suppress had in them an inevitable tendency to increase the evil, by arousing the fears and suspicions both of the soldiery and of the people, and it was patent that among all the sources of rebellion not one was more cogent than terror. "The mismanagement of the disarming at Dinapore," wrote Lord Canning to Mr. Vernon Smith, "is the greatest evil that has befallen us since Delhi was seized. The consequences of it will be that revenue will be more than ever crippled, and that the means of strengthening Havelock's force, Allahabad and Cawnpore, must be directed to pacifying Behar and Bengal. I told you some time ago of the difficulty and risk which would at any time attend the disarming of the Native regiments scattered singly or in detachments through Bengal, at stations far removed from, and, in some cases, inaccessible to European troops. This risk is unfortunately increased by the misconduct of General Lloyd at Dinapore. To some of the sta-

August 8.

tions it is physically impossible to send aid. At 1857.
others, it is a question whether the approach of Europeans will not precipitate the outbreak of the Native troops, and lead to the calamity which it is desired to avert.* Each case has to be judged by itself, and the decision to be taken upon each, together with the general question of weakening the main column of European troops, in order to meet such cases, are subjects of painful anxiety, which will now increase daily."

In the circle of the Bengal Lieutenant-Governor- Rohnee.
ship, other troubles than those in Behar, of which I have written, disturbed the mind of the Governor-General. Some distressing episodes of accomplished facts were, from time to time, reported to him; and there were some peculiar sources of anxiety in the Eastern Bengal districts which kept his mind continually on the rack. I cannot write of all these; but one or two suggestive episodes may be narrated in this place. At Rohnee, in Deoghur, was posted the Fifth Irregular Cavalry. Major Macdonald was commandant. Sir Norman Leslie was Adjutant of the regiment. These officers were sitting one even- June 12.
ing, with the Regimental Assistant-Surgeon Grant, in Macdonald's compound, drinking their tea and talking in all the tranquillity of perfect confidence, when three Sowars, in undress, with swords in their hands, rushed suddenly into the enclosure by the rear of the house and fell upon them with deadly ferocity. One struck at Macdonald's head and scalped him; Grant was severely wounded; and Leslie, who was sitting in an easy-chair, was cut down—or as the Commandant afterwards reported, "literally cut to ribbons." He lived for half an hour, and then

* A very similar opinion was expressed by Sir John Lawrence.

1857. "quietly died." The murderers were detected by the help of some faithful men of the regiment; were tried by a drum-head court-martial; and executed with the utmost promptitude. But Macdonald, who had at first been most reluctant to believe that the assassins were men of his own regiment, still reported that the bulk of the corps were staunch in their fidelity, and would stand by him to the last.*

There was nothing more observable at this time than the fact that, while the British Government were utterly unable to despatch European troops to the outlying stations, the Native regiments posted in those stations were in a fever of alarm, under the belief that the white troops were coming down to disarm or disband—perhaps to fall upon them and massacre them. Propagated by designing persons with fitting circumstantial embellishments, these stories wrought upon the minds of the Sepoys, and made them consider and consult whether it would not be better for their own safety to rise at once before the threatened invasion could come upon them. From

Cuttack. Cuttack came announcements that the Mussulmans

* The cool, almost humorous manner in which Macdonald narrated this tragic incident, so far as regarded himself, is worthy of notice. "I am as fairly and neatly scalped as any Red Indian could do it. Grant got a brace of ugly cuts, but Leslie was literally cut to ribbons; he lived half an hour, poor fellow, and quietly died. We were sitting in front of my house, as usual, at eight P.M., taking our tea, when three men rushed quietly upon us, and dealt us each a crack. I was scalped, Grant cut on the elbow, Leslie, sitting in his easy-chair, appeared to fall at the first blow. I got three cracks in succession on the head, before I knew I was attacked. I then seized my chair by the arms, and defended myself successfully from two of them on me at once; I guarded and struck the best I could, and at last Grant and self drove the cowards off the field. God only knows who they were, and where they came from, but they were practised swordsmen. Leslie was buried with military honours; and had the burial service read over him at Deoghur, in Ronald's garden." In another letter he writes: "When you see my poor old head you will wonder I could hold it up at all. I have preserved my scalp in spirits of wine—such a jolly specimen!"

were tampering in this manner with the Native soldiery. That station being on the extreme southern limits of the Bengal Presidency, was guarded by Madras troops; and the lie was insidiously framed so as to meet the peculiar circumstances of the coast army. They were told that the European troops were coming to disarm them, and then to march them off to a distance of many hundred miles. Now the Madras soldier, as already explained, carries his family with him;* so this was a most alarming rumour. But the thought of the family, if a source of alarm to the soldier, was a source of safety to the State. The Madrassees would not listen to the voice of the charmer, whose wisdom overleapt itself. Some of them answered that they were "bound by both hands; in one they had their wives, in the other their children."† Those wives and children were hostages for their fidelity. If the families of the Bengal Sepoys had followed them in camp and cantonment, they would not have gone into revolt. 1857.

Julpigooree. May—Aug.

But the place of all others, in which the isolation of a body of English officers with a Native regiment, far from any possibility of European support, caused most serious apprehensions to the Government, was Julpigooree, which lies at a short distance from the borders of Bhootan. There Colonel George Moyle Sherer commanded the Seventy-third Regiment. It was a piece of rare good fortune that such a man should have been at the head of the corps. He understood the Sepoys well, and he had the decision

* Vol. i., p. 291. "The family of the Madras soldier followed his regiment, whilst the belongings of his Bengal comrade remained in their native village. The removal of the family from one station to another was a sore trouble and a heavy expense to the Madras Sepoy, and whatever increased the distance to be traversed was, therefore, a grievance to him."

† Letter from Captain W. D. Short, Madras Engineers, in published papers.

1857. June. of character and the conciliatory manners which at once invite respect and confidence. From the first he determined that he would trust his men, and that he would let them know that he trusted them. He felt that vague alarms and groundless suspicions, rather than any discontent or any hatred of the English, were hurrying the Sepoys into rebellion; and that all depended, under Providence, on the belief of his men in the good intentions of the British Government and its officers. For all sorts of rumours were flying about to the effect that European troops were coming in vast numbers to disarm and destroy them. Disarming had come into fashion, not without good reason, and, every time the post was delivered, Sherer expected to receive orders to apply the universal prophylactic to the case of his own men.* But so resolute was he not to betray the least want of confidence, that when the postal wallet was one day being unpacked in his presence, seeing that there was a despatch to his address from Division Head-Quarters, he turned to his second-in-command, and said: "If this, as I suspect, is an order to disarm our men, nothing will induce me to do it; I would rather lose my commission." From this decisive settlement of the grave question some about him dissented, and he was urged by his brother officers to obtain possession of the muskets, to place them on board boats, which would be got ready for them on the Teesta, and to send them off to a place of safety.

As the month of June advanced, sinister rumours of disaffection increased in significance; and it was

* Two troops of Irregular Cavalry, believed to be staunch, were at Julpigooree. Sherer said that they were sharpening their swords, and eager to be led against the Infantry. Two companies of the Seventy-third, who mutinied, were at Dacca.

known that there were emissaries in the Lines from Meerut and Lucknow—one in the well-known guise of a wandering fakeer—who were endeavouring to corrupt the men. But there were no alarming symptoms until the 25th, when these disturbing reports took shape and consistency in the statements of the men of two companies of the Twenty-third, who had arrived from Dacca, and who spoke, as from their own knowledge, of the dangers to come. It was affirmed that two hundred European soldiers were marching from Calcutta to disarm them. There was then great excitement in the Lines. The men were swearing that they would not surrender their arms, and some were meditating an immediate rising. It seemed, indeed, that the time had come when Julpigooree, like other British stations, would be running with Christian blood.

1857. June.

When tidings of this excitement were brought to Sherer on the following day, he at once ordered a parade, sent for his horse and galloped to the Lines. He heard as he approached them that murmur of many voices which bespeaks the general excitement, and he knew that the regiment was in the first throes of a great convulsion. Everything then depended upon the answer given to the question, "Are the men to parade with their arms?" "Yes," replied the Colonel, "by all means—with their arms, loaded as they are." Every man had ten rounds of ammunition in his pouch, and one ready for mischief then in his musket. The parade was formed; and there was not a word spoken or a movement made inconsistent with the strictest discipline. Confidence, in this instance, was triumphant.

But, although the crisis of the hour was past,

1857. June—Aug. and there was less reason to apprehend a general rising of the Sepoys at Julpigooree, the danger was not surmounted. There were, from time to time, signs of individual discontent, and even dribblings of open mutiny. Suspicion, though temporarily allayed, was easily re-awakened. Signs and symptoms were eagerly watched, and commonly misunderstood. When Sherer sent a number of elephants to Darjeeling to bring down the office-establishment of the Lieutenant-Governor, with bag and baggage, to the plains, a rumour ran through the Lines that the carriage had been sent to convey European troops to Julpigooree to overawe the Sepoys and disarm them; and again there was fear of a sudden outbreak. By blended kindness and vigour, by rewarding some and punishing others, Sherer still kept the rebellion of the regiment in check. But there were traitors in the heart of it; and he had to grapple with a succession of plots for the murder of the English officers. The fidelity of some of the Native officers brought these conspiracies to light, and acting on each occasion with the utmost promptitude and decision, he struck terror into the hearts of the disaffected, whilst he encouraged the more loyal of his followers by regimental promotions and pecuniary rewards. Some men were brought, without warning, to court-martial, sentenced to imprisonment and dismissal, and sent in irons to Calcutta. Others, who were known to carry loaded pistols, waiting their opportunity, were attacked in their huts. One man was shot through the head. Another, who in abject fear had malingered in hospital and attempted to starve himself, took to the river and was drowned. And so month followed month, with occasional alarms, but the regiment remained true to the leader whom they loved; and Sherer lived to receive the honours, somewhat overdue, which he had fairly earned by the masterly manner in which, under the most trying circumstances, he had kept his regiment faithful to their colours.* 1857. August.

The Arms Act.

Other troubles had Lord Canning to contend with, at his own doors—new vexations arising from the discontents of the English in Calcutta. It has been said that a General Arms Bill was under consideration. It was thought better that some restrictions should be imposed upon the free possession of offensive weapons. Mr. Barnes Peacock, the Law Member of Council, had sketched out a draft Act, which he enclosed in a letter to Lord Canning. It was brought forward, after some delay, which seemed to bespeak reluctance in the Legislative Council, by Mr. Dorin, and was generally called Mr. Dorin's Act.† But, instead of affording any contentment to the European inhabitants of Calcutta, it filled them with intense disgust. It had the same fatal blot, in their eyes, as the detestable "Gagging Act." It affected all races alike. The Englishman and the Bengalee, if not in the exceptional clauses of the Bill, were alike to provide themselves with licenses for the carrying of arms. It was considered by the Government that, as the Native communities contained large numbers of men of all ranks, who had declared their fidelity to the British Government, and whose substantial interests were so much mixed up with our own as to render it almost a certainty that their pro-

* If it had not been for the institution of the Star of India, Sherer would have gone unrewarded to his grave. It was ruled that as his services were not services against an enemy in the field, he could not receive the honour of the Bath. He did not destroy his regiment, he only preserved it.

† Finally sanctioned Sept. 11.

1857. testations were genuine, it would be an injustice and an insult to our Native fellow-subjects to draw the line that was desired by our own countrymen. Lord Canning, as I have said before, conceived that, as Governor-General of India, he was the protector alike of the black and the white races, and that it was neither just nor politic to impose restrictions only on the latter, at a time when there was nothing to show that the non-military communities of Bengal were not as true to the Government as the Christian populations. And there is nothing plainer than the fact that to have disarmed the Native population, at a time when Government were serving out arms gratuitously to Europeans, would have created a panic of that dangerous kind which is so often the precursor of revolt. But this reasoning was by no means convincing to the European inhabitants of Calcutta. So, whilst Lord Canning was laying up for himself such a store of national honour as has seldom been amassed by any statesman in any period of the world, his name in the mouths of many was always coupled with a term of reproach.

Demand for proclamation of Martial Law.

And there was soon another cause of offence. The Christian communities, in the fulness of their mistrust, were anxious that the whole of the Bengal Provinces should be proclaimed under Martial Law. This Lord Canning firmly resisted. Hints and suggestions were thrown away upon him. So a public memorial was addressed to the Governor-General in Council by two hundred and fifty-three of the inhabitants of Calcutta and the suburbs, setting forth that, having viewed with deep sorrow and alarm the calamities which had overtaken British India in its Bengal Presidency, "they had the painful conviction forced upon their minds that the disturbances might soon extend in all their horrors over the yet quiet portions of Bengal, even to Calcutta itself." They declared that they had no confidence in the Native Police, either of the Mofussil or of Calcutta, on the contrary, total distrust of them, as men who would co-operate with the insurgents; and that as the great Mussulman Festival of the Mohurrum was approaching, the danger had become imminent. The petitioners, therefore, earnestly prayed that his Lordship in Council would be pleased to ordain that Martial Law be at once proclaimed throughout the Bengal Presidency. To this, on the 21st of August, the Governor-General made reply, through Mr. Secretary Beadon, that he had given the most careful consideration to the petition, but that he was "unable to come to the conclusion that the circumstances of Lower Bengal, and especially of Calcutta, were such as to require the proclamation of Martial Law, or that such a measure would in any way be expedient or useful." It was pointed out that large and exceptional powers to deal with heinous offences had already been conceded by the extension of the Acts of May and June to the whole of the Lower Provinces, and by the issue of Commissions in such district for the purpose—that it was wholly impossible that European military troops could take the place of Native Police in the Mofussil, their number being quite inadequate for the purpose, and the interests of the Empire demanding that reinforcements should be otherwise employed. "In Calcutta," it was added, "there are troops enough for the protection of the city and its suburbs against any disturbance. There are also the Volunteer Guards, whose zealous and excellent services the Governor-General in Council is glad to have an opportunity of recognising. And

1857.

1857. there is a numerous and trained Police, a considerable number of whom are Europeans, and all under European direction and control, who, whatever may be the impression entertained of their fidelity and efficiency, have hitherto discharged their duties in a satisfactory manner. The retention in Calcutta of a European Military Force sufficient to take a share in the duties of the Police is impossible, if it were desirable." In fact, it was altogether a wild project to think of proclaiming Martial Law over a vast tract of country, where there were no European regiments to enforce it. Nothing can be clearer than this. But still the Europeans of Bengal resented the refusal, and Lord Canning became more and more unpopular every day.

False reports. Meanwhile he was tantalised by reports of the fall of Delhi, which poured in upon him from time to time, even as early as the month of June. At first, he was disposed to afford some credence to them, and sent home the glad tidings without expressing his doubts of the authenticity of the story. "The latest news from Delhi," he wrote to the President of the Indian Board on the 4th of July, "is that the town was in our hands on the 14th (of June); that there had been great slaughter of the rebels; and that those who remained of them had retreated into the Palace, or Fort. This is by telegraph through Central India."* At that time there seemed—and not only in Calcutta—to be no reason why such news should not be true. And it might have been true, for on that 14th of June an assault upon the city was to have been delivered. But the movement

* Colonel Durand sent the message from Indore, through Major Erskine, who sent it to Mr. Tucker, by whom it was forwarded from Benares.

was arrested by an accident. How the story which anticipated the fact by exactly a quarter of a year first obtained currency it is not easy to discover, but it was believed at the same time in Oude in the Punjab, and in other places, and was the first of a numerous family of false reports of the same kind.* 1857.

Want of information.

And whilst sometimes he was tantalised by tidings of events that never happened, communicated to him perhaps without due discretion by over-zealous functionaries, he was also disturbed by the feeling that what had happened was not always reported to him with the promptitude which he had a right to expect. Whether from accident, or from remissness, he was, for the space of nearly a month, without any communication from the Lieutenant-Governor of the North-Western Provinces; and as many private letters had come in from Agra, Lord Canning was stung by what he conceived to be Mr. Colvin's neglect.† The truth appears to be that the Lieutenant-Governor was deterred from writing by the consideration of the extreme uncertainty of his letters ever reaching Calcutta, and that although he and others might not be greatly concerned about private communications falling into strange and perhaps hostile hands, he thought it expedient not to incur the risk of correspondence of a more important character between two of the highest State functionaries being intercepted by the enemy on its way.

* At Allahabad a royal salute was fired on the 26th of June, for the fall of Delhi.

† Lord Canning to Mr. Vernon Smith. MS. Correspondence, July 4, 1857. On looking over the letters received from Mr. Colvin by Lord Canning, I find an entire blank between the 1st and 21st of June, and as the communication of the latter date begins with the words, "The dawks are so completely closed, that we can only try our chance of a letter reaching you by the circuitous course of the western coast, through Jyepore," I think it very probable that no letters were sent in the interval to the Governor-General.

1857.

Arrival of succours.

But ever was there to be seen, breaking through these great clouds of gloom, some gleams of consolation and encouragement. As time went on the hopes of the Governor-General rose. For he saw at no remote distance the incoming of the ships which were to bring the desired reinforcements, by which he knew that he could tread down mutiny and rebellion in our provinces, so long as the Native States of India should continue true to their allegiance. The great deliverance to which he looked so eagerly was close at hand. From the first day of the outbreak the cry had been, "Send us more English troops;" and now from all quarters were coming the welcome responses, for there was not an Englishman in authority who was not willing to strip his own colony or dependency to succour the great Eastern Empire that was so fearfully endangered. "I cannot express to you," wrote Sir Henry Ward from Ceylon, "the pain with which I have received your despatches by Major Bazeley. The need must, indeed, have been great that made you write so urgently, and I should take shame to myself, as an Englishman, if I were to allow any consideration of responsibility to stand in the way of an immediate compliance with your request to the utmost extent of my power." He had but one regiment—the Thirty-seventh—some eight hundred strong. Of these he despatched to Calcutta four hundred and fifty, with fifty artillerymen from Trincomalee, and a large complement of officers.

Lord Elgin and the China force.

But the most saving help of all that was to come to him was that which he expected to receive from the diversion of the troops, which were on their way to China. It has been shown how earnestly he wrote, on the first outbreak of the rebellion, to Lord Elgin and General Ashburnham, and how manfully he took upon himself the whole responsibility of the diversion.* It does not seem that Lord Elgin, in the first instance, took in the full dimensions of the danger which threatened our Indian Empire. He received the Governor-General's letters at Singapore on the 3rd of June; and on the following day† he replied: "I greatly regret that we can do so little for *you*—but we are doing our best. It is not quite impossible that troubles in India may re-act upon China and add to our difficulties in that quarter. I hope, therefore, that it will not be necessary to remove any troops from Hong-Kong. Indeed, the European force there is so small that it could not, I apprehend, be reduced without positive danger. . . . . I shall await your next letters with the greatest anxiety. Meanwhile, I can only express my earnest hope that you may get well out of your difficulties." This was a hurried private letter. In his subsequent official letter Lord Elgin says, that having since seen a letter from Lord Canning to the Governor of the Straits Settlements, "in which you (the Governor-General) suggest that it might perhaps be expedient that means should be taken to arrest the troop-ships for China in their passage through the Straits of Sunda," he had put himself in communication with the senior naval officer on the station, in order that, with his assistance, he might effect that object. "Such," he added, "are the measures which we have adopted for the moment, subject, of course, to modification in the event of my receiving from your Lordship intelligence to the effect that the pressing necessity for reinforcements in India, which existed when your 1857.

* *Ante*, vol. i. pp. 605—606.

† Probably this should be "on the same day." The original letter, however, is dated June 4. Another (official) communication, also dated June 4, says: "I wrote a hurried line to your lordship yesterday."

1857. Lordship's despatch under acknowledgment was written, had passed away." The regiments which he considered available for the assistance of Bengal were the Fifth from the Mauritius and the Ninetieth from England. Mr. Blundell, the Governor of the Straits Settlements, took resolutely in hand the work of arresting the troop-ships. He chartered a private steamer to proceed at once to Batavia, with a despatch to the Governor-General of Netherlandish India, requesting him to send on board the transport the orders of Lord Elgin and General Ashburnham to stop them on their way through the Straits. The General set his face towards China on that day. The Envoy remained at Singapore, awaiting the arrival of the *Shannon*.

Captain Peel and the *Shannon*.

That vessel was commanded by Captain William Peel—a son of the great Minister, whose career had been cut short by one of those lamentable accidents which at a later period deprived Protestant England of one of the best of her religious teachers. The *Shannon* was "a magnificent ship-of-war carrying sixty sixty-eight-pounders." She was described by her commander as "the fastest sailer he had ever been on board of, and with the best set of officers."* At break of day on the 11th she reached Singapore. On the 24th, having embarked Lord Elgin, she sailed for Hong-Kong, at which place she arrived on the 3rd of July. On the 14th, Elgin received further letters from the Governor-General—not with better, but with worse news of the situation of affairs. It was plain that nothing could be done at that time in China to exact reparation from the Court of Pekin,†

* Lord Elgin's Journal.

† Lord Elgin's motives are so clearly stated in his "Letters and Journals," published by Mr. Walrond, that I need only refer the reader to pp. 194 *et seq.* of that interesting work.

as the French troops had not arrived. So Lord Elgin determined to start for Calcutta in the *Shannon*, and to take council with Lord Canning, who had promised him a most hearty welcome. On board the *Shannon* went also three hundred marines, who had lately arrived on board the *Sanspareil*. 1857.

Lord Elgin at Calcutta.

But the *Shannon*, though a fast sailer, was still but a sailing ship, and Lord Elgin regretted that he was not on board a steamer. He reached the Indian capital on the 8th of August. Lord Canning was rejoiced to welcome his old schoolfellow and brother-collegian. The community of Calcutta equally rejoiced in his appearance. The Governor-General was then in the lowest depths of his unpopularity, and it was insanely thought that Elgin might keep Canning "straight." But Elgin saw at once that his friend needed no help from him. "There was hardly a countenance in Calcutta," he afterwards said, "save that of the Governor-General, Lord Canning, which was not blanched with fear." He had not much speech of the ruler. "Canning is very amiable," wrote Lord Elgin in his journal, "but I do not see much of him. He is at work from five or six in the morning to dinner-time. No human being can, in a climate like this, work so constantly without impairing the energy both of mind and body, after a time. . . . . Neither he nor Lady Canning are so much oppressed by the difficulties in which they find themselves as might have been expected."

But there was an arrival more important than that of the Chinese Commissioner—the vessels which accompanied him to the Hooghly—the *Shannon* commanded by William Peel, and the *Pearl* commanded by Captain Sotheby. They were the backbone of the great Naval Brigade, than which there was

1857. none that held higher place among the succours sent to Calcutta at this time. The idea of this important auxiliary force seems to have emanated from General Ashburnham.* But it was readily adopted by Lord Canning and Sir Patrick Grant, and consented to by Lord Elgin, who wrote to the Governor-General on the 10th of August,† saying, "I have further to state that having learnt from your Lordship and Lieutenant-General Sir Patrick Grant that a body of seamen and marines, though roughly trained as artillerymen, conveying guns of heavy calibre, and commanded by an officer of energy and experience, may render important service at this conjuncture, on the line of communication between Calcutta and Delhi, and possibly at Delhi itself, I am prepared to place Her Majesty's ships *Shannon* and *Pearl*, with their respective crews, at your Lordship's disposal, on the condition that a suitable steamer be provided for the conveyance of myself and suite to China, and for my use there, until I can obtain the requisite accommodation in one of Her Majesty's ships of war." And thus the Naval Brigade, of which much mention will be made hereafter, was formed. And the heart of Lord Canning rejoiced.

* "I hope I have been to some extent instrumental in getting up a demonstration, which I trust will be of service. My great wish was to see a Naval Brigade sent you, which might keep open the river communication with Allahabad, manning and arming some of the river steamers. My plan has as yet been very incompletely followed out; but with Captain Peel once with you, I shall be surprised and disappointed if he does not afford greater assistance than now contemplated. We are both impressed with one idea, and both desire nothing better than to serve you and the imperial interests at stake."—*General A. to Lord C., July* 16, 1857, *MS.* It is worthy of record that in this letter General Ashburnham writes: "Let me also venture to remind you of the dangerous vicinity of Patna, with a large and highly disaffected population."

† The original letter is dated "Calcutta, July 10, 1857," which is obviously a clerical error. I have before observed that errors of this kind are numerous in the correspondence on which this history is based. Sometimes they are very bewildering.

Another source of comfort was this. As the Government needed more troops, so also they needed skilled generals to command them. And news had come that one of the best of India's soldiers was close at hand. Early in the month of June, Sir James Outram, having brought to a successful termination the war in the Persian territory, had received intelligence of the rising of the Bengal regiments. He was then making arrangements for the re-embarkation of his troops, and his own return to the political post which he held as Governor-General's agent in Rajpootana. The stirring news gave a new complexion to his thoughts. He felt that some more active work would be required from him, than that which was likely to arise out of the post to which he stood appointed in the official list; and again his energies were revived by the thought of the coming conflict. But there was, at the same time, much to depress him. "More shocked than surprised,"* as he wrote, by these evil tidings, and seeing clearly the magnitude of the danger, he was torn alike by public and by private anxieties. His wife and son were at Aligurh, in the midst of the disturbed districts, and he wrote that he was "tortured by fears" for their safety. His eagerness to return to India, and to be on the scene of action, was intense. So, having as his first care taken steps to communicate the news to England, through Constantinople, by the electric wire, he made all haste to Bombay, telegraphed thence to the Governor-General for orders, but having received no answer up to the 9th of July,† he embarked on 1857.

* The letter is quoted at p. 242, vol. ii.

† In an autograph memorandum before me, written at the back of a draft letter of that date to Lord Canning, Sir James Outram says: "After my departure from Bombay, the Governor-General telegraphed to Lord Elphinstone on the 15th of June (July) to send me in command

1857. August.

board a steamer bound for Galle, and thence steamed up the bay to Calcutta.

Arrival of Sir James Outram.

On the first day of August Outram arrived at the capital. To the community at large, as to Lord Canning, his appearance was most welcome. It seemed to solve one pressing difficulty arising out of the great failure at Dinapore. "There is no need," wrote the Governor-General to the Chairman of the Court of Directors, "of his services in Rajpootana, and I proposed to him to take the command of the two military divisions of Dinapore and Cawnpore, his first duty being to restore order in Bengal and Behar, for which purpose every European soldier not absolutely necessary for the peace of Calcutta and Barrackpore, would be at his disposal. He undertook the charge eagerly, and left Calcutta on his passage up the river on the 6th. For the moment everything must give way to the necessity of arresting rebellion or general disorder below Benares." And again in another letter: "Outram's arrival was a godsend. There was not a man to whom I could, with any approach to confidence, intrust the command in Bengal and the Central Provinces. Colonel Napier,* lately returned from England, would have been the officer whom I should have selected had Outram not been here, and none more able in his vocation. But he is an engineer, and the work would have been new to him."

From Calcutta Outram wrote to Lord Elphinstone at Bombay, saying: "It will take me a fortnight, they say, to steam up to Dinapore, where I have only a bullock battery. Another (Captain Eyre's) is

of the troops in Central India, but subsequently again telegraphed to send me to Calcutta."

* Afterwards Lord Napier of Magdala and Commander-in-Chief of the Indian Army.

somewhere between that place and Benares. I take up a mountain train with me, but no artillerymen are to be had, and I must extemporise a crew for the guns as best I can from among the sailors and soldiers. You will allow my prospects are not very brilliant, but I will do my best to uphold my honour as a Bombay officer, and to prove myself worthy of the confidence you have always placed in me." In the same letter Outram says: "Lord Canning is bearing up wonderfully under all his anxieties. Sir Patrick Grant is most ably supporting him, and is an excellent fellow.* The Council, too, appear to be cordially aiding, Low especially, who is in better health than when he left England to return here, and he stays till March, to my great delight. Even had his seat in Council been vacant, I should have deemed it my duty to tender my services where they are about to be employed, for action not counsel is now required."† 1857.

On the afternoon of that 6th of August, when Sir James Outram embarked on the river steamer for Dinapore, two officers of high repute in the Bengal Civil Service embarked with him. One was Mr. Samuells, who had been appointed to succeed Mr. Tayler as Commissioner of Patna. He was a man held in great esteem by the Government and by his brethren in the service, as a prudent, sagacious officer, with a judicial cast of mind, one never likely to commit himself by any indiscretions of undue energy, or to compromise the high reputation of his profession by any defects of personal character. He was

The new Patna Commissioner.

* A week after Outram left Calcutta, Sir Colin Campbell arrived and took the chief command of the army. But the deeds of this true soldier belong to another volume.

† Outram had been nominated to succeed Low in the Supreme Council; and, being eager for action, he was sorely afraid of a call to the Board.

1857. not a brilliant man, but it is the nature of brilliancy to contract stains, and Mr. Samuells' good name had not a stain upon it. In a word, he was a safe man, which Mr. Tayler was not; and for purposes of counteraction no better selection could have been made. To assist the new Commissioner in the labours which lay before him, a Mahomedan gentleman of good repute, named Ahman Ali, was appointed as Assistant-Commissioner. It was presumed that the object of this appointment was to signify to the world that Mr. Tayler, in distrusting the Mahomedan population of Patna, had committed a grave error. If it were so, it was a much graver error. But in itself there was nothing that ought to have elicited the yellings and howlings which it drew forth from the European community of Calcutta. No appointment more unpopular among the Europeans of the Presidency was ever made. They were greatly embittered, at that time, against the Native races, and most of all against the Mahomedans, whom they believed to be the prime movers of the insurrection; and they looked upon the elevation of a follower of the Prophet as a declaration of sympathy with the rebel cause. The interpretation was strained and preposterous in the extreme, but there were those who pronounced the head of the Government to be the greatest rebel in the land.

Appointment of Mr. Grant to the Central Provinces.

The other fellow-traveller of Sir James Outram was Mr. John Peter Grant, a member of Lord Canning's Council. It has been said that his great abilities had not up to this time been much tested in situations of exceptional responsibility, demanding from him strenuous action in strange circumstances.*

* *Ante*, vol. i. page 389.

But although his antecedents, and to some extent, indeed, his habits, seemed to fit him rather for the performance of sedentary duties as secretary or councillor, there was a fund of latent energy in him, and he was eager for more active employment than could be found for him in Calcutta. When, therefore, the state of affairs in the Central and Upper Provinces was seen to be such as to require closer supervision and more vigorous control than could be exercised, in such a conjuncture, by the existing local authorities, and Lord Canning determined to despatch a trusted officer of high rank, with a special commission to the disturbed districts beyond the limits of the Lieutenant-Governorship of Bengal, he found Mr. Grant quite prepared to undertake the work at any sacrifice to self, and to proceed at once to the scene of action.* "The condition of the country," wrote the Governor-General to the President of the Board of Control, "about Allahabad and Benares, where we are recovering our own, but where every man is acting after his own fashion, and under no single authority nearer than Calcutta, has made it necessary to put some one in the temporary position of Lieutenant-Governor, all communication between Agra and those districts being indefinitely cut off. There is no man in whose capacity for the task of re-establishing order I have so much confidence as Mr. Grant, and certainly none who will act more in harmony with the military authorities. The punishing, the pardoning, the escheating of lands and the re-appointment of them, need to be superintended by one head, and there is no time to be lost in appointing one. I have, therefore, sent Mr. Grant there in 1857.

* I believe that I am not wrong in saying that Mr. Grant himself suggested the appointment.

1857. the character of Lieutenant-Governor of the Central Provinces. He will exercise precisely the powers which Mr. Colvin would exercise if the latter were not shut up in Agra, without means of communicating with those parts of his Government, and this will continue until Mr. Colvin is set free. Every exertion must now be made to set cultivation going on each acre of ground that we recover. If this be not done, we shall have famine and pestilence upon us in addition to our other calamities; and the chance of doing it depends upon a prudent, temperate, and, where possible, indulgent treatment of the Natives, both proprietors and cultivators. They must be encouraged and won back to their fields without delay, and our local officers, even the best of them, are too much irritated and excited with what has been passing before their eyes to do this as it ought to be done."

It is time now that I should speak of the events referred to in this letter, which had "shut up Mr. Colvin in Agra," paralysed the authority of the Lieutenant-Governor of the North-West Provinces, and rendered it necessary that another high officer should be sent to those districts, below the seat of Government, over which he had ceased to have any but nominal control.

BOOK VIII.—MUTINY AND REBELLION IN THE NORTH-WEST PROVINCES.

[MAY—SEPTEMBER, 1857.]

CHAPTER I.

THE NORTH-WESTERN PROVINCES — MR. COLVIN — CONDITION OF AFFAIRS AT AGRA—COUNCILS AND CONFLICTS—MUTINIES AT ALIGURH—ETAWAH AND MYNPOOREE—ALARM OF THE CHRISTIAN COMMUNITY AT AGRA—MEASURES OF DEFENCE — MR. COLVIN'S PROCLAMATION — OPINIONS OF LORD CANNING—DISARMING OF NATIVE REGIMENTS.

1857. May.

The Government of the North-Western Provinces.

THE "North-Western Provinces of India," as then administratively defined,* extended over an area of more than a hundred and twenty-five thousand miles, comprising the most important and the most interesting part of Hindostan. Stretching along the great valley of the Upper Ganges, they reached from the Kurumnassa on the South-East to the Sub-Himalayahs and the borders of the Punjab in the North-West, and embraced nearly all the great historical cities of Northern India. In the time of the Moguls this country had afforded sites for their palaces and encampments for their armies. And, in later days, it had witnessed the triumphs of our military strength and the successes of our political diplomacy. How

* Major Chesney, in his admirable work on "Indian Polity," very truly says, with reference to the official designation of "North-Western Provinces," "As a geographical expression the appellation 'North-West' is at the present day perfectly inaccurate."

1857. May. first one district and then another had passed by conquest, or by cession, under British rule need not here be narrated. Notwithstanding these diversities of times and circumstances, there was a certain unity and compactness about the whole. The people were, for the most part, composed of the same races, having the same cast of countenance, speaking the same language, and conforming to the same usages. If the population of any part of India Proper could rightly be called a warlike population, the designation might fairly be attached to the inhabitants of these provinces.* They were a handsome, athletic, robust community of men, with finer qualities than those of the timid and astute Bengalees; and they freely supplied our army with fighting men. In no part of the country was there so close an alliance between the military and the agricultural classes; and nowhere, therefore, was a great movement among the former more likely to evoke the sympathies of the latter and to swell into a popular revolt. And in no part of India was the population so dense. Official statistics show that upwards of thirty-three millions of men, women, and children were congregated in the towns and villages.†

The general administration of these great provinces was confided to a Lieutenant-Governor. He was not, like the Governor-General or the Governors of Madras and Bombay, assisted by a Council; nor had he a separate army under his control. The troops located in the North-Western Provinces were components of what had been once correctly designated the Bengal Army, but which by the extension of our Empire had been made wholly to outgrow the term.

* It will be understood that I say India Proper, because the Punjab is not properly a part of India.

† Of these, in round numbers, twenty-eight millions were Hindoos and five millions Mahomedans.

All the most important Divisions of the Army were included in this tract of country, until the Punjab became our border province, and the defence of the frontier against foreign invasion by land became the duty of the regiments that garrisoned it. Still, however, the great Meerut, Cawnpore, and Saugor Divisions were within the circuit of the North-Western Provinces. The Meerut Division of the Army included the great district from which it took its name, and the important territories of Delhi, Rohilkund, and Agra. The Cawnpore Division comprised the Allahabad and Benares districts and the new province of Oude; and in the Saugor Division were Jubbulpoor and Jhansi. The Civil Divisions were more numerous. The administration was entrusted primarily to a number of English Commissioners, members of the privileged Civil Service, under whom were Judges and Magistrates and Collectors of Revenue of the same class. The principal Commissionerships were those of Delhi, Meerut, Rohilkund, Agra, Allahabad, Benares, Jubbulpoor, and Jhansi. The Head-Quarters of the Civil Government were at Agra. 1857. May

The Lieutenant-Governorship of the North-Western Provinces was then held by Mr. John Colvin. He stood high in public estimation as one of the ablest civilians in the country. He had been brought into public notice as the Private Secretary of Lord Auckland, over whom he was supposed to exert an influence far greater than has since been exercised by any officer in the same subordinate position. The disastrous results of the war in Afghanistan, of which he had been supposed to be, if not one of the prime movers, one of the most earnest supporters, had for a time overclouded his reputation. He was held to be, though Mr. Colvin.

1857. May. a clever, a rather unsound and erratic statesman, and he had been sent to outlying protectorates, such as the Tenasserim Provinces, or to far-off frontier residencies like Nepaul, where no especial opportunities of distinguishing himself had been afforded to him. It was not until 1853 that his great administrative capacity was fairly recognised by his appointment to the Agra Government in succession to Mr. Thomason. Then he fully justified the opinion which had been formed of his capacity as an administrator, by the conscientious assiduity with which he superintended the internal affairs of the great provinces which had been committed to his care, and the success which had attended his efforts. Like others of his class, he had profound faith in the security of our Empire, and believed in the popularity of our rule. Perhaps, the recollection of the great historical episode of Caubul had rendered him especially unwilling to interfere in political affairs, and therefore, when news came to him that the Delhi Family were intriguing with Persia, he pigeon-holed the report, and was satisfied that it was all nonsense.* He did not see that the effete Mogul could possibly do us any harm, or that the people could have the least concern about the old dotard's doings. And when suddenly, on a quiet May day, tidings came to Agra to the effect that the Native troops at Meerut had broken into rebellion, he does not seem to have thought of the great political danger of the proximity of the mutineers to Delhi. But when those tidings were supplemented by further news to the effect that Behaudur Shah had been proclaimed Emperor of Hindostan, it was seen at once that the safety of the Empire was imperilled—that a crisis in our fortunes

* See *ante*, vol. ii. p. 38.

had arrived, the like of which had not been seen for a hundred years. Sensible, however, as he was of the magnitude of the danger, he met its first approaches with a calm confidence, not unworthy of the man whose chief lieutenant he was; he looked forth, from the great centre of Agra where the storm found him, over the vast tract of country under his immediate care, and he comprehended, with a steady far-seeing eye, the peculiar perils and necessities of each of the great cities on the banks of the river, and of the outlying stations more remote from its banks. He saw that some of our populous towns, as Benares and Allahabad, were almost wholly barren of European troops, and that other important stations, where the central Civil authority of vast districts was established, the English Government and the English people might be swept away in an hour by the Sepoys, who had been charged with their protection. What the dangers were, and what the efforts made to counteract them, in the two great cities above-named, has already been told. But it was not only to the country below Agra, but all around and above the seat of Government, that Colvin turned his thoughts with apprehensions, every day growing into certainties, of fresh disasters—of mutinies merging into rebellions, of British Administration effaced or paralysed, and society everywhere convulsed.

1857. May.

Meanwhile, at Agra itself, as the month of May advanced, there was great excitement, but no demonstration of active rebellion. This important city in the days of the old Mogul Emperors had been second in grandeur only to Delhi. The sinuous waters of the Jumna flowed beneath the great city, the fortress, and that wonder and delight of the East, the beau-

Agra. May, 1857.

1857. May.

tiful Taj-Mehal. The quarters of our English people lay more inland, extending in something like a semicircle, following the curve of the river, behind the City and the Fort. On the side of the Taj were the British Cantonments, including the barracks of the Europeans, the lines of the Sepoys, the bungalows of the officers, and the Protestant Church. Beyond the city was the civil station, with the Government House, the Government offices, the great Gaol, the College, the Roman Catholic Cathedral and Convent, and the residences of the chief civilians—the whole included within a circuit of some six miles, the Government offices being at one extreme end and the Sepoys' huts at the other. Between the Fort and the City was the bridge across the Jumna, leading to the great roads to Cawnpore and Aligurh.

The military force at Agra.

The military force then posted in the Cantonments of Agra consisted of a mixed body of Europeans and Natives. In the barracks were the Third Regiment of Company's European Infantry, commanded by Colonel Riddell, and near them were the European Artillery—a horse field battery under Captain D'Oyley. The Sepoy regiments were the Forty-fourth and the Sixty-seventh. The whole were commanded by Brigadier Polwhele.

First tidings of disaster.

Intelligence of the great events at Meerut and Delhi reached Agra on the 12th and 13th of May.* On the former day some precautionary measures had been taken. A company of Europeans had been ordered into the Fort,† and Englishmen had begun to look at

* The official report of Mr. Phillipps, magistrate of Agra, says, "On the 14th the news of the massacre at Delhi reached Agra." Mr. Raikes, who quotes from a journal kept at the time, says the 13th. Mr. Reade also gives the 13th as the date. I am inclined, therefore, to accept the latter statement.

† So Mr. Phillipps's official report. Mr. Reade says two companies, and adds, that the merit of the movement is due to Brigadier Polwhele. Mr. Harvey's report says "one com-

their revolvers. If any alarm arose, it was not that there was a doubt of the power to suppress at once all mutiny in the Agra Lines, for an English regiment and a company of English Artillery could have readily disposed of two Sepoy corps. The danger which threatened them was not danger from this source. It was of a twofold character—danger from the great city, the people of which might have risen against us—danger from the outlying districts, in which Sepoy regiments or detachments were posted, without any European troops to hold them in check. It was possible that these might stream down upon Agra — possible, even, that the great rebel force gathered at Delhi might march down to attack the English capital in the North-West. 1857. May.

There were many stout hearts and clear heads in Agra, and Colvin did well in turning them to the best account. Among the leading civilians then at the Head-Quarters of the North-Western Government were Mr. E. A. Reade, Mr. George Harvey, then Commissioner of the Agra Division, Mr. H. B. Harington,* Mr. (the Honourable) R. Drummond, Mr. William Muir, Mr. Charles Raikes, and Mr. Cudbert Thornhill. Never, perhaps, was the Bengal Civil Service, great as it is in history, represented, on one spot, by seven men of greater energy and intelligence. These men, with the higher military authorities—as Brigadier Polwhele, Colonel Fraser, Chief Engineer, and others —were summoned to Government House to attend a Precautionary measures. May 14.

pany." I have since ascertained from Colonel Riddell that only the light company was sent, commanded by Captain Patten.

* Mr. Harington had been appointed a member of the Legislative Council of India, and was preparing for his departure from Agra when intelligence of the outbreak was received. He might easily have proceeded to Calcutta, and thus placed himself and his family in a state of comparative safety; but he cast in his lot with his old comrades, and remained at Agra till the danger was over.

1857. May. Council of War. Mr. Colvin stated that it was his intention, in the face of such great and pressing difficulty, to bring all the Christian families into the Fort, from which the Native regiments were to be entirely removed. The order, indeed, had actually gone forth. But against this measure Mr. Drummond, Mr. Harington, and others vehemently protested, and the order was recalled. It was then resolved that a general parade should be summoned for the following morning, and that the Lieutenant-Governor should address the troops. At the same time, it was determined that a body of European and Eurasian Militia should be raised; and that the minds of the community should be reassured by a system of patrolling which would enable even the most timid to sleep quietly in their beds.

The meeting then broke up. It had not been a decorous one. Men who had been summoned to the Council expressed their opinions with much warmth; and others, who had not been summoned, came unbidden with notes of alarm or warning; whilst letters from outsiders came pouring in, further to embarrass and perplex the Lieutenant-Governor. One who was present writes that Mr. Colvin handed him one of these missives with a smile. "It was from an able public officer, who had great opportunities of knowing what was going on in the city, and contained a solemn warning to His Honour to beware of the knife of the assassin. One officer rushed in to suggest that we should all retire to the Fort, another to ask what was to be done at the Gaol, a third to speak about provisions, a fourth about the Sepoy regiments in cantonments. Every man was anxious to do his best, but to do it in his own way."* It cannot be

* Charles Raikes.

truthfully denied that, even in the midst of the courage and confidence which were generally displayed, there was some trepidation. All men have not the same temperament, and among the large number of Christians at Agra there were some who were not able steadfastly to confront the perils of the situation.

1857. May.

To Mr. Colvin, the multitude of counsellors that assailed him on all sides must have been most distracting and perplexing. He was not merely a Civilian; he was a Civilian of Civilians. He stood by his order; for he had faith in it. And he had reason to have especial faith in the members of that order who surrounded him. But there were men of other experiences, whose counsel he neglected; and it was said that even among his own brethren of the Civil Service, he did not always choose his counsellors wisely. In Mr. Drummond, the Magistrate, he had a colleague able, active, and energetic; and he reposed unstinted confidence in him.* It was Drummond's belief, at the commencement of our troubles, that they would soon subside—that the disaffection was superficial and partial—and that the soundest policy was that which indicated the greatest confidence in the loyalty of the people. It has been said that this in a great measure may have been the growth of his antecedents; for he had served for many years in the Pillibhiet district, where the Mussulman population was abnormally abundant, and he had mixed largely with Mahomedans of the better class—the most thorough gentlemen on the face of the earth—who had made so favourable an impres-

* Writing to Lord Canning on the 29th of May, Mr. Colvin said: "With the invaluable aid of Mr. R. Drummond, the Magistrate here (whose energy, influence, and spirit are beyond all praise), I have been able to maintain order as yet in all the Agra district."—*MS. Correspondence.*

1857. May.

sion upon him, that he was slow to credit the stories of their perversion. When, therefore, unfavourable reports were brought to him—when first one story and then another of treasonable conspiracies in the city reached him—when it was said that even his own Native officials were hatching sedition against the State—he turned a deaf ear to these warnings, and could not be induced either to act or to inquire. It may be assumed that some of these stories were the effusions of an excited imagination; but the general tendency of Mr. Drummond's policy, and therefore of Mr. Colvin's, was to ignore the surrounding danger, and to avert all possible hostility, by appearing to be unconscious of it.

The Engineers at Agra.

There were protests raised against this policy of over-confidence, especially by the Engineer officers at Agra. Of all classes of public functionaries, perhaps, our Engineer officers in India were those whose lives had best fitted them to take an impartial and comprehensive view of the nature of the crisis that threatened the State, and of the best means of combating it. They were the flower, intellectually, of our military service—the *emeriti* of that now-effaced college at Addiscombe, which sent forth so many great men to fight our battles, and to direct our councils. Their duties lay midway between those of the soldier and of the civilian; and they were commonly free from those professional prejudices and jealousies which often raised conflicts of opinion and of action between the two branches of the public service. They had in many, if not in most instances, served in widely different parts of the country, and they had enjoyed peculiar opportunities, when employed in the districts, of ascertaining the feelings of the people. And when it is considered that with this general knowledge were combined their own special scientific qualifications—their knowledge of the theory and often of the practice of modern warfare, and, most of all, of defensive operations—few will hesitate to admit that the crisis at Agra demanded that the advice offered by the Engineer officers should be received by the Lieutenant-Governor with the utmost deference and respect. 1857. May.

It was not so. And yet the Engineer officers at Agra were men of no common merit. The Chief Engineer was Colonel Hugh Fraser—a soldier of high professional attainments, greatly esteemed in his corps; a vigorous, cool-headed man, prompt in action and fertile in expedients. Many anecdotes, illustrative of his courage and energy, were current in the country.* If he lacked anything, it was power of expression to enforce his views in the most effective manner. But what he wanted was largely possessed by Major Weller, his comrade and friend, who ever went hand-in-hand with him, knowing his worth, and feeling that the day would come when it would be fully recognised. There were others of the same distinguished regiment, including Colonel Glasford, who at an early period was appointed Commandant of the Fort, and Captain Norman Macleod, Military

* I cannot abstain from giving the following, in the words of one who knew him well: "Many years before 1857—I think in 1836 or 1837—he was driving along the parade at Cawnpore, when he saw a crowd assembled. Always inquiring, and being very short-sighted, he asked his syce what was the matter. The syce said that there was a row, and Fraser got out of his buggy and walked to the spot. A Sepoy of the Seventh Native Infantry had shot a Havildar, and, having reloaded his musket, was standing at bay threatening to shoot any one who attempted to seize him. Fraser at once pushed through the crowd, and afterwards told me, 'Hang it, ——, what could I do but to collar him?' The man was, of course, tried and hanged; and I think it probable that no one less generally liked could have seized him with impunity." Another characteristic anecdote will be found in a subsequent chapter relating to events at Lucknow.

1857. May. Secretary to the Lieutenant-Governor, whose gallantry had been approved before the gates of Ghuznee at the commencement of the great Afghan campaign.

When Colonel Fraser first learnt that the troops at Meerut had broken into rebellion, he wrote a Minute, or a series of "notes," setting forth the course which, as he conceived, ought to be adopted. The essence of the policy which he advocated was
May 13. contained in the first sentence: "If the news from Meerut is bad, or none arrives from that place by ten A.M., distrust everybody, and recognise the emergency." Mr. Colvin afterwards said that he "recognised the emergency" from the beginning; but he assuredly did not support the policy of mistrusting every one. If Mr. Drummond's notion at this time was not that it would be wise to trust every one, it was assuredly his belief that we should appear to trust every one. But the Engineers thought differently. They recommended that all the treasure should be conveyed to the Fort, and that all the women and children should be ordered to take up their residence within its walls—that the Lieutenant-Governor with his Staff and all important records should also be moved into the Fort—that one half of our Artillery should be garrisoned there, and that "all writers, pensioners, and Eurasians" should be armed and sent thither with "magazine establishment complete." Other detailed suggestions were put forth, and among them one to the effect that the Ninth Native Regiment at Aligurh, believed to be faithful, should be brought down to Agra, and should furnish guards over the Treasury.* It was recommended

* The words are, "March the Ninth Regiment Native Infantry at Aligurh down to the Treasury, put all women and children there, or in

also that General Wheeler, as one of the best Sepoy officers in India, should be summoned to Agra; and that the Cawnpore Brigade, under Brigadier Jack, should be ordered to Aligurh, there to be joined by any troops obtainable from Gwalior, and then to be marched upon Meerut. Viewed by the light of after events, these two last suggestions were of doubtful wisdom; but they were written when nothing more was known than that the Meerut regiments had revolted. Of the recommendations with respect to the internal defence of Agra, I cannot think otherwise than that they were wisely conceived, and that it would have been well if they had been adopted. Had all valuable property, public and private, been removed into the Fort, together with the public records, much would have been saved, the loss of which has since been bitterly deplored alike by individuals and by the State. But it was thought that such precautions would have betrayed a want of confidence, and so the advice of the Engineers was rejected.* 1857. May.

The Lieutenant-Governor's address to the troops, May 15.

On the morning of the 15th, the troops were brigaded in cantonments. The Lieutenant-Governor and all the principal civil officers were present. Mr. Colvin,

nearest adjoining buildings, and let the commanding officer and civil authorities do their best—the civil authorities arranging for Sowar patrols in every direction." This does not seem to be quite consistent with the idea of "distrusting everybody."

* The following is from Mr. (afterwards Sir George) Harvey's official report: "It was unfortunate that occasion was not taken for inviting all residents to send in their valuables for safe custody. It was wholly a mistake to suppose that the Native mind would have imbibed impressions of alarm from such course. It would have been explained by the known occurrences at Meerut and Delhi, the certainty that we should have to wait for European reinforcements, and 'forewarned is forearmed.' Few bulky articles would have been sent in, and the terrible and irreparable destruction of private valuables, libraries, &c., to say nothing of important public records, would not have occurred. Mr. Drummond, a very able, energetic, and intelligent officer, opposed himself strongly to this scheme."

1857. May. standing up in his carriage, first addressed the European regiment on parade. He told the men not to distrust their Native brothers-in-arms, but significantly added that they had murdered a clergyman's daughter at Delhi. The Europeans clutched the butts of their muskets with a firmer grasp, and there was not, perhaps, a man in the ranks who would not fain have loaded at that moment and fired his piece into the thick of the Native battalions. Then Colvin addressed the Sepoys in Hindostanee, telling them that he had full trust in their loyalty, but that if any man wished to leave his colours, or had any complaint to make, it was the desire of the Government that he should come forward. Then the Sepoys set up a shout, or a yell, but no man came to the front. It has been said that they "looked with a devilish scowl" at our people, and it is probable that even then there was rebellion in their hearts. They were merely biding their time—waiting their opportunity—seeing what their brethren would do.

Having done what he thought best, in that first week, to provide for the safety of his capital, Colvin bethought himself of what might best be done for the great country under his charge, or, in other words, for the Empire. He had never taken a desponding view of the situation. He knew that if Delhi were not speedily recovered, the structure of British rule would be shaken to its very foundation; but he did not think that the mutineers even behind the walls of the great city could make an effectual stand against the troops that would be sent down to expel them; and he wrote to General Anson, as Lord Canning and Sir John Lawrence had written, to urge him to lose no time in moving upon and attacking Delhi. Meanwhile, efforts might be made at Agra, to show that the British Government were not stunned or paralysed. If the enemy came down upon them, they would march out to give battle to the rebel force. And, in any case, something might be done to re-open the roads between Agra and Delhi, to give assurance to the neighbouring districts, and to ascertain the actual state of things in the country above. To accomplish these objects, Mr. George Harvey, the Commissioner, was selected by the Lieutenant-Governor. He readily accepted the office, and prepared himself at once to set out on his hazardous mission.* He started on the 20th of May, accompanied by some officers of the Customs departments and some employés of the East India Railway, and on the following morning was at Muttra, where he found a body of Bhurtpore troops. 1857. May.

It was of immense importance in such a conjuncture to secure the support, or, indeed, even the semblance of the support, of the Princes and Chiefs of India, who, at no great distance from Agra, were maintaining their Native Courts, and holding in their pay Native Armies. Although we had taken upon ourselves the entire defence of India, protecting the Native States against Foreign enemies, and not suffering them to make war among themselves, we Support of the Native Chiefs.

* "Mr. Colvin intimated to me a wish that, escorted by two hundred of the Gwalior Contingent and two guns daily expected, I should proceed towards Delhi by the right bank of the river, *viâ* Muttra. It was, he said, very desirable that the Governments of the North-Western Provinces should give some sign of life in this emergency; that the communications between Delhi and, through it, of Meerut should be re-opened; and that the actual truth of rumours causing dangerous excitement should be ascertained—whilst it was of essential importance that the movements and wishes of His Excellency the Commander-in-Chief should be known to Government. I was, on arrival, to take charge of the Delhi Agency, and to remain permanently in the appointment should I desire it."—*Official Report.* The Gwalior troops, however, were required for other service.

1857. May. had permitted these Princes and Chiefs to entertain considerable bodies of troops, partly to give dignity to their rule and partly to support the Civil administration of their respective territories. These had not the high organisation and matured discipline of our own troops; but though, as seen by the outward eye, they lacked much of the military steadfastness and regularity to which we are accustomed, they had some good fighting qualities, and in partisan warfare were by no means to be despised. And, besides these purely Native troops, drilled and equipped after the Eastern fashion, there were in some states bodies of troops, known as Contingents, officered by English officers and disciplined after the English fashion. In the service of the Maharajah Scindiah was a strong force of this description, with its head-quarters at Gwalior — a force, the components of which differed little from those of our own regiments. Of this Contingent I shall presently speak more in detail. In the little state of Kotah, there was also a Contingent, on a much smaller scale; and at Bhurtpore, which lay nearer to Agra than either of those places, there was a Native force in the pay of the Rajah, composed principally of hardy Jháts. The contiguity of these several military powers might be a source of strength or a source of weakness to us at Agra.* In Colvin's eyes it was the former. At that time the movement against the British authority appeared to be mainly a Mussulman movement. At all events, at the great centre of Delhi, it had taken the shape of a Mahomedan revolution, culminating in the restoration of the

* It will be understood that I am speaking here only of those states whose movements especially affected our position at Agra.

Mogul Empire. It was not likely that the Hindoo States would sympathise with this movement. "Scindiah and Bhurtpore," wrote the Lieutenant-Governor on the 15th of May, "will be heartily with us against the new dynasty of the House of Timour." Both Princes responded readily to the call, and, for good or for evil, sent in their military aid. On the 15th Captain Nixon, with a detachment of Bhurtpore troops, occupied Muttra; and on the 16th some details of Cavalry and Artillery from the Gwalior Contingent made their appearance at Agra. Scindiah afterwards manifested his loyalty and good feeling by placing his body-guard at the disposal of the Lieutenant-Governor. It was true that any or all of these might follow, or even lead the way, along the rough road of rebellion; but still the mere fact that their masters had sent them to aid us, and had thus openly arrayed themselves on our side, could not be otherwise than productive of a good moral effect. There was nothing plainer to Colvin than that, if the Princes and Chiefs of India were then to rise against the British, no earthly power could save us from destruction. It was sound policy to trust them—to assume that the interests of the Mahratta, Jhát, and Rajpoot powers were, in that crisis, identical with our own. It flattered their pride to confide in them as faithful allies and to seek their assistance in the hour of our need. The presence of their troops at Agra might be a source to us of immediate weakness rather than of strength, by increasing the numerical preponderance of the Native soldiery; but still, at such a time, there would be gain to our cause throughout the country in this exhibition of the security of our Native alliances; and Colvin was not

1857. May.

1857. May. thinking so much of the safety of the city in which he lived, as of the general welfare of the great provinces committed to his care.

An interval of calm. May 15—21. Days passed, and there were still no overt signs of mutiny. Things went on outwardly much as they had been wont to do before the sound of that ominous word had been heard. The formal routine of public business was not suspended or broken through. The Judge took his seat on the bench, and the Revenue Officer went to his work after the wonted fashion.* The Government and the Missionary schools were attended as numerously as in the most tranquil times. Not a pupil absented himself from his class, not a lesson was foregone or neglected. And though the elder and more thoughtful civil officers went about their work with heavy hearts, thinking of friends and relatives at a distance exposed to the fury of the enemy, the younger military officers took their accustomed rides, played at billiards, swam in the river, and were apparently as joyous and unconcerned by day, and slept as soundly by night in the Sepoys' lines, as though they were not, in all human probability, destined to be the first victims to the savage hatred of the soldiery whom they commanded.† But although the technical business of administration went on with outward regularity, precautionary measures were taken by the authorities to give confidence to the weak and the wavering, and to prepare against any sudden attack. Among these was the formation of a Volunteer Cavalry Corps, for service beyond the limits of cantonments—a corps that afterwards did right good service—and the organisation of patrolling

* Mr. Raikes says with emphatic force, "We had to grant injunctions which nobody attended to, and to pass decrees which no one could execute."

† Raikes.

bands for the immediate defence of Agra, intended to assure the minds of the people if loyal, or to overawe them if they brooded on mischief. It may be said that every Englishman in the place joined one or other of these forces, whilst many Christians of the mixed blood enlisted cheerfully in them. Those who had no ties of wife and children were glad to mount their horses and to scour the surrounding country. Those whose families were in Agra naturally preferred service as town-patrols. 1857. May 21.

The Mutiny at Aligurh.

Affairs were in this state when, on the 21st of May, tidings were brought to Agra that the Native troops at Aligurh,* fifty miles distant, on the other side of the river, had broken into rebellion. The story, as subsequently developed, was this:—Only a small Sepoy force was located at Aligurh. A few companies, with the head-quarters, of the Ninth Sepoy Regiment, under Major Percy Eld, composed the garrison. On the 12th of May, news of the Meerut mutiny reached the station. But the troops did not seem to waver. A week passed away, and the only symptom of disquietude was "the burning of an empty bungalow." But that ever was a sign of coming trouble. Reports of a most alarming and irritating character were in circulation—some wholly false, and some having foundation of fact with a vast superstructure of error. Among the latter there was an exaggerated story of the unfortunate affair of the Sappers and Miners at Meerut.† It was generally said, and currently believed, that the English at that station had been altogether the

* The city is known as Coel, the fort as Aligurh.

† *Ante*, vol. ii. p. 178.

1857. May. aggressors, and that European troops were coming down to destroy the Sepoys at Aligurh.

It was plain, indeed, that, although all was quiet in city and cantonment, it needed but a spark to excite a general conflagration. Before the third week of May was spent, everything was ripe for an outbreak. It was a mere matter of accident what might be the immediate cause to precipitate it. One pitfall was escaped. A party of the Ninth had been
May 16. sent out, under Captain D. M. Stewart, to suppress some alleged disturbances in the district; and with it had gone young Francis Outram, of the Civil Service, with a little party of Sowars, whom he had contrived to pick up at Aligurh. They found the stories of disorder greatly exaggerated—perhaps they were intentional exaggerations for the purpose of diverting our minds from what was passing in the city—and after a day or two they marched back to the station. As they passed through the butchers' quarter of the city, there was much excitement among the people, which communicated itself to the Sepoys, and there was that kind of noise to be heard in the ranks which indicates a suppressed consultation. The detachment, however, marched on, and nothing happened. It was known afterwards that the townspeople had endeavoured to persuade the Sepoys to murder their officers and fly, as the Europeans from Meerut had come in during their absence and massacred their comrades in Cantonments. And they would have fired at once into the backs of their officers, if a drummer of the mixed race had not told them that in a few minutes the Treasury would be in sight, and it would be seen whether the guard was in its accustomed place. So the detachment marched on, and it was presently apparent that

everything was in the condition in which it had been left. 1857. May.

But, although this immediate danger was tided over, it can scarcely be said that the escape delayed the inevitable crisis. Whilst Stewart's detachment had been absent from the station, a new danger had arisen—not in the Sepoys' lines, not in the butchers' quarters, but in the rural districts. In a neigbouring village was a Brahmin of some influence, who had a relative in the Gaol-guard, and who was not unwilling to do service as an ambassador of evil between the villagers and the Sepoys. It was known that there were some seven lakhs of rupees in the Collector's treasury. If the Sepoys would rise, the villagers would come down and share in the plunder. It was proposed that at a given time a crowd of people, simulating a noisy marriage procession, should enter the city, that they should fraternise with the Sepoys, massacre the Europeans, and seize all the property of individuals and of the State.

The Brahmin began his work, and made proposals to two Sepoys, who told the story to their commanding officer. Major Eld ordered them to seize the rebel. They obeyed his orders, and the man was tried by a Native court-martial and sentenced to death. As the sun was setting on that day, the Brahmin was hanged, in the presence of the troops. Up to May 20. that time there was everything to encourage the belief that the Sepoys were true to their salt. But scarcely had swift punishment overtaken the high-caste offender, when the smouldering mutiny in the breasts of the Sepoys of the Ninth broke into a flame. A Brahmin Sepoy stepped from the ranks and cried aloud to his comrades, "Behold a martyr to our faith!" It was like the springing of a mine. The

1857. May. explosion took place at once. All discipline, all fidelity, all loyalty were blown into the air. Only a tender compassion for the officers, who had ever treated them justly and kindly, remained. There was a scene of terrible confusion, such as had been seen before, and was destined often to be seen again. The Sepoys spared the lives of their English commanders; but all were then compelled to escape; all who in any capacity represented the Government or the community of the Christian stranger. Military officers, Civil officers, and independent Europeans or Eurasians, were driven to fly for their lives.

In the little party of Europeans thus expelled from their homes was one, of whom every Englishman must have thought tenderly and affectionately, when he heard that Aligurh was in danger. This was Lady Outram, the wife of the great soldier, who had just brought the war with Persia to a close, and to whose return all men were looking, in this emergency, as to a very present help in trouble. She was making her preparations to spend the hot weather at Nynee-Taal. During the absence of her son with Captain Stewart's detachment, Lady Outram had been residing at the house of Mr. Dumergue, the Judge, whose wife and daughter were the only other English gentlewomen at the station. But, on the day of the outbreak, she had returned to her son's bungalow, in another part of the cantonment, and was superintending the arrangements for her departure, when the regiment broke into rebellion. Frank Outram was, at that critical moment, in the compound of the Magistrate's house, conversing, in absolute peace of mind, with the officers of a detachment of Cavalry from Scindiah's Contingent, which had come in from Gwalior, when some officers of the

Ninth rushed in, crying out that the regiment had "gone." Outram's pony stood saddled close at hand; so he mounted at once and rode for his bungalow, where he found, with joyful surprise, that his mother was safe, and in happy ignorance of the danger that surrounded her. 1857. May.

Lady Outram was at that time, dressed for the evening drive, awaiting the Judge's carriage, which was to call for her. It then seemed that nothing could save her but instant flight. So she mounted the pony behind her son, and they made for the civil lines. The journey was not a long—but it was a dangerous one. They were soon compelled to take to their feet, for the animal they rode resented its double burden and was loth to proceed.* Their road lay through the cantonments, where they saw the Sepoys moving excitedly from place to place, with their arms in their hands, all eager for the plunder of the Christian bungalows. But no man pointed a musket at them. So they passed on, unmolested, to the civil lines, and soon found themselves amidst a little assembly of their countrymen debating what was to be done.

There was nothing to be done—but to seek safety in flight. The Gwalior Cavalry had outwardly remained true, but they were insufficient for the recovery of our position, even if their fidelity could have been relied upon. The only question then was, whether our people should escape to Agra or to Meerut. About this, there was either difference of opinion or misunderstanding as to the decision arrived at, for some went in one direction, some in

* Exaggerated stories of Lady Outram's escape were at one time current. It was said that she escaped, barefooted in her night-dress. She wore the ordinary light costume of the hot weather, with thin shoes, of which the rough road soon dispossessed her.

1857. May. another. Lady Outram had a seat in the Judge's carriage, which took the direction of Agra; whilst Frank Outram and others, headed by Mr. Watson, the Magistrate, all well mounted, took to the Meerut road—a party of Gwalior Cavalry accompanying them. The former party reached Agra in safety. The latter encountered some adventures, and did right good service, to be narrated in a subsequent chapter of this narrative.

The English being thus driven from Aligurh, the mutineers and rebels proceeded to plunder the Treasury and other Government offices, and then to ignite the buildings. The seven lakhs of rupees in the Treasury were shared between the Sepoys and the Rabble. The former, carrying their coin with them, set their faces towards Delhi. The latter remained in possession of the place. The prisoners in the Gaol were set free, and every man helped himself to what he could get. Public and private property fell to the strongest and most active plunderers. The houses of the Europeans were gutted, and everything belonging to them either carried off or destroyed. For a time every trace of English authority was utterly gone from Aligurh. When some time afterwards it was partially re-established, it was seen how great the devastation had been. Of the first return to Aligurh, one present wrote: "A wonderful appearance it presented. The bungalows, gaol, &c., had all been burned and looted. The accumulation of laden bullock-trains and other carts, detained from further progress after the 12th, shared the same fate, and the miscellaneous character of the loot may be imagined. On our approach, the Natives had hastened to clear away all vestiges of booty out of their premises, in fear of search; and the roads for miles round, the jungles, and the wells, were covered and choked by the most extraordinary chaos of articles conceivable, from cases of champagne down to consignments of Holloway's pills (of which there seemed to be a carriage load or two)—from splendid kincaubs down to our old garments, plate, furniture, boxes, supplies of eatables—everything except hard cash."* 1857. May.

Meanwhile, at Etawah, which lies on the road to Meerut, at a distance of seventy-three miles from Agra, the civil officers were watching, with a wise vigilance, the progress of events. A company of the Ninth Sepoys from Aligurh was posted there, but in the earlier part of the month there was no reason to doubt the fidelity of the men. The people of the district were prosperous and contented. Never, indeed, had there been more hopeful and encouraging signs of present tranquillity and future progress.† The Magistrate and Collector was Mr. Allan Hume—a son of the great English reformer—who had inherited the high public spirit and the resolute courage of his father. When news of the mutiny of the troops at Etawah. May, 1857.

* MS. Memorandum. Mr. Bramly's report states that "in this work (of plunder) Regsaal Khan, Khansaman (purveyor) of the Dawk Bungalow (traveller's halting-place), and Meer Khan, mail-coachman, distinguished themselves." It is not improbable that both had tasted the insolence of European travellers.

† "The fatal month of May opened in hopefulness and peace. Never, apparently, had the prospects of the district been so cheering. Crime was and had been for the previous two years steadily decreasing; the Revenue flowed in without a recourse to a single coercive process; public libraries and numerous schools gave rich promise of future progress; new lines of communication were being rapidly opened out; the railroad was fast ripening; the great canal, with its daily multiplying branches, steadily diffusing fertility over an ever-widening area; and all classes of the community, though of course not without their minor grievances, on the whole were singularly happy and contented. Suddenly the mutiny burst upon us, effacing apparently in a day the labour of years."—*Report of Mr. Hume.*

1857. May. Meerut and Delhi arrived from Agra, a day or two after the outburst, Mr. Hume's first thought was that he might arrest some of the mutineers either on their way to their homes or dispersing themselves over the country to corrupt other Sepoy regiments. Patrolling parties were, therefore, sent out to watch the roads, and on the night of the 16th of May a party, seven in number, of the Third Cavalry was arrested. Being well armed with swords and pistols, when taken to the Quarter-Guard and confronted with our soldiery, they made a vigorous resistance, shot Lieutenant Crawford, who commanded, in the shoulder, and would have murdered Lieutenant Allan, but that the assailant was killed by the Kotwal and a Sepoy of the Ninth. The guard was then ordered to turn out, and the mutineers were overpowered. Two were shot dead, two were cut down, and two escaped, one of whom was afterwards captured by the Police. And this was the first retributive blow that fell upon the mutineers of the Third Cavalry. They were all Mahomedans (Pathans) of Futtehpore.

May 18—19. A few days afterwards, another party of fugitives from the Third Cavalry made its appearance in Juswuntnugger, about ten miles from the chief station of Etawah, armed with sabres, pistols, and with a few carbines among them. They had come down in a capacious cart, which was stopped by the patrol upon the road. On being called upon to give up their arms, they first of all made a show of submission, and then shot down their captors. Having done this, they made their way to a Hindoo temple, at the end of a walled grove, and prepared to defend themselves.

When tidings of this movement reached Mr. Hume, he ordered his buggy to be got ready, armed himself as best he could, and, accompanied by Mr. Daniell, started for Juswuntnuggur. It was then nine o'clock in the morning; there was a fierce sun, a hot wind like the blast of a furnace; and neither had broken his fast. A brisk drive of an hour and a quarter brought them before the asylum of the Meerut troopers. It was a strong position in itself, and admirably suited to purposes of defence. Everything was in favour of the mutineers; they had shelter for themselves, a command of observation and a command of fire in all directions; and whichsoever way the intrepid Englishmen turned to reconnoitre the position of the enemy, the Sepoys fired at them from their cover with pistols or carbines. Moreover, the townspeople were on the side of the mutineers. Hume had invested the place with some troopers of the Irregular Cavalry and some of his own Police; but they could or would not keep the people from opening communication with the troopers in the temple, and so the defenders were supplied with food and ammunition. There was no hope, therefore, of starving them into surrender, or rendering them powerless by exhaustion of powder and shot. To carry the place by assault seemed an almost hopeless endeavour. For although there was a large body of armed Police, none would go within reach of the carbines of the troopers. They were content to show their zeal by firing from a distance in the air. Reinforcements had been sent from Etawah, but the detachment of Sepoys despatched to their relief purposely missed their way. So the day wore on in its fiery strength, and Hume and Daniell were without support. The excitement among the townspeople—for the most part a low class of Mahomedans—was increasing. In a little while a rescue might be attempted, and the retreat of the Englishmen might

1857. May.

1857. May. be cut off. So they determined, as the sun was nearing the horizon, to make an effort to carry the place by themselves. Only one man followed them to the door by which an entrance was to be attempted. He paid for his fidelity with his life. Daniell was shot through the face, and fell senseless, amidst a yell of exultation from the townspeople, who were eagerly watching the affray from the side of a neighbouring hill. Then Hume, having vainly endeavoured to rally some of his followers, went to the assistance of his friend, and through the pressing crowd and the uproar of the streets led him safely to the spot where their carriage was posted. That night, in the midst of a violent storm, the mutineers escaped; but the double-barrels of Hume and Daniell had done some execution, for difficult as it had been to reach them, one of their party had been killed and another dangerously wounded.*

This was one of the first of those heroic deeds of which I have before spoken†—great deeds of heroism by which the civil servants of the Company—men not trained to arms or wearing any insignia of the military profession—bore noble witness to the courage and constancy of the national character. This English Magistrate and his Assistant, in the face of an insur-

* The following is Mr. Hume's very modest account of the affair: "Early in the morning of the 19th of May a number of the Third Cavalry were stopped at Juswunt-Nugger, about ten miles from the Sudder Station. On an attempt being made to disarm them, they shot one and wounded three more of the Police, and then took up a position in a neighbouring temple, small, but of great strength. Mr. Daniell and myself proceeded to the spot, and did our best to carry the place, but could obtain no support, owing to the extreme danger attending storming. At last, after a final attempt to force it by ourselves, in which Mr. Daniell was shot through the face, and the only man who accompanied us killed, I thought it advisable (especially as the whole body of the townspeople, mustering some two thousand low-caste Mussulmans, were becoming actively hostile, and the Police proportionately timorous) to return to Etawah."

† *Ante*, chapter ii., p. 116.

gent population, went out, resolute to bring to justice or to avenge themselves on the spot upon men who a few days before had foully murdered our people under the eyes of a brigade of Europeans; and with only a single follower they had laid gallant siege to a strongly defended place of refuge, and then had quietly walked back through the crowd with the confidence of strength and the assumption of victory. Habituated to rule and accustomed to do much great work single-handed, our large-hearted civilians, with any fearful odds against them, still regarded themselves as masters of the situation, and, with their double-barrelled guns or revolvers, made light of their lack of followers, and seldom shrunk from facing, unsupported, a multitude of enemies. It will become a familiar record, as this History advances; and yet so great is the number of these heroic deeds, that, under pressure of historical necessity, some acts of distinguished gallantry may meet with less than their merited applause. 1857. May.

On the following day, the head-quarters of the Ninth Regiment at Aligurh broke into rebellion; and when news of this disaster reached the Government officers, they saw at once that it was their first duty to keep the knowledge of the event from reaching the detachment at Etawah. Accordingly, Mr. Hume took counsel with the senior officer of the company of the Ninth, and it was determined that the detachment should be removed to an isolated position, where they were less likely to hear of the defection of their comrades. It was impossible to keep them long in ignorance of this event; but Hume had written for reinforcements, and it was of primal consequence to gain time. Accordingly, it was resolved that the Sepoys should be marched to May 20. Mutiny of the Ninth.

1857. May. Burpoorah, a police station on the road to Gwalior. They marched out with apparent cheerfulness, but they had not proceeded more than two miles, when the greater number of them threw off the mask, broke into mutiny, and returned to Etawah. A few Native soldiers remained staunch, and, with their officers, the ladies, and the children, marched on to Burpoorah. The mutineers, meanwhile, re-entered Etawah, and, aided by the surrounding rabble, plundered the Treasury, broke open the gaols, released the prisoners, burnt all the public offices and the officers' houses (Mr. Hume's excepted), and for three or four days anarchy in its worst forms was triumphant; every trace of the British Government had disappeared. Happily, Hume's forethought had greatly diminished the evil—for on the first rumour of rebellion he had secured all the most important Government records by bricking them up secretly in a house in the city, and had sent one-half of the treasure to safe custody at Agra.

May 24. On the night of the 24th, our little party at Burpoorah were succoured by the arrival of Major Hennessy with the Grenadier Regiment of the Gwalior Contingent; and as day broke, on the following morning, the whole marched into Etawah and re-occupied the place. A miserable spectacle then presented itself to the eyes of our people. Riot and rapine had held high carnival during our absence, and the predatory classes, of whose inactivity the English Magistrate, a short time before, had great reason to be proud, were now suddenly warmed into new life and vigour. Not only the released convicts of the gaols, but others, who, under the strong arm of authority, had been driven to seek more lawful occupations, had returned to their old courses. Nor were the criminal classes the only persons who were disposed to take advantage of the temporary obscuration of British authority. Those who had suffered by the action of our Civil Courts were also beginning to rouse themselves to reverse the decisions of men, who, it seemed, could no longer enforce them; and in one village, the old Zemindars, who had ousted the proprietor recognised by the British Government, made manful resistance, and were put to the sword.* For a while British authority, as represented by Allan Hume, was again on the ascendant. But it was hard to say how long the Gwalior Grenadiers would continue faithful to the Raj of the Feringhees. We were only maintained in our supremacy by the mercenaries of a Native Prince. 1857. May.

At Mynpooree was another body of the Ninth Sepoys. The head-quarters of the regiment having mutinied, it was not to be expected that the detachment would remain true to its colours. On the evening of the 22nd of May, intelligence of the rising at Aligurh was received, with exaggerated accounts of the murder of the European officers; and at once arrangements were made to convey the Christian families to Agra.† At the same time it was agreed between the civil and military officers Mynpooree.

* See Mr. Hume's official report: "One village fort at Sumpther, where the old Zemindars, who had ousted the proprietor, pertinaciously refused to surrender, though offered pardon, and fired on our emissaries of peace, was carried by storm, burnt, and the garrison put to the sword." This is recorded as a solitary instance; but it is to be remembered that British authority had then been only three days inabeyance.

† Mr. Power, in his report o May 25, says: "Fourteen females, consisting of ladies, sergeants' and writers' wives, with their children (an unlimited number), left the station under the charge of Mr. S. W. Power, the Assistant-Magistrate, who accompanied them a stage towards Agra, which they reached safely in 'shegrams' (native carriages)."

1857. May. that the question of the fidelity of the Sepoys should be at once put to the test by the issue of an order for their immediate march to Bhowgaon.*

The officers of the Ninth with the detachment at Mynpooree were Lieutenant Crawford and Lieutenant De Kantzow. The civil officers were Mr. Arthur Cocks, Commissioner; Mr. Power, Magistrate; his brother, Assistant-Magistrate; and Dr. Watson, Civil Surgeon. The Rev. Mr. Kellner, a missionary, was also at the station. In the early morning of the 23rd, whilst the civilians, with the exception of the younger Power, who was escorting the women and children on their way to Agra, were gathered together discussing the position, the military officers were endeavouring to induce their men to march to Bhowgaon. But they were not to be commanded or persuaded. It was plain that the experiment had failed. The Sepoys were breaking into revolt and threatening the lives of their officers. Upon this Crawford galloped back to the Magistrate's house, told him that the Sepoys were in open mutiny, that he believed that De Kantzow had been killed, and that it was his intention to ride into Agra. What now was to be done? Arthur Cocks, a brave and resolute man, saw that he could do nothing in the immediate crisis, and as Crawford gave it as his opinion that, in a military sense, there was nothing for them but retirement on Agra, and the Sepoys were shouting defiance and firing their muskets to threaten and intimidate the English, he declared that no one was bound to remain at Mynpooree; and presently, accompanied by Mr.

* Mr. Cocks, in his official report, says, that the news came on the 19th. This is obviously an error, as the troops at Aligurh did not mutiny before the evening of the 20th.

Kellner, he set out, in a buggy, for the Jumna, with the intention of returning with reinforcements. But Power, the Magistrate, declared that he had determined to remain at his post; and the younger Power, having returned to the station, cast in his lot with his brother. Dr. Watson determined also to remain at Mynpooree.* 1857. May.

During this time nothing had been heard of De Kantzow. What was he doing? He was stemming single-handed the tide of mutiny. And it was mutiny of the most delirious kind. The Sepoys returned to the station dragging the Lieutenant with them. As they went, they fired into all the houses of Europeans that they passed. They broke open the Magazine—took possession of all the ammunition, amounting to some three hundred rounds a man—and then, proud of their wealth, proceeded to fire wildly in every direction. It was a mercy and a miracle that De Kantzow was not shot dead. Often was the piece of a Sepoy pointed at him, to be struck down or dashed aside by the hand of one of his comrades. The Sepoys had, according to their wont, made for the Treasury, where they were met by the Civil-guard, who would have fired upon the Sepoys had not De Kantzow wisely restrained them. There was then a scene of wild confusion. The Gaol-guards, few in number and badly armed, did all that they could to

* "The Sepoys were now approaching the station and firing off their muskets, and shouting like madmen. Mr. Power seemed to hesitate what he would do. I considered it no time for hesitation. I fairly told him I did not consider any one bound to remain; soon after which I ordered my buggy, and, with the Rev. Mr. Kellner, drove leisurely away, having told the people about that I hoped to return in a day or two with a force."—*Report of Mr. Cocks, November* 16, 1858. "Mr. Cocks and the Rev. Mr. Kellner immediately decided on leaving, and the former tried to induce me to leave also; as I informed him that I did not desire to leave my post, he honoured me by terming my conduct 'romantic,' and immediately departed in company with the Rev. Mr. Kellner."—***Report of Mr. Power, May*** **25, 1857.**

1857. May. resist the Sepoys; but against such a multitude their defence, though faithful, was feeble. It is said to have been "a fearful scene."* But in the midst of this mighty peril, De Kantzow stood, firm and undaunted, imploring the soldiers to consider the wickedness and folly of their course, and showing to the wonder and the admiration of the surging multitude of Sepoys that a single English officer defied them—that they might kill, but that they could not conquer him. And so for three hours the young English soldier breasted alone this great flood of furious mutiny, and overawed his enemies by the consummate gallantry of his bearing.†

When Mr. Power, the Magistrate, heard that De Kantzow was thus perilously situated, he was eager to join him with all the guards he could muster; but he was dissuaded from this both by the Lieutenant himself, who, in the midst of his own tribulation, contrived to send a note to his friend, and by an influential Native gentleman, the Rao Bhowanee Singh (a relative of the Rajah of Mynpooree), who had come in to our assistance with a small body of horse and foot. This man, as brave as he was faithful, went unattended to the spot where De Kantzow stood at bay, and used every art of remonstrance and persuasion to pacify and subdue the mutineers. And after awhile he succeeded. "He drew off and accompanied the rebels to the lines"—and the brave English subaltern was saved, with the treasure which

* Mr. Power's Official Report, May 25, 1857.

† The official account written by Mr. Power says: "Left by his superior officer, unaided by the presence of any European, jostled with cruel and insulting violence, buffeted by the hands of men who had received innumerable kindnesses from him, and who had obeyed him a few hours before with crawling servility, Lieutenant De Kantzow stood for three dreary hours against the rebels, at the imminent peril of his life."

he had so nobly protected. Rife as is this narrative with records of great deeds done by the younger officers of the Company's Services, there is nothing more illustrative than this story of the grand self-reliance and self-devotion so often manifested in the conduct of untried men, when danger suddenly came upon them and girt them round as with rings of fire. Bravery such as this was sure to win the heart of Lord Canning, and to elicit from him prompt words of admiration. So, when he received Power's report he wrote at once to the noble-hearted young subaltern, saying, "I have read it with an admiration and respect which I cannot adequately describe. Young in years, and at the outset of your career, you have given to your brother-soldiers a noble example of courage, patience, good judgment, and temper, from which many might profit. I beg you to believe that it will never be forgotten by me."* 1857. May.

When news of these events reached Agra, there was great consternation among our people. Numbers of the Christian inhabitants rushed wildly to such houses and buildings as seemed most capable of defence. A brave-hearted Englishman then wrote to his brother, saying: "The panic here exceeds anything I have ever witnessed. Women, children, carts, gharries, buggies flying from all parts into the Fort, with loads of furniture, beds, bedding, baskets of fowls, &c. &c. The Europeans have all escaped from Aligurh. Lady Outram came in here, partly on horseback, partly on foot. . . . . One or two civilians here have behaved most shamefully. One of them Agra. Mr. Paterson Saunders. May 22.

* Lord Canning to Lieutenant De Kantzow, June 7, 1857. MS. Records.

1857. May.

went into his office, pale as his own liver, and told all the crannies to save their lives as they best could."*

Measures of defence.

It was now obviously necessary to look the situation very gravely in the face. The Fort had been secured by the detachment of a body of Europeans to garrison it, and arrangements were being made to provision it for six months. There was not much apprehension of danger from the unaided efforts of the citizens; but the Native regiments were of very doubtful loyalty, and if they, or an incursion of the predatory classes in the neighbourhood, should release the prisoners in the gaols, there might be a popular rising. The European quarters, owing to their straggling nature and the wide space which they covered, at a distance from the European barracks, were not easily to be protected. In the Schools, the Convent, and the houses of the married civilians, were large assemblages of women and children. It was expedient, therefore, to organise some system of external defence, and Mr. Reade was called upon by the Lieutenant-Governor to do it. The task could not have been intrusted to better hands. He had,

* It does not appear that this account is at all overstated. Mr. Charles Raikes, in his published volume, gives the following graphic sketch of the general alarm. The picture of the calm steadfastness of the missionaries is very striking: "Every Englishman was handling his sword or revolver—the road covered with carriages, people hastening right and left to the rendezvous at Candaharee Bagh. The city folks running as for their lives, and screaming that the mutineers from Aligurh were crossing the bridge. The Budmashes twisting their moustaches, and putting on their worst looks. Outside the college all alarm, hurry, and confusion. Within calmly sat the good Missionary, hundreds of young Natives at his feet, hanging on the lips which taught them the simple lessons of the Bible. And so it was throughout the revolt. Native functionaries, highly salaried, largely trusted, deserted and joined our enemies, but the students at the Government, and still more the Missionary, Schools, kept steadily to their classes, and when others doubted or fled, they trusted implicitly to their teachers, and openly espoused the Christian cause."

at an earlier period, been of opinion that it would be expedient to intrench the station; but this view had not been supported, and he had abandoned it. He, therefore, projected a system of rendezvous in case of alarm, of defence-posts, and advance-pickets; so that if danger threatened, early announcement of the coming enemy might be received, and every non-combatant might seek an asylum in one of the appointed places of refuge. The principal public buildings, as the Government House, the Post-office, the Agra Bank, the Customs' House, the Medical College, the Convent, and the Candaharee Baugh,* with some of the private houses of civilians, were fixed upon as places of resort, and arrangements were made for their protection, extending from the Taj on one side to the Cutcherry on the other. Defence-posts, ten in number, so as to form a cordon around the places of rendezvous, were to be manned in sufficient strength; and beyond these again another line of defences, describing a larger semicircle, consisting of fifteen outposts, five of which were to be of horsemen, to bring in promptly the first news of approaching danger, was to be established. But it was easier for the Lieutenant-Governor to invite an officer, in whose wisdom he had confidence, to organise a plan of defence, and easier for that officer to perform the important duty intrusted to him, than to induce others to conform to the plan. Ever in such cases is there disunion. Opposition to any scheme is to be expected, unless it comes with all the force of an imperial edict from the highest authority, and there is something that must, not something that may, be done. So it happened that Reade's plan of defence,

1857. May.

* This was a large brick-built house, belonging to the Rajah of Bhurtpore, and then occupied by Mr. Morgan, of the Civil Service.

1857. May. which, read at this distance of time, seems at least to have upon it the stamp of the broad arrow of common sense, was by the multitude of councillors only partially accepted at the time,* and events were taking shape which soon rendered it an anachronism.

Meanwhile, Mr. Drummond, the Magistrate, was doing all that could be done to convert the City Police into a strong defensive force of Horse and Foot. Muskets and side-arms were served out from the Arsenal, and ammunition was freely supplied to them. But it was hard to say whether they were to be trusted, or, if true at the moment, how long they would remain staunch to their employers. Already they had begun "to scowl upon the Christians."†

Mr. Colvin's Proclamation.

Affairs were in this state, when the Lieutenant-Governor, tormented by doubts, seeing clearly what had already been done, and divining what would ere long be done, by mere force of example, in that great flock of Sepoys, whose nature it ever was to follow each other like sheep, bethought himself of doing something authoritatively to restore the fast-waning confidence of the soldiery by a public appeal to them. One of the ablest and most experienced officers of the Sepoy Army had written to him, saying: "Having served, as I trust, faithfully a most liberal Government for upwards of six-and-thirty years, during which long period I have been associated with the Native soldier in every position in which he can be placed (some of them of very great difficulty), I am sanguine enough to believe that I have a correct and extended knowledge of all his habits, customs, and

Colin Troup.

* Mr. Reade himself states that, "It was partially adopted by the Magistrate and other residents—its effectiveness, however, being impaired by want of unity of purpose, by the wilfulness of some, who devised defensive measures of their own, and the neglect and carelessness of others."

† Raikes.

wishes, and, therefore, hesitate not, under the present trying events, to give it as my unqualified opinion, that in all that is said or done to the Native soldier during the present state of excitement no allusion should be made to the retribution or punishment awaiting those who have disgraced the name of soldiers; and I feel certain, if such can be done with propriety, that a proclamation from you to the effect that the past has been forgiven, and that the moment things are more settled those who have proved true to their Government shall not be forgotten, and that a commission of experienced European and Native officers will be formed to inquire into all their wants, and have everything so arranged as to put it out of the power of evil-disposed men to interfere with their rights and privileges for the future, would at this moment do more good than ten thousand European soldiers. For I have satisfied myself beyond all doubt that fear is the principal cause of all that is going on at present among the men of the Native Army." And he added: "Unless this comes direct from yourself or the Government (for the word of any intermediate authority would be of no avail), it will be of little use." The sentiments thus expressed by Colin Troup appear to have made a deep impression upon Colvin's mind. A strong conviction took possession of him that the old soldier was right; that the Native troops had been drawn into mutiny more by their fears than by their resentments, and that it was sound policy, in such a conjuncture, to endeavour by every possible means to reassure the minds of the Sepoys, who were huddling one after another, in panic-stricken confusion, like a flock of sheep, to destruction. And in this I must ever think that he was right. But the question was not whether the thing

1857. May

1857. May. should be done, but how and by whom it should be done. To have reassured the minds of the Sepoys who had not yet broken into rebellion, and to have promised condonation of the offences of those regiments who had only mutinied—who had offended as soldiers, but had not stained their hands with blood—might in that conjuncture have been a wise measure. But it was absolutely necessary that in such a proclamation care should be taken most explicitly and emphatically to shut out from all participation in the promised amnesty every soldier of a regiment which had outraged its officers. And the proclamation should unquestionably have proceeded, not from the subordinate, but from the Supreme Government. But Colvin, though in communication with Calcutta by telegraph, took upon himself, without consulting the officers surrounding him,* to issue a manifesto in the following words, bearing date the 25th of May:

May 25. "PROCLAMATION.

"Soldiers engaged in the late disturbances, who are desirous of going to their own homes, and who give up their arms at the nearest Government civil or military post, and retire quietly, shall be permitted to do so unmolested.

* Mr. Reade says: "Here I must briefly notice the proclamations issued by the Lieutenant-Governor. The first of these is dated May 15, and the original draft was sent to me, Mr. Harington, and others, before publication. It had our hearty concurrence, both for the tone it assumed and the line of policy it indicated. The subsequent proclamation of the 25th of May was framed and issued, so far as I have been able to ascertain, without reference to any one here at Agra. I see it stated in a republication from the Blue-book that it was sent everywhere as being thought by all here likely to have the best effect on the public mind; but this is altogether erroneous. It certainly took most persons at Agra by surprise, not from the objections made by the Supreme Government, which nobody knew of, but generally from its singular contrast with the proclamation issued only a few days before." Mr. Colvin, however, emphatically declared that the proclamation had been "universally approved" in Agra.

"Many faithful soldiers have been driven into resistance to Government only because they were in the ranks and could not escape from them, and because they really thought their feelings of religion and honour injured by the measures of Government. This feeling was wholly a mistake, but it acted on men's minds. A proclamation of the Governor-General now issued is perfectly explicit, and will remove all doubts on these points. Every evil-minded instigator in the disturbance, and those guilty of heinous crimes against private persons, shall be punished. All those who appear in arms against the Government after this notification is known shall be treated as open enemies."

1857. May.

Sentiments of Lord Canning.

These proceedings deeply pained Lord Canning. Only on the 24th he had written to Mr. Colvin in that warm language of gratitude and encouragement which came spontaneously from his generous heart: "I have never yet sufficiently expressed to you my admiration of your cool courage and excellent judgment during all that has been passing. They have, I know for certain, inspired confidence in those around you, and I feel that it would be difficult to appreciate at its true value the service which you have rendered. To myself the satisfaction and comfort of feeling that your charge is in such hands, is incalculable." And now, three or four days afterwards, he was compelled to repudiate, as chief ruler of the country, the most important of the acts of his once-trusted Lieutenant. Writing privately to Mr. Colvin on the 28th, he said: "I never did an act that gave me more distress than that of superseding the proclamation of the 25th. I would have escaped, if I had thought escape possible, and would have made any sacrifice to support the

1857. May. one which had come from you. But I am strongly of opinion that it would not have been safe to leave that proclamation unaltered. The terms of the first paragraph opened escape to every man, and I cannot see that the door was closed to the most heinous offenders by the third paragraph. The soldiers who murdered their officers are not mentioned or indicated. There is no term which includes them among the most guilty. With that proclamation in their hands, every man of the Twentieth and Thirty-eighth Regiments might, so far as we know, have presented himself to you or to the Commander-in-Chief and have claimed liberty to go home. I use no exaggeration when I say that had any of these men availed themselves of it, the Government could never have held up its head again. I can guess, and, indeed, fully understand the difficulties which beset you, and which you have met so calmly, wisely, and with such dignity, but I do not gather that they are such as to compel us yet to offer free pardon to the murderers of our officers. Certainly nothing which you have sent me sets affairs in that light." "Do not suppose," he added, "that, sitting here in Calcutta, I wish to carry things with a high hand, without regarding the embarrassments and unavoidable weaknesses of those who are in the thick of the difficulties. I have no such desire. Menaces are unworthy of a strong and just Government, and dangerous to a weak one. I would use none. The proclamation now sent has less even of menace than your own. It gives even more distinctly a free and unconditional pardon to one section of the mutineers, and marks a difference between regiments, which strictly accords with justice and our duty towards our officers, whilst it may be expected to sow disunion at Delhi."

The proclamation which Lord Canning sent forth to supersede that which had been issued by Mr. Colvin, ran in the following words: 1857. May.

Lord Canning's Proclamation.

"Every soldier of a regiment which, although it has deserted its post, has not committed outrages, will receive a free pardon and permission to proceed to his home, if he immediately delivers up his arms to the civil or military authority, and if no heinous crime is shown to have been perpetrated by himself personally. This offer of free and unconditional pardon cannot be extended to those regiments which have killed or wounded their officers or other persons, or which have been concerned in the commission of cruel outrages. The men of such regiments must submit themselves unconditionally to the authority and justice of the Government of India. Any proclamations offering pardon to soldiers engaged in the late disturbances, which may have been issued by local authorities previously to the promulgation of the present proclamation, will thereupon cease to have effect. But all persons who may have availed themselves of the offer made in such proclamations shall enjoy the benefit thereof."

The Lieutenant-Governor was slow to acknowledge, and, therefore, it may be assumed that he was slow to see—for he was not one to simulate a belief that was not in him—that there was any material difference between the two manifestoes. And, perhaps, as Mr. Colvin intended his own proclamation to be understood, the difference was but slight. Verbally, however, the distinction was great and striking; and practically the embarrassments resulting from a strict interpretation of the Agra manifesto might have been immense. What Colvin had done, unintentionally, it would seem, was to exempt from punishment all but

1857. May. individual Sepoys known to have been "guilty of heinous crimes against private persons;" whereas the proclamation substituted by the Calcutta Government barred whole regiments, any members of which had been guilty of the murder of their officers or others. As it would have been difficult, if not impossible, save in rare instances, to prove blood-guiltiness against individual soldiers, the most probable result of the amnesty issued by the Lieutenant-Governor would have been the escape of numbers of actual murderers, and of many more, guilty in the second degree, as aiders and abettors. Nothing, moreover, could have been more infelicitous than the expression "private persons," for in no sense, with reference to the Sepoys, could their officers be so described. This, however, Lord Canning declared to be but a small part of the offence. "It is not," he wrote, "only a question as to the meaning of the term 'private persons' either in English or in Oordoo. Whatever may be argued on that point (and I confess that I do not like sailing very near the wind in interpretations upon which the lives of men and the honour of the Government depend), the apparent meaning and the real working of the proclamation will be the same. The vice of it, as I have already said by telegraph, does not consist in the words 'private persons' alone.* The whole burden of proof against each man is thrown entirely and at once upon the authority to whom he presents himself. To put a plain case. If twenty men of the

* Mr. Colvin stated afterwards that as rendered in the Native languages, the words literally represented "subjects of Government." Now, as understood in India at that time, "private persons" and "subjects of Government" were different classes of individuals. Mr. Colvin said that his intention was to discriminate between offences against the *State* and offences against persons—but surely offences against the servants of Government were offences against the Government.

Thirty-eighth Regiment leave Delhi and deliver up their arms to the nearest Magistrate, who knows nothing of them but that they belonged to that corps, can their unmolested liberty be refused to them? Assuredly not, unless the promise given in the proclamation is broken."

1857. May.

To such strictures by Lord Canning and others, Mr. Colvin, some weeks afterwards, replied in a letter to his brother: "The proclamation was universally approved here, though much that I have done since has been the cause of much difference of opinion. We here understood the vast extent of the danger that was opening on us, and the sincere and thorough delusion that the mass of the Sepoys were in, about the intentions of Government. Regiments were beginning to give way all round. To prevent the fatal mischief spreading, it seemed the wisest thing that could be done to mark that we desired to be just, and to offer the means of retreat to those not already desperately committed, and who had been betrayed into the rebel ranks by the insane apprehensions about religion, or by the inability of getting away from them. That those who had taken a leading or a deliberately malignant part in the revolt would ever seek to take advantage of the notification, we knew to be quite out of the question. The chance that seemed open (through the proclamation) of escape to such persons was what called forth the heavy censure at many distant points. But we who were nearer the scene, and knew the real spirit of the revolt, could not entertain such a supposition. The attempt to separate the comparatively innocent—to appeal through them to the feelings of the regiments yet in obedience—seemed in my deliberate opinion,

1857. May. and still seems, the right and useful thing to do at that time."*

Upon few events of those troubled times was so much useless controversy expended. For, notwithstanding all this logomachy, the proclamation was a very harmless proclamation. Nothing in effect came from it—except that the adverse criticisms passed upon it in Government House and in other places, high and low, had a wearing and depressing effect upon the Lieutenant-Governor's mind. In such times and in such circumstances, a man even with robust health and a strong nervous system on his side requires some external encouragement to sustain and to keep him up to the athletic standard which is necessary to the right discharge of great responsibilities. But Colvin's health was failing; his nerves were shaken. Whilst day after day, from beyond Agra, fresh tidings of disaffection and disaster came in to increase his perplexities and to aggravate his distresses, the difficulties which presented themselves to him at home, because more immediate and omnipresent, were still more vexatious and annoying. The differences of opinion, which arose among the many able and energetic officers who surrounded him, were continually distracting his mind and ministering to his irresolution. What he suffered no man can tell; but those about him saw more clearly every day that he was growing weaker both in body and in mind. It was plain that the burden upon him was greater than he could bear. He was a brave and honourable Englishman; but his lines had been cast in pleasant places. He had been sage in counsel; but he was not accustomed to face the responsibilities of prompt and strenuous action, and now he began slowly to

* MS. Correspondence.

succumb to the incessant pressure upon his brain; and those who watched him did not think that he would long survive to direct or to control them. 1857. May.

Three weeks had now nearly passed away since the conflagration had commenced in the Upper Provinces of India; but although there had been many alarming rumours, there had been no reality of danger at Agra. The Native regiments had performed their accustomed duties, in obedience to their officers, who for the most part clung to the belief that their men would not turn against them.* And the principal civilians, whose counsels up to this time prevailed, were still preaching the expediency of maintaining an outward show of confidence, though in truth the faith itself, if ever honestly cherished, was rapidly passing away, and the Lieutenant-Governor was beginning to doubt whether he had not been ill-advised from the first. May 30. Mutiny at Muttra.

But before the month of May had closed in upon us, a crisis had arrived in the affairs of Agra. There was a company of one of the Agra regiments (the Forty-fourth) at Muttra, a civil station some thirty-five miles distant; and it had been arranged

* It is probable that this belief was more strongly impressed on the minds of the elder than of the younger officers. When Sir Henry Durand was at Agra, on his way to Indore, at the end of March, he wrote to Lord Canning, saying: "Brigadier Polwhele spoke with dissatisfaction of the opinions and conversation of some of the younger officers, ascribing to unwise assertions on their parts the idea, more or less generally entertained, that the Sepoy corps sympathised with the Nineteenth Native Infantry, and he with a good deal of earnestness denied that the Sepoys here had given the slightest grounds for such a suspicion. There may of course be a lack both of experience and wisdom among young officers, but they are freer in their expression of opinion and the men less on their guard before them. Aged officers like Polwhele are slow to perceive and unwilling to admit anything not flattering to their own influence and authority."—*MS. Correspondence.*

1857. May. that another company of the same regiment, and one also of the Sixty-seventh, should be sent thither, partly to relieve the old detachment, and partly to bring away the bulk of the treasure. This amounted to upwards of six lakhs of rupees. It ought to have been, and it might easily have been, brought away before. Mr. Colvin had been eagerly besought by the Engineer officers to remove the treasure both from Aligurh and Muttra; but these would have been marks of no-confidence, which it was the policy of the Government to disavow. There had been considerable excitement at Muttra. News had come that the Delhi mutineers and others were marching on Agra, and would pass through the Muttra station on their way. The European women and children had, therefore, been sent to the former place. In the middle of the month the arrival of the Bhurtpore force, under Captain Nixon, though it alarmed the Sepoys, did something to restore the general confidence.* It was believed that the Foreign Contingent was to be trusted; but it was merely a question, to be determined by some accident, as to which should be the first to rise. The event proved that in the race of rebellion they were destined to achieve something like a dead heat. When, on the 30th of

* The following is from a letter written by Captain Nixon (Muttra, May 17): "On marching in, we drove very thoughtlessly up to the Treasury-guard, and, on arriving near, the Sepoys turned out in a dreadful fright. The fact is they thought that they were going to be attacked, as I had of course an immense *sowarree* following me. I was put in a very ticklish position, and had to send back my *sowarree*, as I saw the Sepoys commencing to load. However, they immediately stopped all hostile demonstrations on my turning the *sowarree* back, and we went and reassured them and made them 'present arms.' The fact is that my people had evidently been threatening them, and they thought that their time had come. I am glad, for one or two reasons, that this has happened—firstly, because it is now quite clear to me that our Sepoys and the troops of the Native States will never coalesce, and secondly, because they are now frightened by an enemy from another quarter." All this, as will presently be seen, was an entire mistake.

May, the two companies marched in from Agra, there was a sufficient body of Sepoys at the place to seize the treasure without much fear of successful resistance. The moment was opportune; so as soon as the treasure was placed on the carriages, which were to convey it to Agra, the Sepoys broke into open rebellion. Lieutenant Boulton, who was superintending, with others, the transfer of the coin, was shot dead; Lieutenant Gibbon was wounded; and some of the civil officers narrowly escaped the fire of the insurgents. The Sepoys now had the rupee-bags securely in hand, and with them they started off for Delhi.

1857. May.

There was, however, some hope that those plans might be frustrated. At that time the Bhurtpore troops were at Hodul. Mr. Harvey, the Commissioner, was with them. In the early morning of the 31st of May, the Commissioner was apprised, by an incursion of fugitives from Muttra, that the troops had risen and were on their way to Delhi. His first thought was to intercept the progress of the insurgents. A plan of defence was, therefore, agreed upon between the civil and the military officers. The Bhurtpore guns were to be placed in position across the road, by which the mutineers were expected to advance. But all hope of a successful resistance was soon gone. Many of the artillerymen were Poorbeahs, deserters or discharged Sepoys from our own Infantry ranks; and their commanders told our officers that the men were not to be trusted. The Bhurtpore camp, indeed, was declared to be no place of safety for Europeans; and our people were, therefore, exhorted to depart. But they were slow to take this advice. For some hours they exerted themselves most strenuously to induce the regiments to do their duty. They offered

May 31. Mutiny of the Bhurtpore troops.

1857. May 31. liberal rewards on the part of the British Government. They reminded the troops that they would bring disgrace on their own Raj, if they forsook, in the hour of need, the allies whom they had been sent to succour. But no arguments, or persuasions, or promises could avail. The only result of these efforts was, that the Bhurtpore artillerymen pointed some of their guns threateningly at the group of Englishmen. There was now nothing more to be done but either to seek some safer place or to remain in the Bhurtpore camp to be murdered. So the party of Englishmen—some thirty in number—mounted their horses and rode off, carrying nothing with them but the arms in their hands and the clothes on their backs. Scarcely had they started, when the Bhurtpore troops broke into the wonted orgies of rebellion. The tents of the English gentlemen were almost instantly in a blaze. A few bungalows, which had been occupied by Customs' officials in our pay, were fired, one after another; and such property as our people had left behind them was plundered by our allies. And thus was the first rude shock given to our faith in the allied troops of the Native States—thus was all hope of the Agra Commissioner effecting the march to Delhi cut off from him for a time. Harvey's first thought was to endeavour to form a junction with the Sirmoor battalion, which was then moving upon Delhi. This, however, was not accomplished; and he eventually found himself in Rajpootana, where, in co-operation with the political officers in those states, he rendered excellent service to his Government.

Disarming of the Native regiments.

It was to be expected that news of these events would produce great excitement in Agra. The companies which had mutinied belonged to the Agra regiments. There was little doubt that the main bodies would follow the lead of these pioneers into the jungle of rebellion. It was necessary, therefore, to act—and at once. The evil tidings had been brought by a camel-express, and communicated about midnight to Mr. Drummond. The Lieutenant-Governor was at that time sleeping in the Magistrate's house. So Drummond roused him, and insisted that it was necessary to disarm the Sepoy regiments on the coming morning at break of day. If Colvin demurred for a little space, his reluctance was soon overcome by the earnestness of the Magistrate. The order went forth; and at dawn on that Sunday, the 31st of May, the Third Europeans were brought down to the parade-ground, and Captain D'Oyley's battery was drawn up ready for action. When, therefore, the Sepoy regiments found themselves in dangerous proximity to the British Infantry and the guns, they knew that certain destruction was before them if they ventured to resist. The old Brigadier, seated on his white charger, addressed a few words to the Sepoys and gave the word of command. "Silent and sullen" the Sepoys obeyed the order to "pile arms;" and they were marched back to their Lines. Some applied for leave and went to their homes. Others started off without leave for Delhi. But any present danger to be apprehended from them was gone; and, practically, two more regiments were effaced from the Bengal Army List.

1857. May 31.

CHAPTER II.

STATE OF THE DISTRICTS — THE MEERUT AND ROHILKUND DIVISIONS — AFFAIRS AT MOZUFFERNUGGUR AND SAHARUNPORE—THE TWENTY-NINTH AT MORADABAD—MR. CRACROFT WILSON—MUTINY OF THE BAREILLY BRIGADE—KHAN BEHAUDUR KHAN—SHAHJEHANPORE AND BUDAON.

1857. May—June.

So the month of June dawned upon the Lieutenant-Governor and his colleagues, with at least one source of apprehension less. "The greatest good," wrote Mr. Colvin to Lord Canning, on the 1st of June, "has been done by the disarming of the two Native regiments here. Most of the men will slink away, chiefly from fear of what we may do to them, and we are well rid of them." In other parts of the country, this "slinking away" of disarmed Sepoys was called desertion, and men were hanged for the offence.* And wisely, too—for disarmed men, in such a state of things as then confronted us, soon became full-armed men. They had never to go far to re-equip themselves for the battle. And, therefore, a danger removed from Agra, or any central point, was only a danger sent to reappear on some other spot, and perhaps with redoubled cogency for evil. It was commonly said that Sepoys who had mutinied or deserted "went off to Delhi." But many halted by the way, scattering themselves over the

* *Ante*, vol. ii. page 482.

districts, some going straight to their Native villages with such share of the wages of rebellion as they might have succeeded in appropriating to themselves, and spreading abroad everywhere exaggerated stories of the evil intentions of the English, or of the speedy downfall of the British Empire. 1857. May—June.

Indeed, nothing was more certain at this time than that, whatever might be the improvement in the position of Agra itself, the North-Western Provinces were every day sinking into the profoundest depths of disorder. Before the end of May, Mr. Colvin had written to the Governor-General, saying: "The country is in utter disorder; but bold men, holding together, should still make their way through. The real reason, I regret to say, why messages do not get delivered is, that the belief in the permanence of our power has been very deeply shaken, and that men think that there is a better chance for them to take to open plundering than to engage in special risks for our service. . . . . The country north of Meerut (part at least of the Mozuffernuggur district) is at the mercy of the most daring and criminal. There are many good men, whose feelings are with us, but the vicious, the disappointed, and the desperate, are the most bold in all such convulsions of order, and on the whole there is (its police force being dispersed) no support to the Government. . . . . Aligurh and Etah, the two most important districts of the centre Upper Doab, are in a blaze of riot and ravage. . . . . It is melancholy to contemplate the fearful calamities which, at but a short thirty or forty miles from me, are causing the misery of our poor subjects, for whom we have thought and toiled with so many anxious cares. . . . . Such is the state of things in extremely opulent districts, which but three months ago I

1857. May—June. prided myself on having done so much to improve." Some of the more distant manifestations spoken of in this letter I must now proceed to relate.

Above Delhi. In the districts of the North-Western Provinces situated above Delhi, British authority was threatened with greater violence than below. But the danger was not always of the same type. What we have hitherto traced in the shape of overt acts against the Government of the English, have been mutinous risings of the Sepoy soldiery, which their non-military brethren more or less aided and abetted. Into whatsoever dimensions, social or political, the movement may have afterwards swollen, its first activities were purely military. At all our great civil stations were detachments of Native Infantry regiments posted there mainly to protect the Treasury and other property of the Government. The revenue was collected, for the most part, in the silver coinage of the country, and at the head-quarters of every collectorate were treasure-chests groaning with rupees. No one, before the coming of this month of May, ever doubted that, under the charge of a guard of Sepoys, all this wealth was as secure as it would have been in Lothbury. But now it was clear that our strength had become weakness—our security had been turned into danger. The guardians of our public property had become its despoilers; and at most stations were doubt and apprehension, and a general wish that the property of Government and the lives of its servants had been in charge of the Civil Police of the district. But in some of the districts in the Meerut and Bareilly Divisions there was less fear of the soldiery than of the populace. The first threatenings came from the disaffected communities, whilst still the Sepoys were outwardly staunch.

At Saharunpore and Mozuffernuggur, in the Meerut

Division, and at Moradabad and Budaon, in the contiguous Bareilly Division, this was especially apparent. At Saharunpore was a detachment of the Twenty-ninth Sepoy Regiment, its head-quarters being at Moradabad. It was a regiment of good repute, believed to be loyal, and for some time it maintained its character. But the guards at Mozuffernuggur were drawn from the Twentieth that had mutinied at Meerut, and there was, seemingly, small hope of the continuance of its loyalty. It was probable, indeed, that on the arrival of the news from head-quarters, the detachment would break into instant rebellion. For three days, however, the Sepoys were quiet. But those three days were fatal to our rule. Before the soldiery had struck a blow, there were signs of insurrection in the town. The English Magistrate had closed all the public offices, and hid himself in the jungle.* The most exaggerated reports of the total collapse of British rule began to spread through the district. Then all the discontented, the disappointed, and the down-trodden began to take heart. The houses of our public officers were burnt or attacked by armed bands: and it was believed that "the impoverished Syud Zemindars instigated the villagers to commit these excesses."† The example having thus been set by the non-military classes, the Sepoys rose. On the afternoon of the 14th, when it was proposed to move the treasure to a place of greater safety, the guard refused to allow its removal, broke into the chest, and gorged themselves with the plunder.‡ Taking with them as much as they could carry—about one-third, perhaps, of the

1857. May—June.

Mozuffernuggur.

* In the official report by Mr. R. M. Edwards it is significantly said: "Mr. Berford at once ordered that all the public offices should be closed on that day. They were never again opened."

† Official report.

‡ There were eighty-five thousand rupees in the Treasury, and there were only thirty-five Sepoys on the Treasury-guard.

1857. May—June. whole—they marched off triumphantly towards Moradabad. The rest of the coin was plundered by the townspeople, the Magistrate's servants, and it was more than suspected by the Native functionaries of the British Government. "Nobody," says the official report, "raised a finger to prevent them; everybody seems to have been paralysed."

But there was something still more surprising than this. Overcome by unmanly fear for his personal safety, the Magistrate determined to strengthen his own body-guard by releasing the prisoners in the Gaol, and withdrawing the guards that were protecting it. This crowning instance of the paralysis of British authority gave the finishing stroke to all law and order in the district. Whilst the Magistrate was sheltering himself in a suburb of the city, with a guard of Sepoys around the house in which he lay, the Government offices and officers' bungalows were burnt, the public records were exultantly destroyed, the empty Gaol was pulled to pieces, and the doors, and shutters, and railings carried off as plunder by the villagers, and from one end to the other of the district the tidings ran that English rule was at an end, that the English were hiding themselves for fear of their lives, that a reign of anarchy had commenced, that every one might do as he liked, and take what he could get, that the race was to the swift and the battle to the strong, and that every man was his own judge and collector.

Saharunpore. And thus the prevailing faith of Mozuffernuggur soon became the prevailing faith of Saharunpore. I am glad to change the scene, for in the latter district English manhood was not utterly at its last gasp. All men are not alike, and even on the fair countenance of our national manliness may sometimes be seen ugly blotches and unseemly tumours. The difficulties of Saharunpore were increased by the failure of Mozuffernuggur. In the former district there had been some bad symptoms from the commencement, and when it was known that English authority was prostrate in the latter, the audacity of the people increased.* The Magistrate, Mr. Spankie, on first learning that the Meerut troops had risen, summoned a Council, and it was considered whether the English should abandon the station or hold on to the last. There was energy enough in the little conclave to carry a vote in favour of the manlier course. This done, all the ladies and children of the station were sent under safe escort to Mussoorie, on the Hills. There was no expectation that the district would remain quiet. Its population was a dangerous population. Its "plundering tribes" were prominent in its statistics, and a general feeling of the inability of the English any longer to maintain order, stimulated every man to take the law into his own hand. There was a company of the Twenty-Ninth Sepoys in the station, guarding the public property; but the fear was not of the soldiery, but of the populace. Whilst the soldiery were at least outwardly tranquil, among the people were throes and spasms of feverish emotion.

1857. May—June.

* See statements of Mr. Dundas Robertson, Joint-Magistrate of Saharunpore, in his work, entitled "District Duties during the Revolt in the North-West Provinces of India" (1859), one of the best of many valuable books, illustrative of scattered passages of the rebellion. See also Mr. Spankie's official report: "During this period of uncertainty (May 13-14), whilst speaking to several would-be well-disposed Natives, who it was easy to observe visited me more with the view of extracting than of furnishing information, I was much struck with their evident satisfaction in the generally unfavourable nature of the news, and with the promise of misfortune to the English." Again: "In the Mozuffernuggur district (May 18-20), some thirty miles distant, British authority had almost ceased to exist, and was but feebly pulsating in the southern portion of our own, bordering on Mozuffernuggur. . . . The whole surrounding country was in a state of the most complete anarchy."

1857. May—June. Class rose against class; the strong against the weak; the debtor against the creditor; the beaten defendant against the successful plaintiff. The greatest joy of all was to reverse, by stretching forth a mailed hand, the decisions of the English Courts.

Mr. H. D. Robertson. But underlying all this internecine strife there was a hatred, strong though subdued, of British rule. And a shrewd observer—a man equally sagacious and brave, who nobly upheld the British character in Saharunpore—had, before the close of the month, assured himself, by a full consideration of his experiences, that "the Zemindars were one with the lower orders—that rebellion, not plunder alone, actuated the mass of the population." It was as surprising as it was deplorable. "Troops might mutiny," said the Joint-Magistrate, "but I could hardly realise this rapid change amongst peaceful villagers."* The change was sadly apparent everywhere. In the city men were closing their shops and burying their valuables. There was an almost entire suspension of business, whilst on the public roads, which a little time before had been "crowded to excess" with travellers of both races and an extensive traffic, there was now something like a solitude, broken only by a few bands of armed men. There was no longer any security for life or property. The civil power was utterly prostrate. Yet, all this time, there was no danger from the Sepoys. "The Sepoy Treasury-guard continued true to their duty."

Indeed, when towards the end of the month it was proposed to go out and take the offensive, a strong party of Sepoys, accompanying the English gentlemen and the horsemen of the District Police, went out

* Robertson's "District Duties during the Revolt." "A few days preceding the 23rd of May, we ascertained that several of the larger villages had combined to attack us."

to coerce the rebel villages. The detachment of the Twenty-ninth had, by this time, been strengthened by Sepoy reinforcements from Umballah, both Horse and Foot.* Whilst in some parts the authorities were eager to rid themselves of the great danger of the Sepoys, here they were regarded as elements of safety, and our people sought their protection against the enmity of the inhabitants of the towns and villages—and this at no great distance from Meerut and Delhi, where military mutiny was rampant. 1857. May—June.

Meanwhile, in the Rohilkund Division were to be seen similar manifestations of contempt for and defiance of British authority. It was soon apparent throughout the districts that there was an uneasy, restless feeling among the people, and that the national heart was turned against the English. There was, indeed, no part of the country under charge of the Lieutenant-Governor from which accounts were looked for with greater anxiety than from that important province. For there, the Mahomedan population was strong both in numbers and in influence—especially in the great towns. A fine, hardy, warlike race of men were the Pathan Rohillas, and there were chiefs among them with unforgotten hereditary claims and unextinguished hereditary rancours. It was well-nigh certain, therefore, that the bulk of the Mahomedan population would cast in their lot with the military rebels; that if the Rohillas did not, as was probable, set the example of insurrection, they Rohilkund.

* "I felt that I required help from without, and I wrote to Mr. Barnes, Commissioner of Umballah, who did all he could; and Mr. Plowden, Assistant-Commissioner of Umballah, then quartered at Jugadhree, crossed the Jumna with a party of the Fourth Light Cavalry, under Captain Wyld, and a company of Infantry (Fifth Native), under Captain Garsten. The appearance of the troops was most opportune, and confidence for a time restored."—*Mr. Spankie's Report.*

1857. May—June. would instigate the Sepoys to cast off their allegiance to the British Government, and strike for the restoration of the Mogul Empire.

Moradabad. At Moradabad the main body of the Twenty-ninth* Sepoy Regiment was posted; and neither their own officers nor the chief civilians in the district showed any sign of want of confidence in them. There was fortunately then at the station a high civil functionary of immense energy and courage, a man equal to any emergency and capable of any act of daring. Mr. Cracroft Wilson was Judge of Moradabad. In that capacity he had no official control over executive details. But he had large experience of that part of the country; he was highly respected by the Native inhabitants of all classes; and it was with no undue appreciation of his own influence and capacity for good that he applied to the Lieutenant-Governor to enlarge his powers.† The application was promptly granted; and Wilson began his work with characteristic resolution and sagacity. The Twenty-ninth was a regiment of good repute, and it was believed that by firm and judicious management it might be kept true to its allegiance. When news of our disasters at Meerut came in, Wilson, with the consent of the military authorities, went into the Sepoy Lines and conversed freely with the Native officers and privates, telling them that their comrades had been misled by lying reports, and that to follow the noxious example of these misguided men would

* As another instance of the manner in which writers may be misled by following official documents, it may be stated that Mr. Dunlop, in his public reports, calls this regiment the Twenty-third.

† It should be observed that the Magistrate, Mr. C. B. Saunders, had been very recently appointed to Moradabad, and therefore was comparatively unacquainted with the district. He was an officer of the highest promise—since abundantly fulfilled by his attainment to some of the most important political offices under the Government of India.

be to bring ruin upon themselves. Again and again he went among them with reassuring words. And it seemed to him that the majority of the Sepoys were by no means disposed to swerve from their allegiance, although great efforts were being made by some disaffected Mahomedans in the town to induce them to depart from it.* There was, however, a detachment of a Native battery of Artillery, the gunners of which showed from the first unmistakable signs of an inclination to revolt.

1857. May—June.

During the earlier weeks of May the men of the Twenty-ninth continued to obey orders. There was work for them to do, as disorder began to develop itself in the district, in opening the roads which had been closed by the Goojurs, and arresting any dangerous rebels whose designs had become apparent. And for this work they seemed to exhibit no disinclination. But a far greater trial awaited the Twenty-ninth.

* A Hindoo Government translator, who from his propensity to quote Shakspeare may be assumed to have been educated at one of our Government colleges, has written an amusing account of the Moradabad insurrection, which contains the following passage: "An old pretender was now seen going towards the cantonments with a few Mussulman followers to tamper with the Sepoys. It was Newab Niamut-oollah Khan, formerly in Government employ—viz., Moonsiff of Nugeenah in the time of Mr. Judge Okeden, and subsequently a political pensioner. The hoary-headed traitor, emerging from his house in Mohullah Newab-ponah, began to assure the townsfolk that he, being a descendant of a former viceroy, would soon take possession of Moradabad, and govern it in the name of the King of Delhi with justice and peace. In order to gain over the mutinous Twenty-ninth Native Infantry, he sent them a large quantity of parched grain with goor, to serve as breakfast for them. He sent bread and other kinds of food to the Mussulman Sepoys. The Sepoys, after accepting his presents and thanking him, ordered him to leave the lines on pain of death. The ungrateful beast, thus disappointed, returned to his house with indignation and shame." The writer adds, with a self-denying naïveté significant of truth, "Although I knew a great deal, but being an insignificant official, whose task was only to translate into English heavy civil suits, was never asked on any subject, nor in the presence of a large number of cunning Mussulman officers of great influence, I had the pluck to reveal anything successfully. Thus the treason of Newab Niamut-oollah Khan was suffered to pass unnoticed and with impunity, until he openly became a Ghazee, and was shot at Delhi on the day of assault."

1857. May—June. The test was a hazardous one. The detachment of the Twentieth (the mutinous Meerut regiment) which had risen at Mozuffernuggur was coming down upon Moradabad. On the evening of the 18th, intelligence was received of their arrival at the Gangun Bridge. Upon this it was agreed that a party of Irregulars then starting on an expedition to clear the roads should be reinforced by a detachment of the Twenty-ninth. So Captain Faddy and Lieutenant Clifford, two excellent officers, got their men under arms, and accompanied by Mr. Wilson and other civilians, they started for the encampment of the mutineers. It was starlight when they reached their destination. What followed it is not easy accurately to describe. The Sowars, of whose fidelity there was little doubt, had been wisely placed in front, and the detachment of the Twenty-ninth in the rear. The former were spread out so as nearly to surround the mutineers of the Twentieth, who at that time were taking their rest. Their slumbers were soon broken; and they started up surprised and bewildered, and wondering what had come upon them. Then Cracroft Wilson saw that the time had come for the Twenty-ninth to act; so he called upon Captain Faddy to advance. Soon there was a scene of confusion, in the midst of which it was apparent that Faddy's Sepoys, if not against us, were not with us. Some eight or ten of the mutineers were seized, and one was shot dead by a Sowar. The men of the Twentieth were heavily laden with bags of rupees, of which our people made a capture. The fastening cords of one or two of these bags were loosed, and then there was a scramble for the rupees, which put an end to active operations against the insurgents. The prisoners and the coin were carried towards Meerut, and the bulk of the detachment went back to Moradabad, bearing with them the body of the slain mutineer. 1857. May—June.

On the following morning some of the mutineers of the Twentieth, who had escaped from the onslaught on the Gangun, believing that nothing but fraternity would be found there, entered the Lines of Moradabad. But they had miscalculated the amount of security to be found there. One was shot dead by a Sikh Sepoy of the Twenty-ninth, and four were taken alive.* By a fatal error, living and dead were sent to the criminal Gaol.† If they had been placed under a military guard, as was Wilson's desire, they might have escaped, or they might have been released, but they alone would have recovered their liberty. But it happened that the man who had been killed was a relative of one of the Sepoys of the Twenty-ninth, who incited a number of his comrades to proceed with him to the Gaol to rescue the military prisoners and to carry off the body of the slain. Then the Nujeebs of the Gaol-guard fraternised with them, declaring that carriages had been prepared to convey the prisoners to Meerut to be hanged. So the Gaol was entered, the mutineers were released, and with them went forth, cheering and shouting, all the prisoners confined by order of our criminal courts, to carry devastation with them.

When news of this event was brought to Wilson by the European officers, he mounted his horse and accompanied them towards the Gaol. The escaped convicts were then streaming about in all directions,

* Baboo Gunesh Pershad says they were taken "by the City Police."

† The Native chronicler above-quoted says, "By whom and under whose permission Heaven only knows!" Mr. Wilson says that they were sent there by the Adjutant of the Twenty-ninth.

1857. May—June. and it would have been madness to have gone unsupported among them. Remembering, then, that there was in the neighbourhood a party of the Cavalry of the Nawab of Rampore, he rode off towards them and claimed their assistance, but they met him only with insulting refusals. So he rode back to the Lines. Meanwhile, the Adjutant of the Twenty-ninth had mustered a number of well-affected Sepoys, and gone in pursuit of the fugitive prisoners. Learning this, Wilson endeavoured to raise another levy of the same kind, and with a little party of eight or ten Sepoys and a few Rampore Irregulars, he went forth to capture the gaol-birds. These joint efforts were most successful. "A hundred and fifty men were recaptured and lodged in gaol." Returning about an hour after mid-day to the town, he found there an ominous silence. The shops were closed; the streets were deserted. No food had been cooked that day in the Lines. It was evident that every one had been waiting and watching for what was to come next. Wilson looked the crisis in the face. His first effort was to endeavour to enlist some of the principal townspeople on the side of the British Government. But even those on whom he had most relied held back in the hour of his need. So he determined to address the soldiery in the Lines. The Sepoy is easily wrought upon by brave words, aided by a manly presence and a confident demeanour. The resolute courage which the Judge had evinced from the beginning, had made a great impression on the Native soldiery, and now once more it was to be tested. As he rode towards the Lines he passed in front of the Artillery. The Golundauze, whose treachery had been known from the first, laid their guns and lit their portfires. Wilson's clear blue eyes calmly confronted the murderous design. Without a sign of fear on his face, he rode towards the guns, not from them, and waved his hat as a challenge to the gunners. Abashed and overawed by the bearing of the intrepid Englishman they slunk back, and Wilson was saved. Then he went on, accompanied by some officers, to the Quarter-Guard, but not a man had turned out on parade. It seemed that they were held back by a vague suspicion of treachery; but what these few Europeans could have done against so many it is hard to say. Still it was wise to remove the groundless fear; so ball-cartridges were served out to the men of the Twenty-ninth, and they were ordered to assemble with their arms. Thus reassured they were drawn up in a hollow square, and Wilson went into the midst of them and addressed them. He told them that they had committed a great crime in the morning, but that only a portion of the regiment had been implicated, and that it was not right that he and others who had grown grey in the service should be ruined by the excesses of a number of unruly boys; but that if they would swear to behave loyally for the future, he would recommend the Governor-General to forgive them. The Native officers asked if he would swear on the Bible to fulfil what he promised. To this he readily consented; mutual oaths were taken, and confidence was restored for a time. The shops were opened. The streets were thronged. The English ladies, who in this critical conjuncture had been wisely concealed, came forth from their hiding-places. And every one felt as if a load had been taken from his mind.

1857. May—June.

Meanwhile there were great commotions in the district. Against the non-military insurgents the

1857. May—June. Sepoys did their duty well. On the 20th, a party under Lieutenant Clifford, with a few horsemen, went out and captured eighty Goojurs; and on the following day, Cracroft Wilson, having learnt that a disaffected Moulavee had summoned from Rampore a large body of Mahomedans, who were to come down upon Moradabad, raising the green flag, and to plunder the town, went out with a company of the Twenty-ninth, commanded by Captain Faddy, taking some Sowars with him, and arrested their advance. Their leader was cut down,* and several others of their chief people were captured, whilst the rest sought safety in flight.

But another and a far more severe trial was now to be forced upon them. A few days afterwards, news came that the two companies of Sappers, who had been left at Roorkhee, had mutinied on learning how their comrades at Meerut had been treated. These two companies were now marching upon Moradabad. Nothing had made so deep an impression on the minds of the Sepoys in the North-West as the story of the destruction of the Sappers—the story as told, with many exaggerations, in the Lines and Bazaars. A belief was gaining ground that the English intended to deal with all the Native regiments after the same fashion; and the Twenty-ninth had been discussing the incident with no little excitement. It was impossible, therefore, to feel any confidence that

* Mr. Wilson, in his official report, thus relates this incident: "We crossed the river Ram-Gunja at the Bareilly Ghaut, and seeing a man dressed in green on foot, I advanced towards him. Whilst speaking to him I knocked up the pan of his blunderbuss. He put it down. I then laid hold of the muzzle and held it firmly, pointing upwards. The fellow then drew a pistol from his belt, when a Sepoy, by name Kalkae Singh, of the fifth company, who had followed me unperceived, knocked him down; and then the Darogah of the bridge of boats gave him two sword-cuts across the back of his neck."

they would now operate against their comrades. 1857. May—June.
About noon the advancing body of Sappers was seen from the roof of the Court-House. Captain Whish immediately ordered out two hundred men and two nine-pounder guns, and the civilians, with Wilson at their head, got together all the horsemen they could muster and joined the force. They were soon in front of the advanced body of the mutineers. The Sowars went in among the insurgents, endeavouring to persuade them to lay down their arms. The guns were loaded with shrapnel, and the port-fires were lit. But the position of some of our own people (purposely, perhaps) delayed the order to fire; and, when after a time the obstacle was removed, the mutineers "flung down their carbines and ran into the arms of the men of the Twenty-ninth Regiment, which by this time had come to within two hundred yards of the scene from the southward." But what was to be done with the prisoners we had made? Past experience had made us but too well acquainted with the danger of taking them to Moradabad. So they were deprived of their arms and ammunition, their money, and nearly all their clothes, and thus stripped and beggared, were cast adrift upon the world. The majority of them fled to Bareilly.

After this there was an outward appearance of order and discipline in the Lines; but in the surrounding districts there was an almost general defiance of law, and the Sepoys found employment in repeated expeditions to suppress these local disturbances. The Goojurs, the Mehwattees, and others took advantage of the opportunity, and improved the occasion, to the terror of the more peaceful inhabitants, whilst many of the more wealthy inhabitants of the city, though outwardly professing their loyalty

1857. May—June. to Government, secretly intrigued with the Sepoys, and told them that the British Raj was for ever overthrown. So the men of the Twenty-ninth waited and watched, and asked each other, "What news from Bareilly?"

June 1. News from Bareilly.

The month of June dawned ominously upon the little body of brave-hearted Englishmen at Moradabad. Ever since the commencement of our troubles their thoughts had turned anxiously towards Bareilly—the head-quarters of the division—where was a large force of Native troops surrounded by a hostile population. Of these several conditions I shall speak presently, when I come to write of what happened there. Here it need only be said that upon the movements of the Bareilly Brigade depended the safety of Moradabad; and now, on the 1st of June, the first sign of danger in that direction was given by the interruption of postal communication, which, up to that time, had been unintermittent. On that Monday morning no letters came from Bareilly; and there were rumours, both in the Lines and in the public offices, that the brigade had risen. Two hours after midnight, Wilson was roused from his sleep by the arrival of a messenger from the Nawab of Rampore, informing him that there had been mutiny and massacre at Bareilly, and urging him at once to seek safety in flight. To this the English officer demurred, saying that honour forbade such a course. There was no more sleep for him that morning. He rose, and went to the Adjutant of the Twenty-ninth, and at dawn the chief European and Native officers were assembled. Then Wilson stated unreservedly the information he had received, and explained that the only honourable course left for them was "to hold the district until the Bareilly

Brigade came to a distance of twenty miles of them, and that then they should march to Meerut with colours flying, taking guns and treasure with them." To this the Native officers consented, well knowing that the project was one which would never go further than the language in which it was spoken. Our people went to the Lines accompanied by the Native officers, and Wilson's brave words were "met with derision." They believed that to lead them to Meerut would be to take them to their doom, and one man openly reviled Wilson for conceiving this murderous design. Wilson told the man that he lied, which was true, and that he knew it, which perhaps was not true; but all felt that now the game was up at Moradabad, and that there was nothing left for our Christian people but to gird up their loins for flight.

1857. June.

It was a sore trial, but what else could be done? The townspeople were arrayed against us as virulently as the soldiery, and some influential noblemen in the neighbourhood were endeavouring to foment rebellion, and eagerly watching the progress of events in the hope of profiting largely by our discomfiture. There were two Nawabs, said to be men of ruined fortune, men who had been crushed by the padded feet of the English despotism, who now appeared on the scene with rival claims, each hoping to obtain supremacy, on our expulsion, as Governor of Moradabad under the Emperor. Their influence over the townspeople was far greater than that which they exercised over the soldiery, for the Sepoys, thinking that they might lose a portion of the perquisites of rebellion, resented the interference of these pretenders. Still, there was the dispiriting fact that we had no friends on our side, and that it was vain for

1857. June. us to contend against such multiplied antagonism One of the Nawabs, eager to make a short cut to the desired supremacy at Moradabad, recommended the immediate execution of Wilson Sahib as "a great deed, equal to the destruction of half the Europeans in the Presidency of Bengal."* It was plain that from either quarter death might come suddenly; so, as the destruction of the English would have been great gain to the enemy, they came to the resolution above recorded, and prepared promptly for retreat.

But what was to become of the treasure? Virtually it was already lost to us. To carry it off to Meerut was impossible with the resources at our command. The only question was whether it were better to abandon it altogether, to be scrambled for by the soldiery and the townspeople, or to make it over quietly to the former. After some consultation, it was determined that it would be better to remove it from the Treasury, and to place the money-bags in tumbrils, under the Treasury-guard (which was in effect to surrender it to the Sepoys), as such a course "would remove all temptation to the Budmashes of the city to come out and join in the disturbance." So Wilson went to the Treasury with Charles Saunders, the Collector and Magistrate, and after

* The story, as told by the Native writer quoted above, is too characteristic and too amusing not to be recorded here. "The first Thakoor further proposed that it was the wish of his master that Mr. Wilson should be killed, because by killing such a great man and cunning officer, who possessed magic in his words, they would achieve a great deed, equal to the destruction of half the number of Europeans in the Presidency of Bengal. Such was the dread entertained by that villain of our old Mr. Wilson. I could not check myself, so, calling myself a Brahmin, I addressed the artillerymen in their own language, which I can speak very fluently, and used all the artful arguments of a Brahmin, and cited several Sanskrit verses on the impropriety and unrighteousness of the proposal of Abbas Ali. I openly told the artillerymen that Abbas Ali was a mere mean pretender. The Thakoor, being a rustic clown, was quite bewildered, and the artillerymen seemed pleased with my arguments, founded on the doctrines of the *Shasturs*."

some difficulty in forcing the locks, for one of the keys was missing,* they proceeded to empty out its contents. Whilst Wilson was handing out the bags, Saunders was secretly destroying the stamped paper. It was a service of no little danger, for the Sepoys were hungry and impatient, excited and malignant, and the amount of coin in the Treasury was found to be less than they had expected. In this moment of disappointment and exasperation, they would have blown the Treasurer from a gun and shot down the English civilians. Captain Faddy saved the former, and the intervention of some faithful Native officers rescued Wilson and Saunders from death.† There was now nothing left to them but to trust for safety to the horses on which they rode. So they made their way to the house in which they had resided since the commencement of the disturbances, and made their arrangements for a retreat to Meerut. There were four civilians, including the Civil Surgeon, with their wives. An escort of Irregular Cavalry—mostly leave-men—was ready; and so they

1857. June.

* The second key is always kept by the Native Treasurer, who, in this case, not without reason, was slow to appear on the scene.

† Mr. Wilson's striking account of this incident should be given in his own words: "When all the treasure was placed on the tumbrils, the Collector, myself, and the (Native) Treasurer, came out into the eastern verandah, and then began murmurs as to the amount of treasure. The artillerymen forcibly carried off the Treasurer towards the guns, and were in the act of tying him to one of them, when Captain Faddy, who is deservedly a favourite with his men, rescued him. By this time the Collector and myself had mounted our horses, when four young Sepoys of the Treasury-guard levelled their muskets at us. At this instant Bohwance Singh, Soubahdar, and Baldeo Singh, pay-Havildar of the grenadier company, stepped between the muskets and our persons and the former raising his hand said, in an authoritative tone, 'What! do you wish to see the flesh rot from your bones? Did you not take a most solemn oath not to hurt a hair of their heads, and are you now firing at them?' The muskets were lowered, and the Collector and myself rode off." It should be mentioned, with respect to the rescue of the Treasurer, that Mr. Saunders, in his report, says: "I succeeded in rescuing him from the awkward position in which he was placed."

1857. June. made good, without accident, their way to the great military station.*

It had been Mr. Wilson's intention that the officers of the regiment should accompany him to Meerut, and due notice was given to them, but they went off to Nynee-Tal. The distance was shorter, the road was less perilous, and the place itself was more attractive. Thither, therefore, with their wives and children, they bent their way. But the Government clerks were not equally alert nor equally wise. At Moradabad was the usual staff of subordinate officials. Men of this kind—many of them Eurasians—strike deeper root in the local soil than Englishmen, soldiers or civilians, who are subject to more frequent changes of residence. The covenanted servant in the Mofussil is a bird of passage, and always ready for flight. The uncovenanted servant is, more or less, a fixture. He has manifold encumbrances and associations which bind him to the spot. He has relatives and connexions, a little house property and other belongings—the savings of a life—which he is unwilling to abandon, and so he commonly clings to his home to the last. So it had been, and so it was to be in other places. And so it was at Moradabad. When the military officers and the covenanted civilians started for Nynee-Tal and Meerut, the uncovenanted officials thought of their Penates, and were unwilling to gird up their loins for flight. Perhaps they conceived that the fury of the enemy was less likely to descend upon them than upon Christian men of higher degree, or of purer European blood. But it would have been well for them if they had betaken themselves to flight. For some, after a feeble defence

* The escort consisted of a Jemadar's party of the Eighth Irregulars from Bareilly, some twenty leave-men, and a few Sowars attached to the Magistrate of Moradabad.

in the house of an invalid officer named Warwick,* were killed whilst attempting to escape; and others, after outwardly apostatising to Mahomedanism, were carried off captives to Delhi, where some of them, at least, were killed (it is believed, by our own people), at the capture of that fortress. 1857. June.

Bareilly was the chief city of Rohilkund. It was the Head-Quarters of the Civil Establishment—the Head-Quarters of the Military Brigade. It was a busy, stirring place, with no absence of the hum of peaceful industry among the people, though the germs of popular commotion were ever alive within them. The traders were principally Hindoos; the dangerous classes were mostly Mahomedans. The conditions of which I have spoken, in reference to the general state of the province of Rohilkund, were peculiarly observable at the capital. A formidable insurrection had occurred there in 1816, when Mahomedans from different parts of the district—mostly Pathan Rohillas—had arrayed themselves against us, and it had been no easy work to subdue them. "Taxes" were the cause of this popular rising; but there were no military discontents at that time, and the soldiery were with us. But now, forty years afterwards, the English dreaded that dangerous combination which left a handful of European officers at the mercy of thousands of the people. For no Euro- Bareilly.

* Lieutenant Warwick was the only white man in the party. He had married a Native Christian woman, whose influence prevailed to induce him to remain. Being of a very unwieldy figure, and unable to run, he was soon overtaken and cut down. His wife, seeing what had befallen, turned back, and asked the murderer to deal with her in the same manner, and "she instantly fell a corpse at his feet."—*Narrative of Mr. Cracroft Wilson.*

1857. May. pean troops were stationed at Bareilly. The warnings of 1816 had been utterly disregarded.*

In the hot weather of 1857, the troops stationed at Bareilly consisted of the Eighteenth and Sixty-eighth Regiments of Native Infantry, the Eighth Regiment of Irregular Cavalry, and a Native battery of Artillery. Brigadier Sibbald commanded the brigade. But at the first outburst of the mutiny in Upper India he was absent on inspection duty at Almorah, and Colonel Colin Troup, who had served in Afghanistan, and had been one of the British captives there, was then in charge of the station. There was a large cluster of civilians. Mr. Robert Alexander was Commissioner of Bareilly. Mr. David Robertson and Mr. George Davy Raikes were the Judges. Mr. James Guthrie was the Magistrate. There were many others of less rank employed in the Government service; and a considerable number of European or Eurasian merchants and traders. Altogether there were nearly a hundred Christians, exclusive of women and children.

State of the troops in May.

When the news of the risings at Meerut and Delhi first arrived at Bareilly, the temper of the troops appeared to be encouraging. Especial confidence was reposed in the Irregular Cavalry, who were believed to be true as the steel of their own sabres—so true, indeed, that their Commandant had been empowered to increase their numerical strength—and yet they had been largely recruited from among the Pathans

* It is curious to read the following in Hamilton's Gazetteer: "After the insurrection of 1816, Government thought it advisable to erect a small regular citadel on the plain to the south of the town, for the eventual protection of the European inhabitants should any similar commotion again occur. It is of a quadrangular form, has a good ditch, and two bastions projecting from opposite angles, an arrangement which gives the whole rather an odd appearance; but it is quite of sufficient strength for the object contemplated."

of Rohilkund and Delhi. As time advanced, even the Poorbeah regiments, though their demeanour differed from what it had been, were conceived to be rather timorous than malignant—agitated by vague fears, resulting from evil reports of the impending vengeance of the English. If assuring promises could be made to them—if they could be induced to believe that all who had not yet committed themselves would meet, not with punishment, but with favour from Government, all might yet go well. And it was in this conviction that Colonel Troup, with the concurrence of Brigadier Sibbald, addressed to Mr. Colvin the letter quoted in the last chapter.* 1857. May.

Meanwhile, in the city and in the surrounding districts there was visible excitement. The great idea of the "something coming" permeated all strata of society. All kinds of rumours were flying about, disturbing and irritating the public mind, and rendering men ripe for rebellion. On the 20th the Commissioner wrote to the Lieutenant-Governor, saying: "Things here are as uncertain as ever. This statement, as far as the military are concerned, is made on the authority of Colonel Troup. The Brigadier has come in to-day; he is old and ill, and has not the character or intelligence of the Colonel. The city is quiet; but on the *qui vive* at every rumour. The Kotwal behaving excellently. In the Gaol yesterday, a Jemadar was murdered by one of the prisoners. The intelligence of this has caused much sensation throughout the town—some people considering it as the prelude to an outbreak. . . . This morning Native officers have told Colonel Troup that it is believed that the prisoners in this Gaol have been

* *Ante*, page 230.

1857. May. beaten and kept without food for five days, and they say that they must go in and see them. The tale is but a pretext—but of course we are in the power of the men, if in a body they go to the Gaol. I have made a proposal that I should address them, giving them my word and my personal security—*i.e.* my person at their mercy, if a single man of their comrades is now in the Gaol. There is no question but that we must refrain from imprisoning the mutineers."*

May 21. On the following day a general parade was held, and Brigadier Sibbald harangued the troops. He spoke of the uneasy feeling that had recently pervaded all ranks of the Native Army—of the discontent too plainly manifested by their demeanour; but he added that he looked upon all this as the result of their erroneous apprehensions, and that if they would resume the cheerful performance of their duty, the past would be forgiven to them, and the good old relations of mutual confidence would be thoroughly restored. Commissioner Alexander afterwards addressed the Native officers in front of the troops. He told them that they had been led astray by a great delusion, that the intentions of Government towards them were what they had ever been, and he besought them to dismiss from their minds all feelings of distrust and alarm. After this the Brigadier reported

May 23. to Government that the troops were in a more happy and cheerful state, and, in their own words, had "commenced a new life." He asked for a formal assurance from the Lieutenant-Governor that the promises made to the troops would be confirmed. And he added, "were the men under my command

* MS. Correspondence. The wisdom of this is sufficiently proved by what took place at Moradabad—as above recorded—and, indeed, by previous events at Meerut.

fully convinced that the past would be forgotten, I feel convinced that their loyalty and good conduct may be relied upon." The Lieutenant-Governor lost no time in sending the required assurances. The Brigadier was authorised to inform the troops that "nothing that had happened since the commencement of the recent agitation had at all shaken the solid confidence of the Lieutenant-Governor in their fidelity and good conduct." This was written on the 30th of May. Before the letter could reach Bareilly the whole of the Native troops there had revolted, and there was not a living European in the place. 1857. May.

For some days after this general parade there was quietude in the Lines. On the 29th, a crisis was imminent. Some men of the two Infantry regiments, whilst taking their morning bath in the river, had been overheard conversing about the massacre of the English, which they had sworn to perpetrate at midday. So the Irregular Cavalry were got under arms. The cheerfulness and alacrity with which they obeyed, with a full knowledge of the occasion, seemed to indicate that they would be true to the death. The day passed without a rising in the Lines; but it was not an uneventful one. A swarm of mutineers from the Forty-fifth at Ferozepore appeared at Bareilly, scattering about terrifying rumours. Their comrades, already prepared to believe that the English were about to destroy them, grasped with ready credulity the story now told by the refugees, that there was a large body of Europeans—Horse, Foot, and Artillery—collected in the neighbourhood to crush the Native Brigade. After this there was the wildest excitement in the Lines—the intensest anxiety in the bungalows of the British. The thoughts of all our people turned with painful doubt to the attitude of May 29.

1857. May. the Irregular Horse, from whom alone could come the means of deliverance. The hope once entertained of their active succour was now passing away; but it was believed that they would remain neutral, let the Infantry do what they might. There were some, indeed, who still cherished the belief that the regiments would not rise But it was well to be prepared for the worst. So it was agreed that on the first sound of mutiny or rebellion, the English should hasten to the Cavalry Lines and there concert measures for their safety. An influential Mahomedan gentleman, of whom more will be presently narrated, had told Commissioner Alexander that the Sepoys had determined to revolt, and that there was nothing left for him but to "look out for his life." And, indeed, there was nothing else.

May 31. Revolt of the troops. But the 30th of May passed, as its predecessor had passed, without any active demonstrations. And even on the morning of the 31st—the morning of that Sunday, which, it was said, and by many believed, had been fixed upon as the day of simultaneous rising against the white men in all our garrisons and cantonments—some of our chief military officers could not bring themselves to think that their regiments would turn against them. At nine o'clock the delusion prevailed. At eleven there was a sound of firing from the Artillery Lines. It was a signal for general action. The game commenced in the usual way. Parties of Sepoys of the Sixty-eighth went out to fire at the English bungalows. Their first object was to ignite the thatch of our houses. In that dry season of the year the work of incendiarism was easy. Fire and smoke soon rose from the burning straw. A strong, hot wind added fury to the flames, and the work of destruction was accomplished. Then they turned their thoughts towards the destruction of human life; and wheresoever they could meet a white man, they shot him down with a yell of triumph. Brigadier Sibbald, on the first sound of firing, had mounted his horse, and ridden for the appointed place of rendezvous attended by two mounted orderlies. A party of Sepoys met him, and he rode on with a bullet in his body. He is said to have sat his horse till he reached the Cavalry Lines, and then to have fallen lifeless from the saddle.* 1857. May 31.

The chief command then passed, by virtue of seniority, into the hands of Colonel Troup. An abler and a braver officer there was not in the service; but what could he do in such an emergency as this? He had gone down on foot to the appointed place of assemblage, which was near to his own house, and there he found the Commissioner and several other officers, civil and military, congregated beneath a camel-shed. Up to this time it was known only that the Sixty-eighth and the Artillery had revolted. The Eighteenth seem to have hesitated all through the morning; and the Cavalry were making a show of loyalty. The Commandant and Adjutant of the Eighteenth, with some other officers, had gone down to the Lines, and found the men in their normal state of hot weather inactivity—neither armed nor accoutred; and though apparently in a state of excitement, by no means bent upon mischief. They were perplexed and bewildered, and did not know what to do. Whilst they professed loyalty to the Government and fidelity to their officers, they were slow in obeying orders to fall in—little better than

* Some accounts state that he was shot by one of his own orderlies. But it is said also that he was "shot through the chest." If he had been shot by one of his orderlies the presumption is that he would have been shot through the back.

1857. May. "a rabble professing devotion and sorrow,"* but with their hearts in the rebel cause. Meanwhile, the Cavalry were being put to the test. The officers assembled in their Lines had determined to retreat to Nynee-Tal. At first it seemed that the troopers would accompany them. They were mounted and drawn up on parade, and Troup called upon them to follow him. They had scarcely moved off, when Mackenzie represented that his troopers were eager to have "a crack at the mutineers." Troup, though doubtful of the expediency of such an attempt, consented, and the word was given. But the trial was too much for them. There was a fine open space before them, and a charge of cavalry would have been irresistible. But when they fronted the Sixty-eighth they saw the green standard of Mahomedanism, and it was seen at once that the game was up with the English. Whether a sudden impulse seized the troopers, or whether the movement was a preconcerted one, may never be known; but the Eighth Regiment of Irregular Horse forsook their English leaders, and drew up beside the mutineers. A few only found faithful in this emergency prepared to accompany the English in their flight. They were principally Native officers. Their conduct was above all praise. For they left their families and property behind them to succour the English gentlemen.

This important combination having been formed, the insurgent force determined that there should be no defaulters in the great hour of their triumph; and so they turned their guns upon the Eighteenth, which up to this time had been kept together by their officers, threatening to blow them to pieces if they did not join the national standard. Already

* See Captain Gowan's Narrative.

ripe for rebellion and eager for a share of the spoil, they fell in with the mutineers. The whole brigade had now revolted. There was no hope any longer for the officers whom they had deserted. So Major Patterson, Captain Gowan, and others, who had remained at their posts to the last, and who, on the first outbreak of the Eighteenth had been concealed by the men of their regiment, escaped into the country to endure great privations, and, in some cases, eventually to suffer death. It would have been well for them if their corps had revolted in the first instance with the other regiments, for then they would have escaped to Nynee-Tal. But it happened that Major Pearson, with four other officers, were killed by the villagers of Ram-Puttee, whilst Captain Gowan and some others, after months of distressing concealment, were rescued by the heroic exertions of Mr. Cracroft Wilson, of Moradabad.

1857. May 31.

Murder of civilians.

The fate of the civilians was of the same chequered kind. Some were killed—some escaped. Mr. Alexander, the Commissioner, who had been driven to his bed by a severe spasmodic affection, was with difficulty removed from his house in a buggy, but after awhile the emergency of the occasion compelled him to mount a horse, and he reached the Cavalry Lines in safety, eventually to escape to Nynee-Tal. Mr. Guthrie, the Collector and Magistrate, also escaped. The Judges, Mr. D. Robertson and Mr. G. D. Raikes, were both killed. The former, with Dr. Hay and Mr. Orr, took refuge in the house of the Moonsiff, who promised to protect them, but they were both murdered; whilst the latter, accompanied by Dr. Buck, Principal of the College, was, by previous arrangement, sheltered in the house of one Aman Ali Khan, a Mahomedan gentleman of Bareilly. They

1857. May 31. were tracked and put to death by the connivance of a nephew of their host.* The Joint-Magistrates, Mr. Parley and Mr. Currie, escaped. Equally fortunate was Mr. Poynder, the Chaplain. Altogether nine members of the higher class of civilians, with several of the subordinate establishments, were slain. Many merchants and traders, with their wives and children, were massacred at the same time. It need not be added that, attending these murders, was the usual amount of plunder and devastation. The Treasury was emptied; the houses of the Europeans were sacked and burnt; and the Gaol, after a gallant defence by the officer in charge, who paid the penalty of his devotion, as will presently be narrated, was emptied of its criminal inhabitants. In these orgies the people of Bareilly were in nowise behind the military mutineers. The greater number of murders were committed by the former. The dominion of the English was at an end.

There were rival claimants to the Viceroyalty of Rohilkund. Both were of the old stock of Rohilla-Pathans—descendants of those hardy semi-Afghan tribes, against whom Warren Hastings sent our trained soldiery at the infamous bidding of the Wuzeer of Oude. One of these pretenders was Khan Behaudur Khan; the other was named Mobarik Shah. The latter was a man of good family and local influence, and personally possessed of some energy of character. But the former, though older and weaker, had superior claims upon the suffrages of the people, for he was a descendant of that Hafiz Rehmut Khan, who had been the first Pathan ruler

* The story of the English Judges at Bareilly having been subjected to a formal trial and deliberately hanged before Khan Behaudur Khan, seems to be a pure fiction.

of Bareilly, and who had fallen in battle killed by a round shot from an English gun.* He had, therefore, all the strength of old historical traditions on his side. That most iniquitous passage of our Anglo-Indian history, to which I have above referred, had never been forgotten in Rohilkund. Generation after generation may pass away, but the memory of blood feuds of this kind is not obliterated by after-years of peace and friendship and honest dealing. So these men came to the front, hating the English, and all the Mahomedans of Bareilly were ready to become their followers. Mobarik Shah, when he heard the firing that indicated the revolt of the soldiery, started at once for the Kotwali to proclaim himself Viceroy; but Khan Behaudur Khan had anticipated him, and it was plain that the majority of people had accepted him as their chief. So Mobarik Shah, with outward observance of friendship, but with enmity in his heart, joined the party of his rival, who was formally proclaimed. 1857. May 31.

Massacre of Christians.

The first act of the new Mahomedan ruler was to doom to death all the Christian people who had not already perished. This cruel decree had already been so prodigally anticipated by the unauthorised barbarity of lesser men, that there were not many victims to be dragged forth from their hiding-places and to be ruthlessly massacred before the eyes of the old Viceroy. The first to be brought to the shambles

* I have taken this from an official report before me, but if the following passage of Bishop Heber's Journal contain the historical truth, the Rohilla chief must have been killed either by grape-shot or musket-balls. "When his nobles, at the head of their respective clans, either treacherous or timid, gave way, he remained almost alone on a rising ground in the heat of the fire, conspicuous by his splendid dress and his beautiful horse, waving his hand and vainly endeavouring to bring his army back to another charge, till, seeing that all was lost, he waved his hand once more, gave a shout, and galloped on the English bayonets. He fell *shot through and through*."

1857. June 1. were the family of Mr. Aspinall, a merchant. His two children were murdered in the presence of their parents, who were then put to death. To give further effect to this ghastly spectacle, the naked corpses of Englishmen slain in the first outburst of rebellion, having been dragged through the town, were brought into the presence and cast at the foot of the viceregal standard. Next day, Mr. Hansborough, the Superintendent of the Gaol, who had manfully defended himself throughout the whole of Sunday, was captured, and brought before Khan Behaudur Khan. Overcome, but not overawed, the gallant Englishman defied the new ruler, telling him and his followers, in a loud voice, that they might kill him and others, but that they would never destroy the British Government. He was presently cut to pieces. Some others of less note shared the same fate; but the old Rohilla was sorely grieved that there were so few victims for his knife.

Thus the English were in our expressive Anglo-Indian jargon *saf-kar'd*, or cleaned away. After a day or two there was no trace of them or their authority left. So Khan Behaudur Khan began at once to set his house in order—to organise his new Government. He had already made proclamation of his assumption of authority. He had paraded the streets of Bareilly on an elephant, with a number of followers, with bands and banners and other properties and paraphernalia of mock-royalty. And now he began to address himself to the establishment of an administration. The various posts in the Soubah were distributed. Justice was administered, and revenue was collected in the name of the Emperor. It was sound policy to utilise as much as possible of the old agency, and as there were few of our Native officers who were not willing to take the rupees of the restored Mahomedan Government, it was expected that business would go on very much in the old groove. But in this he was disappointed. The turbulent spirit which had been raised did not readily subside. Disorder and violence were rampant everywhere; men rose against each other as ruthlessly as before they had risen against the white men, and were quite as unscrupulous in robbery and murder. 1857. June.

The main source of trouble, at the outset, to Behaudur Khan was the presence of the Sepoy Brigade. The Viceroy was afraid of the soldiery. They had shown no disposition, at the beginning of the rebellion, to fraternise with his political party. Their continuance at Bareilly would have been a source of danger to the new Government. The Native Brigadier was named Bukht Khan—a name afterwards distinguished in the annals of the war—and he had been disposed to favour the pretences of Mobarik Shah rather than those of his more successful rival. The defeated candidate, however, had not given up the game. He might obtain from the Emperor that which he could not secure for himself. So he again opened communications with Brigadier-General Bukht Khan, persuaded him to march the troops to Delhi, and June 11. having made a show of accompanying them, sent a memorial to the Emperor by the hands of his friend, petitioning His Majesty to appoint him Viceroy of Rohilkund; and then he returned to Bareilly.

Whilst these terrible scenes were being enacted at May 31. Bareilly, on that Sunday morning, there was a tragedy Shahjehanpore. in some respects even more painful, though more limited in extent, going on at Shahjehanpore, which

1857. May 31. lies at a distance of some forty-seven miles from the chief station, and had once been but little behind it in importance. Here was posted the Twenty-eighth Sepoy Regiment, commanded by Captain James. Mr. Mordaunt Ricketts* was the Magistrate and Collector. Mr. Charles Jenkins was his Assistant. There was the usual staff of subordinate Government officials, and a few Europeans or Eurasians engaged in the pursuits of mercantile life. There was not, with the exception of the commissioned and non-commissioned officers of the Native regiment, a single English soldier in the place.

When intelligence of the events which had occurred at Meerut and at Delhi first reached Shahjehanpore, there were great excitement and commotion in the city. The English dreaded a rising of the towns-people, but looked with confidence towards the soldiery. It was rumoured—and the Sepoys carried the story to their officers—that, at the time of the Eed Festival, the citizens purposed to rise and to sack the Treasury. So it was determined that the station-guards should be increased, and that the sentries should be doubled. But this, which was intended as a compliment, was regarded as a penalty. Instead of pleasing the Sepoys, by thus manifesting the confidence that was placed in them, it excited their indignation. Vague fears and suspicions had taken possession of their minds. Some associated these extra duties with the greased cartridges; some thought it was a pretext only for keeping them away from the "méla" or great fair, which was being held

* I may avail myself of the mention of Mr. Mordaunt Ricketts's name in this place, to call attention to a clerical error in a note at page 511 of my second volume—where Mr. George Henry Ricketts, Deputy-Commissioner of Loodhianah, is described as Mr. M. Ricketts. The passage is a literal quotation from the "Punjab Mutiny Report," where the error occurred.

in the neighbourhood. And, viewed in this light, it was an outrage on their feelings, for it indicated want of confidence in the Sepoys. On the following day the order for the extra-guards was cancelled; but, although the officers of the Twenty-eighth believed that the bulk of the regiment would remain faithful, the Sepoys, as the month wore on to its close, were waxing every day more rebellious in their hearts, and ever and anon muttering sedition not to be misunderstood. 1857. May 31.

It was only a question of time—and the time soon came. On Sunday, the 31st of May, the troops rose. Many of our people were in church, for it was the hour of morning service, when the revolt commenced. It was the old story over again with scarcely a variation. The bungalows of the English were plundered and burnt. The Treasury was sacked. The Gaol was opened. The prisoners were released. The townspeople made common cause with the mutineers; and the surrounding villagers broke out into rebellion. An English factory, where sugar was refined and rum distilled, was attacked and devastated by the villagers. And, ere night had closed in upon the scene, new Native rulers had been formally proclaimed, and the dominion of the white man was at an end.

The fate of the English residents at Shahjehanpore has now to be recorded. The murder of our people was not a conspicuous feature in the programme of the mutineers of the Twenty-eighth. If the compact had been to destroy the English, root and branch, on that Sunday morning whilst engaged in the offices of their religion, it was very imperfectly fulfilled. A party of mutineers made for the Christian church; but it was to be counted only by units. Armed with

1857. May 31. swords and clubs, they rushed in, yelling. Mordaunt Ricketts was slashed by a Sepoy, but he carried his wound to the outer vestry-door, there to be cut down and slain.* A clerk in the Magistrate's office, named Le Maistre, was killed in this first onslaught. No other member of the congregation stained with his blood the floor of the Christian temple. But the agony of the women was great. These six or seven assassins might be the precursors of hundreds of remorseless insurgents from the Lines and from the city, all thirsting for Christian blood. Was it better, then, to endeavour to escape from the church, or to close the doors and prevent further ingress of the assailants? The Chaplain endeavoured to escape; but he was wounded as he left the church, and was afterwards killed by some villagers, together with a clerk named Smith, at a little distance from Shahjehanpore. After this the doors of the church were closed, and the shuddering women were removed to the Tower, where they abided in safety for a time.

Meanwhile, in the Cantonment, the Sepoys were in a state of wild excitement. But, as often happened, there was division amongst them. Captain James was shot on parade whilst endeavouring to pacify his men. Dr. Bowling, who, returning from his morning visit to the hospital, had found the regiment in rebellion, placed his wife and child and an European female servant in his carriage, and mounting the box beside the coachman, had made for the church. As they went a party of Sepoys fired at them, and Bowling fell dead from the box. Another bullet wounded his wife; but she escaped to reach the

* According to one account, "Mr. Ricketts was pursued and murdered in his own verandah." Mr. Jenkins says: "I saw Mr. Ricketts's body about thirty-five yards from the church vestry-door."

church, where other fugitives were assembling; and their Native servants, true to their salt, were bringing guns and pistols to their masters. If, at this time, there had been united action among the Sepoys, not one of our people could have escaped. But it happened that a party, scarcely less than a hundred strong,* rallied round our officers, and thus the Christian fugitives were saved. With this safeguard, those within and those without the church gathered themselves together and took counsel as to the means of escape. Mr. Jenkins recommended that they should make for Pohwaine beyond the Oude border, where it was believed that the Rajah of that place would shelter them. As by this time several horses and a carriage or two were assembled in the church-compound, the flight was not difficult. So they went. But the Pohwaine man declared his inability to protect them, and they went on to Mohumdee, one of our outstations in Oude. What afterwards befell them may be narrated in another chapter of this history. The tragedy of Shahjehanpore had not yet been acted out. 1857. May 31.

There was another civil station in Rohilkund—Budaon—some thirty miles from Bareilly. The Magistrate and Collector was Mr. William Edwards, who had been for some years attached to the Secretariat, and had been personally familiar with the stirring events of the Governments of Lord Ellenborough and Lord Hardinge. There were few abler and few better men in the service. He had sat at the feet of Thomas Campbell Robertson, and had learnt from him lessons, the wisdom of which was now too miserably apparent. Budaon.

* I believe that these were principally Sikhs.

1857. May. He saw all around him proofs of the errors that had been committed by the new school of civil administrators. The country about him was rising against the British Government, and he had none to help him in the hour of his need.* He stood quite alone. He had not an English friend or comrade near him. There was one great consolation, however, in the thought that, foreseeing the danger to come, he had sent his wife and child to the safety of Nynee-Tal, though he might never see them again.

On the 25th (it was the time of the Eed Festival) it was reported to the Magistrate that there was to be a Mahomedan rising in the town at an appointed hour. So he invited to his house the chief Mussulmans of the place, and there taking counsel with them on the public safety, detained them until the hour was passed. Many of them were fierce and insolent, and all excited. The meeting was a noisy and tumultuous one; but the people calmed down after a time, and the day passed over without an outbreak. There was but one European gentleman to confront all this Mahomedan fury—a single white-faced Christian, a prayerful, God-fearing man, esteemed to be rather a Christian of Christians, with Native converts clustering around him as he ministered to them in his own house. But he was known

* "To the large number of these sales" (sales of estates by decrees of our Civil Courts) "during the past twelve or fifteen years, and the operation of our revenue system, which has had the result of destroying the gentry of the country and breaking up of the village communities, I attribute solely the disorganisation of this and the neighbouring districts. . . . The ancient landed proprietary body of the Budaon district were still in existence, but in the position of tenants, not proprietors. None of the men who had succeeded them as landowners were possessed of sufficient influence or power to give me any aid in maintaining the public tranquillity. . . . On the other hand, those who really could control the vast masses of the rural population were interested in bringing about a state of disturbance and general anarchy."—*Edwards's Personal Narrative.*

also to be a just man, tolerant and compassionate; and he had lifted up his voice fearlessly against the wrongs which had been done by our own Government, and injured himself by his plain-speaking. It might have been a consideration of this fact that saved William Edwards in that hour of danger; or it might have been that some sentiments of chivalry restrained them when they thought of the utter helplessness of that single white man among so many; but that day and the next day passed, and still the solitary Englishman sat and prayed, knowing that he could do nothing unaided, and fearing that no succour would ever come to him from a distance. He had a guard of Sepoys, consisting of about a hundred men of the Sixty-eighth from Bareilly, and these he was beginning to mistrust, for they had cast a covetous eye on the Treasury; and he had little more confidence in the Nujeebs of the Police. He knew that at a signal from the Suddur station the anticipated revolt would at once commence. 1857. May.

But on the third day, as he sat at his lonely dinner, he saw an Englishman ride up towards his house, escorted by a dozen horsemen; and presently he discerned the familiar features of his cousin, Alfred Phillips, the Magistrate of Etah.* He was the bearer of evil tidings; but still it was a joyous meeting—to Edwards most joyous, after those long dreary days of complete isolation. Etah is in the Agra Division of the North-Western Provinces, nearly opposite to Budaon on the other side of the Ganges. The district had risen. In Mr. Colvin's expressive language, it was in "a blaze of riot and ravage,"† and now the May 27. Etah.

* Mr. Phillips in his official report says that he did not reach Budaon till the 29th.

† *Ante*, p. 245. The "riot and ravage" were increasing every day.

1857. May. Magistrate was on his way to Bareilly to ask for military aid. The cry was for more Sepoys to help them against popular insurrections. The little party of the Ninth Regiment, the head-quarters of which were in rebellion at Aligurh and Etawah, with detachments in the same state at Mynpooree, had quietly joined their comrades; and Phillips, thus deserted, with only a few Sowars at his back, had crossed the river in the hopeless errand of obtaining reinforcements from Rohilkund, and passing through a dangerous country, not without risk of his life, had thus joined his cousin at Budaon.* Edwards told him that there was small hope of assistance from Bareilly, as he had himself applied for it in vain. But when it was known to him that the "town and rich mart of Bhilsea" were threatened by the marauders, he made another appeal to the Commissioner, and wrung from him a promise of help. It gladdened the hearts of Edwards and Phillips to learn that a company of Sepoys from the Bareilly Brigade, under the command of an English officer, were coming into the disturbed districts to aid them in the restoration of order. Every day the anarchy was becoming more extensive and more intense; and it was thought that

* Mr. Alfred Phillips distinguished himself greatly on this occasion. At Kasgunj, he encountered a large body of insurgents who had been plundering in the neighbourhood—some armed with muskets, some only with latties, or long clubs. "The whole," Phillips reported, "could not be less than five hundred men." "As soon as they saw us," he adds, "there was some hesitation apparent; on which, calling upon the Sowars to follow, I and the Jemadar charged them. They fired some shots as we advanced, but broke before we reached them. And the whole body took to flight. We followed for some distance outside the town, and killed many, but the ground was difficult for following dispersed footmen, and we were too small a body to separate far. Indeed, with the exception of the Jemadar, and two other Sowars, the rest showed little inclination to go forward. On this occasion the Jemadar behaved with undoubted gallantry. I saw him kill two men." Phillips says nothing of his own exploits, but William Edwards states that his cousin killed "three men with his own hands."

the Sepoys would bring deliverance with them. But 1857. May.
the joy of the English officers was soon turned to mourning. For just as it was supposed that the wished-for succours were at hand, news came that the Bareilly Brigade had revolted, that all the English officers at that Suddur station were either killed or in flight, that the prisoners in the great Gaol had been released, and that the surrounding country was in the wildest state of confusion.

What now was to be done? The news arrived early in the morning; so Edwards at once aroused June 1.
his cousin, who, anxious to return to his post before the roads were closed, mounted his horse and galloped towards the banks of the Ganges. Soon afterwards, the Magistrate was joined by a few of his scattered countrymen from the districts—two indigo-factors and another—which greatly increased the difficulty of his position. Edwards himself determined to remain at his post so long as there was a hope of being useful to his Government. But he called the others together, and after they had joined with him in prayer, exhorted them to seek safety in flight. But they thought that their safety would be best secured by remaining with the Magistrate, and they were unwilling to depart. Up to this time the Sepoys had not broken into revolt. The Treasury-guard at Budaon consisted of a party of the Sixty-eighth Infantry—one of the regiments that had revolted—under the command of a Native officer. When news came that the troops at Head-Quarters had revolted, the Soubahdar, with solemn oaths, assured Edwards that the Sepoys at Budaon had had no communication with their comrades at Bareilly, and that they were determined to defend the treasure against the Budmashes of the city. But on that very evening

1857. June.

the Sepoys rose, and the usual work of plunder and devastation commenced. A party from Bareilly came to fraternise with the Budaon guard; and the released prisoners, some three hundred in number, came yelling around the Magistrate's house. There was nothing now left for him but instant flight. So he mounted his horse, which had been saddled since the morning, in anticipation of a crisis, and, accompanied by three other Englishmen, rode for his life. He had not gone far when a Mahomedan gentleman of position and influence in the neighbourhood met him, with a band of retainers, and persuaded him to turn back and take refuge in his house, which lay at a distance of some three miles from Budaon. Hoping that by these means he might conceal himself until the mutineers and gaol-birds had scattered themselves over the country, and then return to re-establish his authority, Edwards readily accepted the proposal. He passed, as he went, his own house, and found that already it was being plundered—the Chuprassies, who had recently served him, being active in the work.* Thus escorted, he passed on safely to Sheckoopoor, and spent part of the night in the Sheikh's house. But it was obvious that the sole chance of safety lay in his speedy departure, so he went on into the howling wilderness.

The only representative of authority having thus departed, there was the usual license—the usual crime. The Sepoys—the townspeople—the released convicts—the predatory classes from the neighbouring villages scrambled for the spoil of the British Government and its officers, and execrations bitter and deep went up at the thought of the abnormal

* "The first man I saw was one of my own orderlies, and who had been a favourite of mine, with my dress sword on him."

emptiness of the Treasury—for Edwards, seeing what was coming, had wisely refused to receive, for a time, the instalments of revenue due from the Zemindars. But these primal excesses at the central point of action were but a small part of the riotous disorder in which the month of May closed on Budaon. The whole district was in a state of the wildest anarchy and confusion. Men rose against each other—against the existing order of things—against the decrees of the British Government. All our administrative errors then stared us in the face.* Here, as elsewhere, in Rohilkund and in the greater part of the Meerut Division, every trace of British rule was effaced. The Sepoys went off to Delhi, and left the work of rebellion in the hands of the rural population.† The authority of Khan Behaudur Khan was proclaimed and acknowledged. District officers of different grades were appointed; the revenue was collected in the name of the rebel Government; and the whole province remained to be reconquered.

1857. June.

It was necessarily a work of no common difficulty

* "In Budaon the mass of the population rose in a body, and the entire district became a scene of anarchy and confusion. The ancient proprietary body took the opportunity of murdering or expelling the auction-purchasers, and resumed possession of their hereditary estates . . . The rural classes would never have joined the Sepoys, whom they hated, had not these causes of discontent already existed. They evinced no sympathy whatever about the cartridges, or flour said to be made of human bones, and could not then have been acted upon by any cry of their religion being in danger. It is questions involving their rights and interests in the soil and hereditary holdings, invariably termed by them as 'jan see azeez'—*dearer than life*—which excite them to a dangerous degree."—*Edwards's Personal Narrative.*

† "Disturbances broke out in every direction, and anarchy and misrule completely obtained the upper hand. The roads were no longer safe for travellers, and opportunity was taken by the bands of armed men, who scoured the country in all directions, not only to satiate their lust for plunder, but to settle old feuds by an appeal to arms, or more frequently by the committal of cruel murders."—*Mr. Carmichel's Official Report.*

1857. for the new Government at such a time to reconcile all conflicting interests—especially antagonisms of religion. The faith of the dominant party was the faith of a minority. Even in Rohilkund the Mahomedans formed but a small part of the population. The impartiality of the British in dealing with these several races was unquestioned. If they accused us of persecution, as they insanely did at that time, it was persecution of a catholic kind. If the Hindoos did not think that they had more to fear from the bigotry of the Mahomedans than from the bigotry of the Christians, it was sound policy on the part of the new rulers to anticipate such a feeling. So Behaudur Khan issued a proclamation calling upon all, Hindoos and Mahomedans, to combine for the extermination of the Christians, and assuring the first that "if the Hindoos shall exert themselves in the murder of these infidels and expel them from the country, they shall be rewarded for their patriotism by the extinction of the practice of the slaughter of kine." But, in the true spirit of Mahomedanism, these promises were accompanied by threats. "The entire prohibition of this practice," it was added, "is made conditional upon the complete extermination of the infidels from India. If any Hindoo shall shrink from joining in this cause, the evils of revival of this practice shall recoil upon them; and if any person shall be guilty of acting contrary to the requirements of this proclamation, he shall be imprisoned for six months with a fine." The Hindoos of Rohilkund were, for the most part, a quiet, inoffensive people, engaged in industrial work, artificers or agriculturists, or traders of different degrees, little accustomed to the use of arms, and by no means addicted to fighting. But the Mahomedans of that country, on the other hand, were fierce and unscrupulous, skilled in the use of offensive weapons, and ever ready to use them; so, notwithstanding their numerical inferiority, they were dominant in Rohilkund and the adjacent country, and felt that they could issue their mandates without much fear of resistance. 1857. June—Aug.

Still Khan Behaudur Khan and his advisers trusted more to their guile than to their strength. It occurred to them that the Christians might endeavour to checkmate the Mahomedans, by making similar promises to the Hindoos. So they thought it wise to anticipate the movement. "Should the English," said another proclamation, "with a view to neutralise our proposal and make a similar agreement, and urge the Hindoos to rise against the Mussulmans, let the wise Hindoos consider that if the English do so, the Hindoos will be sadly deceived. The English never keep their promises. They are deceitful impostors. The Natives of this country have always been tools in the hands of these deceitful Englishmen. None of you should permit this opportunity to slip. Let us take advantage of it." There is much of this, doubtless, plagiarised from our English modes of assertion. As it was the prevailing faith of Englishmen that the Natives of India were liars, we had no reason to complain that this slander was retaliated upon us. Moreover, we were always reminding the bulk of the people of what they had suffered under Mahomedan rule, and assuring them that their only hopes of happiness and prosperity resided in the permanence of the British Government. It was natural, therefore, and excusable, that the Mahomedans should have copied us also in this matter, and told the Hindoos that their true interests lay in the ex-

1857. June—Aug. termination of the English and the support of Mussulman rule. A Bill of Indictment was brought against us. It was declared that the English were the "destroyers of the creeds of other nations." Then the Hindoos were reminded that we had sanctioned the re-marriage of Hindoo widows*—that we had forcibly suspended the rites of Suttee—that we had pressed the Natives of India to embrace our religion by promises of advancement—and that we "had made it a standing rule, when a Rajah dies, without leaving any male issue by his married wife, to confiscate his territory and not to allow his adopted son to inherit it."† "Hence it is obvious that such laws of the English are intended to deprive the Native Rajahs of their territory and property. They have already seized the territory of Nagpore and Lucknow. Their designs for destroying your religion, O Rajahs, is manifest.‡ . . . Be it known to all of you, that if these English are permitted to remain in India, they will butcher you all and put an end to your religion." And whilst everywhere were going forth these appeals to the religious feelings of the Hindoos, the Mahomedans were called upon, in most inciting language, in prose and in verse, to commence a Jehad, or religious war, against the Feringhees. On the faith of the Koran, all true believers were told that by fighting against the infidels, or paying money to enable others to fight, they would secure to themselves eternal beatitude. It was the old story so often told, with some variations to suit the purposes

* The words were, that we had "promulgated that a Hindoo widow must re-marry."—See vol. pp. 188—189.

† See *ante*, pp. 70, *et seq.*

‡ Here follows a charge against the English with respect to the introduction of the new messing system into the gaols, to which reference is made at pages 195—196 vol. i.

of the hour. I do not know that ever before the commercial element was introduced into a proclamation of Jehad with so much pungency as in one which was found in the "dufter" of Khan Behaudur Khan, and translated by Cracroft Wilson. "He," it was said, "who will willingly give a pice in this cause will get from God on the day of judgment seven hundred pice. And he who will spend a rupee in this cause, and will use his sword also against the infidels, will get from God seven thousand rupees." It may be presumed from this that the "sinews of war" were wanting—that the great difficulty before the new Government was a paucity of rupees. But it is doubtful whether this figurative appeal to the moneyed interest produced the desired effect, for the money came in but slowly to the public Treasury, and more forcible means were resorted to for the abstraction of the public coin than these promises of enormous usufruct on the day of judgment. Still the Native Government went on from day to day, from week to week, from month to month, after a rude fashion of its own; and nothing more was heard of the English except that here and there some wretched fugitive was hiding himself disguised in Oriental costume, and indebted for his life to the exceptional kindness of some Native of the country.

1857. June—Aug.

Furruckabad.

Meanwhile, there was the prologue of a dreadful tragedy in Furruckabad—a district in the Agra Division of the North-Western Provinces. It is bounded on the north by Shahjehanpore and Budaon, from which it is divided by the waters of the Ganges. But though geographically and administratively severed from Rohilkund, the social conditions of the districts were nearly the same. The Mahomedan influences were there especially strong; and the Pathan element

1857. was largely represented among these followers of the Prophet. In the early days of British rule in India, this tract of country had been infamous for its lawlessness—for the supremacy of a race of bandits, who thought robbery insipid if it were not flavoured by murder. All this was gradually effaced under the administration of the English; but although the outward conditions were greatly changed, there was ever beneath the surface the old hatred of the white man—the old desire to extirpate him, root and branch, from the land. They had long been biding their time; and now the time had come.* Before the end of May the whole district was in rebellion. The Native regiment, the Tenth, had not then mutinied. "I traversed a great portion of the district during the first week of June," writes a trustworthy informant to me, "and I saw villages on fire, and being plundered on all sides. At that time the Tenth Native Infantry had not revolted. The rebellion had existed for a full month before the corps mutinied."

March. Inquietudes and alarms.

There had been, indeed, from the early part of the year great excitement in the Furruckabad district. In no part of the country had those monstrous fables of bone-dust flour and polluted wells been circulated more freely or with greater success. And there was at least one story more—one of which I have no knowledge of having been current in any other

* Mr. (afterwards Sir G. F.) Harvey, in his official narrative of events in the Agra Division, one that shows, perhaps, more literary skill than any in the collection, observes: "The (so to speak) Nawabee character of Furruckabad, the vast number of dissolute, desperate, and distressed Mahomedans there; men who had lineage to boast of and old traditions to excite them, who were too proud to labour and too poor not to be discontented; the very indolence and depravity, in short, of a large number of the Bungush family, made me always from the first feel more apprehension for the safety of Futtehgurh (Furruckabad) than for that of any district in the division."

district—it was believed that the English Government had issued rupees of leather silvered over to represent the ordinary coinage of the country. Major Weller, of the Engineers, of whose good services at Agra mention has been made in a preceding chapter, was at Futtehgurh in March. A Native banker called upon him to inquire into the truth of the several stories about the bone-dust and other vile designs of the English to destroy the religion of the people. The English officer explained to him the absurdity of these rumours. But the man was not convinced. "But you know," he said, "that Government are issuing leather rupees, and intend to gather up all the silver of the country." Major Weller laughed at this story. But the credulous banker shook his head, and said that he had seen the leather rupees, and had some in his possession. "Bring them to me," said Weller, "as many as you can, and I will give you fourteen annas for each of them." The Native banker took his departure, but never produced a leather rupee. It is difficult to declare, though it may be easy to conjecture, the origin of this story. It was not a weak invention of the enemy; it was in truth a very crafty device, well calculated to excite the moneyed interests by fears of a depreciation of the currency, and to alarm those who still held to the belief that there was desecration in contact with leather. Nothing could better illustrate the unreasonable alarm pervading the district.

1857.

Futtehgurh.

The English station of Futtehgurh lies at a distance of about six miles from the town of Furruckabad. There was a fort—or some works which were dignified by the name of one—within which was the Gun-carriage Manufactory which Major Robertson of

1857. May—June. the Bengal Artillery then superintended. The Tenth Regiment of Native Infantry was commanded by Colonel George Acklom Smith—a soldier of good repute. The confidence which he felt in his men—a confidence that was shared by most of his officers—was strengthened by the belief that the regiment was generally regarded by the Native Army as a collection of outcasts, with whom their brethren had no sympathy; for they had gone to Burmah across the "black water." In times of violent excitement, however, such distinctions are disregarded; and it was soon apparent that the Tenth were in communication with mutineers from other regiments. Indeed, there were too many scourings of mutiny and rebellion from neighbouring stations to permit any thought of safety. All Oude had risen. Rohilkund was in the throes of a great rebellion. What hope was there for Furruckabad? Not to have taken some precautions would, at such a time, have been madness. So Colonel Smith sent numbers of the women and the children and the non-combatants in boats, to drop down the river, and to make their way to what was then thought a place of safety, the great Cantonment of Cawnpore. On the 3rd of June, under cover of the darkness, some twelve or thirteen boats, "of various sorts and sizes," carried off about a hundred of the residents of Furruckabad, men, women, and children—the majority of them being Christian people, unconnected with the public service.

Occupation of the Fort. Meanwhile the regiment remained in a state of sullen quiescence. But a day, an hour, might change the complexion of affairs. And Colonel Smith, therefore, determined, if mutiny should surround him, to shut himself up in the Fort, with his officers and the Christian people who had either remained at, or had returned to, Futtehgurh. It was hard to say what was the temper of the men of the Tenth. They had behaved well on the occasion of a revolt in the Gaol, and had fired upon the insurgent prisoners, but, on the other hand, they had prevented the removal of the treasure into the Fort. At the end of the second week of June all confidence—all hope—was at an end. The waves of rebellion were closing around Futtehgurh, and it was impossible that the Tenth should resist the power of the great flood. The troops that had mutinied at Seetapore in the Khyrabad Division of Oude* were approaching, and, feasted and flattered on the way by the rebel Zemindars, were holding traitorous correspondence with the Tenth. Colonel Smith then saw the necessity of destroying the bridge of boats across the river; and his regiment, with that strange outward inconsistency which sometimes indicates infirmity of purpose, sometimes conceals deep designs, applied themselves manfully to the work of destruction. This done, a party of Native officers told the Colonel that their "time was up," and that he and all under him had better retreat into the Fort. So he gathered up his people and prepared to defend himself against the multitudes that might rise against him. There was, indeed, a gloomy prospect before them. The Fort was in a most miserable condition for all purposes of defence. There was a glut of gun-carriages and models of all kinds of ordnance. But there was a dearth both of serviceable guns and of ammunition. It is stated that there were six guns on the ramparts and an eighteen-inch howitzer; but that only thirty

1857. June.

* These were the Forty-first Native Infantry, with two regiments of Oude Irregulars, one Cavalry, and one Infantry. The narrative of this outbreak will be found in a subsequent book of this History.

1857. round shots could be mustered. Of small-arm ammunition there was a better supply; but many of the cartridges were blank. Provisions were with difficulty obtained; but after awhile a flock of forty or fifty sheep were driven within the walls by the help of a Sepoy of the Eleventh. There was a population of about a hundred and twenty Christian people in the garrison—one-fourth of whom were men capable of bearing arms. The rest were women and children. There was only one Artillery officer—Major Robertson, of the Gun-carriage Agency—in the Fort. But Colonel Tudor Tucker, of the Cavalry, who had learnt the gun-drill at Addiscombe, was improvised into an Artillery Commandant, and right well he did his work.

June 18. Proclamation of the Nawab.

Whilst Colonel Smith was gathering up his people and concerting measures for their defence, the Sepoys of the Tenth were openly declaring themselves. They tendered their allegiance to the Nawab of Furruckabad, who had cast in his lot against us, and formally placed him on the Musnud under a royal salute. They opened the Gaol, and they seized the treasure, which they had pretended to guard.* But when the new Native Government demanded it, they resolutely refused to surrender a rupee. They were determined not to mutiny for nothing. And when the Sepoys of the Forty-first from Seetapore asked for a share of it, they refused to divide the spoil. From that time there was sharp contention between the two regiments. The Tenth seem to have had more greed for money than for blood. But the Forty-first having tasted the delights of murder, were eager for the

* Among other loot that fell into the hands of the despoilers were the jewels and other property of the Maharajah Duleep Singh, who had an establishment at Futtehgurh. (See note in Appendix.)

destruction of the English in the Fort, and implored the Nawab to order the Tenth to lead the attack on their old officers. Disappointed in this and in their design up the treasure, they set fire to all the houses in the Cantonment, and preluded their attack on the Fort by an internecine conflict, in which several Sepoys on both sides were left dead upon the parade-ground. The Forty-first, when urged to display their own sincerity by leading the attack, said that the omens were not then favourable, but that the 25th would be a propitious day. So on that day action commenced. The Sepoys had two post guns, with which they had pledged themselves to protect the treasure; and the Nawab, who had flung himself, with the deadliest animosity, into the active work of rebellion, spared no pains to supply the besiegers with the munitions of war, and hounded them on to the destruction of the white men. He had received favours from the English Government. He had been rescued from ruin by their kindly exertions. But nothing could efface the traditions of a by-gone supremacy. He had assumed an air of friendliness and an appearance of placidity, when he well knew that the storm was brewing. But now the expected hour had come; and he found himself master of a country in which before he had only been a pensioner.* 1857.

Gallantry of the defence.

With desperate odds against them, our little garrison displayed a sturdy gallantry that could not be surpassed. Day and night they toiled, weary but undaunted, in the batteries. It was no new thing

* His family were in receipt of large compensatory allowances from the British Government. But his predecessors and himself had been ruinously extravagant, and the British Government, by the careful management of the property, had saved the family from absolute beggary.

1857. June. for our people to be driven to use strange ammunition with their artillery. The implements of the Gun Manufactory, as screws, hammers, bolts, and axles, were sewn up in gunny-bags and made to do service as grape-shot. But rude as were these implements of warfare, they did good execution among the besiegers, and many fell beneath the fire of our English rifles. Colonel Smith, a noted marksman, picked off the enemy with an amount of skill that would have done credit to the prizemen of Wimbledon. Tudor Tucker was shot by a Sepoy as he was looking out through an embrasure, or loophole, to see the effect of the last discharge of his gun. The Chaplain, Mr. Frederick Fisher, alternated the duties of a soldier with those of a Christian minister. He preached on the text, "What time I am afraid I will trust in thee;" and then went out to face the enemy. His wife and boy were with him. They were secure in the residence attached to the Gun-carriage Agency, and it is related that little Phil. Fisher and the other children were playing and singing as joyously as if nothing were going on out of the common course of events. The women prayed almost unceasingly for the brave men who were defending them. They bore up bravely in their passiveness—all but one. This was the widow of a sergeant, or conductor, attached to the Clothing Agency, who was shot dead at his post. She was not one to sit down and weep. She went out to work. She took a rifle and posted herself in one of the bastions, whence she is said to have shot down many of the mutineers.* It was a most

* This was the story told to Mr. William Edwards by a Native informant, who, however, added that the woman had been killed at her work. From the official accounts it would appear that Sergeant (Conductor) Ahern was killed in the Fort, but Mrs. Ahern is said to have been murdered at Cawnpore.

1857. June.

unequal conflict. The besiegers were not strong in artillery, and their light guns could not make practicable breaches in the walls of the Fort. They delivered some unsuccessful assaults, and were driven back with heavy loss. But the Sepoys had learnt, from our teaching, lessons of warfare not to be neglected; so they betook themselves to mining operations. They did not fight unaided—for many of the chief Mahomedan people had joined them, and were animating and aiding the assailants. In one of the attacks the foremost man was a Pathan, named Mooltan Khan, who had assisted the escape of Mr. Edwards. The Chaplain, Fisher, shot him dead on the crest of the breach, and those who followed him fell back in dismay. But gallant as were those thirty defenders, the defence could not be protracted with any hope of success or safety to the garrison. Their ammunition had failed, and there was no prospect of the arrival of any succours, though Smith had written imploringly for them. His letters reached Agra.* As the Native regiments there had been disarmed, a detachment of Europeans might have been spared from the seat of Government. Major Weller, who knew the country well, offered to lead it. But the detachment was not sent.† So it was resolved that the besieged should drop down into the boats on the river, under cover of the night.

Evacuation of the Fort.

There were but three boats for the party of a hundred Christian people, and they drifted out forlornly into darkness and unto death. This was the second exodus from Futtehgurh. How it had fared with

* One of them is now before me, written in French—or in such French as an old Indian officer, after years of absence from Europe, can commonly command—in very small characters, and on such thin paper that it might have been conveyed in a quill.

† See Appendix for further information on this point.

1857. June.

the first was not known. But the one idea was to escape to Cawnpore, that cruel Cawnpore, which was to witness the massacre of so many of our Christian people. It was a necessity that there should be some delay in embarking so many women and children with such requisites and appurtenances as could be gathered together for the river voyage. So the shades of night had well-nigh glimmered into dawn before the boats were fairly afloat. The difficulties and dangers of the escape were thus greatly enhanced. Colonel Smith, Colonel Goldie, and Major Robertson commanded severally the three boats. But ere long the three were reduced to two. Colonel Goldie's boat ran upon a shoal, and the rudder was smashed. A vain attempt was made to repair it, the result of which was that the villagers of Soonderpoor came down upon our people in great numbers and fired upon them. The blood of the gallant Englishmen was stirred by this assault. Then a little band of five Christian officers* went out and charged a throng of three hundred Natives, and drove them back to their village with the loss of some of their leaders. But it was plain that they could not wait any longer to refit, so the occupants of Colonel Goldie's boat betook themselves to Colonel Smith, and they pursued their perilous journey down the river.

Pursuit of the enemy.

The pursuit now became more active. The Sepoys took possession of the ferry-boats to follow the fugitives, and a gun was sent down on the right bank of the river to bear upon our unhappy people. The villagers on both banks, especially the dwellers

* These were Captain Vibart (Second Cavalry), Major Munro, Lieutenants Eckford, Sweetenham, and Henderson of the Tenth. Some accounts say that the armed villagers were from four hundred to five hundred in number. They came from three villages.

in the Mahomedan villages, fell upon them with equal ferocity. There had been small chance of escape, from the first, but when Major Robertson's boat grounded on a sand-bank opposite to Singee-Rampore, all hope was abandoned by its inmates. The Sepoys were coming down upon them in their boats, and the banks of the river were lined with enemies. There was acted over again, on a smaller scale, the dreadful scene of the massacre at the Cawnpore Ghaut. Men, women, and children flung themselves into the river, some to be drowned, some to be shot, some to be cut down. Three only of the boat's crew escaped with life and liberty.* Out of the general horror it is difficult to extract the miserable truth of individual calamities. It would seem that the gallant Chaplain, Fisher, severely wounded, leapt into the river with his wife and child in his arms. They were both drowned; but he himself escaped immediate death by hiding himself during the night, and then making his way at dawn to Colonel Smith's boat.† Mrs. Robertson, her child, and Miss Thompson, who accompanied her, also lost their lives at this

1857. June.

* Major Robertson, Mr. Jones, and Mr. Churcher, two badly wounded.

† "Fisher was wounded, a ball passing through his left thigh. The Sepoys then came alongside to board the boat. Major Robertson now urged the ladies and children to get into the water to save themselves. They did so. Jones was still in the boat with other gentlemen, using their muskets. He cannot say to a certainty whether the ladies were mostly shot in the water or were drowned; but when he jumped into the water himself he saw Mrs. Fisher, at some distance, up to her waist in water. The current was strong, and it carried her off her legs several times. Fisher was supporting her, and he had their child in his arms. He (Jones) thinks, from the appearance of the child in his arms, that he (little Philip Fisher) was probably drowned, for this was the fate of many children in the confusion of getting out of the boat. . . . About four o'clock on the morning of the 5th (Sunday), poor Fred. Fisher hailed the boat. He was alone. Directly he got on board he burst into tears, and said, 'My poor wife and child were both drowned in my arms!' Where he had been all night, or what he had been doing, Jones did not hear."—*Rev. Mr. Spry, Chaplain at Allahabad, to Archdeacon Pratt. MS. Correspondence.*

1857. June. place. One of Colonel Goldie's daughters fell at the same time. Major Phillott of the Tenth, and other officers of the same regiment, were also lost here, with several people attached to the Gun-carriage and Clothing Agencies.* Some were taken prisoners, and blown from guns by the Nawab of Furruckabad. Major Robertson, though painfully wounded, escaped with his life, by the generous aid of Mr. David Churcher, an indigo-planter, who secured an oar, on which the two supported themselves in the river until midnight, when they went ashore, and lay hidden in the village of Kulhour, where some herdsmen sheltered them and fed them. Then was witnessed another of those acts of heroic self-devotion of which the annals of the Sepoy War afford so many touching examples. Churcher might have made his escape, but Robertson was in such dire agony both of body and of mind that he could not rouse himself to the activity of flight. So Churcher determined not to leave him. For more than two months he watched over the stricken artilleryman, until death mercifully came to the relief of the sufferer. Then Churcher buried his friend, raised a mound of earth over his remains to mark the spot, and betook himself to the jungle, where Providence mercifully protected him, and enabled him, after awhile, to escape to Cawnpore.

Noble conduct of Churcher.

In the meanwhile Colonel Smith's boat—the last of the little fleet, with all the survivors of the Futtehgurh Fort, dropped down towards Cawnpore—the

* Among those who perished were Dr. and Mrs. Heathcote. Mrs. Heathcote was a niece of Mr. Fisher, and sister of the wife of Major Darcy Todd—daughters of Dr. Sandham, Surgeon of the Sixteenth Lancers, who had married a sister of Mr. F. Fisher and of Colonel Fisher, whose sad fate at Sooltanpore shall afterwards be described. These murdered officers were sons of the Rev. Henry Fisher, Senior Presidency Chaplain for a long series of years.

desired harbour of refuge. And here authentic history fades into dim conjecture. What befel them on the way is not known. But it is too sure that they all perished at the place in which they had thought to find safety and shelter. That they fell into the cruel hands of Doondoo Punt, Nana Sahib, and were butchered at Cawnpore, has been already narrated.* It is known also that those who had preceded them in the flotilla which left Futtehgurh on the 4th of June, had been sent to the shambles before them. In all, more than two hundred Christian people—men, women, and children—who were in or near Futtehgurh at the beginning of June, died miserably on the dreary river voyage or at the place of their destination, where they had hoped to escape the malice of their persecutors.† 1857. June.

The English in Furruckabad having thus been expelled and destroyed, and all trace of their authority effaced, an attempt was made to systematise the restored Native Government. But the Nawab, Tuffoozul Hoosein Khan, was not a chief of superabundant energy and activity, and it is doubtful whether he much delighted in the greatness which had been thrust upon him. He was a man of quiet habits and *dilettante* tastes, fond of painting and illuminating, and like others, both in the East and the West, of the same artistic tendencies, somewhat addicted to epicurean practices. He liked dancing The Nawab of Furruckabad.

* *Ante*, vol. ii. page 353.

† Colonel Williams, in his admirable report of events at Cawnpore, which I have before quoted from, says that those who left Futtehgurh on the 4th of June are supposed to have perished at Cawnpore on the 12th of that month. He states that Colonel Smith's boat reached Bithoor on the 9th of July, that the occupants were seized there and sent into Cawnpore, that the gentlemen (three excepted, Colonels Goldie and Smith and Mr. Thornhill) were killed on the 10th or 11th, and the women and children massacred on the 15th of that month.

1857. July—Aug. girls better than soldiers, and had more pleasure in the society of parasites than of public functionaries. He had a traditional ascendancy in the province, and that was all. He was a weak rather than a bad man, and there were many people about him whose hatred of the English was far more intense than his own. He sat on a throne, and orders were issued in his name for the collection of the revenue, and for the definition of the processes of civil and criminal law. The regulations did not differ much from those which had been ordained in the time of British rule, but they were enforced with greater stringency. It was not to be expected that, here or elsewhere, after long years of depression, Native administrators should suddenly arise with systems and organisations of their own. In such an emergency they were fain to pick up, from the leavings of their predecessors, such crumbs as they could find. Our old Native officials were, for the most part, not unwilling—if not rejoiced—to array themselves under the Native Governments. Not being able to see into men's hearts, I cannot say whether in this there was any spirit of nationality, or whether it was merely an instinct of greed. If they did not obtain higher pay—and in most instances they procured at least the promise of it—they had greater opportunities of illicit gains. Our military retainers were as children, and, like the children of all nations, they were cruel. But our civil functionaries had the astuteness of maturity about them, and were cold and calculating in the midst of the general excitement. It was a necessity of their very existence that they should cast in their lot with the dominant power. And perhaps they did not much care whether the White man or the Black man were triumphant, so long as they retained their places and preserved their pay. Some, however, held back—doubtful as to the final issue of the struggle—far-seeing men, who could afford to wait. And in time they had their reward.* 1857. May—Aug.

Character of the outbreak.

I shall not pause here to attempt a full and impartial inquiry into the inner history—the moral anatomy, I may say—of this great movement against the White Man. But something may be briefly said about the character of the events recorded in the chapter now brought to a close—a chapter, the materials of which have been derived from the official reports of our own civil officers. In many parts of the North-Western Provinces there had been violent rebellion without the aid or presence of Sepoys—where Sepoys were few or none—before they had risen, or after they had left the disturbed districts. And in some instances our Native soldiers had actively aided the authorities in putting down popular insurrections. The violence of the Sepoys was commonly of a superficial kind, and such seeds of rebellion as they sowed took no root in the soil. Having plundered the treasuries, perhaps killed their

* Mr. C. R. Lindsay, in his very able and exhaustive report, says: "The conduct of the officials serving the British Government at the time of the outbreak was not praiseworthy. Out of the six Tehseldars (chief revenue officers) three took service with the Nawab. Out of eleven head police officers six accepted situations under the new Government. Amongst the nine Peshkars (officers next in rank to the Tehseldars), five gave in their adherence to the Nawab. The Canoongoes were all, save one, employed. All the collecting Sowars, with the exception of one, went over to the Nawab *en masse*. Of the other officials, such as Record-keepers, Mohurrers, Nazirs, Burkendauzes, Chuprassies, &c., all, or nearly all, tendered their services to the Government of the time. The Sheristadars of the criminal and revenue departments, and the Nazir of the former, did not accept appointments. The latter official got rather severely handled by the rebels. He was fined and plundered of a portion of his property."

1857. May—Aug. officers and other Christian people, and opened the gaols, they made for their homes or betook themselves to Delhi. It was not on account of the violence of the Sepoys that the Lieutenant-Governor described the provinces under his rule as in "a blaze of ravage and riot," or that the Governor-General wrote officially that they were "lost to us" for the time. Where were no sources of complaint against the British Government other than of a military character, no grievances, no apprehensions, no alarms, where none but our trained soldiers were smarting under injuries, real or supposed, these uprisings made comparatively a slight and transient impression upon the country in respect of its government and administration; and our authority was speedily re-imposed. But there were fears and discontents with which greased cartridges had no connexion, and uprisings not incited by thoughts of the spoliation of the treasure-chests. The fears and discontents of powerful classes, who felt that they had been down-trodden by the English, that their old dynasties had been subverted, their old traditions ignored, their old systems violated, their old usages contemned, and that everywhere the reign of annexation and innovation had commenced, and was threatening to crush out the very hearts of the nations, struck deep root in the soil, and it was a work of time to eradicate the evil growth. And all this, too, in the model provinces, the administrative conduct of which had been vaunted as the greatest triumph of British rule in the East.

It belongs to a later stage of this History, when the events of the Sepoy War shall have been more fully narrated, to prosecute this important inquiry to its legitimate termination. What has been now written is a commentary only on the contents of the present chapter. The brave heart of Lieutenant-Governor Colvin would not have been torn, as it was, if he had thought that the convulsions in the North-Western Provinces were confined to our military Cantonments.

1857. May.

CHAPTER III.

ANXIETIES OF MR. COLVIN—THE NATIVE CHIEFS—SCINDIAH AND HIS CONTINGENT—EVENTS AT GWALIOR—OUTBREAK OF THE CONTINGENT—ESCAPE OF THE ENGLISH—THE NEEMUCH BRIGADE—HOLKAR AND TROOPS—OUTBREAK AT INDORE—WITHDRAWAL OF THE RESIDENT—KOTAH—RAJPOOTANA.

1857. May—June.

COLVIN suffered cruelly, but he bore up bravely, though the silent approaches of death already were casting their dark shadows over him. Much of which I have written was either not known at all, or but dimly perceived at the Head-Quarters of the Supreme Government. But every day brought in some disastrous tidings to the Lieutenant-Governor, whose intimate knowledge of all local circumstances painfully disclosed to him the full significance of the distressing stories that came huddling on each other. Those which I have recorded are but excerpts from the grim catalogue of "ravage and riot" which so distracted and distressed him. And he felt that, bad as was what he saw before him in the Present, there might be worse in the Future to assail him.

To the bearing of the Native chiefs in this conjuncture, and especially of the Maharajah Scindiah of Gwalior, whose capital lay at a distance of only sixty-five miles from Agra, Colvin had looked from the commencement of the rebellion with extreme anxiety, and notwithstanding the promising signs and symptoms above recorded,* he was still racked by most painful doubts, which soon became most distressing realities. That great Mahratta Prince had a Contingent force of more than eight thousand men, with twenty-six guns,† under English officers, and a purely Native force of ten thousand men. The Contingent was little more than a local branch of our own military establishment, and there was small chance of the Gwalior soldiery being proof against the general alarm which was pervading the Native Army in all parts of the country. It was very soon apparent that they were tainted. But an army rebelling against its master, and without an acknowledged head, is one thing; an army led to the battle by its sovereign prince is another thing, and one far more perilous to encounter. Everywhere it was asked, nervously, "What will Scindiah do?" The opportunity that lay before him was a tempting one. He might shake himself loose from the thraldom of the dominant Englishman; he might increase his territory, and increase his army, and become a more powerful and independent ruler than his ancestors had been in the palmiest days of the Raj. Every Native Prince is surrounded, more or less, by a crew of parasites and intriguers, whose game it is to foster the growth of every kind of corruption, and to shut him out from the good influences brought to bear upon him by honest and enlightened advisers. There were those, doubtless, who, still smarting under the losses sustained by their defeat at Maharajpore and

1857. May—June.

* *Ante*, page 208.

† There were two regiments of Irregular Cavalry—1158 men of all ranks—seven regiments of Infantry, aggregating 6412, four field batteries (each comprising five nine-pounders and a twenty-four-pound howitzer), and a garrison battery with two eighteen-pounder iron guns attached for field service. Twenty-six guns in all, with 748 artillery-men. See Appendix.

1857. May—June.

Punniah, would fain have persuaded the young Maharajah to array himself on the side of the enemies of the English now that all things seemed to be in their favour. It was not to be expected that being a man and a Mahratta, he should not, when assailed by the fierce temptation, sometimes have wavered in his allegiance, and, for a little while, yielded inwardly to the allurements that beset him. Perhaps, indeed, there was not a Native chief in India who was not sometimes minded to wait and watch at the outset of the great convulsion. And there were some personal circumstances, peculiar to the Gwalior chief, which rendered it especially likely that he would cast in his lot against the usurping Englishman.

The Maharajah Scindiah.

At this time Scindiah was in his twenty-third year. His passion for military display had grown with his growth, and strengthened with his strength. Had he lived half a century earlier, this ambition might have been pregnant with great events. He might have ripened into a leader of armies, and made for himself a place in the history of the world. But all independent action of this kind had been crushed out of the Native Princes of India by the universal domination of the British. By the introduction of what we called our subsidiary system, it had come to pass that there was but one military power, but one military nation left on the great Indian Peninsula. The English soldier put down all internal conflicts, and took upon himself the general defence of the country. Neither Mahrattas, nor Rajpoots, nor Pathans, nor any other race, Hindoo or Mahomedan, within certain limits, were allowed to fight among themselves. So a Native Prince, with strong military instincts, had nothing to do but to play at soldiering. Of the young Maharajah Scindiah, it was officially reported in 1856, that he "seemed to enjoy no occupation save drilling, dressing, ordering, transforming, feasting, playing with his troops, and the unwearied study of books of evolutions; and he grudged no expenditure connected with this amusement."* 1857. May—June.

A man of this character, if he had fallen into bad hands, might have been dangerous to himself and to others. Fortunately, he fell into good hands—hands that gently but firmly restrained the restlessness of his nature. At the most critical period of his life he had Dinkur Rao at his elbow. That great Native statesman, who has shared with Salar Jung, of Hyderabad, the glory of being the Abul-Fuzl of the nineteenth century, and from whom the best of our English administrators have learnt many lessons of wisdom, exercised a benign influence, not only over the government of the Gwalior territory, which he reformed and consolidated, but over the personal character of Scindiah himself. He could not do this without exciting some jealousy in the mind of the Maharajah, and raising hostile cabals among a less worthy class of Durbar servants. But, encouraged and sustained by the British Political Agent, he triumphed over these difficulties. In Major Charters Macpherson, our Government had at the Court of Gwalior a representative in every way qualified both to conciliate and to restrain a man of Scindiah's temperament. A member of a family, distinguished in many different departments of the public service, he had gained for himself an enduring reputation by his successful efforts to suppress the great abomination of Meriah sacrifice in Southern India. He was one of the good old school of soldier-statesmen, with large

The Dewan Dinkur Rao.

Charters Macpherson.

* Report of Major Charters Macpherson, December 13, 1856.

1857. May—June. human sympathies and broad catholic political views. Few men, whom I have known and conversed with, have had less of that national self-love, which so often over-rides truth and justice in our estimate of and our conduct towards others. Essentially tolerant and many-sided, he could see how much of the evil, which we are wont to condemn in the Native States of India, is the growth of circumstances which have been developed in our own forcing-house. He felt that the young Maharajah was at least as good as, perhaps better than, we had any right to expect him to be; but he exerted himself to make him still better. The relations between the British Officer and the Mahratta Prince were of the most friendly kind. The cordiality between them had been confirmed by their visit to Calcutta in March, 1857, the incidents of which made a strong impression on Scindiah's mind. He saw at our English capital much that was new to him—much that was suggestive and impressive. And he returned to Gwalior with not only an enlarged estimate of the magnificent resources of the British Government, but with a more assured belief than he had ever entertained before of their friendly feelings and just intentions towards him. That was a time of almost general alarm among the rulers of the Native States of India; and Lord Canning saw clearly the necessity of allaying it. So the Maharajah carried back with him to Gwalior the remembrance of assuring words spoken to him by the Governor-General at Calcutta, and had no more fear for the perpetuation of his dynasty. If he did not regard with much complacency the domination of the English, he felt that it was inevitable, and he reconciled himself to it, more contentedly than he could have done, when the air was alive with rumours of the annexation of the Native States.

1857. May—June. Bearing of Scindiah.

It has been seen that, on the first outbreak of revolt, Scindiah had manifested his loyalty by placing his troops at the disposal of the Lieutenant-Governor of Agra. Major Macpherson had always doubted from the first whether the Contingent, composed as it was of the same materials as our own Native Army, would ever act against our Sepoy mutineers; and he represented that in no manner could the Maharajah testify his own devotion to the British so well as by sending to Agra his own body-guard, consisting mainly of Mahratta horsemen "of his own kindred or caste."* To this Scindiah had cheerfully responded. He saw the departure of his favourite phalanx with pride, and rode out some way to their camp. The Contingent, the Maharajah mistrusted as much as Macpherson had done; and he warned the British Agent that they had ceased entirely to be servants of the Government. Their hearts were with the mutineers of the Bengal Army. They were holding nightly meetings—taking oaths upon the Ganges water—receiving emissaries from Calcutta and Delhi—both accepting and propagating monstrous stories of our efforts to destroy the religions of the country and inculcating upon Hindoos and Mahomedans alike the duty of hastening the downfall of the British Government in India. But still Brigadier Ramsay and his officers, like their comrades of the Regular Army, believed in the fidelity of their men. Vainly were the views of the Maharajah and the Political Agent represented to him; he said that they were tinged with Mahratta intrigue and were not to be trusted. Still Macpherson insisted upon the duty of taking some precaution to insure the safety of the

Confidence of the Contingent officers.

* Major Macpherson says of these men, "that they had been Scindiah's companions by day and by night inseparable from his pleasures and State."

1857. May—June. women and children in the event of a sudden outbreak; and to this end it was arranged that the Residency should be fixed upon as a place of refuge, that the Contingent-guard posted there should be withdrawn, and Durbar troops substituted for them. But when the Political Agent represented that it would be expedient for the wives and children of the Contingent officers quietly and gradually to take up their abode in the Residency, the Brigadier protested against the movement as one that would indicate want of confidence in the fidelity of the troops.

May 28. The first panic. But on the next day there was a great panic in Cantonments; and the women and children were flying for their lives to the Residency. It was expected that the troops would rise that night; but it was a false alarm. When tidings of this movement reached Scindiah, he rode down, with a strong escort, to the Residency, posted troops securely around it, and urged upon Macpherson the expediency of bringing all the women and the children to a spacious mansion, built in the English style, attached to the Palace, where they would be protected by his own people. So on the next day they were removed as quietly as possible to the asylum provided for them by the Maharajah; and there they ought to have been suffered to remain. But the Sepoys of the Contingent protested that the removal of our women and children was an imputation on their honour, and they prevailed with their officers to recall their families to Cantonments.*

* Major Macpherson telegraphed to Mr. Colvin to send back Scindiah's body-guard as there was danger of a rising; but Brigadier Ramsay having read this telegram, wrote to the Lieutenant-Governor that all was quiet and confidence increasing, and that he "considered that Scindiah was endeavouring to increase his own services at the expense of the Contingent."

The grievous error that had been committed was soon palpable. No sooner had "confidence been restored" at Head-Quarters than all the Contingent troops posted at the out-stations broke into rebellion. The first two weeks of June saw all the country occupied by the Contingent in a blaze of mutiny and rebellion. One regiment revolted at Neemuch on the 4th, with all the Company's troops. On the 7th, revolt was inaugurated at Jhansi with the most fiendish orgies that the imagination could devise. At Sepree and Jubbulpore, the troops were showing unmistakable signs of a speedy rising; and from our own provinces everywhere came disastrous tidings of regiments in mutiny, of Christian people murdered or flying for their lives, of law and authority prostrate, of districts overrun by unscrupulous marauders. 1857. June.

Temper of the troops.

There was now an almost general impression at Gwalior that the power of the English in India was at its last gasp. Among the very few who did not share this belief were Scindiah and his Minister. The difficulties with which they were beset were of a most embarrassing kind, for there was a constant flood of Mahratta intrigue ever pouring itself upon the Maharajah, and endeavouring to sweep away the influence and ascendancy of the Dewan, who was heart and soul with the English party. His most cherished friends and companions were active upon the other side. They had suffered by our domination; they were eager for the overthrow of Dinkur Rao; and they hoped to persuade Scindiah that, as his power would be vastly aggrandised by the expulsion of the British, it was folly to abstain from casting in his lot with the victorious army. He listened, made plausible answers, and talked of waiting; but he never swerved from his allegiance. Amidst all

1857. June.

these sinister influences he remained true to us; and for awhile the Durbar Army continued to be loyal to its master. But it was plain that the Contingent at Gwalior might at any moment cast off the trammels of mock loyalty and break out into the violence of uncontrolled rebellion.

The outbreak at Gwalior.

The day, indeed, was close at hand. On Sunday, so often a fatal day to the English—Sunday, the 14th of June—our Christian people attended divine service in the church and took the Sacrament of the Lord's Supper. There had been a funeral in the morning. A little son of Captain Murray had been laid in the grave, and many of the European residents of Gwalior had attended the burial. The Sepoys saw them go and depart, and were respectful—almost sympathising in their demeanour. The day passed, and all was outwardly quiet. But on the evening of that Sabbath the Contingent rose. The crisis was precipitated after the wonted fashion. There was a cry that the Europeans were upon them—a panic in the Lines and then a general revolt. The Artillerymen rushed to their guns; the Infantry seized their muskets. The sound of firing and the sight of flames, breaking the stillness and the darkness of the night, proclaimed that the orgies of rebellion had commenced. Shouting, yelling, bugling, the Sepoys of the Contingent, in the wildest confusion, under the influence of a great fear, feeling that the time had come, roused themselves to the work of mischief. Their officers, who, in accordance with the early habits of the East, had either retired to their beds or were preparing for rest, rose up, hastily clothed themselves, and hurried down to the Lines. Many then left their homes never to see them again. All hope of quieting the general excitement had passed away. There was a furious multitude, eager to cast off the domination of the British —some thirsting for the blood of the white-faced Christians. So when our officers went amidst the mutineers, in the darkness and confusion of the night, they were shot down by the men of the Contingent. Every commanding officer then at Gwalior was killed. Hawkins and Stewart of the Artillery, Blake and Sheriff of the Infantry, fell beneath the fire of the insurgents. The truth was soon known to all; and men, women, and children rushed from their houses to find safety where they could, or to perish by the way. The Sepoys in their fury spared none. Hawkins had his sick wife with him, a baby of a few days old at her breast, and four other young children. Mrs. Stewart and her children were also under his care. The fire of the enemy struck down the artilleryman, and when Mrs. Stewart bent over him and took his hand, a volley of musketry killed them both. Three of the children were also murdered. Here, as in other places, the inconsistency of the Sepoy character was marvellously manifested. Captain Stewart himself was wounded in the first nocturnal onslaught. Two of the men of his battery nursed him tenderly through the night; but when he had good hope of deliverance in the morning, he was taken forth and deliberately shot to death. Major Blake, Commandant of the Second Infantry Regiment—an officer much beloved by his men—a man as good as he was brave, who never feared death except for the sake of those he might leave behind him—was shot through the chest as he sat on his charger before the main guard, at the commencement of the outbreak. The Sepoys of his own regiment expressed profound grief, declared that he had been killed by the men of the Fourth, and tried to prove their words by giving him

1857. June 14.

1857. June 15. decent burial. The Superintending Surgeon, Dr. Kirk, was traced to an out-house, in which he had endeavoured to conceal himself, and there killed in the presence of his wife. The Chaplain, Mr. Coopland, having taken refuge with his wife in Major Blake's house, was dragged away from the arms of the beseeching women, hunted through Cantonments amidst volleys of musketry, and finally overtaken and cut down. Altogether on that night were killed seven officers, six sergeants and pensioners, with three women and three children.

A like number of officers—"some under showers of bullets, but favoured by a moonless night"*—escaped. And several ladies and children escaped with them. The majority of these made their way either to the Residency or to Scindiah's Palace. It seemed that, after the first outburst, the Gwalior Sepoys did not lust after the blood of women and children, although their greed compelled them to despoil the ladies of their rings and bracelets, and other ornaments on their persons. A party of five officers' wives—all but one† of whom had been made widows by the tragedy of that Sunday night—escaped in the morning with their children closely packed in a small carriage, which conveyed them in safety to Scindiah's Palace. There sufficient carriage was provided for them, and they were sent on towards the Chumbul. In the Dholepore country they were most generously protected and succoured by the

* Major Macpherson's Report.

† The exception was that of Mrs. Campbell, whose husband, Captain Campbell, was at Agra at the time of the Gwalior outbreak. She was a lady of great personal attractions, and, as she went, she excited the admiration of all—Sepoys and villagers — who saw her; but she was treated with the utmost respect. She had disguised herself in Native costume; but the disguise was soon penetrated. It is related that some who looked upon her exclaimed, with that appreciation of the beauty of small feet that seems to be inherent in nearly all nations: "See how well her feet look in Indian slippers!"

Rajah of that state, who provided them with an escort, and safely conveyed them to Agra, where they arrived on the 19th of June, some of them in a very pitiable plight.* 1857. June.

When the news of these terrible events reached Scindiah in his Palace, he was in an agony of shame and grief, and in dire perplexity as to what was to follow. Macpherson, not without risk of his life, had hastened to join the Maharajah. On his way he was attacked by a party of Ghazees, who would have fired into his carriage, but for the assurance of a Mahratta officer that the British Agent was then on his way to Scindiah's presence as a prisoner, by the express orders of the Chief. When he reached the Palace he found the Maharajah and Dinkur Rao together. Brigadier Ramsay and others, who had escaped from Cantonments, had already arrived at the Phool-bagh. What now was to be done? Scindiah and his Minister confessed their inability to protect our people. Assured of this, they had already ordered carriages and palanquins for the conveyance of the fugitives to the Chumbul, or across it to Agra. A party of the body-guard had been warned to accompany them. Macpherson offered to remain alone with the Maharajah; but against this Scindiah protested. It might have been a needless sacrifice of a precious life. It would certainly have been an embarrassment to the Durbar. But it was important that the Chief and his Minister should take counsel with the British Agent as to what was to be done after his departure. The anxiety of

* MS. Memorandum by Colonel Riddell, who adds: "Accommodation was immediately provided for those who had no friends in the garrison in one of the European barracks, and every comfort attended to as far as our means permitted." The services of the Rajah of Dholepore have been acknowledged by the grant of a knighthood of the Star of India of the highest grade.

1857. June. Scindiah was extreme. To him the crisis was one of almost unexampled difficulty. It was certain that the Contingent had gone. It was doubtful whether the Durbar troops would remain faithful. It was feared that they would coalesce with the mutinous Contingent, and call upon Scindiah to place himself at their head, to march upon Agra, and to drive the English out of the great capital of the North-West. To obviate this difficulty, it was the desire of the Maharajah to feed the mutineers largely with treasure, and to permit them to depart to their homes. But Macpherson saw clearly the evil of such a course. He implored the Maharajah to keep his troops together at Gwalior, and consented on the part of his Government that service should be given to them, so long as they might remain in their Lines. Scindiah promised to do all that could be done to conform with this advice, and for a while the troops of both branches of the service, having expelled the English, were kept together at Gwalior.

But, although there was for the present little apprehension of an attack upon Agra from the Head-Quarters of the Gwalior Force, there was threatened danger from another quarter, which Colvin and his colleagues could not disregard. It was reported that the Neemuch Brigade, which, as before said, had revolted, was about to march down upon Agra. Neemuch was a British Cantonment on the borders of Scindiah's territory, to which it had formerly belonged. It was one of the pleasantest and healthiest places in that part of the country—a "favourite station," at which a large body of troops was constantly posted.* Being on the western boundary of

* Mr. Pritchard, in his very interesting account of the "Mutinies in Rajpootana," says: "It is a very favourite garrison for troops,

the territory administered by the Lieutenant-Governor of the North-Western Provinces, the regiments of the Bombay Army had shared with their comrades of Bengal the duties of garrisoning the station. It was an unlucky circumstance that early in the year some Bombay Infantry corps had been relieved by Bengal regiments. On the first outbreak of the mutiny the force at Neemuch consisted of a troop of Native Horse Artillery, the left wing of the First Light Cavalry, the Seventy-second Regiment of Native Infantry (all of the Bengal Army), and the Seventh Regiment of the Gwalior Contingent. No European troops were in Cantonments, nor any within a distance at which they could be available in an emergency. At Nusseerabad were stationed the Fifteenth and Thirtieth Regiments of Bengal Native Infantry and a Native Horse Field Battery. They had been for some time hovering on the brink of mutiny. But there was a regiment of Bombay Cavalry—the First Lancers, which was believed to be staunch. But when, on the afternoon of the 28th of May, the Bengal troops broke into open mutiny, the half-heartedness of their Bombay comrades was apparent. Ordered to charge and retake the guns, they dashed forward, but when within a few yards of the battery, they turned threes about and left their officers to be slaughtered. Two were killed and two were wounded. The different systems of the several armies under the Company, to which I have more than once referred, was prominently dis-

1857.
May—June
Neemuch and Nusseerabad.

having the reputation of being one of the healthiest stations in the Presidency. The Cantonment is built on an elevated ridge surrounding north-west and south-east; in length about two miles and a half. The soil is well adapted for horticulture, and most of the bungalows had gardens attached to them. A kind of fort, or fortified square, had been erected for the protection of the European inhabitants or garrison, and was generally used, I believe, as a magazine."

1857. June. played. The Bombay troopers had their families with them. They were alarmed for the safety of their wives and children—for if they had used their sabres against the Bengal Sepoys, there might have been a massacre in the Bombay Lines. This accounted for the traitorous inactivity of the Lancers. It was now all over with our unfortunate people. They had nothing left to them but flight—men, women, and children—to Beawur, some thirty miles distant on the road to Deesa — all their property was abandoned; and the Sepoys had their usual "tomasha"—burning and plundering all the public and private buildings, and then marching off for Delhi.

The Nusseerabad troops, having revolted, there was small probability that the Neemuch force, which had long been suspected, would remain true to their colours. On the 3rd of June they broke into open mutiny, and revelled in the wonted plunder and devastation, but they spared their European officers and their families. The only victims to their fury were the wife and children of a Sergeant of Artillery murdered in their own house. The insurgents then made a movement to march on Delhi, taking Agra by the way, intelligence of which caused great consternation. It was soon known by the garrison of that place that the Neemuch Brigade had determined to march down upon them, and that there was little or nothing to interrupt their progress. The distance, however, to be traversed was considerable, and there was an element of consolation in this. More than three hundred miles of country lay between the mutineers and the capital of the North-West. Weeks remained, therefore, to prepare for the reception of the insurgents. Moreover, the well-known vacillating character of the Sepoys rendered it at least possible that they would abandon their design of marching on Agra and strike off at once to Delhi. The danger, though formidable, and one afterwards fearfully realised, was not one of urgent pressure; and in the meanwhile other difficulties might present themselves and other complications were to be considered. Next to the bearing of Scindiah in this emergency, the propinquity of whose dominions was an immediate menace, that of Holkar was to be regarded. It follows, therefore, in due course to speak of the conduct of that chief. 1857. June.

Indore, the capital of the territory over which the Maharajah Holkar had sway, lies to the westward of his dominions, at a distance of four hundred miles from Agra, and some thirty miles less from Bombay. It is the chief seat of the representative of the British Government in Central India. The Residency is there; and the Agent to the Governor-General makes it his home during the greater part of the year. Thirteen miles from the capital, within Holkar's country, is the British Cantonment of Mhow. There in the hot weather of 1857 were posted the Twenty-third Regiment of Native Infantry—and the right wing of the First Native Cavalry. These were our weaknesses. Our strength lay in a Horse Battery of European Artillery commanded by Captain Townsend Hungerford. The commandant of the station was Colonel Platt of the Twenty-third. Indore.

The officiating agent at Indore was Colonel Henry Marion Durand. He had earned for himself a high reputation, nearly twenty years before, when he Colonel H. M. Durand.

1857. June. and Norman Macleod, two splendid young Engineer officers, blew open the gates of Ghuznee. Having returned to England, after the first Afghan campaign, he was, on the nomination of Lord Ellenborough to the Governor-Generalship of India, appointed his Private Secretary.* He went out with the new ruler in the *Cambrian*, and was at the great man's elbow until his recall. He was known then to be a man brave in battle and he was thought to be wise in council. Responsible appointments in the Civil and Political branches of the service were successively bestowed upon him. In 1857, he was acting as Governor-General's Agent in Central India—one of the highest political offices under the Supreme Government. The substantive appointment was held by Sir Robert Hamilton, a Bengal civilian of high repute, whom ill-health had driven to England. The two men were extremely dissimilar. They had different characters and different opinions. Sir Robert Hamilton had much tenderness towards the downtrodden Native princes and chiefs of India. He made great allowances for the evil circumstances surrounding a chief, especially in his younger days; and he conceived that it was his duty, as the representative of the British Government, no less than it was his inclination as a man, to be tolerant, and by toleration to encourage all that was good in a chief rather than to suppress the evil by harshness. But Durand was not tolerant. He was a high-minded, conscientious English gentleman; but he looked at every-

* It appears from the recently published correspondence of Lord Ellenborough that Durand was first appointed A.D.C. to the Governor-General. As mentioned in vol. i., the Private Secretaryship was offered to Lord Canning, and declined. It would seem, from a reference in the Ellenborough Correspondence, that Lord Charles Wellesley also received an invitation. However, Durand eventually became Private Secretary.

thing through the pure crystal of Christianity; he wanted imagination; he could not Orientalise himself. Had his lines been cast in other places, he might have been a great soldier.* He was not a good political officer, because lacking sympathy, he could not make allowances, and expected a Mahratta chief to be as leal as a Percy or a Campbell. This caused him to leap hastily to conclusions—as will presently be shown. 1857. June.

At this time, Holkar was in his twenty-first year.† He was a quiet, well-educated, intelligent man, of no great energy of character, and by no means addicted to warlike pursuits. He had been very carefully trained under the guidance of Sir Robert Hamilton, who placed over the young Maharajah as his immediate preceptor, a clever, well-instructed Brahmin, named Omeid Singh, who had been confidentially employed by Sir George Clerk on the Punjab frontier, and who had afterwards been Government translator at Agra. He was conversant not only with the languages of India, the Mahratta included, but also with English, both as spoken and as written. Sir Robert Hamilton's system was that, which has since been pursued in another Native state, with good promise of the best results.‡ He associated with the young Prince some of the sons of the chief people of Indore—boys of about his own age, who became his class-fellows and friends. When first the Maha- The Maharajah Holkar.

* He was, perhaps, with one exception, the best writer of Military History whom I ever knew. He had not the fire and enthusiasm of William Napier, but no one ever understood more fully or explained more clearly great military operations than Henry Durand.

† Mr. Edward Thornton, in his very valuable *Gazetteer*, says that Holkar attained his majority in 1852. This would have made the Maharajah twenty-three years of age at the time of the mutiny.

‡ In Mysore, where Colonel Malleson is admirably exercising his powers, as guardian of the future ruler of that fine country (1873).

1857. June.

rajah came under tuition he was "an intelligent, bright boy, with an easy, self-possessed manner," but his attainments went little beyond his capacity to trace a few Mahratta characters on sand, after the custom of village schools. But he was exceedingly ductile and eager to learn, and he made good progress with his studies. Ere long he came to read and to understand English, but he never could write it freely. Long after his nonage was at an end—indeed up to the time of Omeid Singh's death—his correspondence was conducted by his old preceptor. But no letter went forth in his name, the contents of which he did not thoroughly understand.

Characteristics of Hamilton and Durand.

It might have been right or it might have been wrong—I think it was right—but Sir Robert Hamilton encouraged the young Maharajah, when he came of age, and the chief people around him, freely to deliver their sentiments on all subjects, even though they might not be, in every case, very flattering to the British Government. It was the habit, therefore, at the Indore Durbar, when Hamilton returned to England, not without some mental inquietude as to the results of his absence, to speak out freely—to ventilate grievances, and to expound the supposed means of remedying them. But Durand could not tolerate this. A man of an imperious temper, with a profound belief in the immense inferiority of the Asiatic races, he esteemed it to be the worst presumption in a Mahratta prince or noble, to openly express an opinion of his own in the presence of the representative of the British Government. And, for this, or for some other reason, which I cannot even conjecture, he seems never to have had any feeling of personal kindness towards the young

Maharajah. There was an antipathy which, perhaps, was reciprocated. But no member of the British agency, during the first two months of trouble, ever spoke of the disloyalty of Holkar. Doubtless, he was sorely troubled in his mind. He knew that at Gwalior the Contingent had revolted. He knew that the British troops at Nusseerabad and Neemuch had declared for mutiny, and, if not drawn away towards Delhi and Agra, might disorganise his whole country. He saw, on his right hand and on his left, most terrible proofs of a general rebellion against the domination of the English. The whole of the North-Western Provinces were slipping away from our grasp. At Delhi we were still besieged by an insolent enemy. At Indore, all except those of his old class-mates, who were still attached to his Government or his person, were openly boasting the downfall of the British Raj, or muttering schemes of hostility, whereby they might rise on the ruins of the British Empire. But Holkar himself, though still young in years, was old enough in wisdom to have full faith in the durability of our power. He knew what were the resources of the State—what the energy of the English character; and there was a strong conviction within him that we should eventually be triumphant. And although he did not love Durand, there were those of our nation whom he did love, and he would not willingly have blackened his face before them.

1857. May—June

Sentiments of Holkar.

So little was Holkar dreaming of war, that his troops were scattered over his country, and everywhere miserably equipped. His arsenal and magazine were almost empty. Early in June the Durbar sought the assistance of the British Agent, who wrote to Lord Elphinstone on the 5th of June for military supplies: "If the arms can be spared," he said,

Arms to Indore.

1857. June. "even to half the amount named,* a thousand fusils, Holkar would be gratified, for his Infantry are badly equipped, and would be much the better for reliable arms. So badly off is this Durbar for warlike preparations, that although they have some good six-pounders and nine-pounders, they have no ammunition; and I have taken upon myself to order that they receive forty rounds per gun for each battery, the ammunition being drawn from the Mhow magazine." No thought had Durand, at that time, that the Indore Government could ever turn against him. He believed Holkar to be true; and he sought to strengthen his powers of defence against the enemies of the British Government.

Up to this time, Durand had received assuring accounts of the state of the brigades at Nusseerabad and Neemuch. But it was impossible not to recognise the magnitude of the crisis. "Sir Robert Hamilton," he wrote to Lord Elphinstone, "escapes a critical period. Central India is as yet all quiet; but men's minds are excited, and anxiously awaiting news from Delhi, which I had hoped to receive to-day. Neemuch and Nusseerabad are reported all quiet, but the officers are evidently anxious, and not very confident. A well-struck blow at Delhi will prove an invaluable sedative. The present is even a more serious crisis than that which your Lordship announced from the signal-post at Madras, when the *Cambrian* hove in sight. It was a serious welcome.†

* The request made by Holkar's Vakeel was for two thousand fusils, three hundred pairs of pistols, and four lakhs of gun-caps.

† The semaphore announced, "Bad news." The *Cambrian* signalled, "What news?" When it was answered, that our troops had been driven out of Afghanistan, Lord Ellenborough drew a long breath of relief, and said to Durand that he had expected something worse—a mutiny of the Native Army.

But Lord Canning's present difficulties and responsibilities are still graver than those which beset all in high authority at the time I had the honour of being presented to you. It is matter of congratulation for all watching the course of events, that one of your Lordship's experience in India is at the head of the Bombay Government, and you may command my services in this sphere of action in any way you may deem necessary to the public service." 1857. June.

Mhow.

But even whilst he was writing that all things were quiet at Nusseerabad and Neemuch, the troops there were in the throes of active rebellion. He then trembled for the safety of Mhow. "I wish," he wrote on the 13th of June, "that I could give you a satisfactory account of the state of the troops at Mhow. The Twenty-third Native Infantry is, I think, more disposed to remain quiet than the wing of the First Cavalry. The troopers of the latter are said to be taunting and urging the Infantry to rise. Both, however, are in fear of the European battery, and also of the troops and guns here. They are in fear, too, of the column from Bombay, which they suspect to have a punitive mission for themselves. The officers are endeavouring to assure them that they have nothing to dread, provided they remain orderly and quiet. If the Mhow troops rise, it will probably be as much owing to the apprehensions so insidiously spread amongst them, of stern measures being in store for suspected corps, as to anything else. We sadly want the capture of Delhi to act as a sedative on Chiefs and People, and the smouldering spirit of Revolt." And so it was from all parts of India, the same despairing cry—Let the English triumph at Delhi, and the head of the great giant

1857. June. Revolt will be crushed under the heel of the Englishman.

And so the month of June wore to a close. The Nusseerabad and Neemuch Brigades were going off to Delhi. But the troops at Mhow had not risen, and no suspicion of the fidelity of Holkar had been entertained. By Colonel Platt, who commanded the station, the confidence system had been consistently maintained; not without some protests from the Artilleryman Hungerford, who urged upon the commanding officer wise, but not obtrusive precautions. All, however, had gone well. But, with the month of June, the prevailing quietude expired. Suddenly, a little before noon on the 1st of July, Colonel Platt received a note from Durand at Indore, saying, "Send the European battery as sharp as you can. We are attacked by Holkar."

July 1. Rising at Indore. The history of this sudden rising at Indore will, perhaps, never be revealed in all its naked truth.* But we know at least this much: on the morning of the 1st of July, Durand was writing a telegram to Lord Elphinstone, when the sound of firing was heard.† It was a startling surprise to him, for the

* Colonel Durand was of opinion that the arrest of General Woodburn's column, which had been ordered to march on Mhow, brought affairs to a crisis; and this is extremely probable. Note the following: "When Lord Elphinstone notified by telegram the countermand of the advance of Woodburn's column, and asked me the probable effect on my charge—*i.e.*, Central India—I replied at once that I could not answer one hour for Central India, when it became known that Woodburn's column was not to advance to Mhow. Unfortunately the contents of the telegram were known in Indore as soon as it arrived, and, being immediately followed by bad news from Delhi, Holkar's troops and city rose, attacked the Residency, &c., &c."—*MS. Memorandum by Colonel Durand.*

† Mr. McMahon and Mr. Butler, and some of the East Indian writers and Telegraph people, were killed. The following account of the Indore mutiny and massacre is borrowed from the letter of an eye-witness, published in a contemporary journal: "The slaughter of the inhabitants of the British Civil Station of Indore by the mutinous troops of Holkar commenced at eight o'clock A.M. on

guns which were roaring out their menaces, were some guns of Holkar's Artillery, which had been brought down, at his own request, for the defence of the Residency and the treasure. It was soon ascertained that they had opened fire upon the pickets of the Bhopal Cavalry, and on the tents of the Bhopal Infantry. Colonel Travers, who commanded the Bhopal Contingent, was soon in the saddle; but with the exception of half a dozen troopers, nearly all Sikhs, his Cavalry would not follow him, when he rode forward to charge the guns. It is a miracle that his life was spared. His horse was shot; the slings of his sword-belt were cut through, but he escaped both the grape-shot and the sabres of his assailants. The Infantry of the Bhopal Contingent were equally inactive. They refused to fire on the enemy—that is, upon those who had fired upon them; but levelled their pieces at the European sergeants, and seemed to be eager for the blood of their officers. Two guns of the Bhopal Contingent were loyally worked; but they made little impression

1857. July 1

the 1st instant. Three guns and the troops sent down by the Rajah for the protection of the Residency were the first to turn against us in the most unexpected and unprovoked manner; nor was the work of murder and destruction stayed until about twenty of the Christian residents had been slaughtered, and the pillage of the Government treasury, as well as the demolition of *all* public and private buildings had been accomplished. The Post Office was one of the first buildings attacked, and the wife, daughter-in-law, and child of the Postmaster, Mr. Beauvais, were shot down in their carriage whilst attempting to escape, before the eyes of the unhappy gentleman and his son, who providentially escaped unhurt amidst volleys of musketry. The following are the names of all those who are known to have escaped in safety from Indore: Colonel and Mrs. Durand; Colonel Travers; Colonel Stockley; Captain Ludlow; Captain Cobbe and wife; Captain Magniac and wife; Captain Waterman; Mrs. Captain Robertson and two children; Dr. Thompson; Mrs. Dutton; Lieut. and Mrs. Shakespeare and child; Dr. and Mrs. Rice; Dr. and Mrs. Knapp; and Messrs. Crawley, Hammond, Galloway, O'Brien, and Collins, of the Electric Telegraph Department."

1857. July 1. on the mutineers; and everything seemed to be against us.*

Departure of the English from Indore. So Durand determined to gather up his people, and to fly from Indore. "Finding," he wrote, "that the Cavalry, who were loyal, though disordered and out of control, would be off on their own score, I very unwillingly gave the order to retire; and, mounting the ladies on the gun waggons, we made an orderly retreat, bringing off every European they had not killed, during the first surprise, and covered our withdrawal with the Bheel corps and the Cavalry of the Bhopal Contingent. The ladies went off from the Residency under a fire of grape from Holkar's guns, followed by a few farewell round-shots—but no damage was done to any of the riders on the waggons, though some had the pleasure of seeing their property burning before they got clear of the Residency."† It was the saddest hour of that brave man's life. "First," he wrote, some time afterwards, "came the humiliation of being forced to withdraw before an enemy that I despised, and who, could I have got anything to fight, would have been easily beaten back. As it was, with only fourteen Golun-

* The conduct of our auxiliaries in this conjuncture may be narrated in Colonel Durand's words: "I never expected to witness such wretched treachery and cowardice as drove us from Indore. . . . The Bhopal and Mehidpore Contingent Infantry would not fire a shot, or obey an order, and threatened to shoot their European officers. The Bhopal Contingent Cavalry never recovered the surprise, were panic-stricken, and from the first quite beyond the control of their officers. As for the Bheels, as fast as I put them behind pillars, or bays of windows, under cover for defence of the Residency, the moment my back was turned, or that of their own European officer, they used to collect together in the centre rooms." . . . "We could have repulsed the attack on the 1st easily, if we had had anything that could fight. But the Bhopal Contingent and Mehidpore Contingent fraternised with Holkar's troops. The Sikh Horse would neither form nor fight, and the only thing they thought of was keeping out of fire and bolting. It was the most painfully disgusting affair I ever underwent."—*MS. Correspondence.*

† Colonel Durand to Lord Elphinstone—Sehore, July 4.—*MS. Correspondence.*

dauze who would stand by their guns, we not only 1857.
held our own for about a couple of hours, but beat July 1.
back their guns and gained temporary advantage." So that "we retired unmolested in the face of superior masses, whose appetite for blood had been whetted by the murder of unarmed men, women, and children. Of all the bitter, bitter days of my life, I thought this the worst, for I never had to retreat, still less to order a retreat myself, and though the game was up, and to have held on was to insure the slaughter of those I had no right to expose to such a fate without an adequate hope or object, still my pride as a soldier was wounded beyond all expression, and I would have been thankful had any one shot me."*

Meanwhile, in the British Cantonment of Mhow, the Native troops, whom Colonel Platt had so greatly trusted, were in the first throes of rebellion. Hungerford, in contemplation of the rising of the Native troops, had urged the Colonel in the month of June, to allow him to take his battery on to the open plain, where they could be immediately manned and prepared for action. This had been granted; but when he further proposed that an artillery gun should be placed at the Fort Gate, and that shelter should be found behind its walls for our women and children, the old confidence cry was repeated. Self-assured of the loyalty of the Sepoys, the Commandant had refused to sanction a measure which might seem to imply suspicion of the fidelity of his men. The guns were parked in front of the barracks, but nothing

* Colonel Durand to Lord Lovaine, September 29, 1857.—*MS. Correspondence.*

1857. July 1. more had been done for our safety, when Hungerford received orders on the 1st of July to march down on Indore, as Holkar's regiments were in rebellion. In a little while his guns were clattering down to the capital.* As no escort had been ordered, two men for each gun and waggon were armed with muskets and mounted on the limbers. But Hungerford had not proceeded more than half-way to Indore, when he met a trooper of the Bhopal Cavalry bringing a pencil-note from Colonel Travers, stating that Durand and other Europeans had evacuated the Residency, and were retreating upon Sehore. The trooper added that Durand had not gone to Mhow, because the Cantonment was in Holkar's dominions, and an attack on our Cantonments was meditated in the course of the night. So the battery was counter-marched, and returned to the Cantonment of Mhow.

Then Hungerford went straightway to the Commandant and met him on the road. Having communicated the strange news, which had reached him on the route to Indore, he besought Colonel Platt to allow him to take his battery into the Fort, as he could defend the place for any time until succours should arrive. But Platt could not be brought to listen to the proposal. Consent was emphatically refused. And so the day wore on; and Hungerford, in spite of frequent refusals, continued persistently to

Mutiny at Mhow.

advocate this course. The day was one of doubt and fear. Even the Commandant, as the shades of evening fell upon Mhow, began to think that he might have been mistaken. He then gave a reluctant assent to the movement, which had been so often pressed upon him; and Hungerford took his battery into the Fort. At this time there were manifest

* See Colonel Durand's statement, *post*, page 344.

signs of an approaching crisis. The mess-house of the Twenty-third was on fire. Other buildings in the Cantonments were blazing and breaking through the darkness of the night. This was ever the old signal for the commencement of action; and soon the ominous sound of firing came from the direction of the Lines. At nine Colonel Platt was writing to Durand, "All right, both Cavalry and Infantry very *khoosh* (happy) and willing." At ten o'clock they were in the spasms of revolt. The delusion was suddenly dispersed. Platt mounted his horse, rode into the Fort, and ordered Hungerford to turn out his guns. He then, accompanied by Adjutant Fagan, rode for the Lines. At the Quarter-Guard he drew rein, and began to address his men. His appeal was cut short by a volley from the faithful Twenty-third; and both the Colonel and the Adjutant fell from their horses, riddled with balls. About the same time Major Harris of the First Cavalry was fired upon by a party of his troopers, deliberately told off for the purpose. The first volley killed his horse. Regaining his legs, he attempted to escape through the darkness—but he was shot down, and then gashed to death by the sabres of his own men. These were the only murders of the night. Other officers had marvellous escapes.

1857. July

Meanwhile Hungerford had been getting his guns ready for action. The process was slower than it would have been, if men and horses had not been wearied by the march and counter-march of the morning. Still, there was but slight delay on the part of Hungerford's gunners. The Artillery Captain had always said that it would take but little time and trouble for him to crush any insurrection of the Native troops, that might confront him at Mhow;

1857. July. and now he went forth, confident of the result. But the difficulty was to find the enemy. As he made for the Lines, half a mile distant from the Fort, he was fired upon through the darkness, but he could not perceive his assailants. The bungalows of the English officers were in a blaze; but the Lines were in total obscurity. He was perplexed, too, by seeing nothing of the Commandant, from whom he had expected to receive orders. He did, therefore, the best thing that could be done. He opened fire upon the Lines. The roar of the guns frightened the Sepoys, Cavalry and Infantry; and they streamed out on the road to Indore, where they fraternised with Holkar's mutinous regiments, clamoured for the blood of our Christian people, and gutted the British Treasury. "Next day their Lines (at Mhow) were found full of their clothes, cooking vessels, &c., and many muskets, coats, &c., were found scattered for a great distance all over the country."* They had fled from our guns in a state of panic and bewilderment. Grape and canister were not to their liking.

Hungerford was now master of the situation. He was the senior officer at Mhow, and right gladly he took the command. The first thing that he did, after burying the bodies of the murdered officers, was to proclaim Martial Law "throughout the station." His first impression was that Holkar might be leagued with the mutineers. Ominous reports reached him, which he did not, over hastily, accept; but for a little space they enfeebled his former strong faith in the Maharajah. So he wrote to Holkar saying, "I understand from many Natives that you have given food to the mutinous troops. I have heard also, but I do not know whether to believe,

* Captain Hungerford's Report to Government, July 17, 1873.

that you have lent them guns and offered them Irregular Cavalry, as assistance. These reports are very probably much exaggerated. I do not believe them. You owe so much to the British, and can be so utterly ruined by showing enmity towards them, that I do not believe that you can be so blind to your own interest as to afford aid and show friendship to the enemies of the British Government." To this Holkar promptly replied: "The accounts, which you seem to have received of my assistance to the enemies of the British Government are, as you suppose, not only exaggerated but entirely false. No one regrets more than I do the heart-rending catastrophes, which befel at Indore and at Mhow. . . . . I have not, even in a dream, ever deviated from the path of friendship and allegiance to the British Government. I know their sense of justice and honour will make them pause before they suspect, even for a moment, a friendly chief, who is so sensible of the obligations that he owes to them, and is ready to do anything for them. But there are catastrophes in the world, which cannot be controlled, and the one that has happened is one of them."* Having written, or caused this to be written, Holkar sent two confidential officers to Mhow to explain all the circumstances of the outbreak of the 1st of July; and Hungerford was satisfied and assured.

1857. July.

July 12.

Conduct of Captain Hungerford.

But it was hard to say what might not happen. No tidings came from Durand. All recognised political authority had swept itself out of the Indore territory. The brave Artilleryman, who had taken

* In this letter Holkar says that the mutineers demanded the heads of a few Europeans, whom he had concealed in the Palace. "I had no alternative," added the Maharajah, "but to offer them my own person, but I would not allow the poor Europeans to be touched before being killed myself."

1857. July. the reins into his own hands, took upon himself the diplomatic, as well as the military, control of affairs. He garrisoned and victualled the Fort. He blew up the magazines in the Lines. He planted guns in the embrasures of the Fort. He prepared himself to stand a month's siege. And he waited for orders—but he waited in vain. No orders came. He wrote to Durand at Sehore—but he received no answers to his letters. So he established himself as representative of the Governor-General in Holkar's dominion, and opened a correspondence with the nearest Government—that of Lord Elphinstone at Bombay. He was one of those men, who, little thought of in quiet times, when opportunities were wanting, rose with the occasion and went boldly to the front. He did what he had "no right to do," and he was afterwards severely rebuked by Durand. But History, rising above all official formalities, must pronounce, that the men who did what they had "no right to do," were those who saved the British Government in India.

Bearing of Holkar. But what was Holkar doing all this time? The roar of the guns surprised him as much as it surprised Durand, and perhaps it bewildered him still more. He could not understand what it portended. He did not know what to do. He knew that some of his guns had opened fire, but for what purpose, and in what direction, was not clearly known to him. All the inmates of the Palace were in the wildest state of tumult and confusion. First one story, then another, was brought to him. No one could give him any clear insight into this most unexpected and most mysterious ebullition. It might have been directed against the English, or it might have been directed against himself. That in the first hour of the outbreak, he was astounded and paralysed is certain. But no one can have followed me so far in this history of the Sepoy War without discerning the patent, the obstreperous truth that English soldiers and statesmen of the highest rank, were sometimes bewildered and paralysed when first the storm burst upon them. If, in the sudden confusion, when there were runnings to and fro at the Palace, and the reports of one man set at naught the reports of another, Holkar thought more of himself and the Raj than of Durand and the British Agency;* he did only that which in like circumstances, any Englishman would have done. His first duty was to his Raj, which he believed to be as much imperilled as the lives of the little cluster of Englishmen at his Court. But before the Maharajah had time to recover himself from the first confusion and stupor of this sudden outbreak, Durand had fled from Indore—no one seemed to know whither.

1857. July.

Still Holkar did not despair; he knew that his face was irretrievably blackened in the eyes of the representative of the British Government at his capital. For Durand could justify his own departure, only by proving the consummate treachery

* Holkar's own words are, "The tumult and confusion which prevailed were such, and alarm and fear so great, that it was impossible to procure an account of what had actually happened. I was utterly ignorant of what had brought about the outbreak, never entertaining for a moment the most distant idea that any troops, which had been posted at the Residency for its protection, had themselves proved mutinous. The first moment that I received even some confused intelligence of what was going on I ordered my Sowarree and was on the point of proceeding to you at once, but at that moment I learnt that you had left the Residency. I never dreamed, could never have dreamed, for one instant that you could have imbibed the shadow of a suspicion against me, or that the attack could have been directed by my orders."

1857. July. of Holkar. Less than two hours had intervened between the first outburst of the guns and the evacuation of the Residency. It must have been a crisis of extraordinary magnitude that compelled the precipitate retreat of so brave and so wise a man with the best blood of England in his veins. All this the Maharajah knew to be fatally against him; but he knew also, that whatsoever might have been done, or not done, during those two delirious hours, there was yet time for him to prove his loyalty to the British Government by casting in his lot with them. And he did it. In what manner will presently be told.

Scarcely had the representative of the British Government turned his back upon Indore, when Holkar, having recovered from the first surprise and confusion attending that most unexpected outburst, began by many outward acts, not to be misunderstood or misinterpreted, to demonstrate his fidelity to the paramount power of India. A few Europeans were still left alive in Indore. The Maharajah concealed them in the Palace, and the insurgents sent to him demanding their heads and those also of some Durbar officers supposed to be friendly to the British. They called on Holkar to come forth and show himself, and he rode out amongst them. They clamoured loudly, but their demands were resolutely rejected. He offered them his own person—but he would not suffer an Englishman to be hurt. They called upon him to place himself at their head, and to lead them against the English. They reminded him of the martial character of his great ancestor, Jeswant Rao, and taunted him with cowardice; but even this did not move him to join the ranks of our enemies. He told the insurgents that it was no part of the traditions of his family that they should murder women and children. He stood out boldly against all the entreaties and all the threats of his own soldiery, and then rode back to the Palace. 1857. July

Already had the Maharajah addressed letters, on the day of the outbreak, to Colonel Durand and to Lord Elphinstone, assuring them of his fidelity, and he urged the immediate advance of the Bombay troops, under General Woodburn, for the suppression of disorder, and the pacification of the country. He gathered up the remains of the English treasure, and sent it under safe escort to Hungerford at Mhow. He sent thither also his own money and jewels, and Government securities and other property, and he despatched his most confidential servants to Hungerford to assure the British officers that he was as true as steel. And of this, the stout-hearted Artilleryman, who had doubted at first, was now fully convinced.

With sore distress and dismay the Maharajah heard that Captain Hutchinson, who held the post of Bheel Agent, under the Indore Resident, had been taken prisoner, with his family, by the Amjheera Rajah, and was confined in his fort. Mrs. Hutchinson was a daughter of Sir Robert Hamilton, and it was in no strain of Oriental hyperbole that the Maharajah declared that he regarded her "as his sister, and the whole family as his relations," for he looked up to Hamilton with filial reverence and affection. So he determined to send out a detachment for their rescue. Amjheera was tributary to Scindiah and to Holkar, therefore, was as foreign country. So he sought instructions from Hungerford, who promptly took upon himself the political responsibility. But Hutchinson and his party were not in captivity.

1857. July. They were at Bhopawur, with other Europeans connected with the Bheel Corps, at the time of the Indore revolt, tidings of which reached them on the 2nd of July, with the addition that Holkar had placed himself at the head of the insurgents. All the smaller chiefs in the neighbourhood were ripe for revolt, and this startling intelligence from Indore made them eager for the affray. At first Hutchinson thought that he could defend himself and his people with the help of a party of loyal Bheels, but this hope soon passed away from him, and he saw no chance of safety but in flight. And even that was doubtful and precarious. They went forth disguised as a party of Parsee merchants, with their families, on the way to Baroda, and made a perilous journey to Jubooah, where they were hospitably entertained by the young chief and his family, who were of good old Rajpoot stock, and would never betray those who had sought sanctuary with them. When this was known, the detachment, which Holkar had sent out, was recalled, and an escort sent forward to bring our people to Indore. "I had such implicit faith in Holkar's friendship," wrote Hutchinson, "that I did not hesitate to place myself and family under the protection of his troops, for the purpose of proceeding to Indore to assume charge of the Residency, during the absence of Colonel Durand, and by my presence and advice to assure and guide Holkar through the crisis." Thus was Hungerford relieved from the political responsibility, which he had undertaken with so much promptitude and acquitted himself of with so much address.

Question of the retreat from Mhow.

Reviewing, after a lapse of years, without prejudice or affection, this question of the retreat from Indore, it appears to me that the grounds upon which the abandonment of the Residency is to be justified are these, as set forth by Durand's friends: "That Holkar's force, which had opened fire on the Residency and attacked our people, and which Holkar was either unable or unwilling to control, were numerous and well-equipped—that the Residency was a building not calculated for purposes of defence—that some of the Contingent troops would not act against the enemy, and that the remainder were too few to resist them—that, by withdrawing at once, and falling back upon such support as he could find elsewhere, he would maintain the independence of the authority which he represented, and would be able to make his influence better felt by the several chieftains under his agency, and even by Holkar himself." The force of these considerations may be readily admitted. But it is added—"that no succour could be obtained from Mhow, where mutiny was known to be imminent, and, in fact, took place on the same day; the mutinous troops marching to Indore and plundering the Government Treasury;" and that "had Colonel Durand decided to remain, he could not possibly have withstood the combined attack of Holkar's troops and the Mhow mutineers. It could only have been by Holkar's being able and willing to control his own troops, and to use them against the Mhow mutineers, that the Residency could have been held." It is evident, however, from what has been already related, that succours from Mhow of the most serviceable kind were available; for Hungerford's European battery was rattling towards Indore, when news met it that Colonel Durand and all his people had departed. Had it

1857. July.

1857. July. arrived whilst the Residency was still occupied, the rising at Indore would most probably have been suppressed, and there would have been no combination of Holkar's troops with the Mhow mutineers. The Sepoys at Mhow were encouraged to revolt by the knowledge that nothing had been done to put down the insurrection at Indore. The evacuation of the Residency naturally caused it to be believed that Holkar was on the side of the insurgents. To have held on for a few hours would have given time for the Maharajah to recover from his first bewilderment, and to declare himself on our side, and it would have brought Hungerford and his battery to Indore.

To this Colonel Durand's answer was—in a letter written to Mr. Talbot, Lord Canning's Private Secretary, on the 16th of August—"I see, by the *Friend of India* of the 30th of July, that that paper, taking up the tone of a letter written from Mhow, talks of my inopportune flight, and repeats the nonsense and mis-statements about Hungerford's proceedings when shut up with the writer of the letter—a Captain Trower, of the Twenty-third Native Infantry—in the Mhow Fort. I should wish the Governor-General to know that Hungerford's battery — though my note to Colonel Platt, despatched from Indore at a quarter to nine, reached Colonel Platt by a quarter to ten—was not ready to move until noon, by the statement of its own officers. It then advanced to Indore at a trot, and had gone to the half-way village of Rao, where obtaining information that we had left Indore, Hungerford returned at a gallop or canter the whole way, and dashed with his battery straight into the Fort at three P.M.—the moment he arrived. Had he continued his course to Indore at the rate he moved away from Mhow, it would have been four P.M. at least before he reached the Residency, for they did not canter out. I retired from the Residency, after a two hours' cannonade, about half past ten."* That is three-quarters of an hour after the call for the battery reached Mhow. Now the battery could not have been equipped, mounted, and brought down to Indore, at full gallop, in three-quarters of an hour. So it is clear that Colonel Durand did not await even the possibility of the arrival, under the most favourable circumstances, of Hungerford and his guns. Indeed, Captain Hungerford's statement is that at eleven A.M. Colonel Platt called on him with a letter from Colonel Durand, begging that the battery under his command might be sent to Indore instantly. "I marched," added Hungerford, "my battery at once on Indore."† So it appears that Hungerford did not get his orders till after Durand had quitted the capital. 1857. July.

It is to the honour of Lord Elphinstone, whose whole conduct, as Governor of Bombay, during this momentous period, was distinguished by as much energy as sagacity, that he supported Hungerford throughout all his irregularities. There is a natural disposition on the part of Governors, where there is an official conflict, to side with the higher authority. Durand, at this time, had a great reputation throughout India. Hungerford was an unknown man—merely a Captain of Artillery—who, in the ordinary routine of regimental duty, had been sent to command a battery at Mhow. But Elphinstone could not resist the conviction that Durand had hastily condemned Holkar, and by his flight from Lord Elphinstone. July.

* MS. Correspondence.

† Captain Hungerford to Adjutant-General, Bombay, July 4, 1857.

1857. July. Indore, had brought matters to this issue—that either the Maharajah was a traitor, or that the British Agent had fled, without good cause, from Indore. That the Governor of Bombay, with all the facts before him, came to the latter conclusion, is certain. At Calcutta, where only the main outline of events was known, the honoured Patriarch of the Political Service, then a member of the Supreme Government, wrote that if the story of the abandonment of Indore were true, Durand ought to be removed from political employment. This was merely a first impression. What I have written will show Durand's reasons for the movements—which Lord Elphinstone could not endorse. But admitting that the sudden retreat was justifiable—or even commendable—I can see nothing to justify the after-treatment of Holkar by the Acting-Resident at Indore. There can be no question that Holkar was sacrificed to the justification of Durand.

Durand and Holkar.

It is certain that in the brief interval between the first thunder of the guns, and the flight from the Residency, there was no time to ascertain, and no attempts made to inquire into the position of affairs, and to investigate the cause of the unexpected explosion. Durand had been warned by Holkar that the Durbar could not rely on the fidelity of their troops. This was not a proof of treachery. But on the 4th of July he wrote to Lord Elphinstone, saying, "The storm burst upon us earlier than I suspected, and from a quarter where gratitude and every other consideration rendered it most improbable. . . . No surprise could have been more complete, as Holkar's guns were there to aid in the defence of the Residency and the Treasury. The Cavalry never recovered from the surprise caused by Holkar's treachery.

Scindiah and Holkar appear to be allies. Scindiah's treachery, if there was any, never was palpable—but Holkar's has been of the true Mahratta stamp." It was Durand's argument, persistently repeated, that a Native Prince is responsible for the conduct of his troops. Whether this opinion be sound or unsound, as applied to ordinary times and circumstances, Justice and Policy should have dictated, at such a period of our history, entire reticence on this question of responsibility. For the great military revolt of 1857 was conceived, born, and developed in our own provinces. Our own disciplined troops led the way to the terrible revolts which convulsed and agonised the country. In the Native States the contagion of rebellion was caught from the Company's Army. It is scarcely to be doubted that the Sepoys of our own regiments at Mhow contaminated Holkar's troops at Indore. But blinded by that intense national self-love, of which I have so often spoken, Durand, like many other good men, could not discern the fact, that the great burden of responsibility for all these troubles was upon our own shoulders. He saw through a glass darkly our own errors and short-comings, but those of the Native States, face to face, or through a magnifying glass of enormous power. He knew that by some negligence or mismanagement of our own, we had set our house on fire and allowed the flames to spread; but when the fire, which we ought to have extinguished, extended to our neighbours, he held them responsible for the conflagration.

1857. July.

The Confiscation of Dhar.

With what tenacity he clung to this doctrine was exemplified by the manner in which, not long afterwards, he treated the petty state of Dhar, when its mercenary troops, in the first days of the minority

1857. July. of the young Rajah, went into rebellion. He recommended the sequestration or the annexation of that ancient principality on the ground of the responsibility of the Durbar. And this most unjust and impolitic sentence would have been executed, but for the interposition of the Court of Directors of the East India Company, who wrote to the Government of India, saying, "We cannot consistently punish this or any other weak state for its inability to control its troops, when it is patent to the whole world that the more powerful states of Gwalior and Indore, and even the British Government itself, were unable to control theirs."*

After long and most deliberate consideration of all the circumstances of Holkar's conduct in that first week of July, I cannot resist the conviction, that he was thoroughly true to the British Government. The charge against him is that within two hours from the time when he was first startled by the roar of the guns, he had not assured the British Agent that he was in nowise concerned in the hostile movement. Durand was new to his work. If he had any knowledge of the Mahratta character it was only a half-knowledge. He had an obscure notion that all Mahrattas were by nature treacherous. But he did not fathom their treachery. He did not seem to know that from the days of Sivajee down to the time of Doondoo Punt, Nana Sahib, a Mahratta has always been most dangerous when simulating friendship. If Holkar had

* I do not know why Mr. Dickenson should so frequently, notwithstanding numerous proofs to the contrary, have called the despatch, from which the above passage is quoted, "Lord Stanley's despatch." I do not question that Lord Stanley, always just and logical, entertained the opinions thus expressed—but the passage was written and sent to India before Lord Stanley was appointed Secretary of State. I ought to be accepted as an authority upon this point of History—as I drafted the despatch myself, for the Court of Directors.

premeditated the attack on the Residency, he would have had a messenger ready to be despatched to Durand to assure the representative of the British Government of his loyalty. That this was not done, within the two first hours of the all-prevailiug confusion, seems to indicate that Holkar was as much surprised as Durand. So strongly impressed was Lord Elphinstone with the conviction that the Maharajah was true to us, that he wrote to Lord Canning on the 13th of July, saying, "It seems clearly proved that Holkar was not implicated in the outbreak. He was unable to control his own troops, who were probably set on by the Bengal Sepoys at Mhow, and who attacked and plundered the Residency. Colonel Durand appears to be under the impression that Holkar had turned against us, and that he was attacked by his orders. This, however, is certainly not the case. On the same evening Holkar wrote to Colonel Durand and to me, protesting his innocence and entreating that the march of General Woodburn's force should be hastened as much as possible."* And some days afterwards he wrote to Colonel Durand, saying, "I am led to believe that you still entertain doubts of Holkar. All that has happened during your absence from Indore tends to acquit him of having been a party to the attack on the Residency. Indeed, if he had been ill-disposed towards us, the whole country would have risen. All the smaller chiefs seem to take their cue from him; and even to the borders of Gujerat, the effects of his conduct would have been apparent. . . . . This comes to me from too many sources to admit of a doubt . . . . . Let me, therefore, beg you not

1857. July.

July 23. 1857

* MS. Correspondence of Lord Elphinstone. He wrote also in the same strain to Vernon Smith on the 14th.

1857. July. to harbour any prejudices against Holkar, to whom I cannot but think that we are very much indebted for the preservation of the peace in Malwa, and also in Gujerat."*

But the prejudice never was overcome in the high places of the Supreme Government. Years passed and he was still more or less a suspect. The Star of India was conferred on him; but that which is most coveted by all as the highest honour—a grant of territory—was withheld from him though granted to Scindiah. He seems never to have recovered from this slight. Meanwhile he saw Durand elevated to the highest offices under the State—Foreign Secretary to Government—Member of Council—Lieutenant-Governor of the Punjab. One of the ablest men and best public servants that India has ever seen, and held deservedly in the highest honour even by those who differed from him in opinion. But we have still to mourn the fact that when the crown of his ambition was gained, Sir Henry Marion Durand died disastrously, in the prime of his life and the fulness of his reputation.

Another pregnant source of anxiety to the Lieutenant-Governor was the condition of that vast tract of country inhabited by the Rajwarrah races, and ruled by a great cluster of Rajpoot chiefs—sympathising little with each other, and many of them living in continual strife with the chief people of the principality—the "Thakoors"—whom they were supposed to govern. There was small chance of these Rajpoot chieftains sympathising with a movement,

* MS. Correspondence of Lord Elphinstone.

which if not in its origin a Mahomedan movement, had culminated in the recognition of the King of Delhi as the sovereign ruler of India. They had, on the whole, been well treated by the British Government, and were grateful in their own way.* But in all parts of the country were turbulent elements of one kind or another, and inconsistencies and discordances were as nothing when there was a common belief to be encouraged—a common object to be gained. In Rajpootana, as elsewhere, there was a prevailing faith that it was the intention of the British Government to destroy the religion of the country; and some openly talked of the restoration of the *Badshah*.† All this was mere ignorance, and nothing was ever likely to come of it. But there was real cause of alarm in the fact that the legions of the great Rajpoot chiefs were composed very much of the same materials as our own Sepoy regiments. They were commanded by officers of our own army—but that had already been shown to be no safeguard. The probability of their breaking into rebellion, when time and opportunity should serve, was too patent to be disregarded by the statesmen of Agra, and they watched the event with the deepest concern.

1857. July.

The Governor-General's Agent in Rajpootana was Colonel George Fitzpatrick Lawrence, brother of Sir Henry Lawrence, whom he had succeeded in that important charge. He had seen more hazardous service and taken part in more exciting adventures than any officer in the country. Hair-breadth es-

* A short time before the outbreak of the mutinies, a report was circulated and published in the Indian papers to the effect that the Rajpoot States were to be annexed. I believe it to have been a malicious, as it was a very mischievous lie. I obtained the permission of the Court of Directors to contradict it on authority.

† See Prichard's "Mutinies in Rajpootana," p. 182.

1857. July. capes from death and long captivities seemed to be his portion. But he bore himself gallantly with a stout heart, a strong frame, and a noble spirit in every way worthy of the name he bore. He was doing his duty well in Rajpootana, when news reached him, on the 19th of May, of the commencement of our troubles. He wrote at once to all the principal officers under his control, urging upon them precautionary measures to be promptly executed. He called for a light field-force from Deesa; and he pressed the Governor of Bombay to send up to Agra, by way of Gujerat and Rajpootana, "all available European troops returning from Persia." But a stronger hand had already been laid upon those troops. They were needed for other more pressing service than the defence of the North-Western capital. Lawrence then issued a proclamation to all the chiefs of Rajpootana calling upon them "to preserve peace within their borders, to intercept rebel fugitives, and to collect their followers on the frontiers." "This," says Lawrence, "was promptly replied to, and in one instance (Jouhdpore) anticipated by the most friendly assurances and promises of aid."*

It is a striking instance of the fact commented upon in an earlier portion of this narrative—the fact that well-nigh every man in authority thought only of the safety of his own immediate charge and of what could be done to insure it, regardless of the interests of others, or of the general welfare of the State—that the Lieutenant-Governor, who had authority over the Governor-General's Agent in Rajpootana, called upon Lawrence early in June "to march with all the European troops, officers, and

* Report of Brigadier-General Lawrence, July 27, 1858.

treasure he could collect, upon Agra, for the defence of that place."* It is impossible to conceive a wilder project than this, or one which would have been more fatal to British interests, if forced into execution. Lawrence was startled by the demand. But he was never for a moment doubtful of the direction in which lay his duty to the State. He would not abandon his charge. Like his brothers, Henry and John, he did not shrink from taking any responsibility upon himself. He saw clearly what would ensue in Rajpootana, if the whole country were evacuated by the British officers, whose influence in such an emergency was all to which we could trust for keeping the chiefs true to their allegiance, and holding the contingents in check. Such a movement, he said, would entail upon us the loss of Ajmere, with its important arsenal and stores, and lead to a general rise in Rajpootana. Representations to this effect, the force of which it was impossible not to recognise, had the expected result. Colvin saw that he had been wrong, and he did not enforce his request. Indeed, he soon perceived that it was his duty to strengthen Lawrence's hands, so he gave him entire command of the troops by appointing him a Brigadier-General.

1857. May—June.

And under George Lawrence worked a noble staff of officers. There was Major William Eden, Political Agent at Jyepore, a man of commanding presence; active and energetic in troubled times—firm, prudent, and sagacious in hours of peace. It may truly be said of him that he was the very backbone of Lawrence's Staff. Then there was Captain Charles Showers, our agent at Oodeypore, a man in whom

* "Reminiscences of Forty-three Years in India," by Lieut.-General Sir George Lawrence, K.C.S.I., C.B.

1857. May—June. some fine qualities were united, but who, lacking others essential to a political officer, marred what he might have made a brilliant career. He had high courage, unquestionable ability, and a rare gift of speech. But he wanted judgment and discretion—especially that kind of discretion which recognises subordination as the main principle of all service and never gives way to the practical egotism, which men of strong convictions are, in defiance of authority, so prone to indulge. Then there was Captain Monck-Mason, Political Agent at Joudhpore—a man shrewd and sagacious, of a firm, well-balanced mind, but not incapable of rising to any height of daring, if strenuous action should be demanded from him. These were our British representatives at the principal ancient courts of Rajpootana. Beneath them were a cluster of younger political officers—many of great promise, who did their duty well and bravely in the emergency that had then risen.

But the most distinguished officer, connected with Rajpootana, was Colonel Dixon, of the Bengal Artillery, who now lay dying at Beawur. He had reclaimed Mhairwarrah from the state of lawlessness and barbarism in which he had found it many years before. The Mhairs were then little better than savages; he had reformed and civilised them. By gentle, kindly measures—by advice and persuasion—by conferring benefits on the people, teaching them what were their true interests, and showing them the blessedness of peace, he had gradually weaned them from their savage habits and converted what had before been a great congeries of robber-clans into a prosperous, thriving community. It was with mingled astonishment and admiration that the Mhairs had witnessed the vast improvement of their country—

and, as years passed, they also continued to improve and never again fell back into their evil ways. And now this wise and good man, stricken in years, lay sick unto death, with all this great turmoil about him. But he felt in his inmost heart that his Mhairs would be true to the Government which had so befriended them. A Mhairwarrah Battalion of trusty fighting men had been formed long ago; and of all the troops in Rajpootana they were those on whom we could most confidently rely. "Do you think," they answered, when an attempt was made to tamper with them, "that we will war against the Government which raised us from the dust and made us what we now are?" Dixon died; and, amidst the clang of arms, little notice was taken of the peaceful end of a man of peace; but he left behind him an abiding monument of his good deeds, such as few have ever reared in India. He did not live to see the staunch loyalty with which the Mhairs followed us everywhere to the battle—but he never doubted it and he died content. 1857. May—June.

The great Meywar chief—the Maharana of Oodeypore—was the acknowledged head of the Rajpoot Confederacy. The traditional veneration in which he was held, caused the other chiefs, in this crisis, to turn their thoughts towards Oodeypore, in expectancy of some sign or portent aiding them the better to shape their own measures. It was not a propitious circumstance that George Lawrence, who had preceded Showers as Political Agent, had been involved in a sharp conflict with the Meywar Durbar, and had recommended military coercion, the deposition of the Maharana and the banishment of some of the principal chiefs under him. The policy then recommended might have been right or might have Oodeypore.

1857. May—June. been wrong. But, right or wrong, its tendency might have been to alienate the confidence, if not to excite the animosity of the Meywar Durbar in this conjuncture. So it happened, that either for this reason, or from a foregone conclusion, that no good thing could come out of Oodeypore, George Lawrence could not believe in the fidelity of the Maharana and the chiefs. But Showers, the Political Agent, though recognising the probabilities of an adverse tone and temper in the Durbar, in no way despaired of success. The Maharana consented to meet him on the margin of the beautiful lake, with its glittering summer palace of white marble, and crossed over to an appointed place in one of his covered gondolas. "The result of this interview," wrote Showers, "was the Maharana giving in his open and declared adhesion to the British cause, and practically proving it by placing the most trustworthy troops at my disposal to take the field, sending his highest chiefs present at the capital and Durbar-officers to accompany me, and calling by proclamation on the loyal chiefs and district officers to afford every aid in our operations."

Whilst still at Oodeypore, tidings came to Showers of the mutiny at Neemuch, and the flight of our people. Barnes of the Artillery and Rose of the Infantry rode into the Residency and reported that a party of more than forty fugitives, women and children included, were gathered together in a village about fifty miles distant. Showers at once made his arrangements to start that night, accompanied by Barnes, with a party of Meywar Horse, for the prompt delivery of the captives. He found them in the last state of destitution—stricken by want and disease—sharing their place of refuge with cattle. He then placed them under the charge of the Rao of Bedla, whom the Maharana had sent with Showers as the most trusted of His Highness's chiefs, whilst he himself pushed on in pursuit of the Neemuch mutineers. The fugitives were brought safely to the capital by the chivalrous Rajpoot, and were lodged in one of the beautiful island-palaces on the lake.

1857. May—June.

Jyepore.

No doubt seems to have been entertained about the fidelity of Jyepore. Eden placed himself at once in communication with the Durbar; and on the 17th of May he wrote to Mr. Colvin saying, "The Maharajah is ready to aid us with the troops to the utmost of his ability and means;" and again, "I feel assured that the Maharajah and the Sirdars will do all in their power to meet the wishes of our Government." At once they placed at Eden's disposal a large body of troops of all kinds, good and bad; the latter greatly preponderating; but it was not easy to decide what was to be done with them. At that moment, however, the moral effect of such a declaration in our favour was, perhaps, of more importance to us than the troops placed at our disposal. The Jyepore detachment under Eden were to protect the Agra frontiers, and he wrote to Colvin for orders; but it was not easy to give any definite instructions, when the agency to be employed was of so uncertain a character. It was eventually resolved that Eden with his five thousand Jyepore troops should march towards the Muttra and Goorgaon districts "to maintain order and aid in the re-establishment of the Civil Government." But it was apparent that the force had in it too large a number of Hindostanees to render success probable, and it soon appeared that they had been tampered with by a discarded minister of the Maharajah. So Lawrence was obliged to admit that

1857. May—June. the assigned "duties were not fully discharged," and Eden, whose personal bearing had been of the most heroic kind, was compelled, after rescuing some European fugitives, to return to Jyepore.

Meanwhile Monck-Mason was calling upon Joudhpore for assistance, and prompt compliance was returned to the requisition. There was no doubt of the fidelity of the Maharajah, but long-standing internal feuds had weakened the State, and there was small likelihood of united action. Some of the great Thakoors, not long before, had been in armed resistance to the Maharajah. He now placed at our disposal two thousand Horse and Foot and six guns, hoping almost against hope that they would be serviceable to us. "Thus in all June and within a fortnight of the receipt of intelligence of the attack," wrote George Lawrence, "were the troops of Bhurtpore, Jyepore, Joudhpore and Ulwar co-operating with us in the field."* All this looked well at the outset, and Colvin's anxieties were relieved for the present by the aspect of affairs; but he clearly discerned the fact that although the Rajpoot Princes had no complicity either in Mussulman or Mahratta intrigues, they gave their daughters in marriage to the House of Delhi, made obeisance to the Mogul and coined money in his name. What the result was will be told in a later chapter of this History.

* It will be seen that there is no mention of Oodeypore in this recital. Oodeypore was ignored and Showers was ignored. But both did right well at the outset. A previous suspicion in the one case and a subsequent sharp contention surely afforded no just ground for the display of antipathies in respect to what had nothing to do with either the one or the other.

CHAPTER IV.

AGRA IN JUNE AND JULY—FRESH ANXIETIES OF THE LIEUTENANT-GOVERNOR—THE STORY OF JHANSI—ADVANCE OF THE NEEMUCH BRIGADE—ILLNESS OF MR. COLVIN—THE PROVISIONAL GOVERNMENT—MUTINY OF THE KOTAH CONTINGENT—THE BATTLE BEFORE AGRA—RETREAT OF THE BRITISH FORCE—DESTRUCTION OF CANTONMENTS—LIFE IN THE FORT.

THE Agra regiments, having laid down their arms, departed peaceably, with money, lawfully their own, in their waistbands. Many are supposed to have gone straightway to their homes; others may have fallen in with their mutinous comrades, and, newly armed by them, gone forth to fight for the Padshah. Whatever may have been the manner in which they disposed of themselves, the Lieutenant-Governor had no more anxiety from that source. They were swept out of Agra and there was an end of them, for the present, as agents of mischief, and an end also of Colvin's anxieties with respect to threatenings of internal revolt. **1857. June.**

But there were many external sources of inquietude. Of the existing Native States within Colvin's circle—of their rulers and their armies—I have already written. Elsewhere were remnants of Native States—prostrate, down-trodden, whose ashes were

1857. June. still smouldering, whose fires a rude touch might at any moment revive. It was too much our wont, in the flush of our strength, in the pride of our egotism, to think that what it had pleased us to extinguish could never burst into a blaze again. But this was only one of our natural delusions. If there be one thing which the Natives of India thoroughly understand, it is the art of waiting. In their hearts, if not on their haunches, they sit *dhurna.* So it was in a Native State, of which I have written—a State our rulers had crushed. And the patience was more malignant, because the remains of sovereignty were represented by a woman.

Jhansi. June, 1857. Jhansi had been formerly a Native State. Lord Dalhousie had annexed it. It was, perhaps, the worst of all his annexations.* It was now to bear its bitter fruit. A pension of five thousand rupees a month, or six thousand pounds a year, had been offered to the Ranee, the widow of the last ruler. She had at first declined, but afterwards accepted, it; and property belonging to her late husband of the value of a lakh of rupees had been placed at her disposal and accepted. But she was thoroughly dissatisfied with her lot. Continuing to brood over the injury and the disgrace of Annexation, she hated the English with the deadliest hatred. And soon she began to cherish new-born grievances. Foremost among these was the killing of cattle by the English—an abomination in the eyes of her late subjects. On this injury she memorialised the British Government. The people of Jhansi did the same; but the answer was a repulse. Again, the Government were guilty of the extraordinary meanness of calling upon her to pay the debts of her late husband.

* In 1854—*ante,* vol. i. page 89 *et seq.*

The Ranee protested against this wrong—and Sir Robert Hamilton urged on Mr. Colvin compliance with Her Highness's request. But the Lieutenant-Governor was inexorable; and part of her pension was resumed or suspended. The Ranee pleaded, very reasonably, that as the debts were not her debts, she was not answerable for their payment out of her personal allowance, and she threatened to write to Government requesting permission to reside at Benares. I do not know what would have been the final issue; but the whole treatment of the Ranee was so ungenerous, and being ungenerous was so unwise, that Colvin must have shuddered, when he thought of the evil fruit that it was developing.* So her resentments grew stronger and stronger. A woman of masculine energy and feminine vindictiveness, she eagerly awaited the rising of the storm, well assured that her time would come. In 1857, she was a well-favoured woman of twenty-nine or thirty years of age. She was endowed with a keen intelligence — strong-minded and quick-witted—quite capable of discussing her affairs with a Commissioner or Governor. If she had any evil dispositions, she knew when to restrain the exhibition of them, and she tried to set bounds on her temper when conversing with a British officer. Evil things were said of her; for it is a custom among us *odisse quem læseris*—to take a Native ruler's king-

1857. June

* Scarcely less irritating as a thorn in the flesh was the following act of spoliation, the circumstances of which are thus recorded in Captain Pinkney's official narrative. "The temple of Luchmee, situated outside the walls to the east of Jhansee, had long been supported by the Native rulers of the country, and an ancestor of Gungahur Rao had made over the revenues of two villages for its support. When he died Captain Francis Gordon, Deputy Commissioner, recommended that this arrangement should continue, but it was ordered that the villages should be resumed. This was strongly objected to by the Ranee and the case again referred to Government, with the same result. But before the resumption order could be carried out the outbreak at Jhansee took place."

1857. May—June. dom and then to revile the deposed ruler or his would-be successor. It was alleged that the Ranee was a mere child under the influence of others, and that she was much given to intemperance. That she was not a mere child was demonstrated by her conversation; and her intemperance seems to be a myth.

The troops posted at Jhansi consisted of a wing of the Twelfth Regiment of Native Infantry, the head-quarters and right wing of the Fourteenth Irregular Cavalry, and a detachment of Golundauze. They were under the command of Captain Dunlop of the Twelfth. The Commissioner, who had held the appointment from the first day of Annexation, was Captain Alexander Skene. How it happened that the Political Officer did not perceive that there were few places in the country where it was necessary at such a time to be cautious and vigilant and mistrustful of every one, that place was Jhansi, it is impossible to conjecture. But it seems never to have been thought that there were any smouldering animosities in high places or in low places—never thought that there was any one within the boundaries of the Commissionership, which had so lately been a petty kingdom, whose interests or antipathies were to be gratified by the subversion of the British power.

May 18. Captain Skene. MS. Correspondence. Skene had no belief that it was the intention of the Sepoys at Jhansi to rise, or that they were likely to be wrought upon by external influences. On the 18th of May he wrote to Agra, saying: "I do not think that there is any cause for alarm about this neighbourhood. The troops here, I am glad to say, continue staunch and express most unbounded abhorrence of the atrocities committed at Meerut and Delhi. They are commanded by a man (Captain

Dunlop) of the right sort, who knows how to manage Sepoys; and I do not anticipate any disaffection among them. As for the small Rajahs and Chiefs, they saw enough of rebellion, fourteen years ago, to give them a salutary dread of it. Then the Oorcha and Chutterpore and Ajeegurh men are children; the Dubbah man is off to Bithoor in a moribund state; the Sumpther man is mad and a prisoner in his own fort; the Chirkaree man and the Punnah men are almost the only chiefs worth mentioning, and they have kept out of everything of the kind hitherto —so I trust we are all safe . . . I am going on the principle of showing perfect confidence—and I am quite sure I am right." On the 30th of May, he wrote again in the same hopeful strain: "All continues quiet here, and the troops staunch. But there is of course a great feeling of uneasiness among the moneyed men of the town, and the Thakoors, who have never been well affected towards any Government, are beginning, it is said, to talk of doing something. All will settle down here, I feel perfectly certain, on receipt of intelligence of success." And again upon the 3rd of June: "We are all safe here as yet. I heard on Monday night of an intended attack on Kunchra by the Puan Thakoors. At midnight I called upon Dunlop to send a party to protect the town, and at eight A.M. a party of Infantry and Cavalry started in high spirits. They reached Kunchra at seven in the evening, but the Thakoors had got wind of the move and did not make the intended chupao. But for the feeling that this mutiny is universal I should say the men here are perfectly staunch." "The Sixty-seventh are the sister corps of my regiment the Sixty-eighth, and I have been watching with intense interest their conduct. I see the Sixty-seventh still pro-

1857. May.

1857. June. mise loyalty. I trust the Sixty-eighth will evince it." And so little was it dreamt that there could be any political danger, that the Ranee obtained permission to entertain a body of armed men, as she said, for her own protection. With the true Mahratta instinct, she pretended that she was in danger from the enemies of the English, and thus intimated that her interests and desires were identical with our own, whilst she was plotting our overthrow.

It is remarkable that although Skene, on the 3rd of June, had expressed his belief in the staunchness of the troops, the wonted unmistakable signs of a coming outbreak had already begun to display themselves. A day or two before, in broad daylight, two bungalows in the Cantonment had been burnt. This was the warning to be ready; and on the 5th "firing was heard." It came from the direction of the Star Fort, which held our magazine and treasure. A party of Sepoys had possession of it and would not surrender it. It was plain now that the mutiny had commenced. So all the non-combatant Europeans betook themselves, with their families and such property as they could carry-off, to the Town Fort, whilst the officers of the Native troops remained in the Cantonments. Dunlop and his brother-officers did their best to soothe and pacify the Sepoys and to instil confidence into their minds. Of course, there was the old story over again. The Sepoys were loyalty itself; a few deluded men might have broken the bonds of discipline by occupying the Star Fort,
June 6. but the rest were true to their salt. A parade was ordered for the following morning. It was attended by the Native officers and men of all arms of the Jhansi force. The men were respectful in their demeanour. What this meant was soon apparent. It

was only intended to lull us into the sense of a false security. On this morning Skene and Gordon left the Fort to visit Dunlop in Cantonments. What the object of the visit or what passed at the conference can never be known. Skene returned at once to the Fort; Gordon breakfasted in his own house and wrote letters to some of the neighbouring chiefs, invoking their aid—letters to which no answer was returned—and then betook himself to the supposed safety of the Fort. Early in the afternoon, the Ranee, and a crowd of people, among whom were her chief adherents, with two banners borne aloft, went in procession from the Town to the Cantonments; and a Mahomedan named Ahsun-Ali called all true believers to prayers.* Then the troops rose at once; and fired upon their officers. All were killed, except Lieutenant Taylor, who, though severely wounded, mounted a horse and rode for the Town Fort.† The massacre of the Cantonment officers having thus been effected, in a manner most gratifying to the mutineers, they released the prisoners from the Gaol, burnt the cutcherry; and then mutineers and gaol-birds, together with the Police and Custom-house officials, streamed into the Town and invested the Fort:

1857. June.

Seizure of the district.

Our people were now most lamentably in the power of the mutineers, the rebels, and the followers of the Queen. They had triumphed over the White Man, who now lay prostrate and writhing at their feet. Another day or two and all would be over. Jhansi would be purged of the presence of the usurpers. So the time had come for the apportioning of the spoils. To whom was Jhansi, recovered after three years of annexation, to belong? On the night of the

* Captain Pinkney's Report. † Colonel Malleson.

1857. June. 6th a meeting was held between the chief officers of the mutineers and certain delegates from the Ranee to settle this momentous question of the future Government of the country. Then came the great standing difficulty, which was doomed, before and afterwards, to cast a great cloud over the triumphant joy of the victors, and sometimes to turn conflicts of opinion into internecine strife. The delegates of the Ranee and of the mutineers, after long disputation, could not come to any terms. The mutineer party bethought themselves of a somewhat clever piece of diplomacy. At Oonao, a village distant about twelve miles from Jhansi, dwelt a kinsman of the late Rajah, who had been one of the claimants to the Guddee of Jhansi. His name was Sadasheo Rao. If in this crisis he could be induced to adhere to the side of the Sepoys and to set himself as a rival of the Ranee, they might make better terms for themselves. So they invited this man to Jhansi. Meanwhile a Proclamation went forth, declaring that "The People are God's; the country is the Padshah's; and the two Religions govern."

The 7th of June was a day of sore tribulation to the ill-fated garrison of the Town Fort. The clouds were thickening above them, and there was small chance of their escaping the full fury of the storm. Their only chance of escape lay in the good offices of the Ranee. The English were reduced to the humiliating necessity of imploring the help of the woman whom they had so grossly wronged. In the morning Captain Skene sent three uncovenanted servants connected with the Commission—Mr. Scott and the two Purcells—to the Ranee to solicit safe-conduct after the exodus of our people from the Fort. They were seized on the way by some of the Ranee's troops and carried to the Palace. The Ranee sent them to our own revolted Sepoys, who deliberately murdered them. Afterwards, another uncovenanted servant, Mr. Andrews, principal Sudder Aumeen, was butchered at the Palace door by the Queen's own servants. Skene and Gordon wrote often to Her Highness on that day—but no trace of their correspondence remains. It was a last hope and it was a vain one. Two hours after noon the insurgents recommenced their attack on the Fort and continued the firing; but they did very little damage, hurting none of our people; whilst some of the insurgents fell under the fire from the Fort. On that night the besiegers were strengthened by the accession of more guns supplied to them by the Ranee; and on the morning of the 8th, with these increased resources now more hopeful of success, they continued their attack on the Fort. They attempted an escalade, but it failed. Too many good shots were in the garrison to render it safe for the assailants to expose themselves.

1857. June.

Now came the last struggle for life—the day of their death or the day of their deliverance. Vigorous and more vigorous became the efforts of the enemy to carry the place by assault; and soon after noon they established themselves on the lower works of the Fort. The crisis of our fate seemed to be approaching. There was treachery within the walls no less than fury without. An attempt was made to open a gate of the Fort so as to admit the ingress of the besiegers. It was happily intercepted in time—though only to defer the final catastrophe for a few hours. The traitors were disposed of by Gordon and Burgess, but not before they had given Powis

1857. June. his death-wound. Meanwhile the siege continued. With all the heroism of despair our people worked on nobly in the defence of the Fort—Skene and Gordon sending many a message of death to the assailants.* But after a while a sad calamity befel us. Captain Gordon was looking through a window over the Fort gate, when his familiar face was observed by one of the enemy's marksmen, who took aim and shot him dead. He is described as "a gallant gentleman and an excellent officer, the life and soul of the garrison." When this lamentable event occurred, a great cloud of despondency gathered over the besieged. Provisions and ammunition were becoming scarce—the enemy were swarming around them. So it was felt that the defence could not be sustained—that there was nothing left for our people but to surrender. So Captain Skene hung out a flag of truce, or otherwise intimated to the besiegers that the garrison would treat for terms.

The leaders of the mutineers and of other insurgents came to the gate, and hearing what Skene had to say, they made oath, with the most solemn and sacred adjurations; a native doctor named Saleh Mohamed being the spokesman, not to hurt a hair of the heads of the British garrison, if they would lay down their arms and surrender the Fort. The terms were accepted; and our hapless people prepared to depart. As soon as they crossed the threshold of the Fort gate the enemy fell upon our unarmed people, and binding their arms, made captives of them. There could be no resistance. They were helpless as sheep. Through the town passed the melancholy procession; when just beyond the city

* It has been stated that Mrs. Skene loaded for them, but I have nothing authentic in proof of this.

walls some Sowars came up and said it was the order 1857.
of the Ressaldar that the whole should be put to June.
death. They then filed down, captors and captives, The end.
to a place near which was a cluster of trees. The Gaol-Darogah, who had been in the confidence of the Superintendent and was never suspected of treachery, was at the head of the party. But, presently a halt was ordered. The murderous work commenced. The Darogah cut down his old master. Then a general massacre ensued. The women and children were separated from the men; but they shared the same sad fate. Not one of those who left the Town-Fort—man, woman, or child—was spared.* The great crime accomplished, the bodies of some three score of our Christian people were left for three days on the road to rot. Then the men were cast into one gravel-pit, the women into another, and lightly covered over. Long afterwards, when we again triumphed at Jhansi, the burial service was read over their remains by a Protestant minister, Mr. Schwabe, and Mr. Strickland, the Roman Catholic priest, attached to Sir Hugh Rose's army.

Thus the curtain fell upon the dismal tragedy which was the antetype of the massacre of Cawnpore. Whether the Ranee instigated this atrocity, or to what extent she was implicated in it, can never be clearly known. I have been informed, on good authority, that none of the Ranee's servants were present on the occasion of the massacre. It seems to have been mainly the work of our own old followers. The Irregular Cavalry issued the bloody mandate and our Gaol-Darogah was foremost in the butchery.

* The number of Christian people slain in this final massacre was between fifty and sixty. The rest were killed in Cantonments or during the siege. Captain Pinkney gives sixty-seven as the total number. Major Erskine, Commissioner of Jubbulpore, says seventy-six.

1857. June. Measures of the Ranee.

So long as the English were cleaned out of Jhansi and the country was left clear for the prosecution of her political intrigues—and she was bent on cleaning them out—it mattered not to her by what means the object was attained. They were all gone now; and the time had come for the settlement of the great political question—"Who is to be the future ruler of Jhansi?" The mutineers had invited Sadasheo Rao to the city and he had gone thither, well disposed to bid for the Guddee. But the Ranee knew that there was nothing they so much coveted as money; so she produced a large sum in coin and promised further donations to the mutineers, who were thus brought to adhere to her cause, and then the Proclamation went forth; "The people are God's; the country is the Padshah's; and the Raj is Ranee Lutchmee Baee's."* This accomplished, she threw all her energy and activity into the work of firmly establishing the Raj. She raised fresh troops; she strengthened her fortified places; she established a mint; and she sent delegates to Doondoo Punt, Nana Sahib, with whom she had previously been in communication. It is stated, and apparently on the most trustworthy authority, that, at the same time, she "endeavoured to keep terms with our Government, by writing to the Commissioner of Jubbulpore and to others, lamenting the massacre of our countrymen; stating that she was in no way concerned in it; and declaring that she only held the Jhansi district till our Government could make arrangements to reoccupy it."† But I have searched Major Erskine's exhaustive Report, and in the four hundred and forty-four para-

* Professedly she was only Regent—her adopted son, then a boy of eight years of age, being nominally the possessor of the Guddee.

† Captain Pinkney.

graphs to which it extends I cannot find a word upon the subject.* 1857. June.

Meanwhile at Naogong, where wings or detachments of the same regiments as those posted at Jhansi —namely, the Head-Quarters of the Twelfth Native Infantry, a wing of the Fourteenth Irregular Horse, and some Golundauze guns—were stationed, under the command of Major Kirke, very contradictory manifestations were apparent in the Sepoy Lines. From the 23rd of May to the 1st of June, it seems that they were waiting and watching. The Irregulars were lounging about in a careless, insolent, half-defiant manner, plainly indicating their belief that the end was near; whilst the Infantry putting on an outer garment of loyalty, protested their allegiance, and gave practical proofs of it, by offering to march against the mutineers at Delhi. On the 5th of June, Major Kirke held a parade of all the troops in Cantonments. He then addressed them, commended them highly for their loyalty, and told them that the troops were in partial mutiny at Jhansi. Then came a most extraordinary scene—a preposterous piece of acting. The Sepoys were quite jubilant in their devotion to the British Government. The Golundauze hugged their guns in a paroxysm of enthusiasm. The Infantry rushed to their colours. The Cavalry, with their wonted demeanour of outward insouciance, merely said that they would be true to their salt.† The officers were "much gratified." They did not seem to see that the violence of these Naogong.

* It should be mentioned here that, finding his claims disallowed, Sadasheo Rao collected some three thousand men, seized the Fort of Kurrara, and issued a proclamation saying, "Maharajah Sadasheo Rao Narain has seated himself on the throne of Jhansi at Kurrara." It was a very uneasy and unstable seat, for the Ranee despatched a body of troops against him and he was fain to escape into Scindiah's territory.

† Captain Scot's Report.

1857. June. spasms clearly denoted the acted lie. For some days everything was quiet. But on the 10th, the play having been played out, the reality commenced. A tall Sikh, followed by two others, walked up to the ground, where the guard of the Twelfth was being relieved, and deliberately shot the Havildar-Major. They then attempted to seize the guns; there was no genuine resistance; the Native Sergeant was overawed and his followers were recreant to the core. Then was heard the rattle of musketry from the Lines, telling the old story. The Sepoys had risen against their British officers, against the British Government; they were mutineers and rebels of the worst kind, working out their ends by means of the basest falsehood and imposture.

The flight. What now was to be done by the handful of British officers thus shamefully deserted? It was hoping against hope to think, for a moment, that any efforts of theirs—any appeals to the Past, any promises for the Future, would lure them back to their allegiance. Some Sepoys of the Twelfth came forward, protesting their fidelity, and mustered in the mess-house of their English officers, but they were not strong enough to turn the tide of affairs in our favour. There was nothing for them, therefore, but to remain at their posts to be massacred, like their comrades at Jhansi, or to attempt to rescue themselves by flight. They chose the latter course—and wisely; but it was a disastrous and a disorderly retreat. The eighty-seven faithful Sepoys accompanied their officers, and the clerks of the Civil Establishment—some burdened with families—were among the number of the fugitives. Their first thought had been to make their way to Allahabad, but this, on account of the state of the country about Banda, had been abandoned, and they next set their faces towards Kalinghur and Mirzapore. The story of their flight has been told in graphic detail by survivors of the retreat. It was a fortnight of misery and horror. The adventures which befel the fugitives on their perilous way much resembled, in many features, those which were encountered by others in like manner driven from their homes. And the same diversities of temperament and character were apparent. Major Kirke soon lost what little power of brainwork he possessed at the first outbreak of the mutiny. It is recorded of him that he had been in feeble health before this event and that "now from want of tea, and beer and wine, he was quite gone"—he sometimes "spoke of a mango, or something to eat and drink as if it were his life"; and he sent back two officers to Naogong to carry off the mess-stores. Occasional strange hallucinations overtook him. The first place to which they made was Chutterpore—a small state governed, like Jhansi, by a widowed Ranee as Regent for her son. It had escaped the great planing-machine of Lord Dalhousie's annexations. The Ranee behaved mercifully and generously to our people; and they passed on with some needed succours. But as they moved forward, it was discovered that Kirke was missing. He fancied that the Sepoys were plotting to murder him and had made off, unattended, by night, to Logassee, where he was received by a friendly chief. At this place Captain Scot and Lieutenant Townsend found him, maundering about new dangers and insisting that the Logassee chief was bent upon his destruction.

1857. June.

Meanwhile the Sepoys had gone on without their officers, greatly distressed by what they supposed to be either their death or their desertion. But on the

1857. June. 16th Kirke made his appearance with the cart-load of beer, wine, and tea, which he had sent his officers back to Naogong to heap up for him, and to satisfy his cravings. They then pressed on to Chirkaree, another friendly Bundelkund state, the chief of which received the fugitives with hospitality, and supplied them with money. The gleam of sunshine was but brief. A powerful gang of Dakoits came down upon them, and under promise of safe conduct to Kalinghur, eased them of a great part of their treasure, and then forthwith began to acquit themselves of their part of the compact, by killing as many of our people as they could. When Kirke and his followers pushed on, without the robber-chief, who had promised to guide them, they were fired upon from behind the cover of a cluster of trees and some adjacent hills. The Sepoys in return fired anywhere. They lost heart, whilst the Dakoits rose in their audacity and fired faster and faster on our people. In this crisis, the Major had a lucid interval of manhood. He went among the Sepoys, and eagerly exhorted them to carry the pass before them. But it was of no use. The brigands were masters of the situation. Their matchlocks carried far and well. Lieutenant Townsend fell dead with a bullet in his body. There was a great panic. The miscellaneous European or Christian community sought safety as best they could in flight—some on horseback, and some on foot—for the Dakoits had seized all our wheeled carriages. It was then necessary that the party should fall back on Mahoba. But Kirke did not live to reach it. After the passing excitement of which I have spoken, a terrible reaction came upon him, and within a few miles from the place of refuge, he fell from his horse and died.

Then Captain Scot became chief of the fugitive band. He was younger, stronger, more active than the Major, and less dependent on mess-stores. He seems, under most trying circumstances, to have worked with almost superhuman energy for the preservation of the people thus committed to his care. But death was busy among them. The fierce rays of the June sun smote them terribly. Some were killed or driven to madness by its power. Some were overcome by extreme exhaustion and fell by the wayside. Others sought shelter, sank into stupor, and were left behind. The great difficulty was the burden of the women. There was but one wife of a commissioned officer among them, but many wives of sergeants and writers with children in their train, whom it was very difficult to succour on the march. There would be something almost ludicrous in the narrative of their adventures, if it were not for the beautiful chivalry of Scot, who went to the rescue of fat barrack-women with as much heroic self-devotion as if they had been princesses in the bloom of their youth and beauty. He had two horses, for he had secured Townsend's, and how best to utilise them was the difficult problem which he had now to solve. Never, perhaps, was back of horse put to stranger uses before. The strangeness culminated in the circumstance that with a nursery of children on one of his horses he was compelled to find room for a wretched woman with but little life left in her—if any. The back of the horse was her death-bed, and the body was left to the vultures.* Nor was Scot alone in these manifesta-

1857. June.

Mrs. Mawe.

* See the following passage of a private letter from Captain Scot: "My work that day was terrible. I had to try to lug along two fat old women, whilst I carried three children on my horse and tried to keep back the Sepoys who were with me. The senior Havildar got more and more savage and wanted me to leave the children and the women; but I

1857. June. tions of the chivalry and self-devotion of the true Christian gentleman. Lieutenant Jackson took up behind him the wife of a Sergeant of the Public Works Department, who rode astride lashed to her preserver, throughout four long days of weariness and pain—on one day riding forty miles—until they reached Adjighur, their numbers sadly diminished by the agonies of that dreadful march.

Before this, the eighty-seven faithful Sepoys had, by agreement, parted from their officers. They had become dissatisfied and hopeless of making good their way to British territory. The people along the line of flight were manifestly hostile to us. It was plain that our officers were encumbered with women and children, and the Sepoys could not appreciate the unselfish chivalry of those who sacrificed themselves to the weaklings who so impeded their progress. They proposed, therefore—whether in good faith or in bad faith it is hard to say—that the Europeans still remaining alive should give up their arms to the Sepoys, who should report everywhere that the white men were prisoners, whom they were taking to Banda. Our officers consented. For a time it succeeded. On pain of the displeasure of the King of Delhi townsfolk and villagers were called upon to supply food and forage to the little camp, and the requisition was obeyed. But the ruse was soon discovered, or the Sepoys said it was; so this state of things was

would not, and thank God, they did not leave us. I came at last to Mr. Smalley sitting beside his wife. She seemed dead, but it was doubtful, so I took her up before me and gave one of the children to my writer, who had got hold of my horse. It was a most arduous task to keep the utterly inert body on the horse, as I placed her as women ride. But after a while she seemed dead. I held a consultation about it and we left the body. I was lame from an awful kick of a horse and had but a strip of cloth on one foot; but poor Smalley was worse, and he got on my horse and Mrs. Tierney behind, her two children got seats upon the horses—and thus I reached the main body."

but of brief duration. The whole country, it was urged, was against us, and it was better that they should separate. So Scot gave them certificates of loyalty and they made their way to Allahabad; whilst the wretched remnant of the Naogong fugitives struggled on to Adjighur, whence they were passed on to Nagode and were saved. Mrs. Mawe, whose husband had died on the march, wandered to Banda, where her little daughter was restored to her by Scot, whose noble exertions had saved the child.* 1857. June.

The month of July dawned darkly and ominously on the defenders of Agra. It was now certain that the Neemuch mutineers, swollen by detachments from other rebel hosts, were rapidly approaching. Colvin, whose health, strong man as he was, had for some time been breaking down under the continued pressure of external anxieties and internal dissensions, and the distressing sleeplessness which they engendered, was now said to be dying. He had many enemies among those who should have been his friends—many opponents among those who should have been his supporters. Some of his own officers, openly or covertly, conducted themselves, in this crisis, in a manner as disgraceful to themselves as it was cruel to their chief. Some were insolent and minacious to his face. Some wrote letters which ought never to have been written. Whilst others, taking advantage of the post by Bombay, addressed July. Agra. Howlings of our people.

* But for the necessities of space, I should gladly have told this story in greater detail, for it is a touching illustration of English heroism of the purest kind. A graphic narrative of the flight was written by Captain Scot and published in the *Times* newspaper of September 11, 1857. Mrs. Mawe, also, recorded her adventures, and the record is said to have been sent to the Queen by Lady Canning.

1857. July. the Governor-General, denouncing the conduct of his lieutenant in no measured language, declaring his incompetency, and beseeching Lord Canning to remove him. Impeachments before Parliament were talked of and forcible arrests—indeed, there were no invectives, no threats, to which his assailants did not resort. Lord Canning spoke of these as "screeches from Agra"—and at Delhi, where many letters were received from these complainants, it was said, "There are the Agra-Wallahs howling again!" The Agra Garrison say that howlings came to them, as frequently from Delhi.

Approach of the Neemuch mutineers.

At the end of June it was clear that the Neemuch mutineers were approaching, and that it was necessary at once to concert detailed measures for their reception. So, on the 30th, a Memorandum was drawn up by the Brigadier, in which he very clearly defined our position and the dangers which threatened us; adding: "It is as well to observe that merely beating the mutineers is *comparatively* no material object gained. From the character of the enemy it does not seem likely that these mutineers would venture upon an attack on us, unless aided by any forces in the present neighbourhood, or by some promise of local treachery here, or by some other aid expected from the westward. The rise of the Chumbul river seems the best security we have against any early hostile movement of the troops at Gwalior." On the following day a Resolution was passed by the Lieutenant-Governor containing explicit instructions as to the movements of all branches of the Agra force; but when the time came for action, circumstances had changed and the Resolution became a dead letter.

Illness of Mr. Colvin.

Colvin had borne all the assaults upon him with

the finest temper and the truest Christian patience. But the malice of his enemies, and the unkindness of his own people struck at the very sources of his life, and on the 3rd of July alarming symptoms of apoplexy presented themselves. He was then compelled to make over the Government, for twenty-four hours, to a Council composed of Mr. E. A. Reade, Brigadier Polwhele, and Captain Macleod, Colvin's military secretary. The Council of Administration assembled on the 4th in the Brigadier's house, where Colvin, attended by his medical adviser, was lying in an adjoining room. Later in the day he brightened up a little and approved generally of the instructions issued by Reade and his colleagues. They made the most of their time and opportunity. One most important point was gained. The first paragraph of the Proceedings of the Council records: "The information regarding the movements of the Neemuch mutineers received through the Police being ambiguous and contradictory, volunteers were called for from the officers, who reported from personal observation the arrival of their camp within a distance of fifteen miles from Agra. Brigadier Polwhele had decided in the event of their advancing nearer, to meet and attack them." This would have been a great point gained, if there had been any certainty of a man, so vacillating as Brigadier Polwhele, clinging to his first resolution. For, a few days before, the Lieutenant-Governor had placed the Brigadier in full possession of all the circumstances of our position, and warned him of the dangers to be encountered. He had told Polwhele to take counsel with his principal officers, receiving their opinions as "to how far it would be prudent to advance from the cantonment and proximity of the Fort to arrest the advance of the enemy; whether it

1857. July 3.

1857. July 3.

would be advantageous to employ the Kotah Contingent then encamped on the left bank of the Jumna, opposite to Agra; and whether it would be advisable to employ a force under our staunch adherent, the Newab Syfoollah Khan, to co-operate with us."

So Polwhele had assembled his officers and consulted them. It was determined that it would not be a wise strategical measure to move out the force so far in advance, as to necessitate its encamping. It would be better to await their coming and then to march out from the barracks to give battle to the enemy.* It was resolved, also, that the Kotah Contingent should be removed within the cantonment, "to take part in the defence," and that the services of Syfoollah Khan should be accepted.†

Mutiny of the Kotah Contingent.

These last questions soon solved themselves. As the Contingent were stationed near the Europeans, it would have been easy to disarm them. This was counselled but the counsel was rejected. Vacillation was all dominant at that time. The Brigadier doubted and hesitated, whilst those whom he should have crushed were girding up their loins and arming themselves for the battle. At last, on the 4th of July, when it was clearly seen that their proximity might be inconvenient, if not dangerous, orders were issued by the Council of Administration for their removal from Agra. It was suggested by Major

* "The entire want of Cavalry with the force here," wrote Mr. Colvin, "was a main motive to this resolution, which I myself thought the best that could be adopted, under all the circumstances of our position."

† The sequel may be given in a note: "Lieutenant Henderson, having brought Nuwab Syfoollah Khan, after midnight, to the railway house to report the desertion of the Bhurtpoor Horse, and the Nuwab having acknowledged that his matchlock infantry were unfit to fight against mutineer soldiers, he was ordered to quit Shagunge at once, and to return to Kerowlee without delay." —*Proceedings of Council of Administration.*

Macleod that a test should be applied to them : "that their guns should remain with the reserve of Europeans left for the protection of Cantonments, while their Infantry and Horse should accompany the force on its march out to meet and attack the mutineers." At first the men of the Contingent seemed to be satisfied with the arrangement; but when orders were given to them to move their camp to the rising ground on the road leading to Futtehpore Sikri, they broke into open mutiny, shot down their European Sergeant-Major, fired at other British officers, and went off to join the Neemuch mutineers, in fear and trembling lest they should be overtaken and cut up. Captain Prendergast, a dashing soldier always on the alert, with a party of Volunteer Horse, got in among them, cut down some of the mutineers and captured their camels and ammunition. On the same evening it was discovered that some of the components of Syfoollah Khan's force were equally treacherous, so all that could be done was to render them harmless as enemies, as they could not be useful as friends.

1857. July 4.

The revolt of the Kotah Contingent rendered it necessary that the Lieutenant-Governor should be moved into the Fort. There was danger of an attack on the Brigadier's house, and a party of volunteers and others had drawn up in front of it for purposes of defence. The Brigadier then insisted upon the removal of Colvin to safer quarters; and the Lieutenant-Governor somewhat reluctantly consented to the change. He was removed under an escort; but when he learnt that the Kotah Contingent had been dispersed, he desired to return to the Brigadier's house that he might be nearer the scene of action. Reade carried the request to the Brigadier, but the

Removal of Colvin into the Fort.

1857. July. old soldier was peremptory and declared that he would not receive him. On the following day Colvin had a relapse so serious as to cause his friends and the general community the greatest anxiety. But he resumed the despatch of business as soon as his medical adviser reluctantly consented to his returning to his work.

July 5. Advance of our troops. It was not then very clearly known at what point the enemy were assembled; but on the 4th of July, it was felt that they must be close upon us. So before sunrise on the 5th, the Engineers, Fraser and Weller, went to Brigadier Polwhele and besought him to go out to meet the advancing enemy. "Give the Europeans their breakfasts," said Fraser, "then march out to find the enemy." But the Brigadier turned a deaf ear to these entreaties. He refused to move out and said that he would hold Agra against all comers. The lives of his Europeans, he said, were very valuable, and he would not needlessly expose them. He was a brave man; but he was obstinate and wanting in judgment, and he was prejudiced against the Engineers. So Fraser and Weller left the Brigadier's quarters—disappointed and crest-fallen—lamenting the failure of their endeavours, but still hoping that another hour might bring forth better results.

Brigadier Polwhele was not the only military officer of rank who had refused advice tendered to him, in the presence of his advisers, and afterwards acted upon it as an original conception. Tidings that the enemy were at Shahgunj were brought in by Ensign F. Oldfield* at seven o'clock; but it was not till two hours later that the Brigadier had determined to move out the troops, and about an hour afterwards

* This promising young officer was afterwards killed on Sir Colin Campbell's first advance on Lucknow.

they were assembled on parade.* When Fraser heard of this he went to the Brigadier and offered his services as second-in-command. As he was the next senior officer in the station this request could not be refused. Weller volunteered at the same time for service and joined the Europeans, as a Volunteer, on foot. But there was still much hesitation and delay; and before the force was ready to move, it was known, not only that the enemy were in sight, but that they had occupied the very position which we ought ourselves to have held. 1857. July 5.

Composition of the enemy.

The rebel force consisted of more than two thousand men; and many of them were among the best Native troops, whom our English officers had disciplined. There was the fourth troop First Brigade of Horse Artillery, known as Murray Mackenzie's troop.† There was the Seventy-second Regiment of Native Infantry, with its rifle company, that had done good service at Mooltan—part of the First Native Cavalry, with four troops of the Mehidpore Horse and the Seventh Regiment of the Gwalior Contingent. And to these was soon added another host, on which we had relied as

* "However, on some information, we did not know what, probably acquired after Colonel Fraser's interview, the Brigadier afterwards decided on going out; for about 9 A.M., when busily engaged in the Fort, I was surprised, on meeting Mr. Thornhill, Secretary to Government, to learn that the Brigadier was going out to fight the Neemuch mutineers. I said it was impossible, as Colonel Fraser had before sunrise failed to persuade him to this course; but on being assured it was true, I at once hurried off to Colonel Fraser, and we went to the parade ground and found the troops assembled. This was between 10 and 11 A.M., and Colonel Fraser at once solicited from the Brigadier the privilege of being his second-in-command, which—as he was the next senior officer in the station—could not of course be refused. I was unable to ride, but I had taken a gun and ammunition, and was allowed by Colonel Riddell, Commanding Third Europeans, to fall in as a volunteer with his regiment."—*MS. Memorandum of Major Weller.*

† At the time of the revolt of the troop, Major Mackenzie was at Delhi. It has been erroneously stated in some narratives, that this troop had rendered itself famous in history, as a component of the "Illustrious Garrison" of Jellalabad. That was a Light Field Battery (No. 6) commanded by Captain Augustus Abbott.

1857. July 5.

our allies. The Kotah Contingent, who had been at our mercy on the preceding day and had gone into revolt, now joined the ranks of the enemy.

The battle of Shahgunj.

The camp of the mutineers was at a distance of some two miles from our Cantonment, planted obliquely on a metalled road with a village of mud-huts for their centre. One half of their Artillery was posted on one flank—one half upon the other—sheltered by low trees and walls, and natural earthworks. The camp and Cavalry were in the rear, hidden from our sight as we advanced. It was nearly two o'clock when Polwhele led his troops to the attack. Forming line and placing one half-battery under Captain D'Oyly on the right, and the other under Lieutenant Pearson on the left, he moved along the sandy plain on the right of the road leading to the enemy's position. Our force consisted of eight hundred and sixteen men, all in fine spirits and eager for the affray. D'Oyly, an excellent officer, and of the highest courage, had unbounded confidence in his guns and his gunners. He believed that it would be small work to silence the enemy's Artillery, and this done, the defeat of the rebels would have been easy. His influence with the Brigadier was great, and it is believed that the plan of attack was in accordance with his suggestions. There was underlying it a wise resolve, not to expose the Europeans. Riddell's regiment was eager for the battle, but it had seen little service, and at a time when the loss of a single English soldier was a calamity, it was deemed expedient to take every precaution against the possible results of rashness and impetuosity. Yet the boldest movement is often the least hazardous. Had the force advanced straight along the metalled road, upon the village, or had it moved in two lines, upon both flanks of the enemy, success would have been certain. But when the mutineers saw our advancing troops, they opened fire upon us, from their cover, and then Polwhele ordered the Infantry to lie down, whilst D'Oyly's guns answered the fire of the rebel artillery. But the enemy were too well posted for us to do them any grievous injury, and the delay enabled them to get our range. They had been firing over our heads; and if we had at once advanced, before they had got their guns to the right elevation, we might have fallen upon them, with comparative immunity, and they could not have stood the rush of the Europeans. But instead of thus utilising all branches of the service, the Brigadier trusted to his guns and wasted his ammunition. 1857. July 5.

Our disasters.

Nothing could have exceeded the gallantry with which D'Oyly and Pearson worked their nine-pounders. But some miserable accidents and miscarriages rendered their good service of but slight avail. D'Oyly's horse was shot under him at an early period of the engagement. This was a small disaster; for he could command on foot, but at a later hour, whilst the intrepid artilleryman was endeavouring to right a gun, one of the wheels of which was in difficulty, a grape-shot from one of the enemy's batteries wounded him dangerously on the side. He was placed upon a tumbril, from which he gave his orders, suffering bravely the severest pain, until exhausted nature could no longer sustain him. Then thinking that the hand of death was upon him, he gasped out "I am done for. Put a stone upon my grave and write that I died fighting my guns."*

* It is doubtful whether this was said on the field of battle or afterwards in hospital. It was probably repeated.

1857. July 5.

Gallantry of the Artillery.

He was carried from the battle-field, and after some hours of pain expired in the Fort. One of his subalterns, Lieutenant Lambe, was dangerously wounded by a grape-shot, which shattered his right thigh.* He lingered for some weeks before death terminated the intensity of his sufferings. Lieutenant Patteson, who commanded the left half-battery, exposed himself with equal audacity. One of his guns was dismantled, the limber was blown up, and the gun-carriage ignited; but he and his men, exposed to a heavy fire, and molested by rushes of Cavalry, went to work to remount it as coolly as if they had been on the parade-ground of Dum-Dum or Meerut on a practice-day. It seemed that this battery, heroically as it was worked, was doomed to disaster, for, before the accident above recorded, a round shot from one of the enemy's guns exploded an ammunition waggon and its limber, and deprived us of that which was the very life of our power of attack, a loss which soon rendered our guns only an encumbrance to us. The rapid firing, with but small effect, at the commencement of our operations, now told most lamentably against us; for before the fortune of the day had been decided, or indeed even before the decisive action had commenced, our guns ceased firing. It is said that they had taken out ninety rounds of ammunition for each gun, but by four o'clock in the afternoon there was scarcely a shot to be fired.

Death of Major Thomas.

Not until D'Oyly had reported that his ammunition was expended, did Colonel Riddell receive orders to advance with his Europeans. Then "two small columns" were thrown forward. The right

* Lambe was with the left half-battery.

was commanded by Major G. P. Thomas* of the Third Europeans, and the left by Colonel Fraser of the Engineers, with whom went his friend and comrade Weller, both "with their shirt-sleeves tucked up." They entered the village with a good English "Hurrah!" all the more eager for having been so long held back. After an obstinate defence, and not without heavy loss on our side, the village was carried. Here Major Thomas, whose horse was shot under him whilst gallantly leading his men, received his death-wound. Fraser's column forcing an entrance into the village, with its "narrow lanes and strong mud huts," was grievously assailed by the firing of the enemy from roofs and doorways. It was truly a critical moment. Fraser was eager to hold the village against all odds, but it was a desperate undertaking; so after taking counsel with Weller, he resolved at least to make an attempt to bring up some guns; Weller, who, although on foot, seems to have acted as staff-officer to the Brigade, and to have been ready for any kind of service, believing that Pearson had still a few rounds of ammunition left, went off to him, to see whether he could bring up his half-battery and render any service in this emergency. But the artilleryman shook his head. So many men and so many horses had been killed, and so much damage had been done, that it was impossible to go to the aid of the Infantry. It was a happy circumstance that, in one important respect, the enemy were in like straits with ourselves; for they also had a scarcity

1857. July 5.

* Major Thomas had been formerly in the Sixty-fourth Native Infantry, in which he had distinguished himself at the commencement of the Second Afghan War. He was a man of consummate courage as a soldier, and, beyond this, he was a man of genius. He was an artist and a poet. I have pleasant recollections of days passed in his society.

1857. July 5.

of Artillery, and their guns had been limbered up for flight.*

Want of British Cavalry.

If then we had not been so miserably weak in the mounted branch all might have gone well. But all the Cavalry we possessed were some sixty mounted militiamen. They were men of all kinds—"military officers, whose regiments had mutinied or had been disarmed, members of the Civil Service holding appointments, salaried clerks in the public offices, sectioners, men drafted from the European regiments, pensioners, Christian drummers, musicians, &c., from Native regiments, and individuals not before in the service of Government."† To this strange list we may add, "horse-riders of a wandering circus from France." They had been exercised only for a space of ten days; but weak as they were in numbers and in discipline they were strong in loyalty and in courage. With such mighty odds against them, they could not conquer, but they took a glorious part in the defeat. Seven of their little party fell mortally wounded—among them Monsieur Jourdan, the chief of the equestrian troupe, who said that he went out to fight *pour l'honneur d'alliance*—and proved his sincerity by his death.

The insurgent Cavalry.

The enemy's Cavalry, on the other hand, were strong in numbers—more than as ten to one. And if they had been well commanded they might have cut us up root and branch. Some dim design of planting themselves between our position and the Fort, so as to cut off our retreat, seems to have been entertained for a time; but it was departed from in

* It seems that they had more sense than we had, and did not fire it all away. This may be gathered from the fact that they fired upon us during our retreat; but it has been stated that the last ammunition used against us consisted of bags of pice

† Memorandum by Mr. E. A. Reade.

favour of another project. It was at that critical 1857. July 5.
period when Weller was endeavouring to bring up Patteson's guns, that large bodies of horse were seen to stream out from behind the village, as if to threaten our rear and to render our retirement on Agra perilous, if not impossible. But afterwards perceiving that our two half-batteries were separated and but imperfectly protected, they determined to make an effort to capture our guns. So they charged down, in two bodies, each on one half-battery—some hundreds strong. Then was it that our mounted militiamen showed the stuff of which they were made. With audacity almost sublime they galloped forward to meet the dense hosts of the enemy, but they were "terribly shattered" and could make no impression on the hostile multitude. But a volley from the British Infantry covering the guns, delivered at a distance of seventy yards from the advancing enemy, threw confusion into their ranks; and they wheeled off to the right, making for the village, where a second volley from the Europeans checked all their forward designs. The few troopers who, with exceptional gallantry, got in among our guns, were easily disposed of by our men.

Meanwhile the conflict in the village had not Conflict in the village.
abated. Our two detachments were separated, and at one time had lost sight of each other. Fraser's column had captured and spiked one of the enemy's guns, and the rest had gone to the rear, limbered up for flight. But the Infantry were strong and bold behind cover. The mud-wall of a tobacco-field gave them great opportunities of carrying on that particular style of warfare in which they most rejoice and are most successful. We were in every way outmatched, and it was soon apparent that we could

1857. July 5.

only destroy our Europeans, every man of whom was of inestimable value at such a time, by continuing the unequal contest. So the attacking columns were withdrawn to join the main body,* and preparations were made for an orderly retreat of the brigade

The retreat

In all the force that went out on this disastrous expedition, there was not a braver man than the old Brigadier. He was always to be seen, conspicuous on his white charger, sitting composedly within reach of the enemy's fire. It was a sore trial to him to be compelled to give the order to fall in. Then there was great tribulation about carriage. Neither Pearson's disabled piece, nor the gun which Fraser had spiked could be carried from the field. Two elephants had been sent from Agra, but they were required to carry off the wounded; and the dead were left where they fell.† But when the Brigade had formed, it moved forward so steadily that the enemy for a time believed that we were returning to our quarters to obtain more ammunition and to renew the conflict. Under this impression, not thinking that the battle had been won and lost, they persistently harassed our retreat. Their Artillery galloped ahead, and with their little remaining ammunition fired into us again and again, whilst their Cavalry also rode forward to within a mile of the Fort, firing upon us from behind walls and village-houses. Still our people marched on "steady and confident, many even cheerful,"‡ halting ever and anon to fire upon the rebel Cavalry. There was very little slaughter in our ranks, and,

* "We found great confusion there—men and officers drinking greedily from a filthy buffalo-pool, which nothing but dire thirst and exhaustion could have induced them to touch."—*MS. Memorandum by an Eye-Witness.*

† A party of volunteers went out next morning; buried the dead bodies, and recovered Pearson's gun. The enemy had carried off their own piece.

‡ MS. Memoranda.

throughout that four miles' march, the column was never really in danger. 1857. July 5.

But although it was an orderly retreat—it was truly a great and pitiable disaster and a dire disgrace. The want of Cavalry was a grievous misfortune. But how often has inferiority of numbers been atoned for by superiority of pluck. It was not this misfortune that destroyed us. We were destroyed by the errors that were committed. The reserve ammunition, though packed, was not sent with our force or after our force; and our Infantry were not brought into action, until our guns had become unserviceable. It was madness of the worst kind to reserve the action of our Infantry until our Artillery had ceased to have the means of supporting them. But even of this madness we must speak tenderly; for D'Oyly paid for it with his life, and Polwhele by the loss of his professional character.

Dismay of the garrison.

With amazement and alarm our people in the Fort had marked the progress of the action. At first they could but dimly conjecture the issue of events from the sounds which reached them from a distance. They heard the booming of the artillery and the crashes of the great explosions, which had so crippled our action; and when the guns ceased firing and an ominous stillness ensued, the pause excited both wonderment and alarm. But, after a while from the Flagstaff, our brigade might be seen retreating, and soon the terrible reality was announced by the appearance of our beaten force making madly towards the Fort—all in the agony of thirst, eager to reach the canteen. There was then a scene of terrible confusion, such as those who witnessed it pray to God that they may never live to see again. It was not

1857. July 5. strange that in such a crisis the hearts of our people failed them through fear. But there were some, principally Eurasians and Portuguese, whose surroundings and belongings were such as to render departure from their old homes difficult and distasteful to them. They said that they had faith in their friends in the city who would protect them, and so they refused to betake themselves to the shelter of the Fort. But they had miserably miscalculated their chances of safety. The enemy's troopers, who had been foremost in the pursuit, had hounded on all the rascality of Agra and the surrounding villages to slaughter and to ravage our Christian people. More than twenty of these helpless ones were killed either on that evening or on the following day, mostly in their own homes. All our houses, except those immediately contiguous to the Fort, were gutted and burnt; the greater part of our public records were destroyed; and by the lurid light of the fires they had ignited might have been seen these savages dancing with frantic delight around the wrecks and ruins they had created. It was a "grand but melancholy sight." The mighty fire disported itself over a space of some six miles, "from the Civil Lines on our extreme right to the Khelat-i-Ghilzee Lines on the left." Everything of a combustible character was in flames; and our people looked out on the illuminated skies with a sickening sense of the sacrifice of their cherished goods, which the great conflagration portrayed.

Burning of Cantonments.

It was a night never to be forgotten. Memorable on many accounts, it was memorable for nothing more than for the deep devotion with which the gentlewomen of Agra ministered to the wants of our wounded and weary fighting men. Ghastly sights were before their eyes to make them shudder and other sights from which feminine delicacy shrinks. But these bravé-hearted, humane women were sustained by a solemn sense of duty to their God, and a great love for their fellow-creatures. "I think I see them now," writes an eye-witness after naming some who might rank with the Florence Nightingales of the Crimean War, "with the skirts of their gowns stuffed through their petticoats, waiting on the weary combatants of the 5th of July, at a table their own hands had prepared, and in turn taking to my poor and almost mortally wounded comrade, Richard Oldfield, lying at one end of the dining-room, or, in an inner room, to the dying hero of that fight, D'Oyly, whose last words were 'Tell them I died fighting my guns.' Never, whilst life lasts, can I forget those exemplars of unabated cheerfulness, active kindness, and readiness for any emergency."* 1857. July 5.

* "Then came the rush of weary soldiers to the canteen, which was close to our room and in the same barrack. Bloody, thirsty, covered with dust and smoke, the soldiers clamoured for drink. Beer, tea, wine and water were hastily given to them by the ladies of our party. I could overhear their remarks. 'Ah, my chummie, my townie!' said one whose comrade had been left dead on the battle-field. 'Faith! and the Major (Thomas) went at 'em grand,' said another. The long string of hospital litters passed through the Fort gates. The gallant D'Oyly was carried in to die. Young Williams was undergoing the amputation of a limb in the hospital. Richard Oldfield, Under-Secretary to Government, was brought faint and steeped in blood to his young wife. I had a small tent near the barracks; in this two wounded officers were lodged. A line of fire in the cantonments showed the course of the retreating enemy. Barracks, private houses, and bazaars, all were in a blaze."—*Raikes*. A touching incident connected with the return of Richard Oldfield has been narrated to me by Mr. E. A. Reade. It cannot be told better than in his own language. "Almost the last man brought in wounded was a relative of mine—R. C. Oldfield, shot down at the same time (as Monsieur Jourdan). His brother, H. T. Oldfield, and Lieutenant Lambe, with the Agra Militia Reserve, of their own accord marched up to the aid of the retreating European Regiment, and formed up as their rear-guard. As they passed up, the wounded brother was carried by (and they were loving brothers). One look was given to the civilian brother, to all appearances dying, and the soldier brother resumed his place at the head of his detachment."—*MS. Memorandum*.

CHAPTER V

LIFE IN THE AGRA FORT—BESTOWAL OF OUR PEOPLE—ADMIRABLE ARRANGEMENTS OF MR. READE AND THE ENGINEERS—THE GOOD WORK OF OUR GENTLEWOMEN—FORAYS OF THE VOLUNTEER HORSE—ANXIETIES FROM THE WESTWARD—DEATH OF MR. COLVIN.

July, 1857.

Population of the Fort.

THERE was nothing now to be looked at but the fact that the English were shut up in the Fort of Agra, defending themselves against an enemy which they had no longer any power to attack. Gathered together within the walls and intrenchments were a mixed population amounting in all to nearly six thousand—men, women, and children. Of these the larger number were Europeans and Eurasians. In the census taken on the 27th of July, nearly fifteen hundred Hindoos and Mahomedans were included. In the earlier part of the month, there had been a smaller body of these suspects in the Fort; but as time went on and inconveniences accumulated, our own people began to doubt whether every man with a dark face must necessarily be an enemy. It was thought at one time that our Europeans might minister to their own wants, or that Native Christians might be employed. But the irksomeness of the one recourse, and the insufficiency of the others, were soon dismally apparent. The theory of self-help is magnificent, but it must severely try an exotic European shut up in a hot fortress in the month of July. The Native Christians who could take service were few, and they proved themselves to be wonderfully unserviceable. So, little by little, we opened our doors to professional Native servants of all classes—to men who could cook, or wait at table, or help us at our toilets, or pull our punkahs, or bring us water, or sweep out and purify our abodes. It was the lesser evil of the two. Thus the number of our "enemies" within the Fort continued gradually to increase until it had attained the height which I have above stated. The Native Christians amounted in all to eight hundred and fifty-eight; but only two hundred and sixty-seven of these were adult males. Of the Europeans and Eurasians nearly half of the number were in this category. There were six hundred and twenty adult females—with some fifteen hundred boys and girls.*

1857. July.

Such was the population of the Agra Fort at the end of the month of July. It must have been difficult to find any accommodation for so large a body of people. It must have been difficult to distribute and assign the quarters without giving offence. But, after a while, these difficulties were overcome, and people shook themselves down in their appointed places, sometimes with an audible growl.† They

* Mr. Raikes says that in this motley assemblage were "unwilling delegates from many parts of Europe and America. Nuns from the banks of the Garonne and the Loire, priests from Sicily and Rome, missionaries from Ohio and Basle, mixed with rope-dancers from Paris, and pedlars from America. Besides these we had Calcutta Baboos and Parsee merchants. Although all the Christians alike were driven by the mutinous legions into the Fort, the circumstances of the multitude were as various as their races."—*Notes on the Revolt in the North-West Provinces of India.*

† On such occasions, much that is good and much that is bad in the human character are frequently evoked. If there was much selfishness there was also some unselfish-

1857. July.

were strange quarters indeed. Some of the best were within the Palace of the Emperor Akbar—improvised little hutches, in the great arcades or galleries, separated from each other by screens of the substantial mat-work of the country,* whilst the different cells and nooks in this stately building were utilised in the most successful manner. Other dwellings were found of less romantic, but probably of a more convenient kind, in the different public buildings provided for the establishments maintained in the Fort. In a tiled barrack, on an elevation known as "the Mound," Brigadier Polwhele, the Sudder Judges, and the Engineers Fraser and Weller, were lodged.

Efforts of the Engineers.

Those stalwart Engineers, and the advice which they offered to the chief military authority, had been thorns in the flesh of the old soldier. But, after the great failure of the 5th of July, he could no longer spurn their counsels. He made Fraser Second-in-Command, and Weller Brigade-Major of Engineers. There was much work to be done in strengthening the defences of the fortress. And from morning to night for weeks these officers laboured to bring the works into such a state as to withstand any possible siege. Embrasures were opened out, guns were mounted on the ramparts, the ground immediately

ness of a high order. One instance may be cited. To Mr. Reade, as next in rank to the Lieutenant-Governor, excellent accommodation was assigned. But, as his family were in England, he refused to make himself comfortable at the expense of others. His quarters were allotted to some wounded officers; and he contented himself with a shake-down on the floor of the marble hall of the palace. An old piano-forte cover and a hassock constituted all his bedding.

* "In huts hastily prepared, amongst the gates and galleries of the old palace of the Emperors, a motley crowd assembled. Matted screens were set up among the marble corridors, which in Akbar's time were hung with the silks of Persia and the brocades of Benares."—*Raikes.*

around the Fort, which might have afforded shelter to the enemy, was cleared. Ammunition was placed ready for immediate use, and the different components of the garrison told-off and warned, so that every man might be at his appointed post as soon as an alarm should be given. But that which was the greatest source of anxiety to the Engineers was the defence of the powder-magazines. It was suspected, and not without reasonable cause of alarm, that there were enemies in the Fort—wandering Fakirs and other birds of passage, who were prowling about to watch our movements, to ascertain the position of our magazines, and opportunity offering, to destroy us by a great explosion. It was proved that people had been tampering with our prepared ammunition. Shot and shell were changed to guns of different calibre, and shell-plugs were jammed home, so as to render the ammunition unserviceable. In this emergency it was above all things necessary to secure our magazines against any hostile devices. There were six or seven of these magazines, of which one only was kept open as an expense magazine. The others were walled round; their roofs were protected by thick coverings of earth, the European sentries over them were doubled, and they were continually visited by the officers, who were responsible for their safety—and who swept away all suspicious Natives who were seen in the neighbourhood of the magazines.

1857. July.

Indeed, from the time of our defeat on the 5th of July, Fraser became in all but name the actual commandant of the fortress. There was no kind of duty which he was not eager to perform. He always went the round of the hospitals to visit and to cheer the sick and the wounded. He had a blunt rough manner, but it was pleasing to our soldiers, and they loved him

1857. July. for his kindness as much as they admired him for his bravery. More than once was he greeted by a sick soldier with the words, "And sure, Colonel, will you soon be tucking up your sleeves again at them mutineers?" He would, on almost every evening, go to Reade and say to him, "Come let us take a turn of the hospitals," and the soldier and the civilian would go out together, distributing kind words and often creature-comforts to the poor fellows, who looked eagerly for these visits, and who sent blessings after them as they went.

Defence of the Fort. I have said that among the defensive measures of Fraser and Weller was the clearing of some space before the Fort, not open to the fire of our guns. Some houses were to be demolished; but it was just, as there was no proof of the enmity of the owners, that they should be compensated for the loss of their property. But who was to go outside the Fort and treat with the possessors? Reade, ever ready for service, undertook the duty. Fraser and Weller thought that the service was a dangerous one, and besought him to take a guard for his protection. But the civilian had no fear. He said laughingly, but logically, "They, at all events, will not kill me until they have got their money!" But the anxieties of the Engineers did not abate. Fraser and Weller were very careful for their friend—very careful for one who, in all civil affairs, was the very life of the defence. So one day when Reade was discussing terms of adjustment with a number of vociferous claimants, whose nature it was all to speak at the same time, a dead silence fell suddenly upon them Turning round upon his saddle Reade saw a detachment of Europeans closely behind him. The householders, not unreasonably, thought that the white troops were coming down to destroy them; Reade thought that they were passing on to recover some property or perform some other duty, in no way connected with himself. But they drew themselves up behind him, and then he learnt that Fraser had sent the guard down for his protection. There was necessarily an end of all business. It was not possible that these Native householders should transact it under the bayonets of the Europeans. So Reade saw that the only thing that he could do was to ride back to the Fort; and he went with the guard behind him. Speaking of it afterwards, he said, "I have no doubt that the Natives thought at the time that they had taken me into custody." 1857. July.

Victualling of the garrison.

Ere long the Fort of Agra was in a state of thorough preparation equally for defence and attack. But even an impregnable fortress is of small use, if it be not well provisioned. Orders had been issued at the end of June for supplying the garrison—to the extent of three thousand Europeans and fifteen hundred Natives—for six months. The general superintendence of this most important business devolved on Reade—the executive details being carried on by Lieutenant Chalmers, the Commissariat Officer. There would have been much difficulty and perplexity in pursuing these operations to a successful issue, if it had not been for the assistance of the great Army contractor, the well-known Jootee-Persaud, whose powers of organisation and extensive machinery of collection were invaluable in such a conjuncture. No one, after what had happened some time before, could blame him for insisting on payment in advance. Supplies were brought in freely; more abundant indeed than, as afterwards appeared, were needed. For when our first fears and suspicions were cast

1857. July.

aside, and we ceased to see a foeman in every Mahomedan or Hindoo, supplies of every kind came in freely from the city. Between the walls of the Fort and the outer intrenchments was a space, which, when cleared, was extremely useful to us, as a sort of repository for our carriages and other heavy goods which had been recovered from the wreck of the cantonments. On this space, little by little, a flourishing Bazaar sprang up: and our people were enabled to purchase almost everything that they might require to satisfy their daily wants.

The women of Agra.

And as time passed, the women of Agra shone forth in all the lustre of good deeds, quietly but vigorously prosecuted. There was much work to be done and they were right willing to do it. Dr. Farquhar represented to Mrs. Charles Raikes that there would be need of the establishment of a Civil Hospital, as the Military Hospital would soon be overcrowded, and he asked her to take the management of it. She consented, and then began to beat up for recruits. There was a little paper published in the Fort, and in this she inserted an advertisement, begging that any women, who wished to take part in this good work, would send in their names. Before evening, numbers of women of all ranks had eagerly offered their help. It was necessary, however, that this beautiful regiment of Dorcases should be well organised and disciplined. So Mrs. Raikes appointed a goodly staff of gentlewomen, who superintended the work of the numerous East Indian females who had no other occupation. Besides visiting the hospital and ministering to the wants of the patients, their principal work was that of making up clothing, bedding, bandages, &c., for the sick. The materials were supplied, by the Financial Commissioner, from the Government stores. It was of necessity that large indents should be made upon Mr. Reade; and he well knew the importance of complying with them. But the Calcutta Financiers took another view of the matter; and ignored this item as a public charge, and pronounced it to be one of "personal responsibility."

1857. July—Aug.

There were others of our English gentlewomen who did their good work in different directions, giving confidence to the desponding by cheerful looks and cheerful words—visiting the sick, teaching the young, and performing other Christian offices. Ominous reports of coming dangers had been set about by men, who, brave as lions themselves, took gloomy views of the position and were not slow to express them. "The space before the house occupied by the Deputy-Commissary," writes one who saw everything that was passing, and who has a rare power of putting his reminiscences into expressive words, "was one of often resort. Here was Lady Outram discussing the thousand and one rumours of the Fort, always cheerful, lightly treating the adventures of a walk, barefooted for many miles, on escaping from Aligurh, given to chaff the Financial Commissioner with some nonsense about our 'chief politician'—'as unshaken as the wind though busy in raising it'—sometimes borne on her 'taun-jaun', her son, Frank Outram, walking beside her. It was a delight to the European soldiers, scattered about Armoury Square, to see her, with her serene face always ready with a kind smile and a kind word. . . . . In Palace Square was Mrs. (now Lady) Muir with her five children, cheery as a sunbeam, energetic in promoting the employment and welfare of the Native Christians, with her neighbour, Mrs. C. B. Thornhill, enlisting other ladies in good work, stirring up

1857. July—Aug. subscriptions for the wounded and destitute of the North-Western Provinces. She and those above-mentioned, leaders in the social scale, were leaders also in the multiplied tasks of urging the well-disposed to active usefulness, relieving the poor, providing guardianships for waifs and strays of humanity, visiting and supporting schools, soothing vain alarms, repressing the vindictive feeling against Natives of the country, promoting charity among all."

I am afraid that this feeling of charity was not universal throughout the Fort. The Roman Catholic community kept themselves scrupulously aloof from the rest of the garrison.* Extensive quarters had been assigned to them—for they had many nuns and school-girls, priests, and monks, with a bishop at their head. This high ecclesiastical functionary, who lived in another part of the Fort, is said to have given much trouble, as he seemed bent upon making political capital out of the situation. At last it was held to be inexpedient to recognise him any longer as our referee, so Father Lewis was appointed to take his place. It has been written of this community that "their inner life was a sealed book. Their outward demonstration was a long promenade of pale sad faces, headed by two monks, whose jolly visages afforded a curious contrast to the rest." And it is added, "I do not remember that any of the nuns served as sisters of charity in the Hospitals; at least I never saw any."*

But our good Protestant Englishwomen knew little and cared less about differences of creed. Unless some accidental circumstance revealed the fact of

* I do not wish to infer that there were no exceptions to this rule. I am informed that Mrs. Vansittart, a Roman Catholic lady, was active in her ministrations.

† MS. Memorandum.

the patient's faith, those who ministered to the wants of the sick or wounded in the Hospitals, had no inkling of the creed of the patient. One poor fellow, whom Mrs. Raikes and others visited in the Hospital, was much pleased with the kindness of his lady-visitors and received them with grateful respect. He was very thankful for any newspapers or light literature that might be offered to him, but he refused to accept any of our religious books and would not listen to the reading of the Bible. One day Mrs. Raikes found his cot empty and saw him kneeling by the bedside of a Roman Catholic comrade to whom a priest was administering extreme unction. This accounted at once for the man's reluctance to listen to the Bible or to read our Protestant books.*

1857. July—Aug.

* Mr. Raikes states in his "Notes on the Revolt," that the ladies were divided into watches and attended day and night. "To avoid teasing the men by too much nursing, they were in a small separate room, and, *at stated periods*, went round to give tea, jelly, soda-water, coffee, soup, or to help in dressing the wounds of the patients. All was done under the orders of the medical officers." There was sometimes a ludicrous side to the pictures of pain and sorrow presented to the eyes of the volunteer nurses. One story I may insert here, for it is so eminently characteristic of the Englishman in India. The man of whom this is told was a common soldier; but I have witnessed similar ebullitions from our English officers—and seen the man beaten for the blunderings of his master. I give the anecdote in the writer's words. The story relates to the period after the battle of the 10th of October, the story of which is reserved for the next volume. "Amongst them was a fine young artilleryman whose leg had been badly crushed by a heavy gun-carriage. His sufferings were intense, and, poor fellow, his temper at first very irritable. Much as I pitied him I could not help feeling amused one day when I found him threatening a hospital coolie who was bringing a chillumchee (brass basin) filled with water. Poor young Cumming was shaking his fists and saying alternately 'Put it down,' and 'Lee-jao' (take it away). The wretched coolie, though anxious to obey, was sorely puzzled by these conflicting orders. First he put down the water, then he took it up. Cumming was furious, until I interposed and said that the coolie did not know what was wanted. 'Yes, he does, lady; he wants to tease me and does it on purpose. I want him to put down the water and *go*, but he won't!' Poor Cumming! what a change came over him at a later day. He was quite a boy, and often spoke of his poor mother. From a lion he became a lamb. His constant words were, 'Don't leave me, dear lady, but offer up a prayer for me!' At last he sunk while joining with us in prayer. One of

1857. July—Aug. There were few, if any, among the women of Agra, who did not gratefully acknowledge the kindly aid, in all matters, rendered to them by Mr. Reade, and especially in the management of the financial affairs of those who were absent from their husbands, or who had been widowed by the great convulsions. To men and women alike shut up in Agra, the cheerful, but systematic manner, in which the "Financial Commissioner," for so they styled him without official sanction, administered the exchequer in a small apartment known as "the hole in the wall," whence he issued his warrants, which were taken to the Treasury and changed into rupees for present use, or if required into bills to be remitted to a distance, must have been very welcome to all his fellow *détenus*. Thus, as there was very little want of necessaries in the Fort, there was little lack of the means of purchasing them. Some special creature-comforts, however, were scarce. It is related that "you could buy millinery or perfumery, but not cheese, beer, wine, or tobacco."* On the whole, the burden of outward suffering to be borne by our people in the Fort was not very heavy or distressing. There were inconveniencies to be encountered, and privations to be endured—especially in respect of household accommodation and the more refined domestic appliances. The greatest evils of all were the over-crowding; the want of privacy on the one hand, and the want of ventilation on the other—the efforts to secure the former being necessarily antagonistic to

us wrote to his mother at Windsor to tell her he died happily. Another poor fellow who was sinking said, 'Lady, pray read to me of Our Lord walking on the water.' The men of the Ninth Lancers were all so gentle, indeed I may say all so gentlemanlike, that it was a rea pleasure to read to them and to nurse them in their sufferings." This also was after the battle of the 10th of October.

* Raikes.

the latter. It was a curious sort of "board-ship life," board-ship life on a gigantic scale, "stuffy, stewy, aud vermin-infested;" with a few state rooms for families, and little side-cabins or hutches for bachelors, and some open places, as cuddies or poop decks, for common resort. Most providentially it happened that the season was an unusually healthy one, and there was probably not more than the average amount of ill-health to distress the occupants of the Fort. Men and women alike missed their ordinary morning or evening rides and drives and "ate the air" under unfavourable circumstances. But the air on the ramparts was wonderfully pure, for the Fort stood high, and the river flowed beneath it, and there was a luxury of their own in the evening promenades. But it must be acknowledged that their employments and diversions were of a somewhat monotonous character. The Engineers had more than enough to do, to keep them at work from sunrise to sundown; and some had business, or made it, in drilling troops for militia or volunteer service, whilst many were driven to the undignified occupation of "loafing." There was no lack of books; but the unwritten contemporary histories were those most discussed, and when the curse of *ennui* sate so heavily upon them, it is not strange that the *gup*, or gossip, market was plentifully supplied, and that sometimes vague, wild rumours passed from mouth to mouth and were embraced or discarded according to the temper of the recipients. But the evening, perhaps, was the pleasantest time, when men met each other at one or other of the numerous messes that had been established, and ate their homely, but abundant fare, with good appetites and cheery faces. One of the best, if not the best of all, was

1857. July—Aug.

1857. July—Aug. that presided over by Machell, the Ordnance Commissariat Officer, who had special means of purveying the best of fare that the place could supply.

Meanwhile, there was little in the aspect of affairs beyond Agra to lighten the burden of trouble that oppressed the Lieutenant-Governor. July passed and August passed; but there was no appearance of the capture of Delhi. Colvin was in close correspondence with Hervey Greathed; but the Commissioner, though of a cheerful nature, could send no tidings to gladden Colvin's heart. Delhi still in the hands of the insurgents and Lucknow unrelieved, there was no prospect of any aid from without to set free the Agra garrison. The fall of the great stronghold of the Moguls might virtually change the condition of affairs throughout the whole of the North-Western Provinces. But, as time went on, Colvin could but see that the state of the country was growing worse and worse. The tidings which came in to him from all parts were not of an assuring character. He had wisely organised an Intelligence Department, of which William Muir had the chief direction. It was highly important at such a time that reliable information should be obtained from the officers of Government themselves in place of the gossip of the bazaars or the confused statements of frightened messengers. And no man could have done the work better than Muir. The demi-official or private correspondence that came in, from day to day, was full of the most instructive and suggestive details. It was said that he was a little over-chary in the dissemination of the intelligence he obtained. But this can scarcely be regarded as a fault when we consider how likely it was, amid such a population as that of the Agra Fort, a story once floated would be exaggerated or distorted, and might rather add to the anxieties than strengthen the confidence of our people. There was, in truth, little or nothing of an exhilarating character to be communicated; so, perhaps, silence, at such a time, was of better metal than speech. 1857. July—Aug.

It was plain, indeed, that the situation was growing more and more perilous. The temper of the soldiery was worse, and their confidence, under the influence of continued success and impunity was waxing stronger every day. In the British districts and in the petty Native States there was a general upheaving of turbulent disorders. It was the great carnival of the dispossessed. And the area of disaffection was spreading largely: not only in the country under Colvin's care, but in other countries beyond the border of the North-Western Provinces; and the political significance of the movement was becoming, every week, more apparent. It had been hoped and, indeed, commonly believed, that the Bombay Army was staunch to the core. It was the fashion to speak of the mutiny of the Bengal Army, engendered by the accident of the greased cartridges. But now, as August dawned upon us, ugly rumours came of an outbreak in the Kolapore country and the mutiny of the Twenty-seventh Regiment. There could be nothing more significant than this. The outbreak did not come out of greased cartridges, but out of the Sattarah Lapse. "In 1849," wrote Lord Dalhousie in his celebrated Farewell Minute, "the principality of Sattarah was included in the British dominions by Right of Lapse."* The Rajah of Sattarah, a descendant of Sivajee, was the acknowledged chief of the Mahrattas. None questioned his su-

* See vol. i. page 71.

1857. July—Aug. premacy. The "Right of Lapse" was not very patiently admitted by the family, who memorialised the East India Company and sent an agent to England to advocate the justice of their claims. It happened that at this time, Azimoollah Khan was advocating, in London, for like purposes, the claims of the Peishwah family, of whom Doondoo-Punt, Nana Sahib, was the chief. To what extent the Mahratta and the Mussulman, not succeeding at all with the Directors of the East India Company, who at that time were the servants not the masters of Lord Dalhousie, took counsel together can only be conjectured. Rungo-Bapojee returned to India, by the help of the East India Company, for he was hopelessly insolvent; and he was soon busily at work in the Southern Mahratta country. That he was in communication with Bithoor may be assumed without any violent straining of the imagination. But whatsover the previous intrigue, on the last day of July the Twenty-seventh Regiment of Sepoys broke into mutiny at Kolapore. After what had happened "on the Bengal side," it was not strange that when tidings of this event reached Bombay there was something like a panic among the Europeans. As in Calcutta, some weeks before, "The European community in Bengal had taken alarm and numbers conveyed their wives and children to the shipping in the harbour. The civilians furnished Volunteer Horse that patrolled the streets at night; meetings were held to discuss points of rendezvous and best modes of defence; every one burnished up his weapons and there was a general feeling of distrust not lessened by the fact that, through the exertions of Mr. Forgett, the excellent and energetic Superintendent of Police, some of the Sepoys in garrison were found to be untrustworthy."* As in Calcutta also, the coolest head and steadiest pulse in Bombay was that of the Governor, Lord Elphinstone. He bethought himself at once of the best measures to be adopted and of the best man to give them effect. The man was Colonel Le Grand Jacob, who had recently returned from the scene of the Persian war, in which he had held command under Sir James Outram. He had a large knowledge of the political affairs of Western India, and he was a soldier of high courage and activity. Lord Elphinstone sent for him and gave him the supreme direction of affairs in the disturbed country. And at the same time he despatched from Bombay, the greater part of the way by sea, a detachment of European Infantry and Artillery. How well Jacob proved that the Governor had placed his confidence in the right man, and how subsequent events in Western India revealed the dangers which were lurking there, will be shown in a later chapter of this narrative. In this place it is enough to say that these tidings of disaffection in the Bombay Army must have fallen heavily upon Colvin. There was at least a likelihood that it would spread, and this likelihood was to be provided against by the Government, whose first duty it was to protect its own people; so there was small chance of the Agra dependencies being relieved, from Bombay, however pressing the need might be. The fidelity of the Bombay Army was a fountain of hope to the Lieutenant-Governor of the North-Western Provinces, and now it was dried up at its source.

1857. July—Aug.

But some stirring spirits were in the Agra garrison Agra.

* "Western India before and during the Mutinies," by Sir G. Le Grand Jacob. I shall write more fully of these Western risings in my next volume. Meanwhile the reader will do well to consult Jacob's book.

1857. July—Aug. who believed that they might do something to help themselves. It was plain that an error had been committed after the battle of Shahgunj in shutting up the Fort so closely as to engender the belief outside that we had no power of further action left in us. The danger anticipated was quite visionary. There was less vitality in the insurgent army than in our own. So far from meditating an attack on the Agra Fort they had been glad to make their way in the direction of Muttra with the utmost possible despatch. The burning and sacking of the cantonments had not been their work. But there were some of our own people, who thought that they could do no better service than by firing wildly down on no one in particular, and thus preventing our friends from obtaining ingress to the Fort and affording us the information we most needed. But now the truth of this had become apparent, and there was a very general desire to go out and do something. Foremost among these were the gentlemen of the Volunteer Horse, who having little or nothing to do in the Fort were eager for some work beyond it. New councils were now prevailing and resolute action was taking the place of the old vacillation and total want of self-reliance that at one time had brought us to feebleness. Brigadier Polwhele had been superseded, and Colonel Cotton had taken his place. There was no cold blood in his veins. He is said, indeed, to have been a somewhat fiery warrior and to have been called "Gun-Cotton" by his comrades. He was easily wrought upon to send out a force to Aligurh to re-occupy that place,* where a rebel Government had

* Mr. Paterson Saunders, of the Volunteer Horse, says that he persuaded Cotton to send out the Force, and, doubtless, he did. But Cotton had no power, except that which was delegated to him by the

been set up by one Ghousa Khan, who proclaimed himself as Soubahdar of the King of Delhi. "The object of this movement was to give protection to the important town of Hatrass, which has hitherto escaped being plundered, to establish authority in this portion of the Aligurh district, to give confidence to the local Talookhdars, whose possessions are in the neigbourhood of Hatrass, and to frustrate the attempts of certain rebels to usurp the authority of the British Government in other parts of the Aligurh district."* 1857. July—Aug.

Action at Aligurh.

Major Montgomery, Brigade-Major of Agra, than whom there was no better officer in the garrison, was appointed to command the Force. On the 20th of August he went out taking with him three companies of Europeans, three guns, a body of Volunteer Horse,† and some Ghat horsemen raised by Thakoor Govind Singh. Arthur Cocks went with them, armed with special powers as Commissioner They started at 4 P.M. on the 20th of October On the 24th they were in the neighbourhood of the insurgents. The enemy were composed chiefly of the

Civil authorities. It is understood that Arthur Cocks, aided by Reade and others, induced Colvin to give his consent. Mr. Saunders' words are: "I persuaded him, Cotton, to send out a party to attack him, (Ghousa Khan), otherwise the Soubahdar would have been his most formidable enemy."

* Memorandum of Instructions by Mr. E. A. Reade. The Lieutenant-Governor was too feeble to draw them up himself. But he countersigned the document.

† The uninstructed reader must be cautioned not to confound the Agra Militia with the Volunteer Horse—I believe that some of both were present. Mr. Reade says: "The Militia is composed of military officers of regiments which have mutinied, or have been disarmed, of members of the Civil Service holding appointments, of salaried clerks in the public offices, of sectioners, of men drafted from the European regiment, of pensioners, of Christian drummers, musicians, &c., from Native regiments, and of individuals not heretofore in the service of Government. It is an additional complication that some of the Agra Volunteer Horse now serve in the Militia, and that some of the Militia have been drafted into the recently constituted Rifle Company."

1857. July—Aug. men raised by Ghousa Khan; but with them were some troopers of the notorious Third Cavalry. They had taken up their position in a walled garden; and it was not easy at first to accurately discern their location. But Saunders, who had ridden round the enclosure, "potted at," as he wrote, "by the enemy lining two sides of the square," carried information to Montgomery, which enabled him to make his dispositions. This was one of those actions of which it is difficult to give a comprehensive account with certainty of accuracy; for every man was so busy with his own work that he knew little of what others were doing at any given moment. The battle raged furiously for some time. All arms of our force fought with distinguished gallantry, and the enemy grappled with them in all the wild energy of desperation. Conspicuous on the field for deeds of daring were the Volunteer Horse; and conspicuous among the horsemen were Saunders and Tandy. Tandy was a man of whom all men knew that he was ready to dash into any dangerous enterprise, and to sell his life, not for the sake of the Government, for which he had less than no love at all, but for the sake of his murdered countrymen and their wives and children. Saunders went into battle with kindred sentiments. When he died, it was said of him that few men had more of the noble chivalry of the old times.* He was a bold, frank man; not chary of speech, and not chary of self. Tandy fell fighting gloriously; Saunders narrowly escaped the bullets to which he unflinchingly exposed himself. Many other brave men did their work well on that day; none better than Captain Murray. Saunders having, as above stated, learnt the

* It should be mentioned that his calling was that of an indigo-planter.

vulnerable point of attack, led that officer to it, and now came the crisis of the action. Murray charged into the midst of Ghousa Khan's people, and was soon engaged in a desperate hand to hand encounter with one of his leading followers. The Englishman slew his man; and the enemy soon lost heart. So completely were they routed that the enterprise was abandoned, and they made the best of their way from Aligurh.

1857. July—Aug.

It too often happens that in narratives of this kind the good deeds of the humbler heroes of the hour find no record. One instance may be cited here. The telegraph wires had been recovered by the activity of the boys of the Department, and a line had been laid between Agra and Aligurh; it being of high importance that all the movements of Montgomery's force should be known in the Fort. One of these boys, named Tayler, sat in a palanquin carriage, close to the field of action, and coolly telegraphed back to Agra all the incidents of the battle as they occurred. There was great rejoicing when it was known that the enemy had fled; and it is to be hoped that the youngster was rewarded.

Last illness of Mr. Colvin.

All this time Colvin was gradually wearing away. After the defeat of our troops on the 5th of July, and our withdrawal into the Fort, he seems to have lost heart and hope. This slow fading away was perceptible to the devoted friends by whom he was surrounded; but he was reluctant to admit that he was breaking down. Perhaps he thought it was sound policy not to confess any apprehensions of the inner dangers that threatened the life of the Lieutenant-Governor. He would not cease to work. No entreaties, no remonstrances could induce him to spare

1857. July—Aug. himself. He had a noble staff of officers under him, who were fully to be trusted; but even in minute details he toiled on to the last. Day after day, from all parts of the provinces, came in reports from his officers—often despairing cries for help, written in French or in Greek characters, and with difficulty to be deciphered. He issued instructions on each. I have them before me, and there are not many not endorsed in his familiar handwriting. Even paltry executive details far beneath the dignity of so high an officer to be concerned with were supervised by the Lieutenant-Governor with a rigid conscientiousness as uncalled for and undesirable as it was praiseworthy in intention. Writing of the month of July, one who served under him, said: "Even now, if I wanted a sword or a pistol from the Magazine, Mr. Colvin's counter-signature was necessary."

Charles Raikes.

This burden of toil alone might not have destroyed him, but it was aggravated a hundredfold by the burden of anxiety that oppressed him. Perhaps of all men in high position during that troubled year, he was the most severely tried. He saw district after district, under his government, passing away from him. He saw hundreds and hundreds of his fellow Christians —men, women, and children—pitilessly massacred. But he could do little to save the country or to rescue our people. Nothing, however, pained him more than the unkindness of those who ought to have sympathised with and aided him. One, who knew better than all others what was on, wrote to me, saying: "He had the mortification to find himself generally unable to exact respect or to enforce obedience. He proposed measure after measure only in too many cases to be met by excuses, evasions, or flat refusals. He attended one or two funerals of officers beyond the entrenchments, he visited the hospitals, traversed the ramparts, and had a kind word for all. But it was of no use, his reception was cold and sullen, when it was not actually disrespectful. He had brutally savage letters in his box." He was emphatically a strong man; but now, in this great extremity, shut up in Agra, with no hope of succour, no chance of deliverance, and little support, he felt that he was helpless as an infant. So as the months of July and August wore on, and the clouds grew darker and denser, it became more patent to those about him, and especially to the chief medical officer, Dr. Farquhar, that he was rapidly breaking down. Yet Colvin himself was slow to acknowledge that he was sensible of any diminution of mental or physical energy, except in regard of some impairment of his old powers of fixing his mind even on small details, which he said greatly distressed him. As far back as the 2nd of July his medical attendant had apprehended an attack of apoplexy, but this had been warded off by judicious prophylactics; and he urged "the necessity of Mr. Colvin's enjoying for a time perfect rest of body and of mind. I am, therefore, desirous that on the first opportunity he should proceed down country, and thence to England, for the recovery of his health."

1857. July—Aug.

But all this was denied to him. Beyond a temporary removal from the Fort to the Cantonment, the purer air of which did him some good, there was no possibility of effecting the desired change, even if Colvin had consented to forego his labours. He knew well that he should never see the old country again. In this knowledge he touchingly quoted to his private secretary, Captain Prinsep, the well-known line of the Æneid: "Nec patriam antiquam nunc est

1857. July—Aug. spes ulla videndi." He was rapidly growing worse, and in the first week of September it was plain that his end was approaching. On the 8th there was a consultation of medical officers, and it was unanimously agreed that "the state of Mr. Colvin's health was such that his continuing to attend to business was dangerous to his life." It was too late. The day of rest was, indeed, approaching—but it was beyond the grave. He was quite prepared for the great change. Mr. French, the Chaplain, who ministered to him at the last, found that he was quite tranquil and assured. He said that he could appeal to all who had watched his career and known his public character—and especially during the last months of sore trial and tribulation—that "he had not shrunk from bearing the burden which God had called upon him to sustain;" that he had performed his duty to the utmost of his ability; and that he had striven "to have always a conscience void of offence towards God and Man." "But it was not," adds the reverend writer, "the consciousness of integrity and honesty of purpose which was the pillow that supported his dying head. . . . He felt in the solemnity of the hour in which he was called to prepare to meet his God, that it was the atonement and intercession of Christ that he found to be 'an anchor of the soul both sure and steadfast.' These words emphatically repeated were some of the last that escaped his lips." He died on the 9th of September, and History rejoices to accord him a place in the front rank of those who died for their country, during that tremendous epoch, more painfully and not less gloriously than those who died on the battle-field—a true Christian hero of whom the nation must ever be most proud.

BOOK IX.—LUCKNOW AND DELHI.

[MAY—SEPTEMBER, 1857.]

CHAPTER I.

GENERAL STATE OF OUDE—CAUSES OF INQUIETUDE—RUIN OF THE INFLUENTIAL CLASSES—THE NOBLES—THE GREAT LANDHOLDERS—THE SOLDIERY—OVERTAXATION OF THE PEOPLE—LUCKNOW IN MAY—THREATENINGS OF REVOLT—PRECAUTIONS OF SIR HENRY LAWRENCE—DEFENSIVE MEASURES—PROGRESS OF MUTINY—THE OUTBREAK IN CANTONMENTS.

1856—57.

General condition of Oude.

FROM one end of India to the other, there was no tract of country, the circumstances of which were to be regarded with more reasonable anxiety and alarm, than the great province of Oude. How, after a long period of misgovernment by its Native rulers, it had passed under the administration of the British, and in what manner it had been governed during the first year after its annexation, has been told in the early part of this History. With the ordinary egotism of the English, blinded by our national self-love, we had looked upon the seizure of Oude as a grand deliverance of the people. It was boasted that a line of Native tyrants had been cut off, and that for their ceaseless cruelty and rapacity had been substituted the just and benevolent sway of the Christian ruler. Law and order, it was said, were to prevail in the place of anarchy and rapine. At the head of the new administration were placed three "experienced

1857. civilians" from the North-Western Provinces, charged with the duty of introducing into Oude the systems which, in that part of the country, it was said, had developed such encouraging results. It has been already shown how these men frittered away their energies in unseemly personal contentions with each other, whilst much of the most important work of Government was neglected, and dangers of all kinds were suffered to gather unheeded around their doors.* Either the sympathetic faculty was wholly absent from their breasts, or they wilfully refused to see what they knew to exist. Their theory was, that the great masses of the people were with them, and that, therefore, the new Government was safe. There could not have been a more fatal error. It is true that the people might have eventually benefited by the new rule. But in India the people have no potential voice.† The *vox populi*, indeed, is little more than a silence. What our statesmen, in such a case, should have considered was, not the feeling engendered by the revolution in the rural population, but the resentments which it was likely to arouse in the breasts of the influential classes of the community. There was a dynasty extinguished—a regal Court erased—a territorial aristocracy demolished—an army disbanded. Out of any one of these might have come "votes for troubles." Out of all combined it would have been strange, indeed, if mighty mischief had not arisen to disturb the "tranquillity" of which the English boasted at the dawn of their dominion in Oude.

* It is pitiable to read the letters addressed by the Chief Commissioner to the Governor-General during the first year of our occupation of Oude. What a relief to turn from them to those of Sir Henry Lawrence!

† It is to be remembered, however, that as the soldiery of the Oude army and the retainers of the great Talookhdars were drawn from the rural population, even that class suffered by the new rule.

1857.

The Court and the nobles.

The fortunes of Wajid Ali, the deposed King, have been traced in previous books of this History. To suppose that any individual sympathies, any tender regrets, any chivalrous feelings of personal devotion, followed the exiled monarch to the British-Indian capital, would be to take a romantic view of the position not probably justified by the fact. But whatsoever the weakness, the selfishness, the profligacy of the man may be, there is always a sort of reverential affection for the King, which neither political imbecility nor moral turpitude can destroy. Oude had seen a succession of Nawabs and Kings of the same family, differing little from each other in their love of self and their disregard of others. But these men, bad as they were, were Native rulers, Mahomedan Princes; and the country had become accustomed even to their abominations. Moreover, there was a large number of people who profited greatly by the extravagance and licentiousness of the Court of Lucknow. Money was freely spent—freely circulated—within the home circuit. It did not go out of the province—scarcely out of the capital. There were shoals of Court functionaries, of Court tradesmen, of titled pensioners, to whom the coffers of the King were accessible; and who were simply ruined when his Majesty was dethroned. The condition of some of these people was truly pitiable. Men and women of high birth, tenderly reared and luxuriously surrounded, were suddenly cast adrift on the world, without the means of subsistence. Some warded off starvation by selling their shawls and trinkets. Some are known to have gone forth into the streets to beg under cover of the darkness of the night.* The

* Mr. Gubbins, the Financial Commissioner, states this in his book with a candour and self-negation worthy of all praise: "But perhaps

1857. usurpation of the English had sunk them into the uttermost depths of humiliation; and there was no one to listen to their despairing cries. Nothing was further from the intention of Government than that these privileged classes should suffer. But the fact remains that they suffered miserably. Whilst the Chief Commissioner and the Financial Commissioner were indulging in contemptible conflicts of authority, the settlement of the Oude Pension List was in abeyance; and nothing was done to provide the pensioners with *ad interim* allowances to keep them from starving. It was, doubtless, a very difficult and complicated business, and the complete disentanglement of it must have been a work of time. The stipends and pensions were of many kinds, drawn from many sources; and in the first year of British administration, work was burdensome and distracting, and much of it had to be learnt by our "experienced civilians." Abler men were not to be found for the performance of administrative duties in our settled provinces; but in a country just rescued, as it was phrased, from Native misrule, they were all astray in the dark. Lacking sympathy with the nobility and gentry of India, they seem to have looked upon the question of the Oude Pension Lists as a problem to be worked out on paper, not as an immediate matter of food and clothing, dignity and modesty, indeed of

the class most entitled to sympathy was the nobility itself, and the numberless relatives and friends who hung upon it. The nobles had received large pensions from the Native Government, the payment of which, never regular, ceased with the introduction of our rule. Government had made liberal provision for their support; but before this could be obtained, it was necessary to prepare careful lists of the grantees, and to investigate their claims. It must be admitted that in effecting this there was undue delay, and that for want of common means of support the gentry and nobility of the city were brought to great straits and suffering. We were informed that families, which had never before been outside the Zenana, used to go out at night and beg their bread."

very life and death, to hundreds, whose misfortune it was to be off-shoots of an effete dynasty—perhaps minions of a corrupt Court—unable to dig and ashamed to beg, and therefore hopelessly stranded after the great wreck of the Native Government.* But Henry Lawrence, who carried with him to Oude the best of heads and the best of hearts, saw at once this terrible omission, and promptly proceeded to redress the wrong. Like many other good deeds done by good men, it was too late. The humiliation had been inflicted, the sufferings had been endured; and the bitter resentments which were festering in the breasts of these down-trodden nobles were not to be eradicated by this tardy instalment of justice. 1857.

And so naturally—reasonably, indeed—the people of the Court, of all kinds, came to hate us with a bitter hatred, and rejoiced when they heard that others had like reason with themselves to long for a day of retribution. They soon found that there were other influential classes who were exacerbated in an equal degree against the new dominion of the white men. Foremost among them were the great baronial land-holders of the country, among whom the English Government had determined to let loose their settlement officers, with instructions to adhere closely to the practice observed in the provinces on the other side of the river. The principles of Bird and Thomason were to have pregnant expression. The Talookhdars were to be crushed down. The opportunity was

The landed aristocracy.

* I do not mean to attribute the immediate executive failure to the Financial Commissioner or his Superior. For the duty of supervising and administering the Pension Lists had been especially intrusted to Captain Fletcher Hayes, who had been appointed Political Assistant to the Chief Commissioner. He was a gallant soldier and an accomplished scholar, but he was dilatory and procrastinating, and he did not get on with his work. This is the official history of the case; but I do not see that it in any way exempts from blame the Chief Commissioner, whose duty it was to see that the work was done by his subordinate.

1857. one most inviting to the disciples of the great levelling school; for, in truth, the Oude Talookhdars had a very evil reputation. Their faces had been blackened, past all hope of purification, by one who held the Thomasonian school in no sort of respect. Colonel Sleeman had printed, for official circulation, two volumes of a "Diary of a Tour in Oude," full of startling revelations of misrule, in which the territorial aristocracy of the country appeared as little better than bandits and outlaws. No one, indeed, had a good word to say for them; so they were sacrificed without remorse. In the new settlement that was made by the English officers they were treated as mere middle-men, and direct engagements were made with village proprietors who had before been content to occupy and to cultivate their lands under the old Talookhdars. Practically, the same results would have followed annexation, if these men had been better landlords and better subjects. But their evil reputation in our eyes, the fame of which had preceded our advent, gave zest to the employment, and barred the sufferers from sympathy. We had not sufficient toleration to discern the essential truth, that great as were the faults, perhaps the crimes of these men, they were the growth of a vicious system, of cankering circumstances, and that it needed only, as was afterwards shown, a better political atmosphere to develop the higher qualities which were latent within them.

But it was not simply through the circumstance of these "estates overthrown" that the germs of future danger lay embedded beneath the ruins of the territorial aristocracy. These great Talookhdars had large bodies of retainers; fighting men armed in a rude sort of way, who had been employed to defy the Government on the one side, and to coerce the cultivators on the other. They had mud forts, with dense jungly enclosures; and mounted guns, which might not have satisfied the critical perceptions of the skilled artillerymen of Dum-Dum and Meerut, but which could do some mischief when occasion required. On the assumption of the Government by the English, these forts were dismantled; these jungly barriers were cleared away; these baronial levies were disarmed and disbanded. Thus was the resentment of the Talookhdars further aroused, and the dangerous classes swollen by the addition of thousands of ruined retainers. The disarming of a country is something that looks well on paper. But in practice it is commonly a delusion. As long as Mother Earth is at hand to receive the iron, back again into her bosom, guns and swords will be buried and give no sign of their existence. It was the theory, too, that these fighting men would, at a moment's notice, return to the plough, and become peaceful tillers of the soil. A few of them, perhaps, did; but the majority were left without employment, chafing under the injury that had been done to them, and sullenly waiting the time to strike. 1857.

No one regarded this as any source of peril to the State; nor, indeed, was it supposed that there was any lurking danger anywhere at the bottom of the great revolution that we had accomplished. But there were other classes than the pensioned nobility and great landed gentry—the feudal Barons of Oude—whom the new supremacy grievously affected. There had been a large Native Army in the service of the King, which had necessarily been disbanded. The soldiery were drawn from the same classes as had recruited our own Army. But as The soldiery.

1857. soldiers they differed, in all essential conditions, from their brethren in the Company's service. The relations between them and the Government were of the most dissolute kind. Master and servant were equally bad. Where is irregularity of payment, there is irregularity of discipline. Under the rule of Wajid Ali, they were a sort of licensed banditti. Sixty thousands of these men had to be disposed of when the British Army was marched into Oude. Some of these—about a quarter of the whole—were taken into the service of the new Government. The rest were cast adrift upon the province with small pensions or gratuities. Sullen, but not despairing, they went off to their native villages, and talked to their brothers and their sons about what was to be lost and what was to be gained by the usurpation of the English. It was natural to them that they should wait and see. Even those who had been dismissed with gratuities had money to spend for the present. And to all had been paid the arrears due by the Oude Government. So there was no need to stir at once. This temporary quiescence was mistaken for permanent content. But when Sir Henry Lawrence was established in the Lucknow Residency, he saw at once that there was danger to be looked for, not only from the disbanded soldiery, but from those who had been taken into the service of the British—especially from the regiments that had been re-enlisted *en masse*. "Our Punjab Irregulars," he wrote to Lord Canning in April, "were mostly either men who had fought under me, or Edwardes, or my brother George, or were new levies recruited from the villages. Here the Irregulars are bodies of men who last year served the King, and who have been taken in masses on their old foundations as regiments with all their old associations. . . . It is quite a mistake to suppose that these regiments like our service better than the King's. The small extra pay (eight annas*) does not cover the extra bother—the pipe-clay, and discipline, and duty. Besides, the officers and men have lost consideration and opportunites of plunder."† 1857.

New taxes.

But the innovations of the English, which thus struck at the very vitals of all the most influential classes in Oude, did not leave untouched the larger masses of the people. From among the causes of seditions set down in the great Baconian analysis, which stands as the motto or text of this work, "Taxes" are not omitted. The enthusiasm of our civil administrators was commonly directed towards the balance sheet. They had learnt, under Lord Dalhousie, that, on the annexation of a new province, it was expected that those, to whose its administration was intrusted, should demonstrate, by figured statements, that it would "pay." Perhaps the old "mercantile bottom" of the East India Company was, in some measure, answerable for this. I do not underrate the importance of the consideration thus suggested. But the mistake always lay in the attempt made to bring out results by a forcing process of unwholesome rapidity. Officers trained in the essential business of "settlement operations" had learnt that their efficiency as public servants was estimated in accordance with the success attending their efforts to screw up the revenue of their several districts to the highest possible pitch of productiveness. As long as the money was got, there was very little thought of the effect that might be produced on the minds of

* A shilling a month.

† Sir Henry Lawrence to Lord Canning, April 18, 1857.—*MS. Correspondence.*

1857. the people by the manner of getting it. The black-and-white of demonstrable figures was greater in their minds than the animosities and resentments of an over-taxed people. So when Jackson and Gubbins went to Oude, they thought that they would gain great credit by making fine figured statements of forthcoming revenue from every possible source. The smoking of opium, or the enjoyment of the narcotic in some form or other, was almost as great a necessity to the people of Lucknow as to the people of Canton. So a heavy tax was laid upon opium. It created intense dissatisfaction. Opium-smoking, or opium-eating, or opium-drinking, is not, to any great extent, a prevailing taste of the English people; so it would have been a miracle if an English administrator, from the Regulation Provinces, had for the nonce put himself into the skin of a citizen of Lucknow, and, taking mentally a loan of his stomach, ascertained by sympathy what would be the effect of raising the price of the acquired necessity to what might be, and was in the case of many, a prohibition price.* Nor was the tax on opium the only financial experiment that pressed heavily on the people, especially of the large towns. The prices of other necessaries were raised, if not by direct imposts, by contract systems, which had equally injurious effects. And whilst our new revenue laws were thus disquieting the people, our new judicial regulations, with their increased formalities, and delays, and expenses, were causing scarcely less uneasiness and scarcely less popular dislike of the new Government,

* Mr. Rees ("Siege of Lucknow") says that "many who could not obtain it at the increased rates actually cut their throats in desperation." I do not vouch for the literal accuracy of this statement. But it is easy to understand the miserable depression of an enervated Asiatic deprived of his accustomed drug.

which was subverting everything with an unsparing hand, and boasting of its beneficent improvements. 1857.

Old and new systems.

No man of healthy intellect can express a doubt that the system of government which the English introduced into Oude was far superior to that which was superseded by it. Order and security are, doubtless, great blessings. But time alone can teach people unaccustomed to such enjoyments thoroughly to appreciate them. Like the beasts of the forest, or the birds of the air, men are slow to conform themselves to the tame domestic conditions. Food may be precarious—life itself may depend upon the will of some stronger animal; but the security, which brings restraints with it, is not appreciable at the outset. We are too prone to bury this fact beneath a heap of platitudes about Humanity and Civilisation, and to complain of the ingratitude of those who do not rush eagerly to embrace our proffered benefits. It is from the intensity of our national ignorance that this great moral cataract proceeds, blinding our eyes to the truth, and causing us to stumble disastrously along the great road of "improvement," which seems to us to be so smooth and open, but which in reality is everywhere beset with impediments and obstructions. We are in too great a hurry to do good after our own fashion. And so we introduce sudden changes, which the people rarely understand, and often resent, until resentment grows into resistance. It is commonly beneath the dignity of our administrators to feel their way to reformation. It is as though a general were to endeavour to force his way into the unknown country of an enemy, without an intelligence department and without pioneers. And so it was with our civilians in Oude. They were not answerable for the system. That originated in Calcutta. It was the

1857. executive work of Mr. George Edmonstone. It bore the impress of the strong brain of Lord Dalhousie. The initial instructions to the Chief Commissioner, dated February 4, 1856, were distinguished by intellectual ability of a high order. They were clear, decided, exhaustive. But lacking the great essential of sympathy, they were utterly unsuited to the purpose. Nobody concerned in drafting the new code seems ever to have thought of the feelings of those whom our system would injuriously affect. There was an utter want of that dramatic perception which enables great statesmen, as it enables great writers, to see into the hearts of men and to know the effects of circumstances upon them. But even with this code before him, a Chief Commissioner of a different stamp—a man such as Outram or Lawrence—with less knowledge of Regulations and more knowledge of Men, might have gradually accommodated the scheme to the changing habits of the people. But these over-zealous civilians, instead of waiting, plunged at once into a great sea of "reformation," and raised a storm which could be subdued only by an overwhelming army.

Lucknow in April and May.

But to Sir Henry Lawrence all these things were clear; and he never ceased to see in them the materials of which revolutions are made. He had always been a great master of the art of "letting people down easily;" and his large sympathies had brought upon him the one great trouble of his life. He saw now with painful distinctness the grievous mistakes which had been committed by our Civilian Government during the first year of British administration; and he deplored, as Lord Canning must then have deplored, the accident which had sent him to Rajpootana, whilst to Mr. Colverly Jackson was intrusted the work of introducing the new system into Oude. In April he had written to the Governor-General, saying: "This city (Lucknow) is said to contain six or seven hundred thousand souls, and does certainly contain many thousands (twenty thousand, I was told yesterday) of disbanded soldiers, and of hungry, nay, starving dependents of the late Government. There *must* be intrigue and disaffection in such a mass. . . . This very morning a clod was thrown at Mr. Ommaney, and another struck Major Anderson whilst in a buggy with myself. . . . The improvements in the city have gone on very fast—too fast and too roughly. Much discontent has been caused by demolitions of buildings, &c., and still more by threats of further similar measures. Also regarding the seizure of religious and other edifices, and plots of ground as Government property. I have visited many of these places and pacified parties, and prohibited any seizures or demolitions without competent authority. The revenue measures, though not as sweeping as represented by the writer, whose letter your Lordship sent me by Colonel Edwardes, have been unsatisfactory. Reductions have been made to the amount of fifteen, twenty, thirty, and even thirty-five per cent., showing how heavy was last year's assessment. The Talookhdars have also, I fear, been hardly dealt with. At least, in the Fyzabad Division they have lost half their villages—some have lost all." Well might he have exclaimed, "All these things are against me!" He derived no comfort from the thought that more than a year had passed without any great demonstration of discontent. For, as he wrote in the letter above quoted, "it is not the

1857. April—May.

1857. April—May.

fashion for Natives to act energetically, or to commit themselves in a hurry." No people in the world know better how to *wait*.

State of the soldiery.

"As long as we can perfectly trust our own people, there will be little danger from any others." This was the one drop of consolation that remained, and it was now fast being dried up. The tranquillity of Oude had been so settled a fact in the minds of our English statesmen, that well-nigh all the European troops had been removed from the province, and such hostilities as might arise from the numerous causes above recited were held in check by Native regiments, Regular and Irregular, at the capital and at the out-stations. At Lucknow there was one weak white regiment—the Thirty-second, under Colonel John Inglis. But such, in the face of so many and great dangers, was the confidence reposed in the general contentment of all classes of the people, that, with the exception of a weak company at Lucknow, there was no European Artillery from one end of Oude to the other. Often had Sir Henry Lawrence, publicly and privately, dwelt, with all the earnestness of his nature, upon the danger of thus falling asleep in the lap of a false security.* And now, as the month of May came in, he saw terribly before him the fulfilment of the old predictions which had been scoffed at by many and unheeded by all. Already has been shown, in an earlier part of this History, what were the first manifestations of an

* See the warnings quoted at page 453, vol. i. The Civilian Chief Commissioner was of opinion that no white troops were required in Oude. A wing of a European regiment was stationed at Cawnpore as a support to the Thirty-second at Lucknow. In the early part of 1857 the military authorities wished to remove this wing, and Mr. Jackson was consulted as to the safety of the measure. His answer was that they might take the wing and also the regiment at Lucknow, as he could hold the province with the Irregulars and the Police.

unquiet spirit in the Lines of Lucknow. Regulars and Irregulars were obviously on the brink of mutiny. Still he did not despair of the Sepoys. He felt that there were some soft spots in them which he would try to reach. If it were right and wise to punish those who had done evil, it was no less right and wise to reward those who had done well. There had been some conspicuous instances of loyalty and devotion to the British Government. Some good might come from a public recognition of these good services, and from an appeal to the better feelings of the general body of the Native soldiery. So the Chief Commissioner determined to hold a grand Durbar. 1857. April—May.

Lawrence was, at this time, resident in the Muriaon Cantonment. The Durbar was to be held in front of his house. At sunset, on the 12th of May, the Chief Commissioner, attended by all his principal military and civil officers, and by some of the chief people of the city, met the officers of the Native Army* in his garden grounds, and, addressing them in Hindostanee, appealed to all their best feelings as soldiers and as comrades. It was an imposing scene. The lawn was carpeted. The seats ranged for the visitors formed three sides of a square. Behind them stood groups of Sepoys eagerly watching the proceedings and listening to the words which fell from the venerable chief. And visible to all were the dresses of honour and the trays of presents that were to be given to the faithful soldiers, who had earned these rewards by their loyalty and devotion. May 12. The Durbar in Cantonments.

"I explained to them," wrote Sir Henry Lawrence, a few days afterwards, "our policy of non-interference with their religious prejudices, and appealed to the history of the last hundred years. I pointed out to

* About fifty privates from each regiment were also present.

1857. May 12. them our strength at home, and the utter madness of their expecting to subvert our power. I showed what we had done, late in the day at Sebastopol, and how that it is equally possible to bring five thousand or thirty thousand Europeans to bear on India. . . . I said that I had come to Oude not for my own profit, but to help them and the country, and that by God's blessing we should get over our present difficulties." All this and much more, he said to them—especially reminding them of the fidelity of generation after generation of Sepoys, who had eaten the Company's salt, and had shared, in mutual confidence and comradeship with their British officers, the dangers and the privations of war. It was the plain, forcible eloquence of genuine sincerity. No words could have been better chosen. They were listened to with rapt attention, and they seemed to make a deep impression on the minds of the hearers. When he ceased, the dresses of honour and the purses of money were distributed, and the Durbar broke up. The English and Native officers conversed with each other; and the latter were voluble in their professions of devotion to the British Government. Perhaps they were sincere at the time.* But the question was, how long would the impression last? Sir Henry Lawrence said that the next fortnight would be one of great anxiety; but he little knew what it would produce.

At this time news was travelling through the country, which, when received from Agra on the 13th, was scarcely credited, in all its length and breadth,

* Mr. Gubbins says: "A number of Sepoys were standing round the space appropriated to the Durbar. We subsequently learnt that the remarks which they were overheard to make were of a different character, and that they attributed the whole proceeding to our fears."

by the Lucknow Commissioner.* At the first blush, 1857.
Lawrence pronounced the account of the disastrous May.
tidings from Meerut to be greatly exaggerated. But the next day brought still more painful and more alarming intelligence. Delhi was in the hands of the mutineers, and the sovereignty of Behaudur Shah had been proclaimed. It has been already told how, on being thus terribly assured of the calamity that had fallen on our people, he had telegraphed to the Governor-General for plenary military power,† and how, in reply, Lord Canning had cheerfully given Lawrence his unstinting confidence, and had placed the chief military command in his hands, with the rank of Brigadier-General. He was one of those who, in all great conjunctures, was eager to take upon himself the largest possible amount of responsibility. He was a man of a sensitive nature, and any proof of confidence in his superiors braced him up to new endeavours to show that it was not misplaced. With this plenary authority in his hands, he now felt that, if, with God's blessing, human agency could save the province—save the lives of our people and

* "We had greatly exaggerated accounts of Meerut doings," he wrote to Lord Canning on the 14th (I quote from his autograph letter). From this I may infer that the Delhi news had not then reached Lucknow. It reached Agra on the 13th or 14th (*ante*, page 198). Sir George Couper, however, writes to me: "We got the telegram on the afternoon of the 13th, and it informed us not only that the insurgents had occupied Delhi, but that they were trying to establish some sort of Government." Lawrence sent for his Secretary (Couper), and asked him what he thought of the news. Couper said that he believed that all the regiments in the army would revolt. Lawrence, who indeed had predicted the rising, seemed to be of the same opinion.

† Vol. i. page 613. It is another curious illustration of the conflicts of authority by which the writer of history is often beset that I have before me, written with reference to a similar assertion in Mr. Gubbins's "Narrative," a note by the man of all others whose testimony, on such a point, I should be most disposed to respect, asserting that Sir Henry Lawrence never did ask for this plenary authority, as it came unsolicited from Lord Canning. The words of Lawrence's telegrams are given in my first volume.

1857. May.

the authority of our Government—he would accomplish this great end. He would strive for the best; but he would prepare himself for the worst. There was little hope now that this epidemic of mutiny could be arrested. Assuredly it was no longer to be talked down. It was too probable, indeed, that the issue was now to be determined by strength alone—strength to do and strength to endure. Still, Sir Henry Lawrence, whilst neglecting no precaution which could contribute to the success of this last appeal, did not wholly abandon the thought that something might be done by conciliatory measures.

Want of European troops.

As a mere conflict of strength, the odds were heavily against us. What was our scanty European force has been shown. The Native force consisted of all arms—Horse, Foot, and Artillery—about seven thousand men.* How to utilise to the utmost our little body of English fighting men had been Henry Lawrence's first care. As it had never been dreamt that the English at Lucknow could ever be put upon the defensive, the troops had been posted here and there with reference to any other considerations than those which now presented themselves to the Chief Commissioner. The military Cantonments lay at a distance of three miles from the city, on the other side of the river. There the Head-Quarters of the Regular Infantry Regiments were planted; and at some distance beyond them were the Lines of the Seventh Cavalry. The road from the city to the Cantonments ran across an iron bridge; there was also a bridge, of masonry, at no great distance from it, and lower down the stream was a bridge

* I take these figures from the report of Captain Hutchinson, Military Secretary. The exact statement, referring to April 30, is six thousand nine hundred Natives and seven hundred Europeans, each exclusive of Artillery. The Native force includes the Police Battalions.

of boats. The iron bridge spanned the river near the Residency;* near the stone bridge was a commanding structure known as the Mutchee-bhawun. The barracks of the European soldiery, the quarters and the mess-house of their officers, lay a little way below the city, within a bend of the river, which there takes a circuitous direction. The Head-Quarters of the European and of the Native Regular troops were, therefore, at the two extremities of our position, with the great city between them. And in the city itself were posted the greater part of the Oude Irregulars, whilst detachments of the Regular Native regiments were continually on duty there, at the various public buildings of Lucknow.

1857. May.

Disposition of the troops.

It was now obvious to Sir Henry Lawrence that such a disposition of the troops was ill calculated to keep the Native soldiery in check, and to overbear them in the event of a sudden rising. It was deter-

* In a previous chapter (*ante*, page 203), reference is made to the extraordinary energy of Colonel Hugh Fraser, who took so distinguished a part in the defence of Agra, and an anecdote connected with Lucknow was then promised. There can be no fitter place than this for its introduction. I give it in the words of a brother officer of Engineers: "In 1842-3 Colonel Fraser was Engineer officer to the King of Oude. A cast-iron bridge had been ordered from England for the river Goomtee, some twenty-five or thirty years before, and its parts had been landed at the mouth of the river, some damaged, some wrecked. No one had ever faced the trouble of putting up this bridge, but Colonel Fraser at once took it in hand. He recovered the wrecked parts, brought all to Lucknow, got made in Calcutta and elsewhere the missing and damaged parts, and, in a few months of intense hard work, the bridge was put up. It was generally supposed the arches would collapse when the centres were struck, and Colonel Fraser, though certain his work had been well done, was very nervous on the subject. However, as he before told me he would do, when the time came for lowering the centre by driving out the wedges, he deliberately placed himself below with the workmen, and himself struck the last blows, with the intention of being crushed with the workmen if his work was to prove a failure. It stood, however, and stands to this day; though, I believe, hardly another officer in India could have been found voluntarily to undertake the work. Certainly many had the opportunity, and some expended large sums in the vain attempt to begin, but nothing really was done, in a long course of years, until Colonel Fraser took it in hand."

1857. May. mined, therefore, as a first precaution, to diminish the number of detached posts, and so to mix up Europeans and Natives as to render the latter comparatively innocuous. Under the old arrangements, the lives of all the European officers in the Cantonments were at the mercy of an insurgent soldiery; and a sudden rising in the city might have placed in the hands of rebels and rioters all the treasure and all the stores of the English; and the general spoliation might have been followed by a general massacre of our people. It was, therefore, determined that the Thirty-second should evacuate their barracks in the suburbs, where they were almost useless for purposes of defence; that a large detachment of them should be posted in the Muriaon Cantonments, and the remainder quartered in those parts of the city which were selected as our chief points of defence. One of these was the British Residency, and the other the Mutchee-bhawun, which lay upon the main road high up the river, at a distance of about a mile from the Residency. The Treasury was within the Residency grounds, close to the Banqueting-hall. In it were thirty lakhs of rupees in coin, and a still larger sum in Government securities. The abandonment of this to the forbearance of a Sepoy-guard seemed to be an invitation to them not readily to be declined. The substitution of an European guard was therefore urged upon the Chief Commissioner by Mr. Gubbins with his wonted energy. In this he was supported by Captain Fletcher Hayes, then Military Secretary; but there was something to be said on the other side, and Sir Henry Lawrence said it. It was not improbable that such a movement would precipitate the anticipated revolt. But when the subject had been discussed with Brigadier Handscombe and Colonel Inglis, and both officers concurred in the propriety of the recommendation, the Chief Commissioner withdrew his objections; and Mr. Gubbins, who had been commissioned to make the necessary preliminary arrangements, now set to work to complete them with the utmost possible despatch.* The first thing to be done was to make room for the new occupants. For not only were these European troops to be provided with accommodation in the Residency buildings, but large numbers of English women and children were to find shelter there. To suit the Residency to these altered conditions it was necessary that new dispositions should be made of well-nigh all the contents of the buildings. Great collections of furniture were to be removed; and the Government records and other materials of the office establishment of the Chief Commissioner, which had been kept in the Banqueting-hall, were to be conveyed to other receptacles. All this could not be done without much outward display of activity, which must have convinced the Sepoys at the Treasury that we were converting the Residency buildings into barracks for European troops. So Gubbins despatched a mounted messenger to the Cantonments with a letter to Lawrence, urging him at once to send a party of the Thirty-second with guns to the Residency; and on the evening of the 17th the desired reinforcements marched in, escorting the women and the sick.

1857. May.

The Mutchee-bhawun.

The Mutchee-bhawun was an extensive edifice, of commanding appearance, the upper story of which is

* It was on the 15th of May that Gubbins first made this proposal to the Chief Commissioner, and on the 16th it was discussed with Brigadier Handscombe, who was then the chief military authority. It is possible that this conflict of opinion *may* have hastened Lawrence's resolution to apply for plenary authority in matters military as well as civil. These contentions, indeed, were frequent, and sometimes of a painfully acrimonious character.

1857. May. described as "towering above the surrounding buildings." It had been a place of no little importance in the earlier history of Lucknow; but in later days it had been used as a storehouse for tents and other public property, and had been suffered to fall into decay. The dilapidated condition of the building rendered it necessary that our Engineers should put forth all their strength in restoring and fortifying it. But it was doubtful whether any human effort could so strengthen the place as to enable it, before its capabilities would be tested, successfully to resist a siege. This at first was better known to the Natives than to ourselves. It was said by them that if the fire of our own guns did not bring down the place about our ears, the fire of an enemy would soon convert it into ruins.* Ere long this became patent to our own people, and the probabilities of the abandonment of the position, at some future period, were contemplated by Sir Henry Lawrence and his colleagues. Meanwhile, this capacious edifice was to be converted into a great storehouse and arsenal. Provisions of all kinds were bought up and carefully stored in it. All our available ordnance and ammunition were gathered up and secured.† The superintendence of

* Take for example the following from a report made by Kulb Ali Khan, extra-Assistant of Seetapore (June 20th), 1827:

"The reason for all these preparations for the attack of Lucknow is, that it is believed to be so weak that if it do not fall from the fire of its own guns, it will easily do so under a fire from the outside."—*MS. Records.*

† Lawrence's efforts are thus epitomised by one of his oldest friends, in a letter to the author, quoted in a former work: "Look at Lucknow. It was Henry Lawrence's foresight, humanly speaking, that saved every one of the garrison. But for him, I do not believe that one would have escaped. Three weeks before any one thought of the possibility of our ever being besieged in Lucknow, he saw that it might be the case. He laid his plans accordingly; got in all the treasure from the city and stations; bought up and stored grain and supplies of every kind; bought up all the supplies of the European shopkeepers; got the mortars and guns to the Residency; got in the powder and small ammunition, all the shot and

this latter work was intrusted to Lieutenant Thomas of the Madras Artillery; whilst Lieutenant James, the Chief Commissariat officer at Lucknow, put forth all his energies, and developed those of his department, in the collection of supplies. In this work he was greatly aided by Mr. Simon Nicolson Martin—a name pregnant with memories of two good men, who, perhaps, did more in their time for the alleviation of human suffering than any who have ever laboured in the East.* Mr. Martin was Deputy-Commissioner of Lucknow, and was well acquainted with the localities and resources of the place. Nor in this work was Captain Carnegy, Chief of the Oude Police, less conspicuous for his activity in collecting the means of a protracted defence. But it was not sufficient at this time to resort only to measures of internal defence. It did not escape the sagacious observation of Henry Lawrence that it was equally necessary to diminish the offensive power of the enemy by destroying such of the surrounding buildings as might afford shelter to our assailants and enable them to fire into our defences. The safety of our garrison demanded this precaution. So its execution was enforced. But Lawrence was a man equally just and tolerant; he had large human sympathies which no amount of wrong-doing on the part of others could repress. The demolition of a citizen's house seemed a harsh measure—but at all events its money value might be reimbursed to the

1857.
May.

shell, and the heavy guns; had pits dug for the powder and grain; arranged for water supply; strengthened the Residency; had outworks formed; cleared away all obstructions close up to the Residency, and made every preparation for the worst; and when, after the fight at Chinhut, the mutineers closed in on the Residency, and the whole population of the city and the province rose against us, they found the little garrison amply supplied with provisions, ammunition, and resources of every kind."

* Mr Martin was the son of Sir Ranald Martin, and godson of Mr. Simon Nicolson, the famous Calcutta physician, whose benevolence was equal to his skill.

1857. May. owner. So he caused all the buildings sentenced to destruction to be appraised, before the work commenced, and every man was fairly reimbursed. But it happened that some of the most commanding buildings, and those most dangerous to the people within our line of defences, were religious edifices—towering mosques—from which a fire might be poured upon us with destructive effect. The expediency of demolishing these buildings was urged upon Lawrence by more than one of his advisers; but his answer was, "Spare the holy places." And the holy places were spared, to bring on us sad requital for our forbearance.

Feverish symptoms.

Meanwhile the Native regiments in Cantonments were in an uncertain state of semi-mutiny. Events had not sufficiently developed themselves elsewhere to encourage a general rising of the troops at Lucknow. There was disunion, therefore, in the Lines. Whilst some were prepared to strike at once, others were for further waiting and watching. Although there were daily reports of a premeditated outbreak, first on one day and then another, the anticipated hour of danger passed again and again, and still the troops were quiescent. Was it possible to keep them so?

Disarming proposed.

No man understood the Sepoy better than Sir Henry Lawrence. But to understand the Sepoy was to have a prevailing sense of his inconsistencies; and those who knew him best were ever the most perplexed as to the mode of treatment best suited to his constitution, whilst the little knowledge of brave and clever men tended to hasty judgment and counselled prompt action of the most hazardous kind. News came of the disarming of the Native regiments at Meean-Meer; and it was considered whether what had been done by a single white regiment in the Punjab might not be done also in Oude.* Lawrence believed that the Thirty-second could overawe the Native troops at Lucknow, and compel them to lay down their arms. But he was not Chief Commissioner of Lucknow—but of Oude; and although he felt that this bold stroke might be successful at the capital, he knew that such a measure would cause a general rising throughout the provinces and endanger our posts on the other side of the Ganges. The suggestion was, therefore, rightly negatived. Another question arose. If we could not overawe the Sepoys, might we not mollify and conciliate them? They had grievances—or they believed that they had grievances. There were many things dear to the Sepoy; but the dearest of all was his *tullub*, or pay. It was considered, therefore, whether a promise to raise the pay of Sepoys—Regular and Irregular—might not bring them round to their old state of contentment. All the chief officers, Civil and Military, in the City and in Cantonments, were consulted. The unanimous opinion was that the pay of the Oude Irregular Army, who did the same duty as the Regulars, should be raised. But with equal unanimity it was resolved that there should be no interference with the pay of the Regular Army.† The

1857. May.

* It must never be forgotten that the Punjab was bristling with European troops, and that what could be done safely in that province would have been dangerous, if not impossible, elsewhere.

† Mr. Gubbins says: "The proposal to raise the pay of the Regulars found no seconder but in the Secretary, Mr. Couper. It was the general opinion that the offer to increase the fixed pay of the Native Army, which had been so long established, would be attributed to fear, and would fail of the object desired. Sir Henry Lawrence probably came to the same conclusion, for the idea was abandoned." But Sir George Couper assures me that Sir Henry Lawrence was always opposed to this project, and that he (Couper) was of the same opinion. The officers consulted were Mr. Ommaney, Mr. Gubbins, Brigadier Gray, Major

1857. May 30.

distinction was obvious. So orders went forth to raise the pay of the Irregulars to a level with that of the Line.

Ripening of revolt.

Again and again it was reported that the Native troops in Cantonments were on the eve of rising, but our people had become so familiar with these reports that little importance was attached to them. Days passed and everything was quiet. The Sepoys, watched by the Europeans, went about their accustomed duties. But on the last day of May but one the long-meditated revolt had ripened. There was still division in the Lines, but the leading mutineers thought that they were strong enough for a successful movement against the Feringhees, and the firing of the nine o'clock gun on that evening was to be the signal for rebellious action. Sir Henry Lawrence was dining with his Staff in the Cantonment Residency House, when a Sepoy rushed in and reported that the game had commenced.* Presently, the sound of firing was heard. Lawrence and his officers at once sent for their horses. As they stood on the steps at the principal entrance in the clear moonlight, the subaltern of the Sepoy-guard at the Residency brought up his thirty men, and asked the General if he should load. "Load! yes, certainly," said Lawrence, "and take care of my property." The order was given, and as the men brought up their muskets in the act of loading, they levelled straight at the little group of officers waiting for their horses on the

Banks, Major Anderson, and Captain Carnegy. Lawrence discussed the question very fully with his Secretary at night—as he often discussed other matters during intervals of sleeplessness—and both concurred in opinion regarding the inexpediency of the measure. See Appendix.

* The first intimation of the intended rising was given to Captain Wilson, Assistant Adjutant-General, by a man of his regiment (the Thirteenth). The informer was one of those whom Lawrence had rewarded for having assisted in the capture of a spy. Nothing more was heard of him after the 30th of May.

steps. And, perhaps, there was not one of them, who did not experience a feeling of relief, when the men shouldered their arms and marched off to defend the gateway.* 1857. May 30.

The horses were brought round. Lawrence and his Staff mounted and rode for the Lines. The most active firing seemed to proceed from the position of the Seventy-first. On the right of that position Lawrence found three hundred men of the Queen's Thirty-second, with four guns of Major Kaye's† battery and two of the Oude Irregular Artillery, ready for action, and so posted as to sweep the Lines of the Seventy-first. At a little distance ran the road from the Cantonment to the city. It was of the utmost importance to command the great thoroughfare, so Lawrence took a company of the Thirty-second, with two guns (afterwards reinforced), and took post on the high road, thus effectually cutting off the communication of the insurgents with Lucknow. Meanwhile, the Sepoys were diligently at work, eager for the destruction of life and property. The red light of burning bungalows soon told the story of their activity as incendiaries, but as murderers they were less successful than they had hoped to be. Knowing that it was the time of the evening meal of the Feringhees, the mutineers rushed to the regimental mess-houses, but the officers on the first sound of the firing had made for their parade-grounds, so the massacre at the dinner-tables was escaped. Some were turned back by the firing; some succeeded in reaching the Lines. It was then apparent that there

* MS. Notes by a Staff Officer.

† Major Kaye himself was absent on leave at the Hills. On the outbreak of the mutiny, he joined the troops proceeding to Delhi, and commanded the detachment which took down the first siege-train. (*Ante*, vol. ii. page 189.) The Lucknow battery was commanded by Lieutenant Alexander, son of Sir James Alexander, K.C.B.

1857. May 30. was division in the regiments. Whilst many Sepoys were bent on plunder and incendiarism, others remained true to their allegiance, followed their officers, and allowed themselves to be drawn up quietly beside the European camp. Most conspicuous among the mutineers were the men of the Seventy-first, but some of them, leaving their comrades, took post "next to the Thirty-second Foot." Three hundred Sepoys of the Thirteenth, under Major Bruere, bringing their colours and their treasure-chest, also fell in beside the Europeans.* The Forty-eighth, less active in their rebellion and less demonstrative in their loyalty, remained on their parade-ground, sullen and obstinate, refusing to march against the mutineers, but not openly siding with them. Vainly did Colonel Palmer endeavour to persuade them to march to the camp of the Thirty-second. Then seeing that they were rapidly deserting, he proposed that they should follow him to the Residency in the city. This proposal met with a nominal consent, and the Colonel and the colours entered Lucknow. But with the head-quarters of the regiment there went but a scanty following. Less than a hundred men marched into the city.

It has been said that, intent as were the mutineers on the murder of their officers, no great success attended their efforts at wholesale massacre. But the night was not without its attendant horrors. On hearing the first sound of the firing, Brigadier Handscombe, with his Staff, had ridden down to the European camping-ground. He had scarcely reached the left flank of the Thirty-second, near which the

* "The treasure was very gallantly saved by Lieutenant Loughnan, assisted by the Sikhs of the regiment." — *Gubbins's "Mutinies in Oudh."*

Seventy-first Sepoys were posted, when a stray shot from the musket of a mutineer took fatal effect, and he fell dead from his horse. Lieutenant Grant, of the Seventy-first, was commanding the main picket in the centre of Cantonments, with a party drawn from different Native regiments, which for a time stood fast. But when a crowd of mutineers swept down upon them, they broke and joined the insurgents, and then Grant was hunted to his death. Vainly did a Soubahdar of the guard, and a few men less cruel than the rest, endeavour to save the white man by concealing him beneath a bed. A Sepoy of the Seventy-first tracked him, with the savage instinct of the bloodhound, and disclosed the hiding-place to his comrades. Then they dragged him out exultingly, and with bullets and bayonets soon completed their work. Lieutenant Chambers, Adjutant of the Thirteenth, whilst endeavouring to save the regimental magazine, was severely wounded. Lying helpless on the ground, he was several times fired upon by his men, but almost miraculously he escaped death. Fortunately, the Cantonment had been well-nigh emptied of its English women and children. One English lady, however, the wife of the Commandant of the Thirteenth Sepoy Regiment, had returned in defiance of orders, and had a narrow escape from violent death. Some Sepoys of the regiment, when the house was assailed in front, made a hole by which she could escape in the rear. Letting herself down through this aperture with her children, she passed the night in a dry ditch, and survived to tell the story of her adventures. 1857. May 30.

The following day was Sunday—that Sunday, the 31st of May, which is thought by many to have been fixed upon for a general rising of the Sepoys during May 31.

1857. May 13—14. the hours of our church service. The Lucknow mutineers had in the course of the night made their way to the race-course, near the Lines of the Seventh Cavalry, and thither the Europeans, with the faithful remnants of the Native regiments, followed at break of day. On reaching the open plain it was seen that a body of mutineers, some twelve hundred strong, were drawn up on the race-course, so our guns opened upon them with round shot, and they were soon in precipitate flight. Then our people gave chase as best they could—Cavalry, and Artillery, and Volunteers—and captured many of the flying enemy. On this day—as, indeed, on the preceding evening—Lieutenant Hardinge, with a body of Irregular Cavalry, did brilliant service, the record of which should not be omitted. "Hardinge," wrote Sir Henry Lawrence to Lord Canning, "is a splendid soldier. He led a few Horse several times through the burning Cantonments and through a crowd of mutineers. One shot at him within a foot, and then bayoneted him through the flesh of the arm. Hardinge shot the fellow dead. Wounded as he was he could not have had an hour's sleep, and yet he was the hero of yesterday's (Sunday's) work; and had we had any good Cavalry he would have cut up all the mutineers."

As it was, too many escaped. The Artillery, after the first discharge, do not seem to have fired a shot at the fugitives, and the Infantry never got within reach of them. A party of the Seventh Cavalry, who had gone out with our force from Cantonments, when they saw their comrades in front of them, went over to the enemy. And the morning's work was rendered memorable in the annals of crime by the brutal murder of a little Cornet of seventeen, who

Cornet Raleigh.

had been only a few weeks with the regiment. Altogether, there was but a poor exhibition of our military strength. One of the finest soldiers who turned out against the enemy on that Sunday morning was, as often happened, a Civilian. Martin Gubbins, the Financial Commissioner, had ridden out from the city to communicate with Sir Henry Lawrence; and when he found there was still some fighting to be done, he attached himself, unarmed as he was, to the Irregular Horse, and was foremost in the pursuit. "Martin Gubbins," wrote Sir Henry Lawrence, "was another hero. He, with three horsemen,* did the work of a regiment, headed the rascals, and brought in six prisoners, for which I have given the men six hundred rupees." But the sun rose; the weather was insufferably hot; the pursuit was ended; the troops were withdrawn; and I am informed that not a single man of the enemy was killed until the hangman took in hand the prisoners whom we had captured. 1857. May 31.

But the foremost hero of the day was Henry Lawrence himself—the grandest act one as yet unrecorded. Our troops had pursued the enemy up to a place known as the "Hubshee-talao," where was a thannah, or police-station. The men were by this time utterly exhausted by heat, hunger, and thirst, and the General, seeing their condition, ordered them back under command of Colonel Inglis. He then rode on, accompanied by George Couper, Secretary and Aide-de-camp, who ever sat beside him in council or rode beside him in war. Couper, never forgetting the inestimable value of his chief's life, represented

* The actual number was four, including Gubbins's own Orderly. Gubbins, during the pursuit, got possession of the sword of a trooper who had surrendered.

1857. May 31. that the enemy might be making a stand at this very place; but Lawrence, taking no heed of the suggestion, rode on, fearless and silent, to the appointed place. He had a great purpose in view. He believed that the mutineers were making for Seetapore, and he wished to write a letter to Mr. Christian, the Commissioner there, to warn him of the coming danger. The Thannadar supplied him with writing materials. The letter was written by Lawrence with a reed pen on the rude paper of the country, copied by Couper, and despatched by a camel-sowar, with offer of a large reward if he should bring back an answer. The man returned next day with the letter itself. It was too late. The troops at Seetapore had already broken into revolt.*

Results of the conflict.

Much had not, in truth, been gained by the incidents of these two days. But if our troops had done little, the enemy had done less. They had run away in fear and confusion, and we had got rid—for a time, at least—of all the dangerous members of the Sepoy force — fortunately or unfortunately, a very large proportion of the troops in Cantonments. Writing on the following day to the Governor-General, Sir Henry Lawrence said: "We are now positively better than we were. We now know our friends and enemies. The latter beggars have no stomach for a fight, though they are capital incendiaries." But there were those who thought that, in this conjuncture, our professing friends might be as dangerous as our open enemies; and Gubbins again lifted up his voice for the disarming of the Native troops.† By this time, however, serious doubts had

* The story of Seetapore and of the fate of Mr. Christian, will be found recorded in the next chapter.

† Mr. Gubbins calculated that out of the four regiments only four hundred and thirty-seven remained faithful on the night of the 30th. Of these two hundred are stated to

begun to be entertained as to whether we were strong enough in Europeans to accomplish such a measure successfully; and, moreover, the military authorities seeing clearly what was before them—feeling that the time was not far distant when the English would be shut up in Lucknow, with an insurgent population around them; for there was rebellion seething in the districts as well as in the capital—knew that they could not hold out with their little handful of Europeans alone. To secure the services of a body of Native troops to take part in the arduous duties of defence, was, therefore, a necessity not to be ignored. So the principal military officers concurred in opinion with Lawrence that it would not be advisable to disarm the Native troops. It was not denied that there were strong arguments in favour of the measure; but, on the whole, it seemed to be more expedient to abstain from adopting it.

1857. May 31.

have been men of the Thirteenth. The numbers are probably somewhat understated. The "Staff Officer," in a revised copy of his book, says that three hundred men of the Thirteenth were true to the State. As he was Assistant Adjutant-General, and an officer of the Thirteenth, his testimony is most reliable.

CHAPTER II.

REVOLT IN THE DISTRICTS—NATURAL HISTORY OF REVOLTS—THE OUTBREAK AT SEETAPORE—MUTINY OF THE FORTY-FIRST—DEATH OF MR. CHRISTIAN—MULLAON AND MOHUMDEE—MASSACRE OF THE REFUGEES FROM SHAHJEHANPORE—THE OUTBREAK AT FYZABAD—DEATH OF COLONEL GOLDNEY—FATE OF THE FUGITIVES—SULTANPORE—EVENTS IN THE BAREITCH DIVISION—ESCAPE OF MR. WINGFIELD—FATE OF THE FUGITIVES—DURRIABAD—AN EPISODE OF CAPTIVITY.

June, 1857. Revolt of the districts. It was now apparent that the worst that had been apprehended, even by the least hopeful, was rapidly overtaking our people in Oude. They had not to contend with the mutiny of a few regiments at the capital, but with a general revolt across the whole length and breadth of the province. "Of what is a Victor Hugo. revolt composed?" asks a great living writer, and proceeds to answer the question. "Of nothing and "of everything—of an electricity suddenly disengaged, of a flame which suddenly breaks out, of a "wandering strength and a passing breath. This "breath meets with heads that talk, brains that "dream, souls that suffer, passions that burn, and "miseries which yell, and carries them off with it. "Whither? it is chance work; through the State, "through the laws, through prosperity and the insolence of others. Irritated convictions, embittered "enthusiasms, aroused indignations, martial instincts "suppressed, youthful courage, exalted and generous "blindnesses; curiosity, a taste for change, thirst "for something unexpected . . . vague hatreds, "rancours, disappointments, every vanity which "believes that destiny has been a bankrupt to "it; straitened circumstances, empty dreams, am-"bitions surrounded with escarpments, every man "who hopes for an issue from an overthrow; and "lastly, at the very bottom, the mob, that mud "which takes fire—such are the elements of riot. "The basest and the most infamous beings who "prowl about beyond the pale of everything while "awaiting an opportunity; gipsies, nameless men, "highway vagabonds, the men who sleep o' nights "in a desert of houses with no other roof but the "cold clouds of heaven, those who daily ask their "bread of chance and not of toil, the unknown men "of wretchedness and nothingness, bare arms and "bare feet, belong to the riot. Every man who has "in his soul a secret revolt against any act of the "State, of life, or of destiny, is on the border line of "riot, and, so soon as it appears, he begins to quiver "and to feel himself lifted by the whirlwind."

1857. June.

The outbreak in the districts.

And so it was in Oude. When it was known that the soldiery had revolted at the capital, their brethren at the out-stations rose at once; and all classes, with any power of rising, rose with them. Day after day the saddest tidings of mutiny and massacre—of English officers murdered, of property pillaged and destroyed, of law and authority extinguished, of anarchy triumphant—came in from the outposts and filled our people in Lucknow with dismay. The new Government had toppled down, like a house built of cards.* It had no more substance or stability. Law-

* I have borrowed this figure from Mr. Gubbins. Coming from such a source the expression is more significant.

1857. June. rence thought that he could clearly see in the movement evidences of general design and consistency. "Everything," he wrote to Lord Canning, with immediate reference to affairs at Fyzabad, "had been conducted with the utmost regularity, the Native civil officers taking prominent places; and the King of Delhi had been proclaimed. In all quarters we hear of similar method and regularity. . . . This quiet method bespeaks some leading influence." And again: "All the outposts are gone, and the rebels and mutineers are said to be closing in on us, though as yet all is quiet at Lucknow. Elsewhere, throughout the province, all is anarchy—the Talookhdars re-occupying the villages of which the summary settlement dispossessed them, and all men asserting their own rights." In the first ten days of June this great anti-revolution had been fully accomplished. Oude, so lately annexed by the British, had now to be conquered by them.

Seetapore. The first place given up to revolt was Seetapore, the head-quarters of the Khyrabad Division. The station was defended by Sepoys of the Forty-first Regiment of Native Infantry and the Ninth and Tenth Oude Irregulars. The chief civil officer was Mr. George Jackson Christian, Commissioner of the Division, whom Sir Henry Lawrence had known, in old times, at Lahore. He was full of cleverness and of courage; but these qualities sometimes manifested themselves in undue self-assertion and impatience of control. Lawrence said of him that, when he was Secretary to the Lahore Board, he "tried to be a member of it;" and the new Oude Government was barely three months old when he was in fierce contention with Mr. Gubbins. Men of this stamp are always good for fighting. "Christian is doing very well and pluckily," wrote Lawrence at Lucknow to Charles Raikes at Agra on the 30th of May. On the very same day Christian had written to Raikes,* saying: "All quiet here; and throughout my division the people seem well disposed, and the regular regiment here, the Forty-first, is quiet; and I have in position nine hundred and fifty men, so that if things go wrong elsewhere, and they are tempted to rise, we could crush them in an hour." He spoke of the Irregulars and the Military Police, on whose fidelity he relied. But he knew that there were sources of danger from which the flames of insurrection might at any time arise. "The village system," he wrote, "which makes all men equal in their poverty, is now fairly on its trial in the disturbed districts, and Government has hardly a single man of influence to look to in them. Their Army is the same, a dead level—no gentlemen, no difference save in military rank. I love neither system; but I hope our eyes will now be opened to Robertson's prophecy on the inevitable tendency of *our* system."† And even as he wrote, events were in the womb of time and well-nigh on the point of development, which opened our eyes very sadly to the fact that we had made a gigantic mistake. The Sepoys, Regular and Irregular, were

1857. June.

* Christian had married a daughter of Charles Raikes.

† He spoke here of the repeated protests of the late Mr. Thomas Campbell Robertson, who had been Lieutenant-Governor of the North-Western Provinces, against the system, so favoured by men of another school, of rooting out the landed aristocracy of the country. I was in habits of the closest intimacy with this excellent man for more than a quarter of a century; and I know well the consistent sagacity with which he dwelt upon the injustice of destroying the influential classes and the evil consequences of such injustice, which we should ourselves experience, if the day of trouble should ever come to us, as he believed that some day it would. And after the insurrections of 1857—58, he spoke, very sorrowfully, of the manner in which his predictions had been fulfilled. Compare Christian's remarks with what is written in book viii., chapter ii., concerning affairs in Rohilkund.

1857. June.

rising on all sides; but if the great landed proprietors had been with us in this conjuncture, we might have held our own against our assailants instead of being helpless as children.

The Forty-first Native Infantry.

At Seetapore, the Sepoys, both of the Regular and of the Irregular Army, protested their loyalty and fidelity, and appeared to be pained by any manifestation of mistrust. An old Native officer, with tears in his eyes, implored his European commandant not to cast away the confidence and to break the bonds of a life of cherished comradeship; and it would have been strange if such appeals as these had not touched the hearts of Sepoy officers, who, in camp and cantonment, and on hard-fought fields, had shared their dangers and privations, and had never known them to murmur. It was natural that, to some extent, this confidence should have been shared by the civil officers. In any case, it was wise to simulate it. There was one precaution, however, which Christian, whatever appearance of mistrust it might create, felt himself bound to take. "I have placed," he wrote to Captain Hutchinson on the 1st of June, "all the ladies, women, and children, except some four, who refuse to leave the Lines of the Forty-first Native Infantry, in my house, and made all secure." But even this might be regarded as a defensive measure against, not the Seetapore regiments, but the muntineers from Lucknow, whom it was supposed, or at least feigned, that their own battalions were eager to attack Indeed, Colonel Birch, who commanded the Forty-first, had marched his men along the road to the capital on the first rumour that the Lucknow mutineers were advancing, and they had kept up a show of fidelity by actually firing on the advanced guard of the declared insurgents.

This had checked the mutineers from Lucknow; and the Forty-first had been marched back to their Lines covered with honour as loyal soldiers. 1857. June.

Thus passed the two first days of June in alternating confidence and doubt. Four guns were posted at Seetapore, and these, flanked by the Irregulars, had been posted between Mr. Christian's house and the Lines of the Forty-first. The house lay in the bend of a deep nullah, so it was free from attack in the rear; but that which prevented the enemy from attacking it, prevented our own people from escaping, and, therefore, it was unwisely chosen as a place of refuge. There had been signs of insubordination on those first two days of the month; on the third they were more unmistakable. On the morning of that day, Mr. Christian was informed by Major Apthorp that the Forty-first were seething into mutiny; but Colonel Birch still believed that the disaffection was only partial. The guns were, however, loaded, and the Irregulars warned; Christian still had confidence in the Oude levies and the Police, and he did not doubt the issue of the conflict. June 3. Mutiny of the troops.

The mutiny commenced in the wonted manner. A company was told off to seize the treasure. The Treasury lay at a distance of a mile from the Sepoy Lines, and whilst the plunderers were marching towards the spoil, the other companies assumed a menacing attitude and advanced in the direction of the guns. Colonel Birch, accompanied by Lieutenant Graves, rode off towards the Treasury, still hoping to arrest the mutinous madness of his men.*

* I have followed in these statements Captain Hutchinson's "Narrative of the Mutinies in Oude." The story is differently told by Mr. Gubbins, who says: "On the morning of the 3rd of June, a cry was raised in the Lines of the Forty-first Regiment that the Tenth Irregulars were plundering the Treasury, and as the men were in a state of ex-

1857. June.

The Colonel was shot dead; the Lieutenant, though wounded, was able to ride back to the Lines and to warn the other English residents in the station that the storm had burst, and that there was nothing for them but to escape with their lives. There was then a scene of terror and confusion, such as even the survivors of that fatal day find it difficult accurately to describe. The Regulars, the Irregulars, and the Mounted Police all fraternised. There were two feelings paramount among them—greed for the spoil, hatred to the Christians. The very name of the Commissioner and his family is said to have been so hateful to them, that the mutineers singled them out for swift destruction. When nothing more could be done by him for the preservation of life and property, Mr. Christian, with his wife and an infant in her arms, walked from his house to the nullah, or river, in its rear, and made for one of its fordable points. He had either crossed, or was preparing to cross the stream, when he fell dead, with his face on the ground, riddled with musket-balls. The poor wife then sat down beside the lifeless body of her husband, still holding her babe in her arms, and in a very little time, mother and child had been killed by the insurgents. Another child, gallantly rescued by Sergeant-Major Morton, was carried safely across the stream, and preserved for awhile, to die afterwards, a little captive in the Kaiser-baugh of Lucknow.*

Death of Mr. Christian.

citement, the Commander, Colonel Birch, who reposed the most entire confidence in his men, called out the two most suspected companies, the Light and Rifle, and led them to the Treasury. All there was found to be quiet, and the Colonel was about to return, when a Sepoy of the guard stepped out of the ranks and shot him in the back."

* Sir Henry Lawrence had pointed out in April the advantage of removing the Forty-first from Seetapore, as well as the Forty-eighth from Lucknow: "I told the Brigadier (Handscombe) that my remedy would be to send the regiment out of Oude. I shall be glad if your Lordship will permit the measure. Brigadier Gray, a Sepoy officer of

Meanwhile, other Christian residents had been effecting their escape or succumbing to the murderous fire of the enemy. Mr. and Mrs. Thornhill were killed. Lieutenant Graves, who had escaped with his life from the first discharge of musketry, was now slain, with his wife and child; Lieutenant Snell, with his wife and child; Lieutenants Dorin, Small, Greene, Dr. Marcus Hill, and others, shared the same fate. Sir Mountstuart Jackson and his two sisters, Mr. and Miss Birch (children of the Colonel of the Forty-first), and Mrs. Dorin, were among those who escaped from Seetapore.* They left behind them one of those scenes of terrible anarchy and outrage, which were even then becoming of such frequent recurrence, that the narrator is compelled to repeat the same story in well-nigh the same words. The houses of the English were gutted. All that was valuable and removable was carried off by the despoilers. The rest was broken or burnt; the buildings were fired, amidst shoutings and yellings, and all utterances of fiendish revelry; and not a Christian man, woman, or child was left alive in the place. 1857. June.

There were two smaller British stations in the Khyrabad Division—Mullaon and Mohumdee. In Mullaon.

forty years' standing, told me this morning that he had suggested the same step to Brigadier Handscombe. Indeed, he went further, and said he should like to see the Forty-first out of Seetapore. So should I; as we have two Oude corps there, and the less the Regulars and Oude Irregulars are together the better, inasmuch as their pay is different, whilst they are mostly men of the same caste and same part of the country. . . . Perhaps the Forty-first might march *viâ* Furruckabad to Meerut, and the Forty-eighth to Cawnpore, either to remain there under its old Colonel (Sir Hugh Wheeler), while one of the corps there is pushed on, or it might move on to Agra or elsewhere." The result of this reference with respect to the Forty-eighth has been already shown (vol. i., pp. 586–7). The same consideration actuated the Chief Commissioner in regard to the Forty-first.

* What befel some of these fugitives will be told in a subsequent part of this narrative.

1857. June. the former, Mr. Capper, of the Civil Service, was Deputy-Commissioner. Detachments of the Forty-first and of the Fourth Oude Irregulars were stationed there. In May, the Deputy-Commissioner had seen reason to doubt their fidelity, and had perceived also ugly symptoms of general fermentation throughout the district. "I wish," he wrote to Mr. Gubbins on the 29th, "that we could hear of the fall of Delhi, for deserters are coming in fast and spreading wonderful reports of the utter cowardice and alarm of the *sahibs* in the North-West. There appear, too, to be a good many corpses of Europeans lying on the Trunk Road; and it is time that they were buried. Their presence seems to cause alarm to all passengers, even more than the Dacoits. Every man who comes here has been thoroughly cleaned out by the Goojurs." Nothing could more strikingly illustrate the progress which the revolt had made, even at that early period, than these simple sentences, written at the end of May by the Deputy-Commissioner at Mullaon. A very few weeks before, a single white corpse lying by the road-side would have created the greatest excitement from one end of the district to the other, and would have been a subject of horrified comment in every English journal in the country. Now these unburied white corpses were spoken of with an indefinite plurality, all the more terrible for the coolness and quietude with which the report was made. Little more than a fortnight of this rough work had so habituated our officers to tales of blood, that the sensation once produced by the murder of one white man was greater than that which now followed the massacre of numbers. The Goojurs, too, the born depredators of the land, had found that their time had come; and with the wonted impartiality of their race were plundering alike friends and foes. It was plain that there was small chance of the British officer holding his own much longer in that isolated station. Still, reluctant to fly, he held to his post for some days after the evacuation of Seetapore; and then, seeing that the troops were on the brink of open mutiny, mounted his horse and rode unharmed to Lucknow. 1857. June.

Mohumdee.

Meanwhile, at Mohumdee, there was the germ of a terrible tragedy. There Mr. J. G. Thomason, who represented the third generation of a family distinguished in our Indian annals for good service, was Deputy-Commissioner. His assistant was Captain Patrick Orr, who had commanded, in the King's time, one of the Oude Regiments. On the 1st of June, the refugees from Shahjehanpore came into Mohumdee;* and thus the European party was largely and dangerously increased. During the two next days there were threatenings of a storm. On the 4th the soldiery rose, sacked the Treasury, and released the prisoners. It was time now for the Europeans to seek safety in flight. The Sepoys were more of the Oude Irregular Force. Captain Orr knew them well, and he obtained from them the most solemn assurances that they would spare the lives of our people. So, that evening, they went forth unharmed, setting their faces towards Aurungabad. The women and children were placed, some in a buggy and the rest on baggage carts; and there seemed good hope of deliverance. But on the following morning it was plain that they had been betrayed. A party of the Oude Irregulars was on their track. About a mile from Aurungabad they declared themselves. Then the carnage began. Resistance was impossible; escape

* The story of Shahjehanpore is told in book viii., chapter ii.

1857. June. almost impossible. One man, however, escaped to tell the tale of the butchery. This was Captain Orr himself. "We all collected under a tree," he says, "and took the ladies down from the buggy. Shots were firing from all directions amidst the most fearful yells. The poor ladies all joined in prayer, coolly and undauntedly awaiting their fate. I stopped for about three minutes among them, but thinking of my poor wife and child here, I endeavoured to save my life for their sakes. I rushed out towards the insurgents, and one of their men, Goordhun, of the Sixth Company, called out to me to throw down my pistol and he would save me. I did so, when he put himself between me and the men, and several others followed his example. In about ten minutes more they completed their hellish work. Poor Lysaght was kneeling out in the open ground, with his hands folded across his chest, and though not using his firearms, the cowardly rascals would not go up to the spot until they shot him; and then rushing up they killed the wounded and children, butchering them in a most cruel way. With the exception of the drummer-boy, every one (of the Shahjehanpore party*) was killed, and besides poor good Thomason and one or two clerks. They denuded the bodies of their clothes for the sake of plunder."

Fyzabad. At Fyzabad, Colonel Philip Goldney, of the Bengal Army, was Commissioner. I have spoken of him

* Captain Orr's list shows that there were eleven commissioned officers from Shahjehanpore, a quartermaster-sergeant, a band-master, and a drummer. There were eight women and four children of the party. Besides these, there were Mr. Jenkins, of the Civil Service, and Lieutenant Sheils, of the Veteran Establishment, who was shot, whilst riding Captain Orr's horse, before the general massacre commenced.

before, with the reverence of an old friendship, as a man of equal courage and capacity.* He had removed himself from Sultanpore, where his head-quarters had been fixed, to Fyzabad, as the "more important position and exposed to the greatest danger." At the latter place were posted the Twenty-second Regiment of Native Infantry, commanded by Colonel Lennox; a light field-battery, under Major Mill, manned by Native gunners; the Sixth Oude Infantry Regiment; and a squadron of the Fifteenth Irregular Horse. After the wonted fashion, these troops, one and all, protested their fidelity. But Goldney, who knew the temper of the Sepoy Army, felt that a crisis could not be far distant, and, in view of the coming danger, tried to rally round him the "friendly Zemindars," and, by the help of a hastily fortified walled enclosure, sufficiently provisioned, to hold out till relief should come to save the lives of the people under his charge. There was talk, too, of sending the women and children to Lucknow. But both projects were abandoned under pressure of stern necessity. The "friendly Zemindars" were not disposed to fight against disciplined troops, and the road to the capital was too dangerous for the contemplated exodus of the helpless ones to be attempted.† 1857. June.

* Vol. i. p. 280, foot-note. Mr. (Sir Charles) Wingfield was at Fyzabad, presiding over an examination committee, when news of the seizure of Delhi and massacre of the English arrived. That evening he dined with Colonel Goldney at the mess of the Twenty-second Regiment, N.I. Almost all the military officers at the station were present. There was no gloom or sadness over the party. They played whist and billiards after dinner according to their wont. But Goldney remarked to Wingfield on this gaiety at such a juncture and in view of the dangers that threatened them, adding, "How many of us will be alive a fortnight hence?" Within three weeks four-fifths of the light-hearted company had perished miserably.

† The state of feeling at Fyzabad in the third week of May is well represented in the following extract of a letter written by the medical officer of the Sixth Oude Infantry:

1857. June.

The Oude Talookhdars.

Our system, as Mr. Christian had said, was on its trial. If the great landholders—the Barons of Oude—had been with us at this time, our position would have been one of comparative strength. But our Revenue measures had hopelessly alienated their affections. The new rule of the English had prostrated them; and though they might conceal their resentments for a time, it was well-nigh certain that the moment would come when they would throw off their disguise, and stand forth as the most bitter and unrelenting of our enemies. Foremost among these great Talookhdars was Maun Singh,* of Shah-gunj.

"Fyzabad, 19th May, 1857.—Here we are, in a jolly state of excitement, as we don't know but that Fyzabad may kick up a row and the Sepoys join in it any hour they like. We have no telegraph to Lucknow, and are dependent upon a foot-postman for news once a day. I need hardly say how we gallop from one bungalow to another when the post arrives, to see who has the latest news. We were certainly surprised at first to hear of the outbreak at Meerut, and then the troops joining the insurgents at Delhi; but there had been signs of discontent for some time past in the Native army. . . . . . The thermometer is eighty-two degrees all night, and in the day (in the shade of course) a hundred degrees, and often more, and this, added to our excitement, keeps us nearly at fever heat. . . . . News just arrived here that we must prepare to make a stand if the worst comes; this is pleasant! and we, that is, all the Europeans, are to be lodged in one large house down by the river—what a spree! Post just in; all the Europeans at Delhi reported to have been murdered in the most horrible manner. People in Lucknow in great agitation." This is characteristic of the high animal spirits of our younger officers, and their confidence in the face of appalling difficulties. Even at a later period, when the danger had thickened around them, the same spirit of confidence was manifested in all their letters.

* Maun Singh was the nephew and adopted heir of the well-known Bukhtawur Singh, often referred to by Colonel Sleeman. "Bukhtawur Singh," wrote the Resident in his journal, under date December 20, 1849, "has always been considered the head of the family, to whom Shah-gunj belongs; but he has always remained at Court, and left the local management of the estate and the government of the districts, placed under their charge in contracts or in trust, to his brothers and nephews. Bukhtawur Singh has no child of his own, but he has adopted Maun Singh, the youngest son of his brother, Dursun Singh, and he leaves all local duties and responsibilities to him. He is a small, slight man, but shrewd, active, and energetic, and as unscrupulous as a man can be. Old Bukhtawur Singh himself is the only member of the family that was ever troubled with scruples of any kind. . . . All his brothers and nephews are thorough-bred ruffians." This, however, must be taken with some limitations. Sleeman's picture of the Oude Talookhdars is much too highly coloured.

The new Revenue system of the English had fallen crushingly upon him, burying him beneath the ruins of an once magnificent estate. The summary settlement had transferred to his tenants a large portion of the broad lands, which he had once owned, and he was declared a defaulter for the non-payment of Government dues which he believed to be illegally demanded from him. Our officers would have arrested him, but he was not to be found. Wronged and humiliated by the arbitrary proceedings of the English, he had gone to the vice-regal capital in search of redress—perhaps of retribution. Avowedly he went to Calcutta to take legal advice as to the possibility of obtaining a reversal of the harsh decrees of the British Government. It is more than probable that he took bitter counsel with Ali Nuckee Khan as to the great question of "what was to be done." What passed at the capital, and whom he saw on his homeward journey, we shall probably never know. He returned to Oude before the outbreaks at Meerut and Delhi, and was soon afterwards arrested and placed in honourable duress by orders from Lucknow.* The outbreak at Fyzabad found

1857. June

* There seems to be some doubt as to the actual cause of Maun Singh's detention. Mr. Gubbins, Financial Commissioner, says: "At the beginning of the month, Rajah Maun Singh, Talookhdar of Shahgunj, was in confinement there. He had been arrested by order of the Chief Commissioner, in consequence of information telegraphed from Calcutta, which accorded with what had reached us at Lucknow." Captain Reid, Deputy-Commissioner of Fyzabad, says: "He was in close, but honourable confinement, having been placed under arrest by the Commissioner in obedience to orders from Lucknow. I was much opposed to this step, as, whatever may have been Maun Singh's conduct since, I had every reason to believe that he was then well affected to our Government." Captain Hutchinson ("Narrative of the Mutinies in Oude") writes, that "Maun Singh was in confinement on a *revenue question*, when Captain Alexander Orr, the Assistant-Commissioner, who had known him for several years, begged his release." One thing, however, is certain, namely, that at the end of May, and at the beginning of June, Maun Singh was under surveillance in Oude, and could not, therefore, have been intriguing at Calcutta. (See *ante*, book vii. page 36.)! But he told Sir Charles Wingfield that he had

1857. June. him under surveillance in that city. With Captain Alexander Orr, the Assistant-Commissioner, he had long been in habits of intimacy, and he now offered, if released from confinement, to shelter and protect Orr and his family in the Fort of Shah-gunj, which lay some twelve miles distant from the British station. Orr hesitated to accept an offer of this exclusive character, and urged that it should be extended to all who would accept it. Colonel Goldney consented to this; and then Captain Reid, the Deputy-Commissioner, accompanied by Orr, proceeded to Maun Singh's house in the city to discuss the whole question with him. Willing as the Rajah professed himself to be to shelter the whole of our women and children, he doubted his ability to do so, and he proposed, therefore, to limit his protection to the families of the civil officers. To this Reid demurred. He could not honourably accept such terms. So at last Maun Singh consented to receive all the families of our officers, on condition that their removal from the station to the Fort should be accomplished with the utmost possible secrecy. But when this decision was communicated to the military officers, they declined to accept the offer. They had more faith in the soldiery than in Maun Singh. They would not trust the one or show mistrust of the other. One only consented to send his wife and children to Shah-gunj, with the families of the civil officers.*

June 7. Escape of the women. On the night of the 7th of June the exode of the women was safely accomplished. On the evening of the 8th the troops rose. Their first movement was to

visited Calcutta earlier in the year, for the purpose of taking legal advice as to whether any remedy were open to him against the injurious measures of the revenue officers of the British Government.

* The family of Captain Dawson, Executive Engineer, who went with his wife and four children to Maun Singh's Fort. The wives and children of the European Staff-sergeants were also sent to Shah-gunj.

seize the guns. The battery was drawn up ready for action, loaded with grape, a company of the Twenty-second on each flank, when the alarm was sounded from the Lines of the Oude Irregulars. The Golundauze lighted their port-fires, but before they could use them, the Infantry rushed in among them and pointed their loaded muskets at the heads of the gunners. Neither the commands nor entreaties of their officers could move them. The main body of the Twenty-second was now moving down, with the usual ominous shouts. It was clear that the game was lost. The Sepoys told the English officers that the guns were theirs, and that they were strong enough to turn us out of the country. They then escorted the officers to the Quarter-guard of the regiment. 1857. June.

Though the lead had been thus taken by the Infantry, the Cavalry were as ever the most vehement in speech and the most murderous in their desires. A Ressaldar of the Fifteenth Irregular Horse appeared to be the chief leader of the revolt. He was clamorous for the blood of the English officers, and the troopers generally accepted the invitation to murder. But the Artillery and Infantry resolutely refused to injure our people. Their forbearance went further than this. They assisted the Europeans to escape. They procured boats for them, and gave them money. All night long the English prisoners remained at the Quarter-guard; and in the morning they were escorted down to the river under an escort of the Twenty-second. The boats were there, but there were no boatmen; so the fugitives took the oars into their hands and left Fyzabad in safety.

But the danger was not yet passed. There are some things in this, as in almost every other narra-

1857. June. tive of regimental revolt, so inconsistent, as to be almost inscrutable. That the mutineers on that morning should have seized the public treasure, and laid their despoiling hands upon the private property of the English, was only in accordance with established rules. The work of plunder went on bravely as a matter of course. But it is not so easy to reconcile with these established rules the Sepoys' treatment of the persons of our officers. They not only permitted Colonel Goldney and his companions to depart unmolested, but aided their departure, as though desirous of securing their safety. Our people were at the mercy of the mutineers. Resistance was wholly impossible. They might have been slaughtered at any moment like a little flock of sheep. Not one could have escaped. But it is stated that scarcely had the English left Fyzabad, when the Twenty-second despatched a messenger charged with instructions to the Seventeenth, who were then on the banks of the Gogra, to intercept the boats, and to slay all the white people in them.* Certain it is that the Christian people were floating down to destruction. For they had scarcely gone thirty miles down the stream, when the inmates of the leading boats perceived that the right bank of the river was lined with Sepoys—Horse and Foot—whose intentions were too apparent. The narrowness of the stream at that point seemed to render escape impossible. The Azimgurh mutineers† opened fire upon them, with

* This is stated very emphatically by Mr. Gubbins: "Begumgunj, where the Seventeenth lay, is on the banks of the Gogra, and the current of the river sweeps underneath it. A messenger had been despatched by the Twenty-second Regiment to the Seventeenth to destroy them. Fearfully was the invitation responded to."

† These were men of the Seventeenth Regiment of Native Infantry, of whose revolt an account is given in vol. ii., 213—216, closing with the statement that, "flushed with success, they marched off to Fyzabad in military array, with all the pomp and panoply of war."

1857. June.

murderous effect, and there was nothing left for them but to endeavour to escape on the opposite shore. But the enemy crossed the river in boats; and it only remained for our people to fly with their lives. So Goldney addressed his companions, exhorting them to save their lives by the only means still open to the fugitives. "I am too old myself to run," he said, "but you should do your best to escape." So they sped across the country whilst the Commissioner prepared himself to die. And death soon overtook him. It is said that, having been carried before the Native officers of the Seventeenth, he asked them if they meant to disgrace themselves by the murder of an old man.* He was shot dead upon the spot. Others from the two leading boats perished in the attempt to escape. Lieutenant Currie, of the Artillery, and Lieutenant Parsons, of the Oude Irregulars, were drowned. It is supposed that Major Mill also was drowned. Adjutant Bright, of the Twenty-second, shared the fate of Colonel Goldney The rest seem to have escaped to Amorah, where they were joined by the fugitives from the fourth boat. The party then consisted of eight. On the morning of the 10th of June they had reached Captan-gunj in safety. Thence they pursued their hazardous journey, with good hope of ultimate deliverance. For the chief people of the villages, through which they passed, had shown a friendly disposition, and some had aided their escape by

Death of Colonel Goldney.

* According to our English estimates of old age, Colonel Goldney was scarcely an old man when he was killed. He entered the service in the year 1820—probably at the age of seventeen; and must have been about fifty-four years old at the time of his death. Mr. Gubbins says: "It would be unjust to the memory of this deserving soldier not to mention that, from every account that has reached me, he maintained a most manly and gallant bearing during these trying scenes at Fyzabad. He believed that he should not survive them. But with a noble, chivalrous feeling he resolved to remain at his post to the last."

1857. June.

giving them money and mounting them on ponies. But these hopes were delusive; for as they sped onwards to the village of Mahwah-dabur,* the people rushed out, armed with swords and matchlocks, and fell mercilessly upon the fugitives. One only escaped to tell the story of this miserable flight. Sergeant-Major Busher outran all his companions, and by sheer bodily activity and power of endurance saved his life. The narrative he has written, which has every appearance of absolute fidelity, is the groundwork of all history relating to this particular episode of our troubles in Oude.†

Escape of Colonel O'Brien.

Thus has a mournful account been rendered of those who embarked in three of the four boats which started from Fyzabad on the morning of the 8th of June. There was yet another party of fugitives occupying the boat described in contemporary narratives as Boat No. 3, of whom no mention has yet been made. This boat was occupied by Colonel O'Brien, of the Oude Irregular Infantry, and by four other commissioned officers. By one of those happy thoughts, which come upon us in critical emergencies almost as divine inspirations, the whole party was saved. Not far below Fyzabad lies Adjoodhea, the ancient capital of Oude. The two leading boats dropped past this place. The third put in to shore, and secured a larger boat and a boat's crew. This enabled our officers to lie down, screened from observation, under the sides of the vessel. The enemy

* This was a Mahomedan village, held by a family that had discharged the office of Kagee. Our unfortunate officers, I am informed, were inveigled into it by two Mahomedan Government Chuprassies. One had preceded the party, declaredly to provide refreshments for them, but in reality to arouse the fanaticism of the people, and to plan the attack on the Christian fugitives.

† This narrative has been published in different shapes. It will be found in Captain Hutchinson's book. The account of the Sergeant-Major's subsequent adventures is extremely interesting and suggestive.

on the river-bank, who had fired on the two leading boats, did not know that the third had any white men in it. So Colonel O'Brien and his companions made good their voyage to Dinapore. 1857. June.

Colonel Lennox and family.

The whole story of the retreat from Fyzabad is not yet told. When the four boats, on the morning of the 9th of June, dropped down the river, Colonel Lennox, Commandant of the Twenty-second, remained with his wife and daughter during the early part of the day, and embarked with them in the afternoon. It appears that Mrs. Mill was to have accompanied the Lennox family, but when the time for embarkation arrived, either purposely or accidentally, she lost the opportunity, and was left behind with her children.* The Lennox family had not gone far down the river, when they were compelled to abandon their boat and to commence a foot journey to Goruckpore. On their way they were made prisoners, and were about to be delivered over to the mutineers, when they were rescued by the followers of Mahmud Hoossein Khan,† who for more than a week sheltered and provided for them, until Mr. Paterson, the Magistrate of Goruckpore, sent an escort to convey them to that place.

Sultanpore.

In command of the station at Sultanpore was Colonel Fisher—familiarly known in India as "Sam

* Mr. Gubbins says: "Unwilling to expose her children to the sun, she had lost the opportunity of leaving the station with Colonel Lennox, and found herself left alone. She succeeded, however, in making her way alone through the country, and at length reached a British station. She had walked the whole way, wandering from village to village. The women in the villages were kind to her, but she lost one of her children from illness and exposure on the way." Some interesting particulars of Mrs. Mill's escape will be found in the Appendix.

† This man afterwards (September, 1857), invaded Goruckpore when that district was abandoned by the Goorkah troops, and established his Government there. He subsequently surrendered himself to the British Government, and in consideration of his having succoured the family of Colonel Lennox, was allowed to go free.

1857. June. Fisher." He was a member of a family which had furnished two generations of good and faithful ministers to the Anglo-Indian Church. His personal qualifications were of a kind to insure for him the highest measure of popularity. He had a splendid seat in the saddle; he was ardent and successful in all the sports of the field; he was a man of kindly and genial temperament, which endeared him alike to his own Christian comrades and to the Native soldiery. An officer of the Queen's Army, he was, I believe, the first man of that service ever appointed to the command of an Irregular regiment under the Company—the Fifteenth Irregular Horse. His second in command was Captain Gibbings. His Adjutant was Lieutenant Charlton Tucker, the youngest member of that family of Indian public servants whose name is synonymous with good work ever bravely done. The Eighth Regiment of Oude Irregular Infantry and a corps of Military Police were also in occupation of Sultanpore. On the 7th, anticipating the coming storm, Fisher despatched all the ladies in the station towards Allahabad, under charge of two officers. On the morning of the 9th, the troops rose. Fisher had gone down to the Lines, and had addressed the men, urging them affectionately to return to their duty, when one of the Nujeebs shot him in the back with a musket, and the fine old soldier, so much honoured, so much beloved, fell mortally wounded before the eyes of his own troopers, not one of whom would go to his aid; Captain Gibbings was also slain beside the dhooly in which Adjutant Tucker had placed the dying body of his Commandant. The death-agony was soon over; and then Tucker, being exhorted to fly for his life, mounted his horse and rode towards the

Death of Colonel Fisher.

Goomtee, where he found hospitable refuge in the house of a Talookhdar of ancient family, who had been unjustly treated in the Settlement, and who, for the evil we had done him, returned to us only good.* Far different was the treatment to which our civil officers were subjected. Mr. Block, of the Covenanted, and Mr. Stroyan, of the Uncovenanted Service, flung themselves on the hospitality of a landholder named Yazeen Khan, of Sultanpore. This man professed friendship and received them into his house. But either with preconcerted treachery, or in an hour of fanatical repentance, he drove them from the shelter that he had offered to them, and caused them both to be shot to death.† 1857. June.

Thus all European authority was swept out of Sultanpore. And the usual festival was held. The houses of the English were sacked; all the portable property carried off; and then for a time the bonfires afforded plentiful amusement to the "baba-logue." This done, the three regiments marched off to Nawab-Gunj, which was fast becoming the rendezvous of all the rebellious troops in the province—with what result will presently be told.

Salone.

There was one other station in the Fyzabad Division. At Salone was posted the main body of the First Regiment of Oude Infantry. Captain R. L. Thompson commanded it. The chief civil officer was Captain Lousada Barrow, an officer of the

* His name was Roostum Sah. Mr. Gubbins says of him, that he deserved all the more credit, "as he had suffered unduly at the Settlement, and had lost many villages, which he should have been permitted to retain." Captain Bunbury of the Police Corps, with Captain Smith, Lieutenant Jenkins, and Dr. O'Donel of the Infantry Regiment, afterwards found shelter under the same roof. The whole were brought safely into Benares by Henry Tucker, the Commissioner of that place.

† Mr. Gubbins says: "This is the only instance of like treachery on the part of a petty Zemindar in Oudh which came to our notice."

1857. June. Madras Cavalry, whose signal administrative capacity afterwards raised him to the Chief Commissionership of the province. All through the month of May and the first week of June the conduct of the troops was orderly, and their temper seemed to be good. In the districts, too, appearances were favourable. The landholders were paying up their Government dues as in the most tranquil times, and there was nothing to bespeak a coming convulsion. But when news came that the troops at Fyzabad and Sultanpore had risen, it was plain that the continued fidelity of the men of the First Irregulars was not to be expected. On the 9th of June there were signs of feverish excitement, and on the 10th the regiment rose—but with none of those worst signs of brutal violence that had distinguished so many similar risings in all parts of the country. The soldiery declared themselves to be masters of the situation, and proceeded to release the prisoners in the Gaol. But they respected the lives of their officers, and escorted them from the station—beyond which they were met by an influential landowner, named Humwunt Singh, who sheltered them for some days, and afterwards, with the aid of some other local gentry, enabled them to reach Allahabad.

Bareitch Division. The Bareitch Division comprised the districts of Bareitch and Gonda, situated upon the left bank of the Gogra, and of Mullapore, on the right bank of the river. Mr. Charles Wingfield* was the Commissioner of the division. A man of generous sym-

* Afterwards Chief Commissioner of Oude, and now (1873) Sir Charles Wingfield, K.C.S.I., representing Gravesend in the House of Commons.

pathies, not at all of the Thomasonian school, he had seen with regret the operation of the new settlement which had struck down the territorial aristocracy of the province; and he had dealt with them more leniently than had others. But when occasion required there had been no want of vigour in his administration. On one memorable occasion, in the preceding year, he had greatly distinguished himself by the pursuit and capture of a recusant Rajah, who had defied the new authority of the British. His ordinary place of residence had been at Bareitch—the chief civil station; but he had removed himself, in the preceding April, to Secrora, an old-established military station in the time of the Native rulers, where were posted in May, 1857, a regiment of Cavalry, a regiment of Infantry,* and a horse battery of the Oude Irregular Force. The troops were commanded by Captain G. W. Boileau. 1857. June.

When news of the disturbances at Meerut and Delhi first arrived, there were the usual appearances, and, indeed, the usual expressions of loyalty; and for some weeks the troops performed their appointed duties with their wonted observance of discipline. It was necessary, however, to watch them closely, and to be prepared for any emergency that might arise; so frequent consultations were held between the chief civil and military functionaries, who freely conversed with the Native officers, and endeavoured to elicit their opinions. But as news came in from station after station, ever with fresh tidings of mutiny and massacre, there seemed to be little hope that the Bareitch Division would be exempt from the great plague of insurrection which was afflicting the whole Secrora.

* He was driven to change his residence by the circumstance that his house at Bareitch was falling down.

1857. June. province. So Wingfield, as a first measure of precaution, provided for the safety of our women, by sending them under a guard of Cavalry, principally Sikhs, to Lucknow; and then he concerted measures for the retirement, in the event of a crisis, of our Christian people to the strongholds of certain friendly chiefs situated on the borders of Nepaul.

A false alarm, which may have been accidental, or may have been designed, precipitated the rising of the troops. News was brought in the night, that the Infantry were arming. Since the departure of the women, the officers had slept at the Commissioner's house, and when this message was brought they went forth into the darkness to the Artillery quarters and turned the guns upon the Infantry Lines. The Golundauze obeyed orders, and seemed to be faithful to their Government; but their was no need to try the strength of their loyalty to the utmost, for the Infantry made no demonstration, and the officers went home to their beds—some declaring it to have been a false alarm, others protesting that a seditious design had been defeated by the attitude we had so promptly assumed.

But a different story gained credence in the Infantry Lines. The Sepoys accused us of a design to massacre them as they slept; and from that time the nameless fear was upon them, that had so often been the precursor of revolt. Then all branches of the Force made common cause. And Boileau soon found that he had ceased to command the troops at Secrora. There was now nothing more to be done for the maintenance of British authority. Sir Henry Lawrence had written to the chief civil and military officers, saying: "Should a mutiny break out or appear to be inevitable, you are at liberty to consult your own safety." So Wingfield mounted his horse, and on pretence of going for his wonted evening ride, galloped with all speed to Gonda, where he found that the regiment posted there had not yet revolted. 1857. June.

Gonda. Everything, indeed, had gone on in the old groove all through the month of May. Our civil courts had seen the wonted number of suitors, and discipline had been maintained in the Lines of the Sepoys. But in the first week of June there was a perceptible change. It was plain that all classes were in a state of feverish excitement, girding themselves up for the coming struggle. The old belief in the indomitable power of the English was fast passing away.* Still there was no outward change. The Sepoys protested that they would remain true to their salt; and the majority of their officers believed them. But when the Commissioner brought in the discouraging news that the troops at Fyzabad and Secrora had revolted, it became evident that the troops, though they still protested their fidelity, would form a junction with their comrades on the first appearance of a mutinous body from either place. As all other roads were now closed, it was proposed that the regiment should be marched to Bulrampore†—some thirty miles distant —with the treasure. To this the men apparently at first consented; but the Sepoys said that they would fight the mutineers, when they might come, June 10.

* Mr. Wingfield says: "It was manifest that confidence in our power was fast departing; and Zemindars who had recovered their villages from Talookhdars at Settlement were writing to propitiate the latter or making preparations for flight. The Tuhseeldars had reported that the Sepoys had been overheard to express their determination not to allow the treasure to be removed," &c. &c.

† Mr. Wingfield had from the first the fullest confidence in the fidelity of the Maharajah of Bulrampore, which was amply justified by after events. He was made a Knight-Commander of the Star of India and a member of the legislative council of the Governor-General.

1857. June. which really meant that they would fraternise with their comrades. So Wingfield with the civil officers rode on to Bulrampore. Captain Miles and his Adjutant, bent on making a last despairing effort to save their men from rebellion, still remained in the Cantonment. But, on the following day, they found that all their efforts were useless; so they also set their faces towards Bulrampore, together with some of the officers from Secrora.

Secrora. One officer, however, still remained at the latter place, when all the rest had abandoned the Cantonment. This was Lieutenant Bonham of the Artillery, who commanded a battery of the Oude Irregular Force. He was a young soldier of great promise, and, for his years, of commanding influence. He kept his company together after the other branches of the service had revolted. But, although his courage commanded the respect and admiration of his men, it could not secure their fidelity. The Commissioner had gone. All the Infantry officers had gone. Everything portended that British authority was utterly extinguished. For a little while, however, the Infantry, without their own officers,* and subdued by the quiet gallantry of the young artilleryman, asked him to take command of them. They "made the most solemn promises never to leave him, and swore to protect him with their lives." Upon this Bonham consented to take command, and at once made his arrangements to march the Infantry and the guns into Lucknow. But these professions of loyalty were but short-lived. The Infantry soon

* I am informed that, on the preceding evening, the Infantry officers had been arrested by their men, and confined together in a house, with a guard over them. In the morning the guard was not relieved, so the men went off to their Lines, and the officers, very wisely, mounted their horses and escaped to Bulrampore.

became insolent in their demeanour, and there was 1857.
a marked change in the bearing of the gunners. Still June.
Bonham clung to his guns; and, when the Infantry advanced upon them, ordered his men to fire. The order was not obeyed, and when Bonham himself went to the battery to do the work, his men pointed their carbines at him. There were some, however, among them who were eager to serve him, and who implored him to leave the place with the European non-commissioned officers. They brought him horses, and they brought him money, and urged him to fly for his life. So at last, with a heavy heart, he turned his back on his cherished guns and started for Lucknow, there to become, as will presently be told, one of the most conspicuous heroes of the memorable defence of that great city.*

Bonham had been cautioned to avoid the principal Bareitch.
ferry across the river, known as the Byram Ghaut, which lay very near to Secrora, for there the main body of the mutineers had taken up their position. Not so our unfortunate people at the Bareitch station, who took flight in that direction. Two companies of the Gonda regiment were posted at the civil station, under Lieutenant Longueville Clarke, a gallant young officer who had shortly before distinguished himself by the capture of a notorious freebooter named Fuzl Ali. Mr. Cunliffe was the Deputy-Commissioner, and with him was Mr. Jordan, an uncovenanted assistant. When they found that the head-quarters of the regiment had revolted, there was no further hope of the fidelity of the detachment; so the Englishmen mounted their horses and rode for Naupara, where

* He was accompanied by Farrier-Sergeant James Bewsey, Assistant-Farrier James Millar, and the Sergeant-Major of the Second Oude Irregular Infantry, of whom Bonham said that they all "behaved remarkably well throughout."

1857. June. they had promise of friendly assistance. Disappointed in this, they turned back and rode for the Gogra, with the intention of making for Lucknow. They had disguised themselves in the costume of the country, and though the approaches to the Byram Ghaut were bristling with mutineers, they managed to escape detection and to gain the river. There they obtained a boat—it was said to be the common ferry-boat—and embarked with their horses. But a cry arose that some Europeans were escaping, and then there was a rush to the river-bank, and the Sepoys fired upon them. On this the Native boatmen took to the water; the Englishmen hid themselves, as best they could, under shelter of the sides of the boat; but powerless in this position to guide the vessel, they made no progress, perhaps they even drifted back, and Cunliffe and Clarke were shot to death. Jordan was dragged out of the boat, and suffered to linger for a few days, at the end of which he shared the fate of his comrades.*

Mullapore. At Mullapore were no Sepoys; so there was no immediate fear of danger. But, after a little while,

* This story depends entirely upon Native evidence. Mr. Gubbins and Sir Charles Wingfield made every exertion to ascertain the truth; but their accounts differ in some respects, though in no material instance. Mr. Gubbins ("Mutinies in Oudh") says: "One of the young officers was engaged to a young lady at Lucknow, and the marriage was to have been shortly celebrated. The betrothed girl would not credit the story, and clung through the weary days of the siege to the hope that her lover would yet be found alive." The history of the great Indian rebellion is too sadly full of such romances. I cannot pass on without narrating a characteristic incident connected with this tragedy. Cunliffe and his companions were accompanied by the Native Deputy-Collector, a man of good parts, whom Mr. Wingfield had taken to Oude. He was a Pathan of an ancient family resident in Rohilkund. It was believed that he had cast in his lot with the European officers. When they turned back from Naupara he was captured with them at Byram Ghaut. His life was spared because he was a Native. He returned to Rohilkund, where family and national influences were too strong for him. He went into rebellion. His defection was proved by his own correspondence; so he was convicted and executed.

the wonted disorganisation of the Civil Government manifested itself in the most unmistakable manner, and our officers, powerless for good, prepared themselves to leave the station. They had been joined by fugitives from Seetapore and other places; and having obtained boats, were bent on making their way—a long river journey—to Calcutta. This hazardous experiment was arrested by information that all the ghauts were closely watched by the mutineers. So they quitted the boats, retraced their steps by land, and made their way to the fortified residence of the young Rajah of Dhowrerah at Mutteeara, where they resided in safety for the space of nearly two months. What were their subsequent adventures will presently be told.* 1857. June.

One more story remains to be told, and it is the more incumbent on me to tell it, as the record is honourable to a brave and good soldier, who did his duty nobly, and rendered good service to the State. Durriabad was a district in the Lucknow Division. The Fifth Regiment of Oude Infantry was stationed there under the command of Captain W. H. Hawes. He was much loved by his men, and he hoped that they would remain staunch. But it was obvious, before the end of May, that there was a growing restlessness among them which might soon be developed into mutinous activity. Some three lakhs of treasure were in Durriabad—an untoward circumstance, which greatly increased the difficulties of the position. Hawes was eager to convey the coin to Lucknow; but he felt that there was danger to Durriabad.

* The party—eleven in number—consisted of Mr. Gonne, Deputy-Commissioner of Mullapore; Captain Hastings, from the same place; Messrs. Brand and Carew, from Shahjehanpore; Captain Hearsey, Mrs. Green, and Miss Jackson, from Seetapore; with Sergeant-Major and Mrs. Rogers, and the stepson of the former; and a clerk in the Mullapore office.

1857. June. others in his leaving the Cantonment.* This was approved by the Chief Commissioner. So Hawes stood fast, and on the 27th he wrote to Lawrence: "I feel my hands getting daily strengthened. . . . I am steadily recovering the former strong hold I had in military discipline and proper subordination." Both the treasure and the prisoners had been brought into Cantonments, and Hawes believed that in a little while he could so restore loyalty to the regiment as to enable him to convey the money to the capital. But these hopes, like many others of the same kind, were delusive. The most favourable symptoms too often presaged a crisis. On the 9th of June he thought that the attempt might be made with safety. The carts were loaded with the treasure. The men marched out of Cantonments with a ringing cheer. But there was division among the Sepoys; and the treasure-escort had not gone more than half a mile towards Lucknow when mutiny broke out in their ranks. There were still some loyal men among them, but they could not resist the stern demands of their comrades, who fired upon them. So the coveted coin was carried back to Durriabad, and there was nothing left for the English but to betake themselves to flight.

They all escaped with their lives. Lieutenants Grant and Fullarton, with their wives and children, went off in an ecka, or Native covered carriage, and,

* "I have every hope," he wrote to Sir Henry Lawrence on the 25th of May, "of being able to hold my own and keep the treasure secure, so long as I can keep everything under my own eye and united; but as any harsh measure would very probably bring on an open revolt, I am desirous, for the sake of the European officers' families, not to show any apparent mistrust, or to bring on the crisis until obliged, or until I have felt my way a little more clearly. I could have taken on the treasure last night, but it would have been at the risk of leaving behind many mutinous spirits."—*MS. Correspondence.*

after some adventures by the way, being sometimes in great peril, they reached Lucknow in safety. Mr. Benson, of the Civil Service, also made good his way to the capital, riding the greater part of the way. The escape of Captain Hawes was a marvel. The Sepoys of his regiment, whom he had so much trusted and so kindly treated, fired upon him from all directions, sometimes by volleys, sometimes by the deliberate aim of single marksmen. But he rode on unharmed, and reached Lucknow without a wound. The English were cleared out of Durriabad. The mutineers remained there for some days, and then set their faces towards the great rebel rallying-ground at Newab-gunj; and the authority of the deposed King of Oude was proclaimed throughout the district.

1857. June—July.

General results.

Such were the principal incidents of mutiny and rebellion at the out-stations of Oude—incidents in their results most disastrous to the lives and property of the English, and most damaging to the fair fame of our nation. Everywhere our authority had collapsed. Everywhere our people, if not feeding the jackals and the vultures, were flying for their lives and imploring the mercy of those whom a little while before they had overawed and commanded. It was plain that we had but few friends in the province. Even those fugitives to whom shelter was given met with but scant courtesy and hospitality. Some, after much toil and travail, made their way to Lucknow; some escaped into Goruckpore, or were fortunate enough to reach Allahabad in safety; others perished by the way. Long time would it take to narrate all the incidents of these adventurous escapes, or the

1857. June—July.

sufferings, often ending in death, endured by our people. One story, however, of captivity in Oude may be briefly told in this place—one episode in the great history of martyrdom.

An episode of captivity.

Among those who escaped from the great massacre at Seetapore were Sir Mountstuart Jackson, a young covenanted civilian, and his two sisters—Georgiana and Madeline Jackson.* The personal attractions and engaging manners of these young people had won all hearts; and there were none whose fates, in this dreadful crisis in Oude, were invested with a wider and deeper interest from one end of the province to the other. In the confusion of the flight, the sisters were separated, and Madeline Jackson alone went with her brother. They were joined by Lieutenant Burnes of the Artillery—a young officer of great gallantry†—and by Sergeant-Major Morton, who had saved little Sophie Christian. These made their way towards Mythowlee, the estate of a "friendly Rajah," to which Captain Philip Orr had already sent his wife and child. On the morning of the 1st of June Mrs. Orr had arrived at Mythowlee, but was presently conveyed to the Fort of Kutchianee, one of those old strongholds defended by belts of jungle, in which the Oude Talookhdars had been wont to resist the authority of the King's officers. It was described as "a most dreary, desolate-looking building, devoid of the most common articles of furniture, and presenting a picture of the utmost discomfiture." In this wretched place Mrs. Orr was joined by her husband, who came in on the 5th of June—worn and weary, his clothes tattered and travel-stained, and with the blood of his

* Children of Sir Keith Jackson, and nephew and nieces of Mr. Colverley Jackson, who had been the first Chief Commissioner of Oude.

† He was son of Dr. Burnes, one of our earliest Scinde diplomatists—and nephew of Sir Alexander Burnes.

murdered comrades still upon them.* Their sojourn in this inhospitable abode was but brief. They were soon sent forth into the more inhospitable jungle. Mountstuart Jackson and his party had arrived, and their custodian alleged that, as the mutineers were approaching, he could not conceal so large a party of Europeans. So the Orrs went forth into the howling wilderness. There they had scanty food and little or no shelter; for if they had sought the shades of the forest the tigers would have been upon them; and at night they were compelled to burn fires in an open space to keep the beasts of prey at a distance from them. 1857. June—July.

Meanwhile, the other party of Seetapore fugitives were received into the Kutchianee Fort. They had gone first to Mythowlee to claim the hospitality of Loonee Singh, but had been refused admittance. Burnes, however, would not be denied, and ere the gate was closed, pushed through, weak and weary as he was, and gained an entrance, to plead the cause of his fellow fugitives. A blow on the head from one of the Rajah's people covered him with blood; and in this plight Loonee Singh took compassion on him, and ordered him and his companions to be received into the Fort. But the hospitality afforded to them was of the most grudging kind. Sorely distressed as they were—wanting everything and altogether in evil plight—they were sent to herd in a wretched cowshed,† and next day were despatched to the gloomy fortress of Kutchianee.

* See the very interesting account of the "English Captives in Oude," compiled from the best sources of information by Captain Patrick Orr's brother. But Captain P. Orr says that the mutineers "let him have a horse and a few clothes" to help him on to Mythowlee.

† Mr. Wylie's Narrative says: "Their condition was sad, indeed, completely worn out, as they were, by fatigue, their clothes in tatters, without any shoes, and their feet lacerated by the thorns of the jungle through which they had passed."

1857. June—July. There, after awhile, the bands of mutineers, who had been hovering about the neighbourhood, having dispersed themselves, the Orrs were again recalled to the Fort. There for some time the whole party dwelt together, hearing from all quarters evil tidings of the success of mutiny and rebellion, and of the sufferings of their fellow-countrymen. One only gleam of sunshine broke through the darkness. News came that Georgiana Jackson, whom her brother and sister had mourned as dead, was alive, but in captivity. And thus miserably passed the time from week to week and from month to month, till all spirit and all hope died within them, and they looked despairingly into one another's faces and said little, for there was no comfort to be interchanged. And thus June passed away and July passed away, and still there was no sign of deliverance. For a little while there was some reasonable expectation that a friend might be found for them in the depths of their sorrow; for the Wakeel of Loonee Singh of Mythowlee owed everything to Patrick Orr, who had raised this man—Zuhoor-ool-Hussun by name—from poverty to wealth by his good offices, and he had hoped that the kindness he had shown him might be returned. But the Wakeel never raised a hand or spoke a word to alleviate the sufferings of his patron, or of those who suffered with him; and after a little while it appeared that the passive friend had become the active enemy of the English captives.

August. In the wilderness. August came, and again there was a rumour of the coming of some detachments of rebel troops, and again the English captives were sent out into the jungle under a lying pretence that they would be safer there than in the Fort. But scarcely had they been driven out into the wilderness, when the Rajah sent a messenger to our enemies to tell them where our people were to be found. It was plainly the design to betray them; but the insurgents never entered the jungle. The cause of their forbearance is not easily explained.* But the result was that the fugitives were left unmolested. Perhaps it was thought that exposure to the sun, the rain, and the wild beasts of the jungle would soon do its work on the white people, and that death would come slowly and painfully, but not less surely, upon them. But death did not come upon them in the jungle, though all that makes life, as health and hope, was crushed out of them. They saw each other drooping day by day, or, as time went on, prostrated by jungle-fever, that left them weaker than before, and returned again and again to rack them. From the 6th of August to the 25th of October, they endured these torments; and then they were ordered to prepare for their departure, none knew whither, under a guard of the people of the Rajah of Mythowlee. Their preparations were very slender—for, in truth, they had nothing to take with them. They had no covering for their heads; no covering for their feet; scarcely any covering for their bodies, except some miserable rags. And when they tried to take with them an old sheet or some scraps of cloth, much prized in their pitiable state, the boon was brutally refused with blows.†

1857. Aug.—Oct.

* The Orr Narrative, already quoted, says: "Will it be believed that two hundred and fifty men were actually afraid to accomplish the mission on which they were sent. They were actually afraid to encounter our small party, expecting a desperate resistance. Such was the report of the Passee—a report subsequently verified by the result, for the troops returned empty-handed to Lucknow, not having dared to penetrate the dreaded jungle, notwithstanding all the remonstrances of the Rajah." I cannot say, however, that I am quite prepared to accept this view of the case.

† "Sergeant-Major Morton begged permission to take with him a piece of cloth which had served as a carpet, but was refused. Mrs. Orr had also wished to carry away a sheet with which to cover her head, as well as that of her daughter, but one of the cowardly ruffians accompanied the refusal with a blow, which felled her to the ground."—*The Orr Narrative. Edited by Macleod Wylie.*

1857. October.

Weak and fever-stricken, they were dragged out of the jungle, and on the roadside two of the common carts of the country were waiting for them. On these they were huddled together, and then they set forth on their nameless journey.

But the measure of their humiliation was not yet full. In a village through which they passed, preparations had been made by Zuhoor-ool-Hussun, who had now himself appeared upon the scene, to send the male prisoners forward in chains. Perhaps it was in bitter remembrance of what had been done by us at Meerut that this last indignity was put upon our people. But whatever the secret cause in the eyes of our persecutors, it was a terrible success. It well-nigh killed one of the captives, and it crazed the brain of another.* It is significantly stated that the ingenious malice of Zuhoor-ool-Hussun reserved the heaviest pair of fetters for his patron; and, although Mrs. Orr went down on her knees to him, she was answered only by a brutal outburst of laughter.

The captives carried to Lucknow.

It was soon apparent that their destination was Lucknow. On they went, a hundred and fifty men and a gun in front of them—a hundred and fifty men and a gun in rear of them. In the villages through which they passed they were made a show to be gazed at and to be mocked by the people. Their food, scanty and nauseous, was thrown to them, as if they had been dogs. Water was given to them grudgingly, or not at all. Nothing was omitted

* "At this gross indignity the mind of poor Burnes received a shock from which it never recovered. Sergeant-Major Morton, at the sight of the fetters, fell into a frightful convulsive fit, from which with difficulty he recovered under the attentions that could be paid to him by his fellow-captives. Death at one time seemed ready to terminate his sufferings."—*The Orr Narrative, ut supra.*

that could enhance their agonies both of body and of mind. And ever as they went on their dreary six days' journey, there was a vague terror upon the captives of what lay before them at Lucknow. As they neared the capital, which was still in possession of the insurgents, a swarm of troops, both Horse and Foot, came out to meet them. The order was that the captives should be taken to the Kaiser-bagh, one of the old palaces of the kings, in which the enemy had a strong position. At a little distance from this place they were made to leave the clumsy vehicles on which they had sat, and to walk, or rather to stagger, through the streets, gazed at by an insolent crowd, which pressed upon them, rejoicing in their humiliation. It was, indeed, a ghastly procession. Orr carried his little daughter in his arms; Burnes carried Sophie Christian; Mountstuart Jackson was so reduced by fever and ague, that he could scarcely crawl to his new prison-house, and he had no sooner entered it than he fell down in a swoon. How the two poor English gentlewomen bore up against such trials it is hard to conceive. It is related that in the agonies of their thirst they shrieked for water, and that when at last their prayer was granted, it was brought to them "in such a vile vessel, that the ladies refused to pollute their lips by touching it."

1857. October.

Here, then, in a small apartment of the Kaiser-bagh the prisoners lay for some weeks. Literally, it may be said that they died daily—for they felt that each hour might be their last. The miserable plight in which they had left the jungle was now greatly aggravated. The men were emaciated and enfeebled both in body and in mind; the women, whose patient courage proved them to be true Christian heroines, tried to bear up bravely, for the

In the Kaiser-bagh.

1857. Aug.—Nov. sake of those they loved; but well-nigh everything most revolting to an English gentlewoman was present to distress them. Their clothes were in rags. They had no appliances of personal cleanliness. That which has been said to be the glory of a woman had now become her shame.* The only comfort that came to them in their tribulation came from the Word of God. They had not a Bible among them; but one day, whilst in the Kaiser-bagh, Mrs. Orr sent for some Native medicines, and they were brought to her wrapped up in a piece of printed paper, which proved to be part of a leaf of the Book of Isaiah. And the message, which came to them through Mahomedan hands, was this:

"*They shall obtain gladness and joy; and sorrow and mourning shall flee away. I, even I, am he that comforteth you; who art thou that thou shouldst be afraid of a man that shall die, and of the son of man that shall be made as grass; and forgettest the Lord thy Maker, that hath stretched forth the heavens and laid the foundations of the earth; and hast feared continually every day because of the fury of the oppressor, as if he were ready to destroy? and where is the fury of the oppressor? The captive exile hasteneth that he may be loosed, and that he should not die in the pit, nor that . . . .*"†

And the words of love, thus strangely and mysteriously sent to them, comforted and strengthened them in the midst of their sorrow. It seemed like a

* "Their clothes even in the jungles had already been in tatters; they were now completely in rags; their hair was completely matted, deprived as they had long had been of combs and brushes."—*Orr Narrative.*

† Isaiah, chap. li., verses 11—14. The paper was torn off before the completion of the last verse. The words are, "nor that his bread should fail."

promise of deliverance; and it was so—but only in part. 1857. November.

For, not long afterwards, the malice of the enemy discharged itself upon our persecuted people in a manner which it is terrible to contemplate. On the morning of the 16th November a party of the Seventy-first Sepoy Regiment, fully armed and equipped, entered the dwelling-place of the captives, and said that they were bidden to take the gentlemen away. With difficulty, in their debilitated state, Jackson and Orr rose from their recumbent position, took a sad and solemn farewell of those who were so near and dear to them, and then with their comrades Burnes and Moreton, calmly suffered themselves to be bound. A rattle of musketry was presently heard; and although the gaolers assured our affrighted gentlewomen that it portended only the execution of some Native prisoners, the terrible truth soon became apparent to them. Our women and children had lost their protectors. Husband, brother, and guardians had been ruthlessly murdered, and the last state of desolation had come upon these poor helpless ones. A few days after this butchery another of the captives was delivered by death. Little Sophie Christian, who had for some time been reduced to an extremity of weakness by the ravages of disease, faded away so gently that those about her scarcely knew the time of her deliverance.* The prisoners in the Kaiser-bagh were now reduced to two

Murder of Jackson, Orr, Burnes, and Moreton.

* "Death passed his hand gently over her; her beautiful blue eyes closed as if in gentle repose, and before her companions were aware of the change her infant spirit had fled for ever from the scenes of danger and misery. Through the kindness of a man of the guard, himself the father of a large family, Mrs. Orr and Miss Jackson had the melancholy satisfaction of knowing that during the dark hours of the ensuing night the remains of the poor little orphan were carefully confided to the earth."—*Macleod Wylie—The Orr Narrative.*

1858. January. women and one child; and such was the insignificance of the party in the estimation of the enemy, that this wretched remnant of the captive band had well-nigh perished from neglect. But time went on, drearily and sadly, until the year wore to a close, and still they lived and prayed and suffered; and great events occurred around them, of which they heard the fearful sounds in the almost incessant roar of the guns, and sometimes the crashing noise which told that the destructive missiles were falling closely around them. Of what all this portended they had but a dim notion, for the information which reached them was either wholly false, or distorted and exaggerated to our disadvantage; but so far as these poor women could understand their miserable environments, it appeared to them that whether the British or the Oude Government should be eventually triumphant, there was equally little prospect of their escape.

Then, whilst they ceased to hope for their own safety, and resigned themselves with Christian patience to whatsoever might be the will of God, their tender hearts were torn by the thought of what might be the fate of the little child who shared their captivity. So they resolved that they would endeavour to effect its deliverance, and cast about in their minds how this might best be accomplished. Among those who guarded them, or had influence over the guardians, were one or two less stern and cruel than the rest. One, indeed, had been their friend from the first of their captivity in the Kaiser-bagh. His name was Wajid Ali, and he was a Darogah of the Native Government. Counsel was now taken with him as to the best means of saving the child. The sympathies of a Native woman—a resident of Lucknow—were enlisted in favour of the child and her mother; and one day, after some earlier schemes had failed, the deliverance was accomplished. They stained the hands and the feet of the little girl so as to resemble those of a Native child, and the woman who was acting this good part wrapped her in a sheet, and with well-simulated weepings and lamentations carried out the precious burden as though she were taking the body of her own little one to burial, and thus eluded the vigilance of the guards. The little captive was taken to the house of Maun Singh, and after some days was conveyed in safety to the British camp in the Alum-bagh.

1858. Jan.—Mar.

Deliverance of the captives.

Then, after this, to the two who were left there was a season of weary suspense. Although British arms had been triumphant on every great occasion of conflict, the enemy still held positions in parts of the city and the suburbs, and might any day sweep in upon them with murderous intent. But Wajid Ali was still true to them, and when it was seen that the Kaiser-bagh was no longer safe, under the vigorous bombardment to which it was now subjected, he placed them in a palanquin, and, not without difficulty, conveyed them to another abode. But this was not beyond the reach of danger, so a second departure became necessary, and now they were housed beneath the same roof as Wajid Ali's wife and children, safe from the fire of our guns, but not secure against the assaults of the enemy. It was feared that the malice of the Moulavee would bring destruction upon them. Renewed exertions were, therefore, to be made to open communications with our people, so Mrs. Orr wrote a letter, to be delivered to the first British officer that could be found, and it was intrusted to the care of the brother-in-law of

1858. March 19. Wajid Ali. Providence favoured the effort. For he had scarcely started when he came upon a detachment of the Goorkah force, accompanied by two English officers. These were Captain M'Neill and Lieutenant Bogle, of the Artillery. To read the letter was to grasp the suggestion of immediate action. They hastened to the house where the captives dwelt, seized a palanquin, placed the Englishwomen in it, improvised a set of bearers from the ever-ready Goorkahs, and under charge of Captain M'Neill were carried through the narrow, tortuous streets, till the welcome sight of General Macgregor's camp at last assured them that they were safe, and soon in a tent pitched for them by the General, where all they needed was supplied to them. They thanked God for their merciful deliverance. Next day they were passed on to the camp of Sir James Outram.

CHAPTER III.

LUCKNOW IN JUNE—SIR HENRY LAWRENCE—HIS FAILING HEALTH—MARTIN GUBBINS—NOMINATION OF A SUCCESSOR—PREPARATIONS AGAINST A SIEGE—THE DISASTERS OF CHINHUT—DESTRUCTION OF THE MUTCHEE-BHAUN—COMMENCEMENT OF THE SIEGE—DEATH OF HENRY LAWRENCE.

ALL these terrible disasters lacerated the heart of Henry Lawrence. He bore up as bravely as he could. But from the very commencement of his employment in Oude he had been in an infirm state of health. He had, indeed, as I have already shown,* intended to visit England in the early part of the year. The summons to Lucknow acted as a stimulant upon him; but stimulants are short-lived in their effects. As the month of June wore on everything around him had a depressing influence upon his exhausted frame and his sensitive mind. It was the worst season of the year. The removal from the Cantonment to the city made the June heats more oppressive to him. He was one who would never willingly spare himself, so long as he had any power of muscular exertion, or any capacity of clear thought. He went about from post to post at all hours, seeing everything with his own eyes, inquiring, examining, directing. His seat had

1857. June.

* Vol. i. page 450.

1857. June.

been on the saddle; it was now on the cushions of his carriage. But the directing power was still the same. Outward action is good for the suppression of inward thought; and perhaps it sustained Lawrence for a time. And there was something that sustained him more—sustained him throughout all his trials—an abounding faith in the goodness of God and the efficacy of prayer. Often was he found upon his knees, by those who entered his room to convey information or to solicit instruction. Thus strengthened, he felt that the great deliverance would come, though he might not live to see it.

Martin Gubbins.

But it was obvious to those around him that he was growing feebler and feebler in body every day, and there was one man in the garrison, who believed, or pretended to believe, that he was growing feebler in mind. This was Mr. Martin Gubbins, the Financial Commissioner.* He was endowed with a high order of genius, nearly allied to madness. It was impossible not to recognise his great intellectual† qualities, as well as his consummate personal bravery; but his intellect was of an impulsive, an erratic character, such as to worry a chief, with all the responsibilities of the situation cast upon him. A man who, being second, thinks that he ought to be first, is a thorn in the flesh of him who has the supreme command. Martin Gubbins was such a

* See the following extract of a letter to Lord Canning: "You sent us a noble-hearted soldier as chief. And with him all promised well until it pleased God to send us this dire calamity. But Sir Henry Lawrence came to us attenuated and weak; and the severe mental anxiety which he has undergone has prostrated him greatly. Sir Henry Lawrence is no longer, I think, firm, nor his mental vision clear. How long, with little sleep, much anxiety, and overwork, any of us will retain clearness of judgment, who can tell?"—*Mr. Martin Gubbins to Lord Canning, June* 2, 1857. *MS. Correspondence.*

† I may say here that he visited me often (I think in 1858), and that I was greatly impressed by his intellectual attainments.

man. He was never quiet. He was never happy unless he was in opposition. It might have been said of him, in imitation of what was said of John Lilburne, that, if he had been the only man left in Lucknow, Martin would have quarrelled with Gubbins, and Gubbins would have quarrelled with Martin. He saw Lawrence fading away, and he hungered for the empty chair. The Chief Commissioner knew it, but he knew also that there was no man in the garrison more unfit to have supreme control. So he telegraphed on the 4th of June to the Governor-General, saying: "If anything happens to me during "present disturbances, I earnestly recommend that "Major Banks succeed me as Chief Commissioner, and "Colonel Inglis in command of the troops, until better "times arrive. This is no time for punctilio as regards "seniority. They are the right men—in fact, the only "men for the places. My Secretary entirely concurs "with me on the above points."* He had at an earlier hour of the same day drawn up a memorandum† in other words, and more limited in its significance. "If anything happens to me during present dis-"turbances, I recommend that Colonel Inglis succeed "me in command, and that Major Banks be appointed "to the command of one of the posts. There should "be *No Surrender*. I commend my children and the "Lawrence Asylum to Government." It is obvious that he had not then fully resolved to recommend Banks as his successor in the Chief Commissionership. It seems to have been an after-thought, or perhaps

1857. June.

Major Banks.

* This is copied from a draft in the handwriting of Sir George Couper, and signed by Sir Henry Lawrence.

† I take this from a copy in the handwriting of Mr. A. Lawrence. It does not seem to have been intended for a telegram, but as a memorandum, in the event of his death, to be read by his Staff and communicated to Government.

1857. June. it was the result of a conference with his sagacious Secretary.

But from whatsoever source the recommendation proceeded, it was a wise and politic one. Major Banks was the Commissioner of the Lucknow Division. A little time before he had been one of Lord Dalhousie's most trusted officers. He was Military Secretary to that great statesman, then heavy with thought of the coming annexation of Oude. In the summer of 1856, the Governor-General was on a visit to the Neilgherry Hills. Thence in the month of June he despatched to the Home Government his exhaustive minute on the vast and still-increasing evils of Native misrule in Oude, and the duty of British interference. Nothing could be done until the decision of the Court of Directors should be communicated to him, but in the meanwhile it was expedient to make secret preparations for the deposition of the reigning prince and the extinction of the existing Government. To this end it was necessary, in the first instance, that a confidential officer should be despatched to Oude, to communicate with General Outram, our Resident at Lucknow, firstly, with regard to "the military preparations that might be necessary; and, secondly, to the civil arrangements which might be subsequently required." For this important duty Major Banks was selected. He received his instructions on the 19th of July, and started on the following day for Calcutta, there to communicate with the President in Council, and afterwards to join Outram in Lucknow. He was a discreet and sagacious man; but still it was Lord Dalhousie's duty to enjoin absolute secrecy.* Banks

* "And as it will be obvious to you that until the order of the Honourable Court shall have been received, entire secrecy should be

did his work well to the absolute satisfaction of the Governor-General, whose former high opinion, evinced by the trust reposed in him, was greatly increased by the manner of its discharge. And not only did the Governor-General entertain respect for his Secretary; he felt a tender affection for him as a man. All the softness of Dalhousie's nature was expressed when he wrote to Banks and his wife. When, therefore, the great project for the extinction of the Native dynasty in Oude had received the assent of the Home Government, and the scheme of British administration had been prepared, it was certain that the man who had been second only to Outram as a pioneer of the great change, should have awarded to him a place in the Government of the newly-acquired province. He was appointed Commissioner of the most important division into which the province was partitioned—the Division of Lucknow—and being therefore at the Head-Quarters of the Government in constant communication with the Chief Commissioner, he soon won the good opinion of his chief, who recognised in him a great combination of prudence, sagacity, firmness, and courage. So Banks obtained, to his exceeding honour, the reversion of the Chief-Commissionership of Oude. 1857. June.

This done, Lawrence felt great mental relief; but the physical weakness was increasing upon him, and he was at last persuaded by Dr. Fayrer—one of the The Provisional Council.

observed in the preparation of measures which the Government may not, after all, be authorised to execute, you are requested to observe absolute silence as to the duty on which you are employed. Here and at Calcutta, it will be a sufficient answer to all curious inquirers, that you are employed by the Governor-General on public business, as to which nobody has any business to ask questions. Your departure from Calcutta may be managed without any one being aware of it. Surmises and suspicions of course cannot be prevented; but no communication for the purpose of your journey need be made except to those already mentioned in this memorandum."—*MS. Document.*

1857. June. brightest ornaments of the Indian medical service—to take a few days of rest. He very reluctantly consented to make over the command, and appointed a Provisional Council, consisting of Mr. Gubbins, Mr. Ommaney, Colonel Inglis, Major Banks, and Major Anderson. But only for two or three days could Lawrence be induced to rest.* The strong spirit asserted itself again; and a certificate was wrung from Fayrer permitting him to return to his work, on condition that he would spare himself as much as was possible. But it was not possible for him to spare himself. The eagerness of his nature forebade him to cease from labour; his deep love for his fellow-men would not suffer him to rest, so long as he thought that he could do anything for them.

The brief interregnum had not been an uneventful one. Gubbins had attempted a "coup" and failed. He had tried, whilst at the head of the Provisional Council, to eliminate the Poorbeah element wholly from the garrison of Lucknow. He had recommended, from the first, the disarming of the Sepoy regiments—but Lawrence had consistently opposed the measure. As chief of the Provisional Council, he now thought that he might carry out this che-

* "It was on the 9th of June that Lawrence appointed this Council. The order ran thus: 'As Dr. Fayrer states that it is imperatively necessary for my health that I should remain perfectly quiet for the next twenty-four hours, I appoint Mr. Gubbins, Mr. Ommaney, Lieutenant-Colonel Inglis, Major Anderson, and Major Banks to be a council to conduct the affairs of the province until I feel myself sufficiently convalescent to resume the Government.—H. M. LAWRENCE, June 9, 1857.' The Council sat on the 10th and 11th. On the morning of the 12th, Lawrence, eager to return to his work, obtained from Dr. Fayrer a certificate, somewhat reluctantly given, to the effect that, although he was capable of resuming his duties, he should be spared as much mental and bodily fatigue as possible. Upon this Mr. Gubbins recommended that the powers of the Council should be continued, but that all important questions should be referred to the General. Against this the other four members voted, and the powers of the Council ceased."—*Lives of Indian Officers.*

rished stratagem. So he obtained the consent of commanding officers to disarm the faithful remnants of their regiments and to send them on leave to their homes. But when Lawrence, to whom everything was promptly reported, was informed of this movement, he resolved at once, as far as was possible, to counteract it. He believed in the fidelity of the Sepoys, who had clung to us through good report and evil report, and he knew that he wanted them to aid in the defence of Lucknow. So it was partly from sentiment, partly from policy, that when he rose from his sick couch and resumed the command, he sent messengers after these home-going Sepoys, and brought numbers of them, with smiling faces, back to their posts.* 1857. June.

Opposition of Mr. Gubbins.

The sudden collapse of the Provisional Council of which Mr. Gubbins was the head, exceedingly disconcerted the energetic financial minister. He expected a longer reign, and he found that he had been "hoist by his own petard." Thus disappointed, he tried to persuade his comrades that Lawrence's policy was feeble, that it would be wise to adopt more vigorous measures, and to strike little blows in every possible direction. Referring to this on the day after his resumption of command, Lawrence wrote to Mr. Colvin at Agra: "Mr. Gubbins is perfectly insane on what he considers energetic manly measures. His language has been so extravagant, that were he not

* In a highly interesting memoir, written by Colonel Wilson (the "Staff Officer," to whom also I am much indebted), and quoted by Mr. Herman Merivale in the second volume of the "Life of Sir Henry Lawrence," it is stated that they "returned with tokens of delight, the honesty of which was verified by their loyalty during the siege." Mr. Merivale, however, quotes another manuscript document, written by Captain Edgell, also a staff-officer, in which it is stated that Lawrence approved of the disarming. That Captain Edgell himself approved of the disarming is certain, for Gubbins writes he was the only officer who supported him. I find that more than two years ago I had written the version of the affair given in the text, after conversing with Colonel Wilson and Sir George Couper.

1857. June. really useful, I should be obliged to take severe measures against him. He is the one malcontent in the garrison. All others, I believe, are satisfied that as much energy has been evinced as circumstances would permit." This has never been questioned by any other than the man against whose counsel this protest was delivered. The true policy at this time was to defend Lucknow, which, it was certain, would be ere long in a state of siege. Concentration, not dispersion, was the great object to be attained. So all the goings-out here and there that Gubbins recommended were for a time totally ignored.

There was one of these recommendations, however, that we are bound to respect—Gubbins thought that assistance might be sent to Cawnpore. How, in the midst of all the tribulation at his own door, Henry Lawrence could still find time to consider, and sympathy to deplore, the dangers and distresses of his brethren at a distance, his correspondence in this month of June largely testifies. It well-nigh broke his heart to think that he could do nothing for Wheeler and the Cawnpore garrison, whatever their straits might be. What these straits were he hardly knew—so difficult was it to obtain correct information from the other side of the Ganges. "We cannot," he wrote, on the 13th, "get certain tidings from Cawnpore, although we have sent many messengers; but we have no reason to doubt that General Wheeler still holds his ground. The mutineers hold the river bank for many miles below and above Cawnpore, and search all passers. They at once seized all the boats and drew them to their own bank. Would that we could help the besieged—but our numbers, and the distance, and the river forbid the thought." Three days afterwards a letter was received from Sir Hugh Wheeler, with an imploring cry for help; and great as was his own need Lawrence would have sent it, if he had believed that the succours could ever cross the river in safety. "Wheeler asks for two hundred Europeans," he wrote on the 16th. "I would risk the absence of so large a portion of our small force, could I see the smallest prospect of its being able to succour him. But no individual here cognisant of facts, except Mr. Gubbins, thinks we could carry a single man across the river, as the enemy holds all the boats and completely commands the river. May God Almighty defend Cawnpore, for no help can we afford!"* Those were days when all men were scrambling for the few Europeans scattered about the country—when many thought of themselves, regardless of the fate of others, and clamoured for help which could be given only by inflicting heavy cost, perhaps ruin on the helpers. It would have been a question, even if it had been possible to cross the river, whether Lawrence would have been justified in sending so large a part of his little force to Cawnpore; but with the impediment, of which he spoke, looming so largely before him, it is simply a certainty that he would have been lamentably wrong; for he would have sent all these men to destruction.

1857. June.

But before the month of June was at an end, an event had occurred which changed the whole com-

Advance of the enemy.

* He repeated this in almost similar words, at a later period, saying: "There was a report that the Nana had offered to escort the Cawnpore garrison to Allahabad, and that an armistice of two days had taken place in consequence. I sincerely trust that no such proposition will be attended to, as it would result in nothing but treachery and disgrace."

1857. June. plexion of affairs at Lucknow. Having received intelligence on the 29th of the month, which left no doubt that the enemy were mustering in great force, about ten or twelve miles from the capital, with intent of marching forward to attack it, Lawrence determined on the following morning to go out in strength to make a reconnoissance, and, at all events, to demonstrate that the English were still capable of action. It was not without much thought and some reluctance, that he resolved to issue orders for a movement, which his ignorance of the actual strength of the enemy seemed to render at least hazardous. The scouts had reported the strength of the insurgent force at nine regiments of Infantry, one regiment of Cavalry, and twelve guns. Mr. Gubbins laughed the estimate to scorn, and wrote "What stuff!" upon the circular which communicated the intelligence to the chief officers of the garrison. That the irrepressible ardour of the Finance Commissioner prevailed over the military circumspection of the Brigadier-General is not to be doubted.* For, weeks past, Martin Gubbins had been urging upon the military authorities the expediency of a forward movement, and had in his letters to the Governor-General and others protested against the prevailing policy of inaction. To these counsels Lawrence yielded at last; and on the morning of the 30th of June, the flower of his force went forth along the road to Chinhut, but rather as a grand military promenade than with any definite thought of meeting the enemy. It was Lawrence's intention, indeed, only to proceed, along the great high road, as far as the Kokaralee Bridge, and

* See a note on this subject in the Appendix. If any further evidence be required, the reader need look back to Mr. Gubbins's letter to Lord Canning previously quoted in this book.

there, if no enemy were seen, to halt the force and to return to Lucknow. 1857. June.

The force that assembled under arms on the last morning of June consisted of three hundred men of the Queen's Thirty-second, under Colonel Case; about two hundred Infantry Sepoys, believed to be faithful to their employers; a hundred and twenty troopers of the Oude Irregular Horse, said to have been principally Sikhs; and a noble little band of Volunteer Cavalry, with the good blood of English gentlemen in their veins. Four guns of a light field battery (Europeans), and six guns of the Oude Native Artillery, with an eight-inch howitzer drawn by an elephant, were equipped to accompany the Force—in all about seven hundred men, one-half of whom were Natives. Sir Henry Lawrence took command of the whole.*

June 30. The march to Chinhut.

The morning was intensely hot; and the march was towards the rising sun. As often happens, some of the Europeans were in that unhinged, shaky condition with which the morning revenges itself on the constitution for the excesses of the preceding night, and nearly all were exhausted with much watching and work.† There are only two things in such a case that can restore the balance of outraged nature—time and

* See Brigadier Inglis's report, from which I have taken the details in the text; but the Staff Officer, a most reliable authority, speaks only of "a hundred and fifty of the Thirty-second from the Mutchee-Bahwun." I conclude that this is merely an accidental omission of those from the cantonment. The Staff Officer says that the howitzer was drawn by "*two* elephants;" Sir George Couper and Dr. Fayrer say by *one*. The point is of little importance except as illustrative of the difficulty of ascertaining the exact truth in respect of military details.

† An eye-witness writes to me: "They were worn out with the excessive labour which had been imposed on them in being under arms all day and all night for some weeks. I remarked to Lawrence as they stood on the Iron Bridge, just as the sun was rising and the word to move on was given, that they looked more like men who had just come off a hard day's work than just starting on one. It is certain they got nothing before starting."

1857. June 30.

further potations. But the stimulant of the morning dram was not served out to the men, and they marched out of Lucknow, for the most part, languid and dispirited, and with little heart for the work before them. Some dropped by the way. Others drooped, but toiled on. It was no thought of the enemy that caused them to flag. For there was a general feeling in the Force that, few as they were in numbers, they were more than a match for any multitude of the enemy that could be brought against them.

Thus the Force marched on to the Kokaralee Bridge, at which point the efforts of the skilled road-makers had ceased, and the onward route was loose and uneven, and muddy with much rain. Here the British Force was halted. No sign of an enemy had been seen; and it was thought that the order would be given for the countermarch to Lucknow. Weary and thirsty, the men looked around for something to refresh them; but there was nothing more supporting for the Europeans than the water in the leather-bags of the bheestees. They were in no mood to go further, on that hot June morning, and joyfully they stood with their faces towards Lucknow. But suddenly the order was issued for an advance to Chinhut.* So the regiments were again countermarched. Lawrence had placed himself at the head of the Force, and was bent on a further reconnoissance. So they struggled along the rugged causeway, and, about nine o'clock, they were approaching the village

The battle of Chinhut.

of Ishmael-gunj. Then it became clear that they were at no great distance from the main body of the insurgent army. Their round-shot were pouring

* Captain Wilson, Assistant-Adjutant-General, was sent with this order to Colonel Inglis.

into our columns. So Lawrence drew up his troops. 1857.
The Thirty-second lay in a hollow to the left of the June 30.
road; in the centre, under charge of Bonham of the Bengal Artillery, the great howitzer was posted; to the right, a little in advance of the heavy ordnance, were the light European guns—and still further to the right the Irregular Cavalry and the Volunteers. For a little while there was a dubious conflict of artillery. The shells from the howitzer were sent bursting into the enemy's camp; and a continual stream of round-shot was poured in from our light batteries, but at too great a range to do much mischief in the ranks of the mutineers. To the fire of the British guns the enemy responded with "beautiful precision." But the battle was not to be fought in this way. After a brief lull, which made our people think that the mutineers were retiring, they were seen to extend themselves out, in both directions, Cavalry, Infantry, and Artillery, as though to outflank us both on the right and on the left. Then, for the first time, the British leaders knew with what they had to contend. The plain between Ishmaelgunj and Chinhut was one "moving mass of men." Steadily and compactly, as though on a field-day under a general of division, the Sepoy regiments, flaunting their standards, advanced to the attack.* Our field-pieces opened on their columns, but with little effect, and soon the battle became a rout.

It was, indeed, impossible to resist the rush of the

* The following is from the very graphic account of an eye-witness, Mr. Lawrence, of the Civil Service, who was serving with the Volunteer Horse: "Regiment after regiment of the insurgents poured steadily towards us, the flanks covered with a foam of skirmishers, the light puffs of smoke from their muskets floating from every ravine and bunch of grass in our front. As to the mass of troops, they came on in quarter-distance columns, the standards waving in their places, and everything performed as steadily as possible. A field-day on parade could not have been better."—*Rees's Siege of Lucknow.*

1857. June 30. swarming enemy. Miserably over-matched as we were, the main hope of our little party of British troops had been in their guns. But, unhappily, the greater number of our field-pieces were manned by Native artillerymen; and their treachery broke out in the hour of our sorest need. Some of the black gunners cut their traces and went off with the horses, overturning the guns upon the field;* whilst the Native Cavalry turned and fled with all speed along the Lucknow Road. We had now only the companies of the Thirty-second, a few English gunners, and the Volunteer Cavalry, upon whom the General could rely to stem the onslaught of the insurgent multitude. The enemy had gained possession of the village of Ishmael-gunj, and were pouring a deadly fire of grape and musketry into our distressed people. Then came the time to storm the village. But it was a forlorn hope. The Colonel was shot down, and two of his officers fell mortally wounded beneath the dreadful fire of the enemy. Seeing this, the men of the Thirty-second, weary, dispirited, and weak for want of sustenance, who had been lying down in a hollow, rose up and fell back.† And the Native Infantry detachments, faithful among the faithless, posted on the right of the British Force, gave back a brisk shower of musket-balls in answer to the musketry of their countrymen.

But it was useless to maintain the unequal conflict. The enemy, having outflanked us, were endeavouring

* The current statement that all the Oude guns were so served, must be accepted with some limitation. I believe that only a part of the battery was served in this manner. One unpublished statement says that only two of the six guns were overturned. Sir George Couper saw Captain Wilson (the "Staff Officer") spike two of them—the carriages of which were not overturned. Wilson did the work with the end of a bayonet.

† One highly credible informant assures me that they did not fire a shot.

to surround our little Force; and had they hemmed us in on all sides, it would have been a merciful—a miraculous deliverance, if a single man had escaped. So Lawrence gave the orders for a retreat. It was a disastrous, but not wholly an inglorious one. To save the guns and the wounded was not possible in the face of such overwhelming numbers. Three field-pieces of the Oude Battery and the heavy howitzer, in spite of all Bonham's heroic efforts, were left in the hands of the enemy.* And many wounded men were left helpless on the field to die where they had fallen, or to be cut to pieces.

1857. June 30.

Death of Colonel Case.

Among these was Colonel Case, who lay, with open eyes, grasping his faithful sword in the agony of death. Captain Bassano, who had sought for his fallen leader among the dead and the dying, had endeavoured to remove him, and had proposed to bring some of the men of his regiment to his aid. But the wounded soldier had rejected all offers of assistance, and when pressed further by his friend, had reminded him, with a chivalry worthy of the dying Sydney,

* The conspicuous gallantry of Lieutenant Bonham on this occasion deserves more than this passing notice. I cannot better repair the omission in the text than by giving the following details from Mr. Gubbins's "Mutinies in Oudh:" "The European artillery limbered up and went to the rear; and Sir Henry Lawrence ordered Lieutenant Bonham to retire with the 8-inch howitzer. Unfortunately, the elephant which was attached to the limber had got frightened when the firing began, and had run off with it. Spare bullocks had been brought out to meet such an accident, but the frightened drivers had let them loose. Lieutenant Bonham seized the limber of a waggon, and mounting on the leading horse brought it up to the howitzer. Dismounting, however, to attach the limber to the gun, the native riders galloped off with it. At this time Captain Hardinge brought up the proper limber with the elephant; but the animal was so restless under fire that the utmost exertions of the untrained gunners failed to attach the trail of the howitzer to the limber. The enemy was pressing on, taking advantage of every break in the ground and of every cover to pour in a murderous fire of musketry. A bullet struck Lieutenant Bonham, who was carried off and put upon a limber, and the howitzer was abandoned. At this time many of the artillery-drivers detached their horses from the guns and ammunition-waggons and took to flight."

1857. June 30. that he was still commanding officer, and had gasped out his last orders by telling Bassano to rejoin his corps. A loving, tender-hearted woman was waiting for his return to the Residency, but the soldier was stronger than the husband in that awful crisis, and he would not take a man from his duty. He was a true-hearted, fine-tempered, English gentleman, of a genial nature, beloved by all who knew him; and there were few better soldiers in our camp.

Sir Henry Lawrence had been forward in the fight. He had moved from point to point unharmed amidst the thick fire of the enemy, and by his side his Secretary, George Couper, sinking the scribe in the soldier, had ridden on the battle-field as the aide-de-camp of his chief. In the crisis of the action, when the Thirty-second were falling fast and the activity of the enemy was at its height, Lawrence brought up a nine-pounder, and, though well knowing that there was not a shot in the tumbril, ordered the artillery-men to serve the gun and to light port-fire. By this timely display of fictitious strength he held the insurgents in check, until the Thirty-second had retired. The excitement of the action over, his physical weakness asserted itself, but the strong will sustained him nobly.* He had ordered out his carriage to meet him, intending, after the reconnoissance, to return in it to Lucknow; but the horses were needed for the guns: so he kept his saddle to the last, and rode on towards Lucknow.† He had been in the

* I am assured that the statement, so often repeated, that Sir Henry Lawrence, at the Kokaralee Bridge, exclaimed, in great anguish of mind: "My God! my God! and I brought them to this!" is a pure invention.

† A different statement to this has been erroneously made, and, I am sorry to say, that in a former work I helped to give it currency. It was said that, after the battle of Chinhut, Lawrence was brought home on a gun-carriage. But Sir George Couper, an undeniable authority, assures me that the General

rear, endeavouring to animate the Thirty-second, until he reached a narrow lane leading straight to the Iron Bridge. He then asked Inglis if he thought he might make a short cut to the Residency without detriment to his reputation as a soldier, to prepare the people there for what was coming and make the necessary arrangements. Inglis answered that in his opinion no possible blame could fall upon the General; so Lawrence left him in command, and accompanied by Wilson and George Couper galloped into the Residency—but they did not anticipate the head of the retreating column by more than a quarter of an hour. 1857. June 30.

At the Kokaralee Bridge, the scene of the morning's halt, a large party of the enemy's Horse, having doubled round our rear, had taken post with the object of cutting off our retreat. At first they were taken for our own Cavalry, and all offensive movements against them were stayed. But when the truth was apparent, Radcliffe's little body of Mounted Volunteers went at them with triumphant audacity and swept away the obstruction. Never was a nobler charge of British horsemen against more tremendous odds. Some thirty-five or forty sabres flashed in the morning sun, as Radcliffe's loud, clear voice gave out the stirring order, followed by that trumpet-note which is dearest to the heroic heart. The enemy did The retreat.

"rode on horseback every yard of the way" to Lucknow. This is another curious instance of the manner in which error is circulated, and may be perpetuated. In Captain Hutchinson's "Narrative of Events in Oude," which may be regarded as an official document, an account of the Chinhut affair is given, as an extract from the report of Brigadier Inglis. In this it is stated that "Sir Henry himself returned on a gun-carriage." But on consulting the work again, and comparing the passage with authenticated versions of Inglis's report, I find that only a portion of Hutchinson's narrative is derived from that source—the latter part of the extract being derived from some private statement, though printed as part of the official document.

1857. June 30. not stand to bear the shock, but fled with their five hundred troopers and two field-guns to cover them.* Nor did the services of the Volunteers on that June morning end with that glorious exploit. It was theirs all along the road to cover the retreat of our Infantry as they fell back upon Lucknow. The heat was excessive; and our men, exhausted and parched with thirst, could scarcely drag their weary limbs along the road. Some jostled for seats on the limbers of the guns and waggons which had been saved; others sought a little help by holding on to the stirrup-leathers of the Volunteers. The water-carriers had deserted, and all sustenance was far from them. Indeed, they were in piteous plight. The insurgent Cavalry were following them—nay, sometimes getting a-head of them, and our wretched people had to fight their way against dreadful odds to the capital. Everything was against them. Even the muskets of the Thirty-second were so foul, that cap after cap exploded to no purpose upon the hammer, and men at last gave up discharging their pieces in despair.†

Weak as we were in European troops, this was a tremendous disaster. A hundred and nineteen of our little body of English soldiers had been struck down by the fire of the enemy or the fierce heat of the morning sun. All further possibility of offensive movements was now gone; and even bare defence was difficult against such odds. The insurgents

* See Mr. Lawrence's "Narrative," quoted by Mr. Rees.

† This is stated by Gubbins (page 212), but another informant assures me that: "They never tried. At least I never saw them, although I heard their officers imploring them to stand and return the enemy's fire." Gubbins refers to the retreat—not to the action at Chinhut—but the pieces must have been foul, when the regiment started, if at all.

came streaming on to the banks of the Goomtee, and as our people entered the Residency, fast and fierce came the round shot from the rebel guns. To those who had remained in Lucknow, whilst this unhappy expedition was in progress, and especially to the Englishwomen in the Residency, who watched the return of our beaten troops from its windows,* the moment was one of intense anxiety. The vast assemblage of the enemy could be clearly seen on the opposite bank of the river. In a little while they might swarm into the city. The Iron Bridge was commanded by the guns of the Redan Battery and the Stone Bridge by the fire from the Mutchee Bhawun.† But there were other means of crossing the river, and it was soon seen that whilst some were planting their batteries on the opposite bank, others were collecting boats lower down for the passage of the Goomtee. Before noon they had invested our positions. The streets were deserted by the people. Contemporary writers describe the aspect of Lucknow as that of a great "city of the silent"—the silence broken only by the boom of the cannon and the rattle of the musketry. The hum of voices and the clatter of wheeled vehicles were gone—and in their place was the roar of the battle. The audacity of the enemy was superb. The passage of the river accomplished, the mutineers speedily occupied the houses, in the most command-

1857. June 30.

* Take as an illustration the following from Lady Inglis's journal. It should be premised that the writer was at the time suffering under the infliction of small-pox. "You may imagine our feelings of anxiety and consternation. I posted myself and watched the poor men coming in; a melancholy spectacle, indeed—no order, one after the other; some riding; some wounded, supported by their comrades; some on guns; some fell down and died from exhaustion not half a mile from our position. The enemy followed them to the bridge close to the Residency, which was defended by a company of the Thirty-second under Mr. Edmonstone, a gallant young officer. I could see the smoke of the musketry and plainly discerned the enemy on the opposite bank of the river."

† Gubbins, p. 215.

1857. June 30.

ing positions, near the Residency and the Mutchee-Bhawun, and loopholing them in the most effective manner, poured in upon us a tremendous shower of musketry that never slackened, day or night.*

In this conjuncture it was one of Sir Henry Lawrence's first thoughts to send off an express to Mr. Tucker at Benares, inclosing a note to Brigadier Havelock, acquainting him with the situation at Lucknow, and urging him to press on to its relief. "This morning," he wrote, "we went out eight miles to meet the enemy, and we were defeated and lost five guns, through the misconduct chiefly of our Native artillerymen, many of whom have deserted. The enemy have followed us up, and we have now been besieged for four hours, and shall probably to-night be surrounded. The enemy are very bold, and our Europeans are very low. I look upon our position as ten times as bad as it was yesterday. Indeed, it is now critical. We shall be obliged to concentrate, if we are able. We shall have to abandon much supplies, and to blow up much powder. Unless we are relieved quickly, say in fifteen or twenty days, we shall hardly be able to maintain our position."† Thus were epitomised the day's disaster and its probable results. Lawrence's anticipations were abundantly fulfilled. Before the new month had commenced the enemy were raging against us on every side; and it had become a matter of necessity to abandon the Mutchee-Bhawun and to concentrate all our force within the walls of the Residency.

Abandonment of the Mutchee-Bhawun.

But how was this concentration to be effected? The ground between the Residency and the Mutchee-

* "The majority of the rebel force crossed at sunset, and it was a beautiful sight the way their Horse Artillery dashed across the bridge."—*MS. Memorandum.*

† MS. Correspondence.

Bhawun was commanded by the enemy. To have sent a messenger with a letter would probably have been to have revealed, and, therefore, to have frustrated, our designs. Fortunately we were not without an alternative. The foresight of Lawrence's engineers had caused the rude machinery of a telegraph to be erected on the roof of the Residency, and the nature of the signals had been agreed upon and was well understood between the inmates of the two buildings.* But it was a service of difficulty and danger so to work this improvised semaphore, as to convey to the garrison of the Mutchee-Bhawun instructions to blow up the building and to withdraw the garrison under cover of the night; for the insurgents, seeing our people actively employed on the roof of the Residency, though probably not understanding the meaning of the movement, poured in such a deadly shower of rifle-balls from a commanding position on the top of the Gaol, that it was not until three hours had been spent, "under a broiling sun and a heavy fire," that, mainly by the personal exertions of Captain Fulton and Mr. George Lawrence, orders were conveyed to the Mutchee-Bhawun. Then there was an interval of intense suspense at the Residency. The movement, upon which so much depended, was to be made at midnight. It was possible that it might be suspected, or if not suspected, it might be discovered by the enemy's sentries or scouts, and our retreat thus intercepted. To avert such a calamity, orders were issued by Lawrence to open, a little before midnight, a distracting fire from all the guns and mortars in our batteries, and thus to cover

1857. June—July.

* "It simply consisted of one post with a bar at the top, from which were suspended in one row black stuffed bags, each having its own pulley to work it."—*Journal of a Staff-Officer.*

1857. July 1. the retirement of the garrison. This was completely successful. By God's providence the hazardous movement was effected without the loss of a man. At the appointed time they marched into the Residency, bringing with them their treasure and their guns.* Had the enemy compassed our designs, it is probable that but few of our party would have escaped with their lives, and it is certain that the guns and the treasure would have fallen into the enemy's hands.

But it was necessary that our people on retiring from the Mutchee-Bhawun should leave much that was dear to us behind them. The building had been appropriated to the uses of a great storehouse and magazine. It was rich with commissariat stores; with powder and with small-arm ammunition. These could not be taken away by the retiring garrison; so arrangements were made to destroy them. The Mutchee-Bhawun and all its contents were to be rendered, so far as a great explosion could render them, unserviceable to the enemy. This work was intrusted to Lieutenant Thomas, of the Madras Artillery, who laid the train—and soon after Colonel Palmer and his men had secured themselves within the Residency-walls, a pillar of fire was seen to rise from the Mutchee-Bhawun. The welcome sight was followed by the sound of a loud explosion; and then presently was seen a great cloud of smoke which hung for some time in mid-air over the shattered building and proclaimed its evacuation. Two hun-

* The enterprise, however, nearly miscarried, owing to a misunderstanding. The story is thus told by the Staff-Officer. "A very serious accident had nearly happened. The leading men, finding the gates closed, shouted out, 'Open the gates,' and the artillerymen at the guns above, which, loaded with grape, covered the entrance, mistook the works for 'Open with grape,' and were already at the guns, when an officer put them right. The whole force came in without a shot being fired."

dred and fifty barrels of gunpowder, with large quantities of small-arm ammunition, had been blown up; and much good food for our people was sacrificed at the same time. But the junction of the garrisons was too great a gain for there to be much disposition to count the cost. The cheers which greeted the arrival of Palmer and his followers showed how intense was the satisfaction in the Residency. Every man felt that a great danger had been escaped—that a great deliverance had come; and thanked God for the providential dispensation.

1857. July 1—2.

July 2. Death of Sir Henry Lawrence.

But a terrible revenge awaited us. On the morrow, nay, on the same morning (for the Mutchee-Bhawun was exploded after midnight), a great calamity overtook not only the Lucknow garrison, but the whole British nation. At dawn of day, Sir Henry Lawrence had risen, and, with his wonted activity, had superintended the new arrangements that had become necessary, owing to the welcome accession of force which the dark hours had brought him. He had seen new detachments posted and new guns planted; and when the morning sun had become oppressive, he had returned to the Residency, and had laid himself down to rest on a couch in his sitting-room—or, more correctly it should be said, to transact business in a recumbent position, for it was only rest of body that was allowed to him. His nephew, George Lawrence, was lying on another couch in the same room. By the General's side stood Captain Wilson, Assistant Adjutant-General, with one knee on the couch, reading an official memorandum, and waiting the orders of his chief. There was also a Native servant in the room. Whilst Wilson was still reading, a crashing noise was heard; then the room was filled with smoke and dust, through which nothing could be

1857. July. seen. The Staff-Officer was thrown to the ground, but, on recovering himself, he cried out, "Sir Henry, are you hurt?" At first there was no answer; but, after a little while, the feeble voice of the Chief Commissioner was heard to say, "I am killed!" And when the smoke cleared away, it was seen that the bed on which Lawrence lay was crimson with his blood. A shell from the howitzer, which Bonham had fought so gallantly at Chinhut, had exploded in the General's room, and a fragment of it had wounded him fearfully on the upper part of the left thigh.*

Dr. Fayrer was at once summoned to the General's assistance by Mr. George Lawrence, the only one in the room who had escaped unhurt. He found that Sir Henry had been removed to a small apartment, not so much exposed, adjoining the drawing-room, and there he lay on a couch near the window, surrounded by his friends. Though he seemed to be under the impression that even then he was in the agonies of death, he was talking quite calmly to the people about him. When Fayrer had examined the wound, Lawrence asked how long he had to live, and when the surgeon replied that his patient might survive for about two days, the sufferer expressed surprise and doubt, for he thought that his end was nearer at hand.† The most that human skill could do for him was to mitigate the pain of his dying hours. The amputation of the mutilated limb would have been fruitless—a doubtful operation on a

* It is a striking instance of the manner in which what is called "the doctrine of chances" may be falsified by actual events, that a shell had burst, on the preceding day, in the same room, between Lawrence and Couper, leaving both unhurt. When the former was exhorted to shift his quarters he answered that it was not likely that another shell would burst in the same room.

† Some accounts say *three*—but Dr. Fayrer assures me that he said "Forty-eight hours."

younger and stronger man, a cruel experiment on one so feeble and worn as the good General. The little life that was left in him might still be serviceable to his countrymen, and it was right to protract it to the utmost. He had work still to do, and he did it with all the firmness and collectedness of health. Death did not steal upon him like a thief in the night. He had already bethought himself of what was to be done in the event of the mortal blow descending upon him, and there was, therefore, no hurry or confusion at the last. He had obtained the sanction of Government to the appointment of Major Banks as his successor in the office of Chief Commissioner; and he now formally made over the charge to him. On Colonel Inglis he conferred the chief military command, associating with him Major Anderson in a kind of council. This done, he prepared himself to give his last instructions to his successors. But the position of the house in which he lay was so exposed to the fire of the enemy, that it was thought best to remove him to another; so he was carried, with all tenderness and care, to Dr. Fayrer's residence, which was less within the reach of the rebel guns, though open to their musketry. There his last hours were passed. There he prepared himself for the great change that was coming upon him.

1857. July 2—4.

And in those last hours, all that was admirable in the soldier, the statesman, and the Christian gentleman, was evinced with a grandeur and beauty of utterance that impressed the understandings and touched the hearts of all who were admitted to his presence, and made even those who had sometimes differed from him in life feel that a great and good man was passing away from the scene. The old

1857. July 2—4. watchword of Derry rung in his dying ears; and his last counsel was, "No surrender!" "Let every man," he said, "die at his post; but never make terms. God help the poor women and children!" The various detailed orders which he issued, some of a public, some of a personal character, were taken down by Major Banks. They showed alike the sagacity and the tenderness of the dying man. He thought much of those about him, now beleaguered in the Lucknow Residency—much also of those at a distance, his children, his kindred, his friends, and those "little ones," for whom he had done so much—the boys and girls of the Lawrence Asylum. When all his dying wishes had been noted down, he bade farewell to his comrades, asking forgiveness if he had offended any one by asperity of speech, and dwelling on the vanity of human greatness and the all-sufficingness of the Saviour's love. There was no one in that garrison so stern or cold as not to be melted to tears in his presence.

Except when, on one or two occasions, chloroform was administered to deaden the sense of pain, he remained in full possession of his faculties nearly to the last. He expressed great interest in the progress of the siege, and earnestly inquired, from time to time, into the events which were passing around him. Neither the booming of the guns, nor the rattle of musketry, seemed greatly to disturb him. The outer sense was deadened by the stronger inward sentiments of love of God and love of Man—strongest of all in his last hours. The sting of death was not in any thought of himself. He believed that he had done his duty; he knew that he had tried to do it. And he desired that on his tomb should be engraven the words, "Here lies Henry Lawrence, who tried to do his duty." He added that he wished to be buried privately, "without any fuss." And so when, on the morning of the 4th of July, after bidding farewell to his comrades, he passed away to his rest, they covered up the body until the shades of night had fallen upon the scene; and then some European soldiers were sent to remove the remains of their late chief to a grave which had been prepared for him in a trench within the Residency grounds. They lifted up the coverlet and kissed him reverentially on the forehead; and then he was laid in the same grave with some men of his old regiment, who had been killed in the course of the day. 1857. July 4.

Character of Sir Henry Lawrence.

The character of Sir Henry Lawrence has been imperfectly sketched at the very commencement of this History. I do not think that I could write anything that can add to a reputation, than which there is none purer or brighter in all the annals of our great Indian Empire. Men of all classes and all characters mourned his death as a personal affliction. And this sympathy, so strong, so general, was but the echo or response to the catholic utterances of his own sympathising nature. All men loved him because he loved all men. It was this sympathy that so especially suited him for the work of Indian Government. Without sympathy we may rule with power; but we cannot govern with wisdom. It has been observed elsewhere that he was wont to say and to write that "it is the due admixture of Romance and Reality that best carries a man through life;" and that what he said and wrote he did—or rather he was. It was the Romance of his nature that placed him in the front rank of our Indian heroes, and to some extent, indeed, has given him a place to himself in the great story of our national heroism. For

1857. July 4. it is a special circumstance of Sir Henry Lawrence's career, that, though it has produced this great impression on the minds of men, it was not wholly a successful one. It was overclouded by failures and embittered by disappointments. And it was not, on the other hand, marked by any salient achievements of peculiar lustre. It had no Trafalgar, no Waterloo; no great peaceful triumph wrought out to the happy end. The student, of a future generation, when asked what Sir Henry Lawrence did, may not always be ready with an answer; but all will tell promptly what he was. And many, perhaps, will say that they do not quite know why of all men, of whom they had ever read in Indian history, he seemed to be the flower; but that they cannot help feeling it. It is a sentiment rather than a conviction, and no one cares to analyse or to explain it.

But that the Romantic did not overlay the Real, in the character of Sir Henry Lawrence, is shown by the estimation in which he was held for good practical work by the Governments under which he served. "We have suffered a sad loss," wrote Lord Canning to the President of the Board of Control. "Poor Henry Lawrence died on the 4th, of a wound received on the 2nd, and I do not know the person who can fill his place. Of all men in India, he is the one whose loss is least reparable at this moment. He would have been invaluable in the pacification of the troubled districts hereafter, both as a soldier and a civilian." And the Home Government paid to him, as a living statesman, the highest tribute that could be paid to one of their Indian servants. On the 22nd of July, a Court of Directors of the East India Company, not then knowing the calamity which had overtaken the nation, passed a Resolution appointing Sir Henry Lawrence to be Provisional Governor-

General "on the death, resignation, or coming away 1857. July.
of Viscount Canning." I never saw so great unanimity in that assembly. No one then present doubted for a moment that Henry Lawrence was the man, pre-eminently qualified above all others, to succeed the ruler who was then bearing up so bravely against the manifold trials by which he was surrounded. And all sorrowed bitterly when they learnt that the commission which had been sent to him, under the most willing sanction of the Crown, had been addressed to one who, ere the letter reached Lucknow, had been many weeks lying in the grave. The sadness was shared by the whole nation. But though the great reward never reached him, not on that account is the example one less to be cherished. It is not less sweetly encouraging, because it "blossomed in the dust."

The Siege and the Defence.

Days passed, and the fury of the siege continued. At every possible point on which guns could be posted, so as to bear upon our position, batteries were erected, and an incessant shower of shot and shell was poured upon the British Residency and its outworks; whilst on all elevated places, as on the summits of mosques and mansions, skilled marksmen were planted, sharp-eyed and steady-handed, watching for the appearance of a white face beyond the cover of our defences.* Those defences had been

* "Our heaviest losses have been caused by the fire from the enemy's sharpshooters stationed in the adjoining mosques and houses of the Native nobility, the necessity of destroying which had been repeatedly drawn to the attention of Sir Henry Lawrence by the Staff of Engineers. But his invariable reply was, 'Spare the holy places and private property too as much as possible;' and we have consequently suffered severely from our very tenderness to the religious prejudices and respect to the rights of our rebellious citizens and soldiery." — *Report of Brigadier Inglis.*

1857. July. greatly strengthened after the rough and ready fashion to which hard necessity had driven us. There was nothing, of whatsoever value, so long as substance and solidity and power of resistance were in it, that was not turned to account by our people for purposes of temporary fortification. Tables and sideboards, wardrobes and chiffonieres, were gathered together and piled up as barricades. And some, when they brought forth the treasures of poor Fletcher Hayes's library,* to receive the assaults of the adversary's ammunition, must have thought, with some bitter-sweet reminiscences of their reading of the "Scotch novels" at home, of the defence of Colonel Mannering's house with the Dominie's cherished folios. Even the records of the Government were dragged from their hiding-places to afford shelter to our garrison, and many ponderous volumes, perhaps of no other value, were put to unexpected uses as muniments of war, making for the besieged paper-walls of serviceable thickness and strength.

Into the work of defence our people—officers and men alike—flung themselves with an amount of vigorous self-devotion seldom paralleled in the military history of the world. There was no duty to which officers, of whatever rank, did not apply themselves

* Captain Fletcher Hayes, of whom mention has been made in earlier parts of this history, had a passion for perilous enterprises. He was always eager to volunteer for some detached service. It has been seen that he was at Cawnpore up to the 26th of May (vol. ii., p. 296). He went thence intending to render assistance to Colonel Smith at Futtehgurh—but was dissuaded from fulfilling this purpose. He went to Mynpooree to take counsel with Mr. Power, whose position at that time (May 30) has been already described—leaving his men (Irregular Cavalry) at Bhowgaon under the command of Lieutenant Barbor. At Mynpooree he learnt that his men were disaffected—but he did not take much heed of the report, and waited till the morning of the 31st to join his troopers at Bhowgaon, accompanied by Captain Carey of the Seventeenth. On the way the troopers fell upon them. Hayes was cut down and massacred. Carey escaped to tell the tale.

with cheerful alacrity; there was no labour, however arduous or revolting, from which they shrunk in the hour of need; there was no danger from without or within to which they were not exposed. Day and night they toiled incessantly, seeing sorrowfully their little garrison diminishing, losing well-nigh every day one or more of their best men, but never faltering, never desponding. The fury of the enemy was but one of the many evils which they had to face. Cholera, Fever, Diarrhœa, Small-pox, the plague of boils and flies, the putrid stench from the rotting carcasses of horses and bullocks, the perpetual heat and the remorseless rain, affected our people more grievously than the fire of the insurgents. All men were soldiers at that time. The civil officers took post and sometimes command in our batteries, and the whole-hearted resolution andun failing fertility of resource which they displayed placed them in the front rank of the warriors of the crisis. Mr. Ommaney, the Judicial Commissioner, whilst visiting the Redan battery, was killed by a round-shot glancing from a tree, which fractured his skull, at the very commencement of the siege. This was a heavy loss, but a still heavier one was in store for the garrison. Little more than two weeks after he had taken into his hands the chief conduct of affairs, Major Banks went out to visit Gubbins's battery. He had ever been active among the active—fearless among the fearless—visiting first one post and then another, in continual personal communication with his chief officers, seeing into all the details of the defence and encouraging the defenders. Thus he had proved himself worthy of the trust reposed in him by his sainted predecessor. But it happened disastrously that, on the 21st of July, he visited Gubbins's battery, where

1857. July.

1857. July. the lion-hearted civilian was working with his wonted energy. It was a great day with the enemy. They were furiously attacking our principal posts, and calling forth all our activities of defence. The works which the Chief Commissioner now visited were greatly exposed. The parapet was only breast-high, and it was necessary, for life's sake, to stoop when the enemy were firing into our battery. Banks had been often cautioned—but he was regardless of all warnings, and on this luckless day he seems to have been more than commonly mindless of his safety. He was a man of no great stature, but walking erect he was a fair mark to the enemy, and ere he had exchanged a word with Gubbins a bullet entered his brain. He fell heavily to the ground and never stirred again. When they tried to move him they found that he was stone-dead. The body was buried that night, sewn up in a white sheet. Death was too busy in the garrison to allow any more coffin-making.*

Others of these soldier-civilians, or civilian-soldiers, though ever under fire, escaped with their lives from the furious raging of the enemy. Mr. Martin Gubbins, the Financial Commissioner, more fortunate than his compeers, lived and served to make for himself a great reputation as a brave soldier and an able leader. The natural pugnacity of his character had now legitimate scope for exercise; and men who had resented his litigiousness on paper could not but respect his audacity under arms. Thornhill and Capper, of the same service, were wounded at their work; and George Couper, the

* We may fairly surmise that the shots which carried off the three chief people of the garrison in a space of less than three weeks were not purely accidental. The enemy, doubtless, had some active spies and tracked the movements of the British leaders.

Secretary, who had begun life as a soldier, was ready for any military duty that might be intrusted to him. And when no inspiriting soldierly work was required from him, he was content to perform the nauseous duties of the scavenger. It was no small thing—no small service to the garrison to look well to its sanitary condition. Many evil influences were against us. It was the hottest season of the year. Death came among our cattle—horses and bullocks—and their rotting carcasses were to be quickly buried. On one occasion, a stack of "bhoosa" had fallen and killed several bullocks, who lay beside it. The disaster of the loss of meat was overborne by the fear of the evil effects of the putrid carrion. So Couper went forth, with one or two staunch comrades, to dig graves and bury the dead. It was the hardest and foulest work that they ever had to do; and as they had neglected to take out with them either the stimulants which are so necessary to insure resistance to poisonous effluvia, or the milder drinks which repair the waste of exhaustion, they suffered fearfully from the unsavoury labour. These were days when men were ready for any kind of work, regardless of self, so that they could help the garrison. And so they toiled on side by side, those robust members of the two great Services; whilst others, whose names were not borne on the rolls of the Company, strove and suffered no less bravely than their enrolled countrymen, and many, who had come to Lucknow only to trade, died with arms in their hands. 1857. July.

But not to the masculine defenders of Lucknow was the heroism of the garrison confined. Numbers of English gentlewomen had followed the fortunes of their husbands to the Oude capital. The Residency The gentlewomen of the Garrison.

1857. July—Aug.

was full of women and children. There was scarcely any kind of suffering—scarcely any kind of privation which they did not uncomplainingly endure. They saw the dead or wounded bodies of their nearest and dearest brought in from the outworks; they felt their children die in their arms. There was no place in which they were secure against the unrelenting fire of the enemy. Disease in its worst forms came upon them, and they bore up bravely against what, in the happiest homes, and with the most bountiful appliances, would have been anguish and bitterness, trying to the utmost the frailty of the flesh. Large numbers of their domestic servants had deserted at the commencement of the siege, and many, accustomed to all the delicacies and luxuries of a life in which every want was supplied, every wish anticipated, had now to perform for themselves menial offices, from which they would before have shrunk with dismay. But week after week, as the siege went on, these English gentlewomen suffered without a murmur. In their patience they were strong. But more than this, they were active in their ministrations. How they comforted and consoled one another—how they tended the sick and wounded—how they soothed the last hours of the dying, and carried help to those who needed it, though needing it themselves, has been gratefully recorded by men who survived the fiery trials of the siege to carry with them to their graves the memory of these gentle ministerings.

Privations of the Garrison.

To one who thinks of the miserable straits to which the Cawnpore garrison were reduced by the total failure of their supplies, of the carrion on which they feasted, of the scanty water, to procure a cup of which might be death, a truthful record of the privations endured by our people at Lucknow must, in comparison, appear faint and feeble. But to Englishmen and Englishwomen accustomed to live delicately and to fare sumptuously every day, the scarcity of wonted food, suited to the condition of those so reared, so spoilt by favouring circumstances, was distressing in the extreme. It was not that hunger gnawed them.* They were not starving. Strong appetites were not to be expected at such a time. But much of the food served out to them was coarse and unwholesome. There was a great want of good bread, for early in the siege the bakers had deserted in a body, and now indigestible chupatties took the place of the accustomed loaf. The gun bullocks for some time supplied meat to the garrison. Indeed, they were often shot by the enemy faster than the garrison could eat them, and it was sore tribulation to our people to dispose of the rotting carcasses. In some houses were good private stores of wine and beer and dainties, such as hermetically-sealed salmon and other European provisions; but, let the generosity of the owner be what it might, what were these among so many? Tea and sugar, of all things most prized by our women, soon became scarce; and ere long there was a failure of rum and tobacco, very distressing to the European fighting man. The loss of the ordinary "smoke" was severely felt. The habit was so strong that rather than smoke nothing many of our soldiers sucked pieces of ignited cane or wood, as schoolboys do, and found some solace in the tasteless substitute. Ever and anon, when some well-

1857. July—Aug.

* This refers to the earlier days of the siege. Speaking of a later period, one of my most trustworthy informants says: "They were next door to it (hunger). *There never was any bread.* And there were no servants to make chupatties of the coarse *bhoosa* (bran), which had therefore to be eaten almost uncooked. It was nearly as indigestible as the grass of the field, although undoubtedly there was enough of it."

1857. July—Aug. furnished officer was struck down, there was a sale of his possessions by public auction, and a sharp competition for every article of food and clothing, at prices well described as "fabulous." At first, comparatively little anxiety on the score of provisions vexed the minds of the besieged; for it was believed that Havelock and Neill would soon bring the looked-for relief. But, as weeks passed, and no succours came, the thoughts of the garrison turned gloomily to a future, in which the supplies would be doled out in smaller and smaller portions, until starvation should stare them in the face.

But amidst these frequent disappointments there was no abatement of heart and hope. The men worked on and the women bore on, sustained by the certainty of a coming deliverance. This certainty seemed to sharpen the imaginations of the garrison, for many thought that they heard firing in the distance, and reported that the succours were coming when they were far-off. How it happened that the relieving force never came no one knew. A letter had been received from Colonel Tytler saying that they might be expected about the 8th of August; but days passed and weeks passed, and still the enemy taunted our people with their helplessness, declaring that they had driven back the relieving force, and would soon expel the garrison from their coverts. Many letters had been sent from Lucknow to which no reply had been received. But there was one man named "Ungud"—a noted scout—who succeeded where others failed. On the 15th of August he brought in a letter dated on the 4th, and partly written in Greek characters, saying: "We march to-morrow morning for Lucknow, having been reinforced. We hope to reach you in four days at furthest. You must aid us in every way, even to cutting your way out, if we can't force our way in. We are but a small force."* But with this letter the scout brought oral information to the effect that the whole of General Havelock's force had fallen back upon Cawnpore. There was great discouragement in this; and the recommendation that the garrison should cut their way out sounded then something like a mockery. The letter was addressed to Martin Gubbins, who took counsel with Colonel Inglis, and the result was that a letter was sent back in reply, stating that, hampered as they were with sick and wounded, with women and children, it was impossible that they should leave their defences. So still they waited and waited, doing their best to bear up against the disappointment, and, duly regarding the uncertainties of the future, husbanding their resources more and more every week. Half rations had become a fact—quarter rations were a prospective certainty, the advent of which could not be very remote.

1857. July.

All through the month of July, the fury of the enemy continued to increase. It was plain to those within our lines of defence that our assailants were not merely the men of the mutinous Sepoy regiments. The great Talookhdars had sent in their contingents, who were aiding the regular soldiery in their unremitting assaults. Now and again new batteries were planted in commanding positions, and our crumbling walls and battered roofs bore terrible witness to the destroying effects of their fire. This added grievously to the sufferings of the weaker portion of our people; for many of the upper rooms were

* As with many of the letters of that period it was written on very thin paper, in minute characters, and rolled up in a quill.

357.
uly.

rendered uninhabitable, and the women and children were forced to crowd together in the lower ones in a manner distressing especially to those whom sickness had rendered helpless and incapable. To the booming of the guns, and the crash of the fallen masonry, they had, by this time, become habituated, and even to the danger, to which they were exposed by the constant intrusions of shot and shell, they were becoming more and more insensible every day.* It is related, indeed, that many of the ladies of the garrison began to take quite a scientific interest in the artillery practice of the enemy, and came to be better judges of the weight of the projectiles which entered our buildings than the officers of the garrison themselves. But brave as they were in the face of all such perils, and patient under pressing privations, it was ard to keep a cheerful countenance under the domestic afflictions with which it pleased God to visit them. As July and August advanced, the children died off rapidly.† Others were born into the garrison—and not the least of the trials of our poor countrywomen were those which came upon them when the inevitable pangs of maternal labour were aggravated by exposure to the dire assaults of a relentless enemy.‡

But soon a greater danger than any that had gone

* "Balls fall at our feet, and we continue the conversation without a remark; bullets graze our very hair and we never speak of them. Narrow escapes are so very common that even women and children cease to notice them."—*Rees's Personal Narrative.*

† *Aug.* 9. "The heat excessive; and children sank rapidly under the effects of want of good air, food, and exercise. Several deaths occurred among them both yesterday and to-day."—*Diary of a Staff-Officer.*—*Aug.* 14. "Many cases of fever and several deaths among the children."—*Ibid.*

‡ *Aug.* 10. "Mrs. Ouseley had a little boy this morning, and Mrs. Barwell yesterday."—*Mrs. Case's Journal* ("Day by Day at Lucknow.") Mrs. Dorin was killed by the fire of the enemy.

before threatened the Lucknow garrison. On the 20th of July, a mine had been sprung by the enemy, near the Redan Battery; but it had done us no injury, and had perhaps been chiefly intended to create confusion and assist the enemy's advance.* Now, it was plain that the insurgents were strenuously endeavouring to undermine our chief positions, in the hope of terminating the siege by some grand explosions. If anything could have stimulated our Engineer officers to increased efforts for the general good, the effect would have been wrought by this stirring intelligence. But in truth no men could have toiled more zealously and assiduously than these had done from the first. Major Anderson was our Chief Engineer. A good officer, highly respected by the garrison, he had recently succumbed to the pressure of sickness, and those who watched him narrowly saw little hope that he would outlive the siege.† Happily, the officer who stood next to him was one of equal energy and capacity. Among the many brave men, whose wisely-directed labours tended so greatly to the security of our position and the salvation of our people, there was not one whose good deeds were more gratefully acknowledged by the garrison than those of Captain Fulton of the Engineers. He had been, from the first, indefatigable in

1857. July.

Mining operations.

Fulton of the Engineers.

* It was intended to destroy the Redan, but failed. The musketry fire was kept up so thickly and persistently that the carrion-birds, attracted by the carcasses of horses and bullocks, fell dead from the surrounding trees.—*Statement of an Eye-Witness* (*MS.*). The Redan Battery was commanded by Captain Lawrence of the Thirty-second Foot, commonly styled in the garrison "Sam Lawrence." Of this hero George Couper writes, "Strange to say, 'Sam,' although commanding one of the most dangerous posts, a volunteer, too, on every sortie, and one of the biggest men in the garrison, escaped throughout without a scratch."—*Notes to Mecham's Sketches.*

† He died on the afternoon of the 11th of August.

1857 August. his endeavours to repair our damaged works, and otherwise to strengthen our defences; and now he had to give his first thoughts to the all-important work of counteracting the designs of the enemy to blow the English into the air. As quietly and guardedly as possible he had set about the preparation of his countermines; but the enemy knew well what he was doing, and did all that lay in their power to obstruct the efforts of our workmen.*

On the 10th of August the enemy sprung a second and a third mine. They made a prodigious noise and alarmed many of the women; but did very little harm so far as human life was affected by the explosion.† Two soldiers were blown into the road beyond our defences, but neither of them was injured. Subsequent experience, indeed, proved that it was a small matter to be blown into the air. But the first explosion did great damage to our masonry and timbers in the part of our defences opposite to Johannes's house.‡ When the smoke cleared away, the enemy pushed forward and occupied the buildings round the Cawnpore Battery; but so warm was the reception they received from our people that they

* *Aug.* 13. "Our mine near Sago's house was pushed on all night with the greatest possible speed. Every possible means was adopted by the enemy to prevent our miners working, and as only a wall and a few feet of ground divided the two parties, they resorted to squibs, rockets, brickbats, and lights at the end of bamboos to annoy our workmen."—*Diary of a Staff-Officer*.

† "About twelve o'clock, as I was sitting at the table writing, Carry washing our things and Mrs. Inglis working, we were suddenly alarmed by what appeared to us a great shaking of the earth, followed by a dreadful noise, such as I never wish to hear again. It was indescribable, and sounded as if the whole earth was coming against us; it was a mine exploding without doing harm."—*Mrs. Case's Journal.*

‡ "It blew in a great part of the house occupied by Mr. Schilling and the Martinière boys, and entirely destroyed our palisades and defences for the space of sixty feet. One of the heaviest timbers was pitched right on the top of the Brigade mess-house, among the officers and men of the Thirty-second, who occupied the post."—*Diary of a Staff-Officer*.

were unable to pass the line of our defences, and after a time fell back in despair. Nor were they more successful at the other point of attack near "Sago's House," where they were driven back with heavy loss and compelled to fire from discreet distances. All day long our garrison were under arms, suffering cruelly from the effects of the exhausting heat, but compelled to be ever on the alert, for the fury of the enemy never ceased even when night fell upon the scene. At nine o'clock, the insurgents, bracing themselves up for a crowning effort, attacked us at several points—at Innes's house, Anderson's and Gubbins's post—and so assured were they of the success of their assaults, that they brought up scaling-ladders with them; but they were compelled to beat a retreat, leaving some of their ladders behind them. In the course of the day's operations, the howitzer, which Bonham had worked so well at Chinhut, and which was supposed to have slain Henry Lawrence, was brought to bear upon our positions, especially upon Innes's outpost. But the result of the day's fighting was that we lost three Europeans and two Sepoys killed, and five or six men wounded. The loss of the enemy must have been considerable, for a heavy fire of shot and shell supplemented the practice of our Infantry and carried slaughter into the Sepoy ranks. That they were greatly disheartened by the failure was believed. On our garrison, on the other hand, the issue had an invigorating effect. It taught them to despise the enemy even more than they had done before; and it renewed their hopes of a successful resistance until the looked-for succours should arrive.

1857. August.

It was soon apparent, however, that the insurgents were resuming their mining operations in the neigh- Countermining.

1857. August. bourhood of Sago's house, so Fulton pushed forward a countermine with the utmost possible despatch, and on the 13th it was reported to be ready. The explosion was successful. The masonry building from which the enemy had started their mine was speedily a heap of ruins, and the groans of those who were buried beneath it declared the work it had done. Foiled at this point, the enemy commenced operations against another—and this time they were more successful. In the early morning of the 18th, they sprung a mine which shattered the outer defences of one of the squares in which the Sikh detachments were posted. A building in one corner of the square, on which we had a look-out post, was blown into the air;* and when the smoke cleared away, it was seen that a breach some ten or twelve yards long had been made in our defences. It was a moment of painful suspense and anxiety. A rebel leader mounted the breach, brandished his sword aloft, and called upon the crowd of insurgents to follow him into the works of the Feringhee. A bullet from the rifle of one of our officers on the roof of the Brigade Mess, where some of our best marksmen were posted, sent this man to his doom. Another rose to take his place, when instantly the same fate overtook him, and he fell beside his countryman in the breach. Then a great panic took possession of those behind their fallen champions, and not another man would advance.

* "By the explosion Lieutenant Mecham and Captain Adolphe Orr and one drummer were thrown into the air, but descended inside the square amidst the *débris* of the building, and escaped with little injury. The fourth, Band-Sergeant Curtain, of the Forty-first Native Infantry, was unhappily thrown outside the works, upon the road, where he was destroyed by the enemy."—*Gubbins.* Eight Christian drummers and a Sepoy were buried under the ruins, and one hurled outside and decapitated by the enemy.—*Couper's Notes.* An account written on the subsequent day and quoted in Wilson's Journal, says "six Christian drummers and a Sepoy.

There was no service, throughout these weary days of the siege, which called more nobly into action all the best qualities of our people, soldiers and civilians, or knit them more closely in the bonds of comradeship, than this work of counteracting the efforts of the enemy to destroy us by their mining operations. It is not easy to convey to the unprofessional reader a right conception of the toil and trouble of these subterraneous workings and explorations. Those who took part in these mole-like burrowings acquired wonderful powers of auscultation. They were continually on the alert to hear the clicking of the enemy's pick-axes, and would sometimes, in the midst of a conversation, suddenly throw themselves down, with one ear on the earth, to catch the suggestive sounds. Then there was the ingress into the shaft of the countermine, sometimes accomplished on all-fours like a beast, and sometimes horizontally on one's stomach, like a reptile; both at great expense of skin and flesh, by unavoidable excoriations. Men, after a time, became accustomed to the trials of the countermine, but a neophyte was sorely perplexed. It must have been a grand sight, if sight were possible, to see the officer in command of the burrowing party, or other "solitary sentinel," sitting, revolver in hand, at the end of the countermine, listening "to the enemy's miner coming closer and closer until his pick-axe actually pierced the gallery and exposed the disconcerted workman to the view." Then there was a crack of the pistol and an end to that man's work.* 1857 Augus Work in mines.

As the month wore on, the labours of the garrison became heavier and heavier. Their numbers had

* See Sir George Couper's admirable descriptive letter-press to Captain Mecham's "Illustrations of the Defence of Lucknow," from which this is mainly taken.

1857. August. greatly diminished, and their work had increased, for the heavy cannonading of the enemy kept up a continual process of destruction, and the necessary business of repairs, both to our residential building and our outworks, became more onerous every day. And ever as the toil increased, the strength of the toilers diminished. For the daywork and the night-work, the want of food and the want of rest, had well-nigh exhausted their powers. Many, indeed, becoming wholly incapable of sustaining this continual pressure upon their bodily and mental energies,* had been compelled to take refuge in the Hospital. A new enemy about this time assailed them. Scurvy, induced by the absence of wholesome food, by hard work and continued exposure, struck heavily our people. Some were invalided; some, who tried to bear up, found their sufferings sadly aggravated, and soon succumbed to death. So great was the debility which accompanied the ravages of this disorder, that it rarely happened that an amputation performed on a scurvy-stricken patient had any other than a fatal termination.

State of the Hospital. And it was a grievous aggravation of the sufferings of the sick and wounded that the Hospital was in a most exposed position. It lay between the Residency and the Baillie Guard, and shot and shell came crashing in at all times, and often with deadly messages to our poor people who lay helpless on

* "We had work nightly for at least three hundred men; as we had the defences to repair daily, supplies to remove from godowns which were fallen in from the effects of the enemy's shot, mines to countermine, guns to remove, barricades to erect, corpses to bury, and rations to serve out; but with our weak, harassed, and daily diminishing garrison, we could seldom produce as working parties more than three fatigue parties of eight or ten men each relief; and the Europeans were capable of little exertion, as from want of sleep, hard work night and day, and constant exposure, their bodily strength was greatly diminished."—*Narrative of an Eye-Witness.*

their beds.* The upper story of the building had been rendered untenable at an early period of the siege. Hence the necessity of crowding and cramming in the basement, which whilst it increased the misery of the inmates, added but little to their security. But they were very patient under all these severe trials. "It was an affecting scene," wrote one who was familiar with every phase of daring and suffering during those "brave days," "to walk through the Hospital. The poor soldiers, and other wounded combatants, destitute as they were of everything that renders pain and disease endurable, were so patient and cheerful under their agony and afflictions, which the pitying beholder could only sympathise with without the power to alleviate. No murmurs, no grumblings were ever heard. If there was any complaint, it was that the sufferers had been incapacitated from taking further part in the desperate and holy struggle. If there was any expression of regret, it was that his fall had entailed additional duty on his dying comrades."† 1857. August.

The mining operations made new demands upon the few sound men with which it was difficult to comply; and the increasing activity of the enemy, whose numbers enabled them to employ a succession of fresh men on every kind of work, kept our people always on the alert. And so, as days passed, and still no tidings of the approach of Havelock's force came to them, they asked each other how long this strain on the resources of the enfeebled garrison could endure—how long thus reduced in number, thus exhausted by work and weakened by privation

* "The sufferers were constantly shot on their beds. In fact there was no spot, either in the sanctuary or throughout the entire defences, where a dying soldier or an ailing woman or child, could feel an instant's security."—*Couper's Notes.*

† Sir George Couper.

1857. August. —they could hold out against an enemy that seemed only to become every day more numerous, more active, and more skilful, whilst not only our physical force, but the genius also which directed it, was rapidly fading away.

For ever as week followed week there was the same grievous catalogue of death and disaster in high places. The casualties in our upper ranks were of many kinds, but always with the same monotonous succession of nocturnal burials. Now, one of our best officers was shot by the enemy—now, by our own people in the confusion of the fight—now, by his own hand in a temporary paroxysm of insanity brought on by long-continued suffering. Thus Bruére of the Thirteenth fell with a rifle-ball through his chest, in the act of picking out a noted marksman of the enemy; thus Birch of the Fifty-ninth, "attached to the Engineer Department," received his death-wound whilst reconnoitring in the darkness, from one of our own European sentries; thus Graham of the Fourth Cavalry blew out his brains with a revolver, not knowing what he did. Others, bearing up bravely as long as Nature could sustain them, sunk at last beneath their wounds or exhausting disease. Among these was Captain Simonds of the Artillery, who, though badly wounded, worked his guns as long as he could, and then laid himself down to die. It is recorded that, during a space of nearly three months, there was only one day in which a funeral party, rudely improvised, did not lay the body of one or more members of our garrison in the grave under cover of the darkness of the night.

Bonham of the Artillery.

Conspicuous among the heroes of the defence was Lieutenant Bonham of the Bengal Artillery. He had been posted with his battery of Oude Irregular

Artillery at Secrora, in the Bareitch Division, when the troops there broke into mutiny, and he had been the last man to leave the station. It was only when he had done all in his power to bring the Native soldiery back to their allegiance, and had been assured by a faithful Soubahdar that not a man would act against his comrades, that Bonham consented to mount a horse that had been brought to him, and accompanied by three European sergeants, to ride for Lucknow. His arrival there was a very serviceable accession of strength, for Artillery officers were much wanted, and Bonham's energies were of the best kind. How he worked the great howitzer at Chinhut has already been told. He was wounded in that action, but wounds did not seem greatly to disturb the robust artilleryman. He was soon at his work again, one of the main pillars of the defence. Fertile of resource, ever active, and regardless of danger, he won the admiring approbation of the whole British garrison. The extraordinary accuracy with which he laid his mortars was a source of continual applause. There was a total absence of howitzers, which was severely felt; but Bonham's ingenuity enabled him to make one, by a clever process of conversion, out of a mortar, and to work it with admirable effect. Reckless of exposure, so long as he could do any good work, he was wounded a second time in the earlier part of the siege; and again a third time, on the 30th of August, when he was struck by a musket-ball, and so severely injured that for awhile his services were lost to the garrison.

1857. August.

Death of Fulton.

Bonham lived—to be neglected. But less or more fortunate, another Addiscombe hero, another member of those great Indian scientific corps, whose doings in peace and in war have shed such lustre upon our

1857. September. reputation in India, men who have led great armies to victory and have constructed vast material works which have given plenty and prosperity to countries often before abandoned to famine and desolation. Fulton died at his work, with the harness on his back. He was the Chief Engineer of the garrison after the death of Anderson, and how, regardless of self, he toiled day and night, has already been told. He was generally to be found working in the mines, often coming into subterranean collision with the enemy, and by well-directed blows from his own hand diminishing the number of the miners; but this did not prevent him from visiting other points of our defences, and bringing his directing mind to bear wheresoever it was wanted. As brave as he was skilful, he was a tower of strength to the garrison; but men asked one another how long this could last in the face of such audacity of exposure. On the 6th of September he had escaped from an explosion,
Sept. 14. with nothing worse than a contusion; but little more than a week afterwards, whilst reconnoitring in Gubbins's battery (for his presence was ubiquitous), the last deadly message came to him. A round shot struck him on the head.* And, perhaps, there was not a man in the garrison whose loss could have been more severely felt or more deeply deplored.

But relief—if not deliverance—was now closely at hand. Havelock's force, having overcome the prodigious difficulties in its way, was now rapidly

* The Staff-Officer, in his Diary, says: "He was a highly-gifted, cool, brave, and chivalrous officer, fertile in resources, and a favourite with both officers and men. His loss was acutely felt." The writer adds, in one of many manuscript notes written for me, which have greatly increased the value of the printed book, "*No one* did more towards our success. He was as brave as he was indefatigable in his endeavours to foil the enemy. He had many personal encounters with our foes underground."

advancing. Outram had joined the Army, whose ranks were swollen by reinforcements from below—and the long looked-for advent was now emerging from the obscure distance. On the 22nd of September, Ungud, the noted scout, brought a letter conveying the glad tidings that the relieving force had crossed the Ganges. The news was at once communicated to the garrison, whose hearts were lightened by the cheering intelligence and who rejoiced outwardly with a great rejoicing. Ungud was the hero of the hour. He was greatly excited by his success; for he had been fired upon as he entered our works and narrowly escaped destruction. He thought, however, that he had had enough of this dangerous service; and he said to Brigadier Inglis, "Now I have got back three times, I will go no more—but live or die with you."* 1857. September.

And in truth the exigencies of the situation demanded that the help in trouble should be speedily present. The rain was falling heavily and rendered more untenable the buildings, already shaken and shattered, to which we looked for some semblance of shelter. Provisions and necessities of all kinds were becoming wofully scarce. Our European soldiery were reduced to a dram a day. At an auction, held at the Residency, of the property of deceased officers, a bottle of brandy was sold for twenty rupees, and a flannel shirt for forty. A few more weeks would have brought us to the direst extremity. The enemy, who seemed to have received intelligence of the advance of our reinforcements, did not slacken in their hostile activity. On the 25th, a sad calamity occurred in our garrison. One of the very best of our officers—one who had been ever foremost in

* MS. Note by the "Staff-Officer."

1857. September.

attack and defence, whose cheerfulness, under all depressing circumstances, had set a gallant example—Captain Radcliffe of the Seventh Cavalry—was mortally wounded, whilst in command of the Cawnpore Battery. Thus another of the younger heroes of Lucknow was swept away from the muster-roll of her defenders.

Arrival of Havelock's Force.

The anxiety of the garrison now became intense. There were many manifest signs, beyond the lines of our defences, that our reinforcements were approaching. There was great commotion among the townspeople. They were seen, huddling about, with bundles in their hands, as if making themselves ready for flight. Our own people, regardless of exposure, flocked to all the best commands of observation, using their glasses or straining their eyes to see all that could be seen in the distance. The enemy, believing that we should make a sortie to meet Havelock's advancing force, kept up an incessant fire upon all our points of egress. It was seen, too—most welcome of signs—that they were firing in a different direction. Soon the glorious sight of our own people, fighting their way through the streets of Lucknow, sent such a thrill of joy through the garrison, as perhaps never had been felt before. "Once fairly seen," wrote one who was present and who still lives to remember it,* "all our doubts and fears regarding them were ended; and then the garrison's long pent-up feelings of anxiety and suspense burst forth in a succession of deafening cheers; from every pit, trench, and battery—from behind the sand-bags piled on shattered houses—from every post still held by a few gallant spirits, rose cheer upon cheer—even from the hospital many of the wounded crawled

* The "Staff-Officer"—now Brigadier-General Wilson.

forth to join in that glad shout of welcome to those who had so bravely come to our assistance. It was a moment never to be forgotten." And then in they came, those glorious Highlanders and Fusiliers—those gallant "blue-caps," alas! without their leader; and then there were all the greetings and hand-grippings of measureless welcome and delight. The women crept forth from their holes and hiding-places and rushed wildly about, grasping and sometimes kissing the hands of the sturdy warriors who had come to their relief, and praying God to bless their deliverers. There were eager inquiries made of what had happened elsewhere, during those long newsless eighty-seven days within the defences of Lucknow when all the rest of the world was a sealed book to the garrison; and the first joy of the happy union was marred by the sad tidings brought to them from without. There were some who wished that they had never lived to see the day.*

1857. September.

Such was the first relief of Lucknow. How Havelock's force fought its way from Cawnpore to Lucknow, achieving many victories, but encountering numerous impediments and obstructions which forbade his turning them to account; how Outram with characteristic chivalry and generosity waived his right of command in favour of the General, who had for so long borne the burden and the heat of the day; how the glorious Neill was struck down on entering Lucknow, at the head of his men, by almost the last unerring shot fired by the enemy from their

Sept. 25.

* "Wives, who had long mourned their husbands as dead were now restored to them; others fondly looking forward to glad meetings with those near and dear to them, now for the first time learnt that they were alone. On all sides eager inquiries for relations and friends were made. Alas! in two many instances the answer was a painful one."—*Journal of a Staff Officer.*

1857. September. walled cover—must be told in another Book of this History. I have now to write of a great event, beside which even this first Relief of Lucknow sinks into comparative insignificance. A few days before Lucknow was relieved by Havelock, Wilson had captured Delhi.

CHAPTER IV

THE DAWN OF SEPTEMBER—ANXIETY FOR THE ASSAULT—WILSON'S CHIEF ASSISTANTS—ARRIVAL OF THE LAST REINFORCEMENTS FROM THE NORTH—THE QUESTION OF ASSAULT DEBATED—WILSON AND BAIRD SMITH—THE FINAL ORDER GIVEN—ERECTION OF THE BREACHING BATTERIES—EFFORTS OF THE ARTILLERY AND ENGINEERS—ALEXANDER TAYLOR.

THE time for resolute action had now come. In the last volume of this History, I brought down the narrative of the so-called "Siege of Delhi" to the end of the month of August. But, up to that time, we had been the Besieged and not the Besiegers. Of the wonderful heroism and the consummate patience—of the gallant actions then performed, of the grievous sufferings then bravely endured, no words can speak in language of sufficient admiration. It was, indeed, this waiting game that tried the metal of our people, all those long months, not of inaction, but of profitless activity—under burning suns, under heavy rains, under constant exposure; wasting human life, only to prove that we had lost nothing of our old vitality. But all this was changed in September. The dawn of that month saw our preparations nearly complete for the delivery of the final assault. John Lawrence had despatched from the Punjab the last of his succours, and, in the estimation of the general camp, the City of the Mogul

1857. September.

1857. September. was doomed—and all who held high carnival in it, in proud defiance of the English.

Neville Chamberlain. There were then, under the Chief Commander of the Delhi Field Force, three men in the very prime of life, who, holding high position in the Army, were working strenuously to accomplish, with the least possible delay, the great final consummation of the assault on the doomed city. There was Neville Chamberlain, who had been severely wounded, but who had lost none of his pristine energy. As chief of the Army Staff, he had been ever ready with sustaining and invigorating counsel; but his vigour was tempered by a clear, sound judgment, and a just appreciation of surrounding circumstances. If, looking from a distance at the work which lay before Anson and Barnard, he took up the Punjabee war-cry, and was disposed to censure what seemed to be the weakness and reluctance of our leaders, a nearer view of the actual difficulties of the position convinced him that he had greatly underrated them. Eager as he had been for the assault, he had not been long on Barnard's Staff before he confessed that, with the scanty means then at our disposal, it was a desperate enterprise. He was the man who first described it, in language often afterwards quoted, as the "gambler's throw." But nothing could have moved him an inch from the ground which we had taken up. The idea of a retrograde movement was an abomination in his eyes. He knew that we needed only a few more companies and a few more guns to make Delhi our own; and he never ceased to do his best, even when least capable of exertion, to persist in this course of action. It was a fortunate circumstance, too, that at this time, when Chamberlain's wound necessarily kept him much in his tent, he had the assistance of a young officer of the highest promise, whose great gifts were fast winning the confidence of his elders. In Captain Norman, of the Adjutant-General's Department, there was a rare combination of those qualities which make a wise counsellor and a man of strenuous action. He had all the enthusiasm and the enterprise of lusty youth, and all the staid intelligence of mature manhood; and there was scarcely a man in Camp who did not recognise in him one of its leading spirits. 1857. September.

Baird Smith.

Then there was Baird Smith, Chief of the Engineer Department, who was also enfeebled by much sickness, and the distresses of a painful wound. He had been struck by the fragment of a shell, when superintending his work in the batteries, and he had been lamed by the blow; but, when he ought to have been on the sick-list, he was in the full swing of active employment; when he ought to have been in his tent, he was busy in the works. Worn to a skeleton by the most weakening of all ailments, he went about, when it was possible for him to go about at all, saturated with opium and brandy, dragging his maimed limb after him, with painful efforts; but never losing his high courage, or the habitual cheerfulness of his demeanour.* Like Chamberlain, he

* See the following, from a private letter written by Baird Smith after the capture of Delhi: "An attack of camp scurvy had filled my mouth with sores, shaken every joint in my body, and covered me all over with livid spots, so that I was marvellously unlovely to look upon. A smart knock on the ankle, from the splinter of a shell which burst in my face—in itself, however, a mere bagatelle of a wound—had been of necessity neglected, under the pressing and incessant calls upon me, and had grown worse and worse, till the whole foot below the ankle became a black mass, and seemed to threaten mortification. I insisted, however, on being allowed to use it until the place was taken, mortification or not; and though the pain was sometimes horrible, I carried my point, and kept up

1857. September. Alexander Taylor.

had an assistant, who was one of the younger heroes of the Camp. In Alexander Taylor, his second in command, he found a man capable of any amount of work, and ready for any heroic enterprise. His energies were unbounded, his spirit unfailing; and it was truly a fortunate circumstance, that when the frailty of the flesh restricted Baird Smith's personal activities, Taylor was ever ready and eager to pass from point to point, and to display his bodily presence, which was always inspiriting and encouraging. There was little or no sympathy between Wilson and Baird Smith. They were men altogether cast in different moulds. But the General fully recognised the great attainments of the Chief Engineer; and though rarely outwardly courteous or orally compliant, practically yielded to his opinions.

John Nicholson.

And now united with these Two, and in daily counsel with them, was John Nicholson, a born soldier, who seemed to have come down to Delhi with a special mission to take it. He had chafed under the long delay, which had left the vast and guilty city so long in the hands of the mutineers. Patience was not one of his virtues. With great ardour commonly some impetuosity is combined. John Nicholson had not the cool temper and calm judgment of Neville Chamberlain. He overlooked all difficulties and ignored all responsibilities; and, perhaps, he did not always make allowance for those who clearly saw the one and were compelled to accept the other. He could not stand still. Active among the active, he was eager to execute any kind of work that might be entrusted to him,

to the last . . . . and to crown the pleasant catalogue, I was worn to a shadow by a constant diarrhœa, and consumed as much opium, with as little effect, as would have done credit to my father-in-law (De Quincey)."—*MS. Correspondence.*

until the day of final retribution should arrive, when he coveted, and believed that he would obtain, the post of honour at the head of the storming party. No man doubted his power, and no man envied his reputation. All felt that a great soldier had come among them, full-brained and lion-hearted; and they looked to him to lead them to victory. 1857. September.

In the early morning of the 4th of September the siege guns, drawn by elephants, appeared upon the Ridge, with an immense assemblage of carts laden with ammunition—sufficient, it was said, "to grind Delhi to powder." On the 6th, the residuary Rifles from Meerut marched into Camp, strong, healthy, and jubilant, welcomed by the inspiring notes of the band of the Fifty-second and the cheers of their old comrades. On the morning of the 8th, the Jummoo Contingent, promised by Gholab Singh and sent down by his son, made their appearance, with Richard Lawrence at their head, and were greeted by the General and the Commissioner. Then the spirits of all men rose, for they saw the beginning of the end. The days of waiting and watching were spent. Every man, every gun, every shot, every shell that could be sent down for the final assault had now reached its destination. There was no pretext for further delay. The waste of a single hour would have been a crime, for our troops were dying fast, and the enemy were escaping. The "real siege of Delhi" was now to commence. Sept. 4–8. Arrival of the last reinforcements.

There are men now living, as I write, who will never forget that crisis; there are others, gone to their rest, who were stirred to the very depths of their natures by a grand enthusiasm, which made Question of assault.

1857. September. them cast aside every consideration of military discipline and decorum, and gird their loins up for that which would have been to them either total ruin or a grand reputation. They thought that the General was wavering; that even then he hesitated to issue the orders for the final assault; and had denial come they were prepared to appeal to the Army, to have put the Commander under arrest, and to have delivered the assault either under the direction of the Chief Engineer, or of a Commander selected by themselves. Eager among the eager was John Nicholson, whose strong impulses were not to be curbed, and who never scrupled to say what others ventured only to think. "The game is completely in our hands," he wrote to John Lawrence on the 11th of September; "we only want the player to move the pieces. Fortunately, after making all kinds of objections and obstructions, and even threatening more than once to withdraw the guns and abandon the attempt, Wilson has made everything over to the Engineers, and they and they alone will deserve the credit of taking Delhi. Had Wilson carried out his threat of withdrawing the guns, I was quite prepared to appeal to the Army to set him aside and elect a successor. The purport of his last Memorandum, in reply to the Engineers, ran thus: 'I disagree with the Engineers entirely. I foresee great, if not insuperable difficulties in the plan they propose; but as I have no other plan myself I yield to the remonstrances of the Chief Engineer.' The above are almost the very words used by him." And, in truth, they were but little wrong.

But it is just that I should pause here for a little space to make clear and intelligible, by reference to documents before me, the facts out of which arose this pregnant talk of the Camp. On the 20th of August, Wilson, then in doubt with respect to the sufficiency of his force for the capture and occupation of Delhi, had written to Baird Smith saying: 1857. September.

GENERAL ARCHDALE WILSON TO COLONEL BAIRD SMITH.

"MY DEAR SMITH,—A letter has been received from the Governor-General urging our immediately taking Delhi, and he seems angry that it has not been done long ago. I wish to explain to him the true state of affairs: that Delhi is seven miles in circumference, filled with an immense fanatical Mussulman population, garrisoned by full 40,000 soldiers armed and disciplined by ourselves, with 114 heavy pieces of artillery mounted on the walls, with the largest magazine of shot, shell, and ammunition in the Upper Provinces at their disposal, besides some 60 pieces of field artillery, all of our own manufacture, and manned by artillerymen drilled and taught by ourselves; that the Fort itself has been made so strong by perfect flanking defences erected by our own engineers, and a glacis which prevents our guns breaking the walls lower than eight feet from the top, without the labour of a regular siege and sap—for which the force and artillery sent against it has been quite inadequate; that an attempt to blow in the gates and escalade the walls was twice contemplated, but that it was considered, from the state of preparation against such an attack on the part of the rebels, such an attempt would inevitably have failed, and have caused the most irreparable disaster to our cause; and that, even if we had succeeded in forcing our way into the place, the small force disposable for the attack would have been most certainly lost in the numerous streets of so large a city, and have been cut to pieces. It was, therefore, considered advisable to confine our efforts to holding the position we now occupy, which is naturally strong, and has been daily rendered more so by our engineers, until the force coming up from below could join to co-operate in the attack. That since the command of the force has devolved on me, I have considered it imperatively necessary to adopt the same plan as the only chance of safety to the Empire, and that I strongly urge upon his

1857. August 20. Lordship the necessity of his ordering General Havelock's or some other force marching upon Delhi as soon as possible. The force under my command is, and has been since the day we took up our position, actually besieged by the mutineers, who, from the immense extent of suburbs, and gardens extending nearly to the walls of the town, have such cover for their attacks, that it has been very difficult to repel them, and at the same time to inflict such a loss as would deter a repetition of them. They have frequently been driven back with loss, but they immediately take refuge under the grape fire of their heavy guns on the city walls, and, on our retirement, reoccupied their former positions; every such attack upon them has entailed a heavy loss upon our troops, which we can ill spare, and has done us little good. I shall be reinforced by a siege train from Ferozepore by the end of this or beginning of next month, when I intend to commence more offensive operations against the city; but I cannot hold out any hope of being able to take the place until supported by the force from below. As an Artillery officer, I have no hesitation in giving my opinion that the attack on Delhi, garrisoned and armed as it now is, is as arduous an undertaking as was the attack on Bhurtpore in 1825-26, for which 25,000 troops and 100 pieces of artillery were not considered too large a force. I enclose a return of the original force which was sent down to capture this strong place, and also a return of the present effective force, including sick and wounded, from which his Lordship will see how desperate would have been any attempt to take the city by assault, more especially as the mutineers keep a large portion of their force encamped outside the city walls, who, on our assaulting the city, could easily attack and capture our camp, with all our hospitals, stores, and ammunition, unless a strong provision was made against it. Something of this sort I intend forwarding to the Governor-General, and shall be glad if you will return this with such remarks and emendations as your experience as Chief Engineer suggests.

"Yours sincerely,

"A. Wilson.

"August 20, 1857."

After the perusal of this letter, Baird Smith drew up a Memorandum stating his reasons most emphatically in favour of immediate action. He contended that although there was always hazard in an assault, the evils of inaction at such a time, were so great, and the chances in our favour were so many, that it would be better to risk the enterprise than to shrink from it. He demonstrated, on scientific grounds, that, although the material resources of the enemy were far greater than our own, the superior forethought and skill, and the perfect union and combination, absent from the designs and operations of the enemy, would give us an immense advantage over them. He represented most urgently to the General that the breaches should be established and the assault should be delivered, with the utmost possible despatch, as the enemy once cognisant of our designs would strengthen their defences without and within the city and render its occupation impossible. To these arguments Wilson reluctantly yielded. The whole responsibility was thrown upon the Chief Engineer. The "ipsissima verba" used by the General were these: "It is evident to me that the results of the proposed operations will be thrown on the hazard of a die; but under the circumstances in which I am placed, I am willing to try this hazard—the more so as I cannot suggest any other plan to meet our difficulties. I cannot, however, help being of opinion that the chances of success, under such a heavy fire as the working parties will be exposed to, are anything but favourable. I yield, however, to the judgment of the Chief Engineer.—A. W." Baird Smith, transcribing the above, observed: "This, I think, every one would allow, places on my shoulders the undi-

1857.
Aug.—Sept.

1857. Aug.—Sept.

vided responsibility for the results of the siege. It would, doubtless, have lightened that burden greatly had I felt assured of the hearty support and concurrence of the General in command; but the withholding of these was no sufficient cause for hesitation, and I was too glad of even a qualified consent to immediate action to be careful as to the terms in which it was given."*

Baird Smith was not a man to shrink from the responsibility thrown upon him. To say that he cheerfully accepted it would be a faint recital of the fact; he eagerly grasped it. And there was not an officer under him, whose heart did not bound with joyous exultation when he knew that the work was to be begun. But Wilson was not wrong when he said that to attempt to erect our batteries so near the city walls, in the face of the enemy's fire from their inexhaustible artillery, was a hazardous undertaking. The eager gallantry of the Engineers believed all things to be possible. And it is by this noble self-reliance that great victories are achieved. But the Engineers, as will presently be shown, had set themselves a task which they could not accomplish. In the midst of that awful but glorious crisis, men saw through a glass darkly. But time has brought them face to face with the Truth. Some of the bravest and best of Wilson's officers, who, heated by the excitements and animosities of the Camp, had condemned this apparent reluctance to order the assault, looking back upon those troublous days, and calmly estimating the difficulties to be encountered and the

* Wilson's remarks are written in pencil on the copy of the "Memorandum by the Chief Engineer," which Baird Smith submitted to the General. It is now before me with Wilson's marginal notes.

responsibilities to be sustained, have since acknowledged that less than justice was done at that time to the Commandant of the Delhi Force. All the principles of warfare were upon his side. But these principles have not been much regarded in India. Everything has been gained by hard blows promptly delivered in defiance of all principles of war.

1857. September. Wilson's address to the Army.

Having once resolved to stand the "hazard of the die," Wilson issued an Address to the Army, manly and spirit-stirring, and wise in the cautions it conveyed.* It spoke of the hardships and privations undergone by the Army, and of the gallantry which they had on all occasions displayed. It expressed a cheerful hope that their great trials were now wearing to a close, and that the grand reward was close at their feet. It called upon the troops of all arms to assist the Engineers in the arduous work that lay before them—in the digging of trenches and the erection of batteries. It appealed to the Artillery, who, it was said, would have "still harder work than they had yet had, and which had been so well and cheerfully performed." Then it spoke wisely and sagaciously of the precautions to be observed after the assault should have been delivered. It warned the soldiers against straggling—it warned them against indiscriminate plundering—it stimulated the worst passions of the soldiery by reminding them (or, as it is customary to say, "I need not remind them") of the atrocious murders and cruelties committed by the enemy, and told them to spare the women and the children, but to give no quarter to the men. And it concluded with the words, "The Major-General calls upon the Officers of the Force to

* It is said to have been written by Baird Smith.

1857. September. lend their zealous aid and efficient co-operation in the erection of the works of the siege now about to be commenced. He looks especially to the regimental officers of all grades to impress upon their men that the work in the trenches during a siege is as necessary and as honourable as to fight in the ranks during a battle. He will hold all officers responsible for their utmost being done to carry out the directions of the Engineers; and he confidently trusts that all will exhibit a healthy and hearty spirit of emulation and zeal, from which he has no doubt that the happiest results will follow in the brilliant termination of all their labours."

And then began a work almost unparalleled in the history of modern warfare. That science, which has taught us how to make the siege of fortified places almost a certainty in the success of its results, was now of no service to us. The approach by parallels, so beautiful upon paper, and so effective in practice, was to us as if War and Science had been wholly divorced. The ring of fire closing in slowly, but surely, upon a doomed fortress, shutting up the garrison within its walls and reducing them to the necessity of surrender, was now to our English officers only a memory of the stirring pages of Napier and Jones. What they saw was an attacking force, scarcely one-third of the numerical strength of the enemy, who had still possession also of some important suburbs, without cover of any well-constructed trenches, bringing their guns within fire of the walls of Delhi, and pouring forth day and night an incessant shower of shot and shell, resolute to atone for the failure of science by gigantic physical efforts and an unexampled display of British pluck.

The plan of attack was that which Baird Smith had projected before he left Roorkhee, and of the efficacy of which his convictions had never been shaken. It was the plan which had commended itself to all our Engineer officers from the first establishment of our Army on the Ridge. Investment with our limited means being impossible, it was necessary to select a front of attack on which all our available breaching power could be brought to bear. The front to be assailed contained the Moree, the Cashmere, and the Water Bastions, with their connecting curtains. These works had, not many years before, been greatly strengthened and improved by our own Engineer officers, so that we well knew the force to be applied to their demolition. There were very important reasons for this selection—Firstly, because our left flank would be protected by the river, thus leaving us only the right flank to guard; secondly, because the flanking fire from the city would thus be comparatively harmless, as only the Moree Bastion commanded the ground in front of it; thirdly, because there was excellent cover to within a short distance of the walls.* The insurgents might have done more to increase both their offensive and their defensive powers, but they had failed to do so; and it was permitted to us, therefore, to take advantage of their neglect.† Some thought, however, that when the enemy should see that we were preparing our batteries in earnest so as to bring a crushing fire from a short distance upon their walls, they would raise cover for a larger number of guns wherewith to

1857. Sept. 7—13. The plan of attack.

* MS. Memorandum by an Engineer Officer.

† Medley, page 73.

1857. Sept. 7—13.

silence our batteries. It was manifest, therefore, that every hour was of the utmost importance to us; and so all our people went to work as if they had never had a day's fighting—never known a day's fatigue.

Construction of the batteries.

Then, night and day, worked the Artillery and the Engineers, as those services, with the lustre of long years of past activities upon them, had never, perhaps, worked before. The first thing was to construct the batteries behind which our guns were to work; the next was to get our heavy guns into position. Brownlow had charge of the Engineer's Park—Hogge of the Park of Artillery. Ever since his first appearance in Camp, Baird Smith had been collecting the materials of the batteries which were to cover the captors of Delhi. Immense supplies of gabions, and fascines, and sand-bags had been prepared, with scaling ladders and all else required for the later operations of the attack. The first heavy battery was traced out on the evening of the 7th,* and all through the night the work was being pressed forward as silently as circumstances would permit; but silence was, indeed, impossible. The large number of camels that were bringing down the *matériel* of the batteries, and the bullocks which were dragging the carts laden with ordnance stores, followed by the heavy guns, each with a team of forty floundering beasts, made such confusion, and the drivers, who are nothing if not clamorous, made such a noise, that it is marvellous that the enemy did not discover our designs and pour an unceasing fire

* There had been a light battery previously (evening of the 6th) erected upon the plateau of the Ridge to the left hand of the Sammy House. The object of this was to keep the ground clear and to protect the operations going on below. This battery contained eight light pieces —six 9-pounders and two 24-pound howitzers—under the command of Captain Remmington.

upon our toiling people. For a time all was secure; and things looked hopeful in the battery, when a heavy shower of grape came in from the Moree, and after a short interval another, too well-directed and too fatally destructive. Then the Engineers must have been much troubled in their minds, what would be the state of the working parties in the morning, if the insurgents should continue thus to molest us all through the night. It was, indeed, a terrible question. But the painful expectation of the renewal of the fire from the bastion soon died away, for there was not another flash, another sound; and the work went on without any further interruption. The carriage, and the cattle, and the drivers, and the camp-followers were cleared away before the morning sun shone upon the scene. The ammunition was stored. The guns were ready for work. But all the exertions of the Engineers, under the vigorous direction of the inexhaustible Alec Taylor, had not sufficed to fix the platforms on which they were to be mounted. No men could have done more; but they had set themselves a task which could not be accomplished in a single night, and so far the doubts of the General were confirmed. He had rightly forecast the difficulty; and when it was reported to him that it had arisen, he was disposed to withdraw the guns. But the man in command was not one to go a step backwards. Let the Moree batteries roar as they might, he would not give the order for the withdrawal of the British Artillery. So they gallantly faced the fire and went on with their work.

1857. Sept. 7—13. No. 1 Battery.

The battery—known as Battery No. 1—was at a distance of seven hundred yards from the enemy's works. It was divided into two parts connected by

Brind's Battery.

1857. Sept. 7—13. Major James Brind.

a trench. The right portion was constructed to cover five heavy guns and a howitzer, the special function of which was to demolish the Moree Bastion —our most obtrusive assailant all through the siege. The left contained four guns, intended to keep down the fire of the Cashmere Bastion. This battery was under the command of Major James Brind, who had virtually, indeed, commanded the heavy Artillery throughout the greater portion of the operations before Delhi,* who had always been foremost where work was to be done, and who, whilst careful in the extreme of his men, had exposed himself in a manner which had called forth the remonstrances of his friends. If there was any fault to be found with him, it was the glorious fault of doing too much. His restless bravery never halted. He did not know what it was to "stand at ease."† But this very activity, though sometimes wasted, suggested, when there was real work to be done, that Brind was the man to do it. He had now the honour, coveted by every artilleryman in the field, of commencing the

* I have before said (vol. ii. pp. 594, 595) that the services of the Foot Artillery, during the period which preceded the actual siege, have been insufficiently recorded. It seems that there were some official misunderstandings as to the authority, whose duty it was to report them, which caused them not to be reported at all.

† It was said of Major Brind that he "never slept"—and the statement was no great exaggeration. I am told that he more than once addressed his men, saying, as he shouldered a musket, "Now, you lie down and rest. Your Commandant will defend the battery." The same informant, himself an officer of the highest gallantry, often mentioned in preceding pages of this narrative, said to me, "We talk about Victoria Crosses — Brind is a man who should be covered with them from head to foot." See also the letters of Major Reid, now (1875) Sir Charles Reid, one of the foremost of the Delhi heroes: "Battery No. 1 was commanded by my dear old friend, Major Brind, who had been constantly on duty with me on the Ridge, and who had given me most able assistance on the night of the Eed attack. Indeed, on all occasions the exertions of this noble officer were indefatigable. He was always to be found where his presence was most required; and the example he set to his officers and men was beyond all praise. A finer soldier I never met."

attack upon those works which had so long defied us. But on that morning, in that unfinished battery, it was a service of extreme danger. The morning light had fully revealed our designs to the insurgents, and laid bare our position. So they poured down from the Moree a pitiless shower of shot and shell, and sent out light guns with riflemen, to endeavour to take the battery in flank, whilst Brind's gunners, animated by his noble example, were working, unshaken and undismayed, to get their pieces into position. Only one gun was mounted when the fire commenced. Then "Brind dragged a howitzer well to the rear and fired over the parapet."* It was but a feeble response that he could return to the bellowing enemy; but he was resolute to give them something, and he knew that he would soon give them something more. Thus, ever as the sun rose higher and higher, the enemy fired and our people fell. But as gun after gun was mounted on its platform, the inequality of the conflict ceased; and then began that of which the insurgents behind their walls had had no former experience—perhaps, indeed, no conception. They had laughed at our long shots. But the close quarters to which we now brought our heavy guns, and the admirable manner in which they were served, gave altogether a new aspect to the operations before Delhi. The insurgents stood manfully to their guns. But the masonry of the Moree soon began to crumble; and ere the heat of the day had passed, the fire of the enemy had slackened, and before sunset it had feebly dwindled away into total quietude. But they had fired to some purpose. Our men were scarce, though our material was abundant, and the result of that first day's work was that

1857. Sept. 7—13.

* Medley.

1857. Sept. 7—13. there were some seventy casualties in our trenches.* Nor was it the fire from the Moree alone that distressed our people in the battery. They were, also, much molested by some light field-pieces and skirmishers of the enemy posted on our right. These enfiladed the battery and sometimes even took it in reverse. To meet these attacks and to protect our position Brind brought down two field guns from the rear. Moreover, the mutineers, inspired probably by our Sappers, who to the number of eight hundred had joined the insurgent force, ran a trench along the plain in front of both sections of the battery, about midway between the city walls and our position, from which they kept up a constant fire and did some damage to us, as the battery had been hastily erected without mantlets and with over-large embrasures.†

Whilst the eighteen-pounders were thus blazing away at the Moree, the twenty-four pounders in the left section of the battery were directing their fire on the Cashmere Bastion. This section of the battery was placed under the command of Major Frank Turner, one of the best Horse Artillery officers in the service. But previous exposure to the sun had broken him down; and an utter failure of his powers of endurance compelled him reluctantly to withdraw from the command. He was succeeded by Major Edward Kaye, who had taken an active part from the beginning in all the

* "No. 1 Battery was unquestionably the key of the attack, and on its success depended the opening of Delhi to our assaulting columns. The progress of the other batteries depended essentially on its efficiency; and but for your moral courage, clear perception, and unwavering resolution in arming and working it, in spite of all obstacles, consequences would have followed causing the greatest embarrassment."—*Colonel Baird Smith to Major Brind.—MS. Correspondence.*

† MS. Memoranda by Engineer and Artillery Officers.

operations on the Ridge. Scarcely had the completion of the parapet enabled him to get his guns in position, when a round shot from the Moree shattered the skull of one of his subalterns—Lieutenant Hildebrand—and Riding-master Budd, of the Horse Artillery, was soon afterwards disabled by the fire of the enemy. But soon our guns were fairly in position, and right good service they did, not only by keeping down the fire of the Cashmere Bastion, but by deluding the enemy into the belief that our assault was to be delivered entirely from the right. During the greater part of three days this left section kept up a continued fire on the enemy's works; but towards noon of the 10th its operations were brought to a close by the internal ignition of the battery. Hastily constructed of fascines, made of very dry brushwood, it caught fire from the blazing of our own guns. Every effort was made to suppress the flames; but the efforts were vain, for water was scarce and had to be brought from a distance; and the water-carriers being much exposed, going and coming, suffered severely from the fire of the enemy. The Infantry on duty in the battery (some details of the Kumaon Battalion) were most zealous in their efforts, and suffered severely from the musketry-fire of the enemy. Several, including Lieutenant Lockhart, who commanded the party, were severely wounded. But, all to no purpose. The fire could not be mastered. So the guns were withdrawn—and made ready for their removal at night to No. 2 Battery. And thus the left section of No. 1 became a thing of the past. It was not, however, a disaster of any moment. For that part of the battery had done its work; and both the guns

1857. Sept. 7—13. No. 1 Battery.

2 O 2

1857. September. and the gunners were wanted for service nearer to the real point of attack.

Sept. 9, 10. No. 2 Battery constructed. For by this time Battery No. 2 had been constructed—the left section immediately in front of Ludlow Castle and the right about eighty yards to the right front of the former. How it happened that the enemy had allowed us to take up such a position, within six hundred yards of the city, no one could explain, except upon the supposition that the insurgents, though never wanting in courage, were greatly wanting in wit. It was expected that we should have a hard fight for the ground, but our occupation of it was never contested. And yet this battery was intended to have, and in effect did have, a most potential effect upon the issue of the war. It was designed to crush the Cashmere Bastion and the adjacent works, and so to breach the walls as to open an entrance for our assaulting columns. It was to comprise, in the right section, cover for seven heavy howitzers and two eighteen-pounders; and in the left for nine twenty-four-pounders. The experiences of the first night had proved the impossibility of completing the battery and getting the guns into position before daybreak on the 9th; so the Engineers went more quietly to work, and there was not, during the darkness, much of a mischievous character from the enemy's guns to impede the operations of our working parties. On the second night the battery was completed and the guns brought into position. The right was to be commanded by Major Kaye; the left by Major J. H. Campbell.

When this Battery No. 2 had been completed,* it

* It was completed on the night of the 10th—11th, and the heavy guns from the left section of No. 1, then joined; others were brought down from the Park.

was not thought advisable immediately to unmask it. It was better to finish the other offensive works for the left attack, so that a simultaneous fire might be opened from both batteries. "The reason," said Baird Smith, "for delaying the opening of this battery until No. 3 has been armed, is that at present the siege works on the left are being carried on with very few casualties in consequence of the apparent ignorance of the enemy that any attack on that side is meditated."* So the works of No. 3 went on apace with little interruption. This battery was erected behind one of the buildings of the Custom House, at a distance of not more than a hundred and eighty yards from the Water Bastion, upon which our guns were to play. It was to cover six eighteen-pounders, under the command of Major Scott, who had commanded No. 14 Light Field Battery throughout the siege. If the building did not much protect our working parties, it greatly obscured the nature of the work on which they were engaged. The enemy never clearly knew what we were doing, but they felt that something was going on that portended mischief, and they poured in such an incessant shower of musketry, with occasional discharges from their mortars, that it was difficult and dangerous to work even under the cover of the night, and impossible after the dawn of day. The workmen were principally Natives and non-combatants, but they faced death as bravely for their Christian employers as if they had been English

1857. Sept. 7–13.

No. 3 Battery.

* Baird Smith had recommended that No. 3 Battery should be commenced before No. 2. (*Memorandum by Chief Engineer*), but General Wilson had objected to this, saying, "The commencement of No. 3 Battery before No. 2 is, I think, objectionable, and will cause a fearful loss of life from the untouched batteries in the Cashmere Bations. It would be much safer to silence the guns on the left bastion before erecting No. 3." (*MS. Notes*). Wilson was right. I am told, however, that in point of fact, No, 2 Battery did open fire before No. 3—indeed, before it was completely constructed.

1857. Sept. 9—11. soldiers.* There is nothing more true than that the calm courage of our Native adherents enabled us to recover India from their own countrymen.

Of a different character was the courage displayed by our allies from beyond the border. Our working parties were composed of men of all races—of all sorts and descriptions of people—whom we could press into our service; for the labour was great and incessant, the heat was intense, and exhaustion soon came upon those who had to lift heavy weights. On the night of the 10th, no Sappers or Pioneers being available, Taylor had been compelled to employ the services of men drawn from two of our European regiments in the heavy howitzer battery. They worked heartily and effectively; but soon after midnight they were failing from sheer exhaustion, and then the Directing Engineer bethought himself of our newly-arrived Jummoo Contingent, and sent a hundred and twenty men down to the battery. Elated with the thought of some fighting, to be followed probably by plunder, they streamed down, armed to the teeth. But when the true nature of the service required from them was explained, they looked askance at the shovels, and the sand, and the sand-bags, and murmured among themselves. So Medley, the Engineer, who had charge of the work, with those immediately under him, began cheerily and lustily to fill the sand-bags, and to do other coolies' work. Then the Commanding Officer of the Jummoo Detachment, feeling some compunctions of shame, followed the lead of the European officers, and presently all his men piled their

* "They were merely unarmed Native Pioneers, and not meant to be fighting men. With the passive courage so common to Natives, as man after man was knocked over, they would stop a moment, weep a little over their fallen friend, pop his body in a row along with the rest, and then work on as before."—*Medley*, pp. 82, 83.

arms and laboured with the heartiest goodwill. All, for some time, was quiet, as they worked under the darkness of the night; but in the hour before the dawn, there came from the enemy's position in front a sharp shower of musketry, which so excited our Dogra friends, that they seized their matchlocks and discharged them with such impetuosity in the direction of their assailants, that they well-nigh shot down all our people who were before them in the battery. It was a mercy and a miracle that a bullet did not go through Medley's head. The danger was too serious to be repeated; so our impulsive allies were told that if they wished to fight they were to go out into the open, but that they had been brought into the battery to work.

1857. September.

The Mortar Battery in the Koodsea Bagh.

Whilst cover was being provided for our heavy guns and howitzers, a powerful mortar battery was in course of construction at the Koodsea Bagh. It was one of the pleasantest places in the neighbourhood, shaded by orange and lemon trees, and odorous with the perfume of the fruit. Sheltered on three sides by a high wall, the position we had taken up, though but two hundred and fifty yards from the city, was but little exposed to the musketry fire of the insurgents. There was some hard work for our people in cutting away the trees; but the axe and the bill-hook were plied with hearty goodwill, and the ground was soon sufficiently cleared for the erection of the battery and the planting of the mortars. They were under the command of Major Tombs, and he was not one to lose a minute in doing good execution with his shells. Before the batteries were completed for the left attack, he was ready to open upon the lines between the Cashmere and the Water Bastions. But his orders were not

1857. Sept. 11.

to commence firing until the morning of the 11th, when it was expected that all the heavy guns and howitzers on the left would be fairly in position. Brind's battery all the time continued to pour in a destructive fire on the right, which so crippled the enemy, that the Moree Bastion and all belonging to it had become little more than a name.

There was great joy throughout the Camp, when it was known that the batteries for the left attack were so far completed that the work of breaching could be commenced. The circumstances of our position were such as to engender impatience. Those who did not know the difficulties with which the Engineers were contending, were disappointed that the breaching operations along the whole line of the enemy's works had not sooner commenced. Doubtless, the first forecast had been somewhat erroneous. Men, who are eager for the realisation of certain results, are wont to be over-sanguine in their calculation of the facilities of accomplishing them. But none could have worked with heartier zeal or more unflagging perseverance than the Artillery and Engineers engaged on that great work.

Scott's Battery.

On the 11th of September, Scott's heavy guns* had been dragged into position, under such a fire of musketry as might have deterred men of fainter hearts; and then, although the battery, from causes

* Norman says: "The establishment of Major Scott's battery within one hundred and eighty yards of the walls, to arm which heavy guns had to be dragged from the rear under a constant fire of musketry, was an operation that could rarely have been equalled in war." Under instructions received from the Chief Engineer, Scott had brought down his guns on the night of the 10th, but on reaching the site of the intended battery, after a difficult march, he found the works incomplete, or rather scarcely commenced. The ground had been cleared, but there were no signs of a battery. To have left the guns within such an easy distance from the enemy would have insured their destruction, so he was compelled to withdraw them before daylight.

to be presently displayed, could not be unmasked, 1857.
there was no longer any reason why the final attack Sept. 11—12.
should be longer deferred. And well was it for us that there was no more delay. Mercifully the intellects of the besieged had been dulled for a time. But before our works were finished, they had woken up to a sense of the expediency of mounting heavy guns along the curtain between the Cashmere and the Water Bastions, from which such a fire could have been poured into our works on the left as to render them wholly untenable.* But God's providence arrested this calamity; the light had broken upon the enemy too late.

At eight o'clock, the fire from our twenty-four-pounders commenced. They were in the left section of No. 2 Battery, under the command of Major Campbell; and all the nine opened at the same moment with terrific effect upon the Cashmere Bastion. When the roar of this great first salvo had ceased, up went three ringing cheers of triumphant delight from the Artillery in the battery. We were now breaching in earnest. When the smoke cleared away, it was seen that the first discharge of our heavy guns had brought down vast masses of masonry, and that a few more such well-aimed blows would reduce their boasted defences to crumbling ruins. The guns on the Cashmere Bastion replied; and the enemy at least had some revenge, for they severely wounded the Commandant of the heavy guns, and sent him crippled from the battery. But a little more of our practice from both sections of the breaching battery, aided by Tombs's mortars on the Koodsea Bagh,

* "So nearly were they being ready, that had the subsequent assault been delayed for forty-eight hours, I believe that we could not have assaulted at all, but must have been driven from our batteries, or had our men knocked to pieces there.—*Medley*.

1857. Sept. 12. soon reduced them to silence. Then it was a grand sight to see the walls of Delhi falling to pieces, as shot and shell rained heavily upon them; the breach widening and widening as the eight-inch shells bursting on its crest, brought down whole yards of parapet, the cruel signs of a future desolation becoming more apparent every hour. It was something which all can understand, apart from circumstances of time and space. But only those who had waited for the great opportunity—who, for months, had been insulted by an enemy behind the walls, who had seen their comrades falling around them, who had toiled day and night under burning suns and drenching rains, and had seemingly made no progress towards the reduction of the great Imperial City, can thoroughly appreciate the glorious excitement of seeing, opening out before them, day after day, the road that was to lead them to the re-occupation of Delhi. It was a turning point in the life of our Anglo-Indian Empire such as not even those who had seen the great crisis at Caubul had ever witnessed before.

Sept 12. No. 3 Battery unmasked. But there was heavier retribution yet to overtake the insurgents. An hour before noon, on the 12th of September, the advanced battery on the left (No. 3) was unmasked. It had been originally designed that it should open fire simultaneously with No. 2 on the preceding day; but it was found that this was impossible. The battery was constructed of sand-bags placed against the masonry of a part of the old Custom House. The walls had been so broken down as to admit of embrasures being made, through which it was intended that our guns should be pointed at the Water Bastion, only a hundred and sixty yards distant. These embrasures had been temporarily filled up with sand-bags, as a blind to the enemy, but, unfortunately, when our people began to remove them, it was found by the morning light that the embrasures, made under cover of the darkness, were so contrived as not to suffer our guns to be brought to bear upon the point intended. To Scott and Taylor this discovery was a bitter disappointment. It was necessary to reconstruct the cheeks of the embrasures, and thus to delay the opening of our guns upon the doomed city. Nothing could be more vexatious and embarrassing. Scott was eager to be first to open fire: so as to dismount the enemy's guns at the very outset; but it was only too probable that if the battery were unmasked at mid-day, the insurgents would direct their heavy guns upon it before we could send in a shot. He was recommended to blow the sand-bags out of the embrasures, but this he refused to do, "being satisfied," as he said, "that the *débris* of the sand-bags would fall inwards, and seriously interfere with the accuracy of our fire." Whilst the question of the best mode of procedure was under discussion, a Sikh sapper, with calm courage, quietly proceeded to throw outwards the sand-bags before his own gun. The example was caught up by the gunners behind the other embrasures, and so rapidly was the work of clearance effected, that our guns opened upon the enemy before they had discovered our designs. Then went forth such a stream of heavy shot from our eighteen-pounders, as within that easy range, even if less skilfully directed, must have soon smashed the enemy's guns and pounded the Water Bastion into ruins. The effect was almost instantaneous. The once symmetrical bastion became a shapeless mass of earth and masonry. Then, for the first time, the enemy learnt what was the cannonade we could keep up, now

1857. Sept. 12.

1857. Sept. 12. that all our guns were in position, and the most sanguine must have despaired. All through the 12th and 13th the batteries on the left continued their breaching operations, under the direction of Kaye, Johnson,* Scott, and Tombs. The roar of fifty heavy pieces of ordnance was to be heard day and night without intermission. Never had our Siege Artillery a greater work before it. Never were guns more nobly served. Our trained gunners were few; but there was not a soldier in the camp who was not eager to handle a sponge-staff, or a portfire, or to bring up the shot and shell to the cannon's mouth. Among these volunteers none were more active than the Lancers. They soon became serviceable gunners, and every officer in charge of a battery was right glad to have their help. It was a service of no little danger, especially in the advanced battery, which was exposed to the incessant musketry fire of the enemy. We could silence their batteries, but we could not stop this skirmishing, and our people were all day long dropping beneath the assaults of the hidden marksmen. The utmost care had been taken to protect the inmates of the battery. Scott had mantlets on all the guns, and he strictly enjoined officers and men to keep themselves well behind them. Thus many lives were saved; but notwithstanding these wise precautions one lamentable casualty in the battery caused a great spasm of grief throughout the whole camp. Whilst working one of the guns, Captain Fagan, of the Artillery, an officer of the highest promise, and, for his years, of great performance, was shot through the head. He had mounted

* Captain (now Sir Edwin) Johnson, Assistant-Adjutant-General of Artillery, had taken the place of Major Campbell, disabled in the left section of No. 2 Battery

a gun-carriage and was looking over the mantlet, when Scott went up to remonstrate with him. It was said in camp, and Fagan himself thought, that he "bore a charmed life." But scarcely had the words of caution been spoken, when a musket-ball entered his temple, and he fell death-stricken at the feet of his commandant.*

1857. Sept. 7—13.

Death of Fagan.

It has been seen how, all this time, our Engineer officers worked, with unflagging perseverance, in the batteries. Alec Taylor was the heart and soul of every movement — always cheery, always active, never sparing himself—inspiring, aiding, animating all by his noble example. It was impossible not to admire—not to endeavour to imitate him. He never complained; he never faltered; almost, it may be said that he never rested. He had the sole executive direction of all the Engineering department of the Siege Batteries, which opened the way to the interior of Delhi. The younger officers of the Engineers swore by him, and in truth there was something almost divine in his wonderful fertility of resource and the self-sacrifice which he continually displayed. He had studied the ground well, and he had seized, with quick soldierly eye, upon the exact points at which it would be desirable to erect our batteries. It was a happy stroke of genius to surprise and divert the enemy by running up a battery (No. 1) in

Alec Taylor.

* "When the enemy discovered the position and object of No. 3 Battery, they at once placed heavy guns in position on the opposite side of the river to take No. 3 in flank and succeeded in dismounting one of the 18-pounders. Traverses were immediately constructed which saved the remainder, but the continuous stream of shot, shell, and bullets, directed on this battery by the enemy from front, flanks, and curtain proved the importance attached to it by them, and it was a matter of astonishment to all present that, thanks to the discipline and untiring devotion of officers and men, the battery was able to open the required breach so rapidly (less than thirty-six hours), so effectively, and at so small a sacrifice of life."—*MS. Memorandum by an Engineer Officer.*

1857. Sept. 7—13. a single night to play upon the Moree Bastion. It was Taylor's unaided idea—as was also the location of No. 3 Battery, the idea of which came suddenly upon him as an inspiration, and was worked out with wonderful promptitude and effect.

Baird Smith and Taylor.

Among the many controversies which have grown out of this story of the Sepoy War, there is not one which it is more difficult to write of than the question as to whether the chief merit of the operations which resulted in the capture of Delhi is due to Colonel Baird Smith or to Captain Alexander Taylor. Such controversies are always painful; for it is not easy to extol the merits of one without seeming to detract from the claims of the other. I believe the real historic truth to be this. Neither could have taken Delhi without the help of the other. Alec Taylor was the necessary supplement of Baird Smith. The large-brained chief of the Engineer Staff required just such a second-in-command to carry his plans into execution as he found in the noble-spirited Field-Engineer. The condition of Baird Smith's health was, as I have already said, such as would have sent most men to their beds. Lame from the effects of a painful and neglected wound on the ankle—suffering acutely from one of the cruel scourges of the country, which compelled him to drench himself with opium and brandy, he could not move about from place to place, so as to become a bodily presence, familiar to the eyes of men of all branches and all ranks of the army.* It has, therefore, sometimes been said: "We

* Baird Smith says that brandy was his daily sustenance, and that it had no other effect upon him than that of increasing his capacity for work. His brain was never clearer or more active. It carried him through the siege—but afterwards, rest and purer air enabled him to lay aside such dangerous diet.

never saw Baird Smith." Taylor, on the other hand, 1857.
though sometimes suffering from fever, was to be seen Sept. 7—13.
everywhere. He had great physical activity and powers of endurance to give practical expression to the zeal and courage which animated him. But the general directions for the conduct of our engineering operations, often even in minute details, emanated from Baird Smith. His thoughtfulness in respect of everything that could in any way contribute to our success is patent in the masses of manuscripts which lie before me. In his own handwriting may be read all his original conceptions and his amended designs; but these last were rare, for it was but seldom, except under pressure of altered circumstances, that he saw any good reason for modifying his first projects. But all these projects might have failed if there had been a less able, a less active, and a less courageous officer than Alec Taylor at the head of the executive officers of the Engineer Brigade. He was one who thought nothing impossible, and all men worked under him with the heartiest goodwill, for he inspired and animated all who came in contact with him in battery or in trench. Those who were above him were equally impressed by his noble exertions. "If I survive to-morrow," said John Nicholson, on the eve of the assault, "I will let all the world know that Alec Taylor took Delhi." This was characteristic of the brave impulsive man, who never lived to tell the story of the siege. But he erred, as he did on a previous occasion of which I have spoken, in not recognising the difference between a responsible and an irresponsible officer, whether at the head of a regiment or the head of an Army.

No one acknowledged Taylor's services more ungrudgingly than Baird Smith himself; but he could

1857. Sept. 7—13. not consent that History should accept the statement that the Chief Engineer had been in the background, doing nothing, whilst his first-assistant had gone to the front and done everything for the direction of the operations of the siege. "I think," he wrote to his wife some time afterwards, "that you may dismiss from your mind all sense of trouble about the injustice done to my work at Delhi. It is just as certain as that I am alive to say so, that from the day I joined, to the day I left, not a single vital act was done but under my orders and on my sole responsibility. And I know well that, but for my resolute determination, humanly speaking, there would have been no siege of Delhi at all; and even that assault which gave value by its success to all the exertions that were made would have ended in deplorable disaster, had I not withstood with effect the desire of General Wilson to withdraw the troops from the city on the failure of Brigadier Campbell's column. Nobody does heartier justice to Taylor's devotion, capacity, and zeal than I do. No personal consideration would, for one moment, induce me to detract, even in the faintest degree, from them. But he was, throughout, my most able and most trusted subordinate, working wholly at my risk and on my responsibility in the one department intrusted to him—namely, the executive duties." And in another letter to a friend in the Royal Artillery he said: "I would not willingly do the very faintest injustice either to Captain Taylor or to any of the other junior officers of the brigade, to whose noble co-operation, given always without reserve and in the most cordial spirit, I was so deeply indebted, and for which I have done my best upon all occasions to express my gratitude. These feelings are especially strong in reference to Taylor, whom I found to be ever, not only the most energetic and competent of seconds, but in all relations a true and right-hearted gentleman. I should be ashamed of myself if I permitted any petty feelings to influence me in estimating his worth; and I feel assured that no credit which may be due to me will ever be really diminished by my doing the amplest and heartiest justice to every man who worked under my orders. But it was with myself alone that the entire responsibility for the conception, progress, and issue of the engineering operations in every essential point rested; and had we failed in our attack, this fact would have been recorded so often and so emphatically, that I should have had none to share the fatal consequences with me."* It is better that, in such a case, Baird Smith should be left to speak for himself. On the subject of responsibility there could be no doubt; and whatsoever question might arise as to the design and execution of the detailed operations of the siege, Alec Taylor was not a man to deny, that as the risk of failure was his chief's, so also should be the credit of success. 1857. September. Alec Taylor.

But the chapter, which I have just completed, is devoted mainly to the exploits of the Artillery. I have written in vain, if I have not shown what tremendous work lay before our gunners throughout that critical week; with what consummate courage they faced the unexampled dangers before them, and with what wondrous patience and calm skill they overcame all obstacles and opened the way for the entrance of the British forces into Delhi. I doubt Services o the Artille

* MS. Correspondence.

1857. September. whether there is any incident of History surpassing in the boldness alike of its conception and of its execution this bombardment of the Imperial City of the Moguls. But this was only the crowning work—the grand culmination of weeks and months of toil upon the Ridge, vexatious, harassing toil, rather demonstrative than effective, little tending to produce any immediate results upon the enemy, to attract the special attention of commanders, or to excite the admiration of comrades. In a little time the heavy-battery service came to be regarded as part of the routine work of the Camp. Its importance in keeping down the fire of the enemy and in arresting their frequent sallies upon our outposts by showing ourselves continually on the alert, could not be overvalued. To have slackened fire would have been to encourage and embolden the insurgents; by leaving them to believe either that our material resources were on the ebb, or that our personal strength was so reduced by death and disease that we were unable to man our batteries. Few but those with scant knowledge of the position talked of this untiring energy as "wasting our ordnance stores." Had our Rear been closed, it would have been wholly different; but as it was, we were never in any real want of ammunition, and we could afford to expend some powder and shot without every discharge from our batteries palpably producing any great material results.

It is among the accidents of the Service, which all good soldiers will cheerfully accept, that whilst one by the very nature of his employment has opportunities of distinguishing himself and finding a niche in some historical episode, by which his name, perhaps, may be remembered in later days, another is condemned to toil on, unnoticed, doing equally good service to the State, but not of a nature to attract the regards of the Official Reporter or of the Military Annalist. So it was, emphatically, with the Bengal Artillery during the long so-called siege of Delhi. The Horse Artillery and the Light Field Batteries had opportunities of distinguishing themselves in dashing charges against the assailants of our outposts; but the Heavy Artillery on the Ridge had no occasion of displaying their high qualities save by their indomitable perseverance and endurance, until the longed-for summons came to go down below and to knock the main defences of the city to pieces. How they did that work, when the time came, I have endeavoured to show. That General Wilson, an old and good Artillery officer, did not appreciate—at least did not acknowledge—the magnificent services of his own branch, as might have been anticipated, alike from his sympathies and his experiences, was generally felt by the regiment. His honesty, if not his discernment, was conspicuous in this. But the omissions apparent in the General's despatches caused much bad feeling in the corps and led to some painful controversy. Brind, with his wonted earnestness and directness of purpose, pleaded the cause of his comrades in language which men in authority were not accustomed to and did not approve. Some wrongs were righted, but others remained unredressed. It is enough to state that the Major Scott of these pages, who fought his Light Battery so nobly, before the day of assault, and then went down to the post of danger, to command the most exposed of the Breaching Batteries, still remains undecorated.

1857. Septembe

CHAPTER V.

THE OCCUPATION OF DELHI—DIFFICULTIES OF THE ENTERPRISE—PLAN OF ASSAULT DEVELOPED—THE STORMING COLUMNS TOLD OFF—DELIVERY OF THE ASSAULT—RESULTS—FIGHTING IN THE CITY—OCCUPATION OF THE PALACE—DELHI TAKEN—ARREST OF THE KING—SLAUGHTER OF THE PRINCES—DEATH OF NICHOLSON.

1857. Sept. 13. Preparations for the assault.

In the meanwhile, in Head-Quarters' Camp, upon the Ridge, Wilson and Baird Smith were taking counsel together as to the organisation of the assaulting columns, which were to move into the city, when the breaches should be pronounced practicable. Chamberlain was still confined to his tent, but he went out sometimes in a dhooly, and was ever ready to put forth sound opinions on all military questions, both of principle and detail. One thing was certain—that the universal voice of the Camp had proclaimed John Nicholson as the man of men to lead the storming columns and to beckon them on to victory. He had come down to Delhi surcharged with the idea that he was ordained to plant the British standard on the proud Palace of the Moguls or to die the soldier's death at the head of his men. The decease of Sir Henry Lawrence had given an increased sobriety—indeed, solemnity—to his demeanour. If, before this, he had been possessed by any vain ambitions; if he had thought of the plaudits of his countrymen and the records of history, all this had passed away. He now thought only of the last words of his dying master—of the words which Lawrence wished to be engraved upon his tomb—and he also "tried to do his duty." He wrote that he wished to "get alongside" of Herbert Edwardes, that he might become more steadfast in his faith and tread more surely in the footsteps of his great exemplar who had died at Lucknow. 1857. Sept. 13.

On the 13th, Taylor announced that the breaches were practicable. All was then ready for the delivery of the assault on the following day. The composition of the several columns had been minutely arranged. Their leaders were nominated. The precise direction which each column was to take, was laid down, and Baird Smith had mapped out on oil-paper for each commander a plan of the operations entrusted to him, and to the other leaders, to be taken with him for his guidance. A meeting of the principal officers was then summoned. All were present at the meeting, except Nicholson, who purposely or accidentally was down in the heavy batteries watching the effect of Scott's guns and Tombs' mortars.* He felt that his position was secured; and knowing that he was too prone to be

* A few days before he had written to the Punjab: "The Engineers have consulted me about the plan of attack though Wilson has not. They tell me they proposed to him that I should be consulted, and that he maintained a chilling silence. I imagine it is as I supposed, that he is afraid of being thought to be influenced by me. I care little, however, whether he receives my suggestions direct or through the Engineers. Like Barnard, he talks about the 'gambler's throw.' I think, however, we have a right to hope for success, and I trust that ere another week passes, our flag will be flying over the Palace minars. Wilson has told me that he intends to nominate me Military Governor, for which I am much obliged, though I would rather he had told me that he intended to give me command of the column of pursuit."—*MS. Correspondence.*

1857. Sept. 13. intemperate in speech, he might have thought it better not to be present at a discussion, in the course of which he might express some divergencies of opinion without becoming moderation. Whatsoever the cause, the meeting was held without his animating presence. Wilson unfolded his plans. Nothing could exceed the clearness of the whole design or the minuteness, which left nothing to be guessed at or puzzled over by commanding officers. Baird Smith's charts, some of which are now before me, were guide-posts which no one could misunderstand. But there were some inquiries to make surety doubly sure—and some minute explanations in reply. Though satisfactory to the inquirers the answers added little to the original information. And the officers upon whom their several responsibilities had been thrown, quitted Wilson's tent eager for the coming struggle, and full of grand expectations of triumphant success.

The force was divided into four columns and a column of Reserve. The First Column commanded by Brigadier General Nicholson, was to consist of—

Her Majesty's 75th Regiment . . .	300	strong.
1st Bengal Fusiliers	250	,,
2nd Punjab Infantry	450	,,

Engineer officers attached, Lieutenants Medley, Lang, and Bingham *

This force was to storm the breach near the Cashmere Bastion and escalade the face of the bastion.

The Second Column was to be commanded by Brigadier Jones, C.B. It consisted of—

* Lieut.-Colonel Herbert commanded the Seventy-fifth, Major Jacob the Fusiliers, and Captain Green the Punjabees.

Her Majesty's 8th Regiment . . .	250 strong.	1857. Sept. 13.
,, 2nd Fusiliers . . .	250 ,,	
4th Sikh Infantry	350 ,,	

Engineer officers attached, Lieutenants Greathed, Hovenden, and Pemberton.*

This column was to storm the breach in the Water Bastion.

The Third Column was placed under Colonel Campbell, of the Fifty-second. It was to assault by the Cashmere Gate after its explosion by the Engineers should have taken effect; and was thus constituted:

Her Majesty's 52nd Regiment . . .	200 strong.
Kumaon Battalion	250 ,,
1st Punjab Infantry	500 ,,

Engineer officers attached, Lieutenants Home, Salkeld, and Tandy.†

The command of the Fourth Column was assigned to Major Charles Reid of the Sirmoor Battalion, who had held so long and so gallantly the post at Hindoo Rao's house. It was to attack and to clear the suburbs of Paharunpore and Kishengunje and to enter the city by the Lahore Gate. Its components were:

Detachments of European and Native Regiments. Sirmoor Battalion. Guides Infantry. Detachment of Dograhs.	860 men, not including Jummoo troops.

Engineer officers attached, Lieutenants Maunsell and Tennant.

* Lieut.-Colonel Greathed commanded the Eighth. The Fusiliers were under Captain Boyd, and Captain Rothney led the Sikhs.

† The Fifty-Second were under Major Vigors, the Kumaon Battalion under Captain Ramsay. Charles Nicholson commanded the Sikhs.

1857. Sept. 13. The Fifth or Reserve Column was commanded by Brigadier Longfield, and was thus composed:

Her Majesty's 61st, 250 men (Lieutenant-Colonel Deacon); 4th Punjab Infantry, 450 men (Captain Wilde); Wing Belooch Battalion, 300 men (Lieutenant-Colonel Farquhar); Jheend Auxiliaries, 300 men (Lieutenant-Colonel Dunsford)—Total, 1300; besides 200 of 60th Rifles, under Lieutenant-Colonel Jones, after they had covered the advance of the stormers.

But there was one thing more to be done before the assaulting columns could be let loose. Captain Taylor had reported that the breaches were practicable. But it was expedient that they should be examined by some picked Engineer officers. It was a service of some danger; but there was not an officer in the brigade who would not have eagerly undertaken the duty. Lieutenants Medley and Lang were to explore the Cashmere breach and Greathed and Home were to examine the breach by the Water Bastion. It was a moonless night, but clear under the broad starlight. And as the gallant subalterns went forth to their appointed work, taking with them a few picked riflemen of the Sixtieth, the guns and mortars from the breaching batteries were still playing upon the enemy's defences, making night hideous with their roar, and well-nigh bringing the services of our exploring parties to a disastrous close. But at ten o'clock there was a lull and the perils of the Engineers were then limited to the assaults of the enemy. "The enemy's skirmishers were firing away on our right," wrote one of the exploring party (Medley), "some thirty yards from us, and the flashes of their muskets lit up the air as if they had been fireflies. The shells and rockets of the enemy at one moment illumined the space around, as they darted over our heads and then left us in total darkness." But the work was done; the desired information was gained and the results of the explorations were duly reported to the Chief Engineer. The breaches would have been better for a little more cannonading; but Baird Smith determined that this would not countervail the evils of further delay; so he despatched a note to Wilson urging immediate action. The General wisely endorsed the recommendation, and the order went forth for the delivery of the assault on the morrow's dawn. 1857. Sept. 13.

Before daybreak the whole assaulting force had assembled near Ludlow Castle, with the exception of Reid's column, which was to advance from the post at Hindoo Rao's and to clear the suburbs of Kishengunje and Paharunpore. Not a man was absent from his post; and few were present who were not eager for the coming affray. After the muster and the dram, they would have rushed at the breaches, with a cheery English hurrah! But, as almost ever happens, there were unexpected causes of delay, and when all were ready for the advance, the signal was not given. No soldiers, seeing their work clearly before them, can bear to wait. Nothing is more depressing than that hour of the "shuddering dawn"—a time when the vital power is ever at its weakest—when men wonder over unexplained delays, and curse their commanders for keeping them waiting. This period of expectancy, as night kindles into day, takes the eagerness for fighting out of them grievously, unless it be sustained by stimulants; and the effect of these, if not renewed, is transient and dangerous.* The reaction may be worse than the first craving. The cause of delay Sept. 14. Muster of the assaulting columns.

* A double dram was served out to them.

1857. Sept. 14. was this. What Baird Smith had anticipated was now coming to pass. The insurgents having discovered our intentions had during the night, when our batteries were quiescent, filled up the main breach by which our columns were to enter Delhi. Skilled engineers were among them, who well knew the use of sand-bags, and moreover could improvise *chevaux-de-frise.* This had been done in the night; so orders went down, in hot haste, to the breaching batteries, to open fire again. This was done promptly and effectually; and soon the ramparts were cleared and our columns awaiting the appointed signal to advance.

Difficulties of the position. Never, in the history of modern warfare, has an officer found himself in a position so environed and embarrassed with difficulties as that which General Wilson was now called upon to confront. The very thought of the responsibility before him had killed one general. A few weeks on the Ridge had sent another to his grave, and despatched a third for very life's sake to Simlah. But not one of them had attempted an assault. The two last had stood on the defensive; and even that was too much for frail humanity to bear up against. But Wilson, who had brought with him to Delhi all the enervating wear-and-tear of the first outbreak at Meerut, following closely upon a critical attack of small-pox, had toiled for months upon the Ridge, during the most trying season of the year, with all responsibilities upon him. His health, as time advanced, had failed him more and more; like Barnard, he was unable to obtain sleep, and some men, in like circumstances, would have followed Reid's example, and betaken himself to the nearest sanitarium.

But Wilson, though feeling painfully, and bitterly deploring, his growing infirmities, determined not to abandon his post. With a candour most honourable to him, he confessed his physical prostration, and the mental disturbances which accompanied it. He was a man always of quick temper; but now, his irritability had become chronic, and he had none of that unfailing urbanity, that unceasing tenderness for others, which had glorified the last days of Sir Harry Barnard.* He was not, therefore, popular with the Army—not even with his own branch of it—and he was often thwarted by men in high places, who knowing his difficulties and responsibilities ought to have condoned his infirmities and supported him. The situation was cast upon him; he did not seek it. And with his high sense of duty and love of country, he would have given over the command to another, with all its high promise of honours and rewards and historical renown, if he had known one of sufficiently high rank equal to the work before him. 1857. Sept. 14.

And now the critical moment had come when a great deed was to be accomplished or a desolating failure was to stain the annals of our country. The strongest brain might have been disturbed—the strongest nerves might have been shaken by the prospect which lay before Wilson on that September morning. With the Heavy Artillery at our disposal it had been no impossible work to breach the defences of the city. With the indomitable pluck of the British soldier it might be no difficult work to carry the breaches thus opened. The difficulty was to commence after the carriage of the defences of the city had been accomplished. It was said that Baird Smith knew

* Vol. ii., pp. 541, 542.

1857. Sept. 14. Delhi well. And in truth he did. He knew the state of the defences thoroughly; but it was doubted whether he knew as much of the interior of the city—the great imperial capital of India, with all its vast piles of buildings, its numerous covered places, its streets, its lanes, and its bazaars. This, however, was a mistake. He knew Delhi well, inside and out.* But had he known the city as it was before the siege, how could he, even with the help of spies, know what changes had been wrought since in May we were expelled from Delhi? Of all our officers the man who knew most was Sir John Metcalfe,† our City Magistrate, ere the storm burst upon us and swept all authority away. His information was ever most reliable, and it was freely given. But even he could not say what might have been done, during those four months of Native occupation; what open streets might have been turned into blind alleys—what houses might have been raised for better command of observation and of fire—what spaces might have been cleared, what batteries erected, in prospect of the inevitable day of assault. We knew only that the enemy relied not on their moral, but on their material resources—not on the number and

* Hear Baird Smith himself on the subject: "I mentioned to you in a former letter that I had been personally familiar with the localities about Delhi for fully sixteen years. Two of the canals under my charge terminate there, on flowing through the heart of the city and throwing out branches in different directions through Delhi. In connexion with this work different plans of improvement or extension had been submitted to me and I made it part of my duty to examine the localities carefully. It was only in the month of September preceding the mutiny that I spent ten days at Delhi, and almost every day was occupied in examining parts of the city. My camp was pitched upon the ground we carried our operations over, and on the whole I had, before I joined the force at all, a tolerably minute knowledge of the important features of the ground both inside and outside the place."—*Letter to General Lefroy, MS.*

† Generally known and described as Sir Theophilus. Theophilus was a family name borne also by Sir Charles and Sir Thomas.

strength of their men, but on the number and strength of their houses. Wilson saw that the crowning victory was to be gained only by overcoming these material resources. His columns had to fight their way to the Palace, to plant the British Standard on its walls, and to secure the person of the King. He knew that our troops had no appetite for street fighting, and he had a causeless lack of confidence in the officers and men of his Force. What wonder then that broken in body and in spirit, by the toil and exposure of months and the ever-present, wearing sense of the responsiblility that lay upon him, he should have shuddered, as he looked down, through the grey dawn of that September morning, on the great city which lay before him; and that thinking of the paucity of troops told off for the assault and the scarcity of available fighting men left for the protection of his Camp on the Ridge, he should have painfully doubted the success of the enterprise on which he was launched.*

1857. Sept. 14.

General design of the assault.

The general design of the attack was this: the Infantry, divided into four columns and a column of Reserve, each guided by Engineer officers,† were to cross the ditch at different points by the aid of scaling ladders, to clear the outer defences of the city, taking possession of all bastions, guns, and gateways, and establishing defensible posts. This having been accomplished, it was to be left to the

* I find in the Laureate's last work, "Queen Mary," the following words, much to my purpose:

"Stupid soldiers oft are bold.
Poor lads, they see not what the general sees,
A risk of utter ruin."

† Nicholson had recommended that two or three Artillery officers, with some gunners, should accompany each of the leading columns to work the captured guns (*MS. Mem.*). The suggestion appears to have been a good one, and it was turned to account.

1857. Sept. 14. discretion of commanding officers, under the general direction of Nicholson, to determine whether, "dependent upon the circumstances of the moment, and the resistance of force," it would be advisable to direct the columns to clear the streets of the city in their front and vicinity, or to wait for the arrival of Artillery to aid them. The roads to the Palace and Selim-Ghur having been rendered practicable, a vigorous bombardment of those places was to be undertaken with the least possible delay, every available mortar being conveyed into the city and placed in the Magazine or other suitable positions.* It was impossible to calculate the amount of resistance except upon the spot, so no one could say how much time it would occupy to clear the inner defences of the city, the streets and squares, and covered buildings, and to bombard the Palace of the Moguls. But it was the general conception that all this might be accomplished, and the person of the King secured, within three or four days from the time of our first delivery of the assault. It was thought, however, that much might be done on the first day; as the enemy, panic-struck and confused, dreading the terrible retribution which would descend upon them, might betake themselves to sudden flight, and clear the way for the advance of the English. Baird Smith's maps had indicated the points within the city at which the several columns, after clearing the outer defences, were to take post; and the Delhi Gate, beyond the Palace, was assigned to the First Column. It will appear, as the narrative advances, how erroneous was this forecast.

The assault commenced. It was a fine still morning. As day broke and the columns took up their positions, awaiting the ap-

* MS. Memorandum in handwriting of General Wilson.

pointed signal, the heavy guns were still thundering at the defences, keeping down the enemy's fire, and enlarging the breaches for our entrance. Nicholson's column was on the left of the Koodsea Bagh. Jones, with the Second Column, was a little space to Nicholson's left. These two formed the Left Attack. Some way to the right on the road leading towards the Cashmere Gate was Campbell with the Third Column; and the Reserve were somewhat behind them. Eager was every man for the signal—the sight of the Sixtieth Rifles rushing to the front, and the sound of their bugle-call. For fast poured the shot from the ramparts of the enemy, and our people of the leading columns were ordered to lie down on the ground and wait. When the time had come for the advance, Nicholson, who directed the general attack, went over to Jones, and, placing his arm on the Brigadier's shoulder in token of comradeship, asked him if he was ready to move. Having received a prompt answer in the affirmative, he rejoined his own column. Then the order was given, and the voice of our heavy guns, which had been roaring at their loudest, suddenly dropped into silence; the Rifles sounded the advance; the regiments started up, and with a cry of exultation surged onward, and, in the teeth of a heavy fire from the enemy's works, steadily went up the slope of the glacis.

1857. Sept. 14.

The Second Column.

Whilst the First Column were thus establishing themselves, the Second under Brigadier Jones of the Queen's Sixty-first were doing their work gallantly and well. The fire of the enemy fell heavily upon them as they ascended the glacis, and the slaughter was terrible among the brave fellows of the ladder party, guided by the Engineers Greathed and Hovenden, who were the first to fall, wounded but not

1857. Sept 14. mortally, beneath the pitiless storm of the insurgents.* The column was divided into three sections. Colonel Greathed, of the Eighth Foot, commanded the first section, of which his splendid regiment formed the principal part. Captain Boyd was at the head of the second; and Brigadier Jones brought up the Reserve. The stormers carrying the ladders were led by Captain George Baynes and Lieutenant Metje of the Eighth. When the signal was given for the advance they rushed forward from a covert of rose-bushes, behind which they had been partially hidden from the sight of the insurgents, who had gathered more thickly on the walls and were ready to sweep us down as we advanced. And awfully they did their work. The Grenadiers of the Eighth went forward manfully with the ladders on their shoulders, but so encumbered could not fire a shot; and they had no covering party.† Thus exposed naked to the fierce fire of the enemy, they fell fast upon the slope of the glacis or the edge of the ditch. One volley brought down five of our ladder-men. When Metje and some of his followers picked up the ladders and went forward they also were struck down and disabled. So fearful, indeed, was the carnage that when Baynes found himself opposite the Water Bastion, the seventy-five men who had started with

* Welby Greathed, when wounded, hid himself among the rose-bushes that his brother might not see him.

† There was a sad mistake about this. One of the leading officers of the column thus explains it. "The supporting party of the Second Bengal Fusiliers instead of following the leading stormers to the left towards the Water Bastion, had gone straight over the breach in the Curtain. This was the result of the divided command in the storming arising from a mixture of regiments. Thus the storming party was left without any support, and their situation would have been very critical, if the company of the Fifty-second Light Infantry, which was sent by Colonel George Campbell to clear his left flank, after he had got into the town, had not cleared the bastion of its defenders, and allowed the remnant of the Eighth stormers to make their way in."—*MS. Memorandum.*

him on their perilous mission were reduced to only 1857.
twenty-five. For two days these twenty-five men, Sept. 14.
without a commissioned officer—for Metje had been carried wounded to the rear and Baynes had been disabled by sharp sickness—held their position in the Water Bastion under Sergeant Walker, and did excellent service.

The escalade.

Then came the difficulties of the escalade. On the crest of the glacis our men were falling fast. So furious was the fire of the enemy, and so heavy the shower of stones and bricks from the crumbling walls, which the maddened insurgents poured upon us, that it was difficult, for a little time, to plant the ladders in the ditch so as to ascend the scarp on the other side. Medley of the Engineers, who led the ladder party of the First Column, received a ball in the fleshy part of the arm. Fortunately the bone escaped; and his brave heart would not suffer him to halt in his work for mere bodily pain, however acute. He went on with the storming party. Two or three ladders, after this brief check, were thrown down into the ditch, and presently the wall beneath the breach was gallantly escaladed. The column was divided into two sections. One composed mainly of the Bengal Fusiliers under Jacob, was personally commanded by Nicholson himself. The other, of which the Seventy-fifth Queen's were the chief components, was led by Colonel Herbert of that regiment. Determined that his leadership should be not a name, but a fact, Nicholson went on in advance of his men, followed by Jacob and Greville of the Fusiliers, and was the first to mount the wall. The other section of the column pushed on with like eagerness. Lieutenant Fitzgerald, of the Seventy-fifth, was the first to ascend, but he was shot

1857. Sept. 14. down, in the moment of victory, and died the hero's death at the head of his men. Others not less gallant and, often, not more fortunate, took his place; and soon both sections of the First Column had gained the ramparts, carried the breach near the Cashmere Bastion, and taken up their position at the Main Guard.

Advance of the Second Column.

The main body of the Second Column went steadily on, and having made good its entrance by the breach in the Cashmere Curtain, went forward, at the double, across the open space, inside the Cashmere Bastion, where they inclined to their Right. Then seeing some men rushing into the city on his Left, Jones cried out to them to "bear away to the right along the ramparts." They were at that time running at the topmost of their speed, the men with Jones being partly of Nicholson's column and partly of his own. As they were proceeding along the road leading to the Caubul Gate, the Brigadier's bugler cried out that the enemy were firing down the streets. This fire was speedily answered, and the insurgents left remaining on the ramparts ran like hares before us and so escaped the fire of our eager soldiery. In the Moree Bastion the gunners made bold resistance; standing to their guns with a gallantry worthy of the great school in which they had been taught. But our English Infantry went in amongst them, bayoneted them as they stood, and cast them dead or dying from the ramparts into the ditch below. Then our people leapt up exultingly on the parapet of the Moree Bastion—that grand defence of the enemy, from which for months an unceasing shower of shot had been poured in upon the besiegers; and waved their caps rejoicingly to their comrades on the Ridge.

Thence they had a prevision of what was going on elsewhere. They saw the Sepoys in their white dresses, huddling on confusedly from Kishengunje, and they saw the Cavalry and Horse Artillery forming up, under Hope Grant, and sustaining a heavy fire from the insurgents in the suburbs. The column then advanced to the Caubul Gate, where Jones having ascended to the summit of it, ordered a party of his men to fire down the streets on each side of the Canal. The order was promptly obeyed, and one of the enemy's deserted guns was turned on the Lahore Gate, from which the enemy had been keeping up a galling fire, whilst the houses adjacent to the Caubul Gate and along both sides of the Canal, were occupied by our own people. The Caubul Gate was now secure, and it remained for us only to plant the British flag on the summit of it. This was done under Jones's orders, by a private of the Sixty-first, whom he rewarded in the presence of his comrades.* The regimental bugle-calls were then sounded; the different corps were gathered together; and men shook hands with and congratulated each other and somewhat marvelled that any were alive.

1857. Sept. 14.

* Unpublished letter from Major-General Jones to Sir Archdale Wilson, March, 1864. This was written, at the suggestion of Colonel (now Sir Edward) Greathed, in consequence of an error in Wilson's Delhi despatch, in which he says: "The firm establishment of the Reserve rendering the assaulting columns free to act in advance, Brigadier-General Nicholson, supported by Brigadier Jones, swept the ramparts of the place from the Cashmere to the Caubul Gates, occupying the bastions and defences, capturing the guns and driving the enemy before him." Wilson sent the letter to me (for which purpose, indeed, it was written) and confirmed the truth of it. Greathed, who commanded the Eighth under Jones, wrote to the latter: "As I was close to you from the time we got up to the top of the breach together, until you had finally caused the troops to re-form and rest at the Caubul Gate, I am perfectly aware that the clearing of the walls, ramparts, and bastions was performed solely under your orders, and that Nicholson did not join us until some time after at the Caubul Gate, when the work had been accomplished."

1857. Sept. 14. The light of these first congratulations was soon darkened by the gloomy thought of their diminished ranks. They had done their work nobly and well; but how many brave men and good soldiers had been left, dead or dying behind them; how many friends and comrades had been lost to them since the dram had been served out in the early morning. The enemy fought well to the last, and the bloody instructions which we had taught, were returning to plague the inventors. Alas! for our shattered columns.

It was not until after the flag had been planted on the Caubul Gate that Nicholson joined the Second Column. He had diverged from the intended line of advance to suppress a brisk fire of musketry, from some houses on his left flank, between the Cashmere and the Moree Bastions, which was severely harassing his people. Having turned aside for the reason stated, as men must at times under heavy pressure of circumstances, and entered the town, he did not meet Jones at the Caubul Gate until more than an hour after the Second Column had reached it. The enemy then observing our inactivity, regained somewhat of their courage and began to pour in a sharp fire of musketry and cannon-shot.* The men of the Second Column were then resting from their work. Misunderstanding the quietude of their demeanour, the young Brigadier-General exclaimed, "The men are not in hand." Upon this Greathed fired up and

* "The Lahore Bastion kept up a steady fire on us from a twelve-pounder, which we could not silence, and a couple of guns were brought to bear on us from a side street; but fourteen men of the Seventy-fifth ran down and took one of them; the other was taken away, and we received no further molestation from that quarter. A gun was also brought to bear upon us from the end of the long straight street which led down directly to our position at the Caubul Gate; and this pelted us throughout the day with round shot and grape. In short our position was a ticklish one."—*MS. Memorandum by an Officer of the Eighth Foot.*

said, "What do you want done? Tell me and I'll soon show you that they are in hand." Nicholson then, whose words had conveyed a meaning beyond what he had probably intended, made some wise suggestions as to the positions of the enemy and the disposition of our troops and then went back to join the First Column. Jones had received orders to remain at the Caubul Gate until he might hear tidings of the fall of the Jumma Musjid; so he got his men well lodged in houses commanding the approaches and waited for the signal to advance.

1857. Sept. 14

Fall of Nicholson.

Meanwhile, a sad misadventure was befalling us in the First Column. Still annoyed by the fire from the Lahore Gate, Nicholson determined to take it, and got together a number of men of different regiments to follow him on this enterprise. It has been said that there were officers without their men and men without their officers, so that they were a "mere rabble." It was a hazardous duty that loomed before them; for the way from the Caubul to the Lahore Gate lay through a narrow lane swept by artillery and commanded by houses occupied by the enemy. If there is one thing to dishearten the British soldier more than all else it is the thought of street-fighting. He can receive a charge of Cavalry with a loud hurrah. He can march steadily on the enemy's blazing batteries and scale their ramparts, or enter the breaches in their walls, as though it were mere play-work. But he is not used to street-fighting. He does not know what barricades may have been suddenly thrown up; he does not know what masked batteries may be erected: and he fancies that every house is full of a hostile soldiery, and that every window is an embrasure, at which a skilled marksman may be placed, and with aim steadied by the sense of his own security.

1857. Sept. 14. And so it was now. Nicholson's column having entered the outskirts of the city, found itself in a long narrow lane lined with marksmen on both sides, and commanded by some more distant positions of the enemy. It was soon obvious that some of the enemy's guns had been brought forward to scatter confusion in our ranks, and, in our helplessness, to send back the advanced columns to the Ridge. The men were falling fast. Major George Jacob of the First Fusiliers, an officer of distinguished gallantry, received his death-wound; but refused to be carried to the rear.* Captain Greville and Lieutenant Speke, doing duty with the Fusiliers, were struck down,† and other officers fell disabled and helpless under the enemy's fire. Then there was something of a waver—a pause. The British soldier found himself in the position which he most hated. It was not fair fighting. He was in a trap. Nicholson saw it all—saw what was depressing the hearts and checking the onward movement of our fighting men. So he drew himself up to his full height, and with his sword raised high above his head, called upon his men to follow him. To some at least of the defenders of Delhi, that face and figure must have been familiar. Others saw a man of commanding presence, whose position at the head of the column, and whose gestures of command, indicated that he was a great

* See a very interesting letter from an officer of the regiment, quoted in Hodson's "Twelve Years of a Soldier's Life": "Again the word was forward, and leading on the men, my glorious friend George Jacob was mortally wounded; he, poor fellow, was shot in the thigh, and died that night. As he lay writhing in agony on the ground, unable to stand, two or three men went to take him to the rear, but a sense of duty was superior to bodily pain, and he refused their aid, desiring them to go and take the guns."

† The writer above quoted says of Speke that he was "gentle everywhere but in the field." Speke never recovered from his wounds. Greville happily was spared.

chief. His lofty stature rendered him so conspicuous, that if he had been a private soldier, some rifleman at a window or on a housetop would have taken deadly aim at him, and he would have sent one more hated Feringhee to his account. But it was not a single life that he took; it was the life of a whole army. 1857. Sept. 14.

Nicholson was shot through the body. He knew at once that he had received his death-wound; but he begged that he might not be carried back to Camp until the capture of Delhi were secure. This, however, was impossible, and he was gently removed to the Hospital on the Ridge. The surgeons who attended him were doubtful of the final issue, for the ball had not touched the lungs. But he had got the death-chill upon him—the worst sign of all; and there was really no hope for him. He could not help chafing, too, under the miserable infliction which had taken him away in the very hour of the grand fulfilment of his hopes, and rendered him helpless as a child. It was a sad addition to his own sufferings to know that his brother, Charles Nicholson, who had commanded the Punjabees, in the First Column, had been brought into Camp with a shattered arm, and that nothing but amputation could save him. He was a fine gallant soldier of high promise, but his lofty stature had made him a sure mark for the enemy, and the promise could never be fulfilled.*

The explosion of the Cashmere Gate.

It was the apportioned duty of the Third Column to enter the city through the Cashmere Gate; and

* Charles Nicholson survived the operation, but he never altogether recovered from the effects of his wounds, and soon passed away. Sir Hope Grant speaks of him as one of three young officers worthy of especial mention—Probyn, Watson, and Nicholson.

1857. Sept. 14. to this end a party of Engineers was told off to blow in the gate with powder-bags. The officers appointed for the performance of this hazardous duty were Lieutenants Home and Salkeld. The non-commissioned officers were Sergeants Carmichael, Burgess, and Smith. With them went a party of Native Sappers. It was broad daylight when they started. Leaving Ludlow Castle at the double, headed by a party of the Sixtieth Rifles, they reached the road leading to the Customs House, where they opened out: the Sappers under Lieutenant Home, and the carrying party with the powder-bags under Lieutenant Salkeld — Sergeant Smith bringing up the rear. Forward they went, at first unseen by the enemy, straight upon the Cashmere Gate, followed by the Sixtieth Rifles and the other components of the column under Colonel Campbell, awaiting the explosion and prepared for the deadly work before them. Home, with his bugler, was first down into the ditch. The danger of the enterprise was then upon them. The designs of the exploding party had been perceived by the enemy; and as they crossed over the broken drawbridge leading from the outer to the inner gate a brisk shower of musketry was poured upon them. But they made good their hazardous march to the point at which the explosion was to be effected. Many were the brilliant episodes of adventure which illustrated the siege of Delhi; but not one more heroic than this. Home had planted his bag, but on Carmichael advancing with his powder on his shoulder, he was shot down by a death-dealing musket-ball. Smith then went forward and placed his dying comrade's bag in position, having also placed his own, and prepared the fuzes for ignition. Salkeld stood ready with a slow match* in his hand, but as he was lighting it, he was struck down; a bullet in his arm and another in his leg had sent their death-messages to him. In falling, he held out the match and called on Smith to take it. Burgess, who stood nearest to Salkeld, took the match but could not ignite the charge. Smith then was in the act of giving him a box of lucifer-matches, when Burgess was shot down by a bullet through the body. Smith was now alone, or thought he was alone, for he had lost sight of Home for some time. The moment was a critical one; but he had succeeded in striking a light and was applying it, when a portfire, which it was thought had been extinguished, went off in his face. There was a confusing fog of smoke and dust as he scrambled down into the ditch, and presently a roar and a crash, significant of a deed accomplished. The gate had been shattered by the explosion, but not with the destructive effect that had been anticipated by the assailants or by those from whom the design had emanated. It was enough, however, for the Third Column, which awaited this signal to advance, and the stirring sounds of the bugle sent them forward to do their work, the Rifles leading the way.† 1857. Sept. 14.

Sliding down into the ditch, his back to the wall, and groping his way amidst the obscuring dust and

* Most accounts state that it was a portfire. It was really a slow-match as stated in the text.

† Lieutenant Medley writes:—"The bugle sounded the advance, and then with a loud cheer the Fifty-second charged through the broken gateway." I wish I could accept this statement unreservedly. But I am bound to add that Sergeant Smith, in an unpublished memorandum given in the Appendix, says: "They did not go fast. Their bugler had sounded fifty times at least, and some ten minutes elapsed before any one came." It was not only known at Head-Quarters, but throughout the army, that there had been some backwardness.

1857. Sept. 14. the masses of falling masonry, Smith placed his hand on some one whom he could not discern and cried out, asking "Who are you?" He was answered by Lieutenant Home, who said he was unhurt. When the dust had somewhat cleared away they went together to minister to Salkeld; but as there was a fire of musketry then bearing upon them, the gallant sergeant told his lieutenant not to expose himself, as he would remain behind to tend the wounded. Having full confidence in Smith and being all eagerness to go forward, Home, after giving some brandy from his flask to Salkeld and Burgess, joined the column and went ahead. Salkeld at first refused to be moved; so Smith and the bugler, who had remained with him, placed the dying officer's head upon a powder-bag and bound up his wounds, as best they could, with improvised bandages torn from a puggery. Smith then went to the rear to obtain some stretchers, and not without threats and the display of a drawn sword succeeded in obtaining the use of two, a third having been taken from him by an officer of the Rifles. Upon one of these Salkeld, now too feeble to resist, was placed, and sent to Camp under charge of the bugler, with strict injunctions not to leave him until he should have seen the wounded man in the hands of a surgeon. But human skill could do nothing for him, and after lingering for a few days the fine young soldier was laid in the grave. Burgess was placed upon the other stretcher and sent under care of a Naick to the hospital, but they had not proceeded far before he died. For these achievements Home, Salkeld, Smith, and the Bugler Hawthorne were promptly rewarded by General Wilson with the Victoria Cross. Neither of the two gallant subalterns lived long to enjoy their honours. Salkeld had passed away from the scene of mortal strife, before Home, on the 1st of October, was killed by the premature springing of a mine, after the capture of the fort of Malagurh. And the explosion well-nigh cost us, in the sequel, another life, which would have been greatly mourned. George Chesney, who was Brigade-Major of Engineers, and one of the most promising of the younger officers of that noble Engineer Corps,* went, after the explosion, with a party of Sappers to restore the broken bridge, of which mention has before been made. Whilst making for the gate, a heavy shell from one of the enemy's batteries at Kishengunje burst in the air, some twenty yards off, severely wounding Chesney, who received a shrapnel bullet through his right side and in his arm.† Renny of the Artillery, whose Native troop had withstood all trials and temptations and shone forth with conspicuous loyalty from first to last,‡ met the Engineer as he was returning. Then he and Fulton of the Artillery finding that the wounded man with some assistance could walk, helped him on to Ludlow Castle, whence he was conveyed to Camp, and by the skill and care of the surgeons saved to do good service to the State.

1857. Sept. 14.

The Third Column.

Having carried the Cashmere Gate, Campbell's

* Now Lieutenant-Colonel Chesney, President of the Engineering College at Cooper's Hill.

† It is stated in MS. accounts that some men of the party were killed. I believe that this was a mistake. Chesney was in advance of his party when the shell burst.

‡ In pursuance of the principle and practice of the time, the guns were taken away from Renny's troop and restored after the fall of Delhi. The gunners were all Hindostanees, but they were as ready to fight against the Poorbeah rebels as if the enemy had been of a different colour and a different race. It is a remarkable illustration of the scant justice done to the Artillery, that no mention was made of Renny's troop in any of the despatches.

1857. Sept. 14. column, followed by the Reserve, streamed onward towards the city. It was a grand sight to see their compact masses, moving forward, like hounds in the hunting-field, and carrying everything before them.* The point to be gained was the Jumma Musjid, which Campbell had been commissioned to take. The capture of this place was to have been the signal for the further advance of the First and Second Columns. But it was a duty of far more difficult accomplishment than it had been thought to be. Campbell, a right-good soldier, intrepid and well-skilled, had the inestimable advantage of the personal guidance of Sir John Metcalfe, who knew neither fear nor pity and was ever eager to push forward in the great work of retribution. He had the plan of the city with all its turns and windings at his fingers' ends; and now he knew well how to lead the column, by a devious way, so as to encounter little opposition on the road. It passed on unharmed until the great street of the Chandna Chouk was reached and the Kotwallee seized by our people. Then fast fell the fire of the insurgents upon them, and it was found impossible to take the Jumma Musjid without such heavy loss as we could ill endure; so the column fell back to the vicinity of the Church and joined the Reserve, which had followed it through the Cashmere Gate and was pressing forward into the heart of the city.

The Fourth Column. Up to this time, if the success of our operations had not been complete, there had been no disastrous

* An officer of the Second Column, who saw the advance says: "The sight at this moment was beautiful. We could see the two columns on our right up the breach and the Cashmere Bastion; like a swarm of bees, or rather like the horses of the Sun all abreast—then like hounds toppi g the fence into a gorse cover they disappeared into the town."—*MS. Journal.*

failure. But the fortune of war was now turning against us on the Right, in a manner little expected. The Fourth Column, commanded by Major Charles Reid, whose gallant and most serviceable exploits in command of the important position at Hindoo Rao's house have been already narrated in this work, was struggling with unforeseen difficulties. It was to have cleared the suburb of Kishengunje and entered the city by the Lahore Gate.* It was an enterprise of no little difficulty and danger. But he had a detachment of the Sixtieth Rifles; a detachment also of the Sixty First and of the Bengal Fusiliers. He had some of Daly's Guides, and he had great reliance on his little Goorkahs. Their indomitable spirit was something beautiful to behold. They had expended themselves so freely, during months of fearless fighting, at the post which they never quitted, that there were but few efficient men, at Hindoo Rao's, on the eve of the assault. The improvised hospital in the back rooms of the building was full of sick and wounded, and all who could move were eager to take part in the coming assault. When Reid went in amongst them, lying, as they were, on the floor, for there were no cots for them, and told them what was to be done on the morrow, sorrowfully adding that he could muster scarcely a hundred of his Goorkahs for service, all sprung up as if the word of command had been given to them and volunteered to

1857. Sept. 14.

* In a letter to the Reverend Mr. Rotton, Chaplain and Historian, Reid says that he was to have entered the city by the *Caubul* Gate. But Norman, who was Deputy-Adjutant-General, has recorded that the Fourth Column was to enter by the Lahore Gate (*ut supra*, 583). The two statements are not irreconcilable. The fact appears to be that the enemy held the Lahore Gate in force and were not disposed to evacuate it. It would have been a dangerous experiment for Reid, weakened by much fighting in the suburbs, to attempt to carry it.

1857. Sept. 14. follow him into the field. Some were wholly unfit for such rough work; but of the hundred and fifty men, who had been reported ineffective, ninety-five mustered for active service on the morning of the assault. So Reid's heart was gladdened by the thought that he was taking with him two hundred of the sturdy little Goorkahs who had clung to him so nobly from the first.

The Jummoo troops. At five o'clock the column was mustered and moved forwards in high spirits. Unfortunately, however, it was overweighted with Jummoo troops. John Lawrence had said that they might be trusted, and in ordinary circumstances they might have been. But their ways were not as our ways; and the great principle of cohesiveness was unknown to them. The original conception of the General had been that this Contingent might act independently, as a substantive force, carrying the Eed Gate and suburb of Paharunpore and spiking the enemy's guns in position there, whilst Reid with his picket was to support this attack, after leaving a sufficient number of men for the defence of Hindoo Rao's house. But Baird Smith saw at once the error of this and asked, "Is the Jummoo Contingent to make this attack as a Principal and not as an Auxiliary Force? It consists of untried troops with no interest in our cause. It is not a Native fashion to take guns, and I greatly fear the results. If Major Reid leads and the Jummoo troops support the attack, I should expect it to be quite successful."* The good sense of the General yielded to this suggestion and the original programme was reversed. But even in this secondary position our allies soon demonstrated their deficiency in those

* Autograph notes by General Wilson and Colonel Baird Smith.

very qualities which we most needed in such a conjuncture. There was a hitch. Reid had been promised three guns, but when the time came there were only gunners enough to man one of them. He was not now going in defiance of the principles of warfare to take a single gun into action, so he ordered the Artillery officer to make inquiries and to endeavour to obtain more gunners. Whilst he was awaiting the result he heard musketry fire to the right, and learnt that the Jummoo troops, on their way down from Camp, had become engaged with the enemy. Any further delay then would have been hazardous in the extreme. So Reid determined to advance without the promised artillery. 1857. Sept. 14.

The enemy had prepared themselves for his reception. When within a short distance from the canal bridge, Reid discovered that the insurgents had erected a breastwork across the road and another running parallel to it. Trained in our English schools of discipline, they knew well the advantage of reserving their fire; so they did not open upon us until our people were within fifty yards of their cover, when they poured in a heavy well-directed volley of musketry from the foremost breastwork. Thus assailed, Reid at once sent forward the British Riflemen and the Sepoys of the Sirmoor Battalion, who headed his column, and dislodged the mutineers from the breastwork and drove them into the road. For some time the enemy stood irresolute, uncertain of the next movement, seemingly hesitating as to whether they should fall back on the further breastwork or should attack our Jummoo allies on the right. Then was seen the result of the miserable accident or mismanagement that had caused the column to go forward without guns. If Reid had been able to open upon the

Confusion of Fourth Column.

1857. Sept. 14. enemy with grape from the Horse Artillery pieces, he could have cleared the road at once and would have hurled back the reinforcements which were pressing onwards to the aid of their comrades. As it was, he presently found himself opposed to some fifteen thousand men, of all kinds, surging on to overwhelm him. In the crisis, which then threatened the gallant leader of the Fourth Column, Reid was making his dispositions, firstly for a false attack upon the enemy, in the front of the Kishengunje batteries, and secondly, for a real one, in front, flank, and rear, when he was smitten down by a bullet, which struck him on his head, and incapacitated him from further command. The officer next in rank was Major Lawrence, who had brought down the Jummoo troops, ten days before, to Delhi. As Reid was being carried to the rear, he met the Punjabee officer, made over the command to him, and explained his plan of attack. "Up to this time," he wrote afterwards, "all was going on admirably; the troops were steady and well in hand, and I made sure of success. I was not a little surprised to hear, about an hour afterwards, that the columns had retreated—that the Jummoo troops had lost their guns and were flying back to Camp."*

* Norman says that "the Cashmere Contingent (Jummoo troops) were so sharply attacked by the insurgents, who were in great force, that, after losing a great number of men, and four guns, they were completely defeated and fell back to Camp. Major Reid's column met with the most strenuous opposition, greatly increased, doubtless, by the failure of the Cashmere Contingent, and the enemy were so numerous and so strongly posted, that after the loss of many men and officers, the Commander, Major Reid, having been carried away severely wounded, Captain Muter, Sixtieth Rifles, the next senior officer, judiciously withdrew the troops to their former post at Hindoo Rao's and the Subzemundee." The variance between these two statements is obvious. It may, perhaps, in some measure, be explained by the fact that Major Lawrence came to Delhi, not in a military but in a political capacity. I find no mention of this affair in Mrs. Muter's interesting volumes.

But although this was a disastrous failure, it was not an ignominious one. There was no better soldier —no braver gentleman, in all the Camp than Charles Reid. Nothing could have been more skilfully devised than his plan of attack, which was unhappily only half developed. Circumstances were against him. He had failed to obtain the light field-pieces, which would have so greatly promoted his success; he had been grievously thwarted by the eccentricities of his Cashmere Allies; and the enemy were not only mighty in numbers but were posted so strongly and so judiciously as to have all the advantages of ground on their side. But our own troops —European and Native—the European detachments, the Goorkahs, and the Guides fought splendidly; and there was more than one of those acts of heroic personal enterprise, which are seldom wanting in such episodes as this, to lighten up the surrounding darkness. One of these incidents, a mournful one, may be narrated here. A party of the enemy sheltered by a breastwork were firing heavily upon our people, when some officers with a handful of men made a rush upon the work to take it. Foremost of these was young Murray of the Guides,* who had been wounded in June and July, who had gone to the Hills to recruit and had returned to Delhi a few days before the assault. Speeding onward with impulsive bravery, the grim message of death met him, in the pride of his youth and the flush of his daring. He was shot through the chest and fell dead upon the field. Almost at the same moment, Captain M'Barnett, attached to the Fusiliers, a good officer,

1857. Sept. 14. Conduct of the troops.

* The Commandant of this distinguished corps, Major Henry Daly, was then at Hindoo Rao's recovering from his wounds He was able to take charge of the Picket for a time, though, as he said, able neither to ride nor to run.

1857. Sept. 14.

ever eager for work, was shot down never to rise* again on this side of the grave—Altogether the loss on our side was heavy. Europeans, Guides, and Goorkahs all suffered severely The sturdy little fellows of the Sirmoor Battalion left forty of their comrades behind them.

Gallantry of the enemy.

The enemy fought well—never better than on this occasion. They were in truth no contemptible opponents. Our finest soldiers are ever the most prompt to acknowledge the merits of their adversaries. On that morning of the 14th of September two of our greatest warriors, crippled in previous fights, and all-eager for the battle, were condemned to be on-lookers only in this momentous crisis. Neville Chamberlain and Henry Daly were at Hindoo Rao's house. Both had carried their wounds thither, thinking that they might be of more service to the State than they could possibly be in Camp. Day had not broken, when Chamberlain went down to the famous Picket to see Reid's column started and to be a present help, if any time of trouble should come. When the operations against the enemy in the suburbs were fairly commenced it was broad daylight. Chamberlain, Daly, and Khan Singh, Rhosa,† went to the top of Hindoo Rao's house and watched the progress of the conflict. From this elevated position a stirring scene was visible below in the early daylight; and Chamberlain, whose quick soldierly eye took in all the details of the struggle below, could not but admire the dashing manner in which the Native officers rode in among the ranks of the mutineers, urging them and leading them on to the battle against the British and

* Captain M'Barnett was an officer of the Fifty-fifth Native Infantry.

† This man was a Sikh chief, who had fought against us at Chillianwallah. He offered his services to us, when the mutiny broke out, and went to Delhi with Daly and the Guides.

the Jummoo troops. Nor was his admiration, in this conjuncture, without some feeling of anxiety. For it seemed at one time that the enemy might break through our Subzee-mundee defences, carry the undefended battery below Hindoo Rao's house, and take possession of the post itself, with its Hospital and its Magazine. So critical, indeed, was the aspect of affairs that Chamberlain summoned the Native guard to the roof of the house, that it might better defend the entrance to the Magazine. And the three wounded officers prepared to take post with muskets in their hands. Happily Reid's people held on, when they reached the Subzee-mundee line of defences and the present danger was averted; so Chamberlain and Daly descended from their plateau and strenuously exerted themselves to keep order among the excited assembly of mixed races below.* It is not questioned that about this time, our position on the Right was in great danger. Reinforcements of any sufficient strength could not be sent from the Camp,† and the Picket at Hindoo Rao's was itself called upon to afford assistance to others in this emergency. It was plain that we had received a severe check, which might have been turned to terrible account against us, and would have been, but for an incident which must now be narrated in detail.

1857. Sept. 14. Chamberlain and Daly.

* Among the troops at Hindoo Rao's house were a part of the Kumaon Battalion. They were in a somewhat disorderly state, when Chamberlain, reproving them for their noise and confusion, addressed them as a *Pultun* (regiment) and called forth an indignant, half-insolent rejoinder: "We are not a regiment, but a battalion." Chamberlain's answer was prompt and to the point: "Then show yourselves worthy of the distinction." Order was at once restored.

† I believe that the Beloochee regiment were first to arrive. They were steadfast in their loyalty and fought well. Captain Bannerman was killed.

1857. Sept. 14. The Cavalry Brigade.

The siege of a fortified city rarely affords much opportunity for a display of the great qualities of the Cavalry branch of an army. It is mainly the work of Engineers, Artillery, and Infantry. But when a city cannot be invested, and therefore the enemy are not shut up within the walls—when, as in this case, they can come out at one end of the place to fight, and go out at the other to escape, the mounted branch may do excellent service.* Seeing clearly the need of our troopers, especially for the protection and support of Reid's column, Wilson had called upon Hope Grant; and Grant, than whom there was no better soldier in Camp, eagerly donned his sabre and his spurs and prepared himself for the battle. The Brigadier took with him two hundred men of the Ninth Lancers, and four hundred Sikh horsemen, and awaited orders from the General. The orders soon came, and Grant marched his men down to a position under the walls of the city, covering the whole of our batteries, which before had been unprotected. At this time the enemy at Kishengunje had just defeated Reid's column, and elated with success were raging furiously against us. Availing themselves of the cover afforded by numerous houses and gardens in the vicinity, they poured

* There was a skirmish on the 11th, in which the Punjab Horse greatly distinguished themselves. The enemy's Cavalry in the Kishengunje suburbs had suddenly attacked one of our pickets; seeing this, Watson, the heroic commander of the First Punjab Cavalry, turned out at once, with his troopers and a few of the Second, and went at the insurgents at "tip-top speed." It was a wild helter-skelter affair; but the enemy could not stand the rush of our horsemen. Some forty of them were left dead on the field. Our own loss was slight, but Watson himself encountering one of the enemy's most intrepid swordsmen in hand-to-hand fight, received a swashing sabre-cut on the head, which glanced off his helmet, and clove his left cheek and upper lip. He was also slightly cut on the shoulder. But he was not a man to take heed of anything much less than a death-wound; so he had his face sewn up, and went about his work as before. The scar will go with him to the grave.

in a brisk shower of musketry upon our line of Cavalry and strove mightily to dislodge us. So Tombs's troop of Horse Artillery was ordered up, to open fire on these mischievous insurgents. This was done, promptly and well, at a range of two hundred yards, and the occupants of the sheltering houses were compelled to fall back. But there was a still more dangerous enemy. The Lahore Gate, which had been a source of such grievous trouble to our Infantry, was still untaken. So the enemy, at a distance of some five hundred yards, turned a twenty-four-pound gun, charged with grape, upon our horsemen, and soon had cause to exult in their success.* 1857. Sept. 14.

It must have been a grand sight then to have seen these troopers and their officers, drawn up in battle array, stern and immovable, to face the deadly fire of the enemy. There they sate, firm in their saddles, "ghastly motionless as if they slept," whilst the unerring grape-shot streamed upon them and made dreadful openings in their ranks. There was scarcely a man, who had not caught the noble spirit of their commanders, Hope Grant, Drysdale of the Lancers,† Tombs of the Artillery, Watson and Probyn of the Punjab Horse. The courage of the Ninth Lancers was never surpassed. Not only were they under the immediate command of an intrepid soldier, but their own Colonel commanded the brigade. When Grant commended their sturdy gallantry under fire,

* It was at this time that Sir Hope Grant says that he saw Nicholson on the ramparts and exchanged greetings with him. "He called out to me that fighting was going on well for us in the town, and that he was on his way to attack the Lahore Gate." I am informed, however, that it was not Nicholson, but Colonel Greathed, who spoke to Hope Grant from the ramparts. Both, however, may have spoken to him.

† Captain Drysdale commanded the detachment of Lancers. Hope Grant says of him that he was "a gallant officer and a thorough Scotchman."

1857. Sept. 14 they replied that they were ready to take as much more of it as he liked. Forty-two men and six officers were struck down. Rosser of the Carabineers, who had been so eager to carry to Delhi the first tidings of the revolt at Meerut, and who now was acting as Hope Grant's aide-de-camp, fell with a bullet in his forehead, which all regarded as his death-wound. Others were slightly wounded. Eleven officers of the Lancers had their horses killed under them. Nor were the Artillery under Tombs less exposed or less steadfast under their exposure. Animated by the noble example of their commander they were equal to any daring and ready to face any danger. The Punjabees, to whom the situation was new, for they were not familiar with grape-shot, lacked nothing of the steadfastness of their white comrades, and never flinched from the merciless fire. Watson's Cavalry lost few men, for they were clothed in slate-coloured uniform, and the neutral tint was of good service to them, placed as they were between the white jackets of the Lancers and the scarlet uniform of Probyn's Horse. For two long hours the brigade stood firm as a rock, and as one after another fell riddled with grape or canister there was no wavering in the ranks. Every man pressed his knees more tightly on his saddle and took a firmer grip of his reins. There was nothing else in their demeanour to distinguish this grand scene of defiance and endurance from an ordinary Cavalry parade. I may be wrong, but I think that this Heroism of Patience is grander far than the active gallantry displayed in a perilous charge. It is far easier to rush at an enemy in the fine enthusiasm of battle, than to stand steadfast on a given spot, for an ungiven period, waiting for the order or the opportunity to move, whilst swept by the fire of a hidden enemy. It is the waiting that tries the man. And never were men more tried, or more patient under trial, than the troopers of Hope Grant's Brigade. 1857. Sept. 14

After a while the enemy's fire began to slacken. Those within the works were, perhaps, diverted by other emergencies, and those in the open were kept back by the guns of Tombs and Campbell, afterwards reinforced by Bourchier. The Brigadier had made a requisition for some infantry to aid him; but only from the Picket at Hindoo Rao's house could any footmen be obtained. A party of two hundred and eighty of the Guides and Goorkahs—staunch as Europeans—were then placed at his disposal, and his nephew, Frank Grant, brought them down to the points where they were most needed.* But there was not much for them to do. The enemy were ceasing to prevail against us, and the General gave orders conditionally to the Cavalry Brigadier to withdraw to the neighbourhood of Ludlow Castle. Grant had done a good morning's work. The presence of the Cavalry Brigade alone prevented the enemy, who had driven back the Fourth Column, from advancing along the open ground between the Ridge and the City, and taking the whole of our Left Attack in flank.

Little more could be done by Infantry or Cavalry against the enemy on that day. Our assaulting columns, though not wholly successful, had done some good work. They were much exhausted by fatigue,

* Sir Hope Grant ("Incidents in the Sepoy War") writes: "Though the officer in command of that post, Chamberlain, who had partially recovered from his wounds, was himself short of men, he placed at my disposal two hundred and eighty men of his little force."

1857. Sept. 14. The afternoon.

and much depressed by the mortality that surrounded them. They saw the dead gathered up and the dying carried off in long strings of doolies to the hospitals in the Camp. Never were our medical officers more saddened by the sights brought before them; never have they shone more brightly in all the best manifestations of professional skill and manly devotion; never have they striven more mightily in the God-like work of alleviating human suffering. The result of that morning's fighting was that sixty European officers and nearly eleven hundred men were either laid in the grave, where burial was possible, or carried disabled to the hospitals.* But among those who remained after that day's carnage, although the desire to avenge their slaughtered comrades was strong, nothing could be done, for exhaustion had disabled them; and they were not fit to undertake the perilous work of penetrating deeper into the city. It would not have been wise to attempt any further offensive operations at such a time; but on the morrow, refreshed and recruited, they might force themselves into the heart of Delhi and plant the British standard on the proud Palace of the Moguls. The Artillery, however, to whom the morning had been comparatively one of inactivity, were eager to lay their mark upon the city itself, as they had before done upon its defences. And Brind, Salt, Renny, Hamilton, and others, under the direction of Wilson, who had fixed his head-quarters in Skinner's house,† turned all

* It would be a very close approximation to the truth to say that the casualty list on the 14th was this: *Europeans*, eight officers killed, fifty-two wounded. Rank and file: one hundred and sixty-two killed and five hundred and ten wounded. *Natives*: killed, one hundred and three; wounded, three hundred and ten.

† A life-like picture of Wilson and his Staff, at this time, is given in the following extract from the Journal of an Artillery Officer: "Towards evening, Frith" (of the Artillery—Wilson's brother-in-law)

their available means to account, in shelling or battering the buildings which it was most important to take or destroy, or in endeavouring to disperse such of the enemy as were still eager to act on the offensive. 1857. Sept. 14.

To a General, strong-bodied and strong-minded in such a juncture, there would have been in the aspect of affairs which presented itself to his eyes and to his understanding, after the assaults of that memorable morning, much to cause the most profound anxiety. To Wilson, feeble as he was at that time, from circumstances already narrated, the half-success of the enterprise was disheartening in the extreme. When he rode down, with his Staff, to the city and, map in hand, learned distinctly all that had happened, his first thought was that the only hope of preserving his army from utter destruction, was to withdraw his columns to their old position on the Ridge. Baird Smith had also gone down to the city. He was at Wilson's elbow, near Skinner's house, when the General put the critical question as to what was then to be done —asking whether he thought we could hold what we

came to me and said, 'The General wishes you to fire some shells just over the top of Skinner's house (in which the General and Staff were), as the enemy had just got into the houses there close by.' I pointed out that I had no regular scales and weights and that it was a ticklish operation, because I knew not what posts were held by us beyond, in the direction of the Moree Bastion. I, therefore, went with him to Skinner's house, and in a large hall I found Johnson, Norman, Anson, and the rest of the Staff and told them I wished to speak about the order I had got. They told me that in that case I had better speak to the General myself, for they had rather not go near him, and pointed to him at the other end of the hall, where he sat balancing himself in a chair, with his face to the wall, on which his feet rested. I told him my errand and he said 'Come, and I will show you what I want, and I followed him to the flat roof of the house, where, creeping to the edge, we looked down on the houses beyond, where we could see the enemy firing at our field guns and a strong picket in the street at the gate, who even came and fired upon us. After looking at the state of affairs and hearing what I had to say, he told me I had better leave it alone; and going back to the hall resumed his old contemplative position."—*MS. Records.*

1857. Sept. 14. had taken. The answer of the Chief Engineer was prompt and decisive, "We *must* do so."* The General, who had before bowed to the decision of a man whose genius he could but recognise, although personally he disliked his "obstinacy," did not now oppose the suggestion. The Chief Engineer had taken, so far as he could take it, the responsibility on himself, and if the aspect of affairs had been still worse, he would not have shrunk from upholding the counsel, which he had tendered when he was more hopeful of immediate success. It is possible that other officers, at a later period, may have urged similar opinions upon the General. Neville Chamberlain from Hindoo Rao's house, sent down a strong appeal in favour of continued action. But it was to Baird Smith's opinion that Wilson deferred, and the merit of the "holding on" is due to the brave pertinacity of the Chief Engineer.†

Sept. 15. Danger of the liquor shops. The morrow was a miserable blank. Delhi was full of spoil—of gold and silver and precious stones and all the rich fabrics of the looms of the East. All these things had been promised to the

* I have the clearest possible proof of this in a memorandum, written for me by a Field Officer, who heard the conversation: "I got some men together," he writes, "and cleared the way for the guns to enter. General Wilson and his Staff passed through the gate soon after this. I joined them, and accompanied them to the vicinity of Skinner's house. Whilst standing there reports were brought to the General that some of the attacking columns had been checked in their advance. . . . Wilson appealed to Colonel Baird Smith, asking him if he thought we could hold what we had taken. The reply was clear and decisive that we *must* do so."

† See *ante*, page 575, for Baird Smith's own statement. I have read in print, some fabulous accounts, with fancy pictures, of the General, propped up by Chamberlain and Seaton, in the city, and forced by them to do what was right. Chamberlain was at Hindoo Rao's house, and Seaton, whose irrepressible desire to see what was going on, took him down to the scene of our operations, was soon sent back to Camp, by the infirmity of the flesh, "so sick and faint that he was more than two hours returning, and when he got to his tent he felt if he should never rise again from his bed."

army as "Prize." Upon the action of the first two days depended, in no small measure, the value of the booty to be divided; for the people were huddling out of the city with all the property they could carry off and burying the rest, with a distant hope that some day they might recover it. But there was one kind of property which all were fain to leave behind and to which our soldiery after that long waiting on the Ridge and the excitement of that fierce assault upon the defences of Delhi was more alluring than all. A black or a green bottle filled with beer or wine or brandy was more precious than a tiara of diamonds. The enemy knew this too well; and with the subtlety of their race had purposely left the immense supplies of intoxicating liquors, stored in the city, open to the hand of the spoiler. The result was more terrible than strange. The Europeans fell upon the liquid treasure with an avidity which they could not restrain. And if the insurgents had then seized the opportunity as cunningly as they had made it, it is hard to say what calamity might have befallen us. But the good Providence, which had so often confounded their wisdom, frustrated their plans, and turned their victories into defeats, now again strangled this pet project in the womb With the great suburb of Kishengunje still in their hands; with the Lahore Bastion and numerous strongholds within the city still held in force by them, whilst our Camp on the Ridge was occupied by a scanty body of troops, many of them invalids or convalescents, a stroke of generalship on the part of the enemy far below genius point, might, at that time, have caught our whole army in the toils, and left the Mogul triumphant. On that miserable Fifteenth of September, a great cloud hung over us. It was the hour

1857. Sept. 15.

1857. Sept. 15. of our sorest peril and our extremest need. For the first and last time during this great struggle the destinies of the English in India trembled in the balance; and no human wisdom could foretell the issue.

It was not strange, therefore, that Wilson, who had doubted, from the first, the expediency of the assault without further reinforcements, and who, on the preceding day, after the failure of the Third Column and the Reserve to penetrate the city, followed by the repulse of Reid's troops, had thought of withdrawing his forces to their old position, should now have felt burdened with a weight of anxiety enough to crush him to the ground. He could scarcely have gone more nearly to the act of withdrawal without positively accomplishing it; for he had made arrangements to cover the retreat of the assaulting columns. But having once recognised the wisdom of the adverse councils tendered to him, he flung away all thought of receding, even if greater disasters should overtake him. It seems to have been little more than a petulant utterance; a hasty inception; the growth of an irritable and nervous temperament wrought upon by hostile circumstances. A little mature thought convinced him of the disgrace and humiliation of going back to be again besieged. What Clive had said a hundred years before, of our position in India, was in this crisis eminently true, "To stand still is danger; to recede is ruin." There was nothing for us, in such a conjuncture, but to go on.

But there could be no going on with any good hope of victory, whilst so many of our fighting men were wallowing like swine in the filth that had been set before them. No sustained efforts could be made for the reduction of the city, until they had been delivered wholly from the temptation of the intoxicating liquor. In a similar emergency Havelock, at Cawnpore, had made over all such stores to the Commissariat. But Wilson could not follow this example. It was necessary to act promptly, and the Commissariat had other duties to perform. It must have been sorely against the grain that the General issued an order for the destruction of the liquid fire, which, if often a baneful enemy, is not seldom a most serviceable friend. But there was clearly no alternative. So the streets ran with spirits, and wine, and beer; the dust licked up the stimulants so much needed for our hospitals,* and a large amount of valuable Prize was sacrificed to the necessities of the hour. 1857. Sept. 16.

The great object was gained. The troops shook themselves free from the humiliating debauch, which, prolonged for another day, might have sent many to the grave and many to the hospital. But there was still the omnipresent thought that, at almost every turning, new stores might be found, as we advanced further into the city; and the fear of such a result sat heavily upon the mind of the General. But on the 16th, though he was obviously suffering under much depression of spirit, he recognised some hopeful appearances in the general aspect of affairs. During the preceding night the enemy had evacuated Kishengunje, and now the great Magazine was falling into our hands. Wilson personally superintended the operations. His experience as an Artillery officer must have been very serviceable at a time, when the chief work was to be done by the scientific branches

* "It was deplorable to see hundreds of bottles of wine and brandy, which were sadly needed for our sick, shivered, and their contents sinking into the ground. Wine which had fallen to threepence the bottle soon rose again to six shillings."—*History of the Siege of Delhi by One who was There.*

1857. Sept. 16 of the Army. And it must have gladdened his heart to see the immense supplies of Ordnance stores which now came into his possession. The grand exploit of the Artilleryman Willoughby* was none the less grand, because the material wealth of the Delhi Arsenal had been but little diminished. It was chiefly the small-arm magazine that had suffered by the explosion in May. It was thought in the British Camp that the insurgents must have been sorely put to it for copper-caps; but large quantities were still in store when the English entered the city. It was no profitless morning's work that placed all these guns and mortars and ammunition again at our disposal; but it did not seem to rouse Wilson, who wrote still in great despondency:

"16th September, 2 P.M.

"We took possession of the Magazine this morning, with the loss of only three men wounded. This advances us a little, but it is dreadfully slow work. Our Force is too weak for this street fighting, when we have to gain our way inch by inch, and of the Force we have, unfortunately there is a large portion besides the Jummoo troops in whom I can place no confidence. . . . . What gives me, however, most trouble, even more than the enemy, is the immense quantity of wines, spirits, and beer which is discovered, and which our fellows, European and Native, get hold of before we can destroy it and make beasts of themselves and incapable of doing their duty. I find myself getting weaker and weaker every day, mind and body quite worn out. The least exertion knocks me down. I walk with difficulty and fully expect in a day or two to be laid altogether on my bed. This is very sad and frets and worries me. . . . The rebels who so long attacked Reid's Picket from Paharunpore, evacuated the place last night, leaving their heavy guns behind. How I wish Reid could have driven them out on the 14th and joined in the attack on the city. . . . . We have a long and

* See vol. ii., pp. 90, 91.

hard struggle still before us. I hope I may be able to see it out." 1857. Sept. 16.

It was in the very nature of things that it should be a long and a hard struggle. Nothing else could be reasonably expected. To think of the great city itself, with all its impediments—of the teeming population, of the military and religious elements, of the still pervading sentiment of loyalty to the House of Delhi even in its decline, was to be convinced of the difficulty of the enterprise. It is a sentiment as old as heroism itself, that the difficulty of an enterprise makes its pleasurable excitement in the hour of action, its glory in the hour of accomplishment. And few men would have felt this more than Wilson, if it had not been for that great failure of the body, to which the mind of every man, great or small, is compelled to succumb. Still, little by little, though his dejection was great at the outset, he began to look more hopefully upon the aspect of affairs. Time was his best ally. There was no sign of any offensive action on the part of the enemy to cause serious inquietude. On the other hand, it was plain that they whose evacuation of the city had been arrested by our inactivity after the assault, had begun to discern the wisdom of flight. A few desperate men, not madmen or "fanatics," but brave soldiers and loyal subjects of the Throne of Delhi, might hold out for a time and die at their posts: but large bodies of soldiers and citizens were flocking out of the city, some with much property and others with only their lives in their hands; whilst our Artillery and Engineers were putting forth their strength, in strenuous endeavours to bombard all the great buildings of Delhi, and to occupy the houses which afforded

1857. Sept. 16. cover to the enemy and impeded our progress into the city. But what seemed the easiest operation of all was in reality a most difficult one—the bombardment of the chief buildings of Delhi. Mortars, and shells, and fuzes were abundant; and there was no lack of experienced gunners; but it perplexed our best artillerymen to determine the elevations, as they could only vaguely surmise the distances, and there was some fear of dropping a loaded shell in the midst of an assembly of our own people, or sending it clean over the building on which it was intended to lodge.*

The Engineer Brigade.

Ever to the front, ever active, ever fertile in resources, the Engineer Brigade had much work to do, and did it well in this conjuncture. It had been terribly shattered during the assault. One after another the subalterns attached to the different columns had fallen beneath the fire of the enemy. Few had escaped the perils to which they had been exposed.† But happily Alexander Taylor was alive, though not unhurt, for a bullet had struck him painfully on the chest on the morning of the assault.‡ And there was work for his active brain in devising the best means of securing what we had gained and in superintending their execution. All the professional resources

* *Ante*, page 617, *note*.

† "I found our Doctor at the General Hospital," writes Medley, "and then heard, as he exclaimed on seeing my bandaged arms, 'What, another of you!' that I was the eighth Engineer officer that had already claimed his good offices to-day." Salkeld and Tandy were killed—the former, as already related; the latter on the withdrawal of the Third Column and Reserve from the attempt on the Jumma Musjid.

‡ As Field-Engineer he had accompanied the Brigadier-General and the First Column of Attack, and when Nicholson, as above related, visited the Second Column, he left the troops immediately under him and all operations that might be necessary to the charge of Captain Taylor, in case the signal were given, during the absence of his chief, for an advance—a contingency which actually occurred. The assault on the breach was delivered under the direction of the Field Engineer.

of "those who were left," were brought into play, to intrench the different commanding positions, as they fell from time to time into our hands. The outer openings, as in the College premises, were closed with sandbags, leaving loopholes for our fire. Barricades were thrown up across the roads, leading to posts likely to be attacked. Houses were garrisoned and loopholed. Implements and stores of all kinds, necessary for immediate use or of probable requirement were furnished, and nothing was left undone that the sagacity of science could suggest, for the retention of the posts which we had captured, but which might be wrested from us.* 1857. Sept. 16.

Sept. 17. State of affairs in the city.

On the evening of the 17th, the general state of affairs was this. Our troops had endeavoured to advance up the streets towards the Palace—the grand object of all our movements—but in almost every instance they had been repulsed. There was still some heart left in the insurgents. Many had evacuated the city by the gates of egress, either in search of the personal safety of the moment, or with some ulterior designs of mischief in other parts; but enough were still left in the city to render the advance of our weak force a work of difficulty. The Magazine and the Bank had been captured and occupied. But the Lahore Bastion† was still in the enemy's hands. No advance had been made in that direction since Nicholson had fallen. It was evident

* This refers to what was done on the day of the assault. After the assault, as already shown, Baird Smith removed his Head-Quarters to the City. He found that his Lieutenant had anticipated all that he desired to be done. Taylor, then worn out with exhaustion from the preceding eight days' hard work in the Batteries, and suffering much from his wound, was compelled to betake himself to his bed until the latter part of the 17th, when he returned to fling himself into his work with all his old energy unabated.

† This is called by some writers the Burn Bastion. It led to the Lahore Gate. I have adhered to uniformity by calling it the Lahore Gate throughout the narrative.

1857. Sept. 17. that the appetite of our troops for this kind of fighting had not improved, and that our attempts to gain our ends by open force must be superseded by some more insidious system of attack. The exposure of our few fighting men was by all means to be avoided. They had seen enough of it already. They courted no more; and if they consented, it was with manifest reluctance.

Taylor's operations. So Taylor, who had returned to the city after his two days' rest in Camp, suggested at Head-Quarters that each brigade should be ordered to work, under the guidance of the Engineer officers attached to it, not along the open streets, but through the sheltered houses, during the advance; using them as means of communication; fortifying all commanding buildings as soon as they could be secured; and placing garrisons in them. The project met with willing concurrence and consent; and Taylor and his subalterns went about their work with the thoughful activity that had characterised all their proceedings. But the progress was not rapid. On
Sept. 18. the evening of the 18th they were little further advanced than on the morning. The cause was not very remote; nor was it very unintelligible. The veterans of the different brigades did not fall in very readily with the views of the young Engineers or cheerfully recognise their temporary supremacy. So situated, Taylor, with the concurrence of the Chief Engineer, went to the General and drew from him an order to the Brigadier commanding at the Caubul Gate to place at the disposal of the Field Engineer a force of some five hundred men, European and Native, to carry out the above-mentioned design; and early on the 19th the advance began in earnest. This was not one of the least of

the great services of Alec Taylor. Some thirty houses, important both by their size and their position, fell into his hands, and were duly barricaded and garrisoned. Nothing could have been more satisfactory than the result, especially as it was attended with but trifling loss on the part of the assailants. The houses thus taken were principally detached houses with surrounding premises, very favourable to our operations, for the occupants were exposed to a flanking and cross fire from the troops occupying the houses which we had already taken in the rear. Working onwards in this insidious but most effective way, our people towards nightfall found themselves in possession of a building, behind the gorge of the Lahore Bastion, which so entirely commanded it that the enemy, seeing their danger, were fain, after firing a few shots, to escape under cover of the night; and so the Bastion became our own. But so great was the terror, which the very name of this formidable work had inspired in the hearts of our men, that although the bastion had fallen thus easily into their hands, and there was no opposition, there was a manifest reluctance on the part of our soldiery to hold what we had taken. It was hard to restrain them from leaving the Bastion. 1857. Sept. 18.

In the meanwhile an attempt had been made to carry the Lahore Gate by assault. Edward Greathed, of the Eighth, who had worked cordially with the Engineers in their house-to-house visitations, was eager to carry the Lahore Gate, which had so long defied us. It appeared that this might be done, without encountering the dreaded opposition of the Lahore Bastion, by a route of a less hazardous nature. Greathed was appointed by Brigadier Jones to command the attack, and Colonel Pelham Burn, who had Attempt on the Lahore Gate.

1857. Sept. 18. been selected to be Military Governor of Delhi after its occupation by the English, was requested to accompany the detachment.* Greathed took with him a party consisting of some details of the Eighth and Seventy-fifth Queen's and of the Bengal Fusilier Regiments, accompanied by a couple of guns. It was arranged that, on the sound of firing being heard, supports should be sent on from the Caubul Bastion by a narrow lane under the ramparts. The force made good its way without difficulty to the narrow street leading into the Chandna Chouk, but the enemy were posted in force behind a gate at the end of it, which was unexpectedly flung open, for we thought that our movements were unknown, and a six-pounder gun was brought to bear upon our advancing detachments.† On this Greathed ordered up a gun under Lieutenant Harington and directed the men of the Seventy-fifth to charge under cover of the smoke, when the gun should be fired. But the Seventy-fifth did not charge. The Eighth were then ordered to the front, but they also refused to charge; and the Artillery were left to be fired at by the insurgents, who exhibited more gallantry than our own people. The noble example of our officers could not induce their men to display that fine onward feeling—that regulated impetuosity—which alone can command success under such trials as this. They hated the kind of work which they were called

* Burn, who had distinguished himself in Afghanistan, and who had afterwards approved himself as an excellent administrator in one of the great Public Departments at the Presidency. He was a general favourite with the Bengal Army. At Delhi he appeared only as a volunteer; and having no fixed position could not avail himself of his rank, But he was very useful as a field officer, and General Wilson spoke of him as one of his best officers. He accompanied Nicholson's column on the morning of the assault.

† In this attack Lieutenant Bristowe of the Seventy-fifth was killed

upon to spring at, and they shrunk back when they ought to have flung themselves upon it. Greathed saw at once the temper of his followers—if followers they could be called who would not follow: he saw the Artillery suffering from the musketry of the enemy; he knew the value of life at such a time too well to needlessly expend it, and wisely, though most reluctantly, he determined to withdraw his men from the unequal encounter before they had sustained any heavy loss. But a new difficulty confronted him, for the men seemed equally unwilling to advance or retire. To give assurance to the rest by covering their advance, Burn had taken the detachment of the First Fusiliers to occupy the houses in the narrow street. So with this aid Greathed was able to withdraw his men in an orderly and creditable manner. It was another illustration of the national character in its soldierly aspects. They did not know what they were fighting against, and the unseen danger assumed, in their imaginations, proportions, the reality of which would have been contemptible in the open field.* 1857. Sept. 18.

Feelings of the General.

There was nothing to exhilarate or to encourage the General in all this. Indeed the crowning misery of all was the thought of the backwardness of the troops under his command. He need not have thought much about numbers, if the hearts of the few were in the right place. Had Wilson been assured of the temper of his men, he might have taken a more cheerful view of the prospect before him. But how this last failure saddened him his letters clearly evince:

* In a letter before me this is described as the "sagacious instinct of the British soldier, which teaches him what can be and what cannot be done." But the *Audace, audace—toujours audace!* is better than this.

1857. Sept. 18.

"Delhi, September 18th, 1857

"We are still in the same position in which we were yesterday. An attempt was made this morning to take the Lahore Gate, but failed from the refusal of the European soldiers to follow their officers. One rush and it would have been done easily, but they refused to make it. The fact is our men have a great dislike to street fighting; they do not see their enemy, and find their comrades falling from shots of the enemy who are on the tops of houses and behind cover, and get a panic and will not advance. This is very sad and to me disheartening. We can, I think hold our present position, but I cannot see my way out at all. I have now only 3100 men (Infantry) in the city—with no chance or possibility of any reinforcement. If I were to attempt to push on into the city they would be lost in such innumerable streets and masses of houses, and would be annihilated or driven back. It is true that a great number of the enemy have bolted, but they have still a large camp out between the Delhi and Ajmere Gate, and those who have bolted may possibly return when they find we cannot make any progress. Again in our favour we have possession of nearly all their guns, shot and shell, except those they have in the bastions still in their possession, and we are bombarding from an easy distance, Selimgurh and the Palace. . . . It has been a hard task imposed upon me, almost too hard; both mind and body are giving way. Since the night of the 13th I have certainly not had five hours' sound sleep, and nature cannot stand it. I trust, however, and think, I have done my duty. May Almighty God still support me in doing so . . . This is a very doleful letter, but the state of my mind and body perhaps make me more depressed than I should be. . . . ."

"Camp before Delhi, 19th September.

". . . . I came up to Camp last night in hopes of getting a good night's sleep—I was not, however, very successful. Brain, nerves, and body have been too much strained to quiet down so quickly. I am going back to the city immediately, but shall try to get back here to-night to sleep. . . . We are progressing more satisfactorily—bombarding the city and gra-

dually seizing strong posts in advance of our present position. 1857.
The King evacuated the Palace yesterday afternoon with most Sept. 19
of his followers, finding it too hot to hold him; report says very few are left in it. He is gone to a place near the *Poorana Killah* (Old Fort), outside the city. We have met with a very heavy loss in taking what we have done. I have not yet seen the returns, but hear the total loss in killed and wounded is full 1150 men, including 46 officers. The killed are only about 250. Brigadier-General Nicholson is a very great loss to me—I have no one who can supply his place. I am very much afraid we shall lose him. He was not going on at all favourably yesterday. . . . ."

But when Wilson returned to his Head-Quarters in the city, glad tidings awaited him. Taylor reported the success of his operations, in working from house to house and making grand progress with little loss. The occupation of the Lahore Bastion was an important step in advance; and the General, determined not to lose what we had gained, sent some officers of his Staff to spend the night in the Bastion, or to remain there as long as might be necessary to secure its continued occupation. But there was no attempt on the part of the enemy to recover it. The night passed peaceably away. When day dawned on the 20th, arrangements were made to resume the tactical operations, which had so far been crowned with such complete success. But those who were on the look-out were struck by the deserted aspect of the streets. Some adventurous explorers then went out to ascertain more certainly the position of affairs in the city, and they found that the place was well-nigh abandoned.

The Lahore Bastion being secured, the fall of the Lahore Gate speedily followed. A body of the Sixtieth Rifles rushed at it; and its defenders, finding

1857. Sept. 19. that "the game was up" with them, from one end of the city to the other, evacuated the work which had so long defied and frustrated the best efforts of our troops. The story of the Lahore Gate is a curious one. It is the story of a lost opportunity. After the first onslaught of the Second Column, the Brigadier, scarcely knowing the importance of the position, found himself on the Lahore Bastion. A bold front, in the confusion and half-panic which had then set in among the defenders, might have carried everything before it and saved all after-trouble and disaster. But Jones had received his orders. He had gone beyond the point at which he had been directed to await tidings of the fall of the Jumma Musjid; so in obedience to orders he fell back and lost the golden opportunity. Emboldened by our inaction at such a time the enemy clung to the work with desperate pertinacity, and for six days held it to the infinite discomfiture of the besiegers. Nicholson had been the only leader of a column, who had, previous to the assault, personally gone down to the breaching batteries, studied the effect of their operations and taken a comprehensive ocular survey of the breaches through which we were to push our way on to victory. But, it may be doubted whether even that "born General" knew much of the position or the designs of the enemy within the ramparts, which Brind, Scott, and others with their heavy guns were battering with such wonderful effect. There were few to whom the advance into the city had not appeared to be a much easier operation than after-events proved that we were justified in anticipating. In affairs of war, it is hard to say what great issues may depend upon some accident of the moment. Had this cruel Bastion and the Lahore Gate, with or without orders, fallen to our arms on the 14th of September, when the Second Column first advanced on these works, Delhi would have fallen sooner; and Nicholson might have survived the siege. 1857. Sept. 20.

Occupation of the Palace.

But, whatsoever the misadventure may have been at the outset, the capture of the defensive works of Delhi was now complete. There was an almost general rush inwards. The cry was "To the Palace! to the Palace!" The occupation by British troops of the great home of the Moguls was the only genuine proclamation of victory. Our scouts had brought us intelligence that the Royal Family had forsaken their old asylum, and had become fugitives and outcasts huddling together in the suburbs, not knowing what to do. The Reality of Indian warfare was now at an end in Delhi; we were about to see the Romance. Hope Grant sent Hodson to the General to convey to him the glad tidings that the city was evacuated.* Wilson sent at once a party under Jones of the Sixtieth Rifles to blow in the gates of the Palace and of the Selim-gurh. The powder-bags aided by our guns, did the work with but little difficulty. A few desperate men remained, moved either by religious enthusiasm or by military devotion, to die at their posts in the Palace of the Moguls. It is related that a sentry was found at each gate, with his musket on his shoulder, grim and immovable, prepared for his doom.† No one found in the imperial premises was left alive. The British standard was hoisted. And the Englishman

* Whether this was the first intimation that reached Head-Quarters I do not know. I follow here only the statement of the Cavalry Brigadier. Sir Thomas Seaton also says that he reported it himself at Head-Quarters. Many others, doubtless, did the same.

† Aitkin of the Artillery shot one of them. See in Appendix, an interesting account of the capture of the Palace and Selim-gurh.

1857. Sept. 20. celebrated his victory by ordering dinner to be laid in the Elysium of the Dewan-Khas, with its lustrous marble walls and lovely arabesques, triumphs of that barbaric art, beside which the best effort of the nineteenth century Englishman is but as a Caliban to an Ariel. I know not whether any harmonious spirit, "tired of war's alarms," celebrated and enlivened the occasion by a burst of song, with the well-known adaptation of the words, which our people now saw around the cornices of the Dewan-Khas, but they knew that the famous "Elysium on Earth" was their resting-place and the enemy who had mocked us was no more.*

To the weary warriors of Delhi the best Elysium at that time must have been Rest. There was little or nothing in the material environments of the place strongly to impress the captors with a sense of its splendour or its beauty. We saw it at the worst in the hour of its decadence and humiliation, with the well-remembered pollution of half a century upon it. But since the early days of May, the Mogul, before a puppet, had become a potentiality; and Delhi, one of our greatest civil and military stations, where the old imbecile King and his multitudinous family had so long lain prostrate at our feet, for four long months, had snorted defiance at us, garrisoned by our own army. But now Delhi again was occupied by our British troops. The usual accompaniments of retribution and spoliation could not be wholly absent from such a siege as this. But if there had been no failures,

* Moore's poetry is better than his authorities. Quoting Franklin, he informs his readers that around the exterior of the Dewan-Khas in the cornice are the following words in letters of gold on a ground of white marble: "If there be a Paradise on earth, it is this, it is this." The inscription is in letters of *black* marble *inside* the hall; and I can find no other account of its having been otherwise.

no checks; if our legions had entered the imperial city, which had so long defied us, with a grand rush, sweeping everything before it, the results would have been terrible. Hatred of the inhabitants and greed for the spoil would have borne their accustomed fruits. But the delays to which we had been compelled to submit gave altogether another character to the first partial and then complete occupation of the city. When on the 20th of September Delhi fell into our hands it was little more than a vast solitude. The cry of *Væ Victis* therefore, was never raised. It was the desertion of the enemy that made us victors at all. There could, happily, therefore, be no wholesale retribution. But during that week of incertitude, when our half-successes were almost counterbalanced by whole failures, and no man knew what might be the issue of these vicissitudes, opportunities arose for the assertion of our retributive strength; and the temptations, if not irresistible, were most difficult to resist. 1857. Sept. 20.

Seldom, if ever, since War began, had there been so much to exacerbate and infuriate an army, as then inflamed the brains and fevered the blood of the men, who found themselves in the blood-stained city. No reader of this narrative needs to be told what were these exciting influences. But when we come to weigh the heavy burden of unutterable guilt, of which our women and children were the victims, against the cruelty and inhumanity of the avenging power, we see how light were our reprisals. Still it must always happen, both in the West and the East, that the miserable consideration still remains that the innocent must suffer for the guilty. Many Treatment of the conquered.

1857. Sept. 14—20. who had never struck a blow against us—who had tried to follow their peaceful pursuits—and who had been plundered and buffeted by their own armed countrymen, were pierced by our bayonets, or cloven by our sabres, or brained by our muskets or rifles. In this instance, I have said, there were aggravations, which have not stirred the hearts of our western warriors. From western warfare there has been absent that which in the East has been most perilous of all, the difference of colour. The very sight of a dark man stimulated our national enthusiasm almost to the point of frenzy. We tolerated those who wore our uniforms and bore our arms, but all else were, in our eyes, the enemies and persecutors of our race. So it sometimes happened that during the first days of our occupation of Delhi, many innocent men were shot down or otherwise massacred. Some of the best and bravest of our officers sanctioned, if they did not take part in these outrages; and it is doubtful whether they could have controlled the excesses of their fighting-men, especially when they were maddened by much drink.

I know only one instance of slaughter on a large scale, which was made the talk of the Camp. Major James Brind, Brind of the Batteries, was sent into the city on the most ungrateful duty of burying the rotting carcases which were polluting the atmosphere of certain parts of Delhi. He took with him a detachment consisting of Artillery and Infantry, mainly, if not wholly, Natives of the country. Among them were forty Sikh artillerymen. The duty thus fixed upon him was of a sanitary, not a retributive character. But it happened that, as he was proceeding to his unsavoury work, news was brought to him of "a brutal attack" which had been made upon a party of Muzbee Sikhs, in one of the lanes between the Delhi and Ajmere Gates. At this time he fell in with Brigadier Jones, who had commanded the Second Column of Attack, and he asked to be reinforced, if needed, by some European Infantry, that he might dispose of the men who had committed these outrages and others which Jones reported. The Brigadier promised to aid Brind, and approved of retributive action. A wounded Sapper was with difficulty persuaded to lead the way to the spot where these "murderers" were located. When Brind got among them he made short work of the chastisement to be inflicted upon them. Among the traitors were "Syuds and various classes of debauchees." Many of the enemy were slain on the spot, and others, "against whom blood-proofs, as also relics of our murdered countrywomen, children, and other Christian residents" were to be found on their persons or in their houses, were reserved for more humiliating punishments. Following the example set by Neill at Cawnpore, he kept these men "to labour in cleansing our polluted lines before their final punishment." The number slain by Brind's detachment ranged from a hundred and fifty to two hundred men. As a pleasant set-off to this, Brind had the satisfaction of reporting that he had "sent out of the city many hundreds of women, children, and helpless male inhabitants—blind and decrepit."* It is not clear whether the men thus "slain" were our revolted Sepoys or civil inhabitants of Delhi. It does not appear to me, however, that the fact of their having certain articles in their possession was any proof of their having murdered the English people, to whom

1857. Sept. 14—20.

* Major James Brind to Colonel Gaitskill, commanding Artillery.—*MS. Correspondence.*

1857. Sept. 14—20. they had belonged. The goods might have been purchased at a prize-auction, or might have come into their possession by some very innocent accident. It was not the first or the last time, when mere possession has been treated as a proof of forcible spoliation attendant on "treacherous murder."* There was not a kinder-hearted, as there was not a braver man in the Delhi army than James Brind; but he was a man of an excitable temperament, and he had been working day and night in the batteries, under a fierce sun, seldom or never sleeping all the time. And he had ever before him the memory of the fact that his brother had been killed at Sealkote by the treacherous connivance of his own servants.†

There is other testimony, which, though not so officially authentic as this, is very strong and reliable, to the effect that many innocent men were destroyed, after the occupation of Delhi, by our infuriated troops. An officer, who served throughout the siege, and who has given us the best account of its chief incidents now before the public, says, "Our men treated these (the women and children) with kindness and sympathy, but many of the citizens were shot, clasping their hands for mercy. It was known, too, that a large proportion of them had all along wished us well."‡ And Colonel Bour-

* There has been a story, long time current, to the effect that a number of wretched villagers were hung up, because they had some new *pice* in their possession (a neighbouring treasury having been looted); but it appeared afterwards that the copper coins had been paid to them, for milk, vegetables, grain, &c., by a detachment of our own people. I have no authentic evidence of the truth of this story—so I merely relate it as something very like truth. In the language of the day every Native of the country was a traitor—if he turned against us. The Sepoys, who had received our pay, and had been drilled and disciplined by us, were, in some sense, rebels and traitors—but all the other inhabitants of Delhi who did *not* strive mightily against us were, assuredly, rebels and traitors. All their loyalty was due to the Mogul.

† *Ante*, vol. ii. p. 629—631.

‡ "History of the Siege of Delhi

chier of the Artillery, in his published narrative 1857.
says: "Some men were caught going out of the Sept. 14—20.
Cashmere Gate disguised as women and were hung; whilst several bheesties, or water-carriers, detected in bringing in drugged liquor for the troops, were likewise disposed of."* The enormity of endeavouring to escape the fury of the assailants by huddling out in petticoats is not very clear. The device was one not altogether unknown, or unpractised, in like emergencies, by our own officers. It might have been better to have given these epicene creatures the benefit of the doubt. It is a pleasure to the Historian to be able to add that from the mass of manuscript documents before him he can clearly derive the one gratifying fact, that the women and children were almost uniformly respected. A stray shot might, now and then, inadvertently have carried death with it; but no intentional outrages were committed. A distinguished officer of the Eighth, which formed part of the Second Column, writes: "The Eighth took possession of a large house, the basement and court of which was filled with women and children, evidently of a respectable rank of life, who were naturally much frightened.† But they had no reason to be so, for our good fellows treated them as if they had been their sisters and passed them out carefully and kindly on their way to the Cashmere Gate, which was all, indeed, we could do for them." I

by an Officer who served there."—This very able writer observes: "Helplessness ought to be respected in either sex, especially in those who have never done us wrong. It is as unmanly for an officer to drive his sword through a trembling old man or a soldier to blow out the brains of a wounded boy, as to strike a woman."

* "Eight Months' Campaign in India against the Bengal Sepoy Army, by Lieutenant-Colonel Bourchier, C.B."—afterwards Sir George Bourchier, K.C.B.

† This was Jung Behaudur's house. The Eighth had afterwards to evacuate it, as the building was required for other purposes.

1857. Sept. 14—20.

could add many other proofs of the forbearance of our soldiery; but this may be taken as a sample of the whole.

Plundering the city.

The reign of unlicensed plundering had begun at an early period. The Sikhs, among whose traditional day-dreams the sack of Delhi had ever been prominent, now found themselves within reach of the realisation of their fondest wishes. No scruples restrained them. They had no conception of a Prize Agency beyond the grand cardinal principle that it was the duty of every man to gather up what spoil he could get and to keep it as long as he could. Their natural astuteness, aided perhaps by some experiences elsewhere, had taught them how to discern the lurking-places of concealed treasure. It might be buried beneath the floors of their houses or bricked up in their walls. In the former case it might be ascertained by pouring water through the crevices, for if the space below were excavated it would soon filter down; if not it would return to the level of the floor. In the latter, the wall might be sounded, as a physician sounds the chest of a patient; and the results of this process of auscultation were very convincing to our Sikh comrades. To what extent their surmises were justified can only be conjectured. But nothing was more patent than the energy of their endeavours, for almost everywhere battered walls and wrenched up floors told plainly what they had done. It was clearly ascertained, too, that large quantities of plunder were handed over the walls to their brethren below, and that afterwards numbers of laden carts passed out at the opposite gates of the city. It has been stated, indeed, that their countrymen would not believe in the fall of Delhi until they had ocular demonstration of the "loot." But it is not to be thought that the Sikhs were the only recipients of unauthorised Prize. Sepoys of other nationalities and camp followers of all, went in remorselessly for what they could clutch. And our own European soldiery in a lesser degree took part in the unlicensed spoliation. But they had not the same discriminating eye for booty as their Sikh comrades, and they were seldom richer in the end for their contempt of the Prize Agents and their evasions of the Provost-Marshal. 1857. Sept. 14—20.

Death of Hervey Greathed.

The Head-Quarters' Staff, Military and Civil, were now fixed in the Palace. But there was one absent from the party, whose work at that time had developed into peculiar interest and importance. It was truly a sad thing that just at this point, when all things were working on, surely if not rapidly, to the complete occupation of Delhi, the subversion of the Mogul, and the proclamation of the Queen's authority, the man who, from the very beginning, had superintended all the political and civil transactions connected with our position at Delhi was suddenly stricken by cholera. The Pestilence that walketh in the darkness had laid the cold hand of death upon Hervey Greathed. He was a man in the prime of his life, with the flush of health on his cheek; with strength and activity in every movement. The published extracts from his family correspondence show how cheerful he was throughout the long months of the siege, how friendly and sociable he was with his comrades, especially his old friends from Meerut, and how lovingly he dwelt with his brothers. It was a luxury during that long dreary period of waiting to have an old friend or relative of any

1857. Sept. 19. degree with whom to converse and to exchange sympathies. But the Greatheds had no such scanty consolation; for the three brothers, Edward, Hervey, and Welby were all in Wilson's camp, performing different duties, but seldom, for a day, apart.* Nothing could be more cheery than the manner in which the civilian wrote of this pleasant family intercourse. And as it did much to sustain the spirits of the Triumviri, so also it must have sustained their health. But the brightest and the lustiest are often those to succumb first to the approaches of cholera; and on the 19th of September, whilst full of hope, eager for the crowning action, and never doubting the final issue of the great contest, all that was mortal of Hervey Greathed lay in the pale stillness of death. He was buried in the graveyard near Ludlow Castle —the first to find a resting-place there.

Capture of the Royal Family. The English had now captured the Palace; but where was the King? If any man in our Army could track him down, that man was Hodson of Hodson's Horse—the famous partisan leader, who had the fierce courage of the tiger unsubdued by any feelings of human compassion—who might have grown

* Much mention is made of Welby Greathed, the Engineer, and of his bold projects for a *coup-de-main*, in Barnard's time, will be found in the second volume of this History. He was severely wounded in the assault (*ante* page 592). Edward Greathed was Lieutenant-Colonel of the Eighth Foot. Wilson, at no time very prodigal of praise, spoke of him as one of his best officers of his force. His subsequent career in India will be detailed in the last volume of this history. He was created a Knight-Commander of the Bath in 1865. Hervey Greathed himself was a man of high promise. He had passed out from Haileybury first of his term, and was held in great estimation by all under whom he served, especially by Mr. Colvin, who was in confidential communication with him almost to the day of the Lieutenant-Governor's death. He was at Meerut, when the mutiny broke out, and went to Delhi with Wilson's force. See vol. ii., pages 68 and 183.

into something good and great, had years, which bring the philosophic mind, taught him the might of mildness and the glory of forbearance. As it is, viewed by such light as is cast by his antecedents on his character and conduct at this time, he appears as a man labouring under a strong sense of intolerable wrong, excited and exasperated by what had befallen him, feeling that he was under a cloud, but firmly resolved to blaze through it, with the light of some heroic enterprise that would cause the past to be forgotten. He had nothing but his character as a fighting man left to him; but this was of the finest temper. He had been dismissed from political employment in the Punjab for truculent injustice to a Native chief and had been pronounced wholly unfit ever to exercise any civil power.* Another grave charge had been brought against him, which I am not competent to discuss. But there was not a stain upon the brightness of his sabre. In critical conjunctures such men are of eminent service to the State. They will do deeds which some would shrink from in fear and others would abstain from on principle. Wilson was not unwilling to give him *carte blanche* to deal with the Royal Family as he might think fit—with the single reservation that the life of the old King was to be spared.

1857. Sept. 18.

Hodson, who had been appointed executive Chief of the Intelligence Department, had done his work right well with the aid of some notable Native spies, the chief of whom was Rujjub Ali, who rendered excellent service to the English by the intelligence and sagacity with which he obtained and communicated information regarding the movements of the

* See *ante*, vol. ii. p. 182.

1857. Sept. 18. enemy throughout the siege. But we owed much also to a traitorous, or as it was the fashion to say a "loyal" member of the House of Delhi, the Meerza Elahee Buksh, who was the father-in-law of the late heir-apparent. This man, who was said to be more "respectable" than the majority of his kinsmen, was also more sagacious. He had no dream of the restoration of the lost honours of the House of Delhi. Believing that the English would triumph in the end, he saw clearly that his own interests would be best served by covertly aiding the Infidels, whilst assuming the part of a friendly adviser of the Mogul. The game which he played was distinguished by no little Oriental astuteness. The leaders of the Army were eager to carry off the King with them. They pleaded that although want of provisions compelled them to leave the city, outside the walls, they could, if it were necessary, ravage the country, supply themselves, and make a great war against the English. And they had well-nigh succeeded, when the wily Meerza, who had persuaded the poor old man to accompany him to his house, where
Sept. 18—19. they spent the night, had not used all his efforts to keep the King from joining the Insurgents. He was satisfied that "a real fidelity required him not to let the King go with the Army." So with "great effort" and "extreme endeavour," when Bukht Khan and other chiefs of the Imperial Army met Behaudur Shah and the Princes at Hoomayoon's Tomb, the Meerza "made so many good arrangements that neither the King nor his sons did ever listen to them, and none of them have ever gone with the officers of the ungrateful regiments."* All this and much more was

* These are a translation of Elahee Buksh's own words as given in a manuscript statement before me.

communicated to Hodson principally through the 1857.
Moonshee Rujjub Ali. It was plain that the wily Sept. 21.
Meerza had got the whole Royal Family in his toils, and that it needed now only that the bold heart and the strong hand should be brought in aid of this crouching treachery. By specious representations Elahee Buksh held them in gentle bondage at the Tomb of the Emperor Hoomayoon with its surrounding structures, a suburb in itself, beyond the modern city. It was the way out of Delhi, and large numbers of the Insurgents were still flocking there for safe egress, carrying off what property they could, but glad to escape even with their lives. It was thought that amidst this crowd of people, the King and his family, swayed by later counsels, might escape. So Hodson galloped down to Head-Quarters and obtained reluctant permission from the General to take a party of his own men to Hoomayoon's Tomb and bring in, without injury or insult, the last of the Mogul Emperors. Taking fifty of his troopers he rode off, elated with the success of his mission, and passing the ruins of the ancient city of Delhi, made his way to the asylum of the prostrate monarch. There was then little risk either of escape or resistance; for the King, under guidance of Zeenut-Mehal, was already treating for his surrender. Still it was hard to say what terrible crisis might not be evolved at such a time, out of the desperation of those about him. It was necessary to move cautiously; so Hodson concealed himself and his men in some ruined buildings near the gateway of the Tomb; whilst he sent his emissaries on to convey his instructions to the royal fugitives. Two weary hours dragged away—hours of painful suspense—before they brought back an answer. The King consented

1857. Sept. 21. to give himself up to Captain Hodson, on assurance received from that officer's own lips that his life would be spared.

Capture of the King. So Hodson went forth from his resting-place and stood out before all, in the open space near the beautiful gateway of the Tomb, a solitary white man, among so many, awaiting the surrender of a King and the total extinction of a dynasty, the most magnificent that the world had ever seen. It was then but a title, a tradition; but still the monarchy of the Moguls was a living influence in the hearts of the Mahomedans of India. And, truly, a grander historical picture was rarely seen than that of the single British subaltern receiving the sword of the last of the Mogul Emperors in the midst of a multitude of followers and retainers grieving for the downfall of the House of Tamerlane and the ruin of their own fortunes. Grand as was the central incident in itself, it was rendered still grander and more impressive by its gorgeous historical background—"the magnificent gateway with the milk-white domes of the Tomb towering up from within"*—the gateway through which, preceded by the Queen and her son, for whom the wretched old man had endured so much and was now perishing, passed the palanquin containing the last poor remnant of royalty on its way to a living tomb. Hodson pricked on with drawn sword, to meet it and called upon the King to give up his arms. The old man asked if he was "Hodson Behaudur," and asked for a renewal from the Englishman's own lips of the promises made by his herald. This was done; and

* See a letter addressed to Hodson's brother in "Twelve Years of a Soldier's Life." The writer is probably Captain M'Dowall, of the Bengal Fusiliers, and second-in-command of Hodson's Horse, who could use his pen as well as his sword.

Hodson formally guaranteed the personal safety of His Majesty and of the son of Zeenut-Mehal. The Imperial arms were then surrendered to the Englishman, who made them over to his orderly, observing that if any attempt were made to rescue his prisoner the King would be shot down like a dog. Then the procession to the city commenced. It was a slow and dismal march along five miles of road; and it might have been a critical one, for a vast crowd followed the palanquins and their escorts during the greater part of the journey. They seemed hushed and overawed—rather wondering than excited—and gradually slunk away as they neared the Lahore Gate. Hodson and his captives then passed up the great street of the Chandna Chouk to the city. Meeting Saunders, the principal civil officer left to us at Delhi, Hodson made over the prisoners to him and went to report himself to the General. Wilson received him in his usual way, with a sort of bluff heartiness, which few in Camp understood, for there was more kindness in his heart than appeared upon the gritty surface; and said, "Well, I am glad you have got him, but I never expected to see him or you again!" But when the royal arms were given up to him Wilson told his subaltern to select any that he wished to possess as memorials of the adventure. One of the swords which he took had adorned the side of Nadir Shah, the other had been worn by the Emperor Jehanguire.

1857. Sept. 21.

Slaughter of the Princes.

I wish that the record of Hodson's exploits had ended with this narrative of the capture of the King. It would have gladdened the heart of the daring subaltern to have been ordered or permitted to shoot Behaudur Shah like a dog or to strike him down like an ox in the shambles. But this congenial occupa-

1857. Sept. 22. tion was not conceded to him. His captive was a miserable, infirm old man, much wrought upon by evil advisers; the slave rather than the master of circumstances, the shadow of a name turned to evil purposes.* To have used brutal violence towards such a poor feeble creature would have been little more manly than the slaughter of a woman. But the game of royalty-hunting had not yet been played out. Some of the King's sons, or near relatives, who were believed to have taken an active part in the insurrection and in the massacre of our people, were still to be tracked down. They were in the prime of life—if life, spent in that great reeking stye of the Delhi Palace could ever be said to have a prime—and no pledges or promises had been made to them. They were lawful game and Hodson knew where to find them. So he got Wilson's permission to hunt down the Shahzadahs and sent to his Second-in-Command, M'Dowall, to bring up a hundred troopers. He promptly obeyed the summons, and Hodson mounted, eager for the affray. The Princes were at Hoomayoon's Tomb where the King had been captured on the preceding day. With them were some thousands of followers, including a number of Mussulman fanatics, who called upon them in the name of the Prophet to resist the infidel intruders; but they thought it better to sue for terms—hoping at least that their lives would be spared. Hodson would grant them no terms—would make no promises of any kind. He commissioned his emissaries† to say that "he had

* Hodson himself spoke of the Behaudur Shah as a mere puppet, a "ruse." "He is old and well-nigh impotent, and is only used as an authority for all the acts of rebellion and barbarity committed by his sons." Yet he admits that he would rather have brought in the king dead than alive.

† These delegates were the notorious Moonshee Rujjub Ali, who was the very life of Hodson's Intelli-

come to seize the Shahzadahs, and intended to do so, dead or alive." After two hours spent in useless negotiation—mere idle talk leading to nothing—the delegates of the British Government as it was then represented by Hodson, reported that the Princes were coming out in covered bullock-carts. Soon the wretched captives appeared, made one last despairing appeal for their lives, and were sent on towards Delhi guarded by our troopers on both sides of the way.* 1857. Sept. 22.

Having seen his prisoners fairly started, Hodson, with his remaining Sowars, passed the precincts of the Tomb, and in a loud voice, called upon the people assembled there to surrender their arms. It is true that the multitude were but the "scum of the Palace," weak, nerveless, heartbroken people, who had seen their King carried off from the midst of them, and yet in their pitiful prostration had not courage to strike a blow in his defence. Still there were at least six thousand of these miserable creatures within the precincts of Hoomayoon's Tomb, and a rush of the surging multitude might have overwhelmed the little body of Hodson's Horse. But the commanding attitude and authoritative utterance of their intrepid leader overawed the congregated numbers; a great fear fell upon them; they felt that it was hopeless to endeavour to resist the power of the White Man, now that he had shattered their defences, dispersed their fighting men, and established

gence Department, and the "loyal" member of the Delhi Family, willing to betray his kinsmen for his own ends.

* Meerza Elahee Buksh had a principal hand in this. "At night," he says, "when I went to Hodson Sahib, he told me to bring to him the Meerza Khazar Sooltan, Meerza Mogul, and Meerza Aboo-Bakr. I answered that I had already made arrangements for that. He might find them any time he liked. . . . Then (22nd September) according to the order of Hodson Sahib, I brought those three above-mentioned from the sepulchre to him. Having taken them with the King's property with him, he returned, and was very pleased with me."—*MS. Records.*

1857. Sept. 22. himself in the Palace of the Moguls. So they submitted almost without a murmur; and in less time than Hodson had dared to anticipate, they were quietly collecting their arms, their horses and carriages, and under the supervision of the troopers gathering them together in the centre of the square.

Up to this time all that had been done by Hodson was worthy of a Christian Warrior. He had captured the Princes; he had disarmed their followers; and in doing so he had confronted great dangers, from the thought of which most men would have shrunk appalled. But, whether he had gone out with any foregone intentions to kill his captives, or whether any sudden emergency arose, which rendered it necessary for the public safety that they should be forthwith executed without the formality of a trial, Hodson resolved that he would shoot them down like dogs. When he left Hoomayoon's Tomb, fearing that some misadventure might have befallen the escort on the road to Delhi, he galloped forward to overtake them. As he neared them a little way outside the city he saw that a crowd was pressing on the guard and he thought that a rescue would be attempted.* Upon this Hodson rode in amongst them, and addressed his troopers, so as to be heard by the multitude, saying that the prisoners were the butchers who had murdered our women and children, and that an outraged Government had now ordained their punishment. So he ordered the Shahzadahs to quit the cart in which they had been placed and strip themselves to their under-vestments. They tremblingly obeyed and were ordered back to the cart. Then either thinking that his Sowars might not obey him,

* It is not stated whether these, or any of these, were armed men.

or rejoicing in the work of carnage, he took a carbine from one of his troopers, and deliberately, with his own hand, shot to death his unarmed and unresisting captives. This done, he rode with his prey into the city, and ordered the corpses of the Princes to be flung out and exposed to public view in front of the Kotwallie. And there they remained till the bodies rotted and stank, and it was necessary, for health's sake, to bury them. 1857. Sept. 22.

Estimate of Hodson's conduct.

I have told this story, briefly and plainly, as it is narrated by the only two European witnesses, who were present at this terrible execution—Hodson himself and his Second-in-Command, M'Dowall. I cannot, for a moment, question the truth of their evidence. But after a full consideration of the incident, as thus recorded and accepted, I cannot resist the conviction that Hodson, in thus stripping and shooting the Princes, committed an act which no good man can, at this distance of time, approve. That the men so suddenly sent to their account were members of the House of Delhi, was shown upon the testimony of that loyal kinsman of the King, who had been bought over, and who had accompanied Hodson for the purpose of identifying his prisoners. But that these identical men were promoters or prime agents of the massacre of our women and children, Hodson seems to have had no satisfactory proof, to justify his summary execution of the suspects. Their trial, probably, would have educed some pregnant truths illustrative of their conduct and of the conduct of other members of the Imperial House—facts now, perhaps, lost to us for ever. It was no uncommon thing in those days to execute the wrong man. I have heard terrible stories of these "mistakes"—stories not to be told unless supported by over-

1857. Sept. 22. whelming evidence. Hodson was the last man in the Camp to trouble himself much about evidence. He believed that it was his mission to take an active personal part in the infliction of dire retribution upon the House of Delhi. On the last day of August he wrote: "If I get into the Palace, the House of Timour will not be worth five minutes' purchase, I ween; but what my share in this work will be no one can say"—and on the 23rd of September he wrote again with exultation; saying, "In twenty-four hours I disposed of the principal members of the House of Timour the Tartar. I am not cruel, but I confess that I did rejoice in the opportunity of ridding the earth of these ruffians." He said that he would sooner have brought in the old King dead than alive. He would fain, indeed, have ridden into Delhi with the head of Behaudur Shah at his saddle-bow.

It is not to be questioned, therefore, that Hodson, as portrayed by himself, was a man of a truculent and sanguinary disposition, delighting in such deeds as this. He was gratified by the execution and proud in the remembrance of such exploits. There is no sign of his having been pained by the thought of them. He scarcely supposed that they required any justification. But as they were altogether of an abnormal character, he felt that the propriety of such an act as the massacre of the Princes might be questioned by men in authority more scrupulous than himself. He set forth therefore, firstly, that the General had told him that he did not wish to be troubled with the prisoners; and, secondly, that if he had not killed them, their adherents would have killed him. But it is not fairly to be assumed that Wilson hinted at the summary execution of the prisoners. He probably meant only that they should be made over at once to the civil authorities. The other plea has certainly much weight, if the emergency was as great as is stated. But at that time the people were so prostrate, and the Princes themselves so powerless for evil or for good, that it is little likely that any serious effort at rescue, resistance, or retaliation would have emanated from such a body, in the presence of Hodson and his well-mounted, well-armed troopers. They had not heart for such an encounter. The fact that so large a body of men had succumbed to Hodson and readily surrendered their arms at Hoomayoon's Tomb, shows the hopeless imbecility to which the adherents of the Imperial House had been reduced. And if Hodson thought that with his heroic band of horsemen he could not have guarded his prisoners and dispersed the mob, with a great slaughter, he must have thought more meanly of his own prowess and of his splended regiment than did any other man in Camp.

1857. Sept. 22.

But what was thought of this achievement by his comrades? "I cannot help being pleased," wrote Hodson, on the 25th of September, "with the warm congratulations I receive on all sides for my success in destroying the enemies of our race. The whole nation will rejoice." But in the February following he wrote in a different strain. "I made up my mind at the time to be abused. I was convinced I was right, and when I prepared to run the great physical risk of the attempt I was equally game for the moral risk of praise or blame." The truth is that, at the time of the capture of Delhi, when men's blood was fevered with anger and hatred, and their faces flushed with shame and indignation at the thought of the

1857. Sept. 22. measureless cruelty of our enemies, some of the best and wisest of our countrymen in India looked with excited approval upon what they came afterwards to regard with calm regret. And although Hodson at one time believed that the "whole nation" would rejoice, I may aver without hesitation, that the general feeling in England was one of profound grief, not unmingled with detestation. I never heard the act approved; I never heard it even defended.

All danger was now at an end. All doubt was now at an end. The King was a captive. The city was a wreck. It had been a week of ceaseless anxiety—of tremendous care. Whatever might have been said or thought at the time, Wilson did not exaggerate the difficulties of the situation. I repeat here at the end, what I said at the beginning, of this narrative of the Siege*—for Justice may reiterate itself without offence—that after the excitements and impetuosities of the hour had passed away, after the eager irresponsible audacities of the younger heroes of the siege had been calmed down by the subduing influence of Time, and that great crisis in our national history had become a tradition, many of the best soldiers of the Delhi Army frankly declared that, the longer they lived, the more convinced they were, that justice had not been done to the General, who had commanded them. Men, whose blood was at fever-heat, looking only from certain fixed stand-points at details within their circumscribed view, and not seeing even the whole significance of those details, were not in a position, neither were they in a temper, at the time, to take a calm and comprehensive view of the great expanse before the General. I have ob-

* *Ante*, pp. 554—555.

served during a period of many years the progress of this reaction. Sooner or later Time will ever bring in its revenges. 1857. Sept. 22.

But the fact that he had taken Delhi did not seem much to rouse him from his depression. He was profoundly thankful to the Almighty for the great deliverance; but he scarcely seemed to rejoice in his victory. There can be no stronger proof of the heavy clouds of gloom which enfolded him, that no thought of honours or rewards—of the realisation of fame or fortune—as the captor of Delhi, seems to have possessed him at this time. He was too much broken down to long for anything but perfect repose. In his private letters he said little of himself. Not a particle of ambition or greed entered into them. Seldom has a man in such a position been so little egotistical:—

"The Palace, Delhi, 22nd September, 2 P.M.

"The plot thickens. Yesterday evening the King and his favourite Begum, Zenut-Mehal, gave themselves up and are now my prisoners. I have not allowed them to return to the Palace, but they are in honourable confinement in Zenut-Mehal's house. To-day Hodson and his Horse surrounded Hoomayoon's Tomb, in which some of the Princes had taken refuge with nearly all the women of the Palace. Three of the Princes, Mirza Moghul, Mirza Abboo Bakr, and Mirza Rezi Sultan, were taken and shot. The two former have been the most virulent against us. Hodson as a partisan officer has not his equal. To-morrow morning a movable column of about 2800 men move in the direction of Muttra, under Colonel Greathed, in pursuit of the flying rebels. If Havelock could only relieve Lucknow and move up this way, the whole rebellion would be put down I believe at once. I have sent a party of Irregular Cavalry in the direction of Meerut to my old battle-ground on the Hindun River to reconnoitre in that direction. I have not a single moment that I can call my own and cannot write you a long letter. . . . . Hod-

1857. Sept. 22—23. son has presented me with the King's sword, dagger, and matchlock . . . . I have just heard the party I ordered to the Hindun (the Mooltanee Horse) have refused to march. You see what materials I have to work with!

"23rd September, Palace, Delhi.

". . . . . We are, I hope, going on smoothly. Order is getting gradually restored, though the discipline of the troops has, I am sorry to say, got sadly disorganised. Such a heterogeneous force as I command was certainly never before collected together—Beloochees, Afghans, Sikhs, Pathans, Dograhs—all of whom have been bred and taught to consider plunder of an enemy legitimate, and will not be restrained. The Europeans are so badly commanded from the loss of most of their old officers, as to be quite as bad, if not worse. I hope, however, it will soon quiet down. Burn is Military Governor of the city and is exerting himself well . . . . I am completely done and can't carry on much longer. I have written to J. Lawrence to tell him I am quite unequal to the task now before me and that I wish some younger and more competent man may be sent to relieve me. . . . . That fine fellow Nicholson died to-day at one o'clock; if he had been spared what an assistance he would have been to me."

Death of John Nicholson. During nine days John Nicholson lay dying in the Camp upon the Ridge. He had been removed to a bungalow for greater comfort and quiet. Now and then, it was said, upon medical authority, that he was a little better. But he chafed under the great misfortune that had fallen upon him. He could not rest for thinking of the doubtful issue of the final struggle. He was continually inquiring how the attack was going on—and was very readily excited by the news that was brought to him. On one occasion the vehement impetuosity of his passionate nature broke through all restraints. When told that there had been some talk of retiring, the dying hero exclaimed, "Thank God, I have still strength enough to shoot that man." 1857. Sept. 14—23.

If he had lived, calmly to review all the events of this momentous siege, with its chances, its perils, its responsibilities, he would never, to himself or to others, have justified such words. And if he had ever got beside Herbert Edwardes, both men would most earnestly have condemned them. But the passionate vehemence of the natural man overbore all restraints, and there may have been something of the delirium of fever which rendered him scarcely responsible for his words. There were few of the more earnest spirits in Camp who were not moved by like seething indignation, at the thought of withdrawal from Delhi; but they did not express their anger and shame in the same truculent language.

These outbursts greatly enhanced his fever and increased his pain, and it was found necessary to give him large doses of morphia to secure him temporary rest. When not under the influence of the drug, he continued to inquire after the progress of our offensive operations, tidings of which Chamberlain, who had gone into the city with Wilson, frequently sent to his dying friend, through the "good Surgeon Mackinnon." And whenever he could leave the city he was beside his friend, gentle as a woman in his ministrations, and ever speaking words of hope and encouragement, to cheer him on his dying bed. Once or twice, as time wore on, warmed, perhaps, by the cheering intelligence which he received from the city, he rallied a little; and again his friends entertained some faint hopes of his recovery. But there was really no hope. He was wearing away to his rest.

And so days passed, and the complete occupation

1857. Sept. 14—23. of the great imperial city was every day approaching the final issue. The tidings brought to Nicholson's bedside were, every day, more and more assuring. He lived to hear that the Palace of the Moguls was occupied by British troops. He lived to hear that Behaudur Shah was a prisoner in our hands. He lived to hear that Hodson had, with his own hands, shot down the Princes like dogs. He lived to hear that Edward Greathed had been ordered to command the column of pursuit—a command which he himself had coveted. But he felt now that the world was passing away from him, and he thought much of those whom he was leaving behind; especially of his aged mother at Lisburne, and of Herbert Edwardes and his wife. "Tell my mother," he said, "that I do not think we shall be unhappy in the next world. God has visited her with a great affliction; but tell her she must not give way to grief." And of Edwardes he spoke, "Say that if at this moment a good fairy were to give me a wish, my wish would be to have him here, next to my mother." This was on the evening of the 22nd of September. On the morrow morning he rendered back his soul to his Maker.

Thus died John Nicholson, in the prime of his life, amidst a great wail of the universal Camp. He was a man *sui generis*. There were features of resemblance in his character to some characteristics of other heroes of the time. He had much of the high sense of duty—the stern conscientiousness of Henry Lawrence, with something more of the impetuosity of temper which that great man so often deplored. There was much also of the fearlessness of responsibility and the contempt of authority that sometimes made Neill a thorn in the flesh of those above him.

But the whole massive manhood of Nicholson had no perfect resemblance, in Camp or in Council, present or past. And the reason was this; his character was not yet fully developed. He was growing into something other than he was when he fell—something more perfect, more complete, more harmonious in its consistency. Some qualities might have been toned down and others might have ripened—each and all for the better. But before the fruit was ripe it fell to the ground. It is not difficult, however, to perceive what would have been the ripening effect of time. The very desire to get nearer to Herbert Edwardes and to think more of Henry Lawrence reveals clearly to us what would have been the growth of the future—what India lost in that final encounter. He had been so much associated with the affairs of Afghanistan and the Punjab, that his comrades and others in Lower India knew but little about his worth. They had a general idea that in the Punjab there was a man of great promise named Nicholson. It has been said that the Queen's officers were jealous of his high reputation. But there were brilliant exceptions to this. Hope Grant said of him as Nicholson lay dying that he was "like a noble oak riven asunder by a thunderbolt.* It must have been painful to the senior officers of the Force to be superseded by so young a man; but there were no complaints, for all admitted the grandeur of his character and his fitness for the work on which he was employed. But it is true that the Punjab was the home of his renown. The Natives of the district which he had governed, regarded him almost as the embodiment of an Avatar—as something little

1857. Sept. 23.

* "Incidents in the Sepoy War," by General Sir Hope Grant.

1857. Sept. 23. short of Godhead itself—as a hero-saint to be adored and worshipped. When he chastised his followers, they regarded it as an honour—for he could do nothing wrong in their eyes. It has been said that such is the prodigal growth of English manhood of the noblest type, in Camp and in Council, that when one great man passes away from the scene, his place is soon filled by one of equal worth. I do not think that it is so. As I write, eighteen years have passed away since Henry Lawrence, Neill, and Nicholson fell beneath the fire of the enemy; but I do not know the men who have replaced them. Nurtured by the grand old East India Company—knowing nothing of purchases and exchanges and Civil Service Commissioners, they went to the front by the unaided force of their own personal heroism. They flung aside, as if it had been a feather, the dead-weight of the seniority system. They knew little, if anything, of the art of war. But they knew how to do the right thing at the right time, and gained victories, when, according to all scientific principles, they ought to have been ignominiously and disastrously beaten.

Then from city to city, from cantonment to cantonment went the chequered tidings; Delhi had fallen, the King was a captive—but John Nicholson was dead.

*** Much that I wished to say in this chapter has unavoidably been left unsaid. But it is proposed to return to Delhi in the first chapter of the next volume. It is but an episode in this story: but it is a very important episode; and demands more than common consideration.

APPENDIX.

NOTES AND ILLUSTRATIONS.

[Vol. iii. p. 9.]

ACT No. XIV. OF 1857.

PASSED BY THE LEGISLATIVE COUNCIL OF INDIA.

(*Received the assent of the Governor-General on the 6th June*, 1857.)

AN ACT *to make further provision for the trial and punishment of certain offences relating to the Army, and of offences against the State.*

WHEREAS it is necessary to make further provision for the trial and punishment of persons who endeavour to excite mutiny and sedition among the Forces of the East India Company, and also for the trial of offences against the State: It is enacted as follows:

I. Whoever intentionally seduces or endeavours to seduce any Officer or Soldier in the service or pay of the East India Company from his allegiance to the British Government or his duty to the East India Company, or intentionally excites or stirs up, or endeavours to excite or stir up, any such Officer or Soldier, or any Officer or Soldier serving in any part of the British Territories in India in aid of the Troops of the British Government, to commit any act of mutiny or sedition; and whoever intentionally causes, or endeavours to cause, any other person to commit any such offence—shall be liable upon conviction to the punishment of death, or to the punishment of transportation for life, or of imprisonment with hard labour for any term not exceeding fourteen years; and shall forfeit all his property and effects of every description.

II. Whoever shall knowingly harbour or conceal any person who shall have been guilty of any offence mentioned in the preceding section, shall be liable to imprisonment, with or without hard labour, for any term not exceeding seven years, and shall also be liable to fine.

III. It shall be lawful for the Governor-General of India in Council, from time to time, by Order in Council, to empower every General or other Officer having the command of Troops in the Service of Her Majesty or of the East India Company, or any of such General or other Officers, to appoint General Courts-Martial for the trial of any person or persons charged with having committed an offence punishable by this Act or by Section I. or Section II. of Act XI. of 1857, and also to confirm and carry into effect any sentence of such Court-Martial.

IV. Any General Court-Martial, which may be appointed under the authority of this Act, shall be appointed by the Senior Officer on the spot, and shall consist of not less than five Commissioned Officers, the number to be fixed by the General or other Officer appointing the Court-Martial. The Order in Council may direct that a General Court-Martial to be appointed under the provisions of this Act shall consist wholly of European Commissioned Officers or wholly of Native Commissioned Officers, or partly of European Commissioned Officers, and partly of Native Commissioned Officers; and in such case the Officer appointing the Court-Martial shall determine whether the same shall consist wholly of European Officers or wholly of Native Officers, or partly of European Officers and partly of Native Officers.

V. Sentence of death or other punishment to which the offender is liable by law, may be given by such Court-Martial, if a majority of the members present concur in the sentence; and any such sentence may be confirmed by, and carried into effect immediately or otherwise by order of, the Officer by whom the Court-Martial shall have been appointed, or, in case of his absence, by the Senior Officer on the spot.

VI. It shall be lawful for the Governor-General in Council to countermand or alter any Order in Council which may be issued under the authority of this Act.

VII. It shall be lawful for the Governor-General in Council, or for the Executive Government of any Presidency or place, or for any person or persons whom the Governor-General in Council may authorise so to do, from time to time to issue a Commission for the trial of all or any persons or person charged with having committed within any district described in the Commission, whether such district shall or shall not have been proclaimed to be in a state of rebellion, any offence punishable by Sections I. and II. of Act XI. of 1857, or by this Act, or any other crime against the State, or murder, arson, robbery, or other heinous crime against person or property.

VIII. The Commissioner or Commissioners authorised by any such Commission, may hold a Court in any part of the district mentioned in the Commission, and may there try any person for any of the said crimes committed within any part thereof, it being the intention of this Act that the district mentioned in the Commission shall, for the purpose of trial and punishment of any of the said offences, be deemed one district.

IX. Any Court held under the Commission shall have power, without the attendance or futwa of a Law Officer, or the assistance of Assessors, to pass upon every person convicted before the Court of any of the aforesaid crimes any sentence warranted by law for such crime; and the judgment of such Court shall be final and conclusive; and the said Court shall not be subordinate to the Sudder or other Court.

X. If a Commission be issued under the authority of this Act, any Magistrate or other Officer having power to commit for trial within the district described in the Commission may commit persons charged with any of the aforesaid crimes within such district for trial before a Court to be held under this Act.

XI. Nothing in this Act shall extend to the trial or punishment of any of Her Majesty's natural born subjects born in Europe, or of the children of such subjects.

XII. This Act shall not extend to the trial or punishment of any person for any offence for which he is liable to be tried by the Articles of War.

XIII. The word "Soldier" shall include every person subject to any Articles of War.

XIV. This Act shall continue in force for one year.

SIR THOMAS MUNRO ON THE INDIAN PRESS.—Page 14.

"Owing to the unnatural state in which India will be placed under the foreign Government, with a Free Press and a Native Army, the spirit of independence will spring up in this army long before it is even thought of among the people. The army will not wait for the slow operation of the instruction of the people, and the growth of liberty among them, but will hasten to execute their own measures for the overthrow of the Government and the recovery of their national independence, which they will soon learn from the press it is their duty to accomplish. The high opinion entertained of us by the Natives, and the deference and respect for authority which have hitherto prevailed among ourselves, have been the main causes of our success in this country, but when these principles shall be shaken or swept away by a Free Press, encouraged by our juries to become a licentious one, the change will soon reach and pervade the whole Native Army. The Native troops are the only body of Natives who are always mixed with Europeans, and they will, therefore, be the first to learn the doctrines circulated among them by the newspapers; for, as those doctrines will become the frequent subject of discussion among the European officers, it will not be long before they are known to the officers and troops. Those men will probably not trouble themselves much about distinctions regarding the rights of the people and forms of government, but they will learn from what they hear to consider what immediately concerns themselves, and for which they require but little prompting. They will learn to compare their own low allowances and humble rank with those of their European officers, to examine the ground on which the wide difference rests, to estimate their own strength and resources, and to believe that it is their duty to shake off a foreign yoke, and to secure for themselves the honours and emoluments which their country yields. If the press be free they must inevitably learn all this and much more. Their assemblage in garrisons and cantonments will render it easy for them to consult together regarding their plans. They will have no difficulty in finding leaders qualified to direct them; their patience, their habits of discipline, and their experience in war, will hold out the fairest prospects of success; they will be stimulated by the love of power and independence, and by ambition and avarice, to carry their designs into execution. The attempts would no doubt be dangerous, but when the contest was for so rich a stake they would not be deterred by the danger."

ESCAPE OF THE CONVICTED SEPOY FROM FORT WILLIAM.—Page 36.

[This incident greatly distressed Lord Canning, who wrote to the President of the Board of Control, saying:]

"It is most deplorable that the man who tampered with the Sepoy, and who, after trial and conviction was placed under guard of the Fifty-third (Queen's), should have escaped. A court-martial is now trying the officer of the guard. But it is probable that he is not so much to blame as the officer who put the prisoner in irons which were too large for him that he slipped his hands and feet out, or as the sentry who failed to keep watch. It will of course be said that the prisoner was allowed to escape as soon as he had turned his evidence to account."

This does not seem to have induced greater caution, for I find Mr. Peacock, on the 17th, calling attention to the disgraceful manner in which things appeared to be managed in the Fort. "It came to my knowledge," he adds, "quite by accident, late last night, that on the previous evening a carriage had been stopped going into the Fort, and some men, who were in it, had been apprehended in endeavouring to carry papers to one of the State prisoners. I also learn that the papers were lying folded up in a piece of paper, not even tied, in the officer's room at the main guard, so that any of them might easily be abstracted during the officer's absence. And this, too, after the escape of the prisoner on Sunday night."—*MS. Records.*

GENERAL LLOYD AT DINAPORE.—Page 110.

[An exculpatory letter from General Lloyd is referred to in a note to page 110, where it is stated that the vindication will be found complete in the Appendix. The extreme length of the communication has, however, suggested the expediency of giving only those passages in which the General explains his own act. The rest merely confirms the accuracy of the narrative given in the text:]

"On the 25th July, 1857, I was far from well, and on that day the crisis occurred here, and in consequence my manner may not have been as firm and decided as it used to be. But my acts will, I think, bear the strictest scrutiny; and although from my gouty feet I am physically unequal to active bodily exertion, I assert that in judgment and intellect I am fully equal, if not superior, to any of the younger commanders at Dinapore. The way I have been vilified and abused by the press forces me thus to assert my own qualifications in a style which might otherwise be thought unbecoming. However, the shortcomings of some of those who had previously talked much, but when the time came did little, have been visited very hardly on me; and the difficult nature of the country, and the peculiar one of the locality of the Dinapore Cantonment at this season, as well as the small available European force at Dinapore, have been quite lost sight of by those who have seen fit to publish their dogmatical opinions as to what should or should not have been done on the occasion of the late outbreak here."

"As I was quite aware of the likelihood of a mutiny of the Native troops here, and feeling sure that in such an event they would make off towards Arrah, I, in June last, issued written instructions relative to the course to be pursued by the European troops acting against them, and this was fully made known to Colonel Fenwick, the commanding officer of the Tenth, who was then the senior. Subsequently, Colonel Huyshe, of the Artillery (senior to Colonel Fenwick, though I was not aware of this till after the 25th July), and I took an early opportunity to inquire from him whether he had made himself acquainted with the orders given and arrangements for meeting an outbreak—whether Lieutenant Smithett had told him all these things—and I received a reply in the affirmative, and the Colonel said the bullocks could be harnessed in a moment, as they were close by, in the tanyard, or old magazine yard, and he would not be caught napping—an expression I particularly remarked."

"I had no horse in Cantonments. My stable was two miles distant, and being unable at the time to walk far or much, I thought I should be most useful on board the steamer with guns and riflemen, in which I proceeded along the rear of the Native lines, the river being only two hundred yards, or thereabouts, distant from the right of the advancing column of guns and Europeans, and expecting to get some shots at the Sepoys on shore, or escaping by the river. Considering that I had fully previously given instructions for the attack and pursuit of the Sepoys by the guns and Her Majesty's Tenth, under their respective commanding officers, I left it to them to follow up the mutineers by land. On embarking, I sent Captain Turner, D.A.A.G., to order the guns to advance, as I thought they were long in setting off, and I sent Lieutenant Nedham, D.A.Q.G., to order the commanding officer of the detachment of Her Majesty's Thirty-Seventh Foot to place himself under Colonel Fenwick's orders."

"The mutineers' position being on the road from Patna *viâ* Phoolwaree towards Arrah, with the road to Gya open in their rear, it was uncertain which road they would take, or they might have taken all three, and visited the three places. Two guns and a detachment were therefore sent off to protect Patna, leaving only five hundred men and four guns at Dinapore. The high road to Arrah was quite impassable for guns, and even the Infantry would have had a difficult and slow march along it to reach the Kholwur Ghaût on the Soane. It is perhaps to be regretted that some were not sent that night or next morning, but only a small party, in comparison to the strength of the mutineers, could have been detached; no guns could have gone, and as the mutineers avoided the road, and kept to the fields, where they could scarcely have been effectively followed by a small party of Europeans, they would probably not have been of much use. However, as the readiest means of following them, to prevent their crossing the Soane, I, next day, the 26th, sent off some riflemen in a steamer up that river, expecting that at this season there would have been sufficient water; but unfortunately the steamer could not get up high enough, and returned in the evening without having effected anything."

"Early next morning the commander of the steamer changed his mind, and said he could not tow two flats, consequently the party had to be reduced by a hundred men, and therefore Colonel Fenwick remained, and sent Captain Dunbar in command, an officer of whose unfitness for such a command I suspect Colonel Fenwick may have been aware; at any rate he subsequently proved himself to be utterly so. He marched his men fasting (though he might have given them a meal, as he had taken three days' provisions with the detachment) towards Arrah, pushed on against advice and common sense in the dark, got his column into an ambuscade from which they were suddenly fired upon by the rebels, and were thrown into utter panic, broken, and scattered."

THE MUTINY AT FUTTEHGURH.

[The subjoined is the letter from Colonel Smith referred to at page 299 :]

"Fort Futtehgurh, July 1st.

"Au magistrat de Mynpoorie, ou à un officier European attaché à une armée de soldats Europeens. Nous avons été fortement assiegés dans le Fort de Futtehghur, par une force d'Insurgents, pendant la dernière semaine et nous avons peu d'espoir de continuer le siege si nous n'avons du secours de suite. Nous sommes en tout 100 personnes: 32 hommes, et 70 femmes et enfans. Nous vous supplions de venir de suite à notre secours, nous sommes en très grand danger. We are in great danger and plead for speedy help. We are more than one hundred—32 men, 70 women and children, against 1000 insurgents.

"G. A. Smith,
"Colonel Commanding."

"R. Thornhill, July."

[This was addressed to "Any Officer commanding or attached to a European Force or to the Magistrate of Mynpoorie or Agra." It was on the receipt of this at Agra, I believe, that Major Weller made the offer mentioned in the text to lead a force to Futtehgurh.]

THE ADVANCE ON CHINHUT.—Page 502.

[In a brief Memoir of Sir Henry Lawrence, written by the author, a few years ago, the following note upon this subject is given, the correspondence being quoted from the originals in his possession :]

"Upon this subject, Mr. Gubbins has written in his book: 'Upon his death-bed Sir Henry referred to the disaster at Chinhut, and said that he had acted against his own judgment from the fear of man. I have often inquired, but I never learnt the name of any one who had counselled the step which resulted in so severe a calamity.' This may be true; but it is not quite the whole truth. It is probable that no one especially recommended this individual movement; but it is certain that Mr. Gubbins himself was continually urging Sir Henry Lawrence to send out a force to meet the enemy. But what he certainly did with respect to this particular affair was to ridicule the idea that the enemy were advancing in any formidable strength. When the news of the advance of the mutineers was first brought in, the circular that went round for the information of the chief officers of the garrison stated that the man who brought the information said he could not speak with certainty as to the numbers, but that he heard there were eight or nine regiments of infantry and one of cavalry, with twelve guns. Mr. Gubbins appended four notes of exclamation to the passage, and wrote beneath it, '*What stuff!*—M. G.;' and not satisfied with this, endorsed the paper with the same words. But we now learn from Mr. Gubbins himself ('Mutinies in Oudh,' pp. 189, 190) that the rebel force consisted of nine and a half regiments of Infantry, twelve guns, and seven or eight hundred Cavalry. It must be added, in the cause of historic truth, that after the death of Sir Henry Lawrence, Brigadier Inglis took some pains to elicit the facts, and that letters were addressed to several staff-officers on the subject. One answered: 'I could not positively state that Mr. Gubbins addressed a letter to the late Sir Henry Lawrence urging him to send troops to Seetapoor, or to Chinhut, or to Cawnpore, or anywhere else, but I have a decided though general impression that he did do so; and, if I am not mistaken, Mahommedabad and Nawabgunje, on the Fyzabad road, might be included in the list of places to which Mr. Gubbins thought it would be beneficial to send troops. . . . . I have so often heard Sir Henry Lawrence talk on this subject, especially dwelling on the pertinacity with which Mr. Gubbins pressed him, that I could, without much difficulty, show, if necessary, the line of argument the Brigadier-General adopted.' Another wrote: 'Several times the Brigadier-General (Lawrence) asked me how I could equip detachments of Europeans which Mr. Gubbins proposed sending to Seetapore, Cawnpore.

Mullcabad, and Nawabgunje; and if it were possible to transport them within certain fixed times on elephants. On these occasions I perfectly remember Sir Henry appeared irritated and annoyed, and always pronounced such expeditions most rash, unsafe, and utterly impracticable. The feasibility of the proposed enterprises was openly discussed by all the members of the Staff, both in Sir H. Lawrence's room, and often at his table, and I always heard that Mr. Gubbins had advocated the movements.' A third said, in reply: 'I have the honour to state, for the information of the Brigadier commanding at Lucknow (Inglis), that I perfectly remember that in the latter part of June last many letters were received by the late Sir H. M. Lawrence from Mr. Gubbins. Several of these letters were given me to read, but not all, as they did not belong to my department, but to that of the Military Secretary. I, however, generally heard the purport of them discussed, which was the advisability of sending an European force over to Cawnpore, at another time to Seetapore and Chinhut, and also the advantages to be gained by sending a force out to meet the rebel army at Nawabgunje. I always heard the late Brigadier-General express himself as strongly opposed to the above movements.' And again another officer, who had peculiar opportunities of observation, said: 'Sir Henry Lawrence did from time to time complain to me that the indomitable personal courage of Mr. Gubbins, his excessive zeal and ardent temperament, had caused him to be the over-earnest, importunate, and too public advocate of military movements which, according to Sir Henry's personal judgment, could only have ended disastrously. He more than once deplored to me, as a calamity which weighed down his spirits, that owing to the chivalric ardour and the eloquent fervour with which Mr. Gubbins urged his views, and the publicity which he gave to them, the Finance Commissioner had come to be regarded by some of the more spirited and less experienced officers of the force, as the real man for the crisis.' Nothing further need be said to explain the meaning of Lawrence's dying words."

CAPTAIN NORMAN AND COLONEL SEATON.

At page 547, mention is made of the high qualities and distinguished services of Captain (afterwards Sir) Henry Norman, Assistant-Adjutant-General of the Army. I gladly avail myself of the opportunity to rectify an error, in which I was led by a previous writer. It is stated at page 573, vol. ii., that Colonel (Sir Thomas) Seaton was, after Chamberlain was wounded, "appointed to officiate as Adjutant-General." No such appointment was ever made. Nor is there any statement to that effect in Colonel Seaton's memoir ("From Cadet to Colonel"). The duties of the Adjutant-General's office were carried on by Captain Norman, under the general direction of Colonel Neville Chamberlain, who, although physically incapacitated by his wound, was never unequal to the duty of giving sound advice and suggesting wise instructions.

HINDOO RAO'S HOUSE.

[The following is portion of a letter from Sir Charles Reid to the author, relating to the famous Picket at Hindoo Rao's house, of which frequent mention has been made in these pages:]

"The true key of our position in front of Delhi, and upon the holding of which the success or failure of the siege depended, was *not* the Subzee-mundee, as stated p. 518, vol. ii., but Hindoo Rao's house. The latter post (which by the way be it said was *not* on the extreme right of my position, there being one battery and two pickets beyond it) commanded the Subzee-mundee by about 150 feet, as well as the Grand Trunk Road. Had the rebels once taken Hindoo Rao's house, a glance at the map will show that our camp lay open to the enemy's guns, and our position would have become an untenable one, and we must have retreated in disgrace. That this was evident to the rebels appears from the extraordinary efforts made by them to obtain possession of the

Ridge, especially the highest point, viz., Hindoo Rao's house, and as Baird Smith remarks, it was 'the one great feature of their operations from which they never departed.' Not less than twenty-six separate attacks were made on the right of the Ridge by the enemy in order to obtain possession of the house—one of which lasted one whole night and a day. I allude to the grand Eed attack on the 1st and 2nd of August, and another from the 6th to the 13th of August, *vide* General Wilson's despatch of the latter date: 'A constant worrying attack night and day by both Infantry and Artillery.' Neither of these you make mention of, which I think must have been an omission. The Eed attack, in my opinion, was the crisis and turning point of the whole siege, and for the sake of the gallant officers and men who served under me I would fain hope it is not too late to mention it, as the history does not go further than the operations in August, in which month it occurred."

"There were several gallant deeds on the part of officers and men who served under me on the Ridge which I made mention of in my letters and notes, and which I cannot but think you would wish to bring forward in your admirable work—viz., Minto Elliot's gallant conduct with a sergeant and a gunner on the 23rd of June, recommended for Victoria Cross."

[No one can regret more than the author of this work, the material exigencies which have compelled him to leave so many brave deeds unrecorded. I have already said that I could not have yielded to my inclinations without extending this work to a length which would scarcely have been acceptable to the reader. It should be remembered that I have not attempted to write a History of the Siege of Delhi, but of the Sepoy War in all parts of the country.]

THE EXPLOSION OF THE CASHMERE GATE.—Page 601.

"Sept. 14, 1857.

"THE party for blowing in the gate, the Sixtieth Rifles leading, went off at a double from the Ludlow Castle, until they arrived at the cross road leading to the Customs, and the men, when they opened out right and left, the Sappers going to the gate led by Lieutenant Home and one bugler, Lieutenant Salkeld, with the party carrying the powder a few paces behind, the three European non-commissioned officers, and nine Natives with twelve bags of 25 lb. each. My duty was to bring up the rear, and see that none of them remained behind. Lieutenant Salkeld had passed through the temporary Burn Gate with Sergeants Carmichael and Burgess, but four of the Natives had stopped behind the above gate and refused to go on. I had put down my bag and taken my gun, and threatened to shoot them, when Lieutenant Salkeld came running back and said, 'Why the d—l don't you come on?' I told him there were four men behind the gate, and that I was going to shoot them. He said, '*Shoot* them—d—n their eyes, *shoot* them!' I said, 'You hear the orders, and I will shoot you,' raising the gun slowly to 'present,' to give fair time, when two men went on. Lieutenant Salkeld said, 'Do not shoot; with your own bag it will be enough.' I went on, and only Lieutenant Salkeld and Sergeant Burgess were there; Lieutenant Home and the bugler had jumped into the ditch, and Sergeant Carmichael was killed as he went up with his powder on his shoulder, evidently having been shot from the wicket while crossing the broken part of the bridge along one of the beams. I placed my bag, and then at great risk reached Carmichael's bag from in front of the wicket, placed it, arranged the fusee for the explosion, and reported all ready to Lieutenant Salkeld, who held the slow match (*not a port-fire,* as I have seen stated). In stooping down to light the quick match, he put out his foot and was shot through the thigh from the wicket, and in falling had the presence of mind to hold out the slow, and told me to fire the charge. Burgess was next him, and took it. I told him to fire the charge, and keep cool. He turned round and said, '*It won't go off, sir; it has gone out, sir*' (not knowing that one officer had fallen into the ditch). I gave him a box of lucifers, and, as he took them, he let them fall into my hand, he being shot through the body from *the wicket also,* and fell over after Lieutenant Salkeld. I was then left alone, and keeping close to the charge, seeing from where the others were shot, I struck a light, when the port-fire in the fuse went off in my face, the light not having gone out as we thought. I took up my gun and jumped into the ditch, but before I had reached the ground the charge went off, and filled the ditch with smoke, so that I saw no one. I turned while in the act of jumping, so that my back would come to the wall to save me from falling. I stuck close to the wall, and by that I escaped being smashed to pieces, only getting a severe bruise on the leg, the leather helmet saving my head.

"I put my hands along the wall and touched some one, and asked who it was; 'Lieutenant Home,' was the answer. I said, 'Has God spared you? Are you hurt?" he said, 'No,' and asked the same from me. As soon as the dust cleared a little we saw Lieutenant Salkeld and Burgess covered with dust; their lying in the middle of the ditch had saved them from being smashed to pieces and covered by the *débris* from the top of the walls, the shock only toppling the stones over, which fell between where we stood and where they lay. I went to Lieutenant Salkeld and called the bugler to help me to remove him under the bridge as the fire had covered upon us, and Lieutenant Salkeld's arms were broken. Lieutenant Home came to assist, but I begged him to keep out of the fire, and that we would do all that could be done. Lieutenant Salkeld would not let us remove him, so I put a bag of powder under his head for a pillow, and with the bugler's puggery bound up his arms and thigh, and I left the bugler to look to him and went to Burgess, took off his sword, which I put on, and done what I could for him. I got some brandy from Lieutenant Home and gave to both, also to a Havildar (Pelluck Singh), who had his thigh shot through, and was under the bridge by a ladder that had been put into the ditch by mistake by the Rifles. Lieutenant Home got out of the ditch, leaving me in charge of the wounded, and went to the front after the Rifles had gone in, and the Fifty-second followed them: THEY DID NOT GO FAST; their bugler *had sounded fifty times at least, and some ten minutes had elapsed before any one came, and the Rifles returned and went in first.* I then went to the rear for three stretchers and brought them, one of which was taken from me for an officer of the Rifles. I had to draw my sword and threaten to run any one through who took the other two. I put them into the ditch, and with the bugler's assistance got Lieutenant Salkeld into one and sent him with him, charging him strictly not to leave him until he had placed him in the hands of a surgeon, and with the assistance of a haick who had come to the Havildar, got Burgess into one and sent the haick with him, I being scarcely able to walk, and in a few minutes he returned to say he was dead, and ask for further orders. I told him to take him to the hospital. After assisting to clear away the gate and make the roadway again, I went on to the front to see what was going on. It will be seen that Carmichael did not live to get up to the gate, and that Sergeant Smith did not run up as he was there and placed the bags and arranged the fuse for the charge, and was there when all were gone or shot down. The bugler took charge of Lieutenant Salkeld at my request, and came to our tents when recommended for the (Victoria) Cross, to thank me in the presence of my comrades for being the means of him getting it.

"JOHN SMITH."

CAPTURE OF THE PALACE AND SELIM-GURH OF DELHI.—

Page 633.

Extract from the Journal of an Artillery Officer.

"Near the Calcutta Gate I met Captain Aitkin with a small party of Wild's Punjabees, who told me he was going on as far as he could, and I returned to the Magazine where we saw Aitkin and his party advance, first to the bridge leading to Selim-gurh, and then right on along the road winding round it, and shortly after we saw them appear in the corner tower whence the last heavy gun had been fired ; and I reported the matter at once. In the mean time Colonel Longfield of the Eighth, a fine old soldier with whom I had marched from Jullundur, came to the Magazine and told me a column was forming to blow in and assault the Palace Gate, and soon after it was blown in and the place captured. But before that Aitkin and his party had got into Selim-gurh, and had spiked the guns there and obtained possession of the gate leading into the Palace, having shot the sentry at the gate on his post. For this act Aitkin has never got the credit he deserved. He afterwards, however, got the V.C. in the more fortunate region of Oude. I sent Lieutenant Evans in after the storming party to report the state of affairs, and then went myself to the Palace Gate, where I found Major R. Ramsay commanding the Kumaon Battalion. While talking to him, word was brought that the enemy were attacking the other, or Duriao-gunge Gate of the Palace, so Ramsay fell in a party of his battalion and we doubled off to the gate, which we found closed, while a large party of the Sixtieth Rifles and Kumaon men formed a semicircle some way off in the yard in front of the gate at which they were firing, while shots were being returned from a small opening between the two leaves of the great iron-covered gate, which did not close completely for the lower four or five feet. We found two of the Sixtieth and three Kumaonees all shot through the legs by this fire, so, getting alongside the wall I ran into the gateway, knowing the gates were musket-proof, and putting the muzzle of my revolver just over the muzzle of a musket that appeared in the chink, I pulled the trigger and the owner of the musket went down with a grunt. Presently after there was a rush and scuffle outside with shouts that we were not to fire, and I found a party of Punjabees had got possession of the gate outside. On opening the gate, we admitted Captain Stewart, whom I did not know, but addressed as Hodson, whom he greatly resembled. And so ended the siege of Delhi, and I flattered myself the troop had done its duty. Afterwards I went to the Jumma Musjid and found Major Brind in possession, having, with characteristic energy, organised and headed the party that pushed on and seized that post.

[The following was published in the last edition of the Second Volume of "The History of the Sepoy War."]

ADDENDA TO VOL. II.

THE CARABINEERS ON THE TENTH OF MAY.

It was stated in the first edition of the second volume that the turning out of the Carabineers at Meerut on the 10th of May, 1857, was delayed by the slow process of a regimental roll-call. This Colonel Custance denied, and supported his denial with an overwhelming amount of documentary evidence. I therefore wrote him the subjoined letter, with permission to publish it:

"Penge, Surrey, Dec. 20, 1870.

"SIR,—I am perfectly convinced, by the documentary evidence which you have afforded me (I should have been satisfied, indeed, with your own denial), that the statement at page 65 of the second volume of my 'History of the Sepoy War,' to the effect that on the 10th of May, at Meerut, there was a roll-call of the Carabineers (then under your command) before they moved out against the Sepoy mutineers, was based upon erroneous information. As the passage was written some years ago, I cannot, without a laborious search, which I have not yet had time to make, ascertain the authority or authorities on which the statement was made; but whatever the authority may have been, I regret that I should have been, however unintentionally, the means of giving publicity to a statement at variance with the fact. I need not add, that I wish to do all that lies in my power to correct the error in future issues of my History; and all the more willingly, as I have reason to believe that the story which I have published was commonly accepted as a fact before the appearance of my book. I may add to this that from a careful perusal and collation of the several documents which you have sent me, containing the evidence of officers and non-commissioned officers of your regiment, it appears that the Carabineers, when proceeding towards the lines of the Native battalions, were countermarched, by order conveyed to you by a staff-officer, and marched towards the gaol, which lies, at a considerable distance, in a different direction. It seems that on reaching the gaol, it was found that the prisoners had already escaped, so the Carabineers were marched back again towards the Native Lines. On their return, darkness having set in, they lost their way, although under the guidance of the staff-officer who had directed you to the gaol. That this was the real cause of the tardiness with which you reported your arrival on the general parade to the Brigadier is sufficiently plain from the evidence which you have afforded me. I have much pleasure in informing you that I am perfectly satisfied of the truth of these statements.

"You may make any use of this letter that you may wish.

"I am yours faithfully,

"J. W. Kaye.

"Major-General Custance, C.B."

[After this had been published, I received another letter on the subject, which I also feel bound to publish; and I am the more willing to give it publicity, because the record is highly honourable to the splendid regiment (though in May, 1857, owing to accidental circumstances, it was not in the height of its splendour) which Colonel Custance then commanded. I thought when I last saw it, on the occasion of Lord Mayo's funeral, that such a regiment might have demolished at least half of the Native Cavalry of Bengal:]

"Junior U.S. Club, Pall Mall, London, Feb. 27, 1871.

"Dear Sir,—On return home I have looked over my memoranda of Meerut and Delhi in 1857, and have carefully read the passage in your History to which Colonel Custance, of the Carabineers, takes objection. As I can personally vouch for certain points, I here state them.

"The Carabineers turned out with extreme rapidity. I ought to know, for it was I who ordered a sergeant of the regiment from the bridge close to the parade of the mutineers to run to Colonel Custance himself, and I sent a rifleman also to the Brigade Office. This was the first intimation given, as the firing, in which Colonel Finnis and others were killed, was then proceeding. This sergeant afterwards told me that Colonel Custance had 'instantly ordered out his regiment,' and, on reaching his house myself a few minutes later, I saw the regiment on its parade rapidly getting ready, *and I heard the roll called in the troop nearest me*, an important duty which no good sergeant will omit on any occasion, as he cannot report his men present if he has not ascertained it.

"Colonel Custance and his regiment had to await 'orders,' and if any delay took place it was, I imagine, owing to the very late arrival on the scene of General Hewitt from his house, distant a long way off, and from whence, half dressed, and upset mentally and physically, he had been brought by Lieutenant Warde, Eleventh Regiment, N.I. He was very old and feeble. The Carabineers were in broad daylight ordered not to the mutineers' parade-ground close by, but to the prison some miles off, and the services of Colonel Custance and of his fine regiment, both of them able and ready to obey any order long before it was issued, were lost *pro tem.* I myself saw the regiment drawn up and ready for orders, and I do not believe the slightest delay occurred when those orders were received by Colonel Custance.

"After the Carabineers had left their parade, I rode across both the parade-grounds of the two mutineer regiments to try to reach the house of Mrs. Chambers. Lieutenant Shelley and another officer wished to accompany me, and the former lent me his Arab. As I crossed, the Sepoys were then plundering my regimental magazine; some on their knees, and all crying, 'Quick, brother, quick! Delhi, Delhi!' and I saw a stream of Sepoys and troopers going off towards the Delhi road.

"The Sepoys took little notice, but I saw several officers lying dead, and one dying raised himself as I passed. I had almost reached the house of Mrs. Chambers, then in her verandah, and looking at me, when five or six Native troopers spread out to cut me off, and forced me back. Even then but few shots were fired at me. I returned to Colonel Custance's house, and then went to the Artillery Lines, and earnestly and repeatedly begged General Hewitt to let me ride to Delhi and give warning. Colonel Smyth and Major Harriott were by, and the latter urged the General to send me, but he refused 'unless I obtained Colonel Wilson's permission.' That officer was actively engaged in the station, a very large one, and I, owing to being misdirected, could not find him; and I corroborate his statement in your History that he did not know that evening for certain 'where the enemy had gone.' You retain General Hewitt's, Colonel Smyth's, and Major Harriott's letters stating that I offered to ride through the mutineers to Delhi; and General Hewitt states I did so at 7.30 P.M., 10th May, 1857, but this was my third and last offer to him, after an hour and a half had been lost by him in sending me again and again to Colonel Wilson for permission!

"The above proves the correctness of your narrative both as to the fact of the 'roll-call,' and that the enemy could have been attacked in broad daylight on their own parades, and followed up to Delhi. That they were in a state of 'scare,' I could myself testify.

"Both Colonel Custance and his fine regiment were in ample time to have attacked the mutineers, and were quite ready for action; and it was, I submit, no fault of either that the regiment was ordered off elsewhere, and our kith and kin left to perish.

"I saw Captain Rosser, Carabineers, late the same evening, and on my stating that I had nearly reached Mrs. Chambers, he said 'I will follow them now with a troop,' and, for aught I know, made the offer, but the enemy had then about four hours' start.

"As I was the only officer who offered to ride through the mutineers to Delhi alone, and who traversed the city early next morning from end to end (alone also), to secure the prisoner alluded to in your History, I naturally felt deeply hurt at my reception by General Hewitt, who insisted I was romancing (until the prisoner corroborated my assertion), and that the city was full of armed men. It is of course possible that there were many armed men, but I did not see them, and they were quiet enough, though a rabble at once surrounded me.

"If you think of referring to Colonel Custance in an introductory chapter to your next volume, or elsewhere, this note —fully corroborating the accuracy of your History—is at your service. If the evidence of an officer in my humble position can be of any avail, you can make what use you please of this letter now or at any time. Thanking you for your personal courtesy to myself, and with best wishes for the success of your important work,

"I remain, yours faithfully,

"H. Le Champion,

"Captain 101st Foot,

"Late Le Champion Möller,

"11th Regiment, N.I."

[I have submitted this letter to General Custance, who writes that the roll-call which Captain Möller heard must have been that of the unmounted men of the regiment. Here I must leave the question for the judgment of the public.]

[As regards Captain Rosser's offer to take a detachment of Cavalry and some Horse Artillery guns to Delhi, on the night of the 10th of May, I should state that I have received a letter from Mrs. Rosser, enclosing one from her husband, written shortly after the outbreak, most distinctly asserting that he made the offer, which has been denied by the authorities; and I must admit that all I have heard, since the first edition of this work was published, strengthens the conviction that the offer was made, though not, perhaps, in accordance with those strict military rules, which though recognised in quiet times, must be departed from in a great crisis.]

THE METCALFE HOUSES.

"6, St. James's-terrace, Harrow-road.
"March 1, 1871.

"DEAR SIR,—There appears to me to be a slight confusion in a matter of detail at p. 543 of the second volume of your Sepoy War, which possibly may be worth mentioning to you in case you wish to inquire further into it. There are *two* Metcalfe houses—one outside the Cashmere Gate, the other at the Kootub, which, you know, is eleven miles from Delhi.

"The former (with which alone you are concerned here) was not, *as far as I know*, an adaptation of, or built on the site of, or in any way connected with a Native building. Lord Lawrence could doubtless tell you all about it. I have only known it since the rebellion; but there is enough of it left to show that it is a thoroughly English building, and I have always understood that Metcalfe built it from top to bottom for himself. I do not think there are even any remains of Native buildings in "Metcalfe's Compound," and the remains in the Koadsiah-bagh somewhat nearer to the Cashmere Gate are, I believe, considerably more recent than the time of Akbar. The rooms in *this* Metcalfe House have never been let at so much a day. One wing of it has been repaired, and is let by the month as an ordinary dwelling-house.

"The Metcalfe House *at the Kootub* is a fine Native tomb adapted to the requirements of a European residence. I cannot find it in our friend Syūd Ahmud's Asaroossunnadeed, but in a small English guide-book I see it is said to have been the tomb of Mohammed Koolee Khan, one of Akbar's foster-fathers. *This* Metcalfe's House is (or *was* a couple of years ago when I was at Delhi) used as a dâk bungalow, some small charge a day being made for the rooms. If I am right in the above, the question as to the removal of the tomb-stone becomes of no importance; but I may mention that though the stone must have been removed from this tomb (for it is not in the centre hall where it ought to be), the passage from Sleeman in your note may refer, and I *suspect* does refer to another tomb close by.

"That other tomb is the burial place of Adum Khan, a man who made a great figure in the reign of Akbar. It would be termed "magnificent," with much more propriety than Metcalfe's tomb. The stone in it has been removed from the centre and placed in the verandah outside, and I have a dim recollection of hearing that it had been removed by one of the Delhi officials many years before, and that the feelings of the people were hurt by the thing. Adum Khan was not the foster-brother of Akbar; but, as you probably are aware, he slew one of Akbar's *foster-fathers*, and was executed in consequence. The story is a long one, and Sleeman may have fallen into some confusion about it. Lord Lawrence, I dare say, could tell you which tomb Blake had done up for himself. Or, if you wish, I could get certain information for you from Delhi or from Syūd Ahmed.

"Assuming that my conjecture is wrong, and that a portion of the Delhi house was a converted tomb with the slab removed, as at the Kootub, I should consider your remarks most just. With the exception of a few celebrated shrines, which are the fashion, and the burial-places of their own families, the Mahomedans are, for the most part, indifferent about the desecration of tombs. The Zemindars often use them as dwelling-houses or as cattle stalls. The fine tomb of Toogluck Shah was occupied in this way until a few years ago, when we swept all the abomination out of it. But though they will stand desecration by others, they are up in arms at once if a European official attempts it, and they are probably right in making the distinction.

"As I am writing to you I may take the opportunity of mentioning, with reference to the words 'baba' and 'beebee' (page 354), that the latter word is universally used by Natives who live in contact with Europeans for our word 'baby,' of which it is no doubt a corruption, while the word 'baba' is used for older children, or for children young and old indifferently. 'Beebee' is used also in its proper sense of a lady or wife, but not *commonly*. A Native would generally speak of a lady as a 'mem sahib.' I speak with reference to the country from Delhi up. It may be otherwise lower down. I do not know whether it is worth while troubling you with this letter; but you seem so anxious to insure accuracy down to the most trifling detail, that even a hint of so slight an inaccuracy may be acceptable.

"Yours truly,

"D. FITZPATRICK,

"Late Officiating Deputy-Commissioner of Delhi.

"J. W. Kaye, Esq.

"P.S.—You do not appear to have seen the papers of the trial of Hajee, the man referred to in your note at page 79. Sir J. Metcalfe almost severed his head from his body at Arah Seran some time after the capture, and left him for dead.* He, however, survived by something scarcely short of a miracle; but the mark, a fearful chasm in his neck—a curiosity from a surgical point of view—enabled us to trace him. I had the satisfaction of committing him for trial just before I left, and he was executed shortly after. I have always understood that he struck the first blow. I think Bucktawur said so on the trial."

* The less said about this affair the better.

END OF VOL. III.

LONDON:
PRINTED BY C. WHITING, BEAUFORT HOUSE, DUKE STREET, LINCOLN'S INN FIELDS.